D1718076

Elmar Waibl – Philip Herdina

Dictionary of Philosophical Terms

Vol 1: German – English

Wörterbuch philosophischer Fachbegriffe

Band 1: Deutsch – Englisch

K·G·Saur – Routledge

1997

First published 1997
by K. G. Saur Verlag
Ortlerstraße 8
D-81373 München

Simultaneously published
in the UK, Australia, New Zealand, South Africa and India
by Routledge
11 New Fetter Lane, London EC4P 4EE
and in the USA and Canada
by Routledge
29 West 35th Street, New York, NY 10001

British Library Cataloguing-in-Publication Data
A catalogue record for this book is available from the British Library

Library of Congress Cataloging-in-Publication Data
Applied for

Die Deutsche Bibliothek - CIP-Einheitsaufnahme

Waibl, Elmar:
Dictionary of Philosophical Terms = Wörterbuch philosophischer
Fachbegriffe / Elmar Waibl-Philip Herdina. - München : Saur ;
London ; New York, NY : Routledge
ISBN 3-598-11329-3 (Saur)
ISBN 0-415-17890-8 (Routledge)

Vol 1. German-English. - 1997
ISBN 3-598-11341-2 (Saur)
ISBN 0-415-17888-6 (Routledge)

Gedruckt auf säurefreiem Papier
Printed on acid-free paper

Printing and binding by Strauss Offsetdruck, Mörlenbach

Vol 1: ISBN 3-598-11341-2 (K. G. Saur)
2-vols set: ISBN 3-598-11329-3 (K. G. Saur)

Vol 1: ISBN 0-415-17888-6 (Routledge)
2-vols set: ISBN 0-415-17890-8 (Routledge)

CONTENTS

INHALT

INTRODUCTION

1. Aims

Multilingual dictionaries are commonplace in most fields of research. Unfortunately this does not appear to be the case in philosophy. This gap is to be filled by the dictionary in hand, which is to provide an instrument for the acquisition of foreign language competence in the field of philosophy.

Since English is increasingly becoming the *lingua franca* of philosophy, as well as of other disciplines, an acquaintance with English technical terminology has become increasingly important in gaining access to the international scientific community. As mobility (in the context of academic exchange programmes and guest professorships) is dependent on foreign language competence, the command of technical English has progressively become an important precondition of participation in the global job market. For the English speaking world the dictionary provides a means to gain better access to the language which is of particular significance to philosophy through thinkers like Kant and Hegel, Nietzsche and Freud, Heidegger and Habermas.

This dictionary aims to open up new possibilities. As this is a pioneering intellectual undertaking and we could not rely on the efforts of past generations of scholars, the editors were confronted with the same difficulties all pioneers have to face: *Pigmei gigantum umeris impositi, plusquam ipsi gigantes vident.*

2. Selection of Terms

The question of a clear demarcation of topic is a crucial one for every dictionary and – as every user knows – is always only successful in part. For the following reasons this issue is a particularly complex one for a technical dictionary of philosophy:

(1) As a foundational science or theory of principles (of being, knowledge, ethics, art etc.) philosophy does not occupy a specific sector in the spectrum of humanities and sciences, but addresses principal questions in virtually all fields. Accordingly, the terminology used in philosophy is correspondingly broad, making the selection of technical terms particularly difficult.

Due to the fact that philosophy touches on so many related subjects it has been considered advisable to include technical terms from related fields as far as they are considered relevant to the philosophical discussion. In keeping with this principle, concepts deriving, for example, from mathematics, economics, technology, and art have been included in so far as they pertain to the *philosophy* of mathematics, the *philosophy* of economics, the *philosophy* of technology, and the *philosophy* of art, whilst technical terms which have no significance outside their specific field are ignored. As the views concerning the necessary terminology of a specific field of philosophy vary, the selection of terms will always contain a certain arbitrariness. What seems a dispensable entry to one user may appear to be of great significance to another for a certain reason. In cases of doubt the experts in the respective fields were consulted. Every selection of terms is based on the knowledge that it is impossible to fulfil every user's expectations. We have also tried to avoid a prescriptive approach, not giving in to the temptation to define what philosophy is and what it is not.

(2) Viewed historically, difficulties derive from the fact that many scientific disciplines were once part of philosophy and only slowly separated from their mother subject. The mathematicians and natural scientists of the past were philosophers, just as the father of modern economics was one. The same holds for theory of law, theory of the state, social theory, theory of art, psychology, and other subjects.

The fact that some terms included can also be found in other general or technical dictionaries can hardly be seen as an argument for the exclusion of the term. Terms that are considered to be philosophically relevant are listed for practical reasons. If one were, for example, to look up *uncertainty principle* in a dictionary of physics, *labour theory of value* in a dictionary of economics, and *high risk technology* in a dictionary of technology, one would require a plethora of reference works containing a very high percentage of entries probably never used in philosophical discussion.

Frequently the impression of a degree of redundancy in the selection of terms is a superficial one. In fact, many entries share a specific philosophical meaning with a general one we might recognise. Thus Heidegger's *Zeug* or *Gestell* might provide such examples. What at first glance seem to be terms derived from everyday language turn out to be concepts taken from philosophical discourse.

But even where the philosophical meaning coincides with everyday meaning, this also constitutes an important piece of information for the user. When this is not the case, this kind of information is also significant. Occasionally ordinary language terms serve as cross-references to technical terms such as *Interesse* to *Erkenntnisinteresse*, *Ironie* to *sokratische Ironie*, *Kolonisation* to *Kolonisation der Lebenswelt*, and so on.

One of the problems to be addressed was the question of how far rare terms associated with particular philosophical schools should be included. With regard to the criterion of a balanced approach, we determined that the question of the significance of entries has to be decided on the basis of immanent criteria by adherents of the respective traditions and schools. To the analytical philosopher Heideggerian terms will largely appear dispensable, whilst Heideggerians will show little interest in the terminology of analytical philosophy. The main aim must be to ensure that the adherent of a school finds the core terms in his or her field of work. Some philosopher may be glad to discover a translation for *angeborene Tötungshemmung* as found in research on aggression and peace studies, the other will be pleased to find *exzentrische Positionalität* in philosophical anthropology and another *Falsifikationismus* in the theory of science, or the metaphysical *Abschiedlichkeit*. The main aim must be to provide every user with an answer to his or her specific query.

Names are only listed if the spelling differs in the respective language (e.g. *Aristoteles•Aristotle*).

Latin and Greek terms were included in so far as these were considered customary terms or expressions that play a significant role in the German technical language of philosophy. The same applies to the selection of *Asian terms* included.

Irrespective of our attempts to ensure a balanced selection of entries the particular problems resulting from the nature of philosophy make it clear that the issue of the subject-related selection of entries will never be solved to everyone's satisfaction. Whoever is required to work with a large number of dictionaries will, however, concede that this problem applies to most fields.

As it is, generally speaking, very difficult to determine the appropriate translations of *philosophical titles,* and these frequently contain information relevant to the entries in the dictionary, a list of titles is contained in the appendix. Where appropriate, the dictionary entries contain cross-references to the titles listed.

3. Mode of Entry

As we assume that a bilingual technical dictionary is only used by people with some command of the target language, the relevant information is presented to the user as succinctly as possible – in accordance with the example set by technical dictionaries in other fields. Each entry is intended to provide as much information as possible with a minimum of words.

- *Order of entries:* The entries are alphabetical, the German umlaut (ä, ö, ü) being treated as a normal vowel (a, o, u). In accordance with the example set by many technical dictionaries, groups of words are sorted word by word, the comma (e.g. in *Tatsache, empirische*) and the hyphen (e.g. in *Tatsache-Wert-Unterscheidung)* being ignored. Compounds, which can also be written as one word and are hyphenated only for better readability (e.g. *Anti-Illusionismus/Antiillusionismus)* are sorted as one term, as the use of hyphens is largely arbitrary and meaningful clusters of entries often result from this sorting algorithm. Heideggerian terms, however, are treated differently, as the words with hyphenated prefixes are generally marked by a change of philosophical meaning compared to the unhyphenated prefixes (e.g. *Ent-fernung* vs. *Entfernung*).

A sample list of entries would therefore run as follows:

Tatsache der reinen Vernunft
Tatsache, empirische
Tatsache-Wert-Unterscheidung
Tatsachenargument

- *Order of items in attribute-head phrases:* In agreement with general lexicographic practice, the entries are generally listed according to the first word to occur (e.g. Nietzsche's *blonde Bestie*), and in other noun and adjective combinations under the most significant word in the entry (e.g. *Seins, Wesen des*). As the significant part of the entry cannot always be clearly determined, some entries occur more than once with a different lemma. This allows the formation of meaningful clusters.

- *Compound nouns and periphrastic genitive constructions:* In German many entries are used both in a compound and in periphrastic form (e.g. *Individuationsprinzip* versus *Prinzip der Individuation*). Where this is the case, frequently both expressions are listed. Generally, however, the entries are selected according to usage.

- *Hyphenation:* Whether a word is written with a hyphenated prefix (such as *Anti-*, *Contra-* or *Pseudo-*) or not is frequently arbitrary. The entries are therefore either hyphenated or not and have neither been systematized nor entered in both the hyphenated and unhyphenated form. Refer to the comments on sorting principles (see *Order of entries* above).

- *Capitalization:* In accordance with grammatical usage, Latin and Greek nouns are capitalized if they are considered part of the German vocabulary; otherwise they are not. There do not appear to be any generally accepted principles even amongst experts. For capitalization in English see *6. Translation Problems*.

- *Singular or plural forms:* Nouns whose singular and plural forms are identical in German are translated by singular terms (e.g. *Hegelianer = Hegelian*). Nouns that usually occur only in the plural are entered in the plural (e.g. *Eigentumsverhältnisse, notiones communes*) and are marked as such (*pl*). Even if a singular form could be derived from the entry, a singular gender marker is not included, in order to preclude misinterpretations of the entry. German plural forms are always preceded by the article *die*. The user is advised to rely on his or her knowledge of the language.

- *Case and gender:* When the entry consists of more then one noun, the gender marker refers to the head (noun) of the phrase and determines which article is to be used with the expression, e.g. *Abschreckungsfunktion des Gesetzes f* means *DIE Abschreckungsfunktion des Gesetzes*. This principle also applies to reordered entries such as *Sprachgeschöpf, Mensch als m* which should be read as *DER Mensch als Sprachgeschöpf*. For reasons of economy the lemma is always provided just as it occurs in the respective expression, e.g. *Werdens, Stufen des*. In attribute-head phrases the adjective is generally given in its inflected form (e.g. *ursprüngliches Sein* instead of *ursprüngliche Sein, das*).

As far as possible in German, gender markers are also attributed to Greek, Latin and Asian terms. Note that these do not always agree with the grammatical gender of the nouns in the languages of origin but refer to the gender attributed to the entries in German, which are generally rendered in italics (e.g. die *lex naturalis*) to indicate that German principles of capitalization are not complied with.

In accordance with the publisher's guidelines and the fact that grammatical and natural gender do not always correspond (cf. *die Person* referring to woman and man alike), the suffix -*in* is not added to the entries where the object of reference might also be female (as in *Logiker*). As the use of the suffix -*in* is not consistent, the entries would have tended to confuse the non-native. We considered it more important to include the specific terminology of feminist philosophy and gender studies.

- *Order of translations:* If more than one translation is provided these occur in a weighted order, the most accurate or most frequently used form being listed first. Entries including a slash indicate ordered sets of alternatives, e.g. *Grenzbegriff m • limit(ing)/boundary/marginal concept/notion* would have to be read as *limit(ing)* or *boundary* or *marginal concept; limit(ing)* or *boundary* or *marginal notion*. The hyphenated alternatives should be read as follows: *normal/bell-shaped distribution* is to be read as *normal distribution* and/or *bell-shaped distribution*, whilst *conflict- generating/producing situation* reads as *conflict-generating situation* and/or *conflict-producing situation*.

- *Identifiers:* Systematic identifiers (e.g. *epi, log, ant* etc; see *4. Abbreviations and Symbols*) are intended to provide an indication of the philosophical field to which the terms are to be attributed. These identifiers serve to distinguish different usages of the same term such as *Primat m/n • primacy (log)*, primate *(nat, ant)* or *Masse f • mass (nat)*, mass, crowd, the masses *(soc)*. As the thematic categorization of philosophical terms is not always unambiguous, it is to be noted that the contextualization provided by the identifiers is only of an approximative nature and neither exclusive nor exhaustive.

- *Identifying names:* Sometimes it appears useful and/or important to add a name to a term to specify with whom the term is generally associated and to provide a more specific contextualization. Although this may indicate the person who actually coined the term, it can also simply mean that the philosopher is generally associated with the expression. The inclusion of a real name is particularly useful in identifying certain translations of a word with the use of a term suggested by a particular philosopher. If the terms suggested differ and are identified with more than one name, more than one philosopher will be listed in brackets. In view of the fact that the user of the technical dictionary is assumed to be acquainted with the field, first names are only given when there is a likelihood of confusion (e.g. *Francis Bacon, Roger Bacon*).

4. Abbreviations and Symbols

a) *Thematic identifiers*:

act	philosophy of action	*his*	philosophy of history
aes	philosophy of aesthetics	*jur*	philosophy of law
AI	artificial intelligence	*lan*	philosophy of language
ant	philosophy of anthropology	*log*	logic
asp	Asian philosophy	*mat*	philosophy of mathematics
cul	philosophy of culture	*met*	metaphysics
dec	decision theory	*min*	philosophy of mind
eco	philosophy of economics	*nat*	philosophy of nature
env	ecological/environmental philoso-	*ont*	ontology
	phy	*pol*	political philosophy
epi	epistemology	*psy*	philosophy of psychology
eso	esotericism	*rel*	philosophy of religion
eth	ethics	*sci*	philosophy of science
fem	feminist philosophy/gender studies	*soc*	social philosophy
gen	general term	*sys*	systems theory
gep	general philosophy	*tec*	philosophy of technology

It is clear that *asp* covering Asian philosophy is not so much a thematic as a geographical marker. This is used since the origin of Asian terms is frequently obscure and the technical terms are often difficult to categorize according to an essentially eurocentric taxonomy.

b) *Other abbreviations and symbols used*:

f   *feminine*
m   *masculine*
n   *neuter*
      Two gender markers separated by a slash indicate that both articles are possible, e.g. *Kalkül m/n*. Two gender markers separated by a comma (e.g. *Erscheinung und Wirklichkeit f,f*) refer to the grammatical gender of both nouns of the respective phrase. Only one gender marker is used, if the expression generally occurs as a pair (e.g. Kant's *Notwendigkeit-Zufälligkeit f*).
pl   *plural*
nt   The English entry is the same as the German one; if *nt* is followed by a number of translations, this means that both the form given in the German and the suggested translations are used.
▷   *as meaning* or *in the meaning of*

etc *and others*, either following or preceding (used in references to philosophers, e.g. *Hegel etc*).

/   The entries preceding and following the slash are exchangeable.

°   *with reservation*, identifies a spurious entry or one inferred rather than found, for reasons that cannot be specified individually.

;   What follows is thematically separated from the preceding, e.g. *Mutualismus m •* mutualism *(nat); (Proudhon) (soc)* < *Tauschbank*: thus the reference to a cognate term only applies to what follows the semicolon, i.e. the sociological interpretation of *mutualism*.

5. Cross-References

In contrast to other technical dictionaries, the editors include cross-references as this provides an informative context to the terms, which should prove of use to the reader. It should make the tracing of particular expressions and undirected search processes much easier. The following symbols are used:

→   refers to synonyms

↔   refers to antonyms

<   refers to cognate terms

< W   refers to index of philosophical titles

Note that synonyms and antonyms are rather generously defined. They may be specified by one of the meanings given for an entry and/or relate to the specific uses of a term by a certain philosopher (e.g. Kant's distinction between *Verstand* ↔ *Vernunft* or Jung's *Animus* ↔ *Anima*).

If an entry includes a synonymous reference to another entry without a translation, the editors wish to indicate that the term listed is not normally used and that the word referred to is the usual equivalent (e.g. *Alienation* → *Entfremdung*). Synonymous back-references are provided (e.g. entry with a reference from *Verhaltensforschung* to *Ethologie* and a reference from *Ethologie* to *Verhaltensforschung*) to show that the two terms are interchangeable. A back-reference is not included, if one of the terms is considered outdated or obsolete, e.g. *Gynaekokratie* refers to *Matriarchat*; *Hylismus* refers to *Materialismus*, but not vice versa. References to expressions without translations are given, if the editors considered the semantic information philosophically relevant. Thus back-references to Latin and Greek terms or expressions are to be found, if they still play a significant role in current philosophical discourse.

The reference to cognate terms < means that the term cited is semantically or historically related to the entry in the cross-reference. This will enable the user to refer to related words, if he or she does not feel the entry at hand is suitable for his or her purposes.

6. Translation Problems

The entries were obtained by diligent research based on primary sources, encyclopedias, glossaries, reference works and current periodicals, which are so numerous that they cannot be listed. The translations were checked and double-checked by multilingual experts in the respective philosophical fields. It is, however, to be emphasized that – in contrast to the technical languages of e.g. medicine or technical science – philosophical terminology appears particularly complex and difficult, which means that it was sometimes impossible to get all the expert opinions to agree. Thus we bear the final responsibility for the correctness of the entries provided.

It is generally assumed that the user of a technical dictionary is sufficiently acquainted with the term he or she is looking up. Therefore the dictionary in hand does not try to explain the terms, but rather attempts to provide equivalents in the respective languages.

- *Unusual terms:* Like German, English technical terminology tends to include unusual words. Lack of acquaintance with the expressions should not lead to the conclusion that these concepts do not exist in English. Just as the native German speaker is not likely to be conversant with all the technical terms found in the language – which is to be explained by the vastness and versatility of natural languages – so the native English speaker is also going to be a stranger to a large number of technical terms in English. All of the terminology given in this dictionary stems from recognized sources. Where this is not the case, as the terms are either inferred or nonce-formations, the entries are marked by the symbol °.

- *Compounds:* The translation of compounds represents a particular problem as for example *Wahrheitstheorie* can be translated as *theory of truth* or *truth theory*. Generally speaking, both forms are possible, but British and US preferences seem to differ frequently in this respect without following a clear principle.

- *Formation of abstract nouns:* Frequently, abstract nouns are derived from adjectival forms. Next to the etymologically plausible suffixes we now also find suffixes the language purist might object to, e.g. *logicality, logicalness.*

- *Obsolete terms:* As the dictionary does not merely include current philosophy, but tries to cover the whole range of philosophical terminology, it also contains obsolete or antiquated terms whose meaning has changed, without them being marked us such, e.g. *politischer Körper - body politic (Hobbes).*

- *Usage:* The sole criterion in the determination of the translations is usage and not the logical consistency of the terminology used. This explains the differences to be found in the details of some terminological clusters. Thus the German *Zufall*, as part of coumpound nouns such as *Zufallselement, Zufallsentdeckung*, is translated once as *random/aleatory element* and then as *chance/accidental discovery*.

- *Spelling:* For pragmatic reasons we have opted for British spelling. The inclusion of both British and American spelling would have made a large number of entries very difficult to read. The American differences of spelling affecting entries such as *behaviour, labour, fulfilment, centre* and others are generally listed in good monolingual dictionaries and have therefore not been specified here. Furthermore, a number of terms allow different spellings (e.g. *medieval/mediaeval*). In such cases we have generally chosen the most common spelling, rather than the etymologically plausible one. Occasionally, alternative spellings are given in brackets referring either to a letter as in *judg(e)ment* or to a syllable as in *dialectic(al), Lamarck(ian)ism* etc.

- *Capitalization of translations:* Similar principles are applied to the question of capitalization, i.e. whether a term is considered a proper noun or not. Again the criterion is that of usage. Non-capitalized or capitalized spellings are generally not listed as alternatives (e.g. *Theatre of the Absurd*). It has occasionally become accepted to use a German term in English. Whether a German word has been assimilated into the English language will determine whether it is capitalized (or not, depending on usage) e.g. *abschiedlichkeit, entwicklungsroman*. These terms are frequently rendered in italics, but this aspect is ignored here.

- *Brackets:* If parts of the translation have been placed in brackets, as in *ontologischer Gottesbeweis m • ontological proof (of the existence of God)*, this indicates that the shorter form as well as the extended form are used in English.

Due to the particular character of any language many expressions can only be rendered by approximation, according with the Italian play on words: *traduttore traditore*. Any user of a technical dictionary should bear this fact in mind.

Acknowledgements

The completion of this technical dictionary would not have been possible without the *Jubiläumsfonds der Oesterreichischen Nationalbank* and the *Stiftung Südtiroler Sparkasse*. The generous financial support of these two institutions has made the realization of this ambitious project possible, for which they cannot be thanked enough.

We would explicitly like to thank *President Dr Herbert Treichl*, the doyen of Austrian banking, whose steadfast support contributed decisively to the initiation of this project. We also wish to express our gratitude to *Senior Senator Dr Hans Rubner*, who backed the project with similar enthusiasm and ensured the continuation of the ambitious undertaking by generous funding. We are particularly grateful to *Dr Albert Galvan*, who helped us overcome recurrent financial problems with an exceptional amount of personal commitment. Special thanks are also due to *Dr Alois Gartner*, executive manager of the *Ausbildungsförderung Alfred Amonn e.V.*, who helped us overcome many a project-related difficulty. We sincerely regret that *Dr Christoph Amonn* was sadly unable to see the project he supported come to fruition.

We also have to thank *Landesrat Dr Bruno Hosp* of the Cultural Department of the South-Tyrolean Provincial Government, *Dr Marjan Cescutti* and *Dr Josef Fontana* of the South-Tyrolean Cultural Institute, *Landesrat Fritz Astl* and *Dr Christoph Mader* of the Cultural Department of the Tyrolean Provincial Government, the *Austrian Forschungsgemeinschaft, Consul Dr Otto Kaspar* of the Bank of Tyrol and Vorarlberg, the *Tiroler Sparkasse*, the *Austrian Students' Union* and the *University of Innsbruck*. Explicit thanks to *Monika Meller*, without whose persistence and help the university would not have been included in the list of sponsors of this undertaking, which will prove to be of great help to both students and graduates .

Further, our gratitude must be expressed to those who consistently worked on the project, in particular *Silvia Breuss, Carl Albert Fähndrich, Heinz Hauffe, Helmut Kalb, Regina Obexer, Thomas Palfrader* and *Wolfgang Pichler* (listed in alphabetical order).

We must also thank those colleagues on whose expert knowledge we relied in establishing the accuracy of many translations. They are listed in alphabetical order: *Allan Janik* (University of Innsbruck and University of Vienna), *Kevin Mulligan* (University of Geneva), *J. C. Nyíri* (University of Budapest), *Graham Parkes* (University of Hawaii at Manoa), *Christian Piller* (University of York), *Peter Simons* (University of Leeds) and last but not least *Barry Smith* (University of Buffalo, State University of New York).

* * *

'Making a dictionary is like painting a bridge: by the time one coat of paint has been applied, the bridge is in need of another.' In view of the necessary incompleteness and scope for improvement of such a complex and ambitious undertaking we are grateful for suggestions concerning additions and amendments.

Elmar Waibl
Department of Philosophy
University of Innsbruck
elmar.waibl@uibk.ac.at

Philip Herdina
Department of English
University of Innsbruck
philip.herdina@uibk.ac.at

VORWORT

1. Zielsetzung

Fachwörterbücher für die globale Wissenschaftssprache Englisch sind für fast jede Disziplin schon lange eine Selbstverständlichkeit. Nicht so für die Philosophie! Das vorliegende Wörterbuch will diese Lücke schließen und ein Instrumentarium für den Erwerb von Fremdsprachenkompetenz im Fachgebiet Philosophie anbieten. Weil nach dem Vorbild anderer Disziplinen Englisch auch für die Philosophie zunehmend zur *lingua franca* wird, ist die Kenntnis der englischen Fachsprache eine entscheidende Bedingung für den Zugang zur internationalen *scientific community*. Mobilität – von Austauschprogrammen bis hin zu Gastprofessuren – ist an Fremdsprachenkompetenz geknüpft, und Mobiltätsbereitschaft ein wichtiger Wettbewerbsfaktor. Kompetenz im Bereich englischer Fachsprache ist daher eine zunehmend wichtige Voraussetzung, um die Chancen eines globalen Arbeitsmarktes nutzen zu können. Für die englischsprachige Welt ist dieses Wörterbuch ein Instrumentarium, um einen vertieften fachlichen Zugang zu derjenigen Sprache zu erschließen, die – durch Denker wie Kant und Hegel, Nietzsche und Freud, Heidegger und Habermas – für die Philosophie bekanntlich von besonderer Bedeutung ist.

Dieses Fachwörterbuch will neue Möglichkeiten auftun. Weil es sich dabei um ein Pionierunternehmen handelt und wir uns folglich nicht auf die Schultern von Vorgängern stellen konnten, waren wir naturgemäß mit allen Schwierigkeiten konfrontiert, die sich beim Betreten von Neuland ergeben: *Pigmei gigantum umeris impositi, plusquam ipsi gigantes vident.*

2. Auswahl

Die Frage der sinnvollen Abgrenzung stellt sich für jedes Wörterbuch und ist – wie jeder Wörterbuchbenutzer aus eigener Erfahrung weiß – immer nur annähernd befriedigend gelöst. Für ein Fachwörterbuch Philosophie ist diese Frage aber besonders schwierig, und zwar aus folgenden Gründen:

(1) Als Grund- und Integrativwissenschaft bzw. als Prinzipienlehre (des Seins, der Erkenntnis, der Ethik, der Kunst usw.) besetzt die Philosophie nicht einen Ausschnitt im Verbund der Wissenschaften, sondern greift mit Grundsatz- und Prinzipienfragen in so gut wie alle Wissens- und Wissenschaftsbereiche ein. Entsprechend breit ist folglich ihr terminologisches Spektrum und damit entsprechend groß die Schwierigkeit der Auswahl und Abgrenzung.

Wegen der vielen Berührungen mit anderen Fächern war es geboten, Fachwörter aus angrenzenden und umliegenden Wissenschaften mit aufzunehmen, wenn sie für die philosophische Diskussion eine Rolle spielen. Entsprechend dieser Richtlinie wurden beispielsweise Termini aus den Bereichen Mathematik, Wirtschaft, Technik, Kunst usw. aufgenommen, sofern sie für die *Philosophie* der Mathematik, für die

Wirtschafts*philosophie*, für die *Philosophie* der Technik und der Kunst relevant sind. Hingegen blieben technische Begriffe, die in diesen Bereichen von bloß disziplinimmanenter Bedeutung sind, ausgeklammert. Die Entscheidung wurde dabei in Absprache mit einschlägig in den einzelnen Bereichen tätigen Fachleuten getroffen. Weil die Auffassungen, welcher Fachwortbestand zu einem bestimmten Themenbereich der Philosophie gehört, selbstredend schwankend und von subjektiven Präferenzen beeinflußt sind, kann die getroffene Auswahl niemals zwingend sein. Was dem einen als entbehrliche Eintragung erscheinen mag, ist für den anderen aus bestimmten Gründen von großer Wichtigkeit. Jede getroffene Auswahl erfolgt somit im Wissen, daß es unmöglich ist, sich mit jedermanns Vorstellung zu treffen. Weil wir unsere Aufgabe als deskriptive Erhebung des Fachvokabulars verstehen, haben wir es vermieden, präskriptive Vorgaben darüber zu machen, was Philosophie zu sein hat.

(2) Historisch gesehen ist die Schwierigkeit der Verzahnung der Philosophie mit anderen Disziplinen angelegt in der Tatsache, daß viele wissenschaftliche Disziplinen ehemals Teil der Philosophie waren und sich erst in einem Prozeß der Ausdifferenzierung zu eigenen Fächern entwickelt haben. Die Mathematiker und Naturwissenschafter von ehemals waren größtenteils Philosophen, ebenso wie der Vater der modernen Wirtschaftswissenschaft Philosoph war. Analoges läßt sich von Rechts- und Staatstheoretikern, von Sozialtheoretikern, Kunsttheoretikern, Psychologen etc. sagen.

Gewisse – in der Regel sehr geringfügige – Überschneidungen mit großen Generallexika bzw. mit einzelwissenschaftlichen Fachwörterbüchern konnten kein Grund sein, die davon betroffenen Termini für dieses Fachwörterbuch auszuklammern. Wir haben es nicht zuletzt aus praktischen Gründen als Aufgabe eines Fachwörterbuchs angesehen, die einzelwissenschaftliche Terminologie, die in die Philosophie hineinspielt und folglich als philosophisch relevant angesehen werden muß, mit aufzunehmen, um dem Benutzer und der Benutzerin den meist sehr mühsamen Umweg über verschiedene, gerade im Ausland oft nur schwer zu beschaffende Auskunftsquellen zu ersparen.

Müßte man z.B. *Unschärferelation* in einem Wörterbuch der Physik, *Arbeitswerttheorie* in einem Fachwörterbuch der Volkswirtschaft und *Hochrisikotechnologie* in einem Wörterbuch der Technik nachschlagen, dann bräuchte man einen Riesenbestand an Wörterbüchern, die aber umgekehrt zu neunzig Prozent rein technische Fachtermini enthalten, die für die philosophische Diskussion mit Sicherheit nie benötigt werden.

Zu beachten ist auch, daß der Eindruck einer gelegentlich redundanten Auswahl oft nur vordergründig besteht. Das ist der Fall bei Eintragungen, die sich auch in Standardwörterbüchern finden, dort aber nicht in fachspezifischer, sondern in alltagssprachlicher Bedeutung (z.B. Heideggers *Zeug* oder *Gestell*). Was scheinbar der Alltagssprache angehört, erweist sich somit bei näherem Hinsehen als fachsprachlich relevant.

Aber auch in Fällen, wo sich die fachspezifische Verwendung eines Wortes mit der alltagssprachlichen deckt, erhält der Benutzer und die Benutzerin die nicht unwesentliche Information, daß die Übersetzung dem alltagsprachlichen Usus folgt. Weil dies in manchen Fällen so ist (siehe die vorhergehenden Beispiele), in anderen Fällen aber nicht, ist diese Klarstellung für die Benutzer von erheblicher Wichtigkeit.

Gelegentlich dienen Wörter der Standardsprache auch als Verweisbrücke für fachsprachliche Bildungen, z.b. *Interesse* für *Erkenntnisinteresse*, *Ironie* für *sokratische Ironie*, *Kolonisation* für *Kolonisation der Lebenswelt*, usw.

Schwierig ist natürlich auch die Frage, inwieweit selten gebrauchte und speziellen Schulen zugehörige Termini berücksichtigt werden sollen. Unter Wahrung des Kriteriums der Ausgewogenheit sind wir der Überzeugung, daß die Frage der Wichtigkeit von Eintragungen von den Vertretern der jeweiligen Richtungen und Schulen immanent entschieden werden muß. Heideggersche Spezialtermini werden einem Vertreter der analytischen Philosophie zum Großteil entbehrlich scheinen – wie umgekehrt Heideggerianer der Terminologie der analytischen Philosophie kaum Wert beimessen werden. Wichtig scheint uns, daß jeder Interessent jeder Richtung den Kernwortschatz vorfindet, den er in seinem Arbeitsbereich benötigt. Dem einen ist die *angeborene Tötungshemmung* der Aggressions- und Friedensforschung wichtig, dem andern die *exzentrische Positionalität* der philosophischen Anthropologie; dem einen der *Falsifikationismus* der Wissenschaftstheorie, dem andern die *Abschiedlichkeit* der Metaphysik. Jeder sollte Antworten auf seine spezifischen Fragen finden.

Personennamen wurden nur aufgenommen, wenn sie im Englischen von der deutschen Schreibung abweichen (z.b. *Aristoteles • Aristotle).*

Lateinische und griechische Termini wurden aufgenommen, sofern es sich um gängige Termini oder Wendungen handelt, die in der deutschen philosophischen Fachsprache eine Rolle spielen. Dasselbe gilt für die getroffene Auswahl aus der Terminologie der *asiatischen Philosophie.*

Bei allem Bemühen um eine angemessene Auswahl von Stichwörtern muß aber angesichts der besonderen Schwierigkeiten, die sich aus dem Charakter der Philosophie ergeben, klar sein, daß das Problem der fachbezogenen Wortauswahl nie endgültig befriedigend gelöst werden kann. Wer viel mit Wörterbüchern arbeitet, wird freilich zugestehen, daß wir mit diesem Problem nicht allein sind.

Da es meist sehr schwierig ist zu eruieren, wie *Werktitel* in der Zielsprache lauten, und Werktitel überdies oft über Wortverwendungen und Übersetzungen Aufschluß geben, wurde eine Auswahl an Werktiteln in einem Appendix zusammengestellt. Wo es aufschlußreich erschien, wurde von einem Stichwort im Hauptteil auf einen thematisch zugehörigen Werktitel im Anhang verwiesen.

3. Eintragungsmodus

Da ein zweisprachiges Fachwörterbuch naturgemäß nur von jemandem benutzt wird, der auf alltagssprachlicher Ebene mit der Zielsprache vertraut ist, wird – nach dem Vorbild von Fachwörterbüchern anderer Disziplinen – im Interesse einer

benutzerfreundlichen Übersichtlichkeit auf alles Entbehrliche verzichtet. Leitend war
für uns die Absicht, durch Eintragungsökonomie mit einem Minimum an Angaben
ein Maximum an Aufschluß zu geben.

- *Anordnung der Stichwörter:* Die Anordnung ist alphabetisch, wobei die Umlaute
(ä, ö, ü) wie die nichtumgelauteten Vokale (a, o, u) eingeordnet werden. Nach dem
Vorbild vieler Fachwörterbücher werden Wortgruppen und Aneinanderreihungen
Wort für Wort sortiert, wobei sowohl der Beistrich (z.b. bei *Tatsache, empirische*)
als auch der Durchkoppelungsbindestrich (z.b. bei *Tatsache-Wert-Unterscheidung*) für
die Sortierung ignoriert werden. Komplexe Wörter, die lediglich um der besseren
Lesbarkeit willen mit Bindestrichen geschrieben werden und wahlweise auch
zusammengeschrieben werden können (z.B. *Anti-Illusionismus/Antiillusionismus*),
werden hingegen als ein Wort sortiert, weil sich dadurch in der Anordnung
gelegentlich aufschlußreiche Begriffscluster ergeben. Nur bei Heidegger, der Binde-
strich-Schreibungen mit philosophischer Bedeutung aufgeladen hat (z.b.
Ent-fernung), wurde – um dieser Intention Rechnung zu tragen – die Eintragung
nicht so gewertet, als wäre wahlweise auch Zusammenschreibung möglich.

Die Anordnung der Eintragungen ist somit exemplarisch folgende:

Tatsache der reinen Vernunft
Tatsache, empirische
Tatsache-Wert-Unterscheidung
Tatsachenargument

- *Wortfolge in mehrteiligen Ausdrücken:* In Übereinstimmung mit dem verbreiteten
lexikographischen Usus erfolgt bei festen Wendungen die Eintragung unter dem
ersten Wort der Wendung (z.b. Nietzsches *blonde Bestie*), bei anderen Wortgruppen
hingegen unter dem bedeutungtragenden Bestandteil (z.b. *Seins, Wesen des*). Weil
der bedeutungtragende Bestandteil nicht immer eindeutig feststeht, wurde in
manchen Fällen eine Doppeleintragung in Kauf genommen. Dieser redundante
Eintragungsmodus ist in manchen Fällen vorteilhaft, weil sich dabei übersetzungstechnisch aufschlußreiche Begriffscluster ergeben.

- *Zusammengesetzte Nomen und Nomen mit Genitivattribut:* Viele Wortverbindungen sind im Deutschen sowohl als Nomen mit Genitivattribut (*z.B. Prinzip der Individuation*) als auch als zusammengesetzte Nomen (z.B. *Individuationsprinzip*) geläufig. Wo dies der Fall ist, wurden oft beide Varianten aufgenommen. Ansonsten
wurde dem üblicheren Gebrauch gefolgt.

- *Bindestrich-Schreibweise:* Ob eine Wortbildung (besonders bei *Anti-, Contra-* und
*Pseudo-*Präfixen) mit oder ohne Bindestrich geschrieben wird, ist häufig arbiträr. Um
dem Rechnung zu tragen, haben wir darauf verzichtet, die Schreibung in eine
Richtung zu vereinheitlichen oder beide Möglichkeiten anzuführen. – Die Hinweise
zur Anordnung sind zu beachten (siehe oben *Anordnung der Stichwörter*)!

- *Groß- und Kleinschreibung:* In Absprache mit Altphilologen wurden lateinische
und griechische Substantive groß geschrieben, wenn sie bereits – oder zumindest
weitgehend – den Charakter von deutschen Fremdwörtern angenommen haben; im

anderen Fall wurde Kleinschreibung gewählt. Es soll aber nicht verschwiegen werden, daß die Handhabung dieses Problems auch unter Fachleuten arbiträr ist. – Zur Groß-Kleinschreibung im Englischen siehe Punkt 6 (Übersetzungsproblematik).

– *Singular/Plural:* Substantive, deren Singular- und Pluralformen im Deutschen identisch sein können (z.b. *Hegelianer*), werden als Singular übersetzt *(Hegelian)*. Substantive, die üblicherweise oder ausschließlich im Plural vorkommen (z.b. *Eigentumsverhältnisse, notiones communes*), sind in der Pluralform angegeben und mit *pl* gekennzeichnet. Es wurde darauf verzichtet, dort, wo Singularformen bildbar wären, das Genus des Singulars in Klammer hinzuzufügen, und zwar deshalb, weil sich für die angegebene Übersetzung daraus gelegentlich Sinnentstellungen ergeben können. Es muß der Sprachkenntnis des Benutzers und der Benutzerin überlassen bleiben, diesbezüglich eigenständig vorzugehen.

– *Genus und Kasus:* Bei Wortgruppen aus zwei Substantiven gilt der Artikel für das Kernsubstantiv der Wortgruppe, z.b. *Abschreckungsfunktion des Gesetzes f: DIE Abschreckungsfunktion des Gesetzes;* aber ebenso für Wortgruppen, bei denen nicht das Kernsubstantiv, sondern das Attribut das relevante Stichwort bildet, wie *Sprachgeschöpf, Mensch als m: DER Mensch als Sprachgeschöpf.* Aus pragmatischen Gründen wird das Lemma im jeweiligen Kasus der Wendung angegeben, z.b. *Werdens, Stufen des.* Auch bei Wortgruppen aus Adjektiv und Substantiv wird das attributive Adjektiv aus ökonomischen Gründen meist in deklinierter Form verwendet (z.b. *ursprüngliches Sein* anstelle von *ursprüngliche Sein, das*).

Lateinische und griechische Termini sowie Termini aus der asiatischen Philosophie wurden – wo es sinnvoll ist – mit Genusangaben versehen, die aber nicht unbedingt das Genus der Herkunftssprache reflektieren, sondern sich nach dem eingebürgerten Fremdwortgebrauch im Deutschen richten. In schriftlicher Verwendung empfiehlt es sich, kleingeschriebene lateinische oder griechische Ausdrücke kursiv zu setzen (z.b. die *lex naturalis),* um der Regel Rechnung zu tragen, daß die Artikel im Deutschen ausschließlich Substantive bestimmen.

Nach Verlagsvorgabe und in Anbetracht des Umstands, daß das grammatikalische Geschlecht nicht unbedingt das natürliche Geschlecht spiegelt (z.b. das Wort *DIE Person,* das Frauen und Männer bezeichnet), wurde darauf verzichtet, bei fraglichen Eintragungen (z.b. *Logiker)* die weibliche Form *(lin*-Variante) dazuzugeben. Es ist dem Benutzer und der Benutzerin überlassen, diese Variante selbst zu bilden. Es war uns wichtiger, das einschlägige Vokabular der feministischen Philosophie und der Gender-Studies anzubieten, als die Genus-Varianten anzuführen, die in der Notation für ausländische Benutzer verwirrend sein können.

– *Reihung der Übersetzungen:* Wo Übersetzungsvarianten anzuführen sind, wird (soweit sinnvoll entscheidbar) durch die Abfolge gewichtet. Eintragungen mit einem Schrägstrich verstehen sich als Reihung von Alternativen. Die Eintragung *Grenz-begriff m • limit(ing)/boundary/marginal concept/notion* wäre beispielsweise zu lesen: *limit(ing)* oder *boundary* oder *marginal concept; limit(ing)* oder *boundary* oder *marginal notion.* Übersetzungsvarianten, die einen Bindestrich aufweisen, sind wie folgt zu lesen: *normal/bell-shaped distribution* als *normal distribution* bzw. *bell-*

shaped distribution, während *conflict- generating/producing situation* zu lesen ist als *conflict-generating situation* bzw. *conflict-producing situation.*

- *Systematische Indikatoren* (z.B. *epi, log, ant;* siehe Liste der Zeichenerklärungen) geben in Kurzform Aufschluß über den thematischen Ort eines Begriffs. In Fällen unterschiedlichen Wortgebrauchs werden durch die Angabe der Verwendungskontexte die Bedeutungsvarianten unterschieden und damit Mißverständnisse vermieden, z.B. bei *Primat m/n* • primacy *(log)*, primate *(nat, ant);* oder bei *Masse f* • mass *(nat)*, mass, crowd, the masses *(soc)*. Weil die thematische Zuordnung philosophischer Termini aber nicht immer eindeutig ist, ist zu beachten, daß die mit den thematischen Kürzeln vorgenommene Kurzkontextualisierung nur approximativen Charakter haben kann und die Zuordnungskürzel in einem weiten Sinn zu verstehen sind.

- *Autoren als Zuordnungsetiketten:* Wo es sinnvoll erschienen ist, verweisen zur weiteren Kontextualisierung in Klammern angeführte Namen auf die Autoren, mit denen die fraglichen Termini maßgeblich in Verbindung gebracht werden (was nicht unbedingt bedeuten muß, daß es sich dabei um die Urheber einer Wortprägung handelt). In manchen Fällen wird ein Name angeführt, um kenntlich zu machen, daß eine bestimmte Übersetzungsvariante im Hinblick auf einen bestimmten Namen gilt. Mehreren Namen werden unterschiedliche Übersetzungen zugeordnet, um die unterschiedlichen Bedeutungen zu spezifizieren, in denen die genannten Autoren einen Ausdruck verwendet haben. – In Anbetracht der Tatsache, daß nur fachlich versierte Benutzer und Benutzerinnen überhaupt in die Situation kommen, nach einem Fachwörterbuch zu greifen, wurde – mit Ausnahme der Fälle, wo Verwechslungsgefahr besteht (z.B. *Francis Bacon, Roger Bacon*) – auf die Nennung der Vornamen verzichtet.

4. Abkürzungen und Zeichen

a) *Kürzel der thematischen Zuordnung*

act	Handlungstheorie	*his*	Geschichtsphilosophie
aes	Ästhetik und Philosophie der Kunst	*jur*	Rechtsphilosophie
AI	Künstliche Intelligenz	*lan*	Sprachphilosophie
ant	Philosophische Anthropologie	*log*	Logik
asp	Asiatische Philosophie	*mat*	Philosophie der Mathematik
cul	Kulturphilosophie	*met*	Metaphysik
dec	Entscheidungstheorie	*min*	Philosophie des Geistes
eco	Wirtschaftsphilosophie	*nat*	Naturphilosophie
env	Ökologie	*ont*	Ontologie
epi	Erkenntnistheorie	*pol*	Philosophie der Politik
eso	Esoterik	*psy*	Psychologie
eth	Ethik	*rel*	Religionsphilosophie
fem	Feministische Philosophie und Gender-Studies	*sci*	Wissenschaftstheorie
		soc	Sozialphilosophie
gen	generelle Bedeutung	*sys*	Systemtheorie
gep	generelle Philosophie	*tec*	Technikphilosophie

Wir sind uns darüber im klaren, daß *asp* für asiatische Philosophie von den anderen Zuordnungen kategorial abweicht. Weil aus westlicher Perspektive die Herkunft der Fachtermini der asiatischen Philosophie häufig schwer zu bestimmen ist, und weil die obigen Zuordnungskategorien nur bedingt auf das asiatische Denken anwendbar sind, ist uns diese Zuordnung sinnvoll erschienen.

b) *Andere Abkürzungen und Zeichen*

f	*Femininum*
m	*Maskulinum*
n	*Neutrum*

Zwei durch Schrägstrich getrennte Kürzel geben an, daß sowohl der eine als auch der andere Artikel möglich ist (z.B. bei *Kalkül m/n*). Zwei mit Beistrichen aneinandergereihte Genuskürzel (z.B. *Erscheinung und Wirklichkeit f,f*) geben das Geschlecht der beiden Substantive an. Bloß ein Genus wird angeführt, wenn eine Wortverbindung geschlossen mit einem Artikel bezeichnet wird (z.B. Kants *Notwendigkeit-Zufälligkeit f*).

pl	*Plural*
nt	Das Wort wird im Englischen identisch übernommen. Steht *nt* und dahinter eine oder mehrere Übersetzung(en), dann bedeutet dies, daß sowohl der unübersetzte Begriff als auch die angeführten Übersetzungen verwendet werden.
▷	*Im Sinn von*
etc	Der Gebrauch erstreckt sich über die genannten Namen hinaus, und zwar chronologisch nach beiden Richtungen (z.B. *Hegel etc*).
/	Die vor und nach dem Querstrich stehenden Eintragungen sind wahlweise möglich.
°	*Mit Vorbehalt*. Die Übersetzung ist entweder unüblich oder erschlossen oder aus Gründen, die nicht im einzelnen spezifiziert werden können, als problematisch anzusehen.
;	Das Nachfolgende ist thematisch vom Vorhergehenden abgesetzt. So bezieht sich ein Verweis nur auf den Teil der Eintragung, der hinter dem Strichpunkt steht, z.B. *Mutualismus m • mutualism (nat); (Proudhon) (soc) < Tauschbank*. Der Verweis nimmt nur auf den Mutualismus im sozialphilosophischen Sinn Bezug.

5. Verweisstruktur

Im Gegensatz zu anderen Fachwörterbüchern beschränkt sich das vorliegende Wörterbuch nicht auf das Anführen der Übersetzungsäquivalenzen, sondern bindet die angebotene sprachliche Information in ein Netzwerk von Verweisen ein. Der Informationsgehalt des Wörterbuchs wird dadurch sowohl inhaltlich als auch übersetzungstechnisch gesteigert. Für die Verweise gelten folgende Zeichen:

→	verweist auf das Synonym
↔	verweist auf das Antonym
<	assoziativer Streuverweis
< W	Verweis auf das Verzeichnis philosophischer Werktitel

Es gilt zu beachten, daß bei Synonym- und Antonymverweisen die Synonymie und die Antonymie oft nicht im engen Sinn zu verstehen sind bzw. sich bei

Mehrdeutigkeit nur auf eine bestimmte Bedeutungsebene beziehen oder auf die spezifische Wortverwendung bestimmter Autoren Bezug nehmen (z.B. Kants *Verstand* ↔ *Vernunft* oder Jungs *Animus* ↔ *Anima*) .

Ohne Übersetzung wird auf das Synonym verwiesen, wenn im Deutschen der fragliche Ausdruck praktisch nicht mehr verwendet wird, z.b. *Alienation* → *Entfremdung.*
Ein rückläufiger Synonymverweis (z.b. *Verhaltensforschung* → *Ethologie, Ethologie* → *Verhaltensforschung*) findet sich, um in beide Richtungen den alternativ gebräuchlichen Terminus anzuzeigen. Auf einen rückläufigen Synonymverweis wurde verzichtet, wenn der Ausgangsbegriff veraltet und obsolet ist (z.b. *Gynäkokratie* für *Matriarchat; Hylismus* für *Materialismus*). Auf Umleitungseintragungen wird dann rückläufig verwiesen, wenn wir der Meinung sind, daß dies für den Benutzer aufschlußreich ist. Auf lateinische und griechische Termini oder Wendungen wird dann rückläufig verwiesen, wenn diese in der rezenten Philosophie noch eine wichtige Rolle spielen.

Der assoziative Streuverweis < versteht sich als weiterführende Gedankenbrücke, die einen assoziativen Fingerzeig geben will bzw. der weiteren Kontextualisierung einer Eintragung dienen soll.

6. Übersetzungsproblematik

Der Stichwortbestand wurde sowohl aus den Primärtexten als auch aus einschlägigen Enzyklopädien, Glossaren, Lexika und aktuellen Fachzeitschriften erhoben, die aus Umfangsgründen hier nicht bibliographisch angeführt werden können. Die Richtigkeit und Gebräuchlichkeit der von uns recherchierten bzw. selbständig erarbeiteten Übersetzungen wurde in der Endphase der Projektarbeit in einem mehrschleifigen Korrekturdurchgang von international anerkannten, in beiden Fachsprachen versierten Wissenschaftern, kritisch überprüft. Es sei allerdings betont, daß sich die philosophische Fachsprache – im Unterschied etwa zu den Fachsprachen der Medizin oder der Technik – durch besondere terminologische Komplexität und Diffizilität auszeichnet, was zur Folge hatte, daß in manchen Fällen auch die Meinungen der Skrutatoren nicht auf einen Nenner zu bringen waren, weshalb die letzte Verantwortung bei uns liegt.

Weil ein Fachwörterbuch kein erläuterndes Lexikon ist, wird bei der Benutzung die Kenntnis des nachgeschlagenen Fachworts vorausgesetzt. Es wurde deshalb vermieden, erläuternde Umschreibungen anstelle von Übersetzungen anzubieten.

- *Ungewöhnliche Bildungen:* So wie das Deutsche neigt auch die englische Fachsprache gelegentlich zu ungewöhnlichen Bildungen. Eine Nichtvertrautheit sollte nicht zur voreiligen Meinung verleiten, daß es diese im Englischen nicht gibt. So wie angesichts der schier unendlichen Komplexität sowie der Wandlungsfähigkeit der Sprache keinem noch so gebildeten Deutschsprachigen alle deutschen Wörter (einschließlich der Fremdwörter) geläufig sind, sowenig gilt dies für englische *native speakers* in bezug auf das Englische. Alle in diesem Wörterbuch angeführten

Fachwörter sind in anerkannten Nachschlagewerken belegt. Wo dies nicht der Fall ist, weil es sich um erschlossene Bildungen oder Kunstwörter handelt, sind die Übersetzungen mit einem kleinen hochgestellten Kreis ° markiert.

- *Zusammensetzungen:* Die Übersetzung zusammengesetzter Wörter (z.B. *Wahrheitstheorie: theory of truth, truth theory*) stellt ein spezifisches Problem dar. Es fällt auf, daß die Präferenzen des britischen und des amerikanischen Englisch diesbezüglich häufig auseinandergehen, ohne in sich einheitlich zu sein.

- *Varianten von Substantivendungen:* Bei abgeleiteten Substantiven finden sich neben den etymologisch naheliegenden Suffixen zunehmend auch Suffixe, die dem Sprachpuristen fraglich erscheinen mögen, z.B. *logicality/logicalness*. Die Eintragungen richten sich nach dem etablierten Gebrauch.

- *Historismen:* Da das Wörterbuch nicht nur die Gegenwartsphilosophie abdeckt, sondern die relevante Nomenklatur der gesamten Ideengeschichte berücksichtigt, kommen – ohne besondere Kennzeichnung – auch sprachlich veraltete Ausdrücke vor bzw. Ausdrücke, deren Bedeutung sich in der Zwischenzeit verändert hat, z.B. *politischer Körper - body politic (Hobbes)* .

- *Gebrauch:* Ausschlaggebend für die Übersetzung ist immer der jeweilige Sprachgebrauch und nicht die Symmetrie der Eintragungen. Dies erklärt die Abweichungen im Detail, die verschiedentlich innerhalb eines Wortclusters zu finden sind. So richten sich z.B. die Übersetzungen von Wortverbindungen mit *Zufall (Zufallselement, Zufallsentdeckung* etc.) nach dem jeweiligen kontextabhängigen Gebrauch (*random/ aliatory element, chance/accidental discovery* etc.).

- *Englisch/Amerikanisch:* Die verwendete Schreibung richtet sich nach den Normen des britischen Englisch. Da eine gleichzeitige Anführung der britischen und der amerikanischen Variante die Lesbarkeit der Eintragungen erheblich beeinträchtigt hätte, wurde darauf verzichtet, beide Varianten zu berücksichtigen. Häufige Abweichungen betreffen Wörter wie *behaviour*, US: *behavior; labour*, US: *labor; fulfilment*, US: *fulfillment; centre*, US: *center* etc.; sie sind mit Leichtigkeit den einsprachigen Standardwörterbüchern zu entnehmen. Eine Anzahl von Begriffen weist verschiedene Schreibweisen auf (z.B. *medieval/mediaeval*). In solchen Fällen wurde die gängigste Schreibweise gewählt und nicht unbedingt die etymologisch naheliegende. Sind einzelne Buchstaben, z.B. bei *judg(e)ment,* oder Wortteile, z.B. bei *dialectic(al)* oder *Lamarck(ian)ism,* in Klammern gesetzt, so sind damit Schreibvarianten angezeigt.

- *Groß-/Kleinschreibung der Übersetzungen:* Die Großschreibung im Englischen richtet sich nach dem Kriterium, ob etwas als Eigenname anerkannt ist oder nicht. Da der Gebrauch das entscheidende Kriterium ist, werden Schreibvarianten (z.B. *Theatre of the Absurd)* nicht berücksichtigt. Die Groß- bzw. Kleinschreibung von Fachwörtern, die aus dem Deutschen ins Englische übernommen wurden (z.B. *abschiedlichkeit, entwicklungsroman*), richtet sich nach dem Grad der Einbürgerung und ist arbiträr. Daß diese Germanismen im Englischen oft kursiv wiedergegeben werden, wurde hier ignoriert.

- *Einklammerungen:* Sind Teile der Übersetzung (Wörter) in Klammern gesetzt, z.B. *ontologischer Gottesbeweis m • ontological proof (of the existence of God),* so wird damit angedeutet, daß der Sachverhalt im Englischen sowohl in der ausführlichen als auch in der verkürzten Variante gebräuchlich ist.

Weil auf Grund der jeweiligen sprachlichen Eigentümlichkeiten und Sprachspiele Sprachen nur bedingt konvertierbar sind *(„traduttore traditore...“),* sind vor allem viele Fachwörter nur approximativ übersetzbar. Jeder Gebrauch eines Fachwörterbuchs hat diesem Umstand Rechnung zu tragen.

Danksagungen

Das vorliegende Wörterbuch wäre ohne den *Jubiläumsfonds der Oesterreichischen Nationalbank* und ohne die *Stiftung Südtiroler Sparkasse* nicht zustande gekommen. Die großzügige finanzielle Förderung dieser beiden Institutionen hat es ermöglicht, unser ehrgeiziges Projekt zu realisieren. Dafür gebührt ihnen unser nachdrücklicher Dank.

Namentlich danken möchten wir dem Doyen der österreichischen Bankwirtschaft, *Generaldirektor a.D. Präsident Dr. Heinrich Treichl,* der mit seiner tatkräftigen Unterstützung entscheidend dazu beigetragen hat, daß für die Projektarbeit die finanziellen Segel gesetzt werden konnten. Gleichermaßen zu Dank verpflichtet sind wir *Altsenator Präsident Dr. Hans Rubner,* der sich ebenso engagiert hinter dieses Projekt gestellt und dafür gesorgt hat, daß dieses große Unternehmen finanziell auf gesichertem Kurs bleiben konnte. Ein besonderer Dank gilt *Dr. Albert Galvan,* der uns mit seinem ganzen persönlichen Einsatz bei der Bewältigung finanzieller Probleme unermüdlich zur Seite gestanden ist. Dasselbe gilt für den Geschäftsführer der Ausbildungsförderung Alfred Amonn e.V., *Dr. Alois Gartner,* der uns mit seinem Entgegenkommen und Engagement über viele Schwierigkeiten hinweggeholfen hat. Wir bedauern zutiefst, daß wir *Dr. Christoph Amonn* unseren Dank für seine vielfältige Unterstützung und Förderung nicht mehr zu seinen Lebzeiten abstatten konnten.

Sehr zu danken haben wir auch *Landesrat Dr. Bruno Hosp* von der Kulturabteilung der Südtiroler Landesregierung, *Dr. Marjan Cescutti* und *Dr. Josef Fontana* vom Südtiroler Kulturinstitut, *Landesrat Fritz Astl* und *Dr. Christoph Mader* von der Kulturabteilung der Nordtiroler Landesregierung, der *Österreichischen Forschungsgemeinschaft, Konsul Dkfm Dr. Otto Kaspar* von der Bank für Tirol und Vorarlberg, der *Tiroler Sparkasse,* der *Österreichischen Hochschülerschaft* sowie der *Universität Innsbruck,* wobei es der Hilfe und Hartnäckigkeit von Frau *Monika Meller* von der Österreichischen Hochschülerschaft zu danken ist, daß unsere Universität sich um die Förderung dieser für die Studierenden und Absolventen so bedeutsamen Initiative zu guter Letzt doch noch Verdienste erworben hat.

Unser Dank gilt – stellvertretend für die vielen Mitarbeiterinnen und Mitarbeiter, die nicht alle namentlich angeführt werden können – auch denjenigen, die über lange Zeit am Projekt mitgewirkt haben (in alphabetischer Reihenfolge): *Silvia Breuss,*

Carl Albert Fähndrich, Heinz Hauffe, Helmut Kalb, Regina Obexer, Thomas Palfrader, Wolfgang Pichler.

Ein besonderer Dank gilt den Kollegen, die für die Überprüfung der Übersetzungen ihre Kompetenz zur Verfügung gestellt haben (in alphabetischer Reihefolge): *Allan Janik* (Universität Innsbruck/Universität Wien), *Kevin Mulligan* (Université de Genève), *J. C. Nyíri* (Universität Budapest), *Graham Parkes* (University of Hawaii at Manoa), *Christian Piller* (University of York), *Peter Simons* (University of Leeds) und *Barry Smith* (University at Buffalo, State University of New York).

* * *

„*Making a dictionary is like painting a bridge: by the time one coat of paint has been applied, the bridge is in need of another.*" Angesichts der unumgänglichen Unabgeschlossenheit und Verbesserungswürdigkeit einer derart komplexen Pionierarbeit sind wir für Verbesserungs- und Ergänzungsvorschläge offen und dankbar.

Elmar Waibl   *Philip Herdina*
Institut für Philosophie   Institut für Anglistik
Universität Innsbruck   Universität Innsbruck
elmar.waibl@uibk.ac.at   philip.herdina@uibk.ac.at

Dictionary of Philosophical Terms

Vol 1: German - English

Wörterbuch philosophischer Fachbegriffe

Band 1: Deutsch - Englisch

A

AAM•IRM *(Lorenz etc) (nat)* →
Mechanismus, angeborener auslösender

a posteriori • *nt (epi)* ↔ a priori < aposteriorisch

a posteriori-Wahrscheinlichkeit *f* • a posteriori probability *(sci, mat, dec)* ↔ a priori-Wahrscheinlichkeit

a posteriori-Wissen *n* • a posteriori knowledge *(Kant etc) (epi)* → Erfahrungswissen ↔ a priori-Wissen < Aposteriorität

a priori • *nt (epi, gep)* ↔ a posteriori < Apriori, das

a priori-a posteriori-Unterscheidung *f* • a priori/a posteriori distinction *(epi, sci)*

a priori-Wahrscheinlichkeit *f* • a priori probability *(sci, mat, dec)* ↔ a posteriori-Wahrscheinlichkeit

a priori-Wissen *n* • a priori knowledge *(Kant etc) (epi)* ↔ a posteriori-Wissen < Apriorismus

Abälard(us) • Abelard

Abarbeitungsmechanismen *pl* • working-off mechanisms *(psy)*

Abart *f* • variety *(gep)*, variety, modification, version *(gen)* → Varietät < Spielart

Abbild *n* • image *(Plato etc) (epi)* → Urbild; image, reflection, copy *(Marx etc) (epi)*, *(Wittgenstein etc) (lan)*, mimesis, depictive representation *(aes)* < Bild, Ektypus, Methexis, Nachbildung, Mimesis, Spiegelbild

abbilden • to represent, to depict *(Wittgenstein etc) (lan)*, to portray *(aes)*

abbildende Beziehung *f* • pictorial relationship, representing relation *(Wittgenstein etc) (lan)*

abbildende Darstellung *f* • mimesis, depictive representation *(aes)*

abbildendes Vermögen *n* • mimetic faculty *(aes)*

Abbildtheorie *f* • picture/copy/representation theory *(Wittgenstein etc)*, image theory *(epi, lan)* < Bildtheorie, Widerspiegelungstheorie, Wissen als Abbild der Wirklichkeit

Abbildtheorie der Erkenntnis *f* • picture/copy theory of knowledge *(Engels, Lenin, Lukács) (epi)* → Widerspiegelungstheorie

Abbildtheorie der Kunst *f* • mimetic/copy theory of art *(aes)* → Widerspiegelungstheorie der Kunst

Abbildtheorie der Sprache *f* • picture theory of language *(Wittgenstein) (lan)*

Abbildtheorie der Wahrheit *f* • picture/copy theory of truth *(epi, lan)*

Abbildung *f* • representation *(epi, lan)*, depiction *(aes)*, mapping *(mat)* < Projektion

abbreviative Definition *f* • abbreviative definition *(log, lan)* < Definition, partielle; Definition, operationale; Definition, implizite; Definition, persuasive

ABC-Kunst *f* • ABC art *(aes)* → Minimal art, Minimalismus

ABC-Waffen *pl* • ABC weapons *(pol)*

Abduktion *f* • abduction *(Peirce etc) (log, sci)*

abduktiver Schluß *m* • abductive inference *(Peirce etc) (log, sci)*

Abduktivismus *m* • abductivism *(log, sci)*

Abelsches Konvergenz-Kriterium *n* • Abel's convergence criterion, Abel's test for convergence *(mat)*

Abendland *n* • the West, the Occident, the Western World *(gen)* < W 1124

abendländische Philosophie *f* • Western/Occidental Philosophy *(gep)*

Abenteurer- und Raubkapitalismus *m* • predatory capitalism, robber-baron capitalism *(Weber) (eco, soc)*

Aberglaube *m* • superstition *(rel, eso)*

Abfolge *f* • succession, sequence (of consecutive terms) *(log, mat)* > Folge

Abfragesprache *f* • query language *(AI)*

Abfuhr *f* • discharge *(Freud) (psy)*

abgeleitetes Wissen *n* • inferred/inferential/mediate/derived knowledge *(epi)*

Abgeschiedenheit *f* • seclusion, retirement *(met, rel)*

abgeschlossen • closed, complete *(log, mat)*

abgeschlossenes System *n* • self-contained/closed system *(sys)* < System, geschlossenes

Abgeschlossenheitsrelation *f* • closure/completeness relation, closure operator/operation° *(mat, log)*

Abgrenzung der Wissenschaft *f* • demarcation of science *(sci)*

Abgrenzungskriterium *n* • demarcation criterion, criterion of demarcation *(sci)* < Sinnkriterium, Überprüfbarkeitskriterien

Abgrenzungsproblem *n* • problem of demarcation *(sci, gep)*

Abgrund *m* • abyss *(Heidegger) (ont)* < ontologische Differenz

Abhandlung *f* • treatise, essay *(gen)* < Essay

abhängige Ereignisse *pl* • dependent events *(mat, sci)* abhängige Variable *f* • dependent variable *(mat, log)* ↔ unabhängige Variable

Abhängigkeit *f* • dependency *(gep)* → Dependenz < Korrelation

Abhängigkeit, kausale *f* • causal dependence/dependency *(sci)* < Bedingtheit

Abhängigkeit, nonkausale *f* • non-causal dependence/dependency *(sci)*

Abhängigkeit, soziale *f* • social dependence/dependency *(soc, pol)*

Abhängigkeitsstruktur *f* • dependence-structure *(sys)*

Abhängigkeitssystem *n* • system of dependences, dependence-system *(Husserl, Reinach, Foucault) (epi, pol)*

Abhängigkeitsverhältnis *n* • dependence-relation, relation of dependence/dependency *(sci, soc, sys)*

Abiogenese *f* • abiogenesis, spontaneous generation *(nat)* → Urzeugung, generatio aequivoca

Abjunktion *f* • abjunction *(log)*

Ablaß *m* • indulgence *(rel)*

Ablaßhandel *m* • selling of indulgences *(rel)*

Ablaufplan *m* • operations plan *(sci)*

Ablaufplanung *f* • operations planning, scheduling *(sys)*

Ableitbarkeit *f* • deducibility, derivability, inferability *(log, lan)*

Ableitbarkeitsbeziehung *f* • derivability relation *(log)*

Ableitbarkeitsfrage *f* • question of derivability *(log, sci)*

ableiten • to deduce, to derive *(log)*

Ableitung *f* • deduction, derivation *(log)*, derivative *(mat)*

Ableitungskomplexität *f* • derivational complexity *(AI, min)*

Ableitungsregel *f* • rule of derivation, inference rule *(log)* < Deduktionsregel, Herleitungsregel

Ableitungsverhältnis *n* • relation of derivability *(log)*

Abneigung *f* • antipathy, aversion *(psy)*

abreagieren • to abreact *(Freud etc) (psy)*

Abreaktion *f* • abreaction *(Freud etc) (psy)* < Katharsis, kathartische Methode

Abreption *f* • abreption° *(rel)* → Trennung der Seele vom Körper

abrichten • to train *(Nietzsche) (psy)*, *(Wittgenstein etc) (lan)*

Abrichtung *f* • training, drill *(Wittgenstein etc) (lan)*; *(Nietzsche) (psy)* < konditionierter Reflex

Abrüstung *f* • disarmament *(pol)* < Friedensbewegung, Antimilitarismus

Abrüstungsverhandlung *f* • disarmament talks/negotiation *(pol)*

Abschattung *f* • profile, shadowing, adumbration, foreshortening, aspect *(Husserl) (met)*

Abschiedlichkeit *f* • abschiedlichkeit, readiness to depart *(Weischedl) (eth, met)*

Abschirmeffekt *m* • screening-off effect *(epi, dec)*

Abschnittsfolge *f* • adjoining sequence, sequence of (initial/final) segments, sequence of partial sums *(log, mat)*

abschreckende Wirkung *f* • deterrent effect *(pol, jur)* < Abschreckungstheorie

Abschreckung, atomare *f* • nuclear deterrence *(pol, eth)* < Vernichtungsdrohung, Terror-Frieden

Abschreckungsfunktion des Gesetzes *f* • deterrent function of law *(jur, pol)*

Abschreckungstheorie *f* • deterrence theory *(pol, jur)* < Gleichgewicht des Schreckens, Präventionstheorie

Abschreckungstheorie der Strafe *f* • deterrence theory of punishment *(jur, pol)*

Abschreckungstheorie des Gesetzes *f* • deterrence theory of law *(jur, pol)*

Absicherung, Grad der *m* • degree of entrenchment *(Goodman) (sci)*, degree of validation/reliability *(sci)*

Absicht *f* • intention, aim, purpose *(act)*

Absicht der Natur *f* • purpose of nature *(Kant etc) (nat, met)* < Naturteleologie

absichtliche Handlung *f* • deliberate/intentional act(ion) *(act)*

Absichtlichkeit *f* • deliberateness, purposiveness, intentionality *(act)* < Intentionalität

Absichtserklärung *f* • declaration of intent *(act)*, statement of intent *(Austin etc) (lan, act)*

absolut notwendiges Wesen *n* • absolutely necessary being *(met, rel)*

absolut Unbedingte, das *n* • (the) absolute unconditioned, that which is absolutely unconditioned *(Kant etc) (met)*

Absolute, das *n* • the absolute *(met)* < Unbedingte, das

Absolute, das unerkennbare *n* • the unknowable absolute *(epi, rel)*

absolute Aktivität *f* • absolute activity *(met)*

absolute Autorität *f* • absolute authority *(pol)*

absolute Dialektik *f* • absolute dialectic *(met)*

absolute Einheit *f* • absolute unity *(Kant etc) (epi, met)*

absolute Idee *f* • absolute idea *(Hegel) (met)*

absolute Identität *f* • absolute identity *(met)*

absolute Indifferenz *f* • absolute indifference *(Hegel) (met)*

absolute Mehrheit *f* • absolute majority *(pol)*

absolute Möglichkeit *f* • absolute possibility *(epi)*

absolute Monarchie *f* • absolute monarchy *(pol)* ↔ konstitutionelle Monarchie

absolute Musik *f* • absolute music *(aes)* ↔ Programmusik

absolute Negativität *f* • absolute negativity *(Hegel) (met)*

absolute Norm *f* • absolute norm *(eth)*

absolute Notwendigkeit *f* • absolute necessity *(Aristotle, Hegel) (met)*

absolute Realität *f* • absolute reality *(met)*

absolute Selbsttätigkeit *f* • absolute self-activity *(Kant etc) (epi, met)*

absolute Totalität *f* • absolute totality *(Kant, Hegel) (epi, met)*

absolute Vernunft *f* • absolute reason *(Hegel) (met)*

absolute Vollständigkeit *f* • absolute completeness *(met)*

absolute Wahrheit *f* • absolute truth *(met, rel)*

absolute Wahrscheinlichkeit *f* • absolute probability *(sci)* ↔ subjektive Wahrscheinlichkeit

absolute Weigerung *f* • absolute refusal *(Marcuse) (soc, pol)*

absoluter Begriff *m* • absolute concept *(met)*

absoluter Geist *m* • absolute spirit *(Hegel) (met)*

absoluter Herrscher *m* • absolute ruler *(pol)*

absoluter Idealismus *m* • absolute idealism *(Hegel etc) (met)*

absoluter Raum *m* • absolute space *(Newton) (nat)*

absoluter Wert *m* • absolute value/worth *(eth)*

absolutes Bewußtsein *n* • absolute consciousness *(met)*

absolutes Gehör *n* • absolute/perfect pitch *(aes)*

absolutes Gut *n* • absolute good *(eth)*

absolutes Ich *n* • absolute I/ego/self *(Fichte etc) (met)* < reines Ich

absolutes Maß *n* • absolute measure *(eth, nat)*

absolutes Moment *n* • absolute moment *(Hegel) (met)*

absolutes Subjekt *n* • absolute subject *(Kant, Hegel) (epi, met)*

absolutes Wissen *n* • absolute knowledge *(Hegel) (epi, met)*

Absolutheitsanspruch *m* • claim to absoluteness *(sci, rel)*

Absolution *f* • absolution *(rel)* → Lossprechung

Absolutismus, staatlicher *m* • state/political absolutism *(pol)*

Absolutsphäre des absoluten Ichs *f* • absolute sphere of the absolute/pure ego *(Husserl etc) (epi, met)*

Absolutsphäre des Bewußtseins *f* • absolute sphere of consciousness *(Husserl) (epi, met)*

Absorptionsgesetz *n* • law of absorption *(nat)*

Abstammung des Menschen *f* • descent of man *(Darwin)*, origin of man *(ant)* < W 27

Abstammungsgruppe *f* • ancestral/descent group *(soc, ant)*

Abstammungslehre *f* → Abstammungstheorie

Abstammungstheorie *f* • theory of evolution/descent, descent theory° *(nat)* → Deszendenztheorie < Evolutionstheorie

Absterben des Staates *n* • withering away of the state *(Marx) (pol)*

Abstimmungsverfahren *n* • voting procedure *(pol, jur)*

Abstinenz *f* • abstinence *(psy)*

Abstinenztheorie *f* • abstinence theory *(eco)*

Abstoßung *f* → Abstoßungskraft

Abstoßungskraft *f* • repulsive force *(Kant) (nat, met)*

abstractio formalis *f* • formal abstraction *(log)*

Abstractum *n* • abstractum, (the) result of abstraction *(gep)* → Abstrakte, das

abstrahieren von • to abstract from *(log, aes)*

abstrakt • abstract *(gep)* ↔ konkret

Abstrakte, das *n* • the abstract *(gep)*

abstrakte Kunst *f* • abstract art *(aes)* → gegenstandslose Kunst, nichtfigurative Kunst

abstrakte Spekulation *f* • abstract speculation *(met)*

abstrakte Struktur *f* • abstract structure *(gep)*

abstrakte Theorie *f* • abstract theory *(sci)*

abstrakter Denker *m* • abstract thinker *(Kierkegaard) (epi, met)*

abstraktes Allgemeines *n* • abstract universal *(met)*

abstraktes Denken *n* • abstract thinking/thought *(epi, ont)* ↔ konkretes Denken

Abstraktheit *f* • abstractedness, abstractness *(gep)*

Abstraktion *f* • abstraction *(gep)*

Abstraktion, formalisierende *f* • formalizing abstraction *(Husserl) (log, lan)*

Abstraktion, generalisierende *f* • generalizing abstraction *(Husserl) (log, lan)*

Abstraktion, idealisierende *f* • idealizing abstraction *(Husserl) (log, lan)*

Abstraktion, isolierende *f* • isolating abstraction *(Husserl) (log, lan)*

Abstraktion, mathematische *f* • mathematical abstraction *(mat)*

Abstraktion, negative *f* • negative abstraction *(sci)*

Abstraktion, positive *f* • positive abstraction *(sci)*

Abstraktion, qualitative *f* • qualitative abstraction *(sci)*

Abstraktion, quantitative *f* • quantitative abstraction *(sci)*

Abstraktionismus *m* • abstractionism *(James) (met)*

Abstraktionsebene *f* • level of abstraction *(gep)*

Abstraktionsgrad *m* • degree of abstraction *(gep)*

Abstraktionsklasse *f* • abstraction class *(Carnap) (log)* < Konstitutionstheorie

Abstraktionsprozeß *m* • process of abstraction *(gep)*

Abstraktionsstufe *f* • level of abstraction *(gep)*

Abstraktionstheorie *f* • abstraction theory *(log, lan, epi)*

Abstraktionsverfahren *n* • method of abstraction *(sci)*

Abstraktionsvermögen *n* • faculty of abstraction, abstractive faculty/ability *(epi, psy)*

Abstraktor *m* • abstraction operator, abstractor *(log)* < Lambda-Abstraktion

Absurde, das *n* • the absurd *(Camus etc) (met)*

Absurden, Philosophie des *f* • Philosophy of the Absurd *(met)*

absurder Held *m* • absurd hero *(Camus) (met)* < Mythos von Sisyphus

absurdes Theater *n* • Theatre of the Absurd *(aes)*

Absurdität *f* • absurdity *(gep)* → Widersinnigkeit, Sinnlosigkeit

Absurdität des menschlichen Daseins *f* • absurdity of the human condition *(Camus) (met)*

Abszisse *f* • abscissa *(mat)*

Abtreibung *f* • abortion *(eth)* → Schwangerschaftsabbruch < Kindstötung

Abtreibung, selektive *f* • selective abortion *(eth)* < pränatale Diagnostik

Abtreibungsbefürworter *m* • pro-choice advocate/supporter *(eth)* ↔ Abtreibungsgegner

Abtreibungsgegner *m* • anti-abortionist, pro-life activist *(eth)* ↔ Abtreibungsbefürworter

Abtrennungsregel *f* • rule of detachment *(log)* → modus ponens

Abwanderung *f* • migration *(soc)*

Abwanderung von Wissenschaft(l)ern *f* • brain drain *(soc)* → Brain Drain, Flucht der Intelligenz

Abwehr *f* • defence *(Freud) (psy)*

Abwehrmechanismus *m* • defence mechanism *(Freud etc) (psy)*

abweichende Meinung *f* • dissenting opinion *(pol, rel)*

abweichendes Verhalten *n* • deviant behaviour *(psy, soc)*

Abweichung *f* • deviance *(soc)*, deviation *(mat)*

Abweichung, mittlere *f* • mean/average deviation *(mat)* < Standardabweichung

Abweichung, primäre *f* • primary deviation *(mat, sci)* ↔ Abweichung, sekundäre

Abweichung, sekundäre *f* • secondary deviation *(mat, sci)* ↔ Abweichung, primäre

Abweichung, statistische *f* • statistical deviation/difference *(mat)*

Abwesenheit von Schmerz *f* • absence of pain *(eth)* < Lust-Unlust-Kalkül

abzählbar • countable, denumerable, enumerable *(mat, log)*

abzählbar unendlich • countably infinite *(mat)*

Abzählbarkeitsaxiom *n* • axiom of countability/numerability° *(mat, log)*

Abzählgrundsätze *pl* • counting principles *(Rawls) (eth)*

Achilles und die Schildkröte-Paradox(on) *n* • Achilles and the tortoise/turtle paradox, paradox of Achilles and the tortoise/turtle *(Zeno) (log)* < Zenos Paradoxien

Achsenzeit *f* • axial/pivotal age *(Jaspers, Blumenberg) (his)* < Krisenzeit der Weltgeschichte, Epochenschwelle

achtfacher Pfad *m* • eightfold way *(Buddha) (asp)*

Achtsamkeit *f* • heedfulness, mindfulness *(Heidegger) (ont)*

achtteiliger Pfad *m* → achtfacher Pfad

Achtung *f* • respect, esteem, reverence *(eth)*

Achtung der Person *f* • respect for the individual *(Kant etc) (eth)*

Achtung vor dem Gesetz *f* • respect/reverence for the law *(Kant) (eth)*

actio et passio *f* • action and passion *(met)*

actio et reactio *f* • action and reaction *(met)*

actio immanens *f* • immanent action/activity *(met)*

Action Painting • *nt (aes)*

actus purus *m* • pure act(uality) *(met, rel)*

actus/potentia *m/f* • *nt (Aristotle etc) (met)* < Akt-Potenz-Lehre, Dynamis und Energeia

Ad-hoc-Hypothese *f* • ad hoc hypothesis *(sci)* < Ad-hoc-Modifikation

Ad-hoc-Modifikation *f* • ad hoc modification *(sci)* < ad-hoc-Hypothese

ad infinitum • *nt (log)* < infiniter Regreß, Regreß, unendlicher

adaequatio intellectus et rei *f* • correspondence of the mind/intellect/thinking and reality *(Aquinas etc) (epi)*

Adaptabilität *f* • adaptability *(ant, psy)* → Anpassungsfähigkeit

Adaptation *f* → Adaption

Adaption *f* • adaption, adaptation, adjustment *(nat, ant)*, adaption, adaptation, accommodation *(soc)* → Anpassung

adaptive Planung *f* • adaptive planning *(sci)*

adaptives System *n* • adaptive system *(sci, sys)*

Adäquanz *f* • adequacy *(gep)* < Angemessenheit

Adäquanzbedingung *f* • adequacy condition *(sci, lan, log)* < Definition, beschreibende

adäquate Ursache *f* • adequate cause *(met)* → causa adaequata < hinreichende Ursache

Adäquatheit *f* • adequacy *(gep)* → Adäquanz

Adäquatheitsbedingung *f* • condition(s) of adequacy *(Hempel, Oppenheim) (sci)*

Adäquatheitskriterien für Definitionen *pl* • aedequacy criteria for definitions *(lan, log)*

Adäquationstheorie der Wahrheit *f* → Korrespondenztheorie der Wahrheit

Additionstheorem *n* • addition theorem *(log, mat)*

additiv • additive *(log, ont)*

Additivitätsproblem *n* • additivity problem *(eth)*

Adel *m* • nobility *(soc, pol)* → Aristokratie

Adel, geistiger *m* • intellectual elite *(cul)*

Adept *m* • adept *(rel, eso)*

adessentia *f* → Allgegenwart Gottes

Adäquation *f* • adequation *(Husserl) (ont)*

Addivität *f* • addivity *(Foucault) (epi, sys)*

Adiaphora *pl* • matter of indifference, adiaphora *(eth, rel)* < Amoralität, moralisch neutral

Adjazenz *f* • adjacency *(AI, min)*

Adjunktion *f* • adjunction *(log)* ↔ Disjunktion

administrative Rationalität *f* • administrative rationality *(Habermas) (soc)*

Advaita *n* • *nt*, non-duality *(asp)*

Adventismus *m* • Adventism *(rel)*

advocatus diaboli *m* • devil's advocate *(rel, sci)*

advokatorisches Denken *n* • advocatory thinking *(Jaspers) (met)*

Affekt *m* • emotion, affect *(psy)*, affect *(Kant) (eth)*, affection, passion *(eth)* < Affektenlehre

Affektambivalenz *f* • affect(ive) ambivalence *(psy)*

Affektenlehre *f* • theory of affects *(Spinoza) (eth)*

Affekthandlung *f* • act committed under the influence of emotion/passion *(act, jur, psy)*

Affektion *f* • affection, affectedness *(eth, psy)* < Wohlwollen

Affektionswert *m* • affective value *(eco)* → Liebhaberwert < Werttheorie, subjektive

affektiver Fehlschluß *m* • affective fallacy *(log)*

Affektlosigkeit *f* • apathy, freedom from passion, emotionlessness *(psy, eth)* → Ataraxie, Leidenschaftslosigkeit < Apathie

Affektstau *m* • emotional block(age) *(psy)*

affektuelles Handeln *n* • affectual action *(Weber) (soc, act)*

Affenkunst *f* • monkey art *(aes)*

Affenmensch *m* • ape-man *(ant)*

Afferenz-Efferenz *f* • afference-efference *(psy, min)*

affine Geometrie *f* • affine geometry *(mat)*

Affinität *f* • affinity *(log, lan, psy)* < Verwandtschaft

Affinität des Mannigfaltigen *f* • affinity of the manifold *(Kant) (epi)*

Affirmation *f* • affirmation *(epi, log)*

affirmative Kultur *f* • affirmative culture *(soc, cul)* ↔ Gegenkultur

affirmativer Charakter der Kultur *m* • affirmative character/nature of culture *(Marcuse) (aes, soc, cul)*

Affiziertwerden der Sinne *n* • affectation of the senses, becoming affected of the senses *(Kant) (epi)*

afrikanische Philosophie *f* • African philosophy *(gep)*

Agape *f* • agape *(rel, eth)* → christliche Nächstenliebe

Agapismus *m* • agapism *(rel, eth)*

agathon *n* • *nt*, the good *(eth)* → Gute, das

Agens *n* • agent, agens *(met)* → treibende Kraft < Movens

Aggregat *n* • aggregate *(Aristotle etc) (ont)* < Einheit

Aggregat der Erscheinungen *n* • aggregate of appearances *(Kant) (epi)*

Aggregateigenschaft *f* • aggregate property *(sys)* < emergente Eigenschaft

Aggregation *f* • aggregation *(nat, soc)*

Aggregatzustand *m* • aggregate state, state of matter *(nat)*

Aggression *f* • aggression *(psy)*

Aggression als Selbstbehauptung *f* • aggression as self-assertion *(psy)*

Aggression, bösartige *f* • malignant aggression *(psy)*

Aggression der Raubtiere *f* • predatory aggression *(Fromm) (psy)*

Aggression, defensive *f* • defensive aggression *(psy)*

Aggression, endogene *f* • endogenous aggression *(psy)*

Aggression, gutartige *f* • benign aggression *(psy)*

Aggression, instrumentale *f* • instrumental aggression *(psy)*

Aggression, interspezifische *f* • interspecies/ interspecific aggression *(nat, psy)* ↔ innerartliche Aggression, intraspezifische Aggression

Aggression, intraspezifische *f* • intraspecies/ intraspecific aggression *(nat, psy)* ↔ interspezifische Aggression

Aggression, konformistische *f* • conformist aggression *(psy)*

Aggression, offene *f* • overt aggression *(psy)*

Aggression, reaktive *f* • reactive aggression *(psy)*

Aggression, spielerische *f* • playful aggression *(psy)*

Aggression, spontane *f* • spontaneous aggression *(psy)* ↔Aggression, reaktive < primäre Feindseligkeit

Aggression, unbeabsichtigte *f* • accidental/ unintentional aggression *(psy)*

Aggression, verdeckte *f* • covert aggression *(psy)*

Aggression, verdrängte *f* • displaced aggression *(psy)*

Aggression, versteckte *f* • hidden/covert aggression *(psy)*

Aggressionskrieg *m* • war of aggression *(pol)*

Aggressionsneigung *f* • inclination to aggression *(psy)*

Aggressionstheorie *f* • theory of aggression, aggression theory *(psy, nat)*

Aggressionstrieb *m* • aggressive instinct/drive, aggression drive *(psy, nat)*

Aggressionsverhalten *n* • aggressive behaviour *(psy, nat)*

Aggressivität *f* • aggressivity, aggressiveness *(psy, nat)*

Aggressor *m* • aggressor *(psy, pol)*

Agieren *n* • acting out *(Freud) (psy)*

Agitprop *f/m* • agitprop *(pol)*

Agitproptheater *n* • agitprop theatre *(aes)*

Agnosie *f* • agnosia, state of not knowing, ignorance *(Plato) (epi, met)* → Nichtwissen, Unwissenheit

Agnostiker *m* • agnostic *(epi, rel)*

agnostischer Atheismus *m* • agnostic atheism *(rel)*

Agnostizismus *m* • agnosticism *(epi, rel)* < Nichtwissen, das

agogisch • agogic *(met, rel)*

Agon *m* • agon°, game, contest *(Burckhardt, Nietzsche etc) (cul, aes)*

Agrarethik *f* • agricultural ethics *(eth)* < ökologische Ethik

Agrargesellschaft *f* • agrarian society *(soc)*

Agrarkapitalismus *m* • agrarian capitalism *(soc, eco)*

Agrarpolitik *f* • agricultural policy *(pol, eco)*

Agrarreform *f* • agrarian reform *(pol, eco)*

Aha-Erlebnis *n* • aha experience *(Bühler) (psy)*

Ahimsa • *nt*, non-injury *(eth, asp)* < Gewaltfreiheit

ahistorisch • ahistorical *(his)*

Ahnenkult *m* • ancestor worship *(cul, rel)* → Manismus

Ahnenverehrung *f* → Ahnenkult

ähnlich • similar *(log)* < verwandt, ident

ähnlich-isomorph • order-isomorphic *(sys)*

ähnliche Mengen *pl* • similar sets *(mat, log)*

Ähnlichkeit *f* • similarity *(gep)*

Ähnlichkeitsbeziehung *f* • similarity relation *(Carnap) (epi, log)*

Ähnlichkeitserinnerung *f* • memory/recollection of similarity *(Carnap) (epi, log)* < Ähnlichkeitskreis, Quasianalyse

Ähnlichkeitsklasse *f* • similarity set *(Carnap) (epi, log)*

Ähnlichkeitskreis *m* • similarity circle *(Husserl, Carnap) (epi, log)*

Ähnlichkeitsmaß *n* • similarity measure *(AI, min)*

Ähnlichkeitsrepräsentation *f* • representation of similarity *(epi, log)*

Ähnlichkeitstransformation *f* • similarity transformation *(log)*

Ähnlichkeitszentrum *n* • centre of similarity/ similitude *(mat)*

Ahnung *f* • presentiment *(met)*

aisthesis *f* → Sinneswahrnehmung

Aitiologie *f* → Ätiologie

Akademie *f* • academy *(aes)* < Platonische Akademie

Akademie der Wissenschaft *f* • academy of science(s), academy of (arts and) sciences *(sci)*

akademische Ethik *f* • academic ethics *(eth)*

akademische Freiheit *f* • academic freedom *(eth)*

akademische Philosophie *f* • academic philosophy *(gep)*

akademische Skeptiker *pl* • academic sceptics *(epi, met)*

akademische Welt *f* • academia, academe, academic world *(gep)*

Akademismus *m* • academicism, academism *(aes, gep)*

Akatalepsie *f* • acatalepsy, incomprehensibility *(epi)* < Skeptizismus, Agnostizismus, Apeiron

akausal • noncausal *(met)*

Akkommodation *f* • accommodation *(Piaget)* *(psy)* < Adaption, Assimilation

Akkulturation *f* • acculturation *(ant, cul)* < Enkulturation, Kulturaneignung, Kulturbegegnung, Sozialisation

Akkumulation des Kapitals *f* • capital accumulation *(Marx) (eco)* → Kapitalakkumulation

Akkumulation, ursprüngliche *f* • original/primitive/primary accumulation *(Marx etc)* *(eco)*

Akkumulationsquote *f* • rate of accumulation *(eco)*

Akkumulationstheorie *f* • accumulation theory *(eco)*

Akosmismus *m* • acosmism *(Fichte etc) (met)* < Idealismus, Antirealismus

akroamatischer Grundsatz *m* • acroamatic principle *(Kant) (log)*

Akt *m* • act, action *(act, met)*

Akt-Potenz-Lehre *f* • act-potentiality theory *(Aristotle, Aquinas) (met)* < Dynamis und Energeia, actus/potentia

Aktcharakter *m* • act-character *(Husserl)* *(act)*

Akteur *m* • actor, agent *(eth, act, dec)* < Aktionsobjekt

akteurzentrierte Moralität *f* • agent-centred morality *(eth)*

Aktionsforschung *f* → Handlungsforschung

Aktionsmalerei *f* • action painting *(aes)*

Aktionsobjekt *n* • object of operation/action *(sci, act, dec)*

Aktionsplanung *f* • planning of action *(sci, act, dec)*

Aktionsvermögen *n* • power/faculty of/for action, active potentialities/powers *(Aristotle etc) (psy, met)*

Aktivismus *m* • activism *(pol)*

Aktivität *f* • activity *(Aristotle, Kant etc) (met)*

Aktlehre *f* • theory of acts/action *(Scheler)* *(met)*

Aktmalerei *f* • nude painting *(aes)*

Aktmaterie *f* • act-matter, act-material *(Husserl)* *(ont, act)*

Aktor *m* • actor, agent *(act, soc)* < W 34

Aktphänomenologie *f* • phenomenology of the act, act-phenomenology *(Geiger) (met, act)*

Aktuale, das *n* • the actual, that which is actual/real *(ont)* < Wirkliche, das

Aktualisierung *f* • actualization *(act, ont)*

Aktualismus *m* • actualism, actual idealism, topicalism *(Gentile etc) (met, cul)*

Aktualität *f* • (▷ Verwirklichung) actualization, realization *(ont)*; (▷ Wirklichkeit) actuality, reality *(Husserl etc) (epi, ont)* < Tatsächlichkeit

Aktualitätsphilosophie *f* → Aktualitätstheorie

Aktualitätstheorie *f* • actuality theory, theory of actuality *(Heraclitus) (ont)*; *(psy)*

aktualunendlich • actual(ly) infinite *(mat, log)*

Aktualwert *m* • actual value *(Meinong) (met)* ↔ Potentialwert

Aktutilitarismus *m* • act utilitarianism *(eth)* → Handlungsutilitarismus ↔ Regelutilitarismus

Akzeptabilität *f* • acceptability *(lan, eth)*

Akzeptabilitätsbedingungen *pl* • conditions of acceptability, acceptability conditions *(lan, act)*

Akzeptanz *f* • acceptance, acceptancy *(gep)*

Akzeptanz- und Verwerfungsregel *f* • acceptance-and-rejection rule *(sci)*

Akzeptanz-Nutzen *m* • acceptance-utility *(Hare etc) (eth)*

Akzeptierbarkeit, idealisierte rationale *f* • idealized rational acceptability *(Putnam)* *(epi, sci)*

Akzeptierungsregel *f* • rule of acceptance *(epi, dec)*

Akzidens *n* • accident *(Aristotle etc) (met)* ↔ Substanz

akzidental → akzident(i)ell

Akzidentalien *pl* • accidents, accidentals *(met)*

Akzidentalismus *m* • accidentalism *(met)* → Zufälligkeit, Theorie der

Akzidentalität *f* • accidentality *(met)* ↔ Substantialität

akzident(i)ell • accidental *(met)*

akzidentielle Aussage *f* • accidental predication *(sci)* < kontingente Aussage

Akzidenz *f* → Akzidens
Albertus Magnus • Albert the Great
Alchemie *f* → Alchimie
Alchemismus *m* → Alchimismus
Alchimie *f* • alchemy *(nat, eso)* < Stein der Weisen
Alchimismus *m* • alchemism *(eso, nat)*
Aleatorik *f* • aleatory *(aes)* < aleatorische Musik
aleatorische Erklärung *f* • aleatory explanation *(sci)*
aleatorische Musik *f* • aleatory/aleatoric music *(aes)*
Aleph null • aleph zero, aleph nought *(mat)*
aleth(e)ische Modalität *f* • alethic/truth modality *(met, log, epi)* < Wirklichkeits-modalität, epistemische Modalität
Aleth(i)ologie *f* • alethiology, alethology *(met)*
Aletheia *f* • aletheia, disclosure, unconcealment, unhiddenness, disclosedness, discoveredness *(Heidegger) (ont)* < Unverborgenheit, Wahrheit, Apeiron
Alexandria, Schule von *f* • School of Alexandria *(gep)* → Alexandrinische Schule
Alexandrinische Philosophie *f* • Alexandrian Philosophy *(gep)*
Alexandrinische Schule *f* • Alexandrian School *(gep)* → Alexandria, Schule von
Alexandrismus *m* • Alexandrianism *(his)*
Algebra der Logik *f* • algebra of logic *(Boole, De Morgan etc) (log, mat)*
algebraische Hülle *f* • algebraic closure/hull *(mat)*
algebraische Struktur *f* • algebraic structure *(mat)*
algorithmische Information *f* • algorithmic information *(log, mat)*
Algorithmus *m* • algorithm *(mat)* < Logarithmus
Alibi *f* • alibi *(act, eth)*
Alienation *f* → Entfremdung
All *n* • space, universe *(nat)*
Allaussage *f* → Allsatz
Allbeseelungslehre *f* → Panpsychismus
Allegorie *f* • allegory *(aes, lan)*
All-Einheit *f* • universal unity/oneness *(met, rel)*
Alleinherrschaft *f* • autocratic rule, (absolute) dictatorship *(pol)*
Alleinvertretungsanspruch *m* • claim to sole representation *(pol)*
alles fließt • everything flows, all is in flow/flux *(Heraclitus) (met)* → panta rhei

alles ist erlaubt • anything goes *(Feyerabend) (sci)* < Anything-goes-Prinzip
Alles-oder-nichts-Annahme *f* • all-or-nothing/none assumption *(sci)*
Alles-oder-nichts-Lösung *f* • all-or-nothing solution *(act, dec)*
Allgegenwart *f* • omnipresence *(rel, met)* → Omnipräsenz
Allgegenwart des Seins *f* • omnipresence of being *(rel, met)*
Allgegenwart Gottes *f* • omnipresence of God *(rel, met)*
Allgemeinbegriff *m* • universal concept, general term/notion/idea *(lan, log)*
Allgemeinbegriffe *pl* → notiones communes
Allgemeinbildung *f* • all-round/general education *(gen)* < Allgemeinwissen
allgemeine Argumentations- und Gewinnregeln *pl* • general rules of argumentation and winning *(dec)* < Gewinnstrategie
allgemeine Gegenstandstheorie *f* • general theory of objects *(Meinong, Husserl) (epi, met)* < formale Ontologie
allgemeine Gesetzgebung des Willens *f* • general legislation of the will, the will's own legislation of universal law *(Kant) (eth)*
allgemeine Gesetzmäßigkeit *f* • (▷ allgemeine Übereinstimmung mit dem Gesetz) universal conformity to law, universal regularity *(Kant) (eth)*; (▷ allgemeines Gesetz) universal law, general principle *(sci)*
allgemeine Gesetzmäßigkeiten des Werdens *pl* • universal laws of becoming *(ont)*, universal laws of development *(nat)*
allgemeine Gleichung *f* • general equation *(mat)*
allgemeine Idee *f* • general idea *(Plato etc) (met)*
allgemeine Logik *f* • general logic *(Kant) (log)*
allgemeine Meinung *f* • general opinion *(gen)* → opinio communis < herrschende Meinung
allgemeine Menschenvernunft *f* • human reason *(epi, eth)* < Gemeinsinn, gemeiner Menschenverstand
allgemeine Modelltheorie *f* • general model theory *(sci, log, sys)*
allgemeine Systemtheorie *f* • general system(s) theory *(Bertalanffy) (sys)*
allgemeine Übereinkunft *f* • general agreement *(soc, jur)*
Allgemeine und das Besondere, das *n* • the general/universal and the particular *(met)*
allgemeine Wesenheit *f* • universal essence *(met)*
allgemeine Wissenschaft *f* • general science *(Lull) (sci)* < ars generalis

allgemeine Wissenschaftsgeschichte *f* • general history of science *(sci)*

allgemeine Wissenschaftstheorie *f* • general philosophy/theory of science *(sci)* ↔ spezielle Wissenschaftstheorie

allgemeine Zustimmung *f* • common/universal consent/agreement/assent *(eth, pol, jur)*

allgemeiner Ausdruck *m* • general term *(lan)*

allgemeiner Begriff *m* → Allgemeinbegriff

allgemeiner Problemlöser *m* • general problem solver, GPS *(Simon) (min, AI)*

allgemeiner Satz *m* • general theorem *(log)*, general sentence *(lan)*, general/universal statement/proposition *(sci)* < Satz, allgemeingültiger; Allsatz

allgemeiner Term *m* • general/universal term *(log, lan)* → Allgemeinbegriff

allgemeiner Wille *m* • general will *(Rousseau etc) (soc, pol)* < volonté générale, Gemeinwille

allgemeines Additionsprinzip *n* • general summation principle *(log, mat)* < Wahrscheinlichkeit

allgemeines Dasein des Menschen *n* • man's general mode of being, the general mode of being human *(Marx etc) (ant, soc)*

allgemeines Gesetz *n* • universal/general law *(nat, sci)*; common law *(jur)* → Gewohnheitsrecht

allgemeines Naturgesetz *n* • universal law of nature *(nat)*

allgemeines Prinzip *n* • universal/general principle *(met, sci)*

allgemeines System der Formation und Transformation der Aussagen *n* • general system of the formation and transformation of statements *(Foucault) (epi, pol, lan)*

allgemeines Teilnehmungsgefühl *n* • universal feeling of sympathy *(Kant) (eth)*

allgemeingültig • universally/generally valid *(log, sci, eth)*

Allgemeingültigkeit *f* • universal/general validity, generality *(log, sci, eth)* → Allgemeinverbindlichkeit < Intersubjektivität

Allgemeingültigkeit der Wahrheit *f* • universal/general validity of truth *(epi, log)*

Allgemeinheit *f* • (▷ Öffentlichkeit) general public *(soc)*; generality, universality *(log)*

Allgemeinheitsbezeichnung *f* • notation/symbolism for/of generality *(Wittgenstein etc) (log)*

Allgemeinheitsstufe *f* • level of universality/generality *(Popper etc) (sci, lan)*

Allgemeinverbindlichkeit *f* • universal/general validity, generality *(log, sci, eth)* → Allgemeingültigkeit < Intersubjektivität

Allgemeinwissen *n* • general/common knowledge *(epi)*

Allgemeinwohl *n* • common wealth/weal, public good/welfare/interest, general good *(soc, eth)* → Gemeinwohl

Allgütigkeit Gottes *f* • omnibenevolence/allbountifulness of God, absolute goodness of God *(Plotin etc) (rel)*

Allheit *f* • allness, the universal *(met)*

Allmacht *f* • omnipotence, unlimited power *(rel, met)* → Omnipotenz

Allmacht Gottes *f* • omnipotence of God *(rel)*

Allmächtigkeit Gottes *f* • omnipotence of God *(rel)*

Allmachtsgefühl *n* • feeling of omnipotence *(psy)*

Allmachtswunsch *m* • desire/wish for omnipotence *(Freud etc) (psy)*

Allmende *f* • common resource/land/property *(eco, soc)*

Allmenge *f* • universal set, universe *(log)*

Allokation *f* • allocation *(eco, eth)*

Allokationseffizienz *f* • allocative efficiency *(eco, soc)* < Ressourcenallokation

Allokationsentscheidung *f* • allocation decision *(eco, eth)*

Allokationsproblem *n* • allocation problem *(eco)*

allokative Gerechtigkeit *f* • allocative justice *(Rawls) (eth)*

Allopathie *f* • allopathy *(nat)* ↔ Homöopathie

Allquantor *m* • universal quantifier *(log)* → Generalisator

Allsatz *m* • universal proposition/statement/sentence *(log, lan)* → Universalurteil

Allschönheit *f* → Pankalie

Allseitigkeit der Entwicklung *f* • universality of development *(Marx) (ant, soc)*

Alltag *m* • everyday life *(gep)* < Uneigentlichkeit; Man, das

alltägliche Umwelt *f* → Lebenswelt

alltäglicher Sprachgebrauch *m* • common/everyday/ordinary (language) use/usage *(lan)*

Alltäglichkeit *f* • everydayness *(Heidegger etc) (ont)*

Alltagsbewußtsein *n* • everyday consciousness *(epi)*

Alltagsdenken *n* • everyday thinking, common sense *(epi)*

Alltagserfahrung *f* • everyday/common experience *(epi)*

Alltagserkenntnis *f* • everyday/common-sense knowledge *(epi)* → Alltagswissen

Alltagskommunikation f • everyday communication *(lan, soc)*

Alltagskontext m • everyday context *(soc)*

Alltagsleben n • everyday/ordinary life *(soc)*

Alltagsobjekt n • everyday object *(Moore etc)* *(epi)*

Alltagspraxis f • everyday practice *(soc)*

Alltagspsychologie f • folk psychology *(psy)*

Alltagssprache f • ordinary language *(lan)*, everyday language *(gen)* → Umgangssprache < Normalsprache

alltagssprachlicher Begriff m • natural/ordinary language concept *(lan)* ↔ theoretischer Term, Fachbegriff

Alltagsverstand m • common sense *(gep)* → gesunder Menschenverstand

Alltagsverständnis n • everyday understanding/interpretation *(epi)*

Alltagswissen n • everyday/common-sense knowledge *(epi)* → Alltagserkenntnis

allumfassend • all-embracing, all-inclusive *(gep)*

allumfassende göttliche Einheit f • all-inclusive divine unity *(rel, met)* < Pantheismus

allumfassendes Göttliches n • all-inclusive divine *(met, rel)*

Allwissenheit f • omniscience *(rel, epi)* → Omniszienz

Allwissenheit Gottes f • omniscience of God *(rel, met)*

Allzeitlichkeit f • omnitemporality *(Husserl)* *(epi, met)*

Almosengeben n • almsgiving *(rel, eth)*

alogisch • alogical *(log)*

Alphabetisierung f • alphabetization *(gen)*

Alphabetisierungskampagne f • literacy campaign *(pol)*

Alphabetisierungsrate f • literacy rate *(soc)*

Alphastrahlen pl • alpha radiation *(nat)*

Als-Ob n • as if *(Kant, Vaihinger etc)* *(met, epi)* < Fiktion, wissenschaftliche < W 770

als-ob-Gesetzmäßigkeit f • as if regularity *(Popper etc)* *(sci)*

Als-Struktur f • as-structure *(Heidegger)* *(ont)*

alte Sprachen pl • classical languages *(lan)*

alter ego n • alter ego, second self *(psy)*

Alternation f • alternation *(log, lan)* < Disjunktion

Alternativ, das n • the alternative *(log)*

Alternativbewegung f • alternative movement *(soc)* < Subkultur, Gegenkultur, Gegenbewegung

Alternative f • alternative *(act)* < Handlungsfreiheit

alternative Ökonomie f • alternative economy *(eco, env)* < nachhaltiges Wachstum, Nachhaltigkeit

Alternativenergiequellen pl • alternative energy sources *(env)*

Alternativgesellschaft f • alternative society *(soc)*

Alternativhypothese f • alternative hypothesis *(sci)* < Nullhypothese

Alternativlösung f • alternative solution *(gep)*

Alternativmedizin f • alternative medicine *(nat)* ↔ Schulmedizin < Ganzheitsmedizin, Komplementärmedizin

Alternator m • alternator *(log)* < Disjunktor

alternierende Folge f • alternation *(sys)* → Wechselfolge

Altersklassensystem n • age class system *(soc, cul)*

Alterspyramide f • age pyramid *(soc)*

Altersstruktur f • age structure/pattern *(soc)*

Altertumskunde f → Archäologie

Althegelianer m • Old Hegelian *(gep)* → Rechtshegelianer ↔ Junghegelianer, Neuhegelianer

Altruismus m • altruism *(eth)* → Selbstlosigkeit, Uneigennützigkeit ↔ Egoismus

Altruismus, reziproker m • reciprocal altruism *(eth)* < Selbstlosigkeit

altruistisches Verhalten n • altruistic behaviour *(eth)*

ambig • ambiguous *(log, lan)* → amphibolisch

Ambiguität f • ambiguity *(log, lan)* → Doppeldeutigkeit, Mehrdeutigkeit, Vieldeutigkeit, Zweideutigkeit, Amphibolie, Äquivokation

Ambiguität, logische f • logical ambiguity *(log)* < Amphibolie

Ambiguität, moralische f • moral ambiguity *(eth)*

Ambiguität, semantische f • semantic ambiguity *(lan)*

Ambiguität, syntaktische f • syntactic ambiguity, amphiboly *(Aristotle)* *(log, lan)*

Ambivalenz f • ambivalence *(log, lan, psy)*

Ambrosius • Ambrose

Amerikanistik f • American studies

Ametrie f • ametry *(aes)* → Disproportion, Mißverhältnis, Ungleichmäßigkeit

Amnesie f • amnesia *(psy)* → Gedächtnisverlust

Amnesie, infantile f • infantile amnesia *(Freud)* *(psy)*

Amnestie f • amnesty *(jur, pol)*

Amor fati *m* • amor fati, willing acceptance/ love of one's fate *(Nietzsche etc) (met)*

Amoral *f* • amorality *(eth)*

amoralisch • amoral *(eth)* < immoralisch, unmoralisch

Amoralismus *m* • amoralism *(eth)*

Amoralität *f* • amorality *(eth)* < Immoralität

Amorphie *f* • amorphism *(nat, aes)* → Amorphismus

Amorphismus *m* • amorphism *(nat, aes)* → Gestaltlosigkeit

amour de soi • *nt*, love of self *(Rousseau) (eth, psy)* → Selbstliebe

amour propre • *nt*, selfishness *(Rousseau) (eth, psy)* → Selbstsucht

Amphibiennatur des Menschen *f* • amphibious nature of man *(Nietzsche) (ant)*

Amphibolie *f* • amphiboly, amphibology, amphibolia *(log, lan)* → Ambiguität

Amphibolie der Reflexionsbegriffe *f* • amphiboly of the concepts of reflection *(Kant) (epi)*

amphibolisch • amphibolous, amphibological *(log, lan)* → ambig

Amtsautorität *f* • authority of office *(Cyprian, Augustine) (jur, rel)*

Amusie *f* • amusia *(aes)*

an sich sein • being in itself *(met)*

an und für sich • in and for itself *(Hegel etc) (met)*

Anachronismus *m* • anachronism *(his)*

Anagnorisis *f* • anagnorisis, recognition *(aes)*

Anagogé *f* • anagoge, anagogy *(rel, log)* ↔ Apagogé

anagogisch • anagogic(al) *(rel, log)*

anagogische Deutung *f* • anagogic interpretation *(Silberer) (psy)*

anagogische Methode *f* • anagogic(al) method *(Plotin etc) (met)*

analer Charakter *m* • anal character *(Freud etc) (psy)*

Analerotik *f* • anal eroticism *(Freud etc) (psy)*

analog • analog(ue) *(AI, mat)* ↔ digital

analoge Gotteserkenntnis *f* • knowledge of God via/by analogy, analogous knowledge of God *(rel)*

analoger Computer *m* • analog(ue) computer *(AI)* ↔ Digitalcomputer < Turing-Maschine

analoges Schließen *n* • analogical inference/ reasoning *(log, AI)*

analogia entis *f* • analogy of being *(Aquinas etc) (ont)*

analogia fidei *f* • analogy of faith/doctrine *(Augustine) (rel)* → Analogie des Glaubens

Analogie *f* • analogy *(log, lan)*

Analogie, arithmetische *f* • arithmetic(al) analogy *(Archytas of Tarent) (mat)*

Analogie des Glaubens *f* • analogy of faith/ doctrine *(Augustine) (rel)* → analogia fidei

Analogie, formale *f* • formal analogy *(lan)*

Analogie, funktionale *f* • functional analogy *(sys)*

Analogie, geometrische *f* • geometrical/ geometric analogy *(Archytas of Tarent) (mat, met)*

Analogie, harmonische *f* • harmonic/harmonical analogy *(Archytas of Tarent) (mat, met)*

Analogie, stoffliche *f* • material analogy *(lan)*

Analogie, strukturelle *f* • structural analogy *(gep)* < Isomorphismus

Analogieargument *n* • argument from analogy *(log)*

Analogiebildung *f* • analogy formation *(gep)*

Analogiedenken *n* • analogical thinking *(gep)*

Analogielehre *f* • doctrine of analogy *(Plato etc) (met)*

Analogien der Erfahrung *pl* • analogies of experience *(Kant etc) (epi)*

Analogieschluß *m* • analogical inference, argument by analogy *(log)* → Analogismus

Analogieverfahren *n* • method of analogy *(Aristotle) (log, sci)*

Analogiezauber *m* • voodoo/sympathetic magic *(rel, eso)*

analogisieren • to analogize *(gep)*

Analogismus *m* • analogism *(log)* → Analogieschluß

analogon rationis *n* • *nt*, analogue of reason *(Wolff, Baumgarten) (epi, aes)*

Analphabetisierungsrate *f* • illiteracy rate *(soc)*

Analphase *f* • anal phase/stage *(Freud etc) (psy)*

Analysand *m* • analysand *(psy)*

Analysator *m* • analyser *(psy, nat)*

Analyse *f* • analysis *(log, mat, psy)*

Analyse abweichender Fälle *f* • deviant case analysis *(mat)*

Analyseparadox *n* • paradox of analysis *(Moore) (log, lan)*

Analysis *f* • analysis *(log, mat)*

Analytik *f* • analytic(s) *(Aristotle etc) (log, epi)* < W 287, 1370

Analytik der Begriffe *f* • analytic of concepts *(Kant) (epi)*

Analytik der Grundsätze *f* • analytic of principles *(Kant) (epi)*

Analytik der teleologischen Urteilskraft *f •* analytic of teleological judg(e)ment *(Kant) (epi)*

Analytik des Erhabenen *f •* analytic of the sublime *(Kant) (epi, aes)*

Analytik des Schönen *f •* analytic of the beautiful *(Kant) (epi, aes)*

Analytik, existentiale *f •* existential analytic *(Heidegger etc) (ont)*

Analytik, transzendentale *f •* transcendental analytic(s) *(Kant) (epi)*

Analytiker *m •* (▷ analytischer Philosoph) analytic philosopher *(log);* analyst *(psy)*

analytisch • analytic(al) *(log)*

Analytisch-Allgemeine, das *n •* (the) analytic universal *(Kant) (epi)*

analytisch in s • analytic in s *(Carnap) (sci)*

analytisch-synthetisch-Unterscheidung *f •* analytic-synthetic distinction *(epi, lan)*

analytische Ästhetik *f •* analytic aesthetics *(aes)*

analytische Aussage *f •* analytic(al) statement *(Frege etc) (lan, log)*

analytische Einheit *f •* analytic(al) unity *(Kant) (epi)*

analytische Ethik *f •* analytical ethics *(eth)*

analytische Geometrie *f •* analytic(al) geometry *(mat)*

analytische Logik *f •* analytic(al) logic *(log)*

analytische Maschine *f •* analytical engine *(Babbage) (mat, tec)* < Differenzmaschine, Rechenmaschine

analytische Metaphysik *f •* analytic(al) metaphysics *(met)*

analytische Methode *f •* analytic(al) method, method of analysis *(epi, sci)* < resolutiv-rekompositive Methode

analytische Notwendigkeit *f •* analytic necessity *(log, lan)*

analytische Opposition *f •* analytic(al) opposition *(Kant) (epi, log)*

analytische Philosophie *f •* analytic(al) philosophy *(gep)*

analytische Psychologie *f •* analytic psychology *(Jung etc) (psy)*

analytische Statistik *f •* analytical statistics *(mat)*

analytische Wahrheit *f •* analytic(al) truth *(epi, log, lan)* < logische Wahrheit

analytische Wissenschaftstheorie *f •* analytic theory/philosophy of science *(sci)*

analytisches Denken *n •* analytic(al) thinking *(epi)*

analytisches Urteil *n •* analytic judg(e)ment *(epi, log)* → Erläuterungsurteil ↔ synthetisches Urteil

analytisches Urteil a priori *n •* analytic a priori judg(e)ment, analytic jugd(e)ment a priori *(Kant) (epi, log)*

Analytizität *f •* analyticity *(log, lan)*

Analytizitätspostulat *n •* analyticity postulate *(Carnap) (log, lan)* < Bedeutungspostulat

Anamnese *f →* Anamnesis

Anamnesis *f •* anamnesis, recollection *(Plato etc) (epi, met)* → Wiedererinnerung

Anamnesislehre *f •* doctrine of recollection *(Plato etc) (epi, met)*

Ananke *f •* destiny, fate *(Parmenides, Plato etc) (met)* → Schicksal

Anapher *f •* anaphora *(lan)*

Anarchie *f •* anarchy *(pol)* → Gesetzlosigkeit < Anomie

Anarchie in der Produktion *f •* anarchy in/of production *(Marx) (eco)*

Anarchismus *m •* anarchism *(Godwin, Proudhon etc) (soc, pol, eth)*

Anarchismus, individualistischer *m •* individualistic anarchism *(Stirner) (pol, met)*

Anarchismus, kommunistischer *m •* communist(ic) anarchism *(Kropotkin) (pol)*

Anarchismus, pazifistischer *m •* pacifist anarchism *(Tolstoi) (pol)*

anarchistische Bewegung *f •* anarchistic movement *(pol)*

anarchistische Erkenntnistheorie *f •* anarchistic epistemology *(Feyerabend) (sci)* < erkenntnistheoretischer Anarchismus, Anything-Goes-Prinzip

Anarchokapitalismus *m •* anarcho-capitalism *(pol)*

Anarchokommunismus *m •* anarcho-communism *(pol)*

Anarchosyndikalismus *m •* anarcho-syndicalism *(pol)*

Anatta • anatta, absence of personal/immortal soul *(asp)*

ancilla theologiae *f •* handmaiden of theology *(gep)* < Philosophie als Magd der Theologie

Andere, das *n •* the other *(Plato, Hegel etc) (ont, met)*

Andere, der *m •* the Other *(Sartre etc) (met)*

Andere, der generalisierte *m •* the generalized other *(Mead) (soc, psy)*

Andere, der phänomenale *m •* the phenomenal other *(soc, psy)*

andere Geschlecht, das *n •* the other sex *(de Beauvoir) (fem)* < W 65

Andersartigkeitsfeminismus *m* • difference feminism *(fem)* → Differenzfeminismus, Geschlechtsfeminismus

Andersgerichtetheit *f* • other-directedness *(soc, psy); (Heidegger) (ont)*

Andersgläubiger *m* • one of a different faith *(rel)*

Andersheit *f* • otherness *(Plato etc) (met)*

Anderssein *n* • being other *(met)*

Änderungsrate *f* • rate of change *(mat, sys)*

Androgynie *f* • androgyny *(nat, psy, fem)*

Androphobie *f* • androphobia *(fem)*

androzentrische Geschlechterpolitik *f* • androcentric gender politics *(fem)*

Androzentrismus *m* • androcentrism *(fem)* < Machismo

Aneignung *f* • appropriation *(Marx etc) (soc)*, assimilation *(Jaspers) (met)*

Aneignung der Wirklichkeit *f* • appropriation of reality *(Marx) (epi, soc)*

Aneignung des Diskurses *f* • appropriation of discourse *(Foucault) (epi, pol)*

Aneignung des menschlichen Wesens *f* • appropriation of (the) human essence *(Marx etc) (ant, soc)*

Aneignung fremder Arbeit *f* • appropriation of alien labour *(Marx) (eco)* → Ausbeutung

Aneignung, ästhetische *f* • aesthetic appropriation *(aes)*

Aneignungsprozeß *m* • process of appropriation *(Marx etc) (soc)*

Anerkennung *f* • acknowledgment *(Hegel etc) (met)*; recognition *(gen)*

Anerkennungserwartung *f* • expectation of recognition *(lan, soc)*

Anerkennungswürdigkeit *f* • worthiness of being recognized *(Habermas) (lan, soc)*

Anfang in der Zeit *m* • beginning in time *(met)*

Anfängergeist *m* • beginner's mind *(asp)*

Anfangsbedingung *f* • initial/boundary condition *(mat, sci)* < Ausgangsbedingung, Rahmenbedingung

Anfangsgrund der Erfahrung *m* • starting point of experience *(Kant etc) (epi)*

Anfangsgrund der Erkenntnis *m* • starting point of knowledge, antecedent ground of knowledge *(Kant) (epi)*

Anfangslosigkeit *f* • beginninglessness *(met, eso)*

Anfangsmenge *f* • initial set *(mat, log)*

Anfangsproblem *n* • initial problem *(gep)*

Anfangsregel *f* • initial/assumption rule *(mat, log)*

Anfangswert *m* • initial value *(sci)* < Ursachenwert

Anfangszustand *m* • initial state *(gep)* ↔ Endzustand

anfechtbar • disputable, contestable *(gep)*

Anfechtbarkeit *f* • defeasibility, contestability, disputability *(gep)* < Widerlegbarkeit

Anführung *f* • mention, quotation, adduction° *(log, lan)*

angeboren • innate, connate *(nat, ant)* < Vererbung

angeborene Aggression *f* • innate aggression *(ant, psy)*

angeborene Disposition *f* • innate disposition *(ant, psy)* < konstitutionelle Bedingungen

angeborene Erkenntnis *f* • innate knowledge *(Descartes etc) (epi)*

angeborene Ideen *pl* • innate ideas *(Descartes etc) (epi)* → eingeborene Ideen

angeborene Neigung *f* • inborn tendency, innate (pre)disposition *(Locke etc) (psy)*

angeborene Tötungshemmung *f* • inborn inhibition against killing/ to kill *(Eibl-Eibesfeld) (ant)*

angeborene Verhaltensdisposition *f* • inborn behavioural disposition *(psy)* < angeborene Neigung

angeborener auslösender Mechanismus *m* • innate releasing mechanism, IRM *(Lorenz etc) (nat)* → AAM

angeborener Begriff *m* • innate concept *(epi, lan)*

angeborenes Verhalten *n* • innate behaviour *(psy)*

angeborenes Wissen *n* • innate knowledge *(epi)*

Angeborenheit *f* • innateness *(nat, ant)* < Nativismus, Genie, Natur oder Kultur, Urvermögen

Angeborenheitshypothese *f* • innateness hypothesis *(Chomsky etc) (lan)*

Angeborenheitsthese *f* • innateness thesis, innatism *(nat, epi)*

Angebot und Nachfrage *n,f* • supply and demand *(eco)* < Marktgesetze, Marktnachfrage

Angebotsknappheit *f* • shortage/scarcity (of supply) *(eco)*

angebotsorientierte Wirtschaft *f* • supply (side) economy, supply-oriented economy *(eco)*

Angelologie *f* → Engellehre

Angemessenheit *f* • appropriateness, adequacy, fittingness *(act, lan, eth)* < Adäquanz

Angemessenheit der Mittel *f* • appropriateness of means *(eth)*

Angenehme, das *n* • the agreeable *(Kant) (aes)*

angepaßte Technologie f • appropriate technology *(tec)*

Angestellter m • employee, white collar worker *(eco)* < Arbeiter

angewandte Ethik f • applied ethics *(eth)* < Bereichsethik

angewandte Forschung f • applied research *(sci)*

angewandte Kunst f • applied/decorative art *(aes)*

angewandte Logik f • applied logic *(log)*

angewandte Mathematik f • applied mathematics *(mat)*

angewandte Psychologie f • applied psychology *(psy)*

angewandte Soziologie f • applied sociology *(soc)*

angewandte Wissenschaft f • applied science *(sci)* ↔ reine Wissenschaft

Angewiesenheit, wechselseitige f • mutual/reciprocal dependency *(soc, eth, sys)*

Angriffskrieg m • war of aggression *(pol)* ↔ Defensivkrieg, Verteidigungskrieg

Angst f • anxiety, anguish, dread *(psy)* < Sorge, Verzweiflung, Furcht

Angst, existentielle f • Angst, existential dread *(met)* < Daseinsangst

Angst vor dem Nichts f • fear of nothingness *(met) (Sartre)*

Angst vor dem Über-Ich f • fear of the superego *(Freud) (psy)*

Angstlust f • thrill, angstlust *(psy)*

Angstneurose f • anxiety neurosis *(Freud etc) (psy)*

Angstsignal n • signal of anxiety *(Freud) (psy)*

Angstzustand m • anxiety state *(psy)*

Anicca • anicca, impermanence *(asp)*

Anima f • anima, female aspect of the human spirit *(Jung) (ant, psy)* ↔ Animus

animal rationale n • rational animal *(Aristotle) (ant)* → vernunftbegabtes Wesen, Vernunftwesen

animal sociale n • social animal *(Aristotle) (ant)* < gesellige Natur, zoon politicon

animalisch • bestial, brutish, animal *(nat, eth)*

animalische Natur des Menschen f • animal/bestial/brutish nature of man *(ant, eth)*

Animalität im Menschen f • animality in man *(Kant) (ant, nat)*

Animation f → Beseelung

Animismus m • animism *(cul, met)* < Spiritismus

Animus m • animus, male aspect of the human spirit *(Jung) (ant, psy)* ↔ Anima

Anklage f • indictment, charge, accusation, inditement° *(jur)* < Beschuldigung

Anlage f • (▷ Talent) talent, natural disposition *(psy)*

Anlage-Umwelt-Kontroverse f • nature-nurture controversy *(ant, psy)* → Natur-Kultur-Kontroverse

Anmaßung des Wissens f • presumption/arrogance of knowledge *(sci)* < Wissenschaftsdiktatur

Anmut f • grace *(psy, aes)* < W 1023

Annäherung f • approximation, approach *(mat, sci)*

Annäherung an die Wahrheit f • approximation to truth *(Popper etc) (epi)*

Annäherungstheorie an die Wahrheit f • approximation theory of truth *(epi, sci)*

Annäherungswert m • approximative/approximation/approximated value *(mat)*

Annahme f • assumption, hypothesis, presumption, supposition *(log, sci)* → Präsumption < Präsupposition, Supposition, Hypothese

Annahme einer Theorie f • acceptance of a theory *(sci)*

Annahme, erwartungswidrige f • contra/counter -intuitive assumption, belief-contravening assumption *(epi, sci)*

Annahme, problematische f • problematic assumption *(epi, sci)*

Annahme, tatsachenwidrige f • counterfactual assumption *(epi, sci)*

Annahmeeinführung f • introduction of an assumption/a hypothesis *(log, sci)*

Annahmenkalkül m/n • calculus of assumptions, assumption calculus *(log)*

Annalen pl • annals *(his)*

Annales-Tradition f • annals tradition *(sci)* < historisch-kritische Methode

Annexionismus m • annexationism *(pol)*

Annihilation f • annihilation *(nat, gep)*

Annihilationismus m • annihilationism *(met)*

Annihilierungsverlangen n • thirst/desire for annihilation *(psy)* < Todestrieb

anomaler Monismus m • anomalous monism *(Davidson) (min)* < Monismus, neutraler

Anomalie f • anomaly *(gep)* < Regelwidrigkeit

Anomie f • anomie, anomy, loss of order *(Durkheim etc) (soc)* < Gesetzlosigkeit, Normlosigkeit

anonyme Gesellschaft f • anonymous society *(soc)*

anonymer Christ m • anonymous Christian *(Rahner) (rel)*

Anonymität f • anonymity *(gen)*

Anordnungen der Äußerungsfolgen *pl* •
orderings of enunciative series *(Foucault)*
(epi, pol)

anorganische Natur *f* • inorganic nature *(nat)*

Anorganismus *m* → unbelebte Natur

Anpassung *f* • accomodation *(soc)*, adaptation,
adjustment *(nat, ant)* → Adaption

Anpassung, soziale *f* • social adjustment/
adaptation, adaptation to society *(soc)*

Anpassung, stammesgeschichtliche *f* • phylo-
genetic/generic adaptation/adjustment *(nat,
ant)*

Anpassungsdruck *m* • adaptation/adjustment
pressure, pressure to adapt/adjust *(psy, soc)*
→ Assimilationsdruck

anpassungsfähiges System *n* • adaptable
system *(sys)*

Anpassungsfähigkeit *f* • adaptability *(ant, psy)*
→ Adaptabiliät < Unspezialisiertheit

Anrecht *n* • entitlement *(jur)*

Anreiz *m* • incentive *(eco, act, psy)*

Anreizstrukturen *pl* • incentive structures
(eco, act, psy)

Anruf *m* • appeal, address *(Heidegger) (ont)*

anschauende Erkenntnis *f* • intuitive know-
ledge/cognition *(epi)*

Anschaulichkeit *f* • vividness, clarity, intuitiveness *(gep)*

Anschauung *f* • intuition, anschauung *(epi)*

Anschauung, ästhetische *f* • aesthetic(al) intui-
tion/anschauung/impression *(Schelling) (aes)*

Anschauung, empirische *f* • empirical intuition/
anschauung/impression *(Kant) (epi)*

Anschauung, göttliche *f* • divine contempla-
tion/intuition/anschauung *(Kant) (met)*

Anschauung, intellektuelle *f* • intellectual
intuition *(Kant, Fichte, Schelling etc) (epi)*

Anschauung, kategoriale *f* • categorial
intuition *(Husserl) (epi, met)*

Anschauung, primäre *f* • primary intuition/
impression *(psy)*

Anschauung, reine *f* • pure intuition/percep-
tion/anschauung *(Kant) (epi)*

Anschauung, sekundäre *f* • secondary intuition/
impression *(psy)*

Anschauung, sinnlich erfahrende *f* • sensuous-
ly experiencing intuition *(Husserl) (epi, met)*

Anschauung, transzendentale *f* • transcendental intuition/perception/anschauung
(Kant, Schelling, Fichte) (met, epi)

Anschauungsbild *n* • eidetic/sensory image
(psy, epi)

Anschauungsform des Raumes *f* • spatial form
of intuition, form of spatial intuition *(Kant)*
(epi)

Anschauungsform, reine *f* • pure form of
intuition/perception° *(Kant etc) (epi)*

Anschauungsformen *pl* • forms of intuition
(Kant) (epi)

Anschauungssatz *m* • intuitive proposition/
clause *(Bolzano) (log, lan)*

Anschauungsvermögen *n* • faculty of intuition
(Kant) (epi)

Anselm von Canterbury • Anselm of
Canterbury

an-sich • (▷ per se) in itself *(lan, ont)*

An-sich-Gute-für-Mich, das *n* • the good-in-
itself-for-me *(Scheler) (eth)*

an-sich-seiend • (being) in itself *(met)*

Ansichsein *n* • being-in-itself *(Hegel,
Heidegger) (met)*

Anspruch *m* • claim, pretension *(jur, eth, psy)*
→ Prätention

Anspruchsrecht *n* • entitlement, claim right
(jur) → Forderungsrecht

Anstaltshandeln *n* • institutional behaviour
(Weber) (soc, act) < Einverständnishandeln,
Gesellschaftshandeln, Verbandshandeln

Ansteckung, emotionale *f* • emotional
contagion *(soc, psy)*

Ansteckung, soziale *f* • social contagion *(soc)*

Antagonismus *m* • antagonism *(log)*

Antecedens *n* → Antezedens

Anteilnahme, Prinzip der *n* • sympathy/
interest/personal responsibility principle
(Gilligan etc) (eth, fem) < weibliche Ethik

Anteprädikamente *pl* • antepredicaments
(Aristotle etc) (log) < Prädikament

Antezedens *n* • antecedent *(log, mat)* ↔
Sukzedens

Antezedensbedingung *f* • antecedent condition
(log, sci)

Antezedentien *pl* • antecedents *(log)*

Anthologie *f* • anthology *(gen)* < Textbuch

Anthropinon *n* • human characteristic *(ant)*

anthropisches Prinzip *n* • anthropic principle
(ant, nat) < Anthropismus, Endzweck des
Kosmos, Mensch als Zweck des Universums

Anthropismus *m* • anthropinism° *(ant, met)*

Anthropodizee *f* • anthropodicy *(his, ant)* <
Kosmodizee, Theodizee

Anthropogenese *f* • anthropogenesis *(ant, nat)*
→ Hominisation < W 73

Anthropogenie *f* → Anthropogenese

Anthropogonie *f* • anthropogeny *(rel)*

Anthropographie *f* • anthropography *(ant)*

Anthropoide *m* • anthropoid *(ape) (nat, ant)*
< Frühmensch; Tiere, höhere

Anthropolatrie *f* • anthropolatry *(rel)*

Anthropologie, philosophische *f* • philosophical anthropology *(ant)*

anthropologische Charakteristik *f* • anthropological characteristic/characterization *(Kant) (ant)*

anthropologische Didaktik *f* • anthropological didactic *(Kant) (ant)*

anthropologische Linguistik *f* • anthropological linguistics *(lan)*

anthropologischer Materialismus *m* • anthropological materialism *(met)*

anthropologischer Wissenschaftsbegriff *m* • anthropological concept of science *(sci)*

Anthropologismus *m* • anthropologism *(Feuerbach) (ant)*

Anthropometrie *f* • anthropometry, anthropometrics *(ant)*

anthropomorph • anthropomorphic *(ant)*

Anthropomorphe *m* → Menschenaffe

anthropomorphisieren • to anthropomorphize *(ant)*

Anthropomorphismus *m* • anthropomorphism *(ant)*

Anthroposophie *f* • anthroposophy *(Steiner) (eso)*

Anthropotheologie *f* • anthropotheology *(Feuerbach etc) (ant, met)*

Anthropozentrismus *m* • anthropocentrism *(ant, met)*

Anthropus *m* → Frühmensch

antianalytisch • anti-analytic *(gep)*

Anti-Atomkraftbewegung *f* • anti-nuclear power movement *(soc)* → Antikernkraftbewegung

antiautoritäre Erziehung *f* • anti-authoritarian education *(Neill etc) (psy, eth)*

Antichrist *m* • *nt (Nietzsche etc) (rel)*

Antidemokrat *m* • antidemocrat *(pol)*

Antideterminismus *m* • antideterminism *(met)*

Antidogmatismus *m* • antidogmatism *(gep)*

Antifaschismus *m* • antifascism *(pol)*

Antifaschist *m* • antifascist *(pol)*

Anti-Held *m* • anti-hero *(aes)*

Antihumanismus *m* • antihumanism *(eth)*

Anti-Illusionismus *m* • anti-illusionism *(met)* < Desillusionismus

anti-illusionistische Kunst *f* • anti-illusionist art *(aes)* < Naturalismus

Anti-Intellektualismus *m* • anti-intellectualism *(gen)*

Antikantianismus *m* • antikantianism *(Stattler etc) (epi, met)*

Antike *f* • antiquity, ancient world *(his)*

Antike, klassische *f* • classical antiquity *(his)*

Antikernkraftbewegung *f* • anti-nuclear power movement *(soc)* → Anti-Atomkraftbewegung

Antiklerikalismus *m* • anticlericalism *(rel)*

Antikommunismus *m* • anticommunism *(pol)*

Antikonzeption *f* • contraception *(eth)* → Empfängnisverhütung

Antikörper *m* • antibody *(nat)*

Antikritik *f* • anticriticism *(gep)*

Anti-Kunst *f* • anti-art *(aes)*

Antiliberalismus *m* • antiliberalism *(pol)*

Antilogie *f* • antilogy, self-contradiction *(Kant etc) (log)* < Paradoxie, Widerspruch

Antilogik *f* • antilogic *(log, met)*

Antilogismus *m* • antilogism *(log)*

Antiloquium *n* • antiloquy *(log, lan)* → Gegenrede, Widerspruch

Antimachiavellismus *m* • antimachiavell(ian)-ism *(Frederick the Great) (pol, soc)*

Antimaterie *f* • antimatter *(nat)*

antimechanistischer Materialismus *m* • non-mechanistic materialism *(met)*

antimetapysisch • antimetaphysical *(met)*

Antimilitarismus *m* • antimilitarism *(pol)* < Abrüstung, Friedensbewegung

Antimoral *f* • antimorality *(Nietzsche etc) (eth)*

Antimoralismus *m* • antimoralism *(Nietzsche etc) (eth)*

Antimoralist *m* • antimoralist *(eth)*

Antinaturalismus *m* • anti-naturalism *(met, aes)*

Antinomie *f* • antinomy *(log, jur)*

Antinomie der Definierbarkeit *f* • antinomy of definability *(Richard) (epi, lan)*

Antinomie der (reflektierenden) Urteilskraft *f* • antinomy of (reflective) judg(e)-ment *(Kant) (epi, aes)*

Antinomie der praktischen Vernunft *f* • antinomy of practical reason *(Kant) (epi, eth)*

Antinomie des Geschmacks *f* • antinomy of taste *(Kant) (aes)*

Antinomie heterologischer Terme *f* • antinomy of heterological terms *(Grelling, Nelson) (epi, lan)*

Antinomien der Mengenlehre *pl* • set-theoretic paradoxes *(mat, log)* < Typentheorie

Antinomien der reinen Vernunft *pl* • antinomies of pure reason *(Kant etc) (epi)*

Antinomien des bürgerlichen Denkens *pl* • antinomies of bourgeois thought *(Lukács) (epi)*

Antinomienlehre *f* • theory/doctrine of the antinomies *(Kant etc) (epi)*

antinomisch • antinomic *(log)* → widersprüchlich

Antinomismus *m* • antinomianism *(rel)*

Antipapismus *m* • antipapism *(rel)*

Antipartikel *n* • anti-particle *(nat)* → Antiteilchen

Antipathie *f* • antipathy *(psy)*

Antiplatonismus *m* • antiplatonism *(met)*

Antipode *m* • (▷ Gegensatz) antipode, exact
opposite *(log)*

Antipositivismus *m* • anti-positivism *(met)*

Antipsychiatrie *f* • anti-psychiatry *(Laing,
Szasz etc) (psy)*

Antiquiertheit des Menschen *f* • obsoles-
cence/antiquatedness of man *(Anders) (soc,
tec)*

Antirealismus *m* • antirealism, anti-realism
(epi, met, aes)

Antirealismus, semantischer *m* • semantic
antirealism *(Dummet) (lan)*

Antisemitismus *m* • antisemitism *(pol, rel)*

Antiskeptizismus *m* • antiscepticism *(epi, met)*

antisozial • anti-social *(soc)*

Antispeziesismus *m* • anti-speciesism *(Singer)
(ant, eth)*

Antiszientismus *m* • anti-scientism *(sci)* < Szientismus

antitechnisch • antitechnological *(tec)* < Technikfeindlichkeit

Antiteilchen *n* • anti-particle *(nat)* → Antipartikel

Antitheater *n* • anti-theatre *(aes)*

Antithese *f* • antithesis *(log, met)*

Antithetik *f* • antithetics *(log, met)*

Antithetik der reinen Vernunft *f* • antithetics
of pure reason *(Kant) (epi)*

antithetisch • antithetic(al) *(log, met)*

Antiutopie *f* • anti-utopia *(soc, pol)* < Dystopie

Antizipation *f* • anticipation *(gep)*

Antizipationen der Wahrnehmung *pl* • antici-
pations of perception *(Kant) (epi)*

antizipierendes Bewußtsein *n* • anticipatory
consciousness *(Bloch) (met, soc)* < Vorschein

antizyklisch • anticyclic(al) *(nat, eco, his)* ↔
prozyklisch

Antonymie *f* • antonymy *(lan)* ↔ Synonymie

Antrieb *m* • impulse, drive *(nat, psy)*

Antriebskraft *f* • motive force *(nat, psy)*

Antriebsorientierung *f* • drive orientation
(Gehlen) (cul) < Bedürfnisorientierung

Antriebsüberschuß *m* • drive surplus *(Gehlen)*
(ant)

Antriebsursache *f* • moving/efficient cause,
source of movement *(Aristotle) (met)*
< Wirkursache

Antwortschema *n* • answer-scheme *(lan)*

Anundfürsichsein *n* • being-in-and-for-itself
(Hegel etc) (met)

Anwendbarkeit *f* → Applikabilität

Anwendungsbereich *m* • range of application
(gen)

anwendungsbezogene Forschung *f* • applied
science *(sci)* ↔ Grundlagenforschung

Anwendungsfeld *n* • field of application *(sci)*

Anwendungsverhältnisse der Gerechtigkeit
pl • circumstances of justice *(Rawls) (eth)*

Anwendungswissen *n* • know-how, practical
knowledge *(epi)* < wissen wie

Anwesenheit *f* • presence *(Heidegger) (ont)*

Anwesenheit Gottes in der Welt *f* • presence
of God in the world *(rel)*

Anything-Goes-Prinzip *n* • anything goes
principle *(Feyerabend) (sci)*

Anziehung *f* • attraction *(nat, psy)* < Attraktion

Anziehungskraft *f* • attraction, appeal *(psy)*,
power/force of attraction, attractive power/
force *(nat)* → Gravitation, Schwerkraft

Äon *m* • eon, aeon *(met, his)* → Weltalter

Apagogé *f* • apagoge *(log)* ↔ Anagogé < reductio ad absurdum

apagogischer Beweis *m* • apagogic(al) proof,
proof via reductio ad absurdum *(Kant) (epi,
log)*

Apartheidpolitik *f* • apartheid policy, segrega-
tionism *(pol)*

Apathie *f* • apathy *(psy, eth)* < Affektlosigkeit,
Ataraxie, Leidenschaftslosigkeit

Apeiron *n* • the unbounded, the unlimited
(Anaximander) (met) → Unbestimmte, das;
Unendlichkeit; Urstoff, ungeformter

Apersonalismus *m* • apersonalism *(met)*

Aperspektivität *f* • aperspectivity *(Gebser)
(met, cul)*

Aphasie *f* • language loss, loss of the faculty of
speech *(psy)*, aphasia *(log)* < Urteilsenthaltung

aphilosophisch • aphilosophical *(gep)* < unphilosophisch

Aphorismus *m* • aphorism *(gep)* < Sinnspruch

aphoristische Philosophie *f* • aphoristic
philosophy *(gep)*

Aphronesis *f* • unreasonableness *(epi, psy)* →
Unvernunft

Apodiktik *f* • apod(e)ictics *(log)*

apodiktisch • apod(e)ictic *(log)*

apodiktische Gewißheit *f* • apod(e)ictic
certainty *(Kant) (epi)*

apodiktischer Satz *m* • apod(e)ictic proposition *(Kant) (epi, log)*

apodiktisches Urteil *n* • apod(e)ictic judg(e)ment *(Kant) (epi, log)*

Apokalypse *f* • apocalypse *(rel)* < Weltuntergang

Apokalypseblindheit *f* • apocalyptic blindness *(Anders) (gep)*

Apokatastase *f* • apocatastasis, restitution *(rel)* < Eschatologie

apokryphe Schriften *pl* • apocrypha *(rel)*

apolitisch • apolitical *(pol)*

apolitische Haltung *f* • apolitical attitude *(pol)*

apollinisch • Appollonian *(aes)* ↔ dionysisch

Apollinische und Dionysische, das *n* • the Apollonian and the Dionysian *(Nietzsche) (aes)*

apollinische und dionysische Kulturen *pl* • Apollonian and Dionysian cultures *(Nietzsche) (cul)*

Apologet *m* • apologist *(gep)*

Apologetik *f* • apologetics *(rel)* → Verteidigung religiöser Lehren

Apologie *f* • apologia, apology *(gep)*

Apophantik *f* • apophantics, logic of proposition *(Husserl) (log)* < apophantisches Als

apophantisches Als *n* • apophantic as, apophantic assertion° *(Heidegger) (epi, ont)*

Aporem *n* • aporeme° *(log)*

Aporetik *f* • aporetics° *(log)*

Aporie *f* • aporia *(log, act)* → Ausweglosigkeit, unlösbares Problem < Paradoxie

Apostasie *f* • apostasy *(rel)*

aposteriorisch • a posteriori *(epi)* < a posteriori

aposteriorisches Urteil *n* • a posteriori judg(e)ment *(epi, log)* ↔ apriorisches Urteil

aposteriorisches Wissen *n* → a posteriori-Wissen

Aposteriorität *f* • a posteriori nature/quality *(epi)* ↔ Apriorität

Apotheose *f* • apotheosis *(rel, pol)*

Apparatemedizin *f* • high-tech(nology) medicine *(nat, eth)*

Apparatschik *m* • apparatchik *(pol)*

Apparenz *f* • appearance *(gep)* → Erscheinung, äußere

appellierende Funktion der Sprache *f* • appellative/appeal function of language *(Bühler) (lan)*

Apperzeption *f* • apperception *(Leibniz etc) (epi)* ↔ Perzeption < Wahrnehmung

Apperzeptionspsychologie *f* • apperception psychology *(Wundt) (psy)*

apperzeptives Bewußtsein *n* • apperceptive consciousness *(min)*

Appetenz-Appetenz-Konflikt *m* • approach-approach conflict *(Lewin) (soc, psy)*

Appetenz-Aversions-Konflikt *m* • approach-avoidance conflict *(Lewin) (soc, psy)*

Appetenz-Aversions-Konflikt, doppelter *m* • double approach-avoidance conflict *(Hovland, Sears) (soc, psy)*

Appetenzverhalten *n* • appetence/appetency behaviour *(nat, psy)*

Appetition *f* • orexis, desire, effort *(Aristotle etc) (psy)*

appetitus intellectualis *m* • intellectual appetite *(Aquinas) (met)*

appetitus naturalis *m* • natural appetite *(Aquinas) (met)*

appetitus sensitivus *m* • sensitivous/sensual appetite *(Aquinas) (met)*

Applikabilität *f* • applicability *(sci)* → Anwendbarkeit

Applikation *f* • application *(met, lan)*

Appräsentation *f* • appresentation *(Husserl) (epi)*

Apprehensibilität *f* • apprehendability, apprehensibility *(epi)* → Begreifbarkeit

Apprehension *f* • apprehension *(epi, psy)* < Wahrnehmung

Appropriation *f* • appropriation *(eco)* → Besitzergreifung

Approximationssatz *m* • approximation theorem *(mat)*

Apriori, das *n* • the a priori *(Kant etc) (epi)* < a priori

apriorisches Urteil *n* • a priori judg(e)ment *(epi, log)* ↔ aposteriorisches Urteil

apriorisches Wissen *n* → a priori-Wissen

Apriorismus *m* • apriorism *(epi)* < reine Erkenntnis

Apriorität *f* • a priori nature/quality, the property of being a priori *(epi)*

Äquidistanz *f* • equidistance *(mat)*

Äquifinalität *f* • equifinality *(Driesch) (met)*

Äquilibrismus *m* • equilibrism *(eth, met)* < Willensfreiheit

äquipollent • equipollent *(log)* → äquivalent, gleichbedeutend

Äquipollenz *f* • equipollence, equipollency *(log, lan)* → Gleichmächtigkeit

Äquipotentialität *f* • equipotentiality *(Driesch) (nat, met)*

Äquiprobabilismus *m* • equi-probabilism *(log, mat)*

äquivalent • equivalent *(log, lan)*

Äquivalenz *f* • equivalence *(log, sci, lan)* → Gleichwertigkeit

Äquivalenz der Form (T) *f* • equivalence of the form (T), (T)-biconditional, (T)-equivalence *(Tarski) (log, lan)*

Äquivalenzformel *f* • equivalence formula *(log, met)*

Äquivalenzklasse *f* • equivalence class *(mat, log)*

Äquivalenzpunkte *pl* • points of equivalence *(Foucault) (epi, pol)*

Äquivalenzprinzip *n* • principle of equivalence *(log, eco)*

Äquivalenzrelation *f* • equivalence relation *(log)*

Äquivalenzschema *n* → Äquivalenzformel

äquivok • equivocal *(log, lan)*

Äquivokation *f* • equivocation *(log, lan)* → Ambiguität

arabische Philosophie *f* • Arabian/Arabic philosophy *(gep)*

arabische Ziffern *pl* • Arabic numerals *(mat)*

Arbeit *f* • labour, work *(eco)*, work *(nat, eco)*

Arbeit, abstrakte *f* • abstract labour *(Marx) (eco)*

Arbeit, allgemeine *f* • general labour *(Marx) (eco)*

Arbeit als Selbstentfremdung *f* • work as self-alienation *(Marx etc) (soc)*

Arbeit als Vermittlung von Mensch und Welt *f* • work as mediation between man and world *(Fichte etc) (met)*

Arbeit, bezahlte *f* • waged work, paid labour *(eco)* ↔ Arbeit, unbezahlte

Arbeit, entfremdete *f* • alienated labour *(Marx etc) (soc)*

Arbeit, kapitalschaffende *f* • capital producing labour *(Marx) (eco)* < Lohnarbeit

Arbeit, kollektive *f* • collective labour *(Marx) (eco)*

Arbeit, konkrete *f* • concrete labour *(Marx) (eco)* → Arbeit, nützliche

Arbeit, lebendige *f* • living labour *(Marx) (eco)* ↔ Arbeit, tote

Arbeit, notwendige *f* • necessary labour *(Marx) (eco)*

Arbeit, nützliche *f* • useful labour *(Marx) (eco)* → Arbeit, konkrete

Arbeit, produktive *f* • productive labour *(Marx) (eco)*

Arbeit, tote *f* • dead labour *(Marx) (eco)* ↔ Arbeit, lebendige

Arbeit, unbezahlte *f* • unwaged work, unpaid labour *(eco)* ↔ Arbeit, bezahlte

Arbeit, unmittelbare *f* • direct labour *(Marx) (eco)*

Arbeit, unproduktive *f* • unproductive labour *(Marx) (eco)*

Arbeit, vergegenständlichte *f* • objectified labour *(Marx) (eco)*

Arbeiter *m* • worker *(eco, soc)*

Arbeiteraristokratie *f* • aristocracy of labour, labour aristocracy *(Marx) (eco, soc)*

Arbeiterbewegung *f* • labour movement *(soc, pol)*

Arbeiterdemokratie *f* • workers' democracy *(pol)*

Arbeiterklasse *f* • working class *(soc, eco)*

Arbeitermitbestimmung *f* • participation of labour *(eco, pol)*

Arbeiterrevolution *f* • proletarian revolution *(pol, soc)* → proletarische Revolution

Arbeiterschaft *f* • workforce, body of workers, employees *(eco, soc)*

Arbeiterselbstverwaltung *f* • worker self-management *(soc)*

Arbeitgeber *m* • employer *(eco, soc)*

Arbeitnehmer *m* • employee *(eco, soc)*

Arbeitnehmermobilität *f* • labour mobility *(soc)*

Arbeitnehmerschaft *f* → Arbeiterschaft

Arbeitsbedingungen *pl* • labour/working conditions, conditions of work *(eco, soc)*

Arbeitseinkommen *n* • labour income, earned income *(eco)*

Arbeitsentlastung *f* • reduction in workload *(eco)*

Arbeitsertrag *m* • labour output, result of/returns for labour *(eco)*

Arbeitsethik *f* • work ethics *(Weber) (eth, soc)*

Arbeitsethos *n* • work ethos/ethic *(eth, soc)* < Arbeitsmoral

Arbeitsfähigkeit *f* • capacity/ability to work, fitness for work *(eco)* < Erwerbsfähigkeit

Arbeitsformen *pl* • forms of work *(eco, soc)*

Arbeitsfrieden *m* • industrial peace *(eco, soc)*

Arbeitshypothese *f* • working hypothesis *(sci)*

Arbeitsintensität *f* • labour intensity *(eco)*

arbeitsintensiv • labour-intensive *(eco)* < kapitalintensiver Wirtschaftssektor

Arbeitskampf *m* • industrial dispute/conflict, labour dispute *(pol)*

Arbeitskapital *n* • working capital *(eco)*

Arbeitskosten *pl* • labour cost(s) *(eco)*

Arbeitskraft, menschliche *f* • manpower, labour power *(eco)*

Arbeitskraft, Verkauf der *m* • sale of labour (power) *(Marx) (eco)*

Arbeitskräfteüberangebot *n* • excess supply of labour *(eco)*

Arbeitslohn *m* • wages *(Marx etc) (eco)*

Arbeitslosenquote *f* • rate of unemployment, jobless rate *(eco, soc)*

arbeitsloses Grundeinkommen *n* • unearned basic income *(eco, soc)*

Arbeitslosigkeit *f* • unemployment *(eco, soc)*

Arbeitslosigkeit, unfreiwillige *f* • involuntary unemployment *(eco)*

Arbeitsmarkt *m* • labour/job market *(eco)*

Arbeitsmittel *n* • means/instrument of labour *(eco)*

Arbeitsmoral *f* • workplace morale, on-the-job morale *(eth, eco)* < Arbeitsethos

Arbeitsnachfrage *f* • demand for labour *(eco)*

Arbeitsplatzbeschaffung *f* • job creation *(eco)*

Arbeitsplatzsicherheit *f* • job security *(eco)*

arbeitsplatzvernichtende Technologie *f* • job-displacing technology *(eco, soc)*

Arbeitsprodukt *n* • product of labour *(eco)*

Arbeitsproduktivität *f* • productivity of labour *(eco)*

Arbeitsprozeß *m* • labour/work process *(eco)*

Arbeitsquanta *pl* • quantities of labour *(Marx) (eco)*

Arbeitsrecht *n* • labour law/legislation *(jur)*

Arbeitstag *m* • working day *(eco)*

arbeitsteilige Wirtschaft *f* • economy resting on the division of labour, specialized economy *(eco, soc)*

Arbeitsteilung *f* • division of labour *(A. Smith etc) (eco, soc)* < W 1116

Arbeitsvermögen *n* • labour capacity, capacity to work *(eco)* < Arbeitskraft, menschliche

Arbeitsvertrag *m* • labour contract *(eco, jur)*

Arbeitswelt *f* • world of work *(eco, soc)*

Arbeitswert *m* • labour value *(eco, soc)*

Arbeitswerttheorie *f* • labour theory of value *(Ricardo, Marx etc) (eco)*

Arbeitszeit *f* • working time, (▷ Arbeitseinheit) man hours *(eco)*

Arbeitszeit, notwendige *f* • necessary labour time *(Marx) (eco)*

Arbeitszeitverkürzung *f* • reduction of working hours *(eco, soc)*

Arbeitszufriedenheit *f* • job satisfaction *(eco, soc)*

Arbeitszwang *m* • obligation/requirement/duty to work *(Marx etc) (eco)* < gleicher Arbeitszwang für alle

Arbiträrität *f* • arbitrariness *(Saussure etc) (lan)*

Arbor Porphyriana *m* • Tree of Porphyry, Porphyrian tree *(log)*

archaischer Stil *m* • archaic style *(aes)*

archaisches Denken *n* • archaic thinking *(epi, cul)*

Archäologie *f* • archeology

Archäologie der Wissensbereiche *f* • archeology of epistemes *(Foucault) (epi)*

Archäologie des Wissens *f* • archeology of knowledge *(epi)*

archäologische Geschichte *f* • archeological history *(Foucault) (epi, his)*

archäologische Isomorphismen *pl* • archeological isomorphisms *(Foucault) (epi, sys)*

arché *f* • origin, beginning, ruling principle *(Thales, Anaximander) (met)* → erster Anfang, Ursprung

Archetyp(us) *m* • archetype *(Jung etc) (psy)*

Archetypenlehre *f* • theory of archetypes *(Jung etc) (psy)*

archetypischer Verstand *m* • archetypical/archetypal intellect *(Kant) (epi)*

Archeus *m* • archeus, vital principle *(Paracelsus etc) (met)*

Archimedischer Punkt *m* • Archimedean point *(met)*

Archimedisches Axiom *n* • Archimedean axiom *(mat)*

Archimedisches Prinzip *n* • Archimedes principle *(nat)*

Architektonik *f* • architectonic, architecture, structure *(aes, sci)*

Architektonik der Begriffe *f* • conceptual architecture *(Kant) (epi)*

Architektonik der reinen Vernunft *f* • (the) architectonic of pure reason *(Kant) (epi)*

architektonische Einheit *f* • architectonic unity *(Kant) (epi)*

Architekturtheorie *f* • theory of architecture *(aes)*

Archologie *f* • archology *(ont)*

Areligiosität *f* • irreligiosity, religiouslessness, religionlessness, irreligiousness° *(rel)* → Religionslosigkeit < Atheismus

Areté *f* → Tugend

Aretologie *f* • aretology, theory of virtue(s) *(eth)* → Tugendlehre

Argument *n* • argument *(lan, log)*

Argument a fortiori *n* • a fortiori argument, argument a fortiori *(lan, log)*

Argument a posteriori *n* • a posteriori argument, argument a posteriori *(lan, log)*

Argument a priori *n* • a priori argument, argument a priori *(lan, log)*

Argument a simili *n* • a simili argument, argument a simili *(lan, log)*

Argument a tuto *n* • a tuto argument, argument a tuto *(lan, log)*

Argument ad baculum *n* • argument ad baculum, appeal to force *(lan, log)*

Argument aus der Feinabstimmung im Universum für die Existenz Gottes *n* • fine-tuning argument for the existence of God *(rel)*

Argument der Absonderlichkeit *n* • argument from queerness *(Mackie) (eth)*

Argument der nicht-unterbrochenen Verursachung *n* • non-interrupted causation argument, argument of non-interrupted causation *(met)*

Argument der offenen Frage *n* • open-question-argument *(Moore) (eth, lan)*

Argument der Relativität *n* • argument from relativity *(Mackie) (eth)*

Argument der schiefen Bahn *n* → Argument der schiefen Ebene

Argument der schiefen Ebene *n* • slippery slope argument, wedge argument *(eth)* → Dammbruch-Argument

Argument des bösen Dämons *n* • evil demon hypothesis *(Descartes) (epi)* < Täuschungs-argument, deus malignus

Argument des unendlichen Regresses *n* • infinite regress argument *(log)*

Argument, elementares *n* • elementary argument, micro-argument *(Toulmin etc) (lan, log)*

Argument, explizites *n* • explicit argument *(log, lan)*

Argument, implizites *n* • implicit argument *(log, lan)*

Argument, modales *n* • modal argument *(min, lan)*

Argument von der unerwarteten technologischen Relevanz *n* • overhead argument, argument from unanticipated technological relevance *(Weinberg) (sci)*

Argument von Gottes Güte *n* • argument from God's benevolence *(Descartes) (met)*

Argumentation *f* • argumentation *(lan, log)*

Argumentationsfehler *m* • error in the argument, argumentation error *(lan, log)*

Argumentationsfeld *n* • field of argument *(lan)*

Argumentationsgemeinschaft *f* • community of argumentation *(Habermas etc) (lan, soc)*

Argumentationslehre *f* • argumentation theory *(lan, log)*

Argumentationsmuster *n* • pattern of argument *(lan, log)*

Argumentationsteilnehmer *m* • participant in argumentation *(lan, soc)*

Argumentationstheorie *f* • argumentation theory *(lan, log)*

Argumentationstruktur *f* • argumentation structure *(lan, log)*

Argumentationstyp *m* • type of argumentation *(lan, log)*

argumentativ • argumentative *(lan, log)*

Argumentausdruck *m* • argument(-expression) *(log)*

Argumentbereich einer Relation *m* • argument domain of a relation *(log)*

Argumentfunktion *f* • function of an argument *(log)*

argumentieren • to argue, to reason *(lan, log)*

Argumentmenge *f* • set of arguments *(log)*

argumentum ad hominem *n* • ad hominem argument *(lan, log)* < argumentum ad personam

argumentum ad ignorantiam *n* • *nt*, argument from ignorance *(lan, log)*

argumentum ad iudicium *n* • *nt (lan, log)*

argumentum ad metum *n* • *nt (lan, log)*

argumentum ad misericordiam *n* • *nt*, appeal to (the emotion) of pity *(lan, log)*

argumentum ad odium *n* • *nt (lan, log)*

argumentum ad personam *n* • *nt*, argument against the person *(lan, log)*

argumentum ad populum *n* • *nt*, appeal to the weight of popular opinion *(lan, log)*

argumentum ad rem *n* • *nt (lan, log)* → Sachargument

argumentum ad superbiam *n* • *nt (lan, log)*

argumentum ad verecundiam *n* •*nt*, appeal to authority *(lan, log)*

argumentum ad veritatem *n* • argument ad veritatem *(lan, log)*

argumentum ad vertiginem *n* • *nt (lan, log)*

argumentum e consensu gentium *n* • *nt*, argument from common consent *(lan, log)*

argumentum e contrario *n* • *nt*, argument from the contrary *(lan, log)*

argumentum e silentio *n* • *nt*, tacit consent argument *(lan)* < stillschweigende Zustimmung

argumentum ex concesso *n* • argument ex concesso *(lan, log)*

argumentum exclusionis *n* • *nt (lan, log)*

argumentum in distans *n* • *nt (lan, log)*

argumentum negativum *n* • *nt (lan, log)*

Argyrokratie *f* → Plutokratie

Arianismus *m* • Arianism *(rel)*

Aristipp • Aristippus

Aristokratie *f* • aristocracy *(soc, pol)* → Adel

Aristokratismus *m* • aristocratism *(soc, cul)*

Aristoteles • Aristotle

Aristotelianismus *m* • Aristotelianism *(gep)* → Aristotelismus

Aristoteliker *m* • Aristotelian *(gep)*

aristotelisch-megarische Modalität *f* • Megaric Aristotelian modality *(sci)*

aristotelische Ethik *f* • Aristotelian ethics *(eth)*

aristotelischer Grundsatz *m* • Aristotelian principle *(Rawls etc) (eth)*

Aristotelismus *m* • Aristotelism *(gep)* → Aristotelianismus

arithmetische Progression *f* • arithmetic progression *(mat)* ↔ geometrische Progression

arithmetisches Mittel *n* • arithmetic(al) mean *(mat)*

arithmetisches Verhältnis *n* • arithmetical ratio *(mat)*, *(Malthus) (soc)*

Arithmetisierung *f* • arithmetization *(mat, sci)*

Arithmoquinieren *n* • arithmoquining *(Hofstadter) (mat, log)*

Arkanum *n* • arcanum *(cul, rel, eso)*

Armen und Entrechteten, die *pl* • the poor and (the) dispossessed *(eco, soc)*

Armengesetze *pl* • poor-laws *(eco, soc)*

Armut, absolute *f* • absolute poverty *(eco, soc)*

Armut, relative *f* • relative poverty *(eco, soc)*

Armutsfalle *f* • poverty trap *(eco, soc)*

Armutsforschung *f* • poverty research *(eco, soc)*

Armutsgrenze *f* • subsistence/survival level *(eco)*

Armutsmigration *f* • poverty migration, economic migration of the poor *(eco, pol)* < Wirtschaftsflüchtling

ars amandi *f* • (the) art of love *(psy)*

ars combinatoria *f* • (the) art of combination *(Lull) (log)*

ars coniecturalis *f* • (the) art of conjecture *(Nicholas of Cusa) (epi)*

ars generalis *f* • general science *(Lull) (sci)* < allgemeine Wissenschaft

ars inveniendi *f* • (the) art of dicovery *(sci)* → Heuristik

ars magna *f* • nt *(mat, sci)*

ars moriendi *f* • (the) art of dying *(met, rel)*

ars poetica *f* • poetic art *(aes)* → Dichtkunst

ars povera *f* • nt *(aes)*

Art brut *m* • art brut, raw art *(aes)*

Art déco *m/n* • art deco, decorative art *(aes)* < dekorative Kunst

Art *f* • kind, natural kind, species *(nat, ant)*, phylum *(nat)*, (▷ Modus) mode *(log)* < Klasse, natürliche; Gattung

Art nouveau *m* • art nouveau *(aes)* → Jugendstil

Art-züchtend • species-breeding *(Nietzsche) (ant)*

Artefakt *n* • artefact, artifact *(aes, tec)*

Artefaktparadigma *n* • artefact/artifact/construct paradigm *(Masterman, Kuhn) (sci, tec)*

arteigen • characteristic of the species, appropriate/peculiar to the species *(nat, ant)*

Arten, gefährdete *pl* • endangered species *(nat, env)* < Artenschutz

Arten, natürliche *pl* • natural kinds *(Quine etc) (log, lan)* → Klasse, natürliche

Artenbildung *f* • speciation *(nat)* → Speziation

Artenreichtum *m* • plurality/diversity of species *(nat)* < Artenvielfalt

Artenschutz *m* • protection of species *(eth, env)* < Arten, gefährdete

Artenschutzabkommen *n* • agreement on the protection of species *(eth, env)*

Artenschwund *m* • species loss *(nat, env)* < Verlust an biologischer Vielfalt

Artentransmutation *f* → Artenumbildung

Artenumbildung *f* • transmutation of species *(Lamarck) (nat)*

Artenvernichtung *f* • extinction of species, species extinction *(eth, env)*

Artenvielfalt *f* • variety/diversity of species *(nat)* < Biodiversi(vi)tät

arterhaltend • species preserving, preservative of the species *(nat)*

Arterhaltung *f* • preservation/survival of the species *(nat)*

artes liberales *pl* • liberal arts *(aes, gep)* → freie Künste ↔ artes mechanicae < Geisteswissenschaften

artes mechanicae *pl* • servile arts *(gep)* → Handwerkskünste ↔ artes liberales, schöne Künste

Artgenosse *m* • member of the same species *(nat, ant)*

artgerechte Tierhaltung *f* • species-appropriate treatment of animals, treatment of animals appropriate to the species *(eth)* ↔ Massentierhaltung

artifizielle Gesellschaft *f* • artificial society *(soc)*

Artistenfakultät *f* • faculty of arts *(gep)* < Geisteswissenschaft, artes liberales

artspezifisches Verhalten *n* • species-specific behaviour *(nat, ant)*

Artunterschied *m* • specific difference *(lan, ont)*, species-specific difference *(nat)*

Artwandel *m* • species change *(Darwin) (nat)*

Ascensus *m* • ascent *(log)* ↔ Descensus

Asebie *f* → Gottlosigkeit

Aseität *f* • aseity *(met)* → Selbstgegründetheit

asiatische Philosophie *f* • Asian philosophy *(gep)* < östliches Denken

asiatische Produktionsweise *f* • Asiatic mode of production *(Marx etc) (eco)*

Askese *f* • asceticism, ascetism° *(eth, rel, asp)* < Bedürfnislosigkeit, Enthaltsamkeit, Lebensentsagung

Askese, innerweltliche *f* • worldly/this-worldly asceticism, inner world asceticism *(Weber) (soc)* ↔ weltabkehrende Askese

Askese, Prinzip der *n* • principle of asceticism, ascetic principle *(eth)*

Asket *m* • ascetic *(eth, rel, asp)*

asketisches Ideal *n* • ascetic ideal *(eth, rel, asp)*

Asketizismus *m* → Askese

Askriptor *m* • ascriptor *(lan)* ↔ Präskriptor

asomatisch • asomatic, asomatous, nonbodily *(met)* → unkörperlich, körperlos

asoziales Verhalten *n* • antisocial/asocial behaviour *(soc, eth)*

Asozialität *f* • asociality *(soc, eth)*

Aspektsehen *n* • aspect seeing, seeing aspects *(psy)*

Assembler *m* • assembler, assembly language *(AI)*

Assertion *f* • assertion *(log, lan)*

Assertive *f* • assertive *(Searle) (lan, act)* → Repräsentative

assertorisch • assertoric, assertory *(log, lan)* < Modalität

assertorischer Imperativ *m* • assertoric imperative *(Kant) (eth)*

assertorisches Urteil *n* • assertoric judg(e)ment *(log)*

Assimilation *f* • assimilation *(psy, nat, soc)*

Assimilationsdruck *m* • assimilation pressure *(psy, soc)* → Anpassungsdruck

Assimilationspolitik *f* • assimilation policy, policy of assimilation *(pol)*

Assimilationsprozeß *m* • assimilation process *(nat, pol)*

Assimilierung *f* → Assimilation

Assoziation *f* • association *(epi, psy, soc)*

Assoziation, freie *f* • free association *(Marx etc) (soc), (Freud) (psy)*

Assoziation, sich selbst verwaltende *f* • self-governing association *(soc)*

Assoziationismus *m* • associationism *(psy)*

Assoziationsgesetz *n* • law of association *(psy)*

Assoziationsmuster *n* • association/associational pattern *(psy)*

Assoziationsprinzipien *pl* • principles of association *(epi, min)*

Assoziationspsychologie *f* • associationist psychology, (psychology of) associationism *(psy)*

Assoziationstheorie *f* • associationist theory *(psy)*

Assoziationsvermögen *n* • power of association *(psy)*

assoziatives Denken *n* • associative thinking/thought *(psy)*

assoziatives Gedächtnis *n* • associative memory *(psy)*

Assoziativgesetz *n* • associative law *(mat, log)*

Assoziieren, freies *n* • free association/associating *(psy)*

Ästhesie *f* • aesthesia, aesthesis *(psy, aes)* → Empfindungsvermögen

Ästhet *m* • aesthete *(aes)*

Ästhetik *f* • aesthetics *(aes)* < Kunstwissenschaft < W 1255, 1262, 1263

Ästhetik, abstrakte *f* • abstract aesthetics *(Bense) (aes)*

Ästhetik, analytische *f* • analytical aesthetics *(aes)*

Ästhetik der Gewalt *f* • aesthetics of violence *(aes)*

Ästhetik des Häßlichen *f* • aesthetics of the ugly *(Rosenkranz) (aes)* < W 90

Ästhetik, empirische *f* • empirical aesthetics *(aes)*

Ästhetik, experimentelle *f* • experimental aesthetics *(aes)*

Ästhetik, formale *f* • formal aesthetics *(aes)* → Formalästhetik

Ästhetik, generative *f* • generative aesthetics *(Bense) (aes)* → Informationsästhetik

Ästhetik, hermeneutische *f* • hermeneutic(al) aesthetics *(Gadamer) (aes)*

Ästhetik, idealistische *f* • idealist aesthetics *(aes)*

Ästhetik, immanente *f* • immanent aesthetics *(aes)*

Ästhetik, informationstheoretische *f* → Informationsästhetik

Ästhetik, kybernetische *f* • cybernetic aesthetics *(aes)*

Ästhetik, marxistische *f* • Marxist aesthetics *(aes)*

Ästhetik, materialistische *f* • materialist(ic) aesthetics *(aes)*

Ästhetik, neomarxistische *f* • neo-Marxist aesthetics *(aes)*

Ästhetik, normative *f* • normative aesthetics *(aes)*

Ästhetik, numerische *f* • numerical aesthetics *(Bense) (aes)*

Ästhetik, phänomenologische *f* • phenomenological aesthetics *(Conrad, Ingarden etc) (aes)*

Ästhetik, politische *f* • political aesthetics *(aes)*

Ästhetik, psychologische *f* • psychological aesthetics *(aes)*

Ästhetik, scholastische *f* • scholastic aesthetics *(aes)*

Ästhetik, semiotische *f* • semiotic aesthetics *(Morris etc) (aes)*

Ästhetik, spekulative *f* • speculative aesthetics *(aes)*

Ästhetik, strukturalistische *f* • structuralist aesthetics *(aes)*

Ästhetik, transzendentale *f* • transcendental aesthetics *(Kant etc) (epi)*

Ästhetiker *m* • aesthetician *(aes)*

ästhetisch • aesthetic(al) *(aes)*

ästhetisch-Erhabenes *n* • the aesthetic(ally) sublime *(aes)*

Ästhetische, das *n* • the aesthetic, the aesthetical *(aes)*

ästhetische Distanz *f* • aesthetic distance *(aes)* < interesseloses Wohlgefallen

ästhetische Eigenschaft *f* • aesthetic property *(aes)*

ästhetische Einstellung *f* • aesthetic attitude *(aes)*

ästhetische Empfänglichkeit *f* • aesthetic receptivity/sensitivity/sensibility/responsiveness *(aes)* < Rezeptivität

ästhetische Erfahrung *f* • aesthetic experience *(aes)*

ästhetische Erziehung *f* • aesthetic education *(Schiller) (aes)* < W 1053

ästhetische Idee *f* • aesthetic idea *(Kant) (aes)* < ästhetische Normalidee

ästhetische Interesselosigkeit *f* • aesthetic disinterestedness *(aes)* → interesseloses Wohlgefallen

ästhetische Intuition *f* • aesthetic intuition *(aes)*

ästhetische Kontemplation *f* • aesthetic contemplation *(aes)*

ästhetische Moral *f* • aesthetic morals/morality *(aes, eth)*

ästhetische Normalidee *f* • aesthetic normal idea *(Kant) (aes)*

ästhetische Objektivation *f* • aesthetic objectivation *(Ingarden) (aes)*

ästhetische Qualität *f* • aesthetic quality *(aes)*

ästhetische Rezeption *f* • aesthetic reception *(aes)* < Rezeptionsästhetik

ästhetische Theorie *f* • aesthetic theory *(Adorno) (aes)* < W 92

ästhetische Urteilskraft *f* • (capacity of) aesthetic judg(e)ment *(Kant) (aes)*

ästhetische Wahrnehmung *f* • aesthetic perception *(aes)*

ästhetische Wertschätzung *f* • aesthetic esteem/appreciation *(aes)*

ästhetische Wertung *f* • aesthetic evaluation *(aes)* < ästhetisches Urteil

ästhetische Wirkung *f* • (▷ unmittelbare Wirkung) aesthetic effect, (▷ Einfluß) aesthetic efficacy/influence *(aes)* < Rezeptionsästhetik

ästhetischer Ausdruck *m* • aesthetic expression *(aes)*

ästhetischer Diskurs *m* • aesthetic discourse *(aes)*

ästhetischer Genuß *m* • aesthetic enjoyment/pleasure *(aes)* < ästhetisches Wohlgefallen

ästhetischer Geschmack *m* • aesthetic taste *(aes)*

ästhetischer Maßstab *m* • aesthetic standard *(aes)*

ästhetischer Schein *m* • aesthetic appearance *(aes)*

ästhetischer Sinn *m* • (▷ Urteilsvermögen) aesthetic sense/feeling *(aes)*

ästhetischer Staat *m* • aesthetic state/nation *(Schiller) (aes, pol, eth)*

ästhetischer Zustand *m* • aesthetic condition/state *(aes)*

ästhetisches Geschmacksurteil *n* • aesthetic judg(e)ment of taste *(Kant) (aes)*

ästhetisches Leben *n* • aesthetic stage of life *(Kierkegaard) (aes)*

ästhetisches Urteil *n* • aesthetic judg(e)ment *(aes)* < ästhetische Wertung, Schönheitsurteil

ästhetisches Wohlgefallen *n* • aesthetic pleasure/enjoyment *(aes)*

ästhetisieren • to aestheticize *(aes)*

Ästhetisierung *f* • aestheticization *(aes)*

Ästhetizismus *m* • aestheticism *(aes)*

Astralgeister *pl* • astral spirits *(Alcmaion etc) (met)*

Astralleib *m* • astral body *(eso)* → Ätherleib

Astralmythologie *f* • astral mythology *(met)*

Astralprojektion *f* • astral projection *(eso)*

Astralreligion *f* • astral religion *(rel)*

Astrobiologie *f* • astrobiology *(nat)*

Astrologie *f* • astrology *(eso)*

Astromantie *f* • astromancy *(eso)*

Astrophysik f • astrophysics *(nat)*

Astrotheologie f • astrotheology *(rel)*

Asylpolitik f • asylum policy *(pol)*

Asylrecht n • right of asylum *(pol)*

Asymmetrie f • asymmetry *(mat, aes)*

asymmetrische Relation f • asymmetric(al) relation *(log, mat)*

asymptotische Annäherung f • asymptotic approximation *(mat)*

Ataraxie f • ataraxia, ataraxy, freedom from disturbance, indifference, imperturbability, tranquillity (of mind), serenity *(Epicurus, Cicero etc) (eth)* → Gelassenheit, Gleichmut, Leidenschaftslosigkeit, Seelenfriede < Affektlosigkeit, Apathie

Atavismus m • atavism *(cul)*

Athanasie f • athanasia, immortality *(rel)* → Unsterblichkeit

Athanatismus m • athanatism°, belief in immortality *(rel)* → Unsterblichkeit der Seele

Atheismus m • atheism *(rel)* → Gottlosigkeit

Atheismus, dogmatischer m • dogmatic atheism *(rel)*

Atheismus, kritischer m • critical atheism *(rel)*

Atheismus, skeptischer m • sceptic atheism *(rel)*

Atheismusstreit m • controversy over atheism *(Fichte) (met, rel)*

atheistischer Humanismus m • atheistic humanism *(Marx etc) (met)*

Athenische Akademie f • Athenian Academy *(gep)*

Äther m • ether, aether *(nat, met, eso)*

Ätherleib m → Astralleib

Ätiologie f • (a)etiology *(met)* → Ursachenlehre

Atman m/n • atman *(asp)*

atomare Abrüstung f • nuclear disarmament *(pol)*

atomare Abschreckung f • nuclear deterrence *(pol, eth)* < Vernichtungsdrohung, Terror-Frieden

atomare Aussage f • atomic proposition/statement *(Russell etc) (log, lan)* < Elementarsatz

atomare Drohung f • nuclear threat *(pol)*

atomare Gesellschaft f • atomic/nuclear society *(soc)*

atomare Kriegsführung f • atomic/nuclear warfare *(pol)*

atomare Tatsachen pl • atomic facts *(epi, sci)*

atomare Vernichtung f • nuclear destruction *(pol)*

atomarer Ausdruck m • atomic expression *(Russell etc) (lan, log)* → einfacher Ausdruck

atomarer Brüter m • breeder reactor *(nat)*

atomarer Overkill m • nuclear overkill *(pol)*

atomarer Sachverhalt m • atomic state of affairs/facts° *(lan, log)* → einfacher Sachverhalt < atomare Tatsachen

atomarer Satz m • atomic sentence *(epi, lan, log)* < Elementarsatz

atomarer Verband m • atomic lattice *(nat)*

atomarer Winter m • nuclear winter *(env)* → nuklearer Winter

atomares Wettrüsten n • nuclear arms race *(pol)* /

Atomenergie f • atomic/nuclear energy *(nat)*

atomisierte Gesellschaft f • nucleated/atomised society *(Cohen etc) (soc)* < Gesellschaft, fragmentierte; Vereinsamung, menschliche

Atomismus m • atomism *(met, nat)* → Atomlehre

Atomismus, logischer m • logical atomism *(Wittgenstein, Russell) (log, lan, sci)*

Atomisten, die pl • the Atomists *(met)*

Atomistik f → Atomismus

atomistische Gesellschaft f → atomisierte Gesellschaft

atomistische Philosophie f • atomistic philosophy *(Leucippus, Democritus etc) (met)*

Atomkrieg m • nuclear war *(pol)* ↔ konventioneller Krieg

Atomlehre f • atomic theory, doctrine of the existence of atoms *(Democritus etc) (met, nat)* → Atomismus

Atommodell n • model of the atom, atomic model *(nat)*

Atommüll m • nuclear waste *(env)*

Atomphysik f • nuclear/atomic physics *(nat)* → Kernphysik < Teilchenphysik

Atomreaktor m • nuclear reactor *(nat, tec)* → Kernreaktor

Atomsatz m • atomic sentence/statement *(Russell etc) (lan, log)* ↔ Molekularsatz < Elementarsatz

Atomspaltung f • atomic/nuclear fission, splitting of the atom *(nat)*

Atomstaat m • nuclear state *(Jungk) (pol, eth)*

Atomteststopp m • atomic/nuclear test ban *(pol)*

Atomtheorie f • atomic theory *(nat)*

Atomtheorie des Universums f • atomic theory of the universe *(Democritus) (met)*

Atomversuche pl • nuclear testing *(nat, pol)*

Atomwaffen pl • nuclear weapons *(pol)*

atomwaffenfreie Zone *f* • nuclear free zone *(pol)*

Atomwaffensperrvertrag *m* • non-proliferation treaty *(pol)* < Proliferation

atonale Musik *f* • atonal music *(aes)*

Atonalismus *m* • atonalism *(aes)*

Atonalität *f* • atonality *(aes)*

Attische Schule *f* • Attic School *(gep)*

Attraktion *f* • attraction *(nat, psy)* < Anziehung ↔ Repulsion

Attraktionsmontage *f* • montage of attractions *(Eisenstein)* *(aes)*

Attraktivität *f* • attractiveness *(aes)*

Attrappenversuch *m* • dummy experiment *(sci)*

Attribut *n* • attribute, predicate *(lan, log, met)* < Prädikat

Attribut-Substanz-Relation *f* • attribute-substance relation *(met, ont)*

Attribute Gottes *pl* • attributes of God *(rel)*

Attributionsanalogie *f* • analogy of attribution *(Cajetan, Aquinas)* *(rel)* < Proportionsanalogie

Attributvariable *f* • predicate variable *(lan, log)*

audiovisuelle Medien *pl* • audio-visual media *(gen)*

Aufeinanderangewiesensein *n* • (state of) being dependent upon each other *(soc, ont)*

Aufenthalt des Seins *m* • dwelling of Being *(Heidegger)* *(ont)*

Auferstehung *f* • resurrection *(rel)* → Resurrektion

Auferstehung des Fleisches *f* • resurrection of the body *(rel)*

Aufgabe *f* • task, item *(gep)*

Aufgabenraum *m* • task space *(min, sci)*

Aufgehen in der Natur *n* • absorption in nature *(Rousseau etc)* *(met)*

Aufgehobene, das *n* • the sublated *(Hegel etc)* *(met)* < aufheben

Aufgehobensein des Gegensatzes *n* • sublation of the opposite/opposition *(Hegel etc)* *(met)*

aufgeklärte Gesellschaft *f* • enlightened/liberal society *(soc)*

aufgeklärter Absolutismus *m* • enlightened absolutism *(pol)*

aufgeklärter Verstand *m* • enlightened intellect *(gep)*

aufgeklärtes Denken *n* • enlightened thinking/thought *(gep)*

aufgeklärtes Selbstinteresse *n* • enlightened self-interest *(eth, act)*

aufgeklärtes Zeitalter *n* • enlightened age *(his)* < Aufklärung, Zeitalter der

aufheben • (▷ emporheben) to sublate, to elevate, to raise, to hold up, to lift up, (▷ bewahren) to preserve, to keep, to save, (▷ negieren) to negate, to abolish, to destroy, to cancel, to annull, to suspend, to overcome *(Hegel)* *(met)*

Aufhebung *f* • (▷ Emporhebung) sublation, raising up, (▷ Bewahrung) preservation, (▷ Negation) negation, abolition, overcoming *(Hegel)* *(met)*

Aufhebung der Arbeit *f* • abolition of labour *(Proudhon etc)* *(soc)*

Aufhebung der Familie *f* • abolition of the family *(Engels)* *(soc)*

Aufhebung des Privateigentums *f* • abolition of private property *(Marx etc)* *(eco, soc)*

Aufhebung des Proletariats *f* • abolition of the proletariat *(Marx etc)* *(pol)*

Aufhebung des Staates *f* • abolition of the state *(Marx etc)* *(pol)*

Aufhebung, dialektische *f* • dialectical sublation *(Hegel)* *(met)*

Aufklärer, philosophischer *m* • philosopher of the Enlightenment *(gep)*

aufklärerisch-emanzipatorische Vernunft *f* • enlightened emancipative reason *(soc)*

aufklärerische Ideale *pl* • Enlightenment ideals *(his)*

Aufklärung *f* • Enlightenment *(his)* < W 113

Aufklärung, Zeitalter der *n* • Age of Enlightenment *(his)* → Vernunftzeitalter

Aufklärungskampagne *f* • educational campaign *(soc)*

Aufklärungsphilosophie *f* • philosophy of the Enlightenment *(gep)*

Auflehnung *f* • revolt *(pol, met)* < Revolte

Aufmerksamkeit *f* • attention, attentiveness *(psy)*

Aufmerksamkeitsleistung *f* • act of attention *(psy)*

Aufmerksamkeitstypen *pl* • types of attention *(psy)*

Aufmerksamkeitswort *n* • head/key word *(Ryle etc)* *(lan)*

Aufnahmefähigkeit *f* • receptivity *(psy)* → Rezeptivität

Aufnahmestopp für Flüchtlinge *m* • ban on immigration *(pol)*

aufrechter Gang des Menschen *m* • erect posture of man *(ant)*

Aufrichtigkeitsbedingung *f* • sincerity condition *(Austin etc)* *(lan)*

Aufrichtigkeitsregel *f* • sincerity rule *(Searle, Grice etc)* *(lan)*

Aufrüstung *f* • armament, arming *(pol)* < Wettrüsten

Aufspaltung *f* → Verzweigung

Aufstand der Massen *m* • revolt of the masses *(Ortega y Gasset) (pol, cul)* < Vermassung des Menschen, Massenmensch, Massengesellschaft < W 102

Aufstand der unterworfenen Wissensarten *m* • insurrection of subjugated knowledge *(Foucault) (epi, pol)*

aufsteigende Bewegung des Lebens *f* • ascending movement of life *(Nietzsche) (met)*

Aufstiegschance *f* • opportunity for social advance *(soc)*

Auftrag der Geschichte *m* • mandate from history *(his)*

Auftragsforschung *f* • commissioned research *(sci)*

Aufwärtsbewegung der Seele *f* • upward movement of the soul *(Plato) (met)*

Aufweis(ung) *m (f)* • demonstration *(Husserl etc) (epi, met)*

aufzählbar • enumerable *(mat)*

Augenblick *m* • moment, instant *(Heidegger etc) (ont)*

Augenzeuge *m* • eyewitness *(his, jur)* < Wahrheitszeuge

Augustinismus *m* • Augustinianism, Augustinism *(gep)*

Augustinus • Augustine

Aura *f* • aura *(Galen, Jung etc) (met, psy)*

Aura der Kunst *f* • aura of art *(Benjamin) (aes)*

aus Pflicht • from duty *(Kant) (eth)* ↔ pflichtmäßig

ausbeuterische Orientierung *f* • exploitative orientation *(Fromm) (psy, soc)*

ausbeuterischer Charakter *m* • exploitative character *(Fromm) (psy, soc)*

Ausbeutung *f* • exploitation *(Marx etc) (eco)* → Aneignung fremder Arbeit, Exploitation, Mehrwerttransfer

Ausbeutung des Menschen durch den Menschen *f* • exploitation of man by man *(Marx etc) (eco, soc)*

Ausbeutungstheorie *f* • theory of exploitation *(Marx etc) (eco, pol)*

Ausblickspunkt *m* • point of view *(Carnap) (epi)*

Ausbürgerung *f* • expatriation *(pol)*

Ausdauer *f* • patience, persistence *(psy)*

Ausdehnung *f* • (▷ Umfang) extension *(nat)*, (▷ Expansion) expansion *(nat)*

Ausdehnung des Universums *f* • expansion of the universe *(nat)* < Doppler-Effekt, Urknall

Ausdehnung, räumliche *f* • spatial extension *(mat, nat, met)*

Ausdeutung *f* • exegesis, interpretation *(gep)* → Exegese < Auslegung

Ausdifferenzierung der Gesellschaft *f* • differentiation of society, social differentiation *(Luhmann) (soc)*

Ausdruck *m* • expression *(lan, log)*

Ausdruck, regulärer *m* • regular expression *(lan, log)*

Ausdruck unendlicher Länge *m* • infinite expression *(mat, lan)*

Ausdrucksbewegung *f* • movement expressing thought/feeling, (facial) expression, gesture *(psy)*

Ausdruckseigenschaft *f* • property of being an expression *(lan, log)*

Ausdrucksform *f* • form of expression *(lan, log)*

Ausdrucksfunktion der Sprache *f* • expressive function of language *(Bühler) (lan)*

Ausdrucksisomorphismus *m* • isomorphism of expressions *(lan, log)*

Ausdruckskalkül *m/n* • statement calculus, calculus of expressions *(lan, log)*

Ausdruckslehre *f* → Ausdruckstheorie

Ausdrucksprinzip *n* • principle of expression *(Klages) (psy)*

Ausdruckspsychologie *f* • psychology of expressive behaviour *(psy)* < Pathognomik

Ausdrucksqualität *f* • expression/expressive quality *(aes)*

Ausdrucksstärke *f* → Expressivität

Ausdruckstheorie *f* • expression theory, theory of expression *(aes)*

Ausdrucksverstehen *n* • understanding of expression *(Scheler etc) (epi, met)*

Ausdrucksweise *f* • mode of expression, way of speaking *(lan)*

Ausfluß *m* → Emanation

Ausgangsbedingung *f* • initial condition *(gen)*

Ausgangsdaten *pl* • initial data *(sci)*

Ausgangswahrscheinlichkeit *f* • initial/prior probability *(mat)*

ausgedehnte Substanz *f* • extended substance *(Descartes) (epi, met)* → res extensa ↔ Substanz, denkende

ausgedehntes Ding *n* → ausgedehntes Objekt

ausgedehntes Objekt *n* • extended object *(epi, met)* → res extensa

Ausgerichtetheit *f* • directedness *(Heidegger) (ont)* < Ausrichtung

ausgeschlossener Widerspruch *m* • non-contradiction *(log)* < Satz vom Widerspruch, Satz vom ausgeschlossenen Dritten

ausgeschlossenes Drittes *n* • excluded middle *(log)*

Ausgleich der Kräfte *m* • balance of power *(pol, nat)*

ausgleichende Gerechtigkeit *f* • retributive/ rectifactory/rectificatory/corrective/commutative justice *(eth, jur)*, compensatory/ poetic justice *(eth, aes)* ↔ distributive Gerechtigkeit < vergeltende Gerechtigkeit

Ausgleichsprinzip *n* • principle of redress *(Rawls) (eth, pol)*

Ausgrenzung, soziale *f* • social exclusion/ marginalization *(soc)* → Marginalisierung, sozialer Ausschluß < Stigmatisierung

Auskristallisierung *f* • cristallization *(nat, cul, aes)* < Posthistoire

Ausländerfeindlichkeit *f* • xenophobia *(pol)*

Ausländerwahlrecht *n* • foreigners' right to vote *(pol)*

Auslegung *f* • interpretation *(lan)* < Ausdeutung

Auslegung des Geistes, Geschichte als *f* • history as exposition of the spirit *(Hegel etc) (his, met)*

Auslegung, enge *f* • narrow interpretation *(lan, sci)*

Auslegung, weite *f* • broad interpretation *(lan, sci)*

Auslegungskunst *f* • art of exegesis *(lan)* → Hermeneutik < Interpretation

Auslegungslehre *f* → Exegese

Auslese *f* • selection *(Darwin etc) (nat)* → Selektion, natürliche Auslese

Ausleseprozeß *m* • selection process *(nat, soc)*

Auslösemechanismus *m* • release mechanism *(psy, tec)*

Ausnahme *f* • exception *(gep)* < Regel und Ausnahme

Ausreißereffekt *m* • runaway effect *(mat)*

Ausrichtung *f* • orientation, direction *(gen)*, directionality *(Heidegger) (ont)* < Ausgerichtetheit

Aussage *f* • (asserted) proposition, statement, utterance *(lan, log)*

Aussage der Kunst *f* • message of art *(aes)*

Aussage, existentielle *f* • existential statement/ proposition *(lan, log)*

Aussage, normative *f* • normative statement *(lan, sci)*

Aussage, universelle *f* • universal statement/ proposition *(lan, log)*

Aussageform *f* • statement form *(lan, log)*

Aussagefunktion *f* • propositional function, statement function *(lan, log)*

Aussagehomogenität *f* • enunciative homogeneity *(Foucault) (epi, lan)*

Aussagengleichung *f* • propositional/statement equation *(log)*

Aussagenkalkül *m/n* • propositional calculus *(log)* < Aussagenlogik

Aussagenkonzeption *f* • propositional conception *(sci)*

Aussagenlogik *f* • propositional/sentential logic *(log)* < Aussagenkalkül

aussagenlogisch • propositional *(log)*

Aussagenvariable *f* • proposition(al) variable *(log)*

Aussageperioden *pl* • enunciative periods *(Foucault) (epi, his)*

Aussagesatz *m* • statement *(lan, log)*

ausschaltende Induktion *f* • eliminative induction *(Mill etc) (log, sci)* → eliminierende Induktion

ausschlaggebende Stimme *f* • deciding vote, decisive voice, tie-breaking vote *(pol)*

Ausschließung *f* • exclusion *(log)* → Exklusion ↔ Inklusion

Ausschlußmethode *f* • method of exclusion *(sci)*

Außen, das *n* • the outside *(Derrida) (met)*

Außenleitung *f* • other-directedness *(Riesman) (soc)*

Außenlenkung *f* → Außenleitung

Außenperspektive *f* • external perspective *(sci)*

Außenseiter, gesellschaftlicher *m* • social outcast, outsider *(soc)* < Paria

Außensteuerung *f* → Außenleitung

Außenwelt *f* • external/outside world *(epi, met)*

Außenweltproblem *n* • problem of the external world *(epi, met)*

Außenweltrealismus *m* • external world realism, realism in regard to the external world *(epi, met)*

Außenwirklichkeit *f* • external reality *(met)*

außer sich • outside/beside oneself *(met)*

äußere Anschauung *f* • outer intuition *(Kant) (epi)*

äußere Erfahrung *f* • outer experience, external experience *(epi)*

äußere Erscheinung *f* • outer appearance *(Kant) (epi)*

äußere Form *f* • external form *(Kant etc) (epi, aes)* ↔ innere Form

äußere Gesetzgebung *f* • external lawgiving *(Kant) (eth, jur)*

äußere Lüge *f* • external lie *(Kant) (eth)*

äußere Objekte *pl* • external objects *(epi, met)*

äußere Sinne *pl* • external senses *(epi)*

äußere Verknüpfung *f* • external link *(log, lan)*

äußere Vorstellung *f* • external representation *(Kant)* *(epi)*

äußere Wahrnehmung *f* • outer/external perception *(epi, psy)*

äußere Widersprüche *pl* • extrinsic contradictions *(Foucault)* *(epi, pol)*

äußere Zweckmäßigkeit *f* • external functionality/appropriateness/fitness/finality *(Kant)* *(epi, nat)* < Zweckmäßigkeit

äußerer Sinn *m* • external/outer sense *(epi, psy)*

äußerer Zwang *m* • external constraint *(act, eth)* < Sachzwang

Äußeres *n* • (the) outer *(epi)*

außereuropäische Philosophie *f* • non-European philosophy *(gep)*

außerirdische Intelligenz *f* • extraterrestrial intelligence *(nat)*

außerirdisches Leben *n* • extraterrestrial life *(met, nat, eso)*

außerkonstitutorische Eigenschaften *pl* • extranuclear properties *(Meinong, Mally)* *(ont)*

außerkörperliche Erfahrung *f* • out-of-the-body experience, OBE *(psy, eso)* < außersinnliche Wahrnehmung, übersinnliche Erfahrungsquelle

Äußerlichkeit *f* • outwardness, externality *(met)*

außernatürlich • preternatural *(eso, rel)*

außerparlamentarische Opposition *f* • extraparliamentary opposition *(pol)*

Außer-Sich, das *n* • the outside-of-itself, the outside oneself *(Hegel, Heidegger)* *(met)*

Außersichsein *n* • being outside oneself, externality *(ont)*

außersinnliche Wahrnehmung *f* • extrasensory perception, ESP *(Rhine etc)* *(eso, psy)*

außersprachlich regulierte Interaktion *f* • extralinguistically regulated interaction *(lan, act)*

Äußerung *f* • utterance, expression *(lan)*

Äußerungsakt *m* • locutionary act *(Austin etc)* *(lan)* → lokutionärer Akt

außerweltlich • extraterrestrial *(met)* < extramundan, transzendent

außerweltliche Spekulation *f* • otherworldly speculation *(met)*

Aussperrung *f* • lockout *(eco)* < Arbeitskampf, Streik

Aussteiger *m* • drop-out *(soc)* < Rückzug aus der Gesellschaft

Austauschbarkeit *f* • interchangeability (salva veritate) *(Leibniz etc)* *(log, lan)* < Synonymität

Austauschbarkeitsprinzip *n* • principle of interchangeability *(Carnap etc)* *(log, lan)*

Austauschregel *f* • exchange rule/law, rule of interchange/interchangeability *(log, lan)* → Substitutionsregel

Austauschverhältnis *n* • exchange relationship *(Marx etc)* *(eco)*

Austeritätspolitik *f* • austerity politics *(eco)*

Australopithecus *m* • australopithecus *(ant)*

Austrofaschismus *m* • Austro-Fascism *(pol)*

Austromarxismus *m* • Austro-Marxism *(pol)*

Auswahlaxiom *n* • axiom of choice *(Zermelo)* *(mat, log)*

Auswahlmethode *f* • method of selection *(sci)*

Auswahlverfahren *n* • selection procedure *(dec, sci)*

Ausweglosigkeit *f* • aporia, paradoxical situation *(log, act)* → Aporie

Auswirkungsanalyse *f* • impact analysis *(sys)*

Autarchie *f* • autarchy *(pol)*

Autarkie *f* • autarky, self-sufficiency *(eco)* < Unabhängigkeit, materielle; Selbstversorgungswirtschaft

authentisches Dasein *n* • authentic existence *(Sartre)* *(met, eth)*

Authentizität *f* • authenticity *(gep)* < Echtheit, Eigentlichkeit

Autismus *m* • autism *(psy)*

autistisches Denken *n* • autistic thinking *(psy)*

Autoaggression *f* • auto/self -aggression *(psy)* < auto-destruktives Verhalten

Autodafé *n* • auto-da-fé, burning at the stake *(rel, pol)*

auto-destruktives Verhalten *n* • auto/self - destructive behaviour *(psy)* → selbstdestruktives Verhalten < Autoaggression

Autodeterminismus *m* • doctrine of self-determination/determinism *(met, eth)* < Autonomie, Selbstbestimmung

Autoevolution *f* • autoevolution *(nat)*

Autofalsifikation *f* • autofalsification, self-falsification *(log, sci)*

Autokatalyse *f* • autocatalysis *(sys)*

Autokinese *f* • autokinesis *(nat)* → Selbstbewegung

Autokratie *f* • autocracy *(pol)*

Autokratismus *m* • autocratic attitude and behaviour *(pol)*

autologischer Begriff *m* • autological concept/term *(Grelling)* *(log, lan)* ↔ heterologischer Begriff

Automat, endlicher *m* • finite-state automaton *(nat, AI)*

Automatentheorie *f* • theory of automata *(sys, nat, met)*

Automation *f* • automation *(tec, eco)*

Automatisation *f* → Automatisierung

automatisches Beweisen *n* • mechanical theorem-proving *(AI, log)*

automatisches Schreiben *n* • automatic writing *(aes)* → écriture automatique

automatisierte Produktion *f* • automated production *(eco)*

Automatisierung *f* • automation, automatization *(tec, eco)*

Automatismus *m* • automatism *(nat, psy, aes, met)*

Automatismus des Instinkts *m* • automatism of instinct *(Nietzsche) (nat)*

Automorphismus *m* • automorphism *(mat)*

autonome Frauenbewegung *f* • autonomous women's movement *(fem)*

autonomes Prinzip *n* • autonomous principle *(Kant) (epi, eth)* ↔ heteronomes Prinzip

autonomes Schichtensystem *n* • multiechelon system *(sys)* < Kontrollhierarchien

Autonomie *f* • autonomy *(eth, met, pol)* → Selbstgesetzlichkeit ↔ Heteronomie < selbstbestimmtes Leben

Autonomie der Ethik *f* • autonomy of ethics *(eth)*

Autonomie der Kunst *f* • autonomy of art *(aes)*

Autonomie der Moral *f* • autonomy of morality *(eth)*

Autonomie der Wissenschaft *f* • autonomy of science *(sci)*

Autonomie des moralisch Handelnden *f* • autonomy of the moral agent *(eth)*

Autonomie des Willens *f* • autonomy of the will *(Kant) (met, eth)*

Autonomie, relative *f* • relative autonomy *(Althusser) (epi, soc)*

Autonomieprinzip *n* • principle of autonomy, autonomy principle *(pol, eth)*

Autonomisierung *f* • autonomization *(eth, pol)*

Autonomismus *m* • autonomism *(met)*

Autophilie *f* → Eigenliebe, Selbstliebe

Autopoiese *f* → Autopoiesis

Autopoiesis *f* • autopoiesis *(Maturana) (sys)* → Selbstorganisation

autopoietische Systeme *pl* • autopoietic systems *(Maturana) (sys)* < selbstorganisierende Systeme, selbsttätige Systeme

Autorenkollektiv *n* • authors' collective *(gen)*

Autorisation *f* • authorization *(jur)*

Autorisierung *f* → Autorisation

autoritäre Gesellschaft *f* • authoritarian/oppressive society *(pol, soc)* < repressive Gesellschaft

autoritäre Persönlichkeit *f* • authoritarian personality *(psy)*

autoritärer Charakter *m* • authoritarian character *(Adorno etc) (psy, soc)* < W 109

autoritärer Kommunismus *m* • authoritarian communism *(Bakunin) (pol)*

autoritärer Staat *m* • authoritarian state *(pol)*

autoritäres Syndrom *n* • authoritarian syndrome *(Adorno etc) (soc)*

Autoritarismus *m* • authoritarianism *(pol)* < Totalitarismus

Autorität *f* • authority *(psy)*

Autorität, abstrakte *f* • abstract authority *(Schelsky) (soc)*

Autorität, äußere *f* • external authority *(Freud etc) (psy)*

Autorität, charismatische *f* • charismatic authority *(Weber) (soc)*

Autorität, delegierte *f* • delegated authority *(soc)*

Autorität, echte *f* • real/true/genuine authority *(Scheler, Hildebrand etc) (eth)*

Autorität, funktionale *f* • functional authority *(soc)*

Autorität, innere *f* • internal authority *(Freud etc) (psy)*

Autorität, künstliche *f* • artificial authority *(psy)*

Autorität, legal-rationale *f* • legal-rational authority *(Weber) (soc)*

Autorität, legitime *f* • legitimate authority *(pol, jur)*

Autorität, literarische *f* • literary authority *(aes)*

Autorität, natürliche *f* • natural authority *(psy)* < Charisma

Autorität, persönliche *f* • personal authority *(psy)*

Autorität, polizeistaatliche *f* • police state authority *(Müller etc) (soc)*

Autorität, primäre *f* • primary authority *(Schelsky) (soc)*

Autorität, religiöse *f* • religious authority *(rel)*

Autorität, staatliche *f* • state authority *(pol)*

Autorität, traditionale *f* • traditional authority *(Weber) (soc)*

Autorität, unechte *f* • inauthentic/false authority *(Scheler etc) (eth)*

Autorität, wissenschaftliche *f* • scientific authority *(sci)*

autoritativ • authoritative *(psy)*

Autoritätsgläubigkeit *f* • belief in authority *(pol, psy)*

Autoritätskritik *f* • criticism of authority *(F. Bacon etc) (sci)*

Autoritätsobjekt *n* • object of authority *(psy)*

Autoritätssubjekt *n* • subject of authority *(psy)*

Autoritätstheorie *f* • theory of authority *(gep)*

Autoritätsträger *m* • bearer/carrier/upholder of authority *(psy, soc)*

Autorschaft *f* • authorship *(gen)*

autosemantisch • autosemantic *(lan)*

Autosuggestion *f* • autosuggestion *(psy)*

Autotelik *f* • autotelicity° *(met)*

Autotheismus *m* • autotheism *(rel, psy)* → Selbstvergötterung

autothelisch • autotelic *(met)*

Avantgarde *f* • avant-garde *(aes)*, vanguard *(gen)*

Avantgarde-Kunst *f* • avant-garde art *(aes)*

Avantgardismus *m* • avant-gardism *(aes, pol)*

Avatara *f* • avatara *(asp)* < Inkarnation

Averroismus *m* • Averr(h)oism *(gep)*

Aversion *f* • aversion *(psy)* → Widerwille

Avidya *f* • avidya, ignorance, lack of wisdom *(asp)*

Axiologie *f* • axiology, theory of values *(eth)* → Wertlehre < Wertwissenschaft

axiologische Ethik *f* • axiological ethics *(eth)* → Wertethik

Axiom der unendlichen Teilbarkeit *n* • axiom of infinite divisibility *(mat, log)*

Axiom *n* • axiom *(log, mat)* < Grundsatz; Satz, grundlegender

Axiom vom ausgeschlossenen Spielsystem *n* • principle of the excluded gambling system *(Mises) (dec)*

Axiomatik *f* • axiomatics *(log)*

axiomatisch-deduktives System *n* • axiomatic deductive system *(sci)* < more geometrico

axiomatische Methode *f* • axiomatic method *(sci)*

axiomatische Ontologie *f* • axiomatic ontology *(ont)*

Axiomatisierbarkeit *f* • axiomatizability *(log)*

Axiomatisierung *f* • axiomatization *(log, sci)*

Axiomatisierung der Wahrscheinlichkeitstheorie *f* • axiomatization of probability theory *(mat, log)*

Axiome der Anschauung *pl* • axioms of intuition *(Kant) (epi)*

Axiomen-Schema *n* • axiom scheme/schema *(mat)*

Axiomensystem *n* • axiom system *(log, mat, sci)*

axonometrisches Bild *n* • axonometric image *(mat)*

azyklisch • acyclical *(nat, eco)* ↔ zyklisch

B

Babouvismus *m* • Babouvism *(soc)* < Jakobinismus

babylonische Sprachverwirrung *f* • a Babel/confusion of languages/tongues *(lan)*

Badische Schule *f* • Baden School, South-West German School *(gep)* → Marburger Schule

Balkendiagramm *n* • bar graph *(mat, sci)*

Banalität des Bösen *f* • banality of evil *(Arendt) (eth)*

Bankokratie *f* • bankocracy, rule by banks *(eco)* < Finanzkapitalismus

Baptismus *m* • baptism *(rel)*

Barbarei, neue *f* • new barbarism *(Horkheimer, Adorno) (soc, pol)*

Barbaren des Geistes *pl* • barbarians of the spirit *(Nietzsche) (met)*

Barbarismus *m* • barbarism *(aes)*

Barcan-Formel *f* • Barcan formula *(log)* < Modallogik

Bardo • in-between state *(asp)*

Barockstil *m* • baroque style *(aes)*

Barockzeit *f* • Baroque era/period *(his, aes)*

Bartergeschäft *n* • barter (trade) *(eco)* < Tauschhandelssystem, Tauschwirtschaft

basale Einzeldinge *pl* • basic particulars *(Strawson) (epi, met)*

Basis und Überbau *f,m* • base/basis and superstructure *(Marx) (eco, soc, epi)*

Basis, empirische *f* • empirical basis *(sci)*

Basis, materielle *f* • material base/basis/foundation *(Marx etc) (eco, soc)* → ökonomische Basis ↔ ideeller Überbau

Basis, ökonomische *f* • economic base/basis/foundation *(Marx etc) (eco, soc)* → materielle Basis ↔ ideeller Überbau

Basis, politische *f* • political basis *(pol)*

Basis-Überbau-Modell *n* • base/basis- superstructure model *(Marx) (eco, soc, epi)*

Basisaussage *f* • basic statement/proposition, test statement *(Popper etc) (sci, lan)* → Basissatz < Beobachtungsaussage, Elementaraussage, Protokollsatz

Basisdemokratie *f* • grass-roots democracy *(pol)*

Basisgemeinde *f* • base/basic community *(rel, soc)*

Basisgruppe *f* • action group *(pol)*

Basishandlung *f* • basic action *(act)*

Basisnorm *f* • basic norm *(Kelsen) (jur, eth)* → Grundnorm

Basissatz *m* • basic statement/proposition, test statement *(Popper etc) (sci, lan)* → Basisaussage < Beobachtungsaussage, Elementaraussage, Protokollsatz

Basissprache *f* • basic language *(lan)*

Basistheorem *n* • basic theorem *(Carnap etc) (sci)*

Basisüberzeugung *f* • basic conviction/belief *(gep)* → Grundüberzeugung

Basisvektor *m* • base/basis vector *(mat)*

Basiswert *m* • basic value *(eth)*, base value *(mat)*

Basiswissen *n* • basic knowledge *(epi)*

bäuerliche Gesellschaft *f* • agrarian/peasant society *(soc)* < traditionelle Gesellschaft

Bauernaufstand des Geistes *m* • peasants' revolt of the mind *(Nietzsche) (met)*

Baum der Entwicklung *m* • tree of evolution, evolutionary tree *(nat)*

Baum der Erkenntnis *m* • tree of knowledge *(epi, rel)*

Baum des Porphyrius *m* • tree of Porphyry, Porphyrian tree *(log, lan)*

Baumdiagramm *n* • tree diagram *(mat, dec)*

baumlogische Systeme *pl* • tree-logic systems *(log)*

Bayesianismus *m* • Bayesianism *(sci, mat)*

Bayessche Rationalitätskonzeption *f* • Bayesian conception of rationality *(sci, mat)*

Bayessche Statistik *f* • Bayesian statistics *(sci, mat)*

Bayessches Theorem *n* • Bayes' theorem *(sci, mat)*

Bedachtsamkeit *f* • deliberation *(eth)*; *(Heidegger) (ont)* < Sorge

Bedarfdeckungswirtschaft *f* • subsistence economy *(eco)* → Subsistenzwirtschaft

Bedarfsbefriedigung *f* • satisfaction of demand *(eco)* < Bedürfnisbefriedigung

Bedarfsdeckung *f* • demand coverage *(eco)* ↔ Bedarfsweckung

Bedarfsdeckungskosten *pl* • subsistence costs *(eco)* → Unterhaltskosten

Bedarfsgüter *pl* • consumer goods *(eco)*

bedarfsorientiert • demand-oriented *(eco)*

Bedarfsweckung *f* • creation of needs *(eco)* ↔ Bedarfsdeckung

Bedenkzeit *f* • time for reflection, time for consideration *(act)*

bedeuten • to mean, to signify, to refer *(lan)*

Bedeutsamkeit *f* • meaningfulness, significance *(lan, gep)* < Sinnkriterium

Bedeutung *f* • meaning, sense, reference, signification *(log, lan)* < W 1115

Bedeutung als Gebrauch *f* • meaning as use *(Wittgenstein) (lan)* < Gebrauchstheorie der Bedeutung

Bedeutung, begleitende *f* • acompanying/ subsidiary meaning *(lan)* → Konnotation

Bedeutung, natürliche *f* • natural meaning *(Grice) (lan)*

Bedeutung, nicht-natürliche *f* • unnatural meaning *(Grice) (lan)*

Bedeutung, übertragene *f* • metaphorical meaning, figurative sense *(lan)*

Bedeutung, wörtliche *f* • literal meaning *(lan)* ↔ metaphorische Bedeutung

Bedeutungsanalyse *f* • analysis of meaning, meaning analysis, semantic analysis *(log, lan)*

Bedeutungsbegriff *m* • concept of meaning *(lan)* < Sinnbegriff

Bedeutungsbereich *m* • range of significance *(Carnap) (lan)*

Bedeutungsbeziehungen *pl* → Sinnrelationen

Bedeutungsblindheit *f* • meaning-blindness *(Wittgenstein) (lan)*

Bedeutungsdefinition *f* • meaning definition *(log, lan)*

Bedeutungserfüllung *f* • meaning-fulfilment *(Husserl) (log)*

Bedeutungsganzes *n* • referential whole *(Heidegger) (ont)*

Bedeutungsgleichheit *f* • synonymy, sameness of meaning *(log, lan)* → Synonymie

Bedeutungshaftigkeit *f* • meaningfulness *(log, lan)* < Bedeutsamkeit

Bedeutungshorizont *m* • horizon of meaning(s) *(lan)*

Bedeutungsintension *f* → Intension

Bedeutungsintention *f* • meaning intention *(Husserl etc) (epi, met)*

Bedeutungskategorie *f* • meaning/semantic category *(Husserl etc) (lan, epi, met)*

Bedeutungskonvention *f* • meaning convention *(lan)*

bedeutungsleer • void/empty of meaning *(lan, sci)*

Bedeutungslehre *f* → Bedeutungstheorie

Bedeutungslosigkeit *f* • meaninglessness, nonsensicality *(lan)* < Sinnkriterium

Bedeutungspostulat *n* • meaning postulate *(Carnap) (log, lan)* < Analytizitätspostulat

Bedeutungsregel *f* • meaning rule *(Hare) (lan)*

Bedeutungsrelation *f* • meaning/sense relation *(lan)*

Bedeutungstheorie *f* • theory of meaning, meaning theory *(lan)*

Bedeutungsverknüpfung *f* • meaning connection, semantic relation *(Husserl) (epi, met)*

Bedeutungsverschiebung *f* • shift of meaning *(lan)*

Bedeutungsverstehen *n* • understanding of meaning *(lan, sci)*

bedeutungsvoll • meaningful *(lan)*

Bedeutungswandel *m* • change of meaning *(lan)*

Bedeutungszusammenhang *m* • context, collocation, interconnection of meaning° *(lan)*

bedingendes Gesetz *n* • conditioning law *(Carnap) (sci)*

bedingt konvergent • conditionally convergent *(mat)* < unterkonvergent

Bedingte, das *n* • the conditional, the contingent *(met)*

bedingte Korrelation *f* • dependent correlation *(mat, sci)*

bedingte Norm *f* • conditional norm *(eth)*

bedingte Notwendigkeit *f* • conditional necessity *(log, met)* → Notwendigkeit, relative

bedingte Prognose *f* • conditional prediction *(sci)*

bedingte Wahrscheinlichkeit *f* • conditional probability *(mat, sci)*

bedingter Reflex *m* • conditioned reflex *(psy)*

bedingter Stimulus *m* • conditional stimulus *(psy)* < bedingter Reflex

bedingter Zusammenhang *m* • conditional relation(ship) *(log, sys)*

Bedingtheit der Existenz *f* • (▷ Kontingenz) contingency of existence, (▷ Bestimmtheit) determinedness of existence *(met)* < Schicksal

Bedingtheit *f* • determinedness, conditionality, contingency *(log, ont)* → Abhängigkeit, kausale

Bedingung *f* • determination, condition *(log, met)*

Bedingung a priori *f* • a priori condition *(Kant) (epi)*

Bedingung der hohen Wahrscheinlichkeit *f* • requirement of high probability *(Hempel etc) (log, sci)*

Bedingung der Möglichkeit *f* • condition of (the) possibility *(Kant etc) (epi, met)*

Bedingung der totalen Evidenz *f* • requirement of total evidence *(log, sci)*

Bedingung der uniformen Interpretation *f* • requirement of uniform interpretation *(log)*

Bedingung, unzureichende f • insufficient/nonsufficient condition (sci, log)

Bedingung, zureichende f • sufficient condition (sci, log)

Bedingungen der Anschauung pl • conditions of intuition (Kant) (epi)

Bedingungen der Erfahrung pl • conditions of experience (Kant) (epi)

Bedingungen der Erkenntnis pl • conditions of knowledge (Kant) (epi)

Bedingungen der Möglichkeit der Erkenntnis pl • conditions of the possibility of knowledge, conditions of possible knowledge (Kant) (epi)

Bedingungen des Denkens pl • conditions of thought/thinking (Kant) (epi)

Bedingungssatz m • conditional clause/proposition/sentence/statement (lan)

Bedingungsurteil n • conditional judg(e)ment (log)

Bedingungsverhältnis n • conditioning relation, relation of interdependence (sys, met)

bedrohte Völker pl • threatened peoples (pol) < ethnische Minderheiten

Bedürfnis n • need, want (eco, psy)

Bedürfnis der Erlösung n • need for redemption (Nietzsche) (met)

Bedürfnisbefriedigung f • satisfaction of needs/wants (eco, psy) < Bedarfsbefriedigung

Bedürfniserfüllung f • fulfilment/satisfaction of needs/wants (eco, psy)

Bedürfnishierarchie f • hierarchy of needs (eco, psy)

Bedürfniskritik f • criticism of needs (eth, soc)

Bedürfnislosigkeit f • absence of (unsatisfied) needs, absence of wants (eco, eth) < Askese

Bedürfnisorientierung f • need orientation (Gehlen) (cul) < Antriebsorientierung

Bedürfnisprinzip n • principle of needs (eco)

Bedürfnisreduktion f • reduction of desires/needs, need reduction (psy, eco, eth)

Bedürfnisse, materielle pl • material needs (eco)

Befehlsmoral f • morality of commands (eth)

Befehlsnotstand m • acting under binding orders (eth, jur)

Befindlichkeit f • disposition, affectedness, state of being/mind, befindlichkeit (Heidegger) (ant) < Grundbefindlichkeit

Befragung, gegabelte f • split ballot (sci, soc)

befreiter Geist m • liberated spirit (Nietzsche) (met) < freie Geister

Befreiung der Frauen f • women's liberation (fem, pol) < Emanzipation der Frau

Befreiung der Tiere f • animal liberation (Singer etc) (eth) < Tier-Ethik

Befreiung von der Wiedergeburt f • liberation from rebirth (asp)

Befreiung von der Zeit f • liberation from time (met)

Befreiungsbewegung f • liberation movement (pol) < Emanzipationsbewegung

Befreiungskampf m • struggle for liberation (pol)

Befreiungskrieg m • war of liberation (pol)

Befreiungsprozeß m • process of liberation (met, pol)

Befreiungstheologie f • liberation theology, theology of liberation (rel, pol)

befriedetes Dasein n • satisfied existence (met, psy) < erfülltes Dasein

Befriedigung f • satisfaction (eco, psy)

Befriedigungserlebnis n • experience of satisfaction (Freud) (psy)

Befriedung f • pacification (pol) → Pazifikation < Friedensstiftung

Begabung f • gift, talent (psy)

begegnen • to encounter (Heidegger) (ont)

Begegnenlassen-von n • to let be encountered (Heidegger) (ont) < Zeugganzheit

Begegnung f • encounter (Goffman) (soc)

Begehren, das n • desire, wish, request (psy) < Verlangen; Wünschen, das

Begehrlichkeit f • conation (psy), covetousness (rel, eth)

Begehrungsvermögen n • faculty of desire (Kant) (epi, ant, psy)

Begierde f • desire, longing, craving (psy) → Kupidität < sinnliche Begierde

Begierde, fleischliche f • sensual/carnal appetite/desire, lust (psy, rel)

Begleiterscheinung f • side-effect, concomitant symptom° (gep)

Begleitursache f • secondary/subsidiary cause (met, sci)

Begreifbarkeit f • comprehensibility (epi)

Begreifen n • comprehension (epi)

begrenzt-endlich • limited-finite (mat)

begrenzte Sinnprovinzen pl → Sinnbereiche, abgeschlossene

Begriff m • concept, conception, notion, term (lan, log, met) < Term

Begriff, abstrakter m • abstract concept (lan)

Begriff, allgemeiner m • universal concept, general term/notion/idea (log, lan) < notiones communes

Begriff, deskriptiver m • descriptive term/concept (lan) ↔ Begriff, normativer

Begriff, einfacher *m* • simple concept *(lan, epi, log)* ↔ Begriff, zusammengesetzter

Begriff, enger *m* • narrow concept *(lan, log)* ↔ Begriff, weiter

Begriff, leerer *m* • empty concept *(Kant) (epi, lan)*

Begriff, normativer *m* • normative term/concept *(lan)* ↔ Begriff, deskriptiver < Wertbegriff

Begriff, substanzieller *m* • substantial/essential concept *(met)*

Begriff, theoretischer *m* • theoretical concept (sci, *log, lan*) → theoretischer Term

Begriff, unendlicher *m* • infinite concept *(log, met)*

Begriff, ungegenständlicher *m* → Begriff, abstrakter

Begriff, vollständiger *m* • complete idea/concept *(Leibniz) (met)*

Begriff, weiter *m* • wide/broad concept *(lan, log)* ↔ Begriff, enger

Begriff, zusammengesetzter *m* • composite term, compound/complex concept *(lan, epi, log)* ↔ Begriff, einfacher

Begriffe, identische *pl* • identical concepts *(log, lan)*

Begriffe, naturalistische *pl* • naturalistic concepts *(lan)*

begriffliche Klarheit und Strenge *f* • conceptual clarity and rigour *(gep)*

begriffliche Nähe *f* • conceptual proximity/relatedness/nearness *(lan)*

begriffliche Revolution *f* • conceptual revolution *(sci)* < Paradigmenwechsel

begriffliche Unmöglichkeit *f* • conceptual impossibility *(Wittgenstein) (lan)*

begriffliche Unterscheidung *f* • conceptual distinction *(log, lan)*

begrifflicher Ansatz *m* • conceptual approach *(sci)*

begrifflicher Rahmen *m* • conceptual framework *(lan, sci)*

begriffliches Denken *n* • conceptual thinking/thought *(epi)*

Begriffs- und Empfindungswurzel *f* • conceptual and sensory/sensible root *(Nietzsche) (met)*

Begriffsabbildung *f* • conceptual mapping *(min, sci)*

Begriffsanalyse *f* • conceptual analysis *(log, lan)*

Begriffsapparat *m* • conceptual apparatus/framework/system *(lan, sci)*

Begriffsarchitektonik *f* • conceptual architectonic *(epi)* → Architektonik der Begriffe

Begriffsbestimmung *f* • definition of terms, conceptual determination/explication *(log, lan)*

Begriffsbildung *f* • concept formation *(log, lan, epi)* < W 391

Begriffsdefinition *f* • conceptual definition, definition of terms/concepts *(log, lan)*

Begriffsdenken *n* • conceptual thinking *(epi)*

Begriffsentwicklung *f* • evolution of concepts, concept evolution *(epi, lan)*

Begriffserklärung *f* • explanation of terms/concepts *(log, lan)*

Begriffsfetischismus *m* • concept fetishism *(gep)*

Begriffsformen *pl* • conceptual forms *(log, lan)*

Begriffsgebäude *n* • structure of concepts *(log)* < Ideengebilde

Begriffsgeschichte *f* • history of concepts, conceptual history *(lan)*

Begriffshierarchie *f* • hierarchy of concepts *(log, lan)*

Begriffsidentität *f* • identity of concepts *(log, lan)*

Begriffsinhalt *m* • conceptual content, meaning, connotation *(log)*, meaning, intension *(log, lan)* < Intension

Begriffskategorie *f* • conceptual category *(epi, sci)* < Kategorienfehler

Begriffsklasse *f* • conceptual category *(log, lan)*

Begriffslogik *f* • logic of concepts/terms *(log)* < Mengenlehre

Begriffslogik, extensionale *f* • extensional logic of terms/concepts *(log)*

Begriffslogik, intensionale *f* • intensional logic of terms/concepts *(log)*

Begriffslosigkeit *f* • conceptlessness, lack of concepts *(epi)*

Begriffsmißbrauch *m* • misuse/abuse of concepts, conceptual misuse/abuse *(sci)*

Begriffsnetz *n* • conceptual net, concept(ual) network, network of concepts *(Quine, Duhem) (epi, lan)*

Begriffsordnung *f* • order of concepts *(log, lan)*

Begriffsphilosophie *f* • philosophy of concepts, conceptual philosophy *(epi, lan)* < Begriffstheorie

Begriffspyramide *f* • pyramid of concepts *(log, lan)*

Begriffsrealismus *m* • concept(ual) realism *(epi, ont)* ↔ Nominalismus

Begriffsrelativismus *m* • conceptual relativism *(log, lan, met)*

Begriffssatz *m* • conceptual proposition (*Bolzano*) (*log, lan*)

Begriffsschema *n* • conceptual scheme (*lan, sci*)

Begriffsschrift *f* • Begriffsschrift, concept(ual) notation (*Frege*) (*log*), logical symbolism (*lan*) < Formalsprache < W 122

Begriffsskelett *n* • conceptual skeleton (*Hofstadter etc*) (*min, sci*)

Begriffsspeicher *m* • concept store, storehouse of concepts (*min*)

Begriffssphäre *f* • conceptual sphere, sphere of concepts (*lan*)

Begriffsstruktur *f* • conceptual structure, structure of concepts (*log, lan*)

Begriffssystem *n* • conceptual system (*log, lan*) < Begriffsapparat

Begriffstheorie *f* • theory of concepts (*epi, lan*)

Begriffsumfang *m* • extension of a concept (*log, lan*) < Extension, Denotation, Referenz

Begriffsverbindung *f* • conjunction of terms (*lan, log*)

Begriffsvermengung *f* • blending/mingling of concepts (*log, lan*)

Begriffsverwirrung *f* • conceptual confusion, confusion of terms (*log, lan*)

Begriffszeichen *n* → Ideogramm

begründen • to give reasons/grounds for, to substantiate, to justify, to account for, to argue for (*gep*)

begründetes Wissen *n* • justified/well-founded knowledge (*epi, sci*)

Begründung *f* • reason, grounds, foundation, justification, argument (*epi, sci, eth*)

Begründungsfrage *f* • question of justification (*epi, sci*)

Begründungspriorität *f* • justificatory priority (*sci*)

Begründungsproblem *n* • justification problem (*epi, sci, eth*)

Begründungsschritte *pl* • steps in/of justification/argumentation (*sci*)

Begründungssystem *n* • system of justification/argumentation (*sci*)

Begründungsverfahren *n* • method of justification, justification procedure (*epi, sci*) < Begründung

Begründungszusammenhang *m* • context of justification (*Reichenbach*) (*sci*) → Rechtfertigungskontext ↔ Entdeckungszusammenhang

Beharrlichkeit *f* • persistence, perseverance (*act, eth, psy*), perdurability, permanence, perdurance (*nat, met*) < Konstanz, Unwandelbarkeit

Behauptbarkeitsbedingungen *pl* • assertability/assertibility conditions (*min, sci*)

Behauptung *f* • assertion, claim, statement, contention (*log, lan*) < Proposition

Behauptungszeichen *n* • assertion sign (*Frege*) (*log*)

Behaviorismus *m* • behavio(u)rism (*psy, act*)

Behaviorismus, logischer *m* • logical behavio(u)rism (*Quine*) (*log, lan*)

Behaviorismus, sprachwissenschaftlicher *m* • linguistic behavio(u)rism (*Bloomfield etc*) (*lan*)

behavioristische Psychologie *f* • behavio(u)ristic psychology (*psy*)

Beherrschung der Leidenschaften *f* • control/mastery of the passions (*eth, rel*)

Behindertenintegration *f* • integration of the disabled/handicapped, integration of the differently abled (*soc, eth*)

Beinahe-Katastrophe *f* • near-tragedy (*tec, nat*)

Beisichsein *n* • being at home/at one with oneself (*Hegel*) (*met*) < Zusich(selbst)kommen

Beisichsein des Geistes *n* • being at home/at one with itself of the spirit (*met*)

Beisichselbstsein *n* • being-in-itself, being-alongside-oneself (*Hegel etc*) (*met*)

Beispiel *n* • example (*gep*) < Paradigma

Beispielhaftigkeit *f* • exemplarity (*gep*)

Beistandsabkommen *n* • treaty of mutual assistance (*pol*)

Bejahung des Lebens *f* • affirmation of life (*met*) → Lebensbejahung

bekannt • familiar (*epi*) < erkannt

Bekanntheitsgrad *m* • degree of familiarity (*gep*)

Bekanntheitsqualität *f* • quality of familiarity (*Höffding*) (*epi, sci*)

Bekenntnisfreiheit *f* • freedom of worship (*rel*) < Religionsfreiheit

Beleg *m* • record, evidence, proof (*jur, sci*)

Beleidigung *f* • insult (*eth*), offence, defamation (*eth, jur*)

Beliebigkeit *f* • arbitrariness (*act, lan*), wilfulness (*act*) < Arbitrarität, Kontingenz

Belletristik *f* • belles lettres (*aes*)

Bellizismus *m* • belligerence, warism (*pol*) ↔ Pazifismus < Kriegslust

bellum iustum • just war (*eth, pol*) → gerechter Krieg

bellum omnium contra omnes → Krieg aller gegen alle

Belohnung *f* • reward (*eth, psy*)

Belohnung, aufgeschobene *f* • deferred gratification (*Schneider, Lysgaard*) (*soc, psy*)

Belohnungs-Bestrafungs-Mechanismen *pl* • reward-punishment mechanisms *(Parsons)* *(soc, psy)*

Benachteiligung, soziale *f* • social disadvantage *(soc, eth)* < Chancengleichheit, Diskriminierung

Benannte, das *n* • named thing, what is named *(lan)* < Referenz

benennen • to name, to designate *(lan)* < bezeichnen

benützerfreundliche Systeme *pl* • user-friendly systems *(tec)* < Fehlerfreundlichkeit

Benutzeroberfläche *f* • user interface *(AI)*

beobachtbare Phänomene *pl* • observable phenomena *(epi, sci)*

beobachtbare Tatsachen *pl* • observable facts *(epi, sci)*

beobachtbares Dingprädikat *n* • observable thing-predicate *(Carnap) (log, lan)*

Beobachtbarkeit *f* • observability *(epi, sci)*

beobachtende Vernunft *f* • observing reason *(Hegel) (epi, met)*

Beobachter *m* • observer *(sci)* < teilnehmender Beobachter

Beobachterperspektive *f* • observer perspective *(sci, act)*

Beobachtung *f* • observation *(epi, sci)*

Beobachtung-Theorie-Unterscheidung *f* • observation-theory distinction *(sci)*

Beobachtungsadäquatheit *f* • observational adequacy *(sci)*

Beobachtungsaussage *f* • observation sentence, observation(al) statement *(sci)* → Beobachtungssatz < Wahrnehmungssatz, Basisaussage, Protokollsatz

Beobachtungsgenauigkeit *f* • precision of observation *(sci)*

Beobachtungsgesetz *n* • observational law *(psy, sci)* < Erfahrungsgesetz

Beobachtungsirrtum *m* • error of observation *(psy, epi, sci)*

Beobachtungsmaterial *n* • observation(al) material *(epi, sci)*

Beobachtungsmerkmal *n* • observable characteristic *(Hempel) (sci)*

Beobachtungsmethode *f* • method of observation *(sci)*

Beobachtungsprädikat *n* • observation predicate *(log, lan)*

Beobachtungssatz *m* • observation sentence, observation(al) statement *(Hempel etc) (sci)* → Beobachtungsaussage < Wahrnehmungssatz, Protokollsatz, Basisaussage

Beobachtungssprache *f* • observational language *(Carnap) (sci, lan)*

Beobachtungstheorie *f* • observation theory *(sci)*

Beobachtungsverfahren *n* • method of observation *(sci)*

Beobachtungswort *n* • observation word *(Quine etc) (lan)*

berechenbar • computable, calculable *(mat, sci, AI)*

berechenbares Verhalten *n* • predictable behaviour *(dec, act)* < Strategiespiel

Berechenbarkeit *f* • computability, calculability, computationality *(mat, sci, AI)*

berechnende Klugheit *f* • calculating prudence *(eth, dec)* < kalkulatorische Vernunft

Berechnung *f* • computation *(mat, AI)*

berechtigtes Interesse *n* • lawful/legitimate/justified interest *(gep)*

Bereicherung der menschlichen Natur *f* • enrichment of human nature *(Marx etc)* *(eth)*

Bereichsethik *f* • ethics applied to a specific field *(eth)* → angewandte Ethik

bereichsspezifisches Wissen *n* • domain-specific knowledge *(sci)*

bereichswissenschaftliche Methodik *f* • specific methodology *(sci)*

Bergpredigt *f* • The Sermon on the Mount *(rel)*

Bergsonismus *m* • Bergsonism *(gep)*

Bernoullische Differentialgleichung *f* • Bernoullian differential equation *(mat)*

Berufsethik *f* • professional ethics *(eth)*

Berufsethos *n* • professional ethos, ethos of the/a profession *(eth)*

Berufsrevolutionär *m* • professional revolutionary *(pol)*

Berufsstände *pl* • trades, professional/vocational groups/guilds *(soc)* < Ständegesellschaft

Berührungsangst *f* • contact anxiety *(psy)*

Berührungstransformation *f* • contact transformation *(nat)*

Beschaffenheit *f* • (▷ Zustand) nature, state, (▷ Eigenschaft) attribute, property *(ont)*

Beschäftigungsgarantie *f* • guarantee of employment *(eco)* < soziale Sicherheit

Beschäftigungstherapie *f* • occupational therapy *(psy)*

Beschaulichkeit *f* • contemplativeness *(aes, psy, met)* < Muße, theoria

Bescheidenheit *f* • modesty *(eth)*

Beschlußfähigkeit *f* • quorum *(pol)*

Beschlußfassung *f* • (passing of a) resolution *(pol)*

Beschränkung der Möglichkeiten *f* • limitation/finiteness of possibilities *(ont, act)*

Beschränkung der Regierungsgewalt *f* • limitation of government/governmental power *(pol)* < Gewaltenteilung

Beschreibbarkeit *f* • describability *(lan, sci)*

beschreibende Definition *f* • descriptive definition *(log, lan)* < Bedeutungsanalyse

beschreibender Satz *m* • descriptive/description statement/proposition *(sci)*

beschreibender Satz durch Definition *m* • description statement/proposition through definition *(log, lan)*

beschreibendes Wort *n* • descriptive word *(Hare) (lan)*

Beschreibung *f* • description *(sci, log, lan)* → Deskription < Kennzeichnung

Beschreibung, bestimmte *f* → Beschreibung, definite

Beschreibung, definite *f* • definite description *(Russell) (log, lan)* < definite Kennzeichnung

Beschreibung, unbestimmte *f* • indefinite description *(Russell etc) (log, lan)*

Beschreibungsadäquatheit *f* • descriptive adequacy *(sci)*

Beschreibungsdualismus *m* • descriptive dualism *(Davidson, Dennett) (min)*

Beschreibungsebene *f* • level of description *(sci)*

Beschreibungskategorien *pl* • categories of description *(sci)*

Beschreibungslogik *f* • description logic *(log, sci)*

Beschreibungstheorie *f* • theory of description *(sci)*, theory of descriptions *(Russell) (log, lan)*

Beschuldigung *f* • accusation, charge *(jur, eth)* < Anklage

Beschwichtigungspolitik *f* • appeasement policy, policy of appeasement *(pol)*

Beschwörungsformel *f* • incantation, magic formula *(eso)*

beseeltes Wesen *n* • animate being *(met)*

Beseelung *f* • animation *(met)*

Beseitigungsregel *f* → Eliminationsregel

Besessenheit *f* • obsession, possession *(psy, eso, rel)* < Exorzismus

Besitz(tum) *m(n)* • possession, ownership *(jur)*

Besitzanspruch *m* • property/proprietary/ownership claim *(eco, jur)* < Possessivität

Besitzbürgertum *n* • propertied middle class, bourgeoisie, property owners *(soc)*

Besitzeinkommen *n* • income from property, unearned income, property income *(eco)*

besitzende Klasse *f* • propertied class *(soc)*

Besitzergreifung *f* • appropriation *(eco)* → Appropriation < ursprüngliche Besitzergreifung

Besitzgier *f* • acquisitive greed *(eco, psy)*

Besitzindividualismus *m* • possessive individualism, individualism of possession *(Locke, Bentham etc) (soc)* < W 807

Besitzrecht *n* • right of ownership *(jur)*

Besitzverhältnisse, individuelle *pl* • (individual) property conditions *(eco, soc)* < Besitzverteilung

Besitzverteilung *f* • distribution of property *(eco, soc)* < Besitzverhältnisse

Besondere, das *n* • the particular, the specific, the singular, the individual *(ont)* < Akzidens

besonderer Satz *m* • specific/particular proposition, singular theorem° *(lan, log)*

Besonderheit *f* • particularity, individuality, characteristic, peculiarity *(gen)* < Einzelnem und Allgemeinem, Einheit von; Einmaligkeit

Besonderheit als ästhetische Kategorie *f* • particularity as an aesthetic category *(Lukács) (aes)*

Besonderheit, historische *f* • historical particularity *(his)*

Besonderung *f* • particularization, specification *(Hegel) (met)*

Besonnenheit *f* • composure, temperance *(eth)*

besorgen • to concern, to provide *(Heidegger) (ont)*

Besorgnis *f* • anxiety, worry *(psy, met)* → Sorge

Besorgung des Seienden *f* • the concern/concerning of (the) Being, concern with Being/beings *(Heidegger) (ont)*

Besserungsfähigkeit *f* • corrigibility *(jur, eth)* < Resozialisierung

Besserungszweck der Strafe *m* • remedial function of punishment *(jur, eth)* < Resozialisationstheorie

Bestand *m* • standing, reserve, stock *(Heidegger)*, subsistence *(Meinong) (ont)* < Existenz

beständige Bewegung *f* • perpetual motion *(nat)* < perpetuum mobile

Beständigkeit *f* • constancy *(eth)*, durability, permanence *(nat)*

Beständigkeit des Daseins *f* • permanence/obstinacy/persistence of being *(met)*

Beständigkeit, Idee der *f* • idea of permanence *(Parmenides etc) (met)*

bestätigbar in Lo • confirmable in Lo *(Carnap etc) (sci)*

bestätigbar in T • confirmable in T *(Carnap etc) (sci)*

Bestätigbarkeit f • confirmability (sci) →
Verifizierbarkeit

Bestätigung f • confirmation (Carnap etc),
corroboration (Popper etc) (sci) → Verifikation < Bewährung, Falsifikationsprinzip,
Hypothesenprüfung

Bestätigung der Wahrheit f • affirmation/
confirmation of (the) truth (epi, sci)

Bestätigungsfähigkeit f → Bestätigbarkeit

Bestätigungsgrad m • degree of confirmation/
corroboration (Carnap, Popper etc) (sci)
< Bewährbarkeitsgrad, Bewährungsgrad,
Prüfbarkeitsgrad, Wahrscheinlichkeitsgrad

Bestätigungsparadox n • paradox of confirmation (Hempel) (sci, log)

Bestätigungstheorie f • confirmation theory,
theory of confirmation/corroboration (sci)
< Verifikationismus

beste aller möglichen Welten f • best of all
possible worlds, best possible world°
(Leibniz) (met)

Bestechlichkeit f • corruptibility (eco, eth)

Bestechung f • bribery, corruption (eco, eth)
→ Korruption

bestehen • (▷ eines Sachverhalts) to obtain, to
exist (Wittgenstein etc) (epi, met) < zutreffen

Bestehen, das n • existence (ont); subsistence,
obtaining (Meinong, Husserl, Wittgenstein
etc) (lan, ont)

bestehende Gesellschaft f • existing society
(soc)

bester Staat m • the best state (Plato etc) (pol)
→ Idealstaat

bestimmbare Grenze f • determinable
boundary (epi, nat, mat)

bestimmbare Wörter pl • determinable words
(lan)

bestimmbarer Begriff m • determinable
(Johnson) (lan)

Bestimmbarkeit f • determinability (log, lan,
sci)

bestimmende Urteilskraft f • determinant/
determining (faculty/power of) judg(e)ment
(Kant) (epi, aes) ↔ reflektierende Urteilskraft

bestimmender Grund m • determining ground/
reason (met)

bestimmendes Gesetz n • determining law
(Carnap) (sci)

bestimmendes Subjekt n • determining
subject° (Kant) (epi) < Autonomie

bestimmte Negation f • determinate negation
(Hegel) (met)

bestimmter Begriff m • determinate concept
(Hegel) (epi, met)

bestimmter Unterschied m • determinate
distinction (Hegel) (met, log)

bestimmtes Sein n • determinate being
(Hegel) (ont)

Bestimmtheit f • definiteness, determinedness,
determinacy (Hegel) (ont)

Bestimmung f • (▷ Determination) determination (log); (▷ Schicksal) vocation, destiny
(met, rel) < Schicksal

Bestimmung der Natur f • purpose of nature
(nat, met) < Naturteleologie

Bestimmung des Menschen f • purpose of man
< W 140, 1234

Bestimmungen, grundlegende pl • basic
predicates/characteristics, determinations
(lan)

Bestimmungslosigkeit der Natur f • inde-
terminacy/indeterminedness of nature (met)

Bestimmungslosigkeit f • (▷ Unbestimmtheit)
indeterminacy (met, nat)

Bestrafung durch den Staat f • punishment by
the state, state punishment (jur, eth) < Gewaltmonopol

Betastrahlen pl • beta rays (nat)

Betrug m • deceit, deception (eth), fraud (jur)
< Täuschung

betrügerischer Gott m → deus malignus

Betrugstheorie f • deception theory (rel)
< Priestertrugstheorie

Beurteilung f • judg(e)ment, evaluation,
estimation (gep)

Beurteilungskompetenz f • judg(e)mental
competence, capacity of judg(e)ment (lan,
sci) < Interpretationskompetenz

Beurteilungskraft f • faculty/power of
judg(e)ment/assessment (Kant) (ant, eth)

Beurteilungskriterium n • evaluation
criterion, appraisal factor (gep)

Bevölkerungsbeschränkung f • population
limitation (pol)

Bevölkerungsdruck m • population pressure
(soc)

Bevölkerungsethik f • population ethics (eth)
< Bevölkerungsexplosion

Bevölkerungsexplosion f • population explosion
(soc) < demographische Zeitbombe, Populationsdynamik

Bevölkerungsgesetz n • principle/law of
population (Malthus) (soc) < W 4, 143

Bevölkerungspyramide f • population pyramid
(soc)

Bevölkerungswachstum n • population growth
(soc)

Bevölkerungszunahme f • increase in population (soc)

bewaffneter Widerstand m • armed resistance (pol)

Bewährbarkeit f • corroborability (Popper) (sci) < Falsifizierbarkeit

Bewährbarkeitsgrad m • degree of corroborability (Popper) (sci) < Bestätigungsgrad

Bewährung f • corroboration (Popper) (sci) < Bestätigung

Bewährung im Diesseits f • proving oneself in this life (rel)

Bewährungsgrad m • degree of corroboration (Popper) (sci)

Bewährungstheorie f • theory of corroboration (Popper) (sci) < empirischer Gehalt einer Theorie, Informationsgehalt, logischer Gehalt, Problemgehalt, Wahrheitsnähe

Bewandtnis f • involvement (Heidegger) (ont)

Bewandtnisganzheit f • involvement whole (Heidegger) (ont)

bewegende Ursache f • motive/efficient/propelling cause (met) → causa movens

Beweger, unbewegter m • unmoved mover (Aristotle) (met, rel) → primum mobile, erster Beweger < causa sui

Beweggrund m → Motiv

Bewegung f • movement (pol, his), motion (nat, met)

Bewegung des Begriffs f • movement of the concept(s) (Hegel) (met)

Bewegung des Werdens f • movement of becoming (Hegel) (his) < Werdensprozeß

Bewegungsenergie f → kinetische Energie

Bewegungsfreiheit f • freedom of movement (pol) < Niederlassungsfreiheit

Bewegungsgesetze pl • laws of motion (nat) < Erhaltung von der Bewegung, Prinzip von der

Bewegungskunst f • art of motion (aes) → Eukinetik

Bewegungslehre f • theory of motion (nat)

Beweis m • proof, demonstration (log, mat), evidence (epi, jur)

Beweis, direkter m • direct proof/demonstration (log)

Beweis, indirekter m • indirect proof/demonstration (log)

Beweis, mathematischer m • mathematical proof/demonstration (mat)

Beweis, ostensiver m • ostensive proof (epi, log)

Beweis, unvollständiger m • incomplete proof (log)

Beweis, vollständiger m • complete proof (log)

Beweisart f • form/type of proof, proof type (log)

beweisbar • provable (mat, log, sci)

beweisbare Aussage f • provable sentence (sci, lan)

Beweisbarkeit f • provability, demonstrability, derivability, provableness° (mat, log, sci)

Beweisbarkeitstheorem n • provability theorem (log)

Beweisfehler m • fallacious proof, error in proof (log) < Fehlschluß, Paralogismus, Trugschluß

Beweisführung f • line of argument(ation), reasoning, proof (log)

Beweisgrund m • reason, argument (epi, log)

Beweiskraft f • cogency, conclusiveness, evidential value, power of proof/demonstration, conclusive force° (log)

beweiskräftig • evidential (sci, jur), conclusive (log)

Beweislast f • burden of proof, onus probandi (jur, gep)

Beweislastumkehr f • reversal of/in the burden of proof, putting the burden of proof on the other side/party/person (jur)

Beweismethode f • method of proof (log, sci)

Beweispflicht(igkeit) f → Beweislast

Beweisregel f • rule of proof (Tarski) (epi, lan)

Beweisrelation f • proof relation (log)

Beweisstück n • exhibit (jur)

Beweistheorie f • proof theory (Hilbert) (log, mat) < Hilbertsches Programm

Bewertung f • (e)valuation, assessment, estimation → Einschätzung, (▷ Erstellen einer Rangordnung) rating (gep) < Wertung

Bewertungsbegriff m • evaluative (concept) (lan, eth) < Wertbegriff

Bewertungskriterium n • evaluation/evaluative° criterion (sci, gep)

Bewertungsmaßstab m • standard of evaluation (gep)

Bewertungsurteil n • evaluative judg(e)ment (log)

bewirken • to cause/produce (an effect) (gep)

bewußt • conscious (psy, min), (▷ absichtlich) deliberate (act, jur)

bewußte Erfahrung f • conscious experience (epi)

bewußtes Denken n • conscious thinking/thought (epi, psy)

bewußtes Wahrnehmungserleben n • conscious perceptual experience (min)

Bewußthaftigkeit f • consciousness, mindfulness, the state of being conscious (met, psy) ↔ Bewußtlosigkeit

Bewußtheit f • awareness (psy, min)

Bewußtlosigkeit *f* • consciouslessness, unconsciousness *(met, psy)* ↔ Bewußthaftigkeit; mindlessness, no-mindness *(asp)* < Leere als Ziel

Bewußtmachung *f* • making aware/conscious *(psy, epi)* < Bewußtwerdung

Bewußtsein *n* • consciousness, awareness *(psy, min)*

Bewußtsein, geistiges *n* • mental consciousness/awareness *(met)*

Bewußtsein, geschichtliches *n* • historical consciousness *(Hegel etc) (epi, his)*

Bewußtsein, neutrales *n* • neutral consciousness *(Husserl) (min)*

Bewußtsein, phänomenales *n* • phenomenal consciousness *(psy)*

Bewußtsein, sinnliches *n* • sense/sensory awareness/consciousness *(Hegel) (epi, met)*

Bewußtsein überhaupt *n* • consciousness-assuch *(Kant) (met)*

Bewußtsein, unabhängiges *n* • independent consciousness *(met)*

Bewußtsein, zweites *n* • secondary consciousness/awareness *(psy, eso)*

Bewußtseinsbildung *f* • consciousness-raising, formation of consciousness *(psy, min)*

Bewußtseinsebene *f* • level of consciousness *(psy, min)*

Bewußtseinserweiterung *f* • expansion of mind/awareness *(psy, eso)*

Bewußtseinsgrade *pl* • degrees of consciousness/awareness *(psy, min)*

Bewußtseinsinhalt *m* • content of consciousness *(psy, min)*

Bewußtseinskategorie *f* • category of consciousness *(met)*

Bewußtseinsphilosophie *f* • philosophy of consciousness *(met)*

Bewußtseinsprozeß *m* • process of consciousness *(psy, min)*

Bewußtseinsspaltung *f* • split consciousness *(min, psy)* < Ichspaltung, Persönlichkeitsspaltung

Bewußtseinsstörung *f* • mental disturbance, disturbance of consciousness *(psy)*

Bewußtseinsstrom *m* • stream/flow° of consciousness *(James, Bergson) (met, psy)* < Erlebnisstrom

Bewußtseinstheorie *f* • theory of consciousness *(psy, min)*

bewußtseinsunabhängige Realität *f* • mind-independent reality *(epi, met)*

Bewußtseinsveränderung *f* • change of the state of mind *(psy)*

Bewußtseinswandel *m* • change of/in consciousness *(psy)*

Bewußtseinswerdung *f* • formation of consciousness *(Jaspers) (met)*

Bewußtseinszustand *m* • state of consciousness *(psy, min)*

Bewußtseinszustand, geänderter *m* • altered state of consciousness/mind *(psy)*

Bewußtwerdung *f* • becoming aware/conscious *(psy, epi)*

bezahlte Arbeit *f* • waged work, paid labour *(eco, soc)* ↔ unbezahlte Arbeit

bezeichnen • to signify/to denote/to designate *(lan)* < benennen

bezeichnende Position *f* • referential position *(Quine etc) (lan)*

Bezeichnete, das *n* • object denoted, denotatum *(log, lan)* → Denotat

Bezeichnung *f* • designation, signification, denotation *(lan)*

Bezeichnung, Theorie der *f* • theory of denoting *(Russell) (lan)*

Bezeichnungsausdruck *m* • designator, denoting expression *(lan)*

Bezeichnungsfunktion *f* • reference function, reference *(lan)*

Bezeichnungswandel *m* • change/alteration of reference *(lan)*

Bezeichnungsweise *f* • mode/method of designation/signification/denotation *(lan)*

Beziehung *f* • relation *(log, soc, sys)*

Beziehungsbeschreibung *f* • relation description° *(Carnap) (sci, lan)*

Beziehungstheorie *f* • theory of personal relations *(psy, soc)* < Bezugsperson

Beziehungsweise *f* • mode of relation/relatedness *(gep)*

Bezug *m* • reference *(lan, ont)* → Referenz

Bezugnahme *f* • reference *(Quine etc) (lan)*

Bezugsfolge *f* • reference sequence *(mat)*

Bezugsgegenstand *m* • reference object, object of reference *(lan, ont)* → Referenzgegenstand

Bezugsgruppe *f* • reference group *(psy, soc)* < Bezugsperson

Bezugsklasse *f* • reference class *(mat)*

Bezugsperson *f* • reference/contact person *(psy, soc)* < Bezugsgruppe

Bezugspunkt *m* • point of reference, reference point *(gen)* < Fixpunkt

Bezugsrahmen *m* • frame of reference *(gep)*

Bezugsrahmen, begrifflicher *m* • conceptual framework *(sci, lan)*

Bezugsrahmen, handlungstheoretischer *m* • action schema *(act, soc)*

Bezugssystem *n* → Bezugsrahmen

Bezugstheorie *f* • theory of reference, reference theory *(lan, log)* → Referenztheorie

bhavachakra • wheel of becoming *(asp)*

Bibelexegese *f* • biblical exegesis, interpretation of the Bible *(rel)*

Bibelkritik *f* • Bible criticism, criticism of the Bible *(rel)*

Bibliographie *f* • bibliography *(gen)*

Bibliotherapie *f* • bibliotherapy *(psy)*

biblische Theologie *f* • biblical theology *(Barth)* *(rel)*

Bifurkation *f* • bifurcation *(gep)*

Bigotterie *f* • bigotry *(rel)* < Wahn, religiöser

Bijunktion *f* • bijunction *(log)*

bikonditional • biconditional *(log)*

Bikulturalität *f* • biculturality *(cul, soc)*

Bilanzsuizid *m* • calculated/premeditated suicide, suicide on the basis of calculation *(eth)* < Negativbilanz

bilateral • bilateral *(gen)* < multilateral

Bild *n* • (▷ Vorstellung) idea, picture, notion *(epi, psy)*, (▷ Gemälde) painting, picture *(aes)*, (▷ Abbild) image, picture → Abbild

Bild der Welt *n* • picture of the world *(met)* → Weltbild

Bildchen-Theorie *f* • theory of impressions *(Empedocles, Epicurus)* *(epi)*

bildende Kunst *f* • visual arts, representational arts *(aes)* → darstellende Kunst

Bilderanbetung *f* • iconolatry, image worship *(rel)* < Idolatrie

Bilderdenken *n* • pictorial thinking *(epi, cul)* < mythisches Denken

Bilderschrift *f* • hieroglyphics, pictography, picture writing *(lan)*

Bildersprache *f* • pictorial language *(lan)*

Bilderstreit *m* • iconoclastic controversy *(rel, aes)*

Bilderstürmerei *f* • iconoclasm *(rel, aes)* → Ikonoklasmus < Bilderstreit

Bildersymbolik *f* • visual/pictorial symbolism/ imagery *(aes)*

Bilderverbot *n* • iconomachy, objection to worship of images *(rel, aes)* < Bilderstreit

Bilderverehrung *f* • image worship, iconolatry, idolatry *(rel, aes)* → Idolatrie

Bildfeld *n* • image field, angle of view *(nat, psy)*

Bildhauerkunst *f* • sculpture, plastic art *(aes)* < Plastik

bildliche Darstellung *f* • pictorial representation *(aes)*

Bildlosigkeit der absoluten Transzendenz *f* • unimaginability of absolute transcendence *(Jaspers)* *(met)* < Chiffrenschrift

Bildphilosophie *f* • philosophy of images/ pictures *(aes)*

Bildsprache *f* • pictorial/pictoral° language *(lan)*

Bildsymbolik *f* • image symbolism *(aes)*

Bildtheorie *f* • picture theory *(lan, met)* < Abbildtheorie

Bildung, formale *f* • formal education *(gen)*

Bildung, theoretische *f* • theoretical education/ training *(gen)*

Bildungsarbeit *f* • educational work *(gen)*

Bildungsbürgertum *n* • educated classes *(soc)*

Bildungschancen *pl* • educational opportunities *(soc, eth)*

Bildungsdrang *m* • desire for education *(gen)* < Wissensdurst

Bildungsgesetz *n* → Bildungsregel

Bildungsgrad *m* • level of education, educational level *(gen)*

Bildungsnotstand *m* • lack of educational opportunities, educational wasteland *(gen)*

Bildungspolitik *f* • educational policy *(pol)*

Bildungsregel *f* • formation rule *(log, mat)*

Bildungsroman *m* • educational novel, novel of character development *(aes)* → Entwicklungsroman

Bildungswesen *n* • educational system *(soc, pol)*

Bildungswissen *n* • educational knowledge *(Scheler etc)* *(epi)* < Heilswissen, Leistungswissen, Wesenswissen

Billigkeit *f* • fairness, justness, reasonableness *(eth)*

Billigung, moralische *f* • moral approval/ approbation *(eth)*

binär • binary *(mat, log)*

binäre Klassifikation *f* • binary classification *(mat, log)*

binäre Opposition *f* • binary opposition *(mat, log, lan)*

binäres Zahlensystem *n* • binary number system *(mat, AI)* → Binärsystem, Dualsystem

Binarismus *m* • binarism *(mat, log)*

Binarität *f* • binarity *(mat, log)*

Binärkode *m* • binary code *(AI)*

Binärnotation *f* • binary notation *(mat, log)*

Binärsystem *n* • binary system *(mat)* → Dualsystem

Bindung *f* • binding *(Freud etc)* *(psy)*

Binomialkoeffizient *m* • binomial coefficient *(mat)*

Binomialsatz *m* • binomial theorem, binomical sentence° *(mat)*

Binomialverteilung *f* • binomial/binomical°
distribution *(mat)*

binomischer Satz *m* → Binomialsatz

Binsenwahrheit *f* → Binsenweisheit

Binsenweisheit *f* • truism, commonplace,
platitude *(gen)* → Gemeinplatz

Biochemie *f* • biochemistry *(nat)*

Biochip *m* • biochip *(AI)*

Biocomputer *m* • biocomputer *(AI)*

Biodiversi(vi)tät *f* • biodiversity *(nat)* < Artenvielfalt

Biodynamik *f* • biodynamics *(nat)*

Bioenergetik *f* • bio-energetics *(Reich) (psy,
eso)*

Bioethik *f* • bioethics *(eth)*

Biofeedback *n* • biofeedback *(eso, psy)*

Biogenese *f* • biogenesis *(nat)*

biogenetisches Grundgesetz *n* • biogenetic
principle *(nat)*

Biogramm *n* • biogram *(nat, ant)*

Biokybernetik *f* • biocybernetics *(sys)*

Bilinguistik *f* • bilinguistics *(lan)*

Biologie *f* • biology *(nat)* → Biowissenschaft

biologische Ästhetik *f* • biological aesthetics
(Spencer, Darwin) (aes)

biologische Kriegsführung *f* • biological
warfare *(pol)*

biologische Struktur *f* • biological structure
(nat)

biologische Uhr *f* • biological clock *(nat)*
< biologische Zeit

biologische Wissenschaften *pl* • biological
sciences, life sciences *(nat)*

biologische Wurzeln der Moral *pl* • biological
roots of morals *(eth)*

biologische Zeit *f* • biological time *(nat)* < biologische Uhr, Biorhythmus

biologischer Determinismus *m* • biological
determinism *(nat, met)*

biologischer Materialismus *m* • biological
materialism *(nat, met)*

biologischer Reduktionismus *m* • biological
reductionism *(nat, sci)*

Biologismus *m* • biologism *(nat, met)* ↔
Kulturismus

Bio-Macht *f* • bio-power *(Foucault) (cul)*

biomedizinische Ethik *f* • biomedical ethics
(eth) < Bioethik

biomorphe Modellbildung *f* • biomorphic
model formation *(Topitsch) (sci)*

Bionik *f* • bionics, biological electronics *(nat,
tec)*

bionome Systeme *pl* • bionomic systems *(Roth-
schuh) (nat, sys)*

Bionomie *f* • bionomics *(nat)*

Bio-Ökonomie *f* • bio-economics *(eco, soc,
nat)*

biophile Ethik *f* • biophilic ethics *(Fromm)
(eth)*

Biophilie *f* • biophilia *(Fromm) (eth, psy)* ↔
Nekrophilie

Biophysik *f* • biophysics *(nat)*

Biopsychismus *m* • biopsychism *(psy, met)*

Biorhythmus *m* • biorhythm *(nat, eso)* < biologische Zeit, innere Uhr

Biosophie *f* • biosophy *(Nietzsche, Bergson etc)*
(met)

Biosoziologie *f* • biosociology *(nat, soc)*

Biosphäre *f* • biosphere *(nat)*

Biotechnik *f* • biotechnology *(nat, tec)* < Bionik

biotechnische Modelle *pl* • biotechnical
models *(sci)*

Biotechnologie *f* • biotechnology *(nat, tec)*

biotische Gemeinschaft *f* • biotic community
(nat, env)

biotisches Potential *n* • biotic potential *(nat)*

Biotod *m* • biological death *(nat)* < Ökozid

Biotop *n* • biotope *(nat, env)*

Biowissenschaften *pl* • life sciences *(nat)*

Biozentrismus *m* • biocentrism *(met)* ↔ Logozentrismus < Zoozentrismus

Bipolarität *f* • bipolarity *(gep)*

Birkhoffsche Formel *f* • Birkhoff formula
(aes) < Informationsästhetik

Bisubjunktion *f* • bisubjunction *(log)*

Bit *m/n* • bit *(AI)*

Bitonalität *f* • bitonality *(aes)*

Bivalenz *f* • bivalence *(log)* → Zweiwertigkeit

Bivalenzprinzip *n* • bivalence principle *(log)*

Black Box *f* • black box *(sci, psy)*

Blackbox-Methode *f* • black box method *(sci,
psy)*

Blanquismus *m* • Blanquism *(pol, soc)*

Blasphemie *f* • blasphemy *(rel)* → Gotteslästerung

bleibende Werte *pl* • enduring values *(eth,
aes, eco)*

bleibender Satz *m* • standing sentence *(Quine)*
(lan) ↔ Gelegenheitssatz

Blickfeld *n* • field of view/vision *(psy)*

Blicklinie *f* • line of view *(Carnap) (epi)*

Blindheit, geistige *f* • mental/psychic blindness
(gep)

Blindtest *m* • blind test *(sci)* < Doppelblindversuch, Placebo-Effekt

Blindversuch *m* → Blindtest

Blindversuch, doppelter *m* • double blind test *(sci)* → Doppelblindversuch

blockfreie Nationen *pl* • non-aligned nations *(pol)*

Blockfreiheit *f* • non-alignment *(pol)*

Blockwelt *f* • blocks world *(Minsky) (min)*

blonde Bestie *f* • blond beast *(Nietzsche) (cul)*

bloßes Aggregat *n* • mere aggregate *(Quine) (epi, lan)*

Blut und Boden-Ideologie *f* • Blut and Boden ideology, blood and soil ideology *(pol)*

Bodenlosigkeit des Geredes *f* • insubstantiality/groundlessness of gossip/idle talk *(Heidegger) (ont)* < Gerede

Bodenreform *f* • land reform *(pol, eco)*

Bodhi • bodhi, enlightenment, supreme knowledge *(asp)*

Bodhisattva *m* • *nt*, one who is enlightened *(asp)* < Buddhaschaft

Bogardus-Skala *f* • social-distance scale *(Bogardus) (soc, mat)*

Bolschewiki *pl* • Bolsheviks *(pol)* ↔ Menschewiki

Bolschewismus *m* • Bolshevism *(pol)*

Bolschewistische Revolution *f* • Bolshevik revolution *(pol, his)*

Bolzano-Weierstrass'sches Theorem *n* • Bolzano-Weierstrass theorem *(nat)* < Weierstrass'sches Approximationstheorem

bona fide • *nt*, genuine, sincere *(gep)*, in good faith *(eth)* → guter Absicht, in

bonum commune *n* • common good/welfare *(eth, soc)* → Gemeinwohl

bonum per se *n* • (the) good in itself *(eth)* → Gutes an sich

Boolesche Algebra *f* • Boolean algebra *(mat, log)*

Boolescher Ring *m* • Boolean ring *(mat, log)*

Boolescher Verband *m* • Boolean lattice *(mat, log)*

booten • booting, bootstrapping *(sys, AI)*

Borelsches Wahrscheinlichkeitsfeld *n* • Borel(ean) field of probability *(mat, log)*

Böse, das *n* • (the) evil *(eth, rel)*

böse Absicht *f* • evil/bad/malevolent intent(ion) *(eth)*

böse Begierden *pl* • evil desires, malevolence *(eth)*

böser Absicht, in • with evil/malevolent intent, with bad intention *(eth)* → mala fide

böser Blick *m* • evil eye *(eso)*

böser Dämon *m* • evil/malignant/malicious demon *(Descartes) (epi)* → deus malignus

böser Geist *m* • evil spirit *(rel, eso)*

böser Glaube(n) *m* • bad faith, mauvaise foi *(Sartre) (met)*

Boshaftigkeit *f* • maliciousness *(eth)*

Bosheit *f* • malignity, badness *(eth)*

Böswilligkeit *f* • ill-will *(eth)*

Bottom-up-Algorithmus *m* • bottom-up algorithm *(AI, mat)* ↔ Top-down Algorithmus

Bourbaki-Programm *n* • Bourbaki programme *(Bourbaki) (mat, sci)*

Bourgeoisie *f* • bourgeoisie, middle class *(soc)*

boustrophedonische Schrift *f* • boustrophedonic writing *(lan)*

Brahma *m* • *nt (asp)*

Brahman *n* • Brahma(n) *(asp)* < Weltseele

Brahmane *m* • Brahman, Brahmin *(asp)*

Brahmanismus *m* • Brahmanism, Brahminism *(asp)*

Brahmismus *m* → Brahmanismus

Brain-Drain *m* • brain drain *(soc)* → Abwanderung von Wissenschaft(l)ern, Flucht der Intelligenz

Brainstorming *n* • brainstorming *(psy)* < freie Assoziation

Brauch *m* • custom, practice, usage *(soc, cul)* < Sitte

Brennpunkt der Interessen *m* • focus of interests *(eth, act)*

Bruch *m* • rupture *(epi, his)*

Bruch zwischen Ideal und Wirklichkeit *m* • split between ideal and reality *(Marx etc) (soc)*

Bruchpunkte *pl* • points of diffraction *(Foucault) (epi, his)*

Brüderlichkeit *f* • fraternity, brotherhood *(eth)*

Brüderlichkeitsethik *f* • ethic of brotherliness *(Weber) (soc, rel)*

Bruitismus *m* • bruitism *(aes)*

Brutalismus *m* • brutalism *(aes)*

Brutreaktor *m* • breeder reactor *(tec, env)*

Buch der Natur *n* • book of nature *(rel, met)*

Buch der Schöpfung *n* • book of genesis/creation *(rel, met)*

Buch des Lebens *n* • book of life *(rel, met)*

Buchstabenwissen *n* • book-learning *(gen)*

Buddha-Natur *f* • Buddha nature *(asp)*

Buddhaschaft *f* • Buddhahood, complete enlightenment *(asp)* < Bodhisattva

Buddhismus *m* • Buddhism *(asp)*

buddhistische Ethik *f* • Buddhist ethics *(eth, asp)*

buddhistische Kunst *f* • Buddhist art *(aes, asp)*

buddhistische Philosophie *f* • Buddhist philosophy *(asp)*

Buddhologie *f* • Buddhology *(asp)*

Bug *m* • bug *(AI)* → Programmfehler < Debugging

Bumerangeffekt *m* • boomerang effect *(sys)*

Bündelmereologie *f* • sheaf mereology *(ont)*

Bündeltheorie *f* • bundle theory *(Searle etc)* *(lan)*

Bündeltheorie des Geistes *f* • bundle theory of (the) mind *(Hume etc)* *(epi, min)*

Bündeltheorie des Selbst *f* • bundle theory of (the) self *(Hume)* *(epi, met)* < Schals Bündel von Wahrnehmungen

Bürde der Zivilisation *f* • pressure/burden of civilization *(Freud)* *(psy, cul)*

Bürden der Vernunft *pl* • burdens of reason *(gep)*

Bürger *m* • citizen *(pol)*

Bürger zweiter Klasse *m* • second-class citizen *(pol)*

Bürgerinitiative *f* • grassroots movement, citizens' initiative *(pol)*

Bürgerkrieg *m* • civil war *(pol)*

bürgerlich • middle-class, bourgeois *(pol, soc)*

bürgerliche Familie *f* • bourgeois family, middle class family *(soc)*

bürgerliche Freiheiten *pl* • civil liberties *(pol, jur, eth)*

bürgerliche Gesellschaft *f* • bourgeois society *(Marx etc)*, civil society *(Hegel etc)* *(soc)* < Zivilgesellschaft

bürgerliche Gesetze *pl* • civil laws *(jur, pol)*

bürgerliche Klasse *f* • bourgeois/middle class *(pol, soc)*

bürgerliche Pflichten *pl* • civil duties *(pol, eth)*

bürgerliche Rechte *pl* • civil/civic rights *(pol, jur)* → Bürgerrechte

bürgerliche Tugend *f* • civic virtue *(eth)*

bürgerliche Vereinigung *f* • civil association *(Rousseau etc)* *(soc, pol)*

bürgerliche Werte *pl* • bourgeois/middle-class values *(soc, eth)* < Bourgeoisie

bürgerlicher Ungehorsam *m* • civil disobedience *(pol)* → ziviler Ungehorsam

bürgerlicher Zustand *m* • civil state *(Hobbes, Rousseau etc)* *(soc, pol)* → status civilis

bürgerliches Eigentumsverständnis *n* • bourgeois understanding of property *(eco, soc)*

bürgerliches Recht *n* • civil law *(jur)*

Bürgerpflicht *f* • civic duty, one's duty as a citizen *(pol)*

Bürgerrechte *pl* • civil/civic rights *(pol, jur)* → bürgerliche Rechte

Bürgerrechtler *m* • civil rights campaigner *(pol)*

Bürgerrechtsbewegung *f* • civil rights movement *(pol)*

Buridans Esel *m* • Buridan's ass *(act, met)* < Äquilibrismus

Bürokratisierung *f* • bureaucratization *(pol, soc)*

Bürokratismus *m* • bureaucratism *(pol)*

Buße *f* • penance, penitence *(rel)* → Pönitenz < Reue

Byte *n* • byte *(AI)*

C

C-Struktur *f* • constituent structure *(lan)* < F-Struktur

Calvinismus *m* • Calvinism *(rel)*

calvinistische Ethik *f* • Calvinist ethics *(eth)*

calvinistisches Ethos *n* • Calvinist ethos *(eth, rel)*

Cambridge Platonisten *pl* • Cambridge Platonists *(gep)*

Camp-Ästhetik *f* • camp aesthetics *(aes)* < Dandyismus

Cantor-Staub *m* • Cantor dust *(mat)*

Cantorsche Menge *f* • Cantor(ian) set *(mat)*

Caritas *f* • charity *(rel, eth)* → Nächstenliebe

Cartesianer *m* • Cartesian *(gep)*

cartesianisch • Cartesian *(gep)*

cartesianische Methode *f* • Cartesian method *(epi)* < geometrische Methode

cartesianischer Dualismus *m* • Cartesian dualism *(met)*, Cartesian bifurcation *(Ryle)* *(min)* < Zwei-Substanzen-Lehre

cartesianischer Zirkel *m* • Cartesian circle *(epi)*

cartesianischer Zweifel *m* • Cartesian doubt *(epi)* < gewisses Wissen

Cartesianismus *m* • Cartesianism *(gep)*

Cartesisch → Cartesianisch

Cartesische Koordinaten *pl* • Cartesian coordinates *(mat)*

Cäsarenwahn *m* • megalomania, Caesarian madness° *(psy)* → Größenwahn, Megalomanie

Cäsarismus *m* • Caesarism *(pol)*

Cäsaropapismus *m* • caesaropapism *(pol, rel)*

Cauchy-Riemannsche Differentialgleichungen *pl* • Cauchy-Riemann equations *(mat)*

Cauchyfolge *f* • Cauchy sequence *(mat)*

causa *f* → Ursache

causa adaequata *f* • adequate cause *(met)* → Ursache, adäquate

causa cognoscendi *f* → Erkenntnisgrund

causa deficiens *f* • insufficient cause *(met)* → nicht-hinreichende Ursache

causa efficiens *f* • efficient cause *(Aristotle)* *(met)* → Wirkursache

causa essendi *f* • cause of being *(met)* → Seinsursache

causa exemplaris *f* • exemplary cause *(met)* → Exemplarursache

causa fiendi *f* • cause of becoming *(met)* → Geschehensursache

causa finalis *f* • final cause *(Aristotle)* *(met)* → Finalursache, Zweckursache

causa formalis *f* • formal cause *(Aristotle etc)* *(met)* → Formursache

causa immediata *f* • immediate cause *(met)* → Ursache, unmittelbare

causa instrumentalis *f* • instrumental cause *(met)* → Instrumentalursache; Ursache, instrumentelle

causa materialis *f* • material cause *(Aristotle etc)* *(met)* → Materialursache, Stoffursache

causa mediata *f* • mediate(d) cause *(met)* → Ursache, mittelbare

causa motiva *f* → causa movens

causa movens *f* • moving cause *(met)* → Ursache, bewegende

causa occasionalis *f* • occasional cause *(Geulincx, Malebranche)* *(met)* → Gelegenheitsursache

causa prima *f* • first cause *(Aristotle)* *(met)* → Ursache, erste

causa principalis *f* • principal cause *(met)* → Ursache, ursprüngliche

causa remota *f* • remote cause *(met)*

causa sufficiens *f* • sufficient cause *(met)* → Ursache, hinreichende

causa sui *f* • *nt*, cause-of-itself *(Aquinas)* *(met, rel)* → Ursache, selbstverursachte < unabhängiger Grund; Ursache, unverursachte; unbewegter Beweger

Certismus *m* • certism° *(sci)* < Gewißheit

ceteris paribus • *nt (epi, sci)*

Chakra *n* • chakra, cacra *(asp)* → Kraftzentrum

Chan-Buddhismus *m* → Zen-Buddhismus

Chancengleichheit *f* • equal opportunities/opportunity, equality of opportunities/opportunity *(eth)* < Gleichbehandlung, Diskriminierung; Benachteiligung, soziale

Chaosforschung *f* • chaos research *(sys, nat)*

Chaosphilosophie *f* • philosophy of chaos *(sys, met)*

Chaostheorie *f* • chaos theory, chaology *(sys, nat, mat)*

chaotische Folge *f* • chaotic sequence *(mat, sys)*

chaotisches System *n* • chaotic system *(sys, AI)* < Chaostheorie

characteristica universalis *f •* *nt,* universal character *(Leibniz etc) (lan)* → Universalsprache

Charakter *m •* character *(psy),* nature *(gen),* moral strength *(eth)*

Charakter, ausbeuterischer *m •* exploitative character *(Fromm) (psy, soc)*

Charakteranalyse *f •* character analysis *(Reich) (psy)* < W 179

Charakteranlage *f •* (character) disposition *(psy)*

Charakterbildung *f •* character formation/building *(psy)*

Charaktereigenschaft *f •* character trait *(psy)* → Charaktermerkmal

Charakterfestigkeit *f •* integrity of character *(eth)*

Charakterisierungsstärke *f •* potency of characterization *(log)* < Formalisierung

Charakteristik *f •* characteristic *(mat),* characteristics *(gep)* → Wesensart

Charakteristikum *n →* Merkmal

Charakteristische, das *n •* that which is characteristic *(aes, gep)* < Typische, das

Charakterkunde *f •* characterology *(psy)*

Charaktermerkmal *n •* character trait, trait *(psy)*

Charakterneurose *f •* character neurosis *(psy)*

Charakterorientierung *f •* character orientation *(Fromm) (psy)* < Charaktertypen

Charakterpanzer *m •* character armour *(Reich) (psy)*

Charakterstruktur *f •* character structure *(psy)*

Charaktertheorie *f •* character theory *(psy)*

Charaktertypen *pl •* character types *(Kretschmer, Freud etc) (psy)*

Charisma *n •* charisma *(psy, rel)* < Autorität, natürliche

Charisma, individuelles *n •* individual charisma *(Weber) (soc)*

Charismatiker *m •* charismatic person *(psy, soc)*

charismatische Autorität *f •* charismatic authority *(Weber) (soc)*

charismatische Bewegung *f •* charismatic movement *(pol, rel)*

charismatische Legitimation *f •* charismatic legitimacy *(Weber) (soc)*

charismatischer Führer *m •* charismatic leader *(Weber) (pol, soc)*

Charta der Vereinten Nationen *f •* Charter of the United Nations *(pol)* < Erklärung der Menschenrechte

Chartismus *m •* Chartism *(pol, soc)*

Chassidismus *m •* Chassidism *(rel)*

Chauvinismus *m •* chauvinism *(fem, pol)* < Ethnozentrismus

Chauvinismus, irdischer *m •* Earth chauvinism *(Hofstadter) (ant)* < Geozentrismus

Checksumme *f •* check sum *(AI)*

Chemie der Begriffe und Empfindungen *f •* chemistry of concepts and sensations *(Nietzsche) (epi)*

chemische Kriegsführung *f •* chemical warfare *(pol)*

cheng *• nt (asp)*

Chi-Quadrat Test *m •* chi-square-test *(mat)*

Chi-Quadrat Verteilung *f •* chi-squared distribution *(mat)*

Chiasmus *m •* chiasmus *(Merleau-Ponty) (ont)*

Chiffer *f →* Chiffre

Chiffre *f •* cipher *(Jaspers) (met)* < verschlüsselter Text

Chiffre der Transzendenz *f •* ciphers of transcendence *(Jaspers) (met)*

Chiffrenschrift *f •* cipher *(Jaspers) (met)*

Chiffreschlüssel *m •* cipher key, cipher code *(Jaspers) (met)*

Chiffrewerden *n •* encipherment *(Jaspers) (met)*

Chiliasmus *m •* chiliasm, millennarianism, millennianism *(rel)* → Millenarismus < Eschatologie, messianische Erwartung

chiliastische Bewegung *f •* chiliastic/millennarian movement *(rel)*

Chimäre *f →* Schimäre

chimärischer Begriff *m •* chimerical concept *(Kant) (lan)*

chinesische Philosophie *f •* Chinese philosophy *(asp)*

Chinesisches-Zimmer-Szenario *n •* Chinese room scenario *(Searle) (AI)*

Chip *m •* chip *(tec)*

Chiropraktik *f •* chiropractic *(eso)*

Choreographie *f •* choreography *(aes)*

Chrematistik *f •* chrematistics *(Aristotle) (eco)* ↔ Ökonomik

Christenglaube *m •* Christian faith *(rel)*

Christenheit *f •* Christendom *(rel)*

Christentum *n •* Christianity *(rel)*

Christenverfolgung *f •* persecution of Christians *(rel)*

Christianisierung *f •* christianization *(rel)*

christliche Anthropologie *f •* Christian anthropology *(rel, ant)*

christliche Morallehre *f •* Christian moral doctrine *(rel, eth)*

christliche Nächstenliebe *f* • Christian love of one's neighbour, (Christian) charity *(rel, eth)* < Agape

christliche Philosophie *f* • Christian philosophy *(gep, rel)*

christliche Soziallehre *f* • Christian social teaching *(rel, soc, eth)*

christlicher Aristotelismus *m* • Christian Aristotelianism *(rel, met)* < Thomismus

christlicher Existentialismus *m* • Christian existentialism *(rel, met)*

christlicher Sozialismus *m* • Christian socialism *(rel, pol)*

Christlichkeit *f* • Christianity, Christianism, Christianness° *(rel)*

Christokratie *f* • Christocracy° *(rel)*

Christologie *f* • Christology *(rel)*

Christus als Erlöser • Christ as Saviour/Redeemer *(rel)*

Church-Turing-These *f* • Church-Turing thesis, CT-thesis *(AI)*

Cineastik *f* • cineastics *(aes)* → Filmkunst

Cinéma-vérité • *nt (aes)*

circulus vitiosus *m* • vicious circle *(log)* → Zirkelschluß, Teufelskreis, petitio principii

Citoyen *m* • citizen *(Bodin, Rousseau, Marx etc) (soc, pol)* ↔ Bourgeois

civitas Dei *f* • *nt (Augustine) (rel)* → Gottesstaat

civitas terrena *f* • terrestial/earthly city *(Augustine) (rel)*

clare et distincte • clearly and distinctly *(Descartes etc) (epi)* < Deutlichkeit, Distinktheit

Cloning *n* • cloning *(nat, eth)* → Klonen

Closed World Assumption *f* • closed world assumption *(AI)*

Cluster *m* • cluster *(nat, lan, aes)*

Clusteranalyse *f* • cluster analysis *(mat)*

Code *m* • code *(mat, lan, AI)*

Codierung *f* • coding, encoding *(lan)* → Kodierung

cogitative Typen *pl* • cogitative types *(Husserl) (sci)*

cogito ergo sum • *nt*, I think, therefore I am *(Descartes) (epi)* < dubito ergo sum, Ichgewißheit, selbstgewisses Ich

Cognitive Science *f* → Kognitionswissenschaft

coincidentia oppositorum *f* • coincidence of opposites *(Kues, Bruno etc) (met)* → Zusammenfallen der Gegensätze

Collage *f* • collage *(aes)*

Commissive *pl* • commissives *(Searle) (lan, act)* < Sprachakttypologie

Common sense *m* → gesunder Menschenverstand, Gemeinsinn

Common sense-Philosophie *f* • common sense philosophy *(Moore etc) (gep)* < Philosophie der normalen Sprache

communes conceptiones *pl* → Gemeinbegriffe

communis opinio *f* • common opinion *(gen)* → allgemeine Meinung, opinio communis < herrschende Meinung

computererfahren • computerate *(AI)*

computergesteuert • computer-controlled *(sys, tec)*

computergestützt • computer- aided/assisted *(sys, tec)*

computergestützte Technik *f* • computer-aided technology *(tec)*

Computerhirn *n* • computational mind *(min, AI)* → Geist als Rechenmaschine

Computerkompetenz *f* • computer literacy *(AI)*

Computerkunst *f* • computer art *(aes)* < elektronische Kunst

Computerlinguistik *f* • computational linguistics *(lan)*

Computermodell *n* • computer/computational model *(AI)*

Computermodellen, Erstellen von *n* • computer-modelling *(AI)*

Computersimulation *f* • computer simulation *(AI)* < virtuelle Realität

Computersprache *f* • computer language *(AI)*

Computertheorie des Geistes *f* • computational theory of mind, CTM *(min, AI)*

Computertheorien der Erkenntnis *pl* • computational theories of cognition *(epi, AI)*

computerunterstütztes Design *n* • computer-aided/assisted design, CAD *(tec)*

computerunterstütztes Fertigen *n* • computer-aided/assisted manufacturing, CAM *(tec)*

computerunterstütztes Lernen *n* • computer-aided/assisted learning, CAL *(AI, psy)*

Computervirus *m* • computer virus *(AI, sys)*

Computerwissenschaft *f* • computer/computational science, computing *(AI)*

Computerzeitalter *n* • computer age, age of computers *(tec, his)*

conceptiones communes *pl* → Gemeinbegriffe

conclusio *f* • conclusion *(log)* → Konklusion

conditio humana *f* • human condition *(ant, met)*

conditio sine qua non *f* → notwendige Bedingung

confutatio *f* • confutation, refutation *(log)* → Widerlegung

consensus gentium • consent of the people *(pol, eth)*

consensus omnium • general consent *(gep)*

Constituante *f* • constituent, assembly *(pol)*

contra legem • against the law *(jur)*

Contract social *m* • social contract *(Rousseau etc) (soc, pol)* → Sozialvertrag

contradictio in adjecto *f* • *nt,* contradiction in terms, inner contradiction° *(log)* < Oxymoron

Copernicus → Kopernikus

corpus juris *n* • (civil) code *(jur)* → Gesetzbuch

Covering-law-These *f* • covering law thesis *(sci)* → Hempel-Oppenheim-Schema < Erklärungsskizze

creatio ex nihilo *f* • creation from nothing, creation ex nihilo *(Aquinas etc) (rel, met)* → Schöpfung aus dem Nichts

credo quia absurdum (est) • *nt (Tertullian°) (rel)*

credo quia impossibile (est) • *nt (Tertullian) (rel)*

credo ut intelligam • I believe in order to understand, I believe that I understand *(Augustine, Anselm) (rel)* ↔ intelligo ut credam

Cybernaut *m* • cybernaut *(AI, tec)*

Cyberpunk *m* • cyberpunk *(AI, tec)*

Cyberspace *m* • cyberspace *(AI, tec)*

Cyberwelt *f* • cyberworld *(AI, tec)*

Cyborg *m* • cyborg *(tec)* < Maschinenmensch, Robobiologie

Cyniker *m* → Zyniker

Cyrenaicer *m* → Kyrenaiker

D

D-S-System *n* → Zustandssystem, diskretes

Da, das *n* • the There *(Heidegger) (ont)*

Da-sein *n* • being there *(Heidegger) (ont)*

Dabeisein *n* • being-(in-)present, being-there-alongside *(Heidegger) (ont)*

Dadaismus *m* • dadaism *(aes)*

Daimon *m* → Dämon

Dammbruch-Argument *n* • slippery slope argument, wedge argument *(eth)* → Argument der schiefen Ebene

Dämon *m* • daemon, daimon(ion) *(Plato)*, demon *(met)*

Dämonion *n* • daemon, daimon(ion) *(Plato)*, demon *(met)* → Dämon

Dämonische, das *n* • the daemonic *(Socrates, Kierkegaard) (met)*

Dämonismus *m* • demonism *(cul, rel)*

Dämonolatrie *f* • demonolatry *(rel)* → Teufelsanbetung

Dämonologie *f* • demonology *(cul, rel)*

Dandyismus *m* • dandyism *(aes)* < Camp-Ästhetik, Snobismus

Dankbarkeit *f* • gratitude, thankfulness *(eth)*

Dao *n* → Tao

Daoismus *m* → Taoismus

darstellende Geometrie *f* • descriptive geometry, theory of projection *(mat)*

darstellende Kunst *f* • representational/imitative/performing art *(aes)* → bildende Kunst

Darstellung *f* • (▷ Abbild) representation *(lan, aes)*, (▷ Präsentation) presentation *(epi)*

Darstellungsfunktion der Sprache *f* • representational function of language *(Bühler) (lan)* < W 931

Darstellungsobjekt *n* • represented object, object of representation *(aes)*

Darstellungsprinzip *n* • principle of representation *(Klages etc) (met)*

Darstellungstheorie der Wahrnehmung *f* • representional/representative theory of perception *(epi)*

Darwinismus *m* • Darwinism *(nat)*

darwinistisch • Darwinian *(nat)*

Darwinsche Theorie *f* • Darwinian theory *(nat)*

Daseiende, das *n* • being-in-existence *(ont)*

dasein • to exist *(met)*

Dasein *n* • Dasein *(Heidegger)*, existence *(Jaspers etc)*, subsistence *(Bolzano) (ont)*

Dasein als Mitsein *n* • Dasein as being with *(Heidegger) (ont)*

Dasein als solches *n* • Dasein as such *(Heidegger) (ant, ont)*

Dasein als Sorge *n* • Dasein as care *(Heidegger) (ont)* < Sorge

Dasein, befriedetes *n* • satisfied existence *(met, psy)* < erfülltes Dasein

Dasein, bestimmtes *n* • determinate being *(Hegel) (met)*

Dasein, eigentliches *n* • authentic Dasein *(Heidegger) (ont)*

Dasein, jeweiliges *n* • current Dasein *(Heidegger) (ont)*

Dasein, menschliches *n* • human existence *(gep)*

Dasein, uneigentliches *n* • inauthentic Dasein *(Heidegger) (ont)*

Daseinsanalyse *f* • existential analysis *(Binswanger, Jaspers) (met)*

Daseinsanalytik *f* • analytic of Dasein *(Heidegger) (ant, ont)*

Daseinsangst *f* • Angst, existential fear/dread *(Kierkegaard) (met)* < Angst, existentielle

Daseinsantrieb *m* • will to exist *(met)*

Daseinsbehauptung *f* • affirmation/assertion of existence *(nat, met)* < Existenzkampf

Daseinsberechtigung *f* • right to exist(ence) *(eth)*

Daseinserhaltung *f* • maintenance of existence *(nat)*

Daseinserhellung *f* • illumination of existence *(Jaspers) (met)*

Daseinsfeld *n* • field of being(-there) *(Janssen) (met)*

Daseinsgemeinschaft *f* • community of existence, common existence *(soc, met)*

Daseinsinteresse *n* • interest in existence *(met)*

Daseinskampf *m* • struggle for existence *(nat, soc)* → Kampf ums Überleben

Daseinskommunikation *f* • communication of existence, mental interchange of existence *(Jaspers) (met)*

daseinsmäßig Seiendes *n* • being in the mode of reality *(ont)*

Daseinsordnung *f* • hierarchy of being/existence *(nat, ont)*

Daseinsprinzipien *pl* • principles of being/existence *(met)*

Daseinssituation *f* • existential situation *(met)* < Geworfenheit

Daseinsverabsolutierung *f* • exaltation of human existence *(met)*

Daseinsweise *f* • mode of being/existence *(met)*

Daseinswelt *f* • world of Dasein *(Heidegger)* *(ont)*

Datenabstraktion *f* • data abstraction *(sci)*

Datenanalyse *f* • data analysis *(AI)*

Datenbank *f* • data bank/base *(AI)*

Datenbasis *f* • database *(sci)*

Datenbereich *m* • data domain *(sci)*

Datenbeschreibung *f* • data description *(sci)*

Datenerfassung *f* • data acquisition *(AI)*

Datenschutz *m* • data protection *(eth, jur)*

Datentyp *m* • data type *(AI)*

Datenverarbeitung *f* • data processing *(AI)*

Datiermethode *f* • dating method *(sci, his)*

Dauer *f* • duration *(Bergson)* *(met)*, length of time *(nat, sci)*

Dauerarbeitslosigkeit *f* • long-term unemployment *(eco)*

dauerhafte Konsumgüter *pl* • consumer durables, durable (consumer) goods *(eco)* < eingebauter Verschleiß

dauernder Krieg *m* • permanent/constant war *(eth, pol)* ↔ ewiger Friede

Dazu, das *n* • the toward(s)-this *(Heidegger)* *(ont)*

dazwischenkommende Intentionalität *f* • intermediary/mediating intentionality *(min, act)*

de dicto-Einstellung *f* • de dicto attitude, attitude de dicto *(gep)*

de dicto-Modalität *f* • modality de dicto *(log)*

De Morgansche Gesetze *pl* • De Morgan's laws *(log, mat)*

de nihilo nihil • nothing (comes/can be created) out of nothing *(met, rel)*

de re-Einstellung *f* • de re attitude, attitude de re *(gep)*

de re-Modalität *f* • de re modality *(log)*

Debugging *n* • debugging *(AI)* < Bug, Irrtumsbeseitigung

Décadence-Instinkte *pl* • decadence instincts *(Nietzsche)* *(met)*

deckungsgleich • congruent *(log, mat)*

decodieren • to decode *(lan, AI)*

Dedekindscher Schnitt *m* • Dedekind cut *(Gentzen)* *(log)*

Deduktion *f* • deduction *(log)* ↔ Induktion

Deduktion der Kategorien *f* • deduction of the categories *(Kant)* *(epi)*

Deduktionslogik *f* • deductive logic *(log)*

Deduktionsregel *f* • deduction rule, deductive rule *(log)*

Deduktionstheorem *n* • deduction theorem *(log)*

deduktiv-nomologische Erklärung *f* • deductive-nomological explanation, covering-law explanation *(Hempel, Oppenheim)* *(sci)* < Hempel-Oppenheim-Schema

deduktiv-nomologische Prognose *f* • deductive-nomological prediction *(sci)*

deduktiv-nomologische Systematisierung *f* • deductive-nomological systematization *(sci)*

deduktiv-nomologisches Modell *n* • deductive-nomological model *(sci)* < Prinzip der Nomologisierbarkeit, Hempel-Oppenheim-Schema

deduktive Erklärung *f* • deductive explanation *(sci)*

deduktive Logik *f* • deductive logic *(log)*

deduktives Argument *n* • deductive argument *(log, sci)*

deduktives Denken *n* • deductive reasoning/thinking *(epi)*

deduktives System *n* • deductive system *(log, sci)*

Deduktivismus *m* • deductivism *(log, sci)*

deduktivistisch • deductivist *(log, sci)*

Deeskalation *f* • de-escalation *(pol)* ↔ Eskalation

Default reasoning *n* → Default-Schluß

Default-Schluß *m* • default inference *(log)*

Defensivkrieg *m* • defensive war *(pol, eth)* → Verteidigungskrieg ↔ Angriffskrieg, Eroberungskrieg

Deficit-Spending *n* • deficit spending *(Keynes)* *(eco)* → Defizitfinanzierung, keyneisianische Wirtschaftspolitik

Definiendum *n* • definiendum *(log)*

Definiens *n* • definiens *(log)*

Definierbarkeit *f* • definability *(log, lan)*

definierende Eigenschaft *f* • defining property *(log)*

definierende Gleichung *f* • defining equation *(log)*

definierter Term *m* • defined term *(log, lan)*

definite Aussage *f* • definite statement *(log, sci)*

definite Beschreibung *f* • definite description *(Russell)* *(log, lan)* → definite Kennzeichnung

definite Deskription *f* → definite Kennzeichnung

definite Kennzeichnung *f* • definite description *(Russell etc) (lan)*

definites Prädikat *n* • definite predicate *(log)*

Definition *f* • definition *(log, lan)*

Definition, abbreviative *f* • abbreviative definition *(log, lan)*

Definition, analytische *f* • analytic(al) definition *(log, lan)*

Definition, beschreibende *f* • descriptive definition *(log, lan)* < Bedeutungsanalyse

Definition, essentialistische *f* • essentialist(ic)/ essential definition *(Aristotle, Popper etc) (log, lan)* < Realdefinition

Definition, genetische *f* • genetic(al°) definition *(log, lan)*

Definition, implizite *f* • implicit definition *(log, lan)*

Definition, kontextuale *f* • contextual definition *(log, lan)*

Definition, operationale *f* • operational definition *(Bridgman) (log, lan)*

Definition, ostensive *f* • ostensive definition *(log, lan)*

Definition, ostentative *f* → ostensive Definition

Definition, partielle *f* • partial definition *(log, lan)*

Definition per genus proximum et differentiam specificam *f* • definition by (proximate) genus and (specific) difference *(log, lan)*

Definition, persuasive *f* • persuasive definition *(Stevenson etc) (log, lan)*

Definition, re-empathische *f* • re-empathic definition *(log, lan)* < Entleerungsdefinition

Definition, rekursive *f* • recursive definition *(log, lan)*

Definition, suggestive *f* • persuasive definition *(Stevenson) (log, lan)*

Definition, syntaktische *f* • syntactic definition *(log, lan)*

Definition, synthetische *f* • synthetic(al°) definition *(log, lan)*

Definitionsbereich *m* • domain (of definition) *(log, lan)*

Definitionsfehler *m* • error of definition, definition error *(log, lan)*

Definitionslehre *f* → Definitionstheorie

Definitionsschema *n* • definition formula° *(log, lan)*

Definitionstheorie *f* • theory of definition, definition theory *(log, lan)*

Definitionsverfahren *n* • definition procedure *(log, lan)*

definitorisch • by definition *(log, lan)*

Defizitfinanzierung *f* • deficit spending *(Keynes) (eco)* → Deficit-Spending

Defizithypothese *f* • deficit hypothesis *(soc, psy)*

deflationäre Wahrheitstheorie *f* • deflationary theory of truth *(epi, met)* → deflationistische Wahrheitstheorie

Deflationismus *m* • deflationism *(epi, lan)* < deflationistische Wahrheitstheorie

deflationistische Wahrheitstheorie *f* • deflationary/deflationist theory of truth *(epi, met)* → deflationäre Wahrheitstheorie

Degeneration *f* • degeneration *(nat, his)* → Dekadenz

Degenerationismus *m* • degenerationism *(his)*

Degenerationserscheinung *f* • sign of degeneration *(nat, his)*

degenerative Forschungsprogramme *pl* • degenerative research programmes *(Lakatos) (sci)*

Dehumanisation *f* • dehumanization *(eth)* → Entmenschlichung

Dehumanisierung der Gesellschaft *f* • dehumanization of society *(Luhmann) (soc)*

Dehumanisierung *f* → Dehumanisation

Deideologisierung *f* • deideologization *(pol)* → Entideologisierung ↔ Reideologisierung

Deifikation *f* • deification *(rel)* < Selbstvergötterung

deiktischer Ausdruck *m* • deictic expression *(lan)* → indexikalischer Ausdruck

Deismus *m* • deism *(rel)* < natürliche Religion, natürliche Theologie

deistisch • deistic *(rel)*

Deixis *f* • deixis *(met, lan)* < Zeigen, das; Indexikalität

Dekadenz *f* • decadence *(cul, his)* → Degeneration < Verfallserscheinung

dekadischer Logarithmus *m* • common logarithm, logarithm (to) base 10 *(mat)*

Dekalog *m* • decalogue *(rel)* → Zehn Gebote

Deklarationen *pl* • declaratives *(Searle) (lan)*

dekodieren • to decode *(lan)*

Dekodierung *f* • decoding *(lan)* ↔ Rekodierung

Dekolonisation *f* • decolonization *(pol)*

Dekolonisierung *f* → Dekolonisation

Dekonstruktion *f* • deconstruction *(Derrida etc) (epi, met)* < Destruktion, Konstruktion

Dekonstruktivismus *m* • deconstructionism *(gep)*

dekorative Kunst *f* • decorative art *(aes)* < Art déco

Dekorum *n* • decorum *(aes)*

Delegation *f* • delegation *(act, dec)* < Planung

Delphisches Orakel n • Delphic oracle *(rel)*

Demarkationismus m • demarcationism *(epi, sci)*

Demarkationskriterium n • criterion of demarcation *(sci)*

Demarkationsproblem n • problem of demarcation *(epi, sci)* < Sinnkriterium

Dematerialisation f • dematerialization *(eso)* ↔ Rematerialisation

Demilitarisierung f • demilitarization *(pol)* ↔ Remilitarisierung

Demiurg m • demiurge *(Plato) (met)* → Weltenschöpfer

Demographie f • demography *(soc)*

demographische Zeitbombe f • demographic time bomb *(soc)* < Bevölkerungsexplosion

demographischer Übergang m • demographic transition *(soc)*

Demokratie f • democracy *(pol)* → Volksherrschaft

Demokratie, direkte f • direct democracy *(pol)* < Volksabstimmung

Demokratie, indirekte f • indirect democracy *(pol)* < Demokratie, repräsentative

Demokratie, parlamentarische f • parliamentary democracy *(pol)*

Demokratie, repräsentative f • representative democracy *(pol)* < Demokratie, indirekte

Demokratiedefizit n • democracy deficit *(pol)*

Demokratietheorie f • democracy theory, theory of democracy *(pol)*

demokratische Entscheidungsfindung f • democratic decision-making *(pol)*

demokratischer Zentralismus m • democratic centralism *(Lenin etc) (pol)*

demokratisches System n • democratic system *(pol)*

Demokratisierung f • democratization *(pol)*

Demokratismus m • democratism *(pol)*

Demokrit • Democritus

Demonstrabilität f • demonstrability *(sci)* < Beweisbarkeit

Demonstrationsobjekt n • object of demonstration *(sci)*

demonstrative Muße f • conspicuous leisure *(Veblen) (eco, soc)*

demonstrative Verschwendung f • conspicuous waste *(Veblen) (eco, soc)*

demonstrativer Konsum m • conspicuous consumption *(Veblen) (eco, soc)* < Eindruckskonkurrenz, Luxuskonsumtion, positionelle Güter, Prestigegüter, Statusgüter

demonstratives Lernen n • learning by demonstration *(psy)*

demonstrierbare Wissenschaft f • demonstrable science *(sci)*

Demotivation f • demotivation *(psy)*

Demut f • humility *(eth, rel)*

demythologisieren • to demythologize *(Bultmann etc) (rel)*

Demythologisierung f • demythologization *(Fichte, Hegel, etc) (met), (Bultmann) (rel)*

Denaturierung f • denaturation, denaturalization, denaturization *(Rousseau etc) (soc)*

Denaturierung des Menschen f • denaturation of man *(Rousseau) (soc)*

Denkakt m • act of thinking/thought, noesis *(Husserl) (epi, min)*

Denkansatz m • starting point (of thinking), approach *(gep)*

Denkanstoß m • impulse, suggestion, initial idea *(gep)*

Denkart f • mentality, way/mode of thinking *(gep)* < Denkstil

Denkbare, das n • the thinkable *(epi)*

denkbare Welt f • conceivable world *(epi, met)* < mögliche Welten

Denkbarkeit Gottes f • conceivability of God *(Aquinas etc) (rel)*

Denken n • thinking, thought, reasoning, reflection, cogitation *(gep)*

denken • to think, to reflect, to reason, to cogitate *(epi)*

Denken, assoziatives n • associative thinking/thought *(psy)* < Bewußtseinsstrom

Denken, eigenständiges n • autonomous thinking/thought *(epi)*

Denken in Begriffen n • conceptual thinking *(epi)* → Begriffsdenken

Denken in Bildern n → Bilderdenken

Denken in Zusammenhängen n → ganzheitliches Denken

Denken, lautes n • thinking aloud *(min)*

Denken, mechanistisches n • mechanistic thought *(epi)*

Denken, produktives n • productive thinking *(epi, psy)*

Denken, systematisches n • systematic thinking/thought *(gep)* < Philosophie, systematische

Denken und Sein, Identität von f • identity of thinking/thought and being *(Parmenides, Hegel etc) (met)*

Denken und Tat, Synthese von f • synthesis of thought and deed/action *(epi, act)*

Denken, wissenschaftliches n • scientific thinking/thought/reasoning *(sci)*

denkende Natur f • thinking nature *(Kant) (met, ant)*

denkende Substanz *f* • thinking substance
(Descartes) (epi, met) → res cogitans ↔
Substanz, ausgedehnte

denkender Verstand *m* • cogitative reason
(Hegel etc) (epi, met)

denkendes Selbst *n* • thinking self *(epi, met)*

denkendes Subjekt *n* • thinking subject *(epi)*

Denkfabrik *f* • think-tank *(gep)*

Denkfähigkeit *f* • faculty of thinking/thought,
capacity to think *(epi)* < Vernunftbegabung

Denkfehler *m* • fallacy, faulty/false reasoning,
error in thought *(epi, log)*

Denkformen *pl* • forms of thought *(epi)*
< Verstandesformen

Denkfreiheit *f* • freedom of thought *(pol)* →
geistige Freiheit < Meinungsfreiheit, Redefreiheit

Denkgegenstand *m* • object of thought, noema
(Husserl, Heidegger) (epi, min)

Denkgesetze *pl* • laws of thought *(log, epi)* <
1127

Denkgesetzen, Lehre von den *f* → Nomologie

Denkgestalt *f* • thought gestalt *(psy, min)*

Denkgewohnheit *f* • thinking habit, habit of
thought/thinking *(psy)*

Denkgrund *m* • ground of thought *(Kant) (epi)*

Denkhemmung *f* • mental block *(psy)*

Denkmethode *f* • method of thinking/thought
(sci)

Denkmodell *n* • model of thought *(sci)*

Denkmöglichkeit *f* • thought possibility,
conceivability, thinkability, conceivable
possibility *(log)*

Denkmuster *n* • pattern of thought, thought
pattern *(epi, psy)* → Paradigma

Denknotwendigkeit *f* → logische Notwendigkeit

Denkökonomie *f* • economy of thought, thought
economy *(epi, psy)*

denkorientiert • thought-oriented *(Jung) (psy)*
↔ empfindungsorientiert, gefühlsorientiert

Denkprojekt *n* • intellectual project *(Kierkegaard) (epi, met)*

Denkprozeß *m* • thought/thinking process *(epi,
min)*

Denkregeln *pl* • rules of reasoning/thinking/
thought *(epi, log)*

Denkschule *f* • school of thought *(gep)*

Denkstil *m* • style of thinking/thought, thought
style *(Fleck) (sci)* < Paradigma

Denktypus *m* • thought type *(Jung) (psy)*

Denkungsart *f* → Denkart

Denkungsart, edle *f* • high-mindedness *(eth)*

Denkunmöglichkeit *f* → Undenkbarkeit

Denkverbot *n* • ban on thinking° *(pol)* < Gedankenkontrolle, Gedankenpolizei, Gedankenverbrechen

Denkvermögen *n* • intellectual power, intelligence *(epi)*

Denkweg *m* • path/way of thinking *(Heidegger) (met)* < Holzweg, Feldweg

Denkweise *f* • mode of thinking/thought *(epi)*
< Denkmuster, Denkart

Denkzwang *m* • obsessive thinking *(psy)*

Denotat *n* • denotatum, referent *(log, lan)* →
Bezeichnete, das

Denotation *f* • denotation *(log, lan)* ↔ Konnotation

Denotation, Theorie der *f* • theory of denotation *(Russell) (log, lan)*

denotativ • denotative *(log, lan)*

denotative Sprache *f* • denotative language
(lan) ↔ emotive Sprache

Denotator *m* • designator, denotator *(log, lan)*

Denuklearisierung *f* → atomare Abrüstung

Deontik *f* • deontics *(log, eth)*

deontische Logik *f* • deontic logic *(log, eth)*

deontischer Operator *m* • deontic operator
(log, eth)

Deontologie *f* • deontology *(eth)* < Pflicht(en)-
ethik < W 196

deontologische Ethik *f* • deontological ethics
(eth) → Pflicht(en)ethik

Deontologismus *m* • deontologism° *(eth)*

Dependenz *f* • dependency, dependence *(gep)*
→ Abhängigkeit

Dependenzgesetze *pl* • laws of dependence,
dependency/dependence laws *(N. Hartmann) (ont)*

Depersonalisation *f* • depersonalization *(psy)*

Depiktion *f* • pictorial/depictive representation
(epi, min)

Deplazierung *f* • displacement *(Foucault) (epi,
pol)*

Depression *f* • depression *(eco, psy)* < Melancholie

Deprivation *f* • deprivation *(Marx (eco); (psy)*

Deregulierung *f* • deregulation *(eco, pol, jur)*

Derivat *n* • derivative *(gep)*

Derivationenlehre *f* • theory of derivation
(Pareto) (epi, soc) < Vorurteilstheorie

derivative Diskursform *f* • derivative form of
discourse, derivative discursive form
(Searle) (lan)

Descensus *m* • descent *(log)* ↔ Ascensus

Desensibilisierung *f* • desensitization *(psy)*

Desertifikation *f* → Verwüstung

Desiderative *pl* • desideratives *(Meinong)* *(epi, min)* < Objekte, Dignitative

Design *n* • design *(aes)* < künstlerische Gestaltung

Design, experimentelles *n* • experimental design *(sci)*

Designat *n* • (the) designated *(lan)* → Signifikat

Designator *m* • designator *(lan)*

Desillusionierung *f* • disillusionment *(psy)*

Desillusionismus *m* • disillusionism *(psy, epi)* < Antiillusionismus

Desinformation *f* • disinformation *(lan, pol)*

Desintegration *f* • disintegration *(sys, soc, pol)*

Desinteresse *n* • disinterest, lack of interest *(Merton)* *(psy)* < Wertfreiheit

Desinteressiertheit *f* • disinterestedness *(psy, sci, aes)* < interesseloses Wohlgefallen, Objektivität, Werturteilsfreiheit

Deskription *f* • description *(sci, log, lan)* → Beschreibung

deskriptive Funktion der Sprache *f* • descriptive function of language *(Austin)* *(lan)*

deskriptive Funktion moralischer Urteile *f* • descriptive function of moral judg(e)ments *(Hare)* *(eth, lan)*

deskriptive Metaphysik *f* • descriptive metaphysics *(Strawson etc)* *(met)*

deskriptive Methode *f* • descriptive method *(sci)*

deskriptive Psychologie *f* • descriptive psychology *(Brentano)* *(psy)* → Psychologie, beschreibende < W 198

deskriptive Statistik *f* • descriptive statistics *(mat)*

deskriptive Theorie *f* • descriptive theory *(sci)*

deskriptiver Ausdruck *m* • descriptive term *(Hare)* *(lan)*

deskriptiver Fehlschluß *m* • descriptive fallacy *(log, lan)*

deskriptiver Gehalt *m* • descriptive content *(Searle)* *(lan)*

deskriptiver Irrationalismus *m* • descriptive irrationalism *(gep)*

deskriptiver Relativismus *m* • descriptive relativism *(sci)* < normativer Relativismus

deskriptiver Term *m* • descriptive term *(lan)*

deskriptives Zeichen *n* • descriptive sign *(lan)*

Deskriptivismus *m* • descriptivism *(Hare etc)* *(lan, eth)* ↔ Präskriptivismus

deskriptiv-normativer Gegensatz *m* • descriptive-normative opposition *(sci)* < Tatsache-Wert-Unterscheidung

Deskriptor *m* • descriptor *(lan, AI)*

Desorientierung *f* • disorientation *(psy)*

Desozialisation *f* • desocialization *(soc)*

Desperatismus *m* • desperatism *(met)* < Pantragismus

Despotie *f* • despotism *(pol)* → Gewaltherrschaft, Willkürherrschaft

Despotismus *m* • despotism *(pol)*

Destabilisierung *f* • destabilization *(pol, sys)*

Destruktion *f* • destruction, deconstruction *(Heidegger etc)* *(ont)* < Dekonstruktion

Destruktion, phänomenologische *f* • phenomenological destruction/ deconstruction *(Heidegger)* *(ont)*

Destruktionstrieb *m* • destructive instinct *(Freud etc)* *(psy)*

destruktives Verhalten *n* • destructive behaviour *(psy)* < W 64

Desublimierung *f* • desublimation *(psy)*

Desurbanisation *f* • disurbanization, deurbanization *(soc)* → Entstädterung

Desymbolisierung *f* • desymbolization *(Lorenzer)* *(psy, lan)* ↔ Resymbolisierung

Deszendenztheorie *f* • theory of descent *(Lamarck, Darwin etc)* *(nat)* → Abstammungstheorie < Evolutionstheorie

Détentepolitik *f* • détente policy, policy of détente *(pol)* → Entspannungspolitik

Determinante *f* • determinant *(mat, sci)*

Determination *f* • determination *(log, psy)* < Spezifikation

Determination, außerkausale *f* • extracausal determination *(N. Hartmann)* *(met)*

Determination, überkausale *f* • supercausal determination *(N. Hartmann)* *(met)*

Determinationskoeffizient *m* • coefficient of determination *(sci, mat)*

Determiniertheit *f* • (▷ Vorbestimmtheit) determinacy, determinedness, (▷ Bestimmtheit) determinateness *(met, lan)*

Determiniertheit des Handelns *f* • determinacy/determinedness of action *(act, eth, met)* ↔ Handlungsfreiheit

Determiniertheit des Willens *f* • determinacy/ determinedness° of (the) will *(met, eth)* ↔ Willensfreiheit

Determinismus *m* • determinism *(met, eth)* < kausale Bedingtheit, Kausalität

Determinismus, biologischer *m* • biological determinism *(nat, met)*

Determinismus, genetischer *m* • genetic determinism *(nat, met)*

Determinismus, harter *m* • hard determinism *(met)*

Determinismus, weicher *m* • soft determinism *(met)*

deterministisch • determinist(ic) *(met)*

deterministische Theorie *f* • determinist(ic) theory *(sci)*

deterministisches Gesetz *n* • deterministic law *(sci)*

Detranszendentalisierung *f* • detranscendentalization *(met)*

deus absconditus *m* • concealed/hidden God *(Goldmann etc) (rel)* → verborgener Gott ↔ deus revelatus

deus ex machina *m* • *nt (aes, met)*

deus malignus *m* • deceiving God *(Descartes) (epi, met)* → böser Dämon

deus revelatus *m* • revealed God *(rel, met)* ↔ deus absconditus

deus sive natura *m,f* • *nt*, God or Nature *(Spinoza) (met)*

Deutlichkeit *f* • distinctness *(epi, met)* < clare et distincte

Deutlichkeit, Grade der *pl* • degrees of clarity *(Leibniz) (epi)*

Deutsche Mystik *f* • German Mysticism *(Eckhart etc) (rel)*

Deutscher Idealismus *m* • German Idealism *(gep)*

Deutschtümelei *f* • German chauvinism *(pol)*

Deutung *f* • interpretation *(gep)* → Interpretation

Deutungshorizont *m* • horizon/frame of interpretation *(gep)*

Deutungsversuch *m* • attempt at (an) interpretation *(gep)*

Devianz *f* • deviance *(Becker, Schur) (mat)*

Dezentralisierung *f* • decentralization *(eco)*, decentralization, devolution *(pol, soc)*

dezentriert • decentred *(sys)*

Dezentrierung *f* • decentration *(Piaget, Habermas) (soc, psy)*

dezimal-binär • decimal-binary *(AI)* < binäres Zahlensystem

Dezimalsystem *n* • decimal system *(mat)*

Dezisionismus *m* • decisionism *(jur, eth)*

Dharma *m/n* • dharma, law *(asp)*

Dharmadhatu *m* • dharmathatu, (Buddhist) meditation centre *(asp)*

Diachronie *f* • diachronic dimension *(Saussure) (lan)* ↔ Synchronie

diachronische Sprachbetrachtung *f* • diachronic view of language *(lan)*

diachronische Sprachwissenschaft *f* • diachronic linguistics *(lan, sci)*

Diagonal-Argument *n* • diagonal argument *(Cantor) (mat)*

Diagonal-Methode *f* • diagonal method *(Cantor) (mat)*

Diagramm *n* • diagram *(mat)*

Dialektik *f* • (▷ objektives Geschehen) dialectic *(met);* (▷ Methode) dialectics *(epi)*

Dialektik der ästhetischen Urteilskraft *f* • dialectic of aesthetic judg(e)ment *(Kant) (epi, aes)*

Dialektik der Aufklärung *f* • dialectic of enlightenment *(Horkheimer, Adorno) (epi, met, soc)* < W 201

Dialektik der Natur *f* • dialectic of nature *(Engels) (nat, met)* < W 202

Dialektik der reinen (praktischen) Vernunft *f* • dialectic of pure (practical) reason *(Kant) (epi, eth)*

Dialektik der teleologischen Urteilskraft *f* • dialectic of teleological judg(e)ment *(Kant) (epi, aes)*

Dialektik des Begriffs *f* • the dialectic of the concept *(Hegel) (met)*

Dialektik des Geistes *f* • the dialectic of the spirit *(Hegel) (met)*

Dialektik des reinen Verstandes *f* • the dialectic of pure reason *(Kant) (epi)*

Dialektik des Scheins *f* • the dialectic of appearance(s) *(Kant) (met)*

Dialektik des Werdens *f* • the dialectic of becoming *(Hegel) (met)*

Dialektik, historische *f* • historical dialectics *(epi, met)*

Dialektik, idealistische *f* • idealistic dialectics *(epi, met)*

Dialektik, materialistische *f* • materialistic dialectics *(epi, met)*

Dialektik, objektive *f* • objective dialectics *(Hegel, Marx etc) (met)*

Dialektik, qualitative *f* • qualitative dialectics *(Kierkegaard) (epi, met)*

Dialektik, revolutionäre *f* • revolutionary dialectics *(Lukács etc) (epi, met)*

Dialektik, subjektive *f* • subjective dialectics *(Marx) (epi, met)*

Dialektik, transzendentale *f* • transcendental dialectic(s) *(Kant) (epi)*

Dialektik von Einzelnem und Allgemeinem *f* • dialectic of the particular and (the) general *(met)*

Dialektiker *m* • dialectician *(gep)*

dialektische Antinomie *f* • dialectical antinomy *(Kant) (epi)*

dialektische Behauptung *f* • dialectical assertion *(Kant) (epi)*

dialektische Bewegung *f* • dialectical movement *(Hegel) (met)*

dialektische Beziehung *f* • dialectical relation *(epi, met)*

dialektische Entwicklung *f* • dialectical development *(his)*

dialektische Logik f • dialectical logic *(log)*

dialektische Methode f • dialectical method *(Plato, Hegel, Marx etc) (epi, met)*

dialektische Opposition f • dialectical opposition *(Kant) (epi)*

dialektische Psychologie f • dialectical psychology *(Kant) (epi, psy)*

dialektische Theologie f • dialectical theology *(Barth) (rel)* < empirische Theologie

dialektischer Dreischritt m • dialectical/dialectic triad, triadicity *(Hegel) (met)* < triadischer Prozeß

dialektischer Gebrauch der reinen Vernunft m • dialectical employment/use of pure reason *(Kant) (epi)*

dialektischer Grundsatz m • dialectical principle *(Kant) (epi)*

dialektischer Materialismus m • dialectical/dialectic materialism *(Marx) (gep)*

dialektischer Prozeß m • dialectical/dialectic process *(his)*

dialektischer Schein m • dialectical appearance/illusion *(Kant) (epi, met)*

dialektischer Schluß m • dialectical inference *(epi)*

dialektischer Sprung m • dialectical/dialectic leap/transition *(Hegel) (met)*

dialektischer Überempirismus m • dialectical hyper-empiricism *(Sartre) (met)*

dialektischer Vernunftschluß m • dialectical inference of reason *(Kant) (epi)*

dialektisches Argument n • dialectical argument *(epi, lan)*

dialektisches Bild n • dialectical/dialectic image *(Benjamin) (met)*

dialektisches Denken n • dialectical/dialectic thinking *(epi)*

dialektisches Theater n • dialectical theatre *(Brecht) (aes)*

Diallele f → Zirkelschluß

Dialog m • dialogue *(Socrates, Plato etc) (gep)*

Dialoge, frühe pl • early dialogues *(Plato) (gep)*

Dialogik f • dialogics *(lan)*

dialogische Logik f • dialogic logic *(Lorenzen etc) (log)*

dialogische Philosophie f • dialogic(al) philosophy *(gep)*

dialogisches Denken n • dialogic(al) thinking *(Buber) (met)*

Diamat m → dialektischer Materialismus

Dianoetik f • dianoetics *(epi, met)*

dianoetische Tugend f • dianoetic(al) virtue *(Aristotle) (eth)* ↔ ethische Tugend < Verstandestugenden

Dianoia f → Verstand, Vernunft

Diätetik f • dietetics *(Aristotle, Hippocrates etc) (eth, aes, nat)* < Euthenik

Dichotomie f • dichotomy *(log)*

Dichter als Lebenserleichterer pl • poets as alleviators of life *(Nietzsche) (aes)*

Dichtkunst f • poetics, art of poetry *(aes)* → Poesie

Didaktik f • didactics *(gen)*

Dienstboten-Rasse f • menial race *(Nietzsche) (soc)*

Dienstleistungsgesellschaft f • service economy/society *(eco)*

Diesheit f • thisness *(Duns Scotus etc) (ont)* → haecceitas

Diesseits n • this life *(rel)*

Diesseitsorientierung f • this-worldly orientation *(rel, soc)*

differentia specifica f • specific difference *(log, lan)* → entscheidendes Merkmal ↔ genus proximum

Differential(kalkül) n(n/m) • differential (calculus) *(mat)*

Differential, semantisches n • semantic differential *(lan)*

Differential- und Integralrechnung f • differential and integral calculus *(mat)*

Differentialgleichung f • differential equation *(mat)*

Differentialkoeffizient m • differential coefficient *(mat)*

Differentialoperator m • differential operator *(mat)*

differentielle Hermeneutik f • hermeneutics of difference *(Gadamer, Derrida etc) (sci)*

differentielle Psychologie f • differential psychology *(psy)*

differentielle Rezeptivität f • differential receptivity *(Foucault) (epi, pol)*

Differenz f • difference *(Hegel etc) (met)*, deference, deferment, différance *(Derrida) (met, lan)* < Nicht-Identität < W 484

Differenz, biologische f • biological difference *(fem)*

Differenz, ontologische f • ontological difference *(Husserl etc) (ont)*

Differenz(en)quotient m • difference quotient *(mat)*

Differenzfeminismus m • difference feminism *(fem)* → Geschlechtsfeminismus ↔ Gleichheitsfeminismus

differenzierbare Funktion f • differentiable function *(mat)*

differenzierte Betrachtung f • differentiated view *(gen)*

Differenzierung *f* • differentiation *(gen)*
< Spezifikation

Differenzierungsmerkmal *n* • distinguishing/
distinctive feature/mark/characteristic *(lan,
log)*

Differenzierungsmethode *f* • method of
difference *(Mill) (sci)*

Differenzmaschine *f* • difference engine
(Babbage) (mat, tec)

Differenzmenge *f* • difference of sets, set-
theoretic difference *(mat)* < Mengendifferenz

Differenzprinzip *n* • difference principle
(Rawls) (eth, pol)

Differenztheorie *f* • difference theory *(fem)*
< Differenzfeminismus

Diffusion *f* • diffusion *(cul)*

Diffusionismus *m* • diffusionism *(cul)*

digital • digital *(mat, AI)* ↔ analog

Digital-Analog-Konverter *m* • digital-
analog(ue) converter *(AI)*

Digitalcomputer *m* • digital computer *(AI, tec)*
↔ analoger Computer

digitale Ästhetik *f* • digital aesthetics *(aes)*
< Informationsästhetik

digitale Technik *f* • digital technology *(AI, tec)*

digitaler Alltag *m* • digital everyday life *(tec,
soc, cul)*

Digitalisierung *f* • digitization *(AI, tec)*

Digitaltechnik *f* → digitale Technik

Dignitative *pl* • dignitatives *(Meinong) (epi,
min)* < Desiderative, Objekte, Objektive

dihairesis *f* • *nt,* division *(Plato etc) (log)*
< Synopse

Diktat der Natur *n* • dictate(s) of nature *(met)*

diktatorisch • dictatorial *(pol)*

Diktatur *f* • dictatorship *(pol)*

Diktatur des Proletariats *f* • dictatorship of
the proletariat *(Marx etc) (pol)*

Diktatur, sanfte *f* • benevolent dictatorship
(pol) < aufgeklärter Absolutismus

Diktion *f* • diction *(lan)*

Dilemma *n* • dilemma *(eth, dec)* < Zielkonflikt

Dilemmatheorie *f* • dilemma/predicament°
theory *(eth, dec)*

Dilettantismus *m* • dilettantism *(aes)*

Dimension, vierte *f* • fourth dimension *(nat,
met)*

dimensionale Kategorie *f* • dimensional
category *(N. Hartmann) (ont)*

Ding *n* • thing, object *(gep)* < Sache, Gegenstand

Ding an sich *n* • thing-in-itself *(Kant) (epi, met)*
→ Noumenon

Dinge aus sich heraus *pl* • things-in-themselves
(Sartre) (ont)

Dinge innerhalb der Welt *pl* • beings within
the world *(ont)* < innerweltlich Seiendes

Dingerfassung *f* • perception/cognition of
things *(epi, psy)* < Objektkonstanz

Dinggestalten *pl* • thing-shapes *(Husserl) (epi,
met)*

Dingqualität *f* • thing-quality *(ont, epi)*

Dingsprache *f* • thing-language *(Carnap) (lan)*
→ Objektsprache

dionysisch • Dionysian *(Nietzsche) (aes)* ↔
apollinisch

Dionysische, das *n* • the Dionysian *(Nietzsche)
(aes)*

Dionysius Areopagita • Dionysius the
Areopagite

direkt evident • directly/immediately evident
(epi)

direkte Demokratie *f* • direct democracy
(pol) < Volksabstimmung

direkte Wahrnehmung *f* • direct/immediate
perception *(epi, psy)*

direkter Beweis *m* • direct proof (demonstration) *(log)*

direktes Schließen *n* • direct/immediate
inference *(log)*

Direktive *pl* • directives *(Searle) (lan)* < Assertive, Expressive, Kommissive

Dirigismus *m* • dirigism(e), statism *(pol, eco)*
< Kommandowirtschaft, Planwirtschaft

Disgregation des Willens *f* • disgregation of
the will *(Nietzsche) (met)*

Disharmonie *f* • discord, disharmony *(aes)*

disjunkt • disjunct *(log, mat)*

disjunkte Mengen *pl* • disjoint sets *(mat)*

Disjunktion *f* • disjunction *(log, mat)* ↔ Adjunktion < Alternation

disjunktive Normalform *f* • disjunctive normal
form *(log)*

disjunktive Synthesis *f* • disjunctive synthesis
(Kant) (epi, log)

disjunktiver Vernunftschluß *m* • disjunctive
inference of reason *(Kant) (epi, log)*

disjunktives Denken *n* • disjunctive reasoning
(log, epi)

disjunktives Urteil *n* • disjunctive judg(e)ment
(epi, log) → Kontravalenz

Disjunktor *m* • disjunctor *(log)* ↔ Adjunktor
< Alternator

diskontinuierliche Objekte *pl* • discontinuous
objects *(ont)*

Diskontinuität *f* • discontinuity *(ont)*

Diskontinuum *n* • (space of) discontinuity *(nat)*

diskrete Größe *f* • discrete magnitude/entity/ quantity, mangitude *(met, nat)*

diskretes Merkmal *n* • discrete property/ characteristic *(mat)*

Diskretisation *f* → Diskretisierung

Diskretisierung *f* • discretization *(mat)*

Diskriminante *f* • discriminant *(mat)*

Diskriminationstechnik *f* → Skalendiskriminationstechnik

Diskriminierung *f* • discrimination *(jur, eth)* < Sonderbehandlung

Diskriminierung am Arbeitsplatz *f* • discrimination in the workplace/at work *(eth, eco)*

Diskriminierung der Alten *f* • ageism *(eth, soc)*

Diskriminierung, umgekehrte *f* • reverse discrimination *(eth, pol)* < Vorzugsbehandlung

Diskriminierungsverbot *n* • prohibition of discrimination *(pol, eth)* < Gleichheitsgebot

Diskurs *m* • discourse *(lan, soc)*

Diskurs der Macht *m* • discourse of power *(Foucault) (epi, pol)*

Diskurs der Moderne *m* • discourse of modernity *(gep)* < W 782

Diskurs, explikativer *m* • explicative discourse *(Habermas) (lan, soc)*

Diskurs, logischer *m* • logical discourse *(lan)*

Diskurs, praktischer *m* • practical discourse *(Habermas) (lan, soc)*

Diskurs, theoretischer *m* • theoretical discourse *(Habermas) (lan, soc)*

Diskursethik *f* • discourse ethics *(Habermas) (eth)* < W 278

diskursiv • discursive *(lan)*

diskursive Arten *pl* • discursive species/kinds/ types *(lan)*

diskursive Beziehungen *pl* • discursive relations *(Foucault) (lan, epi)*

diskursive Erkenntnis *f* • discursive cognition/ knowledge *(epi)*

diskursive Form des Denkens *f* • discursive form of thinking/thought *(epi)*

diskursive Formation *f* • discursive formation *(epi, pol)*

diskursive Grenzen *pl* • discursive limits *(epi, pol)*

diskursive Konsensbildung *f* • discursive consensus formation *(epi, lan)* < Konsenstheorie der Wahrheit

diskursive Ordnung *f* • discursive order *(epi, pol)*

diskursive Regelmäßigkeiten *pl* • unities of discourse *(Foucault) (lan, epi)*

diskursiver Begriff *m* • discursive concept *(Kant) (epi, lan)*

diskursiver Vernunftgebrauch *m* • discursive use/employment of reason *(Kant) (epi)*

diskursives Denken *n* • discursive thinking *(epi)*

diskursives Prinzip *n* • discursive principle *(epi, log)*

Diskursivität *f* • discursivity *(epi)*

Diskursrepresentationstheorie *f* • discourse representation theory, DRT *(Kamp) (min, AI)*

Diskurstheorie *f* • discourse theory *(lan, pol)*

Diskurstheorie der Kunst *f* • discourse theory of art *(aes)*

Diskursuniversum *n* • universe of discourse *(epi, pol)*

Diskurswelt *f* • universe/world of discourse *(lan, soc)*

Diskussionsverbot *n* • ban on (free) discussion *(pol)* < Denkverbot

Diskussionszirkel *m* • discussion circle *(gen)*

Dispens *m* • dispensation *(rel)*

Disposition *f* • disposition *(psy, min)*

dispositionaler Glaube(n) *m* • dispositional belief *(Ryle etc) (epi, min)*

Dispositionsbegriff *m* • dispositional term/ concept *(epi, lan)*

Dispositionsprädikat *n* • dispositional predicate *(Goodman etc) (epi, lan)*

Dispositionssatz *m* • dispositional statement *(log, lan)*

Disproportion *f* • disproportion *(aes)* → Ametrie, Mißverhältnis

Disproportionalität *f* • disproportion(ality) *(aes)*

Disput *m* • dispute *(gep)*

Disputation *f* • disputation *(gep)*

Disputierkunst *f* • art of disputation/argumention *(lan)* < Rhetorik

Disquotation *f* • disquotation *(Quine) (epi, lan)* → Zitattilgung

Disquotationalismus *m* • disquotationalism *(epi, lan)*

Dissensrisiko *n* • risk of disagreement *(lan, act)*

dissipative Selbstorganisation *f* • dissipative self-organization *(sys)* ↔ konservative Selbstorganisation

dissipatives System *n* • dissipative system *(sys)*

Dissonanz *f* • dissonance *(aes)* ↔ Konsonanz

Distanz, ästhetische *f* • aesthetic distance *(aes)* < interesseloses Wohlgefallen

Distanz-Cluster-Analyse *f* • distance-cluster analysis *(Osgood) (lan, nat)*

Distanzierung f • distancing *(aes)* < Verfremdung

Distinktheit f • distinctness *(epi)* < clare et distincte

distributive Gerechtigkeit f • distributive justice *(eth)* → Verteilungsgerechtigkeit

Distributivgesetz n • distributive law *(mat, log)*

Disziplin f • discipline *(eth, sci)*

Disziplin der (reinen) Vernunft f • discipline of (pure) reason *(Kant) (epi)*

disziplinäre Matrix f • disciplinary matrix *(Kuhn) (sci)* < Paradigma

disziplinäre Phase f • disciplinary phase *(Kuhn etc) (sci)* ↔ vordisziplinäre Phase < paradigmatisch

Disziplinargesellschaft f • disciplinary society *(Foucault) (epi, soc)*

Disziplinargewalt f • disciplinary power *(pol)*

Disziplinarordnung f • disciplinary regime *(Foucault) (epi, soc)*

disziplinenübergreifend • interdisciplinary, cross-disciplinary *(gep)* < Interdisziplinarität

Divergenz f • divergence *(log, mat)*

Divergenz der Aussagemodalitäten f • divergence of enunciative modalities *(Foucault) (epi, pol)*

Diversifikation f • diversification *(gep)*

Diversifizierung f → Diversifikation

Divination f • divination *(rel)*

DNS f • DNA *(nat)*

docta ignorantia f • learned ignorance *(met)* < W 134

Dogma n • dogma *(rel)*

Dogmatik f • dogmatics *(rel)*

Dogmatiker m • dogmatist *(gep)*

dogmatische Hermeneutik f • dogmatic hermeneutic(s) *(sci)*

dogmatische Methode f • dogmatic method *(sci)*

dogmatische Wissenschaft f • dogmatic science *(sci)*

dogmatischer Beweis m • dogmatic proof *(Kant) (epi)*

dogmatischer Empirismus m • dogmatic empiricism *(Kant) (epi)*

dogmatischer Idealismus m • dogmatic idealism *(Kant) (epi)*

dogmatischer Schlummer m • dogmatic slumber(s) *(Kant) (epi, met)*

Dogmatismus m • dogmatism *(sci, rel, met)*

Dogmengeschichte f • history of thought/schools *(gep)*, history of dogmatic theology, history of doctrine *(rel)*

Doktrin f • doctrine *(gep)*

Doktrin der Urteilskraft f • doctrine of (the faculty/power of) judg(e)ment *(Kant) (epi)*

doktrinale Auslegung f • doctrinal interpretation *(Kant) (sci, lan)*

doktrinale Methode f • doctrinal method *(Kant) (sci)*

doktrinaler Glaube(n) m • doctrinal faith *(Kant) (epi, rel)* ↔ moralischer Glaube(n), Vernunftglaube

doktrinaler Grundsatz m • doctrinal principle *(Kant) (epi)*

doktrinales Instrument n • doctrinal instrument *(Kant) (sci)*

doktrinär • doctrinaire *(gep)*

Doktrinarismus m • doctrinairism, doctrinarianism *(gep)*

Dokumentarfilm m • documentary film *(aes)*

Dokumentation f • (▷ Aufzeichnungen) documentation, records *(gen)*

Domänenwissen n → bereichsspezifisches Wissen

Domestikation f • domestication *(ant, soc, nat)*

domestiziertes Tier, Mensch als m • man as a domesticated animal *(ant)*

Dominanz, männliche f • male domination *(fem)*

Dominanzprinzip n • principle of dominance *(dec)*

Dominoeffekt m • domino effect *(sys)* < Kettenreaktion, Schneeballeffekt

Dominotheorie f • domino theory *(pol)*

Doppelaspekt-Theorie f • double-aspect theory *(met)*

Doppelbedeutung f • double meaning *(lan)*

Doppelbindungs-Hypothese f • double-bind hypothesis *(Bateson) (min, psy)*

Doppelblindversuch m • double blind test *(sci)* < Blindtest

Doppeldenk m • doublethink *(Orwell) (pol)*

Doppeldeutigkeit f • ambiguity, equivocacy, double meaning/entendre *(lan)* → Ambiguität

Doppelhelix f • double helix *(nat)*

Doppelmoral f • double standard(s), hypocrisy *(eth)*

Doppelnatur des Menschen f • twofold nature of man *(ant, met)*

Doppelnegation f • double negation *(log, lan)* → doppelte Negation, Negation der Negation

Doppelreihe f • double series *(mat)*

Doppelsinn m → Doppeldeutigkeit

doppelsinniger Ausdruck m • double entendre *(lan)* < Doppeldeutigkeit

doppelte Negation f • double negation *(log, met)* → Doppelnegation, Negation der Negation

doppelte Reflexion f • double reflection *(Kierkegaard) (epi, met)*

doppelte Verneinung f → doppelte Negation

doppelte Wahrheit f • double truth, two-fold truth *(Boethius) (rel, epi)*

doppelte Wahrheit, Lehre von der f • doctrine of the two truths *(Averroes°) (rel, epi)*

doppelter Vernunftgebrauch m • twofold use of reason *(Kant) (epi)*

Doppelwirkung f • double effect *(Aquinas etc) (eth)*

Doppelwirkung, moralische f • moral double effect *(eth)*

Doppler-Effekt m • Doppler effect *(nat)*

Dorfgemeinschaft f • village community *(soc)*

Dort, das n • the yonder *(Heidegger) (ont)*

Dorther, das n • the thence *(Heidegger) (ont)*

Dorthin, das n • the thither *(Heidegger) (ont)*

Doxa f • opinion, belief, supposition *(Plato etc) (epi)* → Meinung, Glaube(n)

doxastischer Glaube(n) m • doxastic belief *(epi)* < wissenschaftlicher Glaube(n)

Drama n • drama *(aes)*

Dramaturgie f • dramaturgy *(aes)*

dramaturgisches Handeln n • dramaturgical action *(Goffman, Habermas) (soc, lan, act)*

Drang m • pressure, stress, drive *(psy)* < Trieb

Drehmatrix f • rotation matrix *(mat)*

drei Kennzeichen des Seins pl • three signs of being *(asp)* < Dukkha, Anatta, Anicca

dreidimensionaler Raum m • three-dimensional space *(nat)*

Dreidimensionalität f • three-dimensionality, tridimensionality *(mat)*

Dreieckszahlen pl • triangular numbers *(mat)*

Dreieinigkeit f • trinity *(rel)*

Dreieinigkeitslehre f • trinitarianism, doctrine of the Trinity *(rel)*

dreifache Synthesis f • threefold synthesis *(Kant) (epi)*

Dreiklang m • triad, chord *(aes)*

Dreischritt, dialektischer m • dialectic triad, triadicity *(Hegel) (met)* < triadischer Prozeß

Dreistadiengesetz n • law of (the) three stages *(Comte) (his, soc)*

Dreistadienlehre f • theory of (the) three stages (on life's way) *(Kierkegaard) (met, rel)*

Dreiviertelmehrheit f • three-fourths/three-quarter majority *(pol)*

dreiwertige Logik f • three-value(d) logic *(log)* < mehrwertige Logik

Dritte Welt f • Third World *(pol, soc)* → Entwicklungsländer

dritte Welt f → Welt Drei

Dritte-Welt-Bewegung f • Third World movement *(pol, soc)*

dritter Bereich m • third realm *(Frege, Popper etc) (log, sci, ont)* < Welt Drei

dritter Mensch m • Third Man *(Aristotle, Plato) (met)*

dritter Stand m • third estate *(soc)*

drittes Geschlecht n • third sex/gender *(fem)*

Drittheit f • thirdness *(Peirce) (met, log)*

Drittmittel pl • external funding, sponsoring *(sci)*

drittweltlicher Ansatz m • third-world approach *(Popper) (sci)* < Welt Drei

Drogenabhängigkeit f • drug addiction *(psy)* < psychedelische Erfahrung

Drogenmißbrauch m • drug abuse *(psy)*

Drohgebärde f • threat signal, menacing gesture *(psy)*

Druck der Notwendigkeit m • pressure(s) of necessity *(met)* < Sachzwang

Druck des Daseins m • burden of existence *(Nietzsche) (met)*

Druck und Stoß-Theorie f • theory of (pressure and) impetus *(nat)*

Du n • thou *(met)* < dialogische Philosophie, Ich-Du < W 475

Dualismus m • dualism *(met)* ↔ Monismus

dualistisch-interaktionistische Theorie f • dualistic interactionist theory *(Popper, Eccles) (min)*

dualistische Interpretation der Wahrscheinlichkeit f • dualistic interpretation of probability *(log, mat)* < induktive Interpretation der Wahrscheinlichkeit

dualistisches Geschlechtermodell n • dualistic gender model *(fem)*

Dualität von Geist und Körper f • duality of mind and body *(met)*

Dualitätsprinzip n • principle of duality, duality principle *(mat)*

Dualsystem n • dual/dyadic system *(mat)* → Binärsystem

Dualwirtschaft f • dual economy *(eco)*

dubito ergo sum • I doubt, therefore I exist *(Descartes) (epi)* < cogito ergo sum

Duhemsche These f • Duhem thesis *(sci)* → Quine-Duhem-These

Dukkha • dukkha, suffering *(asp)* < Anicca, Anatta, drei Kennzeichen des Seins

Dummheit *f* • stupidity, ignorance, foolishness *(gen)* < W 134

Dünkel *m* • conceit *(psy)*

Dunkelziffer *f* • dark figure *(gen)*

Durchdringung der Gegensätze *f* • interpenetration of opposites *(Hegel)* *(met)*

Durchdringung von Körpern *f* • (inter)penetration of substances *(met)*

Durchführbarkeit, technologische *f* • technological feasibility *(tec)*

Durchführbarkeitsstudie *f* • feasibility study *(tec)* → Machbarkeitsstudie

Durchschnitt *m* • average, (▷ Schnittmenge) intersection *(mat)*

Durchschnitt, gleitender *m* • moving/sliding average *(mat)*

durchschnittliche Abweichung *f* • mean/average deviation *(mat)* < Standardabweichung

durchschnittliches Seinsverständnis *n* • average understanding of Being *(Heidegger)* *(ont)*

Durchschnittlichkeit *f* • mediocrity *(Nietzsche)* *(soc)* < Man, das

Durchschnittsmensch *m* • average/common man, man in the street *(soc)* → Normalmensch

Durchsetzbarkeit *f* • enforceability *(jur)*

Durchsetzung der Moral *f* • enforcement of morality *(eth)*

Durchsichselbstsein der Natur und des Menschen *n* • the self-mediated being of nature and of man *(Marx)* *(soc, met)*

Durchsichtigkeit *f* • transparency *(log, lan)* → Transparenz ↔ Opakheit

Dynamik *f* • dynamics *(nat, sys, aes)* < Dynamis und Energeia, Dynamismus

Dynamis und Energeia *f,f* → Möglichkeit und Wirklichkeit

dynamisch • dynamic *(gen)*

Dynamisch-Erhabenes der Natur *n* • dynamical sublime of nature *(Kant)* *(nat, aes)*

dynamische Einheit *f* • dynamic(al) unity *(Kant)* *(epi)*

dynamische Gemeinschaft *f* • dynamic(al) community *(Kant)* *(epi, soc)*

dynamische Gewichtung *f* • dynamic(al) weighting *(dec)* < rationale Präferenzbewertung

dynamische Kategorien *pl* • dynamic(al) categories *(Kant)* *(epi)* ↔ mathematische Kategorien

dynamische Kultur *f* • dynamic(al) culture *(cul)*

dynamische Regel *f* • dynamic(al) rule *(Kant)* *(epi)*

dynamische Synthesis *f* • dynamic(al) synthesis *(Kant)* *(epi)*

dynamischer Fluß des Denkens *m* • dynamic(al) flow of thought(s) *(Klages, Jaspers)* *(met)*

dynamischer Vernunftbegriff *m* • dynamic(al) concept of reason *(Kant)* *(epi)*

dynamisches Ganzes *n* • dynamic(al) whole *(Kant)* *(epi, nat, met)*

Dynamismus *m* • dynamism *(met)*

Dysfunktion *f* • dysfunction *(sys)*

Dysteleologie *f* • dysteleology *(met)* < Ziellosigkeit der Natur

Dystopie *f* • dystopia *(soc, his)* → Utopie, schwarze, Antiutopie

E

Eat-art *f* • eat-art *(aes)*

Ebenbild Gottes *n* • God's likeness/image *(rel)*

echte Untermenge *f* • proper subset *(mat)*

Echtheit *f* • genuineness *(aes)* < Authentizität

Echtzeit *f* • real time *(nat, psy, AI)*

écriture *f* • writing *(Barthes) (lan)*

écriture automatique *f* • automatic writing *(aes)* → automatisches Schreiben

Edelmut *m* • magnanimity *(eth)*

edelmütiges Bewußtsein *n* • noble consciousness *(eth)*

Edle, das *n* • the noble *(aes, eth)*

edle Einfalt *f* • noble innocence/simplicity *(Winckelmann) (aes)*

edle Geburt *f* • noble birth *(Plato etc) (soc)*

edler Wilder *m* • noble savage *(Rousseau) (soc)* ↔ zivilisierter Mensch < homme naturel

Effektgesetz *n* • law of effect *(Thorndike) (psy, soc)*

Effektivität *f* • effectiveness *(eco, sys)*

Effektor *m* • effector *(sci)*

Effizienz *f* • efficiency *(eco, sys)*

Egalisierung *f* • equalization *(soc, pol)*

Egalitarismus *m* • egalitarianism *(eth, pol)*

Egalität *f* • equality *(eth, pol)* → Gleichheit

Ego *n* • ego *(psy, met)*

Ego, transzendentales *n* • transcendental ego *(Husserl) (epi, met)*

Ego-Ideal *n* • ego-ideal *(psy)* → Ich-Ideal

Egoismus *m* • egoism, selfishness *(eth)* → Eigennutz, Selbstsucht ↔ Altruismus

egoistisch • egoistic *(eth)*

egoistische Gene *pl* • selfish genes *(nat, ant)*

Egomanie *f* • egomania *(psy)*

Egotismus *m* • egotism *(psy, eth)*

Egozentrik *f* • egocentrism *(psy)* → Ichzentriertheit

ehernes Lohngesetz *n* • iron law of wages *(Marx) (eco)*

Ehre *f* • honour *(eth)*

Ehrerbietung *f* • deference, respect *(eth)* → Respekt

Ehrfurcht vor dem Leben *f* • respect/reverence for life *(Schweitzer etc) (eth)*

ehrfürchtiger Geist *m* • reverential spirit *(Nietzsche) (met)*

Ehrgefühl *n* • sense of honour *(eth)*

Ehrgeiz *m* • ambition *(eth, psy)*

Ehrlichkeit *f* • honesty *(eth)*

Ehrsucht *f* • desire for fame *(eth, psy)*

Eid *m* • oath *(jur, eth)* < Hippokratischer Eid

eidbrüchig • oathbreaking, perjured *(jur, eth)*

eidetische Reduktion *f* • eidetic reduction *(Husserl) (epi, met)*

eidetische Variation *f* • eidetic variation *(Husserl) (epi, met)*

eidetische Wissenschaft *f* • eidetic science *(Husserl etc) (ont)*

eidetischer Sinn *m* • eidetic sense *(Husserl etc) (epi, met)*

eidetisches Bild *n* • eidetic image *(epi, met)*

Eidologie *f* • eidology *(Husserl etc) (epi)*

Eidolon-Theorie *f* • eidolon/phantom theory *(Democritus etc) (epi)*

eidos *n* • *nt*, idea *(Plato, Aristotle, Husserl) (met)* → Idee, Form, Gestalt, Art, Wesen

Eigenbedarfsproduktion *f* • subsistence production *(eco)* → Subsistenzwirtschaft

Eigenbedeutsamkeit *f* • inner significance, significance for itself *(gep)*

Eigendynamik *f* • inherent dynamism, momentum *(sys)* < Schneeballeffekt, Dominoeffekt

eigendynamische Wachstumsprognose *f* • self-fulfilling growth prediction *(sci)* < endogene Wachstumsprognose

Eigenfunktion *f* • characteristic/particular function, eigenfunction *(mat)*

Eigengesetzlichkeit *f* • determination by inherent laws, autonomy *(sys)* → Entelechie

Eigenleiberfahrung *f* • experience of one's own body, own bodily experience *(Schopenhauer) (met, epi)*

Eigenliebe *f* • self-love *(eth, psy)* → Narzißmus, Selbstliebe

Eigenlogik *f* • internal logic *(log)*

Eigenname *m* • proper name/noun *(lan)*

Eigennutz *m* • self-interest *(eth)* → Egoismus

eigennütziges Motiv *n* • selfish motive *(eth)*

eigenpsychischer Gegenstand *m* • autopsychological object *(Carnap) (epi, min)*

Eigenpsychisches *n* • of one's own mind *(Carnap, Scheler) (min, psy)* ↔ Fremdpsychisches

Eigenschaft *f* • property, attribute, feature, characteristic *(gep)*

Eigenschaft, charakteristische *f* • quality *(gep)*

Eigenschaft, unveränderliche *f* • immutable/ unchangeable attribute/property *(ont)* < Wesen, Substanz

Eigenschaften Gottes *pl* • divine attributes, attributes of God *(rel)* → Merkmale Gottes

Eigenschaften, primäre *pl* • primary qualities *(Locke etc) (epi)*

Eigenschaften, sekundäre *pl* • secondary qualities *(Locke etc) (epi)*

Eigenschaftsabstraktion *f* • property abstraction, abstraction of attributes *(Quine) (lan, ont)*

Eigenschaftsbeschreibung *f* • property description *(Carnap etc) (epi, lan)*

Eigenschaftsdualismus *m* • property dualism *(met)*

Eigenschaftsname *m* • property name *(Searle etc) (lan)*

Eigenschaftsvererbung *f* • property inheritance *(log, AI)*

Eigenstaatlichkeit *f* • sovereignty *(pol)* → Souveränität

eigentlich-reale Entitäten *pl* • actual entities/ occasions *(met)*

eigentliche Existenz *f* • actual/real existence *(met)*

eigentliche Natur *f* • true nature *(met)*

eigentlicher Begriff *m* • proper concept *(Carnap etc) (log, lan)*

eigentliches Sein *n* • authentic Being *(Heidegger) (ont)*

eigentliches Selbst *n* • authentic self *(Heidegger) (ont)*

eigentliches Selbstsein *n* • authentic being-as-(one)self *(Jaspers) (met)*

Eigentlichkeit *f* • authenticity *(Heidegger) (ont)* ↔ Uneigentlichkeit < W 497

Eigentlichkeit des Daseins *f* • authenticity of Dasein *(Heidegger) (ont)*

Eigentum *n* • property, ownership *(jur, eco)*

Eigentum als Diebstahl *n* • property as theft *(Proudhon) (eco)*

Eigentum an Produktionsmitteln *n* • ownership of the means of production, ownership of productive assets *(Marx etc) (jur, eco, soc)*

Eigentum, antikes *n* • ancient property *(eco, soc)*

Eigentum durch Arbeit *n* • ownership by/ through labour *(jur, soc)*

Eigentum, feudales *n* • feudal property *(eco, soc)*

Eigentum, fremdes *n* • alien property *(jur, eco)*

Eigentum, Recht auf *n* • right/entitlement to property *(jur, eco)*

Eigentum, selbsterworbenes *n* • (self-)earned property *(eco)*

Eigentum und Arbeit, Trennung von *f* • separation of property and labour *(Marx) (eco, soc)*

Eigentumsanspruch *m* • (▷ Eigentum beanspruchen) property claim, (▷ Recht auf Eigentum) entitlement to property *(jur, eco)*

Eigentumsbedingungen *pl* • conditions of property *(eco, soc)*

Eigentumsbegriff *m* • concept of property *(jur, eco)*

Eigentumsbeschränkung *f* • limitation of property *(jur, eco, soc)*

Eigentumserwerb *m* • acquisition of property *(jur, eco)*

Eigentumsfrage *f* • property question *(eco, soc)*

Eigentumsordnung *f* • property order *(eco, soc, jur)* < Eigentumsverhältnisse

Eigentumsrecht *n* • property right, legal title to property, proprietary right *(jur, eco)* < Privateigentum

Eigentumsstreuung *f* • distribution of property *(eco, soc)* < Verteilungsergebnis

Eigentumsübertragung *f* • transfer of ownership *(jur)*

Eigentumsumverteilung *f* • redistribution of wealth *(soc, eco)*

Eigentumsverhältnisse *pl* • property relations, ownership structure *(eco, soc)*

Eigenverbrauch *m* • private consumption *(eco)*

Eigenwert *m* • intrinsic value *(eth, eco)*, eigenvalue *(mat)*

Eigenwille *m* • self-will *(eth)*

Eigenzeit *f* • proper time *(nat)* < Relativitätstheorie

Eignung *f* • aptitude *(psy)*

Ein-Ebenen-System *n* • one-level-system *(Hare) (eth, sci)*

Einbildung *f* • (▷ Vorstellung) imagination, (▷ irrige Vorstellung) illusion, delusion *(epi, psy)* → Illusion, Täuschung

Einbildungskraft *f* • (faculty/power of) imagination *(Kant) (epi, aes)* < Imagination, Vorstellungskraft

Einbildungskraft, produktive *f* • productive (faculty of) imagination *(Kant) (aes, epi)*

Einbildungskraft, reproduktive *f* • reproductive (faculty of) imagination *(Kant) (aes, epi)*

Einblick *m* • insight *(epi)*

eindeutig • unambiguous, unequivocal, definite *(log, lan)* < Definition, explizite

eindeutig bestimmt • uniquely determined *(log, lan)*

eindeutige Relation *f* • one-to-one relation *(log, lan)* < univok

eindeutige Zuordnung *f* • unambiguous assignment, one to one mapping, injection, unique attribution *(mat)*

Eindeutigkeit *f* • unambiguity, definiteness *(lan, log)* ↔ Mehrdeutigkeit

Eindeutigkeitsprinzip *n* • exclusion principle *(log, mat)*

eindimensionale Gesellschaft *f* • one-dimensional society *(Marcuse) (soc)*

eindimensionaler Mensch *m* • one-dimensional man *(Marcuse) (soc)* < W 220

Eindimensionalität *f* • one-dimensionality *(Marcuse etc) (soc)*

Eindringlichkeit *f* • intensity, urgency, insistence *(gen)*

Eindruck *m* • impression *(Locke, Hume etc) (epi, psy)* < Sinneseindruck

Eindruckskonkurrenz *f* • status competition *(soc, eco)* < demonstrativer Konsum, positionelle Güter

Eine, das *n* • the One *(Plotin etc) (ont)*

Eine und das Viele, das *n* • the One and the Many *(Empedocles etc) (ont)*

einfach geordnet • simply ordered *(mat)*

Einfache, das *n* • the simple *(ont)*

einfache Folgerung *f* • elementary deduction *(log)*

einfache Idee *f* • simple idea *(Descartes, Locke, Leibniz etc) (epi)* ↔ Idee, zusammengesetzte

einfache Naturen *pl* • simple natures *(Descartes etc) (met)*

einfache Substanz *f* • simple substance *(Leibniz etc) (met, ont)* < Monade

einfache Wahrheiten *pl* • simple truths *(epi, met)*

einfache Zeichen *pl* • simple signs *(Wittgenstein etc) (lan)*

einfacher Ausdruck *m* • atomic expression *(lan, log)* → atomarer Ausdruck

einfacher Sachverhalt *m* • atomic fact *(Wittgenstein) (lan, log)* → atomarer Sachverhalt

einfacher Teil *m* • simple part *(epi, ont)* → einfaches Teil

einfacher Term *m* • primitive/basic term *(log, lan)* → primitiver Term

einfaches Teil *n* • einfacher Teil

Einfachheit *f* • (▷ Unteilbarkeit) indivisibility, indivisibleness *(ont)*; simplicity *(aes)*; simplicity *(sci)* < Komplexitätsreduktion

Einfachheit, neue *f* • new simplicity *(met, cul)*

Einfachheitskriterium *n* • simplicity criterion, criterion of simplicity *(Quine etc) (sci)*

Einfall *m* • idea *(gep)* < Aha-Erlebnis

Einfallsreichtum *m* • imaginativeness, inventiveness *(gep)* < Heuristik, Problemlösungskapazität

Einflußbereich *m* • sphere of influence *(pol, soc)* < Machtbereich

Einfühlung *f* • empathy, feeling into° *(Dilthey etc) (psy, aes)*

Einfühlungsästhetik *f* • empathy aesthetics, aesthetics of empathy *(Herder, Vischer, Lipps) (aes)*

Einfühlungstheorie *f* • empathy theory *(Vischer, Lipps) (aes), (epi, sci)*

Einfühlungsvermögen *n* • empathy *(psy, aes)* → Empathie

Einfuhrbeschränkung *f* • import restriction *(eco)*

Einführungsregel *f* • introduction rule *(log)* ↔ Eliminationsregel

Eingabe *f* → Input

Eingabe/Ausgabe *f,f* • input/output, I/O *(sys)*

Eingabeaufforderung *f* • prompt *(AI)*

eingebauter Verschleiß *m* • planned/inbuilt obsolescence *(eco)*

eingeborene Ideen *pl* • innate ideas *(Descartes etc) (epi)* → angeborene Ideen

Eingeborenheit *f* • innateness *(nat, met)*

Eingebung *f* • inspiration *(aes, rel); (sci)* < Entdeckungszusammenhang

Eingebung, göttliche *f* • divine inspiration *(rel)*

Einheit *f* • unity *(met)*, unity element *(mat)*, unit *(ont, mat)* ↔ Vielheit < Entität

Einheit als Einssein *f* • oneness *(met)*

Einheit der Anschauung *f* • unity of intuition *(Kant) (epi)*

Einheit der Apperzeption *f* • unity of apperception *(Kant) (epi)*

Einheit der denkenden Substanz *f* • unity of (the) thinking substance *(Kant) (epi)*

Einheit der Dinge *f* • unity of things *(ont)*

Einheit der Erfahrung *f* • unity of experience *(Kant) (epi)*

Einheit der Erscheinungen *f* • unity of appearances *(Kant) (epi)*

Einheit der Gegensätze *f* • unity/identity of opposites *(Hegel) (met)*

Einheit der Kategorien *f* • unity of the categories *(Kant) (epi)*

Einheit der Maxime *f* • unity of maxim *(Kant) (epi, eth)*

Einheit der Natur *f* • uniformity of nature *(met)*

Einheit der Realität *f* • unity of reality *(Kant)* *(epi, ont)*

Einheit der Vernunft *f* • unity of reason *(Kant)* *(epi, met)*

Einheit der Verstandeserkenntnis *f* • unity in the knowledge of the understanding *(Kant)* *(epi)*

Einheit der Vorstellungen *f* • unity of representations *(Kant)* *(epi)*

Einheit der Wissenschaft *f* • unity of science *(Neurath etc)* *(sci)* < Einheitswissenschaft

Einheit der Zeit *f* • unity of time *(Aristotle etc)* *(aes, ont)*

Einheit der Zwecke *f* • unity of ends *(Kant)* *(epi)*

Einheit des Bewußtseins *f* • unity of consciousness *(epi, min)*

Einheit des Denkens *f* • unity of thought/ thinking *(Kant)* *(epi)*

Einheit des Mannigfaltigen *f* • unity of the manifold *(met)*

Einheit des Menschengeschlechtes *f* • unity of mankind *(Herder)* *(ant)*

Einheit des Raums *f* • unity of space *(Aristotle etc)* *(aes, ont)*

Einheit des Selbstbewußtseins *f* • unity of self-consciousness *(Kant)* *(epi, psy)*

Einheit des Subjekts *f* • unity of the subject *(Kant)* *(epi, met)*

Einheit des Systems *f* • unity of the system *(Kant)* *(sci, epi)*

Einheit des Universums *f* • unity/oneness of the universe *(met)*

Einheit des Verstandes *f* • unity of the understanding *(Kant)* *(epi)*

Einheit des Weltganzen *f* • unity of the cosmical *(Kant)* *(met)*

Einheit des Willens *f* • unity of the will *(Kant)* *(eth, met)*

Einheit in der Mannigfaltigkeit *f* • unity in variety/multiplicity *(met)*

Einheit in der Vielheit *f* • unity in plurality/ diversity *(met)*

Einheit mit dem Universum *f* • oneness with the universe *(met)*

Einheit mit der Natur *f* • oneness with nature *(met, env)*

Einheit, nationale *f* • national unity *(pol)*

Einheit, ontologische *f* • (▷ Element) ontological unit, (▷ Gesamtheit) unity *(ont)*

Einheit und Differenz *f,f* • unity and difference *(met)* < Identität und Differenz

Einheit von Denken und Sein *f* • unity of thinking and being, thought and being as one *(Parmenides, Hegel)* *(met)*

Einheit von Geist und Körper *f* • unity/union of body and mind *(met)*

Einheit von Identität und Differenz *f* • unity of identity and difference *(met)*

Einheit von Leben und Denken *f* • unity of life and thought *(met)*

Einheit von Theorie und Praxis *f* • unity of theory and practice *(Marx etc)* *(soc)*

Einheit von Zeit und Ewigkeit *f* • union of time and eternity *(Jaspers)* *(met)*

Einheitengruppe *f* • group of units *(mat)*

einheitlich • homogeneous *(gen)* < monoton

einheitliche Feldtheorie *f* • unified field theory *(Einstein)* *(nat)*

Einheitlichkeit der Wahrnehmung *f* • unity of (perceptual) experience *(epi, psy)*

Einheitlichkeit der Natur *f* • uniformity of nature *(nat, met)*

Einheitlichkeit der Substanz *f* • homogeneity of substance, unitary character of substance, unicity° of substance *(Leibniz)* *(met)*

Einheitspartei *f* • unity party *(pol)*

Einheitsprinzip *n* • principle of unity *(met)*

Einheitssprache *f* • universal language *(lan, sci)*

Einheitsstaat *m* • centralized state *(pol)*

Einheitsstreben *n* • unitary tendency, striving for unity *(pol)*

Einheitsvektor *m* • unit vector *(mat)*

Einheitswissenschaft *f* • unified/unitary science° *(sci)* < Einheit der Wissenschaft

Einheitswissenschaft, Theorie der *f* • theory of unified science *(sci)* < Einheit der Wissenschaft, Universalwissenschaft

Einigungsprozeß *m* • unification process, process of reaching agreement *(act)*

Einklammerung *f* • bracketing *(epi, met)*

Einklammerung, phänomenologische *f* • phenomenological bracketing *(Husserl)* *(epi, met)* < Epoché

Einklammerungsmethode *f* • method of bracketing *(Husserl)* *(sci)* < Epoché

Einklang *m* • unison, concord *(aes)*

Einklang der Gegensätze *m* • harmony of opposites *(met)*

Einkommensgefälle *n* • income differential *(eco)*

Einkommensgleichheit *f* • equal pay, equality of income *(eco)*

Einkommensniveau *n* • level of income *(eco)*

Einkommenspolitik *f* • income(s) policy *(eco, pol)*

Einkommensumverteilung *f* • income redistribution, redistribution of income *(eco)* → Redistribution

Einkommensverhältnisse *pl* • (▷ Einkommens-höhe) level of income, (▷ Einkommensver-teilung) distribution of income, income levels *(eco)*

Einkommensverteilung *f* • income distribution *(eco)*

Einleitungsparadox *n* • paradox of the preface, preface paradox *(Makinson) (log)*

Einleitungsregel *f* • introduction rule *(log)*

Einmaligkeit *f* • singularity *(ont)*, uniqueness *(aes)*

einräumen • to emplace *(Heidegger) (ont)*

eins-zu-eins-Entsprechung *f* • one-to-one correspondence, one-one correspondence *(log)*

Einsamkeit *f* • loneliness, solitude *(psy)* < atomisierte Gesellschaft

Einschätzung *f* • assessment, estimation *(gen)* → Bewertung

einschließlich • inclusive *(gep)*

Einschränkung *f* • limitation *(gep)*

einseitige Willenserklärung *f* • unilateral statement of intent *(jur)*

Einsfühlung *f* • unipathy, feeling-as-one *(Scheler) (met)*

Einsicht *f* • (▷ Reue) remorse *(eth, psy)*, (▷ Verstehen) insight, understanding *(epi)* < Vernünftigkeit

einsichtiges Lernen *n* → Lernen durch Einsicht

einssein • being one, being at one *(met)*

Einssein, das *n* • oneness, being one *(met)*

Einssein aller Dinge *n* • oneness of all things *(met)* < Einheit der Dinge

Einssein mit dem Universum *n* • being one with the universe, oneness with the universe *(met)*

Einsteinsche Summationskonvention *f* • Einstein's motion convention *(mat)*

einstellige Relation *f* • one-place relation, unary relation *(log)*

einstellige Zahl *f* • one-place figure *(mat)*

einstelliges Prädikat *n* • one-digit predicate *(log, lan)*

Einstellung *f* • attitude, view, set *(psy)*

Einstellung, geistige *f* • mental attitude/view *(psy)*

Einstellung, politische *f* • political attitude/view *(pol)*

Einstellung, propositionale *f* • propositional attitude *(lan, epi, min)*

Einstellungspolitik, bevorzugte *f* • preferential hiring *(eco, eth)*

Einstellungsübernahme *f* • taking of the attitude of the other *(act)*

Einstellungswandel *m* • attitude change, change of attitude *(psy)*

Einstimmigkeit *f* • unanimity *(eth, pol)*

Einstimmigkeitsregel *f* • rule of consensus/unanimity *(pol)*

Einstimmung *f* • (▷ Zustimmung) agreement *(jur)*, (▷ Einfühlung) empathy *(psy)*

Einströmen, das *n* • influx *(Husserl) (met)*

Einteilung *f* • classification *(log, sci)* < Klassifikation

Einteilung der Natur *f* • division of nature *(nat, met)* < W 1058

Einteilungsgrund *m* • principle of classification *(log, lan)*

Eintritt eines Ereignisses *m* • occurrence of an event *(sci)* ↔ Nichteintritt eines Ereignisses

Eintrittsbarriere *f* • barrier to entry *(eco)* < Monopolismus

Eintrittswahrscheinlichkeit *f* • probability of occurrence *(dec, mat)*

Einverleibtheit *f* • incorporatedness *(Nietzsche) (met)*

Einverleibung *f* • incorporation *(jur, pol, nat)*

Einverständnishandeln *n* • consensually oriented action, behaviour based on mutual consent *(Weber) (soc, act)* < Anstaltshandeln, Gesellschaftshandeln

Einwand gegen das Dasein *m* • objection to existence *(Nietzsche) (met)*

Einwelttheorie *f* • one world theory *(Aristotle etc) (met)* ↔ Mehrweltentheorie

Einwortäußerung *f* • one-word utterance *(lan)*

Einzelaussage *f* • singular statement/sentence *(lan)*

Einzelbegriff *m* → Individualbegriff

Einzelding *n* • particular thing *(Quine) (ont)*, individual *(Strawson) (ont)*

Einzelfallstudie *f* • case study *(sci)*

Einzelforscher *m* • isolated/lone researcher *(sci)* < Teamarbeit, Autorenkollektiv

Einzelimplikation *f* • individual implication *(log)*

Einzelne, das *n* • the particular, the individual *(ont)*

Einzelne, der *m* • the individual *(soc)*

Einzelnem und Allgemeinem, Einheit von *f* • unity of the particular and the general, unity of the individual and the universal *(met)* < Besonderheit

Einzelnen im Allgemeinen, Prinzip des *n* • principle of the individual/particular in the general *(ont)*

einzelnes Urteil *n* • particular judg(e)ment *(epi, log)* → Individualurteil

Einzelseele *f* • individual soul *(met, psy)* < Weltseele

Einzelwesen *n* • individual *(met)*

Einzelwille *m* • particular will *(Rousseau) (pol, soc)* → Partikularwille

Einzelwissen *n* • particular knowledge *(epi)* ↔ Allgemeinwissen

Einzelwissenschaft *f* • particular science *(sci)*

Einzigallgemeine, das *n* • unique universal *(met)*

Einzigartigkeit *f* • uniqueness *(gep)* < Singularität

Einzigartigkeit des Kunstwerks *f* • uniqueness of the work of art *(aes)*

Einzigartigkeit künstlerischer Objekte *f* • uniqueness of art objects *(aes)*

eiserner Vorhang *m* • Iron Curtain *(pol)*

Eispende *f* • egg/ovum donation *(nat, eth)* < Reproduktionsmedizin

Ek-sistenz *f* • ek-sistenz *(Heidegger) (ont)*

Ekel *m* • nausea *(Sartre) (ant, met)* < Lebensekel

Eklektiker *m* • eclectic *(gep)*

eklektische Philosophie *f* • eclectic philosophy *(gep)*

Eklektizismus *m* • eclecticism *(aes, gep)*

Ekstase *f* • ecstasy *(Plotinus) (met)*, *(psy)*

Ekstasen der Zeitlichkeit *pl* • ecstasies of temporality *(Heidegger) (ont)*

ekstatische Religion *f* • ecstatic religion *(rel, eso)*

Ektypus *m* • ectype *(met)* → Abbild, Nachbildung

Elan vital *m* • life force, élan vital *(Bergson) (met)* → Lebensschwungkraft

Eleaten *pl* • Eleatics *(gep)*

Eleatische Schule *f* • Eleatic school *(gep)*

Eleatismus *m* • Eleaticism *(gep)*

Elektrakomplex *m* • Electra complex *(psy)* ↔ Ödipuskomplex

Elektrakonflikt *m* • Electra conflict *(psy)*

Elektronengehirn *n* • electronic brain *(AI)* < künstliche Intelligenz

elektronische Kunst *f* • electronic art *(aes)* < Computerkunst

Element *n* • element *(mat, log, ont)*

elementar • elementary, elemental, fundamental *(gen)*

Elementarästhetik *f* • elementary aesthetics *(Fechner) (aes)*

Elementaraussage *f* • elementary proposition *(sci, lan)* < Basissatz, Atomsatz, Protokollsatz

Elementarbegriff *m* • basic concept/idea *(lan, epi)*

Elementarerfahrung *f* → Elementarerlebnis

Elementarerlebnis *n* • elementary experience, elementarerlebnis° *(Carnap etc) (sci)*

elementares Theorieaxiomensystem *n* • elementary system of theoretical axioms *(sci)*

Elementarfarben *pl* • primary colours *(nat, aes)*

Elementargedanke *m* • elementary thought *(Bastian) (cul)*

Elementargeister *pl* • elemental spirits *(eso, met)*

Elementarlehre, transzendentale *f* • transcendental doctrine of elements *(Kant) (epi)* ↔ transzendentale Methodenlehre

Elementarpartikel *n* → Elementarteilchen

Elementarproposition *f* → Elementarsatz

Elementarsatz *m* • elementary proposition *(Wittgenstein) (lan, log)* < atomare Aussage

Elementarteilchen *n* • elementary particle *(nat)* → Partikel, Korpuskel

Elementarteilchenphysik *f* • elementary particle physics *(nat)*

Elemente, die vier *pl* • the Four Elements *(Empedocles etc) (met)*

Elenchus *m* • elenchus, refutation *(log, lan)*

Elenktik *f* • elenctics, art of refutation *(log, lan)*

elenktische Methode *f* • elenctic method *(Socrates) (epi)*

Eleutheriologie *f* → Freiheitslehre

Eleutheronomie *f* • eleutheronomia, eleutheronomy *(Kant) (eth)* → Selbstbestimmung < innere Gesetzgebung

Elfenbeinturm *m* • ivory tower *(gep)*

Elimination *f* • elimination *(sci)*

Eliminationsregel *f* • elimination rule *(log, sci)* ↔ Einführungsregel < Ramsey-Satz

eliminativer Materialismus *m* • eliminative materialism *(Churchland, Stich) (min, ont)*

Eliminativismus *m* • eliminativism *(Churchland, Stich) (min, ont)*

eliminierende Induktion *f* • eliminative induction *(Mill) (log, sci)* → ausschaltende Induktion

Elitarismus *m* • elitism *(soc)*

Elite *f* • elite *(soc)*

Elitedenken *n* • elitist attitude/thinking *(soc)* → Elitarismus

Elitentheorie *f* • theory of elites, elite theory *(Nietzsche, Ortega y Gasset etc) (cul, soc)*

Elitismus *m* → Elitarismus

Ellbogengesellschaft f • competitive society, dog-eat-dog society *(soc)*

Ellipse f • ellipsis *(lan)*

elliptischer Satz m • elliptical sentence *(lan)*

Emanation f • emanation *(met)*

Emanationismus m • emanationism *(Plotinus)* *(met)*

Emanationslehre f • doctrine of emanation *(Plotinus)* *(met)*

Emanzipation der Frau f • women's liberation *(fem, soc)* < Befreiung der Frauen

Emanzipation des Subjekts f • emancipation of the subject *(gep)*

Emanzipationsbewegung f • emancipation movement *(pol)* < Befreiungsbewegung

emanzipatorisches Denken n • emancipatory thinking *(gep)*

emanzipatorisches Interesse n • emancipatory interest *(Habermas)* *(soc)*

Embryo(nen)transfer m • embryo transfer *(nat, eth)* < künstliche Befruchtung, Leihmutterschaft, Reproduktionstechnologie

Embryonenexperiment n • foetal experiment *(nat, eth)*

Embryoversuche pl • embryo experimentation *(nat, eth)*

emergente Eigenschaft f • emergent property *(Morgan, Alexander)* *(met, nat)*

Emergenz f • emergence *(met, nat)*

Emergenzphilosophie f • philosophy of emergence, emergentism, emergence philosophy *(Morgan, Alexander)* *(met, nat)*

Emissionsgrenzwert m • emission threshold/limit *(env)*

Emissionstheorie des Lichts f • emission theory of light *(nat)*

Emotion f • emotion, feeling *(psy)*

emotionaler Ausdruck m • emotional expression *(lan, psy, aes)*

Emotionalismus m • emotionalism *(psy, epi)*

emotive Sprache f • emotive language *(lan)* ↔ denotative Sprache

Emotivismus m • emotivism *(Ayer, Stevenson)* *(eth, lan)* < Non-Kognitivismus

Empathie f • empathy *(psy, aes)* → Einfühlungsvermögen

Empedokles • Empedocles

Empfänger-Sender-Modell n • Shannon-Weaver model *(Shannon, Weaver)* *(lan)*

Empfänglichkeit, ästhetische f • aesthetic receptivity/sensitivity/sensibility/responsiveness/impressionabiliy *(aes)* < Rezeptivität

Empfängnisverhütung f • contraception *(eth)* → Antikonzeption

empfehlende Funktion eines Ausdrucks f • commendatory function of an expression *(Hare)* *(eth, lan)*

Empfehlung f • suggestion, recommendation *(gen)*

empfindendes Wesen n • sentient being *(nat, psy)*

Empfindens, reine Formen des pl • pure forms of sensibility *(Kant)* *(epi)*

Empfindnis f • state of awareness *(Husserl)* *(met)*

Empfindsamkeit f • sensibility, sensitiveness *(aes, psy)*

Empfindsamkeit, Zeitalter der n • the age of sentiment(alism) *(his)*

Empfindung f • sensation, perception, feeling *(epi, psy)* < sinnliche Wahrnehmung, Sinnesdaten < W 10, 56, 129

empfindungsfähige Wesen pl • sentient beings *(nat, psy)*

Empfindungsfähigkeit f • sentience, sensitivity, susceptibility *(nat, psy, aes)* → Empfindungsvermögen

Empfindungsinhalte pl • sense contents *(Carnap)* *(epi)*

Empfindungslosigkeit f • insensitivity *(nat, psy, aes)*

empfindungsorientiert • sensation-oriented *(Jung)* *(psy)* ↔ denkorientiert

Empfindungspsychologie f • sensualistic psychology *(psy)*

Empfindungsqualität f • sensation quality *(Carnap)* *(epi)*

Empfindungsvermögen n • perceptive faculty, sensitivity, sentience *(nat, psy, aes)* → Ästhesie, Empfindungsfähigkeit

Emphase f • emphasis *(psy, lan)*

Empirie f • (▷ Erfahrungswissen) empirical knowledge *(epi)* → Erfahrungswissen; (▷ Erfahrungswissenschaft) empirical science *(sci)* → Erfahrungswissenschaft

Empirik f • empirical experience *(sci)*

Empiriker m • empiricist *(gep)*

Empiriokritizismus m • empiriocriticism *(Avenarius, Mach)* *(epi)* < W 618

Empiriomonismus m • empiriomonism *(Bogdanov)* *(met)*

empirisch • empirical, empiric *(epi, sci)*

empirisch-analytisch • empirical-analytic *(sci)*

empirisch sinnvoll • empirically meaningful *(sci)*

empirisch unterbestimmte Theorie f • empirically under-determined theory *(Quine)* *(sci)*

empirische Adäquatheit f • empirical adequacy *(sci)*

empirische Affektion *f* • empirical affection *(Kant) (epi)*

empirische Affinität *f* • empirical affinity *(epi, psy, nat)*

empirische Allgemeinheit *f* • empirical universality *(Kant) (epi)*

empirische Analyse *f* • empirical analysis *(sci)*

empirische Apperzeption *f* • empirical apperception *(Kant) (epi)*

empirische Ästhetik *f* • empirical aesthetics *(aes)*

empirische Aussage *f* • empirical statement *(sci, lan)*

empirische Beobachtung *f* • empirical observation *(epi, sci)*

empirische Bestätigung *f* • empirical corroboration, evidential support *(sci)*

empirische Daten *pl* • empirical data *(epi, sci)*

empirische Deduktion *f* • empirical deduction *(Kant) (epi)* ↔ transzendentale Deduktion

empirische Einbildungskraft *f* • empirical imagination *(epi)*

empirische Einheit *f* • empirical unity *(Kant) (epi)*

empirische Erfahrung *f* • empirical experience *(epi, sci)* < empirisches Wissen

empirische Erkenntnis *f* • empirical knowledge/cognition *(epi)*

empirische Grundlage *f* • empirical basis *(epi, sci)*

empirische Gültigkeit *f* • empirical validity *(sci)*

empirische Notwendigkeit *f* • empirical necessity *(Kant) (epi, nat)*

empirische Realität *f* • empirical reality *(epi, met)*

empirische Regel *f* • empirical rule *(sci)*

empirische Signifikanz *f* • empirical significance *(sci)*

empirische Sozialforschung *f* • empirical social research/science *(soc, sci)*

empirische Sozialwissenschaft *f* • empirical sociology/social science *(soc, sci)*

empirische Synthesis *f* • empirical synthesis *(Kant) (epi)*

empirische Theologie *f* • empirical theology *(rel)* < dialektische Theologie

empirische Untersuchung *f* • empirical investigation *(sci)*

empirische Urteilskraft *f* • empirical judg(e)-ment *(Kant) (epi)*

empirische Verallgemeinerung *f* • empirical generalization *(sci)* < Induktion, Schluß vom Einzelnen auf das Allgemeine

empirische Wissenschaft *f* • empirical science *(sci)*

empirische Zufälligkeit *f* • empirical contingency *(met, sci)*

empirischer Begriff *m* • empirical concept *(Kant) (epi, lan)*

empirischer Besitz *m* • empirical possession *(Kant) (jur)*

empirischer Charakter *m* • empirical character *(Kant) (epi, met)* ↔ intelligibler Charakter

empirischer Gang der Ideen *m* • empirical progress of ideas *(Foucault) (epi, pol)*

empirischer Gebrauch der Vernunft *m* • empirical use/employment of reason *(Kant) (epi)*

empirischer Gehalt *m* • empirical content *(sci, lan)*

empirischer Gehalt einer Theorie *m* • empirical content of a theory *(sci)* < Informationsgehalt, Bewährungstheorie

empirischer Idealismus *m* • empirical idealism *(Berkeley) (epi, met)* → Idealismus, psychologischer

empirischer Realismus *m* • empirical realism *(Kant etc) (epi, met)*

empirischer Schein *m* • empirical illusion *(Kant) (epi, met)*

empirisches Bewußtsein *n* • empirical consciousness *(Kant) (epi, met)*

empirisches Gesetz *n* • empirical law *(epi, sci)*

empirisches Ich *n* • empirical I/ego/self *(Kant, Fichte) (epi, met)* → phänomenales Ich

empirisches Prinzip *n* • empirical principle *(Kant) (epi, eth)*

empirisches Wesen *n* • empirical essence *(Pfänder) (met)*

empirisches Wissen *n* • empirical knowledge *(epi, sci)* < unvollständiges Wissen

Empirismus *m* • empiricism, empirism, experientialism° *(epi, sci)*

Empirismus im engen Sinn *m* • narrow theory of empiricism, empiricism in the strict sense *(epi, sci)*

Empirismus, logischer *m* • logical empiricism *(Mach, Reichenbach etc) (log, sci)* < logischer Positivismus

Empirismusprinzip *n* • principle of empiricism *(epi)*

empiristischer Fehlschluß *m* → Sein-Sollen-Metabasis

empiristisches Bedeutungskriterium *n* → Sinnkriterium

empiristisches Sinnkriterium *n* • empiricist meaning criterion *(epi, lan)* → empiristisches Bedeutungskriterium

Empirizismus *m* • empiricism *(epi, sci)* < Empirismus

Encoder *m* • encoder *(AI, lan)*

Endabsicht *f* • ultimate/final object/goal/aim/ intention *(act, eth)* < Endzweck

Ende der Geschichte *n* • the end of history *(his)* < Eschatologie, Posthistoire, Vollendung der Geschichte

Ende der Ideologie *n* • the end of ideology *(pol)*

Ende der Kultur *n* • (▷ Ziel) the goal of civilization *(N. Hartmann) (soc, cul)*

Ende der Kunst *n* • the end of art *(Hegel)* *(aes)*

Ende der Metaphysik *n* • the end of metaphysics *(Topitsch) (met)* → Überwindung der Metaphysik < nachmetaphysisches Denken

Ende der Philosophie *n* • the end of philosophy *(gep)*

Ende der Welt *n* • end of the world *(rel)* → Weltende < Eschatologie, Chiliasmus

Endeffekt *m* • final effect/result *(act, nat)* < Endzweck

endgültige Wahrheit *f* • definite/final/ definitive truth *(epi, met)*

endgültiges Ergebnis *n* • definitive result *(sci)*

Endkampf *m* • final struggle, final phase of battle *(Spengler) (his, cul)*

Endlager, atomares *n* • nuclear waste dump/ depot *(env)*

Endlagerung *f* • permanent waste disposal *(env)*

endlich • finite *(mat, met)*

Endliche, das *n* • the finite *(met)*

endliche Erkenntnis *f* • finite cognition/knowledge *(Hegel) (epi, met)*

endliche Gruppe *f* • finite group *(mat)*

endliche Körpererweiterung *f* • finite field extension *(mat)*

endliche Menge *f* • finite set *(mat, log)*

endliche Natur des Menschen *f* • finite nature of man *(ant, met, rel)*

endlicher Automat *m* • finite automaton *(AI, min)*

endlicher Körper *m* • finite field *(mat)*

endliches Ich *n* • finite ego *(Fichte) (met)*

endliches Spiel *n* • finite game *(dec)*

Endlichkeit *f* • finiteness, finitude *(met)* < Zeitlichkeit

Endlichkeit der Existenz *f* • finiteness of existence *(met, rel)*

Endlichkeit, Problem der *n* • problem of finitude *(met)*

Endlichkeitssatz *m* • principle of finiteness/ finitude *(log)* < Prädikatenlogik

Endlosigkeit *f* • (▷ Unbegrenztheit) infiniteness, boundlessness *(met, nat)*

endogene Wachstumsprognosen *pl* • endogenous growth predictions *(sys, sci)* < eigendynamische Wachstumsprognosen, selbsterfüllende Prognose

Endphase des Kommunismus *f* • the final stage of communism *(pol)*

Endursache *f* • final cause *(Aristotle) (met)* → causa finalis

Endurteil *n* • final judg(e)ment *(jur)* < Höchsturteil

Endverbraucher *m* • consumer, end-user *(eco)*

Endzeit *f* • the end of time, the last days/times, eschaton° *(rel)* < Eschatologie

Endzeitstimmung *f* • apocalyptic mood *(cul, rel, psy)*

Endzustand *m* • final state *(gep)* ↔ Anfangszustand

Endzweck *m* • final/ultimate purpose/end *(met, act)* < Finalursache

Endzweck des Kosmos *m* • ultimate aim/goal/ purpose of the universe, cosmological ultimation° *(ant, nat, met)* < anthropisches Prinzip, Anthropismus

energeia *f* • *nt*, activity, actuality *(Aristotle)* *(met)* < Dynamis und Energeia

Energetik *f* • energetics *(Ostwald) (met)*

Energie-Massen-Gleichung *f* • mass-energy equation *(Einstein) (nat)*

Energie, Prinzip von der Erhaltung der *n* → Energieerhaltungssatz

Energie, saubere *f* • clean energy *(env)*

Energiebedarf *m* • power/energy needs/ requirement/demand *(env)*

Energieerhaltungssatz *m* • principle of the conservation of energy *(Newton) (nat)*

Energiefluß *m* • flow of energy, energy flow *(nat, met)*

energieintensiv • energy-intensive *(nat, env)*

Energieknappheit *f* • energy shortage, scarcity of energy *(env)*

Energiekrise *f* • energy crisis *(env)*

Energiepolitik *f* • energy policy *(env, pol)*

Energiesparmaßnahme *f* • energy saving measure *(env)*

Energieverbrauch *m* • energy consumption *(env)*

Energieverschwendung *f* • waste of energy, energy waste *(env)*

Engagement *n* • engagement *(Sartre, Camus)*, commitment *(pol, eth)*

engagierte Kunst *f* • committed art *(aes)*

Engel der Geschichte *m* • the angel of history *(Benjamin) (his)*

Engellehre *f* • doctrine of angels, angelology *(rel)*

enger Gehalt *m* • narrow content *(lan, log)*

Engpaß *m* • bottleneck *(sys)*

Enkulturation *f* • enculturation *(soc, cul)* → Kulturaneignung < Akkulturation, Sozialisation

ens *n* • being *(ont)* < Sein; Seiende, das

ens entium *n* • being of being, essence of essence *(ont)*

ens per se *n* • *nt*, being per se, entity/thing in its own right *(ont)*

ens rationis *n* • *nt*, being of reason, thought-thing *(met)* → Gedankending

ens reale *n* • real being/essence *(ont)*

ens realissimum *n* • most real being/essence, perfect being *(ont)*

Ent-deckung *f* • dis-covery *(Heidegger) (ont)* < Destruktion

Ent-fernung *f* • de-severance, dis-stance *(Heidegger) (ont)*

ent-gegen-wärtigen • to depresentify *(Foucault) (epi)*

entartete Kunst *f* • degenerate art *(aes, pol)* < Unkunst

Entartung *f* • degeneration, degeneracy, decadence *(nat, pol)*

entäußertes Leben *n* • externalized/alienated life *(Marx) (soc)*

Entäußerung *f* • externalization, alienation, estrangement *(Hegel) (met), (Marx) (soc)* < Entfremdung

Entäußerung des menschlichen Wesens *f* • alienation of humanity *(ant, soc)*

entbergen • to dis-cover, to reveal *(Heidegger) (ont)*

Entdeckung, wissenschaftliche *f* • scientific discovery *(sci)*

Entdeckungskontext *m* → Entdeckungszusammenhang

Entdeckungslernen *n* • learning by discovery *(epi, psy)*

Entdeckungssystem *n* • discovery system *(epi, min)*

Entdeckungszusammenhang *m* • context of discovery *(Reichenbach) (sci)* ↔ Begründungszusammenhang

Entdifferenzierung *f* • de-differentiation *(lan, soc)*

Enteignung *f* • dispossession *(eco, jur)* → Expropriation

Entelechie *f* • entelechy *(Aristotle etc) (met)* → Eigengesetzlichkeit

entfernteste Ursache *f* • ultimate/most distant cause *(rel)*

Entfleischung *f* • decarnalization *(Nietzsche) (met)* < Entsinnlichung

entfremdete Arbeit *f* • alienated labour *(Marx etc) (soc)*

entfremdete Gesellschaft *f* • alienated society *(Rousseau, Marx etc) (soc)*

entfremdeter Weltgeist *m* • alienated world spirit *(Hegel) (met)*

entfremdetes Dasein *n* • alienated life *(Marx) (soc)*

entfremdetes Wesen *n* • estranged being *(Marx) (soc)*

Entfremdung *f* • alienation, estrangement *(Hegel) (met)*, Marx etc *(soc)* < Entäußerung

Entfremdung des Menschen vom Menschen *f* • alienation of man from man *(Feuerbach, Marx) (soc)*

Entfremdungseffekt *m* • estrangement effect *(aes)* < Verfremdung

Entfremdungstheorie *f* • theory of alienation, alienation theory *(soc)*

Entgegensetzung *f* • opposition *(gep)*

entgegenwärtigen • to deprive of its character as present, to depresentify° *(Heidegger) (ont), (Foucault) (epi)*

enthalten sein • to be contained/included in *(gen)*, to be a subset of *(mat, log)* < Teilmenge

Enthaltsamkeit *f* • abstinence, continence *(psy, rel)* < Askese

Enthaltung vom Urteil *f* → Urteilsenthaltung

Enthauptungsschlag, atomarer *m* • atomic decapitation *(pol)*

Enthistorisierung *f* • dehistoricisation *(his)*

Enthusiasmus *m* • enthusiasm *(psy)*

Enthusiasmus-Theorie *f* • theory of enthusiasm *(Plato) (aes, rel)*

Enthymem *n* • enthymeme *(Aristotle etc) (log)* → Schluß, unvollständiger

Entideologisierung *f* → Deideologisierung

Entität *f* • entity *(met, ont)* < Einzelding

Entitätenrealismus *m* • entity realism *(Hacking, Cartwright) (epi, met)*

Entkoppelung von System und Lebenswelt *f* • uncoupling of system and lifeworld *(Habermas) (soc)*

Entlarvungspsychologie *f* • unmasking psychology *(psy)*

Entlastung *f* • relief *(Gehlen etc) (ant, soc)*
< Institutionentheorie

Entlastungsfunktion der Kunst *f* • relief/un-
burdening/cathartic function of art *(aes)*
< Katharsis

Entleerungsdefinition *f* • definition of defla-
tion/evacuation *(log, lan)*

Entmannung *f* • emasculation, castration *(cul,
psy)* < Kastrationsangst

Entmaterialisierung *f* • dematerialization *(rel,
eso)*

Entmenschlichung *f* • dehumanization *(eth)* →
Dehumanisation

Entmilitarisierung *f* • demilitarization *(pol)*

Entmündigung *f* • interdiction, legal incapaci-
tation, deprivation of the right of decision
(jur)

Entmythologisierung *f* • demythologization
(rel, soc)

Entnazifizierung *f* • denazification *(pol)*

Enträtsler der Welt *m* • unriddler of the
world *(Nietzsche) (met)*

Entropie *f* • entropy *(nat, sys)* ↔ Negentropie,
negative Entropie < Hitzetod des Univer-
sums, Negentropie, Wärmetod des Weltalls

Entsagung *f* • renunciation *(psy, eth, rel)*
< Weltentsagung, Askese

Entscheidbarkeit *f* • decidability *(act, log)*,
determinability *(log, sci)*

Entscheiden *n* • decision making *(dec)*

entscheidender Augenblick *m* • decisive
moment *(met, rel)* → kairós

entscheidender Grund *m* • conclusive/decisive
reason/factor *(act, epi)*

entscheidendes Experiment *n* • crucial
experiment *(sci)* → experimentum crucis

entscheidendes Merkmal *n* • defining characteristic, distinguishing property *(log, lan)* →
differentia specifica

Entscheidung *f* • decision *(dec)* < Entweder-
Oder, Wahlsituation

Entscheidung unter Risiko *f* • decision/choice
under risk *(dec)*

Entscheidung unter Sicherheit *f* • decision/
choice under certainty *(dec)*

Entscheidung unter Unsicherheit *f* • decision/
choice under uncertainty *(dec)*

Entscheidung, zeitbedingte *f* • temporal
decision *(Jaspers etc) (met)*

Entscheidungsbaum *m* • decision tree *(dec)*

Entscheidungsdruck *m* • decision pressure,
pressure to decide *(dec)*

Entscheidungsfindung *f* • decision-making
(dec, act)

Entscheidungsfreiheit *f* • freedom of choice
(eth, dec)

Entscheidungsgrund *m* • decision motive,
reason for decision *(dec)*

Entscheidungshilfe *f* • aid to decision making
(dec, act)

Entscheidungsknoten *m* • decision/choice node
(dec) < Zufallsknoten

Entscheidungskriterium *n* • decision criterion
(dec, act)

Entscheidungslogik *f* • logic of decision *(dec,
log)* < Praxeologie

Entscheidungsmatrix *f* • decision matrix/table
(dec)

Entscheidungsmechanismus *m* • decision
mechanism *(dec)*

Entscheidungsparameter *m* • decision
parameter *(dec)*

Entscheidungsproblem *n* • decision problem
(dec)

Entscheidungsprozeß *m* • decision process
(dec)

Entscheidungsregel *f* • decision rule *(dec)*

Entscheidungssituation *f* • choice/decision
situation *(dec)* < Entscheidungsproblem,
Wahlsituation

Entscheidungsspielraum *m* • room for
decision, decision space, scope of choice
(dec)

Entscheidungstheorie *f* • decision theory *(dec)*
< Theorie der Wahlakte, Wahlstrategie

Entscheidungsträger *m* • decision maker *(pol)*

Entscheidungsverfahren *n* • decision
procedure *(dec)*

Entschlossenheit *f* • resolut open(ed)ness,
resoluteness *(Heidegger, Kierkegaard) (rel,
ont)*

Entschluß *m* • decision *(act, dec)*, resolution
(pol)

Entschlüsseln *n* • decoding, deciphering *(lan,
met)*

Entschlüsseln der Chiffrenschrift *n* •
decoding the ciphers *(Jaspers) (rel, met)*

Entsinnlichung *f* • desensualization *(Nietzsche)
(met)* < Entfleischung

Entsorgung *f* • (waste) disposal *(env)*

Entspannungspolitik *f* • détente policy, policy
of détente, policy of easing tension *(pol)* →
Détentepolitik

entsprachlichte Steuerungsmedien *pl* • de-
linguistified steering media *(Habermas)*
(soc)

Entstaatlichung *f* • denationalization *(pol)*

Entstädterung *f* • de-urbanization, disurbanization *(soc)* → Desurbanisation

Entstehung der Arten *f* • origin of species *(nat, ant)* → Ursprung der Arten < W 253

Entstehungsgeschichte *f* • genesis *(his, rel, gep)*

Entstehungsursache *f* • original cause *(Aristotle) (met)*

Entstellung *f* • distortion *(psy)*

Entsublimierung *f* • desublimation *(Freud) (psy)*

Enttabuisierung *f* • removal of taboos *(eth, ant, psy)*

Entweder-Oder • either-or *(Kierkegaard) (met, rel)* < Entscheidung, Wahlsituation, < W 256

Entweltlichung *f* • deworlding, deprivation of worldhood *(Nietzsche) (met), (Heidegger) (ont)*

Entwicklung der menschlichen Anlagen, volle *f* • full development of human potentiality *(Marx) (ant)*

Entwicklung der Natur, dialektische *f* • dialectic development of nature *(Engels) (nat, met)*

Entwicklung des Aussagefeldes *f* • development of the enunciative field *(Foucault) (epi, pol)*

Entwicklung des Geistes *f* • development/formation of spirit/mind *(Hegel) (met)*

Entwicklung, innere *f* • inner/internal development *(psy)*

Entwicklungsanalyse *f* • development(al) analysis *(gep)*

Entwicklungsfortschritt *m* • evolutionary progress *(his)*

Entwicklungsgeschichte *f* • evolution *(gep)*

Entwicklungsgesetze der Natur *pl* • laws of natural development, laws of evolution *(Darwin etc) (nat)*

Entwicklungsgesetze, geschichtliche *pl* • laws of historical development *(Vico etc) (his)*

Entwicklungshemmung *f* • retardation/inhibition of development *(psy, eco, soc)* → Retardation

Entwicklungshilfe *f* • development aid, aid to developing countries *(pol, eco)*

Entwicklungsländer *pl* • developing countries *(pol, soc)* → Dritte Welt

Entwicklungslinguistik *f* • developmental linguistics *(lan)*

Entwicklungsniveau *n* • level of development *(psy, ant, his)*

Entwicklungsphase *f* • stage of development, developmental stage *(psy, ant, his)*

Entwicklungsphilosophie *f* • philosophy of development *(eco, pol)*

Entwicklungsprozeß *m* • developmental process *(gep)*

Entwicklungspsychologie *f* • developmental psychology, psychology of development *(psy)*

Entwicklungsroman *m* • developmental novel, novel of character development, entwicklungsroman *(aes)* → Bildungsroman

Entwicklungsstadium *n* • (▷ Phylogenese) evolutionary stage *(nat, ant)*, (▷ Ontogenese) developmental phase/stage *(psy, ant)*

Entwicklungsstörung *f* • developmental disturbance/disorder *(psy)*

Entwicklungsstufe *f* • stage of development, developmental stage *(gep)* → Entwicklungsstadium

Entwicklungstheorie *f* • development(al) theory *(ant, psy, his)*

Entwurf *m* • draft, projection, self-design° *(Heidegger) (ont)*

Entwurzelung *f* • uprootedness *(soc)*

Entzauberung *f* • disenchantment *(Weber) (soc)* ↔ Wiederverzauberung der Welt

entzweites Bewußtsein *n* • bifurcated/divided consciousness *(Hegel) (met)*

Entzweiung *f* • bifurcation *(Hegel) (met)*, split *(gen)*

Environment *n* • environment *(aes)*

Environmentalismus *m* • environmentalism *(ant, soc, env)* < Klimatheorie

Environtologie *f* → Umweltforschung

Enzyklika *f* • encyclical *(rel)*

enzyklopädisches Wissen *n* • encyclop(a)edic knowledge *(gep)* < Universalwissen

Enzyklopädisten *pl* • Encyclopaedists, encyclopédistes *(gep)*

Epagogé *f* • epagoge *(log)* → Induktion

epagogischer Beweis *m* • epagogic/inductive proof *(log)*

Epigenesis der reinen Vernunft *f* • epigenesis of pure reason *(Kant) (sci)*

epigenetische Regeln *pl* • epigenetic rules *(Wilson) (nat, ant)*

Epigonentum *n* • epigonism *(aes)*

Epiktet • Epictetus

Epikur • Epicurus

Epikuräer *m* • Epicurean *(gep)*

epikureisch • Epicurean *(gep)*

Epikureismus *m* • (▷ Lehre) Epicurianism, (▷ hedonistische Einstellung) epicureism *(gep)*

Epimenides-Paradoxon *n* → Lügner-Paradoxon

Epiphanie *f* • epiphany *(rel)*

Epiphänomen *n* • epiphenomen *(gep)* < Begleiterscheinung

Epiphänomenalismus *m* • epiphenomenalism *(min)*

Epiphilosophie *f* • epiphilosophy *(gep)* < Metaphilosophie

Epiphyse *f* • epiphysis *(nat)* → Zirbeldrüse

epische Dichtung *f* • epic poetry *(aes)*

episches Theater *n* • epic theatre *(Piscator, Brecht) (aes)*

Episteme *f* • (scientific) knowledge *(epi)*

epistemisch • epistemic *(epi)* < epistemologisch

epistemische Erkenntnismodalität *f* • epistemic modality of cognition *(sci)*

epistemische Logik *f* • epistemic logic *(log)*

epistemische Mittel *pl* • epistemic resources *(epi)*

epistemische Modalität *f* • epistemic modality *(met, log, epi)* < aleth(e)ische Modalität

epistemische Rechtfertigung *f* • epistemic justification *(epi)*

epistemische Zirkularität *f* • epistemic circularity *(epi)*

epistemischer Zufall *m* • epistemic coincidence/luck *(epi)*

epistemisches Sehen *n* • epistemic seeing *(Dretske) (epi)*

epistemisches Subjekt *n* • epistemic subject *(epi)* → Erkenntnissubjekt

Epistemologie *f* • epistemology *(epi)* → Erkenntnistheorie

epistemologisch • epistemological *(epi)* → erkenntnistheoretisch

epistemologische Geschichte *f* • epistemological history *(Foucault) (epi, his)*

epistemologischer Anarchismus *m* • epistemological anarchism *(Feyerabend) (sci)* < Theorie der Forschungsprogramme

epistemologischer Bruch *m* • epistemological rupture/break *(Althusser, Bachelard) (epi)*

Episyllogismus *m* • episyllogism *(log)* < Prosyllogismus

Epizyklus *m* • epicycle *(nat, sys)*

Epoché *f* • abstention from judg(e)ment, withholding judg(e)ment, absentation of judg(e)ment, epoché *(Pyrrhon, Husserl) (epi)* → Urteilsenthaltung; *(Husserl) (epi)* → phänomenologische Einklammerung

Epoché, phänomenologische *f* • phenomenological epoché/suspension *(Husserl) (epi, met)* < Einklammerungsmethode

Epochenschwelle *f* • threshold of a new age/epoch *(his)* < Achsenzeit, Krisenzeit der Weltgeschichte

Epochenstil *m* • style of an epoch *(aes)*

epsilon-Umgebung *f* • epsilon-neighbourhood *(mat)*

er-leben • to live through, to experience *(Heidegger) (ont)*

Erbanlage-Umwelt-Debatte *f* • nature-nurture debate *(ant, psy)*

Erbauung, moralische *f* • moral edification *(eth, rel)*

Erbauungsbücher *pl* • devotional books *(rel)*

Erbfaktoren *pl* • hereditary factors *(nat)*

Erbfehler *m* • genetic/hereditary defect *(nat)*

Erbfolge *f* • hereditary succession *(jur)*

Erbgutveränderung *f* • genetic changes/mutation *(nat, eth)*

Erblehre *f* • theory of heredity *(Mendel etc) (nat)* < Genforschung

Erblichkeit *f* • heritability *(log, nat, soc)*

Erbrecht *n* • (▷ Anrecht) right of inheritance, (▷ Gesetz) law of inheritance/succession *(jur)*

Erbschaft, geistige *f* • intellectual inheritance *(gep)*

Erbschaftsanspruch *m* • claim to inheritance *(jur)*

Erbsünde *f* • original sin *(rel)* < Sündenfall

Erdenglück *n* • earthly happiness *(eth)*

Erdumdrehung *f* • rotation of the earth *(nat)*

Erdverbundenheit *f* • earthiness *(met)*

Ereignis *n* • event, occurrence, happening *(gep)*, event, outcome *(mat, sys)*, E-vent, event, ereignis, (ap)propriation, *(Heidegger) (ont)*

Ereignisalgebra *f* • algebra of events *(mat)*

Ereigniserklärung *f* • explanation of an event, event explanation *(sci)*

Ereignisfolge *f* • sequence of events *(sci, mat, sys)*

Ereigniskausalität *f* • event causality *(Chisholm) (act, met)*

Ereignislogik *f* • logic of events *(log)*

Ereignisraum *m* • event space *(mat)*

Ereignissatz *m* • event sentence *(lan)*

Ereignistheorie *f* • theory of events *(ont)*

Ereigniswahrscheinlichkeit *f* • event probability *(sci, mat, dec)*

Erfahren, das *n* • experiencing *(epi, psy)*

Erfahrung *f* • experience *(epi, psy)*

Erfahrung, abweichende *f* • deviant experience *(psy)*

Erfahrung, Analogien der *pl* • analogies of experience *(Kant) (epi)*

Erfahrung, ästhetische *f* • aesthetic(al) experience *(aes)*

Erfahrung, äußere *f* • outer experience, external experience *(epi)*

Erfahrung aus erster Hand *f* • first hand experience *(gen)*

Erfahrung aus zweiter Hand *f* • second hand/vicarious experience *(gen)*

Erfahrung des Bewußtseins *f* • experience of consciousness *(min)*

Erfahrung, Begriff der *m* • concept of experience *(Kant, Dewey) (epi)*

Erfahrung, durch • from experience *(epi)*

Erfahrung, erworben durch • acquired from experience *(epi)*

Erfahrung, innere *f* • inner experience, internal experience *(epi)*

Erfahrung, Theorie der *f* • theory of experience *(Kant) (epi)*

Erfahrung, übersinnliche *f* • extrasensory/ supersensory perception *(met, rel, eso)*

Erfahrungsbegriff *m* • empirical concept *(Kant) (epi, lan)*

Erfahrungsbegriffe, elementare *pl* • elementary empirical concepts *(epi, sci)* < Elementarsatz

Erfahrungsdaten *pl* • experiential data *(epi, sci)* < Experiment

Erfahrungserkenntnis *f* • experiential knowledge, knowledge derived from experience *(Kant) (epi)*

Erfahrungsgebrauch *m* • use in experience *(Kant) (epi)*

Erfahrungsgesetz *n* • empirical/experiential law *(sci)*

Erfahrungsproposition *f* • experiential proposition *(lan, sci)* < Wahrnehmungssatz

Erfahrungsquelle, übersinnliche *f* • extrasensory/supersensory source of experience *(rel, eso)*

Erfahrungsregel *f* • rule of experience *(epi, act)*

Erfahrungsreligion *f* • experiential religion *(rel)*

Erfahrungssatz *m* • empirical statement *(lan, sci)* < Beobachtungssatz, Wahrnehmungssatz

Erfahrungstatsache *f* • fact of experience *(epi, sci)*

erfahrungsunabhängige Realität *f* • reality independent of experience *(epi, met)*

Erfahrungsunabhängigkeit *f* • independence of experience *(epi, met)*

Erfahrungswelt *f* • world of experience *(Husserl) (epi)* < Lebenswelt

Erfahrungswert *m* • empirically established value/figure, experience value/figure, pragmatical value *(epi)* < Erfahrungstatsache

Erfahrungswissen *n* • knowledge by experience, empirical knowledge *(epi, sci)* → Empirie, a posteriori-Wissen

Erfahrungswissenschaft *f* • empirical science *(sci)*

Erfaßbarkeit des Seins *f* • apprehensibility of Being *(Heidegger) (ont)*

Erfindungsgabe *f* • inventive faculty, inventiveness, ingenuity, ingenium° *(tec, aes)* → Ingenium

Erfolgsbedingung *f* • condition of success *(act)*

Erfolgsethik *f* • ethics of success, success ethics *(eth)* ethic of consequences, results

erfolgsorientiert • success/achievement -oriented *(psy, soc)*

erfolgsorientierte Einstellung *f* • success-oriented attitude *(Habermas) (act, soc)*

erfolgsorientierte Handlung *f* • success-oriented action, action oriented to success *(Habermas) (act, soc)*

Erfolgsorientierung *f* • success/achievement orientation *(psy, soc)*

Erfolgszeitwort *n* • got-it word *(Ryle) (lan)*

Erfüllbarkeit *f* • satisfiability *(log)*

erfülltes Dasein *n* • full life, meaningful life *(met)*

Erfüllungsbedingung *f* • condition of satisfaction *(lan, act)*

Erfüllungserlebnis *n* • experience of fulfilment *(met, psy)*

Ergänzung *f* • complement *(gen)* < Komplementarität

Ergänzungsfaktor *m* • complementary factor *(gep)*

Erhabene, das *n* • the sublime *(Burke, Kant, Schiller etc) (aes)* < W 138, 788, 1024, 1025

Erhabenheit, dynamische *f* • dynamic sublimity *(Kant) (aes)*

Erhabenheit Gottes *f* • sublimity of God *(rel)*

Erhabenheit, mathematische *f* • mathematical sublimity *(Kant) (aes)*

Erhaltung der Bewegung *f* • conservation of motion/movement/momentum *(nat)*

Erhaltung der Bewegung, Prinzip von der *n* • principle of the conservation/persistence of motion/movement/momentum *(nat)* < Bewegungsgesetze, Trägheit

Erhaltungsgesetz *n* • law of conservation *(Newton) (nat)*

Erhaltungssatz der Energie *m* • law of conservation of energy *(nat)*

Erhaltungssatz der Masse *m* • law of conservation of mass *(nat)*

Erhaltungssatz der Materie *m* • law of conservation of matter *(nat)*

Erhebung *f* • elevation *(met, rel)*, revolt *(pol)*

Erhellung *f* • illumination *(Jaspers) (met)*

Erinnerung *f* • remembrance, recollection *(Ryle) (min)*, memory *(psy)*

Erinnerungsbild *n* • memory image/picture *(psy, aes)*

Erinnerung(sfähigkeit) *f* • memory *(psy)*

Erinnerungsrest *m* → Erinnerungsspur

Erinnerungsspur *f* • mnemic/memory trace *(Freud) (psy)*

Erinnerungsverlust *m* • loss of recall *(psy)* < Gedächtnisverlust

Eristik *f* • eristic *(log, lan)*

Eristiker *m* • eristic *(log, lan)*

eristische Dialektik *f* • eristic(al) dialectic *(log, epi)*

Eriugena, Johannes Scotus • (John Scotus) Eri(u)gena, John the Scot

erkannt • known *(epi)* < bekannt

Erkennbarkeit der Welt *f* • cognizability/ knowability/knowableness of the world *(epi, met)*

Erkennbarkeit des Absoluten *f* • knowability/ knowableness of the Absolute *(Hegel) (epi, met)*

Erkennbarkeit Gottes *f* • knowability/cognizability of God *(rel)*

erkenne dich selbst • know thyself *(epi, eth)*

Erkennen, das *n* • knowing, cognizing *(epi)* < Wahrnehmung, Wissen

Erkennender *m* • man of knowledge *(Nietzsche) (met)*

Erkenntnis *f* • cognition, knowledge *(epi)* → Kognition

Erkenntnis aus Prinzipien *f* • knowledge from principles *(Kant) (epi)*

Erkenntnis durch connaturalitas *f* • knowledge by co-naturality/connateness *(Aquinas) (epi)*

Erkenntnis, abstrakte *f* • abstract(ive) knowledge *(Duns Scotus etc) (epi)* ↔ Erkenntnis, intuitive

Erkenntnis, Anfangsgrund der *m* • starting-point of knowledge, antecedent ground of knowledge *(Kant) (epi)*

Erkenntnis, diskursive *f* • discursive cognition/ knowledge *(epi)*

Erkenntnis, empirische *f* • empirical knowledge/cognition *(epi)*

Erkenntnis, evidente *f* • (self-)evident knowledge *(epi)*

Erkenntnis, intuitive *f* • intuitive knowledge *(Duns Scotus etc) (epi)* ↔ Erkenntnis, abstrakte

Erkenntnis, Mittel der *n* • means of cognition *(epi)*

Erkenntnis, objektive *f* • objective knowledge *(epi)* < W 718

Erkenntnis , prima facie *f* • prima facie knowledge *(epi)*

Erkenntnis, rationale *f* • rational knowledge *(epi)* → Vernunfterkenntnis

Erkenntnis, spekulative *f* • speculative knowledge *(Kant etc) (epi, met)*

Erkenntnis, wahre *f* • true knowledge *(epi)*

Erkenntnisakt *m* • act of cognition, cognitive act *(epi)*

Erkenntnisbasis *f* • foundations/basis of knowledge *(epi)*, knowledge base *(AI)*

Erkenntnisbegründung *f* • justification of knowledge *(epi)* < Wissensbegründung

Erkenntnisbereich *m* • domain/field of knowledge *(epi)*

Erkenntnisdrang *m* • thirst for knowledge, drive to know *(epi)* < Wissensdurst; Eros, philosophischer

Erkenntnisekel *m* • aversion to knowledge *(epi)*

Erkenntniserwerb *m* • acquisition of knowledge *(epi)*

Erkenntnisfähigkeit *f* • cognitive faculty, faculty of cognition *(epi)*

Erkenntnisfortschritt *m* • advance/progress in knowledge *(epi, sci)* < W 542

Erkenntnisgewinn *m* • gain in knowledge *(epi)*

Erkenntnisgrenzen *pl* → Grenzen der Erkenntnis

Erkenntnisgrund *m* • ground of knowledge *(epi)*

Erkenntnisideal, mathematisches *n* • ideal of mathematical cognition *(sci)* < more geometrico

Erkenntnisinteresse *n* • cognitive interest, knowledge interest *(Habermas) (epi, sci)*

Erkenntniskapital *n* • stock of knowledge *(epi)*

Erkenntniskategorie *f* • knowledge category, category of knowledge, epistemological category *(N. Hartmann) (epi)*

Erkenntniskraft *f* • power of cognition/ knowledge *(Kant) (epi)*

Erkenntniskritik *f* • critique of knowledge *(epi)*

Erkenntniskritik, Kantische *f* • Kantian critique of knowledge *(Kant) (epi)*

Erkenntnislogik *f* • epistemic logic, logic of knowledge *(log)*

erkenntnislose Natur *f* • nature without knowledge/cognition *(Leibniz) (met)* erkenntnismäßige Ordnung f • epistemic order (Carnap) (epi, ont)

Erkenntnismetaphysik f • metaphysics of knowledge (N. Hartmann) (epi, met) → Metaphysik der Erkenntnis < W 437

Erkenntnisobjekt n • object of cognition/ knowledge (epi) → Gegenstand der Erkenntnis

erkenntnisorientiert • cognition oriented (Searle etc) (lan, act)

Erkenntnisproblem n • problem of knowledge (epi) < W 274

Erkenntnisprozeß m • cognitive process (epi, sci) < Lernprozeß

Erkenntnispsychologie f • cognitive psychology (psy) → Kognitionspsychologie

Erkenntnisquelle f • source of knowledge/ cognition (epi)

Erkenntnisregel f • rule of/for cognition (epi)

Erkenntnisskepsis f • epistemological scepticism (epi)

Erkenntnissubjekt n • subject of cognition (epi)

Erkenntnissuche f • search for knowledge (epi)

erkenntnistheoretisch • epistemological (epi) → epistemologisch

erkenntnistheoretische Begründung f • epistemological grounding/justification (Husserl) (epi)

erkenntnistheoretische Position f • epistemological position (epi)

erkenntnistheoretischer Anarchismus m • epistemological anarchism (Feyerabend) (epi, sci) ↔ Ratiofaschismus < anarchistische Erkenntnistheorie

erkenntnistheoretischer Konstruktivismus m • (epistemological) constructivism (epi, sci)

erkenntnistheoretischer Realismus m • epistemological realism (epi)

Erkenntnistheorie f • epistemology, theory of knowledge (epi) → Epistemologie

Erkenntnistheorie der Moral f • epistemology of morals (epi, eth)

Erkenntnistheorie, evolutionäre f • evolutionary epistemology (Campbell etc) (epi, sci)

Erkenntnistheorie, genetische f • genetic epistemology (epi)

Erkenntnistheorie, induktivistische f • inductivist theory of cognition, inductivist epistemology (epi)

Erkenntnistheorie, naturalistische f • naturalistic epistemology (Quine, Goldman) (epi)

Erkenntnistrieb m • knowledge drive, drive for knowledge (epi)

Erkenntnisursache f → Erkenntnisgrund

Erkenntnisurteil n • cognitive judg(e)ment (Kant etc) (epi)

Erkenntnisvermögen n • cognitive faculty, faculty of cognition/knowledge (epi)

Erkenntniswert m • cognitive value/ significance (epi)

Erkenntniswissenschaft f • science of knowledge, cognitive science (epi) → Kognitionswissenschaft

Erklären-Verstehen-Kontroverse f • explanation versus understanding controversy (sci) < W 276

erklärende Hermeneutik f • explanatory hermeneutics (Heidegger) (ont)

Erklärung f • explanation (sci), declaration (pol)

Erklärung, deduktiv-nomologische f • covering-law explanation, deductive-nomological explanation (Hempel, Oppenheim) (sci) < Hempel-Oppenheim-Schema

Erklärung, deduktiv-statistische f • deductive-statistical explanation (Hempel) (sci)

Erklärung der Absicht f • purposive explanation (act) < Absichtserklärung

Erklärung der Menschenrechte f • declaration of human rights, declaration of the rights of man (pol)

Erklärung, deterministische f • deterministic explanation (sci)

Erklärung, dispositionale f • dispositional explanation (sci)

Erklärung, funktionale f • functional explanation (sci)

Erklärung, historisch-genetische f • historical-genetic explanation (Dray etc) (sci)

Erklärung, induktiv-statistische f • inductive-statistical explanation (Hempel) (sci)

Erklärung, intentionale f • intentional explanation (min, act)

Erklärung, kausale f • causal explanation (sci)

Erklärung, metaphysische f • metaphysical explanation (Schopenhauer etc) (met)

Erklärung, mögliche f • possible explanation (sci) → Erklärung, potentielle

Erklärung, narrative f • narrative explanation (Danto) (sci)

Erklärung, nichtkausale f • non-causal explanation (sci)

Erklärung, potentielle f • potential explanation (sci) → Erklärung, mögliche

Erklärung, pragmatische f • pragmatic explanation (sci)

Erklärung, statistische f • statistical/ probabilistic explanation (sci)

Erklärung, stochastische *f* • stochastic explanation *(sci)*

Erklärung, subjektive *f* • subjective explanation *(sci)*

Erklärungsadäquatheit *f* • explanatory adequacy *(sci)*

Erklärungskraft *f* • explanatory power *(sci)*

Erklärungskraft von Theorien *f* • explanatory power of theories *(sci)*

Erklärungsmodell *n* • explanatory model, model of explanation *(sci)*

Erklärungsschema *n* → Erklärungsmodell

Erklärungsskizze *f* • explanation sketch *(sci)*

Erklärungstheorie *f* • theory of explanation, explanation theory *(sci)*

Erklärungsvermögen *n* • explanatory power *(sci)*

Erlaubnis *f* • permission, licence *(rel, jur, eth)*

Erlaubte, das *n* • the permitted *(eth, jur)* ↔ Verbotene, das

Erläuterungsurteil *n* • judg(e)ment of explanation/explication *(Leibniz, Kant etc)* *(epi, log, lan)* → analytisches Urteil ↔ Erweiterungsurteil

erleben • to experience *(Dilthey etc) (met)*

Erleben, das *n* • experiencing *(psy)*

Erlebnis *n* • lived experience *(Dilthey) (met, psy)*

Erlebnis, intentionales *n* • intentional experience *(Husserl) (epi, psy)*

Erlebnisgesellschaft *f* • adventure society, thrill-orientated society *(soc, cul)*

Erlebnisphilosophie *f* • philosophy of experience *(gep)*

Erlebnisstrom *m* • stream of experience *(Husserl, Carnap) (epi, met)* < Bewußtseinsstrom

Erlebnisweisen *pl* • modes of experience *(epi, met)*

Erlebniswelt *f* • world of experience *(epi, met)*

Erlebniszeit *f* • experienced time *(psy)* < Zeit, biologische

Erleichterung des Lebens, Mittel zur *n* • means of alleviating life *(Nietzsche) (met)*

Erleuchtete, der *m* • the enlightened-one *(asp)* → Erweckte, der < Buddhismus

Erleuchtung *f* • illumination *(rel, asp)* → satori

Erlösung *f* • salvation, redemption, deliverance *(rel)*

Erlösung vom Willen *f* • redemption/liberation from the will *(Schopenhauer etc) (met, asp)*

Erlösung von sich *f* • delivery from oneself *(Nietzsche) (met)* < Selbsterlösung

Erlösungsbedürfnis *n* • need for redemption/salvation *(met, rel)*

Erlösungsreligion *f* • redemptive religion *(rel)*

Erlösungswissen *n* → Heilswissen

Ermächtigung *f* • empowerment *(jur, pol)*

Ermangelungsschließen *n* • default reasoning *(log, min)*

Ermessen, im eigenen • at one's own discretion *(act)*

Ermessensentscheidung *f* • discretionary decision *(act)*

Ermessensspielraum *m* • scope (for discretion), area for discretion, discretionary powers *(act, pol)*

erneuerbare Energie *f* • renewable energy *(env)*

Ernst *m* • seriousness *(Kierkegaard) (rel, eth, met)*

ernst-komisch → tragikomisch

Eroberung der politischen Macht *f* • conquest of political power *(pol)*

Eroberungskrieg *m* • war of conquest *(pol)* ↔ Verteidigungskrieg

Eros, philosophischer *m* • philosophical eros *(Plato) (epi, met)* < Erkenntnisdrang

Erotomanie *f* • erotomania *(psy)*

Erregungsmuster *n* • arousal pattern *(psy)*

Erregungszustand *m* • state of agitation *(nat)*, state of agitation/arousal *(psy)*

Erreichbarkeitsrelation *f* • attainability relation *(sci)* < Modallogik

Errettung nach dem Tod *f* • salvation after death, after-death salvation *(rel)*

Errungenschaft *f* • achievement *(gen)*

Ersatzbefriedigung *f* • substitute/compensatory satisfaction *(psy)*

Ersatzbildung *f* • substitutive formation *(Freud) (psy)*

Ersatzfamilie *f* • surrogate/substitute family *(soc)*

Ersatzgefühl *n* • ersatz feeling *(psy)*

Ersatzhandlung *f* • displacement activity, redirection activity *(psy)* < Sublimierung

Ersatzmutterschaft *f* • surrogate motherhood *(eth)*

Ersatzreligion *f* • ersatz/surrogate religion *(rel)* < Religionsersatz

Erschaffung der Welt *f* • creation of the world *(rel)* < Genesis

Erschaffung des Menschen *f* • creation of man *(rel)*

Erscheinung *f* • appearance *(met, gep)* < Schein, Sein und Erscheinung

Erscheinung, äußere *f* • outward/outer/external appearance *(aes)*

Erscheinung des Absoluten *f* • appearance of the Absolute *(Hegel) (met)*

Erscheinung und Wirklichkeit *f,f* • appearance and reality *(met)*

Erscheinungsform *f* • manifestation *(met)*

erscheinungsmäßiges Sein *n* → phänomenales Sein

Erscheinungsweise *f* • mode of appearance *(epi, met)*

Erscheinungswelt *f* • phenomenal world, world of appearance(s) *(Plato, Kant etc) (ont)*

Erschleichung *f* → Subreption

Erschlossenheit *f* • open(ed)ness, exploration *(Heidegger) (ont)* < Entschlossenheit

erschöpfbare Ressourcen *pl* • exhaustible resources *(env)*

Erschrecken *n* • alarm *(Heidegger) (ont)*

Ersetzbarkeit *f* • substitutability, substitutivity *(lan)* < Synonymität

Ersetzbarkeit identischer Ausdrücke *f* • substitutablity/substitutivity of equivalent expressions *(Quine) (log, ont)* < Austauschbarkeit

Ersetzungsregel *f* • substitution/replacement rule *(log, lan)* → Substitutionsregel

Ersparnismethode *f* • savings method, method of savings *(sci)*

Erstbegriffe *pl* • initial concepts *(epi, met)*

erste Gewißheit *f* • first certainty *(epi, met)*

Erste Internationale *f* • First International *(pol)*

erste Materie *f* • prime matter *(ont)*

erste Philosophie *f* • first philosophy *(Aristotle etc) (met)* → prima philosophia, Metaphysik

erste Prinzipien *pl* • first principles *(Aristotle) (met)*

erste Prinzipien, unbezweifelbare *pl* • indubitable first principles *(Descartes) (epi)* < fundamentum inconcussum

erste und letzte Dinge *pl* • first and last things *(rel)*

erste Ursache *f* • first cause *(Aristotle) (met)* → causa prima

erste Welt *f* → Welt Eins

ersten Besitzergreifung, Recht der *n* • right of the first occupier *(jur)* < Okkupationstheorie

erster Anfang *m* • prime beginning, origin *(met)* → arché, Ursache

erster Beweger *m* • prime mover *(Aristotle) (met, rel)* → unbewegter Beweger

erstes Gossensches Gesetz *n* • Gossen's first law, law of satiety *(eco)* < Grenznutzen, abnehmender

erstes Prinzip *n* • first principle *(met)*

erstes Verursachtes *n* • first caused *(met)* → prima causatum

Erstgeburtsrecht *n* • primogeniture *(jur)* → Primogenitur ↔ Ultimagenitur

Erstheit *f* • firstness *(Peirce) (met, log)*

Erstschlag *m* • first strike *(pol, eth)* ↔ Zweitschlag, Gegenschlag

Erstschlagdrohung *f* • first strike threat *(pol, eth)* < atomare Drohung

Erstspracherwerb *m* • first language acquisition *(lan, psy)*

Ertragssteigerung *f* • increase in profits, increasing return(s) *(eco)* < Gewinnmaximierung

Ertragssteigerung, landwirtschaftliche *f* • increase of agricultural yield, yield increase *(eco)*

Erwachen *n* • awakening *(asp)*

Erwachsenenbildung *f* • adult education *(gen)* < Weiterbildung

Erwähnung *f* • mention *(lan, log)*

Erwartungshaltung *f* • expectation *(sci, psy)*

Erwartungshorizont *m* • horizon of expectation *(act)*

Erwartungsnutzen *m* • expected utility *(dec)*

Erwartungsnutzenmaximierung *f* • expected utility maximization *(dec)*

Erwartungswert *m* • expected value *(dec)*

Erwartungswert, mathematischer *m* • mathematical expectation *(Popper) (mat)*

Erweckte, der *m* • the awakened-one *(asp)* → Erleuchtete, der < Buddhismus

Erweckung *f* • awakening *(rel)*

Erweiterungsurteil *n* • judg(e)ment of extension *(Leibniz, Kant) (epi)* → synthetisches Urteil ↔ Erläuterungsurteil

Erwerb(ung) *m(f)* • acquisition *(jur, psy)* < Wissenserwerb

Erwerbsarbeit *f* • gainful employment *(eco)* < Kapitaleinkommen

Erwerbsbedingungen *pl* • conditions of appropriation *(eco, jur)*

Erwerbsfähigkeit *f* • fitness to work *(eco)* < Arbeitsfähigkeit

Erwerbsquelle *f* • source of income *(eco)*

Erwerbstätigkeit, selbständige *f* • self-employment, non-salaried occupation *(eco)* < Erwerbsarbeit

Erwerbstätigkeit, unselbständige *f* • gainful employment/occupation *(eco)* < Erwerbsarbeit

Erwerbstrieb *m* • possessive urge *(Weber) (eco, soc)*

Erwerbsunfähigkeit *f* • inability to earn a living *(eco)*

Erwerbswirtschaft *f* • profit(-oriented) economy *(Weber) (eco)*

Erwiderung f • reply, response *(gep)*, replication *(jur)* → Replik

erworbene Eigenschaft f • acquired characteristic *(psy)* < Disposition

erworbene Rolle f • acquired role *(soc, psy)* ↔ zugewiesene Rolle

erworbener Charakter m • acquired character *(psy)*

erworbenes Recht n • acquired right *(jur)*

erworbenes Verhalten n • acquired behaviour *(psy)*

Erzählerperspektive f • narrator-perspective *(lan, act)*

Erzählgedicht n • narrative verse *(aes)*

Erzählliteratur f • (prose) fiction *(aes)*

erzählte Geschichte f • oral history *(his)* < Oralität; Überlieferung, mündliche

erzeugende Funktion f • generating function *(mat)*

Erzeugung einer Gruppe f • generation of a group *(mat)*

Erziehung, ästhetische f • aesthetic education *(Schiller) (aes)* < W 1053

Erziehung zur Einsamkeit f • education in/ toward loneliness *(Nietzsche) (met)*

Erziehung zur Toleranz f • education in/ towards tolerance *(eth)*

Erziehungsautorität f • pedagogical authority *(psy)*

Erziehungsfunktion der Kunst f • educational/ educative function/role of art *(aes)*

Erziehungsroman m • educational novel *(aes)* → Entwicklungsroman, Bildungsroman

Erziehungssystem n • educational system *(soc)*

Erziehungswissenschaft f • pedagogics *(gep)* → Pädagogik

Erzwingbarkeit des Rechts f • enforceability of law/rights *(jur)*

Erzwingung, gesellschaftliche f • social enforcement *(soc)* < Zwangsmaßnahme

Es, das n • the Id *(Nietzsche, Freud) (psy)*

Es-gibt-Aussage f • there-is utterance *(lan, log)* → Existenzaussage

Es-gibt-nicht-Satz m • there-is-not statement, existential negation, non-existence statement *(lan, log)*

Es-gibt-Satz m • there-is statement, existential statement *(lan, log)*

Eschatologie f • eschatology *(rel, met)* < Chiliasmus, Ende der Geschichte, Endzeit, Millenarismus

Eselsbrücke f • pons asinorum *(log)*

Eskalation f • escalation *(pol)* ↔ Deeskalation

Eskapismus m • escapism *(psy)* → Realitätsflucht, Wirklichkeitsflucht

Esoterik f • esoterics, esotericism *(eso)* < Grenzwissenschaft

esoterisches Wissen n • esoteric knowledge *(rel, eso)*

Essay m • essay *(gen)* < Abhandlung

esse est percipi • to be is to be perceived *(Berkeley) (epi, ont)*

essentia f • essence *(met)* → Wesen, das

Essentialismus m • essentialism *(met, ont)* < Wesenslehre

essentialistische Definition f • essentialist(ic)/ essential definition *(Aristotle, Popper etc) (lan)* < Realdefinition

Essentialprädikation f • essential predication *(log, lan)*

essentiell • essential *(met)* → wesensmäßig

Essentifikation f • essentification *(Schelling) (rel, met)*

Essenz f • essence *(met)*

Essenz, bloß begriffliche f • nominal essence *(met)*

Essenz, faktische f • real essence *(met)*

Essenz und Existenz f,f • essence and existence *(met)*

Etatismus m • etatism *(eco, pol)*

Ethik f • ethics *(eth)* → Moralphilosophie < Morallehre, Ethos

Ethik, absolute f • absolute ethics *(Fromm) (eth)*

Ethik, angewandte f • applied ethics *(eth)*

Ethik, argumentative f • argumentative ethics *(Apel, Habermas) (eth)*

Ethik, autonome f • autonomous ethics *(eth)*

Ethik, autoritäre f • authoritarian ethics *(Fromm) (eth)*

Ethik, axiologische f • axiological ethics *(eth)* → Wertethik

Ethik, deontologische f • deontological ethics *(eth)* → Pflichtenethik

Ethik der Technik f • engineering ethics, ethics of technology *(eth, tec)*

Ethik der Verantwortung f • ethics of responsibility *(eth)* → Verantwortungsethik

Ethik des Wir f • ethic of the We *(Sartre) (eth)*

Ethik des Dienens f • ethics of serving *(Gandhi, Rahner etc) (eth)*

Ethik, deskriptive f • descriptive ethics *(eth)* ↔ Ethik, präskriptive

Ethik, dezisionistische f • decisionist ethics *(Weber) (eth)*

Ethik, egoistische f • egoistic ethics *(eth)*

Ethik, emotivistische *f* • emotivist(ic) ethics *(Ayer etc) (eth)*

Ethik, empirische *f* • empirical ethics *(eth)*

Ethik, eudämonistische *f* • eud(a)emonist(ic) ethics *(eth)* < eudämische Ethik

Ethik, evolutionäre *f* • evolutionary ethics *(Spencer etc) (eth)*

Ethik, evolutionistische *f* • evolutionistic ethics *(Moore etc) (eth)* < Ethik, evolutionäre

Ethik, formale *f* • formal ethics *(eth)*

Ethik, geschlechtsspezifische *f* • gender-specific ethics *(eth, fem)*

Ethik, handlungsdeontologische *f* • act-deontological ethics *(Frankena) (eth)* ↔ Ethik, regeldeontologische

Ethik, hedonistische *f* • hedonistic ethics *(eth)*

Ethik, humanistische *f* • humanistic ethics *(Fromm) (eth)*

Ethik, kognitivistische *f* • cognitivistic ethics *(eth)*

Ethik, kollektivistische *f* • collectivist ethics *(Scheler) (eth)*

Ethik, konsequentialistische *f* • consequentalist ethics *(eth)* ↔ Gesinnungsethik

Ethik, konstruktivistische *f* • constructivist ethics *(Kambartel etc) (eth)*

Ethik, männliche *f* • male ethics *(eth, fem)*

Ethik, marxistische *f* • Marxist ethics *(eth)*

Ethik, materiale *f* • material ethics, non-formal ethics *(eth)*

Ethik, medizinische *f* • medical ethics *(eth)* → Medizinethik

Ethik, naturalistische *f* • naturalistic ethics *(eth)*

Ethik, nicht-kognitivistische *f* • non-cognitivist ethics *(eth)*

Ethik, nominalistische *f* • nominalistic ethics *(Scheler) (eth)*

Ethik, normative *f* • normative ethics *(eth)*

Ethik, objektivistische *f* • objectivist ethics *(eth)*

Ethik, phänomenologische *f* • phenomenological ethics *(Brentano etc) (eth)*

Ethik, präskriptive *f* • prescriptive ethics *(eth)* → normative Ethik ↔ Ethik, deskriptive

Ethik, regeldeontologische *f* • rule-deontological ethics *(Frankena) (eth)* ↔ Ethik, handlungsdeontologische

Ethik, relative *f* • relative ethics *(Fromm) (eth)*

Ethik, relativistische *f* • relativistic ethics *(eth)*

Ethik, sozialimmanente *f* • immanent social ethics *(Fromm) (eth)*

Ethik, subjektivistische *f* • subjectivist(ic) ethics *(eth)*

Ethik, teleologische *f* • teleological ethics *(eth)* → Ethik, konsequentialistische

Ethik, theonome *f* • theonomic ethics *(Crusius etc) (eth)*

Ethik, vitalistische *f* • vitalistic ethics *(Scheler) (eth)*

Ethik, weibliche *f* • female ethics *(eth, fem)*

Ethiker *m* • moral philosopher, ethicist *(eth)*

Ethikkode *m* • code of ethics *(eth)*

Ethikkommission *f* • ethics committee/commission *(eth)*

Ethikotheologie *f* • ethico-theology, moral theology *(Kant, Küng) (rel, eth)* < Physiko-theologie

ethisch neutral • ethically neutral *(eth)*

ethische Pflicht *f* • ethical duty *(Kant)* eth ↔ Rechtspflicht

ethische Teleologie *f* • ethical teleology *(Kant) (eth, met)*

ethische Tugend *f* • ethical virtue *(Aristotle) (eth)* ↔ dianoetische Tugend

ethische Unparteilichkeit *f* • ethical impartialism *(eth)*

ethische Verallgemeinerung *f* • ethical generalization *(eth)* < W 1147

ethische Verpflichtung *f* • ethical obligation *(eth)*

ethische Wertung *f* • ethical (e)valuation *(eth)*

ethische Wissenschaft *f* • ethical science *(eth, sci)*

ethischer Intellektualismus *m* • ethical intellectualism *(Socrates) (eth)*

ethischer Konstruktivismus *m* • ethical constructivism *(sci)*

ethischer Relativismus *m* • moral/ethical relativism *(eth)*

ethischer Verhaltenskode *m* • ethical code of conduct *(eth)*

ethischer Voluntarismus *m* • ethical voluntarism *(eth)*

ethischer Wert *m* • (▷ Ideal) ethical value, (▷ Wert einer Sache) ethical worth *(eth)*

ethisches Dilemma *n* • moral dilemma *(eth)* < tragischer Konflikt

ethisches Gemeinwesen *n* • ethical commonwealth *(Kant) (eth)*

ethisches Ideal *n* • ethical ideal *(eth)*

ethisches Leben *n* • ethical life, ethical stage of living, ethical stage on life's way *(Kierkegaard) (eth)* < ethisches Stadium

ethisches Stadium *n* • ethical stage *(Kierkegaard) (eth)* < Dreistadienlehre

ethisches Tunsollen *n* • moral ought-to-do *(Scheler) (eth)*

Ethisierung *f* • ethical rationalization *(Weber)* *(eth, soc)*

ethnische Minderheiten *pl* • ethnic minorities *(pol)* < bedrohte Völker

ethnische Säuberung *f* • ethnic cleansing *(pol)* < Genozid

Ethnizität *f* • ethnicity *(soc)*

Ethnogenese *f* • ethnogeny *(cul)*

Ethnographie *f* • ethnography *(ant, cul)*

Ethnohistorie *f* • ethnohistory *(cul, his)*

Ethnolinguistik *f* • ethnolinguistics *(lan)*

Ethnologie *f* • ethnology *(cul, ant)* → Völkerkunde

Ethnomethodologie *f* • ethnomethodology *(Garfinkel)* *(sci, soc)*

Ethnophilosophie *f* • ethnophilosophy *(ant, cul)*

Ethnopsychologie *f* • ethnopsychology *(psy)*

Ethnozentrismus *m* • ethnocentrism *(pol)* < Chauvinismus

Ethnozid *m* • ethnocide *(pol, eth)* → Völkermord < Genozid

Ethologie *f* • ethology *(nat, psy)* → Verhaltensforschung

Ethos *n* • ethos *(eth)* → Sittlichkeit

Ethos des Genies *n* • ethos/ethics of genius *(eth, aes)*

Ethos-Ethik *f* • ethos-ethics *(Buber)* *(eth)*

Etikette *f* • etiquette *(eth, soc)*

Etikettenschwindel *m* • window dressing, fraudulent labelling *(eco, eth)*

Etwas, das *n* • the something *(ont)* < Sein, Nichts

Etymologie *f* • etymology *(lan)*

etymologisieren • to etymologize *(Heidegger)* *(ont)*

Eubiotik *f* → Lebenskunst

Eubulie *f* • well-advisedness *(Plato etc)* *(gep, eth)* < Einsicht, Vernünftigkeit

Eudämonismus *m* → Eudämonismus

eudämische Ethik *f* • eudemian ethics *(Aristotle)* *(eth)* < eudämonistische Ethik

eudämonistische Ethik *f* • eud(a)emonist(ic) ethics *(eth)*

Eudämonie *f* • eud(a)emonia, happiness *(eth)* → Glückseligkeit

Eudämonismus *m* • eudaimonism *(Plato etc)* *(eth)* → Glückseligkeitslehre

Eugenik, negative *f* • negative eugenics *(nat, eth)*

Eugenik, positive *f* • positive eugenics *(nat, eth)*

Eukinetik *f* • eukinetics *(aes)* → Bewegungskunst

Euklid • Euclid

euklidische Geometrie *f* • Euclidean geometry *(mat)*

euklidischer Raum *m* • Euclidean space *(mat)*

Eule der Minerva *f* • (the) Owl of Minerva *(gep)*

Euler-Diagramm *n* • Euler diagram *(log)*

Eulersche Funktion *f* • Euler function *(mat)*

Eulersches Integral *n* • Euler's integral *(mat)*

Euphemismus *m* • euphemism *(lan)* < Schönfärberei

Eur(h)ythmie *f* • eur(h)ythmy, eur(h)ythmics *(Steiner)* *(aes)*

europäische Philosophie *f* • European philosophy *(gep)*

eurozentrisches Weltbild *n* • eurocentric view of the world *(gep)*

Eurozentrismus *m* • Eurocentrism *(pol)*

Euthanasie *f* • euthanasia *(eth)* < Lebensbeendigung, Lebensrecht, Lebenswertdebatte, schmerzloser Tod

Euthanasie, aktive *f* • active euthanasia *(eth)* < Töten vs. Sterbenlassen

Euthanasie aller Moral *f* • euthanasia of all morals *(Kant)* *(eth)*

Euthanasie der reinen Vernunft *f* • euthanasia of pure reason *(Kant)* *(epi)*

Euthanasie, direkte *f* • direct euthanasia *(eth)*

Euthanasie, freiwillige *f* • voluntary euthanasia *(eth)*

Euthanasie, indirekte *f* • indirect euthanasia *(eth)*

Euthanasie, passive *f* • passive euthanasia *(eth)* < Töten vs. Sterbenlassen

Euthanasie, unfreiwillige *f* • involuntary euthanasia *(eth)*

Euthenik *f* • euthenics *(soc)* < Diätetik

Evaluation *f* • evaluation *(gep)*

Evaluations- und Handlungsforschung *f* • evaluation and action research *(act, sci)*

evaluativ • evaluative *(lan, eth, aes)*

evaluative Äußerung *f* • evaluative expression *(lan)*

Evaluierung *f* → Evaluation

Evidentialismus *m* • evidentialism *(epi)*

evidentielle Relevanz *f* • evidential relevance *(lan, log)*

Evidenz *f* • evidence, intuitiveness, certainty *(log, epi, sci)* < unbezweifelbare Tatsache, zwingende Wahrheit, Gewißheit

Evidenz, absolute *f* • absolute evidence *(epi)*

Evidenz, apodeiktische *f* • apodeictic evidence *(Husserl)* *(epi)*

Evidenz, assertorische *f* • assertoric evidence *(Husserl)* *(epi)*

Evidenz, hypothetische *f* • hypothetical evidence *(epi)*
Evidenz, logische *f* • logical evidence *(log, epi)*
Evidenz, mittelbare *f* • indirect/mediate evidence *(epi)*
Evidenz, psychologische *f* • psychological evidence *(epi, psy)*
Evidenz, unmittelbare *f* • direct/immediate evidence *(epi)*
Evidenzlehre *f* • doctrine of evidence *(epi)*
Evidenztheorie *f* • theory of evidence *(epi)*
evokatives Lernen *n* • evocative learning *(psy)*
Evolution *f* • evolution *(nat)* < Geschichte des Lebens
Evolution, offene *f* • open evolution *(nat, sys)*
evolutionäre Erkenntnistheorie *f* • evolutionary epistemology *(Campbell) (epi, sci)*
evolutionäre Ethik *f* • evolutionary ethics *(Spencer etc) (eth)* < W 303
evolutionäre Veränderung *f* • evolutionary change *(nat, soc)*
evolutionärer Humanismus *m* • evolutionary humanism *(Huxley) (nat, ant)*
evolutionärer Ursprung *m* • evolutionary origin *(nat)*
evolutionärer Vorteil *m* • evolutionary advantage *(nat, ant)*
evolutionärer Wandel *m* • evolutionary change *(nat, soc)*
Evolutionismus *m* • evolutionism *(nat)*
Evolutionsbiologie *f* • evolutionary biology *(nat)*
Evolutionsgeschichte *f* • evolutionary history *(nat, ant)*
Evolutionsgesetze *pl* • laws of evolution *(nat)*
Evolutionsprozeß *m* • evolutionary process *(nat)*
Evolutionsstadium *n* • evolutionary state *(nat)*
Evolutionstheorie *f* • theory of evolution, evolutionary theory *(nat)* < Abstammungstheorie, Deszendenztheorie
evolvierendes System *n* • evolving system *(sys)*
ewige Idee Gottes *f* • eternal idea of God *(met, rel)*
ewige Ideen *pl* • eternal ideas/forms *(Plato) (met)* < unwandelbare Ideen
ewige Schöpfung *f* • eternal generation/ creation *(Origen etc) (rel)*
ewige Wahrheit *f* • eternal truth *(epi, met)*
ewige Wiederkehr des Gleichen *f* • eternal recurrence of the same *(Nietzsche) (met)* < W 525

ewige Wiederkunft *f* • eternal return/recurrence *(Nietzsche) (met, rel)*
ewiger Friede *m* • perpetual/eternal peace *(Kant) (eth, pol)* < universeller Friede, Weltfrieden
ewiger Satz *m* • eternal sentence *(Quine etc) (lan)*
ewiger Wanderer *m* • eternal wanderer *(met, rel)* < homo viator
ewiges Du *n* • eternal Thou *(Buber) (rel)*
ewiges Gesetz *n* • eternal law *(met, rel)*
ewiges Weltauge *n* • eternal world-observer *(met)*
Ewigkeit *f* • eternity *(met)*
Ewigkeit der Naturgesetze *f* • immutability of natural laws, immutability of the laws of nature *(nat, met)*
Ewigkeit Gottes *f* • eternity of God *(rel)*
Ewigkeit in der Zeit *f* • temporal eternity *(met)*
ewigwährende Gegenwart *f* • everlasting present *(met)*
ex definitione • *nt*, by definition *(log, lan)*
ex falso quodlibet • *nt (log)*
ex more • *nt*, according to custom *(soc)*
ex nihilo • *nt*, from nothing *(ont)*
ex nihilo nihil • *nt*, from nothing comes nothing *(ont)*
exakte Wissenschaften *pl* • exact sciences *(sci)*
Exegese *f* • exegesis *(aes, rel)* → Ausdeutung
Exekutive *f* • executive (authority) *(jur)* → Exekutivgewalt < Rechtsvollzug
Exekutivgewalt *f* • executive power, forces of law and order *(jur)* < vollziehender Körper
Exekutivorgan *n* • law-enforcement agency *(jur)*
exemplarische Gültigkeit *f* • exemplary validity *(gep)*
Exemplarismus *m* • exemplarism *(Augustine, Aquinas) (epi, met, rel)*
Exemplarursache *f* • exemplary cause *(Augustine) (met)*
Exemplifikation *f* • exemplification *(sci)*
Exemplifizierung *f* • exemplification *(gep)*
exerzitive Äußerung *f* • exercitive utterance *(Austin) (lan, act)* < Illokution
Exhaustion *f* • exhaustion, removal *(log, mat)*
Exhaustionsmethode *f* • method of removal *(log, mat)*
Exhaustionsregel *f* • removal rule *(log, mat)*
Exilliteratur *f* • literature of exile *(aes, pol)*
existentia *f* • existence *(ont)*
Existential *n* • existential *(ont)*

Existentialanalyse *f* • existential analysis
(Heidegger) (ont)

existentiale Ethik *f* • existential ethics *(eth)*

Existentialismus *m* • existentialism *(gep)*
< W 495

existentialistische Ethik *f* • existentialist ethics
(eth)

existentialistischer Humanismus *m* • existentialist humanism *(Sartre etc) (eth)* < W 495

Existentialität *f* • existentiality *(Heidegger)*
(ont)

Existentialontologie *f* • existential ontology
(Heidegger) (ont)

Existentialphänomenologie *f* • existential
phenomenology *(Heidegger etc) (met)*

Existentialphilosophie *f* → Existenzphilosophie

Existentialsatz *m* • existential sentence/
proposition *(log, lan)* → Existenzsatz

Existentialurteil *n* • existential judg(e)ment/
proposition *(Brentano) (log, min)*

existentielle Bedürfnisse *pl* • existential needs
(eco, soc, met)

existentielle Ironie *f* • existential irony
(Kierkegaard) (met) < sokratische Ironie

existentielle Psychoanalyse *f* • existential
psychoanalysis *(Sartre) (psy)*

existentielle Rede *f* • existential discourse
(met)

existentielle Unwahrheit *f* • existential untruth
(Jaspers, Heidegger) (met)

existentielle Verallgemeinerung *f* • existential
generalization *(log)*

existentielle Wahrheit *f* • existential truth
(met)

existentieller Entschluß *m* • existential resolve
(met)

Existenz *f* • existence *(nat, eco)*, existence,
existenz *(ont)* < Ek-sistenz

Existenz als Seinsstufe *f* • existenz as mode of
being *(Jaspers) (met)*

Existenz, immerwährende *f* • eternal
existence *(met)*

Existenz, kontingente *f* • contingent existenz
(Jaspers) (met), contingent existence *(lan,
ont)*

Existenz, mögliche *f* • potential/possible
existenz *(Jaspers) (met)*, potential/possible
existence *(met)*

Existenz, notwendige *f* • necessary existence
(met)

Existenz, Paradox der *n* • the paradox of
existenz *(Jaspers) (met)*

Existenz, Tiefe der *f* • the depth of existenz
(Jaspers) (met)

Existenzanalyse *f* • existential analysis *(met,
ant)* < Existentialanalyse, Existenzphilosophie

Existenzangst *f* • existential dread, Angst
(psy), subsistence anxiety *(eco, soc)*

Existenzaussage *f* • there-is/existence statement, existential statement/proposition *(lan,
log, ont)*

Existenzaxiom *n* • axiom of existence *(mat)*

Existenzbedingung *f* • existential condition
(met)

existenzbedrohend • life-threatening *(gen)*

Existenzbegriff *m* • existential concept,
concept of existence *(log, lan, ont)*

Existenzberechtigung *f* • right to exist *(eth)* →
Recht auf Leben, Lebensberechtigung

Existenzerhellung *f* • illumination of existenz/
existence *(Jaspers) (met)*

Existenzgrundlage *f* • basis of existence *(eco)*

Existenzial *n* • existentiale, existential
(Heidegger) (ont)

existenziale Analytik des Dasein *f* • existential
analytic/analysis of Dasein *(Heidegger)*
(ont)

existenziale Phänomenologie *f* → Existenzi-
alphänomenologie

existenziale Untersuchungen *pl* • existential
inquiries *(Heidegger) (ont)*

Existenzialien *pl* • existentiales, existentials
(Heidegger) (ont)

Existenzialurteil *n* • existential judg(e)ment
(log, epi)

existenziell • existentiell *(Heidegger) (ont)*

Existenzkampf *m* • struggle for existence *(nat,
soc)* → Kampf ums Dasein < Daseinsbehauptung, Überleben des Tüchtigsten

Existenzlohn *m* • subsistence/minimum income
(eco)

Existenzminimum *n* • subsistence level *(eco)*

Existenzoperator *m* • existential operator
(log) < Existenzquantor, Partikularisator

existenzorientiertes Denken *n* • existence
orient(at)ed thinking/thought *(met)*

Existenzphänomenologie *f* • existential phenomenology *(Heidegger) (ont)*

Existenzphilosophie *f* • existential philosophy
(gep)

Existenzquantor *m* • existential quantifier *(log,
lan)* < Existenzoperator, Partikularisator

Existenzregel *f* • rule of existence *(log)*

Existenzsatz *m* • existence statement *(log, lan)*
→ Existentialsatz

Existenztheologie *f* • existential theology *(rel)*

Existenzverallgemeinerung *f* • existential
generalization *(log)*

Existenzverfassung *f* • existential constitution *(Heidegger) (ont)*

Existenzvoraussetzung *f* • existential/ontological commitment, commitment to existence *(Quine) (ont, lan)*

Existenzweise *f* • way of existing, sphere of existence *(Kierkegaard) (met)*

Exklusion *f* • exclusion *(log)* → Ausschließung ↔ Inklusion

Exklusivität *f* • exclusivity *(gep)*

Exkommunikation *f* • excommunication *(rel)*

Exobiologie *f* • exobiology *(nat)* < extraterrestrisches Leben

Exorzismus *m* • exorcism *(rel, eso)* < Besessenheit

Expansion *f* → Ausdehnung

Expansionspolitik *f* • politics of expansionism *(pol)*

Experiment *n* • experiment *(sci)* < Wiederholbarkeit

Experiment, entscheidendes *n* • crucial experiment *(sci)* → experimentum crucis

Experiment, natürliches *n* • natural experiment *(sci, nat)*

Experimentalfilm *m* • experimental film *(aes)*

Experimentalgruppe *f* • experimental group *(sci)* < Testgruppe

Experimentalmoral *f* • experimental morality *(Nietzsche) (eth)*

Experimentalphilosophie *f* • experimental philosophy *(gep)*

Experimentalwissenschaft *f* • experimental science *(sci)*

Experimentanordnung *f* • experimental design/set-up/arrangement *(sci)*

Experimentator *m* • experimenter, experimentor, experimentator *(sci)*

experimentelle Ästhetik *f* • experimental aesthetics *(aes)*

experimentelle Implikation *f* • experimental import *(sci)*

experimentelle Methode *f* • experimental method *(sci)*

experimentelle Musik *f* • experimental music *(aes)*

experimentelle Psychologie *f* • experimental psychology *(psy)*

experimentieren • to experiment *(sci)*

Experimentierphase *f* • experimental phase/stage *(sci)*

Experimentreihe *f* • experimental series, series of experiments *(sci)*

experimentum crucis *n* • crucial experiment *(sci)* → Experiment, entscheidendes

Expertensystem *n* • expert system *(gep)*

Expertenwissen *n* • expert knowledge, know how *(epi)* → Fachwissen

Expertokratie *f* • expertocracy *(pol)* < Spezialistentum

Explanandum *n* • explanandum *(log)*

Explanation *f* • explanation *(sci)* → Erklärung

Explanationismus *m* • explanationism *(sci)*

Explikandum *n* • explicandum *(log)* ↔ Explikat

Explikans *n* • explicans *(log)*

Explikat *n* • explicatum *(log)* ↔ Explikandum

Explikation *f* • explication *(log)*

Explikationsanspruch *m* • explicative claim *(lan, act)*

explikativer Diskurs *m* • explicative discourse *(Habermas) (lan, act)*

explizit • explicit *(log, lan)* ↔ implizit

explizit performativ • explicitly performative *(Austin) (lan)* < performative Äußerung

explizite Definition *f* • explicit definition *(log, lan)*

explizites Wissen *f* • explicit knowledge *(epi)*

Exploitation *f* • exploitation *(eco)* → Ausbeutung

Exponat *n* • exhibit *(aes)*

Exponentialfunktion *f* • exponential function *(mat)*

exponentionelles Wachstum *n* • exponential growth *(mat, sys)*

Exportationsgesetz *n* • exportation rule *(log)* ↔ Importationsgesetz < Importation

Exposition *f* • exposition *(aes, gep)*

expositive Äußerung *f* • expositive statement *(Austin) (lan)* < Illokution

Expressionismus *m* • expressionism *(aes)*

Expressionismusdebatte *f* • expressionism controversy/debate *(aes)* < Realismustheorie

Expressive *pl* • expressives *(Searle) (act, lan)* < Kommissive

expressive Äußerung *f* • expressive utterance/expression *(lan, act)*

expressive Einstellung *f* • expressive attitude *(lan, act)*

expressive Funktion der Sprache *f* • expressive function of language *(Bühler) (lan, act)* < Organonmodell der Sprache

expressive Sprechhandlung *f* • expressive speech act *(Searle) (lan, act)*

Expressivität *f* • expressivity, expressiveness *(aes, psy)*

Expropriation *f* • expropriation *(eco, jur)* → Enteignung

Expropriation der Exproprriateure *f* • expropriation of expropriators *(Marx) (soc)*

Extension *f* • extension *(log, lan)* ↔ Intension
< Begriffsumfang

extensional • extensional *(log, lan)* ↔
intensional

Extensionalität *f* • extensionality *(log, lan)*

Extensionalitätsaxiom *n* • axiom of extensionality *(log)*

Extensionalitätsthese *f* • law of extensionality *(Carnap etc) (log, lan, sci)*

Extensionsdefinition *f* • definition by extension, extension(al) definition *(log, lan)*

extensive Größen *pl* • extensive magnitudes *(Kant) (epi)*

Externalisation *f* • externalization *(psy, eco)*

Externalismus *m* • externalism *(epi, eth)* ↔ Internalismus

Externalitäten *pl* • externalities *(eco)* < Kostenexternalisierung

externe Frage *f* • external question *(Carnap) (sci)* ↔ interne Frage

extramental • extramental *(min, psy)*

extramundan • extramundane *(met)* < außerweltlich, transzendent

Extrapolation *f* • extrapolation *(mat, log)*

extraterrestrische Intelligenz *f* • extraterrestrial intelligence *(nat, eso)*

extraterrestrisches Leben *n* • extraterrestrial life *(nat, eso)* < Exobiologie

Extraversion *f* • extraversion *(psy)* ↔ Introversion

Extreme *pl* • outliers *(sci)*

Extremismus *m* • extremism *(pol)*

Extremist *m* • extremist *(pol)*

extrinsische Gültigkeit *f* • extrinsic validity *(sci)*

extrinsische Motivation *f* • extrinsic motivation *(psy)*

extrinsischer Wert *m* • extrinsic value *(eth, aes)*

extrinsisches Gut *n* • extrinsic good *(eth)*

Extrovertiertheit *f* → Extraversion

exzentrische Positionalität *f* • eccentric/excentric positionality *(Plessner) (ant)*

Exzentrizität *f* • eccentricity *(nat, psy)*

exzessiver Indeterminismus *m* • excessive indeterminism *(met)*

F

F-falsch • f-false *(Carnap) (log)* ↔ L-falsch

F-Struktur *f* • functional structure *(lan)* < C-Struktur

F-wahr • f-true *(Carnap) (log)* ↔ L-wahr

Fabianismus *m* • Fabianism *(soc, pol)*

Fachausdruck *m* → Fachbegriff

Fachautorität *f* • expert authority *(gep)*

Fachbegriff *m* • technical term/concept, disciplinary/specialist concept *(lan, sci)* < theoretischer Term

Fachgebundenheit *f* • field dependence *(sci)*

Fachsprache *f* • technical language, disciplinary sublanguage, sublanguage *(lan, sci)*

Fachwissen *n* • specialist/technical knowledge *(gep)* → Expertenwissen

Fähigkeit *f* • capacity, ability *(gep)*

Fähigkeitsstruktur *f* • skill structure, structure of competences *(psy)*

Fahrlässigkeit *f* • negligence *(jur, eth)*

fairer Wettquotient *m* • fair betting quotient *(sci, dec)* < Wahrscheinlichkeitstheorie

faires Verfahren *n* • fair/due process *(jur, eth)*

Fakt *m/n* • fact *(gep)* → Faktum, Tatsache

Faktenwissen *n* • factual knowledge, knowledge of facts *(epi)* < positives Wissen

faktisch • factical *(Heidegger) (ont)*, factual *(gep)*

Faktizität *f* • factuality, facticity *(gep)*

Faktor *m* • factor *(mat)* < Variable

Faktor, genereller *m* • general factor, g-factor *(Spearman) (mat)*

Faktorenanalyse *f* • factor analysis *(mat, sci)*

Faktorenanalyse, multiple *f* • multiple factor analysis *(Thurstone) (mat, sci)*

Faktorenladung *f* • factor loading *(mat, sci)*

Faktorzerlegung *f* • factorization *(mat)*

Faktum *n* • factum *(gep)* → Fakt, Tatsache

fakultativ • facultative, optional *(act, eth)* ↔ obligatorisch

Fall sein, der • to be the case *(epi, sci)* < zutreffen (eines Sachverhalts)

Fallazie *f* → Trugschluß

Fallgesetz *n* • law of falling bodies *(nat)* < Gravitationsgesetz

Fallibilismus *m* • fallibilism *(Peirce, Popper etc) (sci)* → Falsifikationismus

fallibilistische Erkenntnistheorie *f* • fallibilist theory of knowledge *(Popper) (epi, sci)*

Fallmethode *f* • case (study) method *(sci)*

Fallstudie *f* • case study *(sci)*

falsch • false, wrong, incorrect *(log, sci)*, devious, insincere *(eth)*, inappropriate *(act, eth)*

falsche Propheten *pl* • false prophets *(gen)*

falsches Bewußtsein *n* • false consciousness *(Marx etc) (epi, soc)*

Falschheit *f* • falsehood, falsity, wrongness, incorrectness *(log, sci)*, (▷ Unaufrichtigkeit) insincerity, deviousness, falsehood, incorrectness *(eth)*, (▷ Unangemessenheit) inappropriateness *(act)*

Falschheitsgehalt *m* • falseness content *(epi, lan, sci)* ↔ Wahrheitsgehalt

Falsifikation *f* • falsification *(Popper etc) (sci)* < Widerlegung < W 307

Falsifikationismus *m* • falsificationism *(Popper etc) (sci)* ↔ Verifikationismus

Falsifikationsimmunität *f* • immunity to falsification *(sci)* < Pseudowissenschaft, Immunisierungsstrategie

Falsifikationskriterium *n* • falsification criterion, criterion of falsification *(sci)* < Falsifizierbarkeitskriterium

Falsifikationsprinzip *n* • principle of falsification *(Popper) (sci)* < Bestätigung, Bewährung

Falsifizierbarkeit *f* • falsifiability *(Popper etc) (sci)* → Widerlegbarkeit < Bewährbarkeit

Falsifizierbarkeitskriterium *n* • criterion of falsifiability, falsifiability criterion *(Popper etc) (sci)*

falsifizieren • to falsify *(Popper etc) (sci)*

familiäre Sozialisation *f* • family socialization *(Habermas) (soc)*

Familienähnlichkeit *f* • family resemblance *(Wittgenstein etc) (lan)*

Familienautorität *f* • family authority *(psy, soc)*

Familienbande *pl* • family ties *(soc)*

Familienplanung *f* • family planning *(soc, pol)*

Familienpolitik *f* • family policy *(pol, soc)*

Familientherapie *f* • family therapy *(psy)*

Fanatismus *m* • fanaticism *(psy, pol)*

Fangfrage *f* • trick/catch question *(lan, log)* → Heterozetesis

Fangschluß *m* • garden path argument *(log)* < Trugschluß, Sophismus

Farbenlehre *f* • theory of colours *(Goethe etc)* < W 1355

Farbenspiel *n* • play of colours *(aes)*

Farbensprache *f* • colour language *(aes)*

Faschismus *m* • fascism *(pol)* < National-sozialismus, Nazismus

faschistisch • fascist *(pol)*

Fast-Gott *m* • the almost god, the near-god *(Nietzsche)* *(met)*

Fatalismus *m* • fatalism *(met, rel)*

faustisches Streben *n* • Faustian ambition *(met)*

Faustregel *f* • rule of thumb *(gen)*

Fauvismus *m* • Fauvism *(aes)*

Feedback *n* • feedback *(AI, sys)*

Feedback-Schleife *f* • feedback loop *(sys, AI)*

Fehlbarkeit *f* • fallibility *(epi, sci, rel)*

Fehlbarkeit der Vernunft *f* • fallibility of reason *(epi)* < Fallibilismus

Fehlbezeichnung *f* • misnomer *(lan)*

Fehler *m* • fault, error *(sys)*, bug *(AI)* < Bug; mistake, error *(gep)* < Irrtum, Verfehlung

Fehler der relativen Häufigkeit *m* • relative frequency error *(mat)*

Fehler erster Art *m* • Type I error *(mat)*

Fehler, mittlerer quadratischer *m* • mean square error, MSE *(mat)*

Fehler zweiter Art *m* • Type II error *(mat)*

Fehleranalyse *f* • error/fault analysis *(sys, AI)*

Fehlerbeseitigung *f* • elimination/removal of faults/errors, debugging *(sys, AI)* < Fehlersuche

Fehlereliminierung *f* → Fehlerbeseitigung

Fehlerfreundlichkeit *f* • fault tolerance *(sys, AI)* < benützerfreundliche Systeme, Toleranz

Fehlerfunktion *f* • error function *(mat, AI)*

fehlerhafte Definition *f* • faulty definition *(log, lan)*

Fehlerhäufigkeit *f* • error frequency *(mat)*

Fehlerkurve *f* • error distribution curve *(mat)*

Fehlerquelle *f* • source of error *(sys, sci)*

Fehlerrechnung *f* • calculus of errors *(mat)*

Fehlersuche *f* • debugging *(AI)*, error/fault tracking/tracing *(sys, tec)*

Fehlerteufel *m* • gremlin(s) *(sys)*

Fehlervermeidung *f* • avoidance of error *(sys)*

Fehlerwahltechnik *f* • error-choice technique *(Hammond)* *(mat)*

Fehlfunktion *f* • malfunction *(sys)* < Störfall

Fehlschluß *m* • erroneous/faulty/fallacious inference, fallacy *(log)* < Beweisfehler, Trugschluß, Paralogismus

Fehlspruch *m* • miscarriage of justice, judicial error, false sentence *(jur)* → Fehlurteil < Rechtsirrtum

Fehltritt *m* • faux pas, lapse *(eth, soc)*

Fehlurteil *n* • misjudg(e)ment *(epi); (jur)* → Fehlspruch

Feindbild *n* • feindbild, concept of the enemy *(soc, pol)*

Feindesliebe *f* • love of one's enemy *(eth, rel)* < Nächstenliebe

Feingefühl *n* • sensibility, sensitivity *(psy)* < Empfindsamkeit

Feld *n* • array, field *(mat)*, field, terrain *(gep)*

Feld der Begleitumstände *n* • field of concomitance *(Foucault) (epi, lan)*

Feld der Präsenz *n* • field of presence *(Foucault) (epi, lan)*

Feld nicht-diskursiver Praktiken *n* • field of non-discursive practices *(Foucault) (epi, lan)*

Feldarbeit *f* • field work *(sci)*

Feldexperiment *n* • field experiment *(sci)*

Feldforschung *f* • field research *(sci)*

Feldstudie *f* • field study *(sci)*

Feldtheorie *f* • field theory *(nat)*

Feldweg *m* • country path *(Heidegger)* *(ant)*

Feminat *n* → Matriarchat

Feminismus *m* • feminism *(fem)* ↔ Maskulinismus

Feministin *f* • feminist *(fem)*

feministische Ästhetik *f* • feminist aesthetics *(fem, aes)*

feministische Bewegung *f* • feminist movement *(fem)*

feministische Erkenntnistheorie *f* • feminist epistemology *(epi, fem)*

feministische Ethik *f* • feminist ethics *(eth, fem)*

feministische Geschichte *f* • feminist history, herstory° *(fem, his)*

feministische Philosophie *f* • feminist philosophy *(fem, gep)*

feministische Theologie *f* • feminist theology *(fem, rel)*

feministische Wissenschaft *f* • feminist science *(fem, sci)*

feministische Wissenschaftstheorie *f* • feminist philosophy/theory of science *(fem, sci)*

feministisches Egalitätskonzept *n* • feminist concept of equality *(fem, eth)*

fensterlose Monaden *pl* • windowless monads *(Leibniz)* *(met)*

Fermatsche Vermutung *f* • Fermat's last theorem *(mat)*

Fermatsches Prinzip *n* • Fermat's principle (of least time) *(nat)* < Quantenphysik

Fernwirkung *f* • action at a distance *(nat)* *(Newton etc)*, long-distance effect *(sys, dec, eth)* < Langzeitwirkung

Fernziel *n* • distant goal *(dec, act)*

feste Größe *f* • fixed magnitude *(sci)*

Festhaltbarkeit des Gegebenen *f* • retainability of the given *(epi)*

Festkörperphysik *f* • solid state physics *(nat)*

festsetzen • to determine *(gep)*

Festsetzung *f* • (conventional) stipulation *(Carnap)* *(log, lan)*, determination *(gep)*

Festwertregelung *f* • regulation of constance, regulation of fixed value *(sci)* < Kybernetik, Rückkoppelung

Fetisch *m* • fetish *(cul)*

fetischisieren • to make a fetish of *(soc, rel, psy)*

Fetischisierung *f* • fetish formation, fetishization *(soc, rel, psy)*

Fetischismus *m* • fetishism *(cul, rel, psy)*

Feudalaristokratie *f* • feudal aristocracy *(Marx etc)* *(soc)*

feudale Eigentumsverhältnisse *pl* • feudal property relations *(eco, soc)*

feudaler Absolutismus *m* • feudal absolutism *(pol)*

feudaler Sozialismus *m* • feudal socialism *(Marx)* *(soc)*

Feudalgesellschaft *f* • feudal society *(soc)*

Feudalismus *m* • feudalism *(soc, his)* → Feudalsystem

feudalistische Produktionsweise *f* • feudal mode of production *(eco, soc)*

Feudalsystem *n* • feudal system *(eco, soc)* → Feudalismus

Feudalwirtschaft *f* • feudal economy *(eco, soc)*

Feudum *n* → Lehen

Feuer als Urelement *n* • fire as the first principle *(Heraclitus)* *(met)*

Feuerbachscher Materialismus *m* • Feuerbachian materialism *(met)*

Fideismus *m* • fideism *(epi)* ↔ Szientismus

Fido-Fido-Prinzip *n* • "Fido"-Fido principle *(lan)*

Figur *f* • figure *(log)*; (▷ Gestalt) figure *(psy, aes)* < Gestaltpsychologie

Figur-Grund-Verhältnis *n* • figure-ground relation *(psy, aes)* < Gestaltwahrnehmung

figuratives Denken *n* • figurative thinking/thought *(Croce)* *(met)*

Fiktion *f* • fiction *(aes, gep)*

Fiktion, wissenschaftliche *f* • scientific fiction *(Vaihinger)* *(sci)* < Als-Ob

fiktionale Rede *f* • fictional discourse *(lan)*

Fiktionalisierung *f* • fictionalization *(gep)*

Fiktionalismus *m* • fictionalism *(Vaihinger)* *(epi, sci, met)*

fiktiver Gegenstand *m* • fictional object *(ont)* < nichtexistierende Gegenstände

Fiktivität *f* • fictitiousness *(gep)*

Fiktivsein *n* • fictiousness *(Ayer etc)* *(epi)* → Fiktivität

Filmästhetik *f* • film aesthetics *(aes)*

Filmkunst *f* • cinematic art *(aes)* → Cineastik

Fin de siècle *n* • fin de siècle *(his, aes)*

Finalismus *m* • finalism *(met)* < Teleologie, Zielgerichtetheit

Finalität *f* • finality *(met, act)*

Finalursache *f* • final cause *(met)* → Zweckursache, causa finalis

Finanzaristokratie *f* • plutocracy *(eco, soc)*

Finanzkapitalismus *m* • finance capitalism *(Lenin etc)* *(eco, soc)*

finite Modelle *pl* • finite models *(log)* ↔ infinite Modelle

Finitismus *m* • finitism *(met)*

finsteres Zeitalter *n* • dark ages *(his)*

Fitneß, individuelle *f* • individual fitness *(nat, ant)*

Fitneß, inklusive *f* • inclusive fitness *(nat, ant)*

Fixationspunkt *m* • fixation point *(Helmholtz)* *(psy, nat)*

Fixelement *n* • fixed element *(mat)*

fixes Kapital *n* • fixed capital *(Marx)* *(eco)*

Fixierung *f* • fixation *(Freud etc)* *(psy)*

Fixpunkt *m* • fixed point *(gen)* < Bezugspunkt

Fixpunktsatz *m* • fixed-point theorem *(mat)*

Flächenstichprobe *f* • area sample *(mat, sci)*

Flaschenhals *m* • bottleneck *(sys)* < Stau

Fleischeslust *f* • sensual desire *(psy)*

Fleischestötung *f* • mortification of the flesh *(rel)*

Flexibilisierung der Arbeitszeit *f* • flexitime, flexibilization of workhours *(eco)* < Teilzeitbeschäftigung

Flexibilität *f* • flexibility *(psy)*

Fliehkraft *f* • centrifugal force *(nat)* → Zentrifugalkraft

Fließgleichgewicht *n* • moving/dynamic equilibrium *(Bertalanffy)* *(sys)* → Gleichgewicht, dynamisches

Flucht der Intelligenz *f* → Brain-Drain

Flucht vor der Freiheit *f* • escape from freedom *(Fromm, Popper etc)* *(pol, eth)*

Flucht vor der Wirklichkeit *f* • escape/flight from reality *(psy)* → Eskapismus, Realitätsflucht

flüchtiger Vorteil *m* • transient advantage *(dec)*

Fluxus *m* • *nt (aes)* < Dadaismus

Föderalismus *m* • federalism *(pol)* < Kommunalismus

föderatives Prinzip *n* • federative principle *(pol)*

Folge *f* • (▷ Nachfolge) succession, (▷ Serie) series, sequence *(mat)* < Abfolge, (▷ Ergebnis) consequence *(gep)* < Konsequenz

Folgebeziehung *f* • entailment *(lan)* < Implikation

Folgeeigenschaft *f* • supervenient property *(log, lan)* < Supervenienz

Folgekosten *pl* • resultant costs, consequential expenses *(eco)*

Folgen, unvorhergesehene *pl* • unanticipated consequences *(act, dec)*

Folgeproblem *n* • resultant problem *(sys)*

Folgerichtigkeit *f* • consistency *(log)*

Folgerung *f* • consequence *(sci)*, deduction, inference *(log)*

Folgerungsbegriff *m* • concept of (logical) consequence *(log)*

Folgerungsbeziehung *f* • relation of consequence *(log)*

Folgerungslehre *f* • theory of consequence *(log)* → Krimatologie

Folgerungsmenge *f* • set of consequences *(log)*

Folgerungssinn *m* • illative sense *(Newman)* *(epi, log)*

Folgerungsvermögen *n* • capacity for deductive reasoning/ratiocination, ratiocinative faculty *(epi, log)*

Folgewidrigkeit *f* • logical inconsistency *(log)* < Widerspruch, logischer

Folgewirkung *f* • aftereffect, consequence effect° *(sys)*

Folgewirkungen, negative *pl* • detrimental effects *(sys)* < Nebenwirkung

Forderung des Gesamtdatums *f* • requirement of total evidence *(Carnap) (epi, sci)*

Forderung maximaler Spezifität *f* • requirement of maximal specifity *(Hempel) (epi, sci)*

Forderungsrecht *n* → Anspruchsrecht

Fordismus *m* • Fordism *(eco)* < Massenproduktion

Form *f* • form *(gep)* < Formenlehre

Form, begriffliche *f* • conceptual form *(epi, lan, met)*

Form der Anschauung *f* • form of intuition/ anschauung *(Kant) (epi)*

Form der Erfahrung *f* • form of experience *(Kant) (epi)*

Form der Erscheinung *f* • form of appearance *(Kant) (epi)*

Form der Natur *f* • form of nature *(Kant)* *(epi, nat)*

Form der Sinnlichkeit *f* • form of sensibility *(Kant) (epi)*

Form der Zweckmäßigkeit *f* • form of functionality /appropriateness/fitness/ purposiveness/finality *(Kant) (epi, met)*

Form des Denkens *f* • form of thought *(Kant)* *(epi)*

Form des Urteils *f* • form of judg(e)ment *(log)* ↔ Materie des Urteils

Form des Verstandes *f* • form of the understanding *(Kant) (epi)*

Form, logische *f* • logical form *(Wittgenstein etc) (log, lan)*

Form und Inhalt *f,m* • form and content *(epi, met)*

Form und Materie *f,f* • form and matter *(met)*

Formalabstraktion *f* • formal abstraction *(log, lan)*

Formalästhetik *f* • formal aesthetics *(aes)* ↔ Inhaltsästhetik

formaldemokratisch • formally democratic *(pol)*

formale Anschauung *f* • formal intuition *(Kant) (epi)*

formale Bedingung *f* • formal condition *(epi, log)*

formale Einheit *f* • formal unity *(epi)*

formale Ethik *f* • formal ethics *(eth)*

formale Logik *f* • formal logic *(log)* ↔ materiale Ontologie

formale Ontologie *f* • formal ontology *(Husserl, Ingarden) (ont)*

formale Operation *f* • formal operation *(log)*

formale Praktik *f* • formal theory of action *(Husserl) (epi, met, act)*

formale Redeweise *f* • formal mode of speech *(Carnap etc) (lan)* ↔ inhaltliche Redeweise

formale Sprache *f* • formal language *(log, lan)* → Formalsprache

formale Wertlehre *f* • formal axiology *(eth)*

formale Zwänge *pl* • formal constraints *(gep)*

formale Zweckmäßigkeit *f* • formal functionality /appropriateness/fitness/ purposeness/inality *(Kant) (met, aes)*

formaler Bruch *m* • breach of form *(aes)* < Stilbruch

formaler Grad *m* • formal degree *(gep)*

formaler Grund *m* • formal ground *(epi, log, met)*

formaler Idealismus *m* • formal idealism *(Kant) (epi, met)* → kritischer Idealismus

formaler Realgrund *m* • formal-real ground *(Kant) (epi, met)*

formaler Satz *m* • formal sentence *(sci)*

formales Prinzip *n* • formal principle *(Kant) (epi, met)*

formales System *n* • formal system *(sci, log)*

Formalisierbarkeit *f* • formalizablity *(log, sci)* < Mathematisierbarkeit

formalisieren • to formalize *(log)*

formalisierte Sprache *f* • formalized language *(Tarski) (lan, epi, log)*

formalisierte Theorie *f* • formalized theory *(sci)*

Formalisierung *f* • formalization *(log)*

Formalisierung, logische *f* • logical formalization *(log)*

Formalismus *m* • formalism *(aes, log, mat)*

Formalist *m* • formalist *(aes, log)*

formalistische Kunsttheorie *f* • formalist theory of art *(aes)*

formalistisches Programm *n* • formalistic programme *(Hilbert) (mat, log)*

Formalontologie *f* → formale Ontologie

Formalpragmatik *f* • formal pragmatics *(Habermas) (soc)*

Formalsprache *f* • formal language *(log, lan)* ↔ Normalsprache < Kunstsprache, Wissenschaftssprache

Formationsregel *f* • formation rule *(lan, log)*

Formationsregeln *pl* • rules of formation *(Foucault) (epi)*

Formationsregeln der Gegenstände *pl* • rules for the formation of objects *(Foucault) (epi)*

Formationssystem *n* • formation system, system of formation *(Foucault) (epi, sys)*

formbare Natur *f* • plastic nature *(nat, ant)*

Formbewußtsein *n* • form(al) consciousness/ awareness *(aes)*

Formel *f* • formula *(lan, log, mat)*

formeller Grund *m* → formaler Grund

Formen der Abfolge *pl* • forms of succession *(Foucault) (epi, his)*

Formen der Koexistenz *pl* • forms of coexistence *(Foucault) (soc, epi, sys)*

Formen der Sinnlichkeit *pl* • forms of sensibility *(Kant etc) (epi, aes)*

formende Kraft *f* • forming power *(Shaftesbury) (aes)*

Formenkanon *m* • canon/set of forms *(aes)*

Formenlehre *f* • theory of forms *(met, aes)*

Formenreihe *f* • series of form, formal series *(Wittgenstein etc) (log)*

Formlosigkeit des Lebens *f* • formlessness of life *(Nietzsche) (met)*

Formtrieb *m* • formal impulse *(Schiller) (aes)* ↔ Stofftrieb

Formursache *f* • formal cause *(Aristotle etc) (met)* → causa formalis

forschende Wahrnehmung *f* • inquiring perception *(Pfänder) (epi)*

Forschung *f* • (scientific) research *(sci)*

Forschung, angewandte *f* • applied research *(sci)*

Forschung, dezentralisierte *f* • decentralized research *(sci)*

Forschung, reine *f* • pure research *(sci)* < Grundlagenforschung

Forschungsarbeit *f* • research work *(sci)*

Forschungsethik *f* • research ethics *(eth)*

Forschungsförderungspolitik *f* • research funding policy *(pol, sci)*

Forschungsforschung *f* • science research *(sci)* < Wissenschaftswissenschaft

Forschungsgegenstand *m* • research subject *(sci)*

Forschungshypothese *f* • research hypothesis *(sci)*

Forschungsmanagement *n* • research management *(sci)* < Wissenschaftsbetrieb

Forschungsmethode *f* • research method *(sci)*

Forschungsmodell *n* • model of research, research model *(sci)*

Forschungsprioritäten *pl* • research priorities *(sci)*

Forschungsprogramm *n* • research programme *(Lakatos etc) (sci)* < Theorie der Forschungsprogramme < W 307

Forschungsprojekt *n* • research project *(sci)*

Forschungsprozeß *m* • research process *(sci)*

Forschungsstand *m* • state of research *(sci)*

Forschungsstrategie *f* • research strategy *(sci)*

Forschungstradition *f* • research tradition *(sci)*

Forschungstypen *pl* • research types *(sci)*

Forschungszentrum *n* • research centre *(sci)*

Fortgang ins Unendliche *m* → infiniter Regreß

fortgeschrittene Gesellschaft *f* • advanced society *(soc)*

Fortpflanzungsfreiheit *f* • procreative liberty *(eth)*

Fortpflanzungsmedizin *f* • reproductive medicine *(nat, eth)*

Fortpflanzungstechnologie *f* • reproductive technology *(nat, eth)*

Fortpflanzungstrieb *m* • reproductive instinct *(nat, psy)*

Fortschreibung *f* • extrapolation *(mat)* → Extrapolation

Fortschritt in der Geschichte *m* • progress in history *(his)*

Fortschrittsdenken *n* • progressivism *(gep)* → Progressismus

Fortschrittsfeindlichkeit *f* • antiprogressive attitude *(soc, psy)* < Maschinenstürmerei

Fortschrittsgläubigkeit *f* • naive belief/faith in progress *(soc, psy)*

Fortschrittsidee *f* • idea of progress *(gep)*

Fortschrittsideologie *f* • ideology of progress *(gep)*

Fortschrittskritik *f* • criticism of progress *(soc)*

fortschrittskritisch • critical of progress *(soc)*

Fortschrittsoptimismus *m* • optimistic belief in progress *(psy)*

Fortschrittstheorie *f* • theory of progress *(gep)*

Fotorealismus *m* • photorealism *(aes)* < Hyperrealismus

Fourier-Transformation *f* • Fourier transformation *(mat)*

Fourierismus *m* • Fourierism *(gep)*

Frag-würdigkeit *f* • questionability *(Heidegger)* *(ont)*

Frage nach dem Sein *f* • the question of Being *(Heidegger etc)* *(ont)* → Seinsfrage < Seinsproblem

Fragebedürfnis *n* • need to ask *(gen)*

Fragmentierung des Lebens *f* • fragmentation of life *(soc)*

Fragwürdigkeit *f* • questionability, doubtfulness *(gen)*

Fraktal *n* • fractal *(mat, sys)* < Mandelbrotmenge

fraktale Geometrie *f* • fractal geometry *(mat)* < Chaostheorie

Frame • frame *(gep)*

Frankfurter Schule *f* • Frankfurt School *(gep)* < kritische Theorie

Französische Sozialisten *pl* • French Socialists *(gep)* < utopischer Sozialismus

französischer Materialismus *m* • French Materialism *(gep)*

Frauenbefreiung *f* • women's liberation *(fem)* → Emanzipation der Frau

Frauenbewegung *f* • women's/feminist/wimmin's° movement *(fem, soc)*

Frauenemanzipation *f* • female emancipation, emancipation of women/wimmin° *(fem, soc, pol)*

Frauenforschung *f* • women's/feminist studies *(fem)* < Geschlechterforschung

Frauenrechtsbewegung *f* • women's rights movement *(fem, jur)*

Frege-Prinzip *n* • Frege's principle *(log)*

Freidenker *m* • freethinker *(rel, pol)*

freidenkerisch • freethinking *(rel, pol)*

freie Arbeit *f* • free labour *(eco, soc)* < Lohnkontrakt, Lohnarbeit

freie Assoziation *f* • free association *(Marx etc)* *(soc); (Freud)* *(psy)* < Brainstorming

freie Geister *pl* • free spirits *(Nietzsche)* *(met)*

freie Künste *pl* • liberal arts *(aes, gep)* ↔ Gebrauchskünste < Geisteswissenschaften

freie Marktwirtschaft *f* • free market economy *(eco)* < Marktwirtschaft, soziale; Wirtschaftsliberalismus

freie Variable *f* • free variable *(mat, log)* ↔ gebundene Variable

freie Willensübereinkunft *f* • voluntary agreement, (free) agreement of will *(act, pol)*

freier Arbeiter *m* • free worker *(Marx)* *(soc)* < Lohnarbeiter

freier Geist *m* • free spirit *(met)* < Freigeist

freier Selbstzwang *m* • free self-compulsion, free self-coercion *(Kant)* *(eth)* < Autonomie des Willens

freier Wettbewerb *m* • free competition *(eco)*

freier Wille *m* • free will *(eth, met)* < W 1200

freies Denken *n* • free thinking *(gep)*

freies Mandat *n* • free mandate *(pol)* ↔ imperatives Mandat

freies Spiel der Kräfte *n* • free play of faculties *(Schiller etc)* *(aes)*; free play of (market) forces *(eco)* < unsichtbare Hand

freies Vorkommen *n* • free occurrence *(log)*

Freigebigkeit *f* • generosity *(eth)* → Großzügigkeit

Freigeist *m* • free spirit *(rel, gep)* < freier Geist

freigeistig • free-spirited *(Nietzsche)* *(met)*

freigestellt • exempt, free *(gen)* → fakultativ

Freihandel *m* • free trade *(eco)*

Freihandelsdoktrin *f* • doctrine of free trade *(eco, pol)* < Manchesterdoktrin

Freiheit *f* • freedom, liberty *(gep)*

Freiheit, absolute *f* • absolute freedom *(Hegel etc)* *(met)*

Freiheit als Abwesenheit von Zwang *f* • liberty as absence of restraint/coercion *(eth, act)*

Freiheit als Autonomie *f* • freedom as autonomy *(Kant)* *(eth, met)*

Freiheit der Wissenschaft *f* • freedom of science *(sci, pol)*

Freiheit des Willens *f* • freedom of will *(eth, met)* < W 818

Freiheit, existenzielle *f* • existential freedom *(Jaspers etc) (met)*

Freiheit, Gleichheit, Brüderlichkeit *f,f,f* • liberty, equality, fraternity *(pol)* → liberté, egalité, fraternité

Freiheitsentzug *m* • deprivation of freedom *(eth, pol)*, imprisonment *(jur)*

Freiheitsgrade *pl* • grades/degrees of freedom *(met, mat)*

Freiheitslehre *f* • theory of freedom *(pol, met)* → Eleutheriologie

Freiheitsrechte *pl* • civil rights and liberties *(jur, pol)*

Freiheit und Notwendigkeit *f,f* • freedom and necessity *(met)*

Freiheit unter dem Gesetz *f* • liberty/freedom under the law *(pol, jur)*

Freiheitsverlust *m* • loss of freedom *(pol)*

Freiheit von der Knechtschaft der Leidenschaften *f* • freedom from (the) servitude of (the) passions *(Spinoza) (eth, met)*

Freiheit von *f* • freedom from *(met)* → negative Freiheit

Freiheit zu *f* • freedom to *(met)* → positive Freiheit

Freiheit zum Tode *f* • freedom for death *(Heidegger etc) (ant)*

Freikörperkultur *f* • nudism *(cul)* < Kulturismus, Kulturistik, Naturismus

Freimaurerei *f* • freemasonry *(eth, pol)* → Freimaurertum

Freimaurerloge *f* • masonic lodge *(eth, pol)*

Freimaurertum *n* • freemasonry *(eth, pol)* → Freimaurerei

Freisetzungsexperiment *n* • experiment in natural surroundings, experiment outside the confines of the laboratory *(sci, eth)* < genetische Manipulation

Freitäter *m* • free-doer *(Nietzsche) (eth)*

Freitod *m* • suicide, voluntary death *(eth)* → Suizid

freiwillige Arbeit *f* • free labour *(soc)* ↔ Zwangsarbeit

freiwillige Handlung *f* • voluntary act(ion) *(act, eth)* < freiwilliger Akt

freiwillige Knechtschaft *f* • voluntary serfdom *(de la Boetie) (eth)*

freiwillige Selbstkontrolle *f* • voluntary self-control *(eth)*

freiwillige Unterwerfung *f* • voluntary submission *(eth, pol)*

freiwilliger Akt *m* • voluntary act *(act, eth)* < freiwillige Handlung

Freiwilligkeit *f* • voluntariness *(act, eth)*

Freizeit *f* • free/leisure/disposable/non-working time *(soc)*

Freizeitgesellschaft *f* • leisure society *(soc)*

Freizeitindustrie *f* • leisure industry *(eco)*

Freizeitverhalten *n* • leisure habits/behaviour/activity *(soc)*

freizügige Gesellschaft *f* • permissive society *(soc, psy)* < Libertinismus

Freizügigkeit *f* • (▷ Permissivität) permissiveness *(pol, eth);* (▷ Niederlassungsfreiheit) freedom of movement and settlement *(pol)* → Niederlassungsfreiheit

Fremdartigkeit in sich selbst *f* • strangeness-in-itself *(met)*

fremdbestimmtes Leben *n* • heteronomous (way of) life *(eth, met)*

Fremdbestimmung *f* • heteronomy *(pol, eth, met)* → Heteronomie ↔ Selbstbestimmung

Fremde *f* • foreign ground *(Husserl) (epi, min, met)* ↔ Heimat

Fremde, das *n* • the alien *(Buber) (rel, met)*

Fremde, der *m* • the stranger *(Camus) (met)* < W 320

Fremdenfeindlichkeit *f* • xenophobia *(eth, pol)* → Xenophobie ↔ Fremdenliebe, Xenophilie

Fremdenliebe *f* • xenophilia *(eth)* → Xenophilie ↔ Fremdenfeindlichkeit, Xenophobie

Fremderfahrung *f* • experience of others *(Husserl) (epi, psy)* < Fremdwahrnehmung

Fremdheit der Welt *f* • alienness of the world, alien character of the world *(met)*

Fremdheit des Menschen in der Welt *f* • man as stranger in the world *(met)*

Fremdherrschaft *f* • foreign rule *(pol)* → Heterarchie, Xenokratie

Fremdpsychisches *n* • of other mind(s) *(Scheler etc) (psy, epi)* ↔ Eigenpsychisches

Fremdwahrnehmung *f* • perception of others *(Husserl) (epi, met)* < Fremderfahrung

Fremdwelt *f* • other world *(Husserl) (epi, met)*

Fremd-Werden *n* → Entfremdung

Frequenztheorie *f* • frequency theory *(mat, sci)* → Häufigkeitstheorie < Wahrscheinlichkeitstheorie

Freud-Leid-Kalkül *n* • pleasure-pain calculus *(dec, eth)* → hedonistischer Kalkül

Freud und Leid *f,n* • pleasure and pain *(psy)*

freudsches Symbol *n* • Freudian symbol *(psy)*

freudsche Fehlleistung *f* • Freudian slip *(psy)*

freudscher Versprecher *m* → Freudsche Fehlleistung

Freund-Feind-Denken *n* • us-and-them attitude *(pol, eth)*

Freundschaft *f* • friendship *(eth)*

Friede als oberster Wert *m* • peace as supreme good/value *(eth)*

Friede des Geistes *m* • peace of mind *(psy)*

Friede des Herzens *m* • peace of heart *(rel)*

Frieden mit der Natur *m* • peace with nature *(env)* ↔ Kampf gegen die Natur < Ökopax

Friede, ewiger *m* • perpetual/eternal peace *(Kant) (eth, pol)* < W 1353

Friedensbewegung *f* • peace movement *(eth, pol)*

Friedensdialog *m* • peace dialogue *(eth, pol)*

Friedensethik *f* • peace ethics *(eth)*

Friedensforschung *f* • peace studies/research *(eth, pol)* < Konfliktforschung

Friedensordnung *f* • peace order *(eth, pol)*

Friedensphilosophie *f* • philosophy of peace *(eth)*

Friedenspolitik *f* • peace policy *(pol)*

Friedenssicherung *f* • securing/protection of (the) peace *(pol)*

Friedensstiftung *f* • peacemaking, pacification *(pol)* < Befriedung

Friedenstheorie *f* • peace theory *(pol, eth)*

Friedfertigkeit *f* • peaceableness *(eth)*

friedliche Koexistenz *f* • peaceful coexistence *(pol)* < Toleranz

friedliche Nutzung der Atomenergie *f* • peaceful use of atomic energy *(tec)*

friedlicher Wandel *m* • peaceful change *(pol)*

Friedman-Gleichung *f* • Friedman-equation *(mat)*

Fristenlösung *f* → Fristenregelung

Fristenregelung *f* • law legalizing abortion (within a time limit), non-punishable termination of pregnancy (during the first three month of pregancy) *(eth)*

fröhliche Wissenschaft *f* • gay/cheerful science *(Nietzsche etc) (met)* < W 321

Frömmigkeit *f* • piety *(rel)*

Frühchristentum *n* • Early Christianity *(his, rel)*

früheres Handeln *n* • former action *(act, asp)* < Karma

Früherkennung *f* • early diagnosis/recognition *(gen)* < pränatale Diagnostik

Frühkapitalismus *m* • early capitalism *(Marx etc) (eco, soc)*

Frühmensch *m* • early man *(ant)* → Anthropus, Präsapiensmensch < Tiere, höhere; Anthropoide

Frühscholastik *f* • early scholasticism *(gep)*

Frühschriften *pl* • early writings *(gen)* ↔ Spätschriften

Frühwarnsystem *n* • early warning system *(tec, pol, sys)*

Frustration *f* • frustration *(psy)*

Frustrations-Aggressions-Hypothese *f* • frustration-aggression hypothesis *(psy, ant)*

Frustrations-Aggressions-Theorie *f* • frustration-aggression theory *(Dollard) (psy)*

Frustrationstoleranz *f* • frustration tolerance *(psy)*

Fühlen, intentionales *n* • intentional (sensitive) consciousness/perception *(Scheler etc) (psy, met)*

Führerautorität *f* • leader authority *(pol, psy)*

Führungsposition *f* • leadership position *(soc)* < Spitzenposition

Fulguration *f* • fulguration *(Leibniz, Fichte, Schelling) (met)*

Fülle der menschlichen Möglichkeit *f* • ful(l)ness of human possibility *(Rousseau) (ant)* < Perfektibilität

Fülle des Lebens *f* • ful(l)ness in life *(Nietzsche) (met)*

Fundamentaldisziplin *f* • foundational discipline *(sci)*

Fundamentalgruppe *f* • fundamental group *(mat)*

Fundamentalismus *m* • fundamentalism *(rel, pol)*

Fundamentalkategorie *f* • fundamental category *(N. Hartmann) (ont)*

Fundamentalontologie *f* • fundamental ontology *(Heidegger etc) (ont)*

Fundamentalphilosophie *f* • fundamental philosophy *(Wolff) (gep)*

Fundamentalsatz *m* • fundamental theorem *(log, mat)*

Fundamentaltheologie *f* • fundamental theology *(Schleiermacher) (rel)*

Fundamentaltheorem *n* • fundamental theorem *(log, mat)*

fundamentum inconcussum *n* • imperturbable basis *(Descartes) (epi)* < erste Prinzipien, unbezweifelbare Gewißheit

fundierte Relation *f* • founded relation *(Carnap) (log, lan)*

Fundiertheit *f* • foundedness *(Carnap etc) (sci)*

Fundierung *f* • reduction, foundation *(ont)*, foundation *(mat)*, support, substantiation *(sci)*

Funktion *f* • function *(log, mat, sys)*

funktional vollständige Menge *f* • functionally complete set *(log, mat)*

funktionale Eindeutigkeit *f* • functional uniqueness *(log, lan)*

funktionale Erklärung *f* • functional explanation *(sci)*

funktionale Kohärenz *f* • functional coherence *(lan)*

funktionale Rationalität *f* • functional rationality *(dec)*

funktionale Rolle *f* • functional role *(soc)*

funktionale Vollständigkeit *f* • functional completeness *(lan)*

Funktionalgleichung *f* • functional equation *(mat)*

Funktionalismus *m* • functionalism *(met, soc, aes)*

funktionalistische Theorie des Geistes *f* • functionalist theory of mind *(min)*

funktionalistische Vernunft *f* • functionalist reason *(epi)*

funktionelle Kunst *f* • functional art *(aes)*

Funktionennetzwerk *n* • function network *(sys, sci)* < Organisationssoziologie

Funktionentheorie *f* • theory of functions, function theory *(sys)*

Funktionsanalyse *f* • function(al) analysis *(sys, sci)*

Funktionslogik *f* • logic of functions *(log, sys)*

Funktionsmodell *n* • working model *(sys, sci)*

Funktionstheorie *f* • theory of function, function(al) theory *(sys, mat)*

Funktionsverhältnis *n* • functional relation, concomitance *(log)*

Funktionsweise *f* • (manner/mode of) functioning *(sys)*

Funktionswert *m* • value of the function *(log, mat)*

Funktionswort *n* • functional word *(Hare)* *(lan)*

Funktionszeichen *n* • function sign *(log)*

Funktor *m* • functor *(log)*

Für und Wider *n,n* • pros and cons *(gen)*

Furcht *f* • fear *(met, psy)* < Angst < W 330

für-sich • for-itself *(Hegel etc)* *(met)*

für sich seiender Wert *m* • self-sufficient value *(met, eth)*

Für-uns-Sein *n* • being-for-us *(Jaspers)* *(met)*

für-uns-selbst-sein • being-for-ourselves *(Sartre)* *(soc, eth)*

Füreinandersein *n* • Being-for-Others *(Sartre)* *(met)*

Fürsichsein *n* • being-for/in-itself *(Hegel etc)* *(met)*

Fürsichselbstsein *n* • Being-for-Itself *(Sartre)* *(met)*

Fürsorge *f* • fürsorge, solicitude, concern *(Heidegger etc)* *(met)*, welfare *(soc)*

Fürsorgeempfänger *m* • welfare recipient *(eth, soc)*

Fürsorglichkeit *f* • thoughtfulness, considerateness, solicitousness *(eth)* < Sorge

Fürst *m* • prince *(pol)* < W 332

Fürwahrhalten *n* • holding(-for)-true, holding-to-be-true *(epi)*

fürwahrhalten • to hold/consider (to be) true *(epi)* < meinen, Glaube(n)

Fusionsenergie *f* • fusion energy *(nat)*

Futurabilien *pl* → Futuribilien

Futuribilien *pl* • future contingents, futurabilia *(Aristotle etc)* *(epi, act, met)*

Futurismus *m* • futurism *(aes)*

Futuristisches Manifest *n* • Futurist Manifesto *(Marinetti)* *(aes)*

Futurologie *f* • futurology *(tec, eco, soc)* < prospektives Wissen, Zukunftsvoraussage

Fuzzy-Logik *f* • fuzzy logic *(Zadeh etc)* *(log)*

Fuzzy-Menge *f* • fuzzy set *(Zadeh etc)* *(log, mat)*

G

Gaia-System *n* • Gaia system *(Margulis, Lovelock) (sci)*

Galileitransformation *f* • Galilean transformation *(nat)*

Gammafunktion *f* • gamma function *(mat)*

ganz Andere, das *n* • the radical other *(Otto) (rel)*

Ganze, das *n* • the whole *(met)*

Ganzes, integrales *n* • integral whole *(mat)*

Ganzheit *f* • wholeness, totality *(met)*, (▷ Einheit) unity *(ont)* < Holismus, Totalität

ganzheitliche Betrachtung *f* • holistic/organic view *(epi)* < Totalität, Holismus

ganzheitliche Sicht *f* → ganzheitliche Betrachtung

ganzheitliches Denken *n* • holistic thinking *(epi)*

Ganzheitsmedizin *f* • holistic/organic medicine *(nat)* → Ganzheitsmedizin < Alternativmedizin, Komplementärmedizin

Ganzheitspsychologie *f* • holistic/organic psychology *(psy)*

Ganzseinkönnen *n* • being-able-to-be-whole, potentiality for being a whole *(Heidegger) (ont)*

Ganzwerdenwollen *n* • will to become whole *(Jaspers) (met)*

Gastmahl *n* • symposium, symposion *(Plato) (gep)* < W 335

Gattung *f* • species, genus, kind *(nat, log)*, genre *(aes)*

Gattung, logische *f* • logical kind/species *(log)*

Gattungsbegriff *m* • generic term *(lan, log)* → Universalbegriff

Gattungsbestimmtheit *f* • generic determination *(log)*

Gattungsbewußtsein *n* • species-consciousness *(Marx etc) (ant)*

Gattungseigenschaft *f* • species property *(ant, log)*

Gattungsentelechie *f* • species entelechy *(met)*

Gattungsform *f* • species form *(Aristotle etc) (nat, ont)*

Gattungsgeschichte *f* • history of the species *(nat, ant)*

Gattungsleben *n* • species life *(Feuerbach, Marx etc) (soc, ant)*

Gattungsname *m* • generic term *(lan, log)* → Gattungsbegriff

Gattungspoetik *f* • poetics of genre *(aes)*

Gattungssein *n* • species-being, being of the species *(Marx etc) (soc, ant)*

gattungsspezifisch • species specific *(gep)*

Gattungstheorie *f* • theory of genres *(aes)*

Gattungsvermögen *n* • species-potential *(Marx etc) (soc, ant)*

Gattungswesen *n* • species-being *(Marx etc) (soc, ant)*

GAU *m* • MCA *(tec)* → größter anzunehmender Unfall

Gaußsche (Glocken-)Kurve *f* • Gaussian curve *(mat)* < Normalverteilung

Gaußsche Verteilung *f* • normal distribution *(mat)* → Normalverteilung < Glockenkurve

Gebärdensprache *f* • gesture/sign language *(lan)* < Zeichensprache

Gebärneid *m* • womb envy *(fem)* ↔ Penisneid

Gebäude der Erkenntnis *n* • edifice of knowledge *(Descartes) (epi)*

Gebiet der Interpositivität *n* • region of interpositivity *(Foucault) (epi, sys)*

Gebietsauswahl *f* • Flächenstichprobe

Gebilde *n* • institution *(Lukács) (pol)*, formation *(ont)*, configuration *(aes)* < Gestalt

gebildete Klassen *pl* • educated/cultured classes *(soc)*

Gebot *n* • command, commandment *(rel)*, law *(jur)*, rule, precept *(eth)*

Gebrauch, situativer *m* • situative use *(lan)*

Gebrauch und Erwähnung *m,f* • use and mention *(Austin etc) (lan)*

Gebrauch von Werturteilen in Anführungsstrichen *m* • inverted-commas use of value-judg(e)ments *(Hare) (lan)*

Gebrauchsdefinition *f* • definition in use *(log, lan)* < Kontextdefinition

Gebrauchskunst *f* • utility/useful art *(aes)* < kommerzielle Kunst

Gebrauchskünste *pl* • useful arts *(aes)* ↔ freie Künste

Gebrauchsmusik *f* • utility music *(Hindemith etc) (aes)*

Gebrauchsnorm *f* • (rule of) use *(lan)*

Gebrauchstheorie der Bedeutung *f* • use theory of meaning *(lan)*

Gebrauchswert *m* • practical value *(gen)*, use value, value in use, utility value *(Marx etc) (soc, eco)* ↔ Tauschwert, Verkaufswert

gebundene Variable *f* • bound variable *(log)*

gebundenes Vorkommen *n* • bound occurrence *(log)*

Geburt Gottes *f* • birth of God *(Nietzsche etc)* *(rel)*

Geburtenkontrolle *f* • birth control *(pol)*

Geburtenrate *f* • birth rate *(soc)* ↔ Sterberate

Geburtsprivilegien *pl* • privileges of/by birth *(pol, soc)*

Geburtsrad *n* • wheel of birth *(asp, rel)*

Geburtsrecht *n* • birthright *(jur, eth)*

Geburtstrauma *n* • birth trauma *(Rank etc)* *(psy)*

Geburtswehen des Geistes *pl* • spiritual birth pangs *(Nietzsche)* *(met)*

Gedachte, das *n* • the thought, the imaginary, thought *(epi, min)*

Gedächtnis *n* • memory *(min, psy, AI)* < Speicher

Gedächtnisbild *n* • memory image *(psy)*

Gedächtnisspur *f* • memory trace *(psy)*

Gedächtnisstütze *f* • memory/recall/mnemonic aid, aid to recollection, aid-mémoire *(psy)*

Gedächtnisverlust *m* • loss of memory, memory loss, amnesia *(psy)* → Amnesie < Erinnerungsverlust

Gedanke *m* • thought *(epi, min)* < Idee

Gedankenassoziation *f* • association of thought(s)/ideas *(psy)* < Ideenassoziation

Gedankenbildung *f* • thought formation *(gep)*

Gedankending *n* • thought-thing *(met, min)* → ens rationis

Gedankenexperiment *n* • thought experiment, gedankenexperiment *(epi, sci)*

Gedankenfigur *f* • figure of thought *(gep)*

Gedankenform *f* • form of thought *(Kant etc)* *(epi)*

Gedankenfreiheit *f* • freedom of thought *(pol)*

Gedankengebäude *n* • edifice/body of thoughts/ideas *(gep)* < Gedankensystem, Ideengebäude

Gedankenkontrolle *f* • thought control, control of thought *(pol, psy)*

Gedankenkraft *f* • thought-force *(met, psy)*

Gedankenlesen *n* • mind-reading, reading thoughts *(eso)*

Gedankenpolizei *f* • thought police *(Orwell)* *(pol)* < Denkverbot, Gedankenverbrechen

Gedankenprozeß *m* • thought process *(min)*

Gedankensystem *n* • system of thought, thought system *(gep)*

Gedankenübertragung *f* • thought transfer(ence) *(eso, psy)* → Telepathie

Gedankenverbrechen *n* • thought crime *(Orwell)* *(pol)* < Gedankenpolizei

Gedankenwelt *f* • world of ideas/thought *(gep)* < Welt Drei

gedankliches System *n* • notional/conceptual system *(gep, sys)*

Gefährdetheit der Existenz *f* • existence at risk *(met)*

gefährlich leben • to live dangerously *(Nietzsche etc)* *(met)* < Wagemut

Gefangenendilemma *n* • prisoner's dilemma *(dec, eth)*

Gefüge *n* • structure *(gep)* → Struktur

Gefühl *n* • emotion, feeling *(psy)*, (▷ Empfindsamkeit) sentiment, sensibility *(met, aes)*

Gefühl der Sittlichkeit *n* • ethical feeling, moral sense *(eth)* < moralischer Sinn < W 995

Gefühlsambivalenz *f* • emotional ambivalence *(psy)*

Gefühlsbindung *f* • emotional tie *(psy)*

Gefühlsdrang *m* • emotional urge *(Scheler)* *(psy)*

Gefühlsglaube *m* • sentimental faith *(Schleiermacher etc)* *(rel)*

Gefühlsleben *n* • emotional life *(psy)*

Gefühlsmoral *f* → Emotivismus

gefühlsorientiert • feeling-oriented *(Jung etc)* *(psy)* ↔ denkorientiert

Gefühlsphilosophie *f* • philosophy of sentiment *(Schleiermacher etc)* *(met)*

Gefühlstheologie *f* • theology of sentiment *(rel)*

gefundenes Objekt *n* → objet trouvé

Gegebene, das *n* • the given *(ont)*

Gegebenheit *f* • givenness *(ont)* → Faktizität

Gegebenheiten *pl* • (▷ Bedingungen, Umstände) conditions *(gep)*

Gegen, das *n* • the counter *(Heidegger)* *(ont)*

Gegenargument *n* • counterargument *(log, lan)*

Gegenaufklärung *f* • counterenlightenment *(his)*

Gegenbeispiel *n* • counterexample *(gep)*

Gegenbewegung *f* • counter-movement *(pol, nat)*

Gegenbeweis *m* • counterevidence, evidence to the contrary *(epi, sci)*, counterproof, proof to the contrary *(log)*

Gegeninstanz *f* • counter-instance *(gep)*

Gegenkultur *f* • counter/alternative culture *(soc, cul)* < Alternativbewegung ↔ affirmative Kultur

Gegenmaßnahme *f* • countermeasure *(act)* < Gegenzug

Gegenpartei *f* • opposition party, the opposition *(pol)*, opponent *(jur)*

Gegenphilosophie *f* • counter-philosophy *(gep)*

Gegenrede f • reply, objection *(gen)* → Antiloquium

Gegenreformation f • Counter-Reformation *(his, rel)*

Gegenrevolution f • counter-revolution *(pol)*

Gegensatz m • opposition, contrariety, contradiction *(log)*, opposition, antithesis *(Hegel)* *(met)*

Gegensatz, dialektischer m • dialectical opposition *(met)*

Gegensatz, kontradiktorischer m • contradictory opposition *(log)* < logisches Quadrat; Gegensatz, konträrer; Gegensatz, subalterner

Gegensatz, konträrer m • contrary opposition *(log)* < logisches Quadrat

Gegensatz, objektiver m • objective opposition/contradiction *(log)*

Gegensatz, polarer m • polar opposition *(log)*

Gegensatz, privativer m • privative opposition *(log)*

Gegensatz, realer m • real opposition *(log)*

Gegensatz, relativer m • relative opposition *(log)*

Gegensatz, subalterner m • subaltern opposition *(log)* < logisches Quadrat

Gegensatz, subkonträrer m • subcontrary opposition *(log)* < logisches Quadrat

Gegensatz von Denken und Sein m • opposition between thought and being *(met)*

Gegensatz von Ich und Nicht-Ich m • opposition of/between ego and non-ego, opposition of/between I and non-I *(Fichte) (met)*

Gegensätze, Einheit der f • unity/identity of opposites *(Hegel) (met)*

Gegensätzliche, das n • the contrary *(log)*

Gegensätze, Streit der m • conflict of opposites *(Heraclitus etc) (met)*

gegensätzliche Auffassung f • opposing view *(gep)*

Gegensätzlichkeit f • contrariety, opposition *(log)*

Gegenschlag m • counterstrike *(pol, act)* → Zweitschlag ↔ Erstschlag

Gegenschlagkapazität f • counterstrike capacity *(pol)* → Vergeltungskapazität

gegenseitig ausschließend • mutually exclusive *(log)*

gegenseitig bedingend • dependent/contingent on each other *(log)*

gegenseitig gesicherte Zerstörung f • mutually assured destruction, MAD *(pol, eth)*

gegenseitige Abhängigkeit f • mutual dependence *(sys)* → Interdependenz

gegenseitige Abschreckung f • mutual deterrence *(pol, eth)*

gegenseitige Hilfe f • mutual assistance *(eth)* < W 345

gegenseitige Verpflichtung f • mutual obligation *(jur, eth, pol)*

gegenseitiges Desinteresse n • mutual disinterest/disinterestedness *(Rawls etc) (eth, pol)*

Gegenseitigkeit f • mutuality, reciprocity *(gep)* → Reziprozität, Wechselseitigkeit

Gegenseitigkeitsabkommen n • reciprocal agreement *(pol)*

Gegenspieler m • antagonist *(pol, act, dec)* → Opponent

Gegenstand m • object, thing *(gep)* < Ding, Sache

Gegenstand, ästhetischer m • aesthetic object *(aes)*

Gegenstand der Erfahrung m • object of experience *(epi)*

Gegenstand der Erkenntnis m → Erkenntnisobjekt

Gegenstand der Vernunft m • object of reason *(epi, met)*

Gegenstand der Wahrnehmung m • object of perception *(epi)*

Gegenstand des Bewußtseins m • object of consciousness/awareness *(epi, psy)*

Gegenstand des Verstandes m • object of understanding *(epi)*

Gegenstand, idealer m • ideal object *(ont)*

Gegenstand, mathematischer m • mathematical object *(mat, ont, log)*

Gegenstand, unmittelbarer m • immediate object *(ont, epi)*

gegenständlich • objective, objectual *(ont)*

Gegenständliche, das n • the concrete, the objective, the objectual *(ont)*

gegenständliche Kunst f • representational/figurative art *(aes)* ↔ gegenstandslose Kunst

gegenständliche Welt f • world of objects, objective world *(ont)*

gegenständliches System n • objective/concrete system *(sys)* < gedankliches System

Gegenständlichkeit f • objectivity *(Hegel etc) (met)*, quality of being an object *(gep)*

Gegenständlichkeitsform f • form of objectivity *(Lukács) (soc, epi)*

Gegenstandsbereich m • domain, universe (of discourse) *(log, ont)*, object *(gep)*

Gegenstandsbewußtsein n • awareness of objects *(ont)*

Gegenstandsbeziehung f • object relation *(Meinong) (ont)*

gegenstandslose Kunst f • abstract/non-representational/non-figural/non-figurative art *(aes)* → abstrakte Kunst, nichtfigurative Kunst ↔ gegenständliche Kunst

Gegenstandstheorie f • theory of objects *(Meinong etc) (ont)* < W 1108

Gegenstandsvariable f • object variable *(log)*

Gegenstück n • counterpart *(gen)*

Gegenübertragung f • counter-transference *(Freud) (psy)*

Gegenwart f • the present, (▷ Anwesenheit) presence *(met)*

Gegenwart des Absoluten f • presence of the absolute *(met)*

Gegenwart, lebendige f • living presence *(Husserl) (met)*

Gegenwärtigen n • gegenwartigen, making present *(Heidegger) (ont)*

gegenwärtiges Zeitalter n • the present age *(his)*

Gegenwärtigkeit f • presence *(met)*

Gegenwärtigkeit des Daseins f • being-present-of-Dasein *(Heidegger) (ont)*

Gegenwärtigkeit des Seins f • presentness of Being, being-present-of-Being *(Heidegger) (ont)*

Gegenwartsdenken n • contemporary thought *(gep)*

Gegenwartshorizont m • horizon of the present, present horizon *(Husserl) (epi, min)*

Gegenwartsphilosophie f • contemporary philosophy *(gep)* < W 448

Gegenwartsschrumpfung f • contraction of the present *(Lübbe) (soc)*

Gegenwirkung f • counteraction, reaction *(nat, met)* < Wirkung

Gegenzug m • countermove, reply *(dec)* < Gegenmaßnahme, Spieltheorie, Spielzug

geglücktes Leben n • perfect life *(eth)*

Gehalt m • meaning *(lan)*, content, import *(aes)*, content *(gen)*

Gehalt, empirischer m • empirical content *(sci, lan)*

Gehalt, intentionaler m • intentional content *(Husserl etc) (lan)*

Gehalt, logischer m • logical content *(log)*

Gehalt, manifester und latenter m • manifest and latent content *(Freud etc) (psy)*

Gehaltenheit f • gehaltenheit, being held *(Heidegger) (ont)*

Gehaltsästhetik f • content aesthetics *(aes)* < Formalästhetik

Gehäuse n • shell *(Jaspers) (met)*

Gehäuse der Hörigkeit n • cage of bondage *(Weber) (soc)*

Geheimlehre f • secret/esoteric doctrine *(eso, rel)* < W 1061

Geheimschriften pl • hermetic writings *(gen)*

Gehirn-Geist-Problem n • mind-brain problem *(min)*

Gehirn im Tank n • brain in a vat *(Putnam) (epi)* < genius malignus

Gehirntod m • brain death *(nat, eth)* < Hirntoddefinition, Organspende

Gehirnwäsche f • brainwashing *(psy)*

Gehirnzustand m • brain state *(min)*

Gehorsam, passiver m • passive obedience *(eth)* < ziviler Ungehorsam

Gehorsamkeitspflicht f • duty/obligation to obey *(jur, eth)*

Gehorsamsverweigerung f • disobedience *(jur, eth)* < Wehrdienstverweigerer

geht gegen unendlich • tends to infinity, approaches infinity *(mat)*

Geist m • spirit, nous *(met, rel)*, mind, intellect, nous *(epi, min)*

Geist, absoluter m • absolute spirit *(Hegel) (met)*

Geist als Organismus m • spirit as organism *(met)*

Geist als Rechenmaschine m • computational mind *(min, AI)* → Computerhirn

Geist als Weltprinzip m • mind as cosmic principle *(Anaxagoras etc) (met)*

Geist als Widersacher der Seele m • the spirit as opponent of the soul *(Klages) (met)* < W 347

Geist der Gesetze m • the spirit of the laws *(jur)* < W 1203

Geist der Zeit m → Zeitgeist

Geist des Kapitalismus m • spirit of capitalism *(Weber) (soc)* < protestantische Ethik

Geist in der Maschine m • Ghost in the machine *(Ryle) (met, min)* → Gespenst in der Maschine

Geist-Körper-Interaktion f • mind-body interaction *(min, met)*

Geist-Körper-Antagonismus m • antagonism/opposition of mind and body/matter *(Descartes etc) (epi, met)*

Geist-Körper-Problem n • mind-body problem *(Descartes etc) (epi, met)*

Geist-Leib-Problem n • mind-body problem *(Descartes etc) (epi, met)* → Leib-Seele-Problem

Geist, nationaler m • national spirit *(Hegel, Fichte etc) (pol)*

Geist, objektiver m • objective mind/spirit *(Hegel) (met)*

Geist, subjektiver m • subjective mind/spirit *(Hegel) (met)*

Geist und Körper *m,m* • mind and body *(min, met)*

Geist und Materie *m,f* • mind and matter *(min, met)*

Geisterglaube *m* • belief in the supernatural *(rel)*; superstition *(eso)*

Geisterwelt *f* • world of spirits, spirit world *(met, eso)*

Geistes, Eigenschaften des *pl* • attributes of the spirit *(met)*

Geistes, Philosophie des *f* • philosophy of spirit/mind *(Hegel) (met)*, philosophy of mind *(min)* < Bewußtseinsphilosophie

Geistes, Unbeschränktheit des *f* • unlimitedness/limitlessness/unboundedness of the spirit *(met)* < geistige Freiheit

Geistesgeschichte *f* • history of ideas *(his)*

Geistesgröße *f* • greatness of mind *(gen)*

Geisteshaltung *f* • attitude of mind, mental attitude *(gep)* → Mentalität

Geisteskraft *f* • power of the mind *(gep)*

Geisteskrise *f* • crisis of the spirit *(gep)*

Geistesleben *n* • life of the mind, intellectual life *(met, cul)*

Geistesphilosophie *f* → Philosophie des Geistes

Geistesschärfe *f* • acuteness of mind *(psy, epi)* ↔ Sinnesschärfe

Geistesschwäche *f* • weakness of mind, mental weakness *(psy, epi)*

Geistestypen *pl* • spiritual types *(Jaspers) (met)*

Geisteswissenschaft(l)er *m* • human scientist, arts scholar, practitioner of the liberal arts *(gep)* < Humanwissenschaften

Geisteswissenschaften *pl* • the humanities, human sciences/studies, the arts, liberal arts ↔ Naturwissenschaft(en) < artes liberales, Kulturwissenschaft < W 98

geisteswissenschaftliche Methode *f* • method of the humanities/human sciences *(sci)*

Geisteszustand *m* • state of mind *(min)*, mental condition *(psy)*

geistig • spiritual, intellectual *(met, min)*

geistig Seiendes *n* • spiritual/intellectual being *(ont, min)* < geistiges Sein

geistig-sittliche Welt *f* • spiritual-moral world *(met, eth)*

Geistige, das *n* • the mental, the spiritual, the mind *(met)*

geistige Abbildung *f* • mental representation/ image *(epi, min)* → mentale Repräsentation

geistige Arbeit *f* • intellectual work, brainwork *(gep)* ↔ körperliche Arbeit, manuelle Arbeit

geistige Besessenheit *f* • spirit(ual) possession, possession by spirits *(eso)*

geistige Eigenschaft *f* • mental property *(met)*

geistige Energie *f* • spiritual energy, mind-energy *(psy, met, eso)*

geistige Entitäten *pl* • mental entities *(min, ont)*

geistige Erfahrung *f* • spiritual insight, intellectual experience *(met, min)*

geistige Erleuchtung *f* • spiritual inspiration/ enlightenment *(rel, asp)*

geistige Freiheit *f* • intellectual freedom/ liberty *(pol, met)* → Denkfreiheit

geistige Geschöpfe *pl* • spiritual creatures *(met)*

geistige Krise *f* • spiritual crisis *(rel, cul)*

geistige Objekte *pl* • mental objects *(min, ont)*

geistige Ruhe *f* • peace of mind, mental quiescence *(met)*

geistige Schönheit *f* • spiritual beauty *(aes)* ↔ sinnliche Schönheit

geistige Substanz *f* • spiritual substance *(Leibniz) (met)*

geistige Tätigkeit *f* • intellectual/mental activity *(gep)*

geistige Vorgänge *pl* • mental/intellectual processes *(min)*

geistige Welt *f* • spiritual/intellectual world *(met)* < Welt Drei

geistige Werte *pl* • spiritual values *(gep)*

geistige Wesenheit *f* • spiritual being/essence *(met)*

geistiger Adel *m* • intellectual élite *(soc)*

geistiger Akt *m* • mental/intellectual act *(Husserl etc) (min)*

geistiger Automat, Seele als *f* • soul as spiritual automaton *(Leibniz etc) (met)*

geistiger Diebstahl *m* • intellectual theft *(eth, jur)* < geistiges Eigentum, Plagiat

geistiger Vorfahre *m* • spiritual ancestor/ (fore)father *(gen)*

geistiger Weg *m* • spiritual way/path *(met)*

geistiger Zustand *m* • mental state *(min)*

geistiges Abbild *n* • mental image *(min)*

Geistiges als Blendwerk *n* • spirit as illusion *(Feuerbach etc) (met)*

geistiges Auge *n* • the mind's eye *(min, met)*

geistiges Eigentum *n* • intellectual property *(jur, eth)* < geistiger Diebstahl, Plagiat

geistiges Ereignis *n* • mental event *(Carnap, Ryle) (min)*

Geistiges in der Gestalt des Materiellen *n* • idea as a product of matter *(Feuerbach etc) (met)*

geistiges Kind *n* • brainchild *(gep)*

geistiges Klima *n* • intellectual climate *(gep)*

geistiges Leben *n* • spiritual life *(met)*

geistiges Sein *n* • (▷ beseeltes Sein) spiritual being *(met, rel)*, (▷ unkörperliches Sein) immaterial/incorporeal/incorporal being *(ont)* < intelligibles Sein < W 830

geistiges Verhalten *n* • mental conduct *(psy)*

geistliche Übungen *pl* • spiritual exercises *(met)* < W 354

Geistmetaphysik *f* • metaphysics of (the) spirit *(met)* < Seinsmetaphysik

Geistperson *f* • spirit person *(met)*

Geistschönes *n* • spiritual beauty *(Hegel etc)* *(aes)* ↔ Naturschönes

Gelassenheit *f* • calmness, imperturbability, composure *(eth)*, gelassenheit, releasement *(Heidegger)* *(ont)* < Seinlassen < W 355

Gelassenheit, heitere *f* • ataraxy, serenity *(Stoics etc)* *(eth)* → Ataraxie

Geldadel *m* • moneyed class *(soc)*

Geldgesellschaft *f* • moneyed/pecuniary society *(Veblen etc)* *(eco, soc)*

Geldgier *f* • greed for money *(eco)* < Mammonismus

Geldherrschaft *f* → Plutokratie

Geldwert *m* • money/currency value *(eco)* < Werttheorie

Geldwertstabilität *f* • monetary/currency stability *(eco)*

Geldwirtschaft *f* • monetary/exchange economy *(soc, eco)* < Tauschwirtschaft

Geldzirkulation *f* • money circulation *(eco)*

gelebte Philosophie *f* • lived philosophy *(gep)*

Gelegenheitssatz *m* • occasion sentence *(Quine)* *(lan)* ↔ bleibender Satz

Gelegenheitsursache *f* • occasional cause *(Geulincx, Malebranche etc)* *(met)* → causa occasionalis < Okkasionalismus

Gelehrtenrepublik *f* • republic of scholars *(Plato etc)* *(soc)*

Gelehrter *m* • scholar *(gep)*

gelehrtes Nichtwissen *n* • learned ignorance, docta ignorantia *(Nicholas of Cusa)* *(epi, met)* < W 134

gelenkte Wirtschaft *f* • controlled economy *(eco)* < Planwirtschaft, Zentralverwaltungswirtschaft

gelichtet • gelichtet, illumined *(Heidegger)* *(ont)*

Gelichtetheit *f* • illuminedness, clearedness *(Heidegger)* *(ont)*

Geltung *f* • (▷ Gültigkeit) validity *(eth, sci)* < Akzeptanz; (▷ Wert) value *(eth)*

Geltung, empirische *f* • empirical validity *(sci)* ↔ Geltung, ideale

Geltung, ideale *f* • ideal validity *(sci)* ↔ Geltung, empirische

Geltungsanspruch *m* • validity claim *(eth, sci)*

Geltungsbasis *f* • validity basis, basis of validity *(eth, sci)*

Geltungsbedürfnis *n* • need/craving for admiration *(psy)* < Geltungstrieb

Geltungsbereich *m* • scope *(log, lan)* → Skopus

Geltungsfrage *f* • question of justification/validity *(sci)*

Geltungsgrund *m* • cause/reason of validity *(met, sci)*

Geltungstheorie *f* • valence theory *(log, sci)*

Geltungstrieb *m* → Geltungsbedürfnis

Gemäßheit *f* • conformity, appropriateness *(gep)* → Angemessenheit, Adäquatheit

Gemeinbegriffe *pl* • general/universal terms/notions *(lan, log)* → notiones communes

Gemeinbild *n* • generic image *(psy)*

Gemeinde *f* → Gemeinschaft

gemeine sittliche Vernunfterkenntnis *f* • ordinary rational knowledge of morality *(Kant)* *(eth)*

Gemeineigentum *n* • collective/communal/common ownership *(jur)*, common property *(eco)*

gemeiner Menschenverstand *m* • plain common sense, common human understanding *(Kant)* *(epi)* → gesunder Menschenverstand

Gemeingefühl *n* • sense of belonging together *(soc)* < Zugehörigkeitsgefühl

Gemeinnützigkeit *f* • public benefit, nonprofit character *(soc, eco, eth)*

Gemeinplatz *m* • commonplace, platitude *(gen)* → Binsenweisheit

gemeinsame Eigenschaft *f* • common property *(lan, ont)*

gemeinsame Interessen *pl* • common/shared/joint interests *(soc)*

gemeinsamer Faktor *m* • common factor *(gen)*

gemeinsamer Markt *m* • common market *(eco)*

gemeinsamer Nenner *m* • common denominator *(mat)*

gemeinsames Gut *n* • common property *(eco)*, common good(s) *(soc, eco)* < Gemeinwohl

gemeinsames Schicksal *n* • common destiny *(gen)* < Schicksalsgemeinschaft

Gemeinsamkeit *f* • common existence *(Weber)* *(soc)* < Gemeinschaft

Gemeinsamkeit der Interessen f • commonness of interests (soc)

Gemeinsamkeitsunterstellung f • supposition of commonality (Habermas) (soc, lan, act)

Gemeinschaft f • community, society (soc); community, gemeinschaft (Tönnies) (soc) ↔ Gesellschaft < W 356

Gemeinschaft der Apperzeption f • community of apperception (Kant) (epi)

Gemeinschaft und Gesellschaft f,f • community and society/association (Tönnies) (soc) < W 356

gemeinschaftliche Produktion f • communal/community production (Marx) (eco)

gemeinschaftlicher Besitz der Produktionsmittel m • common ownership of the means of production (Marx) (eco, pol)

gemeinschaftliches Leben n • communal/common life (Marx etc) (soc)

Gemeinschaftsbeziehung f • communal relationship (soc)

Gemeinschaftsgeist m • community spirit (soc)

Gemeinschaftshandeln n • collective/conventional/communal (social) action (Weber) (soc, act) < Gesellschaftshandeln

Gemeinschaftsleben n • communal life (soc)

Gemeinschaftsordnung f • communal order (soc)

Gemeinschaftsprojekt n • joint venture (eco)

Gemeinschaftssinn m • sense of community (soc)

Gemeinschaftsunternehmen n • joint venture (eco), community project (soc)

Gemeinsinn m • public spirit (pol); common sense (Kant etc) (epi) → gemeiner Menschenverstand < allgemeine Menschenvernunft

Gemeinsprache f • ordinary/standard language (lan)

Gemeinspruch m • common saying (Kant etc) (gep) < W 1042

Gemeinwesen n • commonwealth (Kant) (soc)

Gemeinwesen, staatliches n • national community (pol); commonwealth, body politic (Hobbes etc) (pol) < W 1029

Gemeinwille m • social will (Wundt); general will (Rousseau etc) (pol) → volonté générale, vereinigter Wille; Volkswille; Wille, allgemeiner

Gemeinwirtschaft f • cooperative economy (eco)

Gemeinwohl n • public good/welfare/interest, general good, common weal(th) (soc, eth) → Allgemeinwohl, bonum commune

Gemeinwohlgerechtigkeit f • justice of the common weal (soc, eth)

gemischte Verfassung f • mixed constitution/form of government (pol)

gemischtwirtschaftliches System n • mixed economy (eco)

Gemüt n • (▷ Geist) mind, (▷ Seele) soul, (▷ Gefühl) feeling (epi, psy)

Gemütsbewegung f • emotion, motion of the soul, affect (Kant etc) (psy)

Gemütskräfte pl • enlivened powers, Gemüt's powers° (Kant etc) (psy)

Gemütsruhe f • calmness, peace of mind (psy) < Gelassenheit

Gemütsstimmung f • temper of mind (psy) < Gestimmtheit

Gen-Ethik f • gene ethics (eth)

genau dann und nur dann wenn • if and only if, iff (log)

genau dann wenn • if and only if, if (log)

Genbank f • gene bank (nat, eth)

Gender-Studien pl • gender-studies (fem) < Geschlechterforschung

Gene, egoistische pl • egoistic genes (nat, ant)

Genealogie f • genealogy (gep)

Genealogie der Moral f • genealogy of morals (Nietzsche) (eth) < W 1356

Generalisation f • generalization (gep) → Verallgemeinerung

Generalisator m • universal quantifier (log) → Allquantor

Generalisierung f • generalization (log) < Generalisation

Generalisierungsregel f • rule of generalization (log) < Generalisation

Generalprävention f • general prevention (of crime), general deterrence (jur)

Generalthesis f • general thesis (Husserl) (epi, met)

Generalversammlung f • general assembly (pol)

generatio aequivoca f • nt (nat) → Urzeugung

Generationenfolge f • order of generations (nat, his)

Generationenkonflikt m • generation gap, generational conflict (soc)

Generationenvertrag m • contract of/between generations (soc, eth)

Generationswechsel m • alternation of generations (soc)

generative Ästhetik f • generative aesthetics (Bense) (aes) → Informationsästhetik

generative Grammatik f • generative Grammar (Chomsky) (lan) → Transformationsgrammatik

generative Semantik f • generative semantics (lan) ↔ Semantik, interpretative

generelle Semantik *f* • general semantics
(*Korzybski*) (*lan, cul*)

generisch • generic (*nat, lan*)

Genese *f* • genesis, emergence (*gep*)

Genesis *f* → Genese

Genetik *f* • genetics (*nat*) → Vererbungslehre

genetisch-kulturelle Koevolution *f* • gene-
culture co-evolution (*nat, ant*)

genetisch übertragene Krankheit *f* • gene-
tically transmitted disease (*nat*)

genetische Abweichung *f* • genetic variance/
variation (*nat*) < Mutation

genetische Beratung *f* • genetic counselling
(*nat, eth*)

genetische Epistemologie *f* → genetische
Erkenntnistheorie

genetische Erkenntnistheorie *f* • genetic
epistemology (*Piaget etc*) (*epi*) < W 222

genetische Erklärung *f* • genetic explanation
(*sci*)

genetische Forschung *f* → Genforschung

genetische Information *f* • genetic information
(*nat*)

genetische Manipulation *f* • genetic manipulation (*nat, eth*) → Genmanipulation

genetische Methode *f* • genetic method
(*Fichte etc*) (*sci*)

genetische Mutation *f* • gene/genetic mutation
(*nat*)

genetische Selektion *f* • genetic selection (*nat*)

genetische Überprüfung *f* • genetic screening
(*nat, eth*) → Gentest < Gentechnologie

genetischer Code *m* • genetic code (*nat*)

genetischer Determinismus *m* • genetic
determinism (*nat, met*)

genetischer Fehlschluß *m* • genetic fallacy
(*log*)

genetisches Prinzip des Lukrez *n* • genetic
principle of Lucretius (*sci*) < Kosmologie

Genforschung *f* • genetic research (*nat, eth*)

Genie *n* • genius (*aes, gep*)

genitaler Charakter *m* • genital character
(*Freud etc*) (*psy*)

Genitalerotik *f* • genital eroticism (*Freud etc*)
(*psy*)

Genius *m* → Genie

genius malignus *m* • *nt* (*met*) → böser Dämon

Genmanipulation *f* • gene(tic) manipulation
(*nat, eth*)

Genmaterial *n* • genetic material (*nat*)

Genmaximierung *f* • gene maximization (*nat*)

Genmutation *f* • gene mutation (*nat*)

Genossenschaft *f* • association, cooperative
(*eco, soc*) → Kooperative

Genossenschaftsbewegung *f* • cooperative
movement (*pol*) < Produzentenvereinigung

Genotyp *m* • genotype (*nat*) ↔ Phänotyp

genotypisch • genotypic(al) (*nat*)

Genozid *m* • genocide (*pol, eth*) < ethnische
Säuberung, Ethnozid

Genre *n* • genre (*aes*) → Kunstgattung

Gentechnik *f* • genetic engineering (*nat, eth,
tec*)

Gentechnologie *f* → Gentechnik

Gentest *m* • genetic screening (*nat, eth*)

Gentherapie *f* • gene therapy (*nat, eth*)

Gentzenscher Hauptsatz *m* • Gentzen's
Hauptsatz, Gentzen's principal theorem
(*log*)

Genus *n* → Geschlecht

genus proximum *n* • *nt*, proximate genus,
nearest kind (*log*) < differentia specifica

Genuß *m* • enjoyment, pleasure (*psy, aes*)
< Lustprinzip

Genuß, ästhetischer *m* • aesthetic enjoyment/
pleasure (*aes*) < ästhetisches Wohlgefallen

Genußprinzip *n* • pleasure principle (*eth*)
< hedonistischer Kalkül, hedonistisches
Prinzip

geoffenbarte Religion *f* • revealed religion
(*rel*)

geoffenbarte Wahrheit *f* • revealed truth (*rel*)

Geometrie, affine *f* • affine geometry (*mat*)

Geometrie, analytische *f* • analytic(al)
geometry (*mat*)

Geometrie, euklidische *f* • Euclidean geometry (*mat*) ↔ Geometrie, nichteuklidische

Geometrie, hyperbolische *f* • hyperbolic geometry (*mat*)

Geometrie, nichteuklidische *f* • non-Euclidean
geometry (*mat*) ↔ Geometrie, euklidische

geometrische Beweisführung *f* • geometrical
proof (*mat*)

geometrische Existenz *f* • geometrical existence (*Husserl*) (*ont, log*)

geometrische Methode *f* • geometrical
method (*Descartes, Spinoza etc*) (*epi, eth*)
→ mos gemometricus < Cartesianische
Methode, mathematische Methode < W 295

geometrische Progression *f* • geometrical
progression (*mat, sys*) ↔ arithmetische
Progression

geometrische Reihe *f* • geometric series (*mat*)

geometrischer Körper *m* • geometric object/
body/solid (*mat*)

geometrischer Ort *m* • geometric locus (*mat*)

geometrisches Mittel *n* • geometric mean/
average (*mat*)

geometrisches Verhältnis *n* • geometric(al) ratio *(Malthus etc) (soc)*

Geometrismus in der Kunst *m* • geometrism in art *(aes)*

geordnete Menge *f* • ordered set *(log, mat)*

geordneter Zustand *m* • ordered state *(sys)*

Geowissenschaft *f* • earth science *(nat)*

geozentrisches Weltbild *n* • geocentric conception of the universe *(nat, met)*

Geozentrismus *m* • geocentrism *(nat, met)* ↔ Heliozentrismus < Ptolemäisches System

Geozid *m* • geocide° *(env, eth)* < Ethnozid

gerechte Gesellschaft *f* • just society *(eth)*

gerechte Sache *f* • just cause *(eth)*

gerechte Weltordnung *f* • just world order *(eth, pol)*

gerechten Krieges, Theorie des *f* • theory of just war, just war theory *(eth, pol)*

gerechter Krieg *m* • just war *(eth, pol)* → bellum iustum

gerechter Lohn *m* • fair wage(s) *(eth, eco)*

gerechter Spargrundsatz *m* • just savings principle *(Rawls) (eth, pol)*

Gerechtigkeit *f* • justice, equity, fairness *(eth, jur)*

Gerechtigkeit als Fairneß *f* • justice as fairness *(Rawls) (eth)*

Gerechtigkeit als oberste Tugend *f* • justice as supreme virtue *(eth)*

Gerechtigkeit, allokative *f* • allocative justice *(Rawls) (eth)*

Gerechtigkeit, ausgleichende *f* • rectificatory/rectifactory/corrective/commutative justice *(eth, jur)*, compensatory/poetic justice *(eth, aes)* ↔ distributive Gerechtigkeit < Vergeltungsgerechtigkeit

Gerechtigkeit, distributive *f* • distributive justice *(eth)* → Verteilungsgerechtigkeit

Gerechtigkeit, kommutative *f* • commutative justice *(Aristotle) (eth)* < Tauschgerechtigkeit

Gerechtigkeit, korrektive *f* • corrective justice *(Aristotle) (eth)*

Gerechtigkeit zwischen Generationen *f* • justice between generations *(eth)* → intergenerationelle Gerechtigkeit

Gerechtigkeitsempfinden *n* • feeling for/perception of justice *(jur, eth)* < Rechtsempfinden

Gerechtigkeitsgrundsatz *m* • principle of justice *(eth)*

Gerechtigkeitsideal, abstraktes *n* • abstract ideal of justice *(eth)*

Gerechtigkeitsprinzip *n* • principle of justice *(eth)*

Gerechtigkeitssinn *m* • sense of justice *(eth)*

Gerechtigkeitstheorie *f* • theory of justice *(eth)*

Gerechtigkeitsvorschriften *pl* • precepts of justice *(Rawls etc) (eth)*

Gerede *n* • gossip, idle talk *(Heidegger) (met)* < Geschwätz

Gerichtetheit der Zeichen *f* • directedness/directing of signs *(Heidegger) (ont)*

Gerichtetheit der Zeit *f* • directedness of time *(Brentano etc) (ont)*

Gerichtsbarkeit *f* • jurisdiction *(jur)* → Jurisdiktion, Judikatur, Rechtsprechung

Gerichtshof der Vernunft *m* • court of reason *(Kant) (epi)*

Germanistik *f* • German studies

Gerontokratie *f* • gerontocracy *(pol)*

Gerüst *n* • framework *(Heidegger) (ont)*

Gesamtempfindung *f* • consentience *(psy)*

gesamtes Dasein *n* • totality of existence *(Nietzsche etc) (met)*

Gesamtinteresse *n* • general interest *(soc)*

Gesamtkunstwerk *n* • *nt,* synthesis of the arts, total work of art *(Wagner etc) (aes)*

Gesamtwahrscheinlichkeit *f* → Totalwahrscheinlichkeit

gesatztes Recht *n* • statute/statutory law *(jur)* → geschriebenes Recht, positives Recht

Geschaffenheit *f* • (state-of-)being-created *(Heidegger) (ont)*

Geschehensursache *f* • cause of becoming *(met)* → causa fiendi

Geschichte *f* • history *(his)* < große Erzählung; story *(lan)*

Geschichte als Klassenkampf *f* • history as class struggle *(Marx etc) (his, soc)*

Geschichte als Offenbarung des Absoluten *f* • history as a revelation of the absolute *(Schelling etc) (his, met)*

Geschichte als Seinsgeschichte *f* • history as history of Being *(Heidegger) (his, ont)*

Geschichte der Neuzeit *f* • modern history *(his)*

Geschichte der Philosophie *f* • history of philosophy *(gep)*

Geschichte der reinen Vernunft *f* • history of pure reason *(Kant) (epi)*

Geschichte des Altertums *f* • ancient history *(his)*

Geschichte des Geistes *f* • history of the spirit *(Hegel etc) (met)*

Geschichte des Lebens *f* • history of life *(nat)* < Evolution

Geschichte des Seins *f* • history of Being *(Heidegger) (ont)* → Seinsgeschichte

Geschichte, Entwicklungsgesetze in der *pl* • laws of the development of history *(Vico etc) (his)*

Geschichte, evolutionäre Interpretation der *f* • evolutionary view of history *(his)*

Geschichte von unten *f* • history from below, grassroots history *(his)*

geschichtliche Bewegung *f* • historical movement *(his)*

geschichtliche Erklärung *f* • historical explanation *(his, sci)*

geschichtliche Gewißheit *f* • historical certainty *(his)*

geschichtliche Vorhersage *f* • historical predicton *(his, sci)*

geschichtliche Vorläufer *pl* • historical precursors *(his)*

geschichtlicher Hintergrund *m* • historical background *(his)*

geschichtliches Verstehen *n* • historical understanding *(Dilthey etc) (his, sci)*

Geschichtlichkeit *f* • historicality, historicity *(his)* → Historizität

Geschichtsauffassung *f* • conception of history *(his)*

Geschichtsbegriff, materialistischer *m* • materialist concept of history *(his)* < Historischer Materialismus

Geschichtsbewußtsein *n* • historical consciousness/awareness *(Marx etc) (his)*

Geschichtsbild *n* • view of history *(his)*

Geschichtsdeterminismus *m* • historical determinism *(his)*

Geschichtsdeutung *f* • interpretation of history *(his)*

Geschichtsfälschung *f* • falsification/distortion of history *(his, pol)*

Geschichtsfortschritt *m* • progress in history *(his)*

Geschichtslogik *f* • logic of history *(Spengler etc) (his)*

Geschichtsmetaphysik *f* • metaphysics of history *(his, met)*

Geschichtsoptimismus *m* • historical optimism, optimism in history *(his, psy)*

Geschichtspessimismus *m* • historical pessimism, pessimism in history *(his, psy)*

Geschichtsphilosophie *f* • philosophy of history *(his)*

Geschichtsprozeß *m* • historical process *(his)*

Geschichtsschreibung *f* • historiography, history *(his)* → Historiographie

Geschichtstheorie *f* • theory of history *(sci)*

Geschichtswissenschaft *f* • science of history, historical science *(his, sci)*

Geschichtszeichen *n* • historical symbol *(Kant, Schlegel) (his)*

Geschick *n* • sending, destiny *(Heidegger etc) (met)*

Geschlecht *n* • sex *(nat)*, gender *(fem, lan)* < Geschlechtsidentität, Sex-Gender-Unterscheidung

Geschlechterbeziehung *f* • gender relationship *(fem)*

Geschlechterdifferenz *f* → Geschlechtsdifferenz

Geschlechterdimorphie *f* • sexual dimorphism *(nat, fem)*

Geschlechterforschung *f* • gender studies *(fem)* < Frauenforschung

geschlechtergetrennte Erziehung *f* • single-sex-education *(psy, fem)* ↔ Koedukation

Geschlechterhierarchie *f* • hierarchy of the sexes *(fem)*

Geschlechterkampf *m* • struggle between the sexes, gender-struggle *(soc, fem)*

Geschlechtermoral *f* • gender morality *(Gilligan) (eth, fem)*

Geschlechterproporz *m* • proportional representation of the sexes *(pol, eth, fem)* < Quotenregelung

Geschlechterrolle *f* • gender/sex role *(fem, soc, nat)*

Geschlechtertrennung *f* • gender segregation *(fem)*

geschlechtliche Auslese *f* • sexual selection *(Darwin) (nat, ant)*

Geschlechtscharakter *m* • gender-specific characteristic *(fem)*

Geschlechtsdifferenz *f* • gender/sexual difference, difference between the sexes *(fem, nat)* < sexuelle Differenz

Geschlechtsfeminismus *m* • gender/difference feminism *(fem)* → Andersartigkeitsfeminismus, Differenzfeminismus < Opferfeminismus

Geschlechtsidentität *f* • sexual/gender identity *(nat, fem)*

Geschlechtsmoral *f* • sexual morality *(eth)*

geschlechtsneutral • gender-neutral, gender-free *(fem)*

Geschlechtsneutralität *f* • gender neutrality *(fem)*

Geschlechtsnormen *pl* • gender norms *(fem)*

Geschlechtsrollen *pl* • gender roles *(fem)*

geschlechtsspezifisch • gender/sex specific, gender-coded *(fem)*

geschlechtsspezifische Ausrichtung *f* • gender orientation/bias *(fem)*

geschlechtsspezifisches Verhalten *n* • gender/sex -specific behaviour *(fem, nat, eth)*

Geschlechtsstereotypen *pl* • gender stereotypes *(fem)*

Geschlechtssystem *n* • gender system, sexual caste system *(fem)*

Geschlechtstrieb *m* • sex drive, sexual urge *(nat, psy)*

Geschlechtstypisierung *f* • gender typology, sexual stereotyping *(fem)*

Geschlechtsunterschied *m* • sex difference *(nat)* < Geschlechtsdifferenz

geschlossene Gesellschaft *f* • closed society *(Bergson, Popper etc) (soc)*

geschlossene Gestalt *f* • closed gestalt, compact structure *(aes, epi)* < Gestaltpsychologie

geschlossene Welt *f* • closed world *(met)* < W 1242

geschlossener Handelsstaat *m* • closed commercial state *(Fichte) (soc, eco)* < W 372

geschlossenes System *n* • closed system *(sys)* ↔ offenes System

Geschmack *m* • taste *(aes)*

Geschmack, ästhetischer *m* • aesthetic taste *(aes)*

Geschmack, guter und schlechter *m* • good and bad taste *(aes)*

Geschmacksempfindung *f* • taste-sensation *(epi, psy)*

Geschmacksfrage *f* • question/matter of taste *(aes, gep)*

Geschmackssinn *m* • sense of taste *(aes, psy)*

Geschmackstheorie *f* • theory of taste *(aes)*

Geschmacksurteil *n* • judg(e)ment of taste *(Kant etc) (epi, aes)*

geschriebenes Recht *n* • written law *(jur)* → gesatztes Recht

Geschwätz *n* • chatter *(Kierkegaard etc) (met)* < Gerede

gesellige Natur *f* • social nature, natural sense of community *(Aristotle, Rousseau, Herder etc) (soc)* < animal sociale, zoon politicon

geselliges Tier *n* • social animal *(ant, soc)* → animal sociale, zoon politicon

Geselligkeit *f* • sociability, sociality *(soc, psy)*

Geselligkeitstrieb *m* • gregarious instinct *(soc, psy)* < Herdeninstinkt

Gesellschaft *f* • society, (▷ Assoziation) association *(soc)* ↔ Gemeinschaft < W 356

Gesellschaft, bürgerliche *f* • civil society *(Hegel etc)* bourgeois society *(Marx etc) (pol, soc)* < Zivilgesellschaft < W 1171

Gesellschaft, fragmentierte *f* • fragmented society *(soc)* < atomisierte Gesellschaft

Gesellschaft, geschlossene *f* • closed society *(Bergson, Popper etc) (soc)*

Gesellschaft, offene *f* • open society *(Bergson, Popper etc) (soc)* < W 719

gesellschaftlich • social, societal *(soc)*

gesellschaftliche Aneignung *f* • appropriation by society *(Marx etc) (soc)*

gesellschaftliche Arbeit *f* • social labour *(eco, soc)*

gesellschaftliche Bedürfnisse *pl* • social needs, needs of society *(soc)*

gesellschaftliche Grundgüter *pl* • primary social goods *(soc, eco)*

gesellschaftliche Produktion *f* • production by society *(soc, eco)*

gesellschaftliche Rationalisierung *f* • societal rationalization *(Weber, Adorno etc) (soc)*

gesellschaftliche Stände *pl* • estates of society *(soc, pol)* < Ständegesellschaft

gesellschaftliche Synthesis *f* • social synthesis *(soc)*

gesellschaftliche Ursache *f* • social cause/determinant *(soc)*

gesellschaftliche Verhältnisse *pl* • social conditions *(Marx etc) (soc)*

gesellschaftliche Wünschbarkeit *f* • social desirability *(soc)*

gesellschaftlicher Mensch *m* • social man *(Marx) (soc)* < gesellschaftliches Wesen

gesellschaftlicher Nutzen *m* • social benefit *(soc)*

gesellschaftlicher Reichtum *m* • social wealth *(Marx) (eco, soc)*

gesellschaftlicher Status *m* • social status, position in society *(soc, pol)*

gesellschaftlicher Überbau *m* • social superstructure *(Marx etc) (soc)*

gesellschaftlicher Wert *m* • social/societal value *(soc)*

gesellschaftlicher Zerfall *m* • social decay/dissociation *(soc, pol)* < Anomie, Anarchie

gesellschaftlicher Zusammenhalt *m* • civil unity, social cohesion, (▷ Bindung) social bond/tie *(soc, pol)* < gesellschaftliche Synthesis

gesellschaftlicher Zusammenhang *m* • social context *(soc)*

gesellschaftliches Bewußtsein *n* • social consciousness *(Marx etc) (epi, soc)*

gesellschaftliches Gesetz *n* • law of society, social law *(soc)*

gesellschaftliches Gleichgewicht *n* • social equilibrium *(soc, pol)*

gesellschaftliches Individuum *n* • social individual *(Marx) (soc)*

gesellschaftliches Sein *n* • (▷ Dasein) social existence, (▷ Seiendes) social being *(Marx etc) (soc)* < Sein und Bewußtsein

gesellschaftliches Wesen *n* • social being
(*Marx etc*) (*soc*)

gesellschaftliches Ziel *n* • social goal (*soc, pol*)

Gesellschaftsanalyse *f* • social analysis,
analysis of society (*soc, pol*)

Gesellschaftscharakter *m* • social character
(*Fromm*) (*soc, psy*)

Gesellschaftsgeschichte *f* • history of society
(*his, soc*)

Gesellschaftshandeln *n* • social action, associative behaviour (*Weber*) (*soc, act*) < Einverständnishandeln, Anstaltshandeln,
Verbandshandeln

Gesellschaftskrise *f* • social crisis, crisis of
society (*soc*)

Gesellschaftskritik *f* • social criticism (*soc*)

Gesellschaftsleben *n* • social life (*Marx etc*)
(*soc*)

Gesellschaftslehre *f* → Soziologie

Gesellschaftsmodell *n* • model/idea/concept of
society (*soc, pol*)

Gesellschaftsordnung *f* • social order/system
(*soc, pol*)

Gesellschaftsphilosophie *f* → Sozialphilosophie

Gesellschaftspolitik *f* • social policy (*pol*)

Gesellschaftsstruktur *f* • social structure (*soc,
pol*)

Gesellschaftstheorie *f* • social theory, theory
of society (*soc, pol*)

gesellschaftsverändernd • causing social
change (*soc*)

Gesellschaftsveränderung *f* • social change
(*soc*)

Gesellschaftsvertrag *m* • social contract
(*Hobbes etc*) (*soc, pol*) → Sozialkontrakt
< W 1204

Gesellschaftswissenschaft *f* • sociology, social
science, science of society (*soc*) → Soziologie

Gesetz *n* • law (*nat, jur*), principle (*log*)

Gesetz, allgemeines *n* • universal/general law
(*nat, sci*), common law (*jur*) → Gewohnheitsrecht

Gesetz der ausgeschlossenen Mitte *n* → Gesetz vom ausgeschlossenen Dritten

Gesetz der Geschichte *n* • law of history (*his*)

Gesetz der großen Zahl *n* • law/principle of
large numbers (*mat*)

Gesetz der großen Zahl, starkes *n* • strong
law/principle of large numbers (*mat*)

Gesetz der Identität *n* • law/principle of
identity (*log*)

Gesetz der Kontinuität aller Veränderung *n*
• law of the continuity of all alteration (*Kant*)
(*met*)

Gesetz der Mehrheit *n* • majority rule, rule of
the majority (*pol*)

Gesetz der Natur *n* • law of nature (*nat*)

Gesetz der Negation der Negation *n* • law/
principle of the negation of the negation
(*Hegel, Marx etc*) (*log, met*)

Gesetz der Serie *n* • law of succession (*Leibniz etc*) (*mat, log*)

Gesetz der Spezifikation der Natur *n* • law of
specification of nature (*Kant*) (*met, nat*)

**Gesetz der synthetischen Einheit aller Er-
scheinungen** *n* • law of the synthetic unity of
all appearances (*Kant*) (*epi*)

Gesetz der Vereinigung der Gegensätze *n* •
law of unification of opposites (*Hegel*) (*met*)

Gesetz der Vernunft *n* • law of reason (*Kant*)
(*epi, eth, met*)

Gesetz der Widerspruchsfreiheit *n* • law/
principle of (non-)contradiction (*log*) →
Gesetz vom Widerspruch

Gesetz des Dschungels *n* • law of the jungle
(*soc, pol, eth*)

Gesetz des Effekts *n* → Effektgesetz

Gesetz des geringstmöglichen Aufwandes *n* •
law/principle of least effort (*psy, sys*)

Gesetz des kategorialen Urteils *n* • law of
categorical judg(e)ment (*Thurstone*) (*log,
sci*)

Gesetz des Tages *n* • law of the day (*Jaspers*)
(*met*)

Gesetz des vergleichenden Urteils *n* • law of
comparative judg(e)ment (*Thurstone*) (*log,
sci*)

Gesetz, gefaßtes *n* → Gesetz, geschriebenes

Gesetz, geschriebenes *n* • written law (*jur*)
< positives Recht

Gesetz, göttliches *n* • divine law (*rel*) < göttliches Recht

Gesetz, indeterministisches *n* • indeterministic
law (*sci*)

Gesetz, irdisches *n* • worldly/secular law (*jur*)

Gesetz, moralisches *n* • moral law (*Kant*)
(*eth*)

Gesetz, positives *n* • positive law (*jur*) → gesatztes Recht

Gesetz, reversibles *n* • reversible law (*sci*)

Gesetz, ungeschriebenes *n* • unwritten law
(*jur*) < Gewohnheitsrecht, Naturrecht

Gesetz vom abnehmenden Grenznutzen *n* •
law of diminishing marginal utility, law of
diminishing returns (*eco*)

Gesetz vom ausgeschlossenen Dritten *n* •
law/principle of (the) excluded middle (*log*)
→ Gesetz der ausgeschlossenen Mitte

Gesetz vom Widerspruch *n* • law of contradiction *(log)* → Gesetz der Widerspruchsfreiheit

Gesetz, wissenschaftliches *n* • scientific law *(sci)*

Gesetzbuch *n* • code, statute book *(jur)* → corpus juris

Gesetzbuch der Natur *n* • code of nature *(nat, met)*

Gesetze der Mechanik *pl* • laws/principles of mechanics *(Newton etc) (nat)*

Gesetze des Denkens *pl* → Denkgesetze

Gesetze, kategoriale *pl* • categorical laws *(N. Hartmann) (epi)*

Gesetzes, Abschreckungstheorie des *f* • deterrence theory of law *(jur)*

Gesetzes, Unparteilichkeit des *f* • impartiality of (the) law *(jur, eth)*

gesetzesartiger Satz *m* • lawlike sentence *(Carnap, Goodman, Hempel etc) (sci)*

Gesetzesartigkeit *f* • lawlikeness° *(sci)*

Gesetzesherrschaft *f* • rule of law *(jur, pol)*

gesetzeskonform • law-conforming, in accordance with the law *(jur)*

Gesetzeskraft *f* • legal force *(jur)*

Gesetzeslücke *f* • gap in the law *(jur)*

Gesetzesregel *f* • rule of law, legal rule *(jur)*

Gesetzesrelevanz *f* • nomic relevance *(nat, sci)*

Gesetzessammlung *f* → Gesetzbuch

gesetzgebende Autorität *f* • legislative authority *(jur, pol)*

gesetzgebende Gewalt *f* • legislative power *(jur, pol)*

gesetzgebende Vernunft *f* • lawgiving/legislative reason *(Kant etc) (eth, met)*

gesetzgebender Körper *m* • legislative body *(Rousseau etc) (jur, pol)*

Gesetzgeber *m* • legislator, lawgiver *(jur, pol)*

Gesetzgeber der menschlichen Vernunft *m* • lawgiver/legislator of human reason *(Kant) (epi)*

Gesetzgeber der Natur *m* • lawgiver of nature *(Kant) (epi, met)*

Gesetzgebung *f* • legislation *(jur)* → Legislatur

Gesetzgebung des Willens *f* • lawgiving/legislation of the will *(Kant) (epi, eth)*

gesetzlicher Zwang *m* • legal coercion *(jur)*

Gesetzlosigkeit *f* • lawlessness, anarchy *(jur, pol)* → Anarchie < Anomie, Rechtlosigkeit

Gesetzmäßigkeit *f* • (▷ Regelmäßigkeit) regularity *(gep)* → Regularität; (▷ Legalität) conformity/regularity to law, lawfulness, legality, legitimacy, legitimateness *(jur)*

Gesetzmäßigkeiten der mittleren Reichweite *pl* • middle range laws *(sci)*

gesetzt • posited *(Hegel, Fichte etc) (met)*

gesetztes Recht *n* • statute/statutory law *(jur)* → gesatztes Recht; Gesetz, positives

Gesetztsein *n* • positedness *(Fichte, Hegel, etc) (met)*

Gesetzwidrigkeit *f* → Illegalität

Gesichtlesen *n* • face reading *(eso)*

Gesichtsfeld *n* • field of vision, visual field *(psy, nat)*

Gesichtskreis *m* • field of vision, horizon *(gen)* < Horizont, geistiger

Gesichtspunkt *m* • point of view, viewpoint, angle, aspect *(gep)*

Gesinnung *f* • (▷ Mentalität) mentality, mind, (▷ Haltung) attitude, disposition, (▷ Meinung) opinion, convictions *(gep)*

Gesinnungsethik *f* • ethics of conviction/attitude *(Kant, Weber etc) (eth)* → Intentionalismus ↔ Verantwortungsethik

Gesinnungspazifismus *m* • pacifism of intention *(Scheler) (eth)*

Gesinnungsreligiosität *f* • religiosity of conviction *(Weber) (eth, rel)*

Gesollte, das *n* • the ought *(Kant etc) (eth)*

Gesolltheit *f* • oughtness *(eth)*

Gespenst in der Maschine *n* • ghost in the machine *(Ryle etc) (min)*

Gespensterglaube *m* • belief in ghosts *(met, eso)*

Gesprächstherapie *f* • talking therapy *(psy)*

gesprochene Sprache *f* • spoken language *(lan)*

Gestalt *f* • gestalt, configuration *(epi, psy)*, form *(Aristotle) (ont)* → morphé < Gebilde, Komplex

Gestalt, geschlossene *f* • closed gestalt, compact structure *(aes, epi)* < Gestaltpsychologie

Gestalt, offene *f* • open gestalt/structure *(aes, epi)*

Gestaltfigur *f* • gestalt figure *(psy, aes, epi)*

Gestaltgesetze *pl* • gestalt laws *(psy)*

Gestaltlehre *f* • morphology *(psy, aes)* → Morphologie

Gestaltlosigkeit *f* • amorphism, formlessness *(nat, aes)* → Amorphismus

Gestaltpsychologie *f* • gestalt psychology *(psy, epi)* < Gestalttheorie

Gestaltqualität *f* • gestalt quality *(psy, epi)*, form quality *(aes)*

Gestalttheoretiker *m* • Gestalt-theorist, Gestaltist° *(psy)*

Gestalttheorie f • gestalt theory, gestaltism, configurationism° (Ehrenfels) (epi, psy, aes)

Gestalttherapie f • gestalt therapy (Perls) (psy)

Gestaltung, künstlerische f • artistic design (aes) < Design

Gestaltungskraft f • creative power (aes)

Gestaltungsprinzip n • formative principle, formal principle (aes)

Gestaltungsprozeß m • creative process (aes)

Gestaltverschiedenheit f → Heteromorphie

Gestaltwahrnehmung f • gestalt perception (psy, aes, epi)

Gestaltwandel m • gestalt-switch (psy, aes)

Gestalt-Werden einer Idee n • incarnation of an idea (Hegel) (met)

Gestell n • enframing, gestell, framing (Heidegger) (ont)

gestenvermittelte Interaktion f • gesture-mediated interaction (Mead) (lan)

Gestimmtheit f • attunement, mood (Heidegger) (ont) < Gemütsstimmung, Stimmung, Existential

gesunder Menschenverstand m • common sense (gep) → gemeiner Menschenverstand, Alltagsverstand

Gesundheitsvorsorge f • preventive healthcare (nat) < Vorsorgemedizin

geteilter Bezug m • divided reference (Quine etc) (lan, ont)

Gethmansches Gesetz n • Gethman's rule/law (log)

getrennte Substanzen pl • separate substances (Aquinas) (met)

Gettierproblem n • Gettierproblem (epi)

Geviert n • fourfold (Heidegger) (ont)

Gewalt f • power, force, authority, violence (pol, psy)

Gewalt bezwingt das Recht f • might is right (jur, eth, pol)

Gewaltenteilung f • separation of powers (pol) < Machtbeschränkung, Beschränkung der Regierungsgewalt

Gewaltentrennung f → Gewaltenteilung

Gewaltfreiheit f → Gewaltlosigkeit

Gewaltherrschaft f • despotism, tyranny (pol) → Willkürherrschaft, Despotie

gewaltlose Revolution f • peaceful revolution (soc, pol)

gewaltloser Widerstand m • non-violent resistance (pol, eth) < ziviler Ungehorsam; Widerstand, passiver; Widerstandsrecht; ziviler Ungehorsam

Gewaltlosigkeit f • non-violence (psy, pol, eth)

Gewaltmonopol n • monopoly of power, power monopoly (pol)

gewaltsamer Umsturz m • (▷ gesellschaftlicher Umsturz) violent revolution, (▷ Umsturz einer Regierung) forceable/forcible overthrow, putsch (pol)

Gewässerschutz m • prevention of water pollution (env)

Gewerkschaftsbewegung f • trade unionism, union movement (eco, pol)

Gewesenheit f • character of having-been, been-ness (Heidegger) (ont)

gewichtetes Mittel n • weighted mean (mat)

Gewinn m • profit, gain, return (eco, dec)

Gewinn- und Verlustrechnung f • cost-benefit analysis (eco, dec)

Gewinnbeteiligung f • profit-sharing (eco)

Gewinnchance f • chance of winning (eco, dec)

Gewinnfunktion eines Spiels f • gain/profit function of a game (dec)

Gewinnmaximierung f • maximization of profits/return(s) (eco, dec) < Profitmaximierung

Gewinnstrategie f • winning strategy (dec)

Gewinnstreben n • pursuit of profit (eco)

Gewissen n • conscience (eth)

Gewissen, gutes n • good conscience (eth, rel) → reines Gewissen

Gewissen, reines n • pure/clear conscience (eth, rel) → gutes Gewissen

Gewissen, schlechtes n • bad conscience (eth, rel)

Gewissenhaftigkeit f • conscientiousness, scrupulousness (eth)

gewissenlos • without conscience, unscrupulous, unprincipled (eth)

Gewissenlosigkeit f • unscrupulousness (eth)

Gewissensangst f • moral anxiety (eth), fear of conscience (Freud etc) (psy)

Gewissensautonomie f • autonomy of conscience (eth)

Gewissensbiß m • pang of conscience, sting of conpunction (eth)

Gewissensentscheidung f • decision on a matter of conscience (eth)

Gewissenserforschung f • examination of one's conscience (eth, rel)

Gewissensethik f • ethics of conscience (Aquinas, Weber) (eth)

Gewissensforderung f • demand/requirement of conscience (Freud etc) (psy)

Gewissensfrage f • moral question, question of conscience (eth)

Gewissensfreiheit f • freedom of conscience *(eth)* < Glaubensfreiheit

Gewissensinhalt m • content of conscience *(eth)*

Gewissensprüfung f • examination/test of conscience, self-examination *(eth)*

Gewissensqual f • torment of conscience *(Kierkegaard etc) (eth)*

Gewissensvivisektion f • conscience-vivisection *(Nietzsche) (eth)*

gewisses Wissen n • certain knowledge *(Descartes etc) (epi)* < Cartesianischer Zweifel

Gewißheit f • certainty *(epi)* < sicheres Wissen, Unbezweifelbarkeit, unbezeifelbare Gewißheit < W 1109

Gewißheit der eigenen Existenz f • certainty of one's own existence *(Descartes etc) (epi, met)* < Ichgewißheit

Gewißheit des Wissens f • certainty/certitude of knowledge *(epi)*

Gewißheit, erste f • first truth *(Aristotle etc) (met)*

Gewißheit, sinnliche f • sensual/sensory certainty, sense-certainty *(Hegel etc) (epi)*

Gewißheitsbedingung f • certainty condition, condition of certainty *(epi)*

Gewißheitspostulat n • certainty postulate *(epi)*

Gewohnheit f • habit, habitude *(psy)*

Gewohnheit als Ursprung des Begriffs der Kausalität f • habit as source of the idea of cause *(Hume) (epi)*

gewohnheitsmäßiges Denken n • habitual thought/way of thinking *(gep)*

Gewohnheitsrecht n • customary/common law *(jur)*

Gewöhnung f • habituation *(psy)*

geworfener Entwurf m • thrown projection *(Heidegger) (ont)*

Geworfenheit f • thrownness *(Heidegger) (ant, ont)*

Geziemende, das n • decorum *(Plato, Aristotle etc) (eth, aes)*

Giga-Prinzip n • giga principle *(AI)*

Gildensozialismus m • guild socialism *(soc, pol)*

Glanz m • splendour *(Plotin etc) (met, rel)* < Lichtmetaphysik

Glasnost f • glasnost *(pol)* < Perestroika, vollständige Öffentlichkeit

Glaube(n) m • faith *(rel)*, belief *(epi)* → Doxa

Glaube(n) und Vernunft m,f • faith and reason *(rel)*

Glauben und Wissen m,n • belief and knowledge *(epi)*, faith and knowledge *(rel)*

Glauben, Sprung in den m • leap into faith *(Kierkegaard) (rel)* < Glaubenssprung

Glaubens mit der Vernunft, Übereinstimmung des f • harmony of faith with reason *(rel, met)*

Glaubensartikel m • article of faith *(rel)*

Glaubensaussage f • creed, cre(e)dal statement, affirmation of faith, expression of belief *(rel)*, belief sentence *(lan)*

Glaubensbekenntnis n • credo, creed *(rel)*

Glaubenseinstellung f • (▷ erkenntnistheoretische Grundhaltung) epistemic attitude *(epi)* < Grundhaltung

Glaubensethik f • ethics of belief *(eth)*

Glaubensfreiheit f • religious freedom/liberty *(pol, rel)* < Gewissensfreiheit

Glaubensfunktion f • credence function *(Carnap etc) (log)*

Glaubensgemeinschaft f • religious community, community of fellow believers *(rel)*

Glaubensgewißheit f • certainty of faith *(rel)*

Glaubensgewißheiten pl • (▷ Glaubenstatsachen) facts of faith *(rel)*

Glaubensgrade pl • degrees of belief *(epi)*

Glaubensphilosophie f • philosophy of belief, faith philosophy *(rel)*

Glaubensregel f • rule of faith *(rel)*

Glaubenssache f • matter of faith *(epi, met)*

Glaubenssatz m → Glaubensaussage

Glaubenssprung m • leap of faith *(Kierkegaard) (rel)* → Glauben, Sprung in den

Glaubenssystem n • belief system *(rel, soc)*

Glaubhaftigkeit f • credibility *(Carnap) (sci)*

Glaubhaftigkeitsfunktion f • credibility function *(Carnap etc) (log)*

Glaubwürdigkeit f • credibility *(eth, epi, sci)*, likelihood *(log)* → Plausibilität

Glaubwürdigkeit, wissenschaftliche f • scientific credibility *(sci)*

gleichartige Analyse von Ursachen f → Regularitätsanalyse des Ursachenbegriffs

gleichbedeutend • synonymous *(lan)* → äquipollent

Gleichbehandlung f • equal treatment *(jur, eth)* < Chancengleichheit

Gleichberechtigung f • equal rights, equality (of rights) *(jur)* → Isonomie < Gleichheit vor dem Gesetz

gleicher Arbeitszwang für alle m • equal obligation/requirement for all to work *(Marx etc) (eco)*

Gleichförmigkeit der Natur f • uniformity of nature *(nat, met, sci)* → Gleichmäßigkeit der Natur

Gleichgeartetheit f • sameness *(Aristotle etc)* *(met)*

Gleichgestaltigkeit f → Monomorphie

Gleichgewicht n • balance *(gep)*

Gleichgewicht der Kräfte n • balance of power/forces *(pol)*

Gleichgewicht der Natur n • balance of nature *(met)*

Gleichgewicht des Schreckens n • balance of terror *(pol, eth)* < Abschreckungstheorie, atomare Abschreckung, Kalter Krieg, Terror-Frieden

Gleichgewicht, dynamisches n • dynamic equilibrium *(nat, eco, sys)*

Gleichgewicht, statisches n • static equilibrium *(nat, eco, sys)*

Gleichgewichtsmodell n • equilibrium model *(sys)*

Gleichgewichtspreis m • equilibrium price *(eco)*

Gleichgewichtspunkt m • equilibrium point, centre of gravity *(nat, log)*

Gleichgewichtsstrukturen pl • homeostatic structures *(sys)* < dissipative Strukturen

Gleichgewichtstheorie f • equilibrium/balance theory *(sys, eco)*

Gleichgewichtszustand m • steady state, equilibrium, homeostasis *(sys)* → Homöostase

Gleichgültigkeit f • indifference *(psy, eth)* → Indifferenz

Gleichheit f • identity *(log)*, equality *(jur, soc, pol)* → Egalität; sameness *(fem)* ↔ Andersheit

Gleichheit der Rechte f → Rechtsgleichheit

Gleichheit des Einkommens f → Einkommensgleichheit

Gleichheit vor dem Gesetz f • equality before the law *(jur, eth)* < Gleichberechtigung, Rechtsgleichheit

Gleichheit zwischen den Geschlechtern f • equality between the sexes, sexual equality *(jur, eth, fem)*

Gleichheitsfeminismus m • equity/equality feminism *(fem)* ↔ Differenzfeminismus

Gleichheitsgebot n • equality postulate *(eth, jur)* < Diskriminierungsverbot

Gleichheitsgrundsatz m → Gleichheitsprinzip

Gleichheitsprinzip n • principle of equality *(eth, jur)*

Gleichheitsregel f • rule of identity *(log)*, rule of equality *(eth)*

Gleichheitssymbol n • symbol of equality *(eth, pol)*, equality symbol, identity sign *(log)* < ist gleich

Gleichheitszustand m • state of equality *(soc, jur)* < Naturzustand

gleichlautende Ausdrücke pl • homophones *(lan)*

Gleichmacherei f • egalitarianism, levelling *(soc)*

Gleichmächtigkeit f • equipollence, equipollency, equivalence *(log, mat)* → Äquipollenz

Gleichmächtigkeit von Mengen f • equipollence/equinumerosity of sets, equal cardinality of sets, equivalence of sets *(log, mat)*

Gleichmäßigkeit der Natur f • uniformity of nature *(nat, met, sci)* → Gleichförmigkeit der Natur

Gleichmut m • equanimity *(eth)* → Ataraxie, Gelassenheit

Gleichnis n • simile, allegory, metaphor *(lan, aes)* → Parabel

gleichnishafte Bedeutung f • allegorical/parabolic meaning *(lan)*

Gleichrecht n • equal rights *(jur)*

Gleichschaltung f • forcing into line, co-ordination, gleichschaltung *(pol)*

gleichsetzen • to equate, to equalize *(gen)*

Gleichung f • equation *(log, mat)*

Gleichursprünglichkeit f • equiprimordiality *(met)*

Gleichverteilung f • equal distribution *(eco, soc)*, equal distribution, equidistribution, equiprobability *(mat)*

Gleichverteilungshypothese f • equiprobability hypothesis, assumption/hypothesis of equal/even distribution *(sci, mat, log)*

Gleichwertigkeit f • equivalence *(log)* → Äquivalenz

Gleichzeitigkeit f • simultaneity *(nat, gep)* → Simultaneität, Synchronizität ↔ Ungleichzeitigkeit

Gleichzeitigkeit der Eigenschaften f • parallelism of attributes *(Spinoza etc)* *(met)*

Gliederung, räumliche f • spatial structure/organization *(aes, epi, met)*

globale Erwärmung f • global warming *(env)* ≵ Treibhauseffekt

globale Gerechtigkeit f • global justice *(eth)*

globale Isotropie f • global isotropy *(sci)*

globale Vernunftkritik f • global critique of reason *(Horkheimer, Adorno)* *(met)* < Vernunftkritik

globales Dorf n • global village *(McLuhan)* *(soc)* < Globalisierung, Weltgemeinschaft

Globalisierung f • globalization *(soc)* < globales Dorf, Internationalisierung

Glockenkurve f • bell curve, normal/bell-shaped distribution *(mat)* < Gaußsche Verteilung

Glorifizierung f • glorification *(psy)*

Glück *n* • (▷ Freude) happiness *(psy)*, (▷ Zufall) luck *(psy, met)*

glückbringend • propitious, felicific *(eth)* < hedonistischer Kalkül

Glücksbefriedigung *f* • satisfaction of happiness *(Freud etc) (psy)*

glückseliges Leben *n* • beatific/happy/blissful life *(Augustine etc) (eth)*

Glückseligkeit *f* • happiness, bliss *(psy, eth)* → Eudämonie

Glückseligkeit, ewige *f* • eternal bliss *(rel)*

Glückseligkeitslehre *f* • doctrine of happiness, eudaemonism, eudaimonism *(Platon etc) (eth)* → Eudämonismus

Glückseligkeitsstreben *n* • striving for happiness *(eth)*

Glücksmöglichkeit *f* • possibility of happiness *(Freud etc) (psy)*

Glücksqualität *f* • quality of pleasure *(Bentham etc) (eth)*

Glücksquantität *f* • quantity of pleasure *(Bentham etc) (eth)*

Glücksrad *n* • wheel of fortune *(met)* < Umschwung des Glücks

Glücksstreben *n* • striving/search for happiness *(Freud etc) (psy)*

Glückstheorie *f* • theory of happiness *(eth, psy)*

Gnade *f* • grace *(rel)*

Gnoseologie *f* • gnoseology, gnosiology *(epi)*

Gnosis *f* • gnosis *(epi, rel)*

Gnostik *f* • gnosticism *(epi, rel)*

Gnostiker *m* • gnostic *(epi, rel)*

Gnostizismus *m* → Gnostik

Gödel-Nummer *f* • Gödel number *(Gödel) (log, lan)*

Gödelisierung *f* • Gödelization *(log, mat)*

Gödelscher Beweis *m* • Gödel's proof *(log)*

Gödelscher Satz *m* • Gödel's theorem *(log)*

Gödelscher Unvollständigkeitssatz *m* • Gödel's incompleteness theorem *(log)*

Gödelscher Vollständigkeitssatz *m* • Gödel's completeness theorem *(log)*

Goldbachsche Vermutung *f* • Goldbach's conjecture *(mat)*

Goldene Mitte *f* • golden mean *(Aristotle etc) (eth)* → Mesotes-Regel; Mittelweg, goldener

Goldene Regel *f* • golden rule *(Aristotle etc) (eth)*

Goldener Schnitt *m* • golden section/ratio *(aes, mat)* < Maßästhetik

goldenes Zeitalter *n* • Golden Age *(his)* < Utopie, rückwärtsgewandte

Goodmansche Paradoxie *f* • Goodman's paradox *(epi, log)* < Induktion, neues Problem der

gordischer Knoten *m* • Gordian Knot *(gep)*

Gossensches Gesetz *n* • Gossen's law, law of satiety *(eco)*

Gotik *f* • Gothic period *(aes, his)*

gotischer Stil *m* • Gothic style *(aes)*

Gott als absolutes Wesen *m* • God as absolute being *(rel, met)*

Gott als Betrüger *m* • God as deceiver *(Descartes etc) (epi)* < Traumargument

Gott als Einheit von Denken und Sein *m* • God as identity of thought and being *(Schleiermacher etc) (met, rel)*

Gott als erstes Prinzip *m* • God as first principle *(met, rel)*

Gott als Garant der Gewißheit *m* • God as guarantor of certainty *(Descartes) (epi)*

Gott als höchstes Gut *m* • God as supreme good *(met, rel)*

Gott als moralische Weltordnung *m* • God as moral world order *(Fichte) (met, rel)*

Gott als oberste Vernunft *m* • God as supreme reason *(Malebranche) (met, rel)*

Gott als Prinzip der Selbstentwicklung *m* • God as the principle of self-generation *(Böhme) (met, rel)*

Gott als Raumgeber aller Dinge *m* • God as space of all things *(Arnobius) (met, rel)*

Gott als Wahrheitsgarant *m* • God as guarantor of truth *(met, rel)*

Gott als Zentralmonade *m* • God as central monad *(Leibniz) (met, rel)*

Gott, anschauliches Wissen von *n* • intuitive/demonstrative knowledge of God *(met, rel)*

Gott der Philosophen *m* • (the) God of the philosophers, philosopher's God *(Spinoza) (met, rel)*

Gott in Menschengestalt *m* • God in human form *(rel)*

Gott ist tot • God is dead *(Nietzsche) (met)*

gottähnlich • godlike *(rel)*

Gottähnlichkeit *f* • likeness/similarity to God *(rel)*

Götterdämmerung *f* • twilight of the gods *(Wagner) (met)* < Götzendämmerung

Göttergemeinschaft *f* • community of gods *(rel)*

Götterlehre *f* → Theologie

Gottes Königreich *n* • kingdom of God *(rel)*

Gottes, kosmologisches Argument für die Existenz *n* • cosmological argument for the existence of God *(Al Farabi, Anselm etc) (met, rel)*

Gottes Transzendenz *f* • transcendence of God *(rel)*

Gottesbegriff *m* • idea/concept/conception of God *(rel)* < Gottesbild

Gottesbeweis *m* • proof of the existence of God, argument for the existence of God *(rel)*

Gottesbild *n* • image of God *(rel)* < Gottesbegriff

Gottesdienst *m* • (▷ Dienst an Gott) divine service, (▷ Liturgie) church service *(rel)* → Liturgie

Gottebenbildlichkeit *f* • God's image *(rel)* → Imago Dei

Gotteserfahrung *f* • experience of God *(rel)*

Gotteserkenntnis *f* • perception/knowledge of God *(epi, met, rel)*

Gotteserscheinung *f* • divine manifestation, theophany *(rel)* → Theophanie

Gottesferne *f* • remoteness/distantness/distance of God *(Bultmann) (rel)*

Gottesfinsternis *f* • eclipse of God *(Buber) (rel)* < W 386

Gottesfrage *f* • question of God, God question° *(rel)*

Gottesfügung *f* • act of God *(rel)*

Gottesfurcht *f* • fear of God, godliness, piety *(rel)*

Gottesgesichtspunkt *m* • God's eye view *(Putnam) (epi, met)* < sub specie aeternitatis

Gottesgnadentum *n* • doctrine of divine right *(pol)*

Gottesherrschaft *f* • theocracy, thearchy *(rel, pol)* → Theokratie

Gottesidee *f* • notion of God *(Aquinas etc) (rel)*

Gotteskomplex *m* • God complex *(Richter) (psy)*

Gotteslästerung *f* • blasphemy *(rel)* → Blasphemie

Gotteslehre *f* → Theologie

Gottesleugnung *f* • denial of God, atheism *(rel)* → Atheismus

Gottespartikel *n* • God particle *(Hawking) (nat)*

Gottesstaat *m* • city of God *(Augustine) (rel, pol)* → civitas Dei < W 1206

Gottesurteil *n* • divine judg(e)ment, trial by ordeal *(rel)*

Gotteszwang *m* • obligation imposed on God *(Weber) (rel, soc)*

gottgegeben • God-given, ordained by God *(rel)*

Gottheit *f* • godhead *(rel)*

Göttliche, das *n* • the divine, the godly *(rel)*

göttliche Attribute *pl* • divine attributes, attributes of God *(rel)*

Göttliche außerhalb des Erkennbaren und seinsmäßig Bestimmten, das *n* • Deity above knowledge and being *(rel)*

göttliche Gnade *f* • divine grace *(rel)*

göttliche Regierung *f* • divine government *(rel)*

göttliche Unveränderlichkeit *f* • divine immutability *(rel)*

göttliche Vorsehung *f* • divine providence *(rel)*

göttlicher Ursprung *m* • divine origin *(rel)*

göttlicher Wille *m* • divine will *(rel)*

göttliches Gebot *n* • divine commandment *(rel)*

göttliches Geschlecht *n* • god-like race *(Nietzsche) (ant)*

göttliches Gesetz *n* • divine law *(rel)*

göttliches Recht *n* • divine right *(rel)*

göttliches Recht der Könige *n* • divine right of kings *(jur, pol)*

göttliches Urteil *n* • divine judg(e)ment *(rel)* < Gottesurteil

göttliches Vorwissen *n* • divine foreknowledge *(rel)*

Gottlosigkeit *f* • godlessness, impiety, atheism *(rel)* → Atheismus

Gottmensch *m* • God-Man *(rel)*

Gottwerdung *f* • becoming God *(Scheler etc) (met)*

Götzenbild *n* • idol *(rel)*

Götzendämmerung *f* • twilight of the idols *(Nietzsche)* met < Götterdämmerung < W 389

Götzendienst *m* • idolatry *(rel)* → Idolatrie

Gradation *f* • gradation *(gen)*

Grade des Werdens *pl* • degrees of perfection *(Leibniz etc) (met)*

Gradientenmethode *f* • method of steepest descent, hill-climbing *(sci)*

Grammatik, generative *f* • generative grammar *(Chomsky) (lan)*

Grammatik, spekulative *f* • speculative grammar *(lan)*

Grammatik, universale *f* • universal grammar, UG *(lan)*

Grammatiktheorie *f* • grammar theory, theory of grammar *(lan)*

grammatische Rede *f* • grammatical speech *(Habermas) (lan)*

Grammatologie *f* • grammatology *(Derrida) (epi, lan)* < W 390

Graph *m* • graph *(lan, mat)*

Graphem *n* • grapheme *(lan)*

graphische Benutzeroberfläche *f* • graphical user interface, GUI *(AI, sys)*

graphische Kunst *f* • graphic art *(aes)*

graphische Methode *f* • graphic method *(sci)*

Graphologie *f* • graphology *(psy, eso)*

Gratifikationswert *m* • gratification(al) value *(dec, eth)*

Grausamkeit *f* • cruelty *(eth)*

Gravitation *f* • gravitation, gravity *(nat)* < Anziehungskraft, Schwerkraft, Fallgesetze

Gravitationseffekt *m* • gravitational effect *(nat)*

Gravitationsgesetz *n* • law of gravitation/attraction *(Newton etc) (nat)* < Fallgesetz

Gravitationskraft *f* • gravitational force *(Newton etc) (nat)*

Grazie *f* • grace(fulness) *(aes)*

Grellingsches Axiom *n* • Grelling's axiom *(mat)*

Grenzbegriff *m* • limit(ing)/boundary/marginal concept/notion *(Kant etc) (epi)*

Grenzbestimmung *f* • demarcation *(gep)* < Demarkationskriterium

Grenzbewußtsein *n* • boundary consciousness *(epi, met)*

Grenze *f* • (▷ Beschränkung) bounds, boundary, limit, limitation *(gep)*

Grenze der Staatsgewalt *f* • bounds/limit of state authority *(pol)*

Grenzen der Vernunft *pl* • limits/bounds of reason/rational insight *(Kant etc) (epi, met)*

Grenzen der (sinnvollen) Sprache *pl* • limits of (meaningful) language *(Wittgenstein etc) (lan)*

Grenzen der Erfahrung *pl* • limits/limitations/bounds/boundaries of experience *(Kant etc) (epi)*

Grenzen der Erkenntnis *pl* • limits/limitations/bounds/boundaries of cognition/knowledge *(Kant etc) (epi)* ↔ Möglichkeit der Erkenntnis

Grenzen der Wissenschaft *pl* • limits of/to science *(sci)*

Grenzen des Staates *pl* • (the) limits of the state *(pol)* < Minimalstaat

Grenzen des Wachstums *pl* • limits to growth *(eco, env)* < Wachstumsschranken, ökologische < W 392

Grenzen künstlicher Intelligenz *pl* • limits of artificial intelligence *(AI)*

Grenzenlosigkeit *f* • boundlessness *(met)* < Unendlichkeit, Schrankenlosigkeit

Grenzerfahrung *f* • boundary experience *(met, rel, eso)*

Grenzertrag *m* • marginal return *(eco, sci)* < Grenznutzen

Grenzfall *m* • borderline case *(sci, gep)*

Grenzfrage *f* • marginal question *(sci)*

Grenzlinie *f* • limit *(sci)*

Grenznutzen *m* • marginal/final utility *(eco, dec)* → marginaler Nutzen < Grenzertrag

Grenznutzen, abnehmender *m* • diminishing marginal/final utility *(eco, dec)* < erstes Gossensches Gesetz

Grenznutzentheorie *f* • theory of marginal utility, marginal utility theory *(eco, dec)*

Grenzsituation *f* • ultimate situation *(Jaspers etc) (ant, met)*, boundary situation *(met)* < Grenzerfahrung

grenzüberschreitende Auswirkungen *pl* • cross-boundary/trans-boundary effects *(pol, env)*

Grenzverteilungsfunktion *f* • boundary distribution function *(mat)*

Grenzwert *m* • limit (point) *(mat)*, critical value *(sys, env)* < Schwellenwert

Grenzwertaxiom *n* • axiom of convergence, limit axiom *(log, mat)*

Grenzwissenschaft *f* • esoteric science, marginal science *(sci, eso)* < Esoterik

Grenzzyklus *m* • limit/marginal cycle *(sys, nat)*

griechisch-abendländisches Denken *n* • Hellenistic-Western thought, Greek-Western philosophy *(gep, his)*

griechisch-römische Welt *f* • Gr(a)eco-Roman world *(his)*

griechische Kulturgeschichte *f* • history of Greek culture *(his)* < W 395

Großbürger *m* • member of the haute bourgeoisie, member of the upper (middle) classes *(soc)*

Großbürgertum *n* • haute bourgeoisie, upper (middle) class *(soc)*

Größe *f* • magnitude *(log, lan)*

große Befreiung *f* • great liberation *(Nietzsche) (met)*

große Erneuerung *f* • great instauration *(Bacon) (sci)* < W 397

große Erzählung *f* • grand narrative *(Lyotard) (epi, pol, his)*

große Gesellschaft *f* • large society *(Hayek etc) (soc)*

große Gesundheit *f* • great health *(Nietzsche) (met)*

Größe, historische *f* • historical greatness *(Burkhardt) (his, cul)*

Große Kette des Seins *f* • Great Chain of Being *(Lovejoy) (rel, met)*

Größenwahn *m* • megalomania, delusion(s) of grandeur *(psy)* → Megalomanie, Cäsarenwahn

großer Bruder *m* • Big Brother *(Orwell) (pol)*

großer Mittag *m* • great noontime *(Nietzsche) (met)*

großer Verdacht *m* • great suspicion *(Nietzsche) (met)*

großes Leben *n* • grand life *(Nietzsche) (met)*

Großgesellschaft *f* → große Gesellschaft

Großgrundbesitzer *m* • big landowner *(eco, soc)*

Großkapital *n* • big business *(eco)* < Hochfinanz

Großmachtpolitik *f* • superpower politics *(pol)*

Großmut *f* • magnanimity *(psy, eth)* ↔ Kleinmut

Großmutterneuron *n* • grandmother neuron *(sci)*

größten Glücks, Prinzip des *n* • greatest happiness principle *(Bentham, Mill etc) (eth)*

größter anzunehmender Unfall *m* • maximum credible accident, MCA, China syndrome *(tec)* → GAU

größter gemeinsamer Teiler *m* • greatest common divisor, highest common factor *(mat)* < kleinstes gemeinsames Vielfaches

größtes Glück der größten Zahl *n* • greatest happiness of the greatest number *(Beccaria, Bentham etc) (eth, soc)*

Großzügigkeit *f* • generosity *(eth)* → Freigebigkeit

grot • grue *(Goodman) (epi, sci, lan)* < pathologischer Term

Groteske, das *n* • the grotesque *(aes)*

grünalternativ • Green alternative *(env, pol)*

Grünbewegung *f* • Green Movement *(env, pol)*

Grund *m* • reason, cause, ground *(log, met)*

Grund-Figur-Verhältnis *n* • figure-ground relation(ship) *(aes, psy)*

Grund der Möglichkeit *m* • ground of the possibility *(epi, met)*

Grund, psychologischer *m* • psychological cause/reason *(psy)*

Grund seiner selbst *m* • cause-in-itself *(Aquinas) (met, rel)* → causa sui

Grund, transzendentaler *m* • transcendental ground *(Kant) (epi, met)*

Grundannahme *f* • basic assumption *(gep)*

Grundantinomie *f* • fundamental antinomy, basic inconsistency *(Kant etc) (log, epi)*

Grundbedingung *f* • basic condition *(gep)* < Rahmenbedingung

Grundbedürfnis *n* • basic need *(eco, soc)*

Grundbefindlichkeit *f* • basic disposition *(Heidegger) (ont)* < Befindlichkeit

Grundbegriff *m* • basic concept, primitive notion/idea *(epi, lan)*

Grundeigentum *n* • landed estate, property in land *(eco)*

Grundeinstellung *f* • basic/fundamental attitude *(gep)*

Grundelement *n* • basic element *(Carnap) (log, lan)*

gründender Grund *m* • grounding ground *(Heidegger) (ont)*

Gründerväter *pl* • founding fathers *(pol, rel)*

Grundfrage *f* • basic/leading/fundamental question *(gep)*

Grundfreiheiten *pl* • basic liberties *(pol)*

Grundfürsorge *f* • basic welfare *(eco, soc)*

Grundgegenstand *m* • basic object *(Carnap) (epi, ont)*

Grundgesetze *pl* • basic laws *(jur, log, sci)*

Grundgewißheit *f* • basic certainty *(epi)*

Grundgüter *pl* • basic goods *(eco)* → Primärgüter

Grundhaltung *f* • basic/fundamental attitude *(gep)*

Grundidee *f* • basic/fundamental idea/concept *(gep)*

Grundintention *f* • basic intention *(act)*

Grundkraft *f* • basic/fundamental force *(Kant etc) (nat, met)*

Grundlage *f* • foundation, base, basis, fundament *(gen)*

Grundlagenforschung *f* • basic/pure research *(sci)* ↔ anwendungsbezogene Forschung < Forschung, reine; reine Wissenschaft

Grundlagenkrise *f* • foundational crisis, crisis of fundamentals *(gep)*

Grundlagenkrise der Mathematik *f* • crisis in the foundations of mathematics *(mat)*

Grundlagenskepsis *f* • scepticism concerning the foundations of knowledge *(epi)*

grundlegende Terminologie *f* • basic terminology *(lan)*

Grundlegung *f* • foundation, grounding(s) *(gep)* < W 419

Grundlegung der Erkenntnis *f* • foundation of knowledge *(epi)*

Grundlinien *pl* • elements, outlines *(gep)* < W 420

Grundmaterie *f* • basic stuff/matter *(nat, met)* < Materie, Hyle

Grundmißverständnis *n* • basic misunderstanding *(gen)*

Grundmotiv *n* • basic motive *(psy)*, basic motif *(aes)* < Leitmotiv

Grundnorm *f* • fundamental/basic norm/postulate *(Kelsen) (jur, eth)* → Basisnorm

Grundprinzip *n* • underlying/guiding principle *(gep)*

Grundproblem *n* • basic problem *(gep)*

Grundrecht *n* • fundamental/basic right *(pol, eth)* < Menschenrechte, unveräußerliche Rechte

Grundregel *f* • fundamental/basic rule, ground rule *(gep)*

Grundrelation *f* • fundamental relation *(gep)*

Grundriß *m* • outline(s), sketch *(gep)* < W 425

Grundsatz *m* • principle, fundamental *(gep)*, rule, postulate *(eth)*, axiom *(log, mat)* < Axiom, Lehrsatz

Grundsatz der Beharrlichkeit der Substanz *m* • principle of the permanence of substance *(Kant etc) (met)*

Grundsatz der Bestimmbarkeit *m* • principle of determinability *(Kant etc) (epi, log, lan)*

Grundsatz der Varietät *m* • principle of variety *(Kant etc) (epi, met)*

Grundsatz des gerechten Menschen *m* • rule of (the) just man, rule of (the) just human being *(Augustine) (rel, eth)*

Grundsatz des Zugleichseins *m* • principle of co-existence *(Kant) (met)*

Grundsatzdiskussion *f* • discussion of/on general principles, discussion in principle *(gep)*

Grundsätze der Modalität *pl* • principles of modality *(Kant) (epi)*

Grundsätze der praktischen Vernunft *pl* • principles of practical reason *(Kant) (epi, eth)*

Grundsätze der reinen Anschauung *pl* • principles of pure intuition *(Kant) (epi)*

Grundsätze der reinen Vernunft *pl* • principles of pure reason *(Kant) (epi)*

Grundsätze des reinen Verstandes *pl* • principles of pure understanding *(Kant) (epi)*

Grundsatzgesetzgebung *f* • framework legislation *(pol, jur)*

grundsätzlich → prinzipiell

Grundsatzprogramm *n* • policy statement *(pol)*

Grundschriften *pl* • basic writings *(gep)*

Grundsituation *f* • basic situation *(Heidegger) (ont, ant)*

Grundspaltung *f* • basic dichotomy *(Jaspers etc) (met, ant)*

Grundstimmung *f* • basic/fundamental mood *(Kierkegaard, Heidegger, Jaspers) (ant)*

Grundstruktur *f* • basic structure *(gen)*

Grundthese *f* • basic thesis/assumption/theorem *(sci)*

Grundtugenden *pl* • basic virtues *(eth)*

Grundüberzeugung *f* • basic conviction/belief *(gep)* → Basisüberzeugung

Grundwahrheit *f* • fundamental truth *(epi, met)*

Grundweise *f* • fundamental mode of being *(Jaspers etc) (met)*

Grundwesen *n* • basic essence *(Pfänder) (met)*

Grundwiderspruch *m* • fundamental contradiction *(log)*

Grundwissen *n* • fundamental knowledge *(epi)*

Grundwissenschaft *f* • fundamental/basic/pure science *(sci)* < Grundlagenforschung

grüne Revolution *f* • green revolution *(eco)*

Grüner *m* • environmentalist, green *(pol, env)* < Ökopartei

Gruppe *f* • group *(nat, mat, soc)*, set *(mat)*

Gruppenaggression *f* • group aggression *(soc, psy)*

Gruppenaktion *f* • group action *(act)*

Gruppenanarchie *f* • group anarchy *(soc)*

Gruppenaxiom *n* • group axiom *(mat, log)*

Gruppendynamik *f* • group dynamics *(soc, psy)*

Gruppenegoismus *m* • self-interest of the group *(soc, eth, psy)*

Gruppeneinheit *f* • group unity *(gep)*

Gruppenhierarchie *f* • group hierarchy *(soc)*

Gruppenidentität *f* • group identity *(soc, psy)*

Gruppeninteresse *n* • group interest *(soc, psy)*

gruppeninterne Aggression *f* • in-group aggression *(soc, psy)*

Gruppenkonflikt *m* • group conflict *(soc, psy)*

gruppenmoralischer Status *m* • moral status of groups *(eth, soc)*

Gruppenrechte *pl* • group rights *(eth, jur)* < Minderheitenrechte

Gruppenselektion *f* • group selection *(nat, soc)*

Gruppentafel *f* • group table *(mat)*

Gruppentheorie *f* • group theory *(mat, log)*

gültig • valid, sound *(log, sci)*

gültiger Schluß *m* • valid inference *(log)* ↔ Fehlschluß

Gültigkeit *f* • validity *(log, sci)* → Validität

Gültigkeitsanspruch *m* → Geltungsanspruch

Gültigkeitskriterien *pl* • criteria of validity *(sci)*

Guru *m* • guru *(asp, eso)*

Gut, das höchste *n* • the greatest/supreme good *(rel, met, eth)*

Gut, geistiges *n* • (▷ Eigentum) intellectual property *(eth)* → geistiges Eigentum

gut handeln • to act in accordance with the good, to act correctly/appropriately/rightly *(eth)* < gutes Tun

gut in sich • good in itself *(eth)*

Gut, irdisches *n* • wordly goods *(gep)*

gut und böse • good and evil *(eth, met)*

Gute, das *n* • the good *(eth)* → agathon

gute Absicht *f* • good intention *(eth, act)* < Wille, guter

gutes Leben *n* • the good life *(eth)*

Gute, das vorzügliche *n* • the pre-eminent good *(Kant) (eth)*

Gute, Wahre, Schöne und Gerechte, das *n* • the good, the true, the beautiful and the just *(Plato etc) (eth, aes, met)*

Güte, Prinzip der *n* • principle of charity *(Quine etc) (sci, lan)*

Gütegrad *m* • degree of good *(eth)*, quality level *(eco)*

guter Absicht, in • with good intent/faith *(eth)* → bona fide

guter Glaube(n) *m* • good faith *(act, rel)*

guter Vorsatz *m* → gute Absicht

guter Wille *m* • good will *(Kant etc) (eth)*

Güterabwägung *f* • choice between/among conflicting preferences/goods *(dec, eth, soc)*

Gütergemeinschaft *f* • community of property/goods, communalism *(pol)* < Kommunalismus

Güterlehre *f* • doctrine of goods *(eco)*

Güterordnung *f* → Rangordnung der Güter

Güterproduktion *f* • production/manufacture of goods *(eco)*

Gütertafeln *pl* • tables of values *(Nietzsche) (eth)*

Gütertausch *m* • exchange of goods, barter *(eco)* < Tauschhandelssystem

Güterverteilung *f* • distribution of goods *(eco)* < Verteilungsgerechtigkeit

Gutes an sich *n* • good in itself *(eth)* → bonum per se

gutes Gewissen *n* • good conscience *(eth, rel)* → reines Gewissen

Gutes tun • to do good *(eth)*

Gutheit *f* • goodness *(eth)*

Gutherzigkeit *f* • good-heartedness *(eth)*

Gutwilligkeit *f* • readiness *(eth)*, willingness *(log, eth)*, *(Lorenzen, Kamlah)* < Konsenstheorie der Wahrheit

Gymnosophist *m* → Yogi

Gyn-Ökologie *f* • gyn-ecology *(fem, env)* < Ökofeminismus

Gynäkokratie *f* → Matriarchat

H

H-O-Schema *n* → Hempel-Oppenheim-Schema

Habenmodus *m* • having mode *(Fromm etc)* *(psy)*

Habensinn *m* • having mind *(Fromm etc)* *(psy)* < konsumorientierte Gesellschaft, Pleonexie < W 440

Habgier *f* • greed, avarice *(eth)* → Pleonexie

Habit *m/n* • habit *(psy, soc)* < Natur oder Kultur

Habitualitäten *pl* • habitualities *(Husserl)* *(met)*

Habitus *m* • habitus, disposition, habit *(psy, act)*

Habsucht *f* → Habgier

Hackings Wahrscheinlichkeitsgesetz *n* • Hacking's law of likelihood *(sci)*

Hackordnung *f* • pecking order *(nat, soc)* < Rangordnung

haecceitas *f* • haecceity *(Duns Scotus etc)* *(ont)* → Diesheit < Individuationsprinzip

Haftbarkeit *f* • liability *(jur, eth)*

halbbewußt • half/semi -conscious *(Freud etc)* *(psy)* < unbewußt

halbgeordnete Menge *f* • partially ordered set *(mat)*

Halbgott *m* • demi-god *(rel)*

Halbgruppe *f* • semigroup *(mat)*

Halb-Interpretation *f* • semi-interpretation *(Hofstadter)* *(log)*

Halbmensch *m* • half-man, demi-man *(ant)*

Halbphilosophen *pl* • would-be philosophers *(gep)*

Halbtranszendenz *f* • half-transcendence *(Habermas)* *(lan)*

Halbwahrheit *f* • half-truth *(gep)*

Halbwertszeit *f* • half-life *(nat)*

Halteproblem *n* • halting problem *(AI)* < Turing-Maschine

Hamsterkauf *m* • panic buying, hoarding buying *(eco)*

Hamster-Orientierung *f* • hoarding/hamster orientation *(Fromm)* *(psy, soc)*

Hand- und Kopfarbeit *f* • manual and intellectual labour, work of hand and brain *(eco)*

Handarbeit *f* • manual labour *(Marx)* *(eco)*

Handeln *n* • acting, action *(act, eth)*

Handeln, moralisches *n* • moral action/acting *(act, eth)*

Handeln, probeweises *n* • tentative action *(Freud etc)* *(psy, act)*

Handeln, soziales *n* • social action *(Weber etc)* *(soc, act)*

Handeln wider besseres Wissen *n* • acting against better knowledge *(act, eth)*

handelndes Subjekt *n* • acting subject *(act)*

Handelsschranken *pl* • trade barriers *(eco)*

Handelsstaat *m* • trading state *(eco)* < W 372

handelstreibende Gesellschaft *f* • commercial society *(eco)*

Händler- und Bauernkaste *f* • tradesman and peasant caste *(Nietzsche)* *(soc)*

Handlesekunst *f* • palmistry, ch(e)irogmancy, ch(e)irognomy *(eso)* < Fatalismus

Handlung *f* • action *(act, eth)*

Handlungsablauf *m* • plot, sequence of events *(aes)*, sequence of actions *(act)*

Handlungsabsicht *f* • intention in acting *(act)*

Handlungsanalyse *f* • act analysis *(act)*

Handlungsaufschub *m* • postponement of action *(act)*

Handlungsbereitschaft *f* • readiness/willingness to act *(act)*

Handlungserfahrung *f* → praktische Erfahrung

Handlungserklärung *f* • explanation of action *(act)*

Handlungsfolgen *pl* • consequences of action *(act, eth)* < Konsequentialismus

Handlungsforschung *f* • action research *(act)*

Handlungsfreiheit *f* • freedom of action *(act, eth, met)* ↔ Determiniertheit des Handelns < Wahlvermögen

Handlungsgrundlage *f* • presupposition/foundation(s) of action *(act)*

Handlungshemmung *f* • inhibition to act *(Gehlen)* *(ant, psy)*

Handlungsindifferenz *f* • indifference between actions *(act, dec)* < fairer Wettquotient

Handlungskausalität *f* • agent causality *(Chisholm)* *(act, met)*

Handlungskette *f* • chain of action *(act)*

Handlungskonsequenz *f* • consequence of (an) action *(dec)*

Handlungskoordination *f* • action coordination *(Habermas)* *(act)*

handlungsleitend • action guiding *(act, eth)*

Handlungslernen *n* → Lernen durch Handeln

Handlungslogik f • logic of action (act)

Handlungsmaxime f • maxim of action (Kant etc) (eth)

Handlungsmöglichkeit f • possibility to act/of action (act) < Handlungsfreiheit

Handlungsmuster n • action pattern (act)

Handlungsnorm f • norm of action (act)

Handlungsorientierung f • action orientation (Habermas) (act, soc)

Handlungsperspektive f • action perspective (act)

Handlungsrationalität f • rationality of action (act)

Handlungsraum m • action space (Parsons, Bales) (act)

Handlungsregel f • rule of action (act, eth) → Maxime

Handlungssituation f • action situation (act)

Handlungsspielraum m • scope for/of action (act)

Handlungssystem n • action system (act)

handlungstheoretische Semantik f • act-theoretical semantics, action-theoretic semantics (Grice) (lan) < sprechhandlungstheoretische Semantik

Handlungstheorie f • theory of action, action theory (act)

Handlungsunabhängigkeit f • act-independence (act)

Handlungsursache f • motive, reason (act, met) < Motiv

Handlungsutilitarismus m • act-utilitarianism (eth) → Aktutilitarismus

Handlungsverzicht m • abstention from action (act)

Handlungsweise f • mode/manner/way of acting (act)

Handlungszusammenhang m • context of action, action context (act)

Handwahrsagerei f → Handlesekunst

Handwerkskünste pl • crafts (gep) → artes mechanicae

Hang m • propensity (eth, psy) → Neigung

Happening n • happening (aes)

Häresie f • heresy (rel) → Irrlehre, Heterodoxie, Ketzerei

Harmonie f • harmony (aes) → Wohlklang

Harmonie der Sphären f → Sphärenharmonie

Harmonie der Welt f • harmony of the world (met, aes)

Harmonie des Mannigfaltigen f • harmony of the manifold (Wolff) (met)

Harmonie von Inhalt und Form f • harmony of content and form (aes)

Harmonielehre f • (▷ Theorie) harmonic/harmony theory, (▷ Fach) harmony (aes)

harmonisches Mittel n • harmonic mean (mat)

harte Technologie f • hard technology (tec) < Hochrisikotechnologie

Haß m • hatred, loathing (psy)

Häßliche, das n • the ugly (aes) < Ästhetik des Häßlichen

Hast als Merkmal des Man f • haste as characteristic of the One/They/anyone (Heidegger) (ont, psy)

Häufigkeit f • frequency (mat, log)

Häufigkeitsansatz m • estimate of frequency (Popper etc) (mat, log)

Häufigkeitsfunktion f • frequency function (Carnap) (log, mat)

Häufigkeitsgrenzwert m • frequency limit (mat)

Häufigkeitshypothese f • frequency hypothesis (mat)

Häufigkeitsinterpretation der Wahrscheinlichkeit f • frequency interpretation of probability (mat)

Häufigkeitspunkt m • cluster point (mat)

Häufigkeitstheorie f • frequency theory (mat, sci) → Frequenztheorie

Häufigkeitsverteilung f • frequency distribution (mat)

Häufigkeitswahrscheinlichkeit f • frequency probability (mat)

Häufungspunkt m → Häufigkeitspunkt

Hauptdiagonale f • principal/main diagonal (mat)

Hauptkrümmungslinie f • line of principal curvature (mat)

Hauptnormale f • principal normal (mat)

Hauptsatz m • main proposition, Hauptsatz (Gentzen etc) (mat, log) < Gentzenscher Hauptsatz

Hauptsatz der Funktionstheorie m • Cauchy's theorem for a connected domain (mat)

Haupttugenden pl • principal virtues (eth, rel) < Kardinaltugend

Heautonomie f • heautonomy (Kant) (met)

Hebammenkunst f • maieutic art, midwifery (Socrates) (epi) → Mäeutik, sokratische Methode

Hedonismus m • hedonism (eth)

Hedonismus, evaluativer m • evaluative hedonism (eth)

Hedonismus, psychologischer m • psychological hedonism (eth, psy)

hedonistische Ethik f • hedonistic ethics (eth)

hedonistischer Kalkül *m* • hedonic/ hedonistic/felicific calculus *(Bentham)* *(eth)* →
Freud-Leid-Kalkulation < Genußprinzip,
Lust-Unlust-Kalkül, Maximierung der
Glücksmenge

hedonistisches Prinzip *n* • hedon(ist)ic
principle *(Bentham)* *(eth)*

Hegelianer *m* • Hegelian *(gep)*

Hegelianismus *m* • Hegelianism *(gep)*

Hegelscher Geist *m* • Hegelian spirit *(met)*

Hegelscher Marxismus *m* • Hegelian
Marxism *(gep)*

Hegemonie *f* • hegemony *(pol)*

Heidentum *n* • paganism *(rel)*

heidnische Welt *f* • pagan world *(his)*

Heilige, das *n* • the holy *(rel)* ↔ Profane, das
< W 451

Heilige Schrift *f* • Holy Scripture *(rel)*

Heiligenkult *m* • cult of saints *(rel)*

Heiliger Geist *m* • the Holy Spirit/Ghost *(rel)*

Heiliges Land *n* • the Holy Land *(rel)*

Heiliges Römisches Reich *n* • the Holy Roman
Empire *(his)*

heiliges Wissen *n* • sacred knowledge *(Weber)*
(epi, rel)

Heiligkeit *f* • holiness, sanctity, saintliness,
sacredness *(rel)* < Seligkeit

Heiligkeit des (menschlichen) Lebens *f* • sanctity of (human) life *(eth)* < Lebenswertdebatte < W 453

Heiligkeit des Willens *f* • holiness/sanctity of
will *(Kant)* *(eth, met)*

Heilsgeschichte *f* • salvation history, heilsgeschichte° *(rel, his)*

heilsgeschichtliche Theorie *f* • salvation (type)
theory, theory resting on the idea of salvation *(his)* < lineare Geschichtstheorien,
Fortschrittstheorie, Verfallstheorie

Heilsgewißheit *f* • certainty of salvation *(rel)*

Heilslehre *f* • doctrine of salvation *(rel)*

Heilsordnung *f* • order of salvation *(rel)*

Heilswissen *n* • salvation knowledge, knowledge for salvation *(Scheler)* *(epi)* → Erlösungswissen < Bildungswissen, Leistungswissen

Heimat *f* • home ground *(Husserl)* *(epi, met)*
↔ Fremde

Heimatkunst *f* • folk art *(aes)*

heimatlose Gegenstände *pl* • homeless objects
(Meinong) *(ont)*

Heimwelt *f* • home world *(Husserl)* *(met)*
< Lebenswelt

Heisenbergsches Unbestimmtheitsaxiom *n* •
Heisenberg's axiom of indeterminacy *(nat)*

Heldenverehrung *f* • hero-worship *(soc, pol)*

Heldenzeit *f* • age of heroes *(Vico)* *(his)*
< zyklische Geschichtstheorie

heliozentrisches Weltbild *n* • heliocentric
world view *(nat)* → Kopernikanisches Weltbild

Heliozentrismus *m* • heliocentrism *(nat)* ↔
Geozentrismus

Helldunkel *n* • chiaroscuro *(aes)*

Hellenisierung *f* • hellenization *(his)*

Hellenismus *m* • Hellenism *(his)*

hellenistische Philosophie *f* • Hellenistic/
Hellenic philosophy *(his)* < griechischabendländisches Denken

Hellsehen *n* • clairvoyance *(eso)* < Telegnosis

Hemmung *f* • inhibition *(psy)*

Hemmungslosigkeit *f* • lack of restraint, unscrupulousness *(eth, psy)* → Zügellosigkeit,
Libertinismus

Hempel-Oppenheim-Modell *n* → Hempel-
Oppenheim-Schema

Hempel-Oppenheim-Schema *n* • coveringlaw model (of explanation), Hempel-Oppenheim schema *(Dray)* *(sci)* → H-O-Schema,
Covering-law-These, hypothetisch-deduktives Erklärungsmodell < deduktiv-nomologische Erklärung, deduktiv-nomologisches
Modell

Hempels Rabenparadoxon *n* • Hempel's
paradox of (the) ravens, Hempel's raven
paradox *(Hempel)* *(log, sci)* < Bestätigungsparadox

Hempelsche Paradoxie *f* • paradox of confirmation *(Hempel)* *(log, sci)* → Hempels
Rabenparadoxon

Henotheismus *m* • henotheism *(rel)* < Monotheismus

Heraklit • Heraclitus

Heraklitismus *m* • Heracliteanism *(gep)*

Herdenbewußtsein *n* • herd consciousness
(Nietzsche etc) *(soc)*

Herdenidentität *f* • herd identity *(Fromm etc)*
(soc)

Herdeninstinkt *m* • herd/gregarious instinct
(Nietzsche) *(soc)*, gregariousness *(nat)*

Herdenmoral *f* • herd morality *(Nietzsche)*
(eth) → Sklavenmoral

Herdentier *n* • herd/gregarious animal
(Nietzsche) *(ant)*

Herdentrieb *m* • herd instinct *(nat, psy)*

Herleitungsregel *f* • rule of derivation *(log)*
< Ableitungsregel, Deduktionsregel

Hermeneutik *f* • hermeneutics *(sci)* → Auslegungskunst < W 456

Hermeneutik der Faktizität *f* • hermeneutics
of factual existence *(Heidegger)* *(ont)*

hermeneutische Philosophie *f* • hermeneutic philosophy *(gep)*

hermeneutischer Spalt *m* • hermeneutic gap *(sci)*

hermeneutischer Zirkel *m* • hermeneutic circle *(Gadamer etc) (sci)*

hermeneutisches Als *n* • hermeneutic as *(Heidegger) (met)*

hermetische Form *f* • hermetic form *(aes)*, Hermetian form *(mat)*

hermetische Schriften *pl* • hermetic writings *(eso, rel)*

Hermetismus *m* • hermeticism, hermetism *(aes, eso)*

heroischer Individualismus *m* • heroic individualism *(Nietzsche) (psy)*

heroischer Sinn *m* • sense of the heroic *(psy)*

Heroismus *m* • heroism *(psy)*

Herr der Finsternis *m* • Lord of Darkness *(rel, eso)*

Herr des Schicksals *m* • master of destiny *(met)*

Herr-Knecht-Dialektik *f* • master-slave/servant dialectic *(Hegel) (met, soc)*

Herr-schaft *f* • male rule/domination *(fem)*

Herr und Knecht *m,m* • master and slave/servant *(Hegel etc) (met, soc)* < Herrschaft und Knechtschaft

Herren der Erde *pl* • lords of the earth *(rel, soc)*

Herren- und Sklavenmoral *f* • master and slave morality *(Nietzsche etc) (eth)*

herrenloses Eigentum *n* • ownerless/unclaimed property *(jur)*

Herrenmensch *m* • member of the master race, superior man, herrenmensch *(Nietzsche etc) (soc)* < Übermensch

Herrenmoral *f* • master morality *(Nietzsche) (eth)* → Moral, vornehme ↔ Sklavenmoral

Herrenrasse *f* • master race *(Nietzsche etc) (eth, soc)*

Herrenvolk *n* • herrenvolk *(pol)* → Herrenrasse

Herrschaft *f* • rule, control, power, authority, domination, dominion *(pol)*

Herrschaft der Vernunft *f* → Vernunftherrschaft

Herrschaft des Menschen über den Menschen *f* • power/domination/dominion of man over man *(Marx etc) (soc)*

Herrschaft über die Natur *f* • domination/dominion over/of nature *(met)* → Macht über die Natur, Naturbeherrschung

Herrschaft und Knechtschaft *f,f* • domination and servitude *(soc)* < Herr und Knecht

Herrschaft und Unterordnung, Verhältnis von *n* • relationship of domination and subordination *(soc)*

Herrschafts- und Knechtschaftsverhältnis *n* • master-slave/servant relationship *(Marx) (soc)*

Herrschaftsanspruch *m* • claim to power *(pol)*

Herrschaftsautorität *f* • autority of power *(pol, psy)*

Herrschaftsbedürfnis *n* • desire/need to dominate *(psy)* < Wille zur Macht

Herrschaftsformen *pl* • forms/types of authority/domination/government *(pol)*

herrschaftsfreier Diskurs *m* • discourse free of domination *(Habermas etc) (eth, soc)*

Herrschaftssoziologie *f* • sociology of domination/authority *(Weber etc) (soc)*

Herrschaftssystem *n* • system of rule/government *(pol)*

Herrschaftsvertrag *m* • sovereign-making covenant *(Hobbes etc) (pol)*

Herrschaftswissen *n* • domination knowledge, knowledge for mastery *(Scheler) (epi)* → Machtwissen

herrschende Ideen *pl* • ruling ideas *(gep)*

herrschende Ideologie *f* • dominant ideology *(Marx etc) (soc)*

herrschende Klasse *f* • dominant/ruling class *(Marx etc) (soc)*

herrschende Meinung *f* • ruling/dominant opinion *(gen)* → communis opinio

Herrscher und Beherrschte *m,pl* • (the) ruler and (the) ruled *(pol)*

Herstellbarkeitsvorhersagen *pl* • predictions of implementability *(sci)* < Voraussage, technologische Prognose

Herstellungskosten *pl* → Produktionskosten

Herstellungswissen *n* • poietic knowledge *(epi, tec)* → poietisches Wissen

Herzensbildung *f* • (▷ Großmut) nobleness of the heart, (▷ Erziehung des Herzens) sentimental education *(eth)* ↔ Schulbildung

Hessesche Normalform *f* • Hesse normal form *(log)*

Heterarchie *f* • heterarchy *(pol)* → Fremdherrschaft

Heterodoxie *f* • heterodoxy *(rel)* → Irrlehre, Häresie, Ketzerei

Heterogenität *f* • heterogeneity *(gep)* ↔ Homogenität

Heterogonie *f* • heterogony *(Wundt) (psy, act)*

heterologisch • heterologic(al) *(log, lan)*

heterologischer Begriff *m* • heterologic(al) term/concept *(log, lan)* ↔ autologischer Begriff

Heteromorphie f • heteromorphy (gep)

heteronomer Wille m • heteronomous will (Kant etc) (eth)

heteronomes Prinzip n • heteronomous principle (Kant) (epi, eth) ↔ autonomes Prinzip

Heteronomie f • heteronomy (pol, eth, met) → Fremdbestimmung ↔ Autonomie, Selbstbestimmung

Heterophänomenologie f • heterophenomenology (met)

Heterozetesis f → Fangfrage

Heuchelei f • hypocrisy (eth) < Scheinheiligkeit, Scheintugend

Heuchelei, innere f • inner hypocrisy (Butler) (eth)

heuern und feuern • to hire and fire (eco) < Arbeitsplatzsicherheit

Heuristik f • heuristics (sci)

heuristische Annahme f • heuristic assumption (sci)

heuristische Fiktion f • heuristic fiction (sci)

heuristische Methode f • heuristic method (sci)

heuristischer Begriff m • heuristic concept (Kant) (epi)

heuristischer Grundsatz m • heuristic principle (Kant etc) (sci)

Hexenkunst f • witchcraft (cul, fem)

Hexenverfolgung f • persecution of witches, witch-hunt (rel, his) < Inquisition

hier und jetzt • here and now (met)

Hierarchie f • hierarchy (log, soc)

Hierarchie der Bedürfnisse f • hierarchy of needs (eco, eth)

Hierarchie, terminologische f • terminological hierarchy (lan, log)

Hierarchie von Sprachen f • hierarchy of languages (Tarski) (epi, lan)

Hierarchiegesetz n • hierarchy law (Comte) (met) < Dreistadiengesetz

hierarchisches System n • hierarchical system (sys)

Hieratik f • hieratic art (aes) → religiöse Kunst

Hierokratie f → Priesterherrschaft

Hilbertraum m • Hilbert space (Hilbert) (mat)

Hilbertsches Programm n • Hilbert's programme (mat)

Hilberttyp-Beweis m • Hilbert type proof (log, mat)

Hilflosigkeit des Menschen vor der Natur f • helplessness of man before nature (met)

Hilfshypothese f • auxiliary hypothesis (sci)

Hilfskonstruktion f • auxiliary construction (sci)

Hilfsmaßnahme f • relief action, remedial measure (gen)

Hilfswissenschaft f • complementary/auxiliary science (sci) → Mitwissenschaft

Himmelskörper m • heavenly/celestial body (nat)

Himmelsmechanik f • celestial mechanics (nat)

Himmelsrecht n • heavenly law (rel)

Himmelssphäre f • celestial sphere (nat)

himmlische Sphären pl • celestial spheres (met) < Sphärenharmonie

Hinajana n • nt (asp)

Hinayana n → Hinajana

Hinduismus m • Hinduism (rel)

hinduistische Ethik f • Hindu(istic) ethics (eth, asp)

Hinfälligkeit der menschlichen Natur f • frailty/weakness feebleness of human nature (ant, met) < Gefährdetheit der Existenz

hinreichend • sufficient (gep)

hinreichende Bedingung f • sufficient condition (log, sci) ↔ notwendige Bedingung

hinreichende Ursache f • sufficient cause (met) → causa sufficiens ↔ nicht-hinreichende Ursache

hinreichendes Kriterium n • sufficient criterion (sci) < hinreichende Bedingung

Hintereinanderausführung von Funktionen f • composition of functions (mat)

hinterfragen • to question (gep)

Hintergrundannahme f • background assumption (sci)

Hintergrundideologie f • underlying ideology (soc)

Hintergrundkonsens m • background consensus (Habermas) (lan, act)

Hintergrundstrahlung f • background radiation (nat)

Hintergrundtheorie f • background theory (Quine) (sci) < Rahmentheorie

Hintergrundüberzeugung f • background conviction (epi, soc)

Hintergrundwissen n • background knowledge (epi)

Hinterwelt f • backworld, otherworld (Nietzsche etc) (met)

Hinterweltler m • member of the backworld/ otherworld (Nietzsche etc) (met)

hinweisende Erklärung f • ostensive definition (lan)

Hippokratischer Eid m • Hippocratic oath (eth)

Hippokratismus *m* • Hippocratism *(nat, eth)*

Hirnaktivität *f* • brain activity *(nat, min)*

Hirnlebendefinition *f* • brain life definition *(nat, eth)* ↔ Hirntoddefinition

Hirnpolizei *f* • brain police *(pol)* < Gedanken-polizei

Hirntod *m* • brain death *(nat)*

Hirntoddefinition *f* • brain death definition *(nat, eth)* ↔ Hirnlebendefinition < Todes-feststellung

Histomat *m* → Historischer Materialismus

Historie *f* → Geschichte

Historienmalerei *f* • historical painting *(aes)*

Historiographie *f* • historiography *(his)* → Ge-schichtsschreibung

historisch-hermeneutische Wissenschaften *pl* • historical hermeneutic sciences *(sci)* < Geisteswissenschaften, idiographische Wissenschaften

historisch-kritische Methode *f* • historical-critical method *(sci)*

historische Erkenntnis *f* • historical knowledge *(epi)*

historische Erklärung *f* • historical explanation *(sci)* < deduktiv-nomologische Erklärung

historische Gebundenheit *f* • historical situatedness *(Gadamer) (his)*

historische Methode *f* • historical method *(Bodin, Dilthey etc) (sci)* → Methode, geschichtliche

historische Möglichkeit *f* • historical possibility *(his)*

historische Notwendigkeit *f* • historical necessity *(his)*

Historische Rechtsschule *f* • historical school of jurisprudence *(Savigny, Niebuhr etc) (jur)*

historische Rückbeziehung *f* • historical back-reference, historical retrospection *(Husserl) (epi, met)*

Historische Schule *f* • historical school *(aes, his)*

historische Semantik *f* • historical semantics *(epi, lan, his)*

historische Verlaufsgesetze *pl* • historical laws of development *(sci)*

historische Wahrscheinlichkeit *f* • historical likelihood *(his)*

historische Zyklen *pl* • historical cycles *(Spengler etc) (his)*

historischem Sinn, Mangel an *m* • lack of historical sense, lack of a sense of history *(Nietzsche) (his)*

historischer Glaube(n) *m* • historical faith *(Kant) (rel)* < Offenbarungsglaube

historischer Hintergrund *m* → geschichtli-cher Hintergrund

historischer Horizont *m* • historical horizon *(Husserl) (ont)*

Historischer Materialismus *m* • historical materialism *(Marx etc) (his)* → Histomat < ma-terialistische Geschichtsauffassung

historischer Rückblick *m* • historical retrospec(tion) *(his)* < Retrospektion

historisches Apriori *n* • historical a priori *(Foucault etc) (epi, his)*

historisches Entwicklungsgesetz *n* • law of historical development *(his)*

historisches Individuum *n* • historical individu-al *(his)*

historisches Konstrukt *n* • historical construct *(his)*

historisches Philosophieren *n* • historical philosophizing *(Nietzsche etc) (gep)*

Historisierung *f* • historicization *(his)*

Historismus *m* • historicism, historism *(aes, his)* < W 466

Historizismus *m* • historicism *(Popper etc) (sci, his)*

Historizist *m* • historicist *(Popper etc) (his, sci)*

Historizität *f* • historicity *(his)* → Geschicht-lichkeit

Hitzetod des Universums *m* • heat death of the universe *(nat)* < Entropie

hobbesianischer Rationalismus *m* • Hobbesian rationalism *(epi)*

Hobbesianismus *m* • Hobbesianism *(gep)* → Hobbismus

Hobbismus *m* • Hobbism *(gep)*

Hochbarock *m/n* • High Baroque *(aes, his)*

Hochbourgeoisie *f* • haute/grande bourgeoisie *(soc)*

Hochfinanz *f* • high finance *(eco)* < Groß-kapital

Hochkultur *f* • advanced civilization *(his, cul)*, high culture *(aes)* ↔ Massenkultur

Hochkunst *f* • high art *(aes)* ↔ Volkskunst

hochradioaktiv • highly radioactive *(nat, env)*

Hochrechnung *f* • projection, forecast *(mat)*

Hochrisikotechnologie *f* • high-risk technology *(tec)* < sanfte Technologie; Technologie, harte

Hochschätzung der Arbeit, bürgerliche *f* • bourgeois esteem for work *(soc)* < Arbeits-ethos, protestantische Ethik

Hochscholastik *f* • High Scholasticism *(his)*

höchster Gegenstand *m* • Greatest Being *(Comte) (soc, rel)* < höchstes Wesen

höchster Geist *m* • supreme spirit *(rel)*

höchster Wert *m* • ultimate value *(eth)*

höchster Zweck *m* • highest/ultimate goal/end *(met)*

höchstes Gut *n* • the supreme/highest/prime good *(Aristotle etc) (eth)* → oberstes Gut, summum bonum

höchstes Wesen *n* • Supreme Being *(rel)*

Höchsturteil *n* • high court judg(e)ment/decision *(jur)*

Hochtechnologie *f* • high technology *(tec)*

Hoffnung *f* • hope *(rel, psy)* < W 822

höhere Bedeutung *f* • higher meaning *(lan)*

höhere Bildung *f* • higher learning/education *(gen)*

höhere Einheit *f* • higher unity *(met)* < Dialektik

höhere Geschichte *f* • higher history *(Nietzsche) (his)*

höhere Gewalt *f* • force majeure *(act, jur, met)* < Gottesfügung

höhere Kultur *f* • higher culture *(Nietzsche) (cul)*

höhere Wahrheit *f* • higher form of truth *(epi, met)*

höherer Mensch *m* • higher (type of) man, superior man *(Nietzsche etc) (met)* < Herrenmensch

Höhlengleichnis *n* • allegory/metaphor/simile of the cave *(Platon) (met)*

Höhlenmalerei *f* • cave-painting *(aes)*

Holismus *m* • holism *(met)*

holistische Medizin *f* • holistic medicine *(nat)* → Ganzheitsmedizin

holistische Rechtfertigungstheorie *f* • holistic theory of justification *(epi)*

Holographie *f* • holography *(sci)*

holomorph • holomorphic *(log, mat)*

Holzweg *m* • forest path, blind alley *(Heidegger) (ont)*

Holzwegsatz *m* • garden-path sentence *(lan)* < Fangschluß

Homeostase *f* • homeostasis *(sys)*

homeostatisches System *n* • homeostatic system *(sys)* < selbsterhaltendes System

Homerisches Gelächter *n* • Homeric laughter *(Nietzsche) (met)*

Hominide *m* • hominid *(ant)* < Vormensch

Hominisation *f* • hominization° *(nat, ant)* → Menschwerdung, Anthropogenese

Homizid *m* • homicide *(eth)*

homme civil *m* • civil(ized) man *(Rousseau) (soc)* ↔ homme naturel

homme naturel *m* • natural man *(Rousseau) (soc)* ↔ homme civil < edler Wilder

homo creator *m* • creative man *(ant, cul)*

homo faber *m* • *nt,* man as artisan *(ant, cul)* < werkzeugmachendes Tier, Mensch als

homo homini lupus • *nt,* man is a wolf to man *(Hobbes) (ant)*

homo insciens *m* • ignorant man *(Ortega y Gasset) (ant, cul)*

homo insipiens *m* → homo insciens

homo loquax *m* • loquatious man *(Bergson) (ant, cul)*

homo ludens *m* • *nt (Huizinga) (ant, cul)* < W 469

Homo-mensura-Satz *m* • homo-mensura principle *(Protagoras) (ant, ont)* < Mensch als Maß aller Dinge

homo natura *m* • natural man *(Nietzsche etc) (ant)* < Naturalismus

homo oeconomicus *m* • economic man *(eco, soc)* < Ökonomismus

homo pictor *m* • man as depictor *(Jonas) (ant, cul)*

Homo presapiens *m* • homo praesapiens *(ant)*

Homo sapiens *m* • *nt (ant, cul)*

homo sociologicus *m* • sociological man *(soc)*

homo viator *m* • man as traveller *(Marcel) (ant, rel, cul)* < ewiger Wanderer < W 470

homogen • homogenous *(mat)*

homogene Ausdehnung *f* • homogeneous expansion *(nat)*

homogene lineare Differentialgleichung *f* • homogeneous linear differential equation *(mat)*

Homogenität *f* • homogeneity *(gep)*

Homogenitätsprinzip *n* • homogeneity principle, principle/law of homogeneity *(Kant) (epi, log)* < regulatives Prinzip

Homologie *f* • homology *(eth, nat, mat)*

homomorph • homomorphic *(mat)*

Homomorphismus *m* • homomorphism *(nat, sys, mat)*

homöomorph • homoeomorph(ic) *(mat)*

Homöopathie *f* • homeopathy *(nat)* ↔ Allopathie

Homöostase *f* • homeostasis *(sys)* → Gleichgewichtszustand < statisches Modell

homophone Übersetzung *f* • homophonic translation *(Quine) (lan, epi)*

Homophonie *f* • homophony *(aes)* → Monodie ↔ Polyphonie

homotop • homotopic *(mat)*

Homotyp *m* • homotype *(sci)*

Homunculus *m* • homunculus *(met)*

Horizont *m* • horizon *(mat, met)*

Horizont, geistiger *m* • mental horizon *(gep)*
< Gesichtskreis

Horizontauslegung *f* • horizon interpretation,
horizon exposition *(Husserl) (epi, met)*

Horizontbewußtsein *n* • horizon consciousness
(Husserl) (epi, met)

Horizontgewißheit *f* • horizon-certainty
(Husserl) (epi, met)

Horizonthaftigkeit *f* • horizonality° *(epi, met)*

Horizontintentionalität *f* • horizon intentionality *(Husserl) (epi, met)*

Horizontverschmelzung *f* • fusion/merging of
horizons *(Gadamer) (sci, met)*

Horizontwissen *n* • horizontal knowledge°
(Habermas) (epi, soc)

Hornerschema *n* • Horner's method *(mat)*

horror vacui *m* • *nt (Aristotle etc) (met)*

Human genome project • *nt (nat, eth)*

Humanbiologie *f* • human biology *(nat)*

Humanethologie *f* • human ethology *(nat, ant)*

Humanexperiment *n* • experiment/experi-
mentation on humans/human beings, human
experiment *(eth, nat)* < Versuchskaninchen

Humanisierung der Arbeit *f* • humanization of
work *(soc)*

Humanismus *m* • humanism *(his, eth)*

Humanismus, religiöser *m* • religious
humanism *(eth, rel)*

Humanismus, säkularer *m* • secular humanism
(eth)

humanistische Anthropologie *f* • humanistic
anthropology *(Fromm) (ant)*

humanistische Gesinnung *f* • humanistic
attitude *(eth)*

humanistische Psychologie *f* • humanistic
psychology *(psy)*

Humanitarismus *m* • humanitarianism *(eth)*

Humanität *f* • humanity, humanitarianism *(eth)*
< W 163

Humanitätsideal *n* • ideal of humanity *(eth)*

Humankapital *n* • human capital *(eco)*

Humanökologie *f* • human ecology *(nat, env)*

Humanpsychologie *f* • human psychology *(psy)*

Humanressourcen *pl* • human resources *(gep)*
< Humankapital

Humanwissenschaften *pl* • human sciences
(gep) < Geisteswissenschaft(l)er < W 724

Humes Gesetz *n* • Hume's law *(sci)*

Humesche Welten *pl* • Hume worlds *(epi)*

Humescher Empirismus *m* • Humean
empiricism *(epi)*

Hybris *f* • hubris, hybris *(Aristotle etc) (eth)*
< Stolz

hydraulisches Aggressionsmodell *n* • hydrau-
lic model of aggression *(Lorenz etc) (nat,
psy)*

Hyle *f* • hyle, prime matter *(Aristotle) (ont)* →
Materie, Stoff, Urstoff

Hyle, sensuelle *f* • sensual matter/hyle
(Husserl) (met, psy)

Hylemorphismus *m* • hylomorphism *(Aristotle)*
(met)

Hylismus *m* • hylism, hylicism *(met)* → Materialismus

Hylotheismus *m* • hylotheism *(rel)*

Hylozoismus *m* • hylozoism *(met)*

hylozoistischer Monismus *m* • hylozoistic
monism *(met)*

Hyperbel *f* • hyperbole *(lan)*, hyperbola *(mat)*

Hyperextensionalismus *m* • hyper-exten-
sionalism *(Goodman etc) (lan)*

hyperkomplexes System *n* • hypercomplex
system *(sys)*

Hypermoral *f* • hypermorality *(Gehlen) (eth,
ant)* < W 668

Hyperrealismus *m* • hyper-realism *(epi, aes)*

Hyperrealität *f* • hyper-reality *(met)*

Hyperzyklus *m* • hyper-cycle *(sys, log)*

Hypnose *f* • hypnosis *(psy, eso)*

Hypnotismus *m* • hypnotism *(psy, eso)*

Hypostase *f* • hypostasis *(sci, rel)*

Hypostasen, Lehre von den drei *f* • theory of
the three hypostases *(Plotinus) (met)*

hypostasieren • to hypostasize, to hypostatize
(sci, rel)

Hypostastierung *f* • hypostatization *(sci, rel)*

hypostatische Einheit *f* • hypostatic(al) union
(rel)

Hypotheismus *m* • hypotheism *(rel)*

Hypothese *f* • hypothesis *(sci)* < Annahme

Hypothesenprüfung *f* • hypothesis testing *(sci)*
< Bestätigung, Falsifikation

**Hypothesenüberprüfung, orthodox-stati-
stische** *f* • orthodox statistical hypothesis
testing *(sci)*

Hypothesenwahrscheinlichkeit *f* • probability/
likelihood of a hypothesis *(sci, log)*

hypothetisch • hypothetical *(sci)*

hypothetisch-deduktive Methode *f* • hypothetico-deductive method *(sci)*

hypothetisch-deduktives Erklärungsmodell *n*
• hypothetico-deductive model of explanation *(sci)* → Hempel-Oppenheim-Schema

hypothetische Bedingung *f* • hypothetical
condition *(log, sci)*

hypothetische Entität *f* • hypothetical entity
(ont)

hypothetische Häufigkeit *f* • hypothetical frequency *(mat)*

hypothetische Synthesis *f* • hypothetical synthesis *(Kant) (epi)*

hypothetische Welten *pl* • hypothetical worlds *(mat, ont)* < mögliche Welten

hypothetische Wissenschaft *f* • hypothetical science *(sci)*

hypothetischer Gebrauch der Vernunft *m* • hypothetical employment/use of reason *(Kant) (epi)*

hypothetischer Imperativ *m* • hypothetical imperative *(Kant etc) (eth)* ↔ kategorischer Imperativ

hypothetischer Schluß *m* • hypothetical syllogism *(log)*

hypothetischer Vernunftschluß *m* • hypothetical inference of reason *(Kant) (epi)*

hypothetischer Vertrag *m* • hypothetical contract *(soc, pol)* < Sozialkontraktstheorie

hypothetisches Konstrukt *n* • hypothetical construct *(sci)*

hypothetisches Urteil *n* • hypothetical judg(e)ment *(epi, log)*

Hypotypose *f* • hypotyposis *(Kant) (epi, met)*

hysteron proteron *n* • hysteron-proteron *(log)*

I

Iatromusik *f* → Musiktherapie

Iatrophilologie *f* • iatrophilology *(aes, psy)*

Ich *n* • self, ego, I *(psy, met)* < Selbst, das < W 473, 474, 475, 476

Ich, absolutes *n* • absolute I/ego/self *(Fichte etc) (met)* < reines Ich

Ich als Bündel von Wahrnehmungen *n* • the self as bundle of perceptions *(Hume etc) (epi, met)* < Bündeltheorie des Selbst

Ich als Objekt *n* • I as object *(Kant) (epi)*

Ich als Subjekt *n* • I as subject *(Kant) (epi)*

Ich denke • I think *(Kant) (epi)* < cogito ergo sum

Ich-Du • I-Thou *(Buber etc) (rel)* → Ich und Du

Ich-Du-Beziehung *f* • I-Thou relationship *(Buber) (met)*

Ich, eigentliches *n* • authentic ego *(met)*

Ich, empirisches *n* • empirical I/ego/self *(Kant, Fichte) (epi, met)* → phänomenales Ich

Ich-Es • I-It *(Buber etc) (rel)*

Ich, höheres *n* • higher self *(met)*

Ich, konkretes *n* • concrete self *(Kierkegaard) (met)*

Ich, phänomenales *n* • phenomenal ego/self *(Kant) (epi, met)* → empirisches Ich

Ich, primäres *n* • primary self *(Reininger) (met)* ↔ Ich, sekundäres

Ich, reines *n* • pure self/ego *(Fichte, Husserl etc) (met)*

Ich, sekundäres *n* • secondary self *(Reininger) (met)* ↔ Ich, primäres

Ich, setzendes *n* • positing ego *(Fichte) (met)*

Ich setzt ein Nicht-Ich • the I posits a non-I, the ego posits a non-ego *(Fichte) (met)*

Ich, transzendentales *n* • transcendental I/ego *(Kant) (epi, met)*

Ich, transzendentalphänomenologisches *n* • transcendental-phenomenological self/ego *(Husserl) (met)*

Ich und Du *n,n* • I And Thou *(Buber etc) (rel)* → Ich-Du < Ich-es < W 475

Ich und Nicht-Ich *n,n* • I and non-I, ego and non-ego *(Fichte etc) (met)*

Ich, wollendes *n* • willing/intentional self/ego *(Kant, Fichte) (met, eth)*

Ichbefangenheit *f* • egocentricity *(psy)*

Ichbewußtsein *n* • ego-consciousness *(Fichte etc) (met)*, awareness of the self, self-awareness *(psy, min)* < Selbstbewußtsein

Ich-Entwicklung *f* • ego-development *(Freud etc) (psy)*

Ich-Erlebnis *n* • ego-experience, experience of the self *(psy, met)*

Ichgefühl *n* • ego-feeling *(Freud etc) (psy)*

Ichgewißheit *f* • I-awareness *(Hegel etc) (met)*, I-certainty *(Descartes) (epi, met)* < cogito ergo sum, Gewißheit der eigenen Existenz

Ichheit *f* • I-hood, I-ness, notion of the self *(Heidegger) (met)*

Ich-Ideal *n* • ideal self, ego-ideal *(Freud) (psy)* → Ego-Ideal

Ich-Identität *f* • personal identity, ego-identity *(met, psy)*

ichlos • without ego, selfless *(met, psy)*

ich-loses Bewußtsein *n* • ego-less consciousness *(Habermas) (psy)*

Ichlosigkeit *f* • egolessness *(met, asp)*

Ichpsychologie *f* • ego-psychology *(psy)*

Ichsein *n* • being-a-self *(met)*

Ichspaltung *f* • split identity, splitting of the ego *(Freud) (psy)* → Persönlichkeitsspaltung, Schizophrenie < Bewußtseinsspaltung

Ichtrieb *m* • ego-drive/instinct *(Freud) (psy)*

Ich-Überschreitung *f* • self-transcendence *(met)* < Selbstüberschreitung

Ichverhaftetheit *f* • attachment to the ego *(psy)*

Ichzentriertheit *f* • self-centredness, egocentrism *(psy)* → Egozentrik < Ichbefangenheit

Ideal *n* • ideal *(gep)*

Ideal der (reinen) Vernunft *n* • ideal of (pure) reason *(Kant) (epi, met)*

Ideal der Schönheit *n* • ideal of the beautiful *(Kant) (aes, met)*

Idealbild *n* • ideal image *(psy, aes)*

ideale Anschauung *f* • ideal intuition *(Brentano) (epi, psy)*

ideale Bedingungen *pl* • ideal circumstances *(Rawls etc) (eth, soc)*

Ideale-Beobachter-Theorie *f* • ideal observer theory *(eth)*

ideale Gegenständlichkeit *f* • (property of being an) ideal object *(Husserl) (ont)*

ideale Gesellschaft *f* • ideal society *(soc)* < Idealstaat

ideale Handlung *f* • ideal action *(Searle etc) (lan, act)*

ideale Kommunikationsgemeinschaft *f* • ideal communication community, ideal community of communication *(Mead, Apel, Habermas) (lan, soc)*

ideale Objektivität *f* • ideal objectivity *(Husserl) (epi, ont)*

ideale Sprache *f* • ideal language *(lan, sci)* → Idealsprache

idealer Beobachter *m* • ideal observer *(eth)*

idealer Moralkodex *m* • ideal moral code *(eth)*

idealer Realismus *m* • ideal realism *(Schleiermacher etc) (rel)*

ideales Ich *n* • ideal ego *(Hegel) (met)*

ideales Sein *n* • ideal being *(met)*

ideales Seinsollen *n* • ideal ought-to-be *(Scheler) (eth)*

Idealfaktor *m* • ideal factor *(Scheler) (sci)* < Realfaktor

Idealforderung *f* • ideal demand *(Freud etc) (psy)*

Idealgrund *m* • ideal reason *(Kant etc) (met)* ↔ Realgrund

Idealgruppe *f* • ideal group *(mat)*

Ideal-Ich *n* • ideal ego *(Freud) (psy)*

idealische Norm *f* • ideal norm *(Kant) (met)*

idealischer Charakter *m* • ideal character *(aes)*

idealisieren • to idealize *(gep)*

idealisierende Modelle *pl* • idealizing models *(sci, sys)*

idealisierter Begriff *m* • idealized concepts *(lan, sci)*

idealisierter Handelnder *m* • idealized agent *(eth)*

Idealisierung *f* • idealization *(gep)*

Idealismus *m* • idealism *(gep)*

Idealismus, absoluter *m* • absolute idealism *(Hegel etc) (met)*

Idealismus, akosmischer *m* • acosmic/acosmistic idealism *(Berkeley) (epi, met)* < Idealismus, empirischer

Idealismus, aktualistischer *m* • actualist idealism *(Gentile, Croce) (met)*

Idealismus der Freiheit *m* • idealism of freedom *(Dilthey) (met)*

Idealismus, deutscher *m* • German Idealism *(gep)*

Idealismus, empirischer *m* • empirical idealism *(Berkeley) (epi, met)* → Idealismus, psychologischer

Idealismus, erkenntnistheoretischer *m* • epistemological idealism *(epi)*

Idealismus, kritischer *m* • critical idealism *(Kant) (epi, met)* → Idealismus, transzendentaler

Idealismus, logischer *m* • logical idealism *(Dummett etc) (ont)*

Idealismus, magischer *m* • magical idealism *(met, aes)* < Romantik

Idealismus, metaphysischer *m* • metaphysical idealism *(met)*

Idealismus, methodischer *m* • methodical idealism *(epi, met)*

Idealismus, monistischer *m* • monistic idealism *(Reininger) (met)*

Idealismus, morphologischer *m* • morphological/morphologic idealism *(Friedmann) (met)*

Idealismus, objektiver *m* • objective idealism *(Schelling, Hegel) (met)*

Idealismus, pantheistischer *m* • pantheistic idealism *(met)*

Idealismus, physikalischer *m* • physicalist(ic) idealism *(Lenin) (met)*

Idealismus, praktischer *m* • practical idealism *(met)*

Idealismus, psychologischer *m* • psychological idealism *(Berkeley) (epi, met)* → Idealismus, empirischer

Idealismus, realer *m* • real idealism *(Schleiermacher) (met)*

Idealismus, subjektiver *m* • subjective idealism *(Berkeley, Fichte) (met, epi)*

Idealismus, teleologischer *m* • teleological idealism *(Lotze etc) (met)*

Idealismus, transzendentaler *m* • transcendental idealism *(Kant) (epi, met)* → Idealismus, kritischer < W 978

Idealisten-Mäntel *pl* • idealist cloaks *(Nietzsche) (met)*

idealistische Philosophie *f* • idealist(ic) philosophy *(gep)*

idealistischer Überbau *m* • idealist(ic) superstructure *(Marx etc) (epi)*

Idealität *f* • ideality *(met)* ↔ Realität

Idealkonzept *n* • ideal concept *(aes, gep)*

Idealraum *m* • ideal space *(N. Hartmann etc) (ont)*

Idealrealismus *m* • ideal realism *(Fichte, Kant, Wundt) (met)*

Idealsprache *f* • ideal language *(lan, sci)* ↔ Normalsprache

Idealstaat *m* • ideal state/republic, model city° *(Plato etc) (pol)* < ideale Gesellschaft, platonischer Staat, Staatsideal, Utopie

idealtypisch • ideal-typical, ideal type, of an ideal type *(Weber) (sci)*

idealtypische Definition *f* • ideal-typical definition, ideal type definition, definition by ideal type *(Weber) (sci)*

Idealtypus *m* • ideal type *(Weber etc) (sci)*

Idealzustand *m* • ideal state/condition *(gep)*

Ideat *n* • ideate *(met)*

Ideation *f* • ideation *(met, min)*

Idee *f* • idea, notion, concept *(gep)* < Ideenlehre

Idee der Ausdehnung *f* • idea of extension *(Descartes etc) (met)*

Idee der Freiheit *f* • idea of freedom *(Kant) (epi, eth)*

Idee der reinen Vernunft *f* • idea of pure reason *(Kant) (epi)*

Idee der Vernunft *f* • idea of reason *(Kant, Hegel etc) (met)*

Idee des Guten *f* • idea/form of the good *(Plato etc) (met, eth)*

Idee des Schönen *f* • idea/form of beauty/the beautiful *(Plato etc) (met, aes)*

Idee des Unbedingten *f* • idea of the unconditioned *(Kant etc) (met)* < Unbedingte, das

Idee des Wahren *f* • idea/form of the true/truth *(Plato etc) (met)*

Idee, einfache *f* • simple idea *(Descartes, Locke, Leibniz etc) (epi)* ↔ Idee, zusammengesetzte

Idee, fiktive *f* • fictitious idea *(epi)*

Idee, regulative *f* • regulative idea *(Kant) (epi, met)*

Idee, zusammengesetzte *f* • complex/compound idea *(Locke etc) (epi)* ↔ Idee, einfache

ideeierende Abstraktion *f* • ideation, ideating abstraction *(log, lan)* < Abstraktion, isolierende

ideell • (▷ Idee) ideational, (▷ Ideal) ideal *(gep)*

Ideelle, das *n* • the ideal *(gep)*

ideeller Überbau *m* • ideational superstructure *(Marx) (epi, soc)* ↔ materielle Basis

Ideen, angeborene *pl* • innate ideas *(Descartes etc) (epi)* → eingeborene Ideen

Ideen, erworbene *pl* • acquired ideas *(Descartes etc) (epi)*

Ideen, konstruierte *pl* • constructed ideas *(Descartes etc) (epi)*

Ideen, Reich der *n* • realm of the forms/ideas *(Plato) (met)* → Ideenwelt

Ideenassoziation *f* • association of ideas *(Locke etc) (epi, psy)* < Gedankenassoziation

Ideengebäude *n* • system of ideas *(gep)*

Ideengebilde *n* • set of ideas *(gep)*

Ideengeschichte *f* • history of ideas/thought, intellectual history *(his)* ↔ Realgeschichte < Wissenschaftsgeschichte

Ideengeschichtler *m* • intellectual historian *(his)*

Ideenlehre *f* • theory/doctrine of forms/ideas *(Plato etc) (met)*, ideology *(Condorcet) (epi)*

Ideenlieferant *m* • supplier of ideas *(gen)* < Think-tank

Ideenrealismus *m* • realism of ideas *(epi, met)*

Ideenreichtum *m* • wealth of ideas *(gen)*

Ideenschau *f* • contemplation of (the) forms/ideas *(Plato) (met)*

Ideentheorie *f* • theory of ideas *(met)* < Ideenlehre

Ideenwelt *f* • world of forms/ideas *(Plato etc) (met)* → Ideen, Reich der

idempotentes Element *n* • idempotent element *(mat)*

ident • identical *(log)*

Identifikation *f* • identification *(gep)*

Identifikationssynthese *f* • synthesis of identification *(Husserl) (epi, met)*

identifizieren • to identify *(gep)*

identifizierender Ausdruck *m* • identifying expression/statement *(Searle etc) (lan)*

Identifizierung *f* • identification *(psy)*

identische Punkte *pl* • identical points *(Helmholtz, Wundt) (nat, psy)*

Identität *f* • identity *(log, met, psy)* < Objektkonstanz < W 484

Identität, abstrakte *f* • abstract identity *(Hegel) (met)*

Identität, begriffliche *f* • conceptual identity *(lan)*

Identität, beschädigte *f* • impaired identity *(Goffman) (psy)*

Identität der Apperzeption des Bewußtseins *f* • indentity of apperception of consciousness *(Kant) (epi)*

Identität der Art *f* → Typ-Identität

Identität der Gegensätze *f* • identity of opposites *(Hegel etc) (met)*

Identität des Bewußtseins meiner selbst *f* • identity of the consciousness of myself *(Kant) (epi, met)*

Identität des Geistes *f* • identity of the spirit *(Hegel) (met)*

Identität des Ununterscheidbaren *f* • identity of indiscernibles *(Leibniz etc) (log, met)*

Identität, extensionale *f* • extensional identity *(lan, log)*

Identität, formale *f* • formal identity *(log, met)*

Identität in Differenz *f* • identity in difference *(met)*

Identität, intentionale *f* • intentional identity *(psy, min)*
Identität, konkrete *f* • concrete identity *(psy)*
Identität, kontingente *f* • contingent identity *(log, met)*
Identität, materiale *f* • material identity *(met)*
Identität mit sich *f* → Selbstidentität
Identität, numerische *f* • numerical identity *(mat)*
Identität, persönliche *f* • personal identity *(psy)* < Individualität
Identität, Prinzip der *n* • principle of identity *(log)*
Identität, qualitative *f* • qualititative identity *(psy)*
Identität, reale *f* • real identity *(met, psy)*
Identität, soziale *f* • social identity *(soc)*
Identität und Differenz *f,f* • identity and difference *(met)* < Einheit und Differenz
Identität von Denken und Sein *f* • identity of thinking/thought and being *(Parmenides, Hegel etc) (met)*
Identität von Sein und Wahrnehmung *f* • identity of being and perception *(Berkeley etc) (epi)*
Identitätsbeweis *m* • proof of identity *(log)*
Identitätsbildung *f* • formation of identity *(psy)*
Identitätserlebnis *n* • experience of identity *(Husserl etc) (met)*
Identitätsgefühl *n* • feeling of identity *(Erikson etc) (psy)*
Identitätskrise *f* • identity crisis *(psy)*
Identitätskrise der Kunst *f* • identity crisis of art *(aes)*
Identitätskriterium *n* • identity criterion *(Quine etc) (ont)*
Identitätslosigkeit *f* • lack of identity *(gep)*
Identitätsphilosophie *f* • philosophy of identity, identity philosophy *(Parmenides, Spinoza, Schelling etc) (met)*
Identitätsprinzip *n* • principle of identity *(Schelling etc) (met)*
Identitätsproblem *n* • identity problem *(met, psy)*
Identitätssystem *n* • system of identity *(Schelling) (met)*
Identitätstheorie *f* • identity theory *(log)*
Identitätsverlust *m* • loss of identity *(psy)*
Ideogenese *f* • ideogenesis *(epi)*
Ideogramm *n* • ideogram, ideograph *(lan)*
Ideographie *f* • ideography *(lan)* → Begriffsschrift
Ideologie *f* • ideology *(Destutt de Tracy etc) (epi, pol)* < Ideenlehre < W 486

Ideologiekritik *f* • ideology critique, critique of ideology *(epi, pol)*
ideologisch • ideological *(pol)*
ideologischer Kampf *m* • ideological struggle *(pol)*
ideologischer Überbau *m* • ideological superstructure *(Marx etc) (soc)*
ideologisieren • to ideologize *(pol)*
idiographische Wissenschaft *f* • idiographic science *(Windelband) (sci)* ↔ nomothetische Wissenschaft
Idiolatrie *f* • idiolatry *(psy, rel)* → Selbstvergötterung
Idiolekt *m* • idiolect *(lan)*
idiotes *m* • private person *(Aristotle) (pol)* → Privatmann < zoon politicon
Idolatrie *f* • idolatry *(rel, aes)* → Bilderverehrung, Götzendienst
Idole der Höhle *pl* • idols of the cave/den *(Bacon) (epi)* → Trugbilder der Höhle
Idole des Geistes *pl* • idols of the mind *(Bacon) (epi)*
Idole des Marktes *pl* • idols of the marketplace *(Bacon) (epi)* → Trugbilder des Marktes
Idole des Stammes *pl* • idols of the tribe *(Bacon) (epi)* → Trugbilder des Stammes
Idole des Theaters *pl* • idols of the theatre *(Bacon) (epi)*
Idolenlehre *f* • doctrine of idols *(Bacon) (epi)* < Trugbild
Ignoranz *f* • ignorance *(epi)* < W 134
ignoratio elenchi *f* • nt, ignorance of the point in dispute *(log, lan)*
Ikon *n* • icon *(lan)*
ikonisches Zeichen *n* • iconic sign *(lan)*
Ikonodulie *f* • iconoduly *(rel, aes)* ↔ Ikonoklasmus
Ikonographie *f* • iconography *(aes)*
ikonographisch • iconographic(al) *(aes)*
Ikonoklasmus *m* • iconoclasm *(rel, aes)* → Bilderstürmerei ↔ Ikonodulie
Ikonolatrie *f* • iconolatry, image-worship *(rel, aes)*
Ikonologie *f* • iconology *(aes)* → Ikonographie
Illegalität *f* • illegality, unlawfulness *(jur)* → Ungesetzlichkeit
Illegitimität *f* • illegitimacy *(jur)*
Illiberalität *f* • illiberality, illiberalness°, illiberalism° *(eth)*
Illokution *f* • illocution *(Austin etc) (lan)* < Perlokution
illokutionäre Handlung *f* → illokutionärer Akt

illokutionäre Kraft *f* • illocutionary force
(*Austin etc*) (*lan*) < illokutionäres Ziel

illokutionäre Rolle *f* → illokutionäre Kraft

illokutionärer Akt *m* • illocutionary act
(*Austin, Searle etc*) (*lan*) → Sprechakt,
illokutionärer < lokutionärer Akt

illokutionärer Bindungseffekt *m* • illocutionary binding/bonding effect (*Habermas*)
(*lan, act*)

illokutionärer Erfolg *m* • illocutionary success
(*Austin etc*) (*lan, act*)

illokutionäres Ziel *n* • illocutionary aim
(*Austin*) (*lan, act*)

Illoyalität *f* • disloyalty (*jur, eth*)

Illuminationslehre *f* • doctrine of illumination
(*Augustine etc*) (*rel*)

Illuminismus *m* • illuminism (*Plato, Augustine
etc*) (*rel*)

Illusion *f* • illusion, delusion (*epi, psy*) → Einbildung, Täuschung

Illusion, naive *f* • naive illusion (*Vaihinger*)
(*met*)

Illusionstheorie der Kunst *f* • illusion(ist)
theory of art (*aes*)

imaginär • imaginary (*mat, psy, min*)

imaginäre Befriedigung *f* • imaginary satisfaction (*Freud*) (*psy*)

imaginäre Zahl *f* • imaginary number (*mat*)

imaginäres Museum *n* • the imaginary museum, museum without walls (*Malraux*) (*aes*)

Imagination *f* • imagination (*psy, aes*) < Einbildungskraft, Vorstellungskraft

Imago *f* • imago (*Freud, Jung etc*) (*psy*)

Imago Dei *f* • image of God (*rel*) < Gottebenbildlichkeit

Imitation *f* • imitation (*gep, aes*) < Nachbildung, Mimesis

Imitationslernen *n* • learning by imitation (*epi,
psy*)

immanent • immanent (*gep*)

immanente Gegenständlichkeit *f* • immanent
objectivity/object-quality (*Brentano*) (*ont*)

immanente Gültigkeit *f* • immanent validity
(*Kant*) (*epi, log*)

immanente Kritik *f* • immanent criticism,
immanent critique (*gep*)

immanenter Sinn der Geschichte *m* • immanent sense/meaning of history (*Vico etc*)
(*his*)

immanentes Wirken *n* • immanent causation
(*rel, met*)

Immanenz *f* • immanence (*epi, met*)

Immanenzlehre *f* • doctrine of immanence
(*Avenarius, Schuppe etc*) (*epi*)

Immanenzphilosophie *f* → Immanenzlehre

Immanenzpositivismus *m* • immanence positivism (*Mach, Avenarius etc*) (*epi*)

Immaterialismus *m* • immaterialism (*met*)

Immaterialität *f* • immateriality (*met*)

immaterielle Bedürfnisse *pl* • immaterial
wants/needs (*soc*)

immoralisch • immoral (*eth*) → unmoralisch
< amoralisch

Immoralismus *m* • immoralism (*eth*) < Amoralismus

Immoralität *f* • immorality (*eth*) < Amoralität

Immortalität *f* • immortality (*rel*) → Athanasie, Unsterblichkeit

Immunisierung *f* • immunization (*Lakatos,
Popper etc*) (*sci*)

Immunisierungsstrategie *f* • strategy/strata-
gem of immunization (*Lakatos, Popper etc*)
(*sci*) < Falsifikationsimmunität

Immunitätsrecht *n* • immunity right, right of
immunity (*jur, eth*)

Immutabilität *f* • immutability (*met*) → Unveränderlichkeit

Impenetrabilität *f* • impenetrability (*nat, epi*)
→ Undurchdringlichkeit

Imperativ *m* • imperative (*eth, lan*)

Imperativ der Sittlichkeit *m* • imperative of
morality (*Kant*) (*eth*) < kategorischer Imperativ

Imperativ, hypothetischer *m* • hypothetical
imperative (*Kant etc*) (*eth*) ↔ kategorischer
Imperativ

Imperativ, kategorischer *m* • categorical
imperative (*Kant*) (*eth*) ↔ hypothetischer
Imperativ < universelle Maxime

Imperativ, universeller *m* • universal
imperative (*Hare etc*) (*eth, lan*)

Imperative, strukturelle *pl* • structural
imperatives (*soc, eth*) < Sachzwang

imperatives Mandat *n* • imperative mandate
(*pol*) ↔ freies Mandat

Imperativkomponente (der Bedeutung
moralischer Ausdrücke) *f* • imperative
component (of the meaning of moral terms)
(*Stevenson etc*) (*eth*)

Imperativ-Modus *m* • imperative mode
(*Hare*) (*eth, lan*)

Imperativ-Theorie moralischer Urteile *f* •
imperative theory of moral judg(e)ments
(*eth*)

Imperialismus *m* • imperialism (*pol*) < W 489

Imperialismustheorie *f* • theory of imperialism
(*pol*)

Impersonale *n* • impersonal (*lan*)

Imperzeptibilität *f* • imperceptibility (*psy, epi*)
↔ Wahrnehmbarkeit

Impetustheorie f • theory of impetus (nat)

Implementationsphase f • implementation phase (sci)

Implementierung f • implementation (gep)

Implikat n • implicature (lan)

Implikation f • implication (epi, log, lan)

Implikation, kausale f • causal implication (met, log)

Implikation, logische f • logical implication (log)

Implikation, materiale f • material implication (Frege etc) (log)

Implikator m • implication sign, implicator° (log, lan)

implizit • implicit (log, lan) ↔ explizit

implizit folgernde Vernunfttätigkeit f • implicit reasoning (Newman) (epi, log) < Folgerungssinn

implizite Definition f • implicit definition (log, lan)

implizite Funktion f • implicit function (mat)

implizites Wissen n • implicit knowledge, tacit knowledge (epi) < persönliches Wissen

Imponderabilität f • imponderability (gep) → Unwägbarkeit, Unberechenbarkeit

Imponiergehabe n • display behaviour (nat, psy)

Importation f • importation (log) < Exportationsgesetz

Importationsgesetz n • importation rule (log) ↔ Exportationsgesetz

Impressionismus m • Impressionism (aes)

Improvisation f • improvisation (aes, gep)

improvisierte Musik f • improvised music (aes)

Impulserhaltung f • conservation of momentum (nat)

In-der-Welt-Sein n • being-in-the-world (Heidegger etc) (ont)

In-Sein n • being-in (Heidegger etc) (ont)

In-sich-Sein n • being-in-itself (Heidegger etc) (ont)

In-vitro-Fertilisation f • in-vitro fertilization (nat, eth) < künstliche Befruchtung, Retortenbaby

inadäquates Erkennen n • inadequate cognition (epi) < unvollständiges Wissen

Inadäquatheit f • inadequacy (gep) → Unangemessenheit

Inbegriff aller Erscheinungen m • sum total of all appearances (Kant) (epi)

Inbegriffe pl • collections, sets (Bolzano) (log, lan), aggregates (Stumpf) (sys)

Indefinite, das n • the indefinite (met, log, mat)

Indefinitheit f • indefiniteness (lan, log)

Indeterminabilität f • indeterminability (log) → Unbestimmbarkeit

indeterminierte Formel f → kontingente Formel

Indeterminiertheit der Übersetzung f → Übersetzungsunbestimmtheit

Indeterminismus m • indeterminism (met, eth)

Index librorum prohibitorum m • index of prohibited books (rel) < Zensur

indexikalischer Ausdruck m • index (Peirce), egocentric particular (Russell), token reflexive expression (Reichenbach), indexical expression (Reichenbach, Kripke etc) (lan)

indexikalischer Gedanke m • indexical thought (Frege) (log, lan)

indexikalisches Zeichen n • indexical sign (Peirce) (sci) < ikonisches Zeichen, symbolisches Zeichen

Indexikalität f • indexicality (lan)

indifferente Freiheit des Willens f • indifferent freedom of the will (Schopenhauer etc) (met)

Indifferentismus m • indifferentism (met)

Indifferenz f • indifference (eth, psy) → Gleichgültigkeit

Indifferenzpunkt m • indifference point (psy)

Indikation, ethische f • ethical indication (eth)

Indikation, eugenische f • eugenic indication (eth)

Indikation, kriminologische f • criminological indication (eth)

Indikation, medizinische f • medical indication (eth)

Indikation, soziale f • social indication (eth)

Indikationenlösung f • abortion on medical or social grounds (eth) < Fristenregelung

Indikator m • indicator (lan)

indirekte Demokratie f • indirect democracy (pol) < repräsentative Demokratie

indirekte Mitteilung f • indirect communication/notice (Kierkegaard etc) (rel)

indirekter Beweis m • indirect proof/demonstration (log)

indirekter Nutzen m • indirect benefit/utility (eco) < Umwegrentabilität

indirekter Realitätsbezug m • indirect reference to reality (sci)

Indiscernibilien, Identität der f • identity of indiscernibles (Leibniz) (log, met) → Identität des Ununterscheidbaren

Indische Philosophie f • Indian philosophy (asp)

Indische Weisheit f • Indian wisdom (asp)

Individualbegriff *m* • individual concept *(lan)* ↔ Kollektivbegriff

Individualcharakter *m* • individual character *(psy)*

Individualethik *f* • individual ethics *(eth)* ↔ Sozialethik

Individualien *pl* • individual concepts *(lan)*

Individualisation *f* → Individualisierung

Individualisierung *f* • individualization *(log, lan)*

Individualismus *m* • individualism *(gep)* ↔ Kollektivismus

Individualität *f* • individuality *(log, ont, psy)*

Individualmoral *f* • individual morality *(eth)* ↔ Sozialmoral

Individualontologie *f* • individual ontology *(ont)*

Individualprävention *f* • individual prevention *(jur, soc)* ↔ Sozialprävention

Individualpsychologie *f* • individual psychology *(Adler) (psy)* < W 817

Individualrechte *pl* • individual rights *(jur, eth)*

Individualsphäre *f* • individual sphere *(soc)* < Privatsphäre

Individualstil *m* • individual/personal style *(aes)*

Individualurteil *n* • individual judg(e)ment *(epi, log)* → Urteil, einzelnes

Individuation *f* • individuation *(Quine etc) (ont, lan), (ant, psy)* < Selbstwerdensprozeß

Individuation, Prinzip der *n* → Individuationsprinzip

Individuationsapparat *m* • individuation apparatus *(Quine etc) (lan, ont)*

Individuationsprinzip *n* • principle of individuation *(met)* → principium individuationis

Individuationsprozeß *m* • individuation process, process of individuation *(psy, ant, soc)* < Sozialisationsprozeß

individuelle Freiheit *f* • individual liberty *(pol)*

Individuenbereich *m* • domain of individuals *(log)*

Individuenkonstante *f* • individual constant *(log)* < Prädikatenlogik

Individuenvariable *f* • individual variable *(log)*

Individuum *n* • individual *(log, ont, soc)*

Indiz *n* • (piece of) evidence *(jur)*, sign, indication *(gep)*

Indizienbeweis *m* • (proof based on) circumstantial evidence *(jur)*

Indoktrination *f* • indoctrination *(psy)*

Induktion *f* • induction *(log)* → Epagogé, Schluß vom Einzelnen auf das Allgemeine ↔ Deduktion < empirische Verallgemeinerung

Induktion, abgeleitete *f* • deductive/descending induction *(Mill) (log)*

Induktion, aufzählende *f* • enumerative induction, induction by enumeration *(log, sci)* → Induktion, vollständige

Induktion, eliminative *f* → Induktion, eliminierende

Induktion, eliminierende *f* • eliminative induction *(Mill) (log, sci)* → ausschaltende Induktion

Induktion, hypothetische *f* • hypothetical induction *(log, sci)*

Induktion, mathematische *f* • mathematical induction *(mat, log)*

Induktion durch Aufzählung, Prinzip der *n* • principle of induction by enumeration *(log)* < Induktion, aufzählende

Induktion, transfinite *f* • transfinite induction *(log)*

Induktion, unendliche *f* • infinite induction *(log, sci)*

Induktion, unvollständige *f* • incomplete/imperfect induction *(log, sci)*

Induktion, vollständige *f* • complete induction *(log, sci)* → Induktion, aufzählende

Induktion, voraussagende *f* • predictive induction *(log, sci)*

Induktionsaxiom *n* • induction axiom *(log)*

Induktionslogik *f* • inductive logic *(Carnap etc) (log)* < induktive Logik

Induktionsprinzip *n* • principle of induction *(sci)*

Induktionsproblem *n* • problem of induction *(Hume, Goodman etc) (sci)*

Induktionsregreß *m* • regress in induction *(sci)*

Induktionsschluß *m* → induktiver Schluß

Induktionsskepsis *f* • inductive/inductionist scepticism, scepticism regarding induction *(epi)*

induktiv-statistische Prognose *f* • inductive-statistical prediction *(sci, mat)*

induktiv-statistische Systematisierung *f* • inductive-statistical systematization *(sci, mat)*

induktive Generalisierung *f* • inductive generalization *(log, sci)*

induktive Interpretation der Wahrscheinlichkeit *f* • inductive interpretation of probability *(mat, sci)*

induktive Logik *f* • inductive logic *(Mill etc) (log)*

induktive Metaphysik *f* • inductive metaphysics *(N. Hartmann etc) (met)*

induktive Methode *f* • inductive method *(sci)*

induktive Statistik *f* • inductive/inferential statistics *(mat)*

induktive Verallgemeinerung *f* • inductive generalization *(log, sci)*

induktiver Schluß *m* • inductive inference/ syllogism *(log, sci)*

induktives Argument *n* • inductive argument *(log, sci)*

induktives Denken *n* • inductive reasoning *(epi)*

induktives Schlußfolgern *n* • inferring by induction, inductive inferencing° *(log, sci)*

Induktivismus *m* • inductivism *(sci)*

induktivistisch • inductivist, inductivistic *(sci, log)*

Industrialisierung *f* • industrialization *(eco, soc)*

Industrialismus *m* • industrialism *(eco, soc)*

Industriearchäologie *f* • industrial archaeology *(cul, his)*

Industriedesign *n* • industrial design *(aes)*

Industriegesellschaft *f* • industrial society *(soc, eco)*

Industrielle Revolution *f* • Industrial Revolution *(eco, soc, his)*

industrielle Zivilisation *f* • industrial civilization *(soc)*

industrieller Fortschritt *m* • industrial progress *(eco, soc)*

Industriewelt *f* • industrial world *(eco, soc)*

Industriezivilisation *f* • industrial civilization *(sci)*

Infallibilismus *m* • infallibilism *(rel)*

Infallibilität *f* • infallibility *(rel, gep)* → Unfehlbarkeit

Infantizid *m* • infanticide *(eth)* → Kindstötung < Homizid

inferentielle Begründung *f* • inferential justification *(epi, log)*

Inferenz *f* • inference *(log, epi)*

Inferenz, hypothetisch-deduktive *f* • hypothetic(al)-deductive inference *(sci)*

Inferenz, räumliche *f* • spatial inference *(log, min)*

Inferenzmaschine *f* • inference engine *(Babbage) (mat, tec)*

Inferenzverfahren *n* • inference technique *(log)*

Infinität *f* • infinity *(mat, met)* → Unbegrenztheit

infinite Modelle *pl* • infinite models *(log)* ↔ finite Modelle

infiniter Regreß *m* • infinite regress(ion) *(log, epi, sci)*

Infinitesimalkalkül *m/n* • infinitesimal calculus *(mat, log)*

Infinitesimalrechnung *f* • infinitesimal calculus, calculus of infinitesimals *(mat)* < Differential- und Integralrechnung

Infinitismus *m* • infinitism *(met)*

Inflationismus *m* • inflationism *(epi)*

inflationistische Wahrheitstheorie *f* • inflationary/inflationist theory of truth *(epi, met)*

Inflationsrate *f* • rate of inflation, inflation rate *(eco)* → Teuerungsrate

Informatik *f* • computer science, informatics *(mat, AI)* < Informationstechnologie

Information *f* • information *(gep)*

Information, abweichende *f* • discrepant information *(AI)*

Informationsästhetik *f* • information aesthetics *(Birkhoff, Bense) (aes)* < Birkhoffsche Formel, digitale Ästhetik

Informationsdefizit *n* • information deficit *(gen)*

Informationsgehalt *m* • information content *(lan)*

Informationsgesellschaft *f* • information society *(soc)*

Informationsmenge *f* • amount of information *(mat, AI, min)*

Informationspsychologie *f* • information psychology *(sci, psy)*

Informationstechnologie *f* • information technology, IT *(AI, tec)*

Informationstheorie *f* • information theory *(AI, mat, lan)*

Informationstheorie der Kunst *f* • information theory of art *(aes)*

Informationsträger *m* • information-carrier *(AI)*

Informationsüberlastung *f* • information overload *(AI)*

Informationsverarbeitung *f* • information processing *(AI)*

Informationszeitalter *n* • information age, age of information *(his)*

Informel *n* → informelle Kunst

informelle Formalisierung *f* • informal formalization *(sci)* < Non-statement view von Theorien

informelle Kunst *f* • informal art *(aes)*

informelle Logik *f* • informal logic *(log)* < Logik, nichtmonotone

informierte Einwilligung (der Versuchsperson) *f* • informed consent (of the test subject) *(sci)*

informierte Wahl *f* • informed choice *(act)* < informierte Zustimmung

informierte Zustimmung *f* • informed consent *(act, eth)*

Infragestellung traditioneller Werte *f •* questioning of traditional values *(eth)*

Ingenium *n →* Erfindungsgabe

Inhalt *m •* content *(gen)*

Inhalt der Kunst *m •* content of art *(aes)*

Inhalt des Begriffs *m →* Begriffsinhalt

inhaltlich *•* as regards content *(gen)* < material

inhaltliche Redeweise *f •* material mode (of expression) *(Carnap etc) (lan)* ↔ formale Redeweise

Inhaltsanalyse *f •* content analysis *(lan)*

Inhaltsästhetik *f •* aesthetics of content *(aes)* ↔ Formalästhetik

inhaltsgleiche Prädikatoren *pl •* co-extensive predicators *(log)*

Inhaltsgleichheit *f •* identity of content/meaning/sense *(log, lan)* ↔ Umfangsgleichheit

Inhaltslogik *f •* logic of content, intensional logic *(log)*

Inhaltslosigkeit *f •* emptiness, meaninglessness, lack of content *(lan)*

Inhärentismus *m •* inherentism *(eth)*

Inhärenz *f •* inherence *(met, lan)*

Initiationsritual *n •* initiation rite, rite of transition *(cul, ant, soc)*

Inkarnation *f •* incarnation *(rel) →* Verkörperlichung

inkarnierter Sinn *m •* meaning incarnate *(Merleau-Ponty) (epi, met)*

Inklusion *f •* inclusion *(log)* ↔ Exklusion

Inkohärenz von Wechselwirkungen *f •* incoherence of reciprocal effects *(met)*

Inkommensurabilität *f •* incommensurability *(mat, nat, sci) →* Unvergleichbarkeit

Inkommensuralibilitätsthese *f •* incommensurability thesis *(Kuhn, Feyerabend etc) (sci)*

Inkompatibilismus *m •* incompatibilism *(eth)* ↔ Kompatibilismus < Unvereinbarkeit

Inkompatibilität *f •* incompatibility *(gep) →* Unvereinbarkeit

Imkompatibilität der Begriffe *f •* incompatibility of concepts *(epi, lan)*

Inkompetenzkompensationskompetenz *f •* competence in compensating for incompetence *(Marquard) (gep)*

inkongruentes Gegenstück *n •* incongruent counterpart *(Kant) (met)*

Inkongruenz *f •* incongruence *(log, mat)*

Inkonsistenz *f •* inconsistency *(log)*

Inkorrigibilität *f •* incorrigibility *(gep)*

Inkulturation *f •* enculturation *(cul)*

Innen und das Außen, das *n •* the inner and the outer *(epi, met)* < Inneres und Äußeres, Fremdpsychisches, Innenwelt

Inneneinstellung *f •* inner orientation *(Husserl) (met)*

Innengewandheit *f •* inner direction *(psy)* < Introvertiertheit

Innengruppe-Außengruppe-Unterscheidung *f •* in-group/out-group differentiation *(ant, soc)*

Innenperspektive *f •* internal perspective *(sci)*

Innenschau *f •* introspection *(psy) →* Introspektion

Innenwelt *f •* internal world *(Dilthey) (met, sci)*

innerartliche Aggression *f •* intraspecific/intercommunal aggression *(psy) →* intraspezifische Aggression ↔ interspezifische Aggression

innerbetriebliche Mitbestimmung *f •* industrial democracy/co-determination *(eco)*

Innere, das *n •* the inside, the inner state *(Schleiermacher etc) (met)*

innere Anschauung *f •* inner/internal intuition *(Kant) (epi)*

innere Befreiung *f •* inner/internal liberation *(eth, asp)*

innere Derivationsmodelle *pl •* internal derivation models *(sci)* < semantisches Modell

innere Empfindung *f •* inner sensation, internal sensation *(epi, psy)*

innere Erfahrung *f •* inner experience, internal experience *(epi)*

innere Form *f •* inner/inward form *(Kant, Plotinus, Shaftesbury etc) (epi, aes)* ↔ äußere Form

innere Freiheit *f •* inner/internal freedom *(eth)*

innere Gesetzgebung *f •* internal law-giving, inner legislation *(Kant) (eth)* < Selbstgesetzgebung der Vernunft

innere Harmonie *f •* inner/internal harmony *(rel, psy, eth)*

innere Kolonialisierung *f •* internal colonization *(Habermas) (soc, eth)* < Kolonisierung der Lebenswelt

innere Logik *f •* inner logic *(gep)*

innere Lüge *f •* internal lie *(Kant) (eth)*

innere Möglichkeit *f •* inner/internal possibility *(Kant) (epi)*

innere Natur *f •* inner nature *(ant)*

innere Ruhe *f •* inner stillness/peace *(eth, asp)* < Seelenfriede

innere Uhr *f •* internal clock *(nat)* < Biorhythmus

innere Umkehr *f •* inner conversion *(rel, eth)*

innere Verknüpfung *f •* inner/internal linking *(mat)*

innere Vorausbestimmung *f* • inner/internal predisposition *(Leibniz etc) (met, rel)*

innere Vorstellung *f* • inner/internal representation/impression *(Kant etc) (epi)*

innere Wahrnehmung *f* • inner/internal perception *(Locke, Brentano) (epi, psy)*

innere Zweckmäßigkeit *f* • inner/internal finality *(Kant etc) (met, aes)* < Zweckmäßigkeit ohne Zweck

innerer Dialog *m* • interior/internal dialogue *(aes, psy)*

innerer Feind *m* • the enemy within *(Nietzsche) (eth)*

innerer Friede *m* • inward peace *(rel)*

innerer Gerichtshof *m* • inner forum/court *(Kant) (eth)* < Gewissen

innerer Monolog *m* • interior/internal monologue *(aes, psy)* < Bewußtseinsstrom

innerer Richter *m* • inner judge *(Kant) (eth)*

innerer Sinn *m* • inner/internal/interior sense *(Locke etc) (epi)*, internal meaning *(gep)*

innerer Wert *m* → intrinsischer Wert

innerer Zwang *m* • internal compulsion *(psy)*

inneres Bild *n* • inner picture, internal image *(epi, psy)*

Inneres einer Menge *n* • interior of a set *(mat)*

inneres Erleben *n* • inner/internal experience/life *(Bergson etc) (met)*

inneres Gesetz *n* • inner/innate° law *(Kant) (met, eth)* < innere Gesetzgebung

inneres Leben *n* • internal life *(met)*

inneres Recht *n* • innate right *(Kant) (jur, met)* < Naturrecht

Inneres und Äußeres *n,n* • internal and external *(gep)*

inneres Zeitbewußtsein *n* • internal time consciousness, consciousness of internal time *(Bergson, Husserl etc) (psy)*

Innergruppenaggressivität *f* • ingroup-aggression *(psy, ant)*

Innerlichkeit *f* • inward/interior life, contemplative nature *(met, rel, psy)*

innerstes Leben *n* • innermost life *(met)*

innerweltlich • innerwordly, intrawordly, within-the-world *(met)*

Innerweltlich-Seiendes *n* • beings within the world *(Heidegger) (ont)*

innerweltliche Askese *f* • (this-)worldly asceticism, inner-world asceticism *(Weber) (soc)* ↔ weltabkehrende Askese

Innerweltlichkeit *f* • innerworldliness *(met)*, within-the-worldness *(Heidegger) (ont)*

innerzeitig • within-time *(Heidegger) (ont)*

Innerzeitliches *n* • internality-on-time, what-is-within time *(Heidegger) (ont)*

Innewerden *n* • to become aware, to notice, to perceive *(min)*, becoming-in-contemplation *(Heidegger) (ont)*

Innovationsfähigkeit *f* • faculty of innovation *(eco, tec)*

Innovationsprozeß *m* • innovation process *(eco, tec)*

Input *m* • input *(sys, AI)* ↔ Output

Input-Output-Analyse *f* • input-output analysis *(eco, gen)*

Inquisition *f* • the Inquisition *(rel)*

Insemination, heterologe *f* • heterologous insemination *(nat, eth)*

Insemination, homologe *f* • homologous insemination *(nat, eth)*

Insemination, künstliche *f* → künstliche Befruchtung

Insichsein *n* • being-in-itself *(Sartre) (met)*

Insider-Handel *m* • insider trading *(eco)*

Inspiration *f* • inspiration *(psy)*

Instantialsatz *m* • instantial statement *(lan, sci)*

Instantiation *f* • instantiation *(sci)*

Instanz *f* • instance *(gep)*

Instanzen der Abgrenzung *pl* • authorities of delimitation *(Foucault) (epi, pol)*

Instinkt *m* • instinct, urge, drive *(nat, psy)*

Instinkt der Freiheit *m* • instinct of freedom *(Nietzsche) (met)*

Instinktausstattung *f* • repertoire of instincts *(nat)*

Instinktbegabung *f* • instinctual endowment *(Freud) (psy)*

Instinkt-Entartung *f* • degeneration of instinct *(Nietzsche) (ant)*

instinktgeleitet • instinctual, guided/determined by instinct *(nat, psy)*

instinktgeleitete Verhaltensmuster *pl* • instinctual patterns of behaviour *(nat, psy)*

Instinkthandlung *f* • instinctive act *(nat, psy)*

instinktiv-angeborene Verhaltensweisen *pl* • instinctive (innate) behavioural patterns *(psy, ant)* < Nativismus

instinktive Moralität *f* • instinctive morality *(eth)*

Instinktivismus *m* • instinctivism *(psy)*

Instinktlehre *f* • theory of the instincts *(Freud) (psy)*

instinktorientiert • instinct-oriented *(Jung) (psy)*

Instinktreduktion *f* • instinct reduction *(Gehlen) (ant)*

Instinkttheorie *f* • instinct theory *(nat, psy)*

Institution *f* • institution *(soc, act)*

institutionalisierte Gewalt f • institutionalized violence *(pol)*

institutionalisierter Individualismus m • institutionalized individualism *(Habermas) (soc)*

institutionalisierter Wert m • institutionalized value *(eth, soc)*

Institutionalisierung f • institutionalization *(soc, act)*

institutionell gebundene Sprechhandlung f • institutionally bound speech act(tion) *(Habermas) (lan, act)*

institutionell ungebundene Sprechhandlung f • institutionally unbound speech act(tion) *(Habermas) (lan, act)*

institutioneller Wandel m • institutional change *(pol, soc)*

Institutionentheorie f • theory of institutions *(soc)*

instruktives Lernen n • instructive learning *(psy)*

instrumentale Konditionierung f • instrumental conditioning *(Skinner) (psy)*

Instrumentalisierung f • instrumentalization *(soc, eth)*

Instrumentalismus m • instrumentalism *(Dewey etc) (epi, sci)* < Pragmatismus

Instrumentalmusik f • instrumental music *(aes)* ↔ Vokalmusik

Instrumentalursache f • instrumental cause *(met)* → causa instrumentalis

instrumentelle Systemanalyse f • instrumental systems analysis *(sys)* ↔ maieutische Systemanalyse

instrumentelle Ursache f • instrumental cause *(met)* → causa instrumentalis, Instrumentalursache

instrumentelle Verfügung f • instrumental mastery *(Habermas) (soc, act)*

instrumentelle Verkürzung der Vernunft f • instrumental abridg(e)ment of reason *(Horkheimer, Habermas) (epi, soc)*

instrumentelle Vernunft f • instrumental reason *(Horkheimer etc) (epi, soc)* < Zweckrationalität

instrumentelles Handeln n • instrumental action *(Horkheimer etc) (act, soc)*

Inszenierung f • setting, staging *(aes)*

integraler Bestandteil m • integral part *(sys)*

Integralgleichung f • integral equation *(mat)*

Integralkalkül m/n • integral calculus *(mat)*

Integration f • integration *(soc, pol, mat)*

Integrationsmodell n • integration model *(sci)*

Integrationspolitik f • integration policy *(pol)*

integrative Erklärung f • integrative explanation *(sci)*

integrativer Unterricht m • mixed ability teaching, integrative learning *(psy)*

integrierender Faktor m • integrating factor *(mat)*

integrierte Typen pl • integrated types *(mat)*

Integrität f • integrity *(eth, jur)*

intellectus agens m → Intellekt, handelnder

intellectus archetypus m • archetypal/archetypical/archetypic° intellect *(met)*

Intellekt m • intellect *(epi, met)*

Intellekt, handelnder m • active/acting intellect *(Avicenna etc) (epi, met)* → intellectus agens

Intellektualisierung f • intellectualization *(Weber) (soc)* < Rationalisierung

Intellektualismus m • intellectualism *(gep)*

Intellektualismus, erkenntnistheoretischer m • epistemological intellectualism *(epi)*

Intellektualismus, ethischer m • ethical intellectualism *(Socrates etc) (eth)*

Intellektualismus, metaphysischer m • metaphysical intellectualism *(Leibniz etc) (met)*

Intellektualismus, psychologischer m • psychological intellectualism *(Aristotle, Aquinas etc) (psy)*

intellektuelle Anschauung f • intellectual intuition *(Fichte, Schelling) (epi)*

intellektuelle Lust f • intellectual pleasure *(eth)*

intellektuelle Mode f • intellectual fashion *(gep)*

intellektuelle Schönheit f • intellectual beauty *(Kant) (aes)*

intellektuelle Synthesis f • intellectual synthesis *(Kant) (epi)*

intellektuelle Vorstellung f • intellectual perception *(Locke) (epi)*

intellektuelle Zweckmäßigkeit f • intellectual finality *(Kant) (epi)*

intellektueller Begriff m • intellectual concept *(Kant) (epi, lan)*

intellektueller Gehalt m • intellectual content *(gep)*

intellektuelles Gewissen n • intellectual conscience *(Nietzsche) (eth)*

intellektuelles Interesse n • intellectual interest *(Kant etc) (eth, aes)*

intellektuelles Werterfassen n • intellectual perception of values/morals *(Rickert etc) (eth)*

intelligente tutorielle Systeme pl • intelligent tutoring systems *(AI)* < Expertensystem

Intelligenz f • (▷ Gruppe der Intellektuellen) intelligentsia *(soc)*, (▷ Verstandesvermögen) intelligence *(epi)*

Intelligenz, allgemeine *f •* general intelligence *(epi)*

Intelligenz, künstliche *f •* artificial/machine intelligence *(AI, min)*

Intelligenz, praktische *f •* practical intelligence *(Scheler) (act, gep)*

Intelligenzquotient *m •* intelligence quotient, IQ *(psy)*

Intelligenztest *m •* IQ test, intelligence test(ing) *(psy)*

Intelligibilität *f •* intelligibility *(Kant etc) (epi, met)*

Intelligible, das *n •* (the) intelligible *(Kant) (epi, met)*

intelligible Bedingung *f •* intelligible condition *(Kant) (epi, met)*

intelligible Kausalität *f •* intelligible causality *(Kant) (epi, met)*

intelligible Sphäre *f •* intelligible realm/sphere *(Kant etc) (epi, met)*

intelligible und sinnliche Wirklichkeit *f •* intelligible and sensible reality *(epi, met)*

intelligible Ursache *f •* intelligible cause *(Kant) (epi, met)*

intelligible Welt *f •* intelligible world *(Plato, Kant etc) (epi, met) →* mundus intelligibilis *↔* Sinneswelt

intelligible Zufälligkeit *f •* intelligible contingency *(Kant) (epi, met)*

intelligibler Akt *m •* intelligible act *(met)*

intelligibler Besitz *m •* intelligible possession *(Kant) (jur)*

intelligibler Charakter *m •* intelligible character *(Kant) (epi, met) ↔* empirischer Charakter

intelligibler Gegenstand *m •* intelligible object *(Kant) (epi, met)*

intelligibles Sein *n •* intelligible being *(met)*

intelligibles Wesen *n •* (an) intelligible being *(met)*

intelligo ut credam • I understand in order to believe, I understand that I believe *(Abelard) (rel) ↔* credo ut intelligam

Intension *f •* intension *(log, lan) ↔* Extension < Begriffsinhalt

intensional • intensional *(log, lan) ↔* extensional

intensionale Implikation *f •* intensional implication *(Husserl etc) (log) <* transzendentale Logik

intensionale Semantik *f •* intensional semantics *(log, lan)*

intensionale Zusammensetzungen *pl •* intensional compounds *(Quine) (epi, lan)*

intensionaler Kontext *m •* intensional context *(log, lan)*

intensionales Konditional *n •* intensional conditional *(log, act)*

Intensionalität *f •* intensionality *(log, lan)*

Intensitätsgrad *m •* degree of intensity *(gen)*

intensive Größe *f •* intensive magnitude *(Kant) (epi)*

intensive Tierhaltung *f •* factory farming *(eco, eth) <* Massentierhaltung

Intensivmedizin *f •* intensive care medicine *(nat, eth)*

Intention *f •* intention *(log, epi, act)*

Intention und Ausführung *f,f •* intention and execution *(act, tec, aes)*

intentional • intentional *(act, min)*

Intentionalanalyse *f •* intentional analysis *(Husserl) (epi, met) <* reelle Analyse

intentionale Analyse *f →* Intentionalanalyse

intentionale Einstellung *f •* intentional stance *(Dennett etc) (act, psy)*

intentionale Handlung *f •* intentional act(ion) *(act, min)*

intentionale Semantik *f •* intentional semantics *(lan)*

intentionale Verursachung *f •* intentional causation *(act)*

intentionaler Akt *m •* intentional act *(Husserl) (epi, met)*

intentionaler Gegenstand *m →* intentionales Objekt

intentionaler Gehalt *m •* intentional content *(Brentano, Husserl etc) (epi)*

intentionales Objekt *n •* intentional object *(Husserl) (epi, met), (Ingarden etc) (aes, ont)*

intentionales Verhalten *n •* intentional behaviour *(act) <* zielgerichtetes Verhalten

Intentionalismus *m •* intentionalism *(eth) →* Gesinnungsethik *↔* Konsequentialismus

Intentionalität *f •* intentionality *(Husserl etc) (epi, met, act) <* Absichtlichkeit, W 492

Intentionalität der Wahrnehmung *f •* intentionality of perception *(epi, psy)*

Interaktion *f •* interaction *(soc, psy)*

Interaktion, statistische *f •* statistical interaction *(mat, sci)*

Interaktion von Seele und Körper *f •* interaction of body and soul *(met)*

Interaktionalismus *m •* interactionalism, interactionism *(psy, soc)*

Interaktionismus *m •* interactionism *(Leibniz, Descartes etc) (met), (psy, soc) →* Interaktionalismus

Interaktionismus, symbolischer *m •* symbolic interactionism *(Baldwin, Mead etc) (soc)*

Interaktionsbeziehung *f* • interactive relation *(act, lan)*

Interaktionsebene *f* • level of interaction *(act, lan)*

Interaktionsfolge *f* • sequence of inter-action(s) *(Habermas) (act, lan)*

interaktionsfolgenrelevante Verbindlichkeit *f* • obligation relevant to the sequence of interaction(s) *(Habermas) (act, lan)*

Interaktionskompetenz *f* • interactive competence *(act, lan)*

interaktionssteuernd • interaction-guiding *(act)*

Interaktionsstruktur *f* • interaction structure *(Habermas) (act, lan)*

Interaktionsstufe *f* • stage/level of interaction *(act)*

Interaktionsteilnehmer *m* • participant in interaction *(soc, act)*

Interaktionstyp *m* • type of interaction *(Habermas) (act, lan)*

Interaktionszusammenhang *m* • interaction complex, context of interaction *(Habermas) (soc, act)*

interaktiv • interactive *(AI, sys)*

Interdefinition *f* • interdefinition *(log, lan)*

Interdependenz *f* • interdependence *(sys)* → gegenseitige Abhängigkeit, wechselseitige Abhängigkeit

Interdependenzsystem *n* • interdependence system *(sci, sys)*

interdiskursive Konfiguration *f* • interdis-cursive configuration *(Foucault) (lan, sys)*

interdisziplinäre Forschung *f* • interdiscipli-nary research *(sci)*

Interdisziplinarität *f* • interdisciplinarity *(gep)* < disziplinenübergreifend

Interesse *n* • interest *(gen)* < Erkenntnis-interesse

Interesse der Vernunft *n* • interest of reason *(Kant) (epi)*

interesseloses Anschauen *n* • disinterested contemplation *(aes)*

interesseloses Wohlgefallen *n* • disinterested/uninterested appreciation/pleasure/delight/satisfaction *(Kant, Schiller etc) (aes)* < Di-stanz, ästhetische; Desinteressiertheit

Interesselosigkeit *f* • disinterestedness *(gep)* < interesseloses Wohlgefallen

Interessen(s)ausgleich *m* • reconciliation of interests *(eth, pol)*

Interessenbefriedigung *f* • satisfaction of interests *(psy, act)*

Interessen(s)gegensatz *m* • clash of interests *(eth, pol)*

Interessengemeinschaft *f* • community of interests *(eth, pol, soc)*

Interessenhandeln *n* • action based on self-interest *(act, soc)*

Interessen(s)gruppe *f* • interest group *(pol)* → Lobby

Interessenkomplementarität *f* • complemen-tarity of interests *(Habermas) (lan, soc)*

Interessen(s)konflikt *m* • conflict of interests *(eth, pol)*

Interessensphäre *f* • sphere of interest/influence *(pol)*

Interessen(s)verband *m* • pressure-group *(eco, soc)* → Lobby

Interessenvertretung *f* • representation of interests *(pol)*

Interferenz *f* • interference *(sys)*

intergenerationelle Gerechtigkeit *f* • inter-generational justice *(eth)* → Gerechtigkeit zwischen Generationen ↔ intragseneratio-nelle Gerechtigkeit < Pflichten gegenüber künftigen Generationen, Zukunftsverant-wortung

Interimsregierung *f* • provisional/temporary/interim government *(pol)*

interindividuell • interpersonal *(soc, psy)* ↔ intraindividuell

Interiorisation *f* → Verinnerlichung

interkategorial • intercategorial *(log, epi)*

Interkonfessionalität *f* • interdenomina-tionalism *(rel)*

interkonfessionell • interdenominational *(rel)*

Interkulturalität *f* • inter/cross -culturality *(cul, pol)* < kultureller Pluralismus, Multikul-turalität

interkulturell • inter/cross -cultural *(cul, pol)*

interkulturelle Philosophie *f* • inter/cross-cul-tural philosophy *(gep)*

intermediare Variable *pl* • intervening variables *(Carnap) (epi, sci)*

Intermundien *pl* • intermundia, empty spaces *(Epicurus) (ont)* → Zwischenwelten < lee-rer Raum

Internalisation *f* → Internalisierung

Internalisierung *f* • internalization *(psy)* → Verinnerlichung

Internalisierung sozialer Kosten *f* • interna-lization of social costs *(eco)*

Internalisierung von Normen *f* • internaliza-tion of norms *(jur, eth)*

Internalismus *m* • internalism *(epi, eth)* ↔ Externalismus

Internalismus-Externalismus-Debatte *f* • internalism-externalism debate *(epi)*

Internationale, die *f* • the International *(pol)*

internationale Beziehungen *pl* • international relations *(pol)*

internationale Gerechtigkeit *f* • international justice *(pol, eth)*

Internationaler Gerichtshof *m* • International Court of Justice *(jur, pol)*

Internationaler Stil *m* • the International Style *(aes)*

Internationalisierung *f* • internationalization *(pol)* < Globalisierung

Internationalismus *m* • internationalism *(pol)*

interne Beziehungen *pl* • internal relations *(pol, sys)*

interne Frage *f* • internal question *(Carnap)* *(sci)* ↔ externe Frage

Interpersonalismus *m* • interpersonalism *(epi)*

interpersoneller Nutzenvergleich *m* • interpersonal comparison of utility *(eth, eco)*

Interpolation *f* • interpolation *(lan, mat)*

Interpret *m* • interpreter *(lan, aes)*

Interpretant *m* • interpretant *(Pierce)* *(lan)*

Interpretation *f* • interpretation *(gep)* → Deutung < Hermeneutik

Interpretation, immanente *f* • immanent interpretation *(lan, aes, sci)*

Interpretation, indirekte *f* • indirect interpretation *(Gadamer etc)* *(lan, aes, sci)* < Interpretationshermeneutik

Interpretation, partielle *f* • partial interpretation *(lan, log, sci)*

Interpretation, semantische *f* • semantic interpretation *(Gutzen etc)* *(lan)*

Interpretation, temporale *f* • temporal interpretation *(lan, sci)*

Interpretationismus, methodologischer *m* • methodological interpretationism° *(Lenk, Röd etc)* *(epi, met)*

Interpretationsabbildung *f* • interpretation mapping *(log)* < Prädikatenlogik

Interpretationsabsicht *f* • purpose of (an) interpretation *(sci)*

Interpretationsgegenstand *m* • object of interpretation *(sci)*

Interpretationshermeneutik *f* • interpretative/interpretive hermeneutics *(sci)*

Interpretationskompetenz *f* • interpretative/interpretive competence *(lan)*

Interpretationsleistung *f* • interpretative/interpretive accomplishment *(lan)*

Interpretationsmethode *f* • interpretative/interpretive method *(Dilthey etc)* *(sci)*

Interpretationsmonopol *n* • interpretation monopoly *(sci, soc)* < Machtwissen

Interpretationsregel *f* • rule of interpretation *(log, lan)*

Interpretationssemantik *f* • interpretation(al) semantics *(Tarski)* *(lan)*

Interpretationstheorie *f* • interpretation theory *(sci)*

interpretative Sozialwissenschaft *f* • interpretative/interpretive sociology/social science *(sci)*

interpretative Soziologie *f* • interpretative sociology *(Weber)* *(soc)* → verstehende Soziologie

interpretatives Bezugssystem *n* • interpretative/interpretive framework *(Kuhn)* *(sci)*

interpretierter Kalkül *m* • interpreted calculus *(log)*

Interpunktionsproblem *n* • punctuation problem *(Watzlawick)* *(psy, lan)*

Intersensualität *f* • intersensuality *(Carnap)* *(epi)*

interspezifische Aggression *f* • interspecies/interspecific aggression *(nat, psy)* ↔ intraspezifische Aggression, innerartliche Aggression

intersubjektiv überprüfbar • intersubjectively testable *(sci)*

intersubjektive Anerkennung von Geltungsansprüchen *f* • intersubjective recognition of validity claims *(Habermas)* *(epi, soc)*

intersubjektive Begründbarkeit *f* • intersubjective justifiability *(sci)*

intersubjektive Gültigkeit *f* • intersubjective validity *(sci)*

intersubjektive Überprüfbarkeit *f* • intersubjective testability *(sci)*

Intersubjektivität *f* • intersubjectivity *(epi, sci)* < Allgemeinverbindlichkeit, Objektivität

Intersubjektivitätstheorie der Ethik *f* • intersubjectivity theory of ethics *(eth)* < ethische Verallgemeinerung

Intertextualität *f* • intertextuality *(Kristeva)* *(lan)*

Intervall *n* • interval *(aes, mat)*

intervallische Augmentation *f* • intervallic augmentation *(aes, sys)*

Intervallskala *f* • interval scale *(mat, sci)*

Intervention *f* • intervention *(eco, soc, pol)*

Interventionismus *m* • interventionism *(eco, pol)*

Interview, zentriertes *n* • focused interview *(sci)*

Intimsphäre *f* → Privatsphäre

Intoleranz gegen Mehrdeutigkeit *f* • intolerance of ambiguity *(Fraenkel, Brunswik)* *(mat)*

Intonation *f* • intonation *(aes)*

intragenerationelle Gerechtigkeit *f* • intragenerational justice *(eth)* ↔ intergenerationelle Gerechtigkeit, Gerechtigkeit zwischen den Generationen

intraindividuell • intrapersonal *(soc, psy)* ↔ interindividuell

intramundan → innerweltlich

intransitiv • intransitive *(log, mat)*

intransitive Präferenzen *pl* • intransitive preferences *(dec)*

Intransitivität *f* • intransitivity *(log, lan)*

Intrapersonalismus *m* • intrapersonalism *(epi)*

intraspezifische Aggression *f* • intraspecies/intraspecific aggression *(nat, psy)* → innerartliche Aggression ↔ interspezifische Aggression

intrinsische Bedeutung *f* • intrinsic meaning *(lan)*

intrinsische Motivation *f* • intrinsic motivation *(psy)*

intrinsischer Wert *m* • intrinsic value *(eth)*

intrinsisches Gut *n* • intrinsic good *(eth)*

Introjektion *f* • introjection *(Ferenczi) (psy)*, *(Avenarius) (epi)* < Verinnerlichung

Introspektion *f* • introspection *(psy, min)* → Innenschau

introspektive Methode *f* • introspective method *(sci, min, psy)*

Introversion *f* • introversion *(Jung) (psy)* ↔ Extraversion

Introvertiertheit *f* • introversion, introvertedness *(psy)* < Innengewandtheit

Intuition *f* • intuition *(psy)*

Intuitionismus *m* • intuitionism, intuitionalism *(log, mat); (eth)* < intuitive Ethik

intuitionistische Ethik *f* • intuitionist ethics *(eth)*

intuitionistische Logik *f* • intuitionist/intuitionistic logic *(Brouwer) (log)* < Intuitionismus

intuitionistische Wahrheitskonzeption *f* • intuitionistic concept(ion) of truth *(sci)*

intuitionistisches Kontinuum *n* • intuitionistic continuum *(log)*

Intuitionsethik *f* → intuitive Ethik

intuitive Ebene des moralischen Denkens *f* • intuitive level of moral thinking *(epi, eth)* < intuitive Ethik

intuitive Ethik *f* • intuitional/intuitive ethics *(eth)*

intuitives und diskursives Erkennen *n* • intuitive and discursive cognition *(epi)*

intuitives Verstehen *n* • intuitive understanding *(epi)*

intuitives Wissen *n* • intuitive knowledge *(epi)* < Intuitionismus

Inus-Bedingung *f* • insufficient but non-redundant part of an unnecessary but sufficient condition *(met)*

Invariante *f* • invariant *(mat)*

invariantes Element *n* • invariant element *(mat)*

Invarianz *f* • invariance *(gep)*

inventio medii *f* • inventio medii, introduction of the middle term *(log)*

invers • inverse *(mat)*

inverse Relation *f* • converse relation *(log, mat)*

inverser Schluß *m* • inverse inference *(log)*

Inversion *f* • inversion *(mat)*

Investitionsgüter *pl* • investment/capital goods *(eco)*

Investitionsverweigerung *f* • refusal to invest *(eco)*

Investiturstreit *m* • investiture dispute/struggle *(his, rel)*

Involution *f* • involution *(log)*

Inzesttabu *n* • incest taboo *(psy, cul)*

Ionische Naturphilosophen *pl* • Ionian (natural) philosophers *(gep)*

Ionische Schule *f* • Ionian school *(gep)*

irdische Existenz *f* • earthly existence *(rel)*

irdischer Chauvinismus *m* • Earth chauvinism *(Hofstadter) (ant)* < Geozentrismus

irdisches Gesetz *n* • worldly/secular law *(jur)*

Ironie *f* • irony *(epi, psy)* < sokratische Ironie

Irrationale, das *n* • the irrational *(psy, met)*

irrationale Zahl *f* • irrational number, surd *(mat)*

Irrationalismus *m* • irrationalism *(epi, met)*

Irrationalität *f* • irrationality *(epi, psy)* → Vernunftwidrigkeit

Irrationalität der Gewalt *f* • irrationality of power *(Weber) (soc, pol)*

Irrealität *f* • irreality *(ont)* → Unwirklichkeit

Irreduzibilität *f* • irreducibility *(log, mat)*

irreduzibles Erzeugendensystem *n* • irreducible/irreduncdant system of generators *(mat)*

irreführender Sprachgebrauch *m* • misleading use of language *(lan)*

irrelevanten Alternativen, Axiom der *n* • axiom of the independence of irrelevant alternatives *(dec)*

Irreligiosität *f* • irreligiousness, irreligiosity *(rel)*

irren • to err *(epi)* < Lernen durch Versuch und Irrtum

irrendes Gewissen *n* • erroneous conscience *(rel)*

Irreversibilität *f* • irreversibility *(sys, gep)*
< Unkorrigierbarkeit

irreversibler Prozeß *m* • irreversible process
(sys)

Irrglaube *m* • heterodoxy *(rel)*

Irrlehre *f* • heresy *(rel)* → Häresie, Heterodoxie, Ketzerei

Irrtum *m* • error *(epi, sci)* < Fehler

Irrtumsbeseitigung *f* • error elimination *(epi,
sci)* < Debugging

Irrtumsquellen *pl* • sources of error *(epi, sci)*

Irrtumstheorie *f* • error theory *(Mackie) (eth)*

Irrtumswahrscheinlichkeit *f* • probability of
error *(mat)*

Islam *m* • *nt (rel)* → Mohammedanismus

Islamische Philosophie *f* • Islamic Philosophy
(gep)

Islamische Revolution *f* • Islamic Revolution
(rel, pol)

Islamisierung *f* • Islamization *(rel, pol)*

Isokratie *f* • isocracy *(pol)*

Isolationismus *m* • isolationism *(pol)* → Isolationspolitik

Isolationspolitik *f* • policy of isolation(ism)
(pol) → Isolationismus

Isometrie *f* • isometry *(mat, log)*

Isometrik *f* • isometrics *(eso, nat)*

isometrisch • isometric *(mat, log)*

isomorph • isomorphic *(mat, log)*

isomorphe Struktur *f* • isomorphic structure
(nat, mat)

isomorphes Bild *n* • isomorphic picture/image
(Wittgenstein etc) (lan, ont)

Isomorphie *f* • isomorphism *(sys)* → Strukturgleichheit

Isomorphismus *m* • isomorphism *(nat, mat)*

Isonomie *f* • isonomy *(jur)* → Gleichberechtigung, Gleichheit vor dem Gesetz

Isosthenie *f* • isosthenia *(log)*

Isotopie *f* • isotopy *(mat)*

Isotropie *f* • isotropism, isotropy *(nat)* < lokale
Isotropie, globale Isotropie

ist gleich • is equal to, equals *(log, mat)*
< Gleichheitssymbol

Istwert *m* • present/current value, value at a
time, instantaneous value *(mat, sci)* ↔ Sollwert

Iteration *f* • iteration *(mat, lan, psy)*

Iterationsverfahren *n* • method of iteration
(mat)

ITS → intelligente tutorielle Systeme

ius ad bellum *n* • right for war *(pol, jur)*

ius belli *n* • martial law *(jur)* → Kriegsrecht

ius canonicum *n* • canon law *(rel, jur)* →
kanonisches Recht, Kirchenrecht

ius civile *n* • civil law *(jur)* → Zivilrecht

ius ecclesiasticum *n* → Kirchenrecht

ius gentium *n* → Völkerrecht

ius naturale *n* • natural law *(jur, eth)* → Naturrecht

ius privatum *n* → Privatrecht

ius publicum *n* → öffentliches Recht

J

Ja-Nein-Raum *m* • yes-and-no-space *(Wittgenstein) (ont)*

Jäger und Sammler, die *pl* • hunter-gatherers *(ant, cul)* < Wildbeutergesellschaft, Sammelwirtschaft

Jainismus *m* • Jainism *(rel)*

Jakobiner *m* • Jacobin *(pol, his)*

Jakobinertum *n* → Jakobinismus

Jakobinismus *m* • Jacobinism *(pol, his)*

Jammertal, irdisches *n* • vale of tears *(rel)*

Jansenismus *m* • Jansenism *(rel, gep)*

Japanische Philosophie *f* • Japanese Philosophy *(asp)*

Jasagen zum Leben *n* • affirmation of life *(Nietzsche) (met)* → Lebensbejahung

je-meinige Welt *f* • world that is always mine *(Heidegger) (ont)*

Jedermann *m* • everyman *(gen)* < Man, das

Jemeinigkeit *f* • in each case mine, mineness *(Heidegger) (ont)*

Jenaer Systemkonzept *n* • Jena system concept *(Hegel) (met)*

jenseitiges Leben *n* • afterlife, (the) life hereafter *(rel)*

Jenseits *n* • the hereafter, the beyond, the other world, the world to come *(rel)*

Jenseits in der Kunst, das *n* • the beyond in art *(Nietzsche) (aes)*

jenseits von Gut und Böse • beyond good and evil *(Nietzsche) (eth)* < W 500

Jenseitserwartung *f* • expectation of the hereafter *(rel)*

Jenseitsorientierung *f* • otherworldly orientation *(rel)*

Jesuitenorden *m* • Jesuit order, Society of Jesus *(rel)*

Jesus Christus • Jesus Christ *(rel)*

Jetzt, das *n* • the now *(met)*

Jetztheit *f* • nowness *(met)*

Joachim von Fiore • Joachim of Fioris

Jobeljahr *n* • jubilee year *(rel, eco, soc)*

jokologische Philosophie *f* • jocular philosophy *(gep)*

Jubeljahr *n* → Jobeljahr

Judaismus *m* • Judaism *(rel)* < Semitismus

Judaistik *f* • judaistics *(rel, gep)*

Judentum *n* → Judaismus

Judenverfolgung *f* • persecution of the Jews *(pol, his, rel)* < Pogrom

Judikative *f* • (the) judiciary *(jur)*

Judikatur *f* • judicature *(jur)* → Rechtsprechung, Jurisdiktion

jüdische Mystik *f* • Jewish mysticism *(rel)*

jüdische Philosophie *f* • Jewish Philosophy *(gep)*

jüdischer Glaube(n) *m* • Jewish faith *(rel)*

Jugendarbeitslosigkeit *f* • youth unemployment *(soc)*

Jugendbewegung *f* • youth movement *(cul, soc)*

Jugendkultur *f* • youth culture *(cul, soc, psy)*

Jugendpsychologie *f* • youth/adolescent psychology *(psy)*

Jugendstil *m* • art nouveau *(aes)* → Art nouveau

Junges Deutschland *n* • Young Germany, Young German Movement *(aes)*

Junghegelianer *m* • Young Hegelian *(gep)* → Neuhegelianer, Linkshegelianer ↔ Althegelianer

Jungsche Kugeln *pl* • Jung's spheres *(mat)*

Jungsche Psychologie *f* • Jungian psychology *(psy)*

Jungsozialist *m* • young socialist *(soc)*

Jüngstes Gericht *n* • Judg(e)ment Day, the Last Judg(e)ment *(rel)*

junk art • *nt (aes)*

Junktor *m* • connective *(log)*

Junktorenlogik *f* → Aussagenlogik

Junktorenmenge *f* • set of connectives *(log)*

Jura → Rechtswissenschaft

Jurisdiktion *f* • jurisdiction *(jur)* → Rechtsprechung, Judikatur

Jurisprudenz *f* • jurisprudence *(jur)* → Rechtswissenschaft

juristische Person *f* • legal person/entity *(jur)*

Jus → Rechtswissenschaft

justifikationistische Rechtfertigungsstrategie *f* • justificationist strategy *(sci)* < pankritischer Rationalismus

Justiz *f* • administration of justice *(jur)*

Justizbehörde *f* • legal/judicial authority *(jur)*

Justizgeschichte *f* • history of justice *(jur)*

Justizgewalt *f* • judicial power, judiciary *(jur)*

Justizirrtum *m* • miscarriage of justice, error of justice *(jur)* → Fehlspruch < Fehlurteil

K

Kabbala *f* • kab(b)ala, cab(b)ala *(rel, eso)*

Kabbalistik *f* • cab(b)alism *(rel, eso)*

kafkaesk • Kafkaesque *(aes)*

kairós *m* • nt *(met, rel)* → entscheidender Augenblick

Kakophonie *f* • cacophony *(aes)* < Dissonanz

Kalamargument *n* • kalam argument for the existence of God *(rel)* < ontologischer Gottesbeweis

kalifornische Semantik *f* • Californian semantics *(Putnam)* *(log)*

Kalkül *m/n* • calculus *(log, mat)*, calculus, strategy *(dec)*

Kalkül endlicher Differenzen *m/n* • calculus of finite differences *(mat)*

kalkülartig • computational *(log, mat)*

Kalkulation *f* • calculation, computation *(eco)*, calculation, estimate *(dec)*

kalkulatorische Vernunft *f* • calculatory reason *(eth, dec)* → berechnende Klugheit

Kalkülregel *f* • rule of the calculus *(log, mat)*

Kalkülsprache *f* → Formalsprache

Kalkültheorie *f* • theory of calculus *(log, mat)*

Kalokagathie *f* • unity of beauty and truth *(Plato etc)* *(eth, aes)* < Moralisch-Schöne, das; schöne Seele

Kalter Krieg *m* • the Cold War *(pol)* < Terror-Frieden

Kalvinismus *m* • Calvinism *(rel)*

Kama *n* • nt *(asp)*

Kamaloka *n* • nt *(asp)*

Kameralistik *f* • cameralistics *(eco)*

Kampf als Grenzsituation *m* • struggle as limit/ultimate situation *(Jaspers)* *(met)*

Kampf als Urprinzip *m* • strife as basic principle *(Heraclitus)* *(met)*

Kampf gegen die Armut *m* • struggle with/against poverty *(eco, pol)*

Kampf gegen die Natur *m* • struggle with/against nature *(met, nat, env)* ↔ Frieden mit der Natur

Kampf ums Dasein *m* • struggle for existence *(nat, soc)* → Existenzkampf, Lebenskampf, Daseinskampf < natürliche Auslese, Überleben des/der Tüchtigsten

Kampf ums Überleben *m* • struggle for survival *(nat, soc)* < Überleben des/der Tüchtigsten

Kampf zwischen Kirche und Staat *m* • struggle between church and state *(pol, rel)* → Kulturkampf

Kampfverhalten *n* • aggressive behaviour *(nat, psy)*

Kann-Bestimmung *f* • permissive provision *(eth)* ↔ Mußbestimmung, Sollvorschrift

Kann-Vorschrift *f* → Kann-Bestimmung

Kannibalismus *m* • cannibalism *(cul)*

Kanon *m* • canon *(gep)* < Organon, Proportionslehre

Kanon der reinen (praktischen) Vernunft *m* • canon of pure (practical) reason *(Kant)* *(epi, eth)*

Kanon der Urteilskraft *m* • canon of judg(e)ment *(Kant)* *(epi)*

Kanon des Verstandes *m* • canon of the understanding *(Kant)* *(epi)*

Kanonik *f* • canonic *(Epicurus)* *(log)*

kanonisch • canonical, canonic *(gep)*

kanonische Schreibweise *f* • canonical notation *(mat)*

kanonischer Spielraum *m* • canonical/standard scope *(sci)* < dogmatische Hermeneutik

kanonisches Prinzip *n* • canonical principle *(Kant)* *(epi, log)*

kanonisches Recht *n* • canon law *(rel, jur)* → ius canonicum, Kirchenrecht

Kant-Laplace-Hypothese *f* • Kant-Laplace hypothesis *(nat)* → Nebularhypothese

Kant-Laplace-Raum *m* • Kant-Laplace space *(nat)*

Kantianer *m* • Kantian *(gep)*

Kantianismus *m* • Kantianism *(gep)*

Kantische Philosophie *f* • Kantian philosophy *(gep)*

Kantischer Idealismus *m* • Kantian idealism *(gep)*

Kants kritisches Denken *n* • Kant's critical thought *(gep)*

Kants vorkritisches Denken *n* • Kant's pre-critical thought *(gep)*

Kapazitätsbeschränkung *f* • capacity constraint *(gen)*

Kapital *n* • capital, fund *(eco)* < W 505, 600

Kapital, fixes *n* • fixed capital *(Marx)* *(eco)*

Kapital, produktives *n* • productive capital *(eco)*

Kapital, ursprüngliches *n* • original capital *(eco)*

Kapital, zirkulierendes *n* • circulating capital *(eco)*

Kapitalakkumulation *f* • capital accumulation *(Marx etc) (eco)*

Kapitalbildung *f* • capital formation *(Marx etc) (eco)*

Kapitalertrag *m* • capital yield *(eco)*

Kapitalflucht *f* • capital flight, flight of capital *(eco)*

Kapitalgewinn *m* • return on investment *(eco)*

Kapitalgüter *pl* • capital goods *(eco)*

kapitalintensiver Wirtschaftssektor *m* • capital-intensive sector of the economy *(eco)* < arbeitsintensiv

Kapitalinvestition *f* • capital investment *(eco)*

Kapitalismus *m* • capitalism *(Marx etc) (eco, soc)* < W 837

Kapitalismuskritik *f* • critique/criticism of capitalism *(Marx etc) (eco, soc)*

Kapitalistenklasse *f* • capitalist class *(Marx) (soc)*

kapitalistische Produktionsweise *f* • capitalist mode of production *(Marx etc) (eco)*

kapitalistische Wirtschaftsordnung *f* • capitalist(ic) economic order/economy *(eco, soc)*

Kapitalverbrechen *n* • capital crime *(eth)*

kapriziöse Werte *pl* • caprice/capricious values *(Rousseau) (soc)*

kardinaler Nutzen *m* • cardinal utility *(eth, dec)* ↔ ordinaler Nutzen

Kardinalfrage *f* • cardinal/crucial question *(gep)*

Kardinalskala *f* • cardinal scale *(mat)* ↔ Ordinalskala

Kardinaltugend *f* • cardinal virtue *(eth)*

Kardinalzahl *f* • cardinal number *(mat)*

Karma *n* • karma, fate determining action, law of cause and effect *(asp)* → Vergeltungskausalität < früheres Handeln, Vergeltung der guten Taten, vorausgehende Handlung

Karmamarga *m* • karmamarga *(asp)*

Karman *n* → Karma

karriereorientiert • career-oriented *(soc)*

Karrierismus *m* • careerism *(soc)*

Kartellabkommen *n* • cartel arrangement/ agreement *(eco)* < Marktabsprache, Monopolismus, Wettbewerbsbeschränkung

kartesisch → cartesisch

Kasper-Hauser-Syndrom *n* • Kasper-Hauser syndrome *(ant, psy)* < Wolfskinder

Kassandraruf *m* • prophecy of doom *(gep)* → Unheilsprophezeiung < Dystopie

Kastengeist *m* • caste mentality *(soc)*

Kastengrenze *f* • caste boundary *(soc)*

Kastensystem *n* • caste system *(soc)*

Kastrationsangst *f* • castration anxiety *(Freud) (psy)*

Kastrationskomplex *m* • castration complex *(Freud) (psy)*

Kasualismus *m* • casualism *(met)* ↔ Kausalismus

Kasuistik *f* • casuistry *(eth, jur)* ↔ Situationismus

Katalogisieren *n* • cataloguing *(gen)*

Katastrophensituation *f* • disaster/catastrophe situation *(soc, sys, env)* < GAU

Katastrophentheorie *f* • catastrophe theory *(mat, sys)*, catastrophism *(nat)*

Kategorialanalyse *f* • categorial analysis *(N. Hartmann) (epi, ont)*

kategoriale Anschauung *f* • categorial intuition *(Husserl) (epi, lan)*

kategoriale Kohärenz *f* • categorial coherence *(N. Hartmann) (epi, ont)*

kategoriale Ontologie *f* • categorial ontology *(ont)*

kategoriale Wiederkehr *f* • categorial recurrence *(N. Hartmann) (ont)*

Kategorialgrammatik *f* • categorial grammar, CG *(Husserl, Ajdukiewicz, Lambek) (lan)*

Kategorie *f* • category *(log, epi, met)* < Prädikament

Kategorie der Allheit *f* • category of totality *(Kant) (epi)*

Kategorie der Einheit *f* • category of unity *(Kant) (epi)*

Kategorie der Gemeinschaft *f* • category of community *(Kant) (epi)*

Kategorie der Inhärenz und Subsistenz *f* • category of inherence and subsistence *(Kant) (epi)*

Kategorie der Kausalität und Dependenz *f* • category of causality and dependence *(Kant) (epi)*

Kategorie der Limitation *f* • category of limitation *(Kant) (epi)*

Kategorie der Möglichkeit *f* • category of possibility *(epi)*

Kategorie der Negation *f* • category of negation *(epi)*

Kategorie der Notwendigkeit *f* • category of necessity *(Kant) (epi)*

Kategorie der Realität *f* • category of reality *(epi)*

Kategorie der Substanz *f* • category of substance *(Aristotle, Descartes etc) (met)*

Kategorie der Unmöglichkeit *f* • category of impossibility *(Kant) (epi)*

Kategorie der Vielheit f • category of plurality *(Kant) (epi)*

Kategorie der Zufälligkeit f • category of contingency *(Kant) (epi)*

Kategorie des Daseins f • category of existence *(Kant) (epi)*

Kategorie des Nichtseins f • category of nonexistence *(Kant) (epi)*

Kategorie, existenzielle f • existential category *(met)*

Kategorie, formale f • formal category *(Husserl) (met)*

Kategorie, grammatische f • grammatical category *(Ryle) (lan)*

Kategorie, konstitutive f • constitutive category *(Windelband, Rickert) (epi, met)*

Kategorie, lexikalische f • lexical category *(lan)*

Kategorie, logische f • logical category *(log)*

Kategorie, methodologische f • methodological category *(Rickert) (epi)*

Kategorie, modale f • modal category *(ont, epi)*

Kategorie, reale f • real category *(ont, epi)*

Kategorie, reflexive f • reflective category *(Windelband) (epi)*

Kategorie, semantische f • semantic category *(lan)*

Kategorie, syntaktische f • syntactic category/ type *(lan, log)*

Kategorien *pl* • categories *(Kant) (epi)* → Stammbegriffe

Kategorien der Freiheit *pl* • categories of freedom *(Kant) (epi)*

Kategorien der Modalität *pl* • categories of modality *(epi)*

Kategorien der Qualität *pl* • categories of quality *(epi)*

Kategorien der Quantität *pl* • categories of quantity *(epi)*

Kategorien der Relation *pl* • categories of relation *(epi)*

Kategorien von objektiver Gültigkeit *pl* • categories of objective validity *(Schleiermacher) (met)*

Kategorien, Herleitung von f • deduction of categories *(Plato, Kant) (met)*

Kategorienanalyse f • category analysis *(N. Hartmann) (epi, met)*

Kategorieneigenschaft f • categorical property *(Ryle) (ont)*

Kategorienfehler *m* • category mistake *(log, epi)*

Kategorienlehre f • theory of categories, category theory *(epi, met, mat)* < Topologie < W 99

Kategorienreduktion f • reduction of categories *(N. Hartmann) (met, epi)*

Kategorientafel f • table of categories *(Kant) (epi)*

Kategorientheorie f → Kategorienlehre

Kategorienverwechslung f → Kategorienfehler

kategorische Notwendigkeit f • categorical necessity *(Kant) (epi, met)*

kategorische Synthesis f • categorical synthesis *(Kant) (epi)*

kategorischer Imperativ *m* • categorical imperative *(Kant) (eth)* ↔ hypothetischer Imperativ < universelle Maxime

kategorischer Schluß *m* • categorical syllogism *(log)*

kategorischer Vernunftschluß *m* • categorical inference of reason *(Kant) (epi)*

kategorisches Urteil *n* • categorical judg(e)ment *(log, epi)*

Kategorisierung f • categorization *(gep)*

Kategorizität f • categoricity° *(log, mat)*

Katharsis f • catharsis, purging, purification *(Aristotle) (aes)* → Reinigung von den Leidenschaften < Abreaktion, Entlastungsfunktion der Kunst

Katharsislehre f • doctrine of catharsis *(Aristotle) (aes)*

kathartische Methode f • cathartic method *(Breuer, Freud) (psy)*

Kathederphilosophie f • arm chair philosophy *(Schopenhauer) (gep)*

Kathedersozialismus *m* • professorial socialism, (the) socialism of the chair *(pol, soc)*

Katholische Soziallehre f • Roman Catholic social doctrine *(rel, soc)*

katholischer Existenzialismus *m* • catholic existentialism *(Marcel) (rel, met)*

Katholizismus *m* • Catholicism *(rel)*

Käufersouveränität f • consumer sovereignity *(eco)*

Kaufkraft f • purchasing/spending/buying power *(eco)*

Kaufkraftverlust *m* • loss of purchasing power < Wertverlust

Kaufpreis *m* • purchase price *(eco)*

Kaufrausch *m* • spending spree, splurge *(eco)* < Konsumhysterie

kausal • causal, causative *(gep)*

Kausalanalyse f • causal analysis *(epi, gep)*

Kausalbegriff *m* • causal notion, concept of cause *(epi, met)*

Kausalbeziehung *f* • causal relation(ship)/ nexus *(epi, sci)*

kausale Bedingtheit *f* • causal determinedness *(met)* < Determinismus

kausale Entscheidungstheorie *f* • causal decision theory *(dec)*

kausale Erklärung *f* • causal explanation *(sci)*

kausale Kraft *f* • causal power *(met)*

kausale Nötigung *f* • causal necessitation *(met)*

kausale Notwendigkeit *f* • causal necessity *(met)*

kausale Regularität *f* • causal regularity *(met)*

kausale Verknüpfung *f* • causal link *(met)* < Kausalnexus

kausalen Adäquatheit, Prinzip der *n* • causal adequacy principle *(met, epi)*

kausaler Trugschluß *m* • causal fallacy *(log, epi)*

Kausalerklärung *f* → kausale Erklärung

kausales Relevanzmodell der Erklärung *n* • causal-relevance model of explanation *(sci)*

Kausalgesetz *n* • causal law *(epi, met)* < Kausalität, Gesetz der

Kausalismus *m* • causalism *(met)* ↔ Kasualismus < logischer Intentionalismus

Kausalität *f* • causality *(met)*

Kausalität, akzidentielle *f* • accidental causality *(Suárez) (met)*

Kausalität aus Freiheit *f* • causality of freedom *(Kant) (met, eth)*

Kausalität der Erscheinungen *f* • causality of appearances *(Kant) (epi, met)*

Kausalität der Natur *f* • causality of nature *(Kant) (met)*

Kausalität der Vernunft *f* • causality of reason *(Kant) (epi, met)*

Kausalität durch Freiheit *f* • causality through freedom *(Kant) (met, eth)*

Kausalität, formale *f* • formal causality *(Suárez etc) (met)*

Kausalität, Gesetz der *n* • principle/law of causality/causation *(met)*

Kausalität, globale *f* • global/holistic causality *(met)*

Kausalität, lokale *f* • local causality *(met)*

Kausalität, phänomenale *f* • phenomenal causality *(Hume, Kant etc) (met)*

Kausalität, psychische *f* • psychological/mental causality *(psy)*

Kausalität, substantiell-formale *f* • substantial formal causality *(Suárez etc) (met)*

Kausalitätsgesetz *n* • law of causality *(met)*

Kausalitätsprinzip *n* • causal principle, principle of causality, principle of (universal) cau-

sation *(epi, met)* → Kausalprinzip < Kausalgesetz

Kausalitätsverhältnis *n* → Kausalverhältnis

Kausalkette *f* • causal chain, chain of cause and effect, chain of causation *(met)*

Kausallogik *f* • causal logic *(log)*

Kausalmodell *n* • causal model *(met, sci)*

Kausalnexus *m* • causal nexus/connection/ relation *(met, sci)* → Kausalzusammenhang

Kausalprinzip *n* • causal principle *(epi, met)* → Kausalitätsprinzip

Kausalrealismus *m* • causal realism *(Popper) (ont, sci)*

Kausalreihe *f* • causal series *(met)*

Kausalrelation *f* • causal relation *(sci)*

Kausalsatz *m* • causal clause *(lan, sci)*

Kausaltheorie der Bedeutung *f* • causal theory of meaning *(Kripke) (lan)*

Kausaltheorie der Rechtfertigung *f* • causal theory of justification *(epi)*

Kausaltheorie der Referenz *f* • causal theory of reference *(Kripke) (lan)*

Kausaltheorie der Wahrnehmung *f* • causal theory of perception *(epi)*

Kausaltheorie des Wissens *f* • causal theory of knowledge *(epi)*

Kausalverhältnis *n* • causal relation/nexus *(met)*

Kausalverknüpfung *f* → kausale Verknüpfung

Kausalzusammenhang *m* • causal relationships *(met, sci)* → Kausalnexus < Sinnzusammenhang

Kavaliersdelikt *n* • minor offence, peccadillo, misdemeanour *(eth, jur)*

Kehre, die *f* • the turning *(Heidegger) (ont)* < W 984

Kendo *n* • nt *(asp)*

Kendoka *m* • nt *(asp)*

Kenntnis *f* • knowledge, acquaintance *(epi)*

Kennzeichen *n* • feature, characteristic, mark *(gen)* < Kriterium, Merkmal

kennzeichnende Eigenschaften *pl* • distinctive features, characterizing attributes, distinguishing properties *(lan, ont)*

Kennzeichnung *f* • description, denotation, characterization°, identification *(log, lan)*

Kennzeichnungsoperator *m* • description/ characterization operator° *(Russell) (log)*

Kennzeichnungstheorie *f* • theory of descriptions *(Russell) (log, lan)*

Kern einer Menge, offener *m* • interior of a set *(mat)*

Kernenergie *f* • nuclear/atomic energy *(nat)*

Kernkraftbefürworter *m* • supporter of nuclear/atomic energy/power *(eth)*

Kernkraftgegner *m* • opponent of nuclear/atomic energy/power *(eth)*

Kernkraftwerk *n* • nuclear/atomic power station/plant *(tec)* < Atomstaat

Kernphysik *f* • nuclear/atomic physics *(nat)* → Atomphysik

Kernproblem *n* • crucial/focal problem *(gen)*

Kernreaktor *m* • nuclear/chain° reactor *(tec)* → Atomreaktor

Kernspaltung *f* • nuclear fission *(nat)*

Kernwerte *pl* • core values *(eth)*

Kette *f* • string, chain *(AI)* < Superketten

Kette des Seins *f* • chain of being *(met)*

Ketten von logischen Schlüssen *pl* • chains of inference *(log, sci)*

Kettenbruch *m* • continuous fraction *(mat)*

Kettenreaktion *f* • chain reaction *(nat, sys)* < Dominoeffekt, Schneeballeffekt

Kettenregel *f* • chain rule *(mat)*

Kettenschlußregel *f* • cut rule *(log)*

Ketzerei *f* • heresy *(rel)* → Häresie, Irrlehre, Heterodoxie

Keuschheit *f* • chastity *(eth, rel)*

keynesianische Wirtschaftspolitik *f* • Keynesian economic policy *(eco)* < Deficit-Spending

Kibbutz-Bewegung *f* • kibbutz movement *(pol, soc)*

Kinderarbeit *f* • child labour *(eco, eth)* < Kinderrechte

Kinderphilosophie *f* • philosophy for children *(gep)*

Kinderrechte *pl* • children's/child rights *(eth)*

Kindersterblichkeit *f* • infant mortality *(soc)*

Kindespflicht *f* • filial duty *(eth)*

Kindheitsentwicklung *f* • child development *(psy)*

Kindheitserlebnis *n* • childhood experience *(psy)*

Kindstötung *f* • infanticide *(eth)* → Infantizid < Abtreibung

Kinematik *f* • kinematics *(nat)* → Phoronomie

Kinesis *f* • movement *(nat)*

Kinetik *f* • kinetics *(nat, aes)*

kinetische Energie *f* • kinetic energy *(nat)*

kinetische Kunst *f* • kinetic art *(aes)*

kinetische Rotation *f* • kinetic rotation *(nat)*

Kinoauge *n* • kino-eye *(Vertov)* *(aes)*

Kin-Selektion *f* → Verwandtschaftsselektion

Kirchenaberglaube *m* • church superstition *(rel)*

Kirchenbann *m* • excommunication *(rel)*

Kirchenfeindlichkeit *f* • anti-clericalism *(rel)*

Kirchengeschichte *f* • church/ecclesiastical history *(rel)*

Kirchenglaube *m* • church/ecclesiastical faith *(rel)*

Kirchenkampf *m* → Kulturkampf

Kirchenlehre *f* • church doctrine *(rel)*

Kirchenmusik *f* • sacred/church music *(aes)* ↔ profane Musik

Kirchenpolitik *f* • church policy *(rel, pol)*

Kirchenrecht *n* • canon law *(rel, jur)* → kanonisches Recht

Kirchenreform *f* • church reform *(rel)*

Kirchenspaltung *f* • schism *(rel)* → Schisma

Kirchenstaat *m* • Papal/Pontifical State(s) *(rel, pol)* < Theokratie

Kirchenväter *pl* • the Early/the Church Fathers, the Fathers of the Church *(rel)*

Kismet *n* • kismet *(rel)* < unabwendbares Schicksal

Kitsch *m* • kitsch, trash *(aes)*

kitschig • kitschy, shoddy, trashy *(aes)*

Klangfarbe *f* • timbre, tone colour *(aes)*

klare und distinkte Ideen *pl* • clear and distinct ideas *(Descartes)* *(epi)*

Klarheit *f* • clarity *(epi)* < Distinktheit

Klarheit und Distinktheit *ff* • clarity and distinctness *(Descartes)* *(epi)*

Klasse *f* • class *(soc)*, class, set *(mat, log)*

Klasse, allgemeine *f* • universal class *(Marx)* *(soc)* *(Russell etc)* *(log)*

Klasse, bürgerliche *f* • bourgeois/middle class *(pol, soc)*

Klasse, herrschende *f* • dominant/ruling class *(Marx)* *(pol)*

Klasse, logische *f* • logical class *(log)*

Klasse, natürliche *f* • natural kind *(log, lan)* < Arten, natürliche; Gattung; Art

Klassen, obere *pl* • upper classes *(soc)* < Oberklasse

Klassen, untere *pl* • lower classes *(soc)* < Unterklasse

Klassenantagonismus *m* • class antagonism *(soc, pol)* → Klassengegensatz

Klassenbewußtsein *n* • class consciousness *(Marx etc)* *(soc)* < W 369

Klassenbeziehung *f* • class relation *(Marx)* *(soc)*

Klassenbildung *f* • (▷ Bildung) class culture *(Marx)* *(soc)*, (▷ Formation) class formation *(soc, mat, log)*

Klassendiktatur *f* • class dictatorship *(Marx etc)* *(pol)*

Klasseneigentum *n* • class property *(Marx)*
(soc)

Klassenfeind *m* • enemy of the working class
(soc)

Klassengegensatz *m* • class antagonism *(Marx
etc) (soc)* → Klassenantagonismus

Klassengesellschaft *f* • class society *(Marx)*
(soc) ↔ klassenlose Gesellschaft

Klassengleichung *f* • class equation *(mat)*

Klassengrenze *f* • class boundary *(mat)* < unscharfe Mengen

Klassenhierarchie *f* • class hierarchy *(soc,
mat)*

Klassenidentität *f* • class identity *(soc, mat)*

Klasseninteresse *n* • class interest *(Marx etc)*
(soc) < Partikularinteresse

Klassenkalkül *m/n* • calculus of classes *(mat,
log)*

Klassenkampf *m* • class struggle/war *(Marx
etc) (soc, pol)*

Klassenkonflikt *m* • class conflict *(soc)*

Klassenlogik *f* • logic of classes *(mat, log)*

klassenlose Gesellschaft *f* • classless society
(Marx etc) (soc) ↔ Klassengesellschaft

Klassenlosigkeit *f* • classlessness *(soc)*

Klassenmoral *f* • class morality *(eth, soc)*

Klassenprivileg *n* • class privilege *(soc)*

Klassenschichtung *f* • class stratification *(soc)*

Klassenschranke *f* • class barrier *(soc)*

klassenspezifisch • class specific *(soc)*

Klassenstandpunkt *m* • class view(point)/
standpoint *(soc)*

Klassenstruktur *f* • class structure *(soc)*

Klassentheorie *f* • theory of classes, class
theory *(log, soc)*

Klassentrennung *f* • class segregation *(soc)*

Klassenunterschied *m* • class difference *(soc)*

Klassenverhältnis *n* • set-member relation
(sci)

Klassenvorherrschaft *f* • class domination
(pol, soc)

Klassenvorurteil *n* • class bias/prejudice *(epi,
soc, eth)* → Standesvorurteil < Standortgebundenheit des Denkens

Klassenzugehörigkeit *f* • class membership
(Marx) (soc)

Klassifikation *f* • classification *(gep)*

Klassifikation der Lebensformen *f* •
classification of life forms *(Aristotle) (nat)*

Klassifikationssystem *n* • classificatory system
(sci)

Klassifikator *m* • classifier *(log)*

klassifikatorische Gesetze *pl* • classificatory
laws *(sci)*

klassifikatorischer Begriff *m* • classificatory
concept/category *(lan, log)*

Klassik, die *f* • Classical Age *(aes, his)*

Klassik, deutsche *f* • German Classical Age
(aes, his)

Klassiker, die *pl* • the classics *(aes)*

klassisch • classic(al) *(aes)*

Klassische, das *n* • the classical *(aes)*

klassische Altertumswissenschaften *pl* •
classical studies *(gep)* < Archäologie

klassische Kunst *f* • classical art *(aes)*

klassische Literatur *f* • classical literature
(aes)

klassische Mechanik *f* • classical mechanics
(nat) ↔ Quantenmechanik

klassische Musik *f* • classical music *(aes)*

klassische Philologie *f* • classical
philology/scholarship *(gep)*

klassische Physik *f* • classical physics *(nat)*
< Newtonsche Physik

klassische Termlogik *f* • classical term logic
(log)

klassische Wahrscheinlichkeitsinterpretation
f • classical interpretation of probability
(mat, sci)

klassische Wahrscheinlichkeitstheorie *f* •
classical/conventional probability theory
(Bernoulli, Laplace) (mat, sci)

klassischer wissenschaftlicher Realismus *m* •
classical scientific realism *(epi, sci)*

Klassizismus *m* • classicism *(aes)*

klein ist schön • small is beautiful *(Kohr, Schu-
macher) (tec, pol)* < Verkleinerungswille

kleinbürgerlicher Sozialismus *m* • petty-
bourgeois socialism *(Marx)*

Kleinbürgertum *n* • petty bourgeoisie *(pol,
soc)*

Kleindenker *m* • small-minded person *(gep)*

Kleingläubigkeit *f* • weakness of faith *(rel)*

Kleinmut *f* • faintheartedness, weakhearted-
ness, pusillanimity *(eth, rel)* ↔ Großmut

kleinster gemeinsamer Nenner *m* • lowest
common denominator *(mat)*

kleinstes gemeinsames Vielfaches *n* • least
common multiple *(mat)*

Klerikalismus *m* • clericalism *(rel)*

Klerokratie *f* → Priesterherrschaft

Klerus *m* • clergy *(rel)*

Klimaänderung *f* • climatic change *(env)*

Klimakatastrophe *f* • climate catastrophe
(env)

Klimakonvention *f* • climate convention *(env)*

Klimatheorie *f* • climate theory *(nat, cul)*
< Environmentalismus

Kliometrie *f* • cliometrics *(his)*

Klischee *n* • cliché *(aes, lan)*

Klonen, das *n* • cloning *(nat, eth)* < Serienexistenz

Klugheit *f* • prudence, sagacity, shrewdness *(eth)* < praktische Weisheit

Klumpenstichprobe *f* • cluster-sample *(mat, sci)*

Knappheit *f* • shortage, scarcity *(eco, soc)*

Knappheitsproblem *n* • problem of scarcity *(eco)*

Knoten *m* • node *(AI)*, knot *(gen)* < gordischer Knoten

Knotenpunkt *m* • nodal point *(nat)*

Knotenreihe *f* • nodal series *(mat)*

Knowledge Engineering • knowledge engineering *(AI)*

Koalitionsrecht *n* • right/freedom of combination/association *(pol)*

Koalitionsregierung *f* • coalition government *(pol)*

Koan *n* • koan, nonsensical question *(asp)*

Kochkunst *f* • art of cooking *(Plato, Onfray)* *(aes)*

Kodierung *f* • coding *(lan, AI)*

Kodifizierung *f* • codification *(lan, jur)*, encoding *(lan)*

Koedukation *f* • co-education *(soc)* ↔ geschlechtergetrennte Erziehung

Koeffizient *m* • coefficient *(mat)*

Koevolution *f* • coevolution *(nat)*

Koevolution der Makro- und Mikrosysteme *f* • coevolution of macro- and micro-systems *(sys)*

Koexistenz *f* • coexistence *(ont)* → Zugleichsein

Koexistenz, friedliche *f* • peaceful coexistence *(pol)* < Toleranz

Koexistenzprognose *f* • coexistence prediction *(sci)* < Sukzessionsprognose, Retrodiktionsprognose

kogitative Modelle *pl* • cogitative models *(sci)* < semantisches Modell, Perzeptionsmodelle

Kognition *f* • cognition *(psy, epi)* → Erkenntnis

Kognitionspsychologie *f* • cognitive psychology *(psy)* → Erkenntnispsychologie

Kognitionstheorie *f* → Kognitionswissenschaft

Kognitionswissenschaft *f* • cognitive science, epistemics *(epi, min, AI)*

kognitive Architektur *f* • cognitive architecture *(min)*

kognitive Dissonanz *f* • cognitive dissonance *(Festinger)* *(psy, epi)* ↔ kognitive Konsonanz

kognitive Entwicklung *f* • cognitive development *(psy, epi)*

kognitive Konsonanz *f* • cognitive consonance *(psy, epi)* ↔ kognitive Dissonanz

kognitive Signifikanz *f* • cognitive significance *(epi, lan)*

kognitive Tugend *f* • intellectual/cognitive virtue *(eth)* → dianoetische Tugend

kognitiver Akt *m* • cognitive act *(min)*

kognitiver Prozeß *m* • cognitive process *(min)*

Kognitivismus *m* • cognitivism *(epi, eth)* ↔ Non-Kognitivismus

Kognitivismus, kritischer *m* • critical cognitivism *(Chisholm)* *(epi)*

Kohärentismus *m* • coherentism *(epi)*

Kohärenz *f* • coherence *(log)*

Kohärenz, strikte *f* • strict coherence *(log)*

Kohärenzprinzip *n* • coherence principle, principle of coherence *(log, ont)* < Prinzip der Widerspruchsfreiheit

Kohärenztheorie *f* • coherence theory *(log, sci)*

Kohärenztheorie der Rechtfertigung *f* • coherence theory of justification *(log, sci)*

Kohärenztheorie der Wahrheit *f* • coherence theory of truth *(Leibniz etc)* *(epi, met)*

Kohäsionsvermögen *n* • cohesive force *(psy)*

Koinzidenzsatz *m* → Koinzidenztheorem

Koinzidenztheorem *n* • coincidence theorem *(log)*

Kollegialität *f* • loyalty to one's colleagues *(eth)*

Kollegialprinzip *n* • principle of collective responsibility and competence *(soc)*

Kollegialsystem *n* • collegialism *(pol)*, board system *(eco)*, collegial system *(rel)*

Kollektiv *n* • collective *(soc)*

Kollektivbedürfnisse *pl* • collective needs, social/public wants *(soc)*

Kollektivbegriff *m* • collective term *(lan)* ↔ Individualbegriff

Kollektivbewußtsein *n* • collective consciousness *(Marx, Durkheim)* *(soc)*

kollektive Anschauung *f* • collective intuition *(Kant)* *(epi)*

kollektive Führung *f* • collective leadership *(pol)*

kollektive Gleichgestimmtheit *f* • collective like-mindedness *(Habermas)* *(act)*

kollektive Handlung *f* • collective act(ion) *(act)* < kollektives Handeln

kollektive Identität *f* • collective identity *(soc, psy)*

kollektive Maßnahme *f* • collective measure *(act)*

kollektive Sicherheit *f* • collective security *(pol)*

kollektive Verantwortung *f* → Kollektivverantwortung

Kollektiveigentum *n* • collective ownership *(eco, jur)* < kollektives Eigentum (an Produktionsmitteln)

kollektiver Terminus *m* • collective term *(lan)*

kollektiver Wille *m* • collective will *(act, psy, soc)*

kollektives Bewußtsein *n* → Kollektivbewußtsein

kollektives Eigentum (an Produktionsmitteln) *n* • collective ownership (of the means of production) *(eco, jur)* < Staatseigentum, Kollektiveigentum

kollektives Gedächtnis *n* • collective memory *(psy)*

kollektives Handeln *n* • collective action *(act)* < kollektive Handlung

kollektives Unbewußtes *n* • collective unconscious *(Jung)* *(psy)*

kollektives Verhalten *n* → Kollektivverhalten

Kollektivgüter *pl* • collective/public goods *(eco)*

Kollektivierung (der Landwirtschaft) *f* • collectivization (of agriculture) *(eco, pol)*

Kollektivismus *m* • collectivism *(eco, pol)* ↔ Individualismus

Kollektivität *f* • collectivity *(soc)*

Kollektivpsyche *f* • collective mind *(psy)* < Massenpsychologie

Kollektivpsychologie *f* • collective psychology *(psy, soc)* → Sozialpsychologie

Kollektivschuld *f* • collective guilt *(eth, pol)* < Sippenhaftung, Mitschuld, kollektive Verantwortung

Kollektivstrafe *f* • collective punishment *(eth, pol)*

Kollektivverantwortung *f* • collective responsibility *(eth)* < Kollektivschuld, Sippenhaftung

Kollektivverhalten *n* • collective behaviour *(soc, psy)*

Kollektivvertrag *m* • collective agreement *(eco)*

Kollektivvorstellung *f* • collective idea *(Durkheim etc)* *(soc)* → Kollektivbewußtsein

Kollektivwirtschaft *f* • collective economy *(eco)*

Kolonialismus *m* • colonialism *(eco, pol)*

Kolonisation *f* • colonization *(eco, pol)*

Kolonisierung der Lebenswelt *f* • colonization of the life-world *(Habermas)* *(soc)*

Kolorit *n* • colouring, tone *(aes)*

Kombination *f* • combination *(log, mat)*

Kombinatorik *f* • combinatorics, theory of combinations *(log, mat)*

kombinatorisch • combinatorial, combinative *(log, mat)*

kombinatorische Logik *f* • combinatory/combinatorial logic *(log)*

kombinatorische Topologie *f* • combinatory topology *(mat)*

Komische, das *n* • the comic *(aes)* < W 558

Kommandowirtschaft *f* • command economy, (state) controlled economy, (state-)planned economy *(eco)* < Dirigismus, Planwirtschaft, Zentralverwaltungswirtschaft

kommensurabel • commensurable *(mat, sci)* kompatibel

Kommensurabilität *f* • commensurability *(mat, sci)* → Vergleichbarkeit

kommerzialisierte Unterhaltung *f* • commercialized entertainment *(eco, soc)* < Kulturindustrie

Kommerzialisierung *f* • commercialization *(eco, soc)*

Kommerzialismus *m* • commercialism *(eco)*

kommerzielle Kunst *f* • commercial art *(eco, aes)*

Kommissive *pl* • commissives *(Searle)* *(lan, act)*

kommissive Äußerung *f* • commissive utterance *(Austin)* *(lan, act)* < Illokution

Kommunalismus *m* • communalism *(Merton etc)* *(pol)* < Föderalismus

Kommunikation *f* • communication *(lan)*

Kommunikation, digitale *f* • digital communication *(lan, AI)* < digitaler Alltag

Kommunikation, Ebene der *f* • level of communication, horizon of communication *(Jaspers)* *(lan)* → Kommunikationsebene

Kommunikation, existenzielle *f* • existential communication *(Jaspers)* *(met)*

Kommunikationsbarriere *f* • communication barrier *(lan, soc)*

Kommunikationsbedürfnis *n* • need to communicate, communication need *(psy)*

Kommunikationsebene *f* • level of communication *(lan)*

Kommunikationsforschung *f* • communication research *(lan)*

Kommunikationsgemeinschaft, ideale *f* • ideal communication community, ideal community of communication *(Mead, Apel, Habermas)* *(lan, soc)*

Kommunikationsintention *f* • communicative intention *(Grice)* *(lan, act)*

Kommunikationskultur *f* • culture of communication *(lan, eth)* < Streitkultur

Kommunikationsmittel *n* • means of communication *(lan)*

Kommunikationsmodell *n* • communication model *(lan)*

Kommunikationsprozeß *m* • communication process *(lan)*

Kommunikationsschwierigkeit *f* • communication difficulty *(psy)*

Kommunikationsstörung *f* • disturbance of communication, communication disturbance *(lan, soc)*

Kommunikationssystem *n* • communication system *(lan, tec)*

Kommunikationsteilnehmer *m* • participant in communication *(soc, lan, act)*

kommunikationstheoretische Wende *f* • communication-theoretic turn *(Habermas)* *(sci)* < linguistische Wende

Kommunikationstheorie *f* • theory of communication, communication theory *(lan)*

Kommunikationswille *m* • will/desire to communicate *(psy)*

Kommunikationswissenschaft *f* • communication studies *(lan)*

Kommunikationszusammenbruch *m* • communicative breakdown *(lan)*

kommunikativ erzieltes Einverständnis *n* • communicatively achieved agreement/ consensus *(Habermas)* *(lan, act)*

kommunikative Ethik *f* • commmunicative ethics *(Apel, Habermas etc)* *(eth)*

kommunikative Kompetenz *f* • communicative competence *(Habermas)* *(lan, soc)* < linguistische Kompetenz

kommunikative Praxis *f* • communicative practice *(Habermas)* *(lan, soc)*

kommunikative Rationalität *f* • communicative rationality *(Habermas)* *(lan, soc)*

kommunikative Vergesellschaftung *f* • communicative sociation *(Habermas)* *(lan, soc)*

kommunikative Vernunft *f* • communicative reason/rationality *(Habermas)* *(epi, soc, lan)*

kommunikative Verständigung *f* • communicative understanding *(Habermas)* *(soc, lan, act)*

kommunikatives Handeln *n* • communicative action *(Habermas)* *(lan, act)* < W 670, 1000

kommunikatives Interesse *n* • communicative interest *(Habermas etc)* *(lan, soc)*

Kommunismus *m* • communism *(pol)*

kommunistische Bewegung *f* • communist movement *(pol)*

kommunistische Gesellschaft *f* • communist society *(Marx etc)* *(soc, pol)*

Kommunistische Internationale *f* • Communist International *(pol)*

Kommunistisches Manifest *n* • Communist Manifesto *(Marx/Engels)* *(pol)* < W 517

kommunistische Partei *f* • communist party *(pol)*

kommunistischer Staat *m* • communist state *(pol)*

Kommunitarismus *m* • communitarianism, communitarism *(Sandel, Walzer, Taylor etc)* *(soc, pol)*

kommunitaristische Philosophie *f* • communitarian philosophy *(soc, pol)*

Kommutation *f* • commutation *(log, mat)*

kommutativ • commutative *(log, mat)*

kommutative Vernunft *f* • commutative rationality *(Habermas)* *(epi, soc)*

Kommutativgesetz *n* • commutative law *(mat, log)*

Kommutativregel *f* • commutative rule *(mat, log)*

Komödie *f* • comedy *(aes)*

kompakter Raum *m* • compact (topological) space *(mat)*

Kompaktheitssatz *m* • principle of compactness *(log)*

Komparatistik *f* • comparative literature *(aes)* → Literaturwissenschaft, vergleichende

komparative Philosophie *f* • comparative philosophy *(gep)*

komparativer Begriff *m* • comparative concept *(log, lan)* < komparativer Term

komparativer Term *m* • relative term *(log, lan)* < komparativer Begriff

kompatibel • compatible *(gen)* < kommensurabel

Kompatibilismus *m* • compatibilism *(eth)* ↔ Inkompatibilismus

Kompatibilität *f* • compatibility *(gep)* → Vereinbarkeit

Kompensation *f* • compensation *(psy, eco)*

Kompensationstheorie *f* • compensation theory *(psy, eco)*

Kompensationsthese *f* • compensation thesis *(Ritter, Maquard)* *(soc, cul, aes)*

kompetenter Sprecher *m* • competent speaker *(lan, soc)*

Kompetenz *f* • competence *(lan)* ↔ Performanz

Kompetenzbedingung *f* • competence requirement *(eth)*

Kompetenzkompetenz *f* • competence competence/competency *(jur)* < Inkompetenzkompensationskompetenz

Kompetenzkonflikt *m* • competence conflict *(jur, soc)*

Kompetenzstufe f • level/stage of competence *(Piaget, Habermas) (lan, psy)*

kompetitives Spiel n • competitive game *(dec)*

komplementär • complementary *(mat, log)*

Komplementärfarbe f • complementary colour *(nat, aes)*

Komplementarität f • complementarity *(mat, log)*

Komplementärmedizin f • complementary medicine *(nat)* < Ganzheitsmedizin, Alternativmedizin

Komplex m • complex, syndrome *(sys, psy)*, configuration *(sys)* < Gestalt

komplexe Aussage f • complex proposition/statement *(lan, log)* < molekulare Aussage, Molekularsatz

komplexe Gesellschaft f • complex society *(Hayek) (soc)*

komplexe Ideen pl • complex ideas *(Locke) (epi)*

komplexe Zahl f • complex number *(mat)*

komplexe Zahlenebene f • Argand plane, Gaussian number plane, complex plane *(mat)*

komplexes System n • complex system *(sys)*

Komplexität f • complexity *(sys, gep)* → Multidimensionalität, Vielschichtigkeit

Komplexitätsreduktion f • complexity reduction *(sys, sci)* < Simplifizierung

Komplexitätszuwachs m • complexity increase *(sys, sci)*

Komponenten eines Vektors pl • components of a vector *(mat)*

Komponentenanalyse f • componential/component analysis *(lan)*

Komponentialanalyse f • componential analysis *(lan)*

Komposition f • composition *(aes)*

Komprehension f • comprehension *(log, ont)*

komprehensives Erkennen n • comprehensive cognition *(epi)*

Kompromiß m • compromise *(eth, act)*

Kompromißbereitschaft f • willingness/readiness to compromise *(eth)*

Kompromißbildung f • formation of compromise *(Freud) (psy)*

Kompromißlosigkeit f • uncompromisingness *(eth)*

Kompromißstrategie f • compromise strategy *(dec)*

Kompromißvorschlag m • compromise proposal *(dec)*

Konation f • conation *(psy, act)*

Kondeszendenz f • condescendence *(rel)*

Konditional m • conditional *(lan)* → Konditionalsatz

Konditionalisierung f • conditionalization *(dec, epi)* < Bayessches Theorem

Konditionalismus m • conditionalism *(sci, met)*

Konditionalsatz m • conditional sentence/statement *(lan)*

Konditionalsatz, irrealer m • counterfactual (conditional) *(epi, lan)* → Konditionalsatz, kontrafaktischer

Konditionalsatz, kontrafaktischer m • counterfactual (conditional) *(epi, lan)* → Konditionalsatz, irrealer

Konditionalsatz, kontrafaktualer m → Konditionalsatz, kontrafaktischer

Konditionalschluß m • conditional/hypothetical syllogism *(log)*

Konditionalurteil n • conditional judg(e)ment *(log)*

Konditionierbarkeit f • conditionability *(psy)*

konditionierter Reflex m • conditioned reflex *(Pavlov) (psy)* < Abrichtung

Konditionierung f • conditioning, conditionalization *(psy)*

Konditionierung, klassische f • classical/respondent conditioning *(Pavlov) (psy)*

Konditionierungsregel f • rule of conditionalization *(Pavlov) (psy)*

Konditionierungsstrategien pl • conditioning strategies *(Habermas) (psy)*

Konditionismus m → Konditionalismus

konduktive Äußerung f • behabitive *(Austin) (lan, act)* < Illokution

Konfessionalismus m • confessionalism *(rel)*

konfessionell • confessional *(rel)*

konfessionslos • undenominational, non-denominational, without church affiliation *(rel)*

Konfidenzintervall n • interval of confidence, confidence interval *(mat)*

Konfiguration f • configuration *(Wittgenstein etc) (gep)*

Konfirmierbarkeit f • confirmability *(Carnap, Popper) (epi, log)* < Verifizierbarkeit

Konflikt zwischen Produktivkräften und Produktionsverhältnissen m • conflict between productive forces and the relations of production *(Marx) (eco, soc)*

Konfliktanalyse f • conflict analysis *(soc, psy)*

konflikterzeugende Situation f • conflict-generating/producing situation *(soc, psy)*

Konfliktforschung f • conflict studies *(soc, pol, psy)* < Friedensforschung

Konfliktlösung f • conflict resolution *(soc, psy)*

Konfliktregelung f • conflict management *(soc, psy)*

Konfliktregulierung *f* • conflict regulation (*soc, psy*)

Konfliktsituation *f* • conflict situation (*soc, pol, psy*)

Konflikttheorie *f* • conflict theory (*pol, psy*)

Konfliktvermeidung *f* • conflict avoidance (*soc, psy*)

Konformismus *m* • comformism (*act, soc*)

Konformität *f* • conformity (*eth, soc, psy*)

Konformitätsdruck *m* • pressure to conform, conformity pressure (*soc, psy*)

Konformitätssystem *n* • system of conformity (*Scheler*) (*soc, gep*)

Konfuzianische Ethik *f* • Confucian ethics (*eth, asp*)

Konfuzianismus *m* • Confucianism (*asp*)

Konfuzius • Confucius

Kongregationalismus *m* • Congregationalism (*rel*)

kongruent • congruent (*log, mat*)

Kongruenz *f* • congruence (*log, mat*)

Kongruenzprinzip *n* • congruence principle, principle of congruence/congruity (*mat, log*)

königliche Wissenschaft *f* • royal/kingly science (*Plato*) (*gep*)

Königreich Gottes *n* • kingdom of God (*rel*)

Königsberger Brückenproblem *n* • Königsberg bridge problem, problem of the seven bridges (*log*)

Konjunktion *f* • conjunction (*log, lan*)

konjunktiver Schluß *m* • conjunctive syllogism (*log*)

Konjunktivität *f* • conjunctivity (*log*)

Konjunktor *m* • conjunctor, connective (*log*)

Konjunktur *f* • economic situation/trend, level of economic activity (*eco*), boom (*gen*) < Marktentwicklung

konkludent • conclusive (*jur*); reasoned, conclusive (*log*) → schlüssig

Konklusion *f* • conclusion (*log*)

Konkomitanz *f* • concomitance (*lan, rel*)

konkret • concrete (*gep*) ↔ abstrakt

konkrete Kunst *f* • concrete art (*aes*)

konkrete Poesie *f* • concrete poetry (*aes*)

konkretes Allgemeines *n* • concrete universal (*ont*)

Konkretion *f* • concretion (*gep*) → Verwirklichung

Konkretisierung *f* • concretization (*gep*)

Konkretismus *m* • concretism (*Kotarbinski*) (*met*), (*psy, aes*)

Konkupiszenz *f* • concupiscence (*psy, rel*) < sinnliche Begierde

Konkurrent *m* • competitor, rival (*eco, dec*)

Konkurrenz *f* • competition, rivalry (*eco, soc*)

Konkurrenzdruck *m* • pressure of competition (*eco*)

Konkurrenzgesellschaft *f* • competitive society (*soc*)

Konkurrenzkampf, wirtschaftlicher *m* • economic competition, trade rivalry (*Marx etc*) (*eco*)

Konkurrenzprinzip *n* • competition principle, principle of competition (*eco, soc*)

Konkurrenzsystem *n* • competitive system (*eco, soc*)

Konnektionismus *m* • connectionism (*AI, min*) < neuronales Netz

Konnektivität *f* • connectivity (*AI, sys*)

Konnex *m* • nexus (*log*)

Konnex, kausaler *m* → Kausalnexus

Konnex, logischer *m* • logical nexus (*log*)

Konnotat *n* • connotation (*lan*)

Konnotation *f* • connotation (*lan*) → Nebenbedeutung; Bedeutung, begleitende ↔ Denotation

konnotativ • connotative (*Searle*) (*lan*)

konsekutiv • consecutive (*log, lan*)

Konsens *m* • consent, consensus (*eth, dec*) < Übereinstimmung

Konsensbildung *f* • consensus formation (*eth, dec*)

Konsensbildungsprozeß *m* • process of consensus building (*Habermas etc*) (*soc, dec*)

Konsensentscheidung *f* • consensual decision (*eth, dec*)

Konsenslösung *f* • consensual solution/agreement, solution based on agreement (*eth, dec*)

konsensorientiert • consensus-oriented (*act, eth*)

Konsenspolitik *f* • consensus politics (*pol*)

Konsenstheorie der Wahrheit *f* • consensus theory of truth (*epi, met*)

Konsensualkontrakt *m* • consensual contract (*jur*)

konsensuelle Entscheidung *f* • consensual decision (*dec*)

Konsensus *m* → Konsens

Konsequentialismus *m* • consequentialism (*eth*) ↔ Intentionalismus < Handlungsfolgen

Konsequentialismus, impersoneller *m* • impersonal consequentialism (*eth*)

Konsequentialismus, personeller *m* • person consequentialism (*eth*)

konsequentialistische Ethik *f* • consequentialist ethics (*eth*) ↔ Gesinnungsethik

Konsequenz *f* • consequence (*act, log*) < Folge

konservative Selbstorganisation *f* • conservative self-organization *(sys)*

konservatives System *n* • conservative system *(sys)*

Konservati(vi)smus *m* • conservatism *(pol)* < Traditionalismus

Konservativität *f* • conservatism *(pol)* → Konservat(iv)ismus

Konsistenz *f* • consistency *(log)* → Widerspruchslosigkeit

Konsistenzbedingung *f* • condition of consistency *(log)*

Konsistenzprüfung *f* • proof of consistency, consistency check *(sci)*

Konsonanz *f* • consonance *(aes)* ↔ Dissonanz

konstant • constant *(log, mat)*

Konstante *f* • constant *(log, mat)* → kontinuierliche Größe ↔ Variable

konstantes Summenspiel *n* • constant sum game *(dec)* < Nullsummenspiel

Konstanz *f* • constancy, stability < Beharrlichkeit, Unwandelbarkeit

Konstanz der Natur *f* • uniformity of nature *(nat, met)*

Konstanzphänomen *n* • constancy phenomenon *(psy)*

Konstanzprinzip *n* • constancy principle, principle of constance/constancy *(Freud) (psy)*

Konstatierung *f* • konstatierung, confirmation *(Schlick) (sci)*

Konstativa *pl* • constatives *(Searle) (lan)*

konstative Äußerung *f* • constative utterance/predication *(Austin, Searle etc) (lan)*

konstative Sprechhandlung *f* • constative speech act, constative *(Searle etc) (lan, act)* → Sprechakt, konstativer

Konstellation *f* • constellation *(Adorno etc) (epi, soc)*

Konstituante *f* • constituent *(log, lan)* → Konstituente; constituent assembly *(pol)* → Constituante

Konstituens *n* • constituent *(log, lan)*

Konstituente *f* • constituent *(log, lan)*

Konstituentenanalyse *f* • constituent analysis *(lan)*

Konstitution *f* • constitution *(pol, psy)*

Konstitution, phänomenologische *f* • phenomenological constitution *(Husserl) (met)*

Konstitutionalismus *m* • constitutionalism *(pol)*

konstitutionelle Bedingungen *pl* • constitutional conditions *(nat, psy)* < angeborene Disposition

konstitutionelle Monarchie *f* • constitutional monarchy *(pol)* ↔ Monarchie, absolute

konstitutionelle Regierung *f* • constitutional government *(pol)*

konstitutionelle Veranlagung *f* • constitutional disposition *(psy)*

Konstitutionssystem *n* • constitution-system *(Carnap) (ont)*

Konstitutionstheorie *f* • construction theory *(Carnap)*, constitution theory *(epi, log)* < Abstraktionsklasse, Konstitutionssystem

Konstitutionstypus *m* • constitutional type *(Kretschmer) (psy)* < Typenlehre

konstitutive Prinzipien der Erkenntnis *pl* • constitutive principles of cognition *(Kant) (epi)*

konstitutive Verstandeskräfte *pl* • constitutive powers of the mind *(Kant) (epi)*

konstitutiver Aspekt *m* • constitutive aspect *(gep)*

konstitutives Prinzip *n* • constitutive principle *(Kant) (epi)* ↔ regulatives Prinzip

konstitutorische Eigenschaften *pl* • nuclear properties *(Meinong, Mally) (ont)*

Konstruierbarkeit *f* • constructibility *(sci)*

Konstrukt *n* • construct *(epi, min, sci)*

Konstruktion *f* • construction *(gep)* < Dekonstruktion

Konstruktionsfehler *m* • design fault *(tec, sys)* < Programmfehler

Konstruktivismus *m* • constructivism *(epi, sci, aes)*

Konstruktivismus, kantischer *m* • Kantian constructivism *(Rawls) (eth)*

Konstruktivismus, radikaler *m* • radical constructivism *(epi, sci)*

Konsubstantialität *f* • consubstantiality *(rel)*

Konsubstantiation *f* • consubstantiation *(rel)*

Konsumästhetik *f* • consumer aesthetics *(aes)* < Warenästhetik

konsumentenfreundlich • consumer-friendly *(eco)*

Konsumentenschutz *m* • consumer protection *(eco)*

Konsumentensouveränität *f* • consumer sovereignty *(eco)*

Konsumfreiheit *f* • consumer freedom *(eco)*

Konsumgesellschaft *f* • consumer society *(eco, soc)*

Konsumgewohnheit *f* • consumption pattern, consumer habit *(eco)* → Konsumverhalten

Konsumgüter *pl* • consumer goods *(eco)*

Konsumhaltung *f* → Konsumverhalten

Konsumhysterie *f* • consumer hysteria, shopping madness, shopaholicism° *(eco, soc)* < Kaufrausch

Konsumismus *m* • consumerism *(eco, soc)*
< Überflußgesellschaft

Konsumnachfrage *f* • consumer demand *(eco)*

konsumorientierte Gesellschaft *f* • consumption/consumer -oriented society *(eco, soc)*
< Habensinn

Konsumrausch *m* → Kaufrausch

Konsumterror *m* • pressure of a materialistic society *(eco, soc)*

Konsumverhalten *n* • consumer behaviour *(eco)* → Konsumgewohnheit

Konsumverzicht *m* • consumption abstinence, restraint in consumption *(eco)*

Konsumzwang *m* • compulsion to buy *(eco)*

Konszientialismus *m* • conscientialism *(Leibniz, Fichte etc)* *(epi)*

Kontamination, radioaktive *f* • radioactive/ nuclear contamination *(env)*

Kontemplation *f* • contemplation *(rel, aes)*

Kontemplationstheorie *f* • contemplation theory *(aes)*

Kontemplativ-Erhabenes *n* • contemplative-sublime *(Schiller)* *(aes)*

Konterrevolution *f* • counter-revolution *(pol)*
< W 518

Kontext *m* • context *(gep)* < Kotext

kontextabhängig • context-dependent *(gep)*

kontextabhängige Bedeutung *f* • context-dependent meaning *(lan)*

kontextabhängige Grammatik *f* • context-dependent/sensitive grammar *(lan)* ↔ kontextfreie Grammatik

Kontextdefinition *f* • contextual definition *(log, lan)* < Gebrauchsdefinition

kontextfreie Grammatik *f* • context-free grammar *(lan)* ↔ kontextabhängige Grammatik

Kontextinvarianz *f* • contextual invariance *(lan)*

kontextsensitive Grammatik *f* → kontextabhängige Grammatik

Kontextualismus *m* • contextualism *(lan, eth, cul)*

Kontextualität *f* • contextuality *(lan)*

kontexunabhängige Bedeutung *f* • context-independent meaning *(lan)*

Kontiguität *f* • contiguity *(met, psy)*

Kontiguitätstheorie *f* • contiguity theory *(psy)*

kontingente Aussage *f* • contingent statement/ predication *(lan, log)*

kontingente Existenz *f* • contingent existence *(lan, ont)*, contingent existenz *(Jaspers)* *(met)*

kontingente Formel *f* • contingent formula *(log)* → indeterminierte Formel

kontingente Wahrheit *f* • contingent truth *(epi)*

kontingente Welt *f* • contingent world *(met)*

Kontingenz *f* • contingency *(nat, met, psy)* → Zufälligkeit, Möglichkeit

Kontingenz des Endlichen *f* • contingency of the finite *(met)*

Kontingenz, doppelte *f* • double contingency *(log)*

Kontingenz, Problem der *n* • problem of contingency *(met)*

Kontingenzbeweis *m* • contingency argument, argument from contingency *(Aquinas, Brentano)* *(log)*

Kontingenzerfahrung *f* • contingency experience, experience of contingency *(met, rel)*

Kontingenztheorie *f* • theory of contingency *(Leibniz etc)* *(met)*

kontinuativer Term *m* • mass term *(lan)*

kontinuierliche Größe *f* • continuous quantity/ magnitude *(log, mat)* → Konstante

kontinuierlicher Prozeß *m* • continuous process *(sys)*

Kontinuität *f* • continuity *(gep)*

Kontinuum *n* • continuum *(nat, mat, ont)*
< Raum-Zeit-Kontinuum

Kontinuumsproblem *n* • continuum problem *(sci, mat)* < Logizismus

Kontra-Argument *n* • counter-argument *(log, lan)* → Gegenargument ↔ Pro-Argument

Kontradiktion *f* • contradiction *(log)*

Kontradiktionsprinzip *n* • principle of contradiction *(log)* → Satz vom Widerspruch

kontradiktorischer Gegensatz *m* • contradictory opposition *(log)* < logisches Quadrat

kontradiktorischer Satz *m* • contradictory sentence/proposition/statement *(log)*

kontrafaktische Annahme *f* • counterfactual (assumption) *(log, lan)* → kontrafaktische Aussage

kontrafaktische Aussage *f* • counterfactual *(log, lan)* < kontrafaktischer Konditionalsatz

kontrafaktische Behauptung *f* • counterfactual statement/proposition *(lan)* < Modalbehauptung

kontrafaktische Evidenz *f* • counterfactual evidence *(Pierce)* *(sci)*

kontrafaktische Idealisierung *f* • counterfactual idealization *(log, sci)*

kontrafaktischer Konditionalsatz *m* • counterfactual (conditional) *(log, epi)* → Konditionalsatz, irrealer

kontrafaktischer Konditional *m* • counterfactual/subjunctive conditional *(lan)*

Kontrafaktizität *f* • counterfactuality, counterfacticity *(lan, sci)*

Kontrakt *m* • contract *(jur)*

Kontraktualismus *m* • contractualism *(soc, jur)* < Vertragstheorie, Sozialvertragstheorie

Kontraposition *f* • contraposition, counterposition *(log)*

Kontrapositionsregel *f* • contraposition/counterposition/contrapositive rule *(log)*

Kontrapunkt *m* • counterpoint *(aes)*

konträr • contrary, antithetical, opposite *(log)*

konträrer Gegensatz *m* • contrary opposition *(log)* < logisches Quadrat

konträrer Satz *m* • contrary sentence *(log)*

Kontravalenz *f* • exclusive disjunction *(log)* → disjunktives Urteil

Kontrollgruppe *f* • control group *(sci)* < Testgruppe, Experimentalgruppe

Kontrollhierarchien *pl* • control hierarchies *(sys)*

kontrolliertes Experiment *n* • controlled experiment *(sci)*

Kontrollmaßnahme *f* • control(ling) measure *(sys, sci)*

Kontrollsystem *n* • control system *(sys)*

Konvention *f* • convention *(jur, soc, lan)*

konventionale Handlung *f* • conventional act *(act)*

Konventionalisierung *f* • conventionalization *(log, lan)* < Definition

Konventionalismus *m* • conventionalism *(sci, lan, eth)*

konventionalistische Wendung *f* • conventionalist turn *(Popper) (sci)*

konventionalistischer Einwand *m* • conventionalist argument/objection *(log, lan)*

konventioneller Krieg *m* • conventional war(fare) *(pol)* ↔ Atomkrieg

Konvergenz *f* • convergence *(mat, nat)*

Konvergenzmodell *n* • convergence model *(sci)* < Geisteswissenschaften, Integrationsmodell

Konvergenztheorie *f* • theory of convergence *(pol, eco, soc)*

Konvergenzverhalten *n* • convergence behaviour *(mat)*

Konversationsimplikatur *f* • conversational implicature *(Grice) (lan, act)*

Konversationsmaximen *pl* • maxims of conversation, conversational maxims/principles *(Grice) (lan)*

Konversion *f* • conversion *(Freud) (psy); (log, rel); (eco, pol)* < Rüstungskonversion, Schwerter zu Pflugscharen

Konvivialität *f* • conviviality *(Illich) (eth, env)*

Konzentration des Kapitals *f* • concentration of (the) capital *(Marx) (eco, soc)*

Konzept, funktionales *n* • functional concept *(Natorp) (epi)*

Konzeption *f* • conception *(sci, aes)*

Konzeptkunst *f* • concept art, conceptual art *(aes)*

Konzeptualismus *m* • conceptualism *(lan, ont)* ↔ Nominalismus

Konzil *n* • council *(rel)*

Kooperative *f* • cooperative *(eco)* → Genossenschaft < Produktionsgenossenschaft

kooperativer Deutungsprozeß *m* • cooperative interpretation process, cooperative interpretive process *(Habermas) (lan, act, soc)*

kooperatives Spiel *n* • cooperative game *(dec)*

Koordinatensprache *f* • coordinate language, language of coordinates *(Carnap) (lan, sci)*

Koordinatensystem *n* • coordinate system *(mat)*

Koordinatensystem, betrachterbezogenes *n* • viewpoint reference frame, subjective/observer-relative reference frame *(epi, min)*

Koordinationsbedarf *m* • need for coordination *(soc, sys)*

kopernikanische Revolution *f* → kopernikanische Wende

kopernikanische Wende *f* • Copernican revolution *(Kant) (epi, nat)* < W 522

kopernikanisches (Welt)System *n* • Copernican (world) system *(nat, sci)* < W 359

kopernikanisches Prinzip *n* • Copernican principle *(sci)*

kopernikanisches Weltbild *n* • Copernican world view *(nat)* → heliozentrisches Weltbild

Kopernikus • Copernicus

Kopfarbeiter *m* • brainworker *(Marx etc)*

Kopula *f* • copula *(lan)*

Koran *m* • nt *(rel)*

Körper *m* • body *(nat, ont)*

Körper, atomistische *pl* • atomistic bodies *(Hobbes) (ont)*

Körper, äußerer *m* • external body *(nat, epi, ont)*

Körper-Geist-Problem *n* • mind-body problem *(Descartes, Geulincx, Leibniz etc) (met, min)*

Körper, geometrischer *m* • geometric(al) object/body/solid *(mat)*

Körper, politischer *m* • body politic, political body *(Hobbes, Rousseau) (pol)*

körperbehindert • physically disabled/disadvantaged/handicapped *(soc, eth)*

Körperbewußtsein *n* • body consciousness *(aes, psy)*

Körperbild *n* • body image *(psy)*

Körperkunst *f* • body art *(aes)*

körperlich • (▷ physisches Objekt) corporeal, physical, material *(nat, ont)*, (▷ belebter Körper) corporal *(nat)*

körperliche Arbeit *f* • manual work *(eco)*

körperliche Bewegung *f* • bodily movement *(nat)*

körperliche Empfindung *f* • bodily sensation *(psy)*

körperliche Natur *f* • corporeal nature *(Descartes) (met)*

körperliche Substanz *f* • material/corporeal substance *(Leibniz etc) (met)*

Körperlichkeit *f* • corporeality, corporality *(met, nat)*

körperlos • bodiless, immaterial, incorpor(e)al *(met)* → asomatisch, unkörperlich

Körperpolynom *n* • field polynomial *(mat, nat)*

Körperschaft *f* • corporation *(jur)*

Körpersprache *f* • body language *(lan, psy)*

Körperstrafe *f* • corporal punishment *(jur)* < Todesstrafe

Körpertheorie *f* • field theory *(log, mat)*

Körperwahrnehmung *f* • body perception *(psy)*

Korporativismus *m* • corporatism, corporativism *(pol)* < Ständestaat

Korpuskel *n/f* • corpuscle *(nat)* → Partikel, Elementarteilchen

Korpuskularphilosophie *f* • corpuscular philosophy *(nat, met)*

Korpuskulartheorie der Materie *f* • corpuscular theory of matter *(nat)*

Korrektheitssatz *m* • correctness theorem *(sci, log)* < Vollständigkeitssatz, symbolische Logik

Korrelat *n* • correlate *(log, lan, mat)*

Korrelation *f* • correlation *(log, mat, sys)* → Wechselbeziehung

Korrelation, direkte *f* • direct correlation *(mat)*

Korrelation, kanonische *f* • canonical correlation *(log)*

Korrelation, negative *f* • negative correlation *(mat)*

Korrelation, positive *f* • positive correlation *(mat)*

Korrelationsforschung *f* • correlation research *(Husserl etc) (met, epi)*

Korrelationskoeffizient *m* • correlation coefficient *(mat)*

korrelative Räume *pl* • correlative spaces *(Foucault) (epi, sys)*

Korrelativismus *m* • correlativism *(epi)*

Korrelativität *f* • correlativity *(log, mat, sys)* → Wechselbezüglichkeit < Reziprozität

Korrespondenzprinzip *n* • correspondence principle *(Bohr) (nat)*

Korrespondenzregel *f* • correspondence rule *(Carnap) (log, lan)*

Korrespondenztheorie der Wahrheit *f* • correspondence theory of truth *(epi, met)*

Korruption *f* • corruption *(eth)* → Bestechung < Bestechlichkeit

kosmische Ästhetik *f* • cosmic aesthetics *(aes)*

kosmische Entwicklung *f* • cosmic process *(nat)*

kosmische Harmonie *f* • cosmic harmony *(nat, met)*

kosmische Strahlen *pl* • cosmic rays *(nat, eso)*

kosmisches Rätsel *n* • cosmic riddle *(Nietzsche)*

Kosmodizee *f* • cosmodicy *(Nietzsche) (met, rel)* < Anthropodizee, Theodizee

Kosmogonie *f* • cosmogony *(cul, rel)* → Weltschöpfungsmythos < W 523

Kosmologie *f* • cosmology *(nat)*

kosmologische Dialektik *f* • cosmological dialectic *(Kant) (epi)*

kosmologische Evolution *f* • cosmological evolution *(nat)*

kosmologische Idee *f* • cosmological idea *(Kant) (epi, met)*

kosmologische Paradoxien *pl* • cosmological paradoxes *(ont, nat)*

kosmologischer Gottesbeweis *m* • cosmological proof (of God's existence) *(Aristotle, Augustine) (rel)*

kosmologisches Argument *n* • cosmological argument *(rel)* → kosmologischer Gottesbeweis

kosmologisches Postulat *n* • cosmological postulate *(Milne) (nat)*

Kosmopolitismus *m* • cosmopolitanism *(pol)*

Kosmosophie *f* → Weltweisheit

Kosmotheismus *m* • cosmotheism *(rel)* < Pantheismus, Panentheismus

Kosmotheologie *f* • cosmo-theology *(Kant) (epi, rel)* < Ontotheologie

Kosten-Nutzen-Analyse *f* • cost-benefit analysis, CBA *(eco, dec)* < Nutzenvergleich, Rentabilität, Wirtschaftlichkeitsanalyse

Kosten-Nutzen-Denken *n* • cost-benefit thinking/attitude *(eco, dec)* < Rationalitätsprinzip

Kostenexternalisierung *f* • externalization of costs *(eco)* < Externitäten, Sozialkosten

Kostenrechnung *f* • cost accounting *(eco, dec)*

Kostenvergleich *m* • cost comparison *(eco, dec)*

Kotext *m* • co-text *(Firth) (lan)* < Kontext

Kovarianz *f* • covariance *(mat)*

Kovarianzanalyse *f* • covariance analysis *(mat)*

Kovarianzkonzeption der Repräsentation *f* • covariance conception of representation *(Cummins) (epi, min)*

Kraft *f* • force, power *(met, nat)* < Potenz < W 527

Kraft, treibende *f* • motive/moving/driving force *(met, gep)* → Agens < Movens

Kraftäußerung *f* • manifestation/expression of force *(gep)*

Kräfte *pl* • forces, powers, potencies° *(met, nat)*

Kräfteverhältnis *n* • relation of forces *(nat, pol)* < Gleichgewicht der Kräfte

Kräftevielfalt *f* • plurality of forces *(Nietzsche, Bäumler etc) (met, pol)*

Kraftfeld *n* • force field *(nat, eso)*

Kraftlehre *f* • dynamics *(nat)*

Kraftzentrum *n* • centre of force *(nat); (asp)* → chakra

Krankheit zum Tod *f* • sickness unto/into death *(Kierkegaard) (met)* < W 528

Kränkung *f* • offence, insult *(eth)*

Kränkung, narzißtische *f* • narcissistic/ narcistic insult *(Freud etc) (psy)*

Kreatianismus *m* • creationism *(rel)* < Tradutianismus

Kreatinismus *m* → Kreatianismus

Kreationismus *m* • creationism *(rel)* < Schöpfungslehre

kreativer Prozeß *m* • creative process *(aes)*

kreatives Ich *n* • creative I/ego *(Fichte) (met)*

kreatives Nichts *n* • creative nothing *(Stirner) (met)*

Kreativität *f* • creativity *(aes, psy)*

Kreativitätsforschung *f* • creativity research, study of creativity *(aes, psy)*

Kreatur *f* • creature *(nat, rel)*

kreatürlich • creatural, creaturely *(nat, rel)*

Kreislauf der Wiedergeburt *m* • cycle of rebirth *(asp)* < Reinkarnation

Kreislauftheorie *f* • theory/doctrine of circulation *(nat)*

Kreislauftheorie der Geschichte *f* • circular theory of history *(Polybios, Machiavelli) (his)* < zyklische Geschichtstheorie, Rad des Schicksals

Kreuzmenge *f* → Mengenprodukt

Kreuzprodukt *n* • cross/vector product *(mat)* → Vektorprodukt

Kreuzvalidierung *f* • cross-validation *(mat, sci)*

Krieg aller gegen alle *m* • war of every man against every man *(Hobbes) (soc)* → bellum omnium contra omnes < Kriegszustand

Krieg als Kunstwerk *m* • war as a work of art *(Burckhardt) (cul)*

Krieg der Sterne *m* • star wars *(pol)*

Krieg, gerechter *m* • just war *(eth, pol)* → bellum iustum

kriegerische Seele *f* • warlike soul *(Nietzsche) (psy)*

kriegerisches Zeitalter *n* • warlike age *(Nietzsche) (cul)*

Kriegsbereitschaft *f* • state of preparedness for war *(pol)*

Kriegsdienstverweigerer *m* • conscientious objector *(pol, eth)*

Kriegsdienstverweigerung *f* • refusal to fight in a war, conscientious objection *(pol, eth)*

Kriegsdrohung *f* • threat of war *(pol)* < Abschreckungstheorie

Kriegserklärung *f* • declaration of war *(pol)*

Kriegsgefahr *f* • risk of war *(pol)*

Kriegsgewinnler *m* • war profiteer *(eth, pol)*

Kriegsindustrie *f* • war industry *(eco)*

Kriegskunst *f* • art of war, martial arts *(pol, asp)*

Kriegslust *f* • belligerence, belligerency, bellicosity *(pol, eth)* < Bellizismus

Kriegsneurose *f* • war neurosis *(psy)*

Kriegsrecht *n* • martial/military law *(jur)* → ius belli, Standrecht

Kriegsschuldfrage *f* • question of war guilt *(Jaspers etc) (eth)*

Kriegsschule des Lebens *f* • martial school of life *(Nietzsche) (met)*

Kriegsverbrechen *n* • war crime *(eth)* < Verbrechen gegen die Menschlichkeit

Kriegswirtschaft *f* • war(time) economy *(eco)*

Kriegszustand *m* • state of war *(Hobbes, Locke) (soc)*

Krimatologie *f* • krimatology *(log)* → Folgerungslehre

Kriminalanthropologie *f* • criminal anthropology *(jur, ant)*

Kriminalitätsrate *f* • crime rate *(jur, soc)*

Krischna • Krishna *(asp)*

Krise *f* • crisis *(gep)*

Krise des Subjekts *f* • crisis of the subject *(met, soc)*

Krisenbewußtsein *n* • consciousness/ awareness of crisis *(soc, psy)*

Krisenmanagement *n* • crisis management *(pol, sys)*

Krisentheologie *f* • crisis theology *(Barth etc)* *(rel)* < negative Theologie

Krisentheorie *f* • crisis theory *(Marx) (eco)* < Überproduktionskrise

Krisenwissenschaft *f* • science of crisis *(Habermas) (gep)*

Krisenzeit der Weltgeschichte *f* • pivotal age of world history *(Jaspers) (his)* < Epochenschwelle, Achsenzeit

Krishna → Krischna

Kriterienproblem *n* • problem of the criterion, problem of criteria *(epi, sci)*

Kriterium *n* • criterion *(gep)* < Kennzeichen

Kriterium, gemeinsames *n* • common criterion *(gep)*

Kriteriumsproblem *n* → Kriterienproblem

Kritik *f* • criticism *(gen)*, (▷ kritische Schrift/ systematische Kritik) critique *(gep)*

Kritik der Vernunft selbst *f* • critique of reason itself *(Kant) (epi)*

Kritik des dialektischen Scheins *f* • critique of dialectical illusion *(Kant) (epi)*

Kritik des Geschmacks *f* • critique of taste *(Kant) (epi, aes)*

Kritik, externe *f* • external criticism, external critique *(gep)*

Kritik, immanente *f* • immanent criticism, immanent critique *(gep)*

Kritik, interne *f* → Kritik, immanente

Kritiker *m* • critic *(gen)*

Kritikfähigkeit *f* • faculty of critical thought, ability to think critically *(gep)*

Kritiklosigkeit *f* • uncritical disposition *(gen)*

kritische Auflösung *f* • critical resolution *(Kant) (epi)*

kritische Geschichte *f* • critical history *(his)*

kritische Masse *f* • critical mass *(nat, sys)*

kritische Periode Kants *f* • Kant's critical period *(Kant) (epi)*

kritische Philosophie *f* • critical philosophy *(Kant, Bauer etc) (gep)*

kritische Sozialtheorie *f* • critical social theory *(soc)*

kritische Soziologie *f* • critical sociology *(soc)*

kritische Theorie *f* • Critical Theory *(Horkheimer, Marcuse etc) (sci, soc)* < Frankfurter Schule < W 546

kritischer Idealismus *m* • critical idealism *(Kant) (epi, met)* → formaler Idealismus

kritischer Rationalismus *m* • critical rationalism *(Popper, Albert) (epi, sci)*

kritischer Realismus *m* • critical realism *(epi, sci)*

kritischer Wert *m* • critical value *(mat, sys)* < Schwellenwert

kritisches Bewußtsein *n* • critical consciousness/awareness *(soc)*

kritisches Denken *n* • critical thinking *(gep)*

Kritizismus *m* • criticism, critical philosophy *(Kant) (epi)*

Kübeltheorie des menschlichen Geistes *f* • bucket theory of (the) human mind *(Popper) (epi, sci)* ↔ Scheinwerfertheorie

Kubismus *m* • cubism *(aes)*

Kugelgestalt der Erde *f* • spherical shape of the earth *(nat)*

kuhmäßige Gemütsstille *f* • cow-like/bovine composure *(Nietzsche) (psy)*

Kuhnsche Matrix *f* • Kuhnian matrix *(sci)* → Matrix, disziplinäre

kulinarische Kunstauffassung *f* • culinary conception of art *(aes)*

Kulinarismus *m* • culinarism *(aes)*

Kultbuch *n* • cult book *(aes)*

Kultfigur *f* • cult figure *(aes, soc)*

Kultfilm *m* • cult movie *(aes)*

Kultgemeinschaft *f* • cult/religious community *(rel)*

Kultreligion *f* • cult religion *(rel)*

Kultstatus *m* • cult status *(aes)*

Kultur *f* • culture *(cul)*

Kultur der Differenz *f* • culture of difference *(epi, pol)*

Kultur, Tragödie der *f* • tragedy of culture *(Simmel) (cul)*

Kultur, Wesen der *n* • nature of civilization *(Freud etc) (cul)*

kulturabhängig • culture-dependent *(cul)* < Kulturdeterminismus

Kulturaneignung *f* → Enkulturation

Kulturanthropologie *f* • cultural anthropology *(ant, cul)*

Kulturapologetik *f* • cultural apologetics *(cul)*

Kulturarbeit *f* • cultural work° *(Freud) (psy, cul)*

Kulturaustausch *m* • cultural exchange *(cul, soc)*

Kulturbegegnung *f* • cultural encounter, encounter between cultures *(cul, soc)* → Kulturkontakt

Kulturbegriff *m* • concept of culture, cultural concept *(cul)*

Kulturbesitz *m* • cultural property *(Freud) (cul)* < kulturelles Kapital

Kulturbestrebung *f* • cultural endeavour *(Freud) (cul)*

Kulturdenkmal *n* • cultural monument *(aes)*

Kulturdeterminismus *m* • cultural determinism *(cul)* → Kulturismus

Kultureignung *f* • cultural qualification/disposition, qualification/disposition for culture *(Freud) (psy, cul)*

Kulturelement *n* • cultural element *(cul)*

kulturelle Erbschaft *f* • cultural inheritance *(cul)* < kulturelles Erbe

kulturelle Evolution *f* • cultural evolution *(cul)*

kulturelle Identität *f* • cultural identity *(cul)*

kulturelle Konvention *f* • cultural convention *(cul)*

kulturelle Pseudospeziation *f* • cultural pseudo-speciation *(Erikson, Eibl-Eibesfeld) (cul, ant)*

kulturelle Rationalisierung *f* • cultural rationalization *(Weber) (soc, cul)*

kulturelle Reproduktion *f* • cultural reproduction *(Habermas) (soc, cul)*

kulturelle Revolution *f* • cultural revolution *(pol, cul)* → Kulturrevolution

kulturelle Tradition *f* • cultural tradition *(cul)*

kulturelle Verarmung *f* • cultural impoverishment *(soc, cul)*

kulturelle Verwurzelung *f* • cultural rootedness *(cul)*

kultureller Pluralismus *m* • cultural pluralism *(cul, soc)* → Multikulturalität

kultureller Relativismus *m* • cultural relativism *(cul, eth)* → Kulturrelativismus

kulturelles Kapital *n* • cultural capital *(Bourdieu) (soc, cul)*

kulturelles Erbe *n* • cultural heritage/legacy *(cul)* < kulturelle Erbschaft

kulturelles Universal *n* • cultural universal *(cul)*

Kulturentstehungslehre *f* • theory of the origin of culture *(cul)*

Kulturentwicklung *f* • cultural development, development of civilization *(Freud) (cul)*

Kulturepoche *f* • culture epoch *(cul, his)*

Kulturerwerb *m* • cultural acquisition *(Freud) (cul)* < Enkulturation, Akkulturation

kulturfeindlich • hostile to civilization, anticultural *(cul)*

Kulturforderung *f* • cultural demand/postulate *(Freud) (cul)*

Kulturförderung *f* • patronage of culture *(cul)* < Kultursponsoring

Kulturforschung *f* • cultural research *(cul)*

Kulturfortschritt *m* • cultural progress *(cul)*

Kulturgemeinschaft *f* • cultural community *(Freud) (cul)*

Kulturgene *pl* • cultural genes *(nat, ant)*, culturgenes *(Lumsden, Wilson) (nat, ant)* → kulturerzeugende Mechanismen < Mentifakte

Kulturgeschichte *f* • cultural history, history of culture *(cul, his)*

Kulturgesellschaft *f* • civilized society *(Freud) (cul)*

Kulturgüter *pl* • gifts of civilization, cultural goods *(Freud) (cul)*

Kulturhistoriker *m* • cultural historian, historian of culture *(cul, his)*

Kulturhöhe *f* • level of civilization *(cul)*

Kulturideal *n* • cultural ideal *(Freud) (cul)*

Kulturimperialismus *m* • cultural imperialism *(cul, pol)*

Kulturindustrie *f* • culture industry, cultural industry *(Adorno, Marcuse etc) (aes, eco)* < Massenkonsum, Unterhaltungsindustrie

Kulturismus *m* • culturism° *(cul)* → Kulturdeterminismus ↔ Biologismus < Freikörperkultur, Lebensreformbewegung, Naturismus

Kulturistik *f* • culturism *(aes, cul)* < Freikörperkultur

Kulturkampf *m* • cultural struggle, struggle between state and church *(pol, rel)* < Säkularisierung, Trennung von Kirche und Staat

Kulturkapital *n* • cultural capital *(Bourdieu) (cul, soc)*

Kulturkontakt *m* • culture contact *(cul, soc)* → Kulturbegegnung

Kulturkreis *m* • (▷ geographischer Kulturkreis) cultural area/complex *(cul, ant)*, (▷ Lebenszyklus der Kultur) cultural cycle *(Frobenius, Spengler etc) (cul, ant)* < Kulturseele

Kulturkreistheorie *f* • theory of cultural cycles *(cul, ant)* < Kulturzyklentheorie

Kulturkrieg *m* • cultural war *(cul, pol)*

Kulturkrise *f* • cultural crisis *(cul)*

Kulturkritik *f* • cultural criticism, critique of culture *(Rousseau etc) (cul, soc)*

kultürlich • culturally appropriate *(cul)*

Kulturmensch *m* • civilized man *(Weber, Freud) (cul, ant)*

Kulturmorphologie *f* • cultural morphology *(Frobenius etc) (cul)*

Kulturökologie *f* • cultural ecology, ecology of culture *(cul, env)*

Kulturoptimismus *m* • optimistic view of civilization *(cul)*

Kulturpessimismus *m* • pessimistic view of civilization *(Spengler, Simmel etc) (cul)* < Untergang des Abendlandes

Kulturpflicht *f* • cultural duty/obligation *(cul)* < Kulturforderung

Kulturphilosophie *f* • philosophy of culture, cultural philosophy *(cul)* < W 551

Kulturpolitik *f* • cultural policy *(pol)*

kulturproduzierende Gene *pl* • culturgens *(Lumsden, Wilson) (nat, ant)* → Kulturgene

Kulturprozeß *m* • cultural process, process of civilization *(Freud) (cul, psy)*

Kulturpsychologie *f* • cultural psychology, psychology of culture *(cul, psy)*

Kulturrechte *pl* • cultural rights *(cul, jur)*

Kulturrelativismus *m* • cultural relativism *(cul, eth)* → kultureller Relativismus

Kulturreligion *f* • religion of culture° *(cul, rel)*

Kulturrevolution *f* • cultural revolution *(Mao etc) (pol, cul)*

Kulturschock *m* • culture shock *(cul)*

Kulturseele *f* • cultural soul, soul/spirit of a culture *(cul)* → Paideuma

Kultursoziologie *f* • cultural sociology, sociology of culture *(cul, soc)*

kulturspezifisch • culturally specific *(cul, soc)*

Kultursponsoring *n* • cultural sponsoring *(eco, aes, cul)* < Kulturförderung

Kulturtheorie *f* • theory of culture, cultural/culture theory *(cul, soc)* < W 1331

Kulturträger *m* • culture-bearer, bearer/upholder of culture *(Freud) (cul, psy)*

kulturunabhängig • culture-independent *(cul, soc)*

Kulturverbote *pl* • cultural prohibitions *(Freud) (cul)*

Kulturversagung *f* • cultural frustration *(Freud) (psy, cul)*

Kulturvolk *n* • cultured people, highly civilized nation *(cul)*

Kulturwandel *m* • cultural change *(cul)*

Kulturwesen, Mensch als *m* • man as cultural being *(Freud etc) (cul, ant)*

Kulturwissenschaft *f* • cultural science, cultural/culture studies *(cul)* < Ethnologie

Kulturzyklentheorie *f* • cultural cycle theory *(cul, his)*

kumulativer Prozeß *m* • cumulative process *(sys)*

künftige Gesellschaft *f* • future society *(soc)*

Kunst *f* • art(s) *(aes)*

Kunst als Erscheinung *f* • art as appearance *(aes)*

Kunst als Fetisch *f* • art as fetish *(aes)*

Kunst als Lebenssteigerung *f* • art as life-intensification *(Nietzsche) (aes)*

Kunst als Mittel der Wahrheit *f* • art as vehicle of truth *(Hegel etc) (aes)*

Kunst als Spiel *f* • art as (a) game *(Schiller, Gadamer) (aes)*

Kunst als utopisches Versprechen *f* • art as promise of utopia *(Adorno, Marcuse) (aes, soc)*

Kunst an sich *f* • art as such *(aes)* < reine Kunst, Kunst um der Kunst willen

Kunst aus Überschuß *f* • art as excessive strength *(Nietzsche) (aes)*

Kunst im Zeitalter der technischen Reproduzierbarkeit *f* • art in the age of mechanical reproduction *(Benjamin) (aes)* < W 554

Kunst, Niedergang der *m* • decline/decay of art *(aes)* < Ende der Kunst

Kunst, schöne *f* • fine art *(aes)*

Kunst um der Kunst willen • art for art's sake *(aes)* → L'art pour l'art

Kunstautonomie *f* • autonomy of art *(aes)*

Kunstbolschewismus *m* • Art Bolshevism *(aes, pol)*

Kunstereignis *n* • art event *(aes)*

Kunsterziehung *f* • art/artistic education *(aes)*

Kunstfälschung *f* • forgery/counterfeiting of art *(aes)*

Kunstfehler, medizinischer *m* • medical malpractice *(jur, eth)*

Kunstfertigkeit *f* • artistic skill *(aes)*

Kunstförderung *f* • art sponsoring, patronage of art *(aes)* < Mäzenatentum, Kultursponsoring

Kunstform *f* • art form *(aes)*

Kunstfreund *m* • art lover, lover of the arts *(aes)*

Kunstgattung *f* • genre *(aes)* → Genre

Kunstgegenstand *m* → Kunstobjekt

Kunstgelehrsamkeit *f* • connoisseurship, expertise in art *(aes)*

Kunstgenuß *m* • enjoyment of art, artistic pleasure *(aes)*

Kunstgeschichte *f* • history of art *(his, aes)*

Kunsthandel *m* • art trade *(eco, aes)*

Kunstkenner *m* • art expert/connoisseur *(aes)*

Kunstkritik *f* • art criticism *(aes)*

Künstler *m* • artist *(aes)*

künstlerische Aufrichtigkeit *f* • artistic sincerity/integrity *(aes)*

künstlerische Autonomie *f* • artistic autonomy *(aes)*

künstlerische Berufung *f* • artistic vocation *(aes)*

künstlerische Bewegung *f* • artistic movement *(aes)*

künstlerische Erziehung *f* • artistic education *(aes)*

künstlerische Gestaltung *f* • artistic design *(aes)* < Design

künstlerische Idealisierung *f* • idealization in art *(aes)*

künstlerische Kreativität *f* • artistic creativity *(aes)*

künstlerische Praxis *f* • artistic practice *(aes)*

künstlerische Schöpfung *f* • artistic creation *(aes)*

künstlerische Wahrheit *f* • artistic truth *(aes)*

künstlerischer Gehalt *m* • artistic content *(aes)*

künstlerischer Schein *m* • artistic illusion/ delusion *(aes)*

künstlerischer Wert *m* • artistic value *(aes)*

künstlerisches Schaffen *n* • artistic creation/ work *(aes)* → künstlerische Schöpfung

Künstlerkolonie *f* • artist colony *(aes)*

Künstlerroman *m* • artist novel *(aes)*

künstliche Bedürfnisse *pl* • artificial needs *(eco, soc)*

künstliche Befruchtung *f* • artificial insemination *(nat)* < Embryo(nen)transfer, In-vitro-Fertilisation, Reproduktionstechnologie

künstliche Intelligenz *f* • artificial/machine intelligence *(AI, min)* < W 393

künstliche Sprache *f* • artificial language *(lan)* < ideale Sprache

künstliche Ungleichheit *f* • artificial inequality *(nat, soc)* ↔ natürliche Ungleichheit

künstlicher Mensch *m* • artificial man *(Hobbes) (pol)*, *(nat, tec)* < Maschinenmensch

künstliches Leben *n* • artificial life *(nat, tec)*

Künstlichkeit *f* • artificiality *(aes, tec)*

Künstlichkeit des sozialen Lebens *f* • artificiality of social life *(Rousseau) (soc)*

Kunstmusik *f* • art music *(aes)* ↔ Volksmusik

Kunstobjekt *n* • art object, objet d'art *(aes)*

Kunstphilosophie *f* → Philosophie der Kunst

Kunstproduktion *f* • production of art, creation of art *(aes)*

Kunstpsychologie *f* • psychology of art *(aes, psy)*

Kunstreligion *f* • religion of art *(Hegel etc)* *(aes)*

Kunstrezeption *f* • reception of art *(aes)*

Kunstrichtung *f* • art trend, artistic school *(aes)*

Kunstschönes *n* • beauty in art *(aes)*

Kunstsinn *m* • artistic sense *(aes)* → Kunstverständnis

Kunstsinnigkeit *f* • appreciativeness of art, sensitivity to art *(aes)* < Kunstverständnis

Kunstsoziologie *f* • sociology of art *(aes)*

Kunstsprache *f* • (▷ künstliche Sprache) artificial language *(lan)* ↔ Natursprache < Formalsprache, Normalsprache; (▷ Sprache der Kunst) language of art *(aes)*

Kunsttheorie *f* • theory of art, artistic theory *(aes)* < Ästhetik

Kunsttrieb *m* • art/artistic impulse, artistic drive *(aes)* < Schaffensdrang

Kunstverständnis *n* • understanding of art, artistic sense, appreciation of/for art *(aes)* → Kunstsinn < Kunstsinnigkeit

Kunstwelt *f* • (▷ künstliche Welt) virtual reality *(AI)*, fictitious world *(met)*, (▷ Welt der Kunst) world of art *(aes)*

Kunstwerk *n* • work of art, artwork *(aes)* < W 1197

Kunstwissenschaft *f* • science of art *(aes)* < Kunsttheorie, Ästhetik

Kunstwort *n* • coined/artificial word, technical term *(lan)* < theoretischer Term

Kunstzweck *m* → Zweck der Kunst

Kupidität *f* • cupidity *(psy)* < Begierde, sinnliche Begierde

Kurskorrektur *f* • course correction *(pol)*

Kurve *f* • curve *(mat)*

kurzfristige Planung *f* • short-term planning *(dec)*

kurzfristiger Nutzen *m* • short-term benefit *(dec)*

Kürzungsregel *f* • cancellation rule/law *(mat)*, rule of detachment *(log)*

Kurzzeitgedächtnis *n* • short-term memory *(psy)* ↔ Langzeitgedächtnis

Kybernetik *f* • cybernetics *(sys)* < Systemtheorie

kybernetische Anthropologie *f* • cybernetic anthropology *(sys, ant)*

kybernetische Systemanalyse *f* • cybernetic system analysis *(sys)*

kybernetisches Modell *n* • cybernetic model *(sys)*

Kyniker *m* • Cynic *(gep)* < Zyniker

Kynismus *m* • cynicism *(gep)* < Zynismus

Kyrenaiker *m* • Cyrenaic *(gep)*

L

L-äquivalent • L-equivalent *(Carnap) (epi, log, lan)*

L-Ausdruck *m* • L-expression *(Carnap) (lan)*

L-falsch • L-false *(Carnap) (epi, log, lan)* ↔ F-falsch

L-Semantik *f* • L-semantics *(Carnap etc) (lan)*

L-Struktur *f* • L-structure *(Carnap) (log, lan)*

L-wahr • L-true *(Carnap) (epi, log, lan)* ↔ F-wahr

Lächerliche, das *n* • the ridiculous *(aes)*

Lagrange-Multiplikator *m* • Lagrange multiplier *(mat, sci)*

Laie *m* • layperson, layman *(gen)*

Laiengemeinschaft *f* • lay community *(rel)*

Laienpriester *m* • lay priest *(rel)*

Laissez-faire *n* • laissez-faire *(eco, soc)* < Wirtschaftsliberalismus

Laizismus *m* • laicism *(rel, pol)*

Lamaismus *m* • Lamaism *(asp)*

Lamarckismus *m* • Lamarck(ian)ism *(nat)*

Lambda-Abstraktion *f* • lambda-abstraction *(log)*

Lambda-Kalkül *m/n* • lambda-calculus *(AI)*

Land art *f* • land art *(aes)*

Land der Wahrheit *n* • land of truth *(Kant) (met)* ↔ Ozean des Scheins

Landbesitz *m* • landed property, ownership of land *(eco)*

Landesverteidigung *f* • national defence *(pol)*

Land-Ethik *f* • land ethics *(Leopold) (eth, env)*

Landflucht *f* • urbanization, migration from rural areas *(soc)* ↔ Stadtflucht

Landkarte, kognitive *f* • cognitive map *(Tolman) (min)*

Landreform *f* • land reform *(eco, pol)*

Langage *f* • langage *(Saussure) (lan)* → Spracherwerbsvermögen, Sprachvermögen

langfristige Planung *f* • long-term planning *(dec)*

langfristiger Effekt *m* • long-term effect *(dec)*

langfristiger Nutzen *m* • long-term benefit *(dec)*

Längsschnittuntersuchung *f* • longitudinal study *(sci)* ↔ Querschnittuntersuchung

Langue *f* • langue *(Saussure) (lan)* ↔ Parole

Langzeitarbeitslosigkeit *f* • long-term unemployment *(eco, soc)*

Langzeitgedächtnis *n* • long-term memory *(psy)* ↔ Kurzzeitgedächtnis

Langzeitperspektive *f* • long-term view *(dec)*

Langzeitrisiko *n* • long-term risk *(dec)*

Langzeitstudie *f* • long-range study *(dec)*

Langzeitwirkung *f* • long-term effect *(dec)* < Nachwirkung, Fernwirkung

Lao-Tse • Lao-tzu, Lao-tse

Laplacesche Differentialgleichung *f* • Laplace's differential equation *(mat)*

Laplacesche Hypothese *f* • Laplace's hypothesis *(mat)*

Laplacescher Dämon *m* • Laplace's demon, Laplacean demon *(epi)*

L'art pour l'art • l'art pour l'art, art for art's sake *(aes)* → Kunst um der Kunst willen, reine Kunst

Lassalleanismus *m* • Lassalleanism *(soc)*

Laster *n* • vice *(eth)*

Laster als Tugend *n* • vice as virtue *(Mandeville) (eth)* < W 147

Lasterkatalog *m* • catalogue of vices *(eth, rel)* ↔ Tugendkatalog

latente Bedeutung *f* • latent content *(Freud) (psy)*, latent meaning *(lan)*

latentes Bild *n* • latent image *(epi, psy)*

latentes Wissen *n* • latent knowledge *(epi)*

Latenzperiode *f* • latency period *(Freud) (psy)*

Latenzphase *f* • latency period/stage/phase *(Freud) (psy)*

Latifundienwirtschaft *f* • latifundian agriculture *(eco)*

Laufzeit *f* • runtime *(AI, sys)*

Laune der Natur, der Mensch als *m* • man as whim of nature *(ant)*

Lauschangriff *m* • total surveillance *(pol)* < großer Buder

Law-and-Order-Rationalismus *m* • law-and-order rationalism *(Feyerabend) (sci)* → Ratiofaschismus

Laxismus *m* • laxism *(eth)* < Probabilismus

Leben als Kampf *n* • life as struggle *(Darwin etc) (nat)* < Kampf ums Dasein

Leben des Geistes *n* • life of the mind *(gep)*

Leben Gottes *n* • the life of God *(rel)*

Leben im Modus der Eigentlichkeit *n* • life in the mode of authenticity *(Heidegger) (ont, ant)*

Leben nach dem Tod *n* • after-life, life after death *(rel, met)* < Reinkarnation

Leben, organisches *n* • organic life *(nat)*

Leben, wachsendes und kämpfendes *n* • growing and striving life *(Nietzsche) (met)*

lebende und tote Materie *f* • living and dead matter, animate and inanimate matter *(nat, met)*

lebendig strömende Gegenwart *f* • living streaming present *(Husserl) (epi, min)* < Bewußtseinsstrom

Lebens, oberstes Ziel des *n* • ultimate end of life, highest goal of life *(met)*

Lebensaktivität *f* • life-activity *(psy)*

Lebensalter *n* • (▷ Lebensabschnitt) phase of life, ages of man, (▷ Alter) age *(nat)*

Lebensangst *f* • angst, fear of life, existential dread *(met)*

Lebensanschauung *f* • philosophy/view of life, life view, outlook on life *(gep)*

Lebensart *f* • way/manner of life/living *(cul, aes)* < Lebensstil

Lebensaufgabe *f* • aim in life, life task *(eth)*

Lebensäußerung *f* • manifestation of life *(nat, gep)*

Lebensbaum *m* • tree of life, arbor vitae *(met)*

Lebensbedürfnisse *pl* • basic needs, necessities/necessaries° of life *(eco)*

Lebensbeendigung *f* • termination of life *(eth)* < Euthanasie

lebensbejahend • life-affirming *(met)*

lebensbejahende Einstellung *f* • affirmative attitude toward life *(met)*

Lebensbejahung *f* • affirmation of life *(Nietzsche) (met)* → Jasagen zum Leben, Bejahung des Lebens

Lebensberechtigung *f* • right to live/exist *(eth)* → Existenzberechtigung

Lebensbereich *m* • domain/sphere of life *(gen)*

lebensbestimmend • life-conditioning *(nat, soc)*

Lebensbetrachtung *f* • reflection on life *(met)* < Lebensanschauung

Lebensbewertung *f* • evaluation of life *(eth)* < Lebenswertdebatte

Lebensbezug *m* • affinity to life *(Goethe, Dilthey etc) (met)*

Lebensdauer *f* • life span, duration of life *(nat)*

Lebensdauer, durchschnittliche *f* • average life span *(nat, eco)*

Lebensekel *m* • existential nausea, aversion to life, life-sickness *(met, psy)* < Lebensüberdruß, Widerwärtigkeit des Daseins

Lebensentsagung *f* • denial of life *(rel, eth)* < Askese

Lebenserfahrung *f* • experience of life *(gen)*

lebenserhaltende Funktion *f* • life-sustaining function *(nat, sys)*

lebenserhaltende Macht *f* • life-preserving power *(Nietzsche) (met)*

lebenserhaltende Maßnahme *f* • life-preserving measure *(nat)*

Lebenserhaltung *f* • preservation of life *(nat, eth)*

Lebenserwartung *f* • life-expectancy *(nat, soc)*

lebensfähig • fit for life, capable of life/living, viable *(nat)*

Lebensfähigkeit *f* • viability *(nat)* → Lebenstüchtigkeit < Überlebensfähigkeit

Lebensfeindlichkeit *f* • hostility to life *(eth)*

Lebensfluß *m* • flow of life *(met)*

lebensfördernd • life-advancing, conducive to life *(Nietzsche) (met)*

Lebensform *f* • form of life *(Wittgenstein) (lan)*, form of life *(nat)*; life-form *(Schütz) (soc)* < Lebenswelt

Lebensfrage *f* • question of life and death, fundamental/basic question of life *(met)*

Lebensführung *f* • mode of living, conduct of life *(eth)*

Lebensfunktion *f* • life/vital function *(nat)*

Lebensgefühl *n* • sense/feeling of living/life, vital consciousness *(psy)* < W 1010

Lebensgeist *m* • (▷ Seele) soul, spirit *(psy, met)*, (▷ Lebensfreude) joy of living, joie de vivre, zest (for life) *(psy)*

Lebensgeister *pl* • vitalities *(met)* → spiritus animales

Lebensgemeinschaft *f* • community of life, long-term relationship *(soc)*; symbiosis *(nat)* → Symbiose

Lebensgenuß *m* • enjoyment of life *(eth, aes)*

Lebensgeschichte *f* • biography, life history *(gen)*

Lebensglück *n* • happiness in life *(eth)*

Lebensgrundlage *f* • subsistence, life basis *(eco)*

Lebenshaltung *f* • (▷ Einstellung) (life-)attitude *(psy, met)*

Lebenshaltungskosten *pl* • cost of living *(eco)*

Lebenshorizont *m* • life-horizon *(Dilthey) (met)*

Lebenshunger *m* • hunger/lust for life *(psy)* < Lebenslust

Lebensinhalt *m* • life content, meaning of life *(met)*

Lebensinteressen *pl* • vital/life interests *(psy, eco, eth)*

Lebenskampf *m* • struggle for existence *(nat)* → Kampf ums Dasein

Lebenskategorien *pl* • life categories *(Dilthey)* *(met)*

Lebensklugheit *f* • worldly wisdom *(gep)*

Lebenskraft *f* • vitality *(gen)*, life-force, vital force, elan vital *(Bergson etc) (met)* < Elan vital

Lebenskriterien *pl* • criteria of life, life criteria *(nat)*

Lebenskunst *f* • art of living *(aes, eth)*

Lebenslage *f* • life situation, situation in life *(gen)*

Lebenslauf *m* • course of life, (▷ schriftlicher Lebenslauf) curriculum vitae *(gen)*

Lebenslüge *f* • life-lie, living-lie *(met)*

Lebenslust *f* • lust/zest for life, joie de vivre *(psy)* < Lebensgeist

Lebensmittelknappheit *f* • food shortage *(eco)*

Lebensmüdigkeit *f* • world-weariness, tiredness of life *(psy)*

Lebensmut *m* • faith in life, optimism toward life *(psy)*

Lebensnetz *n* • web of life *(Capra) (nat, sys)*

Lebensnot *f* • crucial affliction/plight *(psy)*

Lebensnotwendigkeiten *pl* • necessities of life, vital necessities *(eco)*

Lebensordnung *f* • order of life *(soc)*

Lebenspfad *m* • path of life *(gen)*

Lebensphilosophie *f* • life-philosophy *(Nietzsche, Bergson, Dilthey) (gep)*, (▷ Lebensanschauung) philosophy of life *(gep)*

Lebensplan *m* • life plan, plan of life *(gen)*

Lebenspraxis *f* • (▷ wirkliches Leben) real life, (▷ gelebtes Leben) life-practice *(gen)* < Lebenserfahrung

Lebensprinzip *n* • principle of life *(met)*

Lebensqualität *f* • quality of life, life quality *(eth)*

Lebensrad *n* • wheel of life *(met)*

Lebensrätsel *n* • riddle of life *(met)*

Lebensraum *m* • living space, Lebensraum *(soc, pol)*, habitat *(nat)*

Lebensrecht *n* • (▷ Recht auf Leben) right to life *(eth, jur)* < Euthanasie, Lebenswertdebatte

Lebensreformbewegung *f* • life-reform movement *(cul)*

Lebensregel *f* • rule of life *(eth)* → Maxime

Lebensschwungkraft *f* → Elan vital

Lebenssinn *m* • meaning of life *(eth, met)*

Lebenssituation *f* → Lebenslage

Lebenssphäre *f* • sphere of life *(gen)*

Lebensstandard *m* • living standard, standard of living *(eco)*

Lebenssteigerung *f* • intensification of life *(Nietzsche) (met)*

Lebensstellung *f* • (▷ Stellung im Leben) position, social status *(soc)* (▷ unkündbare Anstellung) life/permanent position, tenure *(eco)*

Lebensstil *m* • lifestyle *(aes)* < Lebensart

Lebenstechnik *f* • technique of living *(gen)* < Lebenskunst

Lebenstrieb *m* • life instinct *(Freud) (psy)* ↔ Todestrieb < Biophilie

Lebenströstung *f* • consolation in life *(psy)*

Lebenstüchtigkeit *f* • fitness (for life), ability to cope with life *(nat)* → Lebensfähigkeit

Lebensüberdruß *m* • world-weariness, taedium vitae, tedium of life *(psy)* < Lebensekel, Melancholie

Lebensumwelt *f* • surrounding life-world *(Husserl) (epi, met)*

Lebensunfähigkeit *f* • unfitness for life *(nat, psy)*

Lebensunterhalt *m* • livelihood, sustenance *(eco)*

lebensuntüchtig • unfit for life *(nat)* < natürliche Auslese

Lebensverhältnisse *pl* • living-conditions, conditions of life *(eco, soc)*

lebensverlängernd • life- extending/prolonging *(nat, eth, soc)*

Lebensverlängerung *f* • extension/prolongation of life, life extension *(nat, eth)*

lebensverneinend • life-denying *(Schopenhauer, Nietzsche) (met)*

Lebensverneinung *f* • negation of life *(Schopenhauer, Nietzsche) (met)* < neinsagende Haltung zum Leben

Lebenswandel, moralischer *m* • moral conduct *(eth)*

Lebensweg *m* • course of life *(gen)* < W 937

Lebensweise *f* • way of life/living, habit *(gen)*

Lebensweisheit *f* • (▷ Sentenz) words of (wordly) wisdom *(eth)*, (▷ Lebensklugheit) (wordly) wisdom *(eth)* < Weltweisheit

Lebenswelt *f* • lifeworld, lebenswelt *(Husserl, Wittgenstein etc) (met, lan)* < W 950

lebensweltliches Apriori *n* • lifeworld a priori *(epi, met)*

Lebensweltrationalisierung *f* • lifeworld rationalization *(Habermas) (soc)*

Lebenswerk *n* • life/life's work *(gen)*

Lebenswert *m* • value of life *(eth)*

lebenswert • worth living *(eth)*

Lebenswertdebatte *f* • controversy as to the value of life *(eth)* < Euthanasie, Lebensbewertung, Vernichtung unwerten Lebens

lebenswichtiger Bedarf *m* • necessities of life *(eco)*

Lebenswille *m* • will to live *(psy)*

Lebenswissen *n* • knowledge of life *(epi)* → Orientierungswissen ↔ Verfügungswissen

Lebenszeit *f* • lifetime *(met)*

Lebensziel, oberstes *n* • the ultimate/ultimative° aim/goal/end/purpose in/of life *(eth)* → Lebenszweck

Lebenszweck *m* • purpose in life *(met, eth)* → Lebensziel, oberstes

Lebenszyklus *m* • life cycle *(nat)*

Lebewesen *n* • living being *(nat)*

Leere, die *f* • the void, emptiness *(met)* → Sunyata

Leere als Ziel *f* • emptiness as goal *(asp)* < Bewußtlosigkeit

leere Menge *f* • empty/null set *(mat, løg)*

leere Wahrheit *f* • vacuous/empty truth *(epi, lan)*

leere Zeit *f* • empty time *(met)*

leerer Begriff *m* • empty concept *(Kant)* *(epi, lan)*

leerer Raum *m* • empty space, vacuum *(nat)*

leerer Wahn *m* • vain delusion *(gep)*

Leerformel *f* • empty/contentless° formula/phrase *(log, sci)*

Leerheit *f* • emptiness *(nat, met)*

legal • legal *(jur)*

legalisieren • to legalize *(jur)*

Legalismus *m* • legalism *(jur, eth)*

legalistisch • legalistic *(jur, eth)*

Legalität *f* • legality *(Kant etc)* *(jur, eth)* ↔ Moralität

Legalitätsglaube *m* • belief in legality *(Weber)* *(soc)*

Legislative *f* • legislature, legislative *(jur, pol)*

Legislatur *f* • legislation *(jur)* → Gesetzgebung

Legislaturperiode *f* • parliamentary term *(pol)*

Legitimation *f* • legitimation, justification, legitimization *(jur, pol, eth)*

Legitimation durch Verfahren *f* • legitimation by procedure *(Luhmann)* *(pol, eth)* < prozedurale Gerechtigkeit, Verfahrenslegitimität

Legitimationsbedarf *m* • need for justification *(jur, pol, eth)*

Legitimationsdefizit *n* • legitimation deficit, lack of legitimation *(jur, pol, eth)*

Legitimationsforderung *f* • legitimization requirement/demand *(Habermas etc)* *(pol, eth)*

Legitimationsmethode *f* • method of legitimation *(sci)*

Legitimationsmodus *m* • mode of legitimation *(pol, eth)*

Legitimationspotential *n* • legitimation potential *(Habermas)* *(soc)*

Legitimationsproblem *n* • problem of legitimation *(pol, eth)*

Legitimationsstrategie *f* • legitimation strategy *(pol, eth)*

Legitimationstypen *pl* • types of legitimacy *(Weber)* *(soc)*

Legitimationsverfahren *n* • legitimation procedure *(sci, soc)*

Legitimationszwang *m* → Legitimationsforderung

legitime Autorität *f* • legitimate authority *(pol, jur)*

legitime Herrschaft *f* • legitimate sovereignty *(jur, pol)*

legitimer Herrscher *m* • legitimate ruler *(pol)*

Legitimität *f* • legitimacy *(jur)* → Rechtmäßigkeit

Legitimitätsbasis der Gesellschaft *f* • legitimate/rightful basis for society *(jur, pol, eth)*

Legitimitätsprinzip *n* • legitimacy principle *(jur, pol, eth)*

Lehen *n* • fief, fee, feu *(eco)* < Feudalismus

Lehngut *n* → Lehen

Lehnstuhlphilosophie *f* • armchair philosophy *(gep)*

Lehrbarkeit *f* • teachability *(psy)* ↔ Lernbarkeit

Lehrbarkeit der Tugend *f* • teachability of morality *(Plato)* *(eth)*

Lehre *f* • teaching, doctrine, theory *(gep)*

Lehre von Druck und Stoß *f* → Druck und Stoß-Theorie

Lehrfreiheit *f* • freedom of instruction, academic freedom *(pol)*

Lehrgebäude *n* • system of thought *(gep)*, doctrinal system *(rel)*

Lehrmeinung *f* • doctrine *(gep)*

Lehrmethode *f* • teaching method *(gep)*

Lehrplan *m* • curriculum *(gen)*

Lehrsatz *m* • proposition, theorem *(sci)*

Lehrstück *n* • nt, didactic/dialectic play *(Brecht)* *(aes)* < episches Theater

Lehrstuhl *m* • chair *(gep)*

Lehrtätigkeit *f* • teaching (practice), instructional work *(gen)*

Leib-Seele-Dualismus *m* • body-mind dualism *(Descartes etc)* *(met)*

Leib-Seele-Identität *f* • body-mind identity *(met)* < psychophysischer Parallelismus

Leib-Seele-Problem *n* • mind-body problem, body-mind problem *(Descartes etc) (epi, met)* → Geist-Leib-Problem, psychophysisches Problem

leib-seelisch • psychosomatic *(psy)*

Leib und Seele *m,f* • body and soul/mind *(met)* < Leib-Seele-Dualismus

Leibeigenschaft *f* • serfdom, servitude, bondage *(eco, soc)*

Leiberfahrung *f* • bodily experience *(met, psy)*

leibhafte Gegebenheit *f* • bodily givenness *(Heidegger) (ont)*

leibhafte Selbstgegebenheit *f* • authentic self-givenness *(Husserl) (ont)*

leibhafte Wirklichkeit *f* • authentic reality *(Husserl) (ont)*

Leiblichkeit *f* • bodily existence *(met)*

Leibniz-Wolffsche Schule *f* • Leibniz-Wolff school *(gep)*

Leibnizianismus *m* • Leibnizianism *(gep)*

Leibnizsches Gesetz *n* • Leibniz' law *(log)*

Leibnizsches Gesetz der Ununterscheidbarkeit *n* • Leibniz' law of indescernibility *(met)*

Leibphänomen *n* • phenomenon of bodily existence *(met)*

Leichtgläubigkeit, Prinzip der *n* • principle of credulity *(Reid, Swinburne) (epi)*

Leidabwehr *f* • resistance to/avoidance of pain *(Nietzsche, Freud) (psy)*

Leiden *n* • suffering *(psy, met)*

Leiden am Menschen *n* • suffering on man *(Nietzsche) (met)*

Leidenschaft *f* • passion *(psy, eth)*

Leidenschaft der Erkenntnis *f* • (the) passion of knowledge *(Nietzsche) (epi, psy)*

Leidenschaft zur Nacht *f* • passion for the night *(Jaspers) (met)*

Leidenschaftlichkeit *f* • passionateness *(psy)*

Leidenschaftslosigkeit *f* • dispassionateness, ataraxy *(eth)* → Ataraxie, Affektlosigkeit < Apathie

Leidensquelle *f* • source of suffering *(Freud) (psy)*

Leidverhütung *f* • prevention/avoidance/aversion of suffering/pain/harm *(eth)*

Leidvermeidung *f* → Leidverhütung

Leihmutterschaft *f* • surrogate motherhood *(nat, eth)*

Leistungsbereitschaft *f* • willingness to achieve *(eth)*

Leistungsdenken *n* → Leistungsorientierung

Leistungsdruck *m* • pressure to produce results *(psy)* < Konkurrenzgesellschaft

Leistungsfeindlichkeit *f* • hostility towards achievement *(soc)*

Leistungsgesellschaft *f* • achievement-orientated society *(eco, soc)*

Leistungsmotivation *f* • motivation to achieve, achievement/performance motivation *(psy)*

Leistungsorientierung *f* • performance orientation *(eco, soc)*

Leistungsprinzip *n* • achievement/performance principle *(eco, soc)* < Meritokratie

Leistungstest, soziodramatischer *m* • sociodramatic performance test *(soc, sci)*

Leistungsverweigerung *f* • refusal to perform *(eco, psy)*

Leistungswille *m* • will to perform *(eco, psy)* < Leistungsmotivation

Leistungswissen *n* • subject/expert knowledge *(Scheler) (epi)* < Bildungswissen, Heilswissen

Leistungszwang *m* → Leistungsdruck

Leitbild *n* • model *(gep)*

leitendes Prinzip *n* • guiding/leading principle *(gep)*

Leitfaden *m* • guide *(gep)*

Leitfaden, transzendentaler *m* • transcendental clue *(epi, met)*

Leitlinie *f* • directix *(mat)*, guideline *(act)*

Leitmotiv *n* • leitmotif *(aes)* < Grundmotiv

Leitstudie *f* • pilot study *(sci, soc)*

Leittechnologie *f* • leading technology *(tec)*

Lekton *n* • lecton, what can be said *(log, lan)*

Lemma *n* • lemma *(Aristotle etc) (log)* → Prämisse < Syllogismus

Leninismus *m* • Leninism *(pol)*

Lernbarkeit *f* • learnability *(psy)* ↔ Lehrbarkeit

Lernbehinderung *f* • learning disability *(psy)*

Lernen am Modell *n* • learning by model *(psy, epi)*

Lernen am Objekt *n* • object-oriented learning *(psy, epi)*

Lernen durch Beobachtung *n* • observational learning *(Bandura) (psy, epi)*

Lernen durch Einsicht *n* • insightful learning *(Köhler) (psy, epi)*

Lernen durch Handeln *n* • learning by doing *(psy, epi)* → operatives Lernen

Lernen durch Versuch und Irrtum *n* • learning by trial and error, trial-and-error learning *(psy, epi)*

Lernen, soziales *n* • social learning *(psy, soc)*

Lernerfolg *m* • learning achievement/success *(psy)*

Lernprozeß *m* • learning process *(psy)* < Erkenntnisprozeß

Lernstrategie *f* • learning strategy *(psy)*

Lerntheorie *f* • learning theory, theory of learning *(psy)*

lesbische Ethik *f* • lesbian ethics *(eth, fem)*

letztabschließende Erkenntnis *f* • terminal knowledge *(Pfänder) (epi, met)*

Letztbegründung *f* • ultimate justification *(epi, sci)*

Letztbegründung der Logik *f* • ultimate justification of logic *(log)*

Letztbegründung, philosophische *f* • ultimate philosophical justification *(epi, met)*

Letztbegründungsrationalismus *m* • foundationalist rationalism *(Albert) (epi, sci)*

Letztbegründungstheorie *f* • foundationalism *(epi)*

letzte Bedingung *f* • ultimate condition *(gep)*

letzte Dinge *pl* • last things, ultimate entities *(met)*

letzte Mensch, der *m* • the last man *(Nietzsche) (met)*

letzte Wahrheit *f* • ultimate truth *(epi, met)*

letzte Wirklichkeit *f* • ultimate reality *(met)*

letzter Zweck *m* • final/ultimate end/goal *(met, act)*

Leukipp • Leucippus

Lewissches Hauptprinzip *n* • Lewis' principal principle *(epi)*

lex aeterna *f* • eternal law *(rel, met)*

lex divina *f* • divine law *(rel)*

lex naturalis *f* • natural law, law of nature *(jur, eth)*

lex positiva *f* • positive law *(Comte, Kelsen etc) (jur)*

lex talionis *f* → Talionsprinzip

lexikalischer Ausdruck *m* • lexical expression *(lan, log)* < indexikalischer Ausdruck

Li *n* • li, morality, customs *(asp)*

liberale Gesinnung *f* • liberal attitude *(pol, eth)*

Liberalisierung *f* • liberalization *(eco, soc)*

Liberalismus *m* • liberalism *(pol)*

Liberalismus, klassischer *m* • classical liberalism, whiggism *(Locke etc) (pol)* → Libertarianismus

Liberalismus, politischer *m* • political liberalism *(pol)*

Liberalität *f* • liberality, liberalness *(pol, eth)*

Libertär *m* → Libertarier

Libertarianismus *m* • libertarianism *(pol)* → Liberalismus, klassischer

Libertarier *m* • libertarian *(pol)*

Libertarismus *m* • libertarianism *(pol)*

liberté, égalité, fraternité → Freiheit, Gleicheit, Brüderlichkeit

Libertinage *f* • libertinage *(eth, psy)* → Libertinismus, Zügellosigkeit

Libertinismus *m* • libertinism *(eth, psy)* → Libertinage < freizügige Gesellschaft

liberum arbitrium *n* • free judg(e)ment/will, freedom of the will *(eth, met)* → Willensfreiheit

libidinös • libidinous, libidinal *(psy)*

libidinöses Objekt *n* • libido-object *(Freud) (psy)*

Libido *f* • libido *(Freud etc) (psy)*

Libido-Ökonomie *f* • economics of libido *(Freud) (psy)*

Libidostau *m* • damming-up of libido *(Freud) (psy)*

Libidotheorie *f* • libido theory *(Freud) (psy)*

Libidoverschiebung *f* • libido displacement, displacement of libido *(Freud) (psy)*

Licht der Vernunft *n* • light of reason *(met)* → lux rationis

Lichtgeschwindigkeit *f* • velocity of light *(nat)*

Lichtjahr *n* • light-year *(nat)*

Licht-Metapher *f* • light metaphor, metaphor of light *(Plotinus) (met)*

Lichtmetaphysik *f* • metaphysics of light, light metaphysics *(Plotinus etc) (met)*

Lichtung *f* • clearing *(Heidegger) (ont)*

Lichtung des Seins *f* • clearing/lighting of Being *(Heidegger) (ont)*

Liebe Gottes *f* • the love of God *(rel)*

Liebe und Haß *f,m* • love and hate *(psy)* < W 580

Liebe zum Irdischen *f* • love of the earth *(Nietzsche) (met)*

Liebe zur Weisheit *f* • love of wisdom *(gep)*

Liebesbedürfnis *n* • need for/of love *(psy)*

Liebesentzug *m* • withdrawal of affection *(Freud) (psy)* < Liebesverlust

Liebesethik *f* • love ethics, ethic of love *(eth, rel)*

Liebesgott *m* • Eros *(Plato) (met)*

Liebesobjekt *n* • love object, object of love *(Freud) (psy)*

Liebespflichten *pl* • duties of love *(eth)*

Liebesverlust *m* • loss of love *(Freud) (psy)* < Liebesentzug

Liebhaberwert *m* • collector's value, affective value *(eco)* → Affektionswert < Werttheorie, subjektive

Likelihood • likelihood *(log)*

Likert-Skala f • method of summated ratings *(sci, nat)*

Limbus m • limbo *(rel)* → Vorhölle

Limes m • limes *(his)*, limit *(gen)*

Limestheorie f • limit theory *(Mises, Reichenbach) (mat)* < Wahrscheinlichkeit

Limitation f • limitation *(Kant etc) (epi)*

Limitationsbegriff m • concept of limitation *(epi)*

Limitationsprinzip n • principle of limitation *(Kant) (epi)*

linear abhängig • linearly dependent *(mat)* < Korrelation, direkte

linear geordnete Menge f • linearly/completely ordered set *(mat)*

lineare Geschichtstheorie f • linear theory of history *(sci)* < Fortschrittstheorie, Verfallstheorie

lineare Hülle f • linear closure/hull *(mat)*

lineare Optimierung f • linear programming *(mat, sci)*

lineares Denken n • linear thought/thinking *(epi, psy)*

lineares Differentialgleichungssystem n • linear system of differential equations *(mat)*

lineares Modell n • linear model *(sci)*

lineares System n • linear system *(sys)*

Linga(m)kult m • Linga(m) cult *(rel)* → Phalluskult

Linguistik f • linguistics *(lan)*

linguistische Analogie f • linguistic analogy *(Foucault) (lan, sys)*

linguistische Kompetenz f • linguistic competence *(Chomsky) (lan, psy)* ↔ linguistische Performanz < kommunikative Kompetenz

linguistische Performanz f • linguistic performance *(lan, psy)* ↔ linguistische Kompetenz

linguistische Theorie des Apriori f • linguistic theory of the a priori *(lan, epi)*

linguistische Wende f • linguistic turn *(lan)* → sprachphilosophische Wende

linguistischer Imperialismus m • linguistic imperialism *(lan, pol)*

Liniengleichnis n • simile of the line *(Plato) (met)* < Höhlengleichnis, Sonnengleichnis

Linienintegral n • line integral *(mat)*

Linke, die f • the Left *(pol)*

Linker m • leftist *(pol)* ↔ Rechter

links • left-wing *(pol)*

linkseindeutige Relation f • left-unique relation, one-many relation *(mat)*

Linksextremist m • left-wing extremist *(pol)*

linksgerichtet • left(ist) *(pol)*

Linkshegelianer m • left(-wing) Hegelian *(gep)* → Junghegelianer

Linkshegelianismus m • left(-wing) Hegelianism *(gep)*

Linksintellektueller m • left-wing intellectual *(pol)*

Linksnietzscheaner m • left(-wing) Nietzschean *(gep)*

Linksradikalismus m • left(-wing) radicalism *(pol)*

Lipschitz-Konstante f • Lipschitz constant *(mat)*

List der Vernunft f • cunning of reason *(Hegel) (met)*

literarische Bewegung f • literary movement *(aes)*

literarische Wahrheit f • literary truth *(aes)*

literarische Werke pl • literary works *(aes)*

literarischer Text m • literary text *(aes)*

literarisches Kunstwerk n • literary work of art *(aes)*

Literarizität f • literariness *(Jakobson) (aes)*

Literarästhetik f • literary aesthetics *(aes)*

Literaturgeschichte f • history of literature, literary history *(aes)*

Literaturkritik f • literary criticism *(aes)*

Literaturkritiker m • literary critic *(aes)*

Literatursoziologie f • sociology of literature *(aes)*

Literaturtheorie f • theory of literature, literary theory *(aes)*

Literaturwissenschaft f • (▷ Fach) literary studies, (▷ Wissenschaft) literary scholarship/science *(aes)*

Literaturwissenschaft, vergleichende f • comparative literature *(aes)* → Komparatistik

Literaturwissenschaft(l)er m • literary scholar/critic *(aes)*

Litotes f • litotes *(lan)*

Liturgie f • liturgy *(rel)* → Gottesdienst

Lobby f • lobby, pressure-group *(pol)* → Interessen(s)gruppe, Interessen(s)verband < Machtgruppe

Lobbyismus m • lobbyism *(pol)*

Logarithmus m • logarithm *(mat)* < Algorithmus

Loge f • lodge *(rel, eso)* < Freimaurerloge

Logik f • logic(s) *(log)*

Logik, chronologische f → Logik, temporale

Logik, deduktive f • deductive logic *(log)*

Logik, deontische f • deontic logic *(log, eth)*

Logik der ersten Stufe f • first-order logic *(log)*

Logik der Forschung *f* • logic of scientific discovery *(Popper) (sci)* < W 587

Logik der höheren Ordnung *f* • higher-order logic *(log)*

Logik der Imperative *f* • logic of imperatives *(Hare) (log, eth)* → Logik, imperativische

Logik der Modalitäten *f* • logic of modalities *(log)* < Modallogik

Logik der Normen *f* → Normenlogik

Logik der Sozialwissenschaften *f* • logic of social sciences *(Habermas etc) (sci)* < W 1361

Logik der Vagheit *f* → unscharfe Logik

Logik der Wahrheit *f* • logic of truth *(Kant) (log, epi)* ↔ Logik des Scheins

Logik der zweiten Stufe *f* • second-order logic *(log)*

Logik des Herzens *f* • logic of the heart *(Pascal) (rel)*

Logik des Scheins *f* • logic of illusion *(Kant) (log, epi)* ↔ Logik der Wahrheit

Logik des Werdens *f* • logic of becoming *(Hegel) (met)* < Prozeßlogik

Logik, dialektische *f* • dialectical logic *(log)*

Logik, dialogische *f* • dialogic logic *(Lorenzen etc) (log)*

Logik, dreiwertige *f* • three-value(d) logic *(log)* < mehrwertige Logik < W 1103

Logik, elementare *f* • elementary logic *(log)*

Logik, epistemische *f* • epistemic logic *(log)*

Logik, erotematische *f* • erotetic logic *(Tichy etc) (log)*

Logik erster Ordnung *f* • first-order logic *(log)* → zweiwertige Logik

Logik, extensionale *f* • extensional logic *(log)*

Logik, formale *f* • formal logic *(log)*

Logik, hermeneutische *f* • hermeneutic logic *(log)*

Logik, imperativische *f* • imperative logic, logic of imperatives/commands *(Hare) (log, eth)* < Logik, deontische

Logik, induktive *f* • inductive logic *(Mill etc) (log)*

Logik, informelle *f* • informal logic *(log)* < Logik, nichtmonotone

Logik, intensionale *f* • intensional logic *(log, lan)*

Logik, intentionale *f* • intentional logic *(log)*

Logik, intuitionistische *f* • intuitionist/intuitionistic logic *(Brouwer) (log)* < Intuitionismus

Logik, klassische *f* • classical logic *(log)*

Logik, konstruktive *f* • constructive logic *(log)*

Logik, materiale *f* • material logic *(log)*

Logik, mathematische *f* • mathematical logic *(log, mat)* → Logik, symbolische

Logik, mehrwertige *f* • many valued/order logic *(log)*

Logik, monotone *f* • monotonic/monotone logic *(log)*

Logik, nichtklassische *f* • non-classical logic *(log)* < Logik, nichtmonotone

Logik, nichtmonotone *f* • non-monotonic logic *(log)*

Logik, nominalistische *f* • nominalist logic *(log)*

Logik, parakonsistente *f* • paraconsistent logic *(Vasilev etc) (log)*

Logik, produktive *f* • productive logic *(Jaspers) (met)*

Logik, prozedurale *f* • procedural logic *(log)* → Prozeßlogik

Logik, prozessuale *f* • logic of processes *(log)*

Logik, symbolische *f* • symbolic logic *(log)* → Logik, mathematische

Logik, temporale *f* • temporal/tense logic *(log)* → Zeitlogik

Logik, traditionelle *f* • traditional logic *(Aristotle etc) (log)*

Logik, transzendentale *f* • transcendental logic *(Kant) (epi, log)* < W 311

Logik, unscharfe *f* • vague/fuzzy logic *(log)* < Logik, nichtmonotone

Logik von Port Royal *f* • Port Royal Logic *(log)*

Logik, zweiwertige *f* • two-valued/bivalent logic *(log)* → Logik erster Ordnung

Logiker *m* • logician *(log)*

Logikkalkül *m/n* • logic calculus *(log)*

logisch-szientistisches Denksystem *n* • logical scientistic system of thought *(sci)*

logische Ableitbarkeit *f* • logical derivability *(Bolzano etc) (log)*

logische Analyse *f* • logical analysis *(log)*

logische Bedingung *f* • logical condition *(log, sci)*

logische Eigenschaft *f* • logical property *(log)*

logische Falsifizierbarkeit *f* • logical falsifiability *(sci)*

logische Form *f* • logical form *(Wittgenstein etc) (log, lan)*

logische Funktion des Verstandes *f* • logical function of the understanding *(Kant) (epi)*

logische Gewißheit *f* • logical certainty *(log)*

logische Identität *f* • logical identity *(log)*

logische Implikation *f* • logical implication *(log)*

logische Konsistenz *f* • logical consistency *(log)*

logische Konstante *f* • logical constant *(log)*
logische Matrix *f* • logical matrix *(log)*
logische Möglichkeit *f* • logical possibility *(log)*
logische Nähe *f* • logical proximity *(log)*
logische Negation *f* • logical negation *(log)*
logische Notwendigkeit *f* • logical necessity *(log)*
logische Operation *f* • logical operation *(log)*
logische Syntax *f* • logical syntax, syntactics *(log, lan)*
logische Topik *f* • logical topic *(Kant) (log, epi)*
logische Überlegung *f* • logical reflection *(Kant) (log, epi)*
logische Unmöglichkeit *f* • logical impossibility *(log)*
logische Wahrheit *f* • logical truth *(log)* < analytische Wahrheit
logische Wahrscheinlichkeitsinterpretation *f* • logical interpretation of probability *(log, mat)*
logischer Atomismus *m* • logical atomism *(Wittgenstein, Russell) (log, lan, sci)*
logischer Empirismus *m* • logical empiricism *(Mach, Reichenbach etc) (log, sci)* < logischer Positivismus
logischer Fehler *m* • logical error/mistake *(log)* < Fehlschluß
logischer Gegenstand *m* • logical object *(Carnap) (log, epi)*
logischer Grund *m* • logical ground *(log)*
logischer Intentionalismus *m* • logical intentionalism *(act)* < Kausalismus
logischer Kalkül *m* • logical calculus *(log)*
logischer Ort *m* • logical place, place in logical space *(log)* < logischer Raum
logischer Paralogismus *m* • logical paralogism *(Kant) (log, epi)*
logischer Positivismus *m* • logical positivism *(log, sci)* < logischer Empirismus
logischer Raum *m* • logical space *(Wittgenstein) (log)*
logischer Schein *m* • logical illusion/appearance *(Kant) (epi, met)*
logischer Spielraum *m* • logical range *(log)*
logischer Transzendentalismus *m* • logical transcendentalism *(epi, met)*
logisches Bild *n* • logical picture *(Wittgenstein) (lan, log)*
logisches Gatter *n* • logic gate *(log, AI)*
logisches Ich *n* • logical I *(Kant) (epi)*
logisches Kriterium der Wahrheit *n* • logical criterion of truth *(sci, log, lan)*
logisches Nichts *n* • logical nothing *(Kant) (log)*

logisches Partikel *n* • logical particle *(log)*
logisches Prädikat *n* • logical predicate *(log)*
logisches Produkt *n* • logical product *(log, mat)*
logisches Quadrat *n* • square of opposition *(log)* < Gegensatz, kontradiktorischer; Gegensatz, konträrer; Gegensatz, subalterner; Gegensatz, subkonträrer
logisches Rätsel *n* • logical puzzle/riddle *(log)*
logisches Sein *n* • logical being *(log)*
logisches Subjekt *n* • logical subject *(log)*
logisches Wort *n* • logical word *(Hare) (log, lan)* < Moralwort
logisches Zeichen *n* • logical sign *(log, lan)*
logisieren • to logicize *(log, epi)*
Logismus *m* • logism *(log, met)*
Logistik *f* • logistics *(tec, sys)*, logistic *(log)*
Logizismus *m* • logicism *(Frege, Whitehead, Russell etc) (log, epi, mat)*
logizistisches Programm *n* • logisticist/logistical programme *(Frege) (log)*
Logizität *f* • logicality, logicalness *(log)*
Logomachie *f* • logomachy *(lan)*
Logos *m* • logos *(log, lan, met)*
Logos, tätiger *m* • acting/active logos *(met, rel)*
Logotherapie *f* • logotherapy *(Frankl) (psy)*
Logozentrismus *m* • logocentrism, logocentricism *(met)* ↔ Biozentrismus
Logozentrizität *f* • logocentricity *(cul, sci)*
Lohan *m* • nt *(asp)*
Lohn *m* • reward *(gen)*, wage *(eco)*
Lohn-Preis-Spirale *f* • wage-price spiral *(eco)*
Lohnabhängiger *m* • waged employee, (wage-dependent) worker *(eco)*
Lohnangleichung *f* • wage adjustment *(eco)*
Lohnarbeit *f* • labour, wage labour, wage (earning) labour *(Marx etc) (eco)*
Lohnarbeit und Kapital *f,n* • wage-labour and capital *(Marx) (eco)* < W 600
Lohnarbeiter *m* • paid worker, wage worker/labourer *(Marx etc) (eco)* < freier Arbeiter
Lohnempfänger *m* • wage earner *(eco)*
Lohnerhöhung *f* • pay rise, wage increase *(eco)*
Lohnforderung *f* • wage claim *(eco)*
Lohngefälle *n* • wage differential *(eco)*
Lohngleichheit *f* • equal pay *(eco)*
Lohnkampf *m* • wage/pay dispute *(eco)*
Lohnkontrakt *m* • wage contract *(eco)* < freie Arbeit
Lohnkürzung *f* • pay/wage cut *(eco)*
Lohnmoral *f* • morality of reward *(eth)*

Lohnpolitik *f* • pay/wages policy *(eco)*

Lohnsystem *n* • wage system *(Marx etc) (eco)*

Lohntheorie *f* • wage theory *(eco)*

Lohnvertrag *m* • wage/pay agreement *(eco, jur)*

Lokaiata *n* • lokaiata *(asp)*

Lokajata *n* → Lokaiata

lokalendliche Gruppe *f* • locally finite group *(mat)*

lokalkonvexer Vektorraum *m* • locally convex vector space *(mat)*

Lokalpatriotismus *m* • regional/local patriotism/pride, parochialism *(pol)*

Lokalzeichen *n* • local sign *(Lotze, Wundt etc) (psy)*

lokutionärer Akt *m* • locutionary act *(Austin etc) (lan, act)* → Sprechakt, lokutionärer

Lorentz-Kontraktion *f* • Fitzgerald-Lorentz contraction *(nat)* < Relativitätstheorie

Lorentz-Transformation *f* • Lorentz transformation *(Lorentz) (nat)* < Relativitätstheorie

Lossagung vom Irdischen *f* • renunciation of the wordly *(rel)*

Lossprechung *f* • absolution *(rel)* → Absolution

Lösungskurve einer Differentialgleichung *f* • integral curve of a differential equation *(mat)*

Lotosblume *f* • lotus (flower) *(asp)*

Lotossitz *m* • lotus position *(asp)*

Lotterieparadox *n* • lottery paradox *(Kyberg etc) (dec)*

Loyalität *f* • loyalty *(eth)*

Luddismus *m* • Luddism, Ludditism *(tec, pol)* → Maschinenstürmerei

Luftreinhaltepolitik *f* • clean air policy *(env)*

Luft-Schiffahrer des Geistes *pl* • aeronauts of the spirit *(Nietzsche) (met)*

Luftverschmutzung *f* • air pollution *(env)*

Lügenpropaganda *f* • mendacious propaganda *(pol)*

Lügner-Antinomie *f* • liar paradox *(Epimenides) (log)* → Lügner-Paradoxon

Lügner-Paradoxon *n* • liar paradox, the paradox of the liar *(Epimenides) (log)*

Lukrez • Lucretius

Lullus • Lull, Llull, Lully

lumen naturale *n* • light of nature, natural light *(Augustine, Aquinas etc) (rel, met)* → natürliches Licht

Lumpenproletariat *n* • lumpen proletariat, demoralized workers *(Marx) (eco, soc)*

Lust *f* • lust *(Nietzsche) (psy, met)*, pleasure *(psy)* < Lust-Unlust-Kalkül

Lust-Unlust-Erlebnis *n* • pleasure-unpleasure experience *(psy)*

Lust-Unlust-Kalkül *m/n* • pleasure- unpleasure/ pain calculus, calculus of pleasure and pain *(eth)* < hedonistischer Kalkül

Lusterfahrung *f* • pleasurable sensation/ experience *(psy)*

Lustgewinn *m* • pleasure gain, increase in/of pleasure, yield of pleasure *(Freud) (psy)*

Lustmaschine *f* • pleasure machine *(eth)* < Hedonismus

Lustprinzip *n* • pleasure principle *(Freud) (psy)* ↔ Realitätsprinzip < W 498

Lustquelle *f* • source of pleasure *(psy)*

Lustrieb *m* → Libido

Lutheranische Reformation *f* • Lutheran Reformation *(rel, his)*

Lutherismus *m* • Lutheranism *(rel)*

lux rationis *n* → Licht der Vernunft

Luxus *m* • luxury *(eco)* < demonstrativer Konsum

Luxusgüter *pl* • luxury goods *(eco)*

Luxuskonsumtion *f* • luxury consumption *(Marx) (eco)* < demonstrativer Konsum

Lynchjustiz *f* • lynch-law *(jur, eth)*

Lyrik *f* • lyric poetry *(aes)*

lyrisches Subjekt *n* • lyrical subject *(aes)*

Lyssenkoismus *m* • Lysenkoism *(nat)*

M

M-Grammatik *f* • Montague grammar *(lan)*

(m, n)-Matrix *f* • m by n matrix, m x n matrix *(Städtler etc) (log, mat)*

M-Semantik *f* • Montague semantics *(lan)*

Machbarkeit *f* • feasibility, practicability, realizability *(act, tec)*

Machbarkeitsglaube *m* • belief in feasibility/practicability/realizability *(tec)*

Machbarkeitsstudie *f* • feasibility study *(tec)* → Durchführbarkeitsstudie

Machiavellismus *m* • Machiavellism, Machiavellianism *(pol, eth)* < Staatsklugheit

machiavellistisch • Machiavellian *(pol, eth)*

Machismo *m* → Machismus

Machismus *m* • machismo *(cul, fem)* < Männerwelt, Patriarchismus, Androzentrismus

Mach-Prinzip *n* • Mach's principle *(Mach)* *(nat)* → Machsches Prinzip

Machsches Prinzip *n* • Mach's principle *(Mach) (nat)*

Macht *f* • power, might *(pol, psy, met)* < Herrschaft

Macht, absolute *f* • absolute power *(pol)*

Macht als Grundlage der Rechte *f* • power as the basis of rights *(Spinoza) (met, eth)*

Macht, ausschließliche *f* • exclusive power *(pol)*

Macht der Vernunft *f* • power of reason *(met)*

Macht des Kapitals *f* • power of capital *(Marx etc) (eco)*

Macht Gottes *f* • power of God *(rel)*

Macht, instrumentelle *f* • instrumental power *(Hobbes etc) (soc, pol)*

Macht ist Recht *f,n* • might is right *(jur, pol)*

Macht über die Natur *f* • power over nature *(met, nat)* → Herrschaft über die Natur, Naturbeherrschung

Macht, ursprüngliche *f* • original/natural power *(Hobbes etc) (soc, pol)*

Machtakkumulation *f* • accumulation of power *(pol)*

Machtanspruch *m* • claim to power, power claim *(pol, soc)*

Machtbedürfnis *n* • power need, need for power *(psy)* < Machthunger, Machtstreben

Machtbereich *m* • sphere of control/power *(pol)* < Einflußbereich

Machtbeschränkung *f* • limitation of power *(pol, jur)* < Gewaltenteilung

Machtbeziehungen *pl* • power relations *(pol, soc)*

Mächte *pl* • powers *(gep)*

Machtelite *f* • power elite *(Mills) (pol, soc)*

Machtergreifung *f* • seizure of power *(pol)*

Machtgleichgewicht *n* • balance of power *(pol)*

Machtgruppe *f* • power group *(pol, soc)* < Lobby

Machthaber *m* • ruler *(pol)*

Machthunger *m* • hunger for power *(Hobbes etc) (pol, soc, psy)* < Machtstreben

Mächtigkeit *f* • (▷ Anzahl der Elemente einer Menge) cardinality, cardinal number *(Cantor)*, (▷ Hochzahl) power *(mat)*

Machtkampf *m* • struggle for power, power war *(pol, soc)*

Machtkonzentration *f* • concentration of power *(pol, soc)*

Machtlosigkeit *f* • powerlessness *(pol, psy)* → Ohnmacht

Machtmechanismus *m* • mechanism of power *(pol)*

Machtmißbrauch *m* • abuse/misuse of power *(pol, eth)*

Machtmittel *n* • instrument of power *(pol)*

Machtmonopol *n* • monopoly of power *(pol)*

Machtnetz *n* • web of power *(pol)*

Machtorgan *n* • organ of power *(pol)*

Machtpolitik *f* • power politics, (▷ Strategie) power policy *(pol)* < Realpolitik

Machtspiel *n* • power play *(soc, pol)*

Machtstellung *f* • position of power *(pol)*

Machtstreben *n* • striving for power *(pol, psy)* < Machthunger

Machtteilung *f* • power-sharing *(pol)*

Machttyp *m* • type of power *(Foucault) (epi, pol)*

Machtübernahme *f* • assumption of power, takeover *(pol)*

Machtübertragung *f* • transfer of power *(pol)*

Machtverhältnisse *pl* • balance of power, power relations *(pol)*

Machtverteilung *f* • distribution of power *(pol)*

Machtvorteil *m* • power advantage *(pol, psy)*

Machtwechsel *m* • change(-over) of power *(pol)*

Machtwirkungen *pl* • effects of power *(Foucault) (epi, pol)*

Machtwissen *n* • power-knowledge, knowledge-power *(Foucault) (epi, pol)* < Interpretationsmonopol

Mäeutik *f* • maeutics *(Socrates) (epi)* → Hebammenkunst, sokratische Methode

Mafiamethoden *pl* • Mafia methods *(eco, pol)*

Magie, schwarze *f* • black magic *(eso)* < Voodoo

magischer Realismus *m* • magic(al) realism *(aes)*

magisches Quadrat *n* • magic square *(mat)*

Mahajana-Buddhismus *m* • Mahayana Buddhism *(asp)*

maieutische Systemanalyse *f* • maieutic systems analysis *(sys)* ↔ instrumentelle Systemanalyse

maieutischer Zyklus *m* • maieutic cycle *(sci)* < hermeneutischer Zyklus

Maja *f* • maya, illusion *(asp)* < Schleier der Maja

Majoritätsprinzip *n* • majority principle *(pol)*

Makrobiotik *f* • macrobiotics *(eso)*

Makrokosmos *m* • macrocosm *(nat)*

makroskopische Ordnung *f* • macroscopic order *(sys)*

makroskopische Unbestimmtheit *f* • macroscopic indeterminacy *(sys)*

Makrowissenschaft *f* • macro science *(sci)*

mala fide → böser Absicht, in

malerisch • (▷ abbildlich) pictorial, (▷ lieblich) picturesque *(aes)*

Malerische, das *n* • the picturesque *(aes)*

Malthusianismus *m* • Malthusianism *(soc, eco)*

malum *n* • evil, badness, harm *(eth, met)*

Mammonismus *m* • mammonism *(eco)* < Geldgier

Man, das *n* • the They, the One, the anyone *(Heidegger) (ant, ont)* < Durchschnittlichkeit, Jedermann, Massenmensch

Man-selbst, das *n* • the one-self, the they-self *(Heidegger) (ant, ont)*

Manchesterdoktrin *f* • Manchester doctrine *(eco, pol)* < Freihandelsdoktrin

Manchesterliberalismus *m* • Manchester liberalism *(eco, pol)* < Wirtschaftsliberalismus

Mandala *n* • mandala *(asp), (Jung) (psy)*

Mandat, freies *n* • free mandate *(pol)* ↔ Mandat, imperatives

Mandat, imperatives *n* • imperative mandate *(pol)* ↔ Mandat, freies

Mandatarsmacht *f* • mandatory power *(pol)*

Mandelbrotmenge *f* • Mandelbrot set *(mat, sys)* < Fraktal

Mangel *m* • lack, fault, imperfection *(gep)*

Mangelerscheinung *f* • symptom of deficiency, deficiency symptom *(eco, sys)*

Mangelhaftigkeit *f* • defectiveness, faultiness *(gep)*

Mängelwesen, Mensch als *m* • man as imperfect being *(Herder, Gehlen, Portmann) (ant)*

Manichäer *m* • Manichaean *(gep)*

Manichäismus *m* • Manichaeism *(gep)*

Manie *f* • mania *(psy)*

Manierismus *m* • mannerism *(aes)*

Manifest *n* • manifesto *(pol)* < W 517, 613

Manifestation des Willens *f* • manifestation of the will *(Schopenhauer) (met)*

manifeste Bedeutung *f* • manifest content *(Freud) (psy)*

manifester Inhalt *m* • manifest content *(Freud) (psy)*

Manipulation von Symbolen *f* • symbol manipulation *(mat, AI)*

Manismus *m* • manism *(cul, rel)* → Ahnenkult, Totenkult

Manitu *m* • manit(o)u *(rel)*

Männerbefreiung *f* • men's liberation *(soc)*

Männerforschung *f* • men's studies *(psy, fem)*

Männerwelt *f* • world of men, male world *(fem)* < Machismus, Patriarchat

mannigfaltig Gleichartiges *n* • homogeneous manifold *(Kant) (met)*

Mannigfaltige, das *n* • (the) manifold *(met)*

Mannigfaltige der Erscheinung, das *n* • the manifold of appearance *(Kant) (epi)*

Mannigfaltigkeit *f* • manifold *(Kant) (met)*, variety, diversity, multiplicity *(ont, nat, mat)* < Vielfalt, Vielheit

Mannigfaltigkeit des Seins *f* • multiplicity of being *(Aristotle etc) (ont)*

männlich-voreingenommen • male-biased *(fem)*

männlich-weibliche Merkmale *pl* • male-female traits/characteristics *(ant, psy)*

Männlichkeit *f* • maleness *(fem)*, masculinity *(gen)* ↔ Weiblichkeit < Maskulinismus

Männlichkeit der Vernunft *f* • maleness of reason *(fem)* < Phallogozentrismus

Männlichkeitschauvinismus *m* • male chauvinism *(fem)*

Mannschaftsgeist *m* • team spirit *(psy)* → Teamgeist

Mantik *f* • mantic *(eso)* → Wahrsagekunst

Mantra *n* • mantra *(asp)*

Mantrajana *n* • mantrajana *(asp)*

Manu *m* • nt *(asp)*

manuelle Arbeit f • manual work *(eco, soc)* ↔
geistige Arbeit

Manufakturkapitalismus m • manufacture
capitalism *(Marx etc) (eco)*

Maoismus m • Maoism *(pol)*

Marburger Schule f • Marburg School *(Natorp
etc) (gep)* → Badische Schule

marginaler Nutzen m • marginal utility *(eco,
dec)* → Grenznutzen

Marginalisierung f • marginalization *(soc)* →
Ausgrenzung, soziale

Marginalität f • marginality *(soc)*

Mark Aurel • Marcus Aurelius

Markenpiraterie f • product piracy *(eco, eth)*

Marktabsprache f • informal marketing
agreement *(eco)* < Kartellabkommen

Marktanalyse f • market analysis *(eco)*

Marktanteil m • market share *(eco)*

marktbeherrschende Position f • market
dominance *(eco)* → Monopolismus

Marktcharakter m • market character
(Fromm) (soc, psy)

Marktentwicklung f • market tendency/trend
(eco) < Konjunktur

marktfähige Güter pl • marketable goods
(eco) < Ware

Marktfähigkeit f • marketability *(eco)*

Marktforschung f • market research *(eco)*

Marktgesellschaft f • market society *(eco,
soc)*

Marktgesetze pl • laws of the market, market
laws *(eco)* < Angebot und Nachfrage

Marktintervention f • market intervention
(eco)

Marktkräfte pl • market forces *(eco)*

Marktlage f • market conditions *(eco)*

Marktlücke f → Marktnische

Marktmacht f • market power *(eco)*

Marktmechanismus m • market mechanism
(eco)

Marktnachfrage f • market demand *(eco)*
< Angebot und Nachfrage

Marktnische f • market niche *(eco)*

Marktordnung f • market order/organization
(eco), market regulation *(eco, jur)* < Marktregulierung

marktorientiert • market oriented *(eco, soc)*

Marktorientierung f • market orientation
(Fromm) (soc)

Marktpreis m • market price *(eco)*

Marktregulierung f • market regulation *(eco)*
< Marktordnung

Markttugenden pl • virtues of the market
(eco, eth)

Marktversagen n • market failure *(eco)*
< Staatsversagen, unvollkommene Konkur-
renz

Marktwert m • market value *(Marx etc)*
(eco)

Marktwirtschaft f • market economy, free
enterprise system *(eco)* < Wettbewerbswirtschaft

Marktwirtschaft, soziale f • social market
economy *(eco, soc)* < freie Marktwirtschaft

Marktwirtschaft, Verfechter der freien m •
free marketeer *(eco)*

Marktzutrittsschranken pl • market barriers
(eco)

Märtyrer m • martyr *(rel)*

Marxianer m • Marxian *(gep)*

Marxismus m • Marxism *(gep)*

Marxismus-Leninismus m • Marxism-
Leninism *(pol)*

Marxismus mit menschlichem Antlitz m •
Marxism with human face *(Dubcek) (pol)*

marxistisch • Marxist *(gep)*

marxistisch-leninistisch • Marxist-Leninist
(pol)

Marxistische Theorie f • Marxist theory *(gep)*

Marxologie f • Marxology *(gep)*

Marxsche Theorie f • Marxian theory *(gep)*
< Marxistische Theorie

Maschinenästhetik f • machine aesthetics
(aes)

Maschinenkultur f • machine culture *(cul, tec)*

Maschinenmensch m • robot, automaton *(tec,
soc)* < Cyborg; künstlicher Mensch; natürlicher Automat, Mensch als; Robobiologie;
< W 614, 637

Maschinenmetapher f • metaphor of the
machine *(ant, pol)*

Maschinenmodell des Menschen n • machine
model of man *(ant, psy)*

Maschinensprache f • machine language *(AI)*
< Programmiersprache

Maschinenstürmer m • Luddite *(tec, pol)*
< Technikfeindlichkeit

Maschinenstürmerei f • Luddism, Ludditism
(tec, pol) → Luddismus < Fortschrittsfeindlichkeit, Technikfeindlichkeit

Maschinentheorie des (organischen) Lebens f
• machine theory of (organic) life *(Descartes, La Mettrie etc) (met)* → Maschinismus

Maschinenzeitalter n • machine age *(his)*

Maschinismus m → Maschinentheorie des
(organischen) Lebens

Maskulinismus m • masculinism *(psy, fem)* ↔
Feminismus

Masochismus *m* • masochism *(psy)* ↔ Sadismus

Maß *n* • measure *(eth, aes, mat)*

Maßästhetik *f* • aesthetics of proportions *(aes)* < Goldener Schnitt

Masse, die *f* • mass *(nat)*, mass, crowd, the masses *(soc)* < W 102, 615

Maßeinheit *f* • unit of measurement *(mat)*

Massenarbeitslosigkeit *f* • mass unemployment *(eco)*

Massenarmut *f* • mass poverty *(eco)* < Pauperismus

Massenbeeinflussung *f* • propaganda *(pol)*

Massenbeschleunigung *f* • mass acceleration *(nat)*

Massenbewegung *f* • mass movement *(soc)*

Massenbildung *f* • (▷ Erziehung) mass education *(soc)*, (▷ Formation) mass formation *(nat)*

Massenentlassung *f* • mass redundancy *(eco)*

Massenerhaltungssatz *m* • principle of the conservation of mass *(Newton etc) (nat)* → Prinzip von der Erhaltung der Masse

Massengeist *m* • mass attitude *(soc, psy)*

Massengeschmack *m* • mass taste *(aes)*

Massengesellschaft *f* • mass/faceless society *(soc, cul)* < Aufstand der Massen, Vermassung des Menschen

Massenhysterie *f* → Massenwahn

Massenkommunikation *f* • mass communication *(soc)*

Massenkonsum *m* • mass consumerism *(eco, aes)* < Kulturindustrie

Massenkultur *f* • mass culture *(soc, cul)* ↔ Hochkultur < Kulturindustrie

Massenmedien *pl* • mass media *(gen)*

Massenmensch *m* • mass man *(Ortega y Gasset etc) (soc)* < Man, das

Massenproduktion *f* • mass production *(eco)* < Fordismus, Serienfertigung, Taylorismus

Massenpsychologie *f* • mass psychology *(Canetti etc) (psy, soc)* < Kollektivpsyche, < W 616, 617, 845

Massenpsychose *f* • mass psychosis *(psy)* < Massenhysterie

Massenreproduktion *f* • mass reproduction *(aes, tec)*

Massensterben *n* • mass death *(nat, pol)*

Massensuggestion *f* • mass hypnosis/hypnotism *(psy)*

Massenterminus *m* • mass term *(Quine) (lan)*

Massentierhaltung *f* • intensive livestock farming *(eco, eth)* ↔ artgerechte Tierhaltung; intensive Tierhaltung; Tierhaltung, industrielle

Massenträgheitsmoment *n* • moment of inertia *(Newton) (nat)*

Massenverhalten *n* • mass behaviour *(psy, soc)*

Massenvernichtung *f* • mass extermination *(eth, nat)* < ethnische Säuberung

Massenwahn *m* • mass hysteria, collective/mass illusion/delusion *(psy)*

Maßhalten *n* • parsimony *(eth)* → Mäßigung < Mesotes-Regel, Goldene Mitte

Mäßigkeit *f* • moderation, temperance *(eth)*

Mäßigung *f* • self-control, restraint *(eth)* → Maßhalten

Maßlosigkeit *f* • immoderacy *(eth)*, lack of proportion *(aes)*

Maßsetzung *f* • conventional fixing of a unit of measurement *(epi)*

maßstäbliche Abbildung *f* • scale(d) reproduction *(mat)*

materia prima *f* • prime matter *(Aristotle) (ont)*

material • material *(gep)* < inhaltlich

Material *n* • substance *(Carnap) (epi, ont)*

materiale Bedingung *f* • material condition *(Kant etc) (epi, met)*

materiale Ontologie *f* • material ontology *(Husserl) (ont)* → Materialontologie ↔ formale Ontologie < Existentialontologie

materiale Wertethik *f* • material/non-formal ethics of values, material/non-formal value ethics *(Scheler) (eth)* < W 312

materiale Zweckmäßigkeit *f* • material finality *(Kant) (met)*

materialer Idealismus *m* • material idealism *(Kant) (met)*

materialer Realgrund *m* • material-real ground *(Kant) (epi, met)*

materiales Prinzip *n* • material principle *(Kant) (epi, met)*

Materialisation *f* • materialization *(nat, eso)*

materialisieren • to materialize *(nat)*

Materialismus *m* • materialism *(epi, met)*

Materialismus, antimechanistischer *m* • non-mechanistic materialism *(met)*

Materialismus, dialektischer *m* • dialectical/dialectic materialism *(Marx) (epi, met)*

Materialismus, französischer *m* • French Materialism *(gep)*

Materialismus, historischer *m* • historical materialism *(Marx etc) (his)* → Histomat < materialistische Geschichtsauffassung

Materialismus, kritischer *m* • critical materialism *(met)*

Materialismus, mechanischer *m* • mechanical materialism *(met)*

Materialismus, mechanistischer *m* • mechanistic materialism *(met)*

Materialisten, frühe *pl* • early Materialists *(his)*

materialistisch • materialistic *(eco)*

materialistische Geschichtsauffassung *f* • materialist conception of history *(his)* < historischer Materialismus

materialistischer Geschichtsbegriff *m* • materialist concept of history *(his)* < Historischer Materialismus

Materialität *f* • materiality *(nat, met)* ↔ Spiritualität

Materialobjekt *n* • material object *(met)*

Materialontologie *f* • material ontology *(Husserl)* *(ont)* → materiale Ontologie ↔ Formalontologie

Materialursache *f* • material cause *(Aristotle etc)* *(met)* → causa materialis, Stoffursache

Materie *f* • matter *(nat, met)* → Stoff, Hyle < Grundmaterie

Materie, Bewegungslehre der *f* • dynamic theory of matter *(Kant)* *(nat)*

Materie der Anschauung *f* • matter of intuition *(Kant)* *(epi)*

Materie der Erfahrung *f* • matter of experience *(Kant)* *(epi)*

Materie der Erkenntnis *f* • matter of knowledge/cognition *(Kant)* *(epi)*

Materie der Erscheinung *f* • matter of appearance *(Kant)* *(epi)*

Materie der Wahrnehmung *f* • matter of perception *(Kant)* *(epi)*

Materie des Raumes *f* • matter of space *(Kant)* *(epi, met)*

Materie des Urteils *f* • matter/content of judg(e)ment *(log)* ↔ Form des Urteils

Materie, geistige *f* • spiritual matter *(ont)*

Materie, geschaffene *f* • created matter *(ont, rel)*

Materie in Bewegung *f* • matter in motion *(Hobbes)* *(ont)*

Materie, körperliche *f* • corporeal matter *(ont)*

Materie, Monadologie der *f* • monadic(al)/ monadological theory of matter *(Leibniz)* *(ont)*

Materie, schaffende *f* • creating matter *(Aristotle)* *(ont)*

Materie, selbstbewegte *f* • self-moved matter *(ont)*

Materie, stoffliche *f* • (physical) matter *(nat)*

Materie, Theorie der *f* • theory of matter *(met)*

Materie, Wesen der *n* • essence of matter, nature of matter *(gep)*

Materiekondensation *f* • condensation of matter *(nat)*

materielle Basis *f* • material base/basis/ foundation *(Marx etc)* *(eco, soc)* → ökonomische Basis ↔ ideeller Überbau

materielle Kräfte *pl* • material forces *(Marx)* *(soc)*

materielle Lebensbedingungen *pl* • material living conditions *(eco)*

materielle Sicherheit *f* • material security *(eco)*

materieller Lebensstandard *m* • material standard of living *(eco)*

materieller Unterbau *m* → materielle Basis

materielles Ding *n* • material thing *(epi, ont)*

materielles Reichtumsstreben *n* • pursuit of material wealth *(eco)*

materielles Substrat *n* • material substrate *(ont)*

Mathema *n* → Lehrsatz

Mathematik der Erscheinungen *f* • mathematics of appearances *(Kant)* *(epi)*

Mathematik, konstruktive *f* • constructive mathematics *(mat)*

Mathematisch-Erhabenes *n* • mathematical sublime *(Kant)* *(aes)*

mathematische Abstraktion *f* • mathematical abstraction *(mat)*

mathematische Analogie *f* • mathematical analogy *(mat, epi)*

mathematische Entscheidungstheorie *f* • mathematical decision theory *(mat, dec)*

mathematische Gewißheit *f* • mathematical certainty *(Kant)* *(epi)* < more geometrico

mathematische Induktion *f* • mathematical induction *(log, mat)*

mathematische Kategorien *pl* • mathematical categories *(Kant)* *(epi, mat)* ↔ dynamische Kategorien

mathematische Logik *f* • mathematical logic *(log, mat)* → Logik, symbolische

mathematische Methode *f* • mathematical method *(mat, sci)* < geometrische Methode

mathematische Philosophie *f* • mathematical philosophy *(mat)* < W 225

mathematische Physik *f* • mathematical physics *(nat)*

mathematische Wahrheit *f* • mathematical truth *(epi, mat)*

mathematische Zeit *f* • mathematical time *(Newton)* *(nat)*

mathematischer Konstruktivismus *m* • mathematical constructivism *(sci)*

mathematisches Denken *n* • mathematical thinking *(mat)* < W 221

mathematisches Modell *n* • mathematical model *(mat)*

mathematisches Urteil *n* • mathematical judg(e)ment *(Kant) (epi, mat)*

mathematisches Wissen *n* • mathematical knowledge *(mat, epi)*

Mathematisierbarkeit *f* • mathematizability *(log, mat)* < Formalisierbarkeit, Quantifizierbarkeit

Mathematisierung *f* • mathematization *(log, mat)*

Mathematisierung der Welt, die *f* • mathematization of the world *(Husserl etc) (mat)*

Mathematizismus *m* • mathematicism *(mat, log, sci)*

mathesis universalis *f* • *nt (Leibniz, Husserl) (met, mat)* → Universalmathematik

Matriarchat *n* • matriarchy, matriarchate *(Bachofen) (cul)* → Mutterrecht; *(fem)* → Weiberherrschaft ↔ Patriarchat

matrilinear • matrilinear *(fem)*

Matrix, disziplinäre *f* • disciplinary matrix *(Kuhn etc) (sci)* → Kuhnsche Matrix < Paradigma

Matthäus-Effekt *m* • Matthew effect *(Merton) (soc)*

Matthäusprinzip *n* • Matthew principle *(soc, eco)*

mauvaise foi *m* → böser Glaube(n)

Maximalbedingung *f* • maximum condition *(mat)*

maximale Größe *f* • maximal greatness *(Plantinga) (sys, nat)*

maximale Mutmaßlichkeit *f* • maximum likelihood (estimation), MLE *(Fischer) (mat)*

Maximax-Entscheidung *f* • maximax-decision *(dec)*

Maximax-Prinzip *n* • maximax principle *(dec)*

Maxime *f* • maxim *(Kant) (eth)* → Handlungsregel, Lebensregel

Maxime der Handlung *f* • maxim of action *(Kant) (eth)*

Maxime der spekulativen Vernunft *f* • maxim of speculative reason *(Kant) (epi)*

Maxime des Willens *f* • maxim of the will *(Kant) (eth)*

Maximen, vernunftbegründete *pl* • maxims based on/in reason *(Kant) (eth)*

maximieren • to maximize *(gen)*

Maximierung *f* • maximization *(gen)*

Maximierung der Glücksmenge *f* • maximization of the quantity/amount of happiness *(Bentham) (eth)* < hedonistischer Kalkül

Maximierungsgebot *n* • maximization precept *(eth)*

Maximierungspostulat *n* • maximization postulate *(eth)* < Utilitarismus

Maximin-Entscheidung *f* • maximin-decision *(dec)*

Maximin-Prinzip *n* • maximin principle *(dec)* ↔ Minimax-Prinzip

maya *f* • *nt,* illusion *(asp)* → Maja

Mazdaismus *m* • Mazdaism *(Zoroaster) (rel)*

Mäzen *m* • patron *(aes)*

Mäzenatentum *n* • patronage of the arts *(aes)* < Kunstförderung

McCarthyismus *m* • McCarthyism *(pol)*

Mechanik *f* • mechanics *(nat)*

mechanische Erkenntnis *f* • mechanical knowledge *(Kant) (epi)*

mechanische Erklärung *f* • mechanical explanation *(epi, met)*

mechanische Übersetzung *f* • mechanical translation *(AI)*

mechanisches Gesetz *n* • mechanical law *(nat)*

mechanisches Prinzip *n* • mechanical principle *(epi, met)*

mechanisierte Versteinerung *f* • mechanized petrification *(Weber) (soc)*

Mechanisierung *f* • mechanization *(tec)*

Mechanismus *m* • mechanism *(gen)*

Mechanismus, angeborener auslösender *m* • innate releasing mechanism, IRM *(Lorenz etc) (nat)* → AAM

Mechanisten *pl* • mechanists *(pol)* < Organizismus

mechanistische Philosophie *f* • mechanistic/mechanical philosophy *(met)*

mechanistische Weltanschauung *f* • mechanistic world view *(met)*

mechanistischer Materialismus *m* • mechanistic materialism *(met)*

mechanistisches Modell *n* • mechanistic model *(sci)*

mechanistisches System *n* • mechanistic system *(sci)*

mechanistisches Weltbild *n* → mechanistische Weltanschauung

Median *m* • median *(mat)* → Zentralwert

Mediation *f* • mediation *(eth, soc)* < Konfliktlösung

Mediatisierung der Lebenswelt *f* • mediatization of the lifeworld *(Habermas) (soc)*

Mediävistik *f* • medieval studies *(his)*

Medienforschung *f* • media research *(soc)*

mediengesteuerte Interaktion *f* • media-steered interaction *(Habermas) (lan, soc)*

Medienkonzentration *f* • media concentration *(pol, soc)*

Medienkunde *f* • media studies *(soc)*

Medienkunst *f* • media art *(aes)*

Medienkünstler *m* • media artist *(aes)*

Medienmacht *f* • media-power *(pol, soc)*

Medienöffentlichkeit *f* • media public *(Habermas) (lan, soc)*

Medienpädagogik *f* • media pedagogy *(psy)*

Medienwissenschaft *f* • media studies *(soc)* → Medienforschung

Medikamentenmißbrauch *m* • drug abuse *(eth)* < Drogenmißbrauch

Meditation *f* • meditation *(rel, psy)* < W 627

Medium *n* • medium *(lan)*, (spiritualist) medium, psychic *(eso)*

Medizinethik *f* • medical ethics *(eth)*

medizinische Ethik *f* → Medizinethik

Meeresverschmutzung *f* • pollution of the seas *(env)*

Megalomanie *f* • megalomania *(psy)* → Cäsarenwahn, Größenwahn

Megariker *pl* • Megarians *(gep)*

Megarische Schule *f* • Megarian school *(gep)*

Mehrarbeit *f* • surplus labour *(Marx) (eco)*

Mehrarbeitszeit *f* • surplus labour time *(Marx) (eco)* → Surplusarbeitszeit

Mehrdeutigkeit *f* • ambiguity *(lan, log)* → Ambiguität, Äquivokation ↔ Eindeutigkeit

Mehrdeutigkeit der Reichweite *f* • scope ambiguity, ambiguity of scope *(lan)*

Mehrdimensionalität *f* • multidimensionality *(gep)*

Mehrfachentdeckungen *pl* • multiple/simultaneous discoveries *(his, sci)*

mehrgradiger Term *m* • multigrade term *(lan)*

Mehrhabenwollen *n* → Pleonexie

Mehrheitsbeschluß *m* → Mehrheitsentscheidung

Mehrheitsentscheidung *f* • majority decision/vote *(pol)*

Mehrheitsprinzip *n* • majority principle, principle of majority rule *(pol)*

Mehrheitsregel *f* • majority rule *(pol)*

Mehrheitswahlrecht *n* • majority vote system *(pol)*

Mehrparteiensystem *n* • multi-party system *(pol)*

Mehrprodukt *n* • surplus product *(Marx) (eco)*

Mehrproduktion *f* • surplus production *(Marx etc) (eco)*

mehrstellige Zahl *f* • multidigit number *(mat)*

mehrstufiges Experiment *n* • multi-stage experiment *(sci)*

Mehrverbrauch *m* • excess consumption *(eco)*

Mehrweltentheorie *f* • multiple world theory, many worlds theory *(Anaximander) (met)* ↔ Einwelttheorie

Mehrwert *m* • surplus/added value *(Marx) (eco)* → Surpluswert < Neuwert

mehrwertige Logik *f* • many- valued/order logic *(log)* < dreiwertige Logik

Mehrwertigkeit *f* • many-valuedness *(log)* < Zweiwertigkeit

Mehrwertrate *f* • rate of surplus value *(Marx) (eco)*

Mehrwerttheorie *f* • theory of surplus value *(Marx etc) (eco)*

Mehrwerttransfer *m* • transfer of surplus value *(Marx) (eco)* < Ausbeutung

Mehrzahl von Normen *f* • multiplicity of norms *(Nietzsche etc) (eth)*

Mehrzweckverwendung *f* • multi-purpose use *(gen)*

Meidungsverhalten *n* • avoidance behaviour *(nat, psy)* < Konfliktvermeidung

Mein und Dein *n,n* • mine and thine *(soc, jur)*

meinen • to mean *(lan)*, to suppose, to believe, to opine, to have an opinion *(epi)* < fürwahr-halten, Glaube(n)

Meinongsche Gegenstandstheorie *f* • Meinon-gian object theory *(ont)*

Meinung *f* • opinion, view *(gep)*, belief *(epi)* → Doxa

Meinungsaustausch *m* • exchange of views *(gep)*

meinungsbildend • opinion-forming *(soc)*

Meinungsbildner *m* • opinion-leader *(soc)*

Meinungsbildung *f* • opinion formation *(soc)*

Meinungsforscher *m* • opinion pollster/researcher *(soc)*

Meinungsforschung *f* • opinion research *(soc)* < öffentliche Meinung

Meinungsfreiheit *f* • freedom of opinion/ex-pression *(pol)* < Denkfreiheit, Redefreiheit

Meinungsführer *m* • opinion leader *(soc)*

Meinungsklima *n* • climate of opinion *(soc)*

Meinungssache *f* • matter of opinion *(Kant) (epi)*

Meinungsverschiedenheit *f* • disagreement, disparity of views *(gen)*

Meinungsverschiedenheit, inhaltliche *f* • substantial disagreement *(Hare) (gep)*

Meinungsverschiedenheit, moralische f •
moral disagreement (eth)

Meinungsverschiedenheit, verbale f • verbal
disagreement (lan)

Meinungsverschiedenheit, vernünftige f •
rational disagreement, rational difference of
opinion (Rawls etc) (eth)

Meinungswechsel m • change of opinion/mind
(gen)

Meisterdenker m • master-thinker (Glucks-
mann) (gep)

Melancholie f • melancholia, melancholy (psy)
→ Schwermut

Mendelismus m • Mendelism (nat)

Mendelsche Genetik f • Mendelian genetics
(nat)

Mendelsches Gesetz n • Mendel's law (nat)
< Vererbungslehre

Menge f • set (mat), mass, multitude (gen)

Menge, reguläre f • regular set (log)

Mengenbegriff m • mass term (lan), idea/
concept of a set (mat)

Mengenbestimmung f • quantitative determination, measurement (mat, sci)

Mengendifferenz f • set difference (mat)

Mengenlehre f • set theory (Cantor etc) (mat,
log)

Mengenlehre, axiomatische f • axiomatic set
theory (mat)

Mengenprodukt n • Cartesian product (log,
mat)

Mengensystem n • system of sets (mat)

mengentheoretische Semantik f • set-theore-
tical semantics (lan)

mengentheoretisches Prädikat n • set-theore-
tical predicate (log, lan)

Mengentheorie f → Mengenlehre

Mensch m • man, human being, person (ant)
< nichtmenschliches Tier

Mensch als Ebenbild Gottes m • man as image
of God (rel)

Mensch als geschichtliches Wesen m • man as
historical being (ant, his)

Mensch als Marionette Gottes m • man as
God's puppet (met, rel)

Mensch als Maß aller Dinge m • man as
measure of all things (Protagoras) (met, eth)
< Homo-mensura-Satz

Mensch als Selbstzweck m • man as an end in
himself (ant, met)

Mensch als soziales Wesen m • man as social
being (Aristotle etc) (ant, soc)

Mensch als Zweck der Geschichte m • man as
the end of history (ant, his)

Mensch als Zweck des Universums m • man
as the end/goal of the universe (nat, ant,
met) < anthropisches Prinzip

Mensch-Tier-Differenz f • difference between man and beast (ant)

Mensch, ungeselliger m • antisocial man (soc)
< ungesellige Geselligkeit

Menschen, Begriff des m • concept of man
(ant)

Menschen, Bestimmung des f → Bestimmung
des Menschen

Menschen, kennzeichnende Merkmale des pl
• distinguishing characteristics of man (ant)

Menschen, mechanistische Erklärung des f •
mechanical explanation of man (La Mettrie,
Diderot) (ant)

Menschen, Natur des f • the nature of man,
human nature (ant)

Menschen, Naturbedingungen des pl • natural
conditions of man (ant) < angeborenes Verhalten

Menschen, natürliche Schlechtigkeit des f •
natural depravity of man, man bad by nature
(Hobbes) (ant, eth)

Menschen, Perfektionsvermögen des n • the
perfectibility of man (Condillac, Rousseau
etc) (ant)

Menschen, Zweckbestimmung des f • proper
goal/function of man (met, ant)

Menschenaffe m • anthropoid (ape) (ant, nat)
→ Anthropomorphe

Menschenbild n • image/concept of man (ant)

Menschenfeindlichkeit f • misanthropy (eth)
→ Misanthropie ↔ Menschenfreundlichkeit

Menschenfreundlichkeit f • philanthropy (eth)
→ Philanthropie ↔ Menschenfeindlichkeit

menschengerecht • fit/suitable for humans,
appropriate to humans (ant, eth) < Menschlichkeit

Menschengestalt f • human shape (gep)

Menschenkenntnis n • knowledge of human
nature (psy)

Menschenkraft f • human power (gen), manpower (eco)

Menschenliebe f • love of mankind, philanthropy (eth) < Nächstenliebe < W 797

Menschenrechte pl • human rights (pol, eth)
< Grundrecht, Persönlichkeitsrechte, unver-
äußerliche Rechte

Menschenrechte, Erklärung der f • declaration of human rights, declaration of the rights
of man (pol, eth)

Menschenrechtspolitik f • human rights policy
(pol, eth)

Menschenrechtsverletzung f • violation of
human rights (pol, eth)

Menschenseele f • human soul (met) ↔ Tierseele

Menschensohn m • the Son of God, the Son of
man (rel)

menschenunwürdig • unworthy of man, unfit
for man, beneath human dignity (eth)

Menschenverstand, gesunder m • common
sense (gep) → gemeiner Menschenverstand
< Alltagsverstand

Menschenversuch m • experimentation on human beings (eth, nat) → Humanexperiment

Menschenwürde f • dignity of man, human
dignity (eth)

Menschewiki pl • Mensheviks (pol) ↔ Bolschewiki

Menschewismus m • Menshevism (pol)

Menschheit f • mankind, humanity (ant)

Menschheitsentwicklung f • development of
man(kind) (ant, his)

Menschheitsgeschichte f • history of human-
kind/mankind, human history (ant, his)

Menschheitsgeschlecht n • human race (ant)

Menschheitshorizont m • horizon of civilization (Husserl) (ont, epi, met)

Menschheitskultur f • human culture (ant, cul)

Menschheitsreligion f • religion of humanity
(Comte) (soc, rel)

menschliche Fähigkeiten pl • human faculties/
abilities (ant, psy)

menschliche Gattungstätigkeit f • man's
species activity (Marx) (ant, soc)

menschliche Gesellschaft f • human society
(soc) ↔ Tiergesellschaft

menschliche Natur f • human nature (ant)

menschliche Wesenskräfte pl • man's
essential powers (Marx) (ant, soc)

menschliches Individuum n • (human)
individual (ant, soc)

menschliches Potential n • human potential
(ant)

menschliches Verhalten n • human behaviour
(ant)

menschliches Vermögen n • human ability/
capacity (ant)

menschliches Versagen n • human error (eth,
tec)

menschliches Wesen n • (▷ Spezieszugehörigkeit) human being (nat), (▷ Wesenseigenschaft) man's essence (met)

Menschlichkeit f • (▷ Humanität) humaneness,
humanity (eth), (▷ menschliche Natur)
human nature, humanness (ant)

Menschwerdung f • the becoming of man (nat,
ant) → Anthropogenese, Hominisation

Menschwerdung Gottes f • incarnation of God
(rel)

Mensurabilität f → Meßbarkeit

Mentale, das n • the mental (min)

mentale Ereignisse pl • mental events (min)

mentale Konstruktion f • mental construction
(min)

mentale Repräsentation f • mental representation (epi, min) → geistige Abbildung

mentale Retardierung f • mental retardation
(psy) < Unterentwicklung, geistige

mentale Sprache f • language of thought,
mental(ist) language, mentalese (min)

mentale Verursachung f • mental causation
(met, min)

mentale Zustände pl • mental states (min)

mentaler Akt m • mental act (min)

mentaler Monismus m • mental monism (min)

Mentalesisch n • mentalese (lan)

Mentalismus m • mentalism (min)

Mentalität f • mentality (gep) → Geisteshaltung

Mentalitätsgeschichte f • history of mentalities
(his)

Mentifakte pl • mentifacts (Huxley) (nat, ant)
< Kulturgene

Mentor m • mentor (gep)

Mereologie f • mereology (log, met) < Metaphysik, formale

Mereotypologie f • mereotypology (B. Smith,
Varzi) (ont, sys)

Meritokratie f • meritocracy (soc) < Leistungsprinzip, Verdienstadel

Merkantilismus m • mercantilism (eco)

Merkantilsystem n → Merkantilismus

Merkmal n • sign, characteristic, attribute,
feature, mark (lan, ont, log) < Kennzeichen,
Kriterium

Merkmale, deutliche pl • distinct attributes
(Spinoza, Leibniz) (met)

Merkmale, diskrete pl • discrete properties
(mat)

Merkmale Gottes pl • divine attributes, attributes of God (rel) → Eigenschaften Gottes

Merkmale, statistische pl • statistic properties
(mat)

Merkmale, stetige pl • continual properties
(mat)

Merkmalsfolge f • sequence of properties,
property sequence (mat)

Merkmalshäufigkeit f • property frequency
(mat)

Mesmerismus m • mesmerism (nat, psy)

Mesotes-Regel *f* • mesotes rule *(Aristotle etc)*
(eth) → Goldene Mitte; Mittelweg, goldener
< Maßhalten

meßbare Größe *f* • measurable quantity/
magnitude *(mat, sci)*

Meßbarkeit *f* • measurability, mensurability
(mat, sci)

Messen, personenorientiertes *n* • subject-
centred approach *(Torgerson) (sci, soc)*

Messen, reaktionsorientiertes *n* • response-
centred approach *(Torgerson) (sci, soc)*

messianische Erwartung *f* • messianist expectation *(rel)* < Chiliasmus, Milleniarismus

Messianismus *m* • messianism *(rel, pol)*

Meßinstrument *n* • measuring instrument *(sci)*

Meßkonvention *f* • conventional measure
(mat)

Messung *f* • measurement *(sci)*

Messungen, unaufdringliche *pl* • unobtrusive/
noncreative measures *(Webb) (sci, soc)*

Meßwert *m* • measure(d) value, measure *(nat,
mat)*

Meta-Ästhetik *f* • meta-aesthetics *(aes)*

Metabasis *f* • metabasis *(log)*

metabolische Kommunikation *f* • metabolic
communication *(nat)* ↔ neuronale Kommunikation

Metaerzählung *f* • metanarrative *(Lyotard)*
(epi, pol)

Metaethik *f* • metaethics *(eth)*

Metakommunikation *f* • metacommunication
(lan)

Metakritik *f* • metacritique *(gep)* < W 1362

Metalinguistik *f* • metalinguistics *(lan)*

metalinguistische Analyse *f* • metalinguistic
analysis *(lan)*

Metalogik *f* • metalogic° *(log)*

Metamathematik *f* • metamathematics *(mat)*

metamathematische Beweistheorie *f* • meta-
mathematical proof theory *(Hilbert) (sci)*

Metametasprache *f* • metametalanguage *(lan,
sci)*

Metamodell der semantischen Stufen *n* •
metamodel of semantic levels *(mat)*

Metamorphose *f* • metamorphosis *(nat)*

Metamorphosen des Geistes *pl* • metamor-
phoses of the spirit *(Nietzsche) (met)*

Metanoia *f* → Sinnesänderung, innere Umkehr

metaökonomisch • metaeconomic *(eco)*

Metaorganismus *m* • metaorganism *(eso)*

Metapher *f* • metaphor *(lan)*

Metaphilosophie *f* • metaphilosophy *(gep)*

metaphorische Bedeutung *f* • metaphoric(al)
meaning *(lan)* ↔ wörtliche Bedeutung

metaphorische Typen *pl* • metaphoric(al)
types *(Jakobson) (lan)*

metaphorische Wahrheit *f* • metaphoric(al)
truth *(epi)*

metaphorischer Ausdruck *m* • metapho-
ric(al)/figurative expression *(lan)*

Metaphrase *f* • metaphrase *(lan)*

metaphysica specialis *f* → Metaphysik,
spezielle

Metaphysik *f* • metaphysics *(met)* → erste
Philosophie

Metaphysik, allgemeine *f* • general metaphysics *(met)*

Metaphysik als Wissenschaft *f* • metaphysics
as science *(met)* < W 835

Metaphysik, analytische *f* • analytic(al) metaphysics *(met)*

Metaphysik, angewandte *f* • applied metaphysics *(met)*

Metaphysik der Anwesenheit *f* • metaphysics
of presence *(Heidegger, Derrida) (ont)*

Metaphysik der Erkenntnis *f* → Erkenntnismetaphysik

Metaphysik der Natur *f* • metaphysics of
nature *(Kant) (met)*

Metaphysik der Präsenz *f* • metaphysics of
presence *(Derrida) (met)*

Metaphysik der Sitten *f* • metaphysics of
ethics *(Kant) (eth)* < W 419, 649

Metaphysik der spekulativen Vernunft *f* •
metaphysics of speculative reason *(Kant)*
(epi, met)

Metaphysik, deskriptive *f* • descriptive
metaphysics *(Strawson) (met)*

Metaphysik, Ende der *n* • the end of metaphysics *(met)* → Überwindung der Metaphysik < nachmetaphysisches Denken

Metaphysik, formale *f* • formal metaphysics
(met) < Mereologie

Metaphysik, induktive *f* • inductive metaphysics *(met)*

Metaphysik, spekulative *f* • speculative metaphysics *(met)*

Metaphysik, spezielle *f* • special metaphysics
(Wolff) (met)

Metaphysiker *m* • metaphysician *(met)*

Metaphysikkritik *f* • criticism of metaphysics
(met)

metaphysische Deduktion *f* • metaphysical
deduction *(Kant) (epi, met)* < transzendentale Deduktion

metaphysische Erörterung *f* • metaphysical
exposition *(Kant) (epi, met)*

metaphysische Grade *pl* • metaphysical
degrees *(met)*

metaphysische Hinterwelt f • metaphysical otherworldliness *(Nietzsche) (met)*

metaphysische Kunstauffassung f • metaphysical conception of art *(aes)*

metaphysischer Empirismus m • metaphysical empiricism, metaphysical empirism *(met)*

metaphysischer Grund m • metaphysical ground *(sci, met)*

metaphysisches Minimum n • metaphysical minimum *(N. Hartmann) (ont, sci)*

metaphysisches Prinzip n • metaphysical principle *(Kant) (epi, met)*

metaphysisches Wesen Gottes n • metaphysical nature of God *(Aquinas) (rel)*

Metapsychik f → Parapsychologie

Metapsychologie f • metapsychology *(psy)*

Metaregel f • meta-rule *(lan)*

Metasprache f • metalanguage *(lan)*

Metastabilität f • metastability *(sys)*

Metasystem n • metasystem *(sys)*

Metatheorie f • metatheory *(sci)*

Metawissenschaft f • metascience *(sci)* < Forschungsforschung, Wissenschaftswissenschaft

Metempsychose f • metempsychosis, transmigration of the soul *(rel, eso)* → Seelenwanderung < Wiedergeburt

Methexis f • methexis, participation *(Plato) (epi, met)* < Abbild, Urbild

methodäutisch° • methodeutic *(Peirce) (sci)*

Methode, analytische f • analytic(al) method, method of analysis *(sci, epi)* < Methode, resolutiv-rekompositive

Methode, axiomatische f • axiomatic method *(sci)*

Methode, deduktive f • deductive method *(sci)*

Methode der Geisteswissenschaften f → Methode, geisteswissenschaftliche

Methode der Geometrie f → Methode, geometrische

Methode der inneren Wahrnehmung f → Methode, introspektive

Methode der kleinsten Quadrate f • method of least squares, least-square method *(mat, sci)*

Methode der Metaphysik f • method of metaphysics *(met)*

Methode der phänomenologischen Reduktion f • method of phenomenological reduction *(Husserl) (epi, met)*

Methode der Residuen f • method of residues *(Mill) (sci)*

Methode der Übereinstimmung f • method of agreement *(Mill) (sci)*

Methode der Vermeidung f • method/ principle of avoidance *(Rawls) (eth, sci)*

Methode des kritischen Pfades f • critical path method *(sci)*

Methode des nachfühlenden Verstehens f • method of sympathetic understanding *(Dilthey etc) (sci)* < Hermeneutik

Methode des Verstehens f • method of Verstehen, interpretative method *(Dilthey) (sci)* < Hermeneutik

Methode des Zweifels f • method of doubt *(Descartes) (epi)*

Methode, deskriptive f • descriptive method *(sci)*

Methode, dialektische f • dialectical method *(Plato, Hegel, Marx etc) (epi, met)*

Methode, dogmatische f • dogmatic method *(sci)*

Methode, empirische f • empirical method *(sci)*

Methode, geisteswissenschaftliche f • method of the humanities/human sciences *(sci)*

Methode, genetische f • genetic method *(Fichte etc) (sci)*

Methode, geometrische f • geometrical method *(Descartes, Spinoza etc) (epi, eth, sci)* → mos geometricus

Methode, geschichtliche f • historical method *(Bodin etc) (sci)* → Methode, historische < Methode, geisteswissenschaftliche

Methode, hermeneutische f • hermeneutical method *(sci)*

Methode, heuristische f • heuristic method *(sci)*

Methode, historische f • historical method *(Bodin, Dilthey etc) (sci)* → Methode, geschichtliche

Methode, induktive f • inductive method *(sci)*

Methode, introspektive f • introspective method *(psy, sci)*

Methode, isolierende f • isolating method *(sci)*

Methode, kathartische f • cathartic method *(Breuer, Freud) (psy)*

Methode, komparative f • comparative method *(sci)*

Methode, kritische f • critical method *(Kant etc) (sci)*

Methode, mäeutische f • maieutic method *(Socrates) (epi)* → Methode, sokratische

Methode, naturalistische f • naturalist(ic) method *(Kant) (epi, sci)*

Methode, phänomenologische f • phenomenological method *(Husserl etc) (epi, met)*

Methode, reduktive *f* • reductive method *(Husserl) (epi, met)* < Reduktion, phänomenologische

Methode, resolutiv-rekompositive *f* • resolutive-recompositive method *(Zabarella, Hobbes, Descartes) (sci)* < Methode, analytische

Methode, scholastische *f* • scholastic method *(Aquinas) (rel, sci)*

Methode, skeptische *f* • sceptical method *(epi, sci)* < Skeptizismus

Methode, sokratische *f* • Socratic method *(epi)* → Mäeutik, Hebammenkunst

Methode, stochastische *f* • stochastic method *(mat)*

Methode, synthetische *f* • synthetic(al) method *(sci)*

Methode, systematische *f* • systematic method *(sci)*

Methode, transzendentale *f* • transcendental method *(Kant, Cohen etc) (epi, sci)*

Methode, vergleichende *f* • comparative method *(sci)*

Methode von Versuch und Irrtum *f* • method of trial and error *(sci)* < Falsifikationismus

Methode, wissenschaftliche *f* • scientific method *(sci)*

Methoden der Datengewinnung *pl* • methods of obtaining data *(sci)*

Methoden der Transkription *pl* • methods of transcribing *(Foucault) (epi, lan)*

Methodenbewußtsein *n* • methodological awareness *(sci)*

Methodendualismus *m* • methodological dualism, dualism of methods *(sci)*

Methodenkontroverse *f* • methodological controversy *(sci)*

Methodenlehre *f* • methodology, doctrine of method *(sci)* → Methodologie

Methodenlehre, transzendentale *f* • transcendental doctrine of method, transcendental methodology *(Kant) (epi)* ↔ Elementarlehre, transzendentale

Methodenpluralismus *m* • methodological pluralism *(sci)*

Methodenstreit *m* • methodological controversy/debate *(sci)* < Positivismusstreit

Methodentheorie *f* • theory of method(s) *(sci)* → Methodologie

Methodenwahl *f* • choice of method *(sci)*

Methodik *f* • methodology *(sci)*

methodische Analyse *f* • methodical analysis *(sci)*

methodische Einheit *f* • unity of method *(sci)* < Einheitswissenschaft

methodischer und kosmologischer Anfang *m* • methodological and cosmological beginning *(sci, nat)*

methodischer Vorbehalt *m* • methodological reservation/objection *(sci)*

methodischer Zugang *m* • (▷ methodenbezogen) methodological approach, (▷ systematischer Zugang) methodical approach *(sci)*

methodischer Zweifel *m* • methodical doubt *(Descartes) (epi)*

Methodologie *f* • methodology *(sci)* → Methodenlehre

methodologische Regel *f* • methodological rule *(sci)*

methodologischer Falsifikationismus *m* • methodological falsificationism *(Popper) (sci)*

methodologischer Solipsismus *m* • methodological solipsism *(sci)*

methodologischer Szientismus *m* • methodological scientism *(sci)* < moralischer Szientismus

methodologisches Ideal *n* • methodological ideal *(Weber) (sci)*

Metonymie *f* • metonymy *(lan)*

Metrik *f* • metric *(mat)*, metrics *(aes)*

metrische Gesetze *pl* • metric laws *(sci)*

metrische Wissenschaften *pl* • metric sciences *(sci)*

metrischer Raum *m* • metric space *(mat)*

Metrisierung *f* • metrication *(mat)*

Midaskomplex *m* • Midas complex *(psy)*

Migrationstheorie *f* • migration theory *(Ratzel) (cul), (Wagner) (nat)*

Mikroanalyse *f* • microanalysis *(sci)*

Mikrokosmos *m* • microcosm *(nat)* < W 658

Mikromächte *pl* • micro-powers *(Foucault) (pol)*

mildernde Umstände *pl* • mitigating circumstances *(jur)* < Unzurechnungsfähigkeit

Mildtätigkeit *f* • charity *(eth)*

Milesische Schule *f* • Milesian school *(gep)*

Milgram-Experiment *n* • Milgram experiment *(psy, sci)*

Milieueinfluß *m* • environmental influence, milieu influence(s) *(psy, soc)*

milieugeschädigt • environmentally deprived *(psy, soc)*

Milieutheorie *f* • environmentalism *(Helvetius, d'Holbach etc) (soc)* < soziale Umstände

Militärausgaben *pl* • military expenditure *(eco)*

Militärbündnis *n* • military alliance *(pol)*

Militärdiktatur *f* • military dictatorship *(pol)*

Militärethik f • military ethics *(eth)*

militärisch-industrieller Komplex m •
military-industrial complex *(pol, eco)*

Militarismus m • militarism *(pol)*

Militärmacht f • military power *(pol)*

Militärregime n • military regime *(pol)*

Millenarismus m • millenniarism, millenari-
anism, milleniannism, millenialism *(rel)* →
Chiliasmus < Eschatologie

Milleniarismus m → Millenarismus

Mimese f → Mimesis

Mimesis f • imitation, mimesis *(Plato, Aristotle
etc)* *(aes)* → Nachahmung, Nachbildung
< Abbild, Nachahmung der Natur, Nach-
ahmungsvermögen

mimetische Kunst f • mimetic art *(aes)* →
nachahmende Kunst

mimetische Kunstauffassung f • mimetic view
of art/the arts *(aes)*

mimetischer Ausdruck m • mimetic expression *(aes)*

Min-Max-Kriterium n • min-max-criterion
(dec, eco)

Minderheitenfragen pl • minority questions
(soc, pol)

Minderheitenrechte pl • minority rights *(jur,
pol)*

Minderheitenschutz m • protection of
minorities *(pol, eth)*

Minderheitsregierung f • minority government
(pol)

Minderwertigkeitsgefühl n • feeling/sense of
inferiority *(psy)*

Minderwertigkeitskomplex m • inferiority
complex *(Adler etc)* *(psy)* ↔ Überlegenheitskomplex

Mindestanforderungen pl • minimum requirements *(gen)*

Mindesteinkommen n • minimum income
(eco)

Mindestlohn m • minimum wage *(eco)*

Minimal art f • minimal art *(aes)* → Minimalismus, ABC-Kunst < Reduktionismus,
ästhetischer

Minimal music f • minimal music *(aes)*

Minimalismus m • minimalism *(aes)* →
Minimal art, ABC-Kunst

Minimalrecht n • minimal right *(jur, eth)*

Minimalstaat m • minimal state *(Nozick etc)*
(pol) < Grenzen des Staates, Nachtwächterstaat

Minimax-Prinzip n • minimax principle *(dec)*
↔ Maximin-Prinzip < Spieltheorie

Minimax-Theorem n • minimax theorem
(dec)

Minimax-Verfahren n • minimax method
(dec, sci)

Minimax-Verlust m • minimax loss *(dec)*

Minimin-Prinzip n • minimin principle *(dec)*

minoritäres Denken n • minority/marginal
thinking *(epi, pol)*

Minorität f • minority *(pol)*

minus malum n → Übel, kleineres

Misanthropie f • misanthropy *(eth)* → Menschenfeindlichkeit ↔ Philanthropie

mischkategorisch • mongrel-categorical
(Ryle) *(lan)* < pathologisches Prädikat

Mischrasse f • mixed race *(nat, ant)*

Mischverteilung f • mixed distribution *(mat)*

Mischwirtschaft f • mixed economy *(eco)*

Misogynie f • misogyny *(fem)*

Misologie f • misology *(Kant)* *(gep)*

Mißachtung des Gesetzes f • violation of the
law *(eth, jur)*

Mißbrauch der Sprache m • abuse of
language *(lan)* < Sprachkritik

Mißdeutung f • misinterpretation *(lan)*

Mißklang m • discord, cacophony *(aes)*

mißlungene Kommunikation f • failed
communication *(lan)*

Mißton m • discordant note, dissonance *(aes)*

Mißtrauen n • mistrust, distrust, suspicion *(eth)*

Mißtrauensvotum n • vote of no confidence,
vote of censure *(pol)*

Mißverhältnis n • disproportion *(aes)* →
Ametrie, Disproportion

Mißverständlichkeit f • ambiguity *(gen)*

Mißwirtschaft f • mismanagement *(eco)*

mit dem Hammer philosophieren • philosophizing with the hammer *(Nietzsche)* *(gep)*
< Götzendämmerung

Mitarbeiter m • employee, co-worker *(eco)*

Mitarbeiterstab m • staff *(eco)*

Mitbenutzungsrecht n • right of joint use *(jur,
eco)*

Mitbestimmung f • participation, co-determination *(eco, pol)* < Partizipation

Mitbestimmung am Arbeitsplatz f • worker
participation *(eco)* < Wirtschaftsdemokratie

Mitbestimmungsrecht n • right of participation in decisions, co-determination right *(jur,
eco)* < Mitspracherecht, Mitwirkungsrecht

Mitbeteiligung f • co-partnership *(eco)* < Gewinnbeteiligung

Mitbürger m • fellow-cititzen *(pol)*

Mitdasein n • Dasein-with *(Heidegger)* *(ont)*

Miteigentümer m • co-owner, joint owner
(eco, jur)

miteinander fühlen • feeling-with-one another *(Scheler) (psy, soc)*

Miteinander, menschliches *n* • human cooperation *(soc)*

Mitempfindung *f* • concomitant sensation *(eth, psy)* < Sympathie, Synästhesie

mitfühlendes Vorstellen *n* • sympathetic imagination *(Hare etc) (eth)*

Mitgefühl *n* • sympathy, empathy *(psy, eth)* < Mitleid

Mitgeschöpf *n* • fellow creature, animal companion° *(eth)*

Mitgeschöpflichkeit *f* • companionship *(rel)*

Mitgliedsstaat *m* • member state *(pol)*

Mitherrschaft *f* • condominium *(jur)*

Mitläufer *m* • fellow traveller *(pol)*

Mitläufereffekt *m* • bandwagon effect *(pol, soc)*

Mitleid *n* • sympathy, compassion, pity *(psy, eth)* < Mitgefühl

Mitleidsethik *f* • ethics of compassion/ sympathy *(Schopenhauer etc) (eth)*

Mitleidsmoral *f* • morality of compassion/ sympathy *(Schopenhauer etc) (eth)*

Mitmensch *m* • fellow-man *(soc, eth)*

Mitschuld *f* • complicity, joint guilt, accessoriness *(jur, eth)* < Kollektivschuld

Mitsein *n* • the being-with *(Heidegger) (met)*

Mitspracherecht *n* • (right of) say, right to be heard *(pol)* < Mitbestimmungsrecht

Mittäterschaft *f* • complicity *(eth)* < Mitwis-serschaft

Mitteilbarkeit *f* • communicability *(lan)*

Mitteilungszeichen *n* • communication-sign *(lan)*

Mittel *n* • (▷ Durchschnitt) mean, average *(mat)*, (▷ Instrument) means *(act)*

Mittel, begrenzte *pl* • finite/limited means *(eco, env)*

Mittel und Zweck *n,m* • means and ends *(act)*

Mittel zum Leben *n* • means of existence *(eco)*

Mittel zum Zweck *n* • means to an end *(act)*

Mittel-Zweck-Analyse *f* • means-end(s) analysis *(act, dec)*

Mittel-Zweck-Relation *f* • means-end relation *(act, dec)*

Mittel-Zweck-Überlegung *f* • means-ends reasoning *(act, dec)*

Mittelalter *n* • the Middle Ages *(his)*

mittelalterliche Philosophie *f* • medieval philosophy *(gep)*

mittelbare Erkenntnis *f* • mediate knowledge *(epi)*

mittelbare Ursache *f* • mediate(d) cause, caused cause *(met)* → causa mediata

mittelbares Wissen *n* • mediated knowledge *(epi)*

Mittelbegriff *m* • middle term *(log)*

mittelfristige Planung *f* • medium-term planning *(dec)*

Mittelklasse *f* • middle class *(soc)*

Mittelklasse, obere *f* • upper middle class *(soc)*

Mittelklasse, untere *f* • lower middle class *(soc)*

Mittelmäßigkeit *f* • mediocrity *(gen)*

mittelmeerisches Denken *n* • mediterranian thought *(Camus) (gep)*

Mittelpunkt *m* • centre *(gen)*

Mittelstand *m* • the middle classes *(soc)*

Mittelwahl *f* • choice of means *(dec)*

Mittelweg, goldener *m* • the golden mean *(eth)* → Mesotes-Regel

Mittelwert *m* • mean, average, mean/average value *(mat)*

mittlere Abweichung *f* • mean/avarage deviation *(mat)*

mittlerer Weg *m* • Middle/Central Way *(Buddha) (asp)*

mittlerer Zufallsfehler des Mittelwerts *m* • random error *(mat)*

Mitursache *f* • concurring/contributing cause *(sci)*

Mitverantwortlichkeit *f* • co-responsibility, joint responsibility *(eth)*

Mitverschulden *n* → Mitschuld

Mitwelt *f* • co-world, common world *(Husserl) (soc)* < Lebenswelt

Mitwirkung Gottes *f* • participation of God *(rel)*

Mitwirkungsrecht *n* • right to participate *(jur, eth)* < Mitbestimmungsrecht

Mitwissenschaft *f* • co-science *(sci)* → Hilfs-wissenschaft

Mitwisserschaft *f* • complicit knowledge *(jur, eth)* < Mittäterschaft

Mnemotechnik *f* • mnemonics, mnemo-technics, memory training *(min)*

Mobilität *f* • mobility *(cul, soc)*

Mobilitätsbarriere *f* • mobility barrier *(soc)*

Möbiusschleife *f* • Moebius strip/band *(mat, AI)*

Möbiustransformation *f* • Moebius transformation *(mat, AI)*

Modalanalyse *f* • modal analysis *(log, sci)*

Modalbehauptung *f* • modal proposition *(log)* < kontrafaktische Behauptung

modale Prädikatenlogik f • modal predicate logic *(log)*

modale Unterscheidung f • modal distinction *(log)*

modales Urteil n • modal judg(e)ment *(log)*

Modalität f • modality *(log)*

Modalität, aleth(e)ische f • alethic/truth modality *(met, log, epi)* < Wirklichkeitsmodalität, epistemische Modalität

Modalität, apodiktische f • apodictic modality *(Kant etc) (log)*

Modalität, assertorische f • assertoric modality *(log)*

Modalität, deontische f • deontic modality *(log)*

Modalität des Urteils f • modality of judg(e)ment *(Kant) (log)*

Modalität, doxastische f • doxastic modality *(log)*

Modalität, epistemische f • epistemic modality *(log)*

Modalität, kausale f • causal modality *(log)*

Modalität, problematische f • problematic modality *(Kant etc) (log)*

Modalitätsschluß m • modal syllogism/inference *(log)*

Modalkalkül m/n • modal calculus *(log, mat)*

Modallogik f • modal logic *(log)*

modallogisch wahr • true according to modal logic *(log)*

Modaloperator m • modal operator *(log)*

Modalsatz m • modal sentence/proposition *(lan)*

Modalstruktur f • modal structure *(log)*

Modalsystem n • modal system *(log)*

Modalwert m • modal value *(log)*

Modell n • model *(gep, sci)*

Modell, autonomes n • autonomous model *(min)*

Modell, kognitives n • cognitive model *(min)*

Modell, kybernetisches n • cybernetic model *(sys)*

Modell, loglineares n • log-linear model *(log, sci)*

Modell, stochastisches n • stochastic model *(mat, sci)*

Modellbildung f • model building *(sci)*

Modellmenge f • model set, Hintikka-set *(log, mat)*

Modellobjekt n • model object *(sci)*

Modellsprache f • model language *(lan)*

Modellstruktur f • model structure, Kripke structure *(Kripke etc) (log, lan)*

modelltheoretisch • model-theoretic(al) *(sci, log)*

Modelltheorie f • model theory *(sci, log)*

Modephilosophie f • popular/vogue/fashionable philosophy *(gep)*

Moderne f • modernity *(his, aes, soc)* ↔ Postmoderne

moderne Geschichte f • modern history *(his)*

moderne Kunst f • modern art *(aes)*

Moderne, Projekt der n • the project of modernity *(Habermas) (soc, cul)*

Moderne, unvollendete f • unfinished modernity *(soc, cul)*

Moderne, Zeitalter der n • modern age *(Jaspers etc) (his)*

Modernisierung f • modernization *(gen)*

Modernisierungsangst f • fear of modernization, fear of change *(psy, soc)* < Konservativismus

Modernisierungsprozeß m • modernization process *(soc, cul)*

Modernismus m • modernism *(aes, cul)*

Modewort n • in-word, vogue word, buzzword *(lan)*

Modi des Absoluten pl • modes of the Absolute *(Spinoza) (met)*

Modi des Seins pl • modes of being *(met)*

Modul n/m • modulus, module *(mat)*

modulare Logik f • modular logic *(log)*

Modularität des Geistes f • modularity of mind *(Fodor) (min)*

Modularität des Wissens f • modularity of knowledge *(AI)*

Modus m • mode *(log, ont)*, mood *(lan)*

modus significandi m → Bezeichnungsweise

modus (ponendo) ponens m • nt, proposing method° *(log)* → Abtrennungsregel

modus (tollendo) tollens m • nt, removing method° *(log)*

Mögliche, das n • the possible/potential *(met)*

mögliche Begründung f • possible justification *(sci)*

mögliche Erfahrung f • possible experience *(Kant) (epi)*

mögliche Existenz f • potential/possible existenz *(Jaspers) (met)*, potential/possible existence *(met)*

mögliche Positionen des Verlangens im Verhältnis zum Diskurs pl • possible positions of desire in relation to discourse *(Foucault) (psy, lan)*

mögliche Welt f • possible world *(Leibniz, Lewis etc) (epi, met)* ↔ wirkliche Welt < denkbare Welt

mögliche Weltensemantik f • possible world semantics *(Kripke, Putnam) (lan)*

Möglichkeit f • possibility *(act, met)* < W 664

Möglichkeit der Erfahrung f • possibility of experience *(Kant) (epi)*

Möglichkeit der Erkenntnis f • possibility of cognition/knowledge *(Kant etc) (epi)* ↔ Grenzen der Erkenntnis

Möglichkeit und Wirklichkeit f,f • possibility and reality, potency and actuality *(Aristotle etc) (ont)* → Dynamis und Energeia < Potenz-Akt-Lehre

Möglichkeitsbedingung der Erkenntnis f • condition of possible knowledge, condition of the possibility of knowledge *(Kant) (epi)*

Möglichkeitshorizont m • horizon of possibilities *(act, soc)*

Möglichsein n • contingency *(met)* → Kontingenz

Mohammedanismus m • Mohammedanism *(rel)* → Islam

Molekularbiologie f • molecular biology *(nat)*

molekulare Aussage f • molecular proposition/ statement *(lan, log)* < komplexe Aussage, Molekularsatz

Molekularsatz m • molecular proposition *(Russell) (lan, log)* ↔ Atomsatz, Beobachtungssatz

Molekularsprache f • molecular language *(lan, log)*

Molesscher Organismus m • Moles' organism *(sys, lan)*

Moment, das n • (▷ Teil) moment, aspect, element, part *(gep)*, stage of development, factor *(Hegel) (met)*, (▷ Bewegkraft) momentum, moment, motive force *(nat)*

Moment, der m • moment (of time), instant *(gen)*

Monade f • monad *(Leibniz) (met)*

Monadenlehre f → Monadologie

Monadismus m • monadism *(Leibniz) (met)* < Monadologie

Monadologie f • monadology *(Leibniz) (met)* < W 665

Monarchie f • monarchy *(pol)*

Monarchie, absolute f • absolute monarchy *(pol)* ↔ Monarchie, konstitutionelle

Monarchie, konstitutionelle f • constitutional monarchy *(pol)* ↔ Monarchie, absolute

Monastik f • monastic *(Aristotle, Aquinas) (eth)*

mönchisches Leben n • monastic life *(rel)*

Mönchstum n • monasticism *(rel)*

Monem n • moneme *(Martinet) (lan)* < Morphem

Monetarisierung der Arbeitskraft f • monetarization of labour power *(eco, soc)*

Monetarismus m • monetarism *(eco)*

Monismus m • monism *(met)* ↔ Dualismus

Monismus, anomaler m • anomalous monism *(Davidson) (min)* < Monismus, neutraler

Monismus, hylozoistischer m • hylozoistic monism *(met)*

Monismus, naturalistischer m • naturalistic monism *(Häckel) (nat)*

Monismus, neutraler m • neutral monism *(Russell etc) (min)*, *(Hume, Dewey) (met)* < Monismus, anomaler

Monismus, sprachphilosophischer m • (philosophical) linguistic monism *(lan)*

monistische Bewegung f • monistic movement *(Haeckel) (pol, sci)*

monistische Gesellschaft f • monistic society *(pol)* ↔ pluralistische Gesellschaft

monistische Häufigkeitsinterpretation der Wahrscheinlichkeit f • monistic frequency interpretation of probability *(mat)*

Monodie f • monody *(aes)* → Homophonie ↔ Polyphonie

Monogenese f • monogenesis *(nat)* ↔ Polygenese

Monogenismus m • monogenism *(rel)*

Monogramm der reinen Einbildungskraft n • monogram of pure imagination *(Kant) (epi)*

Monographie f • monograph *(gen)*

monokausale Begründung f • mono-causal explanation *(sci)*

monokausale Geschichtstheorie f • mono-causal theory of history *(his)*

Monokratie f • monocracy *(pol)* ↔ Polykratie

monolithische Kultur f • monolithic culture *(cul)*

Monomanie f • monomania, obsession *(psy)*

monomorph • monomorphic, categorical *(log)*

Monomorphie f • monomorphism *(nat)* → Gleichgestaltigkeit

monomythisches Denken n • monomythical thinking *(Marquard) (gep)* ↔ polymythisches Denken

Monophysitismus m • monophysitism *(Averroes) (rel)*

Monopluralismus m • monopluralism *(met)*

Monopol n • monopoly *(eco)* < Monopolstellung

Monopolismus m • monopolism *(eco)* → marktbeherrschende Position < Eintrittsbarriere, Wettbewerbsbeschränkung

Monopolkapitalismus m • monopoly capitalism *(eco)*

Monopolmacht f • monopoly power *(eco, pol)*

Monopolstellung f • monopoly (position) *(eco, pol)*

Monopsychismus m • monopsychism *(psy, met)*

Monotheismus m • monotheism *(rel)* ↔ Polytheismus

Monotheismus, pantheistischer m • pantheistic monotheism *(met, rel)*

monoton • monotonic *(log, mat)*, monotonous *(aes)*

Montage f • cutting, montage *(aes)* < Schnitt

Montague-Grammatik f • Montague grammar *(log, lan)*

Monumentalität f • monumentality *(aes)*

Moral, definitive f • definitive morality/moral code *(Descartes) (eth)* ↔ Moral, provisorische

Moral der Pietät f • morality of piety *(Nietzsche) (eth)*

Moral der Zähmung f • taming morality *(Nietzsche) (eth)*

Moral der Züchtung f • breeding morality *(Nietzsche) (eth)*

Moral des Ressentiment f • morality of resentment/revenge *(Nietzsche, Scheler) (eth)*

Moral, dynamische f • dynamic morality *(Bergson) (eth)* → Moral, offene ↔ Moral, statische

Moral, geschlossene f • closed morality *(Bergson) (eth)* → Moral, statische ↔ Moral, offene

Moral, kritisierende f • critical morality *(Engels) (eth, pol)*

Moral, offene f • open morality *(Bergson) (eth)* → Moral, dynamische ↔ Moral, geschlossene

Moral, provisorische f • provisional morality, provisional moral code *(Descartes) (eth)* ↔ Moral, definitive

Moral, sozialistische f • socialist morality *(eth)*

Moral, statische f • static morality *(Bergson) (eth)* → Moral, geschlossene ↔ Moral, dynamische

Moral, Ursprung der m • origin of morality *(Nietzsche) (eth)* < Genealogie der Moral

Moral, Verbesserung der f • improvement of morals *(eth)*

Moral, vornehme f • noble morality *(Nietzsche) (eth)* → Herrenmoral

Moral, Wandel der m • transformation of morality *(eth)* < Umwertung aller Werte, Wertewandel

Moralbewußtsein, gewöhnliches n • common moral sense/awareness *(eth)*

Moralempfindung f • moral sentiment *(eth)*

Moralempirismus m • moral empiricism *(eth)*

Moralen pl • moralities *(Nietzsche) (eth)*

Moralevolutionismus m • moral evolutionism *(eth)*

Moralin n • hypocrisy, ostentatious morality *(Nietzsche) (eth)*

moralinfreie Tugend f • unpriggish virtue *(Nietzsche) (eth)*

moralisch handelndes Wesen n • moral agent *(eth)* → moralischer Agent

moralisch neutral • morally neutral/impartial/indifferent *(eth)* < Adiaphora, Amoralität

Moralisch-Schöne, das n • moral beauty *(Plato, Shaftesbury, Schiller etc) (aes)* < Kalokagathie, schöne Seele

moralisch verpflichtend • morally obligatory *(eth)*

moralische Absicht f • moral purpose *(eth)*

moralische Begründung f • moral justification *(eth)*

moralische Beschränktheit f • moral narrowness *(Nietzsche) (eth)*

moralische Bestimmung des Willens f • moral determination of the will *(Kant) (eth)*

moralische Billigung f • moral approval/approbation *(eth)*

moralische Doppelwirkung f • moral double effect *(eth)*

moralische Einheit f • moral unity *(Kant) (eth)*

moralische Empfindungen pl • moral sensations/feelings *(eth)*

moralische Entwicklung f • moral development *(eth, psy)*

moralische Forderung f • moral demand *(eth)*

moralische Formen des Bösen pl • moral forms of evil *(Kierkegaard) (rel, eth)*

moralische Gemeinschaft f • moral community *(eth)*

moralische Gesinnung f • moral disposition *(Kant) (eth)*

moralische Gewißheit f • moral certainty *(eth)*

moralische Handlungsanleitung f • guide to moral action *(eth)*

moralische Kosten pl • moral costs *(eth)*

moralische Moden pl • moral fashions *(Nietzsche) (eth)*

moralische Pflicht f • moral duty *(Kant) (eth)* ↔ Rechtspflicht

moralische Qualität f • moral quality *(eth)*

moralische Rechtfertigung f • moral justification *(eth)*

moralische Regel f • moral rule *(eth)*

moralische Reinheit f • moral purity *(Kant) (eth)*

moralische Selbstgenügsamkeit f • moral self-sufficiency *(Kierkegaard) (eth)*

moralische Standfestigkeit *f* • firmness of moral commitment, strength of moral character, moral firmness/virtue *(eth)*

moralische Stärke *f* • moral strength/virtue *(eth)*

moralische Tatsachen *pl* • moral facts *(eth)*

moralische Verpflichtung *f* • moral duty/obligation *(eth)*

moralische Vorstellungskraft *f* • moral imagination *(eth)* < Szenario-Denken

moralische Wahrheit *f* • moral truth *(eth)*

moralische Welt *f* • moral world *(Kant) (eth)*

moralische Weltordnung *f* • moral world order *(eth)*

moralische Welturache *f* • moral cause of the world *(Kant) (eth, rel)*

moralische Werte, absolute *pl* • absolute moral values, moral absolutes *(eth)*

moralische Würde *f* • moral dignity *(eth)*

moralischer Absolutismus *m* • moral absolutism *(eth)*

moralischer Agent *m* • moral agent *(eth)* → moralisch handelndes Wesen

moralischer Begriff *m* • moral concept *(Kant) (eth)*

moralischer Gefühlsdefekt *m* • moral insanity *(eth)*

moralischer Glaube(n) *m* • moral faith *(Kant) (eth, rel)* ↔ doktrinaler Glaube(n)

moralischer Gottesbeweis *m* • moral/ethical argument (for the existence of God) *(Kant) (met, rel)*

moralischer Grund *m* • moral ground *(met, eth)*

moralischer Imperativ *m* • moral imperative *(epi)*

moralischer Pluralismus *m* • moral pluralism *(eth)*

moralischer Preis *m* • moral cost *(eth)*

moralischer Relativismus *m* • moral relativism *(eth)*

moralischer Sinn *m* • moral sense *(Shaftesbury, Hutcheson etc) (eth)* → sittliches Empfinden

moralischer Sinn, fehlender *m* • lack of moral sense *(Shaftesbury) (eth, aes)*

moralischer Standpunkt *m* • moral point of view *(eth)*

moralischer Status *m* • moral status *(eth)*

moralischer Szientismus *m* • moral scientism *(sci, eth)* < methodologischer Szientismus

moralischer Wert *m* • moral value/worth *(eth)*

moralisches Bewußtsein *n* • moral consciousness *(eth)*

moralisches Dilemma *n* • moral dilemma *(eth)*

moralisches Gefühl *n* • moral feeling *(Kant) (eth)*

moralisches Gesetz *n* • moral law *(Kant) (eth)*

moralisches Gut *n* • moral good *(eth)*

moralisches Prinzip *n* • moral principle *(eth)* < Maxime

moralisches Streben *n* • moral striving *(eth)*

moralisches Urteil *n* • moral judg(e)ment *(eth)* < W 673

moralisches Verhalten *n* • moral conduct *(eth)*

moralisches Wissen *n* • moral knowledge *(epi, eth)*

Moralismus *m* • moralism *(eth)*

Moralität *f* • morality *(Kant) (eth)* ↔ Legalität

Moralität und Legalität *f,f* • morality and legality *(Kant) (eth)*

Moralitätskriterium *n* • criterion of morality *(eth)*

Moralkodex *m* • moral code *(eth)*

Morallehre *f* • (▷ einzelne Morallehre) moral doctrine, (▷ allgemeine Morallehre) ethics, moral philosophy *(eth)* < Ethik

Moralphilosophie *f* • moral philosophy *(eth)* < Sittenlehre < W 427

Moralpositivismus *m* • moral positivism *(eth)*

Moralpsychologie *f* • moral psychology *(psy, eth)*

Moral-Sense-Theoretiker *m* • moral sense theorist *(eth)*

Moralstatistik *f* • moral statistics *(eth)*

Moraltheologie *f* • moral theology *(eth, rel)*

Moralurteil *n* • moral judg(e)ment *(eth)*

Moralverbot *n* • moral prohibition *(Nietzsche, Freud) (eth)*

Moralverhalten *n* • moral behaviour *(eth)*

Moralwissenschaft *f* • moral science *(eth)* → Ethik

Moralwort *n* • moral word *(Hare) (log, lan)* ↔ logisches Wort

Mordlust *f* • lust for murder, desire to kill *(Freud) (psy)*

Mordverbot *n* • ban on killing *(Freud) (psy)*

more geometrico • *nt*

Mores *pl* • manners, mores, customs *(eth)* < Sitte

morphé *f* • shape, form *(Aristotle) (met)* → Gestalt, Form

Morphem *n* • morpheme *(lan)* < Monem

Morphemik *f* • morphemics *(lan)*

Morphologie *f* • morphology *(nat, lan, gep)* → Gestaltlehre < W 357

mos geometricus • geometrical fashion *(Spinoza, Descartes etc) (epi, eth, sci)* → Methode, geometrische; Methode, axiomatische; Methode, deduktive < more geometrico

mosaische Gesetze *pl* • Mosaic laws *(rel)*

moslemische Revolution *f* → Islamische Revolution

Motiv *n* • (▷ künstlerische Vorlage) motif *(aes)*, (▷ Veranlassung, Beweggrund) motive, reason, motivation *(psy, act)* → Triebfeder < Handlungsursache

Motivation *f* • motivation *(psy)*

Motivationsforschung *f* • motivation(al) research *(psy)*

Motivationspsychologie *f* • motivation(al) psychology *(psy)*

Motivforschung *f* → Motivationsforschung

motivierender Faktor *m* • motivating factor *(psy)*

motivierender Grund *m* • motivating reason *(psy)*

Motor der Geschichte *m* • motor of history *(his)*

Movens *n* • motive force, motive cause *(ont, nat)* → bewegende Ursache < Agens, bewegende Ursache, treibende Kraft

Müllentsorgung *f* → Abfallbeseitigung

Mülltourismus *m* • garbage tourism *(env)* < Verursacherprinzip

Multidimensionalität *f* • multidimensionality *(gep)* → Vielschichtigkeit, Komplexität

multidisziplinär • multidisciplinary *(sci)*

multifaktoriell • multifactorial *(sci)*

Multifunktionalität *f* • multifunctionality *(sys)*

Multikulturalismus *m* • multiculturalism *(cul, soc)*

Multikulturalität *f* • multiculturality *(cul, soc)* → kultureller Pluralismus < Interkulturalität

multikulturelle Erziehung *f* • multicultural education *(psy, soc)*

multikulturelle Gesellschaft *f* • multicultural society *(cul, soc)*

multikulturelle Identität *f* • multicultural identity *(cul)*

multilateral • multilateral *(gen)* < bilateral

Multilateralismus *m* • multilateralism *(pol, eth)* ↔ Unilateralismus

Multilinearform *f* • multi-linear form *(mat)*

Multilingualismus *m* • multilingualism *(lan)*

Multilinguismus *m* → Multilingualismus

Multimedia *pl* • multimedia *(aes, soc, tec)*

multimedial • multimedia *(aes)*

Multimediashow *f* • multimedia show *(aes)* < Gesamtkunstwerk

multinationale Gesellschaft *f* • multinational company *(eco)*, multiethnic society *(pol, soc)*

multinationaler Konzern *m* • multinational company *(eco)*

Multiple-Choice-Methode *f* • multiple-choice method *(sci)*

Multiple-Choice-Test *m* • multiple-choice test *(sci)*

multiple Korrelation *f* • multiple correlation *(mat)*

multiple Persönlichkeit *f* • multiple personality *(psy, min)*

multiple Persönlichkeitsstörung *f* • multiple personality disorder *(psy, min)*

multiple Quantifikation *f* • multiple quantification *(sci, log)* < Prädikatenlogik, Quantor

Multiplikatoreffekt *m* • multiplier effect *(sys)*

Multiplikatormethode *f* • method of multipliers *(mat)*

multipolare Weltordnung *f* • multi-polar world order *(pol)*

Multivalenz *f* • multivalency *(psy, sci)*

Münchhausen-Trilemma *n* • Münchhausen trilemma *(Albert) (log, epi)* → Trilemma der Begründung

mundan • mundane *(Husserl) (met)*

mündiger Bürger *m* • politically mature citizen *(pol)*

Mündigkeit *f* • age of maturity/consent *(jur)*, self-determinacy/determinedness *(eth, pol)* < Unmündigkeit, selbstverschuldete

mundus intelligibilis *m* • intelligible world *(Plato, Kant etc) (epi, met)* → intelligible Welt ↔ mundus sensibilis

mundus sensibilis *m* • sensible/material world *(Plato, Kant etc) (epi, met)* → Sinneswelt ↔ mundus intelligibilis

Muse *f* • muse *(aes)*

Museologie *f* • museology *(aes, his)*

Museum *n* • museum *(aes, his)* < imaginäres Museum

musikalische Form *f* • musical form *(aes)*

Musikästhetik *f* • music aesthetics *(aes)*

Musikbox-Theorie der Bedeutung *f* • jukebox theory of meaning *(epi)*

Musikdrama *n* • music drama *(Wagner etc) (aes)*

Musikerziehung *f* • music education *(aes)* < Musikpädagogik

Musikethnologie *f* • music ethnology, ethnomusicology *(aes, cul)*

Musikgeschichte *f* • music history, history of music *(aes)*

Musikhistoriker *m* • historian of music, music historian *(aes, his)*

Musikkritiker *m* • music critic *(aes)*

Musikologie *f* → Musikwissenschaft

Musikpädagogik *f* • music pedagogy *(aes, psy)* < Musikerziehung

Musiksoziologie *f* • music sociology, sociology of music *(aes, soc)*

Musikstil *m* • musical style *(aes)*

Musiktheater *n* • music theatre *(aes)*

Musiktheorie *f* • theory of music, music theory *(aes)*

Musiktherapie *f* • music therapy *(psy, aes)*

Musikwerk *n* • musical work, work of music *(aes)*

Musikwissenschaft *f* • musicology *(aes)*

Mußbestimmung *f* • mandatory regulation *(eth, jur)* ↔ Kannbestimmung

Muße *f* • leisure *(psy)* < Beschaulichkeit, theoria

Mußeklasse *f* → müßige Klasse

müßige Klasse *f* • leisure class, leisure(d) class *(Veblen) (soc)*

Müßiggang *m* • idleness, laziness *(psy)* < Oblomowerei

Musterbeispiel *n* • exemplar, example *(sci)* < Paradigma

Mustererkennung *f* • pattern recognition *(AI, psy)* < Gestaltwahrnehmung

Musterhaftigkeit *f* • exemplariness *(gen)*

Mut *m* • courage *(eth)*

Mutation *f* • mutation *(nat)*

Mutmaßlichkeit *f* • likelihood *(log)*

Mutmaßung *f* • speculation *(gen)*

Mutterbindung *f* • mother fixation, mother-tie, maternal bonding *(Freud etc) (psy)*

Muttergesellschaft *f* → Matriarchat

Mutterinstinkt *m* • maternal instinct *(nat, psy)*

Mutterkomplex *m* • mother fixation *(Freud) (psy)* < Ödipus-Komplex

Muttern, das *n* • mothering *(fem)*

Mutterrecht *n* • matriarchy, mother right *(Bachofen) (cul)* → Matriarchat < W 680

Mutterschutz *m* • protection of motherhood *(pol)*

Muttersprache *f* • mother tongue, native language *(lan)*

Mutualismus *m* • mutualism *(nat); (Proudhon) (soc)* < Tauschbank

Mysterienkult *m* • mystery cult *(rel, cul)*

Mysterienreligion *f* • mystery religion *(rel)*

Mysterium *n* • mystery *(rel)*

Mystifikation *f* • mystification *(gen)*

mystifizieren • to mystify *(gen)*

Mystik *f* • mysticism *(rel)*

Mystik, Deutsche *f* • German Mysticism *(Eckhart etc) (rel)*

Mystiker *m* • mystic *(rel)*

Mystische, das *n* • the mystical *(met, eso)*

mystische Einheit *f* • mystical union/unity *(met, rel)*

mystische Erfahrung *f* • mystical experience *(rel, eso)*

mystische Exstase *f* • mystic ecstasy *(rel, eso)*

mystische Unfaßbarkeit *f* • mystical ineffability *(rel)*

mystische Vereinigung *f* • mystic(al) union *(rel, eso)* → unio mystica

Mystizismus *m* • mysticism *(met, rel)*

Mystizismus der praktischen Vernunft *m* • mysticism of practical reason *(Kant) (epi)*

mythenschaffend • mythopoetic, mythopoeic *(cul)*

Mythenschöpfung *f* • mythopoeia, mythmaking *(cul)*

Mythentheorie *f* • theory of myths *(Strauss) (rel, his)*

mythisches Denken *n* • mythical thinking/thought *(epi, cul)* < Bilderdenken

Mythologie *f* • mythology *(rel, cul)* < Mythentheorie

Mythologie, neue *f* • new mythology *(Schelling, Schlegel) (his, aes)*

Mythos *m* • myth *(cul, rel)*

Mythos des Gegebenen *m* • myth of the given *(Sellars) (min)*

Mythos vom Museum *m* • myth of the museum, museum/gallery myth *(Quine) (min, epi)*

Mythos von Sisyphus *m* • myth of Sisyphus *(Camus) (met)* < absurder Held

N

n-dimensional • *nt (mat)*

n-stellig • n-place, n-ary *(log)*

n-stellige Prädikate *pl* • n-place predicates *(log)*

n-wertig • n-order, n-valued *(log)*

„Na und?"-Ethik *f* • „so what?" morality *(Hare) (eth)*

nachahmende Kunst *f* • mimetic art *(aes)* → mimetische Kunst

Nachahmung *f* • imitation, mimesis *(aes)* < Nachbildung

Nachahmung als Wesensprinzip der Kunst *f* • imitation as essence of art *(Plato etc) (aes)*

Nachahmung der Natur *f* • imitation of nature *(Aristotle) (aes)* < Mimesis

Nachahmungseffekt *m* • imitation effect *(psy, act)*

Nachahmungskunst *f* • mimetic art *(aes)*

Nachahmungstheorie *f* • theory of imitation, mimetic theory *(aes, psy)* < Mimesis

Nachahmungstrieb *m* • imitative instinct *(psy)*

Nachahmungsvermögen *n* • imitative faculty, faculty of imitation *(aes, psy)* < Mimesis

Nachbild *n* • after-image, ectype *(psy, epi)*

Nachbildung *f* • (▷ Kopie) copy, imitation; (▷ nachbildende Darstellung) mimesis *(aes)* → Mimesis, Nachahmung < Abbild

Nachdenken *n* → Reflexion

Nachdichtung *f* • adaptation *(aes)*

Nacheinander in der Zeit *n* • succession in time *(nat, met)*

Nachempfindung *f* • (▷ hermeneutische Einfühlung) vicarious experience *(psy, aes)* < Nacherleben, (▷ wahrnehmungspsychologisches Nachbild) after-sensation, time-lag of a sensation *(psy)*

Nacherleben *n* • re-experience, re-experiencing, reliving *(aes, psy)*

Nachfolge *f* • succession *(gep)*

Nachfolge Christi *f* • imitation of Christ *(rel)* < W 685

Nachfolgebewegung *f* • successor movement *(gep)*

Nachfolgeorganisation *f* • successor organization *(pol)*

Nachfrage *f* • demand *(eco)* < Angebot und Nachfrage

Nachfrageseite *f* • demand side *(eco)*

nachfühlen • to feel with, to sympathize with *(psy)* < Einfühlungsvermögen

Nachgeborenen, die *pl* • future generations *(soc, eth)* → nachkommende Generationen < Nachwelt

nachgelassene Schriften *pl* • posthumous writings *(gen)*

nachgeordnet • subordinate *(gen)*

nachgeordnetes Ziel *n* • sub-goal *(dec)*

nachhaltiges Wachstum *n* • sustainable growth *(eco)*

nachhaltige Wirtschaft *f* • sustainable economy *(eco)* < Nachhaltigkeit

Nachhaltigkeit *f* • sustainability *(eco)*

nachindustrielle Gesellschaft *f* • post-industrial society *(Bell) (his, soc)* → postindustrielle Gesellschaft

nachkommende Generationen *pl* • future generations *(soc, eth)* → Nachgeborenen, die < Nachwelt, intergenerationelle Gerechtigkeit

Nachkriegsphilosophie *f* • post-war philosophy *(gep)*

Nachkriegszeit *f* • post-war period *(pol)* ↔ Vorkriegszeit

Nachlaß, wissenschaftlicher *m* • unpublished scientific works, scientific nachlass *(gen)*

nachmetaphysisches Denken *n* • postmetaphysical thought *(met)* < Ende der Metaphysik, < W 686

Nachprüfbarkeit *f* • verifiability *(sci)* < Verifizierbarkeit

Nachprüfung *f* • verification *(sci)*

Nachrichtennetz *n* • communication network *(tec)* < Informationsgesellschaft

Nachrichtensperre *f* • news embargo *(pol)* < Zensur

Nachrüstungsbeschluß *m* • rearmament decision *(pol)* < Aufrüstung

Nachsicht *f* • leniency, indulgence, forebearance *(eth)*

Nachsicht, Recht auf *n* • right to forbearance *(jur)*

Nachsichtigkeitsprinzip *n* • principle of charity *(Wilson, Quine) (lan)* → Prinzip der Nachsicht

Nächste, der *m* • fellow-man, neighbour *(rel, soc)*

Nächstenliebe *f* • love of one's neighbour/fellow-man *(rel, eth)* < Altruismus, Feindesliebe, Menschenliebe

Nächstenliebe, christliche *f* • Christian love of one's neighbour, (Christian) charity *(rel)* → Agape

nächstfolgend • next in order *(gen)*

nächsthöher • next in rank *(gen)*

nachtechnische Gesellschaft *f* • post-technological society *(Marcuse)* *(soc, tec)*

Nachteil *m* • disadvantage *(gen)* < Benachteiligung, soziale

Nachtseiten der menschlichen Existenz *pl* • the dark side(s) of human existence *(Jung)* *(met)*

Nachtwächterstaat *m* • caretaker/nightwatchman state *(pol)* < Minimalstaat

Nachwahrscheinlichkeit *f* • posterior probability *(rel)*

Nachweis *m* • proof, evidence *(log, sci)*

Nachwelt *f* • posterity *(his)* < nachkommende Generationen

Nachwirkung *f* • after-effect, consequence *(gep)* < Langzeitwirkung, Nebenfolge

Nachwirkungsfreiheit *f* • freedom from after-effects *(mat)*

nackte Tatsachen *pl* • bare facts *(sci)*

Nadelstreifsozialismus *m* • pinstripe socialism, bankers' socialism *(pol)* < Salonbolschewismus

Nähe *f* • nearness *(Heidegger)* *(ont)*, vicinity *(gen)*

Nähe, menschliche *f* • human closeness/intimacy *(eth)*

Nähe zu Gott *f* • proximity to God *(rel)*

Näherung *f* • approximation *(mat)* < Annäherungstheorie an die Wahrheit

Näherungsverfahren *n* • approximation technique *(mat)*

Näherungswert *m* • approximative/approximate value *(mat)*

Nahrungskette *f* • food chain *(nat)*

Nahziel *n* • short-term/immediate goal *(dec)*

naiver Determinismus *m* • naive determinism *(met)*

naiver Realismus *m* • naive realism *(epi, met, aes)*

Name *m* • name *(lan)*

Namenstheorie der Sprache *f* • name-relation theory of language, naming theory of language *(lan)*

narrative Kunst *f* • narrative art *(aes)*

narrativer Code *m* • narrative code *(aes, lan)*

Narrativität *f* • narrativity *(aes)*

Narzißmus *m* • narcissism, narcissm *(psy)* → Eigenliebe

Nash-Gleichgewicht *n* • Nash-equilibrium *(eco)*

Nationalbewußtsein *n* • national consciousness *(pol)*

nationale Bewegung *f* • national movement *(pol)*

nationale Identität *f* • national identity *(pol)*

nationaler Geist *m* • national spirit *(Fichte, Hegel etc)* *(pol)*

nationales Interesse *n* • national interest *(pol)*

Nationalgeist *m* • national spirit *(Hegel)* *(met)*

Nationalisierung *f* • nationalization *(eco, pol)* → Verstaatlichung

Nationalismus *m* • nationalism *(pol)*

Nationalitätsprinzip *n* • principle of nationality *(pol)*

Nationalökonomie *f* • political economy *(eco)* → Politische Ökonomie, Volkswirtschaftslehre

Nationalsozialismus *m* • National Socialism *(pol)* → Nazismus < Faschismus

Nationalstaat *m* • nation state, nation, state *(pol)*

Nativismus *m* • nativism *(nat, psy)* < Angeborenheit; Ideen, angeborene; instinktivangeborene Verhaltensweisen

Natur, anorganische *f* • inorganic nature *(nat)*

Natur, Aufgehen in der *n* • absorption in nature *(Rousseau etc)* *(met)*

Natur der Sache *f* • nature of things *(gen)*

Natur des Menschen, ursprüngliche *f* • original nature of man *(ant)*

Natur des Menschen, wahre *f* • true nature of man *(ant, met)*

Natur des Schönen *f* • the nature of beauty/the beautiful *(Kant)* *(aes)*

Natur, entgeistigte *f* • despiritualized nature *(Feuerbach, Schelling)* *(met)*

Natur Gottes, nachfolgende *f* • God's consequent nature *(Whitehead)* *(met)*

Natur Gottes, ursprüngliche *f* • primordial nature of God *(rel, met)*

Natur zum Göttlichen, Beziehung der *f* • relation of nature to Deity/the Divine *(Eckhart)* *(rel)*

Natur-Konvention-Gegensatz *m* • opposition between nature and convention, nature-convention-contradiction *(soc)* → Natur oder Kultur

Natur-Kultur-Kontroverse *f* • nature-culture-controversy *(psy, ant)*

Natur, objektive *f* • objective nature *(Marx etc)* *(met)*

Natur oder Kultur *f,f* • nature versus nurture, heredity versus environment *(psy)* < Angeborenheit

Natur, organische *f* • organic nature *(nat)*

197

Natur, Vergeistigung der *f* • spiritualization of nature *(Plotinus) (met)*

Natur, Zweckmäßigkeit der *f* • finality/purposiveness of nature *(met, nat)* → Naturteleologie

natura naturans *f* • *nt*, self-creating nature *(Spinoza) (met)*

natura naturata *f* • *nt*, created nature *(Spinoza) (met)*

Naturalbezüge *pl* • payment/remuneration in kind *(eco)* < Naturaltausch

naturalisierte Erkenntnistheorie *f* • naturalized epistemology *(Quine, Goldman) (epi)* → naturalistische Erkenntnistheorie

Naturalismus *m* • naturalism *(ant, met, aes)*

Naturalismus, ethischer *m* • ethical naturalism *(eth)*

naturalistische Analyse *f* • naturalistic analysis *(met, aes)*

naturalistische Darstellung *f* • naturalistic depiction *(aes)*

naturalistische Erkenntnistheorie *f* • naturalistic epistemology *(Quine, Goldman) (epi)*

naturalistische Methode *f* • naturalist(ic) method *(Kant) (epi, sci)*

naturalistische Philosophie *f* • naturalistic philosophy *(gep)*

naturalistischer Fehlschluß *m* • naturalistic fallacy *(Moore) (eth)* < Sein-Sollen-Metabasis

Naturaltausch *m* • barter *(eco)* < Tauschwirtschaft

Naturalwirtschaft *f* • barter economy *(eco)*

Naturanlagen *pl* • natural dispositions *(nat, ant)*

Naturauffassung *f* → Naturbegriff

Naturbande *pl* • bonds of nature *(ant, met)*

Naturbedingungen *pl* • natural conditions *(nat, gep)*

Naturbegriff *m* • idea/concept(ion) of nature *(met)*

Naturbeherrschung *f* • mastery of nature *(nat, tec)*

Naturbeobachtung *f* • observation of nature *(nat, sci)*

Naturbetrachtung *f* • contemplation of nature *(aes)*

Naturdialektik *f* → Dialektik der Natur

Nature-nurture-Kontroverse *f* → Natur-Kultur-Kontroverse

Natureingriff *m* • interference with nature *(nat, env)*

Naturerkenntnis *f* • knowledge of nature *(epi, nat)* < Naturverstehen < W 1067

Naturerscheinung *f* • natural phenomenon *(nat)*

Naturforschung *f* → Naturwissenschaften

Naturgeist *m* • natural spirit *(met)*

Naturgeschichte *f* • natural history *(nat, his)* < W 40

Naturgesetz *n* • natural law, law of nature *(nat)* < physikalisches Gesetz

Naturgesetz, moralisches *n* • moral natural law *(eth)*

Naturgesetze, ewige *pl* • eternal laws of nature *(nat)*

Naturgrund *m* • natural ground *(Kant) (epi, nat)*

Naturhäßliche, das *n* • the ugly by nature *(Rosenkranz) (aes)* < Ästhetik des Häßlichen

Naturismus *m* • naturism *(aes, cul)* < Kulturismus, Lebensreformbewegung

Naturkatastrophe *f* • natural disaster/catastrophe *(nat)*

Naturkausalität *f* • causality in nature, natural causality *(Leibniz etc) (met)*

Naturkraft *f* • natural force *(nat, met)*

Naturkräfte *pl* • forces of nature, elements *(nat, met)*

Naturlehre *f* • doctrine of nature *(met, nat)* → Naturphilosophie

natürliche Abbildung *f* • natural projection/mapping *(mat)*

natürliche Auslese *f* • natural selection *(Darwin, Wallace) (nat)* → natürliche Selektion < Kampf ums Dasein

natürliche Autorität *f* • natural authority *(psy)* < Charisma

natürliche Dialektik *f* • natural dialectic *(Kant) (epi)*

natürliche Einstellung *f* • natural attitude *(Husserl etc) (epi, met)*

natürliche Erkenntnis *f* • natural knowledge/cognition *(epi, rel)*

natürliche Freiheit *f* • natural liberty *(Rousseau) (pol)* → ursprüngliche Freiheit

natürliche Geometrie *f* • natural geometry *(mat)*

natürliche Gerechtigkeit *f* • natural justice *(eth)*

natürliche Gutheit *f* • natural goodness *(Rousseau) (eth)*

natürliche Illusion *f* • natural illusion *(Kant) (epi)*

natürliche Lebensgrundlage *f* • natural basis of life *(nat)*

natürliche Ordnung *f* • natural order *(met)* < Naturrecht

natürliche Organisation f • natural organization (sys)

natürliche Rechte pl • natural rights (eth) < Naturrecht

natürliche Religion f • natural religion (Suárez, Cherbury etc) (rel) → natürliche Theologie < Deismus

natürliche Ressourcen pl • natural resources (eco)

natürliche Selektion f • natural selection (Darwin, Wallace) (nat) → natürliche Auslese < Kampf ums Dasein

natürliche Sprache f • natural language (lan) → Normalsprache

natürliche Systeme pl • natural systems (sys)

natürliche Theologie f • natural theology (Suárez) (rel) → natürliche Religion < Deismus

natürliche Ungleichheit f • natural inequality (eth, soc), (Leibniz) (epi, met)

natürliche Vielfalt f • natural variety (nat, env) < Artenvielfalt

natürliche Zahl f • natural number (mat)

natürlicher Automat, Körper als m • the body as natural automaton (Descartes) (nat, met) < Maschinenmensch

natürlicher Grund m • natural ground (met)

natürlicher Kriegszustand m • natural state of war (Hobbes) (soc)

natürlicher Logarithmus m • natural logarithm (mat)

natürlicher Prozeß m • natural process (nat) < Naturprozeß

natürliches Ganzes n • natural whole (ont)

natürliches Licht n • light of nature, natural light (Augustine, Aquinas etc) (rel, met) → lumen naturale

Natürlichkeit f • naturalness (nat, aes)

Naturmechanismus m • mechanism of/in nature (nat)

Naturmensch m • primitive man, child of nature (Rousseau) (cul, soc)

Naturmetaphysik f • metaphysics of nature (Schelling) (met)

Naturnotwendigkeit f • natural necessity (nat, met)

Naturordnung f • natural order (nat, met)

Naturphilosophie f • naturphilosophie (Schelling), natural philosophy, philosophy of nature, nature-philosophy (met, nat) < W 288, 481

Naturprozeß m • natural/physical process (nat, sys)

Naturrecht n • natural law/right, law of nature (jur, eth) → ius naturale < ursprüngliche Rechte < W 409, 693, 694, 695, 696

Naturrechtslehre f • doctrine of natural law/right (jur, eth)

Naturrechtstradition f • tradition of natural law/right (jur, eth)

Naturreligion f • natural religion (rel)

Naturschönes n • the naturally beautiful, natural beauty (Hegel etc) (aes) ↔ Geistschönes

Naturschönheit f • the beauty of nature (aes)

Naturschutz m • (nature) conservation (env) → Umweltschutz

Natursprache f • natural/original language (Böhme etc) (lan) ↔ Kunstsprache

Naturstudium n • study of nature (nat, aes)

Naturteleologie f • teleology of nature (met) → Natur, Zweckmäßigkeit der < Naturzweck, Bestimmung der Natur

Naturverehrung f • nature worship (rel, cul)

Naturverstehen n • understanding of nature (met, nat)

Naturvolk n • primitive people (cul)

Naturvollkommenheit f • perfection of nature (Kant) (nat, met)

Naturwesen n • creature of nature (nat, ant)

naturwidrig • unnatural, against nature, contrary to nature (gen)

Naturwissenschaft(en) f(pl) • (natural) science(s) (nat) ↔ Geisteswissenschaften

naturwissenschaftliche Ethik f • scientific ethics (eth, sci)

naturwissenschaftliche Methode f • scientific method (sci)

naturwüchsige Produktionsinstrumente pl • natural instruments/means of production (Marx) (eco)

Naturzeit f • natural time (nat) < Realzeit

Naturzustand m • natural state, state of nature (Hobbes, Rousseau etc) (soc, pol) → status naturalis < ursprünglicher Zustand, vertragsfreier Zustand, vorbürgerlicher Zustand des Menschen

Naturzustand, reiner m • condition of mere nature (Hobbes etc) (soc, pol)

Naturzweck m • goal/purpose of nature (met) < Naturteleologie

Naziherrschaft f • Nazi rule (pol)

Nazismus m • Nazism (pol) → Nationalsozialismus < Faschismus

Nebenabsicht f • secondary object/goal, ulterior motive (act, eth)

Nebenbedeutung f • connotation, secondary meaning (lan) → Konnotation

Nebeneffekt m → Nebenwirkung

Nebenfolge f • side-effect, spin-off effect (gep) → Nebenwirkung < Nachwirkung

Nebenklasse f • residue class, co-set (mat)

Nebenursache f • secondary cause (met, sci)

Nebenwirkung f • side-effect, spin-off effect (gep) → Nebenfolge

Nebularhypothese f • nebular hypothesis (Kant, Laplace) (nat, met) → Kant-Laplace-Hypothese < Kosmogonie

Negation f • negation (log, mat)

Negation, abstrakte f • abstract negation (log)

Negation als Mangel f • negation as lack (Kant) (epi, log)

Negation, aussagenlogische f • propositional negation (log, lan) < Negation, kontradiktorische

Negation, bloße f • mere negation (Rickert) (log)

Negation der Negation f • negation of the negation (Hegel) (met) < doppelte Negation, Aufhebung, dialektischer Dreischritt

Negation der Negativität f • negation of negativity (Marcuse) (soc, pol)

Negation, immanente f • immanent negation (Adorno) (log, soc)

Negation, kontradiktorische f • contradictory negation (log)

Negation, reine f • pure negation (Sartre) (met)

Negation, schwache f • weak negation (Wright) (log)

Negation, starke f • strong negation (Wright) (log)

Negation, unendliche f • eternal negation (Kierkegaard) (met)

negationsfreie Mathematik f → positive Mathematik

Negationsoperator m • negation connective/operator/function (log)

negativ definit • negative definite (mat)

negativ korreliert • negatively correlated (mat)

Negativbilanz f • negative outcome/result/balance (act)

negative Anthropologie f • negative anthropology (ant)

negative Bedingung f • negative condition (epi, log)

negative Dialektik f • negative dialectics (Adorno) (met, soc) < W 697

negative Einkommensteuer f • negative income tax (eco) < arbeitsloses Grundeinkommen

negative Empfindung f • negative sensation (Wundt) (psy)

negative Entropie f • negative entropy, negentropy (nat, sys) → Negentropie

negative Erziehung f • negative education (Rousseau) (psy)

negative Freiheit f • negative freedom (Kant etc) (met) → Freiheit von

negative Größe f • negative magnitude (Kant) (epi)

negative Korrelation f • negative correlation (mat)

negative Pflicht f • negative duty (Kant etc) (eth)

negative Rückkoppelung f • negative feedback (sys)

negative Theologie f • negative theology (Aquinas, Barth) (rel)

negative Verstärkung f • negative reinforcement (psy) ↔ positive Verstärkung

negatives Bevölkerungswachstum n • negative population growth, NPG (pol)

negatives Nichts n • negative nothing (Kant) (epi, met)

negatives Wachstum n • negative growth (mat, sys)

negatives Wahrheitskriterium n • negative criterion of truth (epi, met)

negatives Wesen der Notwendigkeit n • negative essence of necessity (Scheler) (met)

negatives Wohlgefallen n • negative pleasure/delight (Kant) (aes) ↔ positives Wohlgefallen

Negativität f • negativity (met)

Negator m • negator, negation connective (log)

Negentropie f • negentropy (sys) → negative Entropie ↔ Entropie

Neid m • envy (eth)

Neigung f • pitch (mat), inclination (Kant) (eth) ↔ Pflicht; propensity, inclination, tendency (psy) < Neigungsstruktur

Neigung, Handlung aus f • acting by/out of inclination (Kant) (eth)

Neigung und Pflicht f,f • inclination and duty (Kant etc) (eth)

Neigungsstruktur f • propensity structure (Popper) (sci)

neinsagende Haltung zum Leben f • no-saying/negative attitude to life (Nietzsche) (met) < Lebensverneinung

Nekromanie f → Nekrophilie

Nekromantie f • necromancy (eth, eso)

Nekrophilie f • necrophilia (Fromm etc) (psy) ↔ Biophilie < Todestrieb

Nemesis f • Atrastea (eth) < ausgleichende Gerechtigkeit

Nennwert *m* • nominal value *(eco)* →
Nominalwert

Neo-Darwinismus *m* • Neo-Darwinism *(nat, ant)*

Neofaschismus *m* • Neo-Fascism *(pol)*

Neo-Freudianismus *m* • Neo-Freudianism *(psy)*

Neogotik *f* • Neo-Gothic style *(aes)*

Neo-Hegelianismus *m* • Neo-Hegelianism *(met)*

Neo-Instrumentalismus *m* • neo-instrumentalism *(sci)*

neokantianische Philosophie *f* • Neo-Kantian philosophy *(gep)* → Neukantianismus

Neo-Kantianismus *m* • Neo-Kantianism *(gep)* → Neukantianismus

neoklassische Wirtschaftstheorie *f* • neo-classical economic theory *(eco)*

Neoklassizismus *m* • Neo-classicism *(aes)*

Neokolonialismus *m* • neo-colonialism *(pol)*

Neokonfuzianismus *m* • Neo-Confucianism *(asp)*

Neokonservati(vi)smus *m* • neo-conservatism *(pol)*

Neoliberalismus *m* • neo-liberalism *(pol, eco)*

neolithische Revolution *f* • Neolithic Revolution *(Childe)* *(ant, his)*

Neologismus *m* • neologism *(lan)*

Neo-Malthusianismus *m* • Neo-Malthusianism *(eco, soc)*

Neo-Marxismus *m* • Neo-Marxism *(gep, pol)* < Neue Linke

Neoplatonismus *m* • Neo-Platonism *(Plotinus etc)* *(gep)*

Neopositivismus *m* • neopositivism *(gep)*

neopragmatische Erkenntnistheorie *f* • neopragmatic epistemology *(epi)*

Neopragmatismus *m* • neopragmatism *(Pierce)* *(epi, met)*

Neo-Pythagoräismus *m* • Neo-Pythagoreanism *(gep)*

Neorealismus *m* • neo-realism *(aes)* < Neoverismus

Neo-Scholastik *f* • Neo-Scholasticism *(gep)*

Neostoizismus *m* • neo-stoicism *(his)*

Neothomismus *m* • Neo-Thomism *(gep)*

Neoverismus *m* • neo-verism(o) *(aes)* < Neorealismus

Neovitalismus *m* • neo-vitalism *(Driesch)* *(nat, met)*

Nepotismus *m* • nepotism *(pol, soc)*

Nesthocker, sekundärer *m* • secondary nidicolous animal *(Portmann)* *(ant)* < Spätentwickler

Nettoertrag *m* • net benefit *(eco)*

Netz, logisches *n* • logical net *(log)*

netzförmig • net-like *(sys)*

Netzwerk *n* • network *(sys, soc)*

Neuaristotelismus *m* • Neo-Aristotelianism, Neo-Aristotelism *(gep)*

Neubewertung *f* • reevaluation *(gep)* < Umwertung

neue Armut *f* • new poverty *(eco, soc)* < Schere, soziale; Zweidrittelgesellschaft

Neue Internationale Wirtschaftsordnung *f* • New International Economic Order, NIEO *(pol, eco)*

Neue Linke *f* • New Left *(pol)*

Neue Rechte *f* • New Right *(pol)*

Neue Sachlichkeit *f* • New Objectivity, New Matter-of-Factness *(aes)*

neue Technologien *pl* • new technologies *(tec)*

neue Weltordnung *f* • new world order *(pol)*

Neue Wissenschaft *f* • New Science *(sci)* < W 708, 827

Neuerungssucht *f* • mania/passion for innovation *(psy)*

neues Bewußtsein *n* • new consciousness *(soc)*

neues Problem der Induktion *n* • new riddle/ problem of induction *(Goodman)* *(sci, epi)*

neuester Stand *m* • state of the art *(gep)*

Neufichteanismus *m* • Neo-Fichteanism *(his)*

Neugier *f* • curiosity *(psy)* < Staunen, philosophisches

Neuhegelianer *m* • Neo-Hegelian *(gep)* → Junghegelianer, Linkshegelianer ↔ Althegelianer

Neuheidentum *n* • neopaganism *(Rahner)* *(rel)*

Neukantianismus *m* • Neo-Kantianism *(epi, met)* → Neo-Kantianismus, neokantianische Philosophie

Neuorganisation des diskursiven Feldes *f* • reorganization of the discursive field *(Foucault)* *(epi, lan, pol)*

Neuorientierung *f* • reorientation *(gen)*

neurale Netzwerke *pl* • neural networks *(nat, min)*

Neureicher *m* • nouveau riche *(eco, soc)*

Neurobiologie *f* • neurobiology *(nat)*

neuronale Kommunikation *f* • neural communication *(nat)* ↔ metabolische Kommunikation

neuronales Netz *n* • neural net(work) *(AI, min)* < Konnektionismus

Neurophilosophie *f* • neurophilosophy *(min, AI)*

Neuropsychologie *f* • neuropsychology *(nat, psy)*

neurotisches Arrangement *n* • neurotic arrangement *(Adler) (psy)*

Neurowissenschaft *f* • neuroscience *(nat)*

Neusprech *n* • Newspeak *(Orwell) (pol)*

Neustik *f* • neustic *(Hare) (eth, lan)* ↔ Phrastik

neutrales Element *n* • neutral/identity element *(mat)*

Neutralisierung *f* • neutralization *(gep)*

Neutralismus, methodischer *m* • methodical neutralism *(Carnap) (log, lan)*

Neutralitätserklärung *f* • declaration of neutrality *(pol)*

Neutralitätspolitik *f* • policy of neutrality *(pol)*

Neutralitätsthese *f* • neutrality thesis *(eth)* < Metaethik

Neuwert *m* • additional value *(eco)* < Mehrwert

Neuzeit *f* • modern age *(his)*

neuzeitlich • modern *(gen)*

New Age *n* • nt (*eso)*

New Criticism *m* • nt *(Springarn) (aes)*

New Edge *n* • nt *(his)*

New Wave *n/f* • New Wave, nouvelle vague *(aes)*

Newtons zweites Prinzip *n* • Newton's second principle *(nat)*

Newtonsche Formel *f* • Newton's formula *(Newton) (nat)* < Binomialsatz

Newtonsche Mechanik *f* • Newtonian mechanics *(Newton) (nat)* → klassische Mechanik

Newtonsche Physik *f* • Newtonian physics *(nat)*

Newtonsches Näherungsverfahren *n* • Newton's approximation method *(nat)*

Nexus *m* → Verknüpfung

Nichtanerkennung *f* • non-acknowledgement *(Hegel) (met)* ↔ Anerkennung

Nichtangriffspakt *m* • non-aggression pact *(pol)*

Nichtbefriedigung *f* • nonsatisfaction *(psy)* < Frustration

Nichtbestehen *n* • non-existence, non-obtaining *(ont, epi)*

nicht-doxastischer Glaube(n) *m* • non-doxastic belief *(sci)* → wissenschaftlicher Glaube(n)

Nichteinmischung *f* • non-intervention *(pol)*

Nichteintritt eines Ereignisses *m* • non-occurrence of an event *(sci)* ↔ Eintritt eines Ereignisses

nichten • to nichten/nihilate/noth° *(Heidegger) (ont)*

nichterneuerbare Ressourcen *pl* • non-renewable resources *(env)*

nicht-euklidische Geometrie *f* • non-Euclidean geometry *(mat)*

nichtexistentielle Wahrheit *f* • non-existential truth *(epi)*

Nichtexistenz *f* • non-existence *(met)*

Nichtexistenz, Weisen der *pl* • modes/forms of the non-existent *(Duns Scotus) (met)*

nichtexistierende Gegenstände *pl* • non-existent objects *(ont)*

nicht-extensional • non-extensional *(log)*

nichtfigurative Kunst *f* • non-figurative art *(aes)* → abstrakte Kunst, gegenstandslose Kunst

Nicht-Gesagte, das *n* • the unsaid *(Foucault) (lan)*

nichtgewaltsame Handlung *f* • nonviolent action *(eth, act)*

Nichthandeln *n* • non-action, failure to act *(act)* < Unterlassung

nicht-hinreichende Ursache *f* • deficient/non-sufficient cause *(met)* → causa deficiens ↔ hinreichende Ursache

Nicht-Ich *n* • non-ego, not-self *(Fichte) (met)*

nichtidentisch • non-identical *(log)*

Nichtidentität *f* • non-identity *(log, met)* < Differenz

nichtig • vain, idle, invalid *(gen)*

Nichtigkeit *f* • nullity *(Heidegger) (ont), (jur)*

Nichtigkeitserklärung *f* • declaration of nullity, annulment, nullification, defeasance *(jur, pol)*

nicht-inferentieller Bericht *m* • non-inferential report *(Davidson) (lan)*

nicht-kooperatives Spiel *n* • non-cooperative game *(dec)* < Spieltheorie

nichtkreative Abkürzungsdefinition *f* • non-creative abbreviation definition *(log, lan)*

Nichtkreativität *f* • non-creativity *(log, lan)*

nichtlineares System *n* • non-linear system *(mat, sys)*

nichtmenschliches Tier *n* • nonhuman animal *(eth, ant)* < Mensch

nicht-monotoner Schluß *m* • nonmonotonic inference *(log)*

Nicht-Monotonizität *f* • non-monotonicity *(log)*

nichtparametrischer Test *m* • non-parametric test *(mat)*

nichtparametrisches Verfahren *n* • non-parametric method *(mat)*

nichträumliches Ding *n* • nonspatial thing *(ont)*

Nichts *n* • nothingness, the naught *(Sartre, Jaspers) (ont)*, Nothing, nothingness *(Heidegger) (ont)*, non-being *(Democritus, Hegel) (ont)* ↔ Etwas, Sein < W 891; *(asp)* < Nirwana

Nichtseiende, das *n* • the non-existent, the non-being *(ont)*

nichtseiende Gegenstände *pl* • non-existent objects *(Meinong) (ont)*

Nichtsein *n* • non-being, non-existence *(ont)*

nichtsinnliche Anschauung *f* • nonsensible intuition *(Kant) (epi)*

Nicht-Standardmodell *n* • non-standard model *(sci, log)* < Prädikatenlogik

Nicht-Standard-Zahlentheorie *f* • nonstandard number theory *(mat)*

nicht-teilnehmende Beobachtung *f* • nonparticipant observation *(sci)* ↔ teilnehmende Beobachtung

Nichtübereinstimmung *f* → Inkongruenz

nichtverallgemeinerungsfähiges Interesse *n* • nongeneralizable interest *(Habermas) (eth, soc)*

nichtverbale Kommunikation *f* • non-verbal communication *(lan)*

Nichtverhaftetheit *f* • non-attachment *(asp)*

Nichtverursachung *f* • noncausation *(met)*

Nichtvorhandensein *n* • absence, non-existence, unavailability *(ont)*

nichtwahrheitsfunktional • non-truth-functional *(Quine) (epi, lan)*

Nicht-Widerspruchsprinzip *n* → Prinzip der Widerspruchsfreiheit

Nichtwissen *n* • ignorance, nescience *(epi)* → Agnosie < Agnostizismus

Nichtwollen *n* • non-volition *(psy, eth)*

Nicodsche Funktion *f* • Nicod's function *(log)*

Nicolaus Cusanus → Nikolaus von Kues

Niedergang *m* • decline *(his, cul)*

Niedergang der Moral *m* • decline of morality, moral decadence *(eth)* < Werteverlust

Niedergang des Menschen *m* • man's downfall *(Rousseau) (soc)*

Niedergang des Sozialismus *m* • decline of socialism *(pol)*

Niedergangstheorien *pl* • theories of decadence *(Spengler, Ortega y Gassset etc) (cul, his)* < Untergang des Abendlandes

niedergehende Kulturen *pl* • declining cultures *(cul, his)*

Niederlassungsfreiheit *f* • freedom of movement and settlement *(pol)* → Freizügigkeit < Bewegungsfreiheit

Niemand *m* • the nobody *(Heidegger) (ont)*

Niemandsland *n* • no man's land *(jur)* < Okkupationstheorie

Nietzscheanismus *m* • Nietzscheanism *(gep)*

Nihilismus *m* • nihilism *(met, eth)*

Nikolaus von Kues • Nicholas of Cusa, Nicolaus Cusanus

Nikomachische Ethik *f* • Nicomachean Ethics *(Aristotle) (eth)* < W 714

Nirwana *n* • nirvana *(asp)*

Nirwanaprinzip *n* • Nirvana principle *(Low, Freud) (psy)*

Nivellierung *f* • levelling *(soc)*

Noch-Nicht, das *n* • the not-yet *(Heidegger) (ont)*

Noch-Nicht-Bewußtes *n* • the non-yet-conscious *(Bloch) (met, soc)*

Noch-Nicht-Sein *n* • the not-yet-being *(ont)*, the as-yet-unrealized *(Bloch) (met, his)* < Vorschein

Noema *n* • noema, intentional object of thinking *(Husserl) (epi, met)*

Noematik *f* • noematics *(epi, min)*

Noesis *f* • noesis, intentional act of thinking *(Husserl) (epi, met)*

Noetik *f* • noetics *(log, epi)*

noetische Analyse *f* • noetic analysis *(Husserl) (epi, met)*

Nolens-Volens-Haltung *f* • like it or not attitude *(act)*

Nomadengesellschaft *f* • nomadic society *(cul, soc)*

Nomadismus *m* • nomadism *(cul, soc)* < Nomadengesellschaft

Nomenklatur *f* • nomenclature *(sci, lan)*

Nomenklatura *f* • nomenclatura *(Lenin) (pol)*

nomina ante res *pl* • *nt (epi)* < Universalienstreit

nomina post res *pl* • *nt (epi)* < Universalienstreit

Nominalausdruck *m* • name/noun expression, noun phrase *(lan)* < Name

Nominaldefinition *f* • nominal definition *(log, lan)*

Nominalismus *m* • nominalism *(ont, lan)* ↔ Konzeptualismus, Begriffsrealismus < Universalienstreit

nominalistisch • nominalist(ic) *(ont, lan)*

nominalistische Sprachtheorie *f* • nominalist theory of language *(lan)*

Nominalskala *f* • nominal scale *(mat)*

Nominalwert *m* • nominal value *(eco)* → Nennwert

Nominator *m* • nominator *(log, lan)* → Nominalausdruck

Nomismus *m* • nomism *(jur, rel)*

Nomokratie *f* • nomocracy *(jur, pol)*

Nomologie *f* • nomology *(log, epi, jur)*

nomologische Wissenschaft *f* • nomological science *(sci)*

nomos *m* • nt, law, rule, custom, convention *(eth)* → Gesetz, Sitte

Nomothetik der Natur *f* • nomothetic of nature *(Kant) (epi, nat)*

nomothetische Methode *f* • nomothetic method *(Windelband) (sci)*

nomothetische Wissenschaft *f* • nomothetic science *(Windelband) (sci)* ↔ idiographische Wissenschaft

non sequitur • non-sequitur *(log)*

Nonexistenz *f* • non-existence *(met)* → Nichtexistenz

nonfigurative Kunst *f* → nichtfigurative Kunst

nonfigurativer Gegensatz *m* • non-figurative opposition/contrast *(log)*

Non-Kognitivismus *m* • non-cognitivism *(epi, eth)* ↔ Kognitivismus < Emotivismus

Nonkonformismus *m* • nonconformism *(psy, soc)*

Nonproliferation *f* • non-proliferation *(pol)*

Nonsens *m* • nonsense *(log, lan)*

Non-statement-view von Theorien • non-statement view of theories *(Sneed, Stegmüller) (sci)* < Ramsey-Elimination

nonverbale Kommunikation *f* • non-verbal communication *(lan)*

Noologie *f* • noology *(Plato, Leibniz, Eucken) (met)*

Nord-Süd-Dialog *m* • North-South dialogue *(pol)*

Nord-Süd-Gefälle *n* • North-South divide *(pol)* < wirtschaftliches Ungleichgewicht

Norm *f* • norm *(eth, mat, tec)*

Normalabweichung *f* → Standardabweichung

normale Wissenschaft *f* • normal/ordinary science *(Kuhn) (sci)* < revolutionäre Wissenschaft

normalen Sprache, Philosophie der *f* • philosophy of ordinary language, ordinary language philosophy, OLP *(lan)*

Normalfall *m* • normal case *(gen)*

Normalform *f* • normal form *(log, lan)* < Hessesche Normalform

Normalgleichung *f* • normal equation *(mat)*

Normalisierung *f* • normalisation *(gen)*

Normalität *f* • normality, normalcy *(gen)*

Normalmensch *m* • ordinary man *(soc)* → Durchschnittsmensch

Normalreihe *f* • normal series *(mat)*

Normalsinnigkeit *f* • ordinary suitableness, soundness of mind *(epi, psy)* < Konsenstheorie der Wahrheit

Normalsprache *f* • ordinary language *(log, lan)* → natürliche Sprache ↔ Formalsprache, Idealsprache < Kunstsprache

Normalverbraucher *m* • avarage consumer *(eco)*

Normalverteilung *f* • normal/standard/ Gaussian distribution *(Quetelét) (mat)* → Gaußsche Verteilung < Gaußsche Kurve

Normalverteilung, logarithmische *f* • lognormal distribution *(mat)*

Normalwissenschaft *f* • normal science *(Kuhn etc) (sci)* ↔ revolutionäre Wissenschaft

Normalzahl *f* • normal number *(mat)*

Normalzeit *f* • standard time *(Bergson) (ont)* < Realzeit; Zeit, immanente

normativ • normative, evaluative *(eth, sci, lan)*

normative Aussage *f* • normative statement *(lan, sci)* → Wertaussage

normative Begründung *f* • normative justification *(sci)*

normative Ethik *f* • normative ethics *(eth)* → präskriptive Ethik

normative Geltung *f* • normative validity *(Weber) (eth, soc)*

normative Ordnung *f* • normative order *(eth, soc)* < präskriptive Ethik

normative Philosophie *f* • normative philosophy *(eth, gep)*

normative Wissenschaft *f* • normative science *(sci, eth)*

normativer Irrationalismus *m* • normative irrationalism *(gep)*

normativer Relativismus *m* • normative relativism *(eth)* < deskriptiver Relativismus

normativer Satz *m* • normative sentence/ statement *(eth, lan)*

normatives Sollen *n* • normative ought *(eth)*

Normativismus *m* • normativism *(eth, met)*

Normativität *f* • normativity *(eth, soc)*

Normbefolgung *f* • compliance with a norm *(act, eth, jur)* < Regelbefolgung

normdeskriptive Sätze *pl* • norm-descriptive sentences *(lan, eth)*

Normenbildung *f* • norm formation *(eth, aes)*

Normenethik *f* • ethics of norms *(eth)*

normengeleitete Interaktion *f* • normatively guided interaction *(Mead, Habermas) (act, soc)*

Normenkonflikt *m* • norm conflict *(eth)*

normenkonform • in conformity with norms *(act, eth)* < regelkonform

normenkonforme Einstellung *f* • attitude in conformity with norms, norm-conforming attitude *(act, eth)*

normenkonformes Verhalten *n* • behaviour in conformity with norms, norm-conforming behaviour *(act, eth)*

Normenkonformität *f* • norm-conformity *(act, eth)*

Normenlogik *f* • logic of norms *(eth)*

normenreguliertes Handeln *n* • normatively regulated action *(Habermas) (act, eth)*

Normenvielfalt *f* • plurality/multiplicity of norms *(eth)*

normexpressive Sätze *pl* • norm-expressive sentences *(lan, eth)*

normgebende Kompetenz *f* • normative/norm-giving competence *(eth, soc)*

Normgeltung *f* • normative validity *(act, eth)*

normgemäß → normenkonform

Normierung *f* • norming, normativization, normative regulation *(eth, soc)*, standardization *(tec)*

normkonformes Verhalten *n* → normenkonformes Verhalten

Normlosigkeit *f* • normlessness *(eth)* < Anomie

Normsatz *m* → normativer Satz

normzentrierte Gesellschaft *f* • norm-centred society *(soc)*

Not *f* • need *(Heidegger) (ont)*

Not, soziale *f* • social need *(soc)*

Not- und Verstandesstaat *m* • state based on need and rationality *(Schiller) (pol)* < Notstaat

Notation *f* • notation *(lan, aes)*

Notation, polnische *f* • Polish reverse/inverse notation *(Lukasiewicz) (log)* < polnische Logik

Notgemeinschaft *f* • community bound by/based on need *(soc)*

Notgesetze *pl* • emergency laws *(jur)*

Nötigung *f* • coercion *(eth, jur)*

Notion *f* • notion *(epi, lan)* → Begriff

notionale Welt *f* • notional world *(epi, met)*

notiones communes *pl* • common notions, general/universal terms *(lan, log)* → Gemeinbegriffe < Allgemeinbegriff

Notlüge *f* • white lie *(eth)*

Notmaßnahme *f* • emergency measure *(act)*

Notstaat *m* • state based on need *(Hegel, Schiller) (pol)* < ↔ Vernunftstaat

Notstandsethik *f* • emergency ethics *(Jonas etc) (eth, env)*

Notverordnung *f* • emergency decree *(jur, pol)*

notwendig • necessary *(gep)*

notwendig wahr • necessarily true *(log, epi)*

notwendige aber nicht hinreichende Bedingung *f* • necessary but not sufficient condition *(log, sci)*

notwendige Bedingung *f* • necessary condition *(log, sci)* → conditio sine qua non ↔ hinreichende Bedingung

notwendige Existenz *f* • necessary existence *(met)*

notwendige und hinreichende Bedingung *f* • necessary and sufficient condition *(log, sci)*

notwendige Verbindung *f* → notwendige Verknüpfung

notwendige Verknüpfung *f* • necessary connection *(Hume etc) (log, epi, met)* < Kausalnexus

notwendige Wahrheit *f* • necessary truth *(log, epi)* → zwingende Wahrheit

notwendiges Wesen, Gott als *m* • God as the necessary essence *(Aristotle etc) (met, rel)* < ontologischer Gottesbeweis

Notwendigkeit *f* • necessity *(log, met)* < W 1349

Notwendigkeit, absolute *f* • absolute necessity *(Aristotle, Hegel) (met)*

Notwendigkeit, analytische *f* • analytic necessity *(log, met)*

Notwendigkeit, äußere *f* • outer/external necessity *(Spinoza, Leibniz) (met)*

Notwendigkeit, bedingte *f* • conditional necessity *(log, met)* → Notwendigkeit, relative

Notwendigkeit, blinde *f* • blind necessity *(Kant) (met)*

Notwendigkeit des Bösen *f* • necessity of evil *(Leibniz) (met)*

Notwendigkeit, hypothetische *f* • hypothetical necessity *(Aristotle etc) (met)*

Notwendigkeit, innere *f* • inner necessity *(Spinoza, Leibniz) (met)*, *(Schönberg) (aes)*

Notwendigkeit, kausal-mechanische *f* • causal-mechanical necessity *(Descartes) (met)*

Notwendigkeit, logische *f* • logical necessity *(log)*

Notwendigkeit, materiale und formale *f* • material and formal necessity *(Kant) (met)*

Notwendigkeit, mathematische *f* • mathematical necessity *(Aquinas etc) (met)*

Notwendigkeit, metaphysische *f* • metaphysical necessity *(Kripke) (met)*

Notwendigkeit, moralische *f* • moral necessity *(Kant) (eth)*

Notwendigkeit, natürliche *f* • natural necessity *(met)*

Notwendigkeit, naturwissenschaftliche *f* •
scientific necessity *(sci)*

Notwendigkeit, objektive *f* • objective
necessity *(epi, met)*

Notwendigkeit, physische *f* • physical
necessity *(met)* < Notwendigkeit, reale

Notwendigkeit, reale *f* • real necessity *(met)*

Notwendigkeit, relative *f* • relative necessity
(log, met) → Notwendigkeit, bedingte

Notwendigkeit, subjektive *f* • subjective
necessity *(epi, met)*

Notwendigkeit, unbedingte *f* • unconditioned/
unconditional necessity *(epi, met)*

Notwendigkeit, zufällige *f* • contingent
necessity *(Hegel etc) (met)*

Notwendigkeit-Zufälligkeit *f* • necessity-
contingency *(Kant etc) (met)*

Notwendigkeitslehre *f* • necessitarianism *(met)*

Notwendigkeitstheorie der Naturgesetze *f* •
necessitarian theory of laws of nature *(sci)*

noumenale Welt *f* • noumenal world *(Kant)*
(epi, met)

Noumenon *n* • noumenon *(Plato, Kant) (epi,
met)* → Ding an sich ↔ Phänomen

Nous *n* → Nus

nouvelle vague *f* • *nt (aes)* → New Wave

nukleare Abrüstung *f* • nuclear disarmament
(pol)

nukleare Endlagerung *f* • permanent disposal
of nuclear waste *(env)*

nuklearer Rüstungsstopp *m* • nuclear freeze
(pol)

nuklearer Schlagabtausch *m* • nuclear clash
(pol)

nuklearer Winter *m* • nuclear winter *(env)* →
atomarer Winter

Nuklearethik *f* • nuclear ethics *(eth)*

Nuklearphysik *f* → Atomphysik

Nuklearstrategie *f* • nuclear strategy *(pol)*
< atomare Abschreckung

Nuklearzeitalter *n* • nuclear age *(tec, his)*

Null *f* • zero, null *(mat, log)*

null und nichtig • null and void *(jur)*

Nullbewußtsein *n* • zero-consciousness *(cul)*

nulldimensionale Substanz *f* • zero-dimension-
al substance *(Brentano) (ont)*

Nullgehalt *m* • zero content *(mat, sci)*

Nullhypothese *f* • null hypothesis *(mat, sci)*
< Alternativhypothese

Nullklasse *f* • null set *(log, mat)*

Nullpunkt *m* • zero point, origin *(mat)*

Nullrelation *f* • null/empty relation *(mat)*

Nullrisiko *n* • zero risk *(dec)*

nullstelliger Ausdruck *m* • no-place expression *(log, lan)*

nullstelliges Prädikat *n* • no-place predicate
(log, lan)

Nullsummenspiel *n* • zero-sum game *(dec)*

Nullvektor *m* • null vector *(mat)*

Nullwachstum *n* • zero growth *(eco)* < negatives Wachstum

Nullwachstum der Bevölkerung *n* • zero
population growth, ZPG *(pol)*

Nullwahrscheinlichkeit *f* • zero probability
(mat)

numerische Analyse *f* • numerical analysis
(mat)

numerische Identität *f* • numerical identity
(mat)

numerische Verschiedenheit *f* • numerical
difference/diversity *(mat)*

Numerologie *f* • numerology *(eso)*

Numinose, das *n* • the noumenal *(met, rel)*

Nürnberger Trichter *m* • royal road to
learning *(epi)*

Nus *n* • nous, mind, intellect *(met, epi)*

Nutzanwendung *f* • practical application *(gen)*

Nutzbarmachung *f* • utilization *(act)*

nutzbringend • profitable *(eco, act)*

Nutzeffekt *m* • useful effect, return(s) *(eco,
dec)*

Nutzen *m* • utility *(gep)*

Nutzen, langfristiger *m* • long-term benefit
(dec)

Nutzenfunktion *f* • utility function *(eco, dec)*

Nutzenmaximierung *f* • utility maximization
(eco, dec, eth)

Nutzentheorie *f* • utility theory *(dec)*

Nutzenvergleich *m* • benefit/utility comparison
(eth, dec) < Kosten-Nutzen-Analyse

Nützlichkeit *f* • utility *(gen)*

Nützlichkeitsdenken *n* • utility thinking,
utilitarianism *(dec, eth, eco)* < Utilitarismus

Nützlichkeitserwägung *f* • utility consideration
(dec, eth, eco)

Nützlichkeitskalkül *m/n* • utility calculus
(Bentham) (dec, eth)

Nützlichkeitsmoral *f* • ethics/morality of utility
(eth)

Nützlichkeitsprinzip *n* • principle of utility,
utility/utilitarian principle *(dec, eth, eco)* →
Utilitätsprinzip

Nutzlosigkeit *f* • uselesness *(gen)*

Nutzungsrecht *n* • right of use *(eco)*

Nutzwert *m* • utility (value) *(eco, dec)* →
Gebrauchswert

O

Oberbegriff *m* • generic term *(log)* ↔ Unterbegriff

obere Erkenntnisvermögen *pl* • higher faculties of knowledge *(Kant) (epi)*

obere Schranke *f* • upper bound *(mat)*

Oberflächen- und Zeichenwelt *f* • surface- and sign-world *(Nietzsche) (lan)*

Oberflächengrammatik *f* • surface grammar *(Wittgenstein) (lan)* ↔ Tiefengrammatik

Oberflächenintegral *n* • surface integral *(mat)*

Oberflächenstruktur *f* • surface structure *(Chomsky) (lan)* ↔ Tiefenstruktur

Oberherrschaft *f* • supremacy *(pol)*

Oberklasse *f* • upper class *(soc)*

Oberprämisse *f* • major premise *(log)* → Obersatz

Obersatz *m* • major premise *(log)* → Oberprämisse

Oberschicht, soziale *f* • upper (social) stratum, high society *(soc)*

oberste Monade *f* • supreme monad *(Leibniz) (met, rel)*

oberster Wertmaßstab *m* • the highest standard of value(s) *(eth)*

oberster Zweck *m* • ultimate aim/goal *(eth)*

oberstes Gut *n* • supreme/highest/prime good *(Aristotle etc) (eth)* → höchstes Gut

oberstes Prinzip der Moralität *n* • supreme principle of morality *(Kant) (eth)*

obiectum materiale *n* → Materialobjekt

Objekt *n* • object *(gep)*

Objekt an sich *n* • object in itself *(Kant) (epi)*

Objekt der Erkenntnis *n* → Erkenntnisobjekt

Objekt des Wissens *n* • object of knowledge *(epi)*

Objekt-Subjekt-Spaltung *f* → Subjekt-Objekt-Spaltung

Objektanalyse *f* • object analysis *(sci)*

Objektbewußtsein *n* • object consciousness *(Abraham) (psy)*

Objektbeziehung *f* • object relation *(Freud etc) (psy)*

Objekte *pl* • objects *(Meinong) (epi, min)* < Desiderative, Dignitative, Objektive

Objektfeld *n* • array/field of objects, object-field *(sci)*

objektiv • objective *(sci)*

objektiv gültiges Urteil *n* • objectively valid judg(e)ment *(epi, log)*

Objektiv-Männliche, das *n* • male objectivity *(fem)* ↔ subjektiv-Weibliche, das

Objektivation *f* • objectivation, objectification, objectivization *(met)* → Vergegenständlichung, Reifikation, Verdinglichung

Objektivation des Willens *f* • objectivization/objectification of the will *(Schopenhauer) (met)*

Objektivationen des Geistes *pl* • objectivations/objectifications/objectivizations of mind *(Hegel, N. Hartmann) (met)*

Objektive *pl* • objectives *(Meinong) (epi, min)* < Desiderative, Dignitative

objektive Deduktion *f* • objective deduction *(Kant) (epi, log)*

objektive Deutung *f* • objective interpretation/reading *(sci)* ↔ subjektive Deutung

objektive Dialektik *f* • objective dialectics *(Hegel, Marx etc) (met)*

objektive Eigenschaft *f* • objective property *(epi, ont)*

objektive Einheit des Selbstbewußtseins *f* • objective unity of self-consciousness *(Kant) (epi)*

objektive Erkenntnis *f* • objective knowledge *(epi)* < W 718

objektive Folge *f* • objective succession *(Kant etc) (epi, log)*

objektive Glückseligkeit *f* • objective happiness *(Kant) (eth)*

objektive Gültigkeit *f* • objective validity *(epi, sci)*

objektive Notwendigkeit *f* • objective necessity *(epi, met)*

objektive Realität *f* • objective reality *(met)*

objektive Sittlichkeit *f* • objective ethical practice/life, objective (social/customary) morality, objective sittlichkeit *(Hegel) (eth)*

objektive Wahrscheinlichkeit *f* • objective probability *(mat, sci)*

objektive Zweckmäßigkeit *f* • objective finality *(Kant) (met, aes, nat)*

objektiven Notwendigkeit, Philosophie der *f* • necessitarianism *(Spinoza etc) (met)* → Notwendigkeitslehre

objektiver Geist *m* • objective mind/spirit *(Hegel) (met)*

objektiver Idealismus *m* • objective idealism *(Schelling, Hegel) (met)*

objektiver Zweck *m* • objective end *(met)*

objektives Gut *n* • objective good *(Plato etc)* *(eth)*

objektivierende Einstellung *f* • objectivating/ objectivizing attitude *(epi, psy)*

objektivierter Geist *m* • objectified spirit/ intellect *(met)*

Objektivierung *f* • objectification, objectivization *(epi, sci)* → Vergegenständlichung < Objektivation

Objektivismus *m* • objectivism *(met, epi)*

Objektivismus, bürgerlicher *m* • bourgeois objectivism *(Lenin)* *(epi)*

Objektivismus, ethischer *m* • ethical objectivism *(eth)*

Objektivismus, historischer *m* • historical objectivism *(his)*

objektivistische Wahrscheinlichkeitstheorie *f* • objectivist theory of probability *(mat)* < subjektive Interpretation der Wahrscheinlichkeit

Objektivität *f* • objectivity *(sci)* ↔ Subjektivität < Intersubjektivität, Sachlichkeit, Überparteilichkeit

Objektivität von Tests *f* • objectivity of tests *(sci)* < Validität, Reliabilität

Objektivitätsanspruch *m* • claim to objectivity *(sci)*

Objektivitätsforderung *f* • requirement of objectivity, objectivity requirement *(sci)*

Objektivitätsprinzip *n* • principle of objectivity *(Weber etc)* *(sci)*

Objektkonstanz *f* • object constancy *(Freud, Piaget)* *(psy)* < Wahrnehmungskonstanz; *(ont)* < Identität

Objektkunst *f* • object art *(aes)*

objektorientiert • object-oriented *(AI)*

Objektsein *n* • being-an-object *(Jaspers)* *(met)*

Objektspaltung *f* • splitting of the object *(Klein)* *(psy)*

Objektsprache *f* • object language *(lan)* → Dingsprache

Objektstatus *m* • object status *(epi, soc)*

Objekttriebe *pl* • object-instincts *(Freud)* *(psy)*

Objektwahl *f* • object-choice *(Freud)* *(psy)*

Objektwahrnehmung *f* • object perception *(epi, psy)* < Gestaltwahrnehmung

objet trouvé *n* • *nt (aes)* < Ready-made

Obligation, moralische *f* → moralische Verpflichtung

obligatorisch • obligatory *(jur, eth)* ↔ fakultativ

Oblomowerei *f* • Oblomovianism *(Gontscharow)* *(psy, soc)* < Müßiggang

Obrigkeit *f* • the authorities, the powers that be *(pol)*

Observation *f* • observation *(sci)*

Observationsprädikate *pl* • observation(al) predicates *(lan)*

Obsession *f* • obsession *(psy)*

Obskurantismus *m* • obscurantism *(eso)* < Irrationalismus

Öbszöne, das *n* • the obscene *(aes)*

Obszönität *f* • obscenity *(aes)*

Obversion *f* • obversion *(log)*

Occamismus *m* → Ockhamismus

Occasionalismus *m* → Okkasionalismus

Ochlokratie *f* • ochlocracy *(Aristotle)* *(pol)* → Pöbelherrschaft

Ockham, Wilhelm von • William Ockham/ Occam

Ockhamismus *m* • Ockhamism *(epi, met)* < Nominalimus

Ockhams Parsimoniegesetz *n* • Ockham's principle of parsimony *(ont, sci)* → Ockhams Rasiermesser

Ockhams Rasiermesser *n* • Ockham's razor *(ont, sci)* → Ockhams Parsimoniegesetz < Prinzip der geringstmöglichen Kategorien

ödipale Phase *f* • Oedipal stage *(Freud)* *(psy)*

Ödipuskomplex *m* • Oedipus complex *(Freud etc)* *(psy)* ↔ Elektrakomplex

Ödipuskonflikt *m* • Oedipus conflict *(Freud)* *(psy)*

Ödipusphase *f* → ödipale Phase

offen strategisches Handeln *n* • open strategic action *(Habermas)* *(act)*

Offenbare, das *n* • the apparent, the revealed *(met)*

offenbarer Gott *m* • revealed God *(rel)* ↔ verborgener Gott

Offenbarung *f* • revelation *(rel)*

Offenbarung, außer-verstandesmäßige *f* • revelation above reason *(Plotinus)* *(met)*

Offenbarung, göttliche *f* • divine revelation *(rel)*

Offenbarungsglaube *m* • revealed faith/belief *(rel)*

Offenbarungsreligion *f* • revealed religion *(rel)*

Offenbarungstheologie *f* • revelation theology *(rel)*

Offenbarwerden, das *n* • revelation *(met, rel)*

offene Evolution *f* • open evolution *(nat, sys)*

offene Gesellschaft *f* • open society *(Bergson, Popper)* *(soc)* < W 719

offene Psychiatrie *f* • open psychiatry *(Bassaglia)* *(psy, eth)*

offenen Frage, Argument der *n* • open question argument *(Moore)* *(eth, lan)*

offener Satz *m* • open sentence *(Quine)* *(lan)*

offener Zugang zu Positionen *m* • open access to positions *(Rawls)* *(eth, jur, soc)* < allokative Gerechtigkeit

offenes Interview *n* • open interview *(sci)*

offenes System *n* • open system *(sys)* ↔ geschlossenes System

offenes Wesen, Mensch als *m* • man as open being *(ant)*

Offenheit *f* • openness *(gen)*

öffentliche Anhörung *f* • public hearing *(pol)*

öffentliche Ausgaben *pl* • public spending/ expenditure *(eco)*

öffentliche Gewalt *f* • public power *(pol)*

öffentliche Hand *f* • the public (authorities), the public purse *(pol, eco)*

öffentliche Meinung *f* • public opinion *(soc)*

öffentliche Mittel *pl* • public resources *(eco)*

öffentliche Moral *f* • public morality *(eth)* < Sozialmoral

öffentliche Verantwortung *f* • public responsibility/accountability *(eth)*

öffentliche Wohlfahrt *f* • public welfare/assistance *(eco, pol, soc)* < Wohl, öffentliches

öffentliche Wohlfahrtspolitik *f* • (public) welfare policy *(pol, eth)*

öffentlicher Bereich *m* • public sphere *(pol)*

öffentlicher Diskurs *m* • public discourse *(soc, eth)*

öffentlicher Sektor *m* • public sector *(eco)* ↔ privater Sektor

öffentliches Eigentum *n* • public ownership *(eco)* < Vergesellschaftung, Vergesellschaftung der Produktionsmittel, Verstaatlichung

öffentliches Gut *n* • public good *(eco)*

öffentliches Interesse *n* • public interest *(pol)*

öffentliches Recht *n* • public law *(jur)*

Öffentlichkeit *f* • the public sphere, the public *(soc, pol)* < Strukturwandel der Öffentlichkeit < W 952

Öffentlichkeitsarbeit *f* • public relations, PR *(pol)*

Ohnmacht *f* • impotence *(psy);* powerlessness *(pol, psy)* → Machtlosigkeit

Oikeiosis *f* → Selbsterhaltungstrieb

Okkasionalismus *m* • occasionalism *(Geulincx, Malebranche)* *(met)* ↔ Prästabilismus

Okkulte, das *n* • the occult *(eso)*

okkulte Eigenschaft *f* • occult quality/property *(Gassendi, Descartes etc)* *(met)*

okkulte Entitäten *pl* • occult entities *(lan, met)* < Wahrscheinlichkeit, Propensitäten

okkulte Kräfte *pl* • occult forces *(eso)*

okkulte Phänomene *pl* • occult phenomena *(eso)*

okkulte Qualität *f* → okkulte Eigenschaft

Okkultismus *m* • occultism *(eso)* < Parapsychologie

Okkupationstheorie *f* • occupation theory *(jur, eco)* < Niemandsland, ursprüngliche Besitzergreifung

Öko-Ethik *f* → ökologische Ethik

Ökofeminismus *m* • ecofeminism *(fem, env)* < Gyn-Ökologie

Öko-Flüchtling *m* • eco-refugee, environmental refugee *(env, pol)*

Ökologie *f* • ecology *(env, nat)*

Ökologiebewegung *f* • ecology movement *(env, pol)*

Ökologiebewußtsein *n* • environmental awareness, green-consciousness *(env)*

ökologische Ästhetik *f* • ecological aesthetics *(aes, env)*

ökologische Entwicklungshilfe *f* • ecological development aid *(env)*

ökologische Ethik *f* • ecological ethics *(eth, env)* → Öko-Ethik

ökologische Gerechtigkeit *f* • ecojustice, ecological justice *(eth, env)*

ökologische Krise *f* • ecological crisis *(env)*

ökologische Nische *f* • ecological niche *(env, nat)*

ökologische Potenz *f* • ecological potency *(env)*

ökologische Tragfähigkeit *f* • ecological viability, ecological carrying capacity *(env)* < Umweltverträglichkeit

ökologische Valenz *f* • ecological valency *(env)*

ökologischer Feminismus *m* • ecological feminism *(fem, env)* → Ökofeminismus

ökologischer Landbau *m* • ecological farming, ecologically sound farming/agriculture *(env)*

Ökologismus *m* • immoderate environmental concern *(env)*

Ökonomie der diskursiven Konstellation *f* • economy of the discursive constellation *(Foucault)* *(epi, lan)*

Ökonomie, klassische *f* • classical economics *(eco)*

Ökonomieprinzip *n* • principle of economy, economy principle *(Galilei, Avenarius, Mach)* *(epi), (Fechner, Müller-Freienfels)* *(aes, psy), (eco)* < ökonomisches Prinzip; *(ont)* → Ökonomieprinzip, ontologisches < Ockhams Rasiermesser

Ökonomieprinzip, ontologisches *n* • principle of ontological economy, ontological economy principle *(Ockham, Quine etc) (ont)* → Parsimonieprinzip

Ökonomik *f* • economics *(Aristotle) (eco)* ↔ Chrematistik

ökonomische Basis *f* • economic base/basis/foundation *(Marx etc) (eco, soc)* → materielle Basis ↔ ideeller Überbau

ökonomische Determiniertheit der Geschichte *f* • economic determinacy/determinedness of history *(Marx) (his)* < Geschichtsdeterminismus

ökonomische Freiheit *f* • economic liberty/freedom *(eco)* → Wirtschaftsfreiheit

ökonomische Grundlagen *pl* • economic base *(Marx etc) (eco, soc)* < Basis und Überbau

ökonomische Güter *pl* • economic goods *(eco)* < Ware

ökonomische Interpretation der Geschichte *f* • economic interpretation of history *(Marx) (his)*

ökonomische Klasse *f* • economic class *(Marx) (soc)*

ökonomische Theorie der Moral *f* • economic theory of morality *(eco, eth)*

ökonomischer Determinismus *m* • economic determinism *(Marx etc) (soc)*

ökonomischer Faktor *m* • economic factor *(Marx) (eco, soc)*

ökonomischer Imperialismus *m* • economic imperialism *(eco)*

ökonomischer Intervention(al)ismus *m* • economic interventionism *(eco, soc)*

ökonomischer Liberalismus *m* • economic liberalism *(eco, pol)* → Wirtschaftsliberalismus

ökonomisches Gleichgewicht *n* • economic equilibrium *(eco)*

ökonomisches Prinzip *n* • economy principle, principle of economy, efficiency rule *(eco, act)* < Ockhams Parsimoniegesetz, Parsimonieprinzip

ökonomisches Wachstum *n* • economic growth *(eco)* → Wirtschaftswachstum

Ökonomisierung *f* • economic universalization *(Marx etc) (eco)*

Ökonomismus *m* • economism *(eco)* < homo oeconomicus

Ökopartei *f* • ecology party *(pol, env)* < Grüner

Ökopax *m* • ecopax *(env)* < Frieden mit der Natur

Ökopax-Bewegung *f* • ecopax movement *(env)*

Ökopazifismus *m* • environmental/ecological pacifism *(env, eth)*

Ökosophie *f* • ecosophy *(env)* < Tiefenökologie

ökosoziale Marktwirtschaft *f* • eco-social market economy *(env, eco)*

Ökosystem *n* • ecosystem *(nat, env, sys)*

Ökosystemforschung *f* • ecosystem-research, synecology *(nat, env, sys)*

Ökotechnik *f* • ecological technology, eco-technology° *(env, tec)*

Ökotoxikologie *f* • eco-toxicology, environmental toxicology *(env)*

Ökozentrismus *m* • ecocentrism *(env, pol)*

Ökozid *m* • ecocide *(env)* < Biotod

Ökumene *f* • ecumenicalism, ecumenism, ecumenicity *(rel)*

ökumenische Bewegung *f* • ecumenical movement *(rel)*

Oligarchie *f* • oligarchy *(Aristotle) (pol)*

Oligopol *n* • oligopoly *(eco)*

Ölkrise *f* • oil crisis *(eco)* < Ressourcenknappheit

Omega-Unvollständigkeit *f* • omega-incompleteness *(mat, AI)*

Omega-Widersprüchlichkeit *f* • omega-inconsistency *(mat, AI)*

Omega-Widerspruchsfreiheit *f* • omega-consistency *(mat, AI)*

Omen *n* • omen *(rel, eso)*

Omnipotenz *f* • omnipotence, unlimited power *(pol, rel)* → Allmacht

Omnipräsenz *f* • omnipresence *(rel, met)* → Allgegenwart

Omniszienz *f* • omniscience *(rel, epi)* → Allwissenheit < Gottesgesichtspunkt, absolutes Wissen

ontisch-ontologisch • ontico-ontological *(Heidegger) (ont)*

ontische Wahrheit *f* • ontic truth *(Heidegger) (ont)*

ontisches Schema im Aufbau der Welt *n* • ontic schema in the construction of the world *(N. Hartmann) (ont)*

Onto-Logik *f* • onto-logic *(Heidegger) (ont)*

Ontogenese *f* • ontogenesis, ontogeny *(nat)* ↔ Phylogenese

Ontologie *f* • ontology *(ont)* → Seinslehre

Ontologie des Umfassenden *f* • ontology of the encompassing, periechontology *(Jaspers) (ont)* → Periechontologie

Ontologie, existentiale *f* • existential ontology *(Ingarden) (ont)*

Ontologie, existentielle *f* • existentiell ontology *(Heidegger) (ont)*

Ontologie, existenziale *f* • existential ontology *(Heidegger, Jaspers) (ont)*

Ontologie, formale *f* • formal ontology *(Husserl) (ont)*

Ontologie, regionale *f* • regional ontology *(N. Hartmann etc) (ont)*

ontologische Definition *f* • ontological definition *(Heidegger) (ont)*

ontologische Differenz *f* • ontological difference *(Husserl etc) (ont)*

ontologische Festlegung *f* • ontological commitment *(Church, Quine) (lan, ont)*

ontologische Geltung *f* • ontological import *(ont)*

ontologische Modalitäten *pl* • ontological modalities *(ont)* < Seinsmodalität

ontologische Reduktion *f* • ontological reduction *(Quine) (lan, ont)*

ontologische Relativität *f* • ontological relativity *(Quine) (lan, ont)*

ontologische Voraussetzung *f* • ontological presupposition *(ont)* → ontologische Festlegung

ontologischer Beweis *m* → ontologischer Gottesbeweis

ontologischer Gottesbeweis *m* • ontological argument (for the existence of God), ontological proof (of the existence of God) *(Anselm, Descartes) (rel)*

ontologischer Grund *m* • ontological ground *(ont)*

ontologischer Status *m* • ontological status *(ont)*

ontologisches Kriterium *n* • ontological criterion *(Quine) (lan, ont)*

Ontologismus *m* • ontologism *(Malebranche, Rosmini, Gioberti) (ont)*

Ontosophie *f* • ontosophy° *(Clauberg) (ont)* → Ontologie

Ontotheologie *f* • ontotheology *(Kant, Heidegger etc) (ont, rel)*

ontotheologische Verfaßtheit der Metaphysik *f* • ontotheological conception of metaphysics *(Heidegger) (ont)*

opake Kontexte *pl* • opaque contexts *(Quine) (lan)*

Opakheit *f* • opacity *(Quine etc) (log, lan)* ↔ Transparenz, Perspikuität

Op-art *f* • op-art *(aes)*

operantes Verhalten *n* • operant behaviour *(Skinner) (nat, lan)*

operationale Definition *f* • operational definition *(Bridgeman) (log, lan)*

operationaler Wissenschaftsbegriff *m* • operational concept of science *(sci)*

Operationalisierbarkeit *f* • operationalizability° *(sci)*

Operationalisierung *f* • operationalization° *(sci)*

Operationalismus *m* • operationalism, operationism *(Bridgman) (epi, sci)*

Operationsforschung *f* • operations research *(dec, sci)*

Operationsregel *f* • operational rule *(Habermas) (act, eth)* < Handlungsregel

operative Mathematik *f* • operative mathematics *(mat)*

operative Sprechhandlung *f* • operative speech act *(lan, act)*

operativer Gesichtspunkt *m* • operative aspect *(act, lan)*

operatives Lernen *n* • learning by doing *(psy, epi)* → Lernen durch Handeln

Operator *m* • operator *(log)*

Operator, deontischer *m* • deontic operator *(log, eth)*

Opferfeminismus *m* • victim feminism *(fem)*

opinio communis *f* • common opinion *(gen)* → allgemeine Meinung < herrschende Meinung

Opponent *m* • opponent *(Lorenzen) (log)* ↔ Proponent < Logik, dialogische; opponent *(pol, act, dec)* → Gegenspieler

Opportunismus *m* • opportunism *(eth, pol)* < Wendehals

Oppositionspartei *f* • opposition party *(pol)*

Optical art *f* → Op-art

Optimierungsstrategie *f* • optimization strategy *(dec, sys)*

Optimierungstheorie *f* • optimization theory *(mat)*

optische Täuschung *f* • optical illusion *(epi, psy)*

optische Zeichenerkennung *f* • optical character recognition, OCR *(AI)*

Orakel *n* • oracle *(rel)*

Oralität *f* • orality *(lan)* < erzählte Geschichte

Oralphase *f* • oral stage *(Freud) (psy)*

ordinaler Nutzen *m* • ordinal utility *(eth, dec)* ↔ kardinaler Nutzen

Ordinalskala *f* • ordinal scale *(mat)* ↔ Kardinalskala

Ordinalzahl *f* • ordinal number *(mat)*

Ordnung *f* • order *(gep)* < Chaostheorie

Ordnung der Begriffe *f* • order of concepts *(sci, lan)*

Ordnung der Dinge *f* • order of things *(met)*

Ordnung der Wahrheit *f* • regime of truth *(Foucault) (epi, met)*

ordnungs(ge)treue Abbildung *f* • order-preserving mapping *(mat)*

Ordnungsaxiom *n* • ordering axiom *(mat)*

Ordnungsbegriff *m* → klassifikatorischer Begriff

Ordnungsmechanismus *m* • ordering mechanism *(gep)*

Ordnungsrelation *f* • order relation *(mat, log)*

Ordnungsstruktur *f* • order(ing) structure *(mat, sys)*

Ordnungszahl *f* → Ordinalzahl

Ordo amoris *m* • order of love *(eth, rel)*

Ordoliberalismus *m* • order liberalism *(eco, soc, pol)*

Organentnahme *f* • organ explantation/harvesting° *(nat, eth)*

Organhandel *m* • organ trade *(eth)*

Organik *f* • organics *(Hegel) (met)*

Organisation *f* • organization *(gep)*

Organisationssoziologie *f* • sociology of organizations, organizational sociology *(soc)*

Organische, das *n* • the organic *(nat)*

organische Determination *f* • organic determination *(N. Hartmann) (met)*

organische Einheit *f* • organic unity *(nat, sys)*

organische Maschine *f* • organic machine *(Leibniz) (met)* < Maschinenmensch

organische Natur *f* • organic nature *(nat)*

organische Staatstheorie *f* • organic theory of the state *(Hegel, Spann) (pol)*

organisches Ganzes *n* • organic whole *(nat, sys)* < Holismus

organisches Gesellschaftskonzept *n* • organic concept of society *(pol, soc)*

organisches Leben *n* • organic life *(nat)* ↔ unorganisches Leben < anorganische Natur

organisierter Skeptizismus *m* • organized scepticism *(Merton) (sci, soc)*

Organizismus *m* • organicism *(met, pol)*

Organmangel *m* • organ deficiency *(Gehlen) (ant)* < Mängelwesen, Mensch als

Organon *n* • organon *(log, epi)* < Kanon

Organon der Erkenntnis *n* • organon of knowledge *(Schelling, Hegel) (epi)*

Organon der reinen Vernunft *n* • organon of pure reason *(Kant) (epi)*

Organonmodell der Sprache *n* • organon model of language *(Bühler) (lan)*

Organspende *f* • organ donation *(eth)* < Gehirntod

Organtransplantation *f* • organ transplantation *(nat, eth)* < Zustimmungslösung, Widerspruchslösung

Organverpflanzung *f* → Organtransplantation

orientalische Kunst *f* • oriental art *(aes)*

orientalische Philosophie *f* • Oriental philosophy *(his)*

orientalischer Despotismus *m* • oriental despotism *(Montesquieu, Marx) (pol)*

Orientalistik *f* • oriental studies *(gep)*

Orientierung *f* • orientation *(gep)*

Orientierungskrise *f* • orientation crisis *(cul, met)* < Sinnkrise

Orientierungslosigkeit, existentielle *f* • existential disorientation *(met)*

Orientierungssystem *n* • system of orientation *(met, psy)*

Orientierungswissen *n* • orientation knowledge *(epi)* → Lebenswissen ↔ Verfügungswissen

Originalität *f* • originality *(aes, sci)* < Eingebung

originär gebende Anschauung *f* • original/primal dator intuition *(Husserl) (epi, met)*

originäre Anschauung *f* • originary/primordial intuition, original view *(Husserl) (sci)*

Origines • Origen

Orkus *m* → Totenreich

Orphik *f* • Orphic *(his, gep)*

orphische Religion *f* • Orphic religion *(rel)*

Orphismus *m* • Orphism *(rel, aes)*

Ort der Wahrheit *m* • locus of truth *(met)*

Orteguismus *m* • Ortegism° *(soc)*

orthodox • orthodox *(gep)* < schulmäßig

Orthodoxie *f* • orthodoxy *(rel, sci)* < Fundamentalismus, Strenggläubigkeit

Orthogenese *f* • orthogenesis *(nat)*

Orthopraxie *f* • orthopraxy *(rel)*

orthos logos *m* • right reason *(Stoicism) (met)* < Weltgesetz

Ortsbewegung *f* • locomotion, local motion, local movement *(Aristotle) (nat, met)* < Ortsveränderung

Ortsvektor *m* • position vector *(mat)*

Ortsveränderung *f* • change of place/location *(nat)* < Ortsbewegung, Bewegung

ostensive Definition *f* → ostentative Definition

ostensiver Begriff *m* • ostensive concept *(log, lan)*

ostensiver Beweis *m* • ostensive proof *(epi, log)*

ostentative Definition *f* • ostentative definition, ostensive definition *(lan, log)* < operationale Definition

Ostention *f* • ostention *(lan)*

Österrechische Philosophie *f* • Austrian philosophy *(Neurath, Haller etc) (gep)*

Österreichische Schule *f* • Austrian School *(eco)*

östliche Weisheit *f* • Eastern wisdom *(asp)*
östliches Denken *n* • Eastern thought *(asp)*
 < Asiatische Philosophie
Output *m* • output *(sys)* ↔ Input
Overkill *m* • overkill *(pol, eth)* < Atomkrieg,
 wechselseitig gesicherte Zerstörung
Owenismus *m* • Owenism *(soc)*
Owenisten *pl* • Owenites *(soc)*
Oxymoron *n* • oxymoron *(lan)* < contradictio
 in adjecto

Ozean des Scheins *m* • ocean of illusion *(Kant)*
 (epi, met) ↔ Land der Wahrheit
ozeanisches Gefühl *n* • oceanic feeling *(psy)*
Ozonabbau *m* • ozone depletion *(env)*
Ozonloch *n* • ozone hole *(env)*
Ozonschicht *f* • ozone layer *(nat, env)*
ozonzerstörend • ozone-depleting *(env)*

P

p-adisch • p-adic *(mat)*

Paarung *f* • coupling, pairing *(Husserl) (epi, met)*

Paarvergleich *m* • paired comparison *(sci)*

Paarvergleich von Items *m* • pairing of items *(sci)* < Methode der summierten Beurteilungen, Skalogrammanalyse

Pächter *m* • leaseholder *(eco, soc)* < Leibeigenschaft

Pädagoge *m* • pedagogue, education(al)ist, educational scientist/theorist *(gep)*

Pädagogik *f* • pedagogics, pedagogy, educational sciences → Erziehungswissenschaft

pädagogische Psychologie *f* • educational psychology *(psy)*

Padma *m* • padma *(asp)*

Paganismus *m* • paganism *(rel)*

Paideuma *n* • paideuma *(Frobenius) (cul)* → Kulturseele

Paläoanthropologie *f* • paleoanthropology *(ant)*

Palingenese *f* • palingenesis *(met, rel)* → Wiedergeburt

Palingenesie *f* → Palingenese

Pandaimonion *n* • Pandemonium *(Milton etc) (rel)*

Panentheismus *m* • panentheism *(rel, met)*

Pangenesistheorie *f* • pangenesis theory *(Darwin) (nat)*

Pangermanismus *m* • Pan-Germanism *(pol)*

Panislamismus *m* • Pan-Islamism *(rel)*

Pankalie *f* • pankalia°, the all-beautiful *(Pythagoras etc) (aes)* → Allschönheit

pankritischer Rationalismus *m* • pancritical rationalism *(sci)*

Panlogismus *m* • panlogism *(log, met)*

Panpneumatismus *m* • panpneumatism *(N. Hartmann) (met)*

Panpsychismus *m* • panpsychism *(met)* → Allbeseelungslehre

Panrationalismus *m* • panrationalism *(Epictetus) (sci)*

Pansexualismus *m* • pansexualism *(psy)*

Pansophie *f* • pansophy, pansophism *(his, gep)*

panta rhei • *nt,* everything flows, all is in flux *(Heraclitus) (met)* → alles fließt

Pantheismus *m* • pantheism *(rel)*

Pantheismusstreit *m* • pantheism controversy *(Jacobi) (rel)*

Pantragismus *m* • pantragicism *(met)* < Desperatismus

Panvitalismus *m* • panvitalism *(met)*

Papismus *m* • papism *(rel)* → Papsttum

päpstliche Autorität *f* • papal authority *(rel, pol)* < Unfehlbarkeitsdogma

päpstliche Enzyklika *f* • papal encyclical/encyclic *(rel)*

päpstliche Unfehlbarkeit *f* • papal infallibility *(rel)*

Papsttum *n* • papacy *(rel)* → Papismus

Parabel *f* • parabola *(mat)*, parabole *(aes, lan, nat)*; parable, parabole *(aes)* → Gleichnis

Paradies *n* • paradise *(rel)*

paradiesischer Zustand *m* • paradisic state, state of paradise *(rel)*

Paradigma *n* • paradigm *(Kuhn etc) (sci)* → Denkmuster < disziplinäre Matrix

Paradigmaabhängigkeit *f* • paradigm-dependency *(sci)* < Theorieabhängigkeit

paradigmatisch • paradigmatic *(sci, lan, log)* ↔ syntagmatisch

paradigmatische Reihe *f* • paradigmatic series *(log, lan)*

paradigmatische Serie *f* → paradigmatische Reihe

paradigmatischer Fall *m* • paradigm case *(Moore) (lan)*

Paradigmenfusion *f* • fusion of paradigms *(Habermas) (his, soc)*

paradigmengebundene Wissenschaft *f* • paradigm-bound science *(Kuhn) (sci)*

Paradigmenwechsel *m* • change of paradigm(s) *(Kuhn) (sci)* < Theoriendynamik, Theorienwandel, wissenschaftliche Revolution

Paradox(on) *n* • paradox *(log)*

Paradox, absolutes *n* • absolute paradox *(Kierkegaard) (rel)*

Paradox des Wissenden *n* • paradox of the knower *(Aqvist, Montague, Kaplan) (log)* < Logik, deontische

Paradox, göttliches *n* • divine paradox *(Kierkegaard) (rel)*

Paradoxie *f* • (▷ logische Figur) paradox, (▷ logische Eigenschaft) paradoxicality, paradoxicalness *(log)*

Paradoxien der Mengenlehre *pl* • paradoxes of set theory *(Russell) (log, mat)* < Russell-Paradox

Paradoxien der Modernität *pl* • paradoxes of modernity *(Habermas) (soc, cul)*

Paradoxien des Unendlichen *pl* • paradoxes of infinity/the infinite *(log, mat)*

Paradoxien des Zeno *pl* • Zeno's paradoxes *(log)*

Paradoxon des fliegenden Pfeiles *n* • flying-arrow paradox *(log)*

Parallelenaxiom *n* • parallel postulate *(mat)*

Parallelenpostulat *n* • parallel postulate *(mat)*

Parallelismus, psychophysischer *m* • psychophysical parallelism *(met)*

Parallelität *f* • parallelism *(mat, gep)*

Parallelmontage *f* • parallel montage *(Griffith) (aes)*

Parallelverarbeitung *f* • parallel processing *(AI)* < serielle Datenverarbeitung

Paralogie *f* • paralogy *(log)* → Vernunftwidrigkeit < Paralogismus

Paralogismen der reinen Vernunft *pl* • paralogisms of pure reason *(Kant) (epi)*

Paralogismus *m* • paralogism *(Aristotle etc) (log)* < Fehlschluß, Paralogie

Paralogimus der Personalität *m* • paralogism of personality *(Kant) (epi)*

Paralogismus der reinen Psychologie *m* • paralogism of pure psychology *(Kant) (epi)*

Paralogismus der transzendentalen Psychologie *m* • paralogism of transcendental psychology *(Kant) (epi)*

Paralogismus des reinen Verstandes *m* • paralogism of pure reason *(Kant) (epi, log)*

Paralogistik *f* • paralogistic *(log)*

Parameter *m* • parameter *(mat, sci)*

Parameterdarstellung *f* • parametric representation *(mat, sci)*

Parameterhypothese *f* • parameter hypothesis *(mat)*

Paranoia *f* • paranoia *(psy)* < Verfolgungswahn

paranormales Wissen *n* • paranormal knowledge *(psy, eso)*

Paraphysik *f* • paraphysics° *(nat, eso)*

Parapsychologie *f* • parapsychology *(psy, eso)* < Okkultismus

parasitäre Klasse *f* • parasitic(al) class *(pol, soc)*

Pareto-Optimalität *f* • Pareto optimality *(eco)*

Pareto-Optimum *n* • Pareto optimum *(eco)*

Paria *m* • pariah *(soc)* < Außenseiter, gesellschaftlicher; unberührte Kaste

Pariser Kommune *f* • Paris Commune *(his)*

Pariser Manuskripte *pl* • Paris Manuscripts *(Marx) (eco, soc)* < W 733

Parkettierungsproblem *n* • tiling problem, tessellation problem *(AI)*

Parkinsonsches Gesetz *n* • Parkinson's law *(soc)*

parlamentarische Demokratie *f* • parliamentary democracy *(pol)*

Parlamentarismus *m* • parliamentarianism *(pol)*

Parodie *f* • parody *(aes)*

Parole *f* • parole, speech *(Saussure) (lan)* ↔ Langue

Parser *m* • parser *(lan, AI)*

Parsimonieprinzip *n* • principle of parsimony *(sci)* → Ökonomieprinzip, ontologisches; Ockhams Parsimoniegesetz < ökonomisches Prinzip

Parteilichkeit *f* • partiality, bias *(eth, epi)* < unparteiischer Beobachter, Voreingenommenheit

Parteilinie *f* • party-line *(pol)*

Parteimitgliedschaft *f* • party membership *(pol)*

Parteiprogramm *n* • (party) manifesto, (party) programme *(pol)*

Parteizugehörigkeit *f* → Parteimitgliedschaft

Parthenogenese *f* • parthenogenesis *(nat, rel)*

Partialdefinition *f* • partial definition *(log, lan)*

Partialobjekt *n* • partial object *(Freud etc) (psy)*

Partialtriebe *pl* • partial drives *(Freud) (psy)*

partielle Definition *f* • partial definition *(lan, log)*

partielle Differentialgleichung *f* • partial differential equation *(mat)*

partielle Integration *f* • partial integration *(mat)* < Produktintegration

partielle Interpretation *f* • partial interpretation *(log)*

Partikel *n* • particle *(nat)* → Elementarteilchen, Korpuskel

Partikel, logisches *n* • logical particle *(log)*

Partikuläraussage *f* • particular proposition *(log)* < Syllogismus

Partikulargericht *n* • particular judg(e)ment *(rel)*

Partikularie *f* • particular *(lan, ont)*

Partikularinteresse *n* • special/particular interest *(act, eth)* < Privatinteresse, Klasseninteresse

Partikularisation *f* • particularization *(gep)* → Partikularisierung

Partikularisator *m* • particular/existential quantifier *(log)* < Existenzoperator, Existenzquantor

Partikularisierung *f* • particularization *(gep)* → Partikularisation

Partikularismus *m* • particularism *(epi, met)* ↔ Universalismus; *(Davidson, Danto) (act)* < Kausalismus, logischer Intentionalismus

Partikularität *f* • particularity *(gep)* < Singularität

Partikularität von Ereignissen *f* • particularity of events *(Davidson) (ont)*

Partikularwille *m* • particular will *(Rousseau) (pol, soc)* → Einzelwille

Partition *f* • partition *(log)*

Partitur *f* • (musical) score *(aes)*

Partizipation *f* • participation *(pol)* < Mitbestimmung

Partnerschaft für den Frieden *f* • partnership for peace *(pol)*

Partnerwahl *f* • choice of partner *(nat, soc)* < Selektion, sexuelle

Parusie *f* • parousia, (second) coming *(Plato, Plotinus etc) (met, rel)*

Pascals Wette *f* • Pascal's wager *(met, dec)*

Pascalsches Dreieck *n* • Pascal's triangle *(mat)*

passiver Widerstand *m* • passive resistance *(pol)* < ziviler Ungehorsam

Passivismus *m* • passivism *(psy, asp)* < stoische Gelassenheit

Pastoraltheologie *f* • pastoral theology *(rel)*

Paternalismus *m* • paternalism *(eth)*

Pathetisch-Erhabenes *n* • pathetic-sublime *(Schiller) (aes)*

Pathetische, das *n* • the pathetic *(aes)*

Pathognomik *f* • pathognomy *(Lichtenberg) (met, psy)* < Ausdruckspsychologie

Pathologien der Moderne *pl* • pathologies of modernity *(Habermas) (soc)*

pathologischer Term *m* • pathological term *(lan, sci)* < pathologisches Prädikat

pathologisches Interesse *n* • pathological interest *(Kant) (aes)*

pathologisches Prädikat *n* • pathological predicate *(Goodman) (lan, sci)* < projizierbares Prädikat

Pathos *n* • pathos *(psy, aes)*

Pathos der Distanz *n* • pathos of distance *(Nietzsche) (met)*

Pathosformel *f* • pathos formula *(Warburg) (aes)*

Patientenautonomie *f* • patient autonomy *(eth)* < Zwangsbehandlung

Patientenrechte *pl* • patient rights *(eth)*

Patiententestament *n* • patient's will *(eth, jur)* < Sterbehilfe

patriarchale Gesellschaft *f* • patriarchal society *(soc, fem)*

patriarchale Philosophie *f* • patriarchal philosophy *(fem)*

patriarchales Autoritätsmodell *n* • patriarchal model of authority *(psy, soc)*

patriarchales Denken *n* • patriarchal thought *(fem)*

Patriarchalismus *m* • patriarchalism *(fem, pol, soc)*

Patriarchat *n* • patriarchy *(Bachofen) (soc, fem)* ↔ Matriarchat

patriarchatskritisch • patriarchy-critical *(fem)*

Patriarchismus *m* • patriarchalism *(fem)* → Patriarchalismus

Patriotismus *m* • patriotism *(pol)* → Vaterlandsliebe

Patristik *f* • patristic *(his, rel)*

patristisches Denken *n* • patristic thought *(his, rel)*

Pattsituation *f* • stalemate *(dec)*

Paulinische Doktrin *f* • Pauline doctrine *(rel)*

Pauper *m* • pauper *(eco, soc)*

Pauperisierung *f* • pauperization *(Marx etc) (eco, soc)*

Pauperismus *m* • pauperism *(eco, soc)*

Pauschalurteil *n* • sweeping statement *(gen)*

Pazifikation *f* • pacification *(pol)* → Befriedung

Pazifismus *m* • pacifism *(pol, eth)* ↔ Bellizismus

pazifistische Bewegung *f* • pacifist movement *(eth, pol)*

Peano-Arithmetik *f* • Peano arithmetic *(mat)*

Peanosches Axiomensystem *n* • Peano's axioms, Peano's axiom system, Peano's system of axioms *(mat)*

Peer-group *f* • peer-group *(psy, soc)*

Peircesche Aussage *f* • Peirce's law *(log)*

Pelagianismus *m* • Pelagianism *(met)*

Pelztierfarm *f* • fur farm *(eth)* < Massentierhaltung, artgerechte Tierhaltung

Penisneid *m* • penis envy *(Freud) (psy)* ↔ Gebärneid

per definitionem • *nt,* by definition *(log)*

Perestroika *f* • *nt (pol)* < Glasnost

Perfektibilismus *m* → Perfektionismus

perfekte Korrelation *f* • perfect/complete correlation *(mat)*

Perfektibilität *f* • perfectibility *(gep)* → Vervollkommnungsfähigkeit

Perfektionismus m • perfectionism *(eth)*

Perfektionsgrad m • degree of perfection *(mat, eth)* < Perfektionsstufe

Perfektionsprinzip n • principle of perfection *(Rawls etc) (eth)*

Perfektionsstufe f • degree of perfection *(Leibniz) (met)*

Performance f • performance *(aes, eco, psy)*

Performanz f • performance *(lan)* ↔ Kompetenz

performativ-konstativ • performative-constative *(Austin) (lan)*

performative Äußerung f • performative utterance *(Austin) (lan)*

performative Einstellung f • performative attitude *(lan, act)*

performative Wahrheitstheorie f • performative theory of truth *(Strawson) (epi, met)*

performativer Akt m • performative act *(Austin) (lan)*

performativer Widerspruch m • performative contradiction *(lan, act)*

Periechontologie f • periechontology *(Jaspers) (ont)*

Periode, erzeugende f • generating period *(mat)*

Periodenverdopplung f • period doubling *(sys)*

periodische Gruppe f • periodic group *(mat)*

Periodisierung f • periodization *(his, gep)*

Periodizität f • periodicity *(gep)*

Peripatetiker m • Peripatetic *(gep)*

peripatetische Philosophie f • peripatetic philosophy *(gep)*

Peripatetismus m • peripatetic doctrine *(gep)*

Perlokution f • perlocution *(Austin etc) (lan, act)* < Illokution

perlokutionärer Akt m • perlocutionary act *(Austin) (lan, act)* → Sprechakt, perlokutionärer

perlokutionärer Effekt m • perlocutionary effect *(Austin etc) (lan, act)*

perlokutionärer Erfolg m • perlocutionary success *(Austin etc) (lan, act)*

perlokutionäres Ziel n • perlocutionary aim *(Austin etc) (lan, act)*

permanente Eigenschaften pl • permanent properties *(sci, log)*

permanente Revolution f • permanent revolution *(Trotzky) (pol)*

Permanenz der Kunst f • permanence of art *(Marcuse) (aes)*

Permanenzprinzip n • principle of permanence *(mat)*

permissive Erziehung f • permissive education *(psy, soc)*

permissive Gesellschaft f • permissive society *(soc)*

permissiver Ausdruck m • permissive expression *(lan)*

Permutation f • permutation *(mat, log)* < Assoziativgesetz, Distributivgesetz, Variation

perpetuum mobile n • nt, perpetual motion machine *(nat)*

Perseveranz f • perseverance *(psy, gep)*

Perseveration f • perseveration *(psy)*

Person f • person *(jur, eth)* < Rechtsträger

Person(en)begriff m • concept of person *(eth, ant)*

Person(en)status des Fötus m • personhood of the foetus *(eth)*

personale Erklärung f • personal explanation *(rel)*

personale Identität f • personal identity *(psy, met)*

personaler Gott m • personal God *(rel)*

personaler Idealismus m • personal idealism *(McTaggart) (met)*

personales Leben n • personal life *(met)*

Personalisation f • personalization *(psy)*

Personalismus m • personalism *(Kant, Fichte) (eth), (Nietzsche) (ant), (Scheler etc) (rel)*

Personenkult m • personality cult, cult of personality *(pol)*

Personenname m • personal name, proper noun/name *(lan)*

personenorientiert • person oriented *(Searle) (lan, act)*

Personifikation f • personification *(gep)* → Personifizierung

personifizieren • to personify *(gep)*

Personifizierung f • personification *(gep)* → Personifikation

persönliche Beziehungen pl • personal relationships *(soc)*

persönliche Gewißheit f • personal certainty/certitude *(epi)*

persönliche Identität f • personal identity *(psy)* < Individualität

persönliche Interpretation der Wahrscheinlichkeit f • personal interpretation of probability *(sci)* < Wahrscheinlichkeitsinterpretation, subjektive

persönlicher Wert m • personal value *(eth)*

persönliches Wesen n • personal being *(met, rel)*

persönliches Wissen n • personal knowledge *(Polanyi etc) (epi, sci)*

Persönlichkeit f • personality *(psy)* < Person-Sein

Persönlichkeitsbildung *f* • character formation *(psy)*

Persönlichkeitsentfaltung *f* • personality development *(psy, eth)*

Persönlichkeitsentwicklung *f* → Persönlichkeitsentfaltung

Persönlichkeitspsychologie *f* • psychology of personality *(psy)* < differentielle Psychologie

Persönlichkeitsrechte *pl* • personal rights *(jur)* < Menschenrechte

Persönlichkeitsspaltung *f* • split/multiple personality, schizophrenia *(min, psy)* → Ichspaltung < Bewußtseinsspaltung, Schizophrenie

Persönlichkeitsstörung *f* • personality disorder *(psy)*

Persönlichkeitstest *m* • personality test *(psy)*

Persönlichkeitstyp *m* • personality type *(psy)*

Persönlichkeitsveränderung *f* • personality change *(psy)*

Persönlichkeitsverlust *m* • loss of personality *(psy)* < Selbstverlust

Persönlichkeitswert *m* • value of personality/ the person, value of personhood *(N. Hartmann)* *(eth)*

Person-Sein *n* • personhood *(eth, met)* < Persönlichkeit

Personwert *m* • value as (a) person *(Scheler)* *(met)*

Perspektivansicht *f* • foreshortening *(aes)*

Perspektivenvielfalt *f* • variety of perspectives, perspective variety *(gep)*

Perspektivismus *m* • perspectivism *(epi, met, aes)*

Perspektivität *f* • perspectivity *(mat)*

Perspikuität *f* • perspicuity *(Aristotle)* *(lan)* ↔ Opakheit < Übersichtlichkeit

persuasiv • persuasive *(psy, lan)*

persuasiver Ausdruck *m* • persuasive expression *(lan, eth)*

Perversion *f* • perversion *(psy)*

Perversion der Kunst *f* • perversion of art *(aes)*

pervertiertes Ideal *n* • perverted ideal *(eth)*

Perzeptibilität *f* • perceptibility *(epi, psy)* → Wahrnehmbarkeit < Wahrnehmungsvermögen

Perzeption *f* • perception *(psy)*, *(Leibniz etc)* *(epi)* → sinnliche Wahrnehmung ↔ Apperzeption

Perzeptionalismus *m* • perceptionalism *(Hamilton)* *(epi)*

Perzeptionsmodelle *pl* • perception models *(epi, psy)*

perzipieren • to perceive *(psy, epi)*

Pessimismus *m* • pessimism *(Schopenhauer etc)* *(met, psy)* < Schwarzseher

Peter-Prinzip *n* • Peter Principle *(soc)*

petitio principii *f* • nt, begging the question *(log)* < circulus vitiosus

Pfad, achtfacher *m* • eightfold way *(Buddha)* *(asp)*

Pfad, achtteiliger *m* → Pfad, achtfacher

Pfad der Befreiung *m* • path of liberation *(asp)*

Pfad der Erkenntnis *m* • path of knowledge *(Plato)* *(epi)*

Pfad der Erleuchtung *m* • path to enlightenment *(asp)*

Pfadanalyse *f* • path analysis *(log)*

Pfeildiagramm *n* • arrow diagram *(mat)*

Pfeil-Paradox(on) *n* • arrow paradox *(Zeno)* *(log)*

Pfeilvorschaltung *f* • implication introduction *(log)*

Pflegebedürftigkeit *f* • need of care *(eth)*

Pflegeethik *f* • nursing ethics *(eth)*

Pflicht *f* • duty *(eth)* < Verpflichtung

Pflicht gegen andere *f* • duty to/toward(s) others *(eth)*

Pflicht gegen sich (selbst) *f* • duty to/toward(s) oneself/self *(eth)*

Pflicht, Handeln aus *n* • acting from duty *(Kant)* *(eth)*

Pflicht, Neigung zur *f* • inclination toward duty *(Kant)* *(eth)*

Pflicht und Neigung *f,f* • duty and inclination *(Kant etc)* *(eth)*

Pflicht, vollkommene *f* • perfect duty *(Kant)* *(eth)*

Pflicht(en)ethik *f* • duty ethics, ethics of duty *(Kant etc)* *(eth)* → deontologische Ethik < Deontologie

Pflichtbewußtsein *n* • sense of duty *(eth)* → Pflichtgefühl

Pflichten, bürgerliche *pl* • civil duties *(pol, eth)*

Pflichten des Menschen gegen sich und andere *pl* • duties of man toward himself and others *(eth)*

Pflichten gegenüber künftigen Generationen *pl* • duties towards/to future generations *(eth)* < intergenerationelle Gerechtigkeit

Pflichten, unbedingte *pl* • unconditional duties *(eth)*

Pflichtenkollision *f* • clash/conflict of duties/ obligations *(eth)*

Pflichtenlehre *f* • theory of duties, deontology *(eth)*

Pflichterfüllung *f* • fulfilment of duty, doing one's duty *(eth)*

Pflichtgefühl *n* • sense of duty *(eth)* → Pflicht-bewußtsein

pflichtgemäß • in conformity with duty, according to duty *(eth)*

pflichtmäßig • in accordance with duty, according to duty *(Kant) (eth)* → pflicht-gemäß ↔ aus Pflicht

Pflichtverletzung *f* • breach of duty *(eth)*

Pflichtversäumnis *n* • neglect of duty *(eth)* < Unterlassungshandlung

phallische Phase *f* • phallic stage *(Freud) (psy)*

phallischer Charakter *m* • phallic character *(Freud) (psy)*

Phallogozentrismus *m* • phallogocentrism *(Derrida) (met, fem)* < Männlichkeit der Vernunft

Phallokratie *f* • phallocracy *(fem)*

Phalluskult *m* • phallic cult *(rel)* → Linga(m)-kult

Phänomen *n* • phenomenon *(epi, met)* → Phänomenon

phänomenale Welt *f* • phenomenal world *(Kant) (epi, met)*

phänomenales Ich *n* • phenomenal ego/self *(Kant) (epi, met)* → empirisches Ich

phänomenales Sein *n* • phenomenal being *(Hegel) (met)*

Phänomenalismus *m* • phenomenalism *(epi)*

Phänomenalismus, faktischer *m* • factual phenomenalism *(Mill) (epi)*

Phänomenalismus, konstruktionalistischer *m* • constructivist(ic) phenomenalism *(epi)*

Phänomenalismus, linguistischer *m* • linguistic phenomenalism *(lan)*

phänomenalistische Wahrnehmungstheorie *f* • phenomenalist theory of perception *(epi)*

Phänomenalität, Satz der *m* • principle of phenomenality *(Dilthey) (epi, psy)*

Phänomenimmanenz *f* • immanence of (the) phenomena *(N. Hartmann) (met)*

Phänomenologie *f* • phenomenology *(Lambert, Husserl etc) (epi)*

Phänomenologie der Tat *f* • phenomenology of action/acting *(met, act)*

Phänomenologie des Bewußtseins *f* • phenomenology of consciousness *(met)*

Phänomenologie des Geistes *f* • phenomenology of (the) spirit/mind *(Hegel) (met)* < W 745

Phänomenologie, deskriptive *f* • descriptive phenomenology *(Brentano) (epi)*

Phänomenologie, genetische *f* • genetic phenomenology *(Husserl) (epi, met)*

Phänomenologie, linguistische *f* • linguistic phenomenology *(Austin) (lan)*

Phänomenologie, reine *f* • pure phenomenology *(Husserl) (epi, met)*

Phänomenologie, statische *f* • static phenomenology *(Husserl) (epi, met)*

Phänomenologie, transzendentale *f* • transcendental phenomenology *(Husserl) (epi, met)* < W 531

phänomenologische Analyse *f* • phenomenological analysis *(Husserl) (epi, met)* < logische Analyse

phänomenologische Ästhetik *f* • phenomenological aesthetics *(Konrad, Ingarden etc) (aes)*

phänomenologische Differenz *f* • phenomenological difference *(Husserl etc) (epi, met)*

phänomenologische Einklammerung *f* • phenomenological bracketing *(Husserl) (epi, met)* → Epoché

phänomenologische Einstellung *f* • phenomenological attitude *(epi, met)*

phänomenologische Herkunft *f* • phenomenological derivation *(epi, met)*

phänomenologische Methode *f* • phenomenological method *(Husserl etc) (epi, met)*

phänomenologische Reduktion *f* • phenomenological reduction *(Husserl) (epi, met)*

phänomenologische Wesensschau *f* • intuition of (material) essences *(Stumpf, Husserl) (epi, min)*

phänomenologischer Bruch *m* • phenomenological break *(Husserl) (epi, met)*

Phänomenon *n* • phenomenon *(Plato, Kant) (met)* ↔ Noumenon

Phänotyp *m* • phenotype *(nat)* ↔ Genotyp

phänotypische Plastizität *f* • phenotypic(al) plasticity *(nat, ant)*

Phantasiegebilde *n* • figment of the imagination *(psy, gep)*

Phantasma *n* • phantasm *(psy)*

Phantasmagorie *f* • phantasmagoria *(psy)* → Trugbild

phantastischer Realismus *m* • fantastic realism *(aes)*

Pharisäismus *m* • pharisaism *(rel, eth)*

Phase *f* • phase *(gen)*

Phasenmodell *n* • phase model *(psy, sys)*

Phasenübergang *m* • phase transition *(sys)*

phatischer Akt *m* • phatic act *(Austin) (lan)*

Phem *n* • pheme *(Austin) (lan)*

Philanthropie *f* • philanthropy *(eth)* → Menschenfreundlichkeit ↔ Misanthropie

Philistertum *n* • philistinism *(Nietzsche) (soc)*

Philo von Alexandrien • Philo of Alexandria

Philodoxie f • philodoxy *(Kant) (gep)* ↔ Philosophie

Philologie f • philology *(gep)*

Philosoph m • philosopher *(gep)*

Philosophaster m • philosophaster *(gep)*

Philosophem n • philosopheme, philosophical theorem° *(gep)*

Philosophenkönig m • philosopher-king *(Plato) (pol)*

philosophia perennis f • nt, perennial philosophy *(gep)* → Philosophie, immerwährende

philosophia prima f • first philosophy *(Aristotle) (met)*

Philosophie f • philosophy *(gep)* < Weisheitsliebe

Philosophie als Magd der Theologie f • philosophy as (the) handmaiden of theology *(gep, rel)* < ancilla theologiae

Philosophie, Aufgabe der f • the task/business of philosophy *(gep)*

Philosophie, Begriffssystem der n • conceptual system of philosophy *(gep)*

Philosophie der Aktion f • philosophy of action *(Blondel) (eth)* < Philosophie der Tat

Philosophie der Antike f • philosophy of antiquity, ancient philosophy *(gep)*

Philosophie der Biologie f • philosophy of biology *(nat)*

Philosophie der Differenz f • philosophy of difference *(epi, pol)*

Philosophie der Geisteswissenschaft f • philosophy of the humanities, philosophy of the human sciences *(gep)*

Philosophie der Geschichte f • philosophy of history *(his)* < W 1258

Philosophie der idealen Sprache f • ideal language philosophy *(Carnap etc) (lan)*

Philosophie der Kultur f → Kulturphilosophie

Philosophie der Kunst f • philosophy of art *(aes)*

Philosophie der Logik f • philosophy of logic *(log)*

Philosophie der Mathematik f • philosophy of mathematics *(mat)*

Philosophie der Musik f • philosophy of music *(aes)*

Philosophie der Natur f → Naturphilosophie

Philosophie der Neuen Musik f • philosophy of modern music *(Adorno) (aes)* < W 764

Philosophie der normalen Sprache f • philosophy of ordinary language, ordinary language philosophy, OLP *(lan)*

Philosophie der Politik f • political philosophy, philosophy of politics *(pol)*

Philosophie der Tat f • philosophy of action *(Bauer etc) (gep)*

Philosophie der Technik f • philosophy of technology *(tec)*

Philosophie der technisierten Zivilisation f • philosophy of mechanized civilization *(tec)*

Philosophie des Als-Ob f • philosophy of (the) as if, as-if philosophy *(Vaihinger) (epi, met)* < W 770

Philosophie des Geistes f • philosophy of spirit/mind *(Hegel) (met)*, philosophy of mind *(min)* < Bewußtseinsphilosophie

Philosophie des Geistes, analytische f • analytical philosophy of mind *(min)*

Philosophie des Rechts f • philosophy of law *(jur)* → Rechtsphilosophie

Philosophie des Subjekts f • philosophy of the subject *(met)*

Philosophie des Unbewußten f • philosophy of the unconscious *(E. Hartmann) (psy, met)* < W 775

Philosophie, Ende der n • end of philosophy *(gep)*

Philosophie, Grenzen der pl • limits of philosophy *(gep)*

Philosophie, immerwährende f • perennial philosophy *(gep)* → philosophia perennis

Philosophie, normative f • normative philosophy *(eth, gep)*

Philosophie, praktische f • practical philosophy *(eth, gep)*

Philosophie, scholastische f • scholastic philosophy *(gep)*

Philosophie, sprachanalytische f • linguistic-analytic philosophy, language analytical philosophy *(lan)*

Philosophie, systematische f • systematic philosophy *(gep)*

Philosophie, theoretische f • theoretical philosophy *(gep)*

Philosophiebegriff m • concept of philosophy *(gep)*

Philosophiedidaktik f • didactics of philosophy *(gep)*

Philosophiegeschichte f • history of philosophy *(gep)*

philosophieren • to philosophize *(gep)*

Philosophieren, das n • philosophizing *(gep)*

philosophische Anthropologie f • philosophical anthropology *(ant)*

philosophische Erklärung f • philosophical explanation *(gep)*

philosophische Gewißheit f • philosophical certainty *(epi)*

philosophische Gotteslehre f • philosophical theology *(rel)* philosophische Grammatik *f* • philosophical grammar *(Wittgenstein)* *(lan)*

philosophische Ideengeschichte *f* • history of philosophical ideas *(gep)*

philosophische Spekulation *f* • philosophical speculation *(gep)*

philosophische Theologie *f* • philosophical theology *(rel)*

philosophischer Glaube(n) *m* • philosophical faith *(Jaspers)* *(met)*

philosophischer Idealismus *m* • philosophical idealism *(epi, met)*

philosophischer Realismus *m* • philosophical realism *(epi, met)*

Phlogistontheorie *f* • phlogiston theory *(nat, met)*

Phonetik *f* • phonetics *(lan)*

phonetischer Akt *m* • phonetic act *(Austin)* *(lan)*

Phonozentrismus *m* • phonocentrism *(Derrida)* *(met)*

Phoronomie *f* • phoronomy *(Kant)* *(nat)* → Kinematik

Photorealismus *m* • photorealism *(aes)*

Phraseologie *f* • phraseology *(lan)*

Phrastik *f* • phrastic *(Hare)* *(eth)* ↔ Neustik

Phrenologie *f* • phrenology *(Gall, Lavater)* *(nat, psy)* → Schädellehre < Physiognomik

phronesis *f* • practical wisdom, prudence *(Aristotle)* *(eth)* < Lebensweisheit

Phylogenese *f* • phylogenesis, phylogeny *(nat)* ↔ Ontogenese

Physik *f* • physics *(nat)* < W 794, 796

physikalische Gewißheit *f* • physical certainty *(epi)*

physikalische Möglichkeit *f* • physical possibility *(ont, nat)*

physikalische Notwendigkeit *f* • physical necessity *(ont, nat)*

physikalische Sprache *f* • physical language *(Carnap)* *(lan, sci)*

physikalische Unmöglichkeit *f* • physical impossibility *(ont, nat)*

physikalische Zeit *f* • physical time *(nat)* < Realzeit

physikalischer Monismus *m* • physical monism *(met)*

physikalischer Raum *m* • physical space *(Carnap)* *(epi, ont)*

physikalisches Gesetz *n* • physical law *(nat)* < Naturgesetz

Physikalismus *m* • physicalism *(Neurath, Carnap etc)* *(sci)* < Reduktionismus

physikalistisch • physicalistic *(sci)*

physikotechnische Modelle *pl* • physico-technical models *(mat)*

Physikotheologie *f* • physico-theology *(Kant, Derham etc)* *(met, rel)* < Ethikotheologie

physikotheologischer Gottesbeweis *m* • argument from design *(rel)* → teleologischer Gottesbeweis

Physiognomik *f* • physiognomy, anthroposcopy *(Gall, Lavater)* *(psy)* < Phrenologie

Physiokraten *pl* • Physiocrats *(eco)*

Physiokratismus *m* • physiocratism° *(eco)*

Physiologie *f* • physiology *(nat)*

Physiologie der reinen Vernunft *f* • physiology of pure reason *(Kant)* *(epi)*

Physiologie des menschlichen Verstandes *f* • physiology of human understanding *(Kant)* *(epi)*

Physische, das *n* • the physical *(met, nat)*

physische Teleologie *f* • physical teleology *(Kant)* *(nat, met)*

Pietismus *m* • pietism *(rel)*

pittoresk • picturesque *(aes)*

pittura metafisica *f* • metaphysical painting *(aes)*

Placebo-Effekt *m* • placebo effect *(psy)* < Blindtest

Plagiat *n* • plagiarism *(jur)* < geistiges Eigentum

Planetenbahn *f* • planetary orbit *(nat)*

Planetenbewegung *f* • planetary motion, motion of the planets *(nat)*

Planetenrotation *f* • rotation of the planets *(nat)*

Planetensystem *n* • planetary system *(nat)*

Planung *f* • planning *(act, dec)*

Planungsbürokratie *f* • planning bureaucracy *(soc, pol)*

Planungshorizont *m* • operational horizon *(act, dec)*

Planungsmethode *f* • planning method *(dec)*

Planungsrationalität *f* • planning rationality *(dec, soc)*

Planwirtschaft *f* • planned economy *(eco)* < gelenkte Wirtschaft, Zentralverwaltungswirtschaft

Plastik *f* • (▷ Skulptur) sculpture; (▷ Bildhauerkunst) plastic art *(aes)* → Bildhauerkunst

Plato(n) • Plato

Platoniker *m* • Platonist *(gep)*

Platonische Akademie *f* • Platonic Academy *(gep)*

Platonische Dialoge *pl* • Platonic dialogues *(gep)*

platonische Formen *pl* → platonische Ideen

platonische Ideen *pl* • Platonic forms/ideas *(Plato) (met)*

Platonische Ideenlehre *f* • Platonic theory of forms/ideas *(met)*

platonische Liebe *f* • Platonic love *(psy, gep)*

platonischer Dualismus *m* • Platonic dualism *(met)*

platonischer Idealismus *m* • Platonic idealism *(epi, met)*

platonischer Körper *m* • Platonic solid *(mat)*

platonischer Realismus *m* • Platonic realism *(met)*

platonischer Staat *m* • Platonic state *(pol)* < Idealstaat

platonisches Quadrat *n* • Platonic square *(mat, aes)*

Platonismus *m* • Platonism *(gep)*

Platzhalter *m* • place-holder *(log)*

Plausibilität *f* • plausibility *(epi, sci)*

plausible Welten *pl* • plausible worlds *(epi, ont)* < mögliche Welten

plebejischer Instinkt *m* • plebeian instinct *(Nietzsche) (psy)*

Plebiszit *n* • plebiscite *(pol)* → Volksabstimmung < Demokratie, direkte

Pleonasmus *m* • pleonasm *(lan)* < Tautologie, Redundanz

Pleonexie *f* • greed, acquisitiveness *(eth)* → Habgier < Habensinn, Unersättlichkeit

Plotin • Plotinus

plotinische Metaphysik *f* • Plotinian metaphysics *(met)*

plurale Gesellschaft *f* • plural society *(soc)*

pluralischer Ausdruck *m* • plural term *(Searle) (lan)*

Pluralismus *m* • pluralism *(soc, eth); (ont)* ↔ Singularismus, Monismus

Pluralismus, Faktum des *n* • fact of pluralism *(Rawls) (eth, pol)*

pluralistische Gesellschaft *f* • pluralistic society *(soc)* ↔ monistische Gesellschaft

pluralistische Interpretation der Wahrscheinlichkeit *f* • pluralistic interpretation of probability *(mat)*

Pluralität der Ursachen *f* • plurality of causes *(met)*

Pluriversum *n* • pluriverse *(Schmitt) (pol)*

Plutokratie *f* • plutocracy *(pol)*

Plutoniumgewinnung *f* • plutonium extraction *(env)* < Proliferation

Pneuma *n* • soul *(Stoicism etc) (met, rel)*

Pneumatik *f* • pneumatics *(met, rel)*

Pneumatismus *m* • pneumatism *(Kant etc) (met, rel)*

Pneumatologie *f* • pneumatology *(met, rel)*

Pöbelherrschaft *f* • mob rule *(pol)* → Ochlokratie

Poesie *f* • poetry *(aes)* → Dichtkunst

Poetik *f* • poetics *(aes)* < W 1055

Poetisierung *f* • poeticization *(aes)*

Pogrom *m/n* • pogrom *(pol)* < Judenverfolgung

Poiesis *f* • poiesis *(Aristotle) (aes, tec)*

poietische Philosophie *f* • poietic philosophy *(Plato) (tec)*

poietisches Wissen *n* • poietic knowledge *(epi, tec)* → Herstellungswissen

Pointillismus *m* • pointillism *(aes)*

Poisson-Verteilung *f* • Poisson distribution *(mat)*

Polare *f* • polar line *(mat)*

Polarität *f* • polarity *(gep)*

Polemologie *f* → Konfliktforschung

Polis *f* • city state *(pol)* → Stadtstaat

Politik *f* • politics *(pol)* < W 801

Politik der Differenz *f* • politics of difference *(epi, pol, fem)*

Politik der Wahrheit *f* • politics of truth *(Foucault) (epi, pol)*

Politik des Körpers *f* • politics of the body *(Foucault) (epi, pol)*

Politikberater *m* • political adviser, policy consultant *(pol)*

Politikberatung *f* • political advice, policy consulting *(pol)*

Politikwissenschaft *f* • political science *(pol)* → Staatswissenschaft

politisch korrekt • politically correct *(pol)*

politische Anthropologie *f* • political anthropology *(ant, pol)*

politische Bildung *f* • political education *(pol)*

politische Erziehung *f* → politische Bildung

politische Ideale *pl* • political ideals *(pol)*

politische Korrektheit *f* • political correctness, PC *(pol)*

politische Kultur *f* • political culture *(pol)*

politische Linke *f* • political left *(pol)*

politische Ökonomie *f* • political economy/economics *(eco)* → Volkswirtschaftslehre < W 131, 1112, 1360

politische Philosophie *f* • political philosophy *(pol)*, civil philosophy *(Hobbes) (pol)*

politische Vereinigung *f* • political association *(pol)*

politische Wissenschaft *f* → Politikwissenschaft

politische Zugehörigkeit *f* • political allegiance *(pol)* politischer Körper *m* • body politic, political body *(Hobbes, Rousseau) (pol)*

politischer Zweck der Kunst *m* • political purpose of art *(aes)* < engagierte Kunst

politisches Denken *n* • political thinking/ thought *(pol)*

politisches Tier, Mensch als *m* • man as political animal *(Aristotle) (pol, ant)* < geselliges Tier, soziales Wesen, zoon politikon

Politologie *f* → Politikwissenschaft

Polizeistaat *m* • police state *(pol)* < Überwachungsstaat

polnische Logik *f* • Polish logic *(log)* < Notation, polnische

Polyandrie *f* • polyandry *(fem, cul)*

Polyarchie *f* • polyarchy *(pol)* → Polykratie

Polygamie *f* • polygamy *(fem, cul)*

Polygenese *f* • polygenesis *(nat)* ↔ Monogenese

Polykratie *f* • polycracy, polyarchy *(pol)* → Polyarchie ↔ Monokratie

polymythisches Denken *n* • polymythical thinking *(Marquard) (gep)* ↔ monomythisches Denken

Polynom *n* • polynome, polynomia *(mat)*

Polyphonie *f* • polyphony *(aes)* ↔ Monodie, Homophonie

polysemantisch • polysemantic *(lan)*

Polysyllogismus *m* • polysyllogism *(log)* < Syllogismus

Polytheismus *m* • polytheism *(rel)* ↔ Monotheismus

Polytonalität *f* • polytonality *(aes)*

Polyzentrismus *m* • polycentrism *(pol)*

Pönitenz *f* • penitence *(rel)* → Buße

pons asinorum *m* • *nt (log)* → Eselsbrücke

Pop-art *f* • pop art *(aes)*

Popliteratur *f* • pop literature *(aes)*

Populärkultur *f* • popular/low culture *(cul, aes)* ↔ Hochkultur

Popularphilosophie *f* • popular philosophy *(gep)*

Populärpsychologie *f* • popular psychology *(psy)*

Populärwissenschaft *f* • popular science *(sci)*

Population von Aussagen *f* • population of statements *(Foucault) (lan, sys)*

Populationsdynamik *f* • population dynamics *(nat, soc, sys)* < Bevölkerungsexplosion

Populationsökologie *f* • population ecology *(env)*

Populationstheorie *f* • population theory *(nat, soc)*

Populismus *m* • populism *(pol)*

Pornographie *f* • pornography *(eth, fem, aes)* < Obszönität

Porosität der Begriffe *f* • open texture of concepts *(Waismann) (lan)*

Porphyrischer Baum *m* → Baum des Porphyrius

Porträt *n* • portrait, portrayal *(aes)*

Porträtmalerei *f* • portraiture *(aes)*

Position *f* • position *(gen)*

Position der guten Gründe *f* • good reason approach *(eth)*

positionales Bewußtsein *n* • positional/thetic consciousness/awareness *(Husserl) (epi, met)*

Positionalität, exzentrische *f* • eccentric/ excentric positionality *(Plessner) (ant)*

positionelle Güter *pl* • positional goods *(eco, soc)* → Prestigegüter, Statusgüter < Prestigeobjekt, demonstrativer Konsum

positiv definit • positive definite *(mat)*

Positivbereich *m* • positivity domain *(mat)*

positive Bedingung *f* • positive condition *(epi, log)*

positive Eugenik *f* • positive eugenics *(nat, eth)* ↔ Eugenik, negative

positive Freiheit *f* • positive freedom *(met)* → Freiheit zu

positive Korrelation *f* • positive correlation *(mat)*

positive Mathematik • positive mathematics *(mat)* → negationsfreie Mathematik

positive Pflicht *f* • positive duty *(Kant etc)* *(eth)*

positive Philosophie *f* • positive philosophy *(Schelling, Comte) (met)* < W 810

positive Rechtswissenschaft *f* • positive jurisprudence *(Kelsen) (jur)*

positive Rückkoppelung *f* • positive feedback *(sys)*

positive Verstärkung *f* • positive reinforcement *(psy)* ↔ negative Verstärkung < Sanktion, positive

positive Wissenschaft *f* • positive science *(Comte) (gep)* < Positivismus

positives Recht *n* • positive/enacted law *(jur)* → gesatztes Recht < geschriebenes Gesetz

positives Wissen *n* • positive/factual knowledge *(epi)* < Faktenwissen

positives Wohlgefallen *n* • positive delight *(Kant) (aes)* ↔ negatives Wohlgefallen

Positivismus *m* • positivism *(Comte etc) (gep)*

Positivismus, logischer *m* • logical positivism *(log, sci)* < logischer Empirismus

Positivismus, therapeutischer *m* • therapeutic positivism *(Farrell) (sci)*

Positivismusstreit *m* • positivism dispute/
debate *(sci)* < Methodenstreit, Werturteilsstreit < W 811

positivistische Rechtstheorie *f* • positivistic
theory of law *(jur)* < Rechtspositivismus

Positivitäten *pl* • positivities *(Foucault) (epi,
pol)*

possessiver Charakter *m* • possessive
character *(Fromm) (psy, soc)*

Possessivität *f* • possessiveness *(psy)* < Besitzanspruch

possest • *nt (Nicholas of Cusa) (ont)* → Seinkönnen

Possibilismus *m* • possibilism *(eth, pol)*

post hoc • *nt (log)* ↔ propter hoc

Postexistenz *f* • post-existence *(met)* ↔ Präexistenz

Posthistoire *f* • posthistoire *(cul, aes)* < Auskristallisierung, Ende der Geschichte

postindustrielle Gesellschaft *f* • post-industrial
society *(Bell) (his, soc)* → nachindustrielle
Gesellschaft

Postkolonialismus *m* • post-colonialism *(pol)*

Postkommunismus *m* • post-communism *(pol)*

Postmaterialismus *m* • post-materialism *(soc,
eth)* < Wertewandel

Postmoderne *f* • postmodernism *(aes, his, soc)*
↔ Moderne

postmoderne Kunst *f* • postmodern art, po mo
art° *(aes)*

postmoderne Philosophie *f* • postmodern
philosophy *(gep)*

postmoderne Welt *f* • postmodern world *(gep)*

postmodernes Zeitalter *n* • postmodern era
(his)

Postprädikamente *pl* • postpredicaments
(Aristotle, Kant etc) (log) < Prädikabilien

Poststrukturalismus *m* • poststructuralism
(gep)

Postulat *n* • postulate *(gep)*

Postulat der Freiheit *n* • postulate of freedom
(Kant) (eth, met)

Postulat der Meßbarkeit *n* • postulate of
measurability *(sci)*

Postulat der Notwendigkeit *n* • postulate of
necessity *(Kant) (epi, met)*

Postulat der Unsterblichkeit *n* • postulate of
immortality *(Kant) (met, rel)*

Postulat der Werturteilsfreiheit *n* • postulate
of freedom from value judg(e)ments
(Weber) (sci)

Postulat des Daseins Gottes *n* • postulate of
the existence of God *(Kant) (eth, met, rel)*

Postulate der praktischen Vernunft *pl* •
postulates of practical reason *(Kant) (eth)*

Postulate der reinen praktischen Vernunft *pl*
• postulates of pure practical reason *(Kant)*
(epi, met, eth)

Postulate des empirischen Denkens *pl* • postulates of empirical thought/knowledge *(Kant)*
(epi)

postulierende Methode *f* • postulational
method *(sci)*

Potemkinsches Dorf *n* • Potemkin village
(gen)

potentia *f* → Potenz

Potential *n* • potential *(gep)*

Potentialgleichung *f* • potential equation *(mat)*

Potentialität und Aktualität *f,f* • potentiality
and actuality *(ont)*

Potentialwert *m* • potential value *(Meinong)*
(met) ↔ Aktualwert

potentielle d-n Erklärung *f* • potential d-n
explanation *(sci)*

potentielle Unendlichkeit *f* • potential infinity
(Aristotle) (ont)

Potenz *f* • potency, power *(Aristotle) (met)*
< Kraft, Vermögen

Potenz-Akt-Lehre *f* • potentiality-actuality
theory *(Aristotle) (ont)* < Dynamis und
Energeia, Möglichkeit und Wirklichkeit

Potenzmenge *f* • power set *(mat, log)*

Potenzreihe *f* • power series *(mat)*

Prädestination *f* • predestination *(met, rel)* →
Vorherbestimmung

Prädetermination *f* • predetermination *(met)*

Prädeterminismus *m* • predeterminism
(Aquinas) (rel, met)

Prädikabilien *pl* • predicables, praedicabilia
(Aristotle etc) (log, epi)

Prädikabilien des reinen Verstandes *pl* • pre-
dicables/praedicabilia of pure reason *(Kant)*
(epi)

Prädikabilität *f* • predictability *(sci)* → Vorhersagbarkeit

Prädikament *n* • predicament *(Aristotle, Plato
etc) (log)* < Kategorie

Prädikat *n* • predicate *(log, lan)*

Prädikatenkalkül *m/n* • predicate calculus
(log, mat)

Prädikatenlogik *f* • predicate logic *(log)*

Prädikatenprädikat *n* • second-order
predicate *(log)*

Prädikation *f* • predication *(lan, log)* <
Satzaussage

prädikativer Akt *m* • predicative act *(log, lan)*

prädikativer Kalkül *m* • predicative calculus
(log, mat)

prädikatives Kalkül *n* → prädikativer Kalkül

Prädikator *m* • predicator *(lan, log)*

Prädikatorenvariable *f* • predicate variable *(log)*

Prädikatskonstante *f* • predicate constant *(log)*

Prädiktion *f* • prediction *(sci, gep)* → Vorhersage

Prädisposition *f* • predisposition *(psy, nat, gep)*

Präexistentialismus *m* • pre-existentialism *(met)*

Präexistenz *f* • pre-existence *(met)* ↔ Postexistenz

Präexistenz der Seele *f* • pre-existence of the soul *(Plato, Plotinus etc)* *(met)*

Präferenzlogik *f* • logic(s) of preference(s), preference logic(s) *(log)*

Präferenzmodell *n* • preferential model *(sci)*

Präferenzordnung *f* • preference order, order of preference *(dec)*

Präferenzprogramm *n* • affirmative action *(soc, eth)* < Quotenregelung

Präferenzskala *f* • preference/preferential scale *(dec, eth)*

Präferenzstruktur *f* • preference structure *(dec)*

Präferenzzuordnung *f* • preference ordering *(dec)*

Präfiguration *f* • prefiguration *(psy, met)* < Urbild

Präformation *f* • preformation *(met)*

Pragmatik *f* • pragmatics *(lan, act)*

pragmatische Bedeutung *f* • pragmatic meaning *(lan)*

pragmatische Bedeutungstheorie *f* • pragmatic/pragmatist theory of meaning *(lan)*

pragmatische Ethik *f* • pragmatic ethics *(eth)*

pragmatische Geschichtsschreibung *f* • pragmatic historiography *(his)*

pragmatische Maxime *f* • pragmatic maxim *(Peirce)* *(epi)*

pragmatische Rechtfertigung *f* • pragmatic justification/vindication *(sci)*

pragmatische Rechtfertigungstheorie *f* • pragmatic theory of justification *(James)* *(sci)*

pragmatische Wahrheitstheorie *f* • pragmatic/pragmatist theory of truth *(Peirce etc)* *(epi, met)*

pragmatische Wissenstheorie *f* • pragmatic theory of knowledge *(sci)*

pragmatischer Imperativ *m* • pragmatic imperative *(Kant)* *(eth)*

pragmatisches Argument *n* • pragmatic argument *(lan)*

pragmatisches Denken *n* • pragmatic thinking *(epi, gep)*

pragmatisches Gesetz *n* • pragmatic law *(Kant)* *(epi, eth)*

pragmatisches Wissen *n* • pragmatic knowledge *(epi)* < Verfügungswissen

Pragmatismus *m* • pragmatism, pragmaticism *(Dewey, Peirce etc)* *(epi, sci, eth)* < Instrumentalismus < W 815, 1261

Prägung *f* • imprint *(nat, psy)*

Prägungstheorie *f* • theory of imprinting *(Lorenz etc)* *(nat)*

Prähistorie *f* • prehistory *(his)* → Vorgeschichte

Prähominide *m* • pre-hominid *(nat, ant)* Menschwerdung

Präjudiz *f* • prejudice *(jur, pol)* → Vorurteil

präkapitalistische Gesellschaft *f* • pre-capitalist society *(eco, soc)*

Präkognition *f* • precognition *(epi, psy)* → Vorauswissen < außersinnliche Wahrnehmung

Praktikabilität *f* • practicability *(act, tec)*

Praktiker *m* • practitioner, practical person *(gen)* ↔ Theoretiker

praktisch notwendige Bedingung *f* • practically necessary condition *(Kant)* *(epi, met)*

praktische Absicht *f* • practical intention *(Kant etc)* *(eth, act)*

praktische Anthropologie *f* • practical anthropology *(Kant)* *(ant, eth)*

praktische Erfahrung *f* • practical experience *(gen)*

praktische Ethik *f* • practical ethics *(eth)* < W 816

praktische Falsifizierbarkeit *f* • practical falsifiability *(sci)*

praktische Frage *f* • practical question *(gen)*

praktische Kausalität *f* • practical causality *(Kant)* *(eth, met)*

praktische Maxime *f* • practical maxim *(Kant)* *(eth)*

praktische Notwendigkeit *f* • practical necessity *(Kant)* *(eth, met)*

praktische Philosophie *f* • practical philosophy *(eth, gep)*

praktische Regel *f* • practical rule *(Kant etc)* *(eth)*

praktische Urteilskraft *f* • practical judg(e)-ment *(Kant)* *(eth)*

praktische Vernunft *f* • practical reason *(epi, eth)* ↔ theoretische Vernunft < W 535

praktische Weisheit *f* • practical wisdom *(Aristotle)* *(eth)* < Klugheit

praktischer Begriff *m* • practical concept *(Kant)* *(epi, eth, lan)* praktischer Diskurs *m* • practical discourse *(Habermas) (soc, lan)*

praktischer Gebrauch der (reinen) Vernunft *m* • practical employment/use of (pure) reason *(Kant) (epi, eth)*

praktischer Grund *m* • practical ground *(Kant etc) (epi, eth)*

praktisches Gesetz *n* • practical law *(Kant) (eth)*

praktisches Interesse der Vernunft *n* • practical interest of reason *(Kant) (met, eth)*

praktisches Prinzip *n* • practical principle *(epi, eth)*   *

praktisches Urteil *n* • practical judg(e)ment *(Kant) (epi, eth)*

praktisches Wissen *n* • practical/technical knowledge, know-how *(epi)* < wissen wie

Praktischwerden der Philosophie *n* • philosophy becoming a practical activity *(gep)*

prälogisch • prelogical *(Lévy-Bruhl) (psy, ant)*

prälogisches Denken *n* • prelogical thinking/thought *(Lévy-Bruhl) (ant), (Piaget) (psy)* → vorlogisches Denken < primitives Denken, wildes Denken

Prämeditation *f* • premeditation *(act)* → Vorüberlegung

Prämisse *f* • premise, premiss *(log)* → Lemma

Prämisse, obere *f* • major premise/premiss *(log)*

Prämisse, untere *f* • minor premise/premiss *(log)*

prana *m* • life force, air *(asp)*

pränatale Diagnostik *f* • prenatal diagnostics *(nat, eth)* < Früherkennung, selektive Abtreibung

pränatale Nichtexistenz *f* • prenatal non-existence *(eso)*

pränexe Normalform *f* • prenex normal form *(log)*

präontologisch • preontological *(Heidegger) (ont)*

Präsapiensmensch *m* • pre-sapiens man *(ant)* → Frühmensch

Präsentismus *m* • presentism *(his)*

Präsenzzeit *f* • specious present *(min, psy)*

Präsidentialsystem *n* • presidential system *(pol)*

Präskription *f* • prescription *(eth)*

präskriptiv • prescriptive *(eth, lan)*

Präskriptivaussage *f* • prescriptive statement *(lan)*

präskriptive Ethik *f* • prescriptive ethics *(eth)* → normative Ethik

präskriptiver Ausdruck *m* • prescriptive term/expression *(lan, eth)*

Präskriptivismus *m* • prescriptivism *(lan, eth)* ↔ Deskriptivismus

Präskriptivismus, universeller *m* • universal prescriptivism *(Hare) (eth, lan)*

präskriptivistische Theorie *f* • prescriptivist theory *(sci)*

Präskriptivität *f* • prescriptivity, presciptiveness *(Hare etc) (eth, lan)*

Präskriptor *m* • prescriptor *(Morris) (lan)* ↔ Askriptor

prästabilierte Harmonie *f* • pre-established harmony *(Leibniz) (met)*

Prästabilismus *m* • theory of/belief in pre-established harmony *(met)* ↔ Okkasionalismus

Präsumption *f* • presumption *(log, sci)* → Annahme

Präsupposition *f* • presupposition *(log, lan)* < Voraussetzung, stillschweigende

Präsuppositionstheorie *f* • presupposition theory *(log, lan)*

Prätention *f* • pretension *(eth, jur, psy)* → Anspruch

Präventionstheorie *f* • prevention theory *(jur)* < Abschreckungstheorie, Straftheorie

Präventivkrieg *m* • preventive war *(pol)*

Präventivmaßnahme *f* • preventive measure *(act)* → Vorbeugungsmaßnahme

Präventivmedizin *f* • preventive medicine *(nat)*

Präventivschlag *m* • pre-emptive strike *(pol)*

Praxeologie *f* • praxiology *(Mises) (eco)*, praxeology *(Kotarbinski) (log, act)* < Entscheidungslogik

Praxis *f* • practice *(gen)* < theoretische Praxis

praxisorientiert • practice oriented, practical *(gen)*

Präzedenzfall *m* • precedent *(jur, act)*

Präzision *f* • precision *(gen)*

Preis der Arbeit *m* • price of labour *(eco)*

Preisabsprache *f* • price agreement *(eco, eth)*

Preisbestimmung *f* • price fixing *(eco)*

Preiserhöhung *f* • price increase/rise *(eco)*

Preismechanismus *m* • price mechanism *(eco)* < Angebot und Nachfrage

Preissignal *n* • price signal *(eco)*

Presbyterianer *m* • Presbyterian *(rel)*

Pressefreiheit *f* • freedom of the press *(pol)* < Redefreiheit

Prestigegüter *pl* • prestige goods *(eco, soc)* → positionelle Güter, Statusgüter < demonstrativer Konsum

Prestigeobjekt *n* • prestige object *(eco, soc)* < positionelle Güter

Prestigesucht *f* • desire for prestige *(psy)*

Priesterherrschaft *f* • government by clerics, hierocracy *(rel)* → Hierokratie, Klerokratie

priesterliche Rasse *f* • priestly race *(Nietzsche) (met)*

Priesterreligion *f* • religion of the priests *(Rousseau) (rel)*

Priestertrugstheorie *f* • theory of deception by priests *(soc, rel)*

prima causatum *n* → erstes Verursachtes

Prima-facie-Beweis *m* • prima facie evidence *(jur)*

Prima-facie-Pflicht *f* • prima facie duty *(eth)*

Prima-facie-Prinzip *n* • prima facie principle *(eth)*

Prima-facie-Ursache *f* • prima facie cause *(sci)*

Prima-facie-Verpflichtung *f* • prima facie obligation/duty *(Ross etc) (eth)*

prima philosophia *f* • first philosophy *(Aristotle etc) (met)* → erste Philosophie

Primalitäten *pl* • primalities *(ont)*

primär performative Äußerung *f* • primary/ primitive/implicit performative (utterance) *(Austin) (lan)*

primäre Abstraktion *f* • primary abstraction *(Aquinas etc) (epi)*

primäre Feindseligkeit *f* • primary hostility *(Freud) (psy)* < Aggression, spontane

primäre Sozialisation *f* • primary socialization *(psy, soc)*

primäre Substanzen *pl* • primary substances *(Aristotle) (ont)*

primäre und sekundäre Eigenschaften *pl* • primary and secondary qualities *(Locke) (epi)*

primäre und sekundäre Qualitäten *pl* → primäre und sekundäre Eigenschaften

primäre Wahrheiten *pl* • primary truths *(epi)*

primäre Welt *f* • primary world *(Carnap) (epi, ont)* ↔ sekundäre Welt

primärer Grund *m* • primary reason *(min, act)*

Primärerfahrung *f* • primary experience *(epi, psy)*

Primärgüter *pl* • primary goods *(eco)* → Grundgüter

Primärliteratur *f* • original texts *(gep)* ↔ Sekundärliteratur

Primärtriebe *pl* • primary drives *(psy)*

Primärursache *f* • primary cause *(met)*

Primärvorgang *m* • primary process *(Freud) (psy)* < Sekundärvorgang

Primat *m/n* • primacy *(log)*, primate *(ant, nat)*

Primat der praktischen Vernunft *m/n* • primacy of practical reason *(Kant) (epi, met)*

Primat der Praxis *m/n* • primacy of practice *(Marx etc) (gep)*

Primat des Bewußtseins vor dem Sein *m/n* • primacy of consciousness/mind over matter *(Marx etc) (met)*

Primat des Intentionalen *m/n* • primacy of the intentional *(Brentano, Chisholm) (min)*

Primatenerbe *n* • primate heritage *(ant, nat)*

Primatologie *f* • primatology *(nat, ant)*

primitive Kunst *f* • primitive art *(aes)*

Primitive, semantische *pl* • semantic primitives, semantic primes *(lan)*

primitiver Term *m* • primitive/indefinable term *(log, lan)* → einfacher Term

primitives Denken *n* • primitive thought *(ant, psy)* < prälogisches Denken < W 353

primitives Symbol *n* • primitive symbol *(log)*

Primitivismus *m* • primitivism *(ant, soc, aes)*

Primogenitur *f* • primogeniture *(jur)* → Erstgeburtsrecht ↔ Ultimagenitur, Recht des Letztgeborenen

Primordialsphäre *f* • primordial sphere *(Husserl) (epi, met)*

Primordialursachen *pl* • primordial causes *(met)*

primum mobile *n* • first mover *(Aristotle) (met, rel)* → erster Beweger, unbewegter Beweger

Primzahl *f* • prime number *(mat)*

principium contradictionis *n* • principle/law of (non-)contradiction *(log)* → Satz vom Widerspruch, Widerspruchsprinzip

principium exclusi tertii *n* • principle/law of (the) excluded middle *(log)* → Satz vom ausgeschlossenen Dritten

principium identitatis indiscernibilium *n* • principle of the identitiy of indiscernibles *(Leibniz) (met)* → Prinzip der Identität des Nichtzuunterscheidenden

principium individuationis *n* • principle of individuation *(met)* → Inividuationsprinzip, Prinzip der Individuation

principium rationis sufficientis *n* • principle of sufficient reason *(log, met)* → Satz vom zureichenden Grund

Prinzip *n* • principle *(met)*

Prinzip der Affinität aller Begriffe *n* • principle of the affinity of all concepts *(Kant) (epi)*

Prinzip der Aggregation *n* • principle of aggregation *(Kant) (epi)*

Prinzip der Allgemeingültigkeit *n* • principle of general/universal validity *(Kant) (eth)*

Prinzip der Ausdrückbarkeit *n* • principle of expressibility *(lan)*

Prinzip der Autonomie *n* • principle of autonomy *(Kant) (eth)*

Prinzip der beobachtbaren Arten *n* • principle of observable kinds *(Stace) (epi, lan, ant)*

Prinzip der Beobachtbarkeit *n* • observability principle, principle of observability *(Neurath) (sci)* < Protokollsatz

Prinzip der durchgängigen Bestimmung *n* • principle of complete determination *(Kant) (epi, log)*

Prinzip der Einfachheit *n* • principle of parsimony, Ockham's razor *(sci, ant)* → Ockhams Parsimoniegesetz

Prinzip der Erhaltung der Materie *n* • principle of the conservation of matter *(nat)*

Prinzip der formalen Zweckmäßigkeit der Natur *n* • principle of formal finality of nature *(Kant) (met, nat)*

Prinzip der geringstmöglichen Kategorien *n* • principle of fewest categories *(Goodman) (epi, lan)* < Ockhams Rasiermesser

Prinzip der Gleichförmigkeit der Natur *n* • principle of the uniformity of nature *(nat)*

Prinzip der Glückseligkeit *n* • principle of happiness *(eth)*

Prinzip der Homogeneität *n* • principle of homogeneity *(Kant etc) (epi)*

Prinzip der Identifikation *n* • principle of identification *(Searle etc) (lan)*

Prinzip der Identität des Ununterscheidbaren *n* → Prinzip der Identität des Nichtzuunterscheidenden

Prinzip der Identitität des Nichtzuunterscheidenden *n* • principle of the identity of indiscernibles *(Leibniz) (met)* → principium identitatis indiscernibilium

Prinzip der Individuation *n* • principle of individuation *(met)* → Individuationsprinzip

Prinzip der Kontinuität *n* • principle of continuity *(Kant etc) (epi)*

Prinzip der Nachsicht *n* • principle of charity *(Wilson, Quine etc) (lan)*

Prinzip der Nichteinmischung *n* • principle of non-interference/non-intervention *(pol)* < Isolationismus

Prinzip der Nichtunterscheidbarkeit *n* • principle of indiscernibility *(Leibniz) (met)* → principium identitatis indiscernibilium

Prinzip der Nomologisierbarkeit *n* • principle of lawfulness *(sci)*

Prinzip der Publizität *n* • principle of publicity/publicness *(Kant etc) (soc, pol, eth)* < Transparenz

Prinzip der reflektierenden Urteilskraft *n* • principle of reflective judg(e)ment *(Kant) (epi)*

Prinzip der Reflexion *n* • principle of reflection *(Kant) (epi)*

Prinzip der Sittlichkeit *n* • principle of morality *(Kant) (eth)*

Prinzip der Spezifikation *n* • principle of specification *(Kant) (epi)*

Prinzip der Teleologie *n* • principle of teleology *(Kant) (met)*

Prinzip der Vollkommenheit *n* • principle of perfection *(Kant) (eth)*

Prinzip der Widerspruchsfreiheit *n* • principle of non-contradiction *(log)* < Kohärenzprinzip

Prinzip des geringsten Widerstands *n* • least-action principle, principle of least action *(nat)*

Prinzip des hinreichenden Grundes *n* • principle of sufficient reason *(log)*

Prinzip des sparsamsten Hypothesengebrauchs *n* • principle of economy in the use of hypotheses *(sci)* < Ökonomieprinzip, Ockhams Rasiermesser

Prinzip des unzureichenden Grundes *n* • principle of insufficient reason *(epi, dec)*

Prinzip des Widerspruchs *n* → Widerspruchsprinzip

Prinzip des Wollens *n* • principle of volition *(Kant) (eth)*

Prinzip, konstitutives *n* • constitutive principle *(Kant) (epi)* ↔ regulatives Prinzip

Prinzip, regulatives *n* • regulative principle *(Kant) (epi)* ↔ konstitutives Prinzip

Prinzip universaler Intelligibilität *n* • principle of universal intelligibility *(Aquinas etc) (met)*

Prinzip vom ausgeschlossenen Dritten *n* • principle/law of (the) excluded middle *(log)* → tertium non datur

Prinzip vom zureichenden Grund *n* → Prinzip des hinreichenden Grundes

Prinzip von der Erhaltung der Masse *n* • principle of (the) conservation of mass *(nat)* → Massenerhaltungssatz

prinzipiell • in principle *(gen)*

Prinzipien des gemeinen Wissens *pl* • principles of common-sense knowledge *(Schütz) (soc, epi)*

Prinzipien des Verstandes, reine *pl* • pure principles of the understanding *(Kant) (epi)*

Prinzipien zweiter Ordnung *pl* • second-order principles *(eth, dec)*

Prinzipienentscheidung *f* • decision of principle *(eth, dec)*

Prinzipienstreit *m* • dispute about principles *(gep)*

Priorität *f* • priority *(dec, gep)*

Prioritätenstreit *m* • priority dispute *(gep)*

Prioritätsprinzip *n* • priority principle *(nat, jur)*

Privateigentum *n* • private property/ownership *(eco, jur)* < Eigentumsrecht

Privateigentum an den Produktionsmitteln *n* • private ownership of the means of production *(Marx etc) (eco, soc)*

privater Gegenstand *m* • private entity *(min)*

privater Sektor *m* • private sector *(soc)* ↔ öffentlicher Sektor

privates Wissen *n* • private knowledge *(epi)*

Privatgelehrter *m* • private scholar, freelance scholar *(gep)*

Privatheit *f* • privacy *(epi)* < Privatsprache; *(eth, pol)* < Privatsphäre

Privatinitiative *f* • private initiative *(eco)*

Privatinteresse *n* • private interest *(eco, eth)* < Klasseninteresse, Partikularinteresse

privatio boni *f* • (evil as) the absence of God *(eth, rel)*

Privation *f* • privation *(Husserl) (log, met)* < Deprivation

Privatisierung *f* • privatization, denationalization *(eco, pol)*

Privatmann *m* • private person *(pol)* → Idiotes

Privatmoral *f* • private morality *(eth)* → Individualmoral < Sozialmoral

Privatrecht *n* • private law *(jur)* → ius privatum

Privatsphäre *f* • sphere of privacy, private sphere *(pol, jur)* < Individualsphäre

Privatsprache *f* • private language *(Wittgenstein) (lan)*

Privatsprachenargument *n* • private language argument *(Wittgenstein etc) (lan)*

Privatunternehmen *n* • private enterprise *(eco)*

Privatwirtschaft *f* • private sector (of the economy) *(eco)* < Marktwirtschaft ↔ Staatswirtschaft

Privileg *n* • privilege *(jur, eth)* → Sonderrecht

privilegierte Stände *pl* • privileged classes *(soc)*

privilegierter Zugang *m* • privileged access *(min)*

Pro und Kontra *n* • pros and cons *(gen)*

Pro-Argument *n* • pro-argument *(log, lan)* ↔ Kontra-Argument

Proärese *f* • proairesis, choice, preference *(Aristotle) (act, met)*

Probabilismus *m* • probabilism *(sci, eth, rel)* < Laxismus

probabilistisch • probabilistic *(sci, eth)* < stochastisch

probabilistische Disposition *f* • probabilistic disposition *(epi)* < Propensitätsinterpretation der Wahrscheinlichkeit

probabilistische Ereigniserklärung *f* • probabilistic explanation of an event *(sci)* < probabilistische Tatsachenerklärung

probabilistische Erklärung *f* • probabilistic explanation *(sci)*

probabilistische Tatsachenerklärung *f* • probabilistic explanation of facts *(sci)* < probabilistische Ereigniserklärung

probabilistischer Automat *m* • probabilistic automaton *(Neumann etc) (AI)*

Probabilität *f* • probability *(mat, sci)* → Wahrscheinlichkeit

Problem der Anfangssingularität *n* • problem of singularity of origin *(nat, met)*

Problem der Evidenz *n* • problem of evidence/evidentiality *(sci)*

Problem der Induktion *n* • problem of induction *(sci, log)* → Induktionsproblem

Problem des Bösen *n* • problem of evil *(met, rel)* < Theodizee

Problem des Erkenntnisfundaments *n* • problem of the foundation of knowledge *(sci, epi)*

Problem des Handlungsreisenden *n* • travelling salesman problem *(log)*

problematischer Begriff *m* • problematic(al) concept *(epi, lan)*

problematischer Idealismus *m* • problematic(al) idealism *(Kant) (epi, met)*

problematischer Imperativ *m* • problematic(al) imperative *(Kant) (eth)*

problematisches Urteil *n* • problematic(al) judg(e)ment *(log, epi)*

problematisieren • to problematize, to question *(gep)*

Problemauswahl *f* • problem selection *(gep)*

Problembewußtsein *n* • problem awareness/consciousness *(gep)*

Problemgehalt *m* • problem content *(Popper etc) (sci)*

Problemgeschichte *f* • problem history, history of a/the problem *(his)*

Problemgruppe *f* • problem group *(soc, psy)*

Problemhorizont *m* • problem horizon *(gep)*

Problemkreis *m* • problem cluster *(gep)*

Problemlösen *n* • problem solving *(sci)*

Problemlöser, allgemeiner *m* • general problem solver, GPS *(Simon) (min, AI)*

Problemlösungskapazität *f* • problem-solving capacity *(sci)*

Problemlösungsprozeß *m* • problem-solving process *(sci)*

Problemlösungsverhalten *n* • problem-solving behaviour *(psy, dec)*

problemorientiert • problem-oriented *(gep)*

problemorientierte Sprache *f* • problem-oriented language *(AI)* < Programmiersprache

Problemraum *m* • problem space *(min)*

Problemreduktion *f* • problem reduction *(sci)*

Problemstellung *f* • problem formulation *(gep)*

Problemverkürzung *f* • problem reduction *(epi, sci)* < Reduktionismus

Problemverschiebung *f* • problem shift *(sci)*

Procedere *n* → Prozedere

Produkt, geistiges *n* • intellectual product *(met)*

Produkt, kartesisches *n* • Cartesian product *(mat)*

Produktbeschreibung *f* • product specification *(eco)*

Produkthaftung *f* • product liability *(eco, jur, eth)*

Produktimitation *f* • product imitation *(eco, eth)* → Produktpiraterie

Produktintegration *f* • integration by parts *(mat)*

Produktion des Wissens *f* • production of knowledge *(epi, pol)*

Produktion, geistige und materielle *f* • intellectual and material production *(eco, soc)*

Produktionsakt *m* • act of production *(Marx)* *(eco)*

Produktionsästhetik *f* • production aesthetics *(aes)* ↔ Rezeptionsästhetik

Produktionsbedingungen *pl* • conditions of production *(Marx etc)* *(eco, soc)*

Produktionsfaktoren *pl* • factors of production *(eco)*

Produktionsform *f* • form of production *(eco, soc)* < Produktionsweise

Produktionsgenossenschaft *f* • producer cooperation, collective farm *(eco)* → Kooperative

Produktionsinstrumente *pl* • instruments of production *(eco)*

Produktionskosten *pl* • costs of production, production costs *(eco)*

Produktionsmittel *pl* • productive assets, means of production *(eco)*

Produktionsmitteln, Besitz an *m* • ownership of the means of production, ownership of productive assets *(Marx etc)* *(soc)*

Produktionsniveau *n* • level of productivity *(eco)*

Produktionsprozeß *m* • process of production, production process *(Marx etc)* *(eco)*

Produktionsstufen *pl* • levels of production *(eco)*

Produktionsverfahren *n* • method of production *(eco)*

Produktionsverhältnisse *pl* • relations of production *(Marx etc)* *(eco, soc)*

Produktionsvermögen *n* • productive capacity *(Marx etc)* *(eco)*

Produktionsweise *f* • mode/method of production *(Marx etc)* *(eco, soc)*

produktive Einbildungskraft *f* • productive (faculty of) imagination *(Kant)* *(epi, aes)*

produktive Orientierung *f* • productive orientation *(Fromm)* *(psy, soc)*

produktive Synthesis *f* • productive synthesis *(Kant)* *(epi)*

produktiver Prozeß *m* • productive process *(eco)* < Schaffensprozeß

Produktivität *f* • productivity *(eco)*

Produktivkraft (der Arbeit) *f* • productive power of labour *(eco)*

Produktivkräfte *pl* • forces of production, productive forces *(Marx etc)* *(eco, soc)*, productive powers *(Condillac etc)* *(psy)*

Produktlebensdauer *f* • product life(time) *(eco, env)*

Produktmenge *f* • (Cartesian) product (set) *(mat)*

Produktpiraterie *f* • product piracy *(eco, eth)* → Produktimitation

Produkttechnologie *f* • product technology *(tec)*

Produktwahl *f* • choice of product *(eco)*

Produzentenvereinigung *f* • association of producers *(eco)* < Genossenschaftsbewegung

Profane, das *n* • the profane *(gep)* ↔ Heilige, das < Göttliche, das < W 451

profane Musik *f* • profane music *(aes)* ↔ Kirchenmusik

Profanierung *f* • profanation *(rel)*

Profankunst *f* • secular art *(aes)*

profaschistisch • profascist *(pol)*

Profession *f* • profession *(eco, rel)*

professionelle Deformation *f* • deformation professionelle *(Durkheim)* *(epi, soc)*

Professorenphilosophie *f* • professorial/academic philosophy *(Schopenhauer)* *(gep)* < Schulphilosophie

Profitdenken *n* • profit orientation *(eco)*

Profitgier f • greed for profit, profiteering (eco)

Profitmaximierung f • profit maximization (eco)

Profitmotiv n • profit motive (eco)

profitorientiert • profit oriented (eco)

Profitrate f • rate of profit (Marx etc) (eco)

Profitrate, fallende f • falling/declining profit rate (Marx etc) (eco)

Profitspanne f • profit margin (eco)

Profitstreben n → Profitdenken

Profitsystem n • profit system (eco)

Prognose f • prediction, forecast, prognosis (sci) → Voraussage

Prognosenbildung f • formulation of a prediction (sci) < Szenario-Denken

Prognosendeduktion f • deduction of predictions (sci)

Prognosenskepsis f • prognosis/prognostic scepticism (sci)

Prognosentheorie f • prediction theory (mat, sci)

Prognostik f • prognostics, prognostic science, forecasting, science of prediction (sci)

Prognostizismus m • prognosticism (sci)

Programmatik f • goal, aim (act) < Zielsetzung

Programmfehler m • bug (AI)

Programmiersprache f • programming language (AI)

Programmierung f • programming (AI)

Programmusik f • programme music (aes) ↔ absolute Musik

Progreß m • progress (log)

Progression f • progression (mat, aes)

Progressismus m • progressivism (gep) → Fortschrittsdenken

progressives Forschungsprogramm n • progressive research programme (Lakatos) (sci)

progressive Synthesis f • progressive synthesis (Kant) (epi)

Progressivsteuer f • progressive taxation (eco) ↔ Proportionalsteuer

Progressus m • progression (log) ↔ Regressus

Prohairesis f → Proärese

Projekt der Aufklärung, das n • the enlightenment project (Habermas etc) (soc)

Projektarbeit f • project work (gen)

Projektierbarkeit f • projectibility (Goodman) (log, lan) < Induktionsproblem

Projektion f • projection (psy, min, sci), (▷ Abbildung) mapping, projection function (mat)

Projektionsprinzip n • projection principle (log)

Projekttechnologie f • project technology (tec)

projizierbares Prädikat n • projectible predicate (Goodman) (log, sci) < pathologisches Prädikat

Proklos • Proclus

Prolegomenon n • prolegomenon (gep) < W 835

Proletariat n • proletariat (soc)

proletarische Kunst f • proletarian art (aes) < sozialistischer Realismus

proletarische Revolution f • proletarian revolution (pol, soc) → Arbeiterrevolution

proletarisches Bewußtsein n • proletarian consciousness (Marx etc) (soc)

Proletkult m • proletcult (aes)

Proliferation f • proliferation (pol) < Atomwaffensperrvertrag

Proliferationsprinzip n • principle of proliferation (Feyerabend) (epi, sci)

prometheische Scham f • Promethian shame (Anders) (ant)

prometheisches Gefälle n • Promethian difference/gap (Anders) (ant)

promissorischer Materialismus m • promissive materialism (Popper, Eccles) (min, met)

Propädeutik f • propaedeutics (gep)

Propagandaapparat m • propaganda machine (pol)

Propagandalüge f • propaganda lie (pol)

Propensitäten pl • propensities (mat, sci)

Propensitätsinterpretation f • propensity interpretation (mat, sci)

Propensitätsinterpretation der Wahrscheinlichkeit f • propensity interpretation of probability (Peirce, Popper etc) (mat, sci)

Propensitätstheorie der Wahrscheinlichkeit f • propensity theory of probability (sci)

Propheten, falsche pl • false prophets (gen)

Prophetie f • prophecy (rel, eso) → Weissagung

Prophezeiung f → Prophetie

Proponent m • proponent (log) ↔ Opponent

Proportion f • proportion (mat, aes) → Verhältnis

Proportionalität f • proportionality (gep) → Verhältnismäßigkeit

Proportionalitätsanalogie f • analogy of proportion/proportionality (Cajetan, Aquinas) (met, rel) < Attributionsanalogie

Proportionalsteuer f • proportional taxation (eco) ↔ Progressivsteuer

Proportionsanalogie *f* → Proportionalitätsanalogie

Proportionslehre *f* • theory of proportions
(mat), theory of proportion *(aes)* < Kanon

propositionale Aussage *f* • propositional
statement *(lan)*

propositionale Einstellung *f* • propositional
attitude *(Russell etc)* *(min, act)*

propositionaler Gehalt *m* • propositional
content *(lan)*

propositionaler Wissenschaftsbegriff *m* •
propositional concept of science *(sci)*

propositionales Argumentieren *n* • propositional reasoning *(log, lan)*

propositionales Wissen *n* • propositional knowledge *(epi, lan)*

Propositionskalkül *m/n* • propositional calculus
(log, mat)

proprietates terminorum *pl* • *nt*, properties of
terms *(log, lan)* < Termeigenschaft, Suppositionstheorie

propter hoc • *nt (log)* ↔ post hoc

Prosa *f* • prose *(aes)*

Prosatz *m* • prosentence *(epi, lan)*

Prosatztheorie der Wahrheit *f* → prosententiale Theorie der Wahrheit

prosententiale Theorie der Wahrheit *f* • prosentential theory of truth *(Grover)* *(epi, met)*
< Prosatz

prospektives Wissen *n* • prospective knowledge *(epi, sci)* < Futurologie

Prosperität *f* • prosperity *(eco, soc)* → Wohlstand

Prosyllogismus *m* • prosyllogism *(log)* < Episyllogismus

Protektionismus *m* • protectionism *(eco, pol)*

Protention *f* • protention *(Husserl)* *(epi, met)*
↔ Retention < Intentionalität

protestantische Arbeitsethik *f* • protestant
work ethic *(eco, eth)*

protestantische Ethik *f* • Protestant Ethic(s)
(Weber) *(rel, eth)* < Geist des Kapitalismus
< W 837

Protestantismus *m* • Protestantism *(rel)*

Protestbewegung *f* • protest movement *(pol)*

Protestwähler *m* • protest voter *(pol)*

Prothesengott *m* • prosthetic God *(Freud)*
(psy, rel)

Protokollsatz *m* • protocol/basic statement
(Neurath) *(lan, sci)* < Basissatz, Atomsatz,
Wahrnehmungssatz, Prinzip der Beobacht-
barkeit

Protokollsprache *f* • protocol language
(Neurath) *(lan, sci)* < Theoriesprache

Protologik *f* • protologic *(Lorenzen)* *(log)*

proton pseudos *n* • *nt*, fallacious premise/
premiss *(Aristotle etc)* *(log)*

Protophilosophie *f* • protophilosophy *(gep)*

Protophysik *f* • protophysics *(nat)*

Protophysik der Zeit *f* • protophysics of time
(Janich) *(nat)*

Prototyp *m* • prototype *(sci, tec, lan)* < Methexis, Urbild

Prototypensemantik *f* • prototype semantics
(lan)

Prozedere *n* • procedure *(act)* → Verfahrensweise

prozedural • procedural *(log, sci)*

prozedurale Ethik *f* • procedural ethics *(eth)*

prozedurale Gerechtigkeit *f* • procedural
justice *(eth)* → Verfahrensgerechtigkeit
< Legitimation durch Verfahren

prozedurale Logik *f* • procedural logic *(log)*

Prozeduren der Intervention *pl* • procedures
of intervention *(Foucault)* *(epi, pol)*

Prozeß *m* • process *(sys)*, trial, (court) case
(jur)

Prozeß der Zivilisation *m* → Zivilisationsprozeß

Prozeß des Werdens *m* • process of becoming
(Nietzsche) *(met)* → Werdensprozeß

Prozeßcharakter *m* • process character *(sys)*

Prozeßdenken *n* • process thinking *(min)*

Prozeßkunst *f* • process art *(aes)*

Prozeßlogik *f* • process logic *(log)* → Logik,
prozedurale

prozeßorientiert • process-oriented *(sys)*

Prozeßphilosophie *f* • process philosophy
(Whitehead etc) *(gep)*

Prozeßstruktur *f* • process/procedural
structure *(sys)*

Prozeßtheologie *f* • process theology
(Whitehead etc) *(rel, met)*

prozyklisch • procyclic(al) *(nat, eco, his)* ↔
antizyklisch

Prüfaussage *f* • test utterance *(sci)*

Prüfbarkeit *f* • testability *(sci)* < Verifizierbarkeit

Prüfbarkeitsgrad *m* • degree of testability
(sci) < Bestätigungsgrad

Prüfbarkeitskriterium *n* • testability criterion
(sci) < Falsifizierbarkeit

Prüfsatz *m* • test statement *(Popper)* *(sci)*
< Basissatz

Prüfverfahren *n* • test(ing) procedure *(sci,
tec)*

Pseudomorphose *f* • pseudomorphosis
(Spengler) *(cul)*

pseudonyme Schriften *pl* • pseudonymous writings *(Kierkegaard) (met, rel)*

Pseudophilosophie *f* • pseudo-philosophy *(gep)*

Pseudoproblem *n* • pseudo-problem *(sci)*

Pseudospeziation *f* • pseudo-speciation *(nat, ant)* → Scheinartenbildung

Pseudotatsache *f* • pseudo-fact, bogus fact *(sci)*

Pseudotugend *f* • pseudo-virtue *(eth)*

Pseudowissenschaft *f* • pseudoscience *(Popper) (sci)* < Falsifikationsimmunität, Immunisierungsstrategie

Pseudozufälligkeit *f* • pseudo-randomness *(mat, log)*

Psi-Phänomen *n* • psi-phenomenon *(eso)*

Psittazismus *m* • psittacism *(Leibniz) (lan)*

Psyche *f* • psyche *(psy, rel, met)* → Seele

psychedelische Erfahrung *f* • psychedelic experience *(psy, eso)*

Psychiatrie der Freiheit *f* → offene Psychiatrie

psychisch • psychic, mental *(psy)*

psychische Distanz *f* • psychic/psychological distance *(aes)* < interesseloses Wohlgefallen

psychischer Prozeß *m* • cognitive process *(Carnap) (min)*, mental process *(psy)*

psychischer Zustand *m* • psychological state *(Searle) (min)*, mental state *(min, psy)*

Psychismus *m* • psychism *(psy, met)* → Psychomonismus

Psychoanalyse *f* • psychoanalysis *(Freud etc) (psy)*

psychoanalytische Theorie *f* • psychoanalytic theory *(psy)*

Psychoanthropologie *f* • psycho-anthropology *(Clauß) (ant, soc)*

Psychobiologie *f* • psychobiology *(nat, psy)*

Psychodynamik *f* • psychodynamics *(psy)*

psychogen • psychogenic *(psy)*

Psychogenese *f* • psychogenesis *(psy)*

Psychognosie *f* • psychognostics *(psy)*

Psychohygiene *f* • psycho-hygiene *(psy)*

Psychokinese *f* • psychokinesis *(eso)*

Psychokybernetik *f* • psycho-cybernetics *(Maltz) (eso)*

Psycholamarckismus *m* • psycho-Lamarck-(ian)ism *(nat)* < Psychobiologie

Psycholinguistik *f* • psycholinguistics *(lan, psy)*

Psychologie *f* • psychology *(psy)*

Psychologie, assoziative *f* • associational/associative psychology *(psy)*

Psychologie, beschreibende *f* • descriptive psychology *(Brentano) (psy)* → Psychologie, deskriptive

Psychologie, deskriptive *f* • descriptive psychology *(Brentano) (psy)* → Psychologie, beschreibende

Psychologie, differentielle *f* • differential psychology *(psy)*

Psychologie, empirische *f* • empirical psychology *(psy)*

Psychologie, erklärende *f* • explanatory psychology *(psy)*

Psychologie, genetische *f* • genetic psychology *(Brentano) (psy)*

Psychologie, kognitive *f* • cognitive psychology *(psy)* → Kognitionspsychologie

Psychologie, rationale *f* • rational psychology *(Wolff) (met, psy)*

Psychologie, transzendentale *f* • transcendental psychology *(Kant, Rickert etc) (psy)*

Psychologie, zergliedernde *f* • analytical psychology *(Dilthey) (psy)*

psychologische Kriegsführung *f* • psychological warfare *(psy, pol)*

psychologische Typen *pl* • psychological types *(Jung) (psy)* < W 1052

psychologische Zeit *f* • psychological time *(psy)*

psychologischer Idealismus *m* • psychological idealism *(Berkeley) (epi, met)* → Idealismus, empirischer

psychologisches Ich *n* • psychological I *(Kant) (epi, psy)*

psychologisches Selbst *n* • psychological self *(Husserl) (epi, met)* ↔ transzendentales Selbst

Psychologismus *m* • psychologism *(psy)*

Psychologismusstreit *m* • psychologism debate *(sci)*

Psychometrie *f* • psychometry, psychometrics *(eso)*

Psychomonismus *m* • psychomonism *(met)* → Psychismus

Psychomorphismus *m* • psychomorphism° *(Piaget) (nat, met)*

psychomotorisch • psychomotoric *(psy)*

psychoneurale Identitätstheorie *f* • psycho-neural identity theory *(min, met)*

Psychoontologie *f* • psycho-ontology *(ont)*

Psychophysik *f* • psychophysics *(Fechner etc) (psy)*

Psycho-Physiologie *f* • psychophysiology, physiopsychology *(psy)*

psychophysischer Parallelismus *m* • psycho-physical parallelism *(met)*

psychophysisches Gesetz *n* • psychophysical law *(met)*

psychophysisches Problem *n* • psychophysical problem *(Wundt etc) (psy)* → Leib-Seele-Problem

Psychosynthese *f* • psychosynthesis *(Assagiolio) (psy, eso)*

Psychoterror *m* • psychological terror *(psy)*

Psychovitalismus *m* • psychovitalism *(met)*

Ptolemäisches System *n* • Ptolemaic system *(nat)* < Geozentrismus

Purismus *m* • purism *(aes)*

Puritanismus *m* • puritanism *(rel, psy)*

Pyrrho(n) von Elis • Pyrrho of Elis

Pyrrhonischer Skeptiker *m* • Pyrrhonic sceptic *(epi)*

Pyrrhonismus *m* • Pyrrhonism *(gep)* < Skeptizismus

Pyrrhussieg *m* • Pyrrhic victory *(act)*

pythagoreischer Lehrsatz *m* • Pythagoras' theorem *(mat)*

pythagoreisches Zahlentripel *n* • Pythagorean (number) triples *(mat)*

Pythagoreismus *m* • Pythagoreanism *(gep)*

Q

q.e.d. → quod erat demonstrandum

Quadrat, logisches *n* • square of opposition *(log)* < Gegensatz, kontradiktorischer; Gegensatz, konträrer; Gegensatz, subalterner; Gegensatz subkonträrer

Quadratur des Kreises *f* • squaring the circle *(mat, log)*

Quadrivium *n* • quadrivium *(gep)* < Trivium, artes liberales, Wissenschaftsgeschichte

Qualia *pl* • qualia *(lan, epi)*

Qualiatheorie *f* • qualia theory *(lan, epi)*

Qualifikation *f* • (▷ Befähigung) qualification, eligibility *(eco, soc)*, (▷ Bestimmung, Angabe von Eigenschaften) qualification/determination *(lan, epi)*

Qualifikationsverlust *m* • de-skilling *(eco)*

qualifizierte Mehrheit *f* • qualified majority *(pol)*

Qualität *f* • quality *(ont)*

Qualität des Urteils *f* • quality of judg(e)ment *(log)*

Qualität, primäre *f* • primary quality *(Locke etc) (epi)* ↔ Qualität, sekundäre

Qualität, sekundäre *f* • secondary quality *(Locke etc) (epi)* ↔ Qualität, primäre

Qualitätengliederung *f* • quality space *(Quine) (ont)*

qualitative Änderung *f* • qualitative change *(soc, pol, sys)*

qualitative Analyse *f* • qualitative analysis *(sci, nat)*

qualitative Einheit *f* • qualitative unity *(Kant) (epi)*

qualitative Vielheit *f* • qualitative plurality *(Kant) (epi)*

qualitative Vollständigkeit *f* • qualitative completeness *(Kant) (epi)*

qualitativer Schluß *m* • qualitative syllogism/inference *(log)*

qualitatives Urteil *n* • qualitative judg(e)ment *(log, epi)*

Qualitätsklassen *pl* • quality classes *(Carnap) (lan, epi, ont)*

Qualitätskontrolle *f* • quality control, QC *(eco)*

Qualitätsmaxime *f* • maxim of quality *(Grice) (lan, act)* < Konversationsmaximen

Qualitätssicherung *f* → Qualitätskontrolle

Qualitätsverbesserung *f* • quality improvement *(eco, tec)*

Quantencomputer *m* • quantum computer *(AI, sys)*

Quantenfeldtheorie *f* • quantum field theory *(nat)*

Quantenlogik *f* • quantum logic *(log)*

Quantenmechanik *f* • quantum mechanics *(nat)* ↔ klassische Mechanik < W 790

Quantenphysik *f* • quantum physics *(nat)* < Teilchenphysik

Quantenpostulat *n* • quantum postulate *(Heisenberg) (nat)*

Quantensprung *m* • quantum leap *(nat)*

Quantentheorie *f* • quantum theory *(Heisenberg) (nat)*

Quantenzahl *f* • quantum number *(nat)*

Quantifikation *f* • quantification *(log, mat, sci)* → Quantifizierung

Quantifizierbarkeit *f* • quantifiability *(sci)* < Mathematisierbarkeit

Quantifizieren, das *n* • quantifying *(sci, log)*

Quantifizieren über Objekte *n* • quantifying over objects *(log, lan)*

Quantifizierung *f* • quantification *(sci, log, mat)*

Quantität des Urteils *f* • quantity of judg(e)ment *(log)*

quantitative Analyse *f* • quantitative analysis *(sci, nat)*

quantitatives Verhältnis *n* • quantitative relation *(sci, mat)*

Quantitätsmaxime *f* • maxim of quantity *(Grice) (lan, act)* < Konversationsmaximen

Quantor *m* • quantifier *(log)*

Quantorenlogik *f* • quantum/quantificational logic *(Birkhoff, Neumann) (log)*

Quark *n* • quark *(nat)*

Quasi-Analyse *f* • quasi-analysis *(Carnap) (sci)*

Quasi-Erklärung *f* • quasi-explanation *(Lenk) (sci, log)*

quasigerichtete Menge *f* • quasi-directed set *(mat)*

Quasi-Gesetz *n* • quasi-law *(sci)*

Quasihandlung *f* • quasi-action *(act)*

Quasi-Indikator *m* • quasi-indicator *(Castaneda) (lan)*

Quasi-Induktion *f* • quasi-induction *(Popper) (sci)*

Quasi-Konstituente *f* • quasi-constituent *(Carnap) (log, lan)*

Quasimerkmal *n* • quasi-characteristic/feature *(Carnap) (sci)*

Quasi-Theorie *f* • quasi-theory *(sci)*

Quästion *f* • question of dispute *(lan)* → Streitfrage

quaternio terminorum • *nt,* fallacy of four terms *(log)*

Quell des Lebens *m* • fountain of life *(nat, rel)*

Quellcode *m* • source code *(lan, AI)*

Quelle der Erkenntnis *f* • source of knowledge/cognition *(epi)* → Erkenntnisquelle

Quellenforschung *f* • study of sources *(sci, his)*

Quellenkritik *f* • criticism of sources *(gep)*

Quellensammlung *f* • sourcebook *(gen)*

Quellenverzeichnis *n* • bibliography *(gep)*

quer zur Zeit • athwart time, skew to time *(Jaspers) (met)*

Querschnittuntersuchung *f* • cross-sectional study *(sci)* ↔ Längsschnittuntersuchung

Querwelt(ein)identität *f* • cross-world/transworld identity *(Lewis, Kripke, Putnam) (epi, lan)*

Quidditas *f* → Quiddität

Quiddität *f* • quiddity, quidditas, whatness *(ont)* → Washeit < Wesen, das

Quietismus *m* • quietism *(rel)*

Quine-Duhem-These *f* • Duhem-Quine thesis, Quine-Duhem thesis *(sci)* → Duhemsche These

Quine-Kriterium *n* • Quine's criterion *(sci)*

Quintessenz *f* • quintessence *(gen)*

quod erat demonstrandum • *nt,* QED *(log, mat)*

Quotenauswahlverfahren *n* • quota selection procedure *(sci, mat)*

Quotenregelung *f* • quota regulation/rule *(pol)* < Präferenzprogramm

Quotensystem *n* • quota system *(pol)*

Quotientenmenge *f* • quotient set *(mat)*

Quotientenregel *f* • quotient rule *(mat)*

R

Rabbinismus *m* • rabbinism *(rel)*

Rabenparadoxie *f* • ravens paradox, paradox of the ravens *(Hempel)* *(log, sci)* →
Hempelsche Paradoxie, Hempels Rabenparadoxon < Schwanenparadoxie

Rabulistik *f* • sophistry *(lan)* → Sophisterei

Rache *f* • revenge, vengeance *(rel, jur, eth)*
< Vergeltung

Rache der Schwachen an den Starken *f* •
revenge of the weak upon the strong *(Nietzsche)* *(eth)* < Ressentiment

Rache der Wiederherstellung *f* • restitutional revenge *(Nietzsche)* *(eth, jur)*

Racheengel *m* • avenging angel *(rel)*

Rachsucht *f* • (re)vengefulness, vindictiveness *(eth)*

Rad der Geschichte *n* • wheels of history *(his)*

Rad des Schicksals *n* • wheel of fortune *(met, eso)*

Räderwerk der Macht *n* • wheels of power *(Foucault)* *(pol)*

Radiästhesie *f* • radi(a)esthesia *(eso)*

Radikal *n* • radical *(nat, mat, psy)*

radikal Böses *n* • radical evil *(Kant etc)* *(eth)*

radikale Interpretation *f* • radical interpretation *(Davidson)* *(lan)*

radikale Übersetzung *f* • radical translation *(Quine)* *(lan)* < Unterbestimmtheit der Übersetzung

radikaler Empirismus *m* • radical empiricism *(James etc)* *(epi)*

radikaler Konstruktivismus *m* • radical constructivism *(epi, met)*

radikaler Zweifel *m* • radical doubt *(Descartes)* *(epi)*

Radikalfeminismus *m* • radical feminism *(fem)*

Radikalisierung *f* • radicalization *(pol)*

Radikalismus, politischer *m* • political radicalism *(pol)*

radioaktiver Niederschlag *m* • radioactive/nuclear fall-out *(nat, env)*

Radioaktivität *f* • radioactivity *(nat, env)*

Radioastronomie *f* • radio astronomy *(nat)*
< kosmologische Evolution

Rahmenbedingung *f* • frame/basic/general condition *(gep)*

Rahmengerechtigkeit *f* • background justice *(Rawls)* *(eth)*

Rahmenordnung *f* • frame order *(eco, soc)*

Rahmentheorie *f* • frame theory *(Goffmann)* *(soc)* < Hintergrundtheorie

Rahmenvorschrift *f* • general regulation/provision, outline provision, policy rule *(jur, eth)*

Ramsey-Elimination *f* • Ramsey elimination *(sci)* < Non-statement view von Theorien

Ramsey-Satz *m* • Ramsey sentence *(sci)*

Randbedingung *f* • boundary condition *(log, mat)*, initial/antecedent condition *(sci)*
< Ausgangsbedingung, Antezedens

Randbemerkung *f* • (▷ mündliche) aside, (▷ schriftlich) marginal note *(gen)*

Randgruppe *f* • fringe group *(soc)*

Randomisierung *f* • randomization *(mat)*

Rang, gesellschaftlicher *m* • social rank/status *(soc)*

Rangfolge *f* • rank order *(nat, mat, soc)*

Rangordnung *f* • order of rank, hierarchy *(mat, nat, soc)* < Hackordnung

Rangordnung der Güter *f* • hierarchy of goods *(eco)* < Bedürfnishierarchie

Rangordnung der Werte *f* • hierarchy of values *(N. Hartmann, Scheler etc)* *(eth, ont)*

Rangstreben, soziales *n* • social climbing *(soc)*
< Konkurrenzsystem

Rangunterschied *m* • social distinction, difference in (social) status/rank *(nat, soc)*

Rangzeichen *n* → Statussymbol

Räsonnieren, das *n* • reasoning, arguing *(gep)*

Rasse, kriegerische *f* • warrior race *(Nietzsche)* *(met)*

Rassendiskriminierung *f* • racial discrimination *(eth, pol)*

Rassenforschung *f* • racial research *(nat, ant)*

Rassenhaß *m* • racial hatred *(eth, pol)*

Rassenhygiene *f* • racial hygiene *(pol, nat)*

Rassenkampf *m* • racial conflict *(pol)*

Rassenkunde *f* • racial/race science, the study of race *(nat)*

Rassenphilosophie *f* • racial philosophy *(pol)*

Rassenpolitik *f* • racial/race policy *(pol)*

Rassenpsychologie *f* • race/racial psychology *(Liebenfels)* *(psy)*

Rassenseele *f* • racial soul° *(Helbok etc)* *(pol, psy)*

Rassentheorie *f* • race theory, theory of the race *(nat)*

Rassentrennung *f* • racial segregation *(soc)*

Rassenvorurteil *n* • racial prejudice *(eth)*

Rassismus *m* • racism, racialism *(pol, eth)*

rassistisches Verhalten *n* • racist/racialistic, behaviour *(pol, eth)*

Rastlosigkeit des Geistes *f* • restlessness of mind *(met)*

Räteregierung *f* • government of soviets *(pol)*

Räterepublik *f* • soviet republic *(pol)*

Ratifizierung *f* • ratification *(pol, jur)*

Ratio *f* • reason *(epi, met)* < Vernunft, Verstand

ratio cognoscendi *f* • heuristic rationality/ means *(epi, sci)* < Heuristik

ratio naturalis *f* • nt, natural reason *(epi, met)*

ratio recta *f* • nt, right reason *(epi, met)*

Ratiofaschismus *m* • ratio-fascism *(Feyerabend) (sci)* → Law-and-Order-Rationalismus

rational motivierte Bindung *f* • rationally motivated binding/bonding *(Habermas) (soc)*

rationale Begründung *f* • rational justification/ foundation/grounding *(epi, sci)*

rationale Binnenstruktur *f* • rational infrastructure *(Habermas) (lan, soc)*

rationale Entscheidung *f* • rational decision *(dec)*

rationale Erkenntnis *f* • rational knowledge *(epi)* → Vernunfterkenntnis

rationale Erwartung *f* • rational expectation *(dec, act, epi)*

rationale Handlung *f* • rational action *(dec, act, eth)*

rationale Klugheitswahl *f* • rational prudential choice *(Rawls etc) (eth, dec)*

rationale Physiologie *f* • rational physiology *(Kant) (epi, met)*

rationale Präferenzbewertung *f* • rational preference assessment *(dec)* < dynamische Gewichtung

rationale Psychologie *f* • rational psychology *(Wolff) (met, psy)*

rationale Rekonstruktion *f* • rational reconstruction *(Carnap) (sci)*

rationale Voraussicht *f* • rational foresight *(epi, dec)*

rationale Wahl *f* • rational choice *(dec)*

rationale Wissenschaft *f* • rational science *(sci)*

rationale Zahl *f* • rational number *(mat)*

rationaler Glaube(n) *m* • rational belief *(epi, sci)*, rational faith *(rel)*

rationaler Überzeugungsgrad *m* • degree of rational belief *(sci)*

rationales Denken *n* • rational thinking/thought *(epi, sci)* < vernunftmäßiges Folgern

rationales Handeln *n* • rational action *(dec, act, eth)*

rationales Verhalten *n* • rational behaviour *(dec, act)*

rationales Verstehen *n* • rational interpretation *(Weber etc) (sci)*

rationalisierte Lebenswelt *f* • rationalized lifeworld *(soc)*

Rationalisierung *f* • rationalization *(eco)*, *(Freud) (psy)*

Rationalisierungsgrad *m* • degree of rationalization *(soc, sci)*

Rationalisierungsmaßnahme *f* • efficiency/ rationalization measure *(eco)*

Rationalisierungsprozeß *m* • process of rationalization *(soc, cul)*

Rationalismus *m* • rationalism *(epi, met, sci)*

Rationalismus, klassischer *m* • classical rationalism *(epi, met)*

Rationalismus, kritischer *m* • critical rationalism *(Popper, Albert etc) (epi, sci)*

Rationalismusdebatte *f* • rationalism debate *(epi, sci)*

rationalistische Baukunst *f* • rationalistic architecture *(aes)*

rationalistische Erkenntniskonzeption *f* • rationalist(ic) conception of knowledge *(epi)*

rationalistische Sprachphilosophie *f* • rationalistic philosophy of language *(lan)*

Rationalität *f* • rationality *(epi)*

Rationalitätsannahme *f* • assumption of rationality, rationality assumption *(epi, met)*

Rationalitätsbereich *m* • domain of rationality *(mat, epi, met)*

Rationalitätsdebatte *f* • rationality debate *(sci)*

Rationalitätsgrenzen *pl* • limits of rationality *(sci)* < Grenzen der Wissenschaften

Rationalitätskriterien *pl* • criteria of rationality *(sci)*

Rationalitätspotential *n* • rationality potential *(Habermas) (gep)*

Rationalitätsprinzip *n* • rationality principle *(eco)* < Kosten-Nutzen-Denken

Rationalitätsproblematik *f* • problem of rationality, rationality problem *(gep)*

Rationalitätszuwachs *m* • increase in rationality *(gep)*

rationell • efficient, economical *(eco, act)*

Ratioskalen *pl* • ratio scales *(sci, mat)*

Ratschläge der Klugheit *pl* • councils of prudence *(Kant) (eth)*

Rätsel des Seins *n* • mystery of being *(Marcel) (met)*

Rätsellösen *n* • puzzle solving *(Popper etc) (sci)* < Problemlösen

Rattenfängerpolitik *f* • pied piper policy *(pol)*

Raubbau *m* • overexploitation, wasteful/predatory exploitation, plundering *(env)*

Raubbau an den Ressourcen *m* • overexploitation of resources, resource depletion *(env)*

Raubbauwirtschaft *f* • economy based on overexploitation, robber/plunder economy *(eco, env)*

Raubtiergewissen *n* • predatory conscience *(Nietzsche) (met)*

Raubtiernatur des Menschen *f* • predatory nature of man, man as beast of prey *(Nietzsche) (ant)* < blonde Bestie

Raum *m* • space *(mat, nat, met)*

Raum als Form unserer Anschauung *m* • space as form of our intuition/anschauung *(Kant) (epi)*

Raum, politischer *m* • political sphere *(pol)*

Raum, psychologischer *m* • psychological space *(psy)*

Raum-Spiel-Zeit *f* • space-play-time *(Heidegger) (ont)*

Raum und Zeit *m,f* • space and time *(nat, met)*

Raum-Zeit-Kontinuum *n* • space-time continuum *(nat)*

Raum-Zeit-Punkt *m* • space-time point *(Carnap) (ont)*

Raum-Zeit-Struktur *f* • space-time structure *(nat)* < W 944

Raumanalyse *f* • volumetric analysis *(mat)*

Raumanschauung *f* • intuition of space, spatial intuition *(Kant) (epi)* → räumliche Anschauung

Raumforschung *f* • space research *(nat, tec)*

Raum-geben *n* • to give space *(Jaspers) (met)*

Raumgefüge *n* • space structure *(Carnap) (epi, ont)*

Raumkunst *f* • space art *(aes)* ↔ Zeitkunst

raum-zeitlich • spatio-temporal *(ont)*

raum-zeitlicher Anfang *m* • spatio-temporal beginning *(nat, met)*

raum-zeitliches Ende *n* • spatio-temporal end *(nat, met)*

räumlich-zeitliche Welt *f* • spatio-temporal world *(met)*

räumliche Anschauung *f* • spatial intuition *(Kant) (epi)* → Raumanschauung

räumliche Ausdehnung *f* • spatial extension *(mat, nat, met)*

räumliche Gliederung *f* • spatial structure/organization *(aes, epi, met)*

räumliche Präsenz *f* • spatial presence *(ont, aes)*

räumliche Struktur *f* • spatial structure *(nat, aes)*

Räumlichkeit *f* • spatiality *(met)* ↔ Zeitlichkeit

Raumorientierung *f* • spatial orientation *(psy)*

Raumpunkt *m* • point in space *(Wittgenstein etc) (ont)*

Raumwahrnehmung *f* • perception of space, space/spatial perception *(epi, psy)*

Raumzeit *f* • space-time *(nat)*

Raumzeitalter *n* • space age *(his)*

Rauschen *n* • noise *(lan)* < Informationstheorie

Rauschgifthandel *m* • drug trade/trafficking *(eco)*

Rauschgiftsucht *f* • drug addiction *(psy)*

Rauschzustand *m* • state of intoxication *(Nietzsche, Bollnow etc) (met, psy, aes)* < Genieästhetik

Razor-Search-Methode *f* • razor search method *(Bandler, Macdonald) (sci)*

Ready-made *n* • ready-made *(Duchamp) (aes)*

Reaktion *f* • response, reaction *(psy, act)* < Reiz-Reaktions-Schema; reaction *(pol)*

Reaktion, bedingte *f* • conditioned response, CR *(psy, nat)*

Reaktion, unbedingte *f* • unconditioned response, UCR *(psy, nat)*

Reaktionär *m* • reactionary *(pol)*

reaktionäre Kräfte *pl* • reactionary forces *(pol, soc)*

Reaktionsbildung *f* • reaction-formation *(psy)*

Reaktionsverzögerung *f* • delayed reaction *(psy)*

reaktive Kräfte *pl* • reactive forces *(nat, sys)*

Reaktorkatastrophe *f* • nuclear disaster *(tec, env)* < GAU

real existierender Sozialismus *m* • real-world/existing socialism, actually existing socialism *(pol)*

real und imaginär • real and imaginary *(met)*

Realangst *f* • realistic anxiety *(Freud) (psy)*

Realdefinition *f* • real definition *(log, lan)*

Realdialektik *f* • real dialectics *(N. Hartmann) (met)*

Reale, das *n* • the real *(Kant etc) (met)*

reale Kommunikationsgemeinschaft *f* • real communication community *(Habermas) (soc, lan)* ↔ ideale Kommunikationsgemeinschaft

reale Möglichkeit *f* • real possibility *(epi, met)*

reale Unmöglichkeit *f* • real impossibility *(epi, met)*

Realeinkommen *n* • real income *(eco)*

reales Maß *n* • real measure *(mat)*

reales Prädikat *n* • real predicate *(log, epi)*

Realfaktoren *pl* • real factors *(sci, soc)* < Idealfaktor

Realgeschichte *f* • material history, history of (material) facts, real history *(his)* ↔ Ideengeschichte

Realgrund *m* • real ground *(Kant) (met)* ↔ Idealgrund

Realia *pl* • real things *(ont)*

Realidealismus *m* • real-idealism *(Schelling) (met)* < Identitätssystem

Realismus *m* • realism *(epi, met, aes)*

Realismus, ästimativer *m* • estimative realism *(Rescher) (epi)*

Realismus, blinder *m* • blind realism *(Almender) (epi)*

Realismus, direkter *m* • direct realism *(epi)*

Realismus, emotionaler *m* • emotional realism *(epi, met)* < Realismus, irrationaler

Realismus, epistemologischer *m* • epistemological realism *(Peirce) (epi)*

Realismus, explanatorischer *m* • explanatory realism *(Boyd) (lan)*

Realismus, gemäßigter *m* • moderate realism *(Aristotle etc) (epi)*

Realismus, indirekter *m* • indirect realism *(epi)*

Realismus, interner *m* • internal realism *(Putnam) (epi)*

Realismus, irrationaler *m* • irrational realism *(Scheler, N. Hartmann) (epi)*

Realismus, logischer *m* • logical realism *(log)*

Realismus, metaphysischer *m* • metaphysical realism *(epi, met)*

Realismus, mittelalterlicher *m* • medieval realism *(Duns Scotus etc) (epi)*

Realismus, mittelbarer *m* → Realismus, indirekter

Realismus, naiver *m* • naive realism *(epi, met, aes)*

Realismus, perspektivischer *m* • perspective/ perspectival realism *(McGilvary) (epi)*

Realismus, politischer *m* • political realism *(pol)*

Realismus, psychologischer *m* • psychological realism *(psy)*

Realismus, repräsentativer *m* • representative realism *(Descartes, Locke etc) (epi)*

Realismus, semiotischer *m* • semiotic realism *(lan)*

Realismus, sozialistischer *m* • socialist realism *(aes)*

Realismus, sprachphilosophischer *m* • linguistic realism *(Dummet) (lan)*

Realismus, transzendentaler *m* • transcendental realism *(E. Hartmann) (epi, met)*

Realismus, unmittelbarer *m* → Realismus, direkter

Realismus, volitiver *m* • volitive realism *(epi, met)* < Realismus, irrationaler

Realismus, wissenschaftlicher *m* • scientific realism *(epi, sci)*

Realismustheorie *f* • theory of realism *(aes)* < Expressionismusdebatte

Realistik *f* • realism *(aes)*

Realität *f* • reality *(met)* → Wirklichkeit ↔ Idealität

Realität, akzidentelle *f* • accidental reality *(met)*

Realität der Außenwelt *f* • reality of the external world *(epi, met)*

Realität, existenzielle *f* • existential reality *(met)*

Realität, objektive *f* • objective reality *(met)*

Realität, Sphären der *pl* • spheres of reality *(N. Hartmann) (ont)*

Realitätsbegriff *m* • concept of reality *(met)*

Realitätsbezug *m* • reference/relation to reality *(psy, met)*

Realitätserfahrung *f* • experience of reality *(epi, psy)*

Realitätsflucht *f* • escape/flight/withdrawal from reality *(psy)* → Wirklichkeitsflucht, Eskapismus, Weltflucht

Realitätsgefühl *n* → Realitätssinn

Realitätsprinzip *n* • reality principle *(Freud) (psy)* ↔ Lustprinzip

Realitätsprüfung *f* • reality-testing *(Freud) (psy)*

Realitätssinn *m* • sense of/for reality, sense of realism *(psy)*

Realitätsspaltung *f* • bifurcation of reality *(Descartes etc) (epi, met)*

Realitätsstufe *f* • degree/level of reality *(Leibniz etc) (met)*

Realitätsverlust *m* • loss of (the sense of) reality *(psy, met)*

Realitätsverzerrung *f* • distortion of reality *(psy)*

Realmöglichkeit *f* • real possibility *(N. Hartmann) (ont)*

Realnotwendigkeit *f* • real necessity *(N. Hartmann) (ont)*

Realphilosophie *f* • material/substantial philosophy *(gep)*

Realpolitik *f* • realpolitik *(pol)* < Machtpolitik

Realpsychologie *f* • realpsychologie *(Dilthey etc) (psy)* < Psychologie, erklärende; Psychologie, deskriptive

Realraum *m* • real space *(N. Hartmann) (ont)* ↔ virtueller Raum

Realteil *m* • real part *(mat)*

Realwissenschaft *f* • real science *(sci)* < empirische Wissenschaft

Realzeit *f* • real time *(N. Hartmann) (ont), (Ingarden) (aes), (AI)* < Zeit, biologische; Zeit, immanente; Zeit, physikalische; Naturzeit

Rebirthing *n* • rebirthing *(eso)* → Wiedergeburt

Rechenmaschine *f* • calculating machine *(mat)* < analytische Maschine, Differenzmaschine

Recherche *f* • search, investigation, inquiry *(sci)*

recherchieren • to research/investigate *(sci)*

rechnergestützte numerische Kontrolle *f* • computer-aided numerical control, CNC *(AI)*

rechnerunterstützte Ingenieursarbeit *f* • computer-aided engineering, CAE *(AI)*

rechnerunterstütztes Entwerfen *n* • computer-aided design, CAD *(AI)*

rechnerunterstütztes Übersetzen *n* • computer-aided translation, CAT *(AI)*

Recht *n* • (▷ Anrecht) entitlement, right, (▷ Gesetz) law *(jur)*

Recht aller auf alles *n* • everyone's right to everything *(Hobbes etc) (jur, pol)*

Recht auf Arbeit *n* • right to work *(eth, eco)*

Recht auf Eigentum *n* • right/entitlement to property *(jur, eco)*

Recht auf Freiheit *n* • right to liberty *(jur, eth, pol)*

Recht auf Leben *n* • right to life *(eth, jur)* → Existenzberechtigung, Lebensrecht

Recht auf Verweigerung aus Gewissensgründen *n* • right to conscientious objection *(eth, pol)*

Recht auf Wahlfreiheit *n* • right to choose *(act, eth)*

Recht der ersten Besitzergreifung *n* • right of the first occupant/owner *(jur, eco)* < Okkupationstheorie

Recht des Erstgeborenen *n* → Primogenitur

Recht des Letztgeborenen *n* → Ultimagenitur

Recht des Stärkeren *n* • law of the strongest *(jur)* < Sozialdarwinismus, Verdrängungswettbewerb

Recht, gesatztes *n* • positive/enacted law *(jur)* → positives Recht < Rechtspositivismus

Recht und Ordnung • law and order *(pol)*

Rechte, die *f* • the Right *(pol)* < Rechtsextremismus

rechte Lebensführung *f* • right conduct *(eth, asp)*

rechte Lebensgrundlage *f* • right livelihood *(eth, asp)*

rechte Rede *f* • right speech *(eth, asp)*

Rechte und Pflichten *pl,pl* • rights and duties *(jur, eth)*

rechte Vernunft *f* • right reason *(epi, met)* → recta ratio

Rechter *m* • rightist, right-winger, member of the Right *(pol)* ↔ Linker

rechter Gebrauch *m* → rechtmäßiger Gebrauch

rechtes Verhalten *n* → rechtmäßiges Verhalten

rechtfertigende Kraft *f* • justificatory force *(soc, eth)*

rechtfertigender Grund *m* • justifying/justificatory ground/reason *(eth)*

Rechtfertigung *f* • justification *(gep)*

Rechtfertigungskontext *m* • context of justification/validation *(Reichenbach etc) (sci)* → Begründungszusammenhang

Rechtfertigungstheorie *f* • theory of justification *(sci)*

Rechtfertigungsverfahren *n* • justification procedure *(gep)*

Rechtfertigungsversuch *m* • attempt at justification *(gep)*

Rechtlosigkeit *f* • (▷ Mangel an Rechten) rightlessness, lack of rights *(jur)* < Gesetzlosigkeit, Anarchie

rechtmäßiger Anspruch *m* • legitimate claim, entitlement *(jur, eth)*

rechtmäßiger Gebrauch *m* • rightful use *(eth)*

rechtmäßiges Verhalten *n* • right conduct *(eth)* → richtiges Verhalten

Rechtmäßigkeit *f* • legitimacy *(jur)* → Legitimität

Rechtsanspruch *m* • legal claim *(jur)*

Rechtsbasis *f* • legal basis *(jur)*

Rechtsbegriff *m* • concept of right/law *(jur)*

Rechtsbewußtsein *n* • legal consciousness *(jur)*

Rechtsbruch *m* • breach of law *(jur)*

Rechtschaffenheit *f* • righteousness *(eth)*

Rechtsdenken *n* • legal thought/thinking *(jur)*

Rechtsdurchsetzung *f* • law enforcement *(jur)*

Rechtsempfinden *n* • sense of justice *(jur)* < Gerechtigkeitsempfinden

Rechtsentwicklung *f* • development of law/legal development *(jur, soc)*

Rechtsethik *f* • legal ethics *(eth, jur)*

Rechtsextremismus *m* • right-wing extremism *(pol)* → Rechtsradikalismus

Rechtsfolgen *pl* • legal consequences *(jur)*

rechtsfreier Raum *m* • unregulated/unlegislated sphere *(jur)*

Rechtsfrieden *m* • peace guaranteed by law, law and order, public peace *(jur)*

Rechtsgehorsam *m* • obedience to (the*)* law, law-abidingness *(jur, eth)*

Rechtsgemeinschaft *f* • community bound by law *(jur, pol)* ↔ Solidargemeinschaft

Rechtsgläubigkeit *f* → Orthodoxie

Rechtsgleichheit *f* • equality of rights *(jur, eth)* < Gleichheit vor dem Gesetz

Rechtsgleichheit zwischen allen Menschen *f* • equality of rights among all persons *(jur, eth)*

Rechtsgrundsatz *m* • legal principle, principle of law *(jur)*

Rechtsgüter *pl* • legal values, objects protected by law, objects of legal value *(jur, eth)*

Rechtshandeln *n* • legal action *(jur, act)*

Rechtshegelianer *m* • right(-wing) Hegelian *(gep)* → Althegelianer ↔ Linkshegelianer

Rechtsidee *f* • idea of right/law *(jur)*

Rechtsinhaber *m* → Rechtsträger

Rechtsinstitution *f* • legal institution *(jur, pol)*

Rechtsirrtum *m* • legal error *(jur)* < Justizirrtum, Fehlurteil

Rechtskonzept *n* • concept of law *(jur)*

Rechtskraft *f* • legal force, validity *(jur)*

Rechtslehre *f* • theory of law, legal doctrine, doctrine of right° *(jur)* < Jurisprudenz, Rechtswissenschaft < W 785, 863, 973

Rechtsnorm *f* • legal norm *(jur)*

Rechtsontologie *f* • ontology of law/right *(jur)*

Rechtsordnung *f* • legal order, order of law *(jur)*

Rechtsperson *f* • legal subject/person *(jur)* < Rechtssubjekt

Rechtspflege *f* • administration of justice *(jur)*

Rechtspflicht *f* • legal/juridical duty *(Kant etc)* *(jur, eth)* ↔ ethische Pflicht, moralische Pflicht

Rechtsphilosophie *f* • philosophy of law, legal philosophy *(jur)* < W 854

Rechtspolitik *f* • legal policy *(jur, pol)*

Rechtspositivismus *m* • legal positivism, positivist theory of law *(Kelsen etc)* *(jur)*

Rechtsprechung *f* • jurisdiction, administration of justice *(jur)* → Judikatur, Jurisdiktion

Rechtsprinzip *n* • legal principle, principle of law *(jur)*

Rechtsquelle *f* • source of law *(jur)*

Rechtsradikalismus *m* • right-wing radicalism *(pol)* → Rechtsextremismus

Rechtsrationalismus *m* • rationalism of law *(Weber)* *(jur, soc)*

Rechtssetzung *f* • legal enactment *(jur)*

Rechtssicherheit *f* • legal security/guaranty, certainty of the law *(jur)*

Rechtssoziologie *f* • sociology of law *(jur, soc)*

Rechtsstaat *m* • constitutional state, state bound by the rule of law *(jur, pol)* < Verfassungsstaat

Rechtsstatus *m* • legal status *(jur)*

Rechtsstruktur *f* • legal structure *(jur)*

Rechtssubjekt *n* • legal subject, subject before the law *(jur)*

Rechtssystem *n* • legal system, system of law *(jur)*

Rechtstheorie *f* • legal theory, theory of law, jurisprudence, theory of rights *(jur)*

Rechtstitel *m* • legal title *(jur)*

Rechtstradition *f* • legal tradition, tradition of law *(jur)*

Rechtsträger *m* • bearer of rights *(jur)*

Rechtsübertragung *f* • transfer(ence)/conferment of rights *(jur, pol)*

Rechtsübertragung, wechselseitige *f* • mutual transfer(ence)/transferment/conferment of rights *(jur, pol)*

Rechtsvergleichung *f* • comparative law *(jur)*

Rechtsverhältnis *n* • (▷ Rechtsbeziehung) legal relationship *(jur)* < Vertragsverhältnis, Rechtszustand

Rechtsverletzung *f* • violation of right, offense against the law *(jur, eth)* < Regelverstoß

Rechtsvollzug *m* • enforcement of law *(jur)* < Exekutive

Rechtswissenschaft *f* • jurisprudence, legal studies *(jur)* → Jurisprudenz

Rechtszustand *m* • state of law, legal position *(jur)*

Rechtszweck *m* • purpose of law, legal purpose *(jur)*

recta ratio *f* • right reason *(epi, met)* → rechte Vernunft

Recycling *n* • recycling *(env)* → Wiederverwertung

Rede *f* • talk, telling *(Heidegger)* *(ont)*

Redefigur *f* • figure of speech *(lan)* < Metapher

Redefreiheit *f* • freedom of speech *(pol, eth)* < Denkfreiheit, Meinungsfreiheit, Pressefreiheit

Redeweise *f* • mode/manner of speech, façon de parler *(lan)* < Ausdrucksweise

Redewendung *f* • idiom, idiomatic expression *(lan)*

Redistribution *f* • redistribution *(eco)* < Umverteilung des Einkommens, Einkommensumverteilung

Redlichkeit *f* • honesty, uprightness, probity *(eth)*

Redlichkeit, intellektuelle *f* • intellectual honesty *(eth)*

reductio ad absurdum *f* • *nt*, reduction to impossibility° *(log)*

Reduktion *f* • reduction *(log, epi, sci)* < Reduktion, phänomenologische; Reduzierbarkeit von Theorien

Reduktion des Menschen zur Sache *f* • reduction of human beings to objects *(soc)* < Verdinglichung

Reduktion, eidetische *f* • eidetic reduction *(Husserl)* *(epi, met)*

Reduktion, Husserlsche *f* • Husserl(ian) reduction *(epi, met)*

Reduktion, phänomenologische *f* • phenomenological reduction *(Husserl)* *(epi, met)*

Reduktion, transzendentale *f* • transcendental reduction *(Husserl)* *(epi, met)*

Reduktionismus *m* • reductionism, reductivism° *(epi, sci)* < Problemverkürzung

Reduktionismus, ästhetischer *m* • aesthetic reductionism *(aes)* < Minimal art

reduktionistische Theorie *f* • reductionist theory *(sci)* < Reduktionismus

Reduktionsaussage *f* • reduction sentence *(Hempel)* *(sci, lan)*

Reduktionsproblem *n* • reduction problem *(sci)* < Szientismus

Reduktionssatz *m* • reduction sentence *(Carnap)* *(log, lan, sci)*

reduktive Methode *f* • reductive method *(Husserl)* *(epi, met)* < Reduktion, phänomenologische

reduktive Wissenschaft *f* • reductive science *(sci)*

reduktiver Materialismus *m* • reductive materialism *(min, met)*

Redundanz *f* • redundancy, redundance *(lan, sys)* < Überdeterminiertheit

Redundanz, leere *f* • void/empty redundancy/redundance *(lan, sys)*

Redundanz, nützliche *f* • useful redundancy/redundance *(lan, sys)*

Redundanz, relative *f* • relative redundancy/redundance *(lan, sys)*

Redundanzfreiheit *f* • lack of redundancy/redundance *(lan, sys)*

Redundanztheorie der Wahrheit *f* • redundancy theory of truth, superfluity theory of truth *(Frege etc)* *(epi, met)*

reduzibel • reducible *(mat, log)*

Reduzierbarkeit von Theorien *f* • reducibility of theories *(sci)*

reelle Zahl *f* • real number *(mat)*

re-empathische Definition *f* • re-empathic definition *(log, lan)*

Referent *m* • referent *(lan)*

Referentialität *f* • referentiality *(lan)*

referentielle Sprache *f* • referential language *(lan)*

referentielle Undurchsichtigkeit *f* • referential opacity *(Quine)* *(lan)*

referentieller Rahmen *m* • frame of reference *(lan, sci)*

Referenz *f* • reference *(lan, ont)* → Bezug

Referenzgegenstand *m* • reference object, object of reference *(lan, ont)* → Bezugsgegenstand

Referenzkette *f* • chain of reference *(Kripke)* *(lan)*

Referenzpunkt *m* • reference point *(gep)*

Referenzsemantik *f* • denotational/referential/reference semantics *(lan)*

Referenztheorie *f* • reference theory, theory of reference *(lan, log)* → Bezugstheorie

reflektierende Urteilskraft *f* • reflective/reflecting (faculty of) judg(e)ment *(Kant)* *(epi, aes)* ↔ bestimmende Urteilskraft

reflektierendes Bewußtsein *n* • reflective awareness/consciousness *(Hegel)* *(epi, met)*

reflektierendes Urteil *n* • reflective judg(e)ment *(Hegel)* *(log)*

reflektierte Selbstbeziehung *f* • reflective relation to self *(Habermas)* *(epi, soc)*

Reflex *m* • reflex *(nat, psy)* < bedingter Reflex

Reflexbewegung *f* • reflex action *(nat, psy)*

Reflexion *f* • reflection, reflexion *(epi, nat)*

Reflexion, äußerliche *f* • external reflection *(Hegel)* *(met)*

Reflexion, bestimmende *f* • determining/qualifying reflection *(Hegel)* *(met)*

Reflexion, unendliche *f* • infinite reflection *(Kierkegaard)* *(met)*

Reflexionsbegriff *m* • concept of reflection *(Leibniz, Kant)* *(log, epi, lan)*

Reflexionsbestimmungen *pl* • determinations/qualifications of reflection *(Hegel)* *(log, ont)*

Reflexionsphilosophie *f* • philosophy of reflection, reflective philosophy *(Hegel etc)* *(met)*

Reflexionsschleife *f* • reflexive loop *(psy, sys)* < Feedback-Schleife

Reflexionsurteil *n* • reflective judg(e)ment *(log)*

Reflexionswissenschaft *f* • reflective science *(sci)*

reflexive Funktion *f* • reflexive function *(mat)*

reflexive Relation *f* • reflexive relation *(log, lan)*

reflexive Selbstkontrolle *f* • reflective self-control *(Habermas) (epi, soc)*

reflexives Gleichgewicht *n* • reflective equilibrium *(Rawls) (eth)* → Überlegungsgleichgewicht

reflexives System *n* • reflective system *(sys)* < autopoietisches System

Reflexivität *f* • reflectivity, reflectiveness *(epi)*, reflexivity, reflexiveness *(lan)*

Reformation *f* • reformation *(rel, his)*

Reformbewegung *f* • reform movement *(soc, pol, rel)*

reformierte Erkenntnistheorie *f* • reformed epistemology *(Plantinga) (epi)*

Reformismus *m* • reformism *(soc, pol)*

Reformkommunismus *m* • reform communism *(pol)*

Reformpolitik *f* • reform policy *(pol)*

Regel *f* • rule *(eth, log, lan)*

Regel der (reinen) Vernunft *f* • rule of (pure) reason *(Kant) (epi)*

Regel der doppelten Verneinung *f* • double negation rule *(log)* < Negation der Negation

Regel der Grammatik *f* • rule of grammar *(Wittgenstein) (lan)*

Regel des Richtigen *f* • rule of the right, rule by the right people *(eth)*

Regel, empirische *f* • empirical rule *(sci)*

Regel und Ausnahme *f,f* • rule and exception *(gep)*

Regel vom ausgeschlossenen Widerspruch *f* • rule/law/principle of non-contradiction *(log)*

Regelanarchie *f* • rule anarchy *(eth, sci)*

Regelbefolgung *f* • rule following *(eth, sci)* < Normbefolgung

Regelbewußtsein *n* • rule-consciousness *(eth, act)*

Regelfolgen, das *n* • following a rule *(Wittgenstein) (lan, met)*

Regelfolgeproblem *n* • problem of rule-following *(lan)*

regelgeleitetes Verhalten *n* • rule-governed behaviour *(soc, act)*

Regelkanon *m* • canon (of rules) *(eth)*

Regelkatalog *m* • catalog(ue) of rules, rule catalog(ue) *(eth)*

regelkonform • in conformity with rule *(eth, lan)* < normenkonform

Regellosigkeitsaxiom *n* • axiom of randomness *(mat)*

Regelmäßigkeit *f* • regularity *(gep)* → Regularität

Regelmäßigkeit der Natur *f* • regularity of nature *(nat, met)*

Regeln der Geschicklichkeit *pl* • rules of skill *(Kant) (eth)* < Ratschläge der Klugheit

Regeln des Denkens *pl* • rules of thinking/thought *(log)*

Regelutilitarismus *m* • rule utilitarianism *(eth)* ↔ Aktutilitarismus

Regelverletzung *f* • rule violation, rule-breaking *(jur, eth, lan)*

Regelverstoß *m* • rule violation, breach of (the) rule(s) *(jur, eth, lan)* < Rechtsverletzung

Regelverzeichnis *n* • list of rules *(lan, act)*

Regelwahl *f* • choice of rules *(eth)*

regelwidrig • against the rule(s), irregular *(jur, eth, lan)*

Regelwidrigkeit *f* • irregularity *(jur, eth, lan)* → Anomalie

Regenwaldvernichtung *f* • destruction of the rain forests *(env)* < Waldsterben

Regie *f* • (stage-)direction *(aes)* < Regisseur

Regierungsform *f* • form of government *(pol)*

Regierungsgewalt *f* • governmental power *(pol)*

Regierungssystem *n* • system of government *(pol)*

Regimekritiker *m* • critic of the regime *(pol)*

regionale Ontologie *f* • regional ontology *(N. Hartmann etc) (ont)*

Regionalismus *m* • regionalism *(pol, aes)*

Regionalontologie *f* → regionale Ontologie

Regionen des Seienden *pl* • regions of being *(N. Hartmann, Husserl) (ont)*

Regisseur *m* • stage-manager, director *(aes)* < Regie

Regreß, unendlicher *m* • infinite regress *(log, epi, mat)*

Regression *f* • regression *(psy, eco, nat); (mat)* < Regressionsanalyse

Regressionsanalyse *f* • regression analysis *(mat)*

regressive Synthesis *f* • regressive synthesis *(Kant) (epi)*

regressives Verhalten *n* • regressive behaviour *(psy)*

Regressus *m* • regression *(log)* ↔ Progressus

regulärer Ausdruck *m* • regular expression *(lan, log)*

Regularität *f* • regularity *(gep)* → Regelmäßigkeit < Gesetzmäßigkeit

Regularitätsanalyse des Ursachenbegriffs *f* • regularity analysis of causation *(epi, nat, sci)*

Regularitätstheorie der Naturgesetze *f* • regularity theory of (the) laws of nature *(Hempel, Salmon) (sci)*

Regularitätsthese *f* • regularity hypothesis *(Hume, Mill etc) (epi, met)* < Regelmäßigkeit der Natur

Regulativ *n* • regulative principle *(jur)* → Verordnung

regulative Gerechtigkeit *f* • corrective justice *(eth)*

regulative Idee *f* • regulative idea *(Kant) (epi, met)*

regulative Prinzipien der Erkenntnis *pl* • regulative principles of cognition *(Kant) (epi)*

regulative Sprechhandlung *f* • regulative speech act *(Searle etc) (lan, act)*

regulativer Gebrauch der (reinen) Vernunft *m* • regulative employment/use of (pure) reason *(Kant) (epi)*

regulativer Wahrheitsbegriff *m* • regulative concept(ion) of truth *(epi)*

regulatives Prinzip *n* • regulative principle *(Kant) (epi)* ↔ konstitutives Prinzip

Regulierungsbedarf *m* • need for regulation *(jur)*

Rehabilitierung *f* • vindication, rehabilitation *(soc, jur)*

Rehabilitierung der praktischen Philosophie *f* • rehabilitation of practical philosophy *(gep)*

Reich der Freiheit *n* • realm/kingdom of freedom *(Marx) (soc)* ↔ Reich der Notwendigkeit

Reich der Gnade *n* • realm/kingdom of grace *(Leibniz etc) (rel, met)*

Reich der Natur *n* • realm/kingdom of nature *(Leibniz etc) (rel, met)*

Reich der Notwendigkeit *n* • realm/kingdom of necessity *(Marx) (soc)* ↔ Reich der Freiheit

Reich der Tugend *n* • reign of virtue *(Rousseau) (eth)*

Reich der Zwecke *n* • realm/kingdom of ends *(Kant) (eth, met)*

Reich des Geistes *n* • realm/kingdom of the spirit *(Hegel) (met)*

Reich Gottes *n* • Kingdom of God *(rel)*

Reichtum der menschlichen Bedürfnisse *m* • wealth of human needs *(Marx) (soc)*

Reichtum, menschlicher *m* • human wealth *(Marx) (met)*

Reichtumstransfer *m* • transfer of wealth *(eco)* < Umverteilung des Einkommens

Reideologisierung *f* • reideologization *(pol)* ↔ Deideologisierung

reifer Charakter *m* • mature character *(Fromm) (psy, soc)*

Reifikation *f* • reification, hypostatization *(soc, epi)* → Verdinglichung, Vergegenständlichung, Versachlichung

Reihenkorrelation *f* • serial correlation *(mat, sci)*

rein bezeichnend • purely designative *(Quine) (epi, lan)*

reine Anschauung *f* • pure intuition/perception/anschauung *(Kant) (epi)*

reine Apperzeption *f* • pure apperception *(Kant) (epi)*

reine Beschreibung der diskursiven Ereignisse *f* • pure description of discursive events *(Foucault) (lan, sys)*

reine Dauer *f* • pure duration *(Bergson) (met)* < zeitliche Dauer

reine Erfahrung *f* • pure experience *(asp)* < W 537

reine Erkenntnis *f* • pure cognition/knowledge *(Kant) (epi)* < Apriorismus

reine Form *f* • pure form *(aes)*

reine Form der Anschauung *f* • pure form of intuition *(Kant) (epi)*

reine Formen des Empfindens *pl* • pure forms of sensibility *(Kant) (epi)*

reine Identität *f* • pure identity *(Schelling) (met)*

reine Kategorie *f* • pure category *(Kant) (epi)*

reine Kunst *f* • pure art *(aes)* → L'art pour l'art < Kunst um der Kunst willen

reine Logik *f* • pure logic *(log)*

reine Materie *f* • pure matter *(met)*

reine Mathematik *f* • pure mathematics *(mat)*

reine Moral *f* • pure morality *(Kant) (eth)*

reine Naturgesetze a priori *pl* • pure a priori laws of nature *(Kant) (epi)*

reine Naturwissenschaft *f* • pure natural science *(Kant) (sci)*

reine Objektivität *f* • pure objectivity *(Schelling) (epi, met)*

reine Physik *f* • pure physics *(nat)*

reine Psychologie *f* • pure psychology *(Kant) (epi, psy)*

reine Raumzeitlichkeit *f* • pure space-time *(Husserl etc) (ont)*

reine Rechtslehre *f* • pure theory of law *(Kelsen) (jur)* < W 863

reine Rechtstheorie *f* • pure theory of law *(Kelsen) (jur)*

reine Spontaneität *f* • pure spontaneity *(Kant) (epi)*

reine Synthesis *f* • pure synthesis *(Kant) (epi)*

reine Vernunft *f* • pure reason *(Kant) (epi, met)*

reine Vernunftreligion *f* • pure religion of reason *(Kant) (rel)*

reine Verstandesbegriffe *pl* • pure concepts of the understanding, pure intellectual concepts *(Kant) (epi)*

reine Vorstellung *f* • pure representation *(Kant) (epi)*

reine Wissenschaft *f* • pure science *(sci)* < Grundlagenforschung ↔ angewandte Wissenschaft

reiner Begriff *m* • pure concept *(Kant) (epi, lan)* < Notion

reiner Empirismus *m* • pure empiricism *(Kant etc) (epi, met)*

reiner Gebrauch *m* • pure employment/use *(Kant) (epi)*

reiner Gedanke *m* • pure thought *(epi, met)*

reiner Religionsglaube *m* • pure religious faith *(Kant) (rel)*

reiner Text *m* • pure text *(aes)*

reiner Vernunftbegriff *m* • pure concept of reason *(Kant) (epi, lan)*

reiner Vernunftgebrauch *m* • pure employment/use of reason *(Kant) (epi)*

reiner Verstand *m* • pure intellect/understanding *(Kant) (met, epi)*

reiner Verstandesbegriff *m* • pure concept of the understanding *(Kant) (epi, lan)*

reiner Verstandesgebrauch *m* • pure employment/use of the understanding *(Kant) (epi)*

reiner Wille *m* • pure will *(Kant) (eth)* < W 294

reines Bewußtsein *n* • pure consciousness *(Kant, Husserl etc) (epi, met)*

reines Denken *n* • pure thought *(Kant) (epi)*

reines Geschmacksurteil *n* • pure judg(e)ment of taste *(Kant) (epi, aes)*

reines Gewissen *n* • pure/clear conscience *(eth, rel)* → gutes Gewissen

reines Ich *n* • pure self/ego *(Fichte etc) (met)* < absolutes Ich

reines Interesse *n* • pure interest *(Kant) (eth)*

reines Sein *n* • pure being *(ont)*

reines Subjekt der Erkenntnis *n* • pure subject of knowledge *(Schopenhauer) (epi)*

reines unbestimmtes Sein *n* • pure indeterminate being *(Hegel) (met)*

Reinheit *f* • purity *(Kant) (epi)* < reine Erkenntnis, Apriorität

Reinheit des Geistes *f* • purity of mind/spirit *(rel)*

Reinheit des Gewissens *f* • purity of conscience *(rel)*

Reinheit des Herzens *f* • purity of heart *(Kierkegaard) (rel)*

Reinigung *f* • clarification *(Kant) (epi, met)*

Reinigung des Geistes *f* • purification of the mind *(asp)*

Reinigung von den Leidenschaften *f* • purification of the passions *(Aristotle) (aes, psy)* → Katharsis

Reinkarnation *f* • reincarnation, transmigration of the soul *(rel, eso)* < Wiedergeburt, Kreislauf der Wiedergeburt, Leben nach dem Tod

Reismus *m* • reism *(Brentano, Kotarbinski) (epi)*

Reiz *m* • affection *(Locke, Hume) (epi)*, stimulus *(nat, psy)*

Reiz, bedingter *m* • conditioned stimulus, CS *(Pavlov) (psy, nat)*

Reiz-Reaktions-Beziehung *f* • stimulus-response connection, S-R connection *(psy)*

Reiz-Reaktion-Schema *n* • stimulus-response pattern, S-R pattern *(nat, psy)*

Reiz, unbedingter *m* • unconditioned stimulus, UCS *(Pavlov) (psy, nat)*

reizanalytischer Satz *m* • stimulus-analytic sentence *(Quine) (lan)*

Reizanalytizität *f* • stimulus analyticity *(Quine) (lan)* < Reizbedeutung

Reizbarkeit *f* • excitability, irritability *(nat, psy)*

Reizbedeutung *f* • stimulus meaning *(Quine) (lan)*

Reizeinfluß *m* • stimulation *(nat, psy)*

Reizhunger *m* • hunger for sensation *(psy)*

reizsynonymer Satz *m* • stimulus-synonymous sentence *(Quine) (lan)*

Reizsynonymie *f* • stimulus synonymy *(Quine) (lan)*

Reizwirkung *f* • stimulus effect *(psy)* < Reaktion

Rejektion *f* • rejection *(Peirce etc) (log)*

Rekodierung *f* • recoding *(lan)* ↔ Dekodierung

Rekonstruktion *f* • reconstruction *(gep)*

rekurrentiale Analyse *f* • recurrential analysis *(Foucault) (epi, his)*

Rekurrenz *f* • recurrence *(sys)* < rekursive Funktion

Rekursion *f* • recursion *(mat, AI, log)* < Rekursivität

Rekursionstheorie *f* • recursion theory *(sys, lan, mat)*

rekursiv aufzählbare Menge *f* • recursively enumerable set *(mat)*

rekursiv • recursive, recurrent *(mat, log, lan, sys)*

rekursive Definition *f* • recursive definition *(lan, log)*

rekursive Funktion *f* • recursive function *(sys, mat)*

rekursive Menge *f* • recursive set *(mat)*

rekursive Relation *f* • recursive relation *(log, sys)*

rekursives System *n* • recursive system *(sys)*

rekursives Transitions-Netzwerk *n* • Recursive Transition Network, RTN *(mat, log)*

Rekursivität *f* • recursivity *(mat, AI, log)* < Rekursion

Relation *f* • relation *(log, lan, sys)*

Relation, asymmetrische *f* • asymmetric(al) relation *(log, mat)*

Relation, binäre *f* • binary/two-place relation *(log, mat)* → Relation, zweistellige

Relation der Urteile *f* • relation of judg(e)ments *(Kant) (log, epi)*

Relation, dreistellige *f* • three-place/ternary relation *(log, mat)*

Relation, inverse *f* • converse relation *(log, mat)*

Relation, irreflexive *f* • irreflexive relation *(log, mat)* → Relation, nichtreflexive

Relation, mehrstellige *f* • many-place relation, multiplace relation *(log, mat)*

Relation, nichtreflexive *f* • non-reflexive relation *(log, mat)* → Relation, irrereflexive

Relation, symmetrische *f* • symmetric(al) relation *(log, mat)*

Relation, transitive *f* • transitive relation *(log, mat)*

Relation, zweistellige *f* • two-place relation *(log, mat)* → Relation, binäre

relationales Argumentieren *n* • relational reasoning *(log)*

relationales Wissen *n* • relational knowledge *(Scheler) (epi)* < Wissenssoziologie

Relationallogik *f* • relational logic *(log)*

Relationen, externe und interne *pl* • external and internal relations *(Bradley, McTaggart etc) (epi)*

Relationismus *m* • relationism *(Mannheim) (epi, met)* < Relativismus

Relationsanalyse *f* • relational analysis *(Festinger) (sci)*

Relationsausdruck *m* • relational expression *(log)* < Modellsprache

Relationsprädikat *n* • relational predicate *(log)*

Relationsprodukt *n* • relational product *(log)*

relativ prim • relatively prime *(mat)*

relative algebraische Hülle *f* • algebraic closure *(mat)*

relative Apodiktizität *f* • relative apod(e)icticity *(Husserl) (epi, met)*

relative Autonomie der Kunst *f* • relative autonomy of art *(aes)*

relative Häufigkeit *f* • relative frequency *(mat)*

relative Wahrscheinlichkeit *f* • relative probability *(mat)*

relativer Raum *m* • relative space *(Newton) (nat)*

relativer Terminus *m* • relative term *(Quine) (lan)*

relatives Gut *n* • relative good *(eth)*

relativieren • to qualify, to modify, to relativize *(lan)*

Relativismus *m* • relativism *(gep)*

Relativismus, ethischer *m* • moral/ethical relativism *(eth)*

Relativismus, kognitiver *m* • cognitive relativism *(epi)*

relativistisch • relativistic, relativist *(gen)*

relativistische Semantik *f* • relativistic semantics *(lan)*

relativistische Vernunft *f* • relativist(ic) reason *(Horkheimer) (epi)*

Relativität *f* • relativity *(nat, gep)*

Relativität der Erkenntnis *f* • relativity of knowledge *(epi)*

Relativität der Wahrheit *f* • relativity of truth *(epi)*

Relativitätsprinzip, linguistisches *n* • linguistic relativity principle *(Sapir, Whorf) (lan)*

Relativitätstheorie *f* • relativity theory *(Einstein) (nat)* < W 407

Relativitätstheorie, allgemeine *f* • general theory of relativity *(Einstein) (nat)*

Relativitätstheorie, spezielle *f* • special theory of relativity *(Einstein) (nat)*

relativkomplementärer Verband *m* • relatively complemented lattice *(mat)*

Relevanzdefinition *f* • definition of relevance *(log, lan)*

Relevanzkriterium *n* • relevance criterion *(sci)*

Relevanzmaxime *f* • maxim of relevance *(Grice) (lan)* < Konversationsmaximen

Relevanzprinzip *n* • relevance principle *(gep)*

Reliabilismus *m* • reliabilism *(epi)*

Reliabilität *f* • reliability *(eth, sci)* → Zuverlässigkeit ↔ Unzuverlässigkeit

Religion als Opium des Volkes *f* • religion as the opium of the people *(Marx) (soc)*

Religion des Herzens *f* • religion of the heart *(Pascal etc) (rel)*

Religion innerhalb der Grenzen der Vernunft *f* • religion within the bounds/limits of reason *(Kant) (rel, met)* < Vernunftreligion, < W 868

Religion, natürliche *f* • natural religion *(Suárez, Cherbury etc) (rel)* → natürliche Theologie < Deismus

Religionsersatz *m* • religion substitute *(Feuerbach etc) (rel)* < Ersatzreligion

Religionsethnologie *f* • ethnology of religion *(rel, cul)*

Religionsfreiheit *f* • freedom of religion, religious freedom/liberty *(rel, pol)* < Bekenntnisfreiheit

religionsgeschichtlicher Entzauberungsprozeß *m* • process of disenchantment in the history of religion *(Weber) (his)*

Religionsglaube *m* • religious faith *(Kant) (rel)* < religiöser Glaube(n)

Religionshistoriker *m* • historian of religion, religious historian *(rel, his)*

Religionskriege *pl* • wars of religion *(rel)*

Religionskritik *f* • critique of religion *(rel)*

Religionslosigkeit *f* • religiouslessness, lack of religion *(rel)* → Areligiosität < Atheismus

Religionspädagogik *f* • religious education *(rel)*

Religionsphänomenologie *f* • phenomenology of religion *(Eliade etc) (rel)*

Religionsphilosophie *f* • philosophy of religion *(rel)*

Religionspsychologie *f* • psychology of religion *(rel, psy)*

Religionssache *f* • matter of religion *(Kant) (rel)*

Religionssoziologie *f* • sociology of religion *(Weber etc) (rel, soc)*

Religionsstifter *m* • founder of a religion *(rel)*

Religionstheologie *f* • theology of religion, religious theology *(rel)*

Religionswissenschaft *f* • religious studies/science, science of religion *(rel)* < W 700

Religionszugehörigkeit *f* • religious/church affiliation *(rel)*

religiöse Entfremdung *f* • religious alienation/estrangement *(Marx) (rel, soc)*

religiöse Erfahrung *f* • religious experience *(rel)*

religiöse Kunst *f* • religious art *(aes)* → Hieratik

religiöser Glaube(n) *m* • religious faith/belief, persuasion *(rel)*

religiöser Humanismus *m* • religious humanism *(eth, rel)*

religiöses Bedürfnis *n* • religious need *(rel)*

religiöses Leben *n* • religious life *(rel)*

religiöses Stadium *n* • religious stage *(Kierkegaard) (rel)*

Religiosität *f* • religiosity, religiousness *(rel)*

Rematerialisation *f* • rematerialisation *(eso)* ↔ Dematerialisation

Remilitarisierung *f* • remilitarization *(pol)* ↔ Demilitarisierung

Renaissancephilosophie *f* • Renaissance philosophy *(his)*

Rentabilität *f* • profitability *(eco)* < Kosten-Nutzen-Analyse

Rentabilitätsgesichtspunkt *m* • viewpoint of rentability, rentability aspect *(eco)*

rentierlich • profitable *(eco)*

Replik *f* • replication *(jur, gep)* → Erwiderung

Replikat *n* • copy, replica *(aes)*

Repräsentanz, psychische *f* • psychical representative *(Freud) (psy)*

Repräsentation *f* • representation *(lan, pol)*

Repräsentation, analoge *f* • analog(ue) representation *(log)*

Repräsentation durch Bilder *f* • representation by images *(Duns Scotus) (epi)*

Repräsentation durch Spiegel *f* • representation by mirrors *(epi)* < Widerspiegelungstheorie

Repräsentation durch sprachliche Zeichen *f* • representation by linguistic signs *(Pinborg etc) (epi, lan)*

Repräsentation durch Spuren *f* • vestigial representation *(Aquinas) (epi, lan)* → Repräsentation, vestigiale

Repräsentation, mentale *f* • mental representation *(min)* → geistige Abbildung

Repräsentation, sprachliche *f* • linguistic representation *(lan)*

Repräsentation, vestigiale *f* • vestigial representation *(Aquinas) (epi, lan)* → Repräsentation durch Spuren

Repräsentation, zentralisierte *f* • centralized representation *(Gurwitsch) (epi)*

repräsentationale Theorie des Geistes *f* • representational theory of mind, RTM *(min)*

Repräsentationalismus *m* • representationalism *(min, met)*

repräsentationalistische Theorie des Geistes *f* • representationalist theory of the mind *(min)*

Repräsentationismus *m* • representationalism, representationism *(epi)*

Repräsentationsgehalt *m* • representative content *(lan)*

Repräsentationstheorie *f* • representational theory *(lan, pol)*

Repräsentationstheorie der Wahrnehmung *f* • representative theory of perception *(epi)*

Repräsentative *pl* • representatives *(Searle)* *(lan, act)* → Assertive

repräsentative Demokratie *f* • representative democracy *(pol)*

Repräsentativsystem *n* • representative system, system of representation *(pol)*

Repräsentierbarkeit *f* • representability *(log, lan)*

repressive Entsublimierung *f* • repressive desublimation *(Marcuse)* *(soc, psy)*

repressive Gesellschaft *f* • repressive society *(soc)* < autoritäre Gesellschaft

repressive Toleranz *f* • repressive tolerance *(Marcuse)* *(soc)*

Reprivatisierung *f* • re-privatization, denationalization *(eco)*

Reprobation *f* • reprobation *(rel)* < Prädestination

Reproduktion *f* • reproduction *(nat, epi)*

Reproduktionserfolg *m* • reproductive success *(nat, soc)*

Reproduktionskosten *pl* • cost of reproduction *(Marx)* *(eco)*

Reproduktionsmedizin *f* • reproductive medicine *(nat)*

Reproduktionsprozeß *m* • reproduction process *(Marx)* *(eco)*

Reproduktionsrate *f* • reproduction rate, rate of reproduction *(nat, eco)*

Reproduktionstechnologie *f* • reproductive technology *(nat, eth)*

Reproduktionstreue *f* • fidelity of reproduction *(aes)*

reproduktive Einbildungskraft *f* • reproductive imagination *(Kant)* *(epi)*

reproduktive Synthesis *f* • reproductive synthesis *(Kant)* *(epi)*

reproduktives Denken *n* • reproductive thinking *(gep)*

Reproduzierbarkeit *f* • reproducibility *(tec, aes)* < W 554

Republik *f* • republic *(pol)* < Staat

Republikaner *m* • republican *(pol)*

Republikanische Verfassung *f* • republican constitution *(pol)*

Republikanismus *m* • republicanism *(pol)*

Repugnanz *f* • repugnancy *(log)* → Widerspruch, logischer

Repulsion *f* • repulsion *(nat, psy)* ↔ Attraktion

res cogitans *f* • *nt*, thinking thing/substance *(Descartes)* *(epi, met)* → denkende Substanz ↔ res extensa

res extensa *f* • extended substance *(Descartes)* *(epi, met)* → ausgedehnte Substanz, ausgedehntes Objekt ↔ res cogitans

Reservearmee der Arbeit *f* • reserve army of labour *(Marx)* *(eco)*

Residuum *n* • residue *(mat, eco, psy)*

Résistance *f* • resistance *(pol)* < Widerstand

resolutiv-(re)kompositive Methode *f* • resolutive-(re)compositive method *(Zabarella, Hobbes, Descartes)* *(sci)*

Resonanz *f* • resonance *(nat, aes, psy)*

Resozialisationstheorie *f* • resocialisation theory *(jur, soc)* < Besserungszweck der Strafe

Resozialisierung *f* • resocialisation, rehabilitation *(soc, jur)*

Respekt *m* • respect *(eth)* → Ehrerbietung

Responsivität *f* • responsiveness *(eco, pol)*

Ressentiment *n* • resentment, ressentiment *(Nietzsche, Scheler etc)* *(eth, psy)* < Rache der Schwachen an den Starken, Revanchismus

Ressentiment-Moral *f* → Moral des Ressentiment

Ressourcenallokation *f* • resource allocation, allocation of resources *(eco)* < Allokationseffizienz

Ressourcenerschöpfung *f* • depletion of resources *(eco, env)*

Ressourcenknappheit *f* • scarcity of resources *(eco, env)*

Ressourcenschonung *f* • conservation of resources, resource conservation *(env, eco)*

Ressourcenverschwendung *f* • waste of resources *(eco, env)*

Rest, metaphysischer *m* • metaphysical remainder *(Rickert etc)* *(met, epi)*

Restauration *f* • restoration *(his, pol)*

Restaurationszeit *f* • restoration period *(his)*

Restriktionen der Zivilisation *pl* • restrictions of civilization *(Freud)* *(psy, cul)* < Unbehagen in der Kultur

Restrisiko *n* • residual risk *(tec)*

Restrukturierung *f* • restructuring *(gen)*

Resümee *n* • résumé, summary *(gen)*

Resurrektion *f* • resurrection *(rel)* → Auferstehung

Resymbolisierung *f* • resymbolization *(Cassirer etc)* *(lan, psy)* ↔ Desymbolisierung < Symboltheorie

Retardation *f* • retardation *(psy)* → Entwicklungshemmung

retardierendes Moment *n* • retarding element *(Aristotle)* *(aes)*

Retention *f* • retention *(Husserl)* *(epi, met)* ↔ Protention

Retorsion *f* • retorsion *(act, lan)*

Retortenbaby *n* • test-tube baby *(nat, eth)* < Reproduktionsmedizin, künstliche Befruchtung, In-vitro-Fertilisation

Retortenstadt *f* • new town *(soc)*

Retrodiktion *f* • retrodiction *(sci)*

Retrodiktionsprognose *f* • retrodictive prediction *(sci)*

Retrospektion *f* • retrospection *(gep)* < historischer Rückblick

Retrospektive *f* • retrospective *(aes)*

retrospektive Umgruppierung *f* • retrospective regrouping *(Foucault) (epi, his)*

Rettung der Phänomene *f* • saving the phenomena/appearances *(Simplikios) (nat)*

Reue *f* • remorse, repentance *(rel, eth)*

reumütiger Sünder *m* • penitent/penitant sinner *(rel)*

Revanchismus *m* • revanchism *(pol, eth)* < Ressentiment

Reversibilität *f* • reversibility *(sys)*

Revierkampf *m* • territorial competition/ conflict *(nat, ant)* < territorialer Imperativ

Revisionismus *m* • revisionism *(pol)*

Revolte *f* • revolt, rebellion *(Camus) (pol, met)* < W 518, 634

Revolution des alltäglichen Lebens *f* • revolution of everyday life *(soc, cul)*

Revolution, permanente *f* • permanent revolution *(Trotsky) (pol)*

Revolution, Recht auf *n* • right to/of revolution *(pol)*

Revolution, wissenschaftliche *f* • scientific revolution *(Kuhn) (sci)* < Paradigmenwechsel

Revolutionär *m* • revolutionary, revolutionist° *(pol)*

revolutionäre Praxis *f* • revolutionary praxis *(pol)*

revolutionäre Theorie *f* • revolutionary theory *(pol, sci)*

revolutionäre Wissenschaft *f* • revolutionary science *(Kuhn, etc) (sci)* ↔ Normalwissenschaft

revolutionäres Bewußtsein *n* • revolutionary consciousness *(pol)*

revolutionäres Proletariat *n* • revolutionary proletariat *(pol)*

Revolutionarismus *m* • revolutionism° *(pol)*

Revolutionsarchitektur *f* • revolutionary architecture *(aes)*

Rezeption *f* • reception *(aes, psy)* < ästhetische Erfahrung

Rezeptionsästhetik *f* • aesthetics of reception, reception aesthetics *(Jauss etc) (aes)* < ästhetische Rezeption ↔ Produktionsästhetik

Rezeptionsgeschichte *f* • history of reception, reception history *(gep)* < Wirkungsgeschichte

Rezeptionstheorie *f* • reader-response theory, reception theory *(aes)* < Rezeptionsästhetik

rezeptive Orientierung *f* • receptive orientation *(Fromm) (psy)*

Rezeptivität *f* • receptivity *(Kant) (epi, psy)* ↔ Spontaneität < Empfänglichkeit, ästhetische; Aufnahmefähigkeit

Rezeptivität der Eindrücke *f* • receptivity of impressions *(Kant) (epi)*

Rezipient *m* • recipient *(lan)* < Empfänger-Sender-Modell

reziproke Funktion *f* • reciprocal/inverse function *(mat)*

reziproke Pflicht *f* • reciprocal duty *(eth)*

reziproker Altruismus *m* • reciprocal altruism *(eth)* < Selbstlosigkeit

Reziprozität *f* • reciprocity *(mat, sys, eth)* → Korrelativität, Wechselbezüglichkeit

Reziprozitätsgesetz *n* • law of reciprocity *(mat, sys)* < Wechselbezüglichkeit, wechselseitige Verursachung

Rhapsodie von Wahrnehmungen *f* • rhapsody of perceptions *(Kant) (epi)*

Rhem(a) *n* • rheme *(lan)*

rhetischer Akt *m* • rhetic(al) act *(lan)*

Rhetorik *f* • (art of) rhetoric *(lan)* < Disputierkunst, Überredungskunst < W 870

rhetorische Frage *f* • rhetorical question *(lan)*

Richterrecht *n* • judge-made law, law by judges, law of judg(e)ment, case law *(jur)*

richtiger Gebrauch *m* • correct/right use *(lan)*

richtiges Verhalten *n* • correct/right conduct *(act, eth)*

Richtigkeit *f* • rightness, correctness, exactness *(log, lan)*; appropriateness *(act, lan)*, appropriateness, suitability, properness *(eth)* < Angemessenheit

Richtigkeitsanspruch *m* • rightness claim, claim to correctness *(sci)* < Wahrheitsanspruch

Riemannsches Integral *n* • Riemann integral *(mat)*

rigider Designator *m* • rigid designator *(Kripke) (lan)*

Rigorismus *m* • rigorism, rigour *(Kant) (eth)*

rigoristische Ethik *f* • rigorous ethics *(Kant) (eth)*

Ring *m* • ring *(mat)*

Ringhomomorphismus *m* • ring homomorphism *(mat)*

Ringtheorie *f* • ring theory *(log, mat)*

Risikoabschätzung *f* → Risikoabwägung

Risikoabwägung f • risk assessment (dec, eco, tec) < Technologiefolgenabschätzung

Risikoanalyse f • risk analysis (dec, eco, tec) < Technikfolgenabschätzung

Risikobereitschaft f • readiness/willingness to take risks (act, psy, eco)

Risikobewertung f • risk assessment (dec, eco, tec)

Risikofaktor m • risk factor (dec, sys, tec)

Risikoforschung f • risk research (dec, tec)

Risikogesellschaft f • risk society (Beck) (soc, tec)

Risikogruppe f • high-risk group (soc)

Risikokompensation f • risk compensation (eco)

Risikomanagement n • risk management (eco, dec, tec)

Risikoverhalten n • risk-taking behaviour (psy)

Risikoverteilung f • risk distribution (mat, soc)

Risikowahrnehmung f • risk perception (psy)

Robobiologie f • robot biology° (nat, tec) < Cyborg

Robotertechnik f • robotics (tec, AI)

Rohstoffreserven pl • reserves of raw materials (eco, env) < Ressourcenknappheit

Rokoko n • Rococo (aes)

Rollenerwartung f • role expectation (soc, psy)

Rollenhandeln n • role behaviour (act, psy) < Rollenspiel

Rollenidentität f • role identity (soc, psy)

Rollenkompetenz f • role competence (act)

Rollenkonflikt m • role conflict (soc, psy)

Rollenspiel n • role-play(ing) (soc, psy)

Rollentheorie f • role theory (soc, psy) < symbolischer Interaktionismus

Rollenträger m • role-bearer (soc, psy)

Rollenverteilung f • role allocation (soc, psy)

Rollenvorbild n • role model (psy, soc)

Rollenzuschreibung f • assignment of roles, role ascription (soc, psy)

Rollenzwang m • role coercion (soc, psy)

Romancier m • novelist, novel-writer (aes)

Romanheld m • hero of a novel (aes)

Romanik f • Romanesque period (aes)

romanische Kunst f • Romanesque art (aes)

Romanistik f • Romance philology

Romanliteratur f • fiction (aes)

Romantik f • romanticism (his, aes) < W 805

Romantik, Zeitalter der n • age of Romanticism (his)

romantische Ironie f • romantic irony (aes)

Romantizismus m • romanticism (aes, his)

römische Kunst f • Roman art (aes)

römisches Recht n • Roman law (jur)

römisches Rechtsdenken n • Roman jurisprudence (jur)

Rorschach-Test m • Rorschach test (Rorschach) (psy)

Rosenkreuzerbewegung f • Rosicrucianism (rel, eso)

Rotationsprinzip n • rotation principle (pol)

RTM → repräsentationale Theorie des Geistes

Rückblick, historischer m → historischer Rückblick

Rückkoppelung f • feedback (sys)

Rückkopp(e)lungsprozeß m • feedback process (sys)

Rückmeldung f • feedback (psy), report (gen)

Rückschluß auf die beste Erklärung m • inference to the best explanation (epi, sci)

Rückwärtsentwicklung f • regression (nat, his, eco) → Regression

Rückwärtsverkettung f • backward chaining (AI, log)

Rückwirkung f • retroaction, retroactive effect, reaction, feedback (gep) < Rückmeldung

Rückzug aus der Gesellschaft m • withdrawal from society (soc) < Aussteiger

Ruf des Gewissens m • call of conscience (Kierkegaard etc) (rel, eth)

Rufcharakter des Gewissens m • the appeal character of conscience (Heidegger) (met) < Anruf

Ruhmsucht f • thirst/desire for glory, pursuit of glory (psy, eth)

Russell-Paradox n → Russellsche Antinomie

Russellsche Antinomie f • Russell's paradox (log) < Paradoxien der Mengenlehre

Russischer Formalismus m • Russian Formalism (Jakobson etc) (aes)

Rüstungsbegrenzung f • arms limitation (pol, eth)

Rüstungsbeschränkungsverhandlungen pl • arms limitation talks/negotiations (pol)

Rüstungsgegner m • proponent of disarmament (pol, eth)

Rüstungskontrolle f • arms control (pol)

Rüstungskonversion f • arms conversion (eco, eth) < Schwerter zu Pflugscharen

Rüstungsspirale f → Rüstungswettlauf

Rüstungswettlauf m • arms race (pol)

S

Sa(d)dhu *m* • sad(d)u, holy man *(asp, rel)*

Sabbatjahr *n* • sabbatical year *(rel)*

Sabbatschändung *f* • violation/profanation of (the) Sabbath *(rel)*

Sachargument *n* • factual argument, argument based on fact *(lan)*

Sachbuch *n* • non-fiction title *(gen)*

Sachdarstellung *f* • statement of facts *(gen)*

Sache *f* • (▷ Gegenstand) object, thing, entity, (▷ Thema) subject-matter, topic *(gep)* < Ding, Gegenstand

Sache selbst, die *f* • the thing itself *(gep)*

Sachfrage *f* • factual question/issue, question of fact *(sci)* ↔ Wertfrage

Sachgebiet *n* • subject area *(sci)*

Sachgehalt *m* • factual content *(sci)*

Sachgerechtigkeit *f* • appropriateness *(gen)*

Sachkenntnis *f* → Sachkompetenz

Sachkompetenz *f* • expert knowledge, expertise *(gep)*

Sachlage *f* • circumstance, state of affairs *(gen)*

Sachlichkeit *f* • (▷ pragmatische Einstellung) matter-of-factness, (▷ Unparteilichkeit) impartiality *(gep)* < Objektivität

Sachlichkeit, Neue *f* • New Objectivity, New Matter-of-Factness *(aes)*

Sachverhalt *m* • state of affairs, facts *(gep)* < zutreffen (eines Sachverhalts); Sachverhalt, einfacher

Sachverhalt, einfacher *m* • atomic fact *(Wittgenstein)* *(lan)* < atomarer Sachverhalt

Sachverständiger *m* • expert *(jur, tec)*

Sachwissen *n* • factual knowledge *(epi)*

Sachzwang *m* • practical constraint, inherent necessity *(act)* < äußerer Zwang; Zwänge, gesellschaftliche

Sachzwängen unterliegen • to be constrained by circumstances *(act)*

Sadismus *m* • sadism *(psy)* ↔ Masochismus

Sadomasochismus *m* • sado-masochism *(psy)*

Sage *f* • myth, saga, (▷ Überlieferung) tradition *(cul)*

Sagenwelt *f* • realm of myth *(cul)*

Saint-Simonismus *m* • Saint-Simonianism *(gep)*

Saint-Simonisten *pl* • Saint- Simonians *(gep)*

sakrale Kunst *f* • religious art *(aes)*

Sakrament *n* • sacrament *(rel)*

säkulare Ethik *f* • secular ethics *(eth)*

Säkularisation *f* → Säkularisierung

Säkularisierung *f* • secularization *(rel, pol)* → Verweltlichung < Trennung von Kirche und Staat

Salamitaktik *f* • piecemeal tactics *(act, dec)*

salomonisches Urteil *n* • Solomonic judg(e)-ment/decision *(jur, dec)*

Salonbolschewismus *m* • drawing-room Bolshewism *(pol)* < Nadelstreifsozialismus

saltus in concludendo *m* • *nt*, jumping to conclusions *(log)*

Samariter, barmherziger *m* • good Samaritan *(rel, eth)*

Samenbank *f* • sperm bank *(nat, eth)* < Reproduktionsmedizin

Samenspender *m* • sperm donor *(nat, eth)*

Samenzelle *f* • sperm cell *(nat)*

Sammelbegriff *m* • generic/collective/umbrella/omnibus term *(lan, log)*

Sammelbezeichnung *f* → Sammelbegriff

Sammelwirtschaft *f* • (food-)gathering/collecting economy *(ant, eco)* < Jäger und Sammler

Sammlergesellschaft *f* • food-gathering society *(ant, soc)*

Samsara *n* • samsara, the wheel of life, coming into existence *(asp)* < Lebensrad, Nirwana

sanfte Revolution *f* • velvet revolution *(pol)*

sanfte Technologie *f* • soft technology *(tec)* ↔ Technologie, harte < Hochrisikotechnologie

Sanftmut *f* • gentleness, mildness *(eth)* < Friedfertigkeit

Sanktion *f* • sanction *(jur, pol)*

Sanktion, positive *f* • positive sanction *(jur, eth)* < Verstärkung, positive

Sanktionsbedingungen *pl* • conditions of sanction *(lan, act, jur)*

Sanktionsbedürfnis *n* • need to/of sanction *(jur, eth)*

sanktionserzwungen • enforced by sanction *(jur, eth)*

Sapir-Whorf-Hypothese *f* • Sapir-Whorf-hypothesis *(lan)* < sprachliche Relativitäts-theorie, Sprachrelativismus

Satisfaktionsfähigkeit *f* • qualification/capacity to give satisfaction *(jur, cul)*

Satori *n* • satori, sudden enlightenment *(asp)* < Erleuchtete, der; Zen-Buddhismus

Sättigung *f* • satiation, saturation, satiety *(eco, psy)*

Satz *m* • sentence, statement, clause *(lan)*, proposition *(log)*, theorem, principle *(log, mat)* < Grundsatz

Satz, allgemeiner *m* • general theorem *(log)*, general sentence *(lan)*, general/universal statement/proposition *(sci)* < Satz, allgemeingültiger; Allsatz

Satz, allgemeingültiger *m* • universally valid statement *(log, lan)*

Satz an sich *m* • sentence/proposition in itself, abstract proposition *(Bolzano) (lan, ont)*

Satz, analytischer *m* • analytic(al) statement/proposition *(log, lan)*

Satz, deontischer *m* • deontic statement/sentence *(log, lan)*

Satz, deskriptiver *m* • descriptive statement/sentence *(lan)*

Satz, einfacher *m* • simple statement/proposition *(log, lan)*

Satz, grundlegender *m* • fundamental statement/proposition *(sci, log)* < Axiom

Satz, logisch-falscher *m* • logically false statement/proposition *(log, lan)*

Satz, logisch-wahrer *m* • logically true statement/proposition *(log, lan)*

Satz, logischer *m* • logical statement/proposition *(log, lan)*

Satz, metaphysischer *m* • metaphysical proposition/statement *(epi, lan)*

Satz, normativer *m* • normative statement/sentence *(eth, lan)*

Satz, subjektloser *m* • impersonal sentence, subject-free sentence *(lan)*

Satz, synthetischer *m* • synthetic(al) statement/proposition *(log, lan)*

Satz vom ausgeschlossenen Dritten *m* • principle/law of (the) excluded middle *(log)* → principium exclusi tertii

Satz vom Grund *m* → Satz vom zureichenden Grund

Satz vom Widerspruch *m* • principle/law of (non-) contradiction *(log)* → Widerspruchsprinzip

Satz vom zureichenden Grund *m* • principle of sufficient reason *(log, met)* → principium rationis sufficientis

Satz von Pythagoras *m* • Pythagoras' theorem *(mat)* → Pythagoreischer Lehrsatz

Satz, wahrer *m* • true proposition *(epi, lan)*

Satz, zusammengesetzter *m* • complex statement/proposition *(lan)*

Satzart *f* • kind of sentence *(lan)*

Satzaussage *f* • predication, sentential utterance, assertion *(lan)* < Prädikation

Satzbau *m* • propositional structure, sentence structure/formation *(lan)*

Satzbedeutung *f* • sentence/sentential meaning *(lan)* ↔ Wortbedeutung

Satzform *f* • propositional/sentential form, form of a sentence *(lan)*

Satzfunktion *f* • propositional function *(Russell)*, sentential function *(Frege etc) (log, lan)*

Satzgegenstand *m* • subject *(lan)*

Satzinhalt *m* • proposition, propositional content *(lan)*

Satzlogik *f* • sentence logic, sentential/propositional logic *(log, lan)*

Satzmodus *m* • sentence mode *(lan, log)*

Satzoperator *m* • sentence/sentential/proposition operator *(log, lan)*

Satzradikal *n* • sentence radical *(Wittgenstein) (lan)*

Satzschema *n* • propositional scheme/schema *(lan)*

satzungswidrig • unconstitutional *(jur)*

Satzvariable *f* • sentential/propositional variable, sentence variable *(lan)*

Satzverknüpfung *f* • sentential/propositional combination *(lan)*

Satzwahrheit *f* • truth of a sentence/statement/proposition *(lan)*

Satzzeichen *n* • propositional sign *(Wittgenstein) (lan)*

Säuglingssterblichkeit *f* • infant mortality *(nat)*

Säulenheiliger *m* • stylite *(rel)*

saurer Regen *m* • acid rain *(env)* < Waldsterben

Schablonendenken *n* • stereotyped/stereotypical thinking *(gen)* < Stereotyp, Schwarz-Weiß-Denken

Schädellehre *f* • phrenology *(Gall, Lavater) (nat, psy)* → Phrenologie

Schadenabschätzung *f* • appraisal/estimation of damages *(act, env, tec)*

Schadeneintrittswahrscheinlichkeit *f* • probability of loss *(mat, tec)*

Schadenersatz *m* • compensation, damages *(jur)*

Schadensausmaß *n* • extent of damage(s) *(gen)*

Schadensbegrenzung *f* • limitation of damage(s) *(gen)*

Schadenshäufigkeit *f* • incidence/frequency of loss *(mat)*

Schadensverhütung *f* • prevention of harm *(gen)*

Schadensvermeidung *f* • avoidance of harm *(gen)*

schadstoffarm • low emission *(env)*

Schadstoffbelastung *f* • pollution *(env)*

Schadstoffe *pl* • pollutants, toxic agents *(env)*

Schadstoffemission *f* • harmful emission *(env)*

Schadstoffkonzentration *f* • concentration of harmful substances *(env)*

Schaffen, künstlerisches *n* • artistic creation/ work *(aes)* → künstlerische Schöpfung

Schaffensdrang *m* • creative urge *(aes, psy)* < Kunsttrieb

Schaffensprozeß *m* • creative process *(aes)* < produktiver Prozeß

Schallgeschwindigkeit *f* • speed of sound, sonic velocity *(nat)*

Schallgrenze *f* • sound barrier *(nat)*

Scham *f* • shame *(eth, psy)*

Schamanismus *m* • shamanism *(rel, cul, eso)*

Scharfsinn *m* • mental acuteness, acuteness of mind, acumen *(psy)*

Scharfsinn, wissenschaftlicher *m* • scientific acuteness *(psy, sci)*

Scharia *f* • Sharia *(rel, jur)*

Schattenreich *n* • Hades *(rel)*

Schattenwirtschaft *f* • shadow economy *(eco)*

Schätzung *f* • estimation, estimate *(mat)*

Schau, innere *f* • inner vision *(Schleiermacher)* *(met, rel)*

Schau, religiöse *f* • religious vision *(rel)*

schaubare Symbole *pl* • intuited symbols *(Jaspers)* *(met)*

Schauen, intuitives *n* • intuitive view *(epi, rel)*

Schauen, theoretisches *n* • theoretical view *(met)*

Schauprozeß *m* • show trial *(jur, pol)*

Schein *m* • (▷ Täuschung) illusion, delusion, (▷ Widerschein) reflexion, (▷ Erscheinung) appearance *(met)* < Erscheinung

Schein, ästhetischer *m* • aesthetic appearance *(aes)*

Schein, äußerlicher *m* • external appearance *(epi)*

Schein, dialektischer *m* • dialectical appearance/illusion *(Kant)* *(epi, met)*

Schein, empirischer *m* • empirical illusion *(Kant)* *(epi, met)*

Schein, falscher *m* • false appearance, illusion, delusion *(epi, met)* < Täuschung

Schein, gedanklicher *m* → Schein, logischer

Schein, logischer *m* • logical appearance/ illusion *(Kant)* *(epi, met)*

Schein, schöner *m* • appearance of beauty *(aes)* < Schein, ästhetischer

Schein, sinnlicher *m* • sensory/sensual appearance *(Kant)* *(epi)*

Schein, transzendentaler *m* • transcendental illusion *(Kant)* *(epi, met)*

Schein und Sein *m,n* • appearance and reality *(epi, met)*

Schein, zuverlässiger *m* • reliable appearance *(epi, psy)*

Scheinargument *n* • pseudo-argument, specious/spurious argument *(sci)*

Scheinartenbildung *f* → Pseudospeziation

Scheinbegriff *m* • pseudo-concept *(lan)* < pathologischer Term

Scheinbeweis *m* • pseudo-proof, pseudo-argument, sophism *(log)* → Sophismus

Scheinbild *n* → Trugbild

Scheindemokratie *f* • pseudo-democracy *(pol)*

Scheindemonstration, sophistische *f* • sophistic(al) pseudo-demonstration *(sci)* < Sophismus

Scheindialog *m* • mock dialog(ue) *(lan)*

Scheineigenname *m* • pseudo-proper name, apparent proper name *(Frege)* *(log)*

Scheinfrage *f* • pseudo-question *(Carnap)* *(sci)*

Scheingelehrter *m* • pseudo-scholar *(gep)*

Scheingrund *m* • (▷ scheinbarer Grund), apparent reason *(sci)*, (▷ Vorwand) pretext *(act)*

Scheinheiligkeit *f* • hypocrisy *(eth)* < Heuchelei, Scheintugend

Scheinmotiv *n* • pseudo-motive *(psy)*

Scheinobjekt *n* • virtual object *(ont)*

Scheinphilosophie *f* → Pseudophilosophie

Scheinproblem *n* • pseudo-problem *(Carnap etc)* *(sci)* < W 875

Scheinsatz *m* • pseudo-proposition *(lan)*

Scheintugend *f* • pseudo-virtue, pseudo-morality *(eth)* < Scheinheiligkeit

Scheinwelt *f* • world of appearance(s), virtual reality *(ont)* ↔ wirkliche Welt < virtuelle Realität

Scheinwerfertheorie *f* • searchlight theory, torch theory *(Fleck, Popper etc)* *(sci)* ↔ Kübeltheorie des menschlichen Geistes

Scheinwissen *n* • pseudo-knowledge *(epi)*

Scheinwissenschaft *f* → Pseudowissenschaft

Scheitern *n* • failing, failure *(Jaspers, Kierkegaard, Camus etc)* *(met)*

Scheitern, fruchtbares *n* • productive failure *(Jaspers)* *(met)*

Schema *n* • scheme, schema, pattern, model *(gen)*

Schema der Attribution *n* • schema of attribution *(Foucault)* *(epi, pol)*

Schema der Einbildungskraft *n* • schema of imagination *(Kant)* *(epi)*

Schema der Gemeinschaft *n* • schema of community *(Kant) (epi)*

Schema der Gliederung *n* • schema of articulation *(Foucault) (epi, pol)*

Schema der Größe *n* • schema of quantity *(Kant) (epi)*

Schema der Kausalität *n* • schema of causality *(Kant) (epi)*

Schema der Modalität *n* • schema of modality *(Kant) (epi)*

Schema der Möglichkeit *n* • schema of possibility *(Kant) (epi)*

Schema der Notwendigkeit *n* • schema of necessity *(Kant) (epi)*

Schema der Qualität *n* • schema of quality *(Kant) (epi)*

Schema der Sinnlichkeit *n* • schema of sensibility *(Kant) (epi)*

Schema der Substanz *n* • schema of substance *(Kant) (epi)*

Schema der Wirklichkeit *n* • schema of actuality *(Kant) (epi)*

Schema eines regulativen Prinzips *n* • schema of a regulative principle *(Kant) (epi)*

schematische Hypotypose *f* • schematic hypotyposis *(Kant) (epi, sci)*

schematisieren • to schematize *(gen)*

Schematismus *m* • schematism *(Kant) (epi)*

Schematismus der Kategorien *m* • schematism of the categories *(Kant) (epi, met)*

Schematismus der reinen Verstandesbegriffe *m* • schematism of pure concepts of (the) understanding *(Kant) (epi)*

Schematismus, transzendentaler *m* • transcendental schematism *(Kant) (met)*

Schere, soziale *f* • social rift *(soc)* < neue Armut

Scheuklappendenken *n* • blinkered thinking/thought *(gep)*

Schicht, soziale *f* • social stratum/class *(soc)* < Kastensystem, Klassenschichtung

Schicht(en)ontologie *f* • ontology of strata *(N. Hartmann) (ont)* < Seinsstufen

Schichtarbeit *f* • shiftwork *(eco)*

Schichtenlehre *f* • stratum theory, doctrine of strata *(N. Hartmann, Ingarden) (ont, aes)*

Schichtung, soziale *f* • social stratification *(soc)* < soziale Differenzierung

Schicklichkeit *f* • decency, decorum, propriacy *(eth)* → Angemessenheit

Schicksal *n* • destiny, fate *(met)* → Ananke < Bestimmung

Schicksalsfrage *f* • question of survival, fateful issue *(gen)*

Schicksalsgemeinschaft *f* • community of fate *(soc)* < gemeinsames Schicksal

Schicksalsgläubigkeit *f* → Fatalismus

Schickung des Seyns *f* • destining of Beyng *(Heidegger) (ont)*

Schiedsgericht *n* • arbitration court *(jur)*

schiefen Ebene, Argument der *n* • slippery slope argument, wedge argument *(eth)* < Dammbruchargument

Schiff des Theseus *n* • (the) Ship of Theseus *(Plutarch, Hobbes etc) (ont)* < Mereologie

Schiffsmetapher *f* • Neurath's boat *(Neurath) (sci)* < Schiff des Theseus

Schikane *f* • chicane(ry) *(soc)*

Schildkrötengeometrie *f* • turtle geometry *(mat, AI)*

Schimäre *f* • chimera *(psy, epi)* → Trugbild < Chiffre

Schintoismus *m* • Shinto(ism) *(rel, asp)*

Schisma *n* • schism *(rel, pol)*

Schismogenese *f* • schismogenesis *(Bateson) (sys)*

Schizophrenie *f* • schizophrenia *(psy)* → Ichspaltung < multiple Persönlichkeitsstörung

Schlaf, ewiger *m* • eternal sleep/slumber *(rel, eso)* < Tod

Schlagwort *n* • slogan, catchphrase *(lan)*

schlanke Produktion *f* • lean production *(eco)*

Schlaraffenland *n* • Cockaigne, Cockayne, land of plenty, land of milk and honey *(soc)* < Utopie, goldenes Zeitalter

schlechte Unendlichkeit *f* • bad infinite/infinity *(Hegel) (epi, met)*

schlechter Glaube(n) *m* → böser Glaube(n)

Schlechterstellung *f* • inferior/subordinate position(ing) *(eco, soc)* < Diskriminierung

schlechtes Gewissen *n* • bad conscience *(rel, eth)* < Schuldbewußtsein

schlechteste aller möglichen Welten *f* • worst of all possible worlds *(Schopenhauer) (met)*

schlechtesten aller Möglichkeiten, Annahme der *f* • worst-case assumption/scenario *(dec, eth)* < Schreckensszenario, GAU

schlechthinnige Abhängigkeit *f* • total dependence *(Plotinus) (met)*

schlechthinnige Unendlichkeit *f* • sheer infinity, boundlessness as such, total boundlessness *(aes)*

Schlechtigkeit *f* • depravity, wickedness, badness *(eth)* < Bosheit

Schleier der Erscheinung *m* • veil of appearance *(met)*

Schleier der Maja *m* • veil of maya *(Schopenhauer) (epi, met, asp)*

Schleier des Nichtwissens *m* • veil of ignorance *(Rawls) (eth, soc)* < unparteische Wahl, ursprüngliche Wahl

Schleife *f* • loop *(AI)* < Feedback-Schleife

Schleuderpreis *m* • dumping price *(eco)*

Schlichtheit *f* • plainness, modesty *(aes)* < Schmucklosigkeit

Schließen *n* • reasoning *(log)*

Schließen, approximatives *n* • approximate reasoning *(log)*

Schließen, fallbasiertes *n* • case-based reasoning, CBR *(log)*

Schließen, natürliches *n* • natural deduction *(log)*

Schließen, nicht-monotones *n* • non-monotonic reasoning *(log)*

Schließen, possibilistisches *n* • possibilistic reasoning *(log)*

Schließen, probabilistisches *n* • probabilistic reasoning *(log)*

Schließen, qualitatives *n* • qualitative reasoning *(log)*

Schließen, zeitliches *n* • temporal reasoning *(log)*

Schluß *m* • conclusion, inference, syllogism, argument *(log)* → Schlußfolgerung

Schluß auf die beste Erklärung *m* • inference to the best explanation *(Peirce etc) (sci)*

Schluß, praktischer *m* • practical inference *(Aristotle) (eth, log)*

Schluß, unvollständiger *m* • incomplete inference *(log)* → Enthymem

Schluß vom Allgemeinen auf das Einzelne *m* • inference from the general to the particular *(log)* → Deduktion

Schluß vom Einzelnen auf das Allgemeine *m* • inference from the particular to the general *(log)* → Induktion

Schlüsselbegriff *m* • key term/concept *(lan)*

Schlüsselerlebnis *n* • crucial experience *(psy)*

Schlüsselfrage *f* • core/key question, crucial question *(gen)*

Schlüsselstellung *f* • key position *(soc)*

Schlüsselwerk *n* • key work *(gen)*

Schlüsselwort *n* • keyword *(lan)*

schlußfolgern • to conclude, to infer, to reason, to argue *(log)*

schlußfolgerndes Denken *n* • (inferential) reasoning *(log)*

Schlußfolgerung *f* • conclusion, inference, syllogism, argument *(log)* → Schluß

Schlußfolgerungsdefinition *f* • inferential definition *(Popper) (sci)*

schlüssig • conclusive *(log)* → konkludent

schlüssiger Beweis *m* • conclusive proof/ argument *(log)*, conclusive evidence *(jur)*

Schlüssigkeit *f* • conclusiveness *(log)*

Schlußregel *f* • rule of inference *(log)*

Schlußsatz *m* • conclusion *(log)*

Schmähschrift *f* • (libellous) pamphlet *(gen)*

Schmarotzertum *n* • parasitism *(soc, eth)* < Sozialschmarotzer

Schmerz, seelischer *m* • emotional suffering/ pain *(psy)*

Schmerzempfindung *f* • pain sensation, sensation of pain *(nat, psy)*

schmerzloser Tod *m* • painless death *(eth)* < Euthanasie

Schmerzlosigkeit *f* • painlessness *(nat, psy, eth)* < Hedonismus

Schmerzvermeidung *f* • avoidance of pain *(psy, eth)*

Schmerzwahrnehmung *f* • pain perception, awareness/perception of pain *(psy)*

Schmetterlingseffekt *m* • butterfly effect *(sys)* < Chaostheorie

Schmiergeldzahlung *f* → Bestechung

Schmucklosigkeit *f* • austerity, plainness, lack of ornament *(aes)* < Schlichtheit

Schneeballeffekt *m* • snowball effect *(sys)* < Dominoeffekt, Eigendynamik, Kettenreaktion

Schneeballsystem *n* • snowball system *(sys, soc)*, cumulative returns *(eco)*

schneller Brüter *m* → Brutreaktor

Schnitt *m* • cut, cutting *(aes)* < Montage

Schnitter, der gerechte *m* • the Grim Reaper *(rel)*

Schnittpunkt *m* • (point of) intersection *(mat, log)*

Schnittpunkt der Kulturen *m* • intersection of cultures *(cul)*

Schocktherapie *f* • shock treatment *(psy, nat)*

Schockwirkung *f* • shock effect *(psy)*

Scholastik *f* • scholasticism *(his, rel)*

Scholastiker *m* • scholastic *(his, rel)*

scholastische Methode *f* • scholastic method *(rel, sci)*

scholastische Philosophie *f* • scholastic philosophy *(gep)*

Scholastizismus *m* • Scholasticism *(his, rel)*

Schon-sein-bei *n* • being-already- with/ alongside *(Heidegger) (ont)*

Schon-sein-in (der Welt) *n* • being-already-in (the world) *(Heidegger) (ont)*

Schöne, das *n* • the beautiful/beauty *(aes)*

schöne Kunst *f* • fine art *(aes)*

schöne Künste *pl* • fine/beaux arts *(aes)*

schöne neue Welt *f* • brave new world *(Huxley) (pol, soc)* < W 877

schöne Seele *f* • beautiful soul *(Schiller) (aes)* < Kalokagathie, Veredelung der Seele

Schönen, Idee des *f* • idea/form of beauty/the beautiful *(Plato etc) (met, aes)*

Schönen, Theorie des *f* • theory of beauty *(aes)*

Schönfärberei *f* • glossing things over *(gen)* < Euphemismus

Schöngeist *m* • bel esprit *(aes)* < Ästhetizismus

schöngeistige Literatur *f* • belles-lettres *(aes)*

Schönheit, abhängige *f* • dependent beauty *(aes)*

Schönheit als Symbol der Sittlichkeit *f* • beauty as a symbol of morality *(Kant) (aes, eth)*

Schönheit des Herzens *f* • beauty of the heart *(Shaftesbury) (aes)* < schöne Seele

Schönheit, geistige *f* • spiritual beauty *(aes)* ↔ sinnliche Schönheit

Schönheit, körperliche *f* • physical/bodily beauty *(aes)*

Schönheit, moralische *f* • moral beauty *(aes, eth)*

Schönheit, unabhängige *f* • independent beauty *(aes)*

Schönheitsbegriff *m* • concept of beauty *(aes)*

Schönheitserfahrung *f* • experience of beauty *(aes)*

Schönheitsgenuß *m* • enjoyment of beauty *(aes)* < interesseloses Wohlgefallen

Schönheitsideal *n* • the ideal of beauty, ideal beauty, beau ideal *(aes)*

Schönheitskriterium *n* • criterion of beauty *(aes)*

Schönheitslinie *f* • line of beauty *(Hogarth) (aes)*

Schönheitssinn *m* • sense of beauty *(aes)*

Schönheitssinn, angeborener *m* • inborn sense of beauty *(Hutcheson, Shaftesbury) (aes)*

Schönheitsurteil *n* • judg(e)ment of beauty *(aes)* < ästhetisches Urteil

Schönwetterethik *f* • sunshine ethics *(eth)*

Schöpfer(gott) *m* • the Creator, creator God *(rel)*

Schöpfergeist *m* • creative spark/spirit *(aes)*

Schöpferische, das *n* • the creative *(aes)*

schöpferische Entwicklung *f* • creative development *(aes)*

schöpferische Kraft *f* • creative force *(aes)*

schöpferischer Akt *m* • creative act *(aes)*

schöpferisches Vermögen *n* • creative ability *(aes)*

Schöpfung, die *f* • the Creation *(rel)*

Schöpfung aus dem Nichts *f* • creation out of nothing, creation ex nihilo *(Aquinas etc) (met, rel)* → creatio ex nihilo

Schöpfungsgenuß *m* • creative enjoyment, enjoyment of creation *(Goethe etc) (aes)*

Schöpfungsgeschichte *f* • genesis, history of (the) creation *(rel)*

Schöpfungslehre *f* • doctrine of creation *(rel)* < Kreationismus

Schöpfungsmythos *m* • creation myth, myth of (the) creation *(rel, cul)*

Schöpfungsordnung *f* • order of creation *(rel)*

schottische Aufklärung *f* • Scottish Enlightenment *(his, gep)*

Schranke *f* • boundary *(Kant) (epi)*, bound, limit, barrier *(gep)* < Grenze

Schranken der Produktion *pl* • limits/obstacles in/to production *(Marx) (eco, soc)*

schrankenloser Wettbewerb *m* • free/ unrestricted/unlimited competition *(eco)*

Schreckensherrschaft *f* • reign of terror *(pol)*

Schreckensszenario *n* • worst-case scenario *(dec)* < GAU

Schreibtischforschung *f* • desk research *(sci)*

Schreibtischtäter *m* • armchair culprit° *(pol)*

Schreibverbot *n* • ban on writing *(pol)*

Schrift *f* • (▷ écriture) Writing *(Derrida etc) (lan)*

Schriftauslegung *f* → Exegese

schriftlicher Nachlaß *m* → nachgelassene Schriften

Schriftsinn, mehrfacher *m* • plurality of (text) meanings *(lan)*

Schriftsprache *f* • literary/written language *(lan)* < Umgangssprache

Schriftsteller *m* • writer, author *(aes)*

schrittweise Annäherung *f* • successive approximation *(mat)* < asymptotische Annäherung

Schrödinger-Gleichung *f* • Schrödinger (wave) equation *(nat)*

schrumpfende Ressourcen *pl* • shrinking resources *(eco, env)*

Schulbildung *f* • formal education *(soc)* ↔ Herzensbildung

Schulbildung, höhere *f* • higher education *(soc)*

Schuld *f* • guilt *(jur, eth)*

Schuld, existenzielle *f* • existential guilt *(Jaspers) (eth)*

Schuld, moralische *f* • (▷ Verschulden) moral guilt, (▷ in der Schuld stehen) moral debt *(eth)*

Schuldbekenntnis *n* • confession of guilt *(jur, rel)*

Schuldbeladenheit *f* • sinfulness *(Kierkegaard)* *(rel)* < Sündhaftigkeit

Schuldbewußtsein *n* • consciousness/ awareness of guilt, guilt(y) consciousness *(eth, rel)* < schlechtes Gewissen

Schuldenfalle *f* • debt trap *(eco)* < Zinsknechtschaft

Schuldenhaftung *f* • liability for debts *(eco, jur)*

Schuldenkrise *f* • debt crisis *(eco)* < Schuldenfalle, Schuldenkrise

Schuldennachlaß *m* • debt relief *(eco)*

Schuldentilgung *f* • cancellation of debts *(eco)*

Schuldfrage *f* • question of guilt *(jur, eth)* < W 882

Schuldgefühl *n* • sense/feeling(s) of guilt *(psy)* < Schuldbewußtsein

schuldig sein • to be guilty *(jur, eth)*

schuldig werden • to become guilty *(rel)*

Schuldiger *m* • guilty person, culprit *(jur, eth)*

Schuldigkeit *f* → Pflicht

Schuldkomplex *m* • guilt complex *(psy)*

Schuldlosigkeit *f* • innocence, guiltlessness *(jur)* < Unschuld

Schuldner *m* • debtor *(jur, eco)*

Schuldner-Gläubiger *m,m* • debtor-creditor *(eco)*

Schuldnerländer *pl* • debtor countries *(pol, eco)* < Schuldenkrise

Schuldübernahme *f* • (▷ Verantwortung) assumption of responsibility *(eth)*

Schule von Athen *f* • Athenian School, School of Athens *(his)*

Schulgelehrsamkeit *f* • book learning *(gep)*

schulmäßig • according to rule *(gep)* < orthodox

Schulmedizin *f* • orthodox medicine *(nat)* ↔ Alternativmedizin

Schulmeinung *f* • orthodox/received opinion *(gep)*

Schulmetaphysik *f* • orthodox/school metaphysics *(met)*

Schulphilosophie *f* • orthodox/standard/ accepted philosophy *(gep)*

Schulwesen *n* • educational system *(soc)*

Schulwissen *n* • book learning *(gep)* < Schulphilosophie

Schutzbehauptung *f* • protective assertion, exculpatory statement *(jur, eth)*

Schutzbündnis *n* • defensive alliance *(pol)*

Schutzgeist *m* • guardian spirit *(rel, cul)*

Schutzheiliger *m* • patron saint *(rel)*

Schutzherrschaft *f* • protectorate *(pol)*

Schutzmachtfunktion *f* • protective/protection power function *(pol)*

Schutzmaßnahme *f* • preventive measure *(act)*

Schutzpflicht *f* • duty of protection *(jur, eth)*

Schutzvereinigung *f* • protective association, system of mutual protection *(pol)*

Schutzvorrichtung *f* • safety device *(tec)* → Sicherheitsmaßnahme

schwach vollständig • weakly closed/complete *(mat)*

Schwäche, moralische *f* • moral weakness *(eth)*

schwaches Wissen *n* • weak knowledge *(epi)* ↔ zwingendes Wissen

Schwachsinnigkeit *f* • feeble-mindedness, imbecility *(psy)*

Schwanenparadoxie *f* • swan paradox *(Hempel) (log, epi, sci)* < Rabenparadoxie, Bestätigungsparadox

Schwangerschaftsabbruch *m* • termination of pregnancy *(eth)* → Abtreibung

Schwangerschaftsverhütung *f* • contraception *(nat, eth)*

Schwärmer, religiöser *m* • religious fanatic/ visionary *(rel)*

Schwärmerei *f* • zealotry, zealotism, fanaticism *(psy)*

Schwarz-Weiß-Denken *n* • black-and-white thinking *(gen)* < Schablonendenken

Schwarzarbeit *f* • illicit/illegal work *(eco)* < Untergrundwirtschaft

schwarze Komödie *f* • black comedy *(aes)*

schwarze Liste *f* • black list *(pol)*

schwarze Magie *f* • black magic *(eso)* < Voodoo

schwarzes Loch *n* • black hole *(nat)*

Schwarzfahrerdilemma *n* • free-rider dilemma *(eco, dec, eth)*

Schwarzmarkt *m* • black market *(eco)* < Untergrundwirtschaft

Schwarzsche Ungleichung *f* • Schwarz's inequality *(mat)*

Schwarzseher *m* • pessimist, Cassandra (prophet) *(psy)* < Pessimismus

Schwebe *f* • suspension, indecision *(Jaspers) (met)*

Schweigen *n* • silence *(met)*

schweigende Annahme *f* • tacit assumption *(gep)*

schweigende Mehrheit *f* • the silent majority *(pol, soc)*

Schweigepflicht *f* • oath of confidentiality, pledge/duty of secrecy *(eth)*

Schweigsamkeit *f* • taciturnity, reticence *(psy)*

Schwelle *f* • threshold *(epi)*

Schwelle der Epistemologisierung *f* • threshold of epistemologization *(Foucault) (epi)*

Schwelle der Formalisierung *f* • threshold of formalization *(Foucault) (epi)*

Schwelle der Positivität *f* • threshold of positivity *(Foucault) (epi)*

Schwelle der Wissenschaftlichkeit *f* • threshold of scientificity *(Foucault) (epi)*

Schwellenangst *f* • threshold anxiety *(psy)*

Schwellenländer *pl* • emerging nations *(eco, soc)*

Schwellenwert *m* • threshold (value) *(nat, sys, env)* < Grenzwert, kritischer Wert

Schwere *f* • gravity, weight *(nat)*

Schwerelosigkeit *f* • weightlessness *(nat)*

Schwerkraft *f* • gravitation *(nat)* < Anziehungskraft

Schwermut *f* • melancholy, melancholia *(psy)* → Melancholie

Schwerter zu Pflugscharen *pl* • swords to ploughshares *(rel, eth)* < Rüstungskonversion

Schwesterschaft *f* • sisterhood *(fem)*

Schwierigkeitsgrad *m* • degree of difficulty *(gen)*

Schwingungszahl *f* • vibration frequency, frequency of vibration *(nat)*

schwören bei Gott • to swear by God *(rel)*

Schwungkraft *f* • (angular) momentum, energy (force), drive, torque *(nat)* < Lebensschwungkraft

Schwur *m* • oath *(jur)*

Science-fiction *f* • science fiction *(aes)* < Futurologie

scientia media *f* • middle knowledge *(rel)*

Scotismus *m* • Scotism *(gep)*

sechster Sinn *m* • (the) sixth sense *(eso)*

Seele *f* • soul *(rel, psy)* → Psyche

Seele als substanzielle Monade *f* • (the) soul as a substantial monad *(Leibniz) (met)*

Seele als tabula rasa *f* • (the) soul as tabula rasa, (the) soul as a blank slate/tablet *(Leibniz, Locke) (epi)* < tabula rasa

Seele, doppelte Gestalt der *f* • twofold aspect of the soul *(rel)*

Seele, Postexistenz der *f* • post-existence of the soul *(Plato etc) (met)*

Seele, Präexistenz der *f* • pre-existence of the soul *(Plato, Plotinus etc) (met)*

Seele, schöne *f* • beautiful soul *(Schiller) (aes)* < Veredelung der Seele

Seele, sensitive *f* • sensitive soul *(Aristotle) (met)*

Seele, Unsterblichkeit der *f* • immortality of the soul *(rel)*

Seele, vegetative *f* • vegetative soul *(Aristotle) (met)*

Seelenadel *m* • nobility of mind/soul *(aes, eth)*

Seelenatomismus *m* • indivisibility of the soul *(met)*

Seelenblindheit *f* • mind blindness *(met)*

Seelenforschung *f* → Psychologie

Seelenfriede *m* • peace of mind *(eth, rel)* < Gelassenheit, heitere; innere Ruhe

Seelengröße *f* • greatness of soul *(Nietzsche) (eth)*

Seelenheil *n* • (spiritual) salvation *(rel)*

Seelenleben *n* • inner life *(psy)*

Seelenleiden *n* • mental suffering *(psy)*

seelenloser Zustand *m* • mindless state *(met)*

Seelenruhe *f* → Seelenfriede

Seelenschmerz *m* • mental agony/pain *(psy)*

Seelenstärke *f* • strength of spirit *(psy)* < Willenskraft

Seelenteile, die drei *pl* • the three parts of the soul *(Plato, Aristotle) (met)*

Seelenvermögen *n* • faculty of the soul *(Aristotle, Kant etc) (epi, psy)*

Seelenverwandtschaft *f* • congeniality/affinity of souls/minds *(psy)* < Wahlverwandtschaft

Seelenwanderung *f* • metempsychosis, transmigration (of the soul) *(rel, eso)* → Metempsychose

Seelenzustand *m* • emotional state, psychic condition *(psy)*

seelisches Gleichgewicht *n* • mental equilibrium *(psy)*

Seelsorge *f* • pastoral care *(rel)*

Segen *m* • blessing, benediction *(rel)*

Segment *n* • segment *(mat)*

Segmentierung *f* • segmentation *(soc, sci)*

Segnungen der Zivilisation *pl* • blessings of civilization *(soc, cul)*

Seher *m* • seer, visionary, prophet *(rel, eso)*

Sehergabe *f* • visionary powers *(rel, eso)*

Sehweise *f* • way of seeing *(gen)* < Perspektivismus

seiend • being, existent *(ont)*

Seiende, das *n* • that what/which is, beings, things that are/exist, the existent *(ont)* < ens

Seiendes als Seiendes *n* • being as/qua being *(Heidegger) (ont)*

Seiendheit *f* • beingness *(Aristotle, Wolff, Heidegger) (ont)*

sein • to be, to exist *(ont)*

Sein *n* • being, existence *(ont, met)* < Dasein, Seyn, ens < W 891, 892, 893

Sein, aktuales *n* • actual being, factual being *(ont)*

Sein, akzidentielles *n* • accidental being *(ont)*

Sein als Ich-sein *n* • being-as-self *(Jaspers)*
(met)

Sein als Jetztzeit *n* • Being as nowness
(Heidegger) (ont)

Sein als Objekt-Sein *n* • being-an-object, being
as being an object *(ont)*

Sein als reines Denken *n* • being as pure
thought *(met)*

Sein als Sein *n* • Being as Being *(Heidegger)*
(ont)

Sein als solches *n* → Sein an sich

Sein als Weltzeit *n* • Being as worldtime
(Heidegger) (ont)

Sein an sich *n* • being as such *(ont)* → Sein
selbst

Sein bei *n* • being amidst *(Heidegger) (ont)*

Sein bestimmt Bewußtsein *n* • being determines consciousness *(Marx) (epi)*

Sein der/des Anderen *n* • being of the Other(s)
(Sartre, Derrida) (met)

Sein des Da *n* • the Being of the There
(Heidegger) (ont)

Sein des Daseins *n* • the Being of Dasein
(Heidegger, Jaspers) (ont)

Sein des Seienden *n* • the being of Being, the
being of the existent *(Heidegger) (ont)*

Sein, die Frage nach dem *f* • the question of
Being *(Heidegger etc) (ont)* → Seinsfrage
< Seinsproblem

Sein, ewiges *n* • eternal being *(rel, met)*

Sein-für-Anderes *n* • being-for-another
(Hegel) (met)

Sein für sich *n* • being-for-itself *(Sartre) (met)*
↔ Sein in sich

Sein, gesellschaftliches *n* • (▷ Dasein) social
existence, (▷ Seiendes) social being *(Marx
etc) (soc)* < Sein und Bewußtsein

Sein, ideales *n* • ideal being *(met)*

Sein, immerwährendes *n* → Sein, ewiges

Sein in der Welt *n* → In-der-Welt-Sein

Sein in der Zeit, ursprüngliches *n* • authentic
being in time *(Jaspers) (met)*

Sein in sich *n* • being-in-itself *(Sartre) (met)* ↔
Sein für sich

Sein, intentionales *n* • intentional being *(ont)*

Sein, logisches *n* • logical being *(log)*

Sein, notwendiges *n* • necessary being *(ont)*

sein oder nichtsein • to be or not to be *(ont)*

Sein oder Nichtsein *n* • being or non-being
(ont)

Sein, potentielles *n* • potential being *(ont)*
< Potentialität und Aktualität

Sein, reales *n* • real being *(ont)*

Sein, reines *n* • pure being *(ont)*

Sein-Seiendes-Dichotomie *f* • Being versus
being/that-which-is dichotomy, the dichotomy between being and beings *(ont)* < ontologische Differenz

Sein selbst *n* • being-itself *(ont)* → Sein an sich

Sein-Sollen-Metabasis *f* • is-ought fallacy *(epi,
eth)* < naturalistischer Fehlschluß

Sein-Sollen-Problem *n* • is-ought problem *(sci,
eth)*

Sein-Sollen-Unterscheidung *f* • is-ought
distinction *(sci, eth)* < Tatsache-Wert-
Unterscheidung

Sein, soziales *n* • social being *(Marx) (soc)*

Sein, substanzielles *n* • substantial being,
essential being *(ont)*

Sein, transzendentales *n* • transcendental
being *(ont)*

Sein überhaupt *n* → Sein an sich

Sein und Bewußtsein *n,n* • being and consciousness *(Feuerbach, Marx etc) (epi)*,
matter and mind *(met)*

Sein und Erscheinung *n,f* • being and appearance *(epi, ont, aes)* < Erscheinung, Schein

Sein und Nichts, Einheit von *f* • unity of being
and nothing/non-being *(Hegel) (met)*

Sein und Nichtsein *n,n* • being and non-being
(ont)

Sein und Schein *n,m* • appearance and reality,
fact and fiction *(gep)* < Sein und
Erscheinung

Sein und Sollen *n,n* • is and ought *(eth, epi)*
< Sein-Sollen-Metabasis

Sein und Werden *n,n* • being and becoming
(ont)

Sein und Zeit *n,f* • Being and time *(met)* < W
893

Sein, veritatives *n* • veritative being *(ont)*

Sein, verkörpertes *n* • corporeal being *(ont)*

Sein, virtuelles *n* • virtual being *(ont)*
< Scheinwelt, virtuelle Realität

Sein, wesentliches *n* → Sein, substantielles

Sein zum Seinkönnen *n* • Being-toward(s)-the-
potentiality-for-Being *(Heidegger) (ont)*

Sein zum Tode *n* • Being-unto/toward(s)-death
(Heidegger etc) (ant, ont)

Seinkönnen *n* • potentiality-for-Being, ability to
be *(ont)* → possest < Sein, potentielles

Seinlassen *n* • letting be *(eth, met)* < Gelassenheit

Seinlassen des Seins *n* • the letting-be of Being/
what is° *(Heidegger) (ont)*

Seins, Bedeutung des *f* • meaning of being
(ont)

Seins, Bewußtsein des *n* • consciousness/
awareness of being *(met)*

Seins, Einheit des f • unity of being (ont)

Seins, Geschichte des f → Seinsgeschichte

Seins, Lichtung des f • clearing/lighting of Being (Heidegger) (ont)

Seins, Selbstbewußtsein des n • self-consciousness of being (met)

Seins, Wesen des n • the nature/essence of being (ont)

Seins, zeitliche Deutung des f • temporal interpretation of Being (Heidegger) (ont)

Seinsarten pl • modes of being (ont) → Seinsweisen

Seinsbedingungen pl • conditions of being (met)

Seinsbegriff m • concept of being (ont)

Seinsbestimmung f • (▷ Seinsdefinition) definition of being (ont), (▷ Seinsgeschick) fate, determination of being (met)

Seinsbezug m • reference to being (met)

Seinscharakter m • nature of being (met) < Seinsweise

Seinsdenken n • thinking of Being (Heidegger) (ont)

Seinserkenntnis f • cognition/knowledge of being (met) < Seinswissen

Seinsfrage f • question of being (ont) → Sein, die Frage nach dem

Seinsgebundenheit f • existential determination (Mannheim) (soc, epi) < Standortgebundenheit des Denkens, Wissenssoziologie

Seinsgeltung f • ontic validity (Husserl) (ont)

Seinsgeschichte f • history of being (Heidegger etc) (ont)

Seinsgeschick n • fate of being (met)

Seinsgesetze pl • laws of being (ont)

Seinsgestalten pl → Seinsweisen

Seinsgewißheit f • certainty of Being (Heidegger) (ont)

Seinsgläubigkeit f • faith/confidence in being (met)

Seinsgrade pl • degrees of being (ont)

Seinsgrund m • reason for being, why and wherefore of being (ont)

seinshafte Gegenständlichkeit f • objectivity of being (Jaspers) (met)

Seinshierarchie f • hierarchy of being (ont) < Schicht(en)ontologie

Seinsinkongruenz f • incongruity of being (met)

Seinskategorie f • category of being (N. Hartmann) (ont)

Seinskette f • chain of being (met, nat)

Seinslehre f • doctrine of being (ont) → Ontologie

Seinsmächtigkeit f • power(fulness) of Being (Heidegger) (ont)

Seinsmetaphysik f • metaphysics of being (met) < Geistmetaphysik

Seinsmodalität f • modality of being, existential modality (met) < ontologische Modalität

Seinsmodi pl → Seinsweisen

Seinsmöglichkeit f → Sein, potentielles

Seinsmythologie f • mythology of being (Adorno) (met)

Seinsoffenheit f • the openness of being (ant, ont)

Seinsordnung f • order of being (ont)

Seinsprinzip n • principle of being (N. Hartmann) (ont)

Seinsproblem n • problem of Being (Heidegger) (ont) < Frage nach dem Sein

Seinsrealität f • reality of being (ont)

Seinsrelation f • relation of being (N. Hartmann) (ont)

Seinsschichten pl → Seinsstufen

Seinssinn m • ontic meaning (Husserl) (ont)

Seinsstufen pl • levels/stages of being (ont) < Schicht(en)ontologie

Seinstheorien pl • theories of being/existence (ont)

Seinsursache f • cause of being (met) → causa essendi

Seinsverborgenheit f • concealment of Being (Heidegger) (ont)

Seinsverfassung f • state of being (ont)

Seinsvergessenheit f • forgetfulness of Being (Heidegger) (ont) < erster Anfang

Seinsverhältnis n → Seinsbezug

Seinsverlassenheit f • foresakenness of/by Being (Heidegger) (ont)

Seinsverständnis n • understanding of being (ont)

Seinsverständnis, Eleatisches n • Eleatic conception of being (ont)

Seinsweisen pl • modes/types of being, modi essendi (ont)

Seinsweisen des Daseins pl • ways of being of Dasein (Heidegger) (ont)

Seinswissen n • knowledge of being (epi, ont) < Seinserkenntnis

Seinszeichen n → Existenzquantor

Seinszugehörigkeit f • belongingness to Being, Being-in-clusion (Heidegger) (ont)

Seinszustand m • state of being (ont)

Sektenwesen n • sectarianism (rel, soc)

sekundär wertende Wörter pl • secondarily evaluative words (Hare) (eth, lan)

sekundäre Welt *f* • secondary world *(Carnap)*
(epi, ont) ↔ primäre Welt

sekundärer Nesthocker *m* • secondary
nidicolous animal *(Portmann) (ant)* < Spätentwickler

Sekundärliteratur *f* • secondary literature
(gen) ↔ Primärliteratur

Sekundärvorgang *m* • secondary process
(Freud) (psy) < Primärvorgang

Sekundärwelt *f* • secondary world *(Carnap)*
(epi, ont)

Selbst, das *n* • the self *(met)*

Selbst, der Begriff des *m* • the concept of
(the) self *(Fichte etc) (met)*

Selbst(re)präsentation *f* • (re)presentation of
self *(psy, act)*

Selbstachtung *f* • self-respect/regard *(eth)*
< Selbstwert

selbstähnliche Menge *f* • self-similar set *(mat,
sys)*

Selbstähnlichkeit *f* • self-similarity *(ont, log)*

Selbstanalyse *f* • self-analysis *(Freud etc)*
(psy)

selbständiger Verstand *m* • active/agent intellect *(Aristotle) (met)* → intellectus agens

selbständiges Bewußtsein *n* → Bewußtsein,
unabhängiges

Selbstaufgabe *f* • self-renunciation *(eth)*

Selbstaufopferung *f* • self-sacrifice *(eth)*

Selbstausdruck *m* • self-expression *(psy)*

Selbstbeeinflussung *f* • auto-suggestion *(psy)*

Selbstbefreiung des Proletariats *f* • emancipation of the proletariat, proletarian
(self-)emancipation *(Marx etc) (pol)*

Selbstbegnadigung *f* • self-pardon *(Nietzsche)*
(eth)

selbstbegründet • self-founded, self-evident
(log)

Selbstbegründetheit *f* • having one's founda-
tion/basis in oneself/itself *(met)* → Aseität

Selbstbegründung *f* • self-justification *(epi,
log)*

Selbstbehauptungstrieb *m* • urge for self-
assertion *(psy)*

Selbstbeherrschung *f* • self-control, self-
mastery *(eth, psy)* → Selbstkontrolle

Selbstbejahung *f* • self-affirmation *(psy)*

Selbstbeobachtung *f* • self-observation *(psy)*
< Introspektion

Selbstbesinnung *f* • (self-)contemplation *(psy)*
< Selbstreflexion

Selbstbesitz *m* • self-possession *(jur, met)*

Selbstbesitz des Menschen *m* • self-ownership
of man *(eth)* < Autonomie

selbstbestimmender Wille *m* • self-determin-
ing will *(eth)*

selbstbestimmtes Leben *n* • self-determined
(way of) life *(eth, met)* < Autonomie

Selbstbestimmtheit *f* • self-determinedness
(eth, met)

Selbstbestimmung *f* • self-determination *(pol,
eth, met)* < Eleutheronomie, innere
Gesetzgebung

Selbstbestimmungsrecht *n* • right to self-
determination *(pol, jur)*

Selbstbestimmungsvermögen *n* • faculty of
self-determination, ability to determine
oneself *(eth, met)*

Selbstbetäubung *f* • self-intoxication *(psy)*

Selbstbetrug *m* • self-deception *(psy)* < Selbsttäuschung

Selbstbewegung *f* • autokinesis, self-motion
(nat, eso) → Autokinese

Selbstbewegung der Seele *f* • self-movement
of the soul *(Plato) (met)*

Selbstbewegung des Begriffs *f* • self-movement of the concept *(Hegel) (met)*

Selbstbeweihräucherung *f* • self-glorification
(psy) < Narzißmus

selbstbewußtes Wesen *n* • self-conscious
being *(ant)*

Selbstbewußtheit *f* → Selbstbewußtsein

Selbstbewußtsein *n* • (▷ Selbstvertrauen) self-
confidence *(psy)*, (▷ Ichbewußtsein) self-
consciousness, self-awareness *(met)*

Selbstbezug *m* • self-reference *(lan, sys)*

Selbstbezüglichkeit *f* • self-referentiality *(lan,
sys)*, egocentrism, self-seekingness *(eth)*

Selbstbezwingung *f* • self-mastery/constraint
(Nietzsche) (eth) < Selbstdisziplin

Selbstbild *n* • self-image *(psy)*

Selbstdarstellung *f* • self-presentation *(psy,
soc)*

Selbstdarstellungstrieb *m* • drive to exhibit/
show off oneself *(psy)*

Selbstdenken *n* → Denken, eigenständiges

selbstdenkender Gedanke *m* • thought thinking
itself *(Hegel) (met)*

selbstdestruktives Verhalten *n* • self-destruc-
tive behaviour *(psy)* → auto-destruktives
Verhalten

Selbstdeutung *f* • self-interpretation *(psy)*

Selbstdifferenzierung *f* • self-differentiation
(gep)

Selbstdisziplin *f* • self-discipline *(psy, eth)*

Selbstdressur *f* • self-taming/training *(Nietzsche) (eth)*

Selbsteigentum *n* • self-ownership *(jur, pol)*

Selbsteinschätzung *f* • self-rating, self-appraisal *(psy)*

Selbstempfindung *f* • sensation of self, awareness/feeling of oneself *(psy)* < Selbstwahrnehmung

Selbstentdeckung *f* • self-discovery *(psy)*

Selbstentfaltung *f* • self-realization *(psy)*

selbstentfremdeter Geist *m* • self-alienated spirit *(Hegel) (met)*

Selbstentfremdung *f* • self-estrangement, self-alienation *(Hegel, Marx etc) (met, soc)*

Selbstentfremdung des Geistes *f* • self-estrangement of the spirit/mind *(Hegel) (met)*

Selbstentsagung *f* • self-denial *(psy, eth)*

Selbstentzweiung *f* • self-division, division against oneself *(psy)* < Selbstentfremdung

Selbsterfahrung *f* • experience of oneself *(psy)*

selbsterfüllende Prognose *f* • self-fulfilling prophecy *(sci)* ↔ selbstzerstörende Prognose

selbsterfüllende Prophezeiung *f* → selbsterfüllende Prognose

selbsterhaltendes System *n* • self-maintaining system *(sys)* < homeostatisches System

Selbsterhaltung *f* • self-preservation *(soc, nat)*

Selbsterhaltungsimperativ *m* • imperative of self-preservation *(soc, nat)*

Selbsterhaltungsprozeß *m* • process of self-preservation *(nat, soc)*

Selbsterhaltungstrieb *m* • instinct of self-preservation, survival instinct *(nat, psy)*

Selbsterhellung *f* • self-illumination/enlightenment *(met, rel)*

Selbsterhöhung *f* • self-aggrandizement *(psy)* < Selbsterweiterung

Selbsterkenntnis *f* • self-knowledge, knowledge of oneself, knowing oneself *(met, psy)*

Selbsterklärungseffekt *m* • self-explanation effect *(sci)*

Selbsterlösung *f* • self- salvation/redemption *(rel)*

Selbstermächtigung *f* • self-authorization *(jur, pol)*

Selbsterniedrigung *f* • self-abasement *(rel, eth)* < Selbstherabsetzung

Selbsterschaffung des Menschen *f* • self-creation of man *(Marx) (soc)*

Selbsterweiterung *f* • self-aggrandizement *(Nietzsche) (met)*, extension of the self *(eso)*

selbstevidente Gewißheit *f* • self-evident certainty *(epi)*

selbstevidente Wahrheit *f* • self-evident truth *(epi)* < unzweifelhafte Wahrheit

Selbstevidenz *f* • self-evidence *(epi)*

Selbstfindung *f* • self-discovery *(psy, met)* < Selbstverwirklichung

Selbstgefälligkeit *f* • (self-)complacency *(psy)*

Selbstgefühl *n* • feeling of self, self-feeling *(psy)* < Selbstwahrnehmung

Selbstgenügsamkeit *f* • modesty *(eth)*; self-sufficiency *(eco)* → Autarkie

Selbstgenuß *m* • (self-)indulgence *(psy)*

Selbstgerechtigkeit *f* • self-righteousness *(psy, eth)*

selbstgesetzgebend • self-legislative *(Kant) (met)*

Selbstgesetzgebung der Vernunft *f* • self-legislation of reason *(Kant) (met, eth)*

Selbstgesetzgebung des Willens *f* • self-legislation of the will *(Kant) (met, eth)*

Selbstgesetzlichkeit *f* • autonomy *(eth, met)* → Autonomie

selbstgewisses Ich *n* • self-certain I, self-aware I *(met, epi)* < cogito ergo sum

Selbstgewißheit *f* • self-certainty *(epi)*

Selbstglorifizierung *f* • self-glorification *(psy)* → Selbstverherrlichung

Selbstheit *f* • selfhood *(met)*

Selbstherabsetzung *f* • self-depreciation/depreciation *(psy)* < Selbsterniedrigung

Selbsthilfe *f* • self-help *(act)*

Selbsthilfegruppe *f* • self-help group *(soc, psy)*

Selbsthilfeorganisation *f* • self-help organization *(soc)*

Selbsthypnose *f* • self-hypnosis *(psy, eso)*

Selbstidentität *f* • self-identity *(met, psy)*

Selbstimplikation *f* • self-implication *(log, mat)*

Selbstinteresse *n* • self-interest *(psy, eth)*

Selbstinteresse, aufgeklärtes *n* • enlighted self-interest *(eth, act)*

Selbstkontrolle *f* • self-control *(eth, psy)* → Selbstbeherrschung

Selbstkreuzigung *f* • self-crucifixion *(Nietzsche) (eth, psy)*

Selbstkritik *f* • self-criticism *(psy)*

selbstkritische Einstellung *f* • self-critical attitude *(psy)*

Selbstliebe *f* • love of self, self-love *(psy)*, amour de soi *(Rousseau) (eth, psy)* < Selbstsucht

Selbstlosigkeit *f* • unselfishness *(eth)* → Altruismus

Selbstmitleid *n* • self-pity *(psy)*

Selbstmord *m* • suicide *(eth, psy)* → Suizid, Selbsttötung < W 898

Selbstmord, philosophischer *m* • philosophical suicide *(Camus) (met)*

Selbstmordneigung f • suicidal tendency (psy)

Selbstmordversuch m • attempted suicide, suicide attempt (eth, psy)

Selbstoffenbarung Gottes f • self-relevation of God (Hegel etc) (met, rel)

Selbstorganisation f • self-organization (sys, soc) → Autopoiesis

Selbstorganisation, Verfahren der kreativen n • process of creative self-organization (sys) < autopoietische Systeme

selbstorganisierende Dynamik f • self-organizing dynamics (sys)

selbstorganisierendes System n • self-organizing system (sys) < autopoietisches System, selbstregelndes System

Selbstprüfung f • self-examination (eth, rel)

Selbstrechtfertigung f • self-justification (eth)

Selbstreferentialität f • self-referentiality (log, lan, sys)

selbstreferentiell • self-referential (log, lan, sys)

Selbstreferenz f • self-reference (log, lan, sys)

Selbstreflexion f • self-reflection (epi, psy)

selbstreflexiv • self-reflective (epi, psy), self-reflexive (lan)

selbstregelndes System n • self- regulating/ governing system (sys) < selbstorganisierendes System

Selbstregierung f • self-government, self-rule (pol)

Selbstregulation f → Selbstregulierung

Selbstregulierung f • self-regulation, self-government (sys)

Selbstreproduktion f • self-reproduction (eco)

selbstreproduzierendes System n • self-reproducing system (sys)

Selbstschädigung f • self-damage, self-harm (act)

selbstschaffende Quelle berechtigter Ansprüche f • self-originating source of valid claims (Rawls) (eth, pol)

Selbstschätzung f • self- valuation/appreciation (Nietzsche) (eth)

selbstschöpferisches Wesen n • self-creating being (ant, rel)

Selbstschutz m • self-protection (eth, soc) < Selbsterhaltung

Selbstsein n • being-a-self, self being (met), being-self, being-one's-self, being-its-self (Heidegger) (ont)

Selbstsein als Existenz n • being-a-self as Existenz (Jaspers) (met)

Selbsteinkönnen n • faculty of being-a-self (met)

Selbstsicherheit f • self- confidence/assurance (psy)

selbststeuerndes System n → selbstregelndes System

Selbststudium n • self-instruction (gep)

Selbstsucht f • selfishness (psy), amour propre (Rousseau) (eth, psy) → Egoismus < Selbstliebe

selbsttätige Systeme pl • self-acting systems (sys) → autopoietische Systeme < selbstregelnde Systeme

Selbsttäuschung f • self- deception/delusion (psy)

Selbsttötung f • suicide (eth, psy) → Selbstmord, Suizid

Selbsttranszendenz f • self-transcendence (Jaspers) (met)

Selbstüberschreitung f • self-transgression/ presumption (rel, eth) < Ich-Überschreitung

Selbstüberwindung f • self- overcoming/ surmounting (Nietzsche etc) (eth) < Willenskraft

Selbstüberwindung des Menschen f • self-overcoming/surmounting of the human being (Nietzsche) (met)

Selbstverächter m • self-despiser (Nietzsche) (eth)

Selbstverachtung f • self-contempt (psy)

Selbstverbesserung f • self-betterment (eth)

Selbstverdinglichung f • self-reification/ objectification, reification/objectification of the self (soc)

Selbstvergessenheit f • self-forgetfulness/ oblivion (Nietzsche) (eth, met)

Selbstvergessenheit der Existenz f • disowned mode of existence, self- oblivion/forgetting of existence (Kierkegaard, Heidegger) (ont)

Selbstvergötterung f • self-deification (psy, rel) → Autotheismus, Idiolatrie < Deifikation

Selbstvergottung f → Selbstvergötterung

Selbstverhalten n • self-attitude (psy)

Selbstverherrlichung f • self-glorification (psy)

Selbstverkauf m • the sale of oneself as a commodity (Marx) < Entäußerung

Selbstverleugnung f • self-denial (psy) < Selbstaufopferung

Selbstverlust m • loss of self (psy) < Persönlichkeitsverlust

Selbstverneinung f • self-denial (eth, psy)

Selbstvernichtung f • self-destruction (eth, sys, nat)

Selbstvernichtungsfähigkeit f • faculty of self-destruction (pol) < wechselseitig gesicherte Zerstörung

Selbstverpflichtung *f* • self-obligation *(eth)*

selbstverschuldete Unmündigkeit *f* • self-imposed tutelage, self-incurred immaturity, self-inflicted dependence/dependency *(Kant) (eth, pol)*

Selbstversorgungswirtschaft *f* • self- sufficient/sustaining economy *(eco)* < Autarkie

Selbstverständnis *n* • self- conception/understanding *(psy)* < Selbstidentität

Selbstverstehen *n* • self-understanding *(psy)*

Selbstverteidigungsrecht *n* • right of self-defence *(jur, eth)*

Selbstvertrauen *n* • self- confidence/reliance *(psy)*

selbstverursachte Ursache *f* • self-caused cause *(Aquinas) (met)* → causa sui

Selbstverursachung *f* • self-causation *(met)*

Selbstverwaltung *f* • self-management *(eco)*

Selbstverwandlung *f* • self-transformation *(psy, eso)*

Selbstverwertung des Kapitals *f* • self-valorization of capital *(Marx) (eco)*

Selbstverwirklichung *f* • self- fulfilment/realization/actualization *(psy)* < Selbstfindung

Selbstverwirklichungsbedürfnis *n* • need for self- fulfilment/realization/actualization *(psy)*

Selbstwahrnehmung *f* • self-perception *(epi, psy)*

Selbstwerdensprozeß *m* • process of self-becoming *(psy)* < Individuation

Selbstwert *m* • self-esteem, self-worth° *(eth)* < Selbstachtung

Selbstwertgefühl *n* • self-esteem, sense of one's worth *(psy)*

selbstwiderlegend • self-refuting *(log, sci)*

Selbstwiderlegungsregel *f* • rule of self-refutation, self-denial rule *(log, mat)*

Selbstwiderspruch *m* • self-contradiction *(log)*

Selbstwidersprüchlichkeit *f* • self-contradictoriness *(log)*

Selbstwissen *n* • self-knowledge *(epi)* < Selbsterkenntnis

Selbstzentriertheit *f* • self-centredness *(eth)*

selbstzerstörende Prognose *f* • self-defeating prophecy *(sci)* ↔ selbsterfüllende Prognose

Selbstzerstörung *f* • self-destruction *(psy, sys)*

Selbstzufriedenheit *f* • self-satisfaction, (self-)contentment *(psy)*

Selbstzuschreibung *f* • self-ascription *(psy)*

Selbstzweck *m* • end in itself *(act, eth)*

selbstzwecklich • autotelic, as an end in itself *(act, eth)*

Selektion, genetische *f* • genetic selection *(nat)*

Selektion, natürliche *f* • natural selection *(nat)* → natürliche Auslese

Selektion, organische *f* • organic selection *(nat)*

Selektion, physiologische *f* • physiological selection *(nat)* < Selektion, genetische

Selektion, sexuelle *f* • sexual selection *(nat)* → geschlechtliche Auslese

Selektionsbedingungen *pl* • selection conditions *(nat, sci)* → Selektionskriterien

Selektionsdruck *m* • selection pressure *(nat)*

Selektionskriterien *pl* • selection criteria *(nat, sci)* → Selektionsbedingungen

Selektionsprämie *f* • selection premium *(nat)* < Überlebensqualität

Selektionsprinzip *n* • principle of selection *(nat)*

Selektionsprozeß, natürlicher *m* • natural selection process *(nat)*

Selektionsstrategie *f* • selection strategy *(nat, dec)*

Selektionstheorie *f* • theory of (natural) selection *(nat)*

Selektionsvorteil *m* • selective/selectional advantage *(nat)*

selektive Abtreibung *f* • selective abortion *(eth)* < pränatale Diagnostik

selektive Wahrnehmung *f* • selective perception *(epi, psy)*

Seligkeit *f* • blessedness *(rel)* < Heiligkeit

Seligsprechung *f* • beatification *(rel)*

Semantik *f* • semantics *(lan)*

Semantik der möglichen Welten *f* • possible-world semantics *(Kripke etc) (lan, ont)* → mögliche Weltensemantik

Semantik der natürlichen Sprache *f* • semantics of natural language *(lan)*

Semantik, deskriptive *f* • descriptive semantics *(lan)*

Semantik, formale *f* • formal semantics *(lan, log)*

Semantik, generative *f* • generative semantics *(lan)* ↔ Semantik, interpretative

Semantik, generelle *f* • general semantics *(Korzybsky) (lan, cul)*

Semantik, handlungstheoretische *f* • action-theoretic semantics, act-theoretical semantics *(Grice) (lan)* < sprechhandlungstheoretische Semantik

Semantik, informelle *f* • informal semantics *(Sneed) (lan, sci)*

Semantik, interpretative *f* • interpret(at)ive semantics *(lan)* ↔ Semantik, generative

Semantik, kognitive *f* • cognitive semantics *(lan)*

Semantik, logische *f* • logical semantics *(log, lan)*

Semantik, modelltheoretische *f* • model-theoretic semantics *(lan, log)*

semantisch geschlossene Sprache *f* • semantically closed language *(Tarski)* lan

semantische Antinomien *pl* • semantic antinomies *(lan)*

semantische Implikation *f* • semantic implication/entailment *(lan)*

semantische Konzeption der Wahrheit *f* • semantic conception of truth *(Tarski) (epi, lan)* → semantische Theorie der Wahrheit

semantische Paradoxie *f* • semantic paradox *(lan, log)*

semantische Präsupposition *f* • semantic presupposition *(lan, log)*

semantische Primitive *pl* • semantic primitives *(lan)*

semantische Theorie der Wahrheit *f* • semantic(al) theory of truth *(Tarski) (epi, lan)*

semantische Theorienkonzeption *f* • semantic conception of theories *(Suppes, Sneed etc) (sci, lan)*

semantische Wahrheitstheorie *f* → semantische Theorie der Wahrheit

semantischer Aufstieg *m* • semantic ascent *(Quine) (lan)* < Sinnesbedeutung

semantischer Inhalt *m* • semantic content *(lan)* < Referenz

semantisches Modell *n* • semantic model *(lan)*

semantisches Netz(werk) *n* • semantic net(work) *(lan)*

Semantisierung *f* • semanticization *(lan, soc)*

Semantisierungsprozeß *m* • process of semanticization *(Mead) (lan, soc)*

Semi-Fiktion *f* • semifiction *(Vaihinger) (met)*

Semiologie *f* • semiology *(lan)*

semiologische Analyse *f* • semiological analysis *(Barthes) (lan)*

Semiose *f* • semiosis *(lan)*

Semiotik *f* • semiotics *(Peirce) (lan)* → Zeichentheorie

semiotische Ästhetik *f* • semiotic aesthetics *(Morris etc) (aes)*

semiotisches System *n* • semiotic system *(lan)*

Semitismus *m* • semitism *(rel)* < Zionismus, Judaismus ↔ Antisemitismus

Sender-Empfänger-Modell *n* • Shannon-Weaver model *(lan)* → Empfänger-Sender-Modell

Sendungsbewußtsein *n* • sense of mission *(psy)*

Senizid *m* • senicide *(eth)*

Sensation *f* • sensation *(Locke etc) (epi)* → Sinneseindruck

Sensationsmache *f* • sensationalism *(psy)*

Sensibilität *f* • sensibility, sensivity *(psy)*

Sensibilität, ästhetische *f* • aesthetic sensibility/sensitivity *(aes)*

sensomotorische Phase *f* • sensory-motor phase *(Piaget) (psy)*

sensorisch • sensory *(epi, psy)*

Sensualismus *m* • sensualism, sensationism, sensationalism *(Locke etc) (epi)* < W 705

Sentientismus *m* • sentientism *(eth)*

Sentimentale, das *n* • the sentimental *(aes)*

Sentimentalische, das *n* • the sentimental *(Schiller) (aes)*

Sentimentalität *f* • sentimentality *(psy, aes)*

separable Hülle *f* • separable hull *(mat)*

Separatfrieden *m* • separate peace *(pol)*

Separatismus, politischer *m* • political separatism *(pol)*

Sequenz *f* • sequence *(log)*

Serialität *f* • seriality *(Sartre) (soc)*

Serie *f* • series *(gep)*

serielle Datenverarbeitung *f* • serial data processing *(AI)* ↔ Parallelverarbeitung

serielle Musik *f* • serial music *(aes)*

Serienexistenz *f* • serial existence *(nat, soc)* < Klonen,

Serienfertigung *f* • series production *(eco, tec)* < Massenproduktion, Taylorismus

Seriosität *f* • seriousness *(eth)*

Seßhaftwerdung des Menschen *f* • man's settling, man's becoming settled *(ant, cul)*

Setzen, das *n* • positing *(Fichte, Hegel) (met)*

Setzen des Ich *n* • positing of the Ego *(Fichte) (met)*

setzen • to posit *(Fichte, Hegel) (met)*

Sex-Gender-Unterscheidung *f* • sex-gender distinction *(nat, soc, fem)* < Geschlecht

Sexismus *m* • sexism *(fem, pol)* < politische Korrektheit

Sexualethik *f* • sexual ethics *(eth)*

Sexualforschung *f* • sexology *(nat)*

Sexualmißbrauch *m* • sexual abuse *(eth)*

Sexualmoral *f* • sexual morals/morality *(eth)*

Sexualobjekt *n* • sex object *(Freud etc) (psy)*

Sexualpolitik *f* • sexual politics/policy *(Reich) (psy, pol)*

Sexualtrieb *m* • sex(ual) drive, sexual instinct, libido *(psy)*

Sexualverhalten *n* • sexual behaviour *(psy)*

Sexualwissenschaft *f* • sexology *(sci)*

sexuelle Aufklärung *f* • sex education *(psy)*

sexuelle Belästigung *f* • sexual harassment *(eth, fem)* < Opfer-Feminismus

sexuelle Differenz *f* • sexual difference *(nat, fem)* < Geschlechtsdifferenz

sexuelle Diskriminierung *f* • sexual discrimination *(soc, fem)*

sexuelle Selektion *f* • sexual selection *(nat)* → geschlechtliche Auslese

Seyn *n* • Seyn, Beyng *(Heidegger) (ont)*

Sezession *f* • secession *(pol, aes)*

Sharia *f* • sharia(t), sheria(t) *(jur, rel, pol)*

sich ereignen • to come to one's own, to take place *(Heidegger) (ont)*

sich-nicht-selbst-enthaltende Klasse *f* • nonself-membered class *(log, mat)*

sich-selbst-enthaltende Klasse *f* • selfmembered class *(log, mat)*

sich selbst setzende Idee *f* • self-positing idea *(Hegel, Marx) (met)*

sich-verlieren • to lose oneself *(Nietzsche) (met)*

Sich-vorweg-Sein *n* • being-ahead-of-itself *(Heidegger) (ont)*

sich zeitigen • coming into Being *(Heidegger) (ont)*

Sichaufsichbeziehen *n* → Selbstreferenz

Sichentwerfen *n* • projecting oneself *(Heidegger) (ant, ont)* < Entwurf

sicheres Wissen *n* • certain knowledge *(epi)* < Unbezweifelbarkeit, unbezweifelbare Gewißheit

Sicherheit *f* → Gewißheit

Sicherheit, soziale *f* • social security *(soc)*

Sicherheitsbedürfnis *n* • need for safety, safety need *(psy)*

Sicherheitsbestimmungen *pl* • safety regulations *(tec)*

Sicherheitsgarantie *f* • safety guarantee *(pol)*

Sicherheitsgrad *m* • safety level *(sys)*

Sicherheitsmaßnahme *f* • safety measure *(tec)* → Schutzvorrichtung

Sicherheitspakt *m* • security pact *(pol)*

Sicherheitspolitik *f* • security policy *(pol)*

Sicherheitsstandard *m* • safety standard *(tec)*

Sicherheitssystem, kollektives *n* • collective security system *(pol)*

Sicherungssystem *n* • fail-safe system/device *(sys)* < Metasystem

Sichfinden *n* → Selbstfindung

Sichselbstgleichheit *f* • self-identity, identity with itself/oneself *(log, ont)*

Sicht der Wirklichkeit *f* • perception/view of reality *(gep)*

sichtbare Kirche *f* • visible church *(rel)*

sichtbare Welt *f* • apparent/visible world *(epi, met)*

Sieb des Eratosthenes *n* • Eratosthenes' sieve, sieve of Eratosthenes *(mat)*

Sieben Weisen, die *pl* • the Seven Sages *(gep)*

Siegeswillen *m* • will to win *(psy)*

Sigmafunktion *f* • sigma function *(Weierstrass) (mat)*

Signa *pl* • signa *(Jaspers) (met)* < Chiffre

Signalfunktion der Sprache *f* • signalling function of language *(lan)*

Signalsprache *f* • signal language *(lan)* < Symbolsprache

Signifikant *m* • signifier *(lan)* ↔ Signifikat

Signifikanz *f* • significance *(sci, gep)*

Signifikanz, empirische *f* • empirical significance *(sci)*

Signifikanzgrad *m* • degree of significance *(log, sci)*

Signifikanzniveau *n* • level of significance, significance level *(mat)*

Signifikat *n* • the signified *(lan)* → Designat ↔ Signifikant

Simplifizierung *f* • simplification *(gen)* < Komplexitätsreduktion

Simulation *f* • simulation *(sci, tec)* < Szenario-Denken

Simulationsmodell *n* • simulation model *(sci, tec)*

Simultaneität *f* • simultaneity *(nat, gep)* → Gleichzeitigkeit

singulär • singular *(log, ont)*

singuläre prädiktive Folgerung *f* • singular predictive induction *(log)* < induktive Generalisierung

singulärer Imperativ *m* • singular imperative *(Hare) (eth, lan)*

singulärer Term *m* • singular term *(lan)*

singuläres Gefühl *n* • singular feeling *(epi, psy)*

Singularismus *m* • singularism *(ont)* ↔ Pluralismus

Singularität *f* • singularity *(log, ont, mat)* < Einzigartigkeit, Partikularität

Sinn *m* • (▷ Verständlichkeit) sense, (▷ Bedeutung) sense, meaning, (▷ Perzeptionsfähigkeit) sense, awareness, (▷ Zweck) purpose, point *(gep)* < W 906

Sinn des Daseins *m* • meaning of existence *(met)*

Sinn des Lebens *m* • meaning of life *(met)*

Sinn, innerer *m* • inner/internal/interior sense *(log)* internal meaning *(gep)*

Sinn und Bedeutung *m,f* • sense and reference *(Frege) (log)* < W 1115

Sinn und Zweck *m,m* • sense and purpose *(act)*

Sinn vom Sein des Seienden *m* • the meaning of the being of being *(Plotinus) (met)*

Sinn von Sein *m* • sense/meaning of Being *(Heidegger) (ont)*

Sinnbedeutung *f* • significance *(lan)*

Sinnbegriff *m* • concept of sense *(met)* < Bedeutungsbegriff

Sinnbereiche, abgeschlossene *pl* • finite provinces (of sense/meaning) *(Schütz) (epi, soc)*

Sinnbild *n* → Symbol

sinnbildliche Darstellung *f* • symbolic representation *(aes)*

Sinnbildung *f* • meaning-formation *(Husserl) (epi, met)*

sinndefinit • definite in sense, having determinate meaning/sense *(log, lan)*

Sinndogma *n* • dogma of meaning *(sci)* < Sinnkriterium

Sinne *pl* • senses *(nat, epi)*

Sinneinheit *f* • unit of sense, sense unit *(lan)*

Sinnendinge *pl* → sinnliche Gegenstände

Sinnengenuß *m* • sensual pleasure *(psy, aes)*

Sinnenlust *f* → sinnliche Lust

Sinnenmensch *m* • sensualist *(psy, aes)*

Sinnenphänomene *pl* • sensual phenomena *(epi)*

Sinnenreiz *m* • (sensual) stimulus *(psy)*

Sinnentrug *m* → Sinnestäuschung

Sinnenwelt *f* → Sinneswelt

Sinnesänderung *f* • change of mind *(gep)*

Sinnesanschauung *f* → sinnliche Anschauung

Sinnesbedeutung *f* • sense meaning *(Quine) (lan)* < semantischer Aufstieg

Sinnesbereich *m* • sensory-field *(epi, psy)*

Sinnesbewußtsein *n* • sensory/sense conciousness *(met)*

Sinnesdaten *pl* • sense-data, percepts *(epi, sci)*

Sinnesdatensprache *f* • sense-datum language *(lan)*

Sinnesdatentheorie *f* • sense-data theory, sense-datum theory *(epi)*

Sinnesdatum *n* • sense-datum, percept *(epi, sci)* < Sinneseindruck

Sinneseindruck *m* • sense impression, sensory impression *(epi, psy)* < Sinnesdatum

Sinneserfahrung *f* • sensory/sense experience *(epi)* → sinnliche Erfahrung

Sinnesfreuden *pl* • pleasures of the senses *(psy)*

Sinneshemmung *f* • sensory/sense repression *(psy, epi)*

Sinnesinhalt *m* • sense-content *(psy, epi)*

Sinnesirrtum *m* • sensory error *(epi, psy)*

Sinnesobjekt *n* • sensible object *(psy, epi)*

Sinnesorgan *n* • sense organ *(nat, epi)* < sinnliche Gegenstände

Sinnespsychologie *f* • psychology of sensation *(Brentano) (psy)*

Sinnesqualitäten *pl* • sensible/sensory qualities *(epi)* → sinnliche Qualitäten

Sinnesreiz *m* • sensory stimulus *(psy, epi)*

Sinnesrelationen *pl* • meaning relations, semantic relations, sense relations *(lan, min)*

Sinnesschärfe *f* • acuteness of the senses *(psy, epi)* ↔ Geistesschärfe

Sinnestäuschung *f* • sensory illusion, deception of the senses *(psy, epi)*

Sinneswahrnehmung *f* • sensory/sense perception, sensation *(psy, epi)* → sinnliche Wahrnehmung < Sinneseindruck

Sinneswahrnehmung, Unzuverlässigkeit der *f* • unreliability of sensory/sense perception *(epi)*

Sinneswandel *m* → Sinnesänderung

Sinneswelt *f* • sensible/material world, world of the senses *(Kant etc) (epi, met)* → mundus sensibilis < W 1239

Sinneszentrum *n* • sense/sensory centre *(psy)*

Sinnfrage *f* • the question of meaning *(met)*

Sinngebilde *n* • meaningful structure *(Weber) (soc)*

Sinngebildewissenschaft *f* → Sinnwissenschaft

Sinngebung *f* • giving/imparting meaning *(met)*

sinnhaft adäquat • meaningfully adequate *(Weber) (epi, met)*

sinnhafte Bezogenheit *f* • meaningful relatedness *(Weber) (sci, soc)*

sinnhafte Kausalität *f* • meaningful causality *(Weber) (sci, soc)*

Sinnhaftigkeit *f* • meaningfulness, purposefulness *(gep)*

Sinnigkeit *f* → Sinnhaftigkeit

Sinnkrise *f* • crisis of loss of meaning *(met)* < Orientierungskrise, Sinnverlust

Sinnkriterium *n* • criterion of meaningfulness, meaning criterion *(sci, lan)*

sinnlich wahrnehmbar • (sensibly) perceptible, perceptible by the senses *(epi)*

sinnliche Anschauung *f* • sensory/sensible intuition *(Kant etc) (epi)* → Sinnesanschauung

sinnliche Begierde *f* • sensual desire *(Hegel etc) (met)* → Kupidität

Sinnliche, das *n* • the sensory/sensuous/sensual *(epi, psy)*

sinnliche Erfahrung *f* • sensory/sensible experience *(Kant) (epi)* → Sinneserfahrung sinnliche Gegenstände *pl* • sensual/sensuous/ sensible objects *(epi)* < Sinnesobjekt

sinnliche Gewißheit *f* • sensual/sensory certainty, sense-certainty *(Hegel etc) (epi)*

sinnliche Komponente der Erfahrung *f* • sensory component of experience *(epi)*

sinnliche Leidenschaft *f* • sensuous passion *(psy)*

sinnliche Lust *f* • sensuous pleasure *(psy)* < Epikureismus, Hedonismus, Sinnlichkeit

sinnliche Objekte *pl* → sinnliche Gegenstände

sinnliche Qualitäten *pl* • sensible/sensory qualities *(epi)*

sinnliche Schönheit *f* • sensual/sensible beauty *(aes)* ↔ geistige Schönheit

sinnliche Triebfeder *f* • sensuous motive/ incentive, sensuous motivating force *(Kant)* *(psy, eth)*

sinnliche Vorstellung *f* • sensible representation *(Kant) (epi, psy)*

sinnliche Wahrnehmung *f* • sensory/sense perception *(epi)* → Sinneswahrnehmung, Perzeption

sinnlicher Antrieb *m* • sensuous impulse *(Kant) (eth)*

sinnliches Bewußtsein *n* • sensory/sense consciousness/awareness *(Hegel) (epi)*

Sinnlichkeit *f* • sensibility, sensuousness, sensuality *(epi, aes)*

Sinnlichkeit und Verstand *f,m* • sensibility and understanding *(epi, met)*

Sinnlosigkeit *f* • (▷ Zwecklosigkeit) pointlessness, (▷ Bedeutungslosigkeit) senselessness, meaninglessness *(gep)*

Sinnorientierung *f* • sense orientation *(eth, rel)*

Sinnspruch *m* • device, motto *(lan)* < Aphorismus, Weisheitssprüche

Sinnstiftung *f* → Sinngebung

Sinnsuche *f* • quest/search for meaning *(met)*

Sinntheorem *n* • sense theorem, theorem of sense *(log, sci)* < Sinnkriterium

Sinnvakuum, existentielles *n* • existential vacuum *(met)*

Sinnverlust *m* • loss of meaning *(psy, soc, met)* < Sinnkrise

Sinnvermögen *n* • sensory/sense faculty *(psy)*

Sinnverstehen *n* • interpret(at)ive understanding, understanding (of) meaning *(lan)* < Verstehen

sinnvoller Satz *m* • significant proposition *(Wittgenstein)*, meaningful statement/ sentence *(lan)*

Sinnwidrigkeit *f* • inconsistency, self-contradiction, absurdity *(log, lan)* < Widersprüchlichkeit

Sinnwissenschaft *f* • meaning science *(sci)*

Sinnzusammenhang *m* • meaning context, context of sense/meaning, sense connection, meaningful relationship *(sci, lan)*

Sippenhaftung *f* • collective responsibility, tribal/group liability *(jur)* < Kollektivschuld

Sisyphus, Mythos von *m* • Myth of Sisyphus *(Camus) (met)* < absurder Held < W 684

Sisyphusarbeit *f* • Sisyphean/endless/unavailing task *(Camus) (met, rel)*

Sitte *f* • (▷ Brauch) custom, (▷ Gewohnheit) habit, (▷ sittliches Benehmen) morals, ethics *(eth, soc)* < mores

Sitten und Gebräuche *pl,pl* • manners and customs/mores *(eth, cul)*

Sittengeschichte *f* • history of life and customs *(cul, eth)*

Sittengesetz *n* • ethical/moral law *(Kant) (eth)*

Sittenkodex *m* • moral code *(eth)*

Sittenkomödie *f* • comedy of manners *(aes)*

Sittenlehre *f* • (▷ individuelle Sittenlehre) moral doctrine, (doctrine of) morals, (▷ allgemeine Sittenlehre) moral philosophy, ethics *(eth)* → Morallehre < Moralphilosophie < W 421

Sittenlosigkeit *f* • immorality, profligacy *(eth)*

Sittenrichter *m* • moral judge, censor, moralizer *(eth)*

Sittenverfall *m* • moral decline, corruption of morals *(eth)*

sittenwidriges Verhalten *n* • immoral behaviour, habit contra bonus mores *(eth)*

sittlich • moral, ethical *(eth)*

Sittliche, das *n* • the moral, the ethical *(eth)*

sittliche Pflicht *f* • moral/ethical duty *(Kant) (eth)*

sittliche Weltordnung *f* • moral world-order *(eth, rel)*

sittliches Empfinden *n* • moral sense *(eth)* → moralischer Sinn

Sittlichkeit *f* • ethical/moral practice, ethical life, (social/customary) morality, sittlichkeit *(Hegel etc) (eth)* → Ethos, Moralität

Sittlichkeit der Sitte *f* • morality of custom *(Nietzsche) (eth)*

Sittlichkeitsgefühl *n* → sittliches Empfinden

Sittsamkeit *f* • (▷ Anständigkeit) propriety, correctness, (▷ Keuschheit) chastity *(eth)*

Situation *f* • situation *(act, eth)* < Grenzsituation

Situationen, absolute *pl* • absolute situations *(Jaspers) (met)*

Situationen, kontingente *pl* • contingent situations *(Jaspers) (met)*

Situationismus *m* • situationism *(eth)* ↔ Kasuistik

Situationsabhängigkeit *f* • situation dependency *(gep)*

Situationsanalyse *f* • situational analysis *(dec)*

Situationsbeurteilung *f* • evaluation of a situation, situational evaluation *(dec)*

Situationsethik *f* • situation(al) ethics *(eth)*

Situationslogik *f* • situation(al) logic, logic of situations *(log)*

Situationssemantik *f* • situation semantics *(lan)*

Skalarprodukt *n* • scalar product, dot *(mat)*

Skalendiskriminationstechnik *f* • scale discrimination technique *(Edwards) (sci)*

Skalenniveau *n* • scales of measurement *(mat, sci)*

Skandal der Philosophie *m* • the scandal of philosophy *(Kant) (gep)*

Skepsis, ethische *f* • ethical scepticism *(eth)*

Skepsis, immanenzmetaphysische *f* • immanent metaphysical scepticism *(met, epi)*

Skepsis, logische *f* • logical scepticism *(log)*

Skepsis, methodische *f* → Skeptizismus, methodischer

Skepsis, transzendenzmetaphysische *f* • transcendental metaphysical scepticism *(met, epi)*

Skeptiker *m* • Sceptic *(gep)*

skeptische Haltung *f* • sceptic(al) attitude *(gep)*

skeptische Methode *f* • sceptical method *(epi, sci)* < Skeptizismus

skeptischer Idealismus *m* • sceptical idealism *(Kant) (epi, met)*

Skeptizismus *m* • scepticism *(epi, met)* < Fallibilismus

Skeptizismus, methodischer *m* • (▷ systematischer Skeptizismus) methodical scepticism, (▷ methodenbezogener Skeptizismus) methodological scepticism *(epi, met)*

Skeptizismus, moralischer *m* • moral scepticism *(eth)*

Skeptizismus, organisierter *m* • organized scepticism *(sci)*

Skeptizismus, wissenschaftlicher *m* • scientific scepticism *(sci)*

Sklavenarbeit *f* • slave labour/work *(eco, soc)*

Sklavenaufstand in der Moral *m* • slave-revolt in morality *(Nietzsche) (eth)*

Sklavenbefreiung *f* • emancipation of slaves *(pol)*

Sklavengesellschaft *f* • slave society *(soc)*

Sklavenhaltergesellschaft *f* • slave-owning society *(soc)*

Sklavenmoral *f* • slave-morality *(Nietzsche) (eth)* → Herdenmoral ↔ Herrenmoral

Sklavenseele *f* • servile mind *(psy)*

Sklavenwirtschaft *f* • slave economy *(eco)*

Sklaverei *f* • slavery *(eco, soc)*

Sklaverei, Aufhebung der *f* • abolition of slavery *(pol)*

sklavische Nachahmung *f* • slavish imitation *(aes)* < Epigonentum

sklavische Produktionsweise *f* • slave mode of production *(eco)*

Skopus *m* • scope *(log, lan)* → Geltungsbereich

Skript *n* • script *(AI)*

Skrupelhaftigkeit *f* • scrupulousness *(eth)*

Skrupellosigkeit *f* • unscrupulousness *(eth)*

Slippery-Slope-Argument *n* • slippery slope argument *(eth)* → Argument der schiefen Ebene, Dammbruchargument

Snobismus *m* • snobbery, snobbism, snobbishness *(psy, aes)* < Dandyismus, Camp-Ästhetik

Soforthilfe *f* • first/immediate aid *(eth, eco)*

Sofortmaßnahme *f* • immediate/emergency measure *(act)*

Sokrates • Socrates

Sokratiker *m* • Socratic *(gep)*

Sokratische Ethik *f* • Socratic ethics *(eth)*

sokratische Ironie *f* • Socratic irony *(gep)* < existentielle Ironie

sokratische Methode *f* • Socratic method *(epi)* → Hebammenkunst, Mäeutik

Sokratische Schule *f* • Socratic school *(gep)*

sokratische Tugenden *pl* • Socratic virtues *(Nietzsche) (eth)*

Sokratismus *m* • Socratism *(Nietzsche) (gep)*

Solarenergie *f* • solar energy *(env)* < erneuerbare Energie

Solidargemeinschaft *f* • community bound by solidarity *(soc, eth)* ↔ Rechtsgemeinschaft

Solidarität *f* • solidarity *(eth)*

Solidaritätsgefühl *n* • sentiment/sense/feeling of solidarity *(Camus etc) (eth)*

Solidarpakt *m* • solidarity pact *(eth, pol)*

Solipsismus *m* • solipsism *(epi, met)*

Solipsismus, epistemologischer *m* • epistemological solipsism *(epi)*

Solipsismus, gemäßigter *m* • moderate solipsism *(epi)*

Solipsismus, metaphysischer *m* • metaphysical solipsism *(epi, met)*

Solipsismus, methodischer *m* • methodical solipsism *(Carnap) (epi)*

Solipsismus, methodologischer *m* • methodological solipsism *(Putnam) (epi, min)*

Solipsismus, radikaler *m* • radical solipsism *(Stirner) (met)*

Sollen, das *n* • the ought *(eth)* < Verpflichtung

Sollen und Sein *n,n* → Sein und Sollen

Sollensforderung *f* • obligatory requirement *(eth)*

Sollenssätze *pl* • ought statements *(lan, eth)*

Sollvorschrift *f* • required/binding/obligatory provision *(eth)* ↔ Kann-Bestimmung

Sollwert *m* • nominal/rated/desired value *(mat, sci)* ↔ Istwert

Somnambulismus *m* • somnambulism *(psy, eso)*

Sonderbehandlung *f* • special treatment *(eth, pol)* < Diskriminierung, Privileg

Sonderbestimmung *f* • exceptional/special provision *(jur)* < Sonderregelung

Sonderfall *m* • exception, special/exceptional case *(gen)*

Sonderfrieden *m* → Separatfrieden

Sonderklasse *f* • special class *(gen)*

Sondermüll *m* • toxic/hazardous waste *(env)* < Mülltourismus

Sonderrecht *n* • privilege *(jur, eth)* → Privileg

Sonderregelung *f* • separate ruling/provision *(gen)*

Sonderstatus des Menschen *m* • special status of man/the human race *(ant)*

Sonderstellung *f* • special position/status *(gen)*

Sonderwelt, regionale *f* • special regional world, regional special world *(Husserl) (epi, met)*

Sonnenenergie *f* • solar energy *(env)*

Sonnengleichnis *n* • allegory of the sun *(Plato) (met)* < Liniengleichnis, Höhlengleichnis

Sonnengott *m* • sun-god *(rel)*

Sonnenkollektor *m* • solar panel *(env)*

Sonnenkraftwerk *n* • solar power plant *(env)*

Sonnenspektrum *n* • solar spectrum *(nat)*

Sonnensystem *n* • solar system *(nat)*

Sophia *f* • *nt,* wisdom *(gep)*

Sophisma *n* → Sophismus

Sophismus *m* • sophism *(log)* → Scheinbeweis

Sophist *m* • sophist *(gep)*

Sophisterei *f* • sophistry *(log)*

Sophistik *f* • (▷ Schule) sophist school, the sophists, (▷ Spitzfindigkeit) sophism, sophistry *(gep)*

Sophistikation *f* • sophistication *(epi, log)* < Sophismus

sophistischer Schluß *m* → Fangschluß

Sophrosyne *f* • *nt,* moderation, temperance *(eth)* → Besonnenheit

Sorge *f* • (▷ Besorgnis) care *(Heidegger) (ont)* → Besorgnis; (▷ Kummer) sorrow *(psy)*, (▷ Unruhe) anxiety, worry *(psy)* < Fürsorge, Angst

Sorgepflicht *f* • custody *(jur, eth)*

Sorgerecht *n* • care and custody *(jur)*

Sorglosigkeit *f* • unconcernedness, carelessness *(eth)*

sortale Begriffe *pl* • sortal terms/concepts *(log, lan)*

sortale Terme *pl* → sortale Begriffe

sortaler Ausdruck *m* • sortal expression/term *(lan)*

Sortenlogik *f* • sortal logic, many-sorted logic *(log)*

Sosein *n* • howness, being-so *(Heidegger, Meinong);* suchness, being-so, so-being, howness *(ont)* < Qualität

Sosein des Daseins *n* • the howness/being-so of Dasein *(Heidegger) (ont)*

Souverän *m* • sovereign *(pol)*

souveräne Macht *f* • sovereign power *(pol)*

souveräner Körper *m* • sovereign body *(Rousseau etc) (pol)*

Souveränität *f* • sovereignty *(pol)* → Eigenstaatlichkeit

Souveränitätsdoktrin *f* • sovereignty doctrine *(pol)*

Sowjetkommunismus *m* • soviet-communism *(pol)*

Sowjetsystem *n* • Sovietism, the Soviet system *(pol)*

Soziabilität *f* • sociability *(soc)* < zoon politicon

Sozialabbau *m* • social cuts, cuts in social service(s) *(soc)*

Sozialabgaben *pl* • social security contributions *(eco)*

Sozialanthropologie *f* • social anthropology *(soc, ant)*

Sozialarbeit *f* • social/welfare/community work *(soc)* < soziale Fürsorge

Sozialausgaben *pl* • social spending *(eco)*

Sozialbeitrag *m* → Sozialabgaben

Sozialberuf *m* • caring profession, occupation in social work *(eco, soc)*

Sozialbewußtsein *n* → gesellschaftliches Bewußtsein

Sozialbilanz *f* • (▷ Berücksichtigung sozialer Kosten) social balancing *(eco)*

Sozialbiologie *f* • social biology *(nat, soc)*

Sozialcharakter *m* • social character *(psy, soc)*

Sozialdarwinismus *m* • social Darwinism *(soc)* < Recht des Stärkeren

Sozialdemokratie *f* • social democracy *(pol)*

Sozialdistanz-Skala *f* → Bogardus-Skala

Sozialdynamik *f* • social dynamics *(soc)*

soziale Ausgrenzung *f* • social exclusion/ marginalization *(soc)* → Marginalisierung, sozialer Ausschluß < Stigmatisierung

soziale Bande *pl* • social ties *(soc)*

soziale Differenzierung *f* • social differentiation/stratification *(soc)*

soziale Distanz *f* • social distance *(Simmel) (soc)*

soziale Dynamik *f* → Sozialdynamik

soziale Einheit *f* • (▷ soziale Größe) social unit *(soc)*, (▷ soziale Zusammengehörigkeit) social unity *(soc)*

soziale Entfremdung *f* • social alienation *(Marx) (soc)*

soziale Existenz *f* • social existence *(soc)*

soziale Frage *f* • social question *(soc, pol)*

soziale Fürsorge *f* • social welfare *(soc)* → Sozialfürsorge

soziale Gerechtigkeit *f* • social justice *(eth, soc)*

soziale Institution *f* • social institution *(soc)*

soziale Integration *f* • social integration *(soc, pol)*

soziale Interaktion *f* • social interaction *(act, soc)*

soziale Klasse *f* • social class *(Marx etc) (soc)*

soziale Konditionierung *f* • social conditioning *(psy, soc)*

soziale Kontrolle *f* → Sozialkontrolle

soziale Kosten *pl* → Sozialkosten

soziale Kraft *f* • social force/power *(soc)*

soziale Marktwirtschaft *f* • social market economy *(eco, soc)* < freie Marktwirtschaft

soziale Mißstände *pl* • social grievances *(soc)*

soziale Mobilität *f* • social mobility *(soc)*

soziale Nützlichkeit *f* • social utility *(soc)*

soziale Praxis *f* • social praxis *(Marx) (soc)*

soziale Rangordnung *f* • social rank (order) *(soc)*

soziale Revolution *f* • social revolution *(soc, pol)*

soziale Rolle *f* • social role *(soc)*

soziale Schichtung *f* • social stratification *(soc)* < soziale Differenzierung

soziale Sicherheit *f* • social security *(soc)*

soziale Umstände *pl* • social conditions *(Marx etc) (soc)* < Milieutheorie

soziale Verpflichtung *f* • social duty/obligation/ requirement *(soc)*

soziale Welt *f* • social world *(soc)*

sozialer Abstieg *m* • downward social mobility, social decline *(soc)*

sozialer Aufstieg *m* • upward social mobility, social climbing, social rise *(soc)*

sozialer Ausschluß *m* • social exclusion *(soc)* < soziale Ausgrenzung

sozialer Druck *m* • social pressure *(soc)*

sozialer Friede *m* • social peace *(soc)*

sozialer Kontext *m* • social context *(soc)*

sozialer Organismus *m* • social organism *(soc)*

sozialer Status *m* → Sozialstatus

sozialer Verfall *m* • social disintegration/ decay, social retrogression *(soc, his)*

sozialer Wandel *m* • social change/ transformation *(soc)*

sozialer Wille *m* • social will *(soc)* < volonté générale

sozialer Wohlfahrtsstaat *m* • social welfare state *(soc, pol)*

sozialer Zusammenhalt *m* • social cohesion *(soc)*

soziales Erbe *n* • social heritage *(soc)*

soziales Ganzes *n* • social whole *(soc)*

soziales Gewissen *n* • social conscience *(soc, eth)*

soziales Handeln *n* • social action *(Weber etc) (soc, act)*

soziales Phänomen *n* • social phenomenon *(soc)*

soziales Wesen *n* • social being *(soc)* < Soziabilität, zoon politicon

Sozialethik *f* • social ethics *(eth)* ↔ Individualethik

Sozialeudämonismus *m* • social eudaimonism *(Bentham, Mill etc) (eth)* < Utilitarismus

Sozialexperiment *n* • social experiment *(Popper etc) (soc)*

Sozialforschung *f* • social research *(soc)*

Sozialforschung, empirische *f* • empirical social research/science *(soc, sci)*

Sozialfürsorge *f* • social welfare *(soc)*

Sozialgeschichte *f* • (▷ Geschichte des Sozialen) social history, history of society, (▷ Geschichte von Gesellschaften) societal history *(soc, his)*

Sozialhilfe *f* • (social) welfare *(eco)*

Sozialisation *f* • socialization *(soc)* < Vergesellschaftung

Sozialisation, geschlechtsspezifische *f* • gender/sex-role socialization *(fem, soc)*

Sozialisationsdruck *m* • socializing pressure *(soc)*

Sozialisationsprozeß *m* • socialization process *(soc)* < Individuationsprozeß sozialisatorische Interaktion f • socializatory interaction (Habermas) (soc, act)

Sozialisierung f → Sozialisation

Sozialismus m • socialism (pol)

Sozialismus, wissenschaftlicher m • scientific socialism (Engels) (soc)

Sozialistische Internationale f • Socialist International (pol)

sozialistischer Humanismus m • socialist humanism (eth, pol)

sozialistischer Realismus m • socialist realism (aes)

Sozialkategorie f • social category (soc)

Sozialklima n • social climate (soc, pol)

sozialkognitive Entwicklung f • sociocognitive development (psy, soc)

Sozialkonflikt m • social conflict (soc)

Sozialkonstrukt n • social construct (soc)

Sozialkontrakt m • social contract (Hobbes etc) (soc, pol) → Gesellschaftsvertrag

Sozialkontraktstheorie f → Sozialvertrags-theorie

Sozialkontrolle f • social control (soc)

Sozialkosten pl • social costs (eco) < Kosten-externalisierung

Sozialkritik f • social criticism (soc)

Soziallasten pl • social burdens (soc)

Sozialmoral f • social morality (eth) ↔ Individualmoral

Sozialökologie f • social ecology (nat, env)

Sozialökonomie f • social economy (eco)

Sozialordnung f • social order (soc)

Sozialorganismus m • social organism (soc)

Sozialpartnerschaft f • social partnership (eco, pol) < Wirtschaftsfrieden

Sozialphilosophie f • social philosophy (soc)

Sozialplanung f • social planning (soc, pol) < Sozialtechnik

Sozialpolitik f • social policy (pol, soc)

Sozialprävention f • social prevention (jur) ↔ Individualprävention

Sozialprestige n • social prestige (soc, psy) < Sozialstatus

Sozialpsychologie f • social psychology (soc, psy)

Sozialrecht n • social welfare law (jur, soc)

Sozialreform f • social reform (soc, pol)

Sozialschmarotzer m • social parasite (soc, eth) < Schmarotzertum

Sozialstaat m • welfare state (eco, pol, soc) → Wohlfahrtsstaat

Sozialstatus m • social standing/status (soc) < Sozialprestige

Sozialstruktur f • social structure (soc)

Sozialsystem n • social system (soc)

Sozialtechnik f • social engineering (Popper etc) (soc)

Sozialtechnologie f • social technology (soc) < Sozialtechnik

Sozialtechnologie der kleinen Schritte f • piecemeal social engineering (Popper) (soc)

Sozialtheorie f • social theory (soc) < Sozio-logie

Sozialutopie f • social utopia (soc)

Sozialverhalten n • social behaviour (soc)

Sozialvertrag m → Sozialkontrakt

Sozialverträglichkeit f • social acceptability (soc)

Sozialvertragstheorie f • social contract theory/doctrine (soc, pol)

Sozialwahltheorie f • social choice theory, theory of social choice (dec, soc)

Sozialwesen n → soziales Wesen

Sozialwissenschaft f • social science (soc)

Sozialwissenschaft, empirische f • empirical sociology/social science (soc, sci)

sozialwissenschaftlich • sociological (soc)

Soziobiologie f • sociobiology (nat, soc)

Soziogramm n • sociogram (soc)

soziohistorisch • sociohistorical (soc, his)

soziokulturelle Entwicklung f • sociocultural development (soc, cul)

soziokultureller Prozeß m • sociocultural process (soc, cul)

soziokultureller Wandel m • sociocultural change (soc, cul)

soziokultureller Wissenschaftsbegriff m • sociocultural concept of science (sci)

Soziolinguistik f • sociolinguistics (lan, soc)

Soziologie f • sociology (soc) → Gesellschafts-wissenschaft

Soziologie der Kunst f • sociology of art (aes) → Kunstsoziologie

Soziologie der Moral f • sociology of morals (soc, eth)

Soziologie des Wissens f → Wissenssoziologie

Soziometrie f • sociometry (sci)

soziomorphes Modell n • sociomorphous/sociomorphic model° (soc, sci)

sozioökonomische Bedingungen pl • socioeconomic conditions (eco, soc)

soziopathologisch • sociopathological (soc, psy)

soziotechnische Modelle pl • sociotechnical models (tec, sys, soc)

Spaltung der Objektwelt f • splitting of the world of objects *(Jaspers) (met)* < Umgreifende, das

Spaltungsgesetz der Realmöglichkeit n • cleavage of real possibilities *(N. Hartmann) (met)*

Spannung f • tension, suspense *(aes)*

Spannung, innere f • inner tension *(Bergson) (met)*

Spannungsreduktion f • excitation reduction *(psy)*

Spannungsverhältnis n • tension *(gen)*

Sparmaßnahme f • economy measure *(eco)*

spartanisch leben • lead/live a Spartan life *(eco, eth)* < Askese

Spaßphilosophie f → jokologische Philosophie

Spätaufklärung f • late Enlightenment *(his)*

Spätentwickler m • late developer, late starter *(ant, psy)* < sekundärer Nesthocker

Spätfolge f • delayed effect *(act)*

Spätgeburt f • retarded/post-term birth *(ant)*

Spätkapitalismus m • late capitalism *(eco, soc)*

Spätscholastik f • late scholasticism *(gep)*

Spätschriften pl • later writings *(gen)* ↔ Frühschriften

Spearman-Brown-Formel f • Spearman-Brown prophecy formula *(sci, mat)*

species humana f • human species *(nat, ant)*

Speicher m • memory, store, storage *(AI)* < Gedächtnis

spektrale Zerlegung f • spectral decomposition *(mat)*

Spektralfarbe f • spectral colour *(nat)*

Spektrum n • spectrum *(gen)*

Spekulation f • speculation *(met, eco)*

Spekulationsgewinn m • speculative profit *(eco)*

spekulative Absicht f • speculative intention *(Kant) (epi, met)*

spekulative Einheit aller Erkenntnis f • speculative unity of all knowledge *(Hegel) (epi, met)*

spekulative Erkenntnis f • speculative knowledge *(Kant etc) (epi, met)*

spekulative Erklärung f • speculative explanation *(sci)*

spekulative Idee f • speculative idea *(Hegel) (met)*

spekulative Philosophie f • speculative philosophy *(met)*

spekulative Theologie f • speculative theology *(rel)*

spekulative Vernunft f • speculative reason *(Kant) (met)*

spekulative Wissenschaftstheorie f • speculative theory of science *(sci)*

spekulativer Beweis m • speculative proof *(Kant) (epi, log)*

spekulativer Gebrauch der (reinen) Vernunft m • speculative employment/use of (pure) reason *(Kant) (epi, met)*

spekulatives Interesse der Vernunft n • speculative interest of reason *(Kant) (epi, met)*

Spermatozoon n • spermatozoon *(Thales) (met), (nat)*

Spezialfall m • special case *(gen)*

Spezialisationsanalogie f • analogy of specialization *(nat)*

Spezialisierung f • specialization *(gen)*

Spezialisierung durch Regeln f • specialization by rules *(log, AI)*

Spezialisierungsregel f • rule of specification *(log, AI)*

Spezialistenautorität f • expert authority *(psy)*

Spezialistentum n • specialism, expertise *(gen)* < Expertokratie

Speziation f • speciation *(nat)* → Artenbildung

spezielle Metaphysik f • special metaphysics *(Wolff) (met)*

spezielle Wissenschaftstheorie f • special philosophy/theory of science *(sci)* ↔ allgemeine Wissenschaftstheorie

Spezies f • species *(nat)*

Speziesismus m • speciesism *(Singer) (ant, eth)*

Spezifikation f • specification *(log)*

spezifisch menschlich • specifically human *(ant)* < Anthropinon

spezifisch menschliche Vermögen pl • specifically human capabilities *(Marx etc) (ant)*

spezifisches Quantum n • specific quantity *(nat)* < kritische Masse

Spezifizierung f → Spezifikation

sphärenfremde Sinnesdaten pl • allogeneous sense data *(Carnap) (epi)* ↔ sphärenverwandte Sinnesdaten

Sphärenharmonie f • harmony of the spheres *(Pythagoras) (met, aes)*

Sphärenmusik f • music of the spheres *(met, aes)* < Weltmusik

sphärenverwandte Sinnesdaten pl • isogeneous sense data *(Carnap) (epi)* ↔ sphärenfremde Sinnesdaten

Spiegelbild n • mirror image *(epi, aes)* < Abbild

Spiegelungstheorie f • principle of reflection *(mat)*

Spiel n • game, play *(gen)* < homo ludens

Spiel der freien Phantasie n • play of free phantasy *(aes, psy)* < Kreativität

Spiel der Kräfte *n* • interplay of forces *(nat, pol)*

Spiel der Künste *n* • play of the arts *(aes)*

Spiel der Natur *n* • play of nature *(nat)*

Spiel des Lebens *n* • game of life *(Conway)* *(nat, AI)*

Spielart *f* • variety, type *(gep)* → Varietät

Spielbegriff *m* • concept of (a) game *(aes, cul)*

Spielergebnis *n* • result, outcome (of a game) *(dec)* < Spieltheorie

Spielhandlung *f* → Spielzug

Spielraum *m* • range, room for maneuvre *(mat, lan, dec)* < Interpretation, semantische

Spielraum der Auslegung *m* • range of interpretation *(sci)* < hermeneutischer Spalt

Spielregel *f* • rule (of the game) *(lan, eth)*

Spielsystem *n* • gambling system *(dec, mat, sci)*

spieltheoretische Situation *f* • game-theoretic situation *(dec)*

Spieltheorie *f* • game theory, theory of games *(Neumann, Morgenstern etc)* *(dec, mat)* < W 924

Spieltheorie der Kunst *f* • play theory of art *(aes)*

Spieltheorie, nichtkooperative *f* • non-cooperative game theory, non-cooperative theory of games *(dec)*

Spieltrieb *m* • play instinct *(psy, aes)*

Spielzug *m* • move (in the game) *(dec)* < Gegenzug

Spießbürgertum *n* • philistinism *(soc)*

Spirale der Gewalt *f* • spiral of violence *(psy, soc)*

Spiritismus *m* • spiritism *(psy, eso)* < Animismus

spiritistische Sitzung *f* • seance *(eso)*

Spiritualismus *m* • spiritualism *(met, rel)*

Spiritualität *f* • spirituality *(met)* ↔ Materialität

spiritus animales *pl* • animal spirits *(Decartes)* *(met)* → Lebensgeister

Spitzenleistung *f* • top performance *(psy)*

Spitzenposition *f* • top/pole/number one position *(soc)* < Führungsposition

Spitzfindigkeit *f* • hairsplitting, nit-picking *(gep)* < Sophismus

Splittergruppe *f* • splinter group/party *(pol, soc)*

spontane Aggression *f* • spontaneous aggression *(psy)* ↔ Aggression, reaktive < primäre Feindseligkeit

Spontaneität *f* • spontaneity *(psy)*; *(Kant)* *(epi, psy)* ↔ Rezeptivität < Spontaneität und Passivität

Spontaneität der Anschauung *f* • spontaneity of intuition *(Kant)* *(epi)*

Spontaneität der Begriffe *f* • spontaneity of concepts *(Kant)* *(epi)*

Spontaneität der Erkenntnis *f* • spontaneity of knowledge *(Kant)* *(epi)*

Spontaneität des Dings-an-sich *f* • spontaneity of the thing-in-itself *(Kant)* *(met)*

Spontaneität und Passivität *f,f* • spontaneity and passivity *(Kant)* *(epi, met)*

Sportethik *f* • sport ethics *(eth)*

Sportphilosophie *f* • philosophy of sport *(gep)*

Sprachaberglaube *m* • language/linguistic superstition *(Mauthner)* *(lan)*

Sprachakttheorie *f* → Sprechakttheorie

Sprachakttypologie *f* → Sprechakttypologie

Sprachanalyse *f* • linguistic analysis *(lan)*

sprachanalytische Philosophie *f* • (linguistic) analytic(al) philosophy, analytic(al) philosophy of language *(lan)*

Sprachausdruck *m* • linguistic expression *(Frege etc)* *(lan)*

Sprachbarriere *f* • language barrier *(lan)*

Sprachbedingtheit *f* • linguistic determinedness *(lan)*

Sprachbewußtsein *n* • language/linguistic awareness/consciousness *(lan, psy)*

Sprache *f* • language, speech, vernacular *(lan)* < W 931

Sprache als enérgeia *f* • language as enérgeia/activity *(Humboldt etc)* *(lan)*

Sprache als vermeintliche Wissenschaft *f* • language as putative science *(Nietzsche)* *(lan)*

Sprache der Kunst *f* • language of art *(aes)*

Sprache der Natur *f* • language of nature *(nat, met)*

Sprache des Gefühls, unmittelbare *f* • immediate language of feeling *(Nietzsche)* *(lan)*

Sprache, empiristische *f* • empiristic language *(lan)*

Sprache erster Stufe *f* • first order language *(lan, log)*

Sprache, formale *f* • formal language *(log, lan)* → Formalsprache

Sprache, formalisierte *f* • formalized language *(Tarski)* *(lan, epi, log)*

Sprache, Funktion der *f* → Sprachfunktion

Sprache, gewöhnliche *f* • ordinary language *(lan)* → Sprache, natürliche

Sprache, ideale *f* • ideal language *(lan, sci)* → Idealsprache

Sprache, natürliche *f* • natural language *(lan)* → Normalsprache

Sprache, phänomenalistische *f* • phenomenalistic language *(met, lan)*

Sprache, Philosophie der gewöhnlichen *f* → Philosophie der normalen Sprache

Sprache zweiter Stufe *f* • second order language *(lan, log)*

Spracheigentümlichkeit *f* • idiosyncracy of language *(lan)*

Spracheinheit *f* • (▷ Sprachelement) unit of language *(lan)* < Sprachuniversalien; (▷ Spracheneinheit) unity of language(s)

Sprachengruppe *f* • language group *(lan)*

Sprachentwicklung *f* • language/linguistic development *(lan)*

Sprachenvielfalt *f* • linguistic variety, variety of languages *(lan)*

Spracherkennung *f* • speech/language recognition *(AI, min)*

Spracherwerb *m* • language acquisition *(psy, lan)*, learning to talk/speak *(Quine) (lan)*

Spracherwerbsvermögen *n* • language acquisition capacity, ability to learn a language *(lan)*

Sprachfähigkeit *f* • language/linguistic faculty/ability/capacity *(psy, lan)*

Sprachfamilie *f* • language family, family of languages *(lan)*

Sprachfaschismus *m* • linguistic/language fascism *(lan, pol)*

Sprachform, gemeinsame *f* • common form of language *(lan, soc)*

Sprachforschung *f* • linguistics *(lan)* → Linguistik

Sprachfunktion *f* • language function, function of language *(lan, act)*

Sprachfunktion, appellative *f* • appellative function of language *(Bühler) (lan, act)* < Organonmodell der Sprache

Sprachfunktion, argumentative *f* • argumentative function of language *(lan, act)*

Sprachfunktion, ausdrückende *f* • expressive function of language *(lan, act)*

Sprachfunktion, auslösende *f* • catalytic function of language *(lan, act)*

Sprachfunktion, darstellende *f* • descriptive function of language *(Bühler) (lan, act)* < Organonmodell der Sprache

Sprachfunktion, deskriptive *f* → Sprachfunktion, darstellende

Sprachfunktion, emotive *f* • emotive function of language *(Jakobson) (lan, act)*

Sprachfunktion, ermahnende *f* • admonitive function of language *(lan, act)*

Sprachfunktion, expressive *f* • expressive function of language *(Bühler) (lan, act)* < Organonmodell der Sprache

Sprachfunktion, metasprachliche *f* • metalinguistic function of language *(Jakobson) (lan, act)*

Sprachfunktion, persuasive *f* • persuasive function of language *(lan, act)*

Sprachfunktion, phatische *f* • phatic function of language *(Jakobson) (lan, act)*

Sprachfunktion, poetische *f* • poetic function of language *(Jakobson) (lan, act)*

Sprachfunktion, referentielle *f* • referential function of language *(Jakobson) (lan, act)*

Sprachfunktion, symptomatische *f* • symptomatic function of language *(lan, act)*

Sprachfunktion, überrendende *f* → Sprachfunktion, persuasive

Sprachgebrauch *m* • language use *(lan)*

Sprachgebrauch, deskriptiver *m* • descriptive use of language *(lan)*

Sprachgebrauch, emotiver *m* • emotive use of language *(lan)*

Sprachgemeinschaft *f* • speech/language community *(soc, lan)*

Sprachgeschöpf, Mensch als *m* • man as a product of language *(ant, lan)*

Sprachgruppe *f* • language group *(lan)*

Sprachinsel *f* • language island *(lan)*

Sprachkompetenz *f* • language competence *(lan, psy)*

Sprachkritik *f* • critique of language, language criticism° *(Mauthner, Wittgenstein etc) (lan)*

sprachkritische Analyse *f* • critical linguistic analysis *(lan)*

Sprachkunst *f* • literary/linguistic art, artistic use of language *(aes)*

Sprachkünste *pl* • language arts *(aes)*

Sprachlernfähigkeit *f* • language learning ability *(lan, psy)*

sprachlich organisierter Wissensvorrat *m* • linguistically organized stock of knowledge *(Habermas) (epi, lan)*

sprachlich vermittelte Interaktion *f* • linguistically mediated interaction *(Habermas) (lan, act)*

sprachlich vermitteltes strategisches Handeln *n* • linguistically mediated strategic action *(Habermas) (lan, act)*

sprachliche Modalität *f* • linguistic modality *(lan, ont)*

sprachliche Normierung *f* • linguistic standardization *(lan)*, verbal legislation *(Hare) (eth, lan)*

sprachliche Relativitätstheorie *f* • theory of linguistic relativity *(Sapir) (lan)* < Sapir-Whorf-Hypothese

sprachliche Verfahrensweisen *pl* • linguistic practices *(lan)*

sprachlicher Code *m* • linguistic code *(lan)*

sprachliches Weltbild *n* • linguistic world view *(lan, met)*

sprachliches Zeichen *n* • linguistic sign *(lan)*

Sprachlosigkeit *f* • speechlessness, muteness *(gep)* < Staunen, philosophisches

Sprachneubildung *f* • neologism *(lan)*

Sprachnorm *f* • language/linguistic norm *(lan)*

Sprachphilosophie *f* • philosophy of language, linguistic philosophy *(lan)*

sprachphilosophische Wende *f* • linguistic turn *(lan)* → linguistische Wende

Sprachpraxis *f* • language/linguistic practice *(lan)*

Sprachpurismus *m* • language/linguistic purism *(lan)*

Sprachregel *f* • linguistic/language norm *(lan)* < Regel der Grammatik

Sprachregelung *f* • language regulation *(lan)*

Sprachrelativismus *m* • linguistic relativism/relativity *(lan)* < Sapir-Whorf-Hypothese

sprachschöpferische Tätigkeit *f* • linguistically creative activity *(lan, aes)*

Sprachschöpfung *f* • linguistic creation *(aes)*

Sprachschranke *f* • language barrier *(lan, soc)*

Sprachspiel *n* • language-game, play of language *(Wittgenstein) (lan)*

Sprachstufentheorie *f* • theory of levels of language, language level/hierarchy theory *(lan)* < Metasprache

sprachtheoretische Grundlegung der Sozialwissenschaften *f* • language-theoretic foundation of the social sciences *(Habermas) (lan, soc, sci)* < W 1361

sprachtheoretisches Argument *n* • language-theoretical argument *(lan)*

Sprachtheorie *f* • language theory, theory of language *(lan)*

Sprachuniversalien *pl* • language universals *(lan)*

Sprachverlust *m* • language loss, loss of language *(lan)*

Sprachvermögen *n* • language skills, language/linguistic capacity *(lan)*

Sprachverständnis *n* • language/linguistic understanding *(lan)*

Sprachwissenschaft, allgemeine *f* • general linguistics *(lan)*

Sprachwissenschaft, komparative *f* • comparative philology/linguistics *(lan)*

Sprechakt *m* • speech act *(lan, act)* < W 932, 1365

Sprechakt, direktiver *m* • directive speech act *(lan, act)*

Sprechakt, expressiver *m* • expressive speech act *(act, lan)*

Sprechakt, illokutionärer *m* • illocutionary speech act *(Austin) (lan, act)* → illokutionärer Akt

Sprechakt, kommunikativer *m* • communicative speech act *(lan, act)*

Sprechakt, konstativer *m* • constative speech act, constative *(Searle etc) (lan, act)* → konstative Sprechhandlung

Sprechakt, lokutionärer *m* • locutionary speech act *(Austin etc) (lan, act)* → lokutionärer Akt

Sprechakt, perlokutionärer *m* • perlocutionary speech act *(Austin) (lan, act)* → perlokutionärer Akt

Sprechakt, propositionaler *m* • propositional speech act *(lan, act)*

Sprechakt, referentieller *m* • referential speech act *(lan, act)* < ostensive Definition

Sprechakt, regulativer *m* • regulative speech act *(lan, act)*

Sprechakt, repräsentativer *m* • representative speech act *(lan, act)*

Sprechaktanalyse *f* • analysis of speech acts *(lan, act)*

Sprechaktangebot *n* • speech-act offer *(lan, act)*

Sprechakttheorie *f* • speech-act theory *(Austin, Searle) (lan, act)* < W 1365

Sprechakttypologie *f* • speech-act typology *(Searle) (lan, act)*

sprechhandlungstheoretische Semantik *f* • speech-act-theoretical semantics *(lan, act)*

Sprechsituation, ideale *f* • ideal speech situation *(Habermas) (eth)*

Sprung *m* • leap *(Kierkegaard, Jaspers) (rel)* < transzendentaler Sprung

Sprung in den Glauben *m* • leap into faith *(Kierkegaard) (rel)* → Glaubenssprung

Sprung, transzendierender *m* • transcending leap *(Kierkegaard, Jaspers) (met)*

sprunghaftes Verhalten *n* • erratic behaviour *(act, sys)* < Chaostheorie

Spur *f* • trail *(Derrida) (met)*

Spurenelement *n* • trace element *(nat)*

Staat *m* • (▷ Nationalstaat) state, nation, nation state, (▷ Land) country *(pol)* < W 933

Staat, bürgerlicher *m* • bourgeois state *(Marx etc) (pol)*

Staat, totalitärer *m* • totalitarian state *(pol)* < Totalitarismus

Staatenbund *m* • confederacy, confederation of states *(pol)* < Völkerbund

Staatengemeinschaft, internationale *f* • international community, community of nations *(pol)*

staatliche Kontrolle *f* • governmental control *(pol)*

staatliche Sozialpolitik *f* • public welfare policy *(pol)*

staatlicher Eingriff *m* • state intervention *(eco, pol)* → Staatsintervention

staatlicher Interventionismus *m* • government interventionism *(pol, eco)*

staatliches Strafen *n* → Bestrafung durch den Staat

Staatsapparat *m* • state machinery *(pol)* .

Staatsauffassung *f* • conception/view of the state *(pol)* → Staatsidee

Staatsausgaben *pl* • public spending *(eco)* < Wohlfahrtsökonomie

Staatsbesitz *m* → Staatseigentum

Staatsbürgerpflicht *f* • civic duty *(pol)*

Staatsbürgerrecht *n* • civic/civil rights, rights of citizenship *(pol)*

Staatseigentum *n* • state property *(eco)* < kollektives Eigentum (an Produktionsmitteln)

Staatsfeind *m* • public enemy *(pol)*

Staatsform *f* • form/type of government *(pol)*

Staatsgeheimnis *n* • state secret *(pol)*

Staatsgewalt *f* • executive power *(pol)*

Staatsideal *n* • state ideal *(pol)* < Idealstaat

Staatsidee *f* • idea/concept of the state *(pol)* → Staatsauffassung

Staatsinteresse *n* • interest of the state, public interest *(pol)*

Staatsintervention *f* • state intervention *(eco, pol)*

Staatsinterventionismus *m* • state interventionism *(eco, pol)*

Staatskapital *n* • public/state capital *(eco)*

Staatskapitalismus *m* • state capitalism *(eco)*

Staatskirche *f* • state church *(pol, rel)*

Staatsklugheit *f* • statesmanship, statecraft *(pol)* < Machiavellismus

Staatsmacht *f* • state power *(pol)*

Staatsmonopol *n* • state monopoly *(eco, pol)*

Staatsökonomie *f* → Nationalökonomie

Staatsordnung *f* • system of government *(pol)*

Staatspflicht *f* • governmental duty *(pol)*

Staatsphilosophie *f* • civil philosophy, philosophy of the state *(pol)*

staatspolitisch • relating to national policy *(pol)*

Staatsräson *f* • reasons of state, raison d'état *(pol)*

Staatsrecht *n* • constitutional law, public law *(jur, pol)*

Staatsregierung *f* • government *(pol)*

Staatsreligion *f* • state religion *(pol, rel)*

Staatsschulden *pl* • national debt *(eco, pol)*

Staatssozialismus *m* • state socialism *(pol)*

Staatsstreich *m* • coup d'état *(pol)*

Staatsterrorismus *m* • state terrorism *(pol)*

Staatstheorie *f* • theory of the state *(pol)*

Staatsunternehmen *n* • state-owned enterprise *(eco)*

Staatsverfassung *f* • political constitution *(pol)*

Staatsvergötzung *f* • state-worship, apotheosis/glorification of the state *(pol)* < Etatismus

Staatsversagen *n* • failure of the state *(pol)* < Marktversagen

Staatswirtschaft *f* • state economy, public sector *(eco)* ↔ Privatwirtschaft < Nationalökonomie

Staatswissenschaft *f* • political science *(pol)* → Politikwissenschaft < W 420

stabile Extrapolationen *pl* • stable extrapolations *(sci)*

Stabilitätspolitik *f* • policy of stability *(pol)*

Stadien der Existenz *pl* • stages of existence *(Kierkegaard)* *(met)*

Stadium, metaphysisches *n* • metaphysical stage *(Comte)* *(soc)* < Dreistadiengesetz

Stadium, positives *n* • positive stage *(Comte)* *(soc)* → Stadium, wissenschaftliches < Dreistadiengesetz

Stadium, theologisches *n* • theological stage *(Comte)* *(soc)* < Dreistadiengesetz

Stadium, wissenschaftliches *n* • scientific stage *(Comte)* *(soc)* → Stadium, positives

Stadt und Land, Gegensatz von *m* • opposition of town and country *(Marx)* *(soc)*

Städte, Lebensfeindlichkeit der *f* • hostility of urban life *(cul)*

Stadtflucht *f* • exodus from the cities, reruralization *(soc)* ↔ Landflucht < zurück aufs Land, zurück zur Natur

Stadtplanung *f* • town planning *(aes)*

Stadtstaat *m* • city-state *(pol)* → Polis

Stagnation *f* • stagnation *(eco)*

Stalinismus *m* • Stalinism *(pol)*

Stamm *m* • tribe *(ant, cul, pol)*

Stammbegriffe *pl* • fundamental concepts *(Kant)* *(epi)* → Kategorien

Stammesbewußtsein *n* • tribal spirit *(ant, cul)*

Stammesgemeinschaft *f* • tribal community *(ant, cul, soc)*

Stammesgeschichte *f* • (▷ Geschichte eines Volksstammes) tribal history *(cul);* (▷ Phylogenese) philogeny, philogenesis *(nat, ant)* → Phylogenese

stammesgeschichtliches Erbe *n* • phylogenetic heritage *(ant)*

Stammesgesellschaft *f* • tribal society *(ant, cul, soc)*

Stammeszugehörigkeit *f* • tribal membership *(ant, cul, soc)*

Stand, sozialer *m* • (▷ soziale Position) social position/rank *(soc)* < Sozialstatus; (▷ soziale Klasse) social class *(soc)* < Ständegesellschaft, dritter Stand

Standardabweichung *f* • standard deviation, SD *(mat)* < durchschnittliche Abweichung, Streuung

Standardfehler *m* • standard error *(mat, sci)*

standardisiertes Interview *n* • standardized interview *(sci)*

Standardisierung *f* • standardization *(gen)*

Standardsprache *f* • standard language *(lan)* < Sprachnorm

Standardsprechakt *m* • standard speech act *(lan)*

Standard-Theorienkonzeption *f* • standard conception of theories *(sci)*

Ständegesellschaft *f* • estate/corporate society, society of estates *(pol, soc)* < Ständestaat

Ständeordnung *f* • system of estates *(pol, soc)*

Standesbewußtsein *n* • class/status -consciousness *(soc)*

Standesehre *f* • status honour, social reputation, (▷ Ehre des Berufsstands) professional honour *(soc)*

standesgemäßer Unterhalt *m* • living according to one's social standing, income befitting one's station/status *(Aquinas) (soc, eco)*

Standesprivileg *n* • class privilege *(soc)*

Ständestaat *m* • corporate/corporative state *(pol)*

Standesunterschied *m* • social difference, class-distinction *(soc)*

Standesvorurteil *n* • class bias/prejudice *(epi, soc)* → Klassenvorurteil

Standfestigkeit *f* • steadfastness *(eth)*

ständige Bewegung *f* • perpetual motion *(nat, met)*

Standort *m* • position *(gep)*

Standortbestimmung *f* • determination of (a) position, definition of a position *(gep)*

Standortgebundenheit des Denkens *f* • dependence of thought on perspective, perspectiveness/relativity of thought *(Mannheim) (epi, soc)* < Seinsgebundenheit, Wissenssoziologie

Standpunkt, überwundener *m* • discarded position/standpoint *(gep)*

Standrecht *n* • martial/military law *(jur)* → Kriegsrecht

Stapel *m* • stack *(AI)* < Speicher

Stärke, geistige *f* • mental strength *(gep)*

starke Konvergenz *f* • strong convergence *(mat)*

Stärke, moralische *f* • moral strength/virtue *(eth)*

starre Designation *f* • rigid designation *(Kripke) (lan)*

starrer Designator *m* • rigid designator *(Kripke) (lan)*

Startkapital *n* • starting capital *(eco)* < ursprüngliche Akkumulation

stationäre Wirtschaft *f* • stationary economy *(eco)*

statische Kultur *f* • static culture/civilization *(cul)*

statische Wirtschaftsordnung *f* • static economic order *(eco)*

statisches Modell *n* • static model *(sci)* < Homöostase

statisches Weltbild *n* • static world view *(nat, met)*

Statistik *f* • statistics *(mat)*

statistische Analyse *f* • statistical analysis *(mat)*

statistische Begründung *f* • statistical justification *(epi, mat)*

statistische Erklärung *f* • statistical/probabilistic explanation *(sci)*

statistische Gesetze *pl* • statistical laws/principles *(sci, mat)*

statistische Hypothese *f* • statistical hypothesis *(mat)*

statistische Informationstheorie *f* • statistical information theory *(mat, lan)*

statistische Norm *f* • statistical norm *(mat)*

statistische Tiefenanalyse *f* • statistical depth analysis *(sci, mat)*

statistische Wahrscheinlichkeit *f* • statistical probability *(mat)*

statistischer Gottesbeweis *m* • statistical proof of/argument for the existence of God *(Brentano, Arbuthnot) (mat)*

statistisches Relevanzmodell der Erklärung *n* • statistical-relevance model of explanation *(sci)*

Status *m* • state, status *(soc)* < Stellung, soziale

status civilis *m* • civil state *(Hobbes, Rousseau etc) (soc, pol)* → bürgerlicher Zustand ↔ status naturalis

status naturalis *m* • natural state *(Hobbes, Rousseau etc) (soc, pol)* → Naturzustand ↔ status civilis

status quo *m* • *nt (pol)*

status quo ante *m* • *nt (pol)*

Statusgruppe *f* • status group *(Weber) (soc)*

Statusgüter *pl* • status goods *(eco, soc)* → positionelle Güter, Prestigegüter < demonstrativer Konsum

Statushierarchie *f* • status hierarchy *(soc)*

Statuskonkurrenz *f* • status competition *(soc, eco)* < demonstrativer Konsum

Statusmerkmal *n* • status characteristic *(soc)*

Statussymbol *n* • status symbol *(soc, psy)*

Stau *m* • interruption of flow, jam *(sys)* < Flaschenhals

Staunen, philosophisches *n* • philosophical wonder/astonishment *(gep)*

Stein der Weisen *m* • Philosopher's Stone *(eso)* < Alchemie

Steinzeitmensch *m* • stone age/paleolithic man *(ant)*

Stellenwertbestimmung *f* • ranking *(sci)*

Stellung, soziale *f* • social position *(soc)* → Sozialstatus

Stellvertreterfunktion *f* • proxy function *(log, ont)*

Stellvertreterkrieg *m* • proxy war(fare) *(pol)*

Sterbehilfe *f* • euthanasia *(eth)* < Patiententestament

Sterbehilfegesellschaft *f* • euthanasia society, right-to-die society *(eth)*

Sterberate *f* • mortality/death rate *(soc)* ↔ Geburtenrate

sterblicher Gott *m* • mortal god *(Hobbes) (pol)*

Sterblichkeit *f* • mortality *(nat, met)*

Stereotyp *m* • stereotype *(lan, psy)* < Schablonendenken, Schwarz-Weiß-Denken

Sternbild *n* • constellation *(nat)*, sign of the zodiac *(nat, eso)*

Sterndeutung *f* • astrology *(eso)*

Sternenstaub *m* • star dust *(nat)*

Sternsystem *n* • stellar system *(nat)*

Sternzeichen *n* → Sternbild

stetige Kurve *f* • continuous curve *(mat, sci)*

Stetigkeit *f* • constancy *(eth)*, continuity *(mat)*

Stetigkeit, Gesetz der *n* • law of continuity *(Leibniz) (met)*

Stetigkeitsaxiom *n* • axiom of continuity *(mat)*

Steuerdruck *m* • fiscal burden *(eco)*

Steuerflucht *f* • tax evasion *(eco)*

Steuerfreiheit *f* • tax freedom *(eco)*

Steuergesetzgebung *f* • tax legislation *(eco, jur)*

Steuerhinterziehung *f* → Steuerflucht

Steuerpolitik *f* • taxation policy *(eco, pol)*

Steuerprogression *f* • progressive taxation *(eco)* < Umverteilungspolitik

Steuerreform, ökologische *f* • ecological tax reform *(eco, env)*

Steuerungssystem *n* • control system *(sys)*

Steuerungstheorie *f* • control theory *(sys)* < Kybernetik

Stichhaltigkeit *f* • validity *(sci)* < Validität

Stichprobe *f* • sample *(mat, sci)*

Stichprobenanalyse *f* • random test analysis *(mat)*

Stichprobentheorie *f* • theory of random test *(mat)*

Stichprobenumfang *m* • range of (a) sample *(mat)*

Stigma *n* • stigma *(soc, rel)*

Stigmatisierung *f* • stigmatization *(soc, rel)* < soziale Ausgrenzung

Stil *m* • style *(aes)*

Stilanalyse *f* • style analysis *(aes)*

Stilbruch *m* • breach of style, stylistic inconsistency *(aes)*

Stildynamik *f* • style/stylistic dynamics *(aes)*

Stilelement *n* • stylistic element *(aes)*

Stilistik *f* • stylistics *(aes)*

stilistische Einheit *f* • stylistic unity *(aes)*

stilles Kino *n* • silent movie *(Vertov) (aes)* → Stummfilm

Stillhalteabkommen *n* • standstill agreement *(pol)*

stillschweigende Annahme *f* • tacit/implicit assumption *(act)*

stillschweigende Einwilligung *f* • tacit consent/approval, acquiescence *(jur, eth)* < stillschweigende Zustimmung

stillschweigende Übereinkunft *f* • implicit/tacit understanding, tacit agreement *(jur, soc)*

stillschweigende Übereinstimmung *f* • tacit agreement *(gep)*

stillschweigende Verpflichtung *f* • implied/implicit/tacit obligation *(eth)*

stillschweigende Zustimmung *f* • tacit consent/assent *(pol, jur, eth)* < stillschweigende Einwilligung

Stilmittel *n* • stylistic means *(aes)*

Stilpluralismus *m* • stylistic/style pluralism *(aes)*

Stilvielfalt *f* • variety of styles *(aes)*

Stilwandel *m* • stylistic/style change *(aes)* < Stildynamik

Stimmberechtigung *f* • entitlement/right to vote *(pol)*

Stimme des Gewissens *f* • voice of conscience *(rel, eth)*

Stimmenfang *m* • vote-catching *(pol)*

Stimmengleichheit *f* • equality of votes *(pol)*

Stimmigkeit *f* • consistency, coherence *(log)*, harmony *(aes)* < Harmonie

Stimmrecht *n* → Stimmberechtigung

Stimmung *f* • mood *(Kierkegaard, Heidegger)* *(psy, ont)* < Gestimmtheit

Stimmungsumschwung *m* • change of mood *(psy)*

Stimmvieh *n* • herd of voters *(pol)*

Stimulusbedeutung *f* • stimulus meaning *(Quine) (lan)*

stipulative Definition *f* • stipulative definition *(log, lan)*

Stirlingsche Formel *f* • Stirling('s) formula *(mat)*

Stoa *f* • *nt (gep)* → stoische Schule < Stoizismus

Stochastik *f* • stochastics *(mat)*

stochastisch • stochastic *(mat)*

stochastische Methode *f* • stochastic method *(mat)*

stochastischer Prozeß *m* • stochastic process *(mat, dec)*

Stoff *m* • matter, substance, stuff *(nat, ont)* → Materie < W 527; material *(gen)*

Stofflichkeit *f* • materiality *(ont)*

Stofftrieb *m* • material impulse *(Schiller) (aes)* ↔ Formtrieb

Stoffursache *f* • material cause *(Aristotle etc)* *(met)* → causa materialis

Stoffwechselprozeß *m* • metabolic process *(Marx) (soc)*

Stoiker *m* • Stoic *(gep)*

stoische Gelassenheit *f* • Stoic composure *(eth)*

stoische Haltung *f* • Stoic attitude *(eth)* < Ataraxie

stoische Moral *f* • Stoic morality/ethics *(eth)*

stoische Schule *f* • Stoic school *(gep)* → Stoa

Stoizismus *m* • Stoicism *(gep)*

Stolz *m* • pride *(eth, rel)* ↔ Demut < Hybris

Störaktion *f* • interfering action, (causing) an interference/a disturbance *(pol)*

Störfall *m* • system(s) failure, fault *(tec, sys)* < Fehlfunktion

Störgröße *f* • disruptive factor *(sci)*

strafbare Handlung *f* • punishable act *(jur)*

Strafbarkeit *f* • punishability *(jur)*

Strafbedürfnis *n* • need for punishment *(psy)*

Strafbefugnis *f* • penal authority *(jur)*

Strafe *f* • punishment, penalty *(jur, eth)*

Strafe Gottes *f* • divine punishment *(rel)* < Jüngstes Gericht

Strafe, Legitimation von *f* • justification of punishment *(eth)*

strafende Gewalt *f* • punishing force *(jur)*

Straffreiheit *f* • impunity *(jur)*

Strafgerichtsbarkeit *f* • criminal jurisdiction *(jur)*

Strafgesetzgebung *f* • penal legislation *(jur)*

Strafmaßnahme *f* • punitive measure *(jur)*

Strafpraxis *f* • penal practice *(jur)*

Strafrecht *n* • criminal/penal law *(jur)*

Strafrechtsreform *f* • penal reform, reform of penal law *(jur)*

Strafreform *f* • penal reform *(jur, eth)*

Straftheorie *f* • theory of punishment *(jur, eth)*

Strafvollzug, humaner *m* • humane punishment *(jur, eth)*

Strahlenbelastung *f* • exposure to radiation *(nat, env)*

Strahlendosis *f* • radiation dosage *(nat, env)*

Strahlengeschädigter *m* • radiation victim *(env)*

Strahlenkrankheit *f* • radiation sickness/syndrome *(env)*

Strahlenschutz *m* • radiation protection *(env)*

Strahlenverseuchung *f* • contamination with radiation *(env)*

Strahlungsenergie *f* • radiant energy *(nat)*

Strategie *f* • strategy *(dec)*

Strategie, gemischte *f* • mixed strategy *(dec)*

Strategie, reine *f* • pure strategy *(dec)*

Strategiespiel *n* • strategy game, game of strategy *(dec)* < berechenbares Verhalten

strategische Interaktion *f* • strategic interaction *(act)*

strategische Vorausplanung *f* • strategic planning *(dec)*

strategisches Handeln *n* • strategic action *(act, dec)*

Streben *n* • striving, ambition *(met, eth)* < Teleologie

Strebertum *n* • careerism *(psy)*

Strebsamkeit *f* • assiduity, assiduousness, ambitiousness *(eth)*

Streik *m* • strike *(pol)* < Arbeitskampf, Aussperrung

Streikrecht *n* • right to strike *(pol)*

Streit der Gegensätze *m* • conflict of opposites *(Heraclitus) (met)*

Streitfrage *f* • disputed/controversial question, question of dispute *(gep)* → Quästion

Streitgegenstand *m* • matter in dispute, subject of controversy *(gep)*

Streitgespräch *n* • dispute *(gep)*

Streitkultur *f* • standards of controversy *(eth)* < Kommunikationskultur

Streitschrift *f* • invective, polemic *(gep)*

streng universelle Aussage *f* • strictly universal proposition/statement *(log, lan)*

streng werkimmanente Interpretation *f* • close textual reading *(aes)*

streng wissenschaftlich • strictly scientific *(sci)*

strenge Allgemeinheit *f* • strict universality *(Kant etc) (epi, sci)*

strenge Sitten *pl* • rigid/strict morals, rigid/strict moral code *(eth)*

Strenggläubigkeit *f* • orthodoxy *(rel)* < Orthodoxie, Fundamentalismus

Streubereich *m* • range (of scatter) *(mat)*

Streuung *f* • scatter, dispersion *(mat)* < Standardabweichung

Streuung, soziale *f* • social spread/distribution *(soc)*

Streuungsdiagramm *n* • scatter diagram *(sci, mat)*

Streuungsrelation, statistische *f* • statistical scatter/dispersion, variance relation *(mat)*

strikt konvergent • strictly convergent *(mat)*

strikte Implikation *f* • strict implication *(log)*

strikter Intuitionismus *m* • strict intuitionism *(mat)*

Stringenz *f* • stringency *(log, sci)*

strittiger Punkt *m* • point at issue, controversial issue *(gep)*

Strom der Zeit *m* • flow of time, river of time *(met)*

Strom des Bewußtseins *m* • stream/flow of consciousness *(James, Bergson etc) (psy, met)* → Bewußtseinsstrom

Strömung, geistige *f* • intellectual current/tradition *(his)*

Struktur *f* • structure *(gep)* → Gefüge

Struktur, algebraische *f* • algebraic structure *(mat)*

Struktur der Aneignung *f* • structure of assimilation *(Habermas) (epi, soc)*

Struktur der Spiegelung *f* • structure of reflection *(Habermas) (epi, soc)*

Struktur, externe *f* • external structure *(nat)*

Struktur, interne *f* • inner structure *(nat)*

Struktur, linguistische *f* • linguistic structure *(lan)*

Struktur, logische *f* • logical structure *(log)*

strukturale Anthropologie *f* • structural anthropology *(Lévi-Strauss) (ant)* < W 948

Strukturalismus *m* • structuralism *(lan, sci, cul)* < W 949

strukturalistische Ästhetik *f* • structuralist aesthetics *(aes)*

strukturalistische Theorieexplikation *f* • structuralist explication of theory *(sci)* < Non-statement-view von Theorien

Strukturanalogie *f* • structural analogy *(ant, sys)*

Strukturanalyse *f* • structural analysis *(aes, sys)*

Strukturbeschreibung *f* • structure/structural description *(log, lan)*

strukturbewahrendes System *n* • structure-maintaining system *(sys)*

strukturell-deskriptiver Name *m* • structural-descriptive name *(Tarski) (lan)*

strukturelle Gewalt *f* • structural violence *(Galtung) (pol)*

strukturelle Linguistik *f* • structural linguistics *(lan)*

Strukturformel *f* • structural formula *(nat)*

Strukturfunktionalismus *m* • structural functionalism *(sys)*

Strukturganzes *n* • structural whole *(sys)*

Strukturgleichheit *f* • structural equality *(sys)* → Isomorphie

strukturiertes Interview *n* • structured interview *(sci)* < standardisiertes Interview

Strukturkrise *f* • structural crisis *(sys, eco)*

Strukturmodell der Persönlichkeit *n* • structural model of personality *(Freud) (psy)*

Strukturontologie *f* • structural ontology *(ont)*

Strukturphänomenologie *f* • structural phenomenology *(met)*

Strukturpolitik *f* • structural policy *(pol)*

Strukturpsychologie *f* • structural psychology *(psy)*

Strukturreform *f* • structural reform *(pol, eco)*

Strukturwandel *m* • structural change/transformation *(soc)*

Strukturwandel der Öffentlichkeit *m* • the structural transformation of the public sphere *(Habermas) (soc)* < W 952

Stubengelehrsamkeit *f* • bookmanship *(gep)*

Stückarbeit *f* • piecework *(gen)*

Studentenbewegung *f* • student movement *(pol, cul)*

Studentenrevolte *f* • student(s') revolt *(pol, cul)*

Studienobjekt *n* • subject/object of study *(gep)*

Studium der Natur *n* • study of nature *(nat, aes)*

Stufe der Entwicklung *f* • stage/level of development *(nat, his, psy)* → Entwicklungsstadium

Stufe der Wahrhaftigkeit *f* • level of truthfulness *(Nietzsche) (eth)*

Stufen des Seins *pl* → Seinsstufen

Stufenfolge *f* • gradation, scale, succession (of steps/levels) *(gep)*

stufenweiser Fortschritt *m* • step-by-step/ gradual/graduative° progress *(soc, cul)*

Stummfilm *m* • silent movie/film *(aes)* ↔ Tonfilm

Sturm auf die Bastille *m* • storming (of) the Bastille *(pol, his)*

Sturm und Drang *m* • Storm and Stress, Sturm und Drang *(aes, his)*

sub specie aeternitatis • *nt,* under the perspective of eternity *(Spinoza) (met, eth)*

subaltern • subaltern *(log)* ↔ subkonträr

Subalternation *f* • subalternation *(log)*

subalterne Beziehung *f* • (relation of) subalternation, subaltern relation *(log)*

Subalternmodus *m* • subaltern mood *(log)*

subatomarer Bereich *m* • sub-atomic sphere/ domain *(nat)*

Subjekt *n* • (▷ Person) individual, subject, (▷ Sachgebiet) subject, topic, (▷ Gegenstand) object *(gep)*

Subjekt der Geschichte *n* • subject of history *(his)*

Subjekt des Erkennens *n* • subject of cognition *(epi)*

Subjekt-Objekt-Beziehung *f* • subject-object relation *(epi, met)*

Subjekt-Objekt-Spaltung *f* • subject-object dichotomy/split *(epi, met)*

Subjekt-Objekt-Unterscheidung *f* • subject-object distinction *(epi, met)*

Subjekt-Prädikat-Verbindung *f* • subject-predicate relation *(log, lan)*

Subjektbegriff *m* • subject concept, concept of (the) subject *(log, lan, met)*

subjektiv gültiges Urteil *n* • subjectively valid judg(e)ment *(epi, log)*

subjektiv-Weibliche, das *n* • female subjectivity *(fem)* ↔ objektiv-Männliche, das

Subjektive, das *n* • the subjective (mode) *(gep)*

subjektive Deutung *f* • subjective reading/ interpretation *(sci)* ↔ objektive Deutung

subjektive Einheit des Selbstbewußtseins *f* • subjective unity of self-consciousness *(Kant) (epi)*

subjektive Folge *f* • subjective succession *(Kant etc) (epi, log)*

subjektive Glückseligkeit *f* • subjective happiness *(Kant) (eth)*

subjektive Gültigkeit *f* • subjective validity *(epi, sci)*

subjektive Interpretation der Wahrscheinlichkeit *f* • subjective interpretation of probability *(mat)*

subjektive Logik *f* • subjective logic *(log)*

subjektive Notwendigkeit *f* • subjective necessity *(epi, met)*

subjektive Wahrscheinlichkeit *f* • subjective probability *(epi, mat)*

subjektive Zweckmäßigkeit *f* • subjective finality *(Kant) (epi, aes)*

subjektiver Geist *m* • subjective mind/spirit *(Hegel) (met)*

subjektiver Idealismus *m* • subjective idealism *(Berkeley, Fichte) (met, epi)*

subjektiver Wert *m* • subjective value *(eth, aes)*

subjektiver Zweck *m* • subjective end *(epi, act)*

subjektives Werturteil *n* • subjective value judg(e)ment *(sci, eth, aes)*

Subjektivierung *f* • subjectivization *(gep)*

Subjektivismus *m* • subjectivism *(epi, met, psy)*

Subjektivität *f* • subjectivity *(gep)* ↔ Objektivität

Subjektivität-Objektivität-Dichotomie *f* • objectivity-subjectivity dichotomy/distinction *(met, sci)*

Subjektkonstanz *f* • subject constancy *(psy)* < Identität

Subjektsein *n* • being-a-subject *(Jaspers etc) (met)*

Subjektskonstitution *f* • constitution of subjects *(Foucault) (met)*

Subjektstatus *m* • subject status *(jur, soc)*

subjektunabhängiger Sachverhalt *m* • subject-independent atomic fact *(epi, sci)*

Subjunktion *f* • subjunction *(log)*

Subkategorisierung *f* • subcategorization *(log, min)*

subkonträr • subcontrary *(log)* ↔ subaltern

Subkultur *f* • subculture *(soc, cul)* < Alternativbewegung

subkulturelle Bewegung *f* • subculture movement *(soc, cul)*

Sublimation *f* → Sublimierung

Sublimierung *f* • sublimation *(Freud) (psy)* < Ersatzhandlung

sublunare und translunare Sphäre *f* • sublunar and superlunar/translunar sphere *(nat)*

Subordination f • subordination *(log)*

Subreption f • subreption *(log)*

subreptives Axiom n • subreptic axiom *(Kant)* *(log)*

Subsidiaritätsprinzip n • principle of subsidiarity *(pol, eco, eth)*

Subsistenz f • subsistence *(eco)*

Subsistenzbasis f • basis of subsistence *(eco)*

Subsistenzminimum n • (minimum) level of subsistence *(eco, soc)*

Subsistenzmittel n • means of subsistence *(eco)*

Subsistenzniveau n • subsistence level *(eco)*

Subsistenzwirtschaft f • subsistence economy *(eco)* → Bedarfsdeckungswirtschaft

subsistieren • to subsist *(met)* < Existenz, Bestand

Substantialismus m → Substantialitätstheorie

Substantialität f • substantiality *(met)* ↔ Akzidentialität

Substantialitätstheorie f • substantiality theory, substantialism *(met)*

substantiell • (▷ wesenhaft) essential, (▷ gewichtig) substantial *(gep)*

substantielle Formen pl • substantial forms *(Descartes)* *(met)*

Substanz f • substance *(met)* → Wesen, das ↔ Akzidenz

Substanz, ausgedehnte f • extended substance *(Descartes)* *(epi, met)* → res extensa ↔ Substanz, denkende

Substanz, denkende f • thinking substance *(Descartes)* *(epi, met)* → res cogitans ↔ Substanz, ausgedehnte

Substanz, erste f • first/primary substance *(met)*

Substanz, immaterielle f • immaterial substance *(met, rel)*

Substanz, körperliche f • material/corporeal substance *(Leibniz etc)* *(met)*

Substanz, Prinzip der Beständigkeit der n • law of persistence of substance *(met)*

Substanz, unausgedehnte f • unextended substance *(met)*

Substanz, zweite f • secondary substance *(met)*

Substanzbegriff m • concept of substance *(met)*

Substanzdualismus, cartesianischer m • Cartesian substance dualism *(met)*

Substanzen, Dualität der f • substance dualism, dualism of substances *(Descartes)* *(met)*

Substanzen, einfache und zusammengesetzte pl • simple and compound/complex substances *(Leibniz)* *(met)*

Substanzmetaphysik f • substance metaphysics, metaphysics of substance *(met)*

Substituierung f → Substitution

Substitution f • substitution *(log)*

Substitutionskalkül m/n • substitution calculus *(log, mat)*

Substitutionsmethode f • method of substitution *(sci, mat)*

Substitutionsprinzip n • principle of substitutability/substitutivity *(Leibniz)* *(log, lan)*, substitution principle *(log)*, substitution theorem *(Frege)* *(log)*

Substitutionsregel f • substitution rule *(log, lan)* → Ersetzungsregel, Austauschregel

Substrat n • substrate, substratum *(gep)*

Substratkategorie f • substrate category *(Husserl)* *(met)*

Subsumtion f • subsumption *(log)*

Subsumtionstheorie f • theory of subsumption *(sci)* < Hempel-Oppenheim-Schema

Subsystem n • subsystem *(sys)*

subversive Elemente pl • subversive elements *(pol)*

subversive Ökologie f • subversive ecology *(Roszak)* *(env, pol)*

Suchalgorithmus m • search algorithm *(mat, AI)*

Sucht f • addiction *(psy)*

Suchtmittelmißbrauch m → Drogenmißbrauch

Suchtverhalten n • addictive behaviour *(psy)*

Sufismus m • sufism *(asp)*

Suggestiv-Definition f • persuasive definition *(Stevenson)* *(lan, log)*

Suggestivfrage f • suggestive question *(lan)*

Sühne f • atonement, expiation *(rel, eth)*

Sühneopfer n • expiatory sacrifice *(rel)*

Suizid m • suicide *(eth, psy)* → Freitod, Selbsttötung, Selbstmord

Suizidforschung f • suicide research *(psy)*

Suizidologie f • suicidology *(psy)* → Suizidforschung

Sukzedens n • consequent *(log, mat)* ↔ Antezedens

Sukzession f • succession *(epi, log)*

Sukzessionsprognose f • succession prognosis *(sci)*

sukzessive Synthesis f • successive synthesis *(Kant)* *(epi)*

Summe der Merkmale f • sum of characteristics *(gep)*

Summe der Teile f • sum of parts *(mat, ont)* < Mereologie

summum bonum n • supreme/highest/prime°
good (eth, rel) → höchstes Gut, oberstes Gut

Sünde f • sin, offence (rel)

Sünde als Abfall von Gott f • sin as falling
away from God (rel)

Sünde als Modus des Bösen f • sin as a mode of
evil (Leibniz) (met, rel)

Sündenbabel n • den of iniquity (rel)

Sündenbock m • scapegoat, whipping boy (soc,
psy)

Sündenfall m • the Fall (of man) (rel)

Sündhaftigkeit f • sinfulness, peccability (rel)
< Schuldbeladenheit

Sunyata • sunyata, emptiness, absolute being
(asp) → Leere, die

Supererogation f • supererogation (eth) →
Übertreffen der Pflicht

supererogatorisch • supererogatory (eth)

Superketten pl • superstrings (nat, sys)

Supermacht f • super-power (pol)

Supermann m → Übermensch

Supernaturalismus m • supernaturalism (met)

Superorganismus m • superorganism (nat)

Superstrukturalismus m • superstructuralism
(lan)

Supervenienz f • supervenience (log)

Supposition f • supposition (log, lan)

Suppositionstheorie f • supposition theory (log,
lan)

Supremat des Gewissens m/n • supremacy of
conscience (eth) < Gewissensautonomie

Suprematismus m • suprematism (aes)

Surplusarbeitszeit f • surplus labour/working
time (Marx) (eco) → Mehrarbeitszeit

Surpluskapital n • surplus capital (Marx) (eco)

Surpluswert m • surplus/added value (Marx
etc) (eco) → Mehrwert

Surrealismus m • surrealism (aes)

surrealistische Revolution f • surrealist
revolution (aes)

Surrogat n • surrogate, substitute, ersatz (gen)

Susy Guts pl • supersymmetrical grand unified
theories, Susy Guts (nat, sys)

suum cuique (tribuere) • (to allocate) to each
their own (eth) < Verteilungsgerechtigkeit

Syllogismus m • syllogism (log)

Syllogismus, apodiktischer m • apod(e)ictic
syllogism (log)

Syllogismus, assertorischer m • assertoric
syllogism (log)

Syllogismus, disjunktiver m • disjunctive
syllogism (log)

Syllogismus, hypothetischer m • hypothetical
syllogism (log)

Syllogismus, kontradiktorischer m • contradictory syllogism (log)

Syllogismus, praktischer m • practical
syllogism (log)

Syllogistik f • syllogistics (log)

syllogistische Deduktion f • syllogistic
deduction (log)

Symbiose f • symbiosis (nat)

Symbol n • symbol, emblem (aes, lan) < Zeichen

Symbol-Objekt-Dichotomie f • symbol-object
dichotomy (lan, aes)

Symbolbedeutung f • symbolic meaning (lan,
psy)

Symbolbegriff m • symbolic term (lan)

Symbolfähigkeit f • symbol ability (lan)

Symbolik f • symbolism (lan, aes)

symbolisch vermittelte Interaktion f • symbolically mediated interaction (Mead,
Habermas) (lan, act)

symbolisch vorstrukturierte Wirklichkeit f •
symbolically prestructured reality (Schütz,
Habermas) (lan, ont)

symbolische Äußerung f • symbolic expression
(lan)

Symbolische, das n • the symbolic (Saussure,
Lévi-Strauss, Lacan) (psy)

symbolische Ebene f • symbolic level (aes)
< Schichtenlehre

symbolische Form f • symbolic form
(Cassirer) (cul, aes)

symbolische Handlungskoordinierung f • symbolic coordination of action (Mead) (act)

symbolische Hypotypose f • symbolic
hypotyposis (Kant) (epi)

symbolische Kunst f • symbolic art (aes)

symbolische Logik f • symbolic logic (log) →
Logik, mathematische

symbolischer Interaktionismus m • symbolic
interactionism (Baldwin, Mead etc) (soc)

symbolisches System n • symbolic system (log,
lan)

symbolisches Zeichen n • symbolic sign (lan)

Symbolisierung f • symbolization (aes, gep)

Symbolismus m • symbolism (aes)

Symbolsprache f • symbolic language (lan, AI)
< Zeichensprache

Symboltheorie f • theory of symbols (lan)

Symbolverarbeitung f • symbol processing
(psy)

Symbolwissen n • symbolic knowledge (epi,
sci)

Symmetrie f • symmetry (mat, aes)

Symmetriebruch *m* • breach of symmetry *(sys)*

Symmetrieregel *f* • symmetry rule *(log, mat)*

Symmetriestruktur *f* • symmetric structure *(nat, gep)*

symmetrische Beziehung *f* • symmetric(al) relation(ship) *(log)*

symmetrische Verteilung *f* • symmetric(al) distribution *(mat)*

sympathetisches Weltbild *n* • sympathetic world view *(eth)*

Sympathie *f* • sympathy *(psy, eth)*

Sympathie und Antipathie, Prinzip der *n* • principle of sympathy and antipathy *(Bentham) (eth)*

Sympathisant *m* • sympathizer, partisan *(pol, psy)*

symphilosophieren • to philosophize together *(epi, met)*

Symposion *n* • symposium *(Plato) (soc, cul)* < W 964, (▷ wissenschaftliche Veranstaltung) conference, meeting *(gep)*

symptomatische Funktion der Sprache *f* • symptomatic function of language *(lan, act)*

Symptombekämpfung *f* • symptomatic treatment *(psy, nat, tec)*

Synästhesie *f* • synaesthesia *(psy, aes, lan)*

synchrone Sprachbetrachtung *f* → synchronische Sprachbetrachtung

Synchronie *f* • synchronic dimension *(Saussure) (lan)* ↔ Diachronie

Synchronie der diskursiven Formationen *f* • synchrony of discursive formations *(Foucault) (epi, lan)*

synchronische Sprachbetrachtung *f* • synchronic view of language *(lan, sci)*

Synchronizität *f* • synchronicity *(gep)* → Gleichzeitigkeit

Syndikalismus *m* • syndicalism *(pol)*

synergetischer Effekt *m* • synergetic effect *(sys)*

Synergie *f* • synergy *(sys)*

Synergismus *m* • synergism *(sys)*

Synkretismus *m* • syncretism *(rel, gep)*

Synode *f* • synod *(rel)*

Synökologie *f* → Ökosystemforschung

Synonymie *f* • synonymy *(lan)* → Synonymität, Bedeutungsgleichheit ↔ Antonymie

Synonymität *f* • synonymy, synonymity *(lan)*

Synopse *f* • synopsis *(gen)*

Synopsis des Mannigfaltigen *f* • synopsis of the manifold *(Kant) (epi)*

syntagmatisch • syntagmatic *(lan)* ↔ paradigmatisch

syntagmatische Reihe *f* • syntagmatic series *(lan)*

syntagmatische Serie *f* → syntagmatische Reihe

Syntaktik *f* • syntactics *(Morris) (sci)* < Syntax, Semiotik

syntaktische Ableitbarkeit *f* • syntactic derivability *(lan)*

syntaktische Definition *f* • syntactic definition *(log, lan)*

syntaktische Determiniertheit *f* • syntactical determinacy *(log, lan)*

Syntax *f* • syntax *(lan)*

Syntax, logische *f* • logical syntax/syntactics *(log, lan)*

Syntaxtheorie *f* • theory of syntax, syntactic theory *(lan)*

Synthese *f* • synthesis *(met, nat)*

Synthese von Freiheit und Notwendigkeit *f* • synthesis of freedom and necessity *(met)*

Synthesis der Aggregation *f* • synthesis of aggregation *(Kant) (epi)*

Synthesis der Anschauungen *f* • synthesis of intuitions *(Kant) (epi)*

Synthesis der Apperzeption *f* • synthesis of apperception *(Kant) (epi)*

Synthesis der Apprehension in der Anschauung *f* • synthesis of apprehension in intuition *(Kant) (epi)*

Synthesis der Einbildungskraft *f* • synthesis of imagination *(Kant) (epi)*

Synthesis der Erscheinungen *f* • synthesis of appearances *(Kant) (epi)*

Synthesis der Vorstellungen *f* • synthesis of representations *(Kant) (epi)*

Synthesis der Wahrnehmungen *f* • synthesis of perceptions *(Kant) (epi)*

Synthesis des Gleichartigen *f* • synthesis of the homogeneous *(Kant) (epi)*

Synthesis des Mannigfaltigen *f* • synthesis of the manifold *(Kant) (epi)*

synthetische Einheit der Apperzeption *f* • synthetic unity of apperception *(Kant) (epi)*

synthetische Einheit der Erscheinungen *f* • synthetic unity of appearances *(Kant) (epi)*

synthetische Einheit des Mannigfaltigen *f* • synthetic unity of the manifold *(Kant) (epi)*

synthetische Erkenntnis *f* • synthetic knowledge *(Kant) (epi)*

synthetische Erkenntnis a posteriori *f* • synthetic a posteriori knowledge, synthetic knowledge a posteriori *(Kant) (epi)*

synthetische Erkenntnis a priori *f* • synthetic a priori knowledge, synthetic knowledge a priori *(Kant) (epi)* synthetische Philosophie *f* • Synthetic Philosophy *(Spencer) (soc, met)* < W 976

synthetischer Grundsatz *m* • synthetic principle *(Kant) (epi)*

synthetisches Apriori *n* • synthetic a priori *(Kant) (epi)*

synthetisches Urteil *n* • synthetic judg(e)ment *(Kant) (epi)* → Erweiterungsurteil ↔ analytisches Urteil

synthetisches Urteil a posteriori *n* • synthetic a posteriori judg(e)ment, synthetic judg(e)ment a posteriori *(Kant) (epi)*

synthetisches Urteil a priori *n* • synthetic a priori judg(e)ment, synthetic judg(e)ment a priori *(Kant) (epi)*

Synthetismus *m* • synthetism *(aes)*

Synthetizität *f* • syntheticity *(aes)*

System *n* • system *(sci, sys)*

System der Aussagbarkeit *n* • system of enunciability *(Foucault) (epi, lan)*

System der Bedürfnisse *n* • system of needs *(Hegel) (soc)*

System der kosmologischen Ideen *n* • system of cosmological ideas *(Kant) (epi, met)*

System der Metaphysik *n* • system of metaphysics *(Kant) (epi, met)*

System der Natur *n* • system of nature *(nat)* < W 968

System der reinen Vernunft *n* • system of pure reason *(Kant) (epi, met)*

System der Sittlichkeit *n* • system of ethical life *(Hegel) (eth, met)* < W 975

System der Zwecke *n* • system of ends *(Kant) (eth, met)*

System des Funktionierens *n* • system of functioning *(Foucault) (epi, pol)*

System, formales *n* • formal system *(sci, log)*

System, formalisiertes *n* • formalized system *(sci)*

System, geschlossenes *n* • closed system *(sys)* ↔ offenes System

System kollektiver Sicherheit *n* • system of collective security *(pol)*

System, kybernetisches *n* • cybernetic system *(sys)*

System, offenes *n* • open system *(sys)* ↔ geschlossenes System

System reiner philosophischer Erkenntnisse *n* • system of pure philosophical knowledge *(Kant) (epi)*

System, zielgerichtetes *n* • goal-seeking system *(sys)*

Systemanalyse *f* • systems analysis *(sys)*

Systematik, offenhaltende *f* • open structure *(Jaspers) (met)*

systematisch gestörte Kommunikation *f* • systematically distorted communication *(Habermas etc) (lan, soc)*

systematische Analyse *f* • systematic analysis *(sci)*

systematische Einheit *f* • systematic unity *(gep)*

systematische Handlungswissenschaften *pl* • systematic science of action *(Habermas) (sci, act)*

systematische Vollständigkeit aller Erkenntnisse *f* • systematic completeness of all knowledge *(Kant) (epi, sci)*

systematischer Fehler *m* • systematic error *(mat)*

systematischer Neopragmatismus *m* • systematic neopragmatism *(epi, met)* < neopragmatische Erkenntnistheorie

systematischer Zweifel *m* • systematic doubt *(Descartes) (epi)*

systematisches Denken *n* • systematic thinking/thought *(gep)* < Philosophie, systematische

Systematisierung *f* • systematization *(sci)*

Systematizität *f* • systematicity *(gep)*

Systemautonomie *f* • system(s) autonomy *(sys)*

systembedingt • system dependent, determined by the system *(sys, pol)*

systembildender Effekt *m* • system-building effect *(sys)*

Systembildung *f* • system construction/building *(sys)*

Systemdenken *n* • systems thinking *(gep)*

Systemdifferenzierung *f* • system differentiation *(soc)*

Systemdynamik *f* • system(s) dynamics *(sys)*

Systemeigenschaft *n* • system(ic) property *(sys)*

Systemerfordernisse *pl* • system(s) requirements *(sys, pol)*

systemerfüllendes Modell *n* • model satisfying a system *(log, sci)*

Systemerhaltung *f* • system maintenance *(sys, pol)*

Systemevaluation *f* • system evaluation *(sys)*

Systemfunktionalismus *m* • systems functionalism *(sys)*

systemimmanent • inherent in the system *(sys, pol)*

Systemimmanenz *f* • system immanence *(sys, pol)*

Systemimperativ *m* • system imperative *(sys, pol)*

systemintegrativer Mechanismus *m* • systemintegrative mechanism *(sys, soc)*

systemisch induzierte Lebensweltpathologie *f*
• systemically induced lifeworld pathology
(Habermas) (soc, psy)

Systemkalkül *m/n* • system calculus *(log)*

Systemkohärenz *f* • system coherence *(sys, sci)*

Systemkomplexität *f* • system complexity *(sys)*

Systemkonformität *f* • conformity with the system *(pol)*

Systemkritik *f* • criticism of the system *(pol)*

Systemkritiker *m* • critic of the system *(pol)*

Systemlosigkeit *f* • lack of system, systemless-ness, unsystematicalness° *(sys, act)*

Systemprogramm *n* • system programme *(met, gep)* < W 53

Systemrationalität *f* • systems rationality *(sys, pol)*

Systemsimulation *f* • system simulation *(sys)*

Systemsprache *f* • system language *(Carnap) (lan, sci)*

Systemtechnik *f* • systems engineering *(sys, tec)*

Systemtheorie *f* • system(s) theory *(sys)* < Kybernetik

Systemtheorie, allgemeine *f* • general system(s) theory *(Bertalanffy) (sys)*

Systemüberwindung *f* • overcoming the system *(pol)*

Systemumwelt *f* • system environment *(sys)*

Systemungleichgewicht *n* • systemic disequi-librium *(sys, pol)*

Systemveränderung *f* • change of the system *(pol)*

Systemwettbewerb *m* • system(s) competition *(pol, eco)*

Systemzusammenbruch *m* • system(s) crash *(sys, pol)* < Zusammenbruchstheorie

Szenario-Analyse *f* • scenario analysis *(dec)*

Szenario-Denken *n* • scenario thinking *(dec)*

Szenenabfolge *f* • sequence of scenes *(aes)*

szientifische Methode *f* • scientific method *(Kant) (epi, sci)* → Methode, wissenschaft-liche

szientifischer Vernunftbegriff *m* • scientific concept of reason *(Kant) (epi, sci)*

Szientismus *m* • scientism *(sci)* ↔ Fideismus < Wissenschaftsgläubigkeit

szientistisches Selbstverständnis *n* • scientistic self-understanding *(sci)*

Szientokratie *f* • scientocracy *(sci, soc)*

T

T-Schema *n* • T-schema, Tarski-schema
(Tarski) (epi, lan, sci)

Tabu *n* • taboo, tabu° *(cul, psy)* < Totem
< W 1008

tabuisieren • to taboo, to put under a taboo
(cul, psy)

tabula rasa *f* • *nt*, blank/clean slate *(Leibniz,
Locke) (epi)*

Tabuverletzung *f* • taboo violation *(Freud)*
(cul, psy)

Tachismus *m* • tachism *(aes)*

Tafeln der Unterschiede *pl* • tables of difference *(Foucault) (epi, lan)*

Taglöhner *m* • day labourer *(eco)* < Proletariat

Tagtraum *m* • daydream *(psy)*

Talent der Vernunft *n* • talent of reason
(Kant) (epi)

Talionsprinzip *n* • law of talion, retaliation/
vendetta principle *(eth)* → lex talionis
< Vergeltungsgerechtigkeit

Tantra *n* • tantra *(asp)*

tantrischer Buddhismus *m* • tantric Buddhism
(asp)

Tantrismus *m* • tantrism *(asp)*

Tanzkunst *f* • art of dancing/dance *(aes)*
< Eukinetik, Bewegungskunst

Tao *n* • *nt (asp)* < W 981

Taoismus *m* • Taoism *(asp)*

Tapferkeit *f* • bravery, courage *(eth)* < Unerschrockenheit

Tarski-Semantik *f* • Tarski semantics *(lan)*

Tastempfindung *f* • tactile/tactual sensation
(psy, epi)

Tastsinn *m* • sense of touch *(psy, epi)*

Tat und Täter *f,m* • deed and doer *(act, eth)*

Tatbestand *m* • fact, fact of the matter, observational fact *(Carnap) (epi, sci)*

Tathandlung *f* • fact-act, auto-productive
activity/action *(Fichte) (met)*

tätiger Intellekt *m* → Intellekt, handelnder

tätiger Verstand *m* • active/acting intellect
(Avicenna etc) (epi, met), acting logos
(Aristotle) (epi, met)

Tätigkeit *f* • activity *(act)*

Tatsache *f* • (matter of) fact *(gep)* < W 982

Tatsache der reinen Vernunft *f* • fact of pure
reason *(Kant) (epi, met)*

Tatsache der Vernunft *f* • fact of reason
(Kant) (epi, met)

Tatsache, empirische *f* • empirical fact *(sci)*

Tatsache, institutionale *f* • institutional fact
(pol, soc)

Tatsache, verifizierbare *f* • verifiable fact
(sci)

Tatsache-Wert-Unterscheidung *f* • fact-value
distinction *(sci)* < Positivismusstreit, Sein-
Sollen-Unterscheidung

Tatsachen des Bewußtseins *pl* • facts of
consciousness *(Hegel) (met)*

Tatsachenargument *n* • factual/empirical
argument *(sci)*

Tatsachenaussage *f* • factual statement *(sci)* →
Wirklichkeitsaussage ↔ Wertaussage

Tatsachenbegriff *m* • fact-concept, concept of
fact *(Rickert, Weber) (sci)* ↔ Wertbegriff

Tatsachenerklärung *f* • factual explanation,
explanation of facts *(Hempel, Stegmüller)*
(sci)

Tatsachenfetischismus *m* • fact fetishism *(epi,
psy)*

Tatsachenfrage *f* • question of fact, question
of the facts *(sci)*

tatsachenorientiert • fact-oriented *(gep)*

Tatsachenurteil *n* • factual jugd(e)ment *(sci,
log)*

Tatsachenwahrheit *f* • truth of fact *(epi, met)*
↔ Vernunftwahrheit

Tatsachenwissen *n* • factual knowledge *(sci)*

tatsächlich deontische Modalität *f* • actual
deontic modality *(log, eth)* → tatsächliche
Pflichtmodalität

tatsächliche Pflichtmodalität → tatsächlich
deontische Modalität

Tatsächlichkeit *f* • actuality *(gep)* → Faktizität

Tauschabstraktion *f* • abstraction of exchange
(Lukács) (eco, soc)

Tauschbank *f* • exchange bank *(Proudhon)*
(eco) < Mutualismus

täuschender Schein *m* • deceptive appear-
ance/semblance *(epi, aes)*

tauschfähige Güter *pl* • exchangeable goods
(eco)

Tauschgerechtigkeit *f* • justice in exchange
(eth, eco)

Tauschgesellschaft *f* • barter society *(eco, soc)*

Tauschhandelsystem *n* • barter system *(eco)*
→ Tauschwirtschaft < Bartergeschäft

Tauschmittel *n* • medium/means of exchange
(eco)

Tauschmittelfunktion des Geldes *f* • exchange function of money *(eco)*

Tauschrationalität *f* • exchange rationality *(eco, soc)*

Täuschung *f* • delusion, illusion *(epi, psy)*, deception *(eth)* < Einbildung, Illusion; Schein, falscher

Täuschungsargument *n* • argument from illusion *(Descartes) (epi)* < Argument des bösen Dämons

Tauschwert *m* • exchange value, value in exchange *(Marx etc) (eco)* < Verkaufswert ↔ Gebrauchswert

Tauschwirtschaft *f* • barter/exchange economy *(eco, soc)* < Naturaltausch, Geldwirtschaft

Tautologie *f* • tautology *(log)*

Tautologieeigenschaft *f* • (property of) being a tautology, tautologicality°, tautologousness° *(log)*

tautologisches Urteil *n* • tautological judg(e)ment *(log)*

Taxonomie *f* • taxonomy *(sci)*

Taylorismus *m* • Taylorism *(eco)* < Serienfertigung, Massenproduktion

Teamarbeit *f* • team work *(eco)*

Teamgeist *m* • team spirit *(psy)*

techne logiké *f* • *nt (Husserl etc) (ont)*

Technik *f* • (▷ Fertigkeit) technique, technic, (▷ Technologie) technology *(tec)*

Technik als Modus des Seins *f* • technology as mode of Being *(Heidegger) (ont, tec)*

Technik der Natur *f* • technique/technic of nature *(Kant) (epi, nat)*

Technik der Urteilskraft *f* • technique/technic of judg(e)ment *(Kant) (epi)*

Technikbegeisterung *f* • enthusiasm for technology *(tec)*

Technikbewertung *f* • technology evaluation/assessment *(tec)* < Technikfolgenabschätzung

Techniken der Neubeschreibung *pl* • techniques of rewriting *(Foucault) (epi, lan)*

Technikethik *f* • engineering ethics, ethics of technology *(eth, tec)* → Ethik der Technik

Technikfeindlichkeit *f* • Luddism, Ludditism, anti-technology attitude *(tec, soc)* < Maschinenstürmer, Technophobie

Technikfolgenabschätzung *f* • cost-benefit analysis of (a) technology, technology assessment *(tec, sys)* < Risikoabwägung, Risikoanalyse

Technikkritik *f* • critique of technology, technology criticism *(tec, soc)*

Technikphilosophie *f* • philosophy of technology *(tec)*

technische Wissenschaften *pl* • technical sciences *(sci)*

technischer Fortschritt *m* • technological progress *(tec, his)*

technischer Imperativ *m* • technical imperative *(Kant) (eth)*

technisches Risiko *n* • technological risk *(tec)* < Technikfolgenabschätzung

technisches Urteil *n* • technical judg(e)ment *(Kant) (epi)*

Technisierung der Lebenswelt *f* • technicizing of the lifeworld *(Luhmann, Habermas) (soc)*

Technisierung der Wissenschaft *f* • technicizing of science *(sci)*

Technokratie *f* • technocracy *(tec, soc)*

Technologie *f* • technology *(tec)*

Technologie, angepaßte *f* • appropriate technology *(tec)*

Technologie, fortgeschrittene *f* • advanced technology < Hochtechnologie *(tec)*

Technologie, harte *f* • hard technology *(tec)* ↔ Technologie, sanfte < Hochrisikotechnologie

Technologie, niedrig entwickelte *f* • low (level) technology *(tec)* ↔ Hochtechnologie

Technologie, sanfte *f* • soft technology *(tec)* ↔ Technologie, harte < Hochrisikotechnologie

Technologiefolgenabschätzung *f* → Technikfolgenabschätzung

Technologiekritik *f* → Technikkritik

Technologiepolitik *f* • technology policy *(pol, tec)*

Technologierückstand *m* • technological/technology lag *(tec)*

Technologieschub *m* • technological/technology leap *(tec)*

Technologietransfer *m* • technology transfer, transfer of technology *(tec, eco)*

technologische Innovation *f* • technological innovation *(tec)*

technologische Relevanz *f* • technological relevance *(sci, soc)*

technologischer Fetischismus *m* • technological fetishism *(Marcuse) (soc, tec)*

technologischer Imperativ *m* • technological imperative *(tec, eth)*

technologischer Schleier *m* • technological veil *(Marcuse) (soc, tec)*

technologischer Wandel *m* • technological change *(tec)*

technomorphes Modell *n* • technomorphous model *(tec, soc)*

Technophobie *f* • technophobia *(tec)* → Technikfeindlichkeit

Technosphäre *f* • techno-sphere *(tec)*

Teil-Ganzes-Relation *f* • part-whole relation *(ont, sys)*

Teil und Ganzes *m,n* • part and whole *(ont, sys)*

Teilähnlichkeit *f* • partial similarity *(Carnap) (epi, ont)*

teilbarer Raum *m* • divisible space *(nat, ont)*

Teilbarkeit *f* • divisibility *(mat, ont)*

Teilbarkeit der Materie *f* • divisibility of matter *(nat, ont)* < Atomtheorie

Teilbarkeit, unbegrenzte *f* • infinite divisibility *(mat)*

Teilchenphysik *f* • particle physics *(nat)* < Atomphysik

Teildefinition *f* → Partialdefinition

teilentscheidbarer Satz *m* • unilaterally decidable statement *(log)*

Teilentscheidbarkeit *f* • unilateral decidability *(log)* ↔ Vollentscheidbarkeit

Teilhabe *f* • participation *(Plato) (epi, met), (eco, jur, rel)*

Teilhabe-Idealismus *m* • idealism of participation, participation idealism *(Plato, Berkeley) (epi, met)* < Phänomenalismus

Teilidentität *f* • part identity *(Carnap) (log)*

Teilintegritätsbereich *m* • integral subdomain *(mat)*

Teilinterpretation *f* • partial interpretation *(log, sci)*

Teilmenge *f* • subset *(log, mat)*

teilnehmende Beobachtung *f* • participant observation *(sci)* ↔ nicht-teilnehmende Beobachtung

teilnehmender Beobachter *m* • participant observer *(sci)*

Teilnehmerperspektive *f* • participant perspective *(act)*

teilschematische Abbildung *f* • partial schematic representation *(mat)* ↔ vollschematische Abbildung

teilstrukturiertes Interview *n* • partly structured interview *(sci)*

Teilung der Gewalten *f* → Gewaltenteilung

Teilzeitbeschäftigung *f* • part-time employment *(eco, soc)* < Flexibilisierung der Arbeitszeit

Telearbeit *f* • telework *(eco, tec)*

Telegnosis *f* • telegnosis *(eso)* < Hellsehen

Telekinese *f* • telekinesis *(eso)*

Telematik *f* • telematics *(tec)*

Teleologie *f* • teleology *(met)* < Finalismus, Naturzweck, Zielgerichtetheit, Zweckmäßigkeit der Natur

teleologische Erklärung *f* • teleological explanation *(met)*

teleologische Urteilskraft *f* • teleological judg(e)ment *(Kant) (epi, aes)*

teleologischer Gottesbeweis *m* • teleological argument (for the existence of God), argument from design *(rel)*

teleologischer Grund *m* • teleological ground *(met)*

teleologisches Gesetz *n* • teleological law *(Kant) (met)*

teleologisches Handeln *n* • teleological action *(act)* < strategisches Handeln

teleologisches System *n* • teleological system *(Kant) (met)*

teleologisches Urteil *n* • teleological judg(e)ment *(Kant) (epi, met)*

Teleonomie *f* • teleonomy *(nat, sys)*

Telepathie *f* • telepathy, thought transfer(ence) *(eso, psy)* → Gedankenübertragung

Tendenzkunst *f* • tendentious art *(aes)*

Tendenzliteratur *f* • tendentious/thesis literature, tendency literature *(aes)*

Term *m* • term *(sci)* → Begriff

Term, abgeleiteter *m* • derived term *(log, lan)*

Term, allgemeiner *m* • general/universal term *(log, lan)*

Term, definierbarer *m* • definable term *(log, lan)*

Term, partikularer *m* • particular term *(log, lan)*

Term, singulärer *m* • singular term *(log, lan)*

Term, teilinterpretierter *m* • partially interpreted term *(log, lan)*

Term, theoretischer *m* • theoretical term *(sci, log, lan)*

Term, undefinierbarer *m* • indefinable term *(log, lan)*

Term, universeller *m* → Term, allgemeiner

Termeigenschaft *f* • property of (being) a term *(log, lan)* < proprietates terminorum

Terminalsymbol *n* • terminal symbol *(lan, log, AI)*

Terminismus *m* • terminism *(epi, met)* < Nominalismus

Terminologie *f* • terminology *(lan)*

Terminologie, Primat der *m/n* • primacy of terminology *(Jaspers) (met, rel)* < Umgreifendes

Terminologie, vorzeitige *f* • premature terminology *(Jaspers)* < Chiffre

Terminus *m* • term *(log, lan)*

Terminus technicus *m* • technical term *(lan)*

Termkalkül *m/n* • term calculus *(log)*

Termtheorie *f* • theory of terms *(Searle) (lan)*

territoriale Abgrenzung f • territorial demarcation (pol)

territorialer Imperativ m • territorial imperative (Ardrey) (nat, ant) < Revierkampf

Territorialität f • territoriality (nat, ant, pol)

Territorialverhalten n • territorial behaviour (soc)

Terror-Frieden m • peace of terror (Aron) (eth) < Gleichgewicht des Schreckens, atomare Abschreckung, Kalter Krieg

Terrorherrschaft f • reign of terror (pol)

tertiärer Sektor m • tertiary sector (eco)

tertium non datur • nt (log) → Prinzip vom ausgeschlossenen Dritten < Logik, zweiwertige

Testgruppe f • test group (sci) < Experimentalgruppe, Kontrollgruppe

Testmethode f • test-method (sci)

Teststärke f • power (of a test) (sci)

Testverfahren n • test(ing) procedure (sci)

Teuerungsrate f • inflation rate (eco) → Inflationsrate

Teufel in Menschengestalt, der m • devil incarnate (rel)

Teufelsanbetung f → Dämonolatrie

Teufelskreis m • vicious circle (log) → circulus vitiosus

Textbuch n • textbook (gen) < Anthologie

Textdekonstruktion f • text deconstruction (Derrida etc) (lan, pol)

Texthermeneutik f • text(ual) hermeneutics (lan, sci)

Textinterpretation f • text(ual) interpretation (lan, sci)

Textkritik f • text(ual) criticism (lan)

Texttheorie f • theory of text (Bense) (aes)

Textualität f • textuality (lan)

textueller Kritizismus m • textual criticism (aes)

Thales von Milet • Thales of Miletus

Thanatologie f • thanatology (met)

thaumazein • wonderment, wonder (Heidegger etc) (ant) < Staunen, philosophisches

Theismus m • theism (rel)

Themenbereich m • topic, topic area (gep)

Themenschwerpunkt m • central/main topic (gep)

Themenstellung f • subject, topic (gep) < Subjekt

Theodizee f • theodicy (Leibniz) (met) < Problem des Bösen < W 989

Theodizeeproblem n • theodicy problem (Leibniz) (rel, eth)

Theogonie f • theogony (rel)

Theokratie f • theocracy, thearchy (rel, pol) → Gottesherrschaft

Theologie f • theology (rel)

Theologie der Befreiung f • theology of liberation (Boff etc) (rel)

Theologie, dialektische f • dialectical theology (Barth) (rel) < empirische Theologie

Theologie, dogmatische f • dogmatic theology (rel)

Theologie, geoffenbarte f • revealed theology (rel) ↔ Theologie, natürliche

Theologie, historische f • historical theology (rel)

Theologie, kritische f • critical theology (rel)

Theologie, natürliche f • natural theology (Suárez) (rel) → natürliche Religion < Deismus

Theologie, negative f • negative/apophantic theology (Aquinas, Barth) (rel)

Theologie, philosophische f • philosophical theology (rel)

Theologie, praktische f • practical theology (rel)

Theologie, Prinzip der n • principle of theology (Bentham) (eth)

Theologie, rationale f • rational theology (rel) → Vernunfttheologie

Theologie, spekulative f • speculative theology (rel)

Theologie, systematische f • systematic theology (rel)

Theologie, übernatürliche f • supernatural/supranatural theology (rel)

Theologie, wissenschaftliche f • scientific theology (rel)

Theologik f • theologics° (rel)

theologische Ethik f • theological ethics (rel, eth)

theologische Idee f • theological idea (Kant) (rel)

theologische Tugend f • theological virtue (eth, rel)

Theomanie f • theomania (rel, psy)

Theonomie f • theonomy (rel, eth) < Theokratie

Theophanie f • theophany (rel) → Gotteserscheinung

Theorem n • theorem (log, mat, sci)

Theorembeweiser m • theorem prover (log, AI)

Theoretiker m • theoretician (gep) ↔ Praktiker

theoretische Betrachtungsweise f • theoretical view (gep)

theoretische Erklärung *f* • theoretical explanation *(sci)*

theoretische Konstruktionen *pl* • theoretical constructions/constructs *(Carnap) (epi, sci)* < theoretisches Konstrukt

theoretische Prädikate *pl* • theoretical predicates *(log, lan)*

theoretische Praxis *f* • theoretical praxis/practice *(gep)*

theoretische Schemata *pl* • theoretical schemata *(Foucault) (epi, lan)*

theoretische Signifikanz *f* • theoretical significance *(log, lan, sci)*

theoretische Vernunft *f* • theoretical reason *(Kant) (epi, met)* ↔ praktische Vernunft

theoretische Wissenschaften *pl* • theoretical sciences *(sci)*

theoretischer Begriff *m* • theoretical concept *(sci, log, lan)* → theoretischer Term

theoretischer Diskurs *m* • theoretical discourse *(lan, sci)*

theoretischer Hintergrund *m* • theoretical background *(sci)*

theoretischer Term *m* • theoretical term *(sci, log, lan)* ↔ alltagssprachlicher Begriff

theoretisches Gesetz *n* • theoretical law *(sci, nat)*

theoretisches Konstrukt *n* • theoretical construct *(sci)*

theoretisches Modell *n* • theoretical model *(sci)*

theoretisches Urteil *n* • theoretical judg(e)ment *(log, epi)*

theoretisieren • to theorize *(gep)*

Theoretizität *f* • theoreticity° *(sci)*

Theoria *f* • *nt,* theory *(gep)* < Beschaulichkeit

Theorie *f* • theory *(sci)*

Theorie aufstellen • to put forward/advance a theory *(sci)* < Theoriebildung

Theorie der Forschungsprogramme *f* • theory of research programmes *(Lakatos) (sci)*

Theorie der Gerechtigkeit *f* • theory of justice *(jur, eth)* < W 997

Theorie der Kennzeichnungen *f* → Kennzeichnungstheorie

Theorie der Moderne *f* • theory of modernity *(Habermas) (soc, aes)*

Theorie der Quantifizierung *f* • theory of quantification *(sci)*

Theorie der unscharfen Mengen *f* • fuzzy set theory *(log, mat)*

Theorie der Wahlakte *f* • theory of choice *(dec)* < Entscheidungstheorie

Theorie des eigentlichen Wissens *f* • theory of actual knowledge *(epi, sci, soc)*

Theorie des Geschmacks *f* • theory of taste *(aes)* < Geschmack, ästhetischer

Theorie des idealen Beobachters *f* • ideal observer theory, theory of the ideal observer *(A. Smith) (eth)*

Theorie des kommunikativen Handelns *f* • theory of communicative action *(Habermas) (soc)* < W 1000

Theorie des sozialen Handelns *f* • social action theory, theory of social action *(act)*

Theorie, empirische *f* • empirical theory *(sci)*

Theorie, formale *f* • formal theory *(sci)*

Theorie komplexer Funktionen *f* • complex function theory *(mat)*

Theorie, kritische *f* • Critical Theory *(Horkheimer, Marcuse etc) (sci, soc)* < Frankfurter Schule

Theorie transfiniter Mengen *f* • theory of transfinite sets *(mat)*

Theorie und Praxis *f,f* • theory and practice *(gep)* < W 1002

Theorie und Praxis der Eindämmung *f,f* • theory and practice of containment *(Marcuse) (soc, pol)*

Theorie von allem *f* • theory of everything, TOE *(log, sci)*

Theorieabhängigkeit *f* • theory-dependency *(sci)*

Theorieabhängigkeit der Beobachtung *f* • theory dependency of observation *(sci)* < Theoriebeladenheit der Beobachtung, Theoretizität

Theoriebeladenheit der Beobachtung *f* • theory-ladenness of observation *(Quine, Popper etc) (sci)* < Theorieabhängigkeit der Beobachtung, Theoretizität

Theoriebildung *f* • theory formation *(sci)*

theoriegebunden • theory-bound *(sci)*

Theoriegerüst *n* • theoretical framework, framework for a theory *(Quine etc) (sci)*

Theoriegetränktheit der Beobachtung *f* → Theoriebeladenheit der Beobachtung

Theoriekonstruktion *f* • theory construction *(sci)*

Theorien als Strategien *pl* • theories strategies, theories as strategies *(Foucault) (sci, pol)*

Theorien mittlerer Reichweite *pl* • middle range theories, theories of the middle range *(sci)*

Theoriendynamik *f* • dynamics of theories *(sci)* < Paradigmenwechsel

Theorienentwicklung *f* • theory development *(sci)*

Theorienimmunisierung *f* • immunization of theory *(sci)*

Theorienpluralismus *m* • pluralism of theories, theory pluralism *(Spinner, Kuhn) (sci)*

Theorienstreit *m* • dispute between theories *(sci)*

Theorienunterbestimmtheit *f* • under-determination of theories *(Quine etc) (sci)* < Unterdeterminiertheit

Theorienwandel *m* • theory change *(sci)* < Paradigmenwechsel, wissenschaftliche Revolution

Theoriereduktion *f* • theory reduction *(sci)*

Theoriesprache *f* • theory/theoretical language, language of a theory *(lan, sci)*

Theorieverdrängung *f* • displacement of a theory/theories *(sci)*

Theoriewahl *f* • theory choice, choice of theory *(sci)*

Theosophie *f* • theosophy *(rel, met, eso)*

theosophische Bewegung *f* • theosophical movement *(rel, met, eso)*

therapeutische Kritik *f* • therapeutic critique *(Habermas) (lan, soc)*

Therapeutokratie *f* • therapeutocracy *(Habermas) (soc, pol)*

Thermodynamik *f* • thermodynamics *(nat)*

These *f* • thesis *(sci, log); (Hegel etc) (met)* < dialektischer Dreischritt

Theurgie *f* • theurgy *(rel)*

Think-tank *m* • think tank *(sci, gep)* < Ideenlieferant

Thomas Morus • Thomas More

Thomas von Aquin • Thomas Aquinas

Thomismus *m* • Thomism *(rel, gep)* < christlicher Aristotelismus

Thron und Altar, Allianz von *f* • alliance of throne and altar *(pol, rel)*

Tibetischer Buddhismus *m* • Tibetan Buddhism *(asp)* < tantrischer Buddhismus

Tiefengrammatik *f* • depth grammar *(Wittgenstein) (lan)* ↔ Oberflächengrammatik < Universalgrammatik

tiefenhermeneutisches Verfahren *n* • depthhermeneutic procedure *(Habermas) (lan, sci)*

Tiefeninterview *n* • depth interview *(sci)*

Tiefenökologie *f* • deep ecology *(Naess) (env)* < Ökosophie

Tiefenpsychologie *f* • depth psychology, deep psychology *(psy)*

Tiefenstruktur *f* • deep structure *(Saussure, Chomsky) (lan)* ↔ Oberflächenstruktur < Transformationsgrammatik

Tier im Menschen *n* • animal in man *(ant, eth)*

Tier Mensch, das *n* • animal man *(Nietzsche) (ant, met)*, the human animal *(ant)* < Tierhaftigkeit des Menschen

Tier, nichtmenschliches *n* • nonhuman animal *(eth, ant)* < Mensch

Tiere als Maschinen *pl* • animals as machines, brutes as automata *(Descartes) (met)*

Tiere als mechanische Automaten *pl* • animals as mechanical automata *(Descartes) (met)*

Tiere, höhere *pl* • higher animals *(nat)* < Anthropoide

Tier-Ethik *f* • animal ethics *(eth)* < Befreiung der Tiere

Tiergesellschaft *f* • animal society *(nat, soc)* ↔ menschliche Gesellschaft

Tierhaftigkeit des Menschen *f* • animality of man *(Nietzsche etc) (ant)*

Tierhaltung, industrielle *f* • factory farming, industrial husbandry, animal industry *(eco, eth)* < Massentierhaltung

tierische Aggression *f* • animal aggression *(nat)*

tierische Intelligenz *f* • animal intelligence *(nat)*

tierische Vernunft *f* • animal reason *(nat)*

tierische Vorfahren des Menschen *pl* • animal ancestors of man *(ant)*

tierischer Instinkt *m* • animal instinct *(nat)*

tierisches Bewußtsein *n* • animal consciousness *(Nietzsche) (nat)*

tierisches Erbe *n* • animal heritage *(ant)*

tierisches Verhalten *n* • animal behaviour *(nat, ant)*

Tierkreiszeichen *n* • sign of the zodiac *(eso)* < Sternbild

Tieropfer *n* • animal sacrifice *(rel, cul)*

Tierpsychologie *f* • animal psychology *(psy)* < Verhaltensforschung

Tierquälerei *f* • cruelty to animals *(eth)*

Tierrechte *pl* • animal rights *(eth)*

Tierschutz *m* • animal protection *(eth)*

Tierseele *f* • animal soul *(Aristotle, Descartes) (met)* ↔ Menschenseele

Tierversuch *m* • animal experiment, experimentation on animals *(eth)* < Vivisektion, Versuchstier

tierversuchsfreie Kosmetik *f* • cruelty-free cosmetics, cosmetics without animal testing *(eth)*

Tierwelt *f* • animal world *(nat)*

Tietzes Extensionstheorem *n* • Tietze's extension theorem *(mat)*

Tod *m* • death *(nat, met, rel)* < Vergänglichkeit; Schlaf, ewiger

Tod als Grenzsituation *m* • death as limit situation *(Jaspers) (met)*

Tod der Erkenntnistheorie *m* • death of epistemology *(Rorty etc) (met)*

Tod des Autors *m* • (the) death of the author *(aes)*

Tod Gottes *m* • death of God *(Nietzsche) (met)* < Gott ist tot

Todesangst *f* • (▷ große Angst) mortal fear/ dread; (▷ Angst vor dem Tod) death anxiety, fear of death *(psy)* → Todesfurcht

Todesbereitschaft *f* • readiness to die *(eth)* < Märtyrer

Todesbewußtsein *n* • awareness of death *(ant, met)*

Todesfeststellung *f* • diagnosis of death *(nat, eth)* < Hirntoddefinition

Todesfurcht *f* • fear of death *(psy)* → Todesangst

Todesriten *pl* • death rites *(cul)*

Todessehnsucht *f* • longing for death *(psy)* < Todeswunsch

Todesstrafe *f* • capital punishment, death penalty *(eth)* < Körperstrafe

Todestrieb *m* • death instinct *(Freud) (psy)* ↔ Lebenstrieb < Nekrophilie

Todeswunsch *m* • death-wish *(Freud) (psy)* < Todessehnscht

Todsünde *f* • mortal/deadly sin *(rel)*

Token *n* • token *(lan, log)* ↔ Typ

Token-Identität *f* • token identity *(lan, ont)* ↔ Typ-Identität

Toleranz *f* • tolerance *(eth, sci, nat)* < Koexistenz, friedliche; (▷ Meßgenauigkeit) allowance *(mat)* < Fehlerfreundlichkeit

Toleranzgrenze *f* • tolerance limit *(eth, nat, sci)*

Toleranzprinzip *n* • principle of tolerance *(Carnap) (sci, lan), (pol, eth)*

Tonalität *f* • tonality *(aes)*

Tonfarbe *f* • tone-colour, timbre *(aes)*

Tonfilm *m* • sound film, talkie *(aes)* ↔ Stummfilm

Tonmalerei *f* • tone-painting *(aes)*

Tonsprache *f* • tone-language *(aes)*

Top-down-Algorithmus *m* • top-down algorithm *(AI, mat)* ↔ Bottom-up-Algorithmus

Topik *f* • topic *(Aristotle etc) (lan, log)* < W 1006, *(Kant) (epi)*

Topologie *f* • topology *(log, mat)* < Kategorientheorie

topologische Definition *f* • topological definition *(lan, log)* < Information

topologische Gesetze *pl* • topological laws *(mat)*

topologische Skala *f* • topological scale *(mat)*

Totalabstraktion *f* • total abstraction *(mat)*

totale Verwaltung *f* • total administration *(Marcuse) (soc)*

totaler Krieg *m* • total war *(pol)*

totalitäre Gesellschaft *f* • totalitarian society *(soc, pol)*

totalitärer Staat *m* • totalitarian state *(pol)*

Totalitarismus *m* • totalitarianism *(pol)* < Willkürherrschaft

Totalität *f* • totality, entirety, whole *(gep)* < Ganzheit

Totalität der Erfahrung *f* • totality of experience *(Kant etc) (epi, met)*

Totalität in sich *f* • totality within itself *(Hegel) (met)*

Totalität menschlicher Lebensäußerung *f* • totality of human life-activity *(Marx) (ant, soc)* < universeller Mensch

Totalrelation *f* • total relation *(log, mat)*

Totalwahrscheinlichkeit *f* • total probability *(mat)*

Totalwissen *n* → Universalwissen

Totem *n* • totem *(ant, cul)* < W 1008

Totemismus *m* • totemism *(ant, cul)*

Töten vs. Sterbenlassen *n,n* • killing vs. letting die *(eth)* < Euthanasie, aktive; Euthanasie, passive; Tun und Geschehenlassen

Totenkult *m* • cult of the dead *(cul, rel)* → Manismus

Totenreich *n* • kingdom of the dead *(rel)* → Orkus, Unterwelt

Tötungsabsicht *f* • intention to kill *(jur)*

Tötungsbereitschaft *f* • willingness/ preparedness to kill *(psy, eth)*

Tötungshemmung, angeborene *f* • inborn inhibition against killing/to kill *(Eibl-Eibesfeld) (ant)*

traditionale Autorität *f* • traditional authority *(Weber) (soc)*

traditionale Legitimation *f* • traditional legitimacy *(Weber) (soc)*

traditionales Handeln *n* • traditional action *(Weber) (soc, act)*

Traditionalismus *m* • traditionalism *(pol, cul)* < Konservati(vi)smus

traditionelle Gesellschaft *f* • traditional/folk-society *(soc)*

traditionelle Lebensweise *f* • traditional ways of life, folkways *(soc)*

Traditionsabhängigkeit *f* • dependence/ dependency on tradition *(soc, cul)*

Traditionsbewußtsein n • tradition-consciousness (soc, cul)

Traditionsentbundenheit f • independence/independency from/of tradition (soc, cul) < Traditionsverlust

traditionsgebunden • traditional, tradition-bound (soc)

Traditionsgebundenheit f → Traditionsabhängigkeit

traditionsgeleitet • tradition-directed (soc, cul)

traditionsorientiert • tradition-oriented (soc, cul)

Traditionsverlust m • loss of tradition (soc, cul)

Traduzianismus m • traducianism (rel) < Kreatianismus

Tragfähigkeit f • carrying capacity (env)

Trägheit(skraft) f • inertial force, inertia (nat)

Trägheitsgesetz n • law of inertia (nat)

Trägheitskörper m • inertia(l) field (mat)

Tragiker, die pl • the Tragedians (aes)

tragikomisch • tragicomic(al) (aes)

Tragische, das n • the tragic(al) (aes)

tragische Dichtung f • tragic poetry (aes)

tragische Weltbetrachtung f • tragic world view (Jaspers) (met)

tragischer Held m • tragic hero (aes)

tragischer Konflikt m • tragic conflict (eth) < ethisches Dilemma

tragisches Gefühl n • tragic feeling (aes, psy)

Tragödie, aristotelische f • Aristotelian tragedy (aes)

Tragödie, Theorie der f • theory of tragedy (Aristotle etc) (aes)

Transaktionskosten pl • transaction costs (eco)

Transdisziplinarität f • transdisciplinarity (sci)

transfinit • transfinite (mat)

Transformation f • transformation (gep) < W 1014

Transformationsgrammatik f • transformational grammar (Chomsky) (lan) → generative Grammatik < Tiefenstruktur

Transformationsprozeß m • transformation process (gep)

Transformationsregel f • transformation rule (lan)

transformative Syntax f • transformational syntax (lan)

Transformismus m • transformism (nat) < Deszendenztheorie

transgenes Lebewesen n • transgenic being/life-form, transgene organism (nat, eth)

Transintelligibles n • the trans-intelligible (N. Hartmann) (met)

Transitivität f • transitivity (log, mat)

Transitivitätsgesetz n • transitivity law, law of transitivity (log)

Transitivitätsregel f • transitivity rule, rule of transitivity (log)

Transkribierbarkeitskriterium n • translatability criterion (Quine etc) (sci, epi, lan)

Transobjektivität f • trans-objectivity (N. Hartmann) (ont)

Transparenz f • transparency (Quine etc) (log, lan) → Durchsichtigkeit ↔ Opakheit

Transsubjektivität f • transsubjectivity (met)

Transsubjektivitätsprinzip n • principle of transsubjectivity (epi, sci)

Transsubstantiation f • transubstantiation (rel)

Transsubstantiationslehre f • doctrine of transubstantiation (rel)

transzendent • transcendent (met, rel)

transzendental • transcendental (Kant etc) (epi)

transzendentale Abstraktion f • transcendental abstraction (Kant) (epi)

transzendentale Affinität f • transcendental affinity (Kant) (epi)

transzendentale Analytik f • transcendental analytic(s) (Kant) (epi)

transzendentale Anschauung f • transcendental intuition/perception/anschauung (Kant, Schelling, Fichte) (epi)

transzendentale Apperzeption f • transcendental apperception (Kant) (epi)

transzendentale Ästhetik f • transcendental aesthetic(s) (Kant etc) (epi)

transzendentale Bedeutung f • transcendental meaning (epi)

transzendentale Bedingung f • transcendental condition (Kant) (epi)

transzendentale Behauptung f • transcendental assertion (Kant) (epi)

transzendentale Bejahung f • transcendental affirmation (Kant) (epi)

transzendentale Deduktion f • transcendental deduction (Kant) (epi) ↔ empirische Deduktion

transzendentale Dialektik f • transcendental dialectic(s) (Kant) (epi)

transzendentale Doktrin f • transcendental doctrine (Kant) (epi)

transzendentale Einbildungskraft f • transcendental imagination (Kant) (epi)

transzendentale Einheit der Apperzeption f • transcendental unity of apperception (Kant) (epi)

transzendentale Einheit der Wahrnehmung *f*
→ transzendentale Einheit der Apperzeption

transzendentale Einheit des Selbstbewußt-seins *f* • transcendental unity of self-consciousness *(Kant) (epi)*

transzendentale Elementarlehre *f* • transcendental doctrine of elements *(Kant) (epi)* ↔ transzendentale Methodenlehre

transzendentale Erkenntnis *f* • transcendental knowledge *(Kant) (epi)*

transzendentale Erörterung *f* • transcendental exposition *(Kant) (epi)*

transzendentale Formel *f* • transcendental formula *(Kant) (epi)*

transzendentale Freiheit *f* • transcendental freedom *(Kant) (met)*

transzendentale Gotteserkenntnis *f* • transcendental knowledge of God *(Kant) (epi, rel)*

transzendentale Hypothese *f* • transcendental hypothesis *(Kant) (epi)*

transzendentale Idealität *f* • transcendental ideality *(Kant) (epi)*

transzendentale Idee *f* • transcendental idea *(Kant) (epi)*

transzendentale Kritik *f* • transcendental critique *(Kant) (epi)*

transzendentale Logik *f* • transcendental logic *(Kant) (epi, log)*

transzendentale Methodenlehre *f* • transcendental doctrine of method, transcendental methodology *(Kant) (epi)* ↔ transzendentale Elementarlehre

transzendentale Möglichkeit *f* • transcendental possibility *(Kant) (epi)*

transzendentale Phänomenologie *f* • transcendental phenomenology *(Husserl) (epi, met)*

transzendentale Psychologie *f* • transcendental psychology *(Kant, Rickert etc) (psy)*

transzendentale Realität *f* • transcendental reality *(Kant) (epi, met)*

transzendentale Reduktion *f* • transcendental reduction *(Husserl) (epi, met)*

transzendentale Regeln *pl* • transcendental rules *(Kant) (epi)*

transzendentale Seelenlehre *f* • transcendental doctrine of the soul *(Kant) (epi, psy)*

transzendentale Synthesis *f* • transcendental synthesis *(Kant) (epi)*

transzendentale Theologie *f* • transcendental theology *(Kant) (epi, rel)*

transzendentale Topik *f* • transcendental topic *(Kant) (epi)*

transzendentale Urteilskraft *f* • transcendental judg(e)ment *(Kant) (epi)*

transzendentale Verneinung *f* • transcendental negation *(Kant) (epi)*

transzendentale Vernunft *f* • transcendental reason *(Kant) (epi)*

transzendentale Zahlen *pl* • transcendental numbers *(mat)*

transzendentaler Begriff *m* • transcendental concept *(Kant) (epi)*

transzendentaler Beweis *m* • transcendental proof *(Kant) (epi)*

transzendentaler Gebrauch der Vernunft *m* • transcendental employment/use of reason *(Kant) (epi)*

transzendentaler Grund *m* • transcendental ground *(Kant) (epi, met)*

transzendentaler Grundsatz *m* • transcendental principle *(Kant) (epi)*

transzendentaler Idealismus *m* • transcendental idealism *(Kant) (epi, met)*

transzendentaler Kritizismus *m* • transcendental critical philosophy *(Kant) (epi, met)*

transzendentaler Paralogismus *m* • transcendental paralogism *(Kant) (epi, log)*

transzendentaler Realismus *m* • transcendental realism *(E. Hartmann) (epi, met)*

transzendentaler Schein *m* • transcendental illusion *(Kant) (epi, met)*

transzendentaler Schlüssel *m* • transcendetal clue *(epi, met)*

transzendentaler Sprung *m* • transcendental leap *(Kierkegaard, Jaspers) (met, rel)*

transzendentaler Ursprung *m* • transcendental origin *(Kant) (epi)*

transzendentales Argument *n* • transcendental argument *(Kant etc) (epi)*

transzendentales Bewußtsein *n* • transcendental consciousness *(Kant) (epi)*

transzendentales Gesetz *n* • transcendental law *(Kant) (epi, met)*

transzendentales Ich *n* • transcendental I/ego *(Kant) (epi, met)*

transzendentales Ideal *n* • transcendental ideal *(Kant) (epi, met)*

transzendentales Objekt *n* • transcendental object *(Kant) (epi, met)* < Ding an sich

transzendentales Prädikat *n* • transcendental predicate *(Kant) (epi, lan)*

transzendentales Prinzip *n* • transcendental principle *(Kant) (epi)*

transzendentales Schema *n* • transcendental schema *(Kant) (epi)*

transzendentales Selbst *n* • transcendental ego *(Husserl) (epi, met)* ↔ psychologisches Selbst

transzendentales Subjekt der Gedanken *n* • transcendental subject of thoughts *(Kant)* *(epi)*

transzendentales Substrat *n* • transcendental substrate *(Kant) (epi, ont)*

transzendentales Vermögen *n* • transcendental faculty *(Kant) (epi)*

Transzendentalien *pl* • transcendentals *(met)* < Urbegriffe

Transzendentalismus *m* • transcendentalism *(epi, met)* → Transzendentalphilosophie

Transzendentalismus, logischer *m* • logical transcendentalism *(epi, met)*

Transzendentalität *f* • transcendentality *(Kant) (epi)*

Transzendentalphilosophie *f* • transcendental philosophy *(Kant etc) (epi, met)*

Transzendentalpragmatik *f* • transcendental pragmatics *(Apel) (eth, epi, lan)*

transzendentalpragmatische Letztbegründung *f* • transcendental-pragmatic foundation *(Apel) (eth, epi, lan)*

transzendente Erkenntnis *f* • transcendent knowledge *(Kant) (epi)*

transzendente Idee *f* • transcendent idea *(Kant) (epi)*

transzendente Spekulation *f* • transcendent speculation *(Kant) (met)*

transzendenter Begriff *m* • transcendent concept *(Kant) (epi, met)*

transzendenter Gebrauch *m* • transcendent use *(Kant) (epi)*

transzendenter Grundsatz *m* • transcendent principle *(Kant) (epi, met)*

transzendenter Naturbegriff *m* • transcendent concept of nature *(Kant) (epi, nat, met)*

transzendenter Sinn der Geschichte *m* • transcendent sense of history *(his)*

transzendenter Vernunftbegriff *m* • transcendent concept of reason *(Kant) (epi, met)*

Transzendenz *f* • transcendence *(met, rel)*

Transzendenz des Ich *f* • infinity/transcendence of the Ego *(Fichte) (met)*

Transzendenz Gottes *f* • God's transcendence, transcendence of God *(rel)*

Transzendenzbasis *f* • basis of transcendence *(mat)*

Transzendenzerleben *n* • experience of transcendence, transcendence-experience *(Jaspers) (met)*

Trauerarbeit *f* • (work of) grieving *(psy)*

Trauerspiel *n* • tragedy *(aes)* < Tragödie, Theorie der

Trauma *n* • trauma *(Freud, Breuer etc) (psy)*

Traumarbeit *f* • dream-work *(Freud) (psy)*

Traumargument *n* • dream argument *(Descartes) (epi)*

Traumdeutung *f* • dream-interpretation, interpretation of dreams *(Freud) (psy)* < W 1016

Traumfabrik *f* • dream factory *(aes)* < Kulturindustrie

Traumsymbol *n* • dream symbol *(Freud) (psy)*

Traumsymbolik *f* • dream imagery/symbolism *(psy)*

Traumzensur *f* • censorship of dreams *(Freud) (psy)*

Treffergenauigkeit *f* • predictive accuracy *(mat)* < Vorhersagegenauigkeit

Trefferquote *f* • hit rate, accuracy *(sci)*

treibende Kraft *f* • motive/moving/driving force *(met, gep)* → Agens < Movens

Treibhauseffekt *m* • greenhouse effect *(env)* < globale Erwärmung

Trendwende *f* • trend reversal *(pol, aes)*

Trennung der Produzenten von den Produktionsmitteln *f* • separation/dissociation of producers from the means of production *(Marx) (eco, soc)*

Trennung der Seele vom Körper *f* • separation of the soul from the body *(rel)* → Abreption

Trennung von Geist und Körper *f* • separation of mind and body *(met)*

Trennung von Kirche und Staat *f* • separation of church and state *(pol, rel)* < Kulturkampf, Säkularisierung

Trennungsangst *f* • separation anxiety *(psy)*

Trennungsregel *f* • detachment/separation rule *(log)*

Treppenfunktion *f* • step function *(mat)*

Treue *f* • fidelity, loyalty, faithfulness *(eth)*

triadische Ästhetik *f* • triad(ic) aesthetics *(Morris) (aes)*

triadische Semiotik *f* • triad(ic) semiotics *(Peirce) (lan)*

triadischer Prozeß *m* • triadic process *(Hegel) (met)* < dialektischer Dreischritt

Trichotomie *f* • trichotomy *(log, rel, jur)*

Trichotomismus *m* • trichotomism *(log)*

Trieb *m* • instinct, (instinctive) drive, urge, impulse *(nat, psy)*

Triebanlage *f* • instinctual disposition *(Freud etc) (psy)*

Triebanspruch *m* • instinctual claim *(Freud) (psy)*

Triebbedürfnis *n* • instinctual need *(Freud etc) (psy)*

Triebbefriedigung *f* • (instinctual) gratification/satisfaction *(psy)*

Triebbeherrschung f • instinctual (self-)control *(Freud etc) (psy)*

Triebeinschränkung f • instinctual constraint *(Freud etc) (psy)*

Triebenergie f • instinctual energy *(psy)*

Triebfeder f • incentive, motivating force *(Kant etc) (psy, act, eth)* → Motiv

Triebhandlung f • instinctive act *(psy, jur)*

Triebimpuls m • instinctual impulse *(Freud etc) (psy)*

Triebleben n • libidinal life *(Freud etc) (psy)*

Triebmodell n • drive model *(psy)*

Triebopfer n • sacrifice of instincts *(Freud) (psy)*

Triebregung f • instinctual impulse *(Freud) (psy)*

Triebstruktur f • libidinous structure *(Freud etc) (psy)*

Triebsublimierung f • sublimation of instinct(s) *(Freud) (psy)*

Triebtheorie f • instinct theory *(Freud) (psy)*, drive theory, theory of drives *(psy)*

Triebunterdrückung f • instinct suppression *(Freud) (psy)* < unterdrückte Wünsche

Triebverdrängung f • drive displacement *(Freud) (psy)*

Triebverzicht m • drive renunciation, renunciation of instincts, renunciation of instinctual gratification/satisfaction *(Freud etc) (psy)* < Triebsublimierung

Triebziel n • instinctual aim *(Freud) (psy)*

Trilemma der Begründung n • trilemma of justification/foundation *(Albert) (epi, log)* → Münchhausen-Trilemma

Trinität f • trinity *(rel)*

Trinitätslehre f • doctrine of the trinity *(rel)*

Trittbrettfahrerdilemma n • free-rider dilemma *(soc, eth)*

Trivialkunst f • trivial/trash art, kitsch *(aes)*

Trivialmenge f • trivial set *(mat)*

Trivium n • trivium *(gep)* < Quadrivium, artes liberales

Trope f • trope *(lan)*

Tropus m • trope *(Williams) (ont)*

trostloses Ungefähr n • disconsolate haphazard *(Kant) (epi, psy)*

Trugbild n • idol *(epi, psy)* → Phantasmagorie, Schimäre < Idolenlehre

Trugbilder der Höhle pl • idols of the cave/den *(Bacon) (epi)* → Idole der Höhle

Trugbilder des Marktes pl • idols of the marketplace *(Bacon) (epi)* → Idole des Marktes

Trugbilder des Stammes pl • idols of the tribe *(Bacon) (epi)* → Idole des Stammes

Trugbilder des Theaters pl • idols of the theatre *(Bacon) (epi)* → Idole des Theaters

Trugschluß m • fallacy, fallacious/misleading argument, sophism *(log)* → Fallazie < Fehlschluß, Fangschluß

Trugschluß der Akzidenz m • fallacy of (the) accident *(log)*

Trugschluß der Amphibolie m • fallacy of amphiboly/amphibology/ambiguity *(log)*

Trugschluß der Division m • fallacy of division *(log)*

Trugschluß der Komposition m • fallacy of composition *(log)*

Trugschluß der negativen Prämissen m • fallacy of negative premis(s)es *(log)*

Trugschluß der partikulären Prämissen m • fallacy of particular premis(s)es *(log)*

Trugschluß des Nicht-Folgens m → nonsequitur

Trugschluß des non causa pro causa m • fallacy of non causa pro causa *(log)*

Trugschluß des post hoc ergo propter hoc m • fallacy of post hoc ergo propter hoc, fallacy of false cause *(log)*

Trugschluß, umgekehrter m • reverse fallacy *(log)*

Tugend f • virtue *(eth)*

Tugenden, dianoetische pl • dianoetic(al) virtues *(Aristotle) (eth)* → Verstandestugenden ↔ Tugenden, ethische

Tugenden, ethische pl • ethical virtues *(Aristotle) (eth)* ↔ Tugenden, dianoetische; Verstandestugenden

Tugendepistemologie f • virtue epistemology *(eth, epi)*

Tugendethik f • virtue/aretaic ethics *(eth)*

tugendhaftes Leben n • virtuous life *(eth)*

Tugendhaftigkeit f • virtuousness *(eth)*

Tugendkatalog m • catalogue of virtues *(eth, rel)* ↔ Lasterkatalog

Tugendlehre f • theory of virtues, virtue theory, aretaics *(eth)* → Aretologie

Tugendlehre, christliche f • Christian doctrine of virtues *(eth)*

Tugendpflicht f • duty of virtue *(Kant) (eth)*

Tun und Geschehenlassen n,n • doing and letting happen *(eth)* < Töten vs. Sterbenlassen

Tupel n • tuple *(mat)*

Turing-Maschine f • Turing machine *(Turing) (AI, mat)*

Turing-Test m • Turing test *(Turing) (AI)*

Typ m • type *(lan, log)* ↔ Token

Typ-Identität f • type-identity *(lan, ont)* ↔ Token-Identität

Type-Token-Unterscheidung *f* • type-token distinction *(Peirce) (log, lan)*

Typen und Einzeldinge *pl,pl* • types and tokens *(lan, log, ont)*

Typenhierarchie *f* • type hierarchy *(log, mat)*

Typenlehre *f* • theory of (constitutional) types *(Kretschmer) (psy)* < Konstitutionstypus

Typenlogik *f* • typed logic *(log)* → Typentheorie

Typenlehre der Moral *f* • typology of morals *(Nietzsche) (eth)*

Typenpsychologie *f* • psychology of types *(Jung, Kretschmer) (psy)*

Typentheorie *f* • theory of types, (logical) type theory *(Russell) (log, mat)*

Typenunterscheidung *f* • type difference *(log, mat)*

Typik *f* • typic, typology *(Kant) (epi)*

Typik der (reinen praktischen) Urteilskraft *f* • typic/typology of (pure practical) judg(e)-ment *(Kant) (epi)*

Typik der Begriffe *f* • typic/typology of concepts *(Kant) (epi)*

Typische, das *n* • the typical *(aes)* < Charakteristische, das

Typogenetik *f* • typogenetics *(Hofstadter) (nat, mat)*

typogenetischer Code *m* • typogenetic code *(Hofstadter) (nat, mat)*

Typologie *f* • typology *(gep)*

typologischer Psychologismus *m* • typological psychologism *(psy)*

Tyrannei *f* • tyranny, despotism *(pol)*

Tyrannenmord *m* • tyrannicide *(pol, eth)*

Tyrannei des Unbedingten *f* • tyranny of the unconditional *(Nietzsche) (met, eth)*

U

Übel n • evil (rel, eth)

Übel, kleineres n • (the) lesser evil (eth) →
minus malum

Übel, notwendiges n • necessary evil (eth)

Übeltäter m • evil-doer, wrongdoer,
malefactor (eth, jur)

Übelwollen n • will to evil (eth) < Wille zum
Bösen

übelwollen, jemandem • to be ill-disposed
toward somebody (eth)

Überalterung der Gesellschaft f • super-
annuation of society (soc)

Überangebot n • oversupply, excess supply
(eco)

Überbau m • superstructure (Marx etc) (soc)
↔ Unterbau < ideeller Überbau

Überbevölkerung f • overpopulation (soc)

Überdeterminiertheit f • over-determination
(sci, aes) < Redundanz

Überdeterminierung f → Überdeterminiertheit

Überdrußgesellschaft f • surfeit society (soc)

Übereinkommen n → Übereinkunft

Übereinkunft f • agreement, arrangement (jur)

Übereinkunft von Wissen und Glauben f •
agreement/concord of reason and faith (rel,
epi)

Übereinstimmung f • agreement, correspondence, conformity (gep) < Konsens

Übereinstimmung mit der Natur f • accordance with nature (gep)

Übereinstimmung mit sich selbst f → Konsistenz

Übereinstimmung, strukturelle f • structural
agreement, isomorphism (sys)

**Übereinstimmung und Nichtübereinstim-
mung von Begriffen** f f • agreement and
disagreement of ideas (Locke) (epi)

Übereinstimmungskoeffizient m • coefficient
of agreement (sci, mat)

Überentwicklung f • overdevelopment (eco)
< nachhaltiges Wachstum

Überfluß m • superfluity, superabundance,
excess (eco)

Überflußgesellschaft f • affluent society
(Galbraith) (eco, soc) < Konsumismus,
Wohlstandsgesellschaft

Überflüssigkeit des Seins f • superfluity/
excessiveness of being (Sartre) (met)

Überfremdung f • foreign infiltration, excessive immigration, being swamped by foreigners (pol) < unkontrollierte Einwanderung

Überführungstheorem n • substitution
theorem (log)

Überfülle des Lebens f • superabundance of
life (Nietzsche) (met)

Übergang m • transition (met)

Übergang vom Kapitalismus zum Sozialismus
m • transition from capitalism to socialism
(Marx etc) (soc)

Übergang vom Leben zum Tod m • passage/
transition from life to death (nat, rel)

Übergang von Quantität zur Qualität m →
Umschlag von Quantität in Qualität

Übergangsbestimmungen pl • provisional
regulations (jur, pol)

Übergangslösung f • transitional/provisional
solution (gep)

Übergangsnetzwerk, erweitertes n • aug-
mented transition network, ATN (lan, log)

Übergangsphase f • transition stage/period
(gep)

Übergeordnetheit f • superordination (gep)

übergeschichtlich • transhistorical (his)

Übergeschichtlichkeit f • transhistoricity (his)

Übergreifende, das n • the overreaching
(Jaspers) (met)

übergreifender Konsens m • overlapping
consensus (Rawls etc) (eth, pol)

Über-Ich n • superego (Freud etc) (psy)

Überindividualität f • supra-individuality (met,
soc)

überirdisch • celestial, heavenly, super-
terrestrial (rel)

überkategorial • hyper-categorical (epi, lan)

Überkompensation f • overcompensation (psy)

Überkomplexität f • hypercomplexity (gep)

Überlagerungsraum m • covering space (mat)

Überlassenschaft f • cession (jur)

Überleben des/der Tüchtigsten n • survival of
the fittest (Darwin etc) (nat, soc) < Existenzkampf, Kampf ums Dasein, Kampf ums
Überleben

Überlebenschance f • chance of survival (nat,
eco)

Überlebensfähigkeit f • fitness for survival
(nat)

Überlebensmaschine, Mensch als *m* • man as survival machine *(nat, ant, soc)*

Überlebensqualität *f* • survival quality *(nat)* → Überlebenswert < Selektionsprämie

Überlebensstrategie *f* • survival strategy *(nat, eco)*

Überlebenswahrscheinlichkeit *f* • probability of survival *(nat)*

Überlebenswert *m* • survival value *(nat)* → Überlebensqualität

Überlegenheit einer Kultur *f* • superiority of a culture *(Spengler etc) (cul)*

Überlegenheitskomplex *m* • superiority complex *(psy)* ↔ Minderwertigkeitskomplex

Überlegenheitskonkurrenz *f* • competition for mastery/domination (over others) *(Rousseau etc) (soc)*

Überlegenheitsstreben *n* • striving towards superiority *(Adler etc) (psy)*

Überlegung *f* • deliberation, consideration *(gep)*

Überlegung, rationale *f* • rational deliberation *(epi)*

Überlegungsgleichgewicht *n* • reflective equilibrium *(Rawls) (eth)* → reflexives Gleichgewicht

Überlieferung *f* • tradition *(cul, his)*

Überlieferung, mündliche *f* • oral tradition *(cul, his)* < erzählte Geschichte

Übermacht der Natur *f* • superiority of nature *(nat, met)*

Übermensch *m* • superman, overman *(Nietzsche) (ant, met)*

übermenschlich • superhuman *(Nietzsche) (ant, met)*

Übernahme *f* • takeover *(eco)*

Übernahmeregel *f* • carry-over rule *(log, mat)* → Übertragungsregel

übernational • supranational *(pol)*

übernatürlich • supernatural, supranatural *(rel, met, eso)*

Übernatürliche, das *n* • the supernatural/ supranatural *(rel, met, eso)*

übernatürliche Kräfte *pl* • supernatural powers *(eso)*

übernatürliche Sätze *pl* • non-natural sentences *(eth)*, supernatural statements *(eth, met)*

übernatürliche Zahlen *pl* • supernatural numbers, supernaturals *(mat)*

Übernutzung *f* • over-utilization *(env)*

Überparteilichkeit *f* • supra-partisanism, non-partisan character *(pol)* < Objektivität

Überproduktion *f* • overproduction, excess production *(eco)*

Überproduktionskrise *f* • overproduction crisis *(Marx) (soc)*

Überprüfbarkeit *f* • testability *(sci)*

Überprüfbarkeitskriterien *pl* • testability criteria *(sci)*

Überprüfung, logische *f* • logical verification *(log, sci)*

Überraschungsangriff *m* • surprise attack *(pol, dec)*

Überreaktion *f* • overreaction *(psy)*

überredende Funktion der Sprache *f* • persuasive function of language *(lan)* → Sprachfunktion, persuasive

Überredungskunst *f* • art of persuasion, persuasiveness *(lan)* < Rhetorik, Sophistik

Überreiztheit *f* • over-excitability *(Nietzsche) (psy)*

Überrumpelungstaktik *f* • surpise/rush tactics *(pol, dec)*

Überschuß *m* • surplus *(eco)*

Überschußproduktion *f* • surplus production *(eco)*

Überschußwirtschaft *f* • surplus economy *(eco)*

Überschwang der Gefühle *m* • ecstasy of feelings *(psy)*

Überseele *f* • oversoul *(Emerson) (met)*

Übersetzungsmaxime *f* • maxim of translation *(Quine) (lan)*

Übersetzungsunbestimmtheit *f* • indeterminacy of translation *(Quine etc) (epi, lan)*

Übersichtlichkeit *f* • perspicuity *(Wittgenstein etc) (lan)* < Perspikuität

übersinnlich • extrasensory, supersensory *(met, rel, eso)*

Übersinnliche, das *n* • the supersensory/ supersensual *(met, rel, eso)*

übersinnliche Erfahrungsquelle *f* • extrasensory/supersensory source of experience *(rel, eso)*

übersinnliche Fähigkeiten *pl* • supernatural faculties *(eso)*

übersinnliche Wahrnehmung *f* • extrasensory perception, ESP, supersensory/supersensible perception *(psy, eso)*

übersinnliche Welt *f* • supersensual/ supersensible world *(Kant) (met)*

übersinnliches Objekt *n* • supersensuous object *(met)*

Überstieg *m* • transmigration *(met)*

Übertier *n* • superbeast *(Nietzsche) (ant)*

Übertragsregel *f* • carry-over rule *(log, mat)* → Übernahmeregel

Übertragung *f* • transfer *(Freud) (psy)*

Übertragung von Rechten *f* • transfer of rights *(jur)*

Übertragungsprinzip *n* • principle of transference *(Popper) (epi, sci)*

Übertreffen der Pflicht *n* • supererogation *(eth)* → Supererogation

Übertribunalisierung *f* • overtribunalization *(eth)*

Übervater *m* • overlord *(Freud) (psy)*

Überverallgemeinerung *f* • overgeneralization *(sci)*

Überverdienstlichkeit *f* → Supererogation

Übervereinfachung *f* • oversimplification *(sci)*

Überwachung *f* • surveillance *(Foucault etc) (epi, pol)*

Überwachungsausschuß *m* • watch committee *(pol)*

Überwachungsstaat *m* • surveillance state, big-brother state *(soc)* < Polizeistaat

Überwelt *f* • supra-world *(Nietzsche) (met)*

Überweltlichkeit der Seele *f* • otherworldliness/ultramundanity of the soul *(rel)*

Überwindung der Metaphysik *f* • the overcoming of metaphysics *(met)* → Ende der Metaphysik < nachmetaphysisches Denken

Überzeitlichkeit *f* • timelessness *(met)* → Zeitlosigkeit < Ewigkeit

Überzeugung *f* • belief, conviction *(epi)*

Überzeugung, empirische *f* • empirical belief *(Parsons) (soc)*

Überzeugung, existenzielle *f* • existential belief *(Parsons) (soc, psy)*

Überzeugungskunst *f* • art of persuasion *(lan)*

Überzeugungstäter *m* • conscientious offender, offender acting on grounds of conscience *(jur, eth)*

Überzeugungs-Wert-Matrix *f* • belief-value matrix *(soc, mat)*

Üblichkeitsausdruck *m* → alltäglicher Sprachgebrauch

Uhrenparadox *n* • clock paradox *(Einstein) (nat)* → Zeitparadox

Uhrenvergleich *m* • the universe as a clock, comparison of the universe with a clock *(Leibniz, Spinoza) (met)*

Ultimagenitur *f* • ultimageniture *(jur)* → Recht des Letztgeborenen ↔ Primogenitur

Ultrafilter *m* • ultrafilter *(ont)*

Ultraintuitionismus *m* • ultraintuitionism *(mat)*

Ultralinker *m* • ultra-leftist *(pol)* < Linksradikalismus

Ultrarealismus *m* • ultra-realism, radical realism *(epi, met)*

Ultraschalldiagnose *f* • ultrasound diagnosis *(eth)* < selektive Abtreibung

Ultrastabilität *f* • ultrastability *(sys)*

Um-Willen • the for-the-sake-of *(Heidegger etc) (ont, ant)*

Um-Zu • the in-order-to *(Heidegger) (ont, ant)*

Umbruch, sozialer *m* • social change/upheaval *(soc, pol)*

Umerziehung *f* • re-education *(pol)*

Umfang des Begriffs *m* → Begriffsumfang

Umfangsgleichheit *f* • coextensiveness *(log, lan)* ↔ Inhaltsgleichheit; coincidence *(mat)*

Umfangslogik *f* • logic of extension *(log)*

Umfassende, das *n* • the inclusive *(met, gep)* < allumfassend

umfassende Theorie *f* • enveloping theory *(sci)*

Umfeld, wirtschaftliches *n* • economic environment *(eco)*

Umformung, logische *f* • logical transformation *(log)*

Umformungsregel *f* • transformation rule *(lan)* → Transformationsregel

Umgang *m* • dealing(s) with *(Heidegger) (ont, ant)*

Umgänglichkeit, soziale *f* • sociability *(soc, eth)*

Umgangssprache *f* • everyday language, vernacular *(lan)* → Alltagssprache < Normalsprache

umgangssprachlicher Ausdruck *m* • ordinary language expression, expression of everyday language *(lan)*

umgekehrt proportional • inversely proportional *(log, mat)*

umgekehrte Diskriminierung *f* • reverse discrimination *(eth, pol)* < Vorzugsbehandlung

umgekehrte polnische Notation *f* • reverse Polish notation *(Lukasiewicz) (log)* < Notation, polnische

umgekehrte Teilthese *f* • inverse partial thesis *(sci)* < Prognose

umgekehrter Rassismus *m* • reverse racism *(soc, pol)*

umgekehrtes Verhältnis *n* • inverse relation *(gen)*

Umgreifende, das *n* • the encompassing *(Heidegger, Jaspers) (met, ont)*

umgreifende Seinsweisen *pl* • encompassed modes of being *(Jaspers) (met)*

umgreifendes Ganzes *n* • encompassing whole *(Jaspers) (met)*

Umhafte, das *n* • the aroundness *(Heidegger) (ont)*

Umkehr, innere *f* • inner change/conversion *(Buber etc) (eth, rel)*

Umkehrfunktion *f* • inverse function *(mat)*

Umkehrschluß *m* • inversion of an argument, inverse syllogism *(log)*

Umkehrung *f* • reversal *(gen)*

Umkehrungsfunktion *f* • inversion function *(mat)*

Umlaufmittel *n* • medium/means of circulation *(Marx) (eco)* → Zirkulationsmittel

Umnachtung, geistige *f* • mental derangement *(psy)*

Umraum *m* • surrounding space *(Husserl etc) (met)*

Umschlag von Quantität in Qualität *m* • transformation of quantity into quality *(Hegel, Marx etc) (met)*

Umschreibung *f* • paraphrase, circumscription, periphrasis, paraphrasis *(lan)*

Umschwung des Glücks *m* • turn of fortune *(gep)* < Glücksrad

Umsicht *f* • circumspection, for(e)-sight *(Heidegger) (ont)*, prudence *(rel, eth)*

Umsonst, das *n* • gratuité, gratuity *(Sartre) (met)*

Umstände, mildernde *pl* • mitigating circumstances *(jur)* < Unzurechnungsfähigkeit

Umstände, soziale *pl* • social conditions *(Marx etc) (soc)* < Milieutheorie

Umstrukturierung der Lebenswelt *f* • restructuring of the lifeworld *(Habermas etc) (soc)*

Umsturz *m* • revolution *(pol)*

Umverteilung des Einkommens *f* • redistribution of income *(eco)* → Einkommensumverteilung, Redistribution, Reichtumstransfer

Umverteilungspolitik *f* • redistribution policy *(eco, pol)* < Vermögensverteilung

Umverteilungswirtschaft *f* • redistributive economy *(eco)*

umvolken • to displace population, umvolken° *(pol)* < ethnische Säuberung

Umwegrentabilität *f* • indirect profitability *(eco)* < indirekter Nutzen

Umwelt *f* • environment *(nat, soc, env)* < Umfeld, wirtschaftliches

Umwelt-Erbschaft-Kontroverse *f* • environment-heredity controversy, nature-nurture controversy *(ant, soc)* → Natur-Kultur-Kontroverse

Umwelt, lebenswerte *f* • livable environment *(soc, env)*

Umweltauflage *f* • ecological requirement *(env)*

Umweltauswirkungen *pl* • ecological impact, environmental effects *(env)*

umweltbedingt • environmentally conditioned *(env)*

Umweltbelastung *f* • burden on the environment, ecological damage *(env)*

umweltbewußt • eco-sensitive, ecology-minded, environmentally aware *(env)*

Umweltbewußtsein *n* • environmental/ecological awareness, green consciousness *(env)*

Umweltdeterminismus *m* • environmental/ geographical determinism *(nat, cul)* < Natur-Kultur-Kontroverse

Umwelteinflüsse *pl* • environmental influences *(env)*

Umwelteingriff *m* • intrusion on the environment *(env)*

Umwelterziehung *f* • environmental education *(env)*

Umweltethik *f* • environmental ethics *(eth, env)*

umweltfeindlich • ecologically harmful/ noxious *(env)*

Umweltforschung *f* • environmental research/ studies *(env)* → Umweltwissenschaft

umweltfreundlich • environmentally friendly, eco-friendly *(env)* → umweltverträglich

Umweltgerechtigkeit *f* • environmental justice *(eth, env)*

Umweltgift *n* • environmental pollutant *(env)*

Umwelthaftung *f* • environmental liability *(jur, env)*

Umweltkatastrophe *f* • environmental catastrophe/disaster *(env)*

Umweltkriminalität *f* • environmental crime/ criminality *(jur, env)*

Umweltkrise *f* • ecological/environmental crisis *(env)*

Umweltphilosophie *f* • environmental philosophy *(env)*

Umweltpolitik *f* • ecological/environmental policy *(pol, env)*

Umweltproblem *n* • ecological/environmental problem *(env)*

Umweltqualität *f* • quality of the environment *(env)*

Umweltschaden *m* • environmental/ecological damage *(env)*

umweltschonend → umweltfreundlich

Umweltschutz *m* • environmental protection, environmentalism, protection of the environment, conservationism *(env)* → Naturschutz

Umweltschützer *m* • environmentalist, conservationist *(env)*

Umweltschutzorganisation *f* • environmental protection organization, ecology group *(env)*

Umweltschutztechnik *f* • conservation technology *(tec, env)*

Umweltsteuer *f* • environmental taxation *(eco)*

Umwelttheorie *f* → Milieutheorie

Umweltverschmutzer *m* • polluter *(env)*

Umweltverschmutzung *f* • environmental pollution/contamination *(env)*

umweltverträglich • eco-compatible, environmentally compatible/sound *(env)* → umweltfreundlich

Umweltverträglichkeit *f* • eco-compatibility, environmental compatibility/soundness *(env)*

Umweltverträglichkeitsprüfung *f* • environmental impact evaluation *(env)*

Umweltwirtschaft *f* • environmental industry *(eco, env)*

Umweltwissenschaft *f* • environmental science, ecology *(env)* → Umweltforschung

Umweltzerstörung *f* • environmental damage *(env)*

Umwertung *f* • transvaluation, revaluation *(eth)*

Umwertung aller Werte *f* • transvaluation/revaluation of all values *(Nietzsche) (eth)* < Moral, Wandel der

Unabgeschlossenheitstheorem *n* • incompleteness theorem *(Gödel) (mat, log)* < Unvollständigkeitsbeweis

unabhängige Realität *f* • independent reality *(met)*

unabhängige Variable *f* • independent variable *(mat, log)* ↔ abhängige Variable

unabhängiger Grund *m* • independent reason/cause *(met, rel)* < causa sui

Unabhängigkeit, materielle *f* • material independence/independency *(eco, soc)* < Autarkie

Unabhängigkeit von Axiomen *f* • independence/independency of axioms *(log)*

Unabhängigkeitsbewegung *f* • independence movement *(pol)*

Unabhängigkeitsbeweis *m* • independence proof, proof of independency *(log)*

Unabhängigkeitskrieg *m* • war of independence *(pol)*

Unabhängigkeitserklärung *f* • declaration of independence *(pol)*

unabwendbares Schicksal *n* • inescapable destiny/fate *(met, rel)* < Kismet

Unähnlichkeit *f* • dissimilarity *(gep)* → Ungleichartigkeit

Unanfechtbarkeitsbedingung *f* • incontestability/non-defeasibility condition/clause *(sci)*

Unangemessenheit *f* • inappropriateness, inadequacy *(gep)* → Inadäquatheit ↔ Angemessenheit

unangepaßtes Wesen *n* • unadjusted being *(ant, soc)*

unästhetisch • unaesthetic *(aes)*

unaufhebbare Differenz *f* • insurmountable difference *(met)*

unaufhebbarer Gegensatz *m* • irremediable antagonism, fundamental opposition *(log)*

Unaufrichtigkeit *f* • insincerity *(eth)*

Unaussprechliche, das *n* → Unsagbare, das

unausweichliche Schlußfolgerung *f* • inescapable conclusion *(log)*

Unbedenklichkeitsnachweis *m* • clearance certificate *(env)*

Unbedenklichkeitsüberprüfung *f* • security clearance *(env)*

Unbedingende, das *n* • the unconditioning *(Nietzsche) (met)*

unbedingt • unconditional *(gep)*

Unbedingte, das *n* • the unconditioned *(rel, ont)*

unbedingte Bedingung *f* • unconditioned condition *(Kant) (epi)* < notwendige Bedingung

unbedingte Einheit *f* • unconditioned unity *(Kant) (epi)*

unbedingte Notwendigkeit *f* • unconditioned necessity *(epi, met)*

unbedingter Gehorsam *m* • unconditional obedience *(pol)*

unbedingter Reflex *m* • unconditioned reflex *(psy)*

unbedingter Wert des Sittlichen *m* • unconditional value of morality *(eth)*

unbedingtes Gebot *n* • unconditioned command *(Kant) (eth)*

Unbefangenheit *f* • impartiality *(jur)*

unbefleckte Empfängnis *f* • Immaculate Conception *(rel)*

unbefriedetes Dasein *n* • unfulfilled existence *(Kierkegaard) (rel, ant)*

unbegrenzt • unlimited, limitless, boundless *(gep)*

Unbegrenztheit *f* • unlimitedness, boundlessness *(met)* → Infinität

Unbehagen in der Kultur *n* • unease/discomfort with culture/civilization *(Freud etc) (psy, cul)* < W 1119

unbelebte Natur *f* • inanimate nature/world *(nat)* → anorganische Natur

Unbeirrbarkeit *f* • singlemindedness *(eth, asp)*

Unberechenbarkeit *f* • unpredictability *(dec)* → Imponderabilität

unberührbare Kaste *f* • untouchable caste, the untouchables *(soc)* < Paria

Unbescholtenheit *f* • lack of previous convictions *(jur)*

unbeschränkte Annahmefreiheit *f* • unrestricted freedom of assumption *(Meinong)* *(sci)*

unbeschränkte Herrschaft *f* • unlimited/absolute power, unrestricted domination *(pol)*

unbeseelt • inanimate *(nat, rel)*

unbeseelte Natur *f* • inanimate nature *(met)*

Unbestechlichkeit *f* • integrity, incorruptibility *(eth)*

Unbestimmbarkeit *f* • indeterminability, indeterminacy *(sci, lan, log)* → Indeterminabilität

Unbestimmbarkeit der Referenz *f* • indeterminacy of reference *(lan)*

Unbestimmbarkeit der Übersetzung *f* → Unbestimmtheit der Übersetzung

Unbestimmte, das *n* • (▷ das nicht Festgelegte) the indetermined, the indeterminate; (▷ das Grenzenlose) the indefinite *(met)* → apeiron

unbestimmte Qualität *f* • indeterminate/indefinable quality *(met)*

unbestimmter Ausdruck *m* • indeterminate form *(mat)*

unbestimmter Begriff *m* • indeterminate concept *(Hegel)* *(epi, met)*

Unbestimmtheit *f* • indeterminacy, vagueness *(log, lan)* < Vagheit, unscharfe Menge

Unbestimmtheit der Übersetzung *f* • indeterminacy of translation *(Quine etc)* *(epi, lan)*

Unbestimmtheitsformel *f* • indeterminacy formula *(sci, nat)*

Unbestimmtheitsorte *pl* • loci of indeterminacy *(aes)* < Informationsästhetik

Unbestimmtheitsrelation *f* • uncertainty/indeterminacy principle *(Heisenberg)* *(nat)* → Unschärferelation, Heisenbergsches Unbestimmtheitsaxiom < Quantentheorie

unbewegter Beweger *m* • unmoved mover *(Aristotle)* *(met)* → primum mobile, erster Beweger < causa sui; Ursache, unverursachte

unbeweisbar • unprovable, indemonstrable *(log)*

Unbeweisbarkeit *f* • unprovability, indemonstrability, unprovableness *(log)*

unbewiesene Zukunft *f* • undemonstrated future *(Nietzsche)* *(met)*

unbewußt • unconscious, subconscious, infraconscious° *(psy)* < vorbewußt

Unbewußte, das *n* • the unconscious/subconscious *(psy)* < W 775, 1052, 1336

unbewußte Wünsche *pl* • unconscious desires/wishes *(Freud)* *(psy)*

Unbewußten, Psychologie des *f* • psychology of the unconscious *(Freud etc)* *(psy)*

unbewußter Zustand *m* • unconscious state *(psy)*

unbezweifelbare Gewißheit *f* • unquestionable/indubitable certainty *(Descartes)* *(epi)* < sicheres Wissen

unbezweifelbare Tatsache *f* • undubitable/unquestionable/self-evident fact *(epi)* < Evidenz

unbezweifelbare Wahrheit *f* • indubitable truth *(epi)*

Unbezweifelbarkeit *f* • indubitability *(epi)* < Gewißheit, sicheres Wissen, unbezweifelbare Gewißheit, verläßliches Wissen

unchristlich • unchristian *(rel)*

Undefinierbarkeit *f* • indefinability *(log)* < semantische Primitive

undefinierter Term *m* • undefined/primitive term *(Tarski)* *(lan)* → einfacher Term

Undenkbare, das *n* • the unthinkable *(Wittgenstein etc)* *(epi, met)* < Unfaßbarkeit; Unsagbare, das

Undenkbarkeit *f* • inconceivability, inconceivableness *(epi)*

undifferenzierte Weisen des Existierens *pl* • undifferentiated modes of existence/existing *(Heidegger)* *(ont, ant)*

Undurchdringlichkeit *f* • impenetrability *(met)* → Impenetrabilität

Unechte im Geistesleben, das *n* • the inauthentic/spurious in the life of the spirit *(N. Hartmann)* *(ont)*

Uneigennützigkeit *f* • selflessness *(eth)* → Altruismus, Selbstlosigkeit

uneigentliche Existenz *f* • inauthentic existence *(Heidegger)* *(ant, ont)*

uneigentlicher Begriff *m* • improper concept *(Carnap)* *(epi)*

uneigentlicher Eigenname *m* • degenerate proper name *(lan)*

Uneigentlichkeit *f* • inauthenticity *(Heidegger)* *(ont)* ↔ Eigentlichkeit < Man, das

unendlich • (▷ unbegrenzt) infinite, (▷ unbestimmt) indefinite *(mat, log, met)*

unendlichdimensional • infinite-dimensional *(mat)*

Unendliche, das *n* • the infinite *(met, rel)* < Unendlichkeit

unendliche Gruppe *f* • infinite group *(mat)*

unendliche Teilbarkeit *f* • infinite divisibility *(nat, mat)*

unendliche Teilung *f* • infinite division *(epi, mat)*

unendlicher Gegensatz *m* • infinite contradiction *(met)*

unendlicher Progreß *m* • infinite progress
(*Condillac etc*) (*soc*) < Fortschrittsgläubigkeit

unendlicher Regreß *m* • infinite regress (*log,
epi, mat*)

unendliches Produkt *n* • infinite product (*mat*)

unendliches Spiel *n* • infinite game (*dec*)

Unendlichkeit *f* • infinity, boundlessness,
infinitude, illimitability (*met, mat*) < Apeiron,
Grenzenlosigkeit

Unendlichkeit der göttlichen Substanz *f* • infinity of the divine substance (*Spinoza*) (*met*)

Unendlichkeit der Welt *f* • infinity/
boundlessness of the world (*nat, met*)

Unendlichkeit von Raum und Zeit *f* • infinity
of space and time (*nat, met*)

Unendlichkeitsaxiom *n* • axiom of infinity
(*log*)

Unendlichkeitsbegriff *m* • notion/concept of
infinity (*nat, met*)

Unentscheidbarkeit *f* • undecidability (*log*)

Unerforschbarkeit der Referenz *f* • indeter-
minacy/inscrutability of reference (*Quine
etc*) (*log, lan*)

Unergründliche, das *n* • the inscrutable/
impenetrable/unfathomable (*met*)

Unergründlichkeit *f* • inscrutability,
impenetrability (*epi, met*)

Unergründlichkeit des göttlichen Willens *f* •
inscrutability/impenetrability of the divine
will (*rel*)

Unergründlichkeit des Vorherwissens Gottes
f • inscrutability/impenetrability of divine
foreknowledge (*Malebranche*) (*rel*)

Unerkennbare, das *n* • the unknowable (*epi*)

unerkennbare Sphäre des Ding-an-sich, die *f* •
the inscrutable realm of the thing-in-itself
(*Kant*) (*met*)

Unerkennbarkeit *f* • unknowability (*epi*)

Unersättlichkeit *f* • insatiability (*eco, eth*)
< Pleonexie

Unerschrockenheit *f* • intrepidity, fearlessness
(*psy, eth*) < Tapferkeit

unerwünschte Geburt *f* • unwanted/wrongful
birth (*eth*)

unerwünschtes Leben *n* • unwanted/wrongful
life (*eth*)

Unfähigkeit, trainierte *f* • trained incapacity
(*Veblen*) (*soc, psy*)

Unfaßbarkeit *f* • (▷ Undenkbarkeit) incomprehensibility, inconceivability (*min, met*), (▷
Unaussprechlichkeit) ineffability (*lan*)

Unfehlbarkeit *f* • infallibility (*rel, gep*) → Infallibilität

Unfehlbarkeit, päpstliche *f* • papal infallibility
(*rel*)

Unfehlbarkeitsdogma *n* • dogma of (papal)
infallibility (*rel*)

Unfehlbarkeitslehre *f* • infallibilism (*rel*) →
Infallibilismus

unfreier Wille *m* • unfree will (*met*)

unfreiwillige Handlung *f* • involuntary
act/action (*act, eth*)

Unfreiwilligkeit *f* • involuntariness (*eth*)
< Zwang

Unfrieden *m* • discord, strife (*eth*)

Unfruchtbarkeit *f* • infertility (*nat*) < Reproduktionsmedizin

unfundierte Aussage *f* • unfounded statement/
assertion (*sci*)

ungegenständliche Wahrnehmung *f* • non-
objectual perception (*epi*)

Ungehorsam, ziviler *m* • civil disobedience
(*eth, pol*) < gewaltloser Widerstand;
Widerstand, passiver; Widerstandsrecht

ungerechtes Gesetz *n* • unjust law (*jur*)

Ungerechtigkeit *f* • injustice, unfairness (*eth,
jur*)

ungeschichtliche Tatsache *f* • unhistorical fact
(*his*) < Übergeschichtlichkeit

ungeschriebenes Gesetz *n* • unwritten law
(*jur*) < Gewohnheitsrecht, Naturrecht

ungeschriebenes Recht *n* → ungeschriebenes
Gesetz

ungesellige Geselligkeit *f* • asocial/unsocial
sociability (*Kant*) (*ant, soc, eth*)

Ungeselligkeit *f* • unsociability (*soc, eth*)

Ungesetzlichkeit *f* • illegality, unlawfulness
(*jur*) → Illegalität

Ungewißheit *f* • uncertainty (*epi, sci*)

Unglaube *m* • unbelief (*rel*), disbelief (*gep*)

Ungläubigkeit *f* • infidelity (*rel*)

Ungleichartigkeit *f* • dissimilarity (*gep*) →
Unähnlichkeit

Ungleichbehandlung *f* • unequal treatment,
discrimination (*jur, eth*) → Diskriminierung

Ungleichgewicht *n* • nonequilibrium,
imbalance (*sys*)

Ungleichheit *f* • inequality (*soc, eth, mat*)

Ungleichheit der Geschlechter *f* • gender
inequality, inequality of the sexes (*fem, nat*)
< Differenzfeminismus

Ungleichheit der Menschen *f* • inequality of
man (*soc*)

Ungleichheit, logische *f* • logical inequality
(*log*)

Ungleichheit, natürliche und künstliche *f* •
natural and artificial inequality (*nat, soc*)
< natürliche Ungleichheit, Natur-Kultur-
Kontroverse

Ungleichheiten, menschengemachte *pl* • manmade inequalities *(soc)*

Ungleichheitszeichen *n* • inequality sign/ symbol *(log, mat)*

Ungleichmäßigkeit *f* • irregularity, assymmetry *(gep)* < Ametrie

Ungleichung *f* • inequality *(mat)*

Ungleichzeitigkeit *f* • non-simultaneity *(nat, met)* ↔ Gleichzeitigkeit

Unglück *n* • (▷ soziales Elend) misery, distress, (▷ Unglücksfall) bad luck, (▷ unglücklicher Seelenzustand) unhappiness, misery, distress *(eth, psy)*

unglückliche Äußerung *f* • infelicitous remark/ expression *(lan, act)* < Angemessenheit

unglückliches Bewußtsein *n* • unhappy consciousness *(Hegel) (met)*

Ungnade *f* • disgrace, disfavour *(rel)*

Ungrund *m* • non-ground, Nonground *(Heidegger) (ont)*

ungültig • invalid *(log, jur)*

Ungültigkeit *f* • invalidity *(log, jur)*

Ungültigkeitserklärung *f* • nullification *(jur)* < Widerruf

unharmonisch • inharmonious, discordant *(aes)* < Harmonie

Unheil *n* • harm, disaster *(gen)*

Unheilsprophezeihung *f* • prophecy of doom *(gep)* < Kassandraruf, Dystopie

Unheimlichkeit *f* • unsettledness *(Heidegger) (ont)*, uncanniness *(psy)*

Unhinterfragbarkeit *f* • unquestionability, indubitability, indisputability *(epi, met)*

uniforme Interpretation *f* • uniform interpretation *(lan)*

Uniformität der Natur *f* • uniformity of nature *(nat, met)*

Uniformitätsprinzip *n* • uniformity principle, principle of uniformity *(epi, met)* → Regularitätsprinzip

Unilateralismus *m* • unilateralism *(pol, eth)* ↔ Multilateralismus

uninteressierte Betrachtung *f* • disinterested contemplation *(aes)* < interesseloses Wohlgefallen

uninteressiertes Urteil *n* • disinterested judg(e)ment *(Kant) (log, aes)*

uninteressiertes Wohlgefallen *n* → interesseloses Wohlgefallen

Uninteressiertheit *f* • uninterestedness *(psy)*

unio mystica *f* • mystic(al) union *(rel, eso)* → mystische Vereinigung

Union von Geist und Körper *f* → Einheit von Geist und Körper

universal-deduktive Erklärung *f* • universaldeductive explanation *(sci)*

universal-wahrscheinlichkeitstheoretische Erklärung *f* • universal-probabilistic explanation *(sci)*

Universalbegriff *m* • universal concept, universal *(log, lan)* → Gattungsbegriff < Universalien

universale Eigenschaft *f* • universal property *(met)*

universale Geltung *f* • universal validity *(epi, log)*

universaler Mensch *m* • universal man *(Marx)* *(ant, soc)* → universeller Mensch

Universalgenie *n* • universal genius *(gep)*

Universalgeschichte *f* • universal history *(his)* < Weltgeschichte

Universalgesetz *n* • universal/general law *(nat, sci, eth)*

Universalgrammatik *f* • Universal Grammar, UG *(Chomsky) (lan)* < Tiefengrammatik

Universalien *pl* • universals *(log, lan, met)* < Universalbegriff, Gattungsbegriff

Universalien, evolutionäre *pl* • evolutionary universals *(nat)*

Universalien im Geiste Gottes *pl* • universals in God's mind *(Duns Scotus) (met, rel)*

Universalien, linguistische *pl* • language/ linguistic universals *(lan)*

Universalienlehre *f* • theory of universals *(Abelard etc) (met)*

Universalienproblem *n* • problem of universals *(epi, met)*

Universalienrealismus *m* • realism regarding universals *(epi, met)*

Universalienstreit *m* • universals controversy, debate about universals *(epi, met)*

Universalisierbarkeit *f* • universalizability *(sci, eth)* → Verallgemeinerungsfähigkeit

Universalismus *m* • universalism *(met)* ↔ Partikularismus

universalistische Annahme *f* • universalist assumption *(epi, ont)*

Universalität der Bedürfnisse *f* • universality of needs *(Marx) (soc)*

Universalklasse *f* • universal class *(Russell) (log)*

Universalkunstwerk *n* → Gesamtkunstwerk

Universalmathematik *f* • mathesis universalis *(Leibniz, Husserl) (met, mat)* → mathesis universalis

Universalpoesie *f* • universal poetry *(Schlegel) (aes)*

Universalpragmatik *f* • universal pragmatics *(Apel, Habermas) (lan)*

Universalrechner *m* • Universal Computing Machine *(Neumann) (AI)*

Universalskepsis *f* • universal scepticism *(epi)*

Universalslang *m* • universal slang *(Neurath) (lan)* < Wissenschaftssprache

Universalsprache *f* • universal language *(lan)* → characteristica universalis

Universalurteil *n* • universal statement/ judg(e)ment *(log, lan)* → Allsatz

Universalwissen *n* • universal knowledge *(epi)*

Universalwissenschaft *f* • universal science *(sci)* < Einheitswissenschaft

universelle Maxime *f* • universal maxim *(Kant) (eth)* < kategorischer Imperativ

universelle Normen *pl* • universal norms *(eth)*

universelle Verallgemeinerung *f* • universal generalization *(sci, eth)*

universelle Zeit *f* • universal time *(nat)* < Zeit, absolute

universeller Diskurs *m* • universal discourse *(Habermas etc) (lan, eth)*

universeller Friede *m* • universal peace *(eth, pol)* < ewiger Friede, Weltfrieden

universeller Mensch *m* • universal man *(Marx) (ant, soc)* → universaler Mensch

universeller Zweifel *m* • universal doubt *(Descartes) (epi)*

Universum *n* • universe *(nat)*

Universum der Rede *n* • universe of discourse *(lan, soc)*

univok • univocal, unequivocal *(log)* ↔ äquivok

Unkenntnis *f* • ignorance *(epi)* < docta ignorantia

unkontrollierte Einwanderung *f* • uncontrolled immigration *(pol)* < Überfremdung

unkörperlich • incorporeal *(met)* → asomatisch, körperlos

unkörperliche Intelligenzen *pl* • incorporeal intelligences *(met)*

unkörperlicher Geist *m* • incorporeal spirit *(met)*

unkörperliches Sein *n* • incorporeal being *(met)*

Unkörperlichkeit *f* • incorporeality *(met)*

Unkörperlichkeit des Geistes *f* • incorporeality of the mind *(met, min)*

Unkorrigierbarkeit *f* • incorrigibility *(sci, sys)* < Irreversibilität

Unkunst *f* • non-art *(aes)* < entartete Kunst

Unlogik *f* • illogic, illogicality *(log)*

unlogisch • illogical *(log)*

unlösbares Problem *n* • unsolvable problem *(sci)* → Aporie < Paradoxie, Paradox(on)

Unlust *f* • unpleasure, displeasure *(Freud) (psy)*, reluctance, disinclination, listlessness *(psy)*, displeasure *(psy, eth)* < Lust-Unlust-Kalkül

Unlustvermeidung *f* • avoidance of unpleasure *(Freud) (psy)*

Unmaß *n* • excess *(Aristotle etc) (eth)* < Mesotes-Regel

Unmäßigkeit *f* • immoderation, inordinateness, intemperance *(eth)*

Unmenschlichkeit *f* • inhumanity *(eth)*

unmittelbar-realistische Wahrnehmungstheorie *f* • direct realist theory of perception *(Gibson) (epi)* < naiver Realismus

Unmittelbare, das *n* • the immediate *(gep)*

unmittelbare Arbeit *f* • direct labour *(Marx) (eco)*

unmittelbare Erfahrung *f* • immediate experience *(epi)*

unmittelbare Erkenntnis *f* • immediate/firsthand knowledge *(epi)*

unmittelbare Gegenwart *f* • specious present *(min)*

unmittelbare Gewißheit *f* • immediate certainty *(epi)* < Evidenz

unmittelbare Ursache *f* • immediate cause *(met)*

unmittelbarer Gebrauchswert *m* • immediate use value *(Marx) (eco)*

unmittelbares Bewußtsein *n* • immediate consciousness *(Bergson) (met)*

unmittelbares Dasein Gottes *n* • the immediate being of God *(rel)*

unmittelbares Sein *n* • immediate being *(ont)*

unmittelbares Wissen *n* • immediate knowledge *(epi)* → unmittelbare Erkenntnis

Unmittelbarkeit *f* • immediacy *(met, gep)*

Unmittelbarkeit der Erfahrung *f* • immediacy of experience *(epi)*

Unmittelbarkeit, göttliche *f* • divine immediacy *(rel)*

unmöglich • impossible *(sci)*

Unmöglichkeit *f* • impossibility *(ont)*

unmoralisch • immoral *(eth)* → immoralisch < amoralisch

Unmündigkeit *f* • minority *(jur)*, (mental) immaturity *(psy)*

Unmündigkeit, selbstverschuldete *f* • self-imposed tutelage, self-incurred immaturity, self-inflicted dependence/dependency *(Kant) (eth, pol)*

unorganisches Leben *n* • inorganic life *(nat)* ↔ organisches Leben

unparteiische Wahl *f* • impartial choice *(eth)* < Schleier des Nichtwissens, ursprüngliche Wahl

unparteiischer Beobachter *m* • impartial observer/spectator *(A. Smith, Kant etc) (eth)* < unpersönlicher Standpunkt

unparteiisches Interesse *n* • impartial concern *(Bentham etc) (eth)*

Unparteilichkeit *f* • impartiality *(eth, pol)*

unpersönlicher Standpunkt *m* • impersonal standpoint, impersonal point of view *(eth)* < unparteiischer Beobachter

Unphilosophie *f* • unphilosophy *(Hegel) (gep)*

unphilosophisch • unphilosophical *(gep)* < aphilosophisch

unproduktiv • non-productive *(eco)*

Unrecht *n* • injustice *(eth, jur)*

Unrechtsbewußtsein *n* • awareness of injustice/wrongdoing *(eth, jur, psy)*

Unrichtigkeit *f* • incorrectness *(log)* < Falschheit

Unruhe *f* • disquiet *(Kierkegaard) (ant, rel)*

Unruheherd *m* • storm centre, source of unrest *(pol)*

Unruhen *pl* • riots *(pol)*

Unsagbare, das *n* • the ineffable, the unsayable, the unspeakable *(Plotinus etc) (met)* < Undenkbare, das; Unfaßbarkeit

Unsagbarkeit der Wahrheit *f* • ineffability/unspeakability° of (the) truth *(met)*

Unschärfe *f* • vagueness, fuzziness *(mat, log)* < Vagheit

unscharfe Logik *f* • vague/fuzzy logic *(log)* < Logik, nichtmonotone

unscharfe Menge *f* • fuzzy set *(log)*

Unschärferelation *f* • indeterminacy/uncertainty principle *(Heisenberg) (nat)* → Unbestimmtheitsrelation

Unschuld *f* • innocence *(eth, jur)* < Schuldlosigkeit

Unschuld des Werdens *f* • innocence of becoming *(Nietzsche) (met)*

Unselbständigkeit *f* • dependency, dependence *(soc)* < Herr-Knecht-Dialektik

Unsicherheit der Existenz *f* • insecurity/instability of existence *(eco, soc)*

Unsicherheitsfaktor *m* • uncertainty factor *(dec)*

Unsichtbare, das *n* • the invisible *(nat, met)*

unsichtbare Hand *f* • invisible hand *(A. Smith) (eco, eth)* < freies Spiel der Kräfte

unsichtbare Kirche *f* • invisible church *(rel)*

unsichtbare Welt *f* • invisible world *(met)*

Unsinn *m* • nonsense, senselessness *(lan)*

unsinnig • nonsensical, nonsense, senseless *(lan)*

unsinnige Aussage *f* • senseless statement *(lan)*

unsinnlich • nonsensual *(met, psy)*

Unsittlichkeit *f* • immorality *(eth)*

Unspezialisiertheit *f* • lack of specialization *(ant)* < Anpassungsfähigkeit

unsterbliche Unvernunft *f* • immortal unreason *(Nietzsche) (met)*

Unsterblichkeit *f* • immortality *(rel)* → Immortalität, Athanasie

Unsterblichkeit der Seele *f* • immortality of the soul *(rel)* → Athanatismus

Unsterblichkeit Gottes *f* • immortality of God *(rel)*

Unsterblichkeitsglaube *m* • belief in immortality *(rel)* < Weiterleben nach dem Tod

Unsterblichkeitslehre *f* • doctrine of immortality *(rel)*

unstillbare Bedürfnisse *pl* • insatiable needs *(psy, eco)*

Unteilbarkeit *f* • indivisibility, indivisibleness *(nat, ont)*

Unteilbarkeit der Monaden *f* • indivisibility of monads *(Leibniz) (met)*

Unteilbarkeit des Geistes *f* • indivisibility of mind *(met)*

Unterbau *m* • substructure *(Marx) (soc)* → Basis, ökonomische ↔ Überbau < Basis und Überbau

Unterbegriff *m* • subsumption *(log)*

Unterbeschäftigung *f* • underemployment *(eco)*

Unterbestimmtheit *f* • underdeterminedness *(lan, aes)*

Unterbestimmtheit der Übersetzung *f* • underdetermination of translation *(Quine etc) (sci)* < Unbestimmtheit der Übersetzung, radikale Übersetzung

Unterbewußte, das *n* • the subconscious *(psy)*

Unterbewußtsein *n* • subconsciousness, (the) subconscious *(psy)*

Unterdeterminiertheit *f* • underdetermination *(Quine) (epi, sci), (aes)*

unterdrückte Wünsche *pl* • repressed wishes *(Freud etc) (psy)* < Triebunterdrückung

Unterdrückung *f* • oppression *(pol)*; repression, suppression *(Freud) (psy)* < Triebunterdrückung

Unterdrückung der Frau *f* • oppression of women *(fem, pol)*

Unterdrückung der Geschichte *f* • suppression of history *(Marcuse) (his, pol)*

Unterdrückungssystem *n* • oppressive system *(pol)*

untere Grenze *f* • infimum, (greatest) lower
bound, lower limit *(mat)*

untere Schranke *f* → untere Grenze

unterentwickelte Länder *pl* • underdeveloped
countries *(eco, pol)*

Unterentwicklung *f* • underdevelopment *(eco,
pol)*

Unterentwicklung, geistige *f* • mental
retardation *(psy)* < mentale Retardierung

Unterernährung *f* • malnutrition *(nat, eco)*

Untergang des Abendlandes *m* • decline of the
West *(Spengler) (cul)* < Kulturpessimismus,
Niedergangstheorien < W 1124

untergeordnete Künste *pl* • minor arts *(aes)*

Untergrundwirtschaft *f* • underground economy *(eco)* < Schwarzarbeit, Schwarzmarkt

Unterhalt, standesgemäßer *m* • living according to one's social standing, income befitting
one's status/station/social standing *(Aquinas)*
(soc, eco)

Unterhaltskosten *pl* • subsistence costs/
expenses *(eco)* → Bedarfdeckungskosten

Unterhaltungsindustrie *f* • entertainment
industry *(aes, soc)* < Kulturindustrie

Unterintegritätsbereich *m* • integral
subdomain *(mat)*

Unterklasse *f* • subset, subclass *(mat, log)*;
lower class, underclass *(soc)* < Klassen,
untere; Untermenge; Unterschicht, soziale

unterkonvergent • subconvergent *(mat, log,
lan)* < bedingt konvergent

Unterkörper *m* • subfield *(mat)*

Unterlassung *f* • omission, for(e)bearance
(act, eth, jur) < Nichthandeln

Unterlassungshandlung *f* • deed by omission
(act, eth), (action by) default *(jur)* < Pflichtversäumnis

Unterlassungssünde *f* • sin of omission *(rel)*

Untermenge *f* • subset *(log, mat)* < Unterklasse

Untermensch *m* • subhuman creature *(pol)*

Unternehmensberatung, philosophische *f* •
philosophical consulting *(eco)*

Unternehmensethik *f* • business ethics *(eco,
eth)* < Wirtschaftsethik

Unternehmensführung *f* • management *(eco)*

Unternehmensidentität *f* • corporate identity,
CI *(eco)*

Unternehmenskultur *f* • business/enterprise/
corporate culture *(eco)*

Unternehmensphilosophie *f* • business/
enterprise philosophy *(eco)*

Unternehmensübernahme *f* • take-over,
business acquisition *(eco)*

Unternehmenszusammenschluß *m* • merger
(eco) < Machtkonzentration

Unternehmer *m* • businessman, business-
person, entrepreneur *(eco)*

Unternehmergeist *m* • entrepreneurial spirit
(eco)

Unterprämisse *f* • minor premiss/premise *(log)*
→ Untersatz < Syllogismus

Unterprogramm *n* • subroutine *(AI, sys)*

Untersatz *m* • minor premiss/premise *(log)* →
Unterprämisse < Syllogismus

Unterscheidung *f* • distinction *(log)*

Unterscheidungsschwelle *f* • discrimination
threshold *(Quine) (lan, epi)*

Unterscheidungsvermögen *n* • faculty of discrimination, power of discernment *(epi, psy)*

Unterschicht, soziale *f* • underclass, lower
stratum/class(es) *(soc)*

Unterschied *m* • difference *(log)* < differentia
specifica

Unterschied, eben merklicher *m* • just
noticeable difference, JND *(psy)*

Unterschiedsschwelle *f* • threshold of
(noticeable) difference *(psy)*

Untersuchungskommission *f* • commission of
inquiry, investigating/fact-finding committee
(pol)

Untertanengeist *m* • servile attitude/spirit *(psy,
soc)*

Unterwelt *f* • underworld *(rel)* → Orkus

Unterwerfungsgeste *f* • gesture of submission
(nat, psy)

Unterwerfungsvertrag *m* • contract of submission *(Hobbes) (soc, pol)* ↔ Vereinigungsvertrag

Untugend *f* • vice *(eth)*

Unüberbrückbarkeit von Gegensätzen *f* •
unbridgeability of opposites *(log, pol)*

unumstößliche Gewißheit *f* • irrefutable
certainty *(Descartes) (epi)* < unzweifelhafte
Wahrheit

Unveränderliche, das *n* • the changeless/
unchanging *(Parmenides etc) (ont)*

unveränderliche Wahrheit *f* • immutable/
unchangeable truth *(epi)* < ewige Wahrheit

unveränderlichen Ideen, Reich der *n* • the
realm of unchanging forms *(Plato) (met)*

Unveränderlichkeit *f* • immutability, invaria-
bility, constancy *(gep)* → Immutabilität

Unveränderlichkeit der Substanz *f* • invaria-
bility of substance *(met)*

Unverantwortlichkeit *f* • irresponsibility *(eth,
jur)*

unveräußerliche Rechte *pl* • inalienable rights
(pol, jur) < Menschenrechte

Unveräußerlichkeit der Souveränität *f* •
inalienability of sovereignty *(pol)*

Unverbesserlichkeit *f* • incorrigibility *(jur, eth)*

Unverbindlichkeit *f* • non-commitment, non-
committal nature *(gep)*

Unverborgenheit *f* • unconcealment *(Anaximander, Heidegger) (met)* < Wahrheit

Unverborgenheit des Seins *f* • unconcealment
of Being *(Heidegger) (ont)*

unvereinbare Elemente *pl* • incompatible
elements *(gep)*

Unvereinbarkeit *f* • incompatibility *(gep)* →
Inkompatibilität

Unverfügbarkeit der Folgen *f* • lack of
disposition over consequences *(eth, dec)*

unvergängliche Dinge *pl* • enduring things
(met)

Unvergänglichkeit *f* • everlastingness *(met)*

Unvergleichbarkeit *f* • incommensurability
(gep) → Inkommensurabilität

Unverletzlichkeit der menschlichen Würde *f*
• inviolability of human dignity *(eth, met)*

Unvermeidbarkeit des Fortschritts *f* •
inevitability of progress *(his, soc)*

Unvernunft *f* • unreasonableness, (▷ Torheit)
foolishness *(epi, psy)*

unversehrte Intersubjektivität *f* • undamaged
intersubjectivity *(Habermas) (lan, soc)*

Unvollendete, das *n* • the unfinished
(Keyserling) (ant, met)

unvollendete Projekt der Moderne, das *n* •
the unfinished project of modernity *(soc, his,
gep)*

unvollendete Schöpfung *f* • unfinished creation
(rel)

unvollkommene Konkurrenz *f* • imperfect
competition *(eco)* < Marktversagen

unvollkommene Pflicht *f* • imperfect duty/
obligation *(Kant) (eth)*

unvollständige Induktion *f* • incomplete/
imperfect induction *(log, sci)*

unvollständiges Wissen *n* • imperfect/incom-
plete knowledge *(epi, sci)* < empirisches
Wissen

Unvollständigkeit *f* • incompleteness *(gep)*

Unvollständigkeitsbeweis *m* • incompleteness
proof *(Gödel) (mat, log)*

Unvollständigkeitssatz *m* • incompleteness
theorem *(Gödel) (mat, log)*

Unvollständigkeitstheorem *n* → Unvollständigkeitssatz

Unvoreingenommenheit *f* • impartiality *(eth)*

Unvorhersagbarkeit *f* • unpredictability *(sci,
gep)* < Chaostheorie

Unvorstellbarkeit *f* • non-representability
(Schlick, Carnap) (epi, lan), unimaginable-
ness *(gep)*

Unwägbarkeit *f* • imponderability *(gep)* →
Imponderabilität

Unwahrhaftigkeit *f* • bad faith, mauvaise foi
(Sartre) (met) → böser Glaube(n),
schlechter Glaube(n)

Unwahrheit *f* • falsehood, untruth *(epi, eth)*

unwahrscheinlich • improbable *(gep)*

Unwahrscheinlichkeit *f* • improbability *(gep)*

Unwahrscheinlichkeitsannahme *f* • improbability assumption *(sci)*

Unwandelbare, das *n* • the unchangeable, the
immutable *(met)*

unwandelbare Ideen *pl* •
unchangeable/immutable ideas *(met)* < ewige Ideen

Unwandelbarkeit *f* • immutability *(gep)*

Unwandelbarkeit Gottes *f* • immutability of
God *(rel)*

Unwert *m* • unworth *(eth)* < unwertes Leben

unwertes Leben *n* • worthless life *(eth)*
< Lebenswertdebatte

unwiderlegbare Wahrheit *f* • irrefutable truth
(epi)

Unwiderlegbarkeit *f* • irrefutability *(sci)*
< Immunisierungsstrategie

Unwirklichkeit *f* • unreality *(ont)* → Irrealität

Unwirklichkeit des Raumes *f* • unreality of
space *(met)* < virtuelle Realität

Unwissenheit *f* • ignorance, unknowing(ness)
(epi, met) → Agnosie

Unzurechnungsfähigkeit *f* • unaccountability
(jur), insanity, unsoundness of mind *(psy)* <
mildernde Umstände

unzusammenhängend • (▷ getrennt, abgeson-
dert) discrete *(ont, sys)*, incoherent *(log, lan)*

Unzuverlässigkeit *f* • unreliability *(eth)* ↔
Reliabilität

unzweifelhafte Wahrheit *f* • indubitable truth
(epi) < selbstevidente Wahrheit, unumstößliche Gewißheit

Unzweifelhaftigkeit *f* → Unbezweifelbarkeit

Uranfang *m* • first beginning *(nat, rel)* < Urknall

Urbegriffe *pl* • proto-concepts *(met)* < Transzendentalien

Urbestimmungen *pl* • proto-conditions *(met)*

Urbild *n* • prototype, archetype *(Plato etc)*
(met, psy) < Prototyp, Methexis ↔ Abbild,
Nachbild

Urchristentum *n* • early Christianity *(rel)*

Ureinheit *f* → Monade

Urelement *n* • urelement, individual, element that is not a set *(mat)*

Urerlebnis *n* • primal experience *(Freud etc)* *(psy)*

Urfaktum *n* • original fact *(Fichte)* *(met)*

Urfamilie *f* • primal family *(Freud etc)* *(psy)*

Urgeschichte *f* • prehistory *(his)*

Urgesellschaft *f* • primitive society *(soc)*

Urgrund *m* • primal ground *(Heidegger etc)* *(ont)*

Urgrund der Welt *m* • (ultimate) origin/source of the world, (ultimate) foundation of the world *(rel, met)*

Urheber der Geschichte, Mensch als *m* • man as originator of history *(his)*

Urhorde *f* • primal group *(Freud etc)* *(ant, psy)*

Ur-Ich *n* • original ego *(Fichte)* *(met)*

Urinstinkt *m* • basic instinct *(psy)*

Urknall *m* • big bang *(nat)* < Uranfang

Urknalltheorie *f* • big bang theory/hypothesis *(nat)*

Urkraft *f* • basic/elementary force *(nat, met)*

Urmaterialien *pl* • primal materials *(Husserl)* *(ont)*

Urmaterie *f* • prime matter *(nat, met)* → Urstoff

Urmensch *m* • primeval/primitive man *(Freud etc)* *(ant, psy)*

Urpflanze *f* • *nt,* archetypal plant *(Goethe)* *(nat, met)*

Ursache *f* • cause *(met)*

Ursache, adäquate *f* • adequate cause *(met)* → causa adaequata < hinreichende Ursache

Ursache, Bestimmung der *f* • definition of cause *(Locke)* *(met)*

Ursache, bewegende *f* • motive/efficient/propelling cause *(met)* → causa movens

Ursache, effektive *f* • efficient cause *(met)* → Wirkursache

Ursache, erste *f* • first cause *(Aristotle)* *(met)* → causa prima

Ursache, finale *f* • final cause *(met)* → Finalursache, causa finalis

Ursache, formale *f* • formal cause *(Aristotle)* *(met)*

Ursache, hinreichende *f* • sufficient cause *(met)* → causa sufficiens ↔ nicht-hinreichende Ursache

Ursache, instrumentelle *f* • instrumental cause *(met)* → causa instrumentalis

Ursache, materiale *f* • material cause *(met)* → Materialursache

Ursache, mittelbare *f* • mediate(d) cause, caused cause *(met)* → causa mediata

Ursache, nächste *f* • proximate cause *(met)*

Ursache, nicht-hinreichende *f* • deficient/non-sufficient cause *(met)* → causa deficiens

Ursache, selbstverursachte *f* • self-caused cause *(Aquinas)* *(met, rel)* → causa sui

Ursache, unmittelbare *f* • immediate cause *(met)* → Ursache, unverursachte

Ursache und Wirkung *f,f* • cause and effect *(met)*

Ursache, unverursachte *f* • uncaused cause *(Aquinas)* *(met, rel)* → causa sui; Ursache, unmittelbare < unbewegter Beweger

Ursache, ursprüngliche *f* • principal/original/prime cause *(met)* → causa principalis < erste Ursache

Ursache-Wirkung-Analyse *f* • cause-and-effect analysis *(met, sys)*

Ursache-Wirkung-Kette *f* • cause-and-effect chain *(met)*

Ursachen, Lehre von den vier *f* • doctrine of the four causes *(Aristotle)* *(met)*

Ursachenkette, unendliche *f* • infinite chain of causes *(met)*

Ursachenlehre *f* • etiology *(met)* → Ätiologie

Ursachenwert *m* • seed value *(sys)* < Anfangswert

ursächlich • causal *(met)*

ursächlicher Zusammenhang *m* • causal relation *(met)*

Ursächlichkeit *f* • causality *(met)* < Verursachung

Ursächlichkeit, göttliche *f* • divine causality *(Spinoza)* *(met)*

Urschlamm *m* • primeval mud/slime *(Anaximander)* *(met)* < Urstoff, Urmaterie

Urschrei *m* • primal scream *(Janov)* *(psy)*

Urschrift *f* • archewriting *(Derrida)* *(met)*

Ursein *n* • primordial being *(Schelling)* *(met)*

Urspaltung *f* • original split *(met)*

Ursprache *f* • proto-language *(lan)*

Ursprung *m* • origin *(met)* → arché < W 701; intersection *(mat)*

Ursprung der Kunst *m* • origin of art *(aes)*

Ursprung des Lebens *m* • origin of life *(nat, met)*

Ursprung des Übels *m* • origin/cause of evil *(eth, rel)*

ursprüngliche Akkumulation *f* • original/primitive/primary accumulation *(Marx etc)* *(eco)* < Wertbildung

ursprüngliche Apperzeption *f* • original/originary apperception *(Kant)* *(epi)*

ursprüngliche Auslegung *f* • primordial interpretation *(Heidegger)* *(met)*

ursprüngliche Besitzergreifung *f* • primary occupation *(eco)* < Okkupationstheorie

ursprüngliche Erwerbung *f* • original acquisition *(Kant, Marx etc) (jur, met)*

ursprüngliche Freiheit *f* • original liberty *(soc, pol)* → natürliche Freiheit

ursprüngliche Position *f* • original position *(Rawls) (dec, eth)*

ursprüngliche Rechte *pl* • aboriginal rights *(Locke etc) (pol, jur)* < Naturrecht

ursprüngliche Situation *f* • original situation *(Rawls) (dec, eth)*

ursprüngliche Ursache *f* • principal/original/ prime cause *(met)* → causa principalis < erste Ursache

ursprüngliche Wahl *f* • original choice *(Rawls) (dec)* < Schleier des Nichtwissens

ursprünglicher Zustand *m* • primitive condition *(pol)* < Naturzustand, vertragsfreier Zustand, vorbürgerlicher Zustand des Menschen

ursprüngliches Sein *n* • primordial/originary Being *(Heidegger) (ont)*

ursprüngliches Seinsverständnis *n* • primordial understanding of Being *(Heidegger) (ont)*

ursprüngliches Verstehen *n* • primordial understanding *(Heidegger) (ont)*

ursprüngliches Wesen der Wahrheit *n* • primordial essence/nature of truth *(Heidegger) (ont)*

Ursprünglichkeit *f* • originality, authenticity *(Jaspers, Kierkegaard) (met)*

Urspung der Arten *m* • origin of species *(nat, ant)* → Entstehung der Arten < W 253

Urstoff *m* • prime/primeval matter *(Thales etc) (met)* → Hyle

Urstoff, ungeformter *m* • unformed prime/ primeval matter *(met)* < Apeiron

Ursünde *f* → Erbsünde

Urteil *n* • judg(e)ment, proposition *(epi, log),* (▷ Entscheidungsurteil) decision *(dec),* judg(e)ment, sentence *(jur, gep)*

Urteil, allgemeines *n* • general judg(e)ment *(epi, log)*

Urteil, analytisches *n* • analytical judg(e)ment *(Kant) (epi, log)* → Erläuterungsurteil ↔ synthetisches Urteil

Urteil, apodiktisches *n* • apod(e)ictic judg(e)ment *(Kant) (epi, log)*

Urteil, aposteriorisches *n* • a posteriori judg(e)ment *(epi, log)*

Urteil, apriorisches *n* • a priori judg(e)ment *(epi, log)*

Urteil, assertorisches *n* • assertoric judg(e)ment *(log)*

Urteil, ästhetisches *n* • aesthetic judg(e)ment *(aes)* < Schönheitsurteil

Urteil, bejahendes *n* • affirmative judg(e)ment *(epi, log)*

Urteil, besonderes *n* • particular judg(e)ment *(epi, log)*

Urteil, disjunktives *n* • disjunctive judg(e)ment *(epi, log)*

Urteil, einzelnes *n* • particular judg(e)ment *(epi, log)* → Individualurteil

Urteil, empirisches *n* • empirical judg(e)ment *(epi, log)*

Urteil, hypothetisches *n* • hypothetical judg(e)ment *(epi, log)*

Urteil, kategorisches *n* • categorical judg(e)- ment *(epi, log)*

Urteil, normatives *n* • normative judg(e)ment *(log, eth, aes)*

Urteil, problematisches *n* • problematic(al) judg(e)ment *(epi, log)*

Urteil, synthetisches *n* • synthetic judg(e)ment *(Kant) (epi, log)* → Erweiterungsurteil ↔ analytisches Urteil

Urteil, unendliches *n* • infinite judg(e)ment *(epi, log)*

urteilen • to judge *(log)* < Beurteilung

Urteils, Materie des *f* • matter/content of judg(e)ment *(log)* ↔ Form des Urteils

Urteilsenthaltung *f* • abstention from judg(e)- ment, withholding judg(e)ment *(Pyrrhon, Husserl) (epi)* → Epoché < Einklammerung, phänomenologische; Aphasie

Urteilsfähigkeit *f* → Urteilskompetenz

Urteilsform *f* • type/form of judg(e)ment *(log)*

Urteilsfunktion, logische *f* • logical function of judg(e)ment *(log)*

Urteilsinhalt *m* • judg(e)ment content, content of judg(e)ment *(log)*

Urteilskategorie *f* • judg(e)ment category, category of judg(e)ment *(log)*

Urteilskompetenz *f* • judg(e)mental competence, faculty of judg(e)ment/ discrimination *(epi)*

Urteilskraft *f* • (faculty/power of) judg(e)- ment *(Kant) (epi, eth, aes)* < W 539

Urteilstafel *f* • table of judg(e)ments *(Kant) (epi, log)*

Urteilstheorie *f* • theory of judg(e)ment *(epi, log)*

Urteilsvermögen *n* • faculty of judg(e)ment *(Kant) (epi)* → Urteilskompetenz

Urtrieb *m* • basic instinct/drive, primal instinct *(Freud) (psy)* < Urinstinkt

urtümliche Wesenheit *f* • primal entity *(Jaspers) (ont)*

Urvater *m* • primal father *(Freud) (psy, cul)*

Urverbrechen *n* • primal crime *(Freud etc)* *(psy)*

Urverdrängung *f* • primal repression *(Freud)* *(psy)*

Urvermögen *n* • original/innate ability *(ant, met)* < Angeborenheit, Genie

Urvertrauen *n* • basic/fundamental trust *(psy)*

Urwahrheit *f* • primary truth *(met)*

Urwesen *n* • primal being *(Freud) (ant, psy)*

Urzeichen *n* • primitive sign *(lan)*

Urzeit *f* • primitive age, prehistory *(his)*

Urzeugung *f* • original/primal creation *(rel);* spontaneous generation *(nat)* → Abiogenese, generatio aequivoca

Urzustand *m* • original/primordial state *(ant, soc)*

Utilitarismus *m* • utilitarianism *(eth)* < Regelutilitarismus, Aktutilitarismus, Lust-Unlust-Kalkül < W 1145

Utilitarismus, negativer *m* • negative utilitarianism *(eth)*

Utilitarist *m* • utilitarian *(eth)*

utilitaristische Ethik *f* • utilitarian ethics *(eth)*

Utilitätsprinzip *n* • utility principle, principle of utility *(dec, eth, eco)*

Utopie *f* • utopia *(pol, soc)* < Idealstaat; < W 348, 486, 1146

Utopie, rückwärtsgewandte *f* • retrograde utopia *(pol, soc)* < goldenes Zeitalter

Utopie, schwarze *f* → Dystopie

utopisch • utopian, unrealistic *(pol, soc)*

utopischer Sozialismus *m* • utopian socialism *(Engels) (pol, soc)* ↔ wissenschaftlicher Sozialismus

utopisches Bewußtsein *n* • utopian consciousness *(gep)*

utopisches Denken *n* • utopian thought *(soc)*

utopisches Ideal *n* • utopian ideal *(pol)*

Utopismus *m* • utopianism *(pol, soc)*

Utopist *m* • utopian *(pol, soc)* < Weltverbesserer

V

Vagantenbewegung *f* • vagrant movement *(soc, cul)* < Jugendbewegung

Vagheit *f* • vagueness *(mat, log)* < Unbestimmtheit, Unterdeterminiertheit, Unschärfe

Vagheit, intensionale *f* • intensional vagueness *(lan)*

Vakuum, existentielles *n* • existential vacuum *(met)*

Valenztheorie *f* • valency theory *(mat)*

Valenzzahl *f* • valency/equivalent number *(mat)*

Validität *f* • validity *(log, sci)* → Gültigkeit < Stichhaltigkeit

Validität, experimentelle *f* • experimental validity *(sci)*

Validität, externe *f* • external validity *(sci)* ↔ Validität, interne

Validität, interne *f* • internal validity *(sci)* ↔ Validität, externe

Validität theoretischer Konstrukte *f* • validity of theoretical constructs, construct validity *(sci)*

Variable *f* • variable *(log, mat)* ↔ Konstante

Variable, abhängige *f* • dependent variable *(mat, log)* ↔ Variable, unabhängige

Variable, freie *f* • free variable *(mat, log)* ↔ Variable, gebundene

Variable, gebundene *f* • bound/bounded° variable *(mat, log)* ↔ Variable, freie

Variable, unabhängige *f* • independent variable *(mat, log)* ↔ Variable, abhängige

Variable, versteckte *f* • hidden variable *(sci)*

Variablenbindung *f* • binding of variables *(log, mat)*

Variablenfeld *n* • array/field of variables *(log, mat)*

Variablenreduktion *f* • reduction of variables *(log, mat)*

Varianz *f* • variance *(mat)*

Varianzanalyse *f* • analysis of variance, ANOVA *(mat)*

Variation *f* • variation *(aes);* variation, permutation *(mat)* < Permutation

Variationsrechnung *f* • calculus of variation(s) *(mat)*

Varietät *f* • variety *(nat, gep)* < Abart, Spielart

Vater-Sohn-Konflikt *m* • father-son conflict/hostility *(psy)* < Ödipuskonflikt, Elektrakonflikt, Generationenkonflikt

Väterautorität *f* • authority of the fathers *(gep)*

Vaterersatz *m* • father substitute *(Freud)* *(psy)*

Vaterfigur *f* • father figure *(psy)*

Vaterfixierung *f* • father fixation *(psy)*

Vaterland *n* • fatherland, motherland *(pol)*

vaterländische Gesinnung *f* • patriotic frame of mind, patriotic mentality *(pol)*

Vaterlandsliebe *f* • love of one's country *(pol)* → Patriotismus

Vaterlandsverräter *m* • traitor to one's country *(pol)*

väterliches Recht *n* • paternal right *(jur)* < Paternalismus

vaterlose Gesellschaft *f* • fatherless society *(Mitscherlich) (soc, psy)*

Vatermord *m* • patricide *(Freud) (psy, cul)*

Vatikanisches Konzil *n* • Vatican Council *(rel)*

Veda *m* • veda *(asp)*

Vedantaphilosophie *f* • vedanta philosophy *(asp)*

Veganismus *m* • veganism *(eth, eso)*

Vegetarismus *m* • vegetarianism *(eth)*

Vektor *m* • vector *(mat)*

Vektordarstellung *f* • vector representation *(mat)*

Vektorprodukt *n* • vector/cross product *(mat)* → Kreuzprodukt

Venn-Diagramm *n* • Venn diagram *(log, mat)*

Ventilfunktion der Künste *f* • outlet function of the arts *(aes)* < Sublimation

verabsolutieren • to make absolute, to absolutize° *(gep)*

Verabsolutierung *f* • making absolute, absolutization° *(gep)*

Verächter des Leibes *m* • despiser of the body *(Nietzsche) (met)*

Verachtung *f* • contempt, disdain *(eth)*

Verallgemeinerung *f* • generalization *(gep)* → Generalisation < W 1147

Verallgemeinerungsfähigkeit *f* • generalizability, universalizability *(sci, eth)* → Universalisierbarkeit

Verallgemeinerungsregel *f* • generalization rule *(eth)*

Verallgemeinerungstest *m* • generalization test *(eth, sci)*

Veränderung f • change *(met)* < Werden, das; Vergehen, das

Veränderung, qualitative f • qualitative change *(gep)*

Veränderung, quantitative f • quantitative change *(gep)*

Veränderungspotential n • potential for change *(soc, pol, sys)*

Veranlagung f • disposition, constitution *(psy)*, investment *(eco)*

Veranlassung f • reason, motive *(psy, act)* → Motiv

Veranschaulichung f • visualization *(gen)*

Verantwortlichkeit f • responsibility *(eth)*

Verantwortlichkeit, verminderte f • diminished responsibility *(jur)*

Verantwortung der Wissenschaft f • responsibility of science *(sci, eth)* < Wissenschaftsethik

Verantwortungsbewußtsein n • sense of responsibility *(eth)*

Verantwortungsethik f • ethics of responsibility *(Weber) (eth)* ↔ Gesinnungsethik

Verarmung f • impoverishment, pauperization *(eco, soc)* < Verelendung

Verästelung f • branching, bifurcation *(log, AI)* → Verzweigung

Veräußerlichung f • exteriorization *(Hegel) (met)*

Veräußerungsrecht n • right of disposal *(jur)*

Verbalisierung f • verbalization *(lan)* < Oralität

Verbalverhalten n • verbal behaviour *(Skinner) (lan, soc)*

Verband m • lattice *(mat)*, association *(soc)*, (corporate) group *(Weber etc) (soc)* < Korporativismus

Verbandshandeln n • group behaviour *(Weber) (act, soc)* < Gesellschaftshandeln, Gemeinschaftshandeln

Verbandshomomorphismus m • homomorphism of lattices, lattice homomorphism *(mat)*

Verbandstheorie f • lattice theory *(mat, log)*

Verbergung des Seins f • concealment of Being *(Heidegger) (ont)*

Verbindlichkeit f • (▷ Einklagbarkeit) obligation, liability *(jur)*, (▷ Verläßlichkeit) reliability, commitment *(eth)*

Verbindung f • (▷ Einheit) union, combination, synthesis *(met)*, (▷ Gemeinsamkeit) association, union *(soc, pol)* < Verband, Vereinigung

Verbindung, chemische f • chemical compound *(nat)*

Verbindung, politische f • political association *(pol)*

Verbindungsregel f • joining rule *(log)*

Verblendung f • delusion *(psy)*

verborgene Inwendigkeit f • hidden inwardness *(Kierkegaard) (ont, rel)*

verborgener Gott m • hidden God *(rel)* → deus absconditus ↔ offenbarer Gott

Verborgenheit des Seins f → Verbergung des Seins

Verborgensein des Grundes n • hiddenness of the ground *(Jaspers) (ont)*

Verbot n • ban, prohibition *(eth, jur)*

Verbotene, das n • the forbidden *(eth, jur)* ↔ Erlaubte, das

verbraucherfreundlich • consumer-friendly *(eco)*

Verbraucherschutzrecht n • consumer protection law *(jur, eco)*

Verbrechen gegen die Menschlichkeit n • crime against humanity *(eth, pol)*

Verbrechen ohne Opfer n • victimless crime *(Mill) (eth)*

Verbrechensbekämpfung f • fight against crime *(jur)*

Verbrechensprävention f • crime prevention *(jur, soc)* < Präventionstheorie

verbrieftes Recht n • vested right *(jur)*

Verbundenheitsgefühl n → Solidaritätsgefühl

Verbürgerlichung f • embourgeoisement *(Engels) (soc, pol)*

Verdammnis, ewige f • eternal damnation *(rel)*

Verdammung zur Freiheit f • condemnation to freedom *(Sartre) (met)*

verdeckt strategische Handlung f • concealed strategic action *(Habermas) (act)*

Verderbnis, sittliche f • moral depravity *(eth)*

Verdichtung f • condensation *(Freud) (psy), (nat)*

Verdienst n • merit, deserts *(eth)*

Verdienstadel m • life peerage *(soc)* < Meritokratie

Verdienstethik f • meritocratic ethics *(eth)*

Verdienstspanne f → Profitspanne

verdiktive Äußerung f • verdictive utterance *(Austin) (lan, act)* < Illokution

verdinglichendes Denken n • reifying thought *(epi)*

Verdinglichung f • reification, objectification *(Marx etc) (epi, soc)* → Reifikation, Vergegenständlichung < Reduktion des Menschen zur Sache

Verdinglichungseffekt m • reifying effect *(soc)*

Verdrängung f • repression (psy)

Verdrängungswettbewerb m • cut-throat competition, driving-out competition° (eco)

Veredelung der Seele f • refinement of the soul (Schiller) (aes) < schöne Seele

Verehrungskult m • cult of adoration (rel, cul)

Vereinbarkeit f • compatibility (gep) → Kompatibilität

Vereinbarkeit von Wissenschaft und religiösem Glauben f • compatibility of science and religious faith/belief (gep, rel)

vereinfachende Annahme f • simplifying assumption (sci)

Vereinfachung f • simplification (gep) < Komplexitätsreduktion

Vereinheitlichung f • standardization, integration (sci)

vereinigter Wille m • corporate will (Rousseau) (soc, pol) < Gemeinwille

Vereinigung f • unification (mat, pol)

Vereinigungsmenge f • union set (log, mat)

Vereinigungsvertrag m • contract of convention (Hobbes) (soc, pol) ↔ Unterwerfungsvertrag

Vereinsamung, menschliche f • human isolation (soc, psy) < atomisierte Gesellschaft

Vereinte Nationen pl • United Nations (pol) < Weltstaat, Völkerbund

Verelendung f • impoverishment, immiseration, pauperization (eco)

Verelendung, absolute f • absolute impoverishment/immiseration (Marx) (eco, soc)

Verelendung des Proletariats f • impoverishment/immiseration of the proletariat (Marx) (soc)

Verelendung, relative f • relative impoverishment/immiseration (Marx) (eco, soc)

Verelendungstheorie f • doctrine of impoverishment/immiseration (Marx) (eco, soc)

Vererbung f • inheritance (log, jur), heredity (nat)

Vererbung von (erworbenen) Eigenschaften f • inheritance of (acquired) properties/characteristics (nat, log)

Vererbungslehre f • genetics (nat) → Genetik < Mendelsches Gesetz

Vererbungstheorie f → Vererbungslehre

Verewigung f • immortalization (rel, aes)

Verfahren n • process, method, procedure (sci)

Verfahren der nachträglich bestimmten Abstände n • method of successive intervals (sci, mat)

Verfahren der transferierten Einschätzungen n • unfolding technique (Coombs) (sci)

Verfahren, experimentelles n • experimental method/procedure (sci)

Verfahren, generalisierendes n • generalizing method/procedure (sci)

Verfahren gleich erscheinender Abstände n • Thurstone scale (sci, mat)

Verfahren, idiographisches n • idiographic method (Windelband) (sci)

Verfahren, vergleichendes n • comparative method (sci)

Verfahrensethik f → prozedurale Ethik

Verfahrensgerechtigkeit f • procedural justice (Rawls etc) (eth) → prozedurale Gerechtigkeit

Verfahrenslegitimität f • procedural legitimacy, legitimacy through procedure (jur, soc, pol) < Legitimation durch Verfahren

Verfahrensregeln pl • rules of procedure (sci, jur)

Verfahrensweise f • mode of procedure (sci, dec)

Verfall, sittlicher m • moral decline (eth)

Verfallen-an n • falling-to, lapsing-to (Heidegger etc) (ant) < Man, Uneigentlichkeit

Verfallenheit f • fallenness (Heidegger) (ant), (Jaspers) (met)

Verfallserscheinung f • symptom of decline/decay (his) < Dekadenz

Verfallssymptom n → Verfallserscheinung

Verfallstheorie f • theory of decay (cul, soc) < zyklische Geschichtstheorie

Verfassung f • constitution, make-up (Heidegger etc) (ont) < Seinsverfassung

Verfassung, geistige f • state of mind (psy)

Verfassung, geschriebene f • written constitution (pol, jur)

Verfassung, staatliche f • constitution (pol, jur)

Verfassung, ungeschriebene f • unwritten constitution (pol, jur)

Verfassungsentwurf m • constitutional project (pol) < W 261

Verfassungsganzheit f • constitutive totality (Heidegger) (ont)

verfassunggebende Versammlung f • constituent assembly (pol, jur)

Verfassungsgericht n • constitutional court (jur)

Verfassungskreislauf m • constitutional cycle (pol) < Verfassungstypen

Verfassungsrecht n • constitutional law (jur)

Verfassungsreform f • constitutional reform (jur)

Verfassungsschutz m • protection of the constitution (jur, pol)

Verfassungsstaat *m* • constitutional state *(pol, jur)* < Rechtsstaat

Verfassungstypen *pl* • constitutional types, types of constitution *(Aristotle etc) (pol, jur)*

verfassungswidrig • unconstitutional *(jur)*

Verfehlung *f* • transgression, failing *(eth)*

Verfehlung, methodische *f* • methodological error *(sci)*

Verfolgungswahn *m* • persecution complex *(psy)* < Paranoia

Verfremdung *f* • alienation *(soc, aes)*

Verfremdungseffekt *m* • alienation effect *(Brecht) (aes)* < Lehrstück; estrangement effect *(Marcuse) (soc)*

Verfügbarkeit des Wissens *f* • availability of knowledge *(sci)*

Verfügungsgewalt *f* • power of disposition *(jur)*

Verfügungsrecht *n* • right of disposal *(jur)*

Verfügungswissen *n* • disposable/usable knowledge *(epi)* ↔ Orientierungswissen, Lebenswissen < pragmatisches Wissen, Erfahrungswissen

Verführung der Sprache *f* • seduction of language *(Mauthner) (epi, lan)*

Verführungstheorie *f* • seduction theory *(Freud) (psy)*

Vergangenheitsbewältigung *f* • coming to terms with the past, coping with the past *(pol)*

Vergänglichkeit *f* • transitoriness, transience *(met)*

Vergänglichkeit des Daseins *f* • transitoriness/transience of existence *(met)*

Vergeblichkeit *f* • futility *(gep)*

Vergebung *f* • forgiveness *(eth)*

Vergebung der Sünden *f* • forgiveness/remission of sins *(rel)*

vergegenständlicht • objectified, reified *(Hegel, Marx etc) (met)*

vergegenständlichte Arbeitszeit *f* • objectified working time *(Marx) (eco)*

Vergegenständlichung *f* • objectification, reification *(Hegel, Marx etc) (met)* → Objektivation, Reifikation

vergegenwärtigen • to re-present, to make present *(Husserl etc) (ont)* < gegenwärtigen

Vergegenwärtigung *f* • re-presentation *(Husserl etc) (ont)*, recall *(gen)*

Vergehen *n* • offence *(jur, eth)* < Verstoß

Vergehen, das *n* • passing away *(ont)* ↔ Werden, das < W 1105

Vergeistigung *f* • spiritualization *(met, rel)*

vergeltende Gerechtigkeit *f* → Vergeltungsgerechtigkeit

Vergeltung *f* • retaliation, retribution *(eth, jur)* < Rache

Vergeltung der guten Taten *f* • recompense for good actions *(eth, rel)* < Karma, ausgleichende Gerechtigkeit

Vergeltungsangriff *m* • retaliatory attack *(pol)*

Vergeltungsdrohung *f* • retaliatory threat, threat of retaliation *(pol, act)*

Vergeltungsgerechtigkeit *f* • retributive/retaliatory justice *(eth)* < ausgleichende Gerechtigkeit, Talionsprinzip

Vergeltungsjustiz *f* • retributive justice *(jur)*

Vergeltungskapazität *f* • retaliatory capacity *(pol)* → Gegenschlagkapazität

Vergeltungskausalität *f* • retributive causality *(eth)* → Karma

Vergeltungsmaßnahme *f* • retaliatory measure *(eth, jur)*

Vergeltungsstraftheorie *f* • retributivist theory of punishment *(eth, jur)* < Präventionstheorie, Resozialisationstheorie

vergesellschafteter Mensch *m* • socialized/social man *(Rousseau) (soc)*

Vergesellschaftung *f* • socialization, sociation° *(soc)* → Sozialisation

Vergesellschaftung der Produktionsmittel *f* • socialization/nationalization of (the) means of production *(Marx) (eco)* < öffentliches Eigentum

Vergesellschaftung des Subjekts *f* • socialization of the individual *(soc)*

Vergessenheit des Seins *f* → Seinsvergessenheit

Vergessenskurve *f* • forgetting curve *(min, epi, psy)*

Vergewaltigung *f* • rape *(eth)* < Sexualmißbrauch

Vergleichbarkeit *f* • comparability *(gep)*, commensurability *(sci)* → Kommensurabilität

vergleichende Ethik *f* • comparative ethics *(eth)*

vergleichende Geschichte *f* • comparative history *(his)*

vergleichende Linguistik *f* • comparative linguistics *(lan)*

vergleichende Literaturwissenschaft *f* • comparative literature *(aes)* → Komparatistik

vergleichende Methode *f* • comparative method *(sci)*

vergleichende Philosophie *f* • comparative philosophy *(gep)*

vergleichende Psychologie *f* • comparative psychology *(psy)*

vergleichende Religionswissenschaft *f* •
comparative religion *(rel)*

vergleichende Untersuchung *f* • comparative
study *(sci)*

vergleichende Verhaltensforschung *f* • (comparative) ethology *(nat, psy)* < Ethologie

Vergleichsebene *f* • level of comparison *(gep)*

Vergleichsklasse *f* • comparison class *(log, sci)*

Vergleichskriterium *n* • criterion of comparison *(gep)*, comparison test *(mat)*

Vergleichsmaßstab *m* • standard of comparison *(gep)*

Vergleichsverhalten *n* • competitive behaviour *(psy)*

Vergötterung *f* • deification *(rel, psy)*

Vergöttlichung *f* • apotheosis, deification *(rel)*

Verhalten *n* • behaviour *(psy)*

Verhalten, regelgeleitetes *n* • rule-governed
behaviour *(soc, act)*

Verhalten, unzulässiges *n* • impermissible
behaviour *(eth)*

Verhalten, zulässiges *n* • permissible behaviour *(eth)*

Verhaltenheit *f* • comportment *(Heidegger)*
(ont)

Verhaltensänderung *f* • behaviour modification *(psy)*

Verhaltensansteckung *f* • behaviour contagion
(soc, psy)

Verhaltensdisposition *f* • behaviour disposition
(psy)

Verhaltensformung *f* • behaviour shaping
(Skinner) (psy) → Konditionierung

Verhaltensforschung *f* • ethology, behavioural
science *(nat, psy)* → Ethologie

Verhaltenskode *m* • code of conduct *(eth)*

Verhaltenskonsistenz *f* • consistency of
behaviour *(act)*

Verhaltenskontrolle *f* • behavioural control
(act, psy)

Verhaltensmaxime *f* • maxim of action,
maxim/principle of behaviour *(Kant) (eth)*,
maxim of manner *(Grice) (lan)*

Verhaltensmuster *n* • behaviour(al) pattern
(psy, nat)

Verhaltensmutation *f* • mutation of behaviour
(nat, psy)

Verhaltensnorm *f* • norm of conduct *(eth)*

Verhaltensprinzip *n* • principle of conduct
(eth), behavioural principle *(nat)*

Verhaltensrepertoire *n* • behavioural
repertoire/repertory *(psy)*

Verhaltensschema *n* • behaviour scheme *(nat,
psy)* → Verhaltensmuster

Verhaltensstörung *f* • behaviour(al) disorder/
disturbance, maladjustment *(psy)*

Verhaltenstheorie *f* • behaviour theory *(psy)*
< Behaviorismus

Verhaltenstherapie *f* • behaviour(al) therapy
(psy)

Verhaltenswissenschaft *f* → Verhaltensforschung

Verhältnis *n* • ratio *(mat)* → Proportion

Verhältnis von Kunst und Leben *n* • relationship of art to life *(aes)*

Verhältnis von Teil und Ganzem *n* • part-
whole relation *(ont, aes)*

Verhältnis von Theorie und Praxis *n* • relation
of theory and practice/praxis *(gep)*

Verhältnis zwischen Denken und Sein *n* •
relation of thought and being *(met)*

Verhältnismäßigkeit *f* • (▷ Angemessenheit)
appropriateness *(eth, act)*; (▷ richtiges Verhältnis) proportionality *(gep)* → Proportionalität

Verhältnismäßigkeit der Mittel *f* • appropriateness of means *(act, eth)*

Verhältnisschätzung *f* • ratio estimation *(sci)*

Verhältnisskala *f* • ratio scale *(mat)*, relation
scale *(eth, dec)*

Verhältniswahlsystem *n* • proportional
representation *(pol)*

Verhandeln *n* • bargaining *(eco, dec)*

Verhängnis *n* • (▷ Unglück) misfortune,
calamity, (▷ Schicksal) fate *(met)*

Verheißung *f* • promise *(rel)*

Verheißung, Land der *n* • promised land *(rel)*
< Goldenes Zeitalter

Verifikation *f* • verification *(sci)* → Bestätigung

Verifikationismus *m* • verificationism *(sci)* ↔
Falsifikationismus < Bestätigungstheorie

Verifikationskriterium *n* • verifiability/verifi-
cation criterion *(sci)* < Wahrheitskriterium

Verifikationskriterium der Bedeutsamkeit *n*
• verifiability/verification criterion of
meaningfulness *(lan)* < Verifikationstheorie
der Bedeutung

Verifikationsmethode *f* • method of
verification *(sci)*

Verifikationsprinzip *n* • principle of
verification, verification/verifiability
principle *(sci)*

Verifikationstheorie *f* • verification(ist) theory
(sci)

Verifikationstheorie der Bedeutung *f* • verifi-
cation(ist) theory of meaning *(lan)* < Verifikationskriterium der Bedeutsamkeit

Verifizierbarkeit *f* • verifiability *(sci)* < Bestätigbarkeit, Nachprüfbarkeit, Prüfbarkeit

Verifizierbarkeitskriterium *n* • criterion of verifiability *(lan, sci)*

verifizierende Begründung *f* • verificatory/ verifying justification *(epi)*

Verinnerlichung *f* • internalization, introjection *(psy)* → Interiorisation < Introjektion

Verirrung, religiöse *f* • religious aberration *(rel)*

Verismus *m* • verism, verismo *(aes)*

Verkaufsförderung *f* • consumer promotion *(eco)* < Konsumismus, Überflußgesellschaft

Verkaufswert *m* • market value *(eco)* ↔ Gebrauchswert < Tauschwert

Verkehrsverhältnisse *pl* • commercial relationships *(Marx etc) (eco, soc)*

verkehrte Welt *f* • inverted world *(Hegel) (met)*

verkehrtes Bewußtsein *n* • inverted consciousness *(Marx) (soc)*

Verkehrungsprozeß *m* • process of inversion *(Marx) (soc)*

verkettete Prognosen *pl* • concatenated/ chained predictions/prognoses *(sci)*

Verkettung *f* • sequence *(Derrida etc) (epi, pol)*

Verklärung *f* • transfiguration *(rel)*

Verkleinerungswille *m* • will to diminution *(Kohr) (soc)* < klein ist schön

Verknüpfung *f* • connection, integration, nexus *(log, mat)*

Verknüpfung von Vorstellungen *f* • association of ideas *(Hume) (epi, psy)*

Verknüpfungsregeln *pl* • laws of connection, principles of concatenation, concatenation rules *(epi, log, lan)* < Assoziationsprinzipien

Verkommenheit, moralische *f* • moral depravity *(eth)*

Verkörperlichung *f* • incarnation *(rel)* → Inkarnation

verkörperte Kreatur *f* • embodied creature *(met)*

verkörperter Geist *m* • embodied mind *(met)*

verkörpertes Bewußtsein *n* • embodied consciousness *(Husserl) (epi, met)*

Verkörperung *f* • embodiment *(gep)*

Verkümmerung der Individualität *f* • atrophy of individuality *(Horkheimer, Adorno etc) (soc)* < Verlust des Subjekts

Verkündigung *f* • word of God *(rel)*

Verkürzungsregel *f* • thinning rule, rule of thinning, shortening rule *(log)*

Verlagerungen *pl* • shifts *(Foucault etc) (epi, his)*

Verlangen *n* • desire, longing, craving *(psy)* < Begehren

Verlängerungsregel *f* • addition rule, rule of addition, lengthening rule° *(log)*

Verlassenheit *f* • abandonment *(Heidegger, Sartre) (ant)* < Geworfenheit

verläßliches Wissen *n* • reliable knowledge *(epi)* < Unbezweifelbarkeit

Verläßlichkeit *f* • reliability *(sci, eth)*

Verläßlichkeit der Sinne *f* • reliability of the senses *(epi)*

Verläßlichkeitstheorien *pl* • theories of reliability *(sci)* < Reliabilismus

Verleumdung *f* • defamation, libel, slander *(jur)*

Verliebtheit *f* • amorousness *(psy)* < Eros, philosophischer

Verlogenheit *f* • mendacity *(eth)*

verlorene Generation *f* • lost generation *(G. Stein) (cul)*

Verlust an biologischer Vielfalt *m* • loss of biological diversity *(nat, env)* < Artenschwund

Verlust der Lebenswelt *m* • loss of life world *(cul)*

Verlust des Subjekts *m* • loss of the subject *(met, soc)* < Selbstverlust

Verlustangst *f* • loss anxiety *(psy)*

Vermächtnis, geistiges *n* • intellectual heritage/legacy *(gep)*

Vermassung *f* • massification°, depersonalization, stereotyping *(soc, cul)*

Vermassung des Menschen *f* • massification° of man *(Ortega y Gasset) (cul)* < Massengesellschaft, Massenmensch, Aufstand der Massen

Vermehrung der Bedürfnisse *f* • multiplication of needs *(Marx) (eco, soc)*

Vermeidungslernen *n* • avoidance learning *(psy)*

Vermeidungsverhalten *n* • avoidance behaviour *(nat, act, psy)*

vermenschlichte Natur *f* • humanized nature *(Marx) (ant)*

Vermenschlichung des Menschen *f* • humanization of man *(met, soc)*

vermitteltes Wissen *n* • mediated knowledge *(epi)*

Vermittlung *f* • mediation, mediacy *(Hegel) (met)*

Vermittlung, dialektische *f* • dialectical mediation *(met)*

Vermittlung, historische *f* • historical mediation *(his)*

Vermögen *n* • (▷ Besitz) fortune, wealth, property *(eco)*, (▷ Fähigkeit) faculty, ability, capacity, power *(psy)* < Potenz

Vermögen der Begriffe *n* • faculty of
concepts *(Kant) (epi)* < Verstand als
Vermögen der Begriffe

Vermögen der Ideen *n* • faculty of ideas
(Kant) (epi) < Vernunft als Vermögen der
Ideen

Vermögen der Prinzipien *n* • faculty of
principles *(Kant) (epi)*

Vermögen der Regeln *n* • faculty of rules
(Kant) (epi)

Vermögen unter Regeln zu subsumieren *n* •
faculty of subsuming under rules *(Kant) (epi,
log)* < Urteilskraft

Vermögensbildung *f* • creation of wealth,
capital/wealth formation *(eco)*

Vermögensgegenstand *m* • property asset
(eco)

Vermögenskonzentration *f* • concentration of
wealth *(eco)*

Vermögenspolitik *f* • property policy *(eco,
pol)*

Vermögensverhältnisse *pl* • financial/
pecuniary circumstances *(eco)*

Vermögensverteilung *f* • distribution of wealth
(eco) < Umverteilungspolitik

Vermögenswert *m* • asset *(eco)*

Vermutungscharakter *m* • conjectural/
speculative character/nature *(sci)*

Vermutungswissen *n* • conjectural knowledge
(epi, sci)

Vernachlässigung der Pflicht *f* • neglect of
duty *(eth)* < Pflichtverletzung

Verneinung *f* • negation, denial *(log, lan)*

Verneinung des Daseins *f* • denial of existence
(met)

Verneinung des Willens *f* • denial of the will
(Schopenauer) (met)

Verneinung des Willens zum Leben *f* • denial
of the will to live *(Schopenhauer) (met)*

Verneinungssatz *m* • negation (statement)
(lan)

vernetztes Denken *n* • network(ed) thinking
(sys, min)

Vernichtung unwerten Lebens *f* • extinction
of unworthy life *(eth, pol)* < Lebenswertdebatte

Vernichtungsangst *f* • annihilation anxiety
(psy) < atomare Drohung

Vernichtungsdrohung *f* • threat of annihilation
(pol, eth) < atomare Abschreckung

Vernichtungskrieg *m* • war of extermination
(pol)

Vernunft *f* • (faculty of) reason *(epi, met)* ↔
Verstand

Vernunft, absolute *f* • absolute reason *(Hegel)*
(met)

Vernunft, abwägende *f* • deliberative
rationality *(Rawls) (eth)*

Vernunft als Vermögen der Ideen *f* • reason
as the faculty of ideas *(Kant) (epi, met)*

Vernunft, ästhetische *f* • aesthetic reason
(aes)

Vernunft, diskursive *f* • discursive reason
(Habermas etc) (lan, epi, soc)

Vernunft, Grenzen der *pl* • limits/bounds of
reason/rational insight *(Kant etc) (epi, met)*

Vernunft, instrumentelle *f* • instrumental reason *(Horkheimer etc) (epi, soc)* < Zweckrationalität < W 1359

Vernunft, intuitive *f* • intuitive reason *(epi,
met)*

Vernunft, praktische *f* • practical reason *(epi,
eth)* ↔ Vernunft, theoretische < W 535

Vernunft, reine *f* • pure reason *(Kant) (epi,
met)* < W 538

Vernunft, Stimme der *f* • voice of reason
(met, eth)

Vernunft, theoretische *f* • theoretical reason
(epi, met) ↔ Vernunft, praktische

Vernunft, transzendierende *f* • transcending
reason *(epi, met)*

Vernunft, universelle *f* • universal reason *(epi,
met)*

Vernunft, Zeitalter der *n* → Vernunftzeitalter

Vernunftappell *m* • appeal to reason *(gep)*

vernunftbegabtes Wesen *n* • rational being/
creature *(ant)* < animal rationale

Vernunftbegabung *f* • rationality, endowed-
ness with reason, being endowed with
reason *(epi, ant)*

Vernunftbegriffe *pl* • concepts of reason
(Kant) (epi, met)

Vernunftbeweis *m* • rational proof *(met, rel)*
< Gottesbeweis

Vernunfterkenntnis *f* • rational cognition/
knowledge *(epi, met)* → Erkenntnis,
rationale

Vernunftgebrauch *m* • use of reason *(epi,
met, eth)*

Vernunftgefühl *n* • rational sentiment *(aes)*

Vernunftgegenstand *m* → Gegenstand der
Vernunft

vernunftgeleitet • governed by reason *(gep)*

Vernunftgesetze, ewige *pl* • eternal laws of
reason *(epi, met)*

Vernunftglaube *m* • rational faith/belief *(Kant
etc) (rel)*

Vernunftgrund *m* • (▷ Basis der Vernunft)
ground/foundation (of reason, (▷ vernünftiger Grund) reasonable argument/ground
(gep)

Vernunftherrschaft *f* • rule of reason *(met)*

Vernunftidee *f* • idea of reason *(Kant) (epi, met)*

vernünftig • rational, reasonable *(epi, gep)* < Vernunftbegabung

vernünftige Selbstprüfung *f* • rational self-examination *(epi, psy)*

vernünftige Zustimmung *f* • reasonable agreement *(eth, soc)* < Vertragstheorie

vernünftiger Grund *m* • rational reason *(log)*

Vernünftigkeit *f* • reasonableness *(act, eth),* rationality *(epi, ant)*

Vernunftkritik *f* • (▷ Kritik der Vernunft) critique of reason, (▷ Kritik durch Vernunft) rational critique/criticism *(Kant) (epi, met)*

vernunftmäßiges Folgern *n* • ratiocination *(epi)*

Vernunftphilosophie *f* • rational philosophy *(met)*

Vernunftpostulate *pl* • postulates of reason *(Kant) (epi, met)* < Postulate der praktischen Vernunft

Vernunftreligion *f* • rational religion *(rel)*

Vernunftschluß *m* • rational inference/argument, inference of reason *(epi, log)*

Vernunftseele *f* • rational soul *(Aristotle) (met)*

Vernunftstaat *m* • rational state, state based on reason *(Schiller) (pol)* ↔ Notstaat

Vernunfttheologie *f* • rational theology *(rel)* → Theologie, rationale

vernunfttranszendierend • reason-transcending *(met)*

Vernunftvermögen *n* • faculty of reason *(Kant) (epi)*

Vernunftwahrheit *f* • truth of reason *(Leibniz, Hume) (epi, met)* ↔ Tatsachenwahrheit

Vernunftwesen *n* • rational being/creature *(epi, ant)* → animal rationale

vernunftwidrig • unreasonable, irrational, contrary to reason *(epi, met)*

Vernunftwidrigkeit *f* • illogicality, illogicalness *(log)* → Paralogie; unreasonableness, irrationality *(epi, psy)* → Irrationalität

Vernunftwissen *n* • rational knowledge *(epi)* ↔ Verstandeswissen

Vernunftzeitalter *n* • the age of reason *(his)* → Aufklärung, Zeitalter der

Verordnung *f* • order, ordinance, regulation *(jur)* → Regulativ

Verpflichtung *f* • obligation *(eth, jur)* < Pflicht; Sollen, das

Verpflichtung eingehen • to enter (into) an obligation *(eth, jur)*

Verpflichtung erfüllen • to honour/fulfil an obligation *(eth)*

Verpflichtung, moralische *f* • moral duty/obligation *(eth)*

Verpflichtung, soziale *f* • social duty/obligation/requirement *(soc)*

Verpflichtungsgrund *m* • source of obligation *(eth)*

Verrechtlichung *f* • juridification, regulation by law, legal regulation, bringing within the orbit of the legal system *(jur, soc)*

Verrechtlichungsschub *m* • wave of juridification/legal regulation *(Habermas etc) (jur, soc, pol)*

Versachlichung *f* • (▷ Vergegenständlichung) objectification, reification *(epi)* → Reifikation; (▷ Ent-Emotionalisierung) objectification *(lan, sci)*

Versagensangst *f* • fear of failure, failure anxiety *(psy)*

Versagung *f* • refusal, denial *(psy)*

Versammlungsfreiheit *f* • freedom of assembly *(pol)*

Versammlungsrecht *n* • right of assembly *(pol, jur)*

Versäumnis von Pflichten *n* → Pflichtversäumnis

verschachtelte Intervalle *pl* • nested intervals *(mat, sys)*

Verschanzung *f* • entrenchment *(Goodman) (sci)* < Immunisierungsstrategie

Verschiebung *f* • displacement *(Freud etc) (psy)* < Verdrängung

Verschiedenartigkeit *f* • (▷ Mannigfaltigkeit) variety, diversity < Vielfalt, (▷ Andersartigkeit) difference, heterogeneity, disparateness *(gep)* → Verschiedenheit

Verschiedenheit *f* • dissimilarity, difference, disparateness *(gep)* → Heterogenität

Verschiedenheit, numerische *f* • numerical difference/diversity *(mat)*

Verschleierung von Tatsachen *f* • veiling/dissimulation/cover-up of facts *(gep)*

Verschlüsseln *n* • encoding *(sys, mat)* ↔ Entschlüsseln

verschlüsselter Text *m* • enciphered text, cypher/cipher text *(lan)* < Chiffre

verschmähtes Dasein *n* • unrequited existence *(Kierkegaard) (ant, rel)*

Verschmelzung mit dem Einen *f* • fusion/amalgamation with the One *(Plotinus) (ont, rel)*

Verschmelzungsgesetz *n* • law of absorption *(mat)*

Verschönerung *f* • beautification *(aes)*

verschüttetes Wissen *n* • buried knowledge *(epi)*

Verschwendung *f* • waste *(eco, env)*

Verschwendungssucht *f* • wastefulness, extravagance *(eco, env, psy)*

Verschwiegenheit *f* • discretion, secrecy *(eth)* < Schweigepflicht

Verschwinden des Menschen *n* • the disappearance of man *(soc)*

verschwommene Begriffe *pl* • fuzzy/vague/indistinct concepts *(sci)*

Verschwörung des Geistes gegen die Seele *f* • conspiracy of (the) mind against (the) soul *(Klages) (cul)* < Geist als Widersacher der Seele

Verschwörungstheorie *f* • conspiracy theory *(soc, pol)*

verselbständigter Tauschwert *m* • autonomous exchange value *(Marx) (eco)*

Versenkung in Gott *f* • immersion in God *(Plotinus, Eckhart etc) (rel)*

Versinnbildlichung *f* • representation, symbolization *(aes, lan)* < Repräsentation

versinnlichter Geist *m* • sensualized mind *(Hegel) (met)*

Versklavung *f* • enslavement *(pol, soc)*

Versöhnung *f* • reconciliation *(eth, rel)*

Versöhnung der Gegensätze *f* • reconciliation of opposites/contradictions *(Fichte, Hegel) (met)*

Versöhnung von Eros und Erkenntnis *f* • reconciliation of eros and knowledge *(Adorno) (aes, cul)*

Versorgungslage *f* • supply position/situation *(eco)*

verspätete Nation *f* • latecomer-nation, delayed nation *(pol)*

Verspottung Christi *f* • derision/mockery of Christ *(Kierkegaard) (rel)*

Versprachlichung des Sakralen *f* • linguistification of the sacred *(Durkheim) (lan, rel)*

Versprechen *n* • avowal, promise *(eth)*

Versprecher, freudscher *m* • Freudian slip *(psy)*

verstaatlichte Industrie *f* • nationalized industries *(eco)*

verstaatlichte Wirtschaft *f* • state/nationalized economy *(eco, pol)*

Verstaatlichung *f* • nationalization *(eco, pol)* < Vergesellschaftung der Produktionsmittel

Verstädterung *f* • urbanization *(soc)*

Verstand *m* • (faculty of) understanding, intellect *(Kant, Hegel etc) (epi, met)*, reason, mind *(min)* ↔ Vernunft

Verstand als Urteilsfähigkeit *m* • intellect as faculty of judg(e)ment *(Kant) (epi)*

Verstand als Vermögen der Begriffe *m* • understanding as the faculty of concepts *(Kant) (epi)*

Verstand, tätiger *m* • acting/active intellect *(Avicenna)*, acting logos *(Aristotle) (epi, met)* → Intellekt, handelnder; intellectus agens

Verstandesbegriff *m* • concept of the understanding, intellectual concept *(Kant) (epi, lan)*

Verstandesbegriffe, reine *pl* • pure concepts of the understanding, pure intellectual concepts *(Kant) (epi)*

Verstandesdenken *n* • intellectual reasoning *(epi)*

Verstandesformen *pl* • intellectual forms *(Kant) (epi)* < Denkformen

Verstandesgebrauch *m* • use of intellect *(met)*

Verstandeskategorien *pl* • categories of the understanding *(Kant) (epi)*

Verstandeskraft *f* • intellectual faculty, faculty of the understanding *(epi)*

verstandesmäßig • rational, intellectual *(epi)*

Verstandesmetaphysik *f* • metaphysics of intellect *(met)*

Verstandesschluß *m* • inference of the understanding *(Kant) (epi)*

Verstandestugenden *pl* • intellectual/rational virtues *(Aristotle) (eth)* → Tugenden, dianoetische

Verstandeswelt *f* • world of the understanding, intelligible world *(Kant) (epi, met)* → intelligible Welt < noumenale Welt < W 1239

Verstandeswissen *n* • intellectual knowledge *(epi)* ↔ Vernunftwissen

Verständigungsabsicht *f* • communicative intent *(lan, soc)*

Verständigungsform *f* • form of understanding, form of establishing agreement *(lan, soc)*

Verständigungsfriede *m* • negotiated peace *(pol, eth)*

verständigungsorientierte Einstellung *f* • attitude oriented to reaching understanding *(Habermas) (act, soc)*

verständigungsorientierte Handlung *f* • action oriented to reaching understanding *(Habermas) (lan, act)*

Verständigungspolitik *f* • rapprochement policy *(pol)*

Verständigungsprozeß *m* • process of (reaching) understanding *(lan, soc)*

Verständigungsschwierigkeit *f* • communication problem *(lan)* < Interpunktionsproblem

Verstärkung, positive *f* • positive reinforcement *(psy)* < Feedback-Schleife; Sanktion, positive

Verstehen *n* • understanding, intellection *(epi, sci)*, verstehen *(Dilthey)* *(sci)* < Hermeneutik, Sinnverstehen

Verstehen, geschichtliches *n* • historical understanding *(Dilthey etc)* *(his, sci)*

Verstehen, linguistisches *n* • linguistic understanding *(epi, lan)*

Verstehen, psychoanalytisches *n* • psychoanalytical understanding *(psy)*

Verstehen, sinnliches *n* • sensual/sensory understanding *(epi)*

verstehende Erklärung *f* • interpretative explanation *(Weber)* *(sci)*

verstehende Methode *f* • method of Verstehen/understanding *(Dilthey etc)* *(sci)*

verstehende Psychologie *f* • interpretative psychology, psychology of Verstehen *(psy)*

verstehende Soziologie *f* • interpretative sociology, sociology of Verstehen *(Weber)* *(soc)*

Verstehens, Theorie des *f* • theory of understanding *(epi, sci, met)*

Verstehensakt *m* • act of understanding/comprehension *(epi)*

Verstelltheit *f* • disguisedness, being covered-over *(Heidegger)* *(ont)*

Verstofflichung *f* • materialization *(met)*

Verstoß *m* • offence, violation *(eth, jur)* < Vergehen

Verstrahlung *f* • nuclear contamination *(nat, env)*

verstreuter Gegenstand *m* • scattered object *(Cartwright)* *(ont)* < diskontinuierliche Objekte

Versuch und Irrtum *m,m* • trial and error *(sci)*

Versuchs-Irrtums-Lernen *n* • learning by trial-and-error, trial-and-error learning *(psy)*

Versuchsanordnung *f* • experimental design *(sci)*

Versuchsbedingung *f* • experimental condition, test condition *(sci)*

Versuchsergebnis *n* • test result(s) *(sci)*

Versuchskaninchen *n* • guinea pig *(eth, sci)* < Humanexperiment

Versuchsmodell *n* • test model *(sci)*

Versuchsperson *f* • test person, test/experimental subject *(sci)*

Versuchsreihe *f* • test series *(sci)*

Versuchsstadium *n* • experimental stage *(sci)*

Versuchstier *n* • laboratory/vivisectional animal *(nat, eth)* < Tierversuch

Versuchszweck *m* • experimental/test purpose *(sci)*

Versuchung *f* • temptation, trial *(rel)*

Versündigung gegen das göttliche Gebot *f* • sin against the Divine law *(rel)*

Verteidiger des Glaubens *m* • defender of the faith *(rel)*

Verteidigung religiöser Lehren *f* • defence of religious doctrines *(rel)* → Apologetik

Verteidigungsausgaben *pl* • defence expenditure *(pol, eco)*

Verteidigungsbündnis *n* • defensive alliance *(pol)*

Verteidigungsfähigkeit *f* • defence capability/capacity *(pol)*

Verteidigungsgemeinschaft *f* • defence community *(pol)*

Verteidigungskrieg *m* • defensive war *(pol)* → Defensivkrieg ↔ Angriffskrieg, Eroberungskrieg

Verteidigungsschrift *f* • written defence, apologia *(gep)*

Verteidigungssystem *n* • defensive system *(pol)*

Verteilung *f* • distribution *(mat, eco)*

Verteilungseffekt *m* • distribution effect *(eco, soc)*

Verteilungsergebnis *n* • result of distribution *(eco)* < Eigentumsstreuung

Verteilungsfunktion *f* • distributive function *(mat)*

Verteilungsgerechtigkeit *f* • distributive justice *(eth)* → distributive Gerechtigkeit

Verteilungskampf *m* • struggle over distribution, distributive battle, allocation competition *(eco)*

Verteilungsprinzip *n* • principle of distribution *(eco, eth)*

Verteilungsproblem *n* • distribution problem *(eco, eth)*

Verteilungsschlüssel *m* • allocation formula/key *(eco, eth)*

Vertrag *m* • contract *(jur)*

vertragliche Vereinbarung *f* • contractual agreement *(jur)*

vertraglicher Austausch *m* → Vertragstausch

Verträglichkeit *f* • (▷ Friedfertigkeit) peaceableness *(eth)*; (▷ Vereinbarkeit) compatibility *(nat, log)* → Kompatibilität

Vertragsabschluß *m* • conclusion of a contract, completion of an agreement *(jur)*

Vertragsbedingungen *pl* • contractual terms *(jur)*

Vertragsbeziehungen *pl* • contractual relations *(jur, soc)*

Vertragsbruch *m* • breach of contract *(jur, eth)* → Vertragsverletzung

vertragsfreier Zustand *m* • contract-free state *(soc)* < Naturzustand, Anarchie

Vertragsfreiheit *f* • freedom of contract *(jur, soc)*

Vertragsgegenstand *m* • object of agreement *(jur)*

Vertragsindividualismus *m* • contractarian individualism *(eth, soc)*

Vertragsmacht *f* • treaty power *(jur, pol)*

Vertragspartei *f* • contracting party *(jur, pol)*

Vertragspartner *m* • partner in contract, contractee *(jur)*

Vertragsrecht *n* • law of contract, contract law *(jur)*

Vertragstausch *m* • contractual exchange *(jur, soc)*

Vertragstheorie *f* • contract theory *(jur, soc)* < Kontraktualismus, Sozialvertragstheorie

Vertragstreue *f* • contractual fidelity/commitment *(jur, eth)*

Vertragsverhältnis *n* • contractual relationship *(jur, pol)* < Rechtsverhältnis

Vertragsverletzung *f* • violation/infringement of contract *(jur, eth)* → Vertragsbruch

Vertrauensbereich *m* • confidence limit *(mat)*

Vertrauensbeweis *m* • proof/mark of confidence *(eth)*

vertrauensbildende Maßnahmen *pl* • confidence-building measures, CBM *(pol)*

Vertrauensbruch *m* • breach of confidence/trust/faith *(eth)*

Vertrauenskrise *f* • crisis of confidence, confidence crisis *(psy)*

Vertrauensschwund *m* • loss of confidence *(psy)* → Vertrauensverlust

Vertrauensstellung *f* • position of trust *(soc)*

Vertrauensverhältnis *n* • relationship of mutual trust *(soc)*

Vertrauensverlust *m* • loss of confidence *(psy)*

Vertrauensvorschuß *m* • advance trust, trust in advance *(psy, eth)*

Vertrauenswürdigkeit der Sinne *f* • reliability/truthworthiness of the senses *(epi)*

Vertraulichkeit *f* • confidentiality *(eth)*

Vertrautheit *f* • familiarity *(epi, met)* < Lebenswelt

Vertreibung aus dem Paradies *f* • expulsion from paradise, expulsion from the Garden of Eden *(rel)*

Vertretung *f* • representation *(jur, pol)*

Verunreinigung *f* • pollution, contamination *(env)* < Umweltverschmutzung

Verursacher aller Ereignisse *m* • cause/creator of all things *(rel)*

Verursacherprinzip *n* • polluter-pays principle *(eco, env)*

Verursachung *f* • causation *(nat, met)*

Verursachung, intentionale *f* • intentional causation *(min)*

Verursachung, mentale *f* • mental causation *(min, met)*

Verursachung, nicht verursachte *f* • non-causal/uncaused causation *(met)*

Verursachungsprinzip *n* → Verursacherprinzip

Verurteilung, moralische *f* • moral condemnation *(eth)*

Vervielfältigung *f* • multiplication *(ont)*, reproduction *(nat)*

Vervollkommnung *f* • perfection *(eth, rel)*

Vervollkommnungsfähigkeit *f* • perfectibility, capacity for self-improvement *(gep)* → Perfektibilität

Vervollkommnungsfähigkeit des Menschen *f* • perfectibility of man *(met)*

vervollständigte Systeme *pl* • completed systems *(sys)*

verwaltete Welt *f* • administered world *(Adorno) (soc, pol)*

Verwaltungsorgan *n* • administrative body *(pol)*

Verwandlung von Geld in Kapital *f* • transformation of money into capital *(eco)*

verwandt • related, similar *(log, ont)* → ähnlich < ident

verwandte Disziplinen *pl* • cognate/related disciplines *(sci)*

Verwandtschaft *f* • kinship *(ant, cul)*, relationship, connection, relation *(gep)* < Affinität

Verwandtschaftsbeziehung *f* • relation of kinship *(Carnap) (epi, ont)* < Familienähnlichkeit

Verwandtschaftsgruppe *f* • kin-group *(cul, soc)*

Verwandtschaftsselektion *f* • kin-selection *(cul, soc)*

Verwandtschaftssystem *n* • kinship system *(ant, cul)*

Verwegenheit *f* • boldness *(eth)*

Verweis *m* • reference *(lan)*

Verweisungsbezug *m* • referential relation *(lan, ont)*

Verweisungscharakter des Zeugs *m* • referential character of equipment, equipmental nexus *(Heidegger) (ont)*

Verweisungsganzheit *f* • referential whole *(Heidegger) (ont)*

Verweisungszeichen *n* • mark of reference *(lan)*

Verweisungszusammenhang *m* • context of reference *(lan)*

Verweltlichung *f* • secularization *(rel, pol)* → Säkularisierung

Verwendung *f* • use *(gep)*

Verwendung eines Ausdrucks *f* • use of an expression *(lan)*

Verwendungstheorie der Bedeutung *f* • use theory of meaning *(lan)*

Verwerfung *f* • repudiation, foreclosure *(Lacan, Freud) (psy)*, rejection *(Brentano) (log)*, rejection, refutation, denial *(gep)*

Verwertungsprozeß *m* • process of valorization, valorization process *(Marx) (eco)*

Verwestlichung *f* • occidentalization, westernization *(cul)*

Verwindung der Metaphysik *f* • transformation/overcoming of metaphysics *(Heidegger) (ont)* < Ende der Metaphysik

Verwirklichung *f* • actualization *(Hegel) (met)*, realization *(gep)* → Konkretion

Verwirklichung des menschlichen Vermögens *f* • realization of human potential *(Rousseau, Marx etc) (ant, soc)*

verworrene Begriffe *pl* • indistinct/confused concepts *(Leibniz) (epi, met)*

verwurzelt im Glauben • rooted in faith *(rel)*

Verwurzelung, kulturelle *f* • cultural rootedness *(soc, cul)*

Verwüstung *f* • (▷ Desertifikation) desertification *(env)*

Verzeitlichung *f* • temporalization *(rel, met)*

verzerrte Optik *f* • distorted view *(epi, psy)* < optische Täuschung

Verzichtserklärung *f* • disclaimer, renunciation *(jur)*

Verzichtsleistung *f* • renunciation *(psy, jur)*

Verzögerungstaktik *f* • delaying tactics *(dec, act)*, filibustering *(pol)*

Verzweiflung *f* • despair *(Kierkegaard etc) (met)*, desperation *(psy)* < Angst

Verzweiflung, existentielle *f* • existential despair/desperation *(Kierkegaard etc) (ant, rel)*

Verzweiflung, stille *f* • silent despair *(Kierkegaard) (rel)*

Verzweigung *f* • bifurcation *(log, AI)* → Verästelung

Vetorecht *n* • right/power of veto, veto power *(jur)*

Vexierbild *n* • picture puzzle *(psy)*

Videoinstallation *f* • video installation *(aes)*

Videokunst *f* • video art *(aes)*

Vieldeutigkeit *f* • ambiguity, equivocation *(log, lan)* < Ambiguität, Zweideutigkeit

Vielen, die *pl* • the many *(Plato etc) (pol)*

Vielfalt *f* • multiplicity, variety, plurality *(gep)* < Verschiedenartigkeit

Vielgeisterei *f* • multi-spiritedness *(Nietzsche) (met)*

vielgestaltig • polymorphic *(met, aes)*

Vielgötterei *f* → Polytheismus

Vielheit *f* • plurality, manifoldness *(ont)* ↔ Einheit < Vielfalt, Mannigfaltigkeit

vielschichtiges Modell *n* • multi-layered model *(sci)*

Vielschichtigkeit *f* • multi-layeredness, complexity, intricacy *(gep)* → Multidimensionalität, Komplexität

Vielseitigkeit *f* • versatility, versatileness *(gen)*

Vielvölkerstaat *m* • multi-ethnic state *(pol)*

Vielwisser *m* • know(-it)-all *(gen)* < enzyklopädisches Wissen

Vier Wahrheiten, die edlen *pl* • the four noble truths *(asp)*

vierfache Wurzel des zureichenden Grundes *f* • fourfold root of sufficient reason *(Schopenhauer) (met)*

vierte Dimension *f* • fourth dimension *(nat)*

Vierter Stand *m* • fourth estate *(pol, soc)* < Ständestaat

Vierursachenlehre *f* • doctrine of the four causes, four-cause theory *(Aristotle) (met)*

virtuelle Realität *f* • virtual reality *(AI)* < Scheinwelt, Vorstellungswelt

virtueller Raum *m* • virtual space, cyberspace *(AI)* ↔ Realraum < Cyberspace

Virtuosität *f* • virtuosity *(aes)*

Visionär *m* • visionary *(gep)*

visionär • visionary *(gep)*

visuelle Kommunikation *f* • visual communication *(aes, lan)*

visuelle Reize *pl* • visual stimuli *(nat, epi)*

visuelle Wahrnehmung *f* • visual perception *(epi)*

Vitalismus *m* • vitalism *(met)* < W 1190

Vitalseele *f* • vital soul *(Aristotle) (met)*

Vivisektion *f* • vivisection *(nat, eth)* < Tierversuch

Vogel-Strauß-Politik *f* • head-in-the-sand policy, ostrich policy *(pol)*

Vokalmusik *f* • vocal music *(aes)* ↔ Instrumentalmusik

Volk *n* • (▷ Einwohner) people, Volk, (▷ Nation) nation, Volk, (▷ Rasse) race *(pol)*

Völkerbund *m* • league/federation of nations *(pol)* < Staatenbund, Vereinte Nationen, Weltbund

Völkerfriede *m* • international peace *(pol)*

Völkergemeinschaft *f* • community of nations *(pol)*

Völkerkunde *f* • ethnology *(cul, ant)* → Ethnologie

Völkermord *m* • genocide *(pol, eth)* → Ethnozid

Völkerpsychologie *f* • ethnopsychology *(cul)* < W 1191

Völkerrecht *n* • international law, law of nations *(jur)* → ius gentium

Völkerverständigung *f* • international understanding *(eth, pol)*

Völkerwanderung *f* • migration *(pol, soc)* < Armutsmigration

völkisch • racial *(pol)*

Volksabstimmung *f* • plebiscite, referendum *(pol)* → Plebiszit < Demokratie, direkte

Volksaufklärung *f* • public information (campaign) *(pol)*

Volksbegehren *n* • (petition for a) referendum *(pol)*

Volksbildung *f* • people's/popular education *(pol)* < Volksaufklärung

Volksbildungsprogramm *n* • people's/popular education programme *(pol)*

Volkscharakter *m* • national character *(cul)* < Klimatheorie

Volksdemokratie *f* • people's democracy *(pol)*

Volkseinkommen *n* • national income *(eco)*

Volksempfinden, gesundes *n* • sound popular instinct *(pol)*

Volkserhebung *f* • national uprising *(pol)*

Volksetymologie *f* • popular/folk etymology *(lan)*

Volksfront *f* • popular front *(pol)*

Volksgeist *m* • national spirit, spirit of the people, volksgeist *(Hegel etc)* *(met, his)* < Völkerpsychologie

Volksgemeinschaft *f* • national community, folk community *(pol)*

Volksgesundheit *f* • public health *(nat)*

Volksgruppe *f* • ethnic group *(pol)*

Volksherrschaft *f* • rule of the (common) people *(pol)* → Demokratie

Volkskommune *f* • people's commune *(Mao)* *(pol)*

Volkskultur *f* • popular culture *(cul)*

Volkskunde *f* • folklore *(cul)* < Ethnologie, Völkerkunde

Volkskunst *f* • folk art *(aes)* ↔ Hochkunst

Volksmeinung *f* • public/popular opinion *(pol)*

Volksmetaphysik *f* • popular/folk metaphysics *(met)*

Volksmusik *f* • folk music *(aes)* ↔ Kunstmusik

Volkspsychologie *f* • folk psychology *(psy)*

Volksreligion *f* • folk religion *(Herder, Hölderlin, Hegel etc)* *(rel)*

Volksrepublik *f* • people's republic *(pol)*

Volksschicht *f* • social class/stratum *(soc, pol)*

Volksseele *f* • soul of the nation *(cul)* < Volksgeist

Volkssouveränität *f* • popular sovereignty *(pol)*

Volksstamm *m* • tribe *(cul)*

Volkstum *n* • nationality, national characteristics *(cul)*

Volksverführer *m* • demagogue *(pol)*

Volksverhetzung *f* • popular agitation *(pol)*

Volksvermögen *n* • national wealth *(eco)*

Volksversammlung *f* • national/people's assembly, public meeting *(pol)*

Volkswille *m* • popular will, the people's will, will of the people *(Rousseau)* *(pol)* < Gemeinwille

Volkswirtschaftslehre *f* • political economy/economics *(eco)* → politische Ökonomie

Volkswohlfahrt *f* • public welfare *(eco)*

Vollbeschäftigung *f* • full employment *(eco)*

Vollendung der Geschichte *f* • fulfilment of history *(his)* < Eschatologie, Ende der Geschichte

Vollentscheidbarkeit *f* • complete decidability *(log)* ↔ Teilentscheidbarkeit

vollentwickeltes menschliches Leben *n* • fully developed human life *(Rousseau, Marx etc)* *(ant)*

Voll-Fiktion *f* • full-fiction *(Vaihinger)* *(met)*

vollkommene Pflicht *f* • perfect duty *(Kant)* *(eth)*

vollkommene Zahl *f* • perfect number *(mat)*

vollkommener Wettbewerb *m* • perfect competition *(eco)*

vollkommenes Gleichgewicht *n* • perfect equilibrium *(nat, eco)*

vollkommenes Wesen *n* • perfect being *(met, rel)*

vollkommenes Wissen *n* • perfect knowledge *(epi)*

Vollkommenheit *f* • perfection *(met, eth, aes)*

Vollkommenheitsethik *f* • ethics of perfection *(Wolff etc)* *(eth)*

Vollkommenheitsgrade *pl* • degrees of perfection *(rel, ont)*

vollschematische Abbildung *f* • complete schematic representation *(sci)* ↔ teilschematische Abbildung

vollständig • complete *(mat)*

vollständig individuierte Person *f* • fully individuated person *(Mead etc) (soc, psy)*

vollständige Definition *f* • complete definition *(lan, sci)*

vollständige Hülle *f* • completion, complete hull *(mat)*

vollständige Induktion *f* • complete induction *(log, sci)* → Induktion, aufzählende

vollständige Öffentlichkeit *f* • complete transparency *(Rawls etc) (eth, pol)* < Glasnost

vollständige Verifizierbarkeit *f* • complete verifiability *(Hempel) (sci)*

vollständiger Grund *m* • complete reason *(met)*

vollständiges Differential *n* • total differential *(mat)*

vollständiges Gut *n* • complete good *(Kant) (eth)*

vollständiges System der reinen Vernunft *n* • complete system of pure reason *(Kant) (epi)*

Vollständigkeit *f* • completeness *(log, mat)*

Vollständigkeitsaxiom *n* • axiom of completeness, completeness axiom *(Gödel) (log, mat)* → Vollständigkeitssatz

Vollständigkeitsergebnis *n* • completeness result *(mat, log)*

Vollständigkeitsnachweis *m* • completeness proof *(log, mat)*

Vollständigkeitsrelation *f* • completeness relation *(mat)*

Vollständigkeitssatz *m* • completeness theorem *(Gödel) (log, mat)* → Vollständigkeitsaxiom

vollstetiger Operator *m* • completely/uniformly continuous operator *(mat)*

Vollstreckung *f* • execution *(jur)*

Vollsubstanz *f* • total substance *(rel, met)*

Vollversammlung *f* • plenary/general assembly *(pol)*

vollziehender Körper *m* • executive body *(Rousseau etc) (pol, jur)* < Exekutivgewalt

Vollzug des Seins *m* • enactment/realization/completion of Being *(Heidegger) (ont)* < Ereignis

Vollzugsgewalt *f* • executive power *(pol, jur)*

volonté de tous *f* • will of all *(Rousseau) (pol)* ↔ volonté générale < Wille aller

volonté générale *f* • general will *(Rousseau) (pol)* → Gemeinwille < Wille, allgemeiner

Voluntarismus *m* • voluntarism *(met, psy)*

Voluntarismus, psychologischer *m* • psychological voluntarism *(met, psy)*

Voodoo *m* • voodoo *(rel, eso)* < schwarze Magie

Vor- und Nachteil *m,m* • advantage and disadvantage *(act, dec)*

Vorabdruck *m* • preprint *(gen)*

Vorahnung *f* • presentiment *(psy)*

Vorausbestimmung *f* → Vorherbestimmung

vorausdenken • to think ahead *(gep)* < Futurologie

vorausgehende Absicht *f* • prior intent(ion) *(act, jur)*

vorausgehende Handlung *f* • previous action *(act)* < Karma

Vorausplanung *f* • (forward) planning, planning ahead *(act)*

Voraussagbarkeit *f* • predictability *(sci)*

Voraussage *f* • prediction *(sci)* → Prognose < Retrodiktion < W 982

voraussagende Funktion *f* • predictive function *(Peirce) (sci)*

Voraussagerelevanz *f* • predictive relevance *(sci)*

Voraussagestudie *f* • prediction study *(sci)*

Voraussetzung *f* • presupposition, (pre)condition *(sci)* → Präsupposition < Vorgegebenheit

Voraussetzung, formale *f* • formal presupposition/(pre)condition *(gep)*

Voraussetzung, materiale *f* • material presupposition/(pre)condition *(gep)*

Voraussetzung, ontologische *f* • ontological commitment *(Church, Quine) (lan, ont)*, ontological presupposition *(ont)*

Voraussetzung, stillschweigende *f* • tacit/implicit presupposition *(gep)*

Voraussetzung, transzendentale *f* • transcendental presupposition *(epi)*

Voraussetzungen, geistige *pl* • mental presuppositions *(gep)*

Voraussetzungen, kulturelle *pl* • cultural preconditions *(cul)*

Voraussetzungen, metaphysische *pl* • metaphysical presuppositions/preconditions *(met)*

Voraussetzungen, wirtschaftliche *pl* • economic (pre)conditions *(eco)*

voraussetzungslose Wissenschaft *f* • presuppositionless science, science without presuppositions *(Husserl) (sci, met)*

Voraussetzungslosigkeit *f* • presuppositionlessness *(sci, met)*

Voraussicht, göttliche *f* • divine foresight *(rel)*

Vorauswissen *n* • foreknowledge, precognition *(epi, psy)* → Präkognition

Vorbedingung der Freiheit *f* • precondition of freedom *(met)*

Vorbegriff *m* • preliminary/inchoate concept *(epi, met)*

vorbegriffliche Ebene f • preconceptual level *(Foucault) (epi, lan)*

vorbereitender Mensch m • preparatory man *(Nietzsche) (ant, met)* < Übermensch

vorbestimmte Harmonie f → prästabilierte Harmonie

Vorbeugung f • prevention *(act)*

Vorbeugungsmaßnahme f • preventive measure *(act)* → Präventivmaßnahme

vorbewußt • preconscious *(Freud) (psy)* < unbewußt

Vorbewußtsein n • preconsciousness *(Freud) (psy)*

Vorbild n • model, pattern, paradigm *(gep)* < Rollenvorbild

vorbürgerliche Verhältnisse pl • pre-bourgeois conditions *(soc, his)*

vorbürgerlicher Zustand des Menschen m • pre-civil condition of man *(Hobbes, Locke, Rousseau) (pol, soc)* < Naturzustand, Wildheit

vorchristliches Denken n • pre-Christian thought *(rel, his)*

Vordenker m • intellectual pioneer *(gep)* < Vorläufer, Wegbereiter

vordisziplinäre Phase f • pre-disciplinary phase *(Kuhn etc) (sci)* ↔ disziplinäre Phase

Vordringlichkeit f • priority *(dec)* < Priorität

Voreingenommenheit f • biased/prejudiced attitude *(eth)* < Parteilichkeit, vorgefaßte Meinung, Vorurteil

Vorentscheidung f • preliminary decision *(act, dec)*

vorfindliche Welt f • present/current/received world *(Heidegger) (ont)*

Vorgangsweise f • (mode of) procedure *(gep)*

vorgefaßte Meinung f • preconceived opinion *(eth)* → Vorurteil < Voreingenommenheit

vorgegebener Weltentwurf m • predetermined world-design *(met)*

Vorgegebenheit f • givenness *(ont, sci)* < Voraussetzung

Vorgeschichte f • prehistory *(his)* → Prähistorie

vorgesellschaftliche Rechte pl • pre-social rights *(jur)* → Naturrecht, vorpositives Recht

Vorgriff m • fore-conception *(Heidegger) (ont)*

Vorgriff auf Vollkommenheit m • anticipation of completeness *(Gadamer) (met)*

Vorhabe f • fore-having *(Heidegger) (ont)* < Vorsicht

Vorhandenes, bloß n • what is merely present to hand *(Jaspers, Heidegger) (ont)*

Vorhandenheit f • occurrentness, presence at hand *(Heidegger) (ont)* < Zuhandenheit

Vorhandensein n • being-on-hand, (objective) presence *(Heidegger) (ont)*

Vorherbestimmung f • preordination, preordainment, predetermination *(rel, met)* → Prädestination

Vorherrschaft f • (pre)dominance, superiority *(pol, gep)*

vorherrschende Werte pl • dominant values/ethic *(eth)*

Vorhersagbarkeit f • predictability *(sci)* → Prädiktabilität

Vorhersage f • prediction *(sci, gep)* → Prädiktion

Vorhersagegenauigkeit f • predictive accuracy *(sci)*

Vorhersagekraft f • predictive power *(sci)*

Vorhersageparadoxon n • prediction paradox *(log)*

Vorhersagetheorie f • theory of prediction, prediction theory *(sci)*

Vorherwissen n • foreknowledge *(epi, eso)*

Vorhölle f • limbo *(rel)* → Limbus

vorindustrielle Gesellschaft f • pre-industrial society *(eco, his)*

vorinterpretiert • preinterpreted *(lan)*

Vorkriegszeit f • pre-war period, antebellum *(pol)* ↔ Nachkriegszeit

vorkritische Periode f • precritical period *(Kant) (epi, met)*

vorkritische Schriften pl • precritical writings *(Kant) (gep)*

Vorlaufen zum Tod n • forerunning to death *(Heidegger) (ant, ont)*

vorlaufende Entschlossenheit f • precursive resoluteness *(Heidegger) (ant, ont)*

Vorläufer m • precursor *(gen)* < Vordenker

Vorläuferphilosophie f • precursor philosophy *(gep)*

vorläufiges Verstehen n • precursive understanding *(Heidegger) (ont)* < ursprüngliches Verstehen

Vorläufigkeit f • anticipatoriness, primordiality *(ont)*, provisionality *(gep)*

vorlogisches Denken n • pre-logical thinking/thought *(Lévy-Bruhl) (ant)*, → wildes Denken; *(Piaget) (psy)* → prälogisches Denken

Vormachtstellung f • supremacy *(soc, pol)*

Vormensch m • pre-human *(ant)* < Hominide

Vornehmheit des Geistes f • nobility of spirit *(Nietzsche) (met)*

vorontologisch • pre-ontological *(Heidegger) (ont)*

vorparadigmatisch • pre-paradigmatic *(Kuhn)* *(sci)*

vorphilosophischer Mensch *m* • pre-philosophical man *(gep)*

vorpositives Recht *n* • pre-positive right *(jur)* → Naturrecht, vorgesellschaftliche Rechte

vorprädikative Erfahrung *f* • pre-predicative experience *(Husserl)* *(epi)*

Vorrangsregel *f* • rule of priority *(eth)*

Vorrangstellung *f* • priority position, superiority, preeminence *(soc, pol)*

Vor-Schein, ästhetischer *m* • aesthetic anticipation *(aes)*

Vorschein *m* • anticipation *(Bloch)* *(met, soc)* < antizipierendes Bewußtsein, Noch-Nicht-Sein

Vorschein der Apokalypse *m* • anticipation of the apocalypse *(cul)* < atomare Vernichtung

Vorscholastik *f* • pre-scholasticism *(gep)*

Vorscholastiker *m* • pre-scholastic *(gep)*

vorschreibende Sprache *f* • prescriptive language *(lan)* < Präskriptivismus

Vorsehung *f* • providence *(rel)*

Vorsehungsplan *m* • providential plan *(rel)*

Vorsicht *f* • foresight, fore-sight *(Heidegger)* *(ont)*

Vorsokratik *f* • the Presocratic school/period *(gep)*

Vorsokratiker *m* • Presocratic *(gep)*

Vorsokratiker, die *pl* • Presocratics *(gep)*

vorsokratische Philosophie *f* • Presocratic philosophy *(his)*

Vorsorgemedizin *f* • preventive medicine *(nat)*

Vorstellung *f* • idea, conception, image *(epi, psy)*, representation *(Hegel)* *(met)*, presentation *(Brentano)* *(min, psy)* < Abbild

Vorstellung an sich *f* • idea in itself/as such *(Bolzano)* *(ont)*

Vorstellung, bildhafte *f* • visual image/imagination/representation *(epi, aes, psy)*

Vorstellung geistiger Bilder *f* • idea/representation of mental images *(epi, min)*

Vorstellung, körperliche *f* • physical notion *(epi, psy)*

Vorstellungen als Abbilder von Eindrücken *pl* • ideas as images of impressions *(Hume)* *(epi)*

Vorstellungen der göttlichen Vernunft *pl* • ideas of Divine reason *(rel)*

Vorstellungen, Verknüpfung von *f* • association of ideas *(Hume)* *(epi, psy)*

Vorstellungskraft *f* • (power of) imagination *(epi, psy)*

Vorstellungsvermögen *n* • powers of imagination, faculty of representation *(epi, psy)* < W 1167

Vorstellungswelt *f* • world of imagination *(epi, min)* < virtuelle Realität

Vorteil, persönlicher *m* • personal advantage *(eth)*

Vorüberlegung *f* • preliminary/preparatory consideration *(gep)* → Prämeditation

Voruntersuchung *f* • preliminary test/investigation *(sci)*

Vorurteil *n* • prejudice, preconception *(eth, sci)* → vorgefaßte Meinung, Präjudiz < Voreingenommenheit

Vorurteil der Gelehrten *n* • prejudice of the learned *(Nietsche)* *(epi)*

vorurteilsfrei • unprejudiced, unbiased *(eth, sci)*

Vorurteilslosigkeit *f* • unbiasedness, lack of prejudice *(eth, sci)*

Vorurteilstheorie *f* • prejudice theory *(Spencer)* *(soc)*

Vorverständnis *n* • preconception *(sci)*, foreconception, pre-understanding *(Heidegger)* *(ont)*

vorweltlich • before time *(nat)*

Vorwissen *n* • precognition *(epi, psy)*, preknowledge *(sci)*

Vorwissenschaft *f* • pre-science *(Stumpf)* *(sci)*

vorwissenschaftlich • pre-scientific *(sci)*

Vorzeichen *n* • sign *(mat, eso)*

Vorzeit *f* • prehistory, prehistoric times *(his)*

Vorzeitigkeit *f* • anteriority *(ont)*

Vorzeitmensch *m* • prehistoric man *(ant)*

Vorzensur *f* • precensorship *(pol)*

Vorzugsaxiom *n* • axiom of preference *(log)*

Vorzugsbehandlung *f* • preferential treatment *(eth)* < Diskriminierung, umgekehrte

Vulgärdarwinismus *m* • vulgar Darwinism *(nat, pol)*

Vulgarismus *m* • vulgarism *(aes)*

Vulgärmarxismus *m* • vulgar Marxism *(pol)*

W

W-Schema *n* • T-schema *(Tarski) (epi, lan, sci)*

Wachstum, arithmetisches *n* • arithmetic growth *(mat, sys)*

Wachstum, exponentielles *n* • exponential growth *(mat, sys)*

Wachstum, geometrisches *n* • geometric growth *(mat, sys)*

Wachstum, lineares *n* • linear growth *(mat, sys)* → Wachstum, stetiges

Wachstum, negatives *n* • negative growth *(mat, sys)*

Wachstum, nichtlineares *n* • non-linear growth *(mat, sys)* → Wachstum, unstetiges

Wachstum, progressives *n* • progressive growth *(mat, sys)*

Wachstum, stetiges *n* • stable/steady growth *(mat, sys)* → Wachstum, lineares

Wachstum, unstetiges *n* • unstable/unsteady growth *(mat, sys)* → Wachstum, nichtlineares

wachstumsfördernd • conducive to growth, growth-promoting *(eco)*

Wachstumsgesellschaft *f* • growth-oriented society *(eco)*

wachstumshemmend • growth-retarding *(eco)*

Wachstumsideologie *f* • growth ideology *(eco)*

Wachstumsimpuls *m* • growth impulse *(eco)*

Wachstumskritik *f* • critique/criticism of growth *(eco)*

wachstumsorientiert • growth-minded/oriented *(eco, soc)*

Wachstumsphase *f* • growth phase *(eco, nat, psy)*

Wachstumspolitik *f* • growth policy *(eco)*

Wachstumsrate *f* • rate of growth, growth rate *(eco, nat)*

Wachstumsschranken, ökonomische *pl* • barriers to economic growth *(eco)* < Grenzen des Wachstums

Wächter, die *pl* • the guardians *(Plato) (pol)*

Wächterstaat *m* • state of guardians *(Plato) (pol)*

Wachtraum *m* → Tagtraum

Wachzustand *m* • wakeful state (of mind) *(psy)*

Wadschrajana *n* • vajrayana *(asp)*

Waffen der Vernunft *pl* • weapons of reason *(Kant) (epi)*

Waffenausfuhrverbot *n* • ban on arms exports *(pol, eth)*

Waffengewalt *f* • force of arms *(pol)*

Waffenindustrie *f* • arms/armaments industry *(eco, eth)* < Rüstungskonversion

Waffenruhe *f* • ceasefire *(pol)*

Waffenstillstand *m* • armistice, truce *(pol)*

Waffenstillstandsabkommen *n* • armistice agreement *(pol)*

Wagemut *m* • spirit of adventure, courage, daring *(eth)* < gefährlich leben

Wagnerianer *m* • Wagnerite, Wagnerian *(aes)*

Wagnerianisches Gesamtkunstwerk *n* • Wagnerian Gesamtkunstwerk, Wagnerian synthesis of the arts, Wagnerian total art work *(aes)*

Wagner(ian)ismus *m* • Wagner(ian)ism *(aes)* < Gesamtkunstwerk

Wagnis, Philosophie als *f* • philosophy as venture *(Jaspers) (gep)*

Wahl *f* • choice *(dec)*

Wahl der Hoffnungslosigkeit *f* • choice of despair *(Kierkegaard) (ant, rel)*

Wahl der Mittel *f* • choice of means *(act)*

Wahl, freie *f* • free choice *(act, eth)*

Wahl, rationale *f* • rational choice *(dec)*

Wahl unter Unsicherheit *f* • choice under uncertainty *(dec)*

Wahl, ursprüngliche *f* • original choice *(Rawls) (dec)* < Schleier des Nichtwissens

Wahlaxiom *n* • axiom of choice, multiplicative axiom *(mat)*

Wählbarkeit *f* • eligibility *(pol)*

Wahlberechtigung *f* • right/entitlement to vote *(pol)*

Wählerschaft *f* • electorate, (▷ lokale Wählerschaft) constituency *(pol)*

Wählerverhalten *n* • voter behaviour *(pol)*

Wahlfreiheit *f* • freedom of choice *(act, dec)*

Wahlgeheimnis *n* • secrecy of the ballot *(pol)*

Wahlkampagne *f* • election campaign *(pol)*

Wahlmöglichkeit *f* • option, choice *(act, dec)*

Wahlpropaganda *f* • election propaganda, electioneering *(pol)*

Wahlrationalität *f* • rationality of choice *(Weber) (dec)*

Wahlrecht, aktives *n* • right to vote *(pol)*

Wahlrecht, allgemeines *n* • universal suffrage *(pol)*

Wahlrecht, passives *n* • eligibility, right to run for office *(pol)* < Wählbarkeit

Wahlsituation *f* • choice situation *(dec)* < Entscheidungssituation, Entscheidungstheorie

Wahlstrategie *f* • choice strategy *(dec)* < Entscheidungstheorie

Wahlsystem *n* • electoral system *(pol)*

Wahlverhalten *n* • voting behaviour *(pol)*

Wahlvermögen *n* • ability/capacity to choose, faculty of choice *(act, eth)* < Handlungsfreiheit

Wahlverwandtschaft *f* • elective affinity *(nat)* < Seelenverwandtschaft

Wahn, religiöser *m* • religious mania/insanity *(rel)* < Bigotterie

Wahnsinn *m* • insanity, lunacy, madness *(psy)* < W 1265

Wahnvorstellung *f* • delusion, hallucination *(psy)*

wahr • true *(log, lan)*

Wahre, das *n* • the true *(met)*

wahre Gesellschaft *f* • true community *(Marx)* *(soc)*

wahre Kunst *f* • true art *(aes)*

wahre Natur *f* • true nature *(met)*

wahrer Sozialismus *m* • true socialism *(soc)*

wahres Sein des Menschen *n* • man's true being *(Marx)* *(soc)*

Wahrhaftigkeit *f* • veracity, veridicality, truthfulness *(eth)* < Wahrheitsliebe

Wahrhaftigkeit als Wahrheitskriterium *f* • veracity as criterion of truth *(Descartes)* *(epi, met)*

Wahrhaftigkeit Gottes *f* • veracity of God *(rel)*

Wahrhaftigkeitsanspruch *m* • claim to truthfulness/sincerity *(epi, act, eth)*

Wahrheit *f* • truth *(epi, met)*

Wahrheit, absolute *f* • absolute truth *(met, rel)*

Wahrheit als Gewißheit *f* • truth as certainty *(epi)*

Wahrheit als Übereinstimmung von Denken und Sein *f* • truth as agreement of being and thought *(epi, met)*

Wahrheit, analytische *f* • analytic(al) truth *(epi, log, lan)*

Wahrheit des Seins *f* • truth of Being *(Heidegger)* *(ont)*

Wahrheit, doppelte *f* • double truth, twofold truth *(Boethius)* *(rel, epi)*

Wahrheit, empirische *f* • empirical truth *(epi, lan)*

Wahrheit, Evidenztheorie der *f* • evidence theory of truth *(Brentano)* *(epi, met)*

Wahrheit, ewige *f* • eternal truth *(epi, met)*

Wahrheit, immergültige *f* • everlasting/sempiternal truth *(epi, rel)* → Wahrheit, ewige

Wahrheit, Kohärenztheorie der *f* • coherence theory of truth *(Leibniz etc)* *(epi, met)*

Wahrheit, Konsenstheorie der *f* • consensus theory of truth *(epi, met)*

Wahrheit, Korrespondenztheorie der *f* • correspondence theory of truth *(epi, met)*

Wahrheit, notwendige *f* • necessary truth *(log, epi, met)*

Wahrheit, objektive *f* • objective truth *(epi, sci)*

Wahrheit, performative Theorie der *f* • performative theory of truth *(Strawson etc)* *(epi, met)* → performative Wahrheitstheorie

Wahrheit, prosententiale Theorie der *f* • prosentential theory of truth *(Grover etc)* *(epi, met)* < Prosatz

Wahrheit, Redundanztheorie der *f* • redundancy theory of truth, superfluity theory of truth *(Frege etc)* *(epi, met)*

Wahrheit, relative *f* • relative truth *(epi, sci)*

Wahrheit, selbstevidente *f* • self-evident truth *(Descartes etc)* *(epi)* < unzweifelhafte Wahrheit

Wahrheit, subjektive *f* • subjective truth *(epi, sci)*

Wahrheit, Trieb zur *m* • drive to truth *(Nietzsche)* *(epi)*

Wahrheit, unveränderliche *f* • immutable/unchangeable truth *(epi)*

Wahrheit, Verifizierbarkeitstheorie der *f* • verifiability/verification(ist) theory of truth *(epi, met)* < Verifikationstheorie der Bedeutung

Wahrheit, vier Arten von *pl* • four kinds of truth *(Schopenhauer)* *(epi, met)* < vierfache Wurzel des zureichenden Grundes

Wahrheit, Zitattilgungstheorie der *f* • disquotation(al) theory of truth *(Quine)* *(epi, sci)* < T-Schema

Wahrheitsähnlichkeit *f* • verisimilitude, truthlikeness *(Popper)* *(epi, sci)* < Wahrheitsnähe

Wahrheitsanspruch *m* • truth claim, claim to truth *(epi)*

Wahrheitsargument *n* • truth argument *(epi, log, lan)*

Wahrheitsbedingung *f* • truth condition *(epi, sci)* < Wahrheitskriterium

Wahrheitsbegriff *m* • concept of truth *(epi)* < Wahrheitsverständnis < W 1271

Wahrheitsbegriff, objektiver *m* • objective concept of truth *(epi)*

Wahrheitsbegriff, subjektiver *m* • subjective concept of truth *(epi)*

Wahrheitsbeweis *m* • proof of truth *(epi, sci)*

Wahrheitsbewußtsein *n* • awareness of truth *(met)*

Wahrheitsblindheit *f* • blindness to truth *(met)*

Wahrheitsdefinition *f* • truth definition *(Tarski etc) (log, lan)* < Wahrheitstheorie, semantische

Wahrheitsfanatismus *m* • truth fanatism *(gep)*

Wahrheitsfindung *f* • discovery of truth *(epi, sci)*

Wahrheitsfunktion *f* • truth function *(log)*

wahrheitsfunktional • truth functional *(log)*

Wahrheitsgehalt *m* • truth content *(epi, lan, sci)* ↔ Falschheitsgehalt

wahrheitsgetreu • truthful *(jur, eth)*

Wahrheitsgrund *m* • truth-reason *(Popper) (epi, sci)*

Wahrheitskombination *f* • truth-combination *(Wittgenstein) (lan)*

wahrheitskonservierend • truth-preserving *(log, lan)*

Wahrheitskriterium *n* • criterion of truth *(epi, sci)* < Verifikationskriterium

Wahrheitsliebe *f* • love of truth *(epi, eth)* < Wahrhaftigkeit

Wahrheitsmodalität *f* → aleth(e)ische Modalität

Wahrheitsmöglichkeiten *pl* • truth-possibilities *(Wittgenstein) (epi, lan)*

Wahrheitsnähe *f* • approximation to truth *(epi, sci)* < Wahrheitsähnlichkeit

Wahrheitsoperation *f* • truth operation *(log)*

Wahrheitsoperator *m* • truth operator *(log)*

Wahrheitspathos *n* • truth pathos *(Nietzsche) (epi, met)*

Wahrheitspotential *n* • truth potential *(epi, met)*

Wahrheitsproblem *n* • the problem of truth, truth problem *(epi, met)*

Wahrheitsregel *f* • rule of truth, truth rule *(Carnap) (log)*

Wahrheitssemantik *f* • truth semantics *(Tarski) (lan)*

Wahrheitssinn *m* • sense for truth *(Nietzsche) (epi)*

Wahrheitsskepsis *f* • truth scepticism *(epi)*

Wahrheitsstreben *n* • pursuit of/striving for truth *(epi, met)*

Wahrheitssuche *f* • quest/search for truth *(epi, met)* < Heuristik

Wahrheitstabelle *f* • truth table *(Carnap etc) (epi, log)*

Wahrheitstafel *f* • truth table *(epi, log)*

Wahrheitstest *m* • test of truth *(sci)*

Wahrheitstheorie *f* • theory of truth, truth theory *(epi, met)*

Wahrheitstheorie, deflationistische *f* • deflationary/deflationist theory of truth *(epi, met)*

Wahrheitstheorie, inflationistische *f* • inflationary/inflationist theory of truth *(epi, met)*

Wahrheitstheorie, pragmatische *f* • pragmatic/pragmatist theory of truth *(Peirce) (epi, met)*

Wahrheitstheorie, semantische *f* • semantic(al) theory of truth *(Tarski) (epi, lan, met)*

Wahrheitsträger *m* • truth bearer/vehicle *(log, lan)*

Wahrheitsverständnis *n* • conception of truth *(epi, sci)* < Wahrheitsbegriff

Wahrheitswert *m* • truth value *(log, lan)*

Wahrheitswertanalyse *f* • truth-value analysis *(log)*

Wahrheitswertbelegung *f* • attribution of truth value *(epi, sci)*

Wahrheitswertfunktion *f* • truth(-value) function *(log)*

Wahrheitswertlücke *f* • truth-value gap *(Quine) (log)*

Wahrheitswertoperator *m* → Wahrheitsoperator

Wahrheitswerttabelle *f* → Wahrheitstafel

Wahrheitswille *m* • will to truth *(met)*

Wahrheitszeuge *m* • truth witness, witness to the truth *(gep)* < Augenzeuge

Wahrmacher *m* • truth-maker *(Mulligan, Simons, B. Smith) (ont),* truth-bearer *(lan)*

wahrnehmbare Eigenschaft *f* • perceptible property *(epi)*

Wahrnehmbarkeit *f* • perceptibility *(epi, psy)* → Perzeptibilität ↔ Imperzeptibilität

wahrnehmendes Subjekt *n* • perceiving subject *(epi)*

Wahrnehmung *f* • perception *(epi)* → Apperzeption

Wahrnehmung, ästhetische *f* • aesthetic perception *(aes)*

Wahrnehmung, äußere *f* • outer/external perception *(epi, psy)* ↔ Wahrnehmung, innere

Wahrnehmung durch Hörensagen *f* • perception by hearsay *(Spinoza) (epi)*

Wahrnehmung, Grade der Deutlichkeit der *pl* • degrees of clarity of perception *(Leibniz) (epi)*

Wahrnehmung, innere f • inner/internal perception (*Locke, Brentano*) (*epi, psy*)

Wahrnehmung, objektive f • objective perception (*epi*)

Wahrnehmung, subjektive f • subjective perception (*epi*)

Wahrnehmung, transzendentale f • transcendental apperception (*Leibniz*) (*epi*)

Wahrnehmungseinheit f • perceptual unit (*epi, psy*)

Wahrnehmungserlebnis n • perceptual/perceptive experience (*epi, psy*)

wahrnehmungsfähiges Wesen n • sentient being (*nat, psy*)

Wahrnehmungsfeld n • perceptual field (*epi, psy*)

Wahrnehmungsinhalt m • perceptual content (*epi, psy*)

Wahrnehmungskonstanz f • perceptual invariance/constancy (*epi, psy*) < Objektkonstanz

Wahrnehmungslehre f → Wahrnehmungstheorie

Wahrnehmungsmethode f • method of perception (*epi*)

Wahrnehmungsobjekt n • object of perception (*epi*)

Wahrnehmungsprotokoll n • observation protocol (*sci*) < Protokollsatz

Wahrnehmungspsychologie f • psychology of perception, perceptual psychology (*psy*)

Wahrnehmungsraum m • perceptual space (*epi, psy*)

Wahrnehmungsrealismus m • perceptual realism (*epi*)

Wahrnehmungssatz m • perception statement (*sci*) < Beobachtungssatz, Protokollsatz, Beobachtungsaussage

Wahrnehmungsstil m • style of perception (*aes*)

Wahrnehmungstäuschung f • perceptual illusion (*psy*)

Wahrnehmungstheorie f • theory of perception, perception theory (*epi, psy*)

Wahrnehmungsurteil n • judg(e)ment of perception (*epi*)

Wahrnehmungsvermögen n • faculty of perception, perceptive faculty (*epi, psy*)

Wahrnehmungsvermögen, sinnliches n • faculty of sensory/sensuous perception (*epi*)

Wahrnehmungsverzerrung f • perceptual bias/distortion (*epi, psy*)

Wahrnehmungswissen n • perceptual knowledge (*epi*)

Wahrnehmungszustand m • perceptive/perceptual state (*epi, psy*)

Wahrsagekunst f → Mantik

Wahrsagerei f • prophecy, fortune-telling (*eso*)

Wahrscheinlichkeit f • probability, likelihood (*mat, sci*) → Probabilität

Wahrscheinlichkeit, bedingte f • conditional probability (*mat, sci*)

Wahrscheinlichkeit, Grad der m • degree of probability (*mat, sci*)

Wahrscheinlichkeit von E unter der Bedingung, daß H f • probability of E given H (*sci*)

Wahrscheinlichkeitsansatz m • probabilistic approach (*sci*)

Wahrscheinlichkeitsaussage f • probability statement (*sci*)

Wahrscheinlichkeitsauswahlen pl • probability choices (*mat, dec*)

Wahrscheinlichkeitsberechnung f • calculation of probabilities (*mat*)

Wahrscheinlichkeitserklärung f • probabilistic explanation (*mat, sci*)

Wahrscheinlichkeitsfunktion f • probability/likelihood function (*sci, log, mat*)

Wahrscheinlichkeitsgrad m • degree of probability (*sci*) < Bestätigungsgrad

Wahrscheinlichkeitsinterpretation f • interpretation of probability (*mat, sci*)

Wahrscheinlichkeitsinterpretation, subjektive f • subjective interpretation of probability (*mat, sci*)

Wahrscheinlichkeitskalkül m/n • probability calculus (*log, sci*)

Wahrscheinlichkeitslogik f • probability logic, logic of probability (*log, sci*)

Wahrscheinlichkeitsrechnung f • probability calculus (*mat*)

Wahrscheinlichkeitsschluß m • probability inference (*log*) < stochastische Methode

Wahrscheinlichkeitsstandpunkt m → Probabilismus

Wahrscheinlichkeitstheorie f • probability theory, theory of probability, probabilistic theory (*mat, sci*)

Wahrscheinlichkeitsverteilung f • probability distribution (*sci, epi, dec*)

Wahrscheinlichkeitswert m • probability (value) (*sci, mat*)

Wahrtraum m • true dream (*eso*)

Währungspolitik f • monetary policy (*eco*)

Währungssystem n • monetary system (*eco*)

Waldsterben n • forest dieback, dieback, waldsterben° (*env*)

Wandel der Zeiten m • changing times (*cul*)

Wandel des Überbaues m • superstructural changes (*Marx*) (*soc*)

Wandel, kultureller *m* • cultural change *(cul)*

Wandel, sozialer *m* • social change/ transformation *(soc)*

Wandelbare, das *n* • the changing *(Heraclitus etc) (met)* < alles fließt

Wandelbarkeit *f* • mutability *(gep)*

Wandelbarkeit des Menschen *f* • mutability/ malleability of human nature *(ant)* < Anpassungsfähigkeit

Wanderleben *n* • vagrant life *(Rousseau etc) (cul, soc)* < Jugendbewegung, Vagantenbewegung

Wanderlust *f* • wanderlust *(cul)*

Wanderprediger *m* • itinerant preacher *(rel)*

Wandlung *f* • change, transformation *(gep)* < Mutation; transubstantiation, consecration *(rel)* → Transsubstantiation

Wandlungsfähigkeit der Materie *f* • mutability of matter *(nat, met)*

Wankelmütigkeit *f* • inconstancy *(eth)* < Inkonsistenz

Ware *f* • commodity, merchandise, goods *(eco)* < marktfähige Güter, ökonomische Güter

Ware, Geld als allgemeine *n* • money as universal commodity *(Marx) (eco)*

Warenästhetik *f* • commodity aesthetics *(aes)* < Konsumästhetik

Warenaustausch *m* • trade, exchange of commodities *(eco)*

Warencharakter der Kunst *m* • commodity status of art, art as commodity *(aes)*

Warenfetischismus *m* • commodity fetishism, fetishism of commodities *(Marx) (soc, eco)*

Warengesellschaft *f* • commodity society *(Marx) (eco, soc)*

Warenmarkt *m* • commodity market *(Marx etc) (eco)*

Warenpreis *m* • commodity price *(eco)*

warenproduzierende Gesellschaft *f* • commodity economy *(Marx) (eco)*

Warenwirtschaft *f* • commodity economy *(eco)*

Wärmetod des Weltalls *m* • (the) heat death of the universe *(nat)* < Entropie

Warum-Frage *f* • why-question *(lan)*

Was-ist-Frage *f* • what-is question *(lan)*

Washeit *f* • whatness *(Heidegger) (ont)* → Quiddität

Wassein *n* • what-being *(Heidegger) (ont)*

Wassermann-Zeitalter *n* • Age of Aquarius *(eso)* < New Age

Wechselbeziehung *f* • correlation, interrelation, reciprocal relation *(gep)* → Korrelation

Wechselbeziehung von Männlichem und Weiblichem *f* • female-male interrelation *(asp)* < Yin-Yang

Wechselbezüglichkeit *f* • correlativity *(gep)* → Korrelativität, Reziprozität

Wechselfolge *f* • alternation *(sys)* → alternierende Folge

wechselseitig gesicherte Zerstörung *f* • mutually assured destruction, MAD *(pol, eth)* < Overkill, Selbstvernichtungsfähigkeit

wechselseitige Abhängigkeit *f* • mutual/reciprocal dependence *(sys)* → Interdependenz

wechselseitige Determinierung *f* • mutual determination *(sys, met)*

wechselseitige Sicherheit *f* • mutual security *(pol)*

wechselseitige Verursachung *f* • reciprocal causation *(met, sys)* < Reziprozität

wechselseitiger Vorteil *m* • mutual advantage *(eco, eth)*

wechselseitiger Zwang *m* • mutual coercion *(eth)*

wechselseitiges Fürsorgeverhältnis *n* • relationship of reciprocal care *(eth, soc)*

wechselseitiges Versprechen *n* • mutual promise *(eth)*

Wechselseitigkeit *f* • mutuality, reciprocity *(gep)*

Wechselverhältnis *n* • interrelation(ship) *(gep)*

Wechselwirkung *f* • interaction, reciprocity *(sys, gep)* → Reziprozität

Wechselwirkung, psychophysische *f* • psychophysical interaction *(psy, met)*

Wechselwirkung von Substanzen *f* • interaction of substances *(Descartes) (met)*

Weg *m* • path *(mat)*, path, road *(gep)*

Weg der Befreiung *m* • way of liberation *(met)*

Weg des Geistes *m* → geistiger Weg

Wegbereiter *m* • pioneer, precursor *(gep)* < Vordenker, Gründerväter

Wegkomponente *f* • path component *(mat)*

wegunabhängig • route independent *(mat, sys)*

Wegwerfgesellschaft *f* • obsolescent/wasteful/ throw-away society *(eco, env)*

Wehrdienstverweigerer *m* • conscientious objector *(eth)* < ziviler Ungehorsam

Wehrpflicht, allgemeine *f* • conscription *(pol)*

Weibergemeinschaft *f* • community of women *(Marx) (soc)*

Weiberherrschaft *f* • gynocracy, gynaecocracy, petticoat-government *(fem)* → Matriarchat

Weibliche, das *n* • the female, the feminine *(fem)*

weibliche Ästhetik *f* • female aesthetics *(aes)*
< feministische Ästhetik

weibliche Ethik *f* • female ethics *(eth)*

weibliche Identität *f* • feminine identity *(fem)*

weibliche Qualität *f* • feminine quality *(fem)*

Weiblichkeit *f* • femininity *(fem)*

Weibsästhetik *f* • female aesthetics *(Nietzsche)*
(aes, fem)

Weierstrass'sches Approximationstheorem
n • Weierstrass theorem of approximation,
Weierstrass approximation theorem *(mat)*

Weigerung, große *f* • great refusal *(Marcuse)*
(soc)

Weise des Daseins, durchschnittliche *f* • average mode of Dasein *(Heidegger) (ont)*

Weisen des Existierens *pl* • modes of
existence *(Heidegger) (ont)*

Weisen des Seins *pl* → Seinsweisen

Weisen des Umgreifenden *pl* • modes of
encompassing *(Jaspers) (met)*

Weisheit *f* • wisdom *(eth)*

Weisheit, Buch der *n* • Book of Wisdom *(rel)*

Weisheit der Natur *f* • wisdom of nature *(nat,
met)*

Weisheitsliebe *f* • love of wisdom *(gep)* < Philosophie

Weisheitssprüche *pl* • proverbs/words of
wisdom *(gep)*

Weissagung *f* • prophecy *(rel, eso)* → Prophetie

Weiterbestand der Gesellschaft *m* • continuance/continued existence of society *(soc)*

Weiterbestand der Kultur *m* • continuance/
continued existence of culture *(cul)*

Weiterbildung *f* • further education *(gen)*
< Erwachsenenbildung, Volksbildungsprogramm

Weiterentwicklung, technische *f* • technical
development *(tec)* < Innovationsprozeß

Weitergabe von Atomwaffen *f* → Proliferation

Weiterleben nach dem Tod *n* • life after
death, afterlife *(rel)* < Unsterblichkeitsglaube

Weitsichtigkeit *f* • farsightedness *(gep)*

Wellenmechanik *f* • wave mechanics *(nat)*

Wellentheorie *f* • wave theory *(nat)*

Welt als ästhetisches Phänomen *f* • world as
an aesthetic phenomenon *(Nietzsche) (aes)*

Welt als Idee *f* • world as idea *(Schopenhauer)*
(met)

Welt als Kunstwerk *f* • world as a work of art
(Nietzsche) (aes)

Welt als Wille und Vorstellung *f* • world als
will and idea *(Schopenhauer) (met)* < W
1291

Welt der Endlichkeit *f* • world of finiteness
(met, rel)

Welt der Erfahrung *f* • world of experience
(Kant) (epi)

Welt der Erscheinung *f* • world of appearance(s) *(Kant etc) (epi, met)* → Welt,
phänomenale

Welt der Ideen *f* • world of forms/ideas
(Plato) (met)

Welt der Kunst *f* • art world, world of art
(aes)

Welt der Unendlichkeit *f* • world of infinity
(met, rel)

Welt der Vorstellung *f* • ideational world,
world of imagination *(Nietzsche) (epi, met)*

Welt der Wissenschaft *f* • world of science,
scientific realm *(sci)*

Welt des Seienden *f* • world of being *(ont)*

Welt Drei *f* • world three, third world
(Popper) (sci) < drittweltlicher Ansatz,
Gedankenwelt, geistige Welt

Welt Eins *f* • world one, first world *(Popper)*
(sci)

Welt, hintere *f* → Hinterwelt

Welt, intelligible *f* • intelligible world *(Kant
etc) (met)*

Welt, kontemplative *f* • contemplative world
(Schleiermacher etc) (rel)

Welt, mögliche *f* • possible world *(Leibniz,
Lewis etc) (epi, met)* ↔ wirkliche Welt

Welt, phänomenale *f* • phenomenal world
(Kant etc) (epi, met)

Welt weltet • the world worlds *(Heidegger)*
(ont)

Welt Zwei *f* • world two, second world
(Popper) (sci)

Weltabgewandtheit *f* • reclusiveness *(met, rel)*
< Weltflucht

weltabkehrende Askese *f* • asceticism which
renounces the world *(Weber) (rel, soc)* ↔
innerweltliche Askese

Weltall *n* • universe, cosmos *(nat)*

Weltalter *n* • world-age *(nat)*, world-epoch
(his) < Äon < W 1290

Weltangst *f* • world-angst, weltangst
(Spengler) (met)

Weltanschauung *f* • world view, weltanschauung *(met)* → Weltsicht < Lebensanschauung
< W 846

Weltanschauung, Typen der *pl* • types of
weltanschauung *(Dilthey) (met)*

Weltanschauungsanalyse *f* • analysis of worldviews *(Jaspers, Topitsch) (met, soc)*

Weltanschauungsgemeinschaften *pl* • ideological communities *(soc, met)*

Weltauslegung *f* • interpretation of the world *(met)*

Weltbegriff *m* • concept of the world, world-concept *(met)* < W 641

Weltbeherrschung *f* → Weltherrschaft

Weltbeschaffenheit *f* • nature of the world *(met)* < Weltzustand

Weltbewußtsein *n* • world consciousness *(met)*

Weltbezug *m* • relatedness to the world *(gep)*

Weltbild *n* • world view/picture *(nat, met)* < W 1292

Weltbund *m* • international union *(pol)* < Völkerbund

Weltbürgerrecht *n* • cosmopolitan right *(Kant) (jur)*

Weltbürgerschaft *f* • world citizenship *(Kant etc) (pol)*

Weltbürgertum *n* • cosmopolitanism *(pol)*

Weltdeutung *f* • world interpretation, interpretation of the world, world reading *(met)*

Welteinstellung *f* • world view, view of (the) world *(Husserl) (met)*

Weltende *n* • end of the world *(rel)* → Ende der Welt, das

Weltenschöpfer *m* • demiurge, maker of the world *(Plato etc) (met)* → Demiurg

Weltensystem *n* • world system *(nat)*

Weltentsagung *f* → Weltflucht

Weltentwurf *m* • projection of the world *(met)*

Welterfahrung *f* • worldly wisdom *(gep)* < Weltweisheit

Welterkenntnis *f* • world knowledge *(gep)*

Welterklärung *f* • world explanation, explanation of the world *(met)* < Weltdeutung

Welterleuchter *m* • world-illuminator *(rel)*

Welterlöser *m* • world-redeemer *(rel)*

Welterzeugung *f* • worldmaking *(Goodman etc) (epi)* < W 1289

Weltflucht *f* • flight from reality, escapism, escape from the world *(psy, rel)* < Realitätsflucht, Askese

Weltformel *f* • world formula *(nat)* < Superketten, Susy Guts

Weltfremdheit *f* • otherworldliness, unworldliness *(gep)*

Weltfrieden *m* • world/universal/global peace *(pol, eth)* < ewiger Friede, universeller Friede

Weltfriedensordnung *f* • world/universal/global peace order *(pol)*

Weltgebäude *n* • cosmic system *(met)*

weltgebundene Individuen *pl* • world-bound individuals *(Lewis) (ont)*

weltgebundene Variablen *pl* • world-bound variables/individuals *(log, ont)* < Modallogik

Weltgeist *m* • world-spirit *(Hegel) (met)*

Weltgeist, entfremdeter *m* • alienated world-spirit *(Hegel) (met)*

Weltgeltung *f* • international acclaim/standing *(gen)*

Weltgemeinschaft *f* • world community *(soc)* < Weltstaat, globales Dorf

Weltgericht *n* • last jugd(e)ment *(rel)*, judg(e)ment of the world *(Hegel) (his, rel)*

Weltgeschichte *f* • world history, universal history *(his)* < Universalgeschichte

weltgeschichtliche Individuen *pl* • world-historical individuals *(Hegel) (his)*

Weltgesellschaft *f* • world society *(pol)*

Weltgesetz *n* • cosmic law *(nat, met)* < Universalgesetz

Weltgestalter *m* • world-shaper *(Brentano) (met)*

Weltgestaltung *f* • world-shaping *(met)*

Weltgrund *m* • world ground *(met)*

Welthandelssystem *n* • world trade system *(eco)*

Welthaß *m* • hatred of the world *(met)* ↔ Weltliebe

Weltherrschaft *f* • world domination *(pol)*

Welthilfssprachenbewegung *f* • artificial interlanguage movement *(lan, pol)*

Welthorizont *m* • world-horizon *(Husserl) (epi, met)*

Welthunger *m* • world hunger *(eco)*

Weltkirchenrat *m* • World Council of Churches *(rel)*

Weltklugheit *f* → Weltweisheit

Weltkonzepte *pl* • world concepts *(Popper, Habermas etc) (epi, met)*

Weltkultur *f* • world culture *(cul)*

Weltlauf *m* • way of the world *(his)*

Weltlehre *f* → Kosmologie

weltliche Autorität *f* • secular authority *(pol, rel)*

weltliche Mächte *pl* • secular powers *(pol, rel)*

weltliche Pflichten *pl* • worldly obligations *(eth)*

weltliches Leben *n* • worldly life *(gen)*

Weltlichkeit *f* • worldliness *(gep)*

Weltlichkeit der Welt *f* • worldness/worldliness/worldhood of the world *(Heidegger) (ont)*

Weltliebe *f* • love of the world *(met)* ↔ Welthaß

Weltlinie *f* • world line *(Carnap) (epi, ont)*

Weltliteratur *f* • world literature *(aes)*

Weltmacht *f* • great/world power, superpower *(pol)*

Weltmachtpolitik *f* • great power policy *(pol)* < Imperialismus

Weltmarkt *m* • global market *(eco)*

Weltmonopol *n* • global/world monopoly *(eco)*

Weltmusik *f* • world music *(aes)* < Sphären-musik

Weltoffenheit *f* • open-mindedness *(psy)*

Weltordnung *f* • world order *(pol)* < neue Weltordnung

weltorientierendes Denken *n* • world-orienting thought *(Jaspers) (met)*

Weltorientierung *f* • world orientation *(Hoffman) (met)*

Weltorientierung, philosophische *f* • philosophical world-orientation *(Jaspers) (met)*

Weltphänomen *n* • world phenomenon *(Husserl) (epi, met)*

Weltpolitik *f* • world politics *(pol)*

Weltpolizei *f* • world police *(pol)*

Weltpunkt *m* • world point *(Carnap) (epi, ont)*

Welträtsel *n* • riddle of the universe *(met)* < W 903, 1296

Weltraum *m* • (outer) space *(nat)*

Weltreligion *f* • world/global religion *(rel)*

Weltrevolution *f* • world revolution *(pol)*

Weltschmerz *m* • world weariness, welt-schmerz, sentimental pessimism *(psy)*

Weltschöpfungsmythos *m* • creation myth *(cul, rel)* → Kosmogonie

Weltseele *f* • world-soul *(Plato, Schelling etc) (met)* < W 1250

Weltsicht *f* • world-view *(met)* → Weltan-schauung

Weltsicht, dynamische *f* • dynamic world-view *(nat, met)*

Weltsicht, statische *f* • static world-view *(nat, met)*

Weltstaat *m* • world state *(pol)* < globales Dorf, Völkerbund, Weltgemeinschaft

Weltsystem *n* • world system, system of the world *(met)*

Weltüberdruß *m* • world-weariness *(psy)*

weltumspannende Organisation *f* • global organization *(pol)*

Weltuntergang *m* • end of the world, apoca-lypse *(rel)* < Apokalypse

Weltverbesserer *m* • world changer, would-be universal reformer, starry-eyed idealist, utopian *(eth, soc)* < Utopist

weltverklärend • world-transfiguring *(Nietzsche) (met)*

Weltverlust *m* • world loss, loss of the world *(met)*

Weltverneinung *f* • denial of the world *(met, rel)*

Weltvernichter *m* • world destroyer *(rel)*

Weltverständnis *n* • understanding of the world *(gep)*

Weltvorräte *pl* • global reserves *(eco, env)*

Weltweisheit *f* • world(ly)/secular wisdom *(gep)*

Weltwende *f* • turning-point in (world) history *(his)*

Weltwirtschaft *f* • world economy *(eco)*

Weltwirtschaftskrise *f* • world economic crisis *(eco)*

Weltwirtschaftsordnung *f* • international economic order, world trade order *(eco)*

Weltwunder *n* • wonder of the world *(gen)*

Weltzeit *f* • world-time, global/universal time *(nat)*

Weltzustand *m* • state/condition of the world *(pol)*, state of nature/the world *(dec)*

Wendehals *m* • turncoat, opportunist *(pol)* < Opportunismus

Wendepunkt *m* • point of inflexion *(mat)*, turning point *(gen)*

wenn p, dann q • if p, then q *(log)*

wenn und nur dann wenn • if and only if, iff *(log)*

Werden, das *n* • (the) becoming, (the) coming to be *(ont)* ↔ Vergehen, das

Werden und Vergehen *n,n* • coming to be and passing away *(ont)*

Werdens, Prozeß des *m* • process of becoming *(Nietzsche) (met)*

Werdens, Stufen des *pl* • degrees of becoming *(Aquinas) (met, rel)*

Werdensgrund *m* • reason for becoming *(Aristotle) (met)*

Werdensprozeß *m* • process of becoming, being in process *(gep)*

Werk *n* • (▷ Tat) work, deed, action, (▷ Leistung) achievement, (▷ künstlerisches Werk) opus *(act, aes)*

Werk, künstlerisches *n* • work of art *(aes)*

Werkgenese *f* • work genesis *(aes)*

werkimmanente Interpretation *f* • text-based interpretation *(aes)*

Werkinstinkt *m* • instinct of workmanship *(Veblen) (soc)*

Werktreue *f* • faithfulness (to the original), faithful rendition *(aes)*

Werkzeug *n* • instrument, tool *(Heidegger)* *(ont)* < Zeug

Werkzeug Gottes *n* • God's instrument, God's passive agent *(rel)*

Werkzeuggebrauch *m* • use of tools, tool use *(ant, tec)*

werkzeugmachendes Tier, Mensch als *m* • man as toolmaking animal *(ant, tec)* < Homo faber

Wert *m* • value, worth, asset *(eco)*, merit, value, worth *(eth, rel)*

Wert, ästhetischer *m* • aesthetic value *(aes)*

Wert, äußerlicher *m* → Wert, extrinsischer

Wert des Lebens *m* • value of life *(eth)* < Lebenswertdebatte < W 906

Wert, extrinsischer *m* • extrinsic value *(eth, aes)*

Wert, immanenter *m* • immanent value *(eth, aes)*

Wert, innerer *m* → Wert, intrinsischer

Wert, intrinsischer *m* • intrinsic value *(eth)*

Wert, künstlerischer *m* • artistic value *(aes)*

Wert, logischer *m* • logical value *(log)*

Wertanalyse *f* • value analysis *(eco, eth)*

Wertannahme *f* • normative/value assumption *(eth)*

Wertantagonismus *m* • antagonism of values *(Weber)* *(eth)*

Wertausdruck *m* • evaluative term *(lan, eth, aes)*

Wertaussage *f* • value statement *(lan, sci)* → normative Aussage ↔ Tatsachenaussage

Wertbegriff *m* • value concept, concept of value *(Lotze etc)* *(lan, sci)* < Begriff, normativer ↔ Tatsachenbegriff

wertbeladener Ausdruck *m* • value-laden term *(lan, sci)* < Wertbegriff

Wertbereich *m* • domain of values, domain of quantification *(log)*

Wertbeständigkeit *f* • stability of value *(eco)*

Wertbestimmender *m* • determiner of values *(Nietzsche)* *(eth)*

Wertbestimmung *f* • value determination, (e)valuation *(eth, aes, eco)*

Wertbewußtsein *n* • sense of value(s) *(eth, eco)*

wertbezogen • related to values *(eth)*

Wertbezogenheit *f* • value-relatedness *(eth, soc)*

Wertbildung *f* • formation of assets *(eco)* < ursprüngliche Akkumulation

Wertbindung *f* • value commitment *(soc, eth)*

Werte, System der *n* • system/hierarchy of values *(Rickert)* *(eth)* < Wertsystem, Werthierarchie

Werte, Ursprung der *m* • source of values *(gep)*

Wertebereich *m* • (value) range, range (of values) *(sci)*

Wertebeständigkeit *f* • stability of values *(eth, cul)* < Werteverfall

wertender Ausdruck *m* • evaluative term *(lan, eth)*

wertender Vergleich *m* • evaluative comparison *(eth)*

Wertentscheidung *f* • normative decision, decision as to values *(eth, dec)*

Werterfahrung *f* • value experience *(eth, met)*

Wertergründung *f* • value inquiry *(eth)*

Wertesystem *n* • system of values, value system *(eth, rel, aes)* → Wertsystem

Wertetafel *f* • table of values *(Nietzsche)* *(eth)*

Wertethik *f* • value ethics *(eth)* → axiologische Ethik

Wertethik, materiale *f* • material/non-formal value ethics, material/non-formal ethics of values *(Scheler)* *(eth)* < W 312

Werteverfall *m* • decline of values *(eth)*

Werteverlust *m* • loss of values *(eth)* < Niedergang der Moral

Wertewandel *m* • value change, change/transformation of values *(eth, cul)* < Moral, Wandel der

Wertform *f* • form of value *(Marx)* *(eco)*

Wertfrage *f* • value question *(sci)* ↔ Sachfrage

wertfreie Wissenschaft *f* • value-free science *(sci)* < Werturteilsfreiheit

wertfreier Raum *m* • value-free sphere *(gep)*

Wertfreiheit *f* • value-freedom, value-free condition *(Weber)* *(sci)*

Wertfreiheitspostulat *n* • postulate of value-freedom, value-freedom postulate *(Weber)* *(sci)*

Wertfreiheitsthese *f* • value freedom thesis *(Weber)* *(sci)*

Wertfühlen *n* • value-feeling *(Scheler)* *(eth)*

Wertgefühl *n* • value-feeling, feeling for values *(eth)*

Wertgegebenheiten *pl* • value facts *(eth)*

Werthierarchie *f* • value hierarchy, hierarchy of values *(eth)* < Wertsystem

Wertigkeit *f* • valency *(log, mat, nat)*, valence *(nat)*

Wertigkeitsskala *f* • value scale *(nat)*

Wertimplikation *f* • value implication *(eth)*

Wertinhalt *m* • value content *(eth)*

Wertinternalisierung *f* • value internalization *(eth, soc)*

Wertinterpretation *f* • value-interpretation *(Weber etc)*

Wertkonflikt *m* • conflict of values, value conflict *(eth)*

Wertkonsens *m* • value consensus, consensus regarding values *(eth)*

Wertkrise *f* • value crisis *(eth, cul)*

Wertkritik *f* • criticism of values *(eth, aes)*

Wertlehre *f* • axiology, value theory *(Scheler etc) (eth)* → Axiologie < W 416

Wertmaß(stab) *n(m)* • standard/measure of value *(eth)*

wertneutral • value-neutral *(eth, sci)*

Wertorientierung *f* • value-orientation *(eth)*

Wertphilosophie *f* • philosophy of value(s) *(gep)* < Philosophie, normative < W 1284

Wertpluralismus *m* • value pluralism, pluralism of values *(eth)*

Wertpostulat *n* • value postulate *(eth)*

Wertpräferenz *f* • value preference *(eth)*

wertrationales Handeln *n* • value-rational action *(Weber) (act, soc)*

wertrationales Verhalten *n* • value-rational conduct *(Weber) (act, soc)* < zweckrationales Verhalten

Wertrationalität *f* • value rationality *(act)* ↔ Zweckrationalität

Wertrealismus *m* • value realism, realism of values *(Brentano, Scheler etc) (eth, met)*

Wertrelativismus *m* • value relativism *(eth)*

wertschaffende Arbeit *f* • value producing labour *(Marx) (eco)*

wertschaffende Tätigkeit *f* • value creating activity *(eco)*

Wertschätzung *f* • esteem, appreciation *(eth)*

Wertschluß *m* • evaluative inference *(log, eth)*

Wertschöpfung *f* • net product, (real) net output *(eco)*, creation of values *(Nietzsche) (eth)*

Wertsetzung *f* • positing of norms *(eth)*

Wertsinn *m* → Wertbewußtsein

Wertskala *f* • value scale, scale of value(s) *(eth)*

Wertstandard *m* • standard of value *(eth, soc)*

Wertsystem *n* • system of values, value system *(eth, rel, aes)* < Werthierarchie

Werttheorie *f* • theory of value(s), value theory *(eth, eco)* < W 977

Werttheorie, materiale *f* • material theory of value *(N. Hartmann) (eth)*

Werttheorie, objektive *f* • objective theory of value *(eco)*

Werttheorie, subjektive *f* • subjective theory of value *(eco)* < Liebhaberwert, Affektionswert, Zahlungsbereitschaft

Wertung *f* • (e)valuation *(gep)* < Bewertung

Wertungsweise *f* • mode of evaluation/valuating° *(Nietzsche) (eth)*

Wertunterscheidung *f* • value distinction *(eth)*

Wertunterschied *m* • value difference *(eth)*

Wertuntersuchung *f* • value inquiry/enquiry *(eth, met)*

Werturteil *n* • value judg(e)ment *(eth, aes, sci)*

Werturteil, nicht-moralisches *n* • non-moral value judg(e)ment *(eth)*

werturteilsfrei • free from value jugd(e)ments, non-normative *(sci)*

Werturteilsfreiheit *f* • freedom from value judg(e)ments, non-normativity *(sci)* < wertfreie Wissenschaft

Werturteilsstreit *m* • value controversy *(Weber) (sci)* < Positivismusstreit

Wertvergleich *m* • value comparison *(eth, aes, eco)*

Wertverhältnis *n* • value relationship *(eco)*

Wertverlust *m* • depreciation (in value), loss of/in value, (value) depreciation *(eco)*

Wertverwirklichung *f* • value actualization, realization of value *(eth, soc)*

Wertvision *f* • value vision *(eth, met)*

Wertvorstellung *f* • (concept of) value *(eth)* < Wertannahme

Wertwissenschaft *f* • science of values, value science *(eth, met)* < Axiologie

Wertwort *n* • value word *(eth, lan)* < Begriff, normativer

Wesen, das *n* • nature, essence *(gep)* → Substanz, essentia; < Eigenschaft, unveränderliche

Wesen der Erscheinung *n* • essence of appearance *(Kant) (met)*

Wesen der Kunst *n* • essence of art *(aes)*

Wesen der Wahrheit *n* • essence of truth *(met)*

Wesen des Christentums *n* • the essence of Christianity *(rel)* < W 1303

Wesen des Menschen, das eigentliche *n* • man's essential being *(Marx) (ant)*

Wesen, höchstes *n* • Supreme Being *(rel)*

Wesen, menschliches *n* • (▷ Spezieszugehörigkeit) human being *(nat)*, (▷ Wesenseigenschaft) man's essence *(met)*

wesenhafte Beschaffenheit *f* • essential nature/characteristic *(gep)*

Wesenhaftigkeit *f* • essentiality, intrinsicality, substantiality *(met)*

Wesenheit *f* • essentiality, essential being *(met)* < Substantialität

Wesensanschauung *f* • essential intuition/ anschauung *(Husserl) (epi, met)*

Wesensart *f* • nature, character *(gep)* → Charakteristik

Wesensattribute *pl* • attributes of being, essential attributes *(met)*

Wesensbegriff *m* • essence-concept, concept of essence *(met)*

Wesensbestimmung *f* • determination of essence *(met)*

Wesensdefinition *f* • definition of essence *(lan)*

Wesensgleichheit *f* • essential likeness/ similarity *(gep)*

Wesensgrund *m* • ground of being *(met)*

Wesenslehre *f* • doctrine of essences *(met)* < Essentialismus

wesensmäßig • essential *(met)* → essentiell

Wesensmöglichkeit *f* • essential possibility *(N. Hartmann) (met)*

Wesensnotwendigkeit *f* • essential necessity *(N. Hartmann, Reinach) (met)*

Wesensphilosophie *f* • philosophy of essence *(met)*

Wesensschau *f* • essential intuition, insight into essences *(Husserl) (epi, met)*

Wesenswissen *n* • knowledge of essences *(Scheler) (epi, met)* < Bildungswissen

Wesenszusammenhang *m* • essential relationship/structure/connection, relationship of essence *(Husserl, Reinach) (met)*

wesentliche Reichhaltigkeit *f* • essential richness *(epi, lan)*

Wesentlichkeit *f* • essentialness *(Hegel) (met)*

westlich orientiert • occidentalist, western-oriented/orientated *(pol, cul)*

westliches Denken *n* • Western thought *(gep, cul)*

Wettbewerb, freier *m* • free competition *(eco)*

Wettbewerb, unlauterer *m* • unfair competition *(eco, jur)*

Wettbewerbsbeschränkung *f* • restraint of trade *(eco)* < Monopolismus

Wettbewerbsfähigkeit *f* • competitiveness *(eco)*

Wettbewerbsfreiheit *f* • freedom of competition *(eco)*

Wettbewerbsverzerrung *f* • distortion of competition *(eco)*

Wettbewerbsvorteil *m* • competitive advantage, advantage in competition *(eco)*

Wettbewerbswirtschaft *f* • competitive economy *(eco)* < Marktwirtschaft

Wette *f* • wager, bet *(dec, mat)* < Pascals Wette

Wettquotient *m* • betting quotient *(Carnap) (dec)*

Wettrüsten *n* • arms race *(pol)*

Widerlegbarkeit *f* • refutability, disprovability *(sci)* → Falsifizierbarkeit < Anfechtbarkeit

Widerlegbarkeit, logische *f* • (logical) refutability *(log)*, defeasibility *(gep)*

Widerlegung *f* • refutation, disproof, confutation, refutal° *(log)*, disconfirmation *(sci)* < Falsifikation

Widerlegung des Idealismus *f* • refutation of idealism *(Kant) (epi, met)*

Widerlegungsregel *f* • refutation rule *(log)*

Widerrechtlichkeit *f* • illegality, unlawfulness *(jur)*

Widerruf *m* • revocation, recantation *(rel, jur)* < Ungültigkeitserklärung

widersinnig • paradoxical, nonsensical, absurd *(log, lan)*

Widersinnigkeit *f* • countersense, nonsense, absurdity *(log, lan)* < Absurdität

Widerspenstigkeit *f* • defiance *(Kierkegaard) (rel)*

Widerspiegelung *f* • reflection *(epi)*

Widerspiegelungstheorie *f* • image/reflection theory, theory of reflection *(Lenin) (epi)* → Abbildtheorie der Erkenntnis

Widerspiegelungstheorie der Kunst *f* → Abbildtheorie der Kunst

Widerspruch *m* • contradiction *(log)*

Widerspruch, dialektischer *m* • dialectical contradiction *(log, met)*

Widerspruch in sich *m* • self-contradiction *(log)* < Widerspruch, innerer

Widerspruch, innerer *m* • internal contradiction *(log)*

Widerspruch, logischer *m* • logical contradiction *(log)*

Widersprüche des/im Kapitalismus *pl* • contradictions of capitalism *(Marx etc) (eco, soc)*

widersprüchlich • inconsistent, contradictory *(log)* → antinomisch

Widersprüchlichkeit *f* • inconsistency, contradictoriness *(log)* → Inkonsistenz < Sinnwidrigkeit

widerspruchsfrei • non-contradictory, consistent, contradiction-free *(log, sci)* < Kohärenz

Widerspruchsfreiheit *f* • consistency *(log)* → Widerspruchslosigkeit, Konsistenz

Widerspruchsgeist *m* • spirit of contradiction *(gen)*

Widerspruchslosigkeit *f* • freedom from contradiction, consistency *(log)* → Widerspruchsfreiheit, Konsistenz

Widerspruchslösung *f* • rule of implicit consent *(eth, jur)* ↔ Zustimmungslösung < Organtransplantation

Widerspruchsprinzip *n* • principle of (non-) contradiction *(log)* → Satz vom Widerspruch, Kontradiktionsprinzip

Widerstand *m* • resistance, opposition *(pol)* < Résistance

Widerstand, passiver *m* • passive resistance *(pol)* < ziviler Ungehorsam

Widerstandsbewegung *f* • resistance movement *(pol)*

Widerstandsrecht *n* • right of resistance *(jur, pol)* < ziviler Ungehorsam

Widerstandsrecht gegen die Staatsgewalt *n* • right of resistance to the (power of the) state *(pol, jur, eth)*

Widerstreit *m* • antagonism, conflict, opposition, contrast *(gep)*

widerstreitende Interessen *pl* • conflicting interests, clash of interests *(gep)*

Widerwärtigkeit des Daseins *f* • ugliness/ offensiveness/unpleasantness of existence *(psy)* < Lebensekel

Widerwille *m* • aversion, dislike *(psy)* → Aversion

widrige Umstände *pl* • untoward circumstances *(act)*

Wie-sein *n* • how-being *(Heidegger) (ont)*

Wieder-holung *f* • repetition *(Heidegger) (ont)*

Wiederaufbau *m* • reconstruction *(eco, pol)* < Wirtschaftswunder

Wiederaufbereitungsanlage *f* • reprocessing plant *(tec, env)*

Wiederauferstehung des Körpers *f* • resurrection of the body *(rel)*

Wiederaufrüstung *f* • rearmament *(pol)*

Wiedererinnerung *f* • remembrance, recollection *(epi, psy)*

Wiedererinnerung, Erkenntnis als *f* • knowledge as remembrance *(Plato) (epi)* → Anamnesis

Wiedererinnerungslehre *f* • theory of remembrance/anamnesis *(Plato) (epi)* < Anamnesis

Wiedererkennung *f* • recognition *(epi)*

Wiedererstattung *f* • retribution, reimbursement *(jur)*

Wiedergabetreue der Kunst *f* • fidelity/ authenticity of reproduction in art *(aes)*

wiedergeboren • born again *(eso)* < Rebirthing

Wiedergeburt *f* • rebirth, reincarnation *(met, rel)* → Palingenese < Seelenwanderung, Rebirthing, Reinkarnation

Wiedergutmachung *f* • restitution, reparation, compensation *(eth, jur)*

Wiederherstellung des Rechts *f* • restitution of law *(jur)*

Wiederholbarkeit *f* • repeatability *(sci)* < Experiment

Wiederholung der Seinsfrage *f* • repetition of the question of Being *(Heidegger) (ont)*

Wiederholungstäter *m* • recidivist, persistent offender *(jur)*

Wiederholungszwang *m* • repetition-compulsion, compulsion to repeat *(psy)*

Wiederkehr, ewige *f* • eternal recurrence *(Nietzsche) (met)* < ewige Wiederkehr des Gleichen

Wiederkunft *f* • Second Coming *(rel)*

Wiedervereinigung *f* • reunification *(pol)*

Wiedervereinigung des Christentums *f* • reunion of Christendom *(Leibniz) (rel)*

Wiedervergeltungsrecht *n* • law of retaliation *(jur, eth)*

Wiederverwertung *f* • recycling *(env)* → Recycling

Wiederverzauberung der Welt *f* • reenchantment of the world *(Marquard) (aes)* ↔ Entzauberung

Wiege der Philosophie *f* • cradle of philosophy *(gep)*

Wiege des Menschen *f* • cradle of man *(ant, met)*

Wiener Kreis *m* • Vienna Circle *(sci)*

Wiener Schule *f* • Vienna/Viennese School *(aes)*

Wiener Schule der Nationalökonomie *f* • Vienna School of political economy *(eco)*

Wilcoxon-Test *m* • signed rank-test *(sci)*

Wildbeutergesellschaft *f* • game hunter society *(ant, soc, cul)* < Jäger und Sammler

Wilder, edler *m* • noble savage *(Rousseau) (soc)* ↔ zivilisierter Mensch

wildes Denken *n* • savage reasoning *(Lévi-Strauss) (ant)* → vorlogisches Denken < W 1316

Wildheit *f* • savageness, savagery *(cul)* < Naturzustand

Wilhelm von Ockham • William of Ockham/ Occam

Wille *m* • intention, volition *(act)*, will *(psy, met)* < Wollen, das

Wille aller *m* • will of all *(pol)* → volonté de tous

Wille, allgemeiner *m* • general will *(Rousseau etc) (soc, pol)* → volonté générale, Gemein- wille

Wille als Ding an sich *m* • will as thing-in-itself *(Schopenhauer) (met)*

Wille, blinder *m* • blind will *(Schopenhauer) (met)*

Wille des Volkes *m* → Volkswille

Wille, freier *m* • free will *(eth, met)*

Wille, guter *m* • good will *(Kant etc) (eth)* < gute Absicht

Wille, letzter *m* • last will (and testament) *(jur, rel)*

Wille zum Bösen *m* • will to evil *(eth)* < Übel- wollen

Wille zum ewigen Leben *m* • will to eternal life *(rel)*

Wille zum Leben *m* • will to life *(Nietzsche) (met)*

Wille zum Nichts *m* • will to nothingness *(Nietzsche) (met)* < Nihilismus

Wille zum Wissen *m* • will to know/knowledge *(Foucault) (epi, pol)*

Wille zur Macht *m* • will to power *(Nietzsche) (met)* < W 1318

Willen, Loskommen vom *n* • liberation from the will *(Schopenhauer, Nietzsche) (met)*

Willenlosigkeit *f* • lack of will(-power) *(psy)*

Willensakt *m* • volitional act, (act of) volition, act of will(ing) *(met)*

Willensäußerung *f* • declaration of intent/ intention/will *(jur, pol)*

Willensbestimmung *f* • determination of (the) will *(Kant) (eth, met)*

Willensbildung *f* • formation of will/volition *(pol)*

Willensentscheidung *f* • volition *(psy)*

Willenserklärung *f* → Willensäußerung

Willensfreiheit *f* • free will, freedom of the will *(eth, met)* → liberum arbitrium

Willenskraft *f* • willpower, strength of will *(psy, act)* < Seelenstärke, Selbstüberwin- dung

Willensmetaphysik *f* • metaphysics of the will *(Schopenhauer) (met)*

Willensschwäche *f* • weak will, weakness of (the) will, lack of willpower, akrasia, incontinence *(Aristotle etc) (eth, act)*

willentlich • wilful, deliberate, intentional *(act, jur)*

Willigkeit *f* • willingness *(psy)*

Willkür *f* • arbitrariness, caprice *(act)*

Willkürakt *m* • arbitrary action *(act)*

Willkürherrschaft *f* • arbitrary rule, despotism *(pol)* → Despotie < Totalitarismus

Willkürlichkeit des Zeichens *f* • arbitrariness of the sign *(Saussure) (lan)*

Wir-Bewußtsein *n* • we-consciousness *(Sartre) (met)*

Wir-Gefühl *n* • we-sentiment° *(psy)* < Solida- ritätsgefühl, Zugehörigkeitsgefühl

Wirkfaktor *m* • power factor *(nat)*

wirklich Seiendes *n* • real entities *(Ayer) (ont)* < Wesenheit

Wirkliche, das *n* • the real/actual/true/genuine *(gep)*

wirkliche Welt *f* • real/actual world *(met)* ↔ mögliche Welten, Scheinwelt

Wirklichkeit *f* • reality, actuality *(met)* → Realität < W 664

Wirklichkeit, Ebenen der *pl* • levels of reality *(Plato etc) (met)*

Wirklichkeit, existenzielle *f* • existential reality *(Jaspers) (met)*

Wirklichkeit, feststellbare *f* → Faktizität

Wirklichkeit, geistige *f* • spiritual reality *(met)*

Wirklichkeit, materielle *f* • material reality *(met)*

Wirklichkeit, Stufen der *pl* • degrees of reality *(met)*

Wirklichkeit, substanzielle *f* • substantial reality *(met)*

Wirklichkeit und Erscheinung *f f* • reality and appearance *(Hegel etc) (met)*

Wirklichkeitsaussage *f* • reality statement, assertion of reality *(sci)* → Tatsachen- aussage ↔ Wertaussage

Wirklichkeitsbewußtsein *n* • consciousness of reality, reality consciousness *(met)*

Wirklichkeitsbezug *m* • reference to reality, real world reference *(psy)*

Wirklichkeitserkenntnis *f* • knowledge/ cognition of reality *(epi)*

Wirklichkeitsferne *f* • distance from reality *(met)*

Wirklichkeitsflucht *f* • escapism *(psy)* → Eskapismus

wirklichkeitsfremd • unrealistic, otherworldly *(psy)*

Wirklichkeitsmodalität *f* • alethic modality, real modality *(sci)*

Wirklichkeitssinn *m* • sense of reality *(psy)*

Wirklichkeitsspaltung *f* → Realitätsspaltung

Wirklichkeitsstufe *f* → Realiätsstufe

Wirklichkeitsverlust *m* → Realitätsverlust

Wirklichkeitsverständnis *n* • understanding/ concept(ion) of reality *(met)*

Wirkmächtigkeit *f* • efficacy *(gep)*

Wirkung f • (▷ Einfluß) efficacy, influence *(cul, soc)*; effect, consequence, action *(nat, met)* < Gegenwirkung, Ursache und Wirkung

Wirkung, ästhetische f • (▷ unmittelbare Wirkung) aesthetic effect; (▷ Einfluß) aesthetic efficacy/influence *(aes)* < Rezeptionsästhetik

Wirkung der Kunst f • effect of art *(aes)*

Wirkung der Willenskräfte f • efficacy of volitions *(Berkeley) (met)*

Wirkungsgeschichte f → Rezeptionsgeschichte

wirkungsgeschichtliches Bewußtsein n • effective historical consciousness *(Gadamer) (cul)*

Wirkungsgrad m • (degree of) efficiency, effectiveness, efficacy *(gep)*

Wirkungslosigkeit f • inefficacy, ineffectiveness *(gep)*

Wirkungssteigerung f • efficiency increase, increase in efficiency *(eco, sys, tec)* < Rationalisierung

Wirkungsvermögen n • effectiveness *(gep)*

Wirkungsweise f • mode of action *(gep)*

Wirkursache f • efficient cause *(Aristotle) (met)* → causa efficiens

Wirkursächlichkeit f • efficient causation *(met)*

Wirtschaft, die Welt der f • business world, (world of) industry and commerce *(eco)*

wirtschaftliche Betrachtungsweise f • economic approach *(eco)*

wirtschaftliche Effizienz f • economic efficiency *(eco)*

wirtschaftliche Entwicklung f • economic development *(eco)*

wirtschaftliche Ressourcen pl • economic resources *(eco)*

wirtschaftliche Sicherheit f • economic security *(eco, soc)*

wirtschaftlicher Anreiz m • economic incentive *(eco)*

wirtschaftliches Gleichgewicht n • economic equilibrium *(eco)*

wirtschaftliches Ungleichgewicht n • economic disequilibrium *(eco)* < Nord-Süd-Gefälle

Wirtschaftlichkeitsanalyse f • analysis of profitability *(eco)* < Kosten-Nutzen-Analyse

Wirtschaftsbeziehungen pl • economic relations *(eco)*

Wirtschaftsdemokratie f • industrial democracy *(eco, pol)* < Mitbestimmung am Arbeitsplatz

Wirtschaftsethik f • business ethics *(eco, eth)* < Unternehmensethik

wirtschaftsfeindlich • antibusiness, antimarket *(eco)*

Wirtschaftsflüchtling m • economic refugee *(eco, pol)* < Armutsmigration

Wirtschaftsform f • economic system, type of economy *(eco)*

Wirtschaftsfreiheit f • economic liberty *(eco)* → ökonomische Freiheit

Wirtschaftsfrieden m • industrial peace *(eco, pol)* < Sozialpartnerschaft

Wirtschaftsgeschichte f • economic history *(eco)* < W 1322

Wirtschaftshilfe f • economic aid *(eco)* < Entwicklungshilfe

Wirtschaftshistoriker m • economic historian *(eco, his)*

Wirtschaftsimperialismus m • economic imperialism *(eco, pol)*

Wirtschaftskraft f • economic power *(eco)*

Wirtschaftskrise f • economic crisis *(eco)*

Wirtschaftslage f → Konjunktur

Wirtschaftslenkung f • governmental control (of the economy) *(eco, pol)* < Planwirtschaft

Wirtschaftsliberalismus m • economic liberalism *(eco, pol)* < freie Marktwirtschaft, Manchesterliberalismus, Laissez-faire

Wirtschaftsmacht f • economic power *(eco)*

Wirtschaftsordnung f • economic order *(eco)*

Wirtschaftspolitik f • economic policy *(eco, pol)*

Wirtschaftspsychologie f • industrial psychology *(eco, psy)*

Wirtschaftssystem n • economic system *(eco)*

Wirtschaftstheorie f • economic theory *(eco)*

Wirtschaftswachstum n • economic growth *(eco)* < Grenzen des Wachstums

Wirtschaftswissenschaft f • economics, economic science(s) *(eco)*

Wirtschaftswunder n • economic miracle *(eco)*

Wißbarkeit f • knowability *(epi)*

Wißbegierde f → Wissensdurst

Wissen n • knowledge *(epi)*, knowing, learning, erudition *(gep)* < Wissen, theoretisches; Wissen, praktisches; Wissenserwerb

Wissen a posteriori n • a posteriori knowledge, knowledge a posteriori *(epi)* → aposteriorisches Wissen

Wissen a priori n • a priori knowledge, knowledge a priori *(epi)* → apriorisches Wissen

Wissen, absolutes n • absolute knowledge *(Hegel) (epi, met)*

Wissen als Abbild der Wirklichkeit *n* • knowledge as a copy/an image of reality *(epi)* < Abbildtheorie, Widerspiegelungstheorie

Wissen als Prüf(ungs)wissen *n* • examiner's view of knowledge *(Hacking) (epi)*

Wissen, anschauliches *n* • intuitive/demonstrative knowledge *(epi)*

wissen daß • knowing that *(Ryle etc) (epi, min)* ↔ wissen wie

Wissen, deklaratives *n* • declarative knowledge *(epi, AI)* ↔ Wissen, prozedurales

Wissen durch Bekanntschaft *n* • knowledge by acquaintance *(Russell etc) (epi)*

Wissen durch Beschreibung *n* • knowledge by description *(Russell etc) (epi)*

Wissen, explizites *n* • explicit knowledge *(epi)*

Wissen, implizites *n* • implicit knowledge, tacit knowledge *(epi)* < persönliches Wissen

Wissen, intuitives *n* • intuitive knowledge *(epi)* < Intuitionismus

Wissen ist Macht *n,f* • knowledge is power *(Bacon) (gep)*

Wissen ist Tugend *n,f* • knowledge is virtue *(Socrates) (eth)*

Wissen, objektives *n* • objective knowledge *(epi)* < W 718

Wissen, partikuläres *n* • particular knowledge *(epi)*

Wissen, phänomenales *n* • phenomenal knowledge *(Husserl) (epi, met)*

Wissen, praktisches *n* • practical/technical knowledge, know-how *(epi)*

Wissen, prozedurales *n* • procedural knowledge *(epi, AI)* ↔ Wissen, deklaratives

Wissen, sicheres *n* • certain knowledge *(epi)* < Unbezweifelbarkeit, unbezweifelbare Gewißheit

Wissen, sinnliches *n* • sensible/sensitive knowledge *(Aristotle etc) (epi)*

Wissen, subjektives *n* • subjective knowledge *(epi)*

Wissen, theoretisches *n* • theoretical knowledge *(epi)*

Wissen und Gewissen *n,n* • knowledge and belief *(gep)*

Wissen und Gewissen, nach bestem • to the best of one's knowledge *(eth, jur)*

Wissen und Glaube(n) *n,m* • knowledge and belief *(epi)*, knowledge and faith *(rel)*

Wissen und Meinung *n,f* • knowledge and opinion *(epi)*

Wissen, vegetatives *n* • vegetative knowledge *(Aristotle) (epi)*

Wissen von geistigen Zuständen *n* • knowledge of mental states *(Ayer) (min)*

Wissen, wahres *n* • true knowledge *(epi)*

wissen wer • knowing who *(epi, min)*

wissen wie • knowing how *(Ryle) (epi, min)* ↔ wissen daß < Anwendungswissen; Wissen, praktisches; Wissen, prozedurales

wissen wieso • knowing why *(epi, min)*

Wissens, Begrenzung des *f* • limitation of knowledge *(epi)* < Wissens, Grenzen des

Wissens, Formen des *pl* • forms of knowledge *(Kant etc) (epi)*

Wissens, Grenzen des *pl* • limits to/bounds of knowledge *(epi)*

Wissens, Grundlage der Gewißheit des *f* • knowledge as basis of certitude/certainty *(Augustine) (epi)* < systematischer Zweifel

Wissens, Relativität des *f* • relativity of knowledge *(epi)* < Wissenssoziologie, Standortgebundenheit des Denkens

Wissensanspruch *m* • knowledge claim, claim to knowledge *(epi, sci)*

Wissensarchäologie *f* • intellectual archeology *(Foucault) (epi, pol)*

Wissensarten *pl* • knowledges, forms of knowledge *(Foucault etc) (epi, pol)*

Wissensbasis *f* • knowledge base *(epi, AI)*

Wissensbedingung *f* • condition of knowledge *(epi)*

Wissensbegriff *m* • concept of knowledge *(epi)*

Wissensbegründung *f* • justification of knowledge *(epi)* < Erkenntnisbegründung

Wissensbereich *m* • range/domain/area of knowledge *(epi, sci)*

Wissenschaft *f* • science *(sci)* < Geisteswissenschaften, Naturwissenschaft(en), Forschung

Wissenschaft der Logik *f* • science of logic *(Hegel) (log)* < W 1325

Wissenschaft, Errungenschaften der *pl* • achievements of science *(sci)*

Wissenschaft, Grenzen der *pl* • limits to/of science *(sci)*

Wissenschaft vom Menschen *f* • human sciences, science of man, anthropology *(ant, cul)* < Anthropologie, philosophische

Wissenschaft von den Grenzen menschlicher Vernunft *f* • science of the limits of human reason *(Kant) (epi, met)*

Wissenschaft von den Zeichen *f* • science of signs *(lan)* < Zeichentheorie

Wissenschaft(l)er *m* • scientist, researcher, scholar *(sci)*

Wissenschaften, Unterscheidung der *f* • differentiation of (the) sciences *(sci)*

wissenschaftliche Aussage *f* • scientific statement *(sci)*

wissenschaftliche Eliten *pl* • scientific elites *(sci)*

wissenschaftliche Entdeckung *f* • scientific discovery *(sci)*

wissenschaftliche Erklärung *f* • scientific explanation *(sci)*

wissenschaftliche Forschung *f* • scientific research *(sci)*

wissenschaftliche Gesellschaft *f* • learned society *(gep)*

wissenschaftliche Handlungserklärung *f* • scientific explanation of action *(sci, act)*

wissenschaftliche Hypothese *f* • scientific hypothesis *(sci)*

wissenschaftliche Legitimation *f* • scientific legitimation *(sci)*

wissenschaftliche Methode *f* • scientific method *(sci)*

wissenschaftliche Revolution *f* • scientific revolution *(Kuhn) (sci)* < Paradigmenwechsel < W 947

wissenschaftliche Theorie *f* • scientific theory *(sci)*

wissenschaftliche Untersuchung *f* • scientific investigation *(sci)*

wissenschaftlicher Durchbruch *m* • scientific breakthrough *(sci)* < wissenschaftliche Revolution

wissenschaftlicher Fortschritt *m* • scientific progress, progress in science *(sci, his)*

wissenschaftlicher Glaube(n) *m* • scientific belief *(sci)* → nicht-doxastischer Glaube(n) < doxastischer Glaube(n)

wissenschaftlicher Materialismus *m* • scientific materialism *(Marx etc) (met, sci)*

wissenschaftlicher Realismus *m* • scientific realism *(epi, sci)*

wissenschaftlicher Sozialismus *m* • scientific socialism *(Engels) (soc)* ↔ utopischer Sozialismus

wissenschaftliches Denken *n* • scientific thinking/thought/reasoning *(sci)*

wissenschaftliches Fehlverhalten *n* • scientific misconduct *(eth)* < Wissenschaftsethik

wissenschaftliches Verstehen *n* • scientific understanding *(sci)*

wissenschaftliches Wissen *n* • scientific knowledge *(epi, sci)*

wissenschaftliches Zeitalter *n* • scientific age, age of science *(his, sci)*

Wissenschaftlichkeit *f* • scientific nature/character, scientificality, scientificity *(sci)*

Wissenschaftsbetrieb *m* • institutionalized research *(sci)* < Forschungsmanagement

Wissenschaftsdekonstruktion *f* • deconstruction of science *(epi, pol)*

Wissenschaftsdifferenzierung *f* • differentiation of the sciences *(sci)*

Wissenschaftsdiktatur *f* • dictatorship of science *(soc)* < Anmaßung der Wissenschaft

Wissenschaftsentwicklung *f* • scientific development *(sci)*

Wissenschaftsethik *f* • ethics of science *(eth)* < Verantwortung der Wissenschaft

Wissenschaftsfeindlichkeit *f* • hostility to science *(psy, soc)*

Wissenschaftsforschung *f* • theory of science *(sci)*

Wissenschaftsfreiheit *f* → Freiheit der Wissenschaft

Wissenschaftsgegenstände *pl* • objects of science, science-objects *(sci)*

Wissenschaftsgemeinde *f* • scientific community *(sci)*

Wissenschaftsgeschichte *f* • history of science *(sci, his)* < Ideengeschichte

Wissenschaftsgeschichte, externe *f* • external history of science *(sci, his)*

Wissenschaftsgeschichte, interne *f* • internal history of science *(sci, his)*

Wissenschaftsgläubigkeit *f* • faith in science *(psy, soc)* < Szientismus

Wissenschaftsideal *n* • scientific ideal *(sci)*

Wissenschaftskritik *f* • criticism of science *(sci)*

Wissenschaftskultur *f* • culture of science *(sci)*

Wissenschaftslehre *f* • science of knowledge *(Fichte) (met)* < W 1334; theory of science *(Bolzano) (log)* < Wissenschaftstheorie < W 1333 < W 362, 408, 426, 1041

Wissenschaftspark *m* • science park *(sci)*

wissenschaftsphilosophisch • pertaining to the philosophy of science *(sci)*

Wissenschaftspolitik *f* • science policy *(sci, pol)*

Wissenschaftspraxis *f* • practice of science, scientific practice *(sci)*

Wissenschaftsprosa *f* • scientific prose *(sci, lan)* < Wissenschaftssprache

Wissenschaftssoziologie *f* • sociology of science *(sci, soc)*

Wissenschaftssprache *f* • scientific language *(sci, lan)* < Formalsprache

wissenschaftstheoretisch • pertaining to the theory of science *(sci)* < Methodologie

Wissenschaftstheorie *f* • theory/philosophy of science, science studies° *(sci)*

Wissenschaftstheorie, allgemeine *f* • general philosophy/theory of science *(sci)*

Wissenschaftstheorie, evolutionäre f • evolutionary theory of science *(Popper, Campbell etc) (sci)*

Wissenschaftstheorie, konstruktive f • constructive theory of science *(Lorenzen) (sci)*

Wissenschaftstheorie, spezielle f • special philosophy/theory of science *(sci)*

Wissenschaftswissenschaft f • science of science, metascience *(sci)* < Metawissenschaft, Forschungsforschung

Wissensdurst m • thirst for knowledge *(epi)* < Bildungsdrang, Erkenntnisdrang

Wissenserwerb m • acquisition of knowledge *(epi)*

Wissensform f • form of knowledge *(sci, soc)*

Wissensgebäude n • edifice of knowledge *(epi)*

Wissensgebiet n • field of knowledge *(epi)*

Wissensgegenstand m • object of knowledge *(epi)*

Wissensgrade pl • degrees of knowledge *(Locke) (epi)*

Wissenshintergrund m • background of knowledge *(epi)*

Wissensparadoxie f • paradox of knowledge *(epi)*

Wissensquelle f • source of knowledge *(epi)*

Wissensrelativismus m • knowledge relativism *(epi)*

Wissensrepräsentation f • representation of knowledge *(AI)*

Wissensschatz m • treasure house of knowledge, store of knowledge *(epi)*

Wissenssoziologie f • sociology of knowledge *(Mannheim, Scheler etc) (sci)* < Standortgebundenheit des Denkens; Wissens, Relativität des < W 834

Wissenstypen pl • types of knowledge *(epi, soc)*

Wissensvermögen n • faculty of knowing *(epi)*

Wissenszuwachs m • growth of knowledge *(epi)*

Witz m • joke, pleasantry, wit *(gen)* < jokologische Philosophie < W 1336

Wohin und Wozu des Menschen, das n • the Wherefore and Whither of mankind *(Nietzsche) (met)*

Wohl, öffentliches n • public weal/good *(pol)* → Gemeinwohl < öffentliche Wohlfahrt

Wohlfahrt, allgemeine f • general welfare/well-being, civic good *(eth, pol)* < Allgemeinwohl

Wohlfahrt, öffentliche f • public welfare/assistance *(eco, pol, soc)* < Wohl, öffentliches

Wohlfahrtsbürokratie f • welfare bureaucracy *(soc, pol)*

Wohlfahrtseinrichtung f • welfare institution *(pol)*

Wohlfahrtsfunktion f • welfare function *(eth, eco)*

Wohlfahrtsökonomie f • welfare economics *(eco)*

Wohlfahrtsorganisation f • welfare organization *(eco, pol)*

Wohlfahrtsrechte pl • welfare rights *(eco, pol, jur)*

Wohlfahrtsstaat m • welfare state *(eco, soc, pol)* → Sozialstaat

Wohlgefallen n • delight, satisfaction, pleasure *(aes)*

Wohlgefallen, interesseloses n • disinterested/uninterested appreciation/pleasure/delight/satisfaction *(Kant, Schiller etc) (aes)*

Wohlgeformtheit f • well-formedness *(log, lan, aes)*

Wohlgefühl n • pleasant sentiment/feeling *(eth, aes, psy)*, well-being *(psy)*

wohlgeordnete Gesellschaft f • well-ordered society *(soc, eth)*

wohlgeordnete Seele f • well-ordered soul *(Plato) (met)*

Wohlgeratenheit f • well-constitutedness *(Nietzsche) (ant, aes)*

wohlgestaltet • well-shaped, well-turned *(aes)*

Wohlklang m • harmony, euphony *(aes)* → Harmonie

Wohlordnungssatz m • well-ordering theorem *(mat)*

Wohlstand m • affluence, wealth, prosperity *(eco)* → Prosperität

Wohlstandsförderung f • furtherance/promotion of the welfare/well-being of man *(eco)*

Wohlstandsgesellschaft f • affluent society *(Galbraith) (eco)* < Überflußgesellschaft

Wohlstandsverwahrlosung f • waywardness caused by affluence *(soc)*

Wohltätigkeit f • charity *(eth)*

Wohltätigkeitsorganisation f • charity/charitable organization *(eth)*

wohlüberlegtes Urteil n • considered judgement *(gep)*

Wohlwollen n • benevolence *(eth)*

Wohlwollens, Prinzip des n • principle of benevolence/beneficence *(eth)*

Wohnkultur f • living style *(aes)*

Wolfskinder pl • wolf children *(ant, psy)* < Kaspar-Hauser-Syndrom

Wollen, das n • will, volition *(eth, met, act)* < Wille, Voluntarismus, Absicht

wollendes Ich n • willing/intentional self/ego *(Kant, Fichte) (met, eth)*

Wollust *f* • voluptuousness, lust *(psy)*

Woraufhin, das *n* • the uponwhich, that in-terms of which *(Heidegger) (ont)*

Wort *n* • word, term *(lan)* < Begriff, Term

Wort Gottes *n* • the word of God *(rel)*

Wortbedeutung *f* • word meaning *(lan)* ↔ Satzbedeutung

Wortbildung *f* • word formation *(lan)*

wortbrüchig sein • to break one's word *(eth, jur)*

Wortfamilie *f* • word family *(lan)*

Wortfeld *n* • word field/cluster *(lan)*

Wortklasse *f* • word class *(lan)*

wörtliche Bedeutung *f* • literal meaning *(lan)* ↔ metaphorische Bedeutung

Wortmalerei *f* • word painting *(aes)*

Wortschatz *m* • vocabulary *(lan)*

Wortschöpfung *f* • neologism *(lan)*

Wortspiel *n* • pun, play on words *(lan)*

Wortverbindung *f* • compound *(lan)*

Worumwillen, das *n* • the wherefore, the fore-the-sake-of-which *(Heidegger) (ont)*

Wucher *m* • usury *(eco)* < Zinsverbot

Wucherpreis *m* • exorbitant price *(eco)*

Wunder *n* • miracle, wonder *(rel)*

Wunder der Technik *n* • engineering marvel *(tec)*

Wunderglaube *m* • faith in miracles *(rel)*

Wunderheilung *f* • miracle healing *(esp)*

Wundertat *f* • miracle, miraculous deed *(rel)*

Wundertäter *m* • miracle worker *(rel)*

Wundertätigkeit *f* • miracle working *(rel)*

Wunder-Ursprung *m* • miracle source *(Nietzsche) (met)*

Wunderzeichen *n* • miraculous sign *(rel)*

Wunschbefriedigung *f* • satisfaction of desire, desire satisfaction *(psy)*

Wunschbild *n* • wishful image *(psy)* < Utopie

Wunschdenken *n* • wishful thinking *(psy)*

Wünschen, das *n* • wishing, wanting *(psy)* < Begehren

Wunscherfüllung *f* • wish-fulfilment, want satisfaction *(Freud) (psy)*

Wunschtraum *m* • wishful dream, wish-fulfilling fantasy *(psy)*

Würde *f* • dignity, honour *(eth)* < W 1023, 1099

Würde, menschliche *f* • human dignity *(eth)*

Würdigkeit, glücklich zu sein *f* • worthiness to be happy *(Kant) (eth)*

Würfelverdoppelung *f* • duplication of the cube *(mat)*

Wurzel *f* • root *(mat)*

Wu-wei • wu-wei, non-doing, non-action *(asp)* ↔ Yu-wei

X

x eins • x one, x sub(script) one *(log, mat)*
x (ist) gleich y • x equals y, x (is) equal to y
(log, mat)
x (ist) identisch mit y • x (is) identical with y,
x (is) equal to y *(log, mat)*
x (ist) ungleich y • x (is) unequal to y, x (is) not
equal to y, x does not equal y *(log, mat)*
x Index eins → x eins
X-Koordinate *f* • x-coordinate *(mat)* ↔ Y-
Koordinate

Xenokrates • Xenocrates
Xenokratie *f* • xenocracy *(pol)* → Fremdherrschaft
Xenophilie *f* • xenophilia *(eth, pol)* → Fremdenliebe
Xenophobie *f* • xenophobia *(eth, pol)* → Fremdenfeindlichkeit
XOR-Problem *n* • XOR (exclusive 'or')
problem *(log)*

Y

Y-Koordinate *f* • y-coordinate *(mat)* ↔ X-
Koordinate
Yggdrasill *m* • Yg(g)drasil, World-Ash *(rel)*
Yin-Yang *n* • yin-yang *(asp)* < Wechselbe-
ziehung von Männlichem und Weiblichem
Ymir der Riese *m* • Ymir the Giant *(rel, cul)*
Yoga *m/n* • yoga *(asp)*

Yogacara *n* • yogacara *(asp)*
Yogi(n) *m* • yogi *(asp)* → Gymnosophist
Yogini *f* • yogini *(asp)*
Yuppi *m* • yuppie *(soc, cul)*
Yu-wei • yu-wei, arbitrary action *(asp)*

Z

Zahlbegriff *m* • number concept, concept of number *(mat)*

Zahlendarstellung *f* • representation of a number *(mat)*

Zahlenmystik *f* • number mysticism *(eso)*

Zahlentheorie *f* • theory of numbers, number theory *(Fermat, Gauss, Cantor etc) (mat)*

Zahlungsbereitschaft *f* • willingness to pay *(eco)* < Werttheorie, subjektive

Zahlungsvermögen *n* • ability to pay *(eco)*

Zähmung des Menschen *f* • the taming of man *(Nietzsche) (ant)*

Zarathustra • Zarathustra, Zoroaster

Zazen *n* • zazen, zen meditation *(asp)*

Zehn Gebote, die *pl* • The Ten Commandments *(rel)* → Dekalog

Zehnt *m* • tithe *(eco, soc)*

Zeichen *n* • sign, mark, token, symbol *(lan, log)* < Symbol < W 1342

Zeichen und Bezeichnetes *n,n* • signifier and signified, sign and significatum *(lan)*

Zeichenbegriff *m* • concept of (a) sign *(lan)*

Zeichen-erfindender Mensch *m* • sign-inventing man *(Nietzsche) (ant)*

Zeichenhaftigkeit *f* • significance, sign-character *(Heidegger) (ont)* < Verweisungszusammenhang, Referentialität

Zeichenkette *f* • chain of signification *(aes, lan, log)*

Zeichenphilosophie *f* • philosophy of signs *(lan)* < Semiotik

Zeichenregel *f* • rule for a symbol *(Wittgenstein) (lan, log)*

Zeichenreihe *f* • string sequence of symbols *(log)*

Zeichenrelation *f* • relation of symbols *(lan)*

Zeichensprache *f* • sign language, symbolism *(lan)* < Gebärdensprache, Symbolsprache

Zeichensystem *n* • sign system *(Saussure) (lan)*

Zeichentheorie *f* • theory of signs *(lan)* → Semiotik < W 415, 1343

Zeichenträger *m* • sign vehicle *(lan)*

Zeichenverbindung *f* • combination of signs/symbols *(Wittgenstein) (lan)*

Zeigehandlung *f* • deictic act *(Kamlah, Lorenzen) (act)*

Zeigen, das *n* • pointing *(Augustine, Wittgenstein etc) (lan)* < Deixis, Ostention

Zeiger *m* • pointer *(AI, sys)*

Zeit *f* • time *(nat, ont)*

Zeit, absolute *f* • absolute time *(ont)*

Zeit als Anschauungsform a priori *f* • time as a priori form of intuition/perception *(Kant) (epi)*

Zeit als Horizont des Seinsverständnisses *f* • time as horizon of the understanding/interpretation of Being *(Heidegger) (ont)*

Zeit als innere Wahrnehmung *f* • time as inner sense *(met)*

Zeit, außerhalb der • outside time *(met)*

Zeit, außerzeitliche Erfahrung der *f* • extra-temporal experience of time *(Bergson) (met)*

Zeit, biologische *f* • biological time *(psy, nat)* < biologische Uhr, Biorhythmus

Zeit, Geschichte der *f* • history of time *(nat)*

Zeit, immanente *f* • immanent time *(met, aes)*

Zeit, objektive *f* • objective time *(nat)*

Zeit, physikalische *f* → Realzeit

Zeit und Raum *f,m* • time and space *(nat, met)*

Zeit, ursprüngliche *f* • original time *(Heidegger, Bergson) (ont)*

Zeit, Ursprungserfahrung der *f* • original experience of time, lived time, durée *(Bergson) (met)*

zeitabhängiges Verhalten *n* • time-dependent behaviour *(sys)*

Zeitalter der Aufklärung *n* • age of Enlightenment *(his)*

Zeitbegriff *m* • concept(ion) of time *(met)*

Zeitbestimmtheit *f* → Zeitlichkeit

Zeitbewußtsein *n* • consciousness/awareness of time, time consciousness/awareness *(psy)*

Zeitdiagnose *f* • diagnosis of the age/time(s) *(cul)*

Zeitdilatation *f* • time dilatation *(Einstein etc) (nat)*

Zeiterfahrung *f* • experience of time *(psy)* → Zeiterleben, Zeitwahrnehmung

Zeiterleben *n* • experiencing of time, psychological time *(psy)*

Zeitfluß *m* • flow of time, temporal flux *(met)*

Zeitgebundenes *n* • the time-bound *(Husserl) (ont)*

Zeitgeist *m* • spirit of the age/time(s), zeitgeist *(Hegel etc) (met, his)*

Zeitgenosse *m* • contemporary *(his)*

zeitgenössische Philosophie *f* • contemporary philosophy *(gep)*

Zeitgeschichte *f* • contemporary/modern history *(his)*

Zeitgeschichtler *m* • contemporary/modern historian *(his)*

Zeithorizont *m* • temporal horizon *(Husserl)* *(met)*

zeitigen • to temporalize *(Heidegger)* *(ont)*

Zeitigung *f* • bringing about temporality, temporalization, bringing to maturity *(Heidegger, Sartre)* *(ont, ant)*

Zeitigungsmodi *pl* • modes of bringing about temporality, modes of temporalization, modes of bringing to maturity *(Heidegger)* *(ont, ant)*

Zeitkontinuum *n* • continuum of time, time continuum *(ant, met)*

Zeitkrankheit *f* • disease of the time(s) *(Kierkegaard)* *(rel)*

Zeitkunst *f* • process art *(aes)* ↔ Raumkunst

zeitliche Dauer *f* • temporal duration *(Bergson)* *(ont)*

zeitliche Reichweite *f* • time range *(nat)*

Zeitlichkeit *f* • temporality *(Kierkegaard, Heidegger)* *(ont)*, (▷ zeitliche Beschränktheit) temporarity, (▷ Vergänglichkeit) transitoriness *(ont)* < Endlichkeit

Zeitlichkeit als Sinn der Sorge *f* • temporality as the sense of care *(Heideger)* *(ont)*

Zeitlichkeit der Wahrheit *f* • temporality of truth *(epi, met)*

Zeitlogik *f* • tense *logic (log)* → Logik, temporale

zeitlose Dinge *pl* • atemporal things *(met)* < nichträumliches Ding

zeitlose Gewißheit *f* • timeless certainty *(epi, sci)*

zeitlose Probleme *pl* • timeless/eternal problems *(gep)* < philosophia perennis

zeitlose Strukturen *pl* • timeless structures *(met)*

zeitlose Wahrheit *f* • timeless truth *(epi, met)*

zeitloser Satz *m* • eternal sentence *(Quine)* *(lan)*

Zeitlosigkeit *f* • timelessness *(met, gep)* < Überzeitlichkeit

Zeitmanagement *n* • time management *(eco)*

Zeitparadox *n* • time paradox *(Einstein)* *(nat)* → Uhrenparadox

Zeitpräferenz *f* • time preference *(dec)*

Zeitpunkt *m* • point in time *(nat, met)*

Zeitreihe *f* • time series *(mat)*

Zeitreihenanalyse *f* • time series analysis *(sci)*

Zeitsinn *m* • sense of time *(psy)*

Zeittheorie *f* • theory of time *(met, nat)*

Zeitverhältnis *n* • time relation *(epi, nat)*

Zeitwahrnehmung *f* • time/temporal perception *(psy)* < Zeiterfahrung

Zeitzeuge *m* • contemporary witness *(his)*

Zellbiologie *f* • cell biology *(nat)*

Zellularautomat *m* • cellular automaton *(nat, AI)*

Zen-Buddhismus *m* • Zen Buddhism *(rel, asp)*

Zendo • zendo, meditation room *(asp)*

Zeno von Elea • Zeno of Elea

Zenos Paradoxien *pl* • Zeno's paradoxes *(log)* < Achilles und die Schildkröte-Paradoxon, Pfeil-Paradoxon

Zensur *f* • censorship *(pol, aes, psy)*

Zensur der Vernunft *f* • censorship of reason *(Kant)* *(epi)*

Zentraldetermination *f* • central determination *(N. Hartmann)* *(met)*

zentrale Recheneinheit *f* • central processing unit, CPU *(AI, tec)*

zentrale Werte *pl* • core values *(eth)*

Zentralkörper *m* • central body *(nat)*

Zentralverwaltungswirtschaft *f* • centrally administered/planned economy *(eco)* < gelenkte Wirtschaft, Planwirtschaft

Zentralwert *m* • median *(mat)* → Median

Zentrifugalkraft *f* • centrifugal force *(nat)* → Fliehkraft ↔ Zentripetalkraft

Zentripetalkraft *f* • centripetal force *(nat)* ↔ Zentrifugalkraft

Zentrum, politisches *n* • the political centre *(pol)*

zerlegbares Element *n* • reducible/decomposable element *(mat)*

Zerlegung *f* • decomposition *(log)*

Zerlegungskörper *m* • decomposition field *(mat)*

Zerrbild *n* • distorted image *(psy)*

zerrissenes Bewußtsein *n* • divided/split/rent consciousness *(Hegel)* *(met)*

Zerrissenheit *f* • dismemberment, disjointedness *(Hegel)* *(met)*

Zerstörungstrieb *m* • destructive urge/impulse *(psy)*

Zerstreuung *f* • dispersion *(Foucault)* *(epi, pol)*

Zertrümmern der alten Wertetafeln *n* • breaking the old tables/tablets of values *(Nietzsche)* *(eth)* < Umwertung aller Werte

zetetische Hermeneutik *f* • zetetic hermeneutics *(sci)*

Zeug *n* • equipment *(Heidegger)* *(ont)*

Zeugenschaft der Wahrheit *f* • witness of truth *(rel, his)*

Zeugganzheit f • equipmental whole/totality *(Heidegger) (ont)*

zeughaft-Seiendes n • Being-as-equipment *(Heidegger) (ont)*

Zeugnis n • testimony *(jur)*

Zeugnisse, geschichtliche pl • historical documents *(his)*

Zeugung f • generation, procreation, reproduction *(nat)* < Reproduktionsrate

Zick-Zack-Theorie f • zig-zag theory *(Russell) (sci)*

Zieharmonika-Effekt m • accordion effect *(sys)*

Ziel n • goal, end, purpose, aim *(act, dec)*

Ziel-Mittel-Problem n • means-ends problem *(sys, dec)*

Zielbildungsprozeß m • goal setting process *(act, dec)*

Zielerreichung f • goal attainment *(dec)*

Zielfindung f • goal finding *(act, dec)*

Zielfindungsprozeß m • goal finding process *(act, dec)*

zielführende Strategie f • effective/purposive strategy *(act, dec)*

zielgehemmte Liebe f • aim-inhibited love *(Freud) (psy)*

zielgerichtetes Handeln n • goal-directed action *(act, dec)*

zielgerichtetes Verhalten n • goal-directed behaviour/action *(act, dec)* < intentionales Verhalten

Zielgerichtetheit f • goal-directedness *(act, dec)* < Teleologie

Zielgruppe f • target group *(psy, eco, soc)*

Zielhemmung f • aim inhibition *(Freud) (psy)*

Zielhierarchie f • goal hierarchy *(dec, log)*

Zielkonflikt m • goal conflict *(act, eth)* < Dilemma

Ziellosigkeit der Natur f • purposelessness of nature *(met)* < Dysteleologie

Zielmodell n • goal model *(sci)*

zielorientiertes Verhalten n • purposive behaviour *(act, dec)*

Zielsetzung f • goal setting, setting one's goal/target *(act, dec)* < Programmatik, Ziel

Zielstrebigkeit (in) der Natur f • teleology in nature *(met)*

Zielstruktur f • nt, aim-structure *(act, met, sys)*

Zielvorstellung f • purposive idea, representation of a goal *(psy)*

Zinseszins m • compound interest *(eco)*

Zinsknechtschaft f • interest slavery *(eco)* < Schuldenfalle

Zinsnehmen n • charging interests *(eco, eth)*

Zinsverbot n • ban on usury, ban on interest *(eco, rel)* < Wucher

Zionismus m • Zionism *(pol, rel)*

Zirbeldrüse f • pineal gland *(Descartes) (nat)* → Epiphyse

Zirkel, hermeneutischer m • hermeneutic circle *(Gadamer etc) (sci)*

Zirkel, logischer m • logical circle *(log)*

Zirkelbeweis m • circular proof *(log)*

Zirkeldefinition f • circular definition *(log)*

zirkelförmig → zirkulär

Zirkelschluß m • circular argument, vicious circle *(log)* → circulus vitiosus

Zirkelstruktur f • circular structure *(log)*

zirkulär • circular *(log)*

zirkuläre Definition f • circular definition *(log)*

zirkuläres Begründen n → zirkuläres Denken

zirkuläres Denken n • circular reasoning/thinking *(log)*

Zirkularität f • circularity *(log)*

Zirkularität dialektischer Untersuchungen f • circularity of dialectical investigation(s) *(Albert) (sci)*

Zirkulation, einfache f • simple circulation *(Marx etc) (eco)*

Zirkulationsmittel n • medium/means of circulation *(Marx) (eco)* → Umlaufmittel

Zitattilgung f • disquotation *(Quine) (epi, lan)* → Disquotation

Zivilcourage f • moral/civil courage *(eth, pol)*

Zivildienst m • obligatory community service (as an alternative to military service) *(eth, soc)*

ziviler Ungehorsam m • civil disobedience *(pol)* → bürgerlicher Ungehorsam < gewaltloser Widerstand, Widerstandsrecht; Widerstand, passiver

Zivilgesellschaft f • civil society *(pol, soc)* < bürgerliche Gesellschaft

Zivilisation f • civilization *(soc, cul)*

Zivilisationskrankheit f • disease of civilization, civilizational disease *(soc, cul)*

Zivilisationskritik f • critique of civilization *(soc, cul)*

Zivilisationsprozeß m • process of civilization *(soc, cul)*

zivilisatorischer Fortschritt m • progress of/in civilization *(his)* < Kulturprozeß

zivilisierter Mensch m • civilized man *(Rousseau etc) (soc)* ↔ edler Wilder

Zivilrecht n • civil law *(jur)* → ius civile

Zivilreligion f • civil religion *(Rousseau) (pol, rel)*

Zölibat *m/n* • celibacy *(rel)*

zoon politikón *n* • *nt*, political/social animal *(Aristotle) (soc, pol)* < politisches Tier, Mensch als; soziales Wesen

Zoozentrismus *m* • zoocentrism *(eth, env)* < Biozentrismus

Zoroastrismus *m* • Zoroastrianism *(rel)*

zu den Sachen selbst • to the things themselves *(Husserl) (epi, met)*

Zu-fall *m* • be-falling *(Heidegger) (ont)*

Zu-kunft *f* • the future as coming towards *(Heidegger) (ont)*

zu sich selbst kommen • coming to oneself/ itself *(Hegel) (met)*

Zubehör der Maschine, Mensch als *m* • man as appendage of the machine *(Marx etc) (soc)*

Zucht und Züchtung *f,f* • breed and breeding *(Nietzsche) (nat, met)*

Züchtigung *f* • chastisement *(Nietzsche) (eth)*

Zuchtwahl, natürliche *f* • natural selection *(Darwin) (nat)* → natürliche Auslese

Zufall *m* • chance, accident, incident, contingency, coincidence *(mat, sys, met)*

Zufall und Notwendigkeit *m,f* • chance and necessity *(met)* < W 1349

zufällig • by chance/accident *(mat, sys, met)*

Zufällige, das *n* • the accidental *(met)* < W 77

Zufälligkeit *f* • contingency *(nat, met)* → Kontingenz

Zufälligkeit, Theorie der *f* • accidentalism *(met)* → Akzidentalismus

Zufälligkeitsrelation *f* • relation of coincidence *(Carnap) (epi, ont)*

Zufallsanordnung *f* • chance set-up *(sci)*

zufallsartige Ereignisfolgen *pl* • random (sequence of) events *(sci)*

zufallsartige Folge *f* • random/chance sequence *(mat, sys)*

Zufallsauswahl *f* • random sample *(mat, sci)*

Zufallselement *n* • random/aleatory element *(mat, sys)*

Zufallsentdeckung *f* • chance/accidental discovery *(sci)*

Zufallsereignis *n* • random/chance event *(mat, met)*

Zufallsfehler *m* • random error *(mat, sci)*

Zufallsfolge *f* • random sequence *(mat)*

Zufallskette *f* • chain/sequence of chance events *(met)*

Zufallsknoten *m* • chance/random node *(dec)* < Entscheidungsknoten

Zufallslehre *f* • accidentalism, casualism *(met)* → Kasualismus

Zufallsprinzip *n* • principle of contingency *(mat, met)*

Zufallsstichprobe *f* • random sample *(mat, sci)*

Zufallstheorie *f* • theory of chance(s) *(met, mat)* < Wahrscheinlichkeitstheorie

Zufallsvariable *f* • random variable, variate *(mat, sci)*

Zufallswahrscheinlichkeit *f* • coincidence probability *(mat)*

Zufallszahl *f* • random number *(mat)*

Zufallszahlengenerator *m* • random number generator *(sys, mat)*

Zugehörigkeitsgefühl *n* • feeling of belonging *(psy, soc)* < Gemeingefühl, Wir-Gefühl

Zügellosigkeit *f* • intemperateness, dissoluteness, lack of restraint *(eth, psy)* → Hemmungslosigkeit, Libertinage

zugewiesene Rolle *f* • ascribed role *(soc, psy)* ↔ erworbene Rolle

Zugleichsein *n* • co-existence, co-occurence *(Kant) (ont)* → Koexistenz

Zugriffszeit *f* • access time *(sys)*

zugrundeliegende Struktur *f* • underlying structure *(gep)*

Zuhandene, das *n* • the ready-to-hand *(Heidegger) (ont)*

Zuhandenheit *f* • readiness-to-hand, availableness *(Heidegger) (ont)* < Vorhandenheit

Zuhandensein *n* • being-at-hand *(Heidegger) (ont)* < Vorhandensein

Zuhause *n* • the at-home *(Heidegger) (ont)*

zukünftige Generationen *pl* • future generations *(soc)* < intergenerationelle Gerechtigkeit

zukünftige Wahrheit *f* • future truth *(met)*

Zukunftsangst *f* • fear of the future *(psy)*

Zukunftsethik *f* • future ethics *(eth)*

Zukunftsforschung *f* • futurology *(gep)* → Futurologie

Zukunftsoptimismus *m* • optimism about the future *(psy)*

zukunftsorientiert • future-oriented *(gen)*

Zukunftspessimismus *m* • pessimism about the future *(psy)*

Zukunftsverantwortung *f* • responsibility for the future *(eth)* < intergenerationelle Gerechtigkeit

Zukunftsvoraussage *f* • prediction of the future *(gep)* < Futurologie, Zukunftsforschung

Zulassen des Bösen *n* • authorization of evil *(Leibniz) (met)* < Theodizee

Zulässigkeit *f* • permissibility, admissibility *(eth, jur)*

Zulassungsverfahren *n* • admission/certification/approval procedure *(jur)*

Zunft *f* • guild *(Weber) (soc)*

Zunftzwang *m* • guild coercion *(soc)*
< Zwangsmitgliedschaft

Zuordnungsdefinition *f* • definition of classification *(Reichenbach) (log)*

Zuordnungsregel *f* • attribution rule, assignment rule, coordination rule *(log, lan)* →
Korrespondenzregel; mapping rule *(mat)*

Zur-Erscheinung-Kommen *n* • coming into appearance *(Hegel, Heidegger etc) (ont)*

Zurechnung *f* • imputation *(jur, eth)*

Zurechnungsfähigkeit *f* • soundness of mind *(psy)*, responsibility, accountability *(jur, eth)*

zureichender Grund *m* • sufficient reason *(log)*

zurück aufs Land • back to the land *(soc)*
< Stadtflucht, zurück zur Natur

zurück zur Natur • back to nature *(Rousseau) (soc)*

Zurückführbarkeitsbeziehung *f* • relation of reducibility *(Carnap) (epi, ont)*

Zurückführung *f* • reduction, transformation *(Carnap) (log, sci)* < Reduktionismus

Zusammenbruch des Kapitalismus *m* • collapse/breakdown of capitalism *(Marx) (eco)*

Zusammenbruchstheorie *f* • breakdown theory *(Marx etc) (eco)* < Systemzusammenbruch

Zusammenfallen der Gegensätze *n* • coincidence of opposites *(met)* → coincidentia oppositorum

Zusammengehörigkeitsgefühl *n* • communal spirit, feeling of solidarity *(psy, soc)*

zusammengesetze Zeichen *pl* • composite signs *(Wittgenstein etc) (lan)*

zusammengesetzte Dinge *pl* • composite things *(ont)*

zusammengesetzte Handlung *f* • composite action *(act)*

zusammengesetzte Hypothese *f* • composite hypothesis *(sci)*

zusammengesetzte Natur der Erkenntnis *f* • compound nature of cognition *(Kant) (epi)*

zusammengesetzte Naturen *pl* • composite natures *(Descartes) (met)*

zusammengesetzte Substanz *f* • compound/complex substance *(Leibniz) (met)*

Zusammenhangslosigkeit *f* • incoherence *(log)*, disjointedness, unconnectedness *(ont)*

Zusammenleben, menschliches *n* • human co-existence, social life *(soc)*

Zusammentreffen *n* → Begegnung

Zusatzannahme *f* • additional assumption *(sci)*

Zusich(selbst)kommen *n* • coming to itself/oneself *(Hegel) (met)*

Zustand, innerer *m* • internal state *(psy)*

Zustandsbeschreibung *f* • state description *(Carnap etc) (sci)*, description of a situation *(gen)*

Zustandsindikator *m* • state indicator *(gep)*

Zustandsraum *m* • state space *(ont, sci, AI)*

Zustandssystem, diskretes *n* • discrete state system *(sys)*

Zustandsvektor *m* • state vector *(sys, sci)*

Zustimmung *f* • assent, agreement, approval *(pol, jur)*

Zustimmungslösung *f* • rule of assent *(eth, jur)*
↔ Widerspruchslösung < Organtransplantation

zutreffen • (▷ es ist der Fall) to obtain *(epi, sci)* < Fall sein, der

Zuverlässigkeit *f* • reliability *(eth, sci)* → Reliabilität

Zuverlässigkeitstheorie der Rechtfertigung *f* • reliability theory of justification *(sci)*

Zuverlässigkeitstheorie des Wissens *f* • reliability theory of knowledge *(epi)*

Zwang *m* • coercion, necessitation *(pol, eth)*
< Befehlsnotstand, Unfreiwilligkeit

Zwang des Notwendigen *m* • constraint of the necessary *(Nietzsche) (met)* < Sachzwang

Zwänge, gesellschaftliche *pl* • social constraints/restraints *(soc)* < Sachzwang

zwanglose Vernunft *f* • unconstrained reason *(Kant) (epi)*

zwanglose Verständigung *f* • unconstrained understanding *(Habermas) (lan, soc)*

Zwangsarbeit *f* • forced labour *(jur, eco, pol)*
↔ freiwillige Arbeit

Zwangsautorität *f* • coercive authority *(soc)*

Zwangsbehandlung *f* • compulsory treatment *(eth)* < informierte Zustimmung, Patientenautonomie

Zwangscharakter *m* • compulsive character *(psy)*

Zwangsdenken *n* • obsessive/compulsive/insistent/coercive thinking *(psy)*

Zwangsgewalt *f* • coercive power *(pol)*

Zwangshandlung *f* • compulsive act *(psy, act)*

Zwangsmaßnahme *f* • compulsory measure *(act)*

Zwangsmitgliedschaft *f* • compulsory/obligatory membership *(soc)* < Zunftzwang

Zwangsneurose *f* • obsessional/compulsion neurosis *(Freud) (psy)*

Zwangsverhalten *n* • obsessive behaviour *(psy)*

Zwangsvorstellung *f* • obsession, obsessive/compulsive idea, idée fixe *(psy)*

Zweck *m* • end, purpose, aim, goal, scope *(act, met)*

Zweck an sich selbst *m* • end in itself *(Kant)* *(met, eth)* → Zweck in sich

Zweck der Kunst *m* • aim/purpose of art *(aes)*

Zweck der Schöpfung *m* • purpose of creation *(rel)*

Zweck in sich *m* • end in itself *(act, gep)*

Zweck-Mittel-Relation *f* • means-end relation *(dec, eth)*

Zweck und Mittel *m,n* • ends and means *(act)*

Zweckbegriff *m* • concept of purpose *(act, met)*

Zweckbestimmung *f* • (determination of) purpose, application *(act, met)*

Zweckdienlichkeit *f* → Zweckmäßigkeit

Zwecke, Reich der *n* • realm/kingdom of ends *(Kant)* *(eth, met)*

zweckfrei • without purpose *(act, met)*

zweckgerichtetes Verhalten *n* • purposive behaviour *(act)*

Zweckgerichtetheit *f* → Zielgerichtetheit

Zweckmäßigkeit *f* • purposiveness *(act)*

Zweckmäßigkeit der Dinge *f* • fit(ted)ness of things *(met)*

Zweckmäßigkeit der Natur *f* • finality/purposiveness of nature *(met, nat)* → Naturteleologie

Zweckmäßigkeit ohne Zweck *f* • finality without an end, purposiveness without purpose *(Kant)* *(aes)*

Zweckmodell *n* → Zielmodell

Zweckorientiertheit *f* • means-end/instrumental/purposive orientation *(act)*

Zweckprinzip *n* • principle of means-end/instrumentality/purpose *(met)*

zweckrationales Handeln *n* • purposive-rational action *(Weber etc)* *(act, soc)*

zweckrationales Verhalten *n* • instrumental conduct, conduct by means-end rationality, goal-oriented conduct *(Weber)* *(act, soc)* ↔ wertrationales Verhalten

Zweckrationalität *f* • means-end/instrumental/purposive rationality *(Weber etc)* *(act, soc)* < instrumentelle Vernunft

Zwecksetzung *f* • determination of aims *(act)*

Zwecktätigkeit *f* • purposive activity *(act)*

Zweckursache *f* • final cause *(met)* → Finalursache, causa finalis

Zweckverhalten *n* • purposive behaviour *(act)* < zweckrationales Verhalten

Zwei-Aspekten-Lehre *f* • double-aspect theory *(met)* < Leib-Seele-Problem

zwei Kulturen, Theorie der *f* • theory of the two cultures *(Snow)* *(cul, sci)*

Zweideutigkeit *f* • ambiguity *(lan)* → Ambiguität, Mehrdeutigkeit, Vieldeutigkeit

Zweidrittelgesellschaft *f* • *nt (soc)* < neue Armut

zweifaches Interesse der Vernunft *n* • twofold interest of reason *(Kant)* *(epi, met)*

Zweifel *m* • doubt *(epi)*

Zweifel, radikaler *m* • radical doubt *(Descartes)* *(epi)*

Zweifel, religiöser *m* • religious doubt(s) *(rel)*

Zweifels, Methode des *f* • method of doubt *(Descartes)* *(epi)*

Zweiheitslehre *f* → Dualismus

Zweiklassengesellschaft *f* • two-tier society *(soc)*

Zwei-Reiche-Lehre *f* • doctrine of two kingdoms *(Augustine)* *(pol, rel)*

Zweisprachigkeitsbedingung *f* • bilingualism requirement *(pol)*

Zweistufentheorie der Sprache *f* • two-tier/level theory of language *(lan)*

Zwei-Substanzen-Lehre *f* • two-substance theory, doctrine of the division of substances *(Descartes)* *(met)* < cartesianischer Dualismus

Zweitbegriffe *pl* • second-order concepts *(met)*

Zweite Internationale *f* • Second International *(pol)*

zweite Natur *f* • second nature *(ant)*

zweite Welt *f* → Welt, Zwei

Zweiteilung der Welt *f* • division of the world into two *(met)*

zweiter Hauptsatz der Thermodynamik *m* • second principle of thermodynamics *(nat)*

zweites Gesicht *n* • second sight *(eso)*

Zweitheit *f* • secondness *(Peirce)* *(met, lan)*

Zweitschlag *m* • second strike, retaliation *(pol)* → Gegenschlag ↔ Erstschlag

Zweitschlagdrohung *f* • second-strike threat, retaliation/retaliatory threat *(pol)* < Gegenschlag

Zweitschlagfähigkeit *f* • second-strike/retaliatory capacity/capability *(pol)*

Zweitspracherwerb *m* • second language acquisition, SLA *(psy, lan)*

Zweiweltenlehre *f* • two-world theory *(met)*

zweiwertige Logik *f* • two-valued/bivalent logic *(log)* → Logik erster Ordnung

Zweiwertigkeit *f* • bivalence *(log)* → Bivalenz < Mehrwertigkeit

Zweiwertigkeitsprinzip *n* • principle of bivalence, bivalent principle, two-value principle *(log)*

Zwietracht *f* • discord *(eth)*

Zwillingsparadox *n* • twin paradox *(Einstein)* *(nat)*

zwingende Macht *f* • coercive power *(Hobbes etc)* *(pol)*

zwingende Wahrheit *f* • cogent/compelling truth *(log, epi)* → notwendige Wahrheit < Evidenz

zwingender Beweis *m* • irrefutable proof, compelling evidence *(epi, log, jur)*

zwingender Grund *m* • compelling reason *(gep)*

zwingendes Wissen *n* • cogent knowledge *(epi)* ↔ schwaches Wissen

Zwischen, das *n* • the between, betweenness *(Heidegger)* *(ont)*

zwischenmenschliche Beziehungen *pl* • interpersonal/social relation(ship)s *(soc)*

Zwischenwelten *pl* • interworlds *(ont)* → Intermundien

Zwischenwertsatz *m* • intermediate value theorem *(mat)*

Zwischenzustand *m* • intermediate state *(gep)*

Zwitterwort *n* • hybrid word *(lan)*

Zwölftonmusik *f* • twelve-tone/dodecaphonic music *(Hauer, Schönberg)* *(aes)*

zyklisch • cyclic(al) *(nat, eco)* ↔ azyklisch

zyklische Bewegung *f* • cyclic(al) movement *(eco, nat)*

zyklische Entwicklung *f* • cyclic(al) development/progression *(Vico etc)* *(met, his)*

zyklische Geschichtstheorie *f* • cyclic(al) theory of history *(Vico etc)* *(his)* < Kreislauftheorie der Geschichte

zyklische Organisation *f* • cyclic(al) organization *(sys)*

Zyklothymie *f* • cyclothymia *(Kretschmer)* *(psy)*

Zyklus der Wiedergeburt *m* • cycle of rebirth/ reincarnation *(rel, asp)*

Zylinderuniversum *n* • cylinder universe *(nat)*

Zyniker *m* • cynic *(gep)* < Kyniker

Zynismus *m* • cynicism *(psy)* < Kynismus < W 540

INDEX OF PHILOSOPHICAL TITLES
GERMAN - ENGLISH

The following index provides a selection of important philosophical titles whose translations are difficult to trace. Note that the dictionary refers to titles related to specific entries, thus providing a further contextualization. The translation marked with an ° indicates that the title is not to be found in the common bibliographies but is generally quoted in this form in English reference works and secondary literature.

The list of translated titles does not list the Christian names of the authors, if there is no danger of confusion.

The titles are sorted according to RAK (rules of general cataloguing). The article is found in initial position but ignored in the alphabetical sorting process (e.g., *Der Abbau des Menschlichen* is to be found under *A*). Other prepositions do, however, affect the position of the entry (e.g., *Über das Erhabene* is to be found under the letter *U*, and *Zur Logik der Sozialwissenschaften* under *Z*).

VERZEICHNIS PHILOSOPHISCHER WERKTITEL
DEUTSCH - ENGLISCH

Das nachfolgende Verzeichnis stellt eine Auswahl philosophischer Werktitel zusammen, deren Übersetzung oft nur sehr schwer zu eruieren ist. Darüber hinaus wird im Begriffsteil an geeigneten Stellen auf Werktitel verwiesen, um einen Terminus und seine Übersetzung zusätzlich zu kontextualisieren. Mit ° gekennzeichnete Übersetzungen sind solche, die nicht belegt sind, aber von englischen Autoren in Nachschlagewerken oder in der Sekundärliteratur in dieser Weise angeführt werden.

Da ein Verzeichnis philosophischer Werktitel nur für Fachleute aufschlußreich ist, wurde – wie im Wörterverzeichnis – bei den Namen auf die Nennung der Vornamen verzichtet, wenn eine Verwechslungsgefahr auszuschließen ist.

Sortierung nach *RAK* (Regeln allgemeiner Katalogisierung): Der Artikel wird vorangestellt, wird aber für die alphabetische Anordnung nicht berücksichtigt (z.B. *Der Abbau des Menschlichen* entsprechend dem leitenden Substantiv unter *A*). Präpositionen sind hingegen sortierungsrelevant (z.B. *Über das Erhabene* unter *U; Zur Logik der Sozialwissenschaften* unter *Z*).

1. Der Abbau des Menschlichen *(Lorenz)* • The Waning of Humaneness
2. Die Abenteuer der Dialektik *(Merleau-Ponty)*, orig. Les aventures de la dialectique • Adventures of the Dialectic
3. Abenteuer der Ideen *(Whitehead)* • orig. Adventures of Ideas
4. Abhandlung über das Bevölkerungsgesetz, oder Eine Untersuchung seiner Bedeutung für die menschliche Wohlfahrt in Vergangenheit und Zukunft; *auch:* Versuch über das Bevölkerungsgesetz und seine Auswirkungen auf die künftige Verbesserung der Gesellschaft *(Malthus)* • orig. An Essay on the Principle of Population, as it Affects the Future Improvement of Society
5. Abhandlung über das erste Prinzip *(Duns Scotus)*, orig. Tractatus de primo principio • Treatise on the First Principle
6. Abhandlung über das freie Denken *(Collins)* • orig. A Discourse of Free-Thinking
7. Abhandlung über den Geist des Positivismus *(Comte)*, orig. Discours sur l'esprit positif • Discourse on the Positivist Outlook
8. Abhandlung über den Ursprung der Sprache *(Herder)* • Essay on the Origin of Language
9. Abhandlung über die Argumentation *(Perelman, Olbrechts-Tyteca)*, orig. La nouvelle rhétorique. Traité de l' argumentation • The New Rhetoric: A Treatise on Argumentation

10. Abhandlung über die Empfindungen *(Condillac), orig.* Traité des sensations • Condillac's Treatise on the Sensations

11. Abhandlung über die Evidenz in metaphysischen Wissenschaften *(Mendelssohn)* • Essay on Evidence in Metaphysical Science

12. Abhandlung über die Gesetze und Gott als Gesetzgeber *(Suárez), orig.* Tractatus de legibus ac Deo legislatore • A Treatise on the Law and God the Lawgiver

13. Abhandlung über die Methode des richtigen Vernunftgebrauchs und der wissenschaftlichen Wahrheitsforschung *(Descartes), orig.* Discours de la méthode pour bien conduire sa raison, et chercher la vérité dans les sciences • Discourse on Method for the Well Guiding of Reason and the Discovery of Truth in the Sciences; *also:* Discourse on the Method of rightly conducting the Reason and seeking for Truth in the Sciences; *also:* Discourse on the Method of Rightly Conducting One's Reason and Reaching the Truth in the Sciences

14. Eine Abhandlung über die Natur und das Verhalten der Leidenschaften und Affekte mit Erläuterungen zum Moralempfinden *(Hutcheson)* • *orig.* An Essay on the Nature and Conduct of the Passions and Affections with Illustrations on the Moral Sense

15. Eine Abhandlung über die Prinzipien der menschlichen Erkenntnis *(Berkeley)* • *orig.* A Treatise concerning Human Knowledge; *also:* Principles of Human Knowledge

16. Abhandlung über die Toleranz anläßlich des Todes von Jean Calas *(Voltaire), orig.* Traité sur la tolerance à l'occasion de la mort de Jean Calas • Treatise on Tolerance

17. Abhandlung über die Unsterblichkeit der Seele *(Pomponazzi), orig.* Tractatus de immortalitate animae • On the Immortality of the Soul

18. Abhandlung über die Verbesserung des Verstandes *(Spinoza, postum), orig.* Tractatus de intellectus Emendatione • Treatise on the Emendation of the Intellect

19. Abhandlung über die Weltgeschichte *(Bossuet), orig.* Discours sur l' histoire universelle • Discourse on Universal History

20. Abhandlung über Dynamik *(d'Alembert), orig.* Traité de dynamique • Treatise of Dynamics

21. Abhandlung von den Verbrechen und Strafen *(Beccaria), orig.* Dei delitti e delle pene • On Crimes and Punishments

22. Abhandlung zur Metaphysik *(Voltaire, postum), orig.* Traité de metaphysique • Treatise on Metaphysics

23. Abhandlungen über das Naturrecht *(Locke, postum)* • Essays on the Law of Nature

24. Abschied von der bisherigen Geschichte *(A. Weber)* • Farewell to European History: or, The Conquest of Nihilism

25. Abschließende unwissenschaftliche Nachschrift zu den Philosophischen Brocken/Brosamen/Bissen *(Kierkegaard), orig.* Afsluttende Efterskrift til de philosophiske Smuler • Concluding Unscientific Postscript to Philosophical Fragments

26. Die Absichten der Philosophen *(Al-Ghazzali), orig.* Maqäsid al-faläsifah • The Intentions of Philosophers

27. Die Abstammung des Menschen und die geschlechtliche Zuchtwahl *(Darwin)* • *orig.* The Descent of Man, and Selection in Relation to Sex

28. Acht Bücher von Natur- und Völkerrecht *(Pufendorf), orig.* De iure naturae et gentium libro octo • Of the Law of Nature and Nations

29. Die acht Todsünden der zivilisierten Menschheit *(Lorenz)* • Civilized Man's Eight Deadly Sins

30. Der achtzehnte Brumaire des Louis Bonaparte *(Marx)* • The Eighteenth Brumaire of Louis Bonaparte

31. Aesthetica in nuce *(Hamann)* • Aesthetics in a Nutshell

32. Die Agonie des Christentums *(Unamuno), orig.* La Agonía del cristianismo • The Agony of Christianity

33. Akademische Abhandlungen *(Cicero), orig.* Academici libri quattuor • Academics

34. Aktor, Situation und normatives Muster *(Parsons)* • *orig.* Actor, Situation and Normative Pattern

35. Die Aktualität des Schönen *(Gadamer)* • The Relevance of the Beautiful and Other Essays

36. Alciphron oder der winzige Philosoph *(Berkeley)* • *orig.* Alciphron, or the Minute Philosopher

37. Allgemeine Erkenntnislehre *(Schlick)* • General Theory of Knowledge

72. Der Antichrist. Fluch auf das Christentum *(Nietzsche)* • The Antichrist; *also:* The Anti-Christ

73. Anthropogenie *(Haeckel)* • The Evolution of Man

74. Die Anweisung zum seligen Leben (oder auch die Religionslehre) *(Fichte)* • The Way Towards the Blessed Life; *also:* The Way to the Blessed Life or The Doctrine of Religion; *also:* Guide to the Blessed Life

75. Aphorismen zur Lebensweisheit *(Schopenhauer)* → Parerga und Paralipomena

76. Apokalypse *(Derrida)*, orig. Pas d'apocalypse, pas maintenant • No Apocalypse, Not Now

77. Apologie des Zufälligen *(Marquard)* • In Defense of the Accidental

78. Apologie oder Schutzschrift für die vernünftigen Verehrer Gottes *(Reimarus, postum)* • Apology for or Defence of the Rational Worshippers of God

79. Arbeit am Mythos *(Blumenberg)* • Work on Myth

80. Die Archäologie des Frivolen *(Derrida)* • The Archeology of the Frivolous: Reading Condillac

81. Archäologie des Wissens *(Foucault)*, orig. L'Archéologie du savoir • Archeology of Knowledge

82. Die Archetypen und das kollektive Unbewußte *(Jung)* → Über die Archetypen des kollektiven Unbewußten

83. Die Arroganz der Satten *(Galbraith)* • *orig.* The Affluent Society

84. Das Aschermittwochsmahl *(Bruno)*, orig. La cena de la ceneri • The Ash Wednesday Supper

85. Aspekte der Syntax-Theorie *(Chomsky)* • *orig.* Aspects of the Theory of Syntax

86. Aspekte wissenschaftlicher Erklärung und andere Aufsätze zur Wissenschaftsphilosophie *(Hempel)* • *orig.* Aspects of Scientific Explanation and Other Essays in the Philosophy of Science

87. Ästhetik *(Baumgarten)*, orig. Aesthetica • Aesthetics

88. Ästhetik *(Beardsley)* • *orig.* Aesthetics. Problems in the Philosophy of Criticism

89. Ästhetik als Wissenschaft des Ausdrucks und allgemeine Linguistik *(Croce)*, orig. Estetica come scienza dell' esspressione e linguistica generale • Aesthetics as Science of Expression and General Linguistic; *also:* The Aesthetic as the Science of Expression of the Linguistic in General

90. Ästhetik des Häßlichen *(Rosenkranz)* • Aesthetics of the Ugly°

91. Ästhetik des reinen Gefühls *(Cohen)* • Aesthetics of Pure Feeling

92. Ästhetische Theorie *(Adorno, postum)* • Aesthetic Theory

93. Atheismus im Christentum *(Bloch)* • Atheism in Christianity: The Religion of the Exodus and the Kingdom

94. Der Atheismus und seine Geschichte im Abendlande *(Mauthner)* • Atheism and its History in the Western World

95. Die Atombombe und die Zukunft des Menschen *(Jaspers)* • The Future of Mankind

96. Auch eine Philosophie der Geschichte zur Bildung der Menschheit *(Herder)* • Another Philosophy of History for the Education of Mankind

97. Auf den Gipfeln der Verzweiflung *(Cioran)* • On the Heights of Despair

98. Der Aufbau der geschichtlichen Welt in den Geisteswissenschaften *(Dilthey)* • Formation of the Historical World in the Human Sciences°; *also:* The Construction of the Historical World in the Human Studies°

99. Der Aufbau der realen Welt. Grundriß der allgemeinen Kategorienlehre *(N. Hartmann)* • The Construction of the Real World: Outline of the General Doctrine of Categories

100. Die Aufgabe unserer Zeit *(Ortega y Gasset)*, orig. El tema de nuestro tiempo • The Modern Theme

101. Aufsätze zu Wissenschaft und Philosophie *(Whitehead)* • *orig.* Essays in Science and Philosophy

102. Der Aufstand der Massen *(Ortega y Gasset)*, orig. La revolución de las masas • The Revolt of the Masses

103. Der Aufstieg der wissenschaftlichen Philosophie *(Reichenbach)* • *orig.* The Rise of Scientific Philosophy

104. Der Augenblick *(Kierkegaard)* • The Instant

105. Aurora oder Morgenröte im Aufgang *(Böhme)* → Morgenröte im Aufgang

106. Aus Staatsraison *(Chomsky)* • *orig.* For Reasons of State

107. Ausdruck und Bedeutung *(Searle)* • *orig.* Expression and Meaning

108. Ausführliche Darstellung der Gründe der Moral und Politik *(Ferguson)* • *orig.* Principles of Moral and Political Science; *also:* (The) Principles of Moral and Social Science

109. Der autoritäre Charakter *(Adorno et al.)* • *orig.* The Authoritarian Personality

110. Axiomatik der relativistischen Raum-Zeit-Lehre *(Reichenbach)* • Axiomatization of the Theory of Relativity

111. Der von der Akademie Dijon im Jahre 1750 mit dem Preis gekrönte Diskurs über die von derselben Akademie gestellte Frage: ob der Fortschritt der Wissenschaften und Künste zur Läuterung der Sitten beigetragen habe *(Rousseau), orig.* Discours qui a remporté le prix à l'Académie de Dijon. En l'année 1750. Sur cette question proposée par la même Académie: Si le rétablissement des Sciences et des Arts a contribué à épurer les mœurs • Discourse on the Sciences and Arts

112. Der Baum der Erkenntnis *(Maturana, Varela)* • *orig.* The Tree of Knowledge: The Biological Roots of Human Understanding

113. Beantwortung der Frage: Was ist Aufklärung? *(Kant)* • An Answer to the Question: What is Enlightenment?

114. Die Bedeutung des Protestantismus für die Entstehung der modernen Welt *(Troeltsch)* • Protestantism and Progress

115. Bedeutung und Notwendigkeit. Eine Studie zur Semantik und modalen Logik *(Carnap)* • *orig.* Meaning and Necessity: A Study in Semantics and Modal Logic

116. Befreiung der Tiere. Eine neue Ethik zur Behandlung der Tiere *(P. Singer)* • *orig.* Animal Liberation: A New Ethics for Our Treatment of Animals

117. Der Begriff Angst *(Kierkegaard), orig.* Begrebet Angest • The Concept of Anxiety; *also:* The Concept of Dread

118. Der Begriff der Natur *(Whitehead)* • *orig.* Concept of Nature

119. Der Begriff des Geistes *(Ryle)* • *orig.* The Concept of Mind

120. Der Begriff des Politischen *(C. Schmitt)* • The Concept of the Political

121. Der Begriff des Rechts *(Hart)* • *orig.* The Concept of Law

122. Begriffsschrift (eine der arithmetischen nachgebildete Formelsprache des reinen Denkens) *(Frege)* • Concept-notation and related articles

123. Behemoth oder Das lange Parlament *(Hobbes, postum)* • *orig.* Behemoth or the Long Parliament

124. Behemoth: Struktur und Praxis des Nationalsozialismus *(Neumann)* • *orig.* Behemoth: The Structure and Practice of National Socialism

125. Die beiden Grundprobleme der Erkenntnistheorie *(Popper)* • Knowledge and the Body-Mind Problem

126. Die beiden Grundprobleme der Ethik *(Schopenhauer)* • The Two Fundamental Problems of Ethics

127. Die beiden Quellen der Moral und der Religion *(Bergson), orig.* Les deux sources de la morale et de la religion • The Two Sources of Morality and Religion

128. Beiträge zu einer Kritik der Sprache *(Mauthner)* • Critique of Language

129. Beiträge zur Analyse der Empfindungen *(Mach)* • Contributions to the Analysis of Sensations; *also:* The Analysis of Sensations and the Relation of the Physical to the Psychical

130. Beiträge zur Berichtigung der Urteile des Publicums über die französische Revolution *(Fichte)* • Contributions Designed to Correct the Judg(e)ment of the Public on the French Revolution

131. Beiträge zur Kritik der politischen Ökonomie *(Marx)* • Contributions to the Critique of Political Economy

132. Bekenntnisse *(Augustine), orig.* Confessiones • Confessions

133. Die Bekenntnisse *(Rousseau, postum), orig.* Les Confessions • Confessions

134. Die belehrte Unwissenheit *(Nicholas of Cusa), orig.* De docta ignorantia • Of Learned Ignorance

135. Bemerkungen über die Farben *(Wittgenstein)* • Remarks on Colour

136. Bemerkungen über die Grundlagen der Mathematik *(Wittgenstein)* • Remarks on the Foundations of Mathematics

137. Bemerkungen über die Philosophie der Psychologie *(Wittgenstein)* • Remarks on the Philosophy of Psychology

138. Beobachtungen über das Gefühl des Schönen und Erhabenen *(Kant)* • Observations on the Feeling of the Beautiful and Sublime
139. Beschreibung der drei Prinzipien göttlichen Wesens *(Böhme)*, *orig.* De tribus principiis oder Beschreibung der Drey Principien Göttlichen Wesens • Description of the Three Principles of Divine Essence
140. Die Bestimmung des Menschen *(Fichte)* • The Vocation of Man
141. Betrachtungen über die Französische Revolution und über die Reaktion gewisser Londoner Kreise auf dieses Ereignis *(Burke)* • *orig.* Reflections on the Revolution in France, and on the Proceedings in Certain Societies in London relative to that Event
142. Betrachtungen über die Ursachen von Größe und Untergang der Römer *(Montesquieu)*, *orig.* Considérations sur les causes de la grandeur des Romains et de leur décadence • Considerations on the Romans
143. Das Bevölkerungsgesetz *(Malthus)* → Abhandlung über das Bevölkerungsgesetz
144. Das Bewegungsbild: Kino 1 *(Deleuze)* • Cinema One: Movement-Image
145. Beweis, daß das Christentum so alt als die Welt sei *(Tindal)* • *orig.* Christianity as Old as Creation
146. Beweise und Widerlegungen *(Lakatos)* • *orig.* Proofs and Refutations
147. Die Bienenfabel oder private Laster, öffentliche Vorteile *(Mandeville)* • *orig.* The Fable of the Bees: or, Private Vices, Public Benefits
148. Bildnerei der Geisteskranken *(Prinzhorn)* • Artistry of the Mentally Ill
149. Die Bildung des wissenschaftlichen Geistes. Beitrag zu einer Psychoanalyse der objektiven Erkenntnis *(Bachelard)*, *orig.* La formation de l' esprit scientifique. Contribution à une psychanalyse de la connaissance objective • The New Scientific Spirit
150. Biologie und Erkenntnis *(Piaget)*, *orig.* Biologie et connaissance • Biology and Knowledge
151. Das Blaue Buch *(Wittgenstein)* • *orig.* The Blue Book
152. Der Blick aus der Ferne *(Lévi-Strauss)*, *orig.* Le regard eloigne • The View from Afar
153. Der Bourgeois *(Sombart)* • The Quintessence of Capitalism
154. Das Braune Buch *(Wittgenstein)* • *orig.* The Brown Book
155. Ein Brief über den Enthusiasmus *(Shaftesbury)* • *orig.* A Letter concerning Enthusiasm
156. Brief über den Humanismus *(Heidegger)* • Letter on Humanism
157. Brief über die Blinden zum Gebrauch für die Sehenden *(Diderot)*, *orig.* Lettres sur les aveugles à l' usage de ceux qui voient • The Letter of the Blind for the Benefit of Those Who See
158. Brief über die Toleranz *(Locke)* • *orig.* Epistola de tolerantia • Letters concerning Toleration
159. Briefe an Serena *(Toland)* • *orig.* Letters to Serena
160. Briefe über die ästhetische Erziehung des Menschen *(F. Schiller)* → Über die ästhetische Erziehung des Menschen in einer Reihe von Briefen
161. Briefe über die Empfindungen *(Mendelssohn)* • Letters on Sensations
162. Briefe über die englische Nation *(Voltaire)* • *orig.* Letters concerning the English Nation; *also:* Letters on England
163. Briefe zur Beförderung der Humanität *(Herder)* • Letters for the Furtherance of Humanity
164. Bruno oder über das göttliche und natürliche Princip der Dinge *(Schelling)* • Bruno: or, On the Divine and Natural Principle of Things
165. Das Buch der Erkenntnis *(Maimonides)*, *orig.* Sefer Ha-Madda • Book of Knowledge
166. Buch der Genesung *(Avicenna)*, *orig.* Kitäb as-Shifä' • Canon of Medicine
167. Das Buch der göttlichen Tröstung *(Meister Eckhart)* • Book of Divine Consolation
168. Buch der Grundlehren *(Albo)*, *orig.* Sefer ha-Iqqarim • The Book of Roots
169. Das Buch der Pflichten des Herzens *(Ibn Paquda)*, *orig.* Kitab al-Hidaya ila fara'id al-qulub • Duties of the Heart
170. Das Buch vom Liebenden und Geliebten *(Lullus)*, *orig.* Libre d'amic e amat • The Book of the Lover and the Beloved
171. Ein Buch von der großen Kunst *(Cardano)*, *orig.* Artis magnae, sive de regulis algebraicis • The Great Art: or, The Rules of Algebra; *also:* Ars magna or the Rules of Alegbra
172. Das Buch von der Malerei *(Da Vinci, postum)*, *orig.* Trattato della pittura • The Notebooks of Leonardo Da Vinci

209. Differenz des Fichteschen und Schellingschen Systems der Philosophie *(Hegel)* • Difference Between Fichte's and Schelling's System of Philosophy; *also:* Difference between the Philosophical Systems of Fichte and Schelling

210. Differenz und Wiederholung *(Deleuze), orig.* Différence et répétition • Difference and Repetition

211. Diskurs über den Ursprung und die Grundlagen der Ungleichheit unter den Menschen *(Rousseau), orig.* Discours sur l' origine et les fondements de l' inégalité parmi les hommes • Discourse on the Origin and Foundation of Inequality Among Mankind

212. Diskurs über die unwandelbaren Pflichten der Natürlichen Religion und die Wahrheit und Gewißheit der Christlichen Offenbarung *(Clarke)* • *orig.* A Discourse concerning the Unchangeable Obligations of Natural Religion and the Truth and Certainty of the Christian Revelation

213. Drei Abhandlungen zur Sexualtheorie *(Freud)* • Three Essays on the Theory of Sexuality

214. Drei Dialoge zwischen Hylas und Philonous *(Berkeley)* • *orig.* Three Dialogues between Hylas and Philonous

215. Das dreigeteilte Werk *(Meister Eckhart), orig.* Opus tripartitum • Opus tripartitum

216. Ecce Homo *(Nietzsche)* • nt

217. Eduard Allwills Briefsammlung *(Jacobi)* • Edward Allwill's Collected Letters

218. Eichmann in Jerusalem. Ein Bericht von der Banalität des Bösen *(Arendt)* • *orig.* Eichmann in Jerusalem: A Report of the Banality of Evil

219. Der Einbruch der sexuellen Zwangsmoral. Zur Geschichte der sexuellen Ökonomie *(Reich)* • The Sexual Revolution: Toward a Self-Regulating Character Structure

220. Der eindimensionale Mensch. Studien zur Ideologie der fortgeschrittenen Industriegesellschaft *(Marcuse)* • *orig.* The One-Dimensional Man. Studies in the Ideology of Advanced Industrial Society

221. Einführung in das mathematische Denken. Die Begriffsbildung der modernen Mathematik *(Waismann)* • Introduction to Mathematical Thinking. The Formation of Concepts in Modern Mathematics

222. Einführung in die genetische Erkenntnistheorie *(Piaget), orig.* L' epistemologie genetique • Genetic Epistemology

223. Einführung in die Kybernetik *(Ashby)* • *orig.* Introduction to Cybernetics

224. Einführung in die Logik *(William of Sherwood), orig.* Introductiones in logicam • William of Sherwood's Introduction to Logic

225. Einführung in die mathematische Philosophie *(Russell)* • *orig.* Introduction to Mathematical Philosophy

226. Einführung in die Metaphysik *(Heidegger)* • An Introduction to Metaphysics

227. Einführung in die Philosophie *(Jaspers)* • Way to Wisdom

228. Einführung in die Philosophie der Naturwissenschaft *(Carnap)* • Philosophical Foundations of Physics

229. Einführung in die Prinzipien der Moral und der Gesetzgebung *(Bentham)* • *orig.* An Introduction to the Principles of Morals and Legislation

230. Einführung in die symbolische Logik *(Carnap)* • Introduction to Symbolic Logic and Its Application

231. Einleitung in die Geisteswissenschaften *(Dilthey)* • Introduction to the Human Sciences

232. Einleitung in die Kategorien *(Porphyry), orig.* Eisagoge; *also:* Peri tön pente phonön • Isagoge

233. Einleitung in die Musiksoziologie *(Adorno)* • Introduction to the Sociology of Music

234. Einübung im Christentum *(Kierkegaard), orig.* Indövelse i Christendom • Training in Christianity

235. Einzelding und logisches Subjekt *(Strawson)* • *orig.* Individuals: An Essay in Descriptive Metaphysics

236. Der einzig mögliche Beweisgrund zu einer Demonstration des Daseins Gottes *(Kant)* • The Only Possible Argument in Support of a Demonstration of the Existence of God; *also:* The One Possible Basis for a Demonstration of the Existence of God

273. Erkenntnis, Maschinen, Verstehen. Zur Neugestaltung von Computersystemen *(Winograd, Florens)* • *orig.* Understanding Computers and Cognition

274. Das Erkenntnisproblem in der Philosophie und Wissenschaft der neueren Zeit *(Cassirer)* • The Problem of Knowledge, Philosophy, Science, and History since Hegel; *also:* The Problem of Knowledge in the Philosophy and Science of the Modern Era

275. Erklären und Verstehen *(Wright)* • *orig.* Explanation and Understanding

276. Die Erklären-Verstehen-Kontroverse in transzendentalpragmatischer Sicht *(Apel)* • Understanding and Explanation: A Transcendental Pragmatic Perspective

277. Erklärung und Verstehen *(Dilthey)* • Explanation and Understanding

278. Erläuterungen zur Diskursethik *(Habermas)* • Justification and Application: Remarks on Discourse Ethics

279. Das Erlebnis und die Dichtung *(Dilthey)* • Poetry and Experience

280. Die Eroberung des Brotes *(Kropotkin)* • The Conquest of Bread

281. Eroberung des Glücks *(Russell)* • *orig.* The Conquest of Happiness

282. Erörterung der Frage nach dem Bösen *(Aquinas), orig.* Questio disputatae de malo • Disputed Question on Evil

283. Erörterungen der Fragen nach der Macht Gottes *(Aquinas), orig.* Questiones disputatae de potentia Dei • On the Power of God

284. Erörterungen der Fragen nach der Wahrheit *(Aquinas), orig.* Questiones disputatae de veritate • Truth and Disputed Questions on Truth

285. Der Erretter aus dem Irrtum *(Al-Ghazzali), orig.* Al-Munqid min ad al-dalal • Freedom and Fulfilment: An Annotated Translation of Al-Ghazali's Al-Muniqdh min ad-dalal and other Relevant Works of Al-Ghazali

286. Erscheinung und Wirklichkeit. Ein metaphysischer Versuch *(Bradley)* • *orig.* Appearance and Reality: A Metaphysical Essay

287. Die Erste Analytik *(Aristotle), orig.* Analytika protera • Prior Analytics

288. Erster Entwurf eines Systems der Naturphilosophie *(Schelling)* • First Sketch of a System of the Philosophy of Nature

289. Die Erziehung des Menschengeschlechts *(Lessing)* • Education of Mankind

290. Die Erziehung, intellektuell, moralisch und physisch *(Spencer)* • *orig.* Education: Intellectual, Moral and Physical

291. Ein Essay über Metaphysik *(Collingwood)* • *orig.* (An) Essay on Metaphysics

292. Essays *(Montaigne), orig.* Essais • The Essays

293. Ethik *(N. Hartmann)* • Ethics

294. Ethik des reinen Willens *(Cohen)* • Ethics of the Pure Will

295. Die Ethik nach geometrischer Methode dargestellt *(Spinoza, postum), orig.* Ethica ordine geometrico demonstrata • Ethic: demonstrated in geometrical Order and divided into five Parts; *also:* Ethics demonstrated according to the Geometrical Order

296. Ethik oder über die Kardinaltugenden *(Geulincx), orig.* Gnothi seauton, sive ethica • Ethica

297. Ethik. Eine Untersuchung der Tatsachen und Gesetze des sittlichen Lebens *(Wundt)* • Ethics: An Investigation of the Facts and Laws of the Moral Life

298. Ethik: Die Erfindung des moralisch Richtigen und Falschen *(Mackie)* • *orig.* Ethics: Inventing Right and Wrong

299. Eudemische Ethik *(Aristotle), orig.* Ethika Eudemeia • Eudemian Ethics

300. Eudemos oder Von der Seele *(Aristotle), orig.* Eudemos ē Peri tēs psychēs • Eudemos, or On the Soul

301. Euthydemos *(Plato)* • *nt*

302. Euthyphron *(Plato)* • *nt*

303. Evolution und Ethik *(Huxley)* • *orig.* Evolution and Ethics

304. Die Existenz Gottes *(Swinburne)* • *orig.* The Existence of God

305. Experimentum mundi *(Bloch)* • *nt*

306. Der Fall Wagner *(Nietzsche)* • The Case of Wagner; *also:* The Wagner Case

307. Falsifikation und die Methodologie wissenschaftlicher Foschungsprogramme *(Lakatos)* • *orig.* Falsification and the Methodology of Scientific Research Programmes
308. Die fatalen Strategien *(Baudrillard), orig.* Les strategies fatales • Fatal Strategies
309. Die Fehlbarkeit des Menschen. Phänomenologie der Schuld I *(Ricoeur), orig.* Finitude et culpabilité. I. L'homme faillible • Fallible Man
310. Formale Philosophie *(Montague, postum)* • *orig.* Formal Philosophy
311. Formale und transzendetale Logik. Versuch einer Kritik der logischen Vernunft *(Husserl)* • Formal and Transcendental Logic
312. Der Formalismus in der Ethik und die materiale Wertethik *(Scheler)* • Formalism in Ethics and Non-Formal Ethics of Values
313. Die Frage nach dem Ding *(Heidegger)* • What is a Thing?
314. Fragen der Ethik *(Schlick)* • Problems of Ethics
315. Fragmente einer Sprache der Liebe *(Barthes), orig.* Fragments d'un discours amoureux • A Lover's Discourse: Fragments
316. Die Frau und der Sozialismus *(Bebel)* • Woman in the Past, Present and Future
317. Freges Grundlagen der Arithmetik *(Austin)* • Foundations of Arithmetic
318. Freie Wissenschaft und freie Lehre *(Haeckel)* • Freedom in Science and Teaching
319. Freiheit und Vernunft *(Hare)* • *orig.* Freedom and Reason
320. Der Fremde *(Camus), orig.* L' Etranger • The Stranger
321. Die fröhliche Wissenschaft *(Nietzsche)* • The Gay Science; *also:* The Joyful Science
322. Führer der Unschlüssigen *(Maimonides), orig.* Dalalat al-Ha' irin • Guide to/of the Perplexed/ Doubting
323. Fundamental-Anthropologie *(Landmann)* • Fundamental Anthropology
324. Fünf Bücher über das Schicksal *(Pomponazzi), orig.* De fato • On Fate
325. Fünfzehn Predigten *(Butler)* • *orig.* Fifteen Sermons
326. Die Funktion der Vernunft *(Whitehead)* • *orig.* Function of Reason
327. Die Funktion des Orgasmus *(Reich)* • The Function of Orgasm: Discovery of the Orgone
328. Funktion und Begriff *(Frege)* • Function and Concept
329. Für Marx *(Althusser), orig.* Pour Marx • For Marx
330. Furcht und Zittern *(Kierkegaard), orig.* Frygt og Baeven • Fear and Trembling
331. Die Furcht vor der Freiheit *(Fromm)* • *orig.* Escape from Freedom
332. Der Fürst *(Machiavelli, postum), orig.* Il Principe • The Prince

333. Die Gabe. Form und Funktion des Austauschs in archaischen Gesellschaften *(Mauss), orig.* Essai sur le don • Gift: Forms and Functions of Exchange in Archaic Societies
334. Gang der Weltgeschichte. Aufstieg und Verfall der Kulturen *(Toynbee)* • *orig.* A Study of History
335. Gastmahl *(Plato), orig.* Symposion • Symposium or Supper; *also:* The Drinking Party
336. Der Gebrauch von Argumenten *(Toulmin)* • *orig.* The Uses of Arguments
337. Die Geburt der Klinik. Eine Archäologie des ärztlichen Blicks *(Foucault), orig.* Naissance de la clinique: une archéologie du regard médical • The Birth of the Clinic: An Archeology of Medical Perception
338. Die Geburt der Tragödie aus dem Geiste der Musik *(Nietzsche)* • The Birth of Tragedy from the Spirit of Music
339. Gedanken *(Pascal, postum), orig.* Les Pensées de M. Pascal sur la religion et sur quelques autres sujets • Thoughts; *also:* Pensées
340. Gedanken über die Erziehung *(Locke)* • *orig.* Some Thoughts concerning Education
341. Gedanken über Tod und Unsterblichkeit *(Feuerbach)* • Thoughts on Death and Immortality
342. Gedanken zur Interpretation der Natur *(Diderot), orig.* Pensées sur l' interpretation de la nature • On the Interpretation of Nature
343. Gegen Celsus *(Origen), orig.* Kata Kelsu • Contra Celsum
344. Gegen die Christen *(Porphyry), orig.* Kata Christianon • Against the Christians

345. Gegenseitige Hilfe in der Tier- und Menschenwelt *(Kropotkin)* • Mutual Aid: A Factor of Evolution
346. Das Geheimnis Hegels *(Stirling)* • orig. The Secret of Hegel
347. Der Geist als Widersacher der Seele *(Klages)* • The Mind as Adversary of the Soul
348. Geist der Utopie *(Bloch)* • Spirit of Utopia
349. Geist und Natur: Eine notwendige Einheit *(Bateson)* • orig. Mind and Nature: A Necessary Unity
350. Geist, Hirn und Wissenschaft *(Searle)* • orig. Minds, Brains and Science
351. Geist, Identität und Gesellschaft. Aus der Sicht des Sozialbehaviorismus *(Mead, postum)* • orig. Mind, Self, and Society, from the Standpoint of a Social Behaviorist
352. Die geistige Situation der Zeit *(Jaspers)* • Man in the Modern Age
353. Die geistige Welt der Primitiven *(Lévy-Bruhl)*, orig. La mentalité primitive • Primitive Mentality
354. Geistliche Übungen *(Ignatius Loyola)*, orig. Exercitia spiritualia • Spiritual Exercises
355. Gelassenheit *(Heidegger)* • Discourse on Thinking
356. Gemeinschaft und Gesellschaft *(Tönnies)* • Community and Association
357. Generelle Morphologie der Organismen *(Haeckel)* • General Morphology of Organisms°
358. Genese und Struktur der Gesellschaft *(Gentile, postum)*, orig. Genesi e struttura della società • Genesis and Structure of Society
359. Die Genesis der kopernikanischen Welt *(Blumenberg)* • The Genesis of Copernican World
360. Der Genius des Christentums oder die Schönheit der christlichen Religion *(Chateaubriand)*, orig. Génie du christianisme ou Beauté de la religion chrétiennes • The Genius of Christianity
361. Gesammelte Aufsätze *(Schlick)* • Collected Essays
362. Gesammelte Aufsätze zur Wissenschaftslehre *(M. Weber)* • Methodology of the Social Sciences
363. Geschichte als System und über das römische Imperium *(Ortega y Gasset)*, orig. Historia como sistema • History as a System
364. Geschichte der Ästhetik *(Bosanquet)* • orig. (A) History of Aesthetics
365. Geschichte der ökonomischen Analyse *(Schumpeter)* • orig. History of Economic Analysis
366. Geschichte der Sexualität *(Foucault)*, orig. Histoire de la sexualité • The History of Sexuality
367. Geschichte des Materialismus und Kritik seiner Bedeutung in der Gegenwart *(Lange)* • The History of Materialism: Criticism of Its Present Importance
368. Geschichte und Eschatologie *(Bultmann)* • orig. History and Eschatology
369. Geschichte und Klassenbewußtsein *(Lukács)* • History and Class Consciousness
370. Geschichte und Utopie *(Cioran)* • History and Utopia
371. Geschlecht und Charakter *(Weininger)* • Sex and Character
372. Der geschlossene Handelsstaat *(Fichte)* • The Closed Commercial State
373. Die Gesellschaft der Individuen *(Elias)* • The Society of Individuals
374. Die Gesellschaftslehre des sowjetischen Marxismus *(Marcuse)* • orig. Soviet-Marxism: A Critical Analysis
375. Gesetz, Kausalität und Wahrscheinlichkeit *(Schlick)* • Law, Causality and Probability
376. Das Gesetzbuch der Natur oder der zu allen Zeiten vernachlässigte oder verkannte, wahrhafte Geist ihrer Gesetze *(Morelly)*, orig. Code de la nature ou le véritable esprit de ses lois de tout temps négligé ou méconnu • The Code of Nature
377. Gesetze *(Plato)*, orig. Nomoi • Laws
378. Gespräche über die natürliche Religion *(Hume, postum)* • orig. Dialogues Concerning Natural Religion
379. Gevierteilt *(Cioran)* • Drawn and Quartered
380. Glauben und Verstehen *(Bultmann)* • Faith and Understanding
381. Der Gödelsche Beweis *(Nagel, Newman)* • orig. Gödel's Proof
382. Der goldene Zweig. Das Geheimnis von Glauben und Sitten der Völker *(Frazer)* • orig. The Golden Bough: A Study in Magic and Religion
383. Die Goldwaage *(Galilei)*, orig. Il Saggiatore • The Assayer
384. Gorgias *(Plato)* • nt

385. Gott und der Staat *(Bakunin), orig.* Dieu et l'état • God and the State
386. Gottesfinsternis *(Buber)* • Eclipse of God
387. Gotteslicht *(Crescas), orig.* Or Adonai • The Light of the Lord
388. Göttliche Unterweisungen *(Lactantius), orig.* Divinae institutiones • Divine Institutes
389. Götzen-Dämmerung oder Wie man mit dem Hammer philosophiert *(Nietzsche)* • Twilight of the Idols
390. Grammatologie *(Derrida), orig.* De la Grammatologie • Of Grammatology
391. Die Grenzen der naturwissenschaftlichen Begriffsbildung *(Rickert)* • The Limits of Concept Formation in Natural Science
392. Die Grenzen des Wachstums *(Meadows et al.)* • *orig.* The Limits of Growth
393. Die Grenzen künstlicher Intelligenz. Was Computer nicht können *(Dreyfus)* • *orig.* What Computers Can't Do - The Limits of Artificial Intelligence
394. Die Grenzen und der Ursprung menschlicher Erkenntnis *(Czolbe)* • The Limits and Origin of Human Knowledge
395. Griechische Kulturgeschichte *(Burckhardt)* • History of Greek Culture
396. Große Didaktik *(Comenius), orig.* Didactica Magna • The Great Didactic
397. Große Erneuerung *(F. Bacon)* → Über die Würde und die Fortschritte der Wissenschaften, Neues Organon
398. Große Katechese *(Gregory of Nyssa), orig.* Logos katechetikos ho megas • The Catechetical Oration
399. Die große Kette der Wesen. Geschichte eines Gedankens *(Lovejoy)* • *orig.* The Great Chain of Being: A Study of the History of an Idea
400. Große Therapeutik *(Galenos), orig.* Therapeutike methodos • On the Therapeutic Method
401. Großer Kommentar zur Metaphysik *(Averroes), orig.* Tafsïr mä ba' d at-tabï'ah • Long Commentary on Aristotle's Metaphysics
402. Größeres Werk, Kleineres Werk, Drittes Werk *(R. Bacon), orig.* Opus maius, Opus minus, Opus tertium • Greater Work, Lesser Work, Third Work
403. Grundbegriffe der Glaubenslehre *(Melanchthon), orig.* Loci communes rerum theologicarum • Melanchthon on Christian Doctrine
404. Grundformen und Erkenntnis menschlichen Daseins *(Binswanger)* • Basic Forms and Conditions of Human Existence
405. Grundfragen der allgemeinen Sprachwissenschaft *(Saussure, postum), orig.* Cours de linguistique générale • Course in General Linguistics
406. Grundgesetze der Arithmetik *(Frege)* • The Basic Laws of Arithmetic; *also:* Fundamental Laws of Arithmetic
407. Die Grundlage der allgemeinen Relativitätstheorie *(Einstein)* • The Principle of Relativity
408. Grundlage der gesamten Wissenschaftslehre *(Fichte)* • Foundation of the Entire Doctrine of Science; *also:* Foundation of the Complete Theory of Knowledge; *also:* Basis of the Entire Theory of Science; *also:* Foundations of the Entire Wissenschaftslehre
409. Grundlage des Naturrechts *(Fichte)* • Foundation/Basis of Natural Right
410. Die Grundlagen der Arithmetik *(Frege)* • The Foundations of Arithmetic
411. Die Grundlagen der Charakterkunde *(Klages)* • The Science of Character
412. Die Grundlagen der Geometrie *(Hilbert)* • (The) Foundations of Geometry
413. Grundlagen der Logik und Mathematik *(Carnap)* • Foundations of Logic and Mathematics
414. Grundlagen der Mathematik *(Hilbert, Bernays)* • Foundations of Mathematics
415. Grundlagen der Zeichentheorie *(Morris), orig.* Foundations of the Theory of Signs
416. Die Grundlagen einer wissenschaftlichen Wertlehre *(Kraft)* • Foundations for a Scientific Analysis of Value
417. Grundlagen. Abhandlungen zur Philosophie, Logik, Mathematik und Wirtschaftswissenschaft *(Ramsey, postum)* • *orig.* Foundations: Essays in Philosophy, Logic, Mathemathics and Economics
418. Grundlegung und Aufbau der Ethik *(Brentano, postum)* • The Foundation and Construction of Ethics

419. Grundlegung zur Metaphysik der Sitten *(Kant)* • Groundwork of/Grounding for/Foundations of the Metaphysic(s) of Morals
420. Grundlinien der Philosophie des Rechts oder Naturrecht und Staatswissenschaft im Grundriß *(Hegel)* • Foundations/Outlines of the Philosophy of Right; *also:* Natural Right and Political Science in Outline
421. Grundlinien einer Kritik der bisherigen Sittenlehre *(Schleiermacher)* • Outlines of a Critique of the Doctrine of Morals up to Present
422. Grundprobleme der Ethik *(Moore)* • *orig.* Ethics
423. Die Grundprobleme der Phänomenologie *(Heidegger)* • The Basic Problems of Phenomenology
424. Grundriß der Geschichte der Philosophie *(Überweg)* • A History of Philosophy, from Thales to the Present Time
425. Grundriß der Psychologie *(Wundt)* • Outlines of Psycholgy
426. Grundriß des Eigentümlichen der Wissenschaftslehre in Rücksicht auf das theoretische Vermögen *(Fichte)* • Outline of the Distinctive Character of the Wissenschaftslehre with Respect to the Theoretical Faculty
427. Grundsätze der Moralphilosophie *(Ferguson)* • *orig.* Institutes of Moral Philosophy
428. Grundsätze der Philosophie der Zukunft *(Feuerbach)* • Principles of the Philosophy of the Future
429. Grundzüge der Ansichten der Bürger der vollkommenen Stadt *(Al-Farabi), orig.* Mabädi' ärä' ahl al-madïna al-fädila • On the Perfect State
430. Grundzüge der Lehre Newtons *(Voltaire), orig.* Eléments de la philosophie de Newton • Elements of Sir Isaac Newton's Philosophy
431. Grundzüge der Logik *(Quine)* • *orig.* Methods of Logic
432. Grundzüge der Naturphilosophie *(Schlick, postum)* • Philosophy of Nature
433. Grundzüge der Philosophie *(Hobbes)* → Vom Körper; Vom Menschen; Vom Bürger
434. Grundzüge der physiologischen Psychologie *(Wundt)* • Principles of Physiological Psychology
435. Grundzüge der theoretischen Logik *(Hilbert, Ackermann)* • Principles of Mathematical Logic
436. Die Grundzüge des gegenwärtigen Zeitalters *(Fichte)* • (The) Characteristics of the Present Age
437. Grundzüge einer Metaphysik der Erkenntnis *(N. Hartmann)* • Principles of a Metaphysics of Knowledge
438. Die gute Sache der Freiheit (und meine eigene Angelegenheit) *(B. Bauer)* • The Good Cause of Freedom
439. Die Gutenberg-Galaxis: Das Ende des Buchzeitalters *(McLuhan)* • *orig.* The Gutenberg Galaxy: The Making of Typographic Man

440. Haben oder Sein. Die seelischen Grundlagen einer neuen Gesellschaft *(Fromm)* • *orig.* To Have or to Be?
441. Hand-Orakel und Kunst der Weltklugheit *(Gracián), orig.* Oráculo manual y arte de prudencia • The Oracle: A Manual of the Art of Discretion
442. Handbuch der physiologischen Optik *(Helmholtz)* • A Treatise on Physiological Optics
443. Handbuch der Religionsphilosophie und der philosophischen Aesthetik *(Fries)* • Handbook of the Philosophy of Religion and of Philosophical Aesthetics
444. Handbüchlein der Ethik *(Epictetus), orig.* Encheiridion • The Echiridion
445. Handbüchlein eines christlichen Streiters; *auch:* Handbüchlein des christlichen Soldaten *(Erasmus), orig.* Enchiridion militis Christiani • Enchiridion militis Christiani
446. Die Hauptfragen der Philosophie *(Ayer)* • *orig.* The Central Questions of Philosophy
447. Hauptlehren *(Epicurus), orig.* Kyriai doxai • Principal Doctrines
448. Hauptströmungen der Gegenwartsphilosophie *(Stegmüller)* • Main Currents in Contemporary German, British and American Philosophy
449. Der heilige Eros *(Bataille), orig.* L' érotisme • Eroticism
450. Die heilige Familie oder Kritik der kritischen Kritik *(Marx, Engels)* • The Holy Familiy
451. Das Heilige und das Profane *(Eliade)* • The Sacred and the Profane: The Nature of Religion

452. Das Heilige: Über das Irrationale in der Idee des Göttlichen und sein Verhältnis zum Rationalen *(Otto)* • The Idea of the Holy: An Inquiry into the Non-rational Factor in the Idea of the Divine and Its Relation to the Rational

453. Die Heiligkeit des Lebens in der Medizin. Eine philosophische Kritik *(Kuhse)* • *orig.* The Sanctity-of-Life Doctrine in Medicine: A Critique

454. Die Heilkunst *(Galenos), orig.* Techne iatrike • On the Therapeutic Method

455. Hemmung, Symptom und Angst *(Freud)* • Inhibitions, Symptoms, and Anxiety

456. Hermeneutik *(Schleiermacher)* • Hermeneutics

457. Heroische Leidenschaften und individuelles Leben *(Bruno), orig.* De gli eroici furori • Heroic Frenzies

458. Herrn Eugen Dührings Umwälzung der Wissenschaft *(Engels)* • Anti-Dühring: Herrn Eugen Dühring's Revolution in Science

459. Himmlische Geheimnisse *(Swedenborg), orig.* Arcana coelestia • Heavenly Secrets

460. Hippias I *(Plato)* → Hippias maior

461. Hippias maior *(Plato)* • Greater Hippias

462. Hippias II *(Plato)* → Hippias minor

463. Hippias minor *(Plato)* • Lesser Hippias

464. Historik. Vorlesungen über Enzyklopädie und Methodologie der Geschichte *(Droysen)* • Outline of the Principles of History

465. Historisches und kritisches Wörterbuch *(Bayle), orig.* Dictionnaire historique et critique • A General Dictionary, Historical and Critical; *also:* A Historical and Critical Dictionary: Selections

466. Der Historismus und seine Überwindung *(Troeltsch)* • *orig.* Christian Thought, Its History and Application

467. Die Hochzeit der Philologie und des Merkur *(Martianus Capella), orig.* De nuptiis Philologiae et Mercurii • Concerning the Marriage of Mercury and Philology

468. Die höfische Gesellschaft *(Elias)* • The Court Society

469. Homo ludens. Vom Ursprung der Kultur im Spiel *(Huizinga)* • Homo Ludens: A Study of the Play Element in Culture

470. Homo viator. Philosophie der Hoffnung *(Marcel)* • Homo Viator. Introduction to a Metaphysic of Hope

471. Humanismus *(F. C. S. Schiller)* • *orig.* Studies in Humanism

472. Humanismus und Terror *(Merleau-Ponty), orig.* Humanism et terreur • Humanism and Terror: An Essay on the Communist Problem

473. Das Ich und das Es *(Freud)* • The Ego and the Id

474. Das Ich und die Abwehrmechanismen *(A. Freud)* • The Ego and the Mechanisms of Defence

475. Ich und Du *(Buber)* • I and Thou

476. Das Ich und sein Gehirn *(Popper, Eccles)* • *orig.* The Self and Its Brain. An Argument for Interactionism

477. Die Idee der Phänomenologie *(Husserl)* • (The) Idea of Phenomenology

478. Die Idee der Sozialwissenschaft und ihr Verhältnis zur Philosophie *(Winch)* • *orig.* The Idea of a Social Science and Its Relation to Philosophy

479. Idee zu einer allgemeinen Geschichte in weltbürgerlicher Absicht *(Kant)* • Idea for a Universal History from a Cosmopolitan Point of View; *also:* Idea for a Universal History with a Cosmopolitan Intent

480. Ideen zu einem Versuch, die Grenzen der Wirksamkeit des Staats zu bestimmen *(W.v.Humboldt)* • The Limits of State Action

481. Ideen zu einer Philosophie der Natur *(Schelling)* • Ideas concerning a Philosophy of Nature

482. Ideen zu einer reinen Phänomenologie und phänomenologischen Philosophie *(Husserl)* • Ideas Pertaining to a Pure Phenomenology and to a Phenomenological Philosophy; *also:* Ideas for a pure Phenomenology and phenomenological Philosophy

483. Ideen zur Philosophie der Geschichte der Menschheit *(Herder)* • Reflections on the Philosophy of the History of Mankind; *also:* Ideas for the Philosophy of the History of Mankind

484. Identität und Differenz *(Heidegger)* • Identity and Difference
485. Identität und Wirklichkeit *(Meyerson), orig.* Identité et réalité • Identity and Reality
486. Ideologie und Utopie *(Mannheim)* • Ideology and Utopia: An Introduction to the Sociology of Knowledge
487. Illuminationen *(Benjamin)* • Illuminations
488. Die Imagination *(Sartre), orig.* L'imagination • The Imagination
489. Der Imperialismus als höchstes Stadium des Kapitalismus *(Lenin), orig.* Imperializm, kak vys§aja stadija kapitalizma • Imperialism as the Highest Stage of Capitalism
490. Individuum und Kosmos in der Philosophie der Renaissance *(Cassirer)* • Individual and the Cosmos in Renaissance Philosophy
491. Integraler Humanismus. Zeitliche und geistige Probleme einer neuen Christenheit; *auch:* Christlicher Humanismus. Politische und geistige Fragen einer neuen Christenheit; *auch:* Die Zukunft der Christenheit *(Maritain), orig.* Humanisme intégral. Problémes temporels et spirituels d'une nouvelle chrétienté • Integral Humanism
492. Intentionalität: Eine Abhandlung zur Philosophie des Geistes *(Searle)* • *orig.* Intentionality: An Essay in the Philosophy of Mind
493. Ion *(Plato)* • nt
494. Irrwege der Vernunft *(Feyerabend)* • *orig.* Farewell to Reason
495. Ist der Existenzialismus ein Humanismus? *(Sartre), orig.* L'existentialisme est un humanisme • Existentialism and Humanism

496. Ja und Nein *(Abaelard), orig.* Sic et non • For and Against
497. Jargon der Eigentlichkeit *(Adorno)* • The Jargon of Authenticity
498. Jenseits des Lustprinzips *(Freud)* • Beyond the Pleasure Principle
499. Jenseits von Freiheit und Würde *(Skinner)* • *orig.* Beyond Freedom and Dignity
500. Jenseits von Gut und Böse. Vorspiel einer Philosophie der Zukunft *(Nietzsche)* • Beyond Good and Evil. Prelude to a Philosophy of the Future
501. Jerusalem oder über religiöse Macht und Judentum *(Mendelssohn)* • Jerusalem, or on Religious Power and Judaism

502. Die Kämpfe Gottes *(Lewi ben Gerschom/Gersonides), orig.* Milchamot Adonai • (The) Wars of the Lord
503. Kant und das Problem der Metaphysik *(Heidegger)* • Kant and the Problem of Metaphysics
504. Das Kapital lesen *(Althusser), orig.* Lire le Capital • Reading Capital
505. Das Kapital. Kritik der politischen Ökonomie *(Marx)* • Capital: A Critique of Political Economy
506. Kapitalismus, Sozialismus und Demokratie *(Schumpeter)* • *orig.* Capitalism, Socialism and Democracy
507. Die Katholische Wahrheit oder die theologische Summe *(Aquinas)* → Summe der Theologie
508. Kerygma und Mythos *(Bultmann)* • Kerygma and Myth
509. Klage des Friedens *(Erasmus), orig.* Querela pacis • The Complaint of Peace
510. Kommentar über die wahre und falsche Religion *(Zwingli), orig.* De vera et falsa religione commentarius • Commentary on the True and False Religion
511. Kommentar zu Peri hermeneias *(Aquinas), orig.* Sententia in librum Peri hermeneias • Aristotle on Interpretation
512. Kommentar zum Buch des Boethius über die Trinität *(Aquinas), orig.* Expositio super librum Boetii De Trinitate • Division and Methods of the Sciences
513. Kommentar zum Buch über die Seele *(Aquinas), orig.* Sententia in librum De anima • Commentary on Aristotle's De Anima
514. Kommentar zur Metaphysik *(Aquinas), orig.* Sententia in librum Metaphysicae • Commentary on the Metaphysics of Aristotle
515. Kommentar zur Nikomachischen Ethik *(Aquinas), orig.* Sententia in librum Ethicorum • Commentary on the Nicomachean Ethics

516. Kommentar zur Physik *(Aquinas), orig.* Sententia in librum Physicae • Commentary on Aristotle's Physics

517. Das Kommunistische Manifest *(Marx, Engels)* → Manifest der Kommunistischen Partei

518. Konterrevolution und Revolte *(Marcuse)* • *orig.* Counterrevolution and Revolt

519. Die Kontingenz der Naturgesetze *(Boutroux), orig.* De la contingence des lois de la nature • The Contingency of the Laws of Nature

520. Kontingenz, Ironie und Solidarität *(Rorty)* • *orig.* Contingency, Irony, and Solidarity

521. Konventionen: Eine sprachphilosophische Studie *(Lewis)* • *orig.* Convention: A Philosophical Study

522. Die Kopernikanische Revolution *(Kuhn)* • *orig.* Copernican Revolution: Planetary Astronomy in the Development of Western Thought

523. Kosmogonie *(Ehrenfels)* • Cosmogony

524. Kosmopolis. Die unerkannten Aufgaben der Moderne *(Toulmin)* • *orig.* Cosmopolis. The Hidden Agenda of Modernity

525. Kosmos und Geschichte. Der Mythos der ewigen Wiederkehr *(Eliade), orig.* Le mythe de l' éternal retour. Archétypes et répétition • Cosmos and History. The Myth of the Eternal Return

526. Kosmos. Entwurf einer physischen Weltbeschreibung *(A. v. Humboldt)* • Cosmos: A Sketch of a Physical Description of the Universe

527. Kraft und Stoff *(Büchner)* • Force and Matter

528. Die Krankheit zum Tode *(Kierkegaard), orig.* Sydommen til Døden • The Sickness into/unto Death

529. Kratylos *(Plato)* • *nt*

530. Krieg und Frieden aus der Sicht der Verhaltensforschung *(Eibl-Eibesfeld)* • The Biology of Peace and War

531. Die Krisis der europäischen Wissenschaften und die transzendentale Phänomenologie. Eine Einleitung in die phänomenologische Philosophie *(Husserl)* • The Crisis of European Sciences and Transcendental Phenomenology: An Introduction to Phenomenological Philosophy

532. Kritias *(Plato)* • *nt*

533. Kritik der dialektischen Vernunft *(Sartre), orig.* Critique de la raison dialectique • Critique of Dialectical Reason

534. Kritik der kollektiven Vernunft *(Toulmin)* • *orig.* The Collective Use and Evolution of Concepts

535. Kritik der praktischen Vernunft *(Kant)* • Critique of Practical Reason

536. Kritik der praktischen Vernunft *(Nelson)* • Critique of Practical Reason

537. Kritik der reinen Erfahrung *(Avenarius)* • Critique of Pure Experience

538. Kritik der reinen Vernunft *(Kant)* • Critique of Pure Reason

539. Kritik der Urteilskraft *(Kant)* • Critique of Judg(e)ment

540. Kritik der zynischen Vernunft *(Sloterdijk)* • Critique of Cynical Reason

541. Kritik des Gothaer Programms *(Marx)* • Critique of the Gotha Program

542. Kritik und Erkenntnisfortschritt *(Lakatos)* • *orig.* Criticism and the Growth of Knowledge

543. Kritik und Gemeinsinn *(Walzer)* • *orig.* The Company of Critics: Social Criticism and Political Commitment in the Twentieth Century

544. Kritik und Wahrheit *(Barthes), orig.* Critique et vérité • Criticism and Truth

545. Der Kritiker *(Gracián), orig.* El Criticón • The Critick

546. Kritische Theorie *(Horkheimer, postum)* • Critical Theory

547. Kriton *(Plato)* • Crito

548. Die Kultur der Renaissance in Italien *(Burckhardt)* • The Civilization of the Renaissance in Italy

549. Kultur und Anarchie *(Arnold)* • *orig.* Culture and Anarchy

550. Kultur und Gesellschaft *(Marcuse)* • Negations: Essays in Critical Theory

551. Kulturphilosophie *(Schweitzer)* • The Philosophy of Civilization

552. Kulturwissenschaft und Naturwissenschaft *(Rickert)* • Science and History

553. Kunst als Erfahrung *(Dewey)* • *orig.* Art as Experience

554. Das Kunstwerk im Zeitalter seiner technischen Reproduzierbarkeit *(Benjamin), orig.* L'œuvre d'art à l'époque de sa reproduction mécanisée • Art in the Age of Mechanical Reproduction

555. Kurze Abhandlung von Gott, dem Menschen und dessen Glück *(Spinoza, postum), orig.* Tractatus de Deo et homine eiusque felicitate • Short Treatise on God, Man and his Well-being

556. Eine kurze Geschichte der Zeit *(Hawking)* • *orig.* A Brief History of Time

557. Kybernetik: Regelung und Nachrichtenübertragung im Lebewesen und in der Maschine *(Wiener)* • *orig.* Cybernetics, or Control and Communication in the Animal and the Machine

558. Das Lachen. Versuch über die Bedeutung des Komischen *(Bergson), orig.* Le rire. Essai sur la signification du comique • Laughter: An Essay on the Meaning of the Comic

559. Laches *(Plato)* • *nt*

560. Die Lage der arbeitenden Klasse in England *(Engels)* • The Condition of the Working Class in England

561. Der Laie über die Weisheit, den Geist und die Versuche mittels der Waage *(Nicolas de Cusa), orig.* Idiota de sapientia, de mente, de staticis experimentis • The Idiot

562. Laokoon: oder über die Grenzen der Malerei und Poesie *(Lessing)* • Laocoon: An Essay on the Limits of Painting and Poetry

563. Das Leben der Vernunft oder die Phasen menschlichen Fortschritts *(Santayana)* • *orig.* The Life of Reason or the Phases of Human Progress

564. Das Leben Jesu (kritisch bearbeitet) *(D. F. Strauss)* • Life of Jesus Critically Examined

565. Leben und Meinungen berühmter Philosophen *(Diogenes Laertios), orig.* Philosophon bion dogmaton synagoge • The Lives and Opinions of Eminent Philosophers

566. Die lebendige Metapher *(Ricoeur), orig.* La métaphor vive • The Rule of Metaphor°

567. Die Lebensanschauungen der großen Denker *(Eucken)* • The Problem of Human Life

568. Lebensformen *(Spranger)* • Types of Men

569. Lebensquelle, vom ersten Teil der Weisheit das ist die Wissenschaft von der universellen Materie und Form *(Ibn Gabirol), orig.* Yanbu' alhayya• The Fountain of Life

570. Legitimationsprobleme im Spätkapitalismus *(Habermas)* • Legitimation Crisis

571. Die Legitimität der Neuzeit *(Blumenberg)* • The Legitimacy of the Modern Age

572. Die Lehre vom richtigen Recht *(Stammler)* • The Theory of Justice

573. Lehre vom Satz *(Aristotle), orig.* Peri tes hermeneias • On Interpretation

574. Lehren der Naturphilosophen *(Theophrast), orig.* Physikon doxai • Opinions of the Natural Philosophers

575. Der Lehrer *(Augustine), orig.* De magistro • The Teacher

576. Die Leidenschaften der Seele *(Descartes), orig.* Les passions de l'âme • (The) Passions of the Soul

577. Letzte Schriften über die Philosophie der Psychologie *(Wittgenstein, postum)* • *orig.* Last Writings on the Philosophy of Psychology

578. Leviathan, oder Stoff, Form und Gewalt eines bürgerlichen und kirchlichen Staates *(Hobbes)* • *orig.* Leviathan, ore the Matter, Forme, and Power of a Commonwealth, Ecclesiasticall and Civill

579. Liebe als Passion. Zur Codierung von Intimität *(Luhmann)* • Love as Passion: The Codification of Intimacy

580. Liebe und Haß *(Eibl-Eibesfeld)* • Love and Hate: The Natural History of Behaviour Patterns

581. Linguistik und Poetik *(Jakobson)* • *orig.* Linguistics and Poetics

582. Das literarische Kunstwerk. Eine Untersuchung aus dem Grenzgebiet der Ontologie, Logik und Literaturwissenschaft *(Ingarden)* • The Literary Work of Art. An Investigation on the Borderlines of Ontology, Logic and Theory of Literature

583. Literarischer Anzeiger *(Kierkegaard)* • The Literary Anouncement

584. Lob der Torheit *(Erasmus), orig.* Morias Enkomium seu Laus Stulticiae • The Praise of Folly

585. Logik *(Wundt)* • Logic

586. Logik als Wissenschaft vom reinen Begriff *(Croce), orig.* Logica come scienza del concetto puro • Logic as the Science of the Pure Concept

587. Logik der Forschung. Zur Erkenntnistheorie der modernen Naturwissenschaft *(Popper)* •
Postscript to the Logic of Scientific Discovery
588. Die Logik der heutigen Physik *(Bridgman)* • *orig.* The Logic of Modern Physics
589. Logik der reinen Erkenntnis *(Cohen)* • Logic of Pure Reason
590. Logik des Sinns *(Deleuze), orig.* Logique du sens • The Logic of Sense
591. Die Logik oder die Kunst des Denkens *(Arnauld, Nicole), orig.* La logique ou l'art de penser •
Logic or the Art of Thinking
592. Logik, Sprache, Philosophie *(Waismann, postum)* • The Principles of Linguistic Philosophy
593. Der logische Aufbau der Welt *(Carnap)* • The Logical Structure of the World
594. Logische Syntax der Sprache *(Carnap)* • The Logical Syntax of Language; *also:* Philosophy and
Logical Syntax
595. Logische Untersuchungen *(Frege)* • Logical Investigations
596. Logische Untersuchungen *(Husserl)* • Logical Investigations
597. Logische Untersuchungen *(Trendelenburg)* • Logical Inquiries
598. Die logischen Grundlagen der exakten Wissenschaften *(Natorp)* • The Logical Foundations of
the Exact Sciences
599. Lohn, Preis und Profit *(Marx)* • Wages, Price and Profit
600. Lohnarbeit und Kapital *(Marx)* • Wage-Labour and Capital
601. Ludwig Feuerbach und der Ausgang der klassischen deutschen Philosophie *(Engels)* • Ludwig
Feuerbach and the End/Outcome of Classical German Philosophy
602. Die Lust am Text *(Barthes), orig.* Le plaisir du texte • The Pleasure of the Text
603. Lysis *(Plato)* • nt

604. Macht *(Russell)* • *orig.* Power
605. Die Macht der Computer und die Ohnmacht der Vernunft *(Weizenbaum)* • *orig.* Computer Power
and Human Reason
606. Macht oder Ohnmacht der Subjektivität? *(Jonas)* • On Faith, Reason and Responsibility
607. Macht und Gewalt *(Arendt)* • *orig.* On Violence
608. Magia naturalis, oder Haus-, Kunst- und Wunderbuch *(Della Porta), orig.* Magiae naturalis sive
de miraculis rerum naturalium libri III • Natural Magic
609. Magische Werke; *auch:* Drei Bücher über die okkulte Philosophie oder Über die Magie *(Agrippa
v. Nettesheim), orig.* De occulta philosophia libri III sive de magia• Three books of occult
philosophy; *also:* The Philosophy of Natural Magic
610. Mahnrede *(Iamblichus), orig.* Protreptikos • Exhortation to Philosophy
611. Mahnrede an die Heiden *(Clement of Alexandria), orig.* Protreptikos pros Hellenas • The
Exhortation to the Greeks
612. Mahnschrift *(Aristotle), orig.* Protreptikos • Protrepticus
613. Manifest der Kommunistischen Partei *(Marx, Engels)* • The Communist Manifesto
614. Die Maschine Mensch *(La Mettrie), orig.* L'homme machine • Man a Machine
615. Masse und Macht *(Canetti)* • Crowds and Power
616. Die Massenpsychologie des Faschismus *(Reich)* • The Mass Psychology of Fascism
617. Massenpsychologie und Ich-Analyse *(Freud)* • Group Psychology and the Analysis of the Ego
618. Materialismus und Empiriokritizismus *(Lenin), orig.* Materializm i Empiriokriticizm • Materialism
and Empirio-Criticism
619. Materie und Gedächtnis *(Bergson)* • Matter and Memory
620. Materie und Gedächtnis. Abhandlung über die Beziehung des Körpers zum Geist *(Bergson),
orig.* Matière et mémoire. Essai sur la relation du corps à l'esprit • Matter and Memory
621. Mathematik, empirische Wissenschaft und Erkenntnistheorie *(Lakatos)* • *orig.* Mathematics,
Science and Epistemology
622. Mathematik, Wahrheit und Wirklichkeit *(Brouwer), orig.* Wiskunde, Waarheid, Werkelijkheid •
Intuitionism and Formalism

623. Mathematische Prinzipien der Naturlehre *(Newton), orig.* Philosophiae naturalis principia mathematica • Mathematical Principles of Natural Philosophy

624. Mechanik des Himmels *(Laplace), orig.* Traité de mécanique céleste • Celestial Mechanics

625. Die Mechanik in ihrer Entwicklung historisch-kritisch dargestellt *(Mach)* • The Science of Mechanics: A Critical and Historical Account of its Development

626. Die Mechanisierung des Weltbildes *(Dijksterhuis)* • The Mechanization of the World Picture

627. Meditationen über die Grundlagen der Philosophie *(Descartes), orig.* Meditationes de prima philosophia • Meditations on First Philosophy

628. Das Medium ist Massage *(McLuhan, Fiore)* • *orig.* The Medium is the Massage

629. Menexenos *(Plato)* • *nt*

630. Menon *(Plato)* • *nt*

631. Der Mensch als Maschine *(La Mettrie)* → Die Maschine Mensch

632. Der Mensch eine Maschine *(La Mettrie)* → Die Maschine Mensch

633. Der Mensch im Kosmos *(de Chardin), orig.* Le phénomène humain • The Phenomenon of Man

634. Der Mensch in der Revolte *(Camus), orig.* L'Homme révolté • The Rebel: An Essay on Man in Revolt

635. Der Mensch und der Staat *(Maritain)* • *orig.* Man and the State

636. Der Mensch und die Technik. Beitrag zu einer Philosophie des Lebens *(Spengler)* • Man and Technics: A Contribution to a Philosophy of Life

637. Mensch und Menschmaschine. Kybernetik und Gesellschaft *(Wiener)* • *orig.* The Human Use of Human Beings. Cybernetics and Society

638. Der Mensch. Seine Natur und seine Stellung in der Welt *(Gehlen)* • Man. His Nature and Place in the World

639. Menschenkenntnis *(Adler)* • Understanding Human Nature

640. Die menschliche Natur, ihr Wesen und ihr Verhalten. Eine Einführung in die Sozialpsychologie *(Dewey)* • *orig.* Human Nature and Conduct. An Introduction to Social Psychology

641. Der menschliche Weltbegriff *(Avenarius)* • The Human Concept of the World

642. Das menschliche Wissen *(Russell)* • *orig.* Human Knowledge. Its Scope and Limits

643. Menschliches, Allzumenschliches *(Nietzsche)* • Human, All Too Human

644. Der Mensch in der Evolution, Naturwissenschaft und Religion *(Thorpe)* • Science, Man and Morals

645. Metaphysik *(Albertus Magnus), orig.* Metaphysica • Metaphysics

646. Metaphysik *(Aristotle), orig.* Ta meta ta physika • Metaphysics

647. Metaphysik *(Baumgarten), orig.* Metaphysica • Metaphysics

648. Metaphysik als strenge Wissenschaft *(Scholz)* • Metaphysics as an Exact Science

649. Die Metaphysik der Sitten *(Kant)* • The Metaphysics of Morality/Ethics; *also:* Metaphysics of Morals

650. Metaphysik, oder Vernünftige Gedanken von Gott, der Welt und der Seele des Menschen, auch allen Dingen überhaupt *(Wolff)* • Rational Ideas of God, the World and the Soul of Man

651. Metaphysische Abhandlung *(Leibniz, postum), orig.* Discours de métaphysique • Discourse on Metaphysics

652. Metaphysische Anfangsgründe der Logik im Ausgang von Leibniz *(Heidegger)* • The Metaphysical Foundations of Logic

653. Metaphysische Anfangsgründe der Naturwissenschaft *(Kant)* • Metaphysical Foundations of Natural Science; *also:* Metaphysical First Principles of Natural Sciences

654. Metaphysische Disputationen *(Suárez), orig.* Disputationes metaphysicae • Metaphysical Disputations

655. Meteorologie *(Aristotle), orig.* Meteorologika • Meteorologics

656. Die Methode der Soziologie *(Durkheim), orig.* Les règles de la méthode sociologique • The Rules of Sociological Method

657. Die Methoden der Ethik *(Sidgwick)* • *orig.*The Methods of Ethics

658. Mikrokosmos. Ideen zur Naturgeschichte und Geschichte der Menschheit *(Lotze)* • Microcosm: An Essay concerning Man and His Relation to the World

659. Mikromegas *(Voltaire), orig.* Micromégas • Micromegas
660. Minima Moralia. Reflexionen aus dem beschädigten Leben. *(Adorno)* • Minima Moralia
661. Die mitbedeutenden Wörter *(William of Sherwood), orig.* Syncategoremata • Treatise on Syncategorematic Words
662. Die moderne Industriegesellschaft *(Galbraith)* • *orig.* The New Industrial State
663. Der moderne Kapitalismus *(Sombart)* • A History of the Econonomic Institutions of Modern Europe
664. Möglichkeit und Wirklichkeit *(N. Hartmann)* • Possibility and Actuality
665. Monadologie *(Leibniz, postum), orig.* Principes de la Philosophie ou Monadologie • Monadology
666. Der Monismus als Band zwischen Religion und Wissenschaft *(Haeckel)* • Monism as Connecting Religion and Science: The Confession of Faith of a Man of Science; *also:* Monism as Link between Religion and Science
667. Monologen *(Schleiermacher)* • Soliloquies; *also:* Monologues
668. Moral und Hypermoral *(Gehlen)* • Morality and Hypermorality°
669. Moral und Politik *(Russell)* • *orig.* Human Society in Ethics and Politics
670. Moralbewußtsein und kommunikatives Handeln *(Habermas)* • Moral Consciousness and Communicative Action
671. Moralische Briefe an Lucilius *(Seneca), orig.* Epistulae morales ad Lucilium • Moral Epistles to Lucilius
672. Moralische Schriften *(Plutarch), orig.* Ethika • Moralia
673. Das moralische Urteil beim Kinde *(Piaget), orig.* Le jugement moral chez l'enfant • The Moral Judg(e)ment of the Child
674. Moralisches Denken: seine Ebenen, seine Methode, sein Witz *(Hare)* • *orig.* Moral Thinking: Its Levels, Method and Point
675. Die Moralisten, eine philosophische Rhapsodie *(Shaftesbury)* • *orig.* The Moralists, a Philosophical Rhapsody
676. Morgenröte *(Nietzsche)* • Daybreak; *also:* The Dawn of Day
677. Morgenröte im Aufgang. Von den drei Prinzipien. Vom dreifachen Leben *(Böhme)* • The High and Deep Searching out of the Threefold Life of Man through the Three Principles; *also:* Aurora, or the Rising Dawn
678. Morgenstunden *(Mendelssohn)* • Morning Hours
679. Mutmaßlicher Anfang der Menschengeschichte *(Kant)* • Conjectural/Speculative Beginning of Human History
680. Das Mutterrecht *(Bachofen)* • Mother Right
681. Mystik und Logik *(Russell)* • *orig.* Mysticism and Logic
682. Mythen des Alltags *(Barthes), orig.* Mythologies • Mythologies
683. Mythos der Maschine. Kultur, Technik und Macht *(Mumford)* • *orig.* The Myth of the Machine
684. Der Mythos von Sisyphos. Ein Versuch über das Absurde *(Camus), orig.* Le Mythe de Sisyphe. Un raisonnement absurde • The Myth of Sisyphus

685. Die Nachfolge Christi *(Thomas à Kempis), orig.* De imitatione Christi • The Imitation of Christ
686. Nachmetaphysisches Denken *(Habermas)* • Postmetaphysical Thinking
687. Name und Notwendigkeit *(Kripke)* • *orig.* Naming and Necessity
688. Die Natur *(Emerson)* • *orig.* Nature
689. Das Naturbild der heutigen Physik *(Heisenberg)* • Physicist's Conception of Nature
690. Naturgeschichte *(Plinius Secundus the Older), orig.* Historia naturalis • Natural History
691. Naturgeschichte der Religion *(Hume)* • *orig.* The Natural History of Religion
692. Naturgeschichte der Seele *(La Mettrie), orig.* Histoire naturelle de l'âme • Natural History of the Soul
693. Naturrecht auf dem Grunde der Ethik *(Trendelenburg)* • Natural Right on the Foundation of Ethics
694. Naturrecht und allgemeines Staatsrecht in den Anfangsgründen *(Hobbes, postum)* • *orig.* The Elements of Law, Natural and Political

695. Naturrecht und Geschichte *(L. Strauss)* • *orig.* Natural Right and History
696. Naturrecht und menschliche Würde *(Bloch)* • Natural Law and Human Dignity
697. Negative Dialektik *(Adorno)* • Negative Dialectics
698. Die Nemesis der Medizin. Von den Grenzen des Gesundheitswesens *(Illich)* • *orig.* Medical Nemesis. The Expropriation of Health
699. Neu-Atlantis *(F. Bacon, postum)* • *orig.* New Atlantis
700. Die Neubelebung der Religionswissenschaft *(Al-Ghazzali), orig.* Ihyā' 'ulum ad-dïn • The Revival of the Religious Sciences
701. Neue Abhandlung über den Ursprung der Ideen *(Rosmini-Serbati), orig.* Nuovo saggio sull' origine delle idee • Certainty: The Origin of Thought
702. Neue Abhandlungen über den menschlichen Verstand *(Leibniz, postum), orig.* Nouveaux essais sur l'entendement humain • New Essays on the Human Understanding
703. Neue Astronomie oder Physik des Himmels *(Kepler), orig.* Astronomia nova, Aitiologetos, seu physica coelestis • A New Astronomy Based on Causes, or A Physics of the Sky
704. Eine neue Auffassung von der Gesellschaft *(Owen)* • *orig.* A New View of Society
705. Neue Darstellung des Sensualismus *(Czolbe)* • New Exposition of Sensualism
706. Neue Wege der Ontologie *(N. Hartmann)* • New Ways in Ontology
707. Neues Christentum *(Saint-Simon), orig.* Le nouveau christianisme • The New Christianity
708. Neues Organon der Wissenschaften *(F. Bacon), orig.* Novum organum sive indica vera naturae (Part II of "Instauratio magna") • New Organon
709. Neues Organon oder Gedanken über die Erforschung und Bezeichnung des Wahren und dessen Unterscheidung vom Irrtum und Schein *(Lambert)* • New Organon/Thoughts on the Investigation and Induction of Truth and the Distinction between Error and Appearances
710. Neues System der Natur und der Verbindung der Substanzen sowie der Vereinigung zwischen Seele und Körper *(Leibniz), orig.* Système nouveau de la nature et de la communication des substances, aussi bien que de l'union qu'il y a entre l'âme et le corps • New System of Nature and of the Interaction of Substances
711. Neunheiten *(Plotinus), orig.* Enneades • Enneads
712. Neunzehnhundertvierundachtzig *(Orwell)* • *orig.* Nineteen Eighty-Four
713. Nietzsche contra Wagner *(Nietzsche)* • Nietzsche versus Wagner
714. Nikomachische Ethik *(Aristotle), orig.* Ethika Nikomacheia • Nicomachean Ethics
715. Norm und Handlung *(Wright)* • *orig.* Norm and Action
716. Das Normale und das Pathologische *(Canguilhem), orig.* Le normal et le pathologique • The Normal and the Pathological
717. Noten zur Literatur *(Adorno)* • Notes to Literature

718. Objektive Erkenntnis. Ein evolutionärer Entwurf *(Popper)* • *orig.* Objective Knowledge. An Evolutionary Approach
719. Die offene Gesellschaft und ihre Feinde *(Popper)* • *orig.* The Open Society and Its Enemies
720. Ökologie des Geistes. Anthropologische, psychologische, biologische und epistemologische Perspektiven *(Bateson)* • *orig.* Steps to an Ecology of Mind
721. Die Ökonomie des Wunsches *(Lyotard), orig.* Économie libidinale • Libidual Economy
722. Ökonomisch-philosophische Manuskripte aus dem Jahre 1844 *(Marx, postum)* • The Economic and Philosophical Manuscripts of 1844
723. Ontologische Relativität und andere Schriften *(Quine)* • *orig.* Ontological Relativity and Other Essays
724. Die Ordnung der Dinge. Eine Archäologie der Humanwissenschaften *(Foucault), orig.* Les mots et les choses. Une archéologie des sciences humaines • The Order of Things. An Archeology of the Human Sciences
725. Die Ordnung des Diskurses *(Foucault), orig.* L'ordre du discours • The Discourse on Language
726. Organismus und Freiheit *(Jonas)* • *orig.* The Phenomenon of Life
727. Organon *(Aristotle)* • Organon

728. Das Pantheistikon *(Toland), orig.* Pantheisticon, sive formula celebrande Sodalitatis Socraticae • Pantheisticon, or The Form of Celebrating the Socratic-Society

729. Paradoxien des Unendlichen *(Bolzano, postum)* • The Paradoxes of the Infinitite

730. Parapsychologie *(Driesch)* • Psychical Research

731. Der Parasit *(Serres), orig.* Le parasite • The Parasite

732. Parerga und Paralipomena *(Schopenhauer)* • Parerga and Paralipomena

733. Pariser Manuskripte *(Marx)* • Paris Manuscripts → Ökonomisch-philosophische Manuskripte aus dem Jahre 1844

734. Pariser Quästionen *(Meister Eckhart), orig.* Quaestiones Parisienses • Parisian Questions and Prologues

735. Parmenides *(Plato)* • nt

736. Das Passagen-Werk *(Benjamin)* • (The) Arcades Project

737. Persische Briefe *(Montesquieu), orig.* Lettres persanes • (The) Persian Letters

738. Pfade in Utopia *(Buber)* • Paths in Utopia

739. Die Pflichten des Menschen und des Bügers nach dem Naturgesetz *(Pufendorf), orig.* De officio hominis et civis iuxta legem naturalem libri duo • On the Duty of Man and Citizen According to Natural Law

740. Phaedon oder über die Unsterblichkeit der Seele *(Mendelssohn)* • Phaedon, or the Death of Socrates

741. Phaidon *(Plato)* • nt

742. Phaidros *(Plato)* • nt

743. Phänomenologie der Schuld *(Ricoeur)* → Die Fehlbarkeit des Menschen, Symbolik des Bösen

744. Phänomenologie der Wahrnehmung *(Merleau-Ponty), orig.* Phénoménologie de la perception • Phenomenology of Perception

745. Phänomenologie des Geistes *(Hegel)* • The Phenomenology of Mind/Spirit

746. Die Phänomenologie *(Lyotard)* • Phenomenology

747. Die Phänomenologie und die Fundamente der Wissenschaft *(Husserl)* • Phenomenology and the Foundations of the Sciences

748. Phänomenologische Psychologie *(Husserl)* • Phenomenological Psychology

749. Philebos *(Plato)* • nt

750. Philolosophisches Tagebuch *(Berkeley)* • *orig.* Philosophical Commentaries

751. Philosophie *(Jaspers)* • Philosophy

752. Philosophie als strenge Wissenschaft *(Husserl)* • Philosophy as Rigorous/Strict Science

753. Philosophie auf neuem Wege *(Langer)* • *orig.* Philosophy in a New Key

754. Philosophie aus den Sinnen hergeleitet *(Campanella), orig.* Philosophia sensibus demonstrata • Philosophy Derivated by the Senses°

755. Philosophie der Arithmetik *(Husserl)* • The Philosophy of Arithmetic

756. Philosophie der Geschichte *(F. Schlegel)* • The Philosophy of History

757. Die Philosophie der induktiven Wissenschaften *(Whewell)* • *orig.* The Philosophy of the Inductive Sciences

758. Philosophie der Kunst *(Schelling)* • The Philosophy of Art

759. Philosophie der Kunst *(Taine), orig.* Philosophie de l'art • Lectures on Art

760. Philosophie der Logik *(Quine)* • *orig.* Philosophy of Logic

761. Philosophie der Mythologie *(Schelling, postum)* • Philosophy of Mythology

762. Philosophie der Natur *(N. Hartmann)* • Philosophy of Nature

763. Philosophie der Naturwissenschaften *(Hempel)* • *orig.* Philosophy of Natural Science

764. Philosophie der neuen Musik *(Adorno)* • Philosophy of Modern Music

765. Philosophie der Offenbarung *(Schelling, postum)* • Philosophy of Revelation

766. Philosophie der Praxis. Oekonomik und Ethik *(Croce), orig.* Filosofia della pratica. Economia ed etica • (The) Philosophy of the Practical

767. Philosophie der Raum-Zeit-Lehre *(Reichenbach)* • The Philosophy of Space and Time

768. Philosophie der symbolischen Formen *(Cassirer)* • Philosophy of Symbolic Forms
769. Philosophie des Abendlandes. Ihr Zusammenhang mit der politischen und sozialen Entwicklung *(Russell)* • *orig.* History of Western Philosophy and Its Connection with Political and Social Circumstances from the Earliest Times to the Present Day
770. Die Philosophie des Als Ob *(Vaihinger)* • The Philosophy of As If
771. Philosophie des Geldes *(Simmel)* • The Philosophy of Money
772. Philosophie des Lebens *(F. Schlegel)* • The Philosophy of Life
773. Die Philosophie des Nein. Versuch einer Philosophie des neuen wissenschaftlichen Geistes *(Bachelard), orig.* La philosophie du non. Essai d'une philosophie du nouvel esprit scientifique• The Philosophy of No: A Philosophy of the New Scientific Mind
774. Philosophie des Organischen *(Driesch)* • *orig.* The Science and Philosophy of the Organism
775. Philosophie des Unbewußten. Versuch einer Weltanschauung *(E. v. Hartmann)* • (The) Philosophy of the Unconscious
776. Philosophie und Religion *(Schelling)* • Philosophy and Religion
777. Philosophisch-politische Profile *(Habermas)* • Philosophical Political Profiles
778. Philosophische Aufsätze *(Putnam)* • *orig.* Philosophical Papers
779. Philosophische Bemerkungen *(Wittgenstein)* • Philosophical Remarks
780. Philosophische Briefe über Dogmaticismus und Kriticismus *(Schelling)* • Philosophical Letters on Dogmatism and Criticism
781. Philosophische Brocken/Brosamen/Bissen *(Kierkegaard), orig.* Philosophiske Smuler eller En Smule Philosophi • Philosophical Fragments
782. Der philosophische Diskurs der Moderne *(Habermas)* • The Philosophical Discourse of Modernity
783. Der philosophische Glaube angesichts der Offenbarung *(Jaspers)* • The Perennial Scope of Philosophy
784. Philosophische Grammatik *(Wittgenstein)* • Philosophical Grammar
785. Philosophische Rechtslehre *(Fries)* • Philosophical Theory of Right
786. Philosophische Untersuchungen *(Wittgenstein)* • *orig.* Philosophical Investigations
787. Philosophische Untersuchungen über das Wesen der menschlichen Freiheit *(Schelling)* • Philosophical Investigations concerning the Nature of Human Freedom
788. Philosophische Untersuchungen über den Ursprung unserer Begriffe vom Erhabenen und Schönen *(Burke)* • A Philosophical Enquiry into the Origin of our Ideas of the Sublime and Beautiful
789. Philosophische Versuche über die menschliche Natur und ihre Entwicklung *(Tetens)* • Philosophical Essays on Human Nature and Its Development
790. Die philosophischen Grundlagen der Quantenmechanik *(Reichenbach)* • *orig.* Philosophic Foundations of Quantum Mechanics
791. Philosophischer Versuch über die Wahrscheinlichkeit *(Laplace), orig.* Essai philosophique sur les probabilités • A Philosophical Essay on Probabilities
792. Philosophisches Taschenwörterbuch *(Voltaire), orig.* Dictionnaire philosophique portatif • Philosophical Dictionary
793. Physik und Philosophie *(Heisenberg)* • Physics and Philosophy: The Revolution in Modern Science
794. Physik und Realität *(Einstein)* • Physics and Reality
795. Die physikalische Sprache als Universalsprache der Wissenschaft *(Carnap)* • The Unity of Science
796. Physikvorlesung *(Aristotle), orig.* Physike akroasis • Physics
797. Physiognomische Fragmente zur Beförderung der Menschenkenntnis und Menschenliebe *(Lavater)* • Physiognomical Fragments for the Promotion of the Knowledge and Love of Man; *also:* Essays on Physiognomy
798. Pilgerbuch der Seele zu Gott *(Bonaventure), orig.* Itinerarium mentis in Deum • The Minds Road/Journey to God; *also:* Journey of the Mind to God; *also:* The Mind's Journey onto God

799. Die platonische Theologie über die Unsterblichkeit der Seelen *(Mars. Ficino), orig.* Theologia platonica de immortalitate animorum XVIII libris comprehensa • (The) Platonic Theology of the Immortality of Souls

800. Die Poetik der Träumerei *(Bachelard), orig.* La poétique de la rêverie • Poetics of Reverie

801. Politik *(Aristotle), orig.* Politika • (The) Politics

802. Politik als Beruf *(M. Weber)* • The Profession and Vocation of Politics; *also:* Politics as a Vocation

803. Politik, methodisch dargestellt *(Althusius), orig.* Politica methodice digesta atque exemplis et profanis illustrata • Politics Methodically Arranged and Illustrated by Holy and Profane Examples

804. Politische Diskurse *(Hume)* • *orig.* Political Discourses

805. Politische Romantik *(C. Schmitt)* • Political Romanticism

806. Politische Theologie *(C. Schmitt)* • Political Theology

807. Die politische Theorie des Besitzindividualismus *(McPherson)* • *orig.* The Political Theory of Possessive Individualism

808. Polycraticus oder über die Zerstreuung der Höflinge und die Kennzeichen der Philosophen *(John of Salisbury), orig.* Policraticus sive De nugis curialium et vestigiis philosophorum • The Stateman's Book; *also:* Policraticus, or Of the Frivolities of Courtiers and the Footprints of Philosophers

809. Populäre Schriften *(Boltzmann)* • Popular Writings

810. Die positive Philosophie *(Comte), orig.* Cours de philosophie positive • Course in Positivist Philosophy; *also:* Course of Positive Philosophy

811. Der Positivismusstreit in der deutschen Soziologie *(Adorno et al.)* • Positivist Dispute in German Sociology

812. Positivistischer Katechismus *(Comte), orig.* Catéchisme positiviste • The Catechism of Positive Religion

813. Die Postkarte von Sokrates bis an Freud und jenseits *(Derrida), orig.* La carte postale de Socrate à Freud et au-delà • The Post Card: From Socrates to Freud and Beyond

814. Das postmoderne Wissen *(Lyotard), orig.* La condition postmoderne. Rapport sur le savoir • The Post-Modern Condition

815. Der Pragmatismus. Ein neuer Name für alte Denkmethoden *(James)* • *orig.* Pragmatism: A New Name for Some Old Ways of Thinking

816. Praktische Ethik *(Singer)* • *orig.* Practical Ethics

817. Praxis und Theorie der Individualpsychologie *(Adler)* • The Practice and Theory of Individual Psychology

818. Preisschrift über die Freiheit des Willens *(Schopenhauer)* • On the Freedom of the Will

819. Preisschrift über die Grundlage der Moral *(Schopenhauer)* • On the Basis of Morality

820. Principia Ethica *(Moore)* • *nt*

821. Principia Mathematica *(Whitehead, Russell)* • *nt*

822. Das Prinzip Hoffnung *(Bloch)* • The Principle of Hope

823. Das Prinzip Verantwortung. Versuch einer Ethik für die technologische Zivilisation *(Jonas)* • The Principle of Responsibility. An Attempt at an Ethic for Technological Civilization; *also:* The Imperative of Responsibility. In Search of an Ethics for the Technological Age

824. Die Prinzipien der Philosophie *(Descartes), orig.* Principia philosophiae • Principles of Philosophy

825. Die Prinzipien der physikalischen Optik. Historisch und erkenntnis-psychologisch entwickelt *(Mach)* • The Principles of Physical Optics. A Historical and Philosophical Treatment

826. Die Prinzipien der Psychologie *(James)* • *orig.* The Principles of Psychology

827. Prinzipien einer neuen Wissenschaft über die gemeinsame Natur der Völker *(Vico), orig.* Principj di una scienza nuova intorno alla natura delle nazioni • Principles of a New Science Concerning the Common Nature of Nations

828. Prismen - Kulturkritik und Gesellschaft *(Adorno)* • Prisms

829. Das Problem der Relevanz *(Schütz)* • Reflections on the Problem of Relevance

830. Das Problem des geistigen Seins *(N. Hartmann)* • The Problem of Spiritual Being

831. Die Probleme der Geschichtsphilosophie. Eine erkenntnistheoretische Studie *(Simmel)* • The Problems of the Philosophy of History. An Epistemological Essay

832. Probleme der Philosophie *(Russell)* • *orig.* The Problems of Philosophy

833. Die Probleme der Philosophie in ihrem Zusammenhang *(Schlick)* • The Problems of Philosophy in Their Interconnection

834. Probleme einer Soziologie des Wissens *(Scheler)* • Problems of a Sociology of Knowledge

835. Prolegomena zu einer jeden künftigen Metaphysik, die als Wissenschaft wird auftreten können *(Kant)* • Prolegomena to any Future Metaphysic that will be able to Present itself as a Science

836. Protagoras *(Plato)* • *nt*

837. Die protestantische Ethik und der Geist des Kapitalismus *(M. Weber)* • The Protestant Ethic and the Spirit of Capitalism

838. Provinzialbriefe *(Pascal), orig.* Les provinciales • The Provincial Letters

839. Prozeß und Realität. Entwurf einer Kosmologie *(Whitehead)* • *orig.* Process and Reality. An Essay in Cosmology

840. Die Psyche des Menschen *(Eccles)* • *orig.* The Human Psyche

841. Psychoanalyse des Feuers *(Bachelard), orig.* Psychanalyse du feu • Psychoanalysis of Fire

842. Psychoanalyse und Ethik *(Fromm)* • *orig.* Man for Himself. An Inquiry into the Psychology of Ethics

843. Psychologie als Wissenschaft *(Herbart)* • Psychology as a Science

844. Psychologie *(James)* • *orig.* Principles of Psychology

845. Psychologie der Massen *(Le Bon), orig.* La psychologie des foules • The Crowd: A Study of the Popular Mind

846. Psychologie der Weltanschauungen *(Jaspers)* • Psychology of World Conceptions; *also:* Psychology of Worldviews

847. Psychologie und Geisteskrankheit *(Foucault), orig.* Maladie mentale et Psychologie • Mental Illness and Psychology

848. Psychologie vom empirischen Standpunkt *(Brentano)* • Psychology from an Empirical Standpoint

849. Pyrrhoneische Grundzüge *(Sextus Empiricus), orig.* Pyrrhoneion hypotyposeis • Outlines of Pyrrhonism; *also:* Pyrrhonean Sketches

850. Quelle der Erkenntnis *(John Damascene), orig.* Pege gnoseos • Fount of Wisdom

851. Randgänge der Philosophie *(Derrida), orig.* Marges de la philosophie • Margins of Philosophy

852. Raum und Zeit in der gegenwärtigen Physik. Zur Einführung in das Verständnis der Relativitäts- und Gravitationstheorie *(Schlick)* • Space and Time in Contemporary Physics: An Introduction to the Theory of Relativity and Gravitation

853. Recht, Gesetzgebung und Freiheit *(Hayek)* • Law, Legislation, and Liberty

854. Rechtsphilosophie *(Hegel)* • Philosophy of Right

855. Rede über die Unsicherheit und Eitelkeit der Wissenschaften und Künste und über die Erhabenheit des Gotteswortes *(Agrippa v. Nettesheim), orig.* De incertitudine et vanitate scientiarum et artium atque excellentia verbi Dei delamatio • Of the Vanitie and Incertaintie of Artes and Sciences

856. Reden an die Deutsche Nation *(Fichte)* • Addresses to the German Nation

857. Reflexionen oder Sentenzen und moralische Maximen *(La Rochefoucauld), orig.* Réflexions ou sentences et maximes morales • Maxims

858. Reflexionen über die Sprache *(Chomsky)* • *orig.* Reflections on Language

859. Reformation des Himmels *(Bruno), orig.* Spaccio de la bestia trionfante • The Expulsion of the Triumphant Beast

860. Regeln und Repräsentationen *(Chomsky)* • *orig.* Rules and Representations

861. Regeln zur Ausrichtung der Erkenntniskraft *(Descartes, postum), orig.* Regulae ad directionem ingenii • Rules for the Direction of the Understanding/Mind

862. Das Reich der Zeichen *(Barthes), orig.* L'empire des signes • The Empire of Signs

863. Reine Rechtslehre *(Kelsen)* • Pure Theory of Law; *also:* Introduction to the Problems of Legal Theory

864. Reinigungen *(Empedocles), orig.* Katharmoi • Purifications

865. Relativitätstheorie und Erkenntnis Apriori *(Reichenbach)* • The Theory of Relativity and A Priori Knowledge

866. Die Religion *(Simmel)* • Sociology of Religion

867. Religion der Vernunft aus den Quellen des Judentums *(Cohen)* • Religion of Reason out of the Sources of Judaism

868. Die Religion innerhalb der Grenzen der bloßen Vernunft *(Kant)* • Religion Within the Limits of Reason Alone; *also:* Religion Within the Boundary of Pure Reason; *also:* Religion within the Limits of Bare Reason

869. Repräsentation und Realität *(Putnam)* • *orig.* Representation and Reality

870. Rhetorik *(Aristotle), orig.* Techne rhetorike • (Art of) Rhetoric

871. Das Rohe und das Gekochte *(Lévi-Strauss), orig.* Le cru et le cuit • The Raw and the Cooked

872. Die Rückseite des Spiegels *(Lorenz)* • Behind the Mirror: A Search for Natural History of Human Knowledge

873. Sammlung der pythagoreischen Lehren *(Iamblichus), orig.* Synagoge ton Pythagoreion dogmaton • The Pythagorean Sourcebook and Library

874. Sätze aus der erotischen Philosophie *(Baader)* • Propositions from the Erotic Philosophy

875. Scheinprobleme in der Philosophie. Das Fremdpsychische und der Realismusstreit *(Carnap)* • Pseudoproblems in Philosophy

876. Die Schlafwandler *(Koestler)* • *orig.* The Sleepwalkers

877. Schöne neue Welt *(Huxley)* • *orig.* Brave New World

878. Schöpferische Entwicklung *(Bergson), orig.* L' évolution créatrice • Creative Evolution

879. Schöpferische Treue *(Marcel), orig.* De refus à l'invocation • Creative Fidelity

880. Die Schrift und die Differenz *(Derrida), orig.* L' écriture et la différence • Writing and Difference

881. Schriften *(Lacan), orig.* Écrits • Ecrits: A Selection

882. Die Schuldfrage - ein Beitrag zur deutschen Frage *(Jaspers)* • The Question of German Guilt

883. Sechs Bücher über den Staat *(Bodin), orig.* Les six livres de la république • Six Books of the Republic; *also:* The Six Bookes of a Commonweale

884. Sechs Bücher über die Politik oder über die Lehre von der Politik *(Lipsius), orig.* Politicorum sive civilis doctrinae libri sex • Sixe Bookes of Politickes or Civil Doctrine

885. Das Sechstagewerk *(Bonaventure), orig.* Collationes in hexameron • Commentary on the Sentences°

886. Die Seele im technischen Zeitalter *(Gehlen)* • Man in the Age of Technology

887. Die Seele und die Formen *(Lukács)* • Soul and Form

888. Seelenprobleme der Gegenwart *(Jung)* • Modern Man in Search of a Soul; *also:* The Spiritual Problem of Modern Man

889. Die seelische Energie *(Bergson), orig.* L'energie spirituelle. Essais et conférences • Mind-Energy

890. Das Seiende und das Wesen *(Aquinas), orig.* De ente et essentia • On Being and Essence

891. Das Sein und das Nichts. Versuch einer phänomenologischen Ontologie *(Sartre), orig.* L' être et le néant. Essai d'ontologie phénoménologique • Being and Nothingness. An Essay on Phenomenological Ontology

892. Sein und Haben *(Marcel), orig.* Etre et avoir • Being and Having

893. Sein und Zeit *(Heidegger)* • Being and Time

894. Selbstbegrenzung. Eine politische Kritik der Technik *(Illich)* • *orig.* Tools for Conviviality

895. Selbstbetrachtungen *(Marcus Aurelius), orig.* Ta eis heauton • Meditations

896. Selbstgespräch *(Anselm of Canterbury), orig.* Monologion • Soliloquy

897. Selbstgespräche *(Augustine), orig.* Soliloquia • Soliloquies

898. Der Selbstmord *(Durkheim), orig.* Le Suicide • Suicide: A Study in Sociology
899. Das semiologische Abenteuer *(Barthes), orig.* L'aventure semiotique • The Semiotic Challange
900. Semiotik und Philosophie der Sprache *(Eco)* • Semiotics and the Philosophy of Language
901. Sexualität und Wahrheit *(Foucault), orig.* Histoire de la sexualité • The History of Sexuality
902. Das Sichtbare und das Unsichtbare *(Merleau-Ponty, postum), orig.* Le visible et l'invisible • The Visible and the Invisible
903. Die Sieben Welträtsel *(du Bois-Reymond)* • The Seven Riddles of the Universe
904. Das Siebentagewerk *(Pico della Mirandola), orig.* Heptaplus de septiformi sex dierum geneseos • Heptaplus
905. Sinn und Sinneserfahrung *(Austin, postum)* • *orig.* Sense and Sensibilia
906. Der Sinn und Wert des Lebens *(Eucken)* • The Meaning and Value of Life
907. Der sinnhafte Aufbau der sozialen Welt *(Schütz)* • (The) Phenomenology of the Social World
908. Die sittliche Idee des Rechts *(Trendelenburg)* • The Moral Idea of Right
909. Skepsis *(Russell)* • *orig.* Sceptical Essays
910. Skeptizismus und Naturalismus *(Strawson)* • *orig.* Skepticism and Naturalism. Some Varieties
911. Das sogenannte Böse *(Lorenz)* • On Aggression
912. Die Soiréen von Petersburg oder Gespräche über die zeitliche Herrschaft der göttlichen Vorsehung *(De Maistre), orig.* Les soirées de Saint-Petersbourg ou Entretiens sur le government temporel de la providence • Evenings at St. Petersburg; *also:* Saint Petersburg Evenings
913. Sonnenklarer Bericht an das größere Publicum über das eigentliche Wesen der neueren Philosophie *(Fichte)* • A Report, Clear as the Sun, for the General Public on the Real Essence of the Latest Philosophy
914. Der Sonnenstaat oder Idee einer philosophischen Republik *(Campanella), orig.* La città del sole • The City of the Sun, or the Ideal Organisation of the Human Society
915. Sophist *(Plato), orig.* Sophistes • Sophist
916. Sophistische Widerlegungen *(Aristotle), orig.* Peri tön sophistikön elenchön • On Sophistical Refutations
917. Die Soziallehren der christlichen Kirchen und Gruppen *(Troeltsch)* • The Social Teaching of the Christian Churches
918. Sozialpädagogik *(Natorp)* • Social Education
919. Soziologie und Anthropologie *(Mauss), orig.* Sociologie et Anthropologie • Sociology and Anthropology
920. Soziologie und Philosophie *(Durkheim), orig.* Sociologie et philosophie • Sociology and Philosophy
921. Soziologie. Untersuchungen über die Formen der Vergesellschaftung *(Simmel)* • The Sociology of Georg Simmel
922. Soziologische Aufklärung *(Luhmann)* • The Differentation of Society°
923. Der Spiegel der Natur. Eine Kritik der Philosophie *(Rorty)* • *orig.* Philosophy and the Mirror of Nature
924. Spieltheorie und wirtschaftliches Verhalten *(Neumann, Morgenstern)* • *orig.* Theory of Games and Economic Behavior
925. Die Sprache der Mode *(Barthes) orig.* System de la mode • The Fashion System
926. Die Sprache der Moral *(Hare)* • *orig.* The Language of Morals
927. Sprache und Geist *(Chomsky)* • *orig.* Language and Mind
928. Sprache, Denken, Wirklichkeit *(Whorf)* • *orig.* Language, Thought and Reality
929. Sprache, Wahrheit und Logik *(Ayer)* • *orig.* Language, Truth and Logic
930. Sprachen der Kunst. Ein Ansatz zu einer Symboltheorie *(Goodman)* • *orig.* Languages of Art. An Approach to a Theory of Symbols
931. Sprachtheorie. Die Darstellungsfunktion der Sprache *(Bühler)* • Theory of Language. The Representational Function of Language
932. Sprechakte. Ein sprachphilosophischer Essay *(Searle)* • *orig.* Speech Acts. An Essay in the Philosophy of Language
933. Der Staat *(Plato), orig.* Politeia • Republic

934. Staat und Revolution *(Lenin)* • State and Revolution
935. Staatlichkeit und Anarchie *(Bakunin), orig.* Gosudarstvennost i Anarchija • Statism and Anarchy
936. Der Staatsmann *(Plato), orig.* Politikos • Statesman
937. Stadien auf dem Lebensweg *(Kierkegaard), orig.* Stadier paa Livets Vei • Stages on Life's Way
938. Die Stellung des Menschen im Kosmos *(Scheler)* • Man's Place in Nature
939. Der Stern der Erlösung *(Rosenzweig)* • The Star of Redempt(at)ion
940. Die Stimme und das Phänomen *(Derrida), orig.* La voix et la phénomène • Speech and Phenomena
941. Streifzüge: Gesetz, Form, Ereignis *(Lyotard)* • *orig.* Peregrinations: Law, Form, Event
942. Der Streit der Fakultäten *(Kant)* • The Conflict of the Faculties
943. Der Streit um die Existenz der Welt *(Ingarden), orig.* Spór o Istnienie Swiata • Time and Modes of Being
944. Die Struktur der Raum-Zeit *(Schrödinger)* • *orig.* Space-Time Structure
945. Die Struktur des Verhaltens *(Merleau-Ponty), orig.* La structure du comportement • The Structure of Behavior
946. Die Struktur sozialen Handelns *(Parsons)* • *orig.* The Structure of Social Action
947. Die Struktur wissenschaftlicher Revolutionen *(Kuhn)* • *orig.* The Structure of Scientific Revolutions
948. Strukturale Anthropologie *(Lévi-Strauss), orig.* Anthropologie structurale • Structural Anthropology
949. Der Strukturalismus *(Piaget), orig.* Le structuralisme • Structuralism
950. Strukturen der Lebenswelt *(Schütz, Luckmann)* • The Structures of the Life-World
951. Strukturen der Syntax *(Chomsky)* • *orig.* Syntactic Structures
952. Strukturwandel der Öffentlichkeit *(Habermas)* • The Structural Transformation of the Public Sphere
953. Studien zur Entwicklungsgeschichte des modernen Kapitalismus *(Sombart)* • Luxury and Capitalism
954. Die Stufen des Wissens oder Durch Unterscheidung zur Einung *(Maritain), orig.* Distinguer pour unir ou Les degrés du savoir • Distinguish to Unite of The Degrees of Knowledge
955. Substanzbegriff und Funktionsbegriff *(Cassirer)* • Substance and Function
956. Summe der Logik *(William of Ockham), orig.* Summa totius logicae • Summa logicae
957. Summe der Theologie *(Albertus Magnus), orig.* Summa theologiae • Handbook of Theology
958. Summe der Theologie *(Aquinas), orig.* Summa theologica • Summa of Theology
959. Summe gegen die Heiden *(Aquinas), orig.* Summa contra Gentiles • Against the Errors of the Infidels; *also:* On the Truth of the Catholic Faith; *also:* Summa against the Gentiles
960. Summe über die Geschöpfe *(Albertus Magnus), orig.* summa de creaturis • Handbook of Doctrine concerning Creatures
961. Symbolik des Bösen. Phänomenologie der Schuld II *(Ricoeur), orig.* Finitude et culpabilité. II. Symbolique du mal • Symbolism of Evil
962. Symbolik und Realität *(Morris)* • *orig.* Symbolism and Reality: A Study in the Nature of Mind
963. Der symbolische Tausch und der Tod *(Baudrillard), orig.* L' échange symbolique et la mort • For a Critique of the Political Economy of the Sign
964. Symposion *(Plato)* • Symposium
965. System der deduktiven und induktiven Logik. Eine Darlegung der Grundsätze der Beweislehre und der Methoden wissenschaftlicher Forschung *(Mill)* • *orig.* A System of Logic, Ratiocinative and Inductive. Being a Connected View of the Principles of Evidence, and the Methods of Scientific Investigation
966. System der Logik als Theorie des Erkennens *(Gentile), orig.* Sistema di logica come teoria del cognoscere • System of Logic as a Theory of Knowledge°
967. System der Metaphysik *(Fries)* • System of Metaphysics
968. System der Natur oder von den Gesetzen der physischen und moralischen Welt *(d'Holbach), orig.* Système de la nature, ou, des lois du monde physique et du monde moral • The System of Nature, or The Laws of the Moral and Physical World

969. System der Philosophie *(Lotze, postum)* • Lotze's System of Philosophy
970. System der Philosophie *(Wundt)* • System of Philosophy
971. System der philosophischen Ethik und Pädagogik *(Nelson, postum)* • System of Ethics
972. System der positiven Politik, oder Abhandlung über die Soziologie zur Errichtung der Religion der Humanität *(Comte), orig.* Système de politique positive, ou traité de sociologique instituant la réligion de l'humanité • System of Positive/Positivist Polity
973. Das System der Rechtslehre *(Fichte, postum)* • The Science of Rights
974. Das System der Sittenlehre nach den Principien der Wissenschaftslehre *(Fichte)* • The Science of Ethics, as Based on the Science of Knowledge; *also:* System of the Doctrine of Ethics; *also:* The System of Ethical Theory
975. System der Sittlichkeit *(Hegel, postum)* • System of Ethical Life 1802-03 and First Philosophy of Spirit (part III of the System of Speculative Philosophy 1803-04
976. System der synthetischen Philosophie *(Spencer)* • *orig.* A System of Synthetic Philosophy
977. System der Werttheorie *(Ehrenfels)* • System of Value Theory
978. System des transzendentalen Idealismus *(Schelling)* • The System of Transcendental Idealism

979. Tagebuch des Verführers *(Kierkegaard)* • The Diary of the Seducer
980. Tagebücher *(Kierkegaard), orig.* Papirer • Journals and Papers
981. Das Tao der Physik *(Capra)* • *orig.* The Tao of Physics
982. Tatsache, Fiktion, Voraussage *(Goodman)* • *orig.* Fact, Fiction and Forecast
983. Die Tatsachen in der Wahrnehmung *(Helmholtz)* • The Facts of Perception
984. Die Technik und die Kehre *(Heidegger)* • The Question concerning Technology
985. Technik und Wissenschaft als "Ideologie" *(Habermas)* • Technology and Science as "Ideology"
986. Teleologisches Denken *(N. Hartmann, postum)* • Teleological Thought
987. Texte zur Phänomenologie des inneren Zeitbewußtseins *(Husserl)* • Phenomenology of Internal Time-Consciousness; *also:* On the Phenomenology of the Consciousness of Internal Time
988. Theaitetos *(Plato)* • nt
989. Die Theodizee *(Leibniz), orig.* Essais de theodicée sur la bonté de Dieu, la liberté de l'homme et l'origine du mal • Theodicy. Essays on the Goodness of God, the Freedom of Man and the Origin of Evil
990. Theologie vom höchsten Gut oder Abhandlung über die göttliche Einheit und Dreieinigkeit *(Abelard), orig.* Theologia summi boni sive tractatus de unitate et trinitate divina • Theologia Summi Boni
991. Theologisch-politischer Traktat *(Spinoza), orig.* Tractatus theologico-politicus • Treatise on Theology and Politics; *also:* Theological-Political Treatise
992. Theologische Elementarlehre *(Proclus), orig.* Stoicheiosis theologike • The Elements of Theology
993. Theologische Jugendschriften *(Hegel, postum)* • Early Theological Writings
994. Theoretische Biologie *(Uexküll)* • Theoretical Biology
995. Theorie der ethischen Gefühle *(A. Smith)* • *orig.* The Theory of Moral Sentiments
996. Theorie der feinen Leute *(Veblen)* • *orig.* The Theory of the Leisure Class
997. Eine Theorie der Gerechtigkeit *(Rawls)* • *orig.* A Theory of Justice
998. Theorie der politischen und religiösen Macht in der bürgerlichen Gesellschaft *(Bonald), orig.* Théorie du pouvoir politique et religieux dans la societé civile • Theory of Political and Religious Power in Civil Society
999. Theorie der vier Bewegungen und der allgemeinen Bestimmungen *(Fourier), orig.* Théorie des quatre mouvements et des destinées générales • Theory of the Four Movements and of General Destinies
1000. Theorie des kommunikativen Handelns *(Habermas)* • The Theory of Communicative Action
1001. Die Theorie des Romans *(Lukács)* • Theory of the Novel
1002. Theorie und Praxis *(Habermas)* • Theory and Practice
1003. Theorien und Dinge *(Quine)* • *orig.* Theories and Things
1004. Thesen über Feuerbach *(Marx)* • Theses on Feuerbach

1042. Über den Gemeinspruch: Das mag in der Theorie richtig sein, taugt aber nicht für die Praxis *(Kant)* • On the Common Saying: This May Be True in Theory, But It Does Not Apply in Practice; *also:* On the Proverb: That May Be True in Theory, But Is of No Practical Use

1043. Über den Grund unseres Glaubens an eine göttliche Weltregierung *(Fichte)* • On the Ground of Our Belief in a Divine World-Order; *also:* On the Basis of Our Belief in a Divine Governance of the World

1044. Über den Himmel *(Aristotle), orig.* Peri uranu • On the Heavens

1045. Über den Intellekt *(Al-Kindi), orig.* Fi ʾl-ʿaql • Al-Kindi's Treatise on the Intellect

1046. Über den Prozeß der Zivilisation. Soziogenetische und psychogenetische Untersuchungen *(Elias)* • The History of Manners: The Civilizing Process

1047. Über den richtigen Gebrauch des Verstandes *(Locke)* • *orig.* The Conduct of the Understanding

1048. Über den Ungehorsam *(Fromm)* • *orig.* On Disobedience and other Essays

1049. Über den Ursprung des Übels *(Augustine), orig.* De ordine • Divine Providence and the Problem of Evil

1050. Über den Willen in der Natur *(Schopenhauer)* • On the Will in Nature

1051. Über die älteste Weisheit der Italer, zu gewinnen aus den Ursprüngen der lateinischen Sprache *(Vico), orig.* De antiquissima Italorum sapiente ex lingua latinae originibus eruenda • On the Most Ancient Wisdom of the Italians

1052. Über die Archetypen des kollektiven Unbewußten *(Jung)* • The Archetypes and the Collective Unconscious

1053. Über die ästhetische Erziehung des Menschen in einer Reihe von Briefen *(F. Schiller)* • Letters on the Aesthetic Education of Mankind; *also:* On the Aesthetic Education of Man

1054. Über die Demokratie in Amerika *(Tocqueville), orig.* De la démocratie en Amérique • Democracy in America

1055. Über die Dichtkunst *(Aristotle), orig.* Peri poietikes • Poetics

1056. Über die eigene und vieler Leute Unwissenheit *(Petrarca), orig.* De sui ipsius et multorum ignorantia • On His Own Ignorance and That of Many Others

1057. Über die Einheit des Verstandes gegen die Averroisten *(Aquinas), orig.* De unitate intellectus contra Averroistas • On the Unity of the Intellect Against the Averroists

1058. Über die Einteilung der Natur *(Erigena) orig.* De divisione naturae • On the Division of Nature

1059. Über die Existenz der Übel *(Proclus), orig.* De malorum subsistentia • The Existence of Evils

1060. Über die Freiheit *(J. S. Mill)* • *orig.* On Liberty

1061. Über die Geheimlehren *(Iamblichus), orig.* Peri mysteriön logos • On the Mysteries

1062. Über die Gesetze *(Cicero), orig.* De legibus • On (the) Laws

1063. Über die getrennten Substanzen *(Aquinas), orig.* De substantiis separatis • Treatise on Seperate Substances

1064. Über die Gewalt *(Arendt)* • On Violence

1065. Über die Gewalt *(Sorel), orig.* Réflexions sur la violance • Reflections on Violence

1066. Über die göttlichen Namen *(Dionysius the Areopagite), orig.* Peri theion onomaton • On the Divine Names

1067. Über die Grenzen der Naturerkenntnis *(Du Bois-Reymond)* • The Limitations of Natural Knowledge

1068. Über die Heilmittel wider Glück und Unglück *(Petrarca), orig.* De remediis utriusque fortunae • Petrarch's Remedies for Fortune Fair and Foul; *also:* Remedies Against One and the Other Fortune

1069. Über die Irrtümer und über die Wahrheit *(Saint-Martin), orig.* Des erreurs et de la vérité • Of Errors and Truth

1070. Über die kabbalistische Kunst *(Reuchlin), orig.* De arte cabalistica • On the Art of Kabbalah

1071. Über die Klarheit unserer Gedanken *(Peirce)* • *orig.* How to Make Our Ideas Clear

1072. Über die Konstitution der Atome und Moleküle *(Bohr)* • *orig.* On the Constitution of Atoms and Molecules

1073. Über die Kreisbewegungen der Weltkörper *(Kopernikus), orig.* De revolutionibus orbium coelestium libri VI • On the Revolution of the Celestial Orbs

1074. Über die Liebe zu Gott *(Bernard of Clairvaux), orig.* De diligendo Deo • On Loving God

1075. Über die Moral *(Malebranche), orig.* Traité de morale • A Treatise of Morality

1076. Über die mystische Theologie *(Dionysius the Areopagite), orig.* Peri mystikes theologias • On the Mystical Theology

1077. Über die naive und sentimentalische Dichtung *(F. Schiller)* • On the Naive and Sentimental in Literature; *also:* On Naive and Sentimental Poetry

1078. Über die Natur *(Empedocles), orig.* Peri physeös • On Nature

1079. Über die Natur *(Epicurus), orig.* Peri physeös • On Nature

1080. Über die Natur *(Parmenides), orig.* Peri physeös • On Nature

1081. Über die Natur der Dinge gemäß den ihnen eigenen Prinzipien *(Telesio), orig.* De rerum natura iuxta propria principia • On the Nature of Things According to Their Principles

1082. Über die Naturgeschichte der Tiere *(Aristotle), orig.* Peri ta zöa historia • Progression of Animals

1083. Über die Pflicht zum Ungehorsam gegen den Staat *(Thoreau)* • *orig.* On the Duty of Civil Disobedience

1084. Über die platonische Götterlehre *(Proclus), orig.* Peri tes kata Platöna theologias • The Platonic Theology

1085. Über die Prozeßeinrede gegen die Häretiker *(Tertullian), orig.* De praescriptione haereticorum • On the 'Prescription' of Heretics

1086. Über die Psychologie des Unbewußten *(Jung)* • Psychology of the Unconscious

1087. Über die Rangordnung im Himmel *(Dionysius the Areopagite), orig.* Peri tes uranias hierarchias • Celestial Hierarchy

1088. Über die Religion. Reden an die Gebildeten unter ihren Verächtern *(Schleiermacher)* • On Religion. Speeches to its Cultured Despisers

1089. Über die Revolution *(Arendt)* • *orig.* On Revolution

1090. Über die Seele *(Aristotle), orig.* Peri psyches • On the Soul

1091. Über die Seele *(William of Auvergne), orig.* De anima • On the Soul

1092. Über die Stufen von Demut und Hochmut *(Bernard of Clairvaux), orig.* De gradibus humilitatis et superbiae • The Steps of Humility and Pride

1093. Über die Teile der Tiere *(Aristotle), orig.* Peri zöön moriön • Parts of Animals

1094. Über die Verbindung des Physischen und Moralischen in dem Menschen *(Cabanis), orig.* Rapports du physique et du moral de l'homme • On the Relations Between the Physical and Moral Aspects of Man

1095. Über die Verschiedenheit des menschlichen Sprachbaues und ihren Einfluß auf die geistige Entwicklung des Menschengeschlechts *(W. v. Humboldt, postum)* • Linguistic Variability and Intellectual Development

1096. Über die vierfache Wurzel des Satzes vom zureichenden Grunde *(Schopenhauer)* • On the Fourfold Root of the Principle of Sufficient Reason

1097. Über die Vorsehung, das Schicksal und den freien Willen *(Proclus), orig.* De providentia et fato et eo quod in nobis • On Providence and Fate

1098. Über die Welt *(Pseudo-Aristotle), orig.* Peri kosmu • On the Cosmos

1099. Über die Würde des Menschen *(Pico della Mirandola), orig.* De hominis dignitate • On the Dignity of Man

1100. Über die Würde und die Fortschritte der Wissenschaften *(F. Bacon), orig.* De dignitate et augmentis scientiarum • Of the Proficience/Dignity and Advancement of Learning

1101. Über die Zeit *(Elias)* • Time: An Essay

1102. Über die Ziele des menschlichen Handelns; *auch:* Über das höchste Gut und das höchste Übel *(Cicero), orig.* De finibus bonorum et malorum • On the Ends/Ultimates Among Goods and Evils

1103. Über dreiwertige Logik *(Lukasiewicz), orig.* O logice trójwartosciowej • On Three-Valued Logic

1104. Über ein vermeintes Recht aus Menschenliebe zu lügen *(Kant)* • On a Supposed Right to Lie from Benevolent/Altruistic Motives

1105. Über Entstehen und Vergehen *(Aristotle), orig.* Peri geneseös kai phtoras • On Coming-To-Be and Passing-Away

1106. Über Erkenntnis und Freiheit *(Chomsky)* • *orig.* Problems of Knowledge and Freedom: The Russell Lectures

1107. Über formal unentscheidbare Sätze der Principia Mathematica und verwandter Systeme *(Gödel)* • On Formally Undecidable Propositions of Principia Mathematica an Related Systems

1108. Über Gegenstandstheorie *(Meinong)* • The Theory of Objects

1109. Über Gewißheit *(Wittgenstein)* • *orig.* On Certainty

1110. Über Helden und Heldenverehrung *(Carlyle)* • *orig.* On Heroes, Hero Worship, and the Heroic in History

1111. Über Philosophie und Christentum *(Feuerbach)* • On Philosophy and Christianity

1112. Über politische Ökonomie *(Rousseau), orig.* Economie ou oeconomie - morale et politique • Discourse on Political Economy

1113. Über Ressentiment und moralisches Werturteil *(Scheler)* • Ressentiment

1114. Über Sein und Urteil *(Hölderlin)* • On Being and Judg(e)ment

1115. Über Sinn und Bedeutung *(Frege)* • On Sense and Meaning

1116. Über soziale Arbeitsteilung *(Durkheim), orig.* La division du travail social, étude sur l'organisation des societés supérieures • The Division of Labor in Society

1117. Über tierisches und menschliches Verhalten *(Lorenz)* • Studies in Animal and Human Behaviour

1118. Überwachen und Strafen. Die Geburt des Gefängnisses *(Foucault), orig.* Surveiller et punir. La naissance de la prison • Discipline and Punish. The Birth of the Prison

1119. Das Unbehagen in der Kultur *(Freud)* • Civilization and Its Discontents

1120. Die Unfähigkeit zu trauern *(Mitscherlich)* • The Inability to Mourn: Principles of Collective Behaviour

1121. Universelle Harmonie, enthaltend die Theorie und Praxis der Musik *(Mersenne), orig.* Harmonie universelle contenant la theorie et la pratique de la musique • Harmonie Universelle: The Books on Instruments

1122. Unpopuläre Betrachtungen *(Russell)* • *orig.* Unpopular Essays

1123. Unser Wissen von der Außenwelt *(Russell)* • *orig.* Our Knowledge of the External World as a Field for Scientific Method in Philosophy

1124. Der Untergang des Abendlandes (Umriß einer Morphologie der Weltgeschichte) *(Spengler)* • The Decline of the West (Outline of a Morphology of World History)

1125. Unterhaltung über Metaphysik und Religion *(Malebranche), orig.* Entretiens sur la métaphysique et sur la religion • Dialogues/Conversations on Metaphysics and on Religion

1126. Unterredungen und mathematische Demonstrationen über zwei neue Wissenszweige, die Mechanik und die Fallgesetze betreffend *(Galilei), orig.* Discorsi e dimonstrazioni matematiche intorno a due nuove scienze attenti alla mecanica e i movimenti locali • Dialogues concerning Two New Sciences

1127. Eine Untersuchung der Gesetze des Denkens *(Boole)* • *orig.* An Investigation of the Laws of Thought

1128. Untersuchung der Natur und Ursachen des Volkswohlstands *(A. Smith)* • *orig.* An Enquiry into the Nature and Causes of the Wealth of Nations

1129. Eine Untersuchung über Bedeutung und Wahrheit *(Russell)* • *orig.* An Inquiry into Meaning and Truth

1130. Untersuchung über den menschlichen Geist nach den Grundsätzen des gemeinen Menschenverstandes *(Reid)* • *orig.* An Inquiry into the Human Mind on the Principles of Common Sense

1131. Eine Untersuchung über den menschlichen Verstand *(Hume)* • *orig.* An Enquiry concerning Human Understanding

1132. Eine Untersuchung über den Ursprung unserer Ideen von Schönheit und Tugend *(Hutcheson)* • *orig.* An Inquiry into the Original of Our Ideas of Beauty and Virtue

1133. Untersuchung über die Deutlichkeit der Grundsätze der natürlichen Theologie und der Moral *(Kant)* • An Inquiry into the Distinctness of the Principles of Natural Theology and Morals/Morality; *also:* Concerning the Clarity of the Principles of Natural Theology and Ethics

1134. Eine Untersuchung über die Prinzipien der Moral *(Hume)* • *orig.* An Enquiry concerning the Principles of Morals

1167. Versuch einer neuen Theorie des menschlichen Vorstellungsvermögens *(Reinhold)* • Attempt at a New Theory of the Human Faculty of Representation, *also:* Essay on an New Theory of the Faculty of Representation of the Human Mind

1168. Ein Versuch über den Menschen *(Pope)* • *orig.* An Essay on Man

1169. Versuch über den menschlichen Verstand *(Locke)* • *orig.* An Essay concerning Human Understanding

1170. Versuch über den Ursprung der menschlichen Erkenntnis *(Condillac), orig.* Essai sur l'origine des connoissances humaines • Essay on the Origin of Human Knowledge

1171. Versuch über die Geschichte der bürgerlichen Gesellschaft *(Ferguson)* • *orig.* An Essay on the History of Civil Society

1172. Versuch über die Gleichgültigkeit in Religionssachen *(Lamennais), orig.* Essai sur l'indifférence en matière de religion • Essay on Indifference in Matters of Religion

1173. Versuch über die Grundlagen der Psychologie und ihre Beziehung zum Studium der Natur *(Maine de Biran, postum), orig.* Essai sur les fondements de la psychologie et sur ses rapports avec l' étude de la nature • Essay on the Foundation of Psychology

1174. Versuch über die Hauptelemente der Vorstellung *(Hamelin), orig.* Essai sur les éléments principaux de la représentation • Essay on the Principal Elements of Representation

1175. Versuch über die Transcendentalphilosophie *(Maimon)* • An Essay on Transcendental Philosophy

1176. Versuch über die Ungleichheit der Menschenrassen *(Gobineau), orig.* Essai sur l'inégalité des races humaines • The Moral and Intellectual Diversity of Races

1177. Versuch über die Weltgeschichte, über die Sitten und den Geist der Völker von Karl dem Großen bis auf unsere Zeit *(Voltaire), orig.* Essai sur l' histoire générale et sur les mœurs et l'esprit des nations depuis Charlemagne jusqu' à nos jours • Essay on the Manner and Morals of Nations; *also:* An Essay on General History and on the Manners and Spirit of Nations from Charlemagne up to Our Days

1178. Versuch über eine neue Theorie des Sehens *(Berkeley)* • *orig.* An Essay towards a New Theory of Vision

1179. Versuch, das Endspiel zu verstehen *(Adorno)* • Trying to Understand Endgame

1180. Versuche über die geistigen Vermögen des Menschen *(Reid)* • *orig.* Essays on the Intellectual Powers of Man

1181. Die Verteidiger des Friedens *(Marsilius of Padua), orig.* Defensor pacis • The Defender of Peace

1182. Verteidigung des Christentums *(Tertullian), orig.* Apologeticum • Apology; *also:* Apologetical Works

1183. Eine Verteidigung des Common Sense *(Moore)* • *orig.* A Defence of Common Sense

1184. Die Verteidigung des Sokrates *(Plato), orig.* Apologia Sokratus • Apology

1185. Verteidigung des Wuchers *(Bentham)* • *orig.* In Defence of Usury

1186. Verteidigungsschrift für Galilei *(Campanella), orig.* Apologia pro Galileo • The Defence of Galileo

1187. Die Vielfalt religiöser Erfahrung *(James)* • *orig.* The Varieties of Religious Experience

1188. Vier Bücher der Lehrmeinungen *(Petrus Lombardus), orig.* Libri quattuor sententiarum • Book of Sentences

1189. Vita activa oder vom tätigen Leben *(Arendt)* • The Human Condition

1190. Der Vitalismus als Geschichte und als Lehre *(Driesch)* • The History and Theory of Vitalism

1191. Völkerpsychologie *(Wundt)* • Psychology of Peoples

1192. Vom Berufe unserer Zeit für Gesetzgebung und Rechtswissenschaft *(F. C. v. Savigny)* • On the Vocation of our Age for Legislation and Jurisprudence

1193. Vom Bürger *(Hobbes), orig.* De cive • Philosophical Rudiments concerning Government and Society

1194. Vom Denken und anderen Dingen *(Goodman)* • *orig.* Of Mind and Other Matters

1195. Vom dreieinigen Gott *(Augustine), orig.* De trinitate • On the Trinity

1196. Vom Elend der menschlichen Lage *(Segni), orig.* De miseria humanae conditionis • On the Misery of the Human Condition

1233. Von den Prinzipien *(Origen), orig.* Peri archön • On First Principles
1234. Von der Bestimmung des Menschen *(Berdiajew), orig.* O nazuazcemij czeloveka • The Destiny of Man
1235. Von der Bewegung der Tiere *(Aristotle), orig.* Peri zoon kinëseos • On the Movement of Animals
1236. Von der Dreifaltigkeit *(William of Auvergne), orig.* De trinitate • On the Trinity
1237. Von der Erforschung der Wahrheit *(Malebranche), orig.* De la recherche de la vérité • The Search after/for Truth
1238. Von der Erziehung *(Milton)* • *orig.* Of Education
1239. Von der Form der Sinnes- und Verstandeswelt und ihren Gründen *(Kant), orig.* De mundi sensibilis atque intelligibilis forma principiis • Dissertation on the Form and Principles of the Sensible and Intelligible World
1240. Von der Freiheit der Meere *(Grotius), orig.* De jure praedae commentarius • The Freedom of the Seas
1241. Von der Freiheit eines Christenmenschen *(Luther)* • (Treatise on) The Christian Liberty; *also:* The Freedom of a Christian
1242. Von der geschlossenen Welt zum unendlichen Universum *(Koyré), orig.* Du monde clos a l' univers infini • From the Closed World to the Infinite Universe
1243. Von der mannigfachen Bedeutung des Seienden nach Aristoteles *(Brentano)* • On the Several Senses of Being in Aristotle; *also:* On the Manifold Meanings of Being in Aristotle
1244. Von der Natur der Dinge *(Lucretius), orig.* De rerum natura • On the Nature of Things
1245. Von der Philosophie *(Aristotle), orig.* Peri philosophias • On Philosophy
1246. Von der Schau Gottes *(Nicolas de Cusa), orig.* De visione Dei • The Vision of God
1247. Von der Ursache, dem Prinzip und dem Einen *(Bruno), orig.* De la causa, principio et uno • Cause, Principle and Unity
1248. Von der Wahrheit *(Antiphon), orig.* Aletheia • On Truth
1249. Von der Wahrheit *(Jaspers)* • On Truth; *also:* Truth and Symbol
1250. Von der Weltseele. Eine Hypothese der höheren Physik *(Schelling)* • On the World-Soul
1251. Von der Zeugung der Tiere *(Aristotle), orig.* Peri zöön genëseös • Generation of Animals
1252. Von einem logischen Standpunkt *(Quine)* • *orig.* From a Logical Point of View: Nine Logico-Philosophical Essays
1253. Vorlesungen *(Wittgenstein)* • *orig.* Lectures
1254. Vorlesungen über das Wesen der Religion *(Feuerbach)* • Lectures on the Essence of Religion
1255. Vorlesungen über die Ästhetik *(Hegel, postum)* • Aesthetics: Lectures on Fine Art
1256. Vorlesungen über die Geschichte der Philosophie *(Hegel, postum)* • Lectures on the History of Philosophy
1257. Vorlesungen über die Menschen- und Tierseele *(Wundt)* • Lectures on Human and Animal Psychology
1258. Vorlesungen über die Philosophie der Geschichte *(Hegel, postum)* • Lectures on the Philosophy of History
1259. Vorlesungen über die Philosophie der Religion *(Hegel, postum)* • Lectures on the Philosophy of Religion
1260. Vorlesungen über Gastheorie *(Boltzmann)* • Lectures on the Theory of Gases
1261. Vorlesungen über Pragmatismus *(Peirce)* • *orig.* Lectures on Pragmatism
1262. Vorschule der Aesthetik *(Jean Paul)* • Introduction to Aesthetics
1263. Vorschule der Ästhetik *(Fechner)* • Introduction/Propaedeutics to Aesthetics
1264. Vorspiel zur Pansophie *(Comenius), orig.* Prodromus pansophiae • A Reformation of Schooles

1265. Wahnsinn und Gesellschaft. Eine Geschichte des Wahns im Zeitalter der Vernunft *(Foucault), orig.* Folie et déraison. Histoire de la folie à l' âge classique • Madness and Civilization: A History of Insanity in the Age of Reason
1266. Das wahre vernünftige System des Universums *(Cudworth)* • *orig.* The True Intellectual System of the Universe

1303. Das Wesen des Christentums *(Feuerbach)* • The Essence of Christianity
1304. Wesen und Formen der Sympathie *(Scheler)* • The Nature of Sympathy
1305. Wider den Methodenzwang. Skizze einer anarchistischen Erkenntnistheorie *(Feyerabend)* • *orig.* Against Method. Outline of an Anarchistic Theory of Knowledge
1306. Die Widersprüche der Philosophen *(Al-Ghazzali), orig.* Tahäfut al-faläsifah • The Incoherence of the Philosophers
1307. Die Widersprüche der Widersprüche *(Averroes), orig.* Tahäfut-at-tahäfut • The Incoherence of the Incoherence
1308. Die Widersprüche der Nationalökonomie oder Philosophie des Elends *(Proudhon), orig.* Système des contradicions économiques, ou philosophie de la misère • System of Economic Contradictions, or the Philosophy of Misery/Poverty
1309. Der Widerstreit *(Lyotard), orig.* Le différend • The Different: Phrases in Dispute
1310. Wie entsteht Religion? *(Whitehead)* • *orig.* Religion in the Making
1311. Wie unsere Ideen zu klären sind *(Peirce)* • *orig.* How to Make Our Ideas Clear
1312. Wie wirklich ist die Wirklichkeit? Wahn, Täuschung, Verstehen *(Watzlawick)* • *orig.* How Real is Real? Confusion, Disinformation, Communication
1313. Die Wiederentdeckung des Geistes *(Searle)* • The Rediscovery of the Mind
1314. Die Wiederholung *(Kierkegaard), orig.* Gjentagelsen • Repetition
1315. Der Wiener Kreis. Der Ursprung des Neo-Positivismus *(Kraft)* • The Vienna Circle, the Origin of Neo-Positivism
1316. Das wilde Denken *(Lévi-Strauss), orig.* La pensée sauvage • Savage Mind
1317. Der Wille zum Glauben und andere popular-philosophische Essays *(James)* • *orig.* The Will to Believe and Other Essays in Popular Philosophy
1318. Der Wille zur Macht. Versuch einer Umwertung aller Werte *(Nietzsche, postum)* • The Will to Power: An Essay towards the Transvaluation of all Values
1319. Das Willentliche und das Unwillentliche *(Ricoeur), orig.* Le volontaire et l'involontaire • The Voluntary and the Involuntary
1320. Wirkungsquantum und Naturbeschreibung *(Bohr)* • Atomic Theory and the Description of Nature
1321. Wirtschaft und Gesellschaft. Grundriß der verstehenden Soziologie *(M. Weber, postum)* • Economy and Society: An Outline of Interpretive Sociology; *also:* The Theory of Social and Economic Organization
1322. Wirtschaftsgeschichte *(M. Weber, postum)* • General Economic History
1323. Wissen, Glaube und Ahndung *(Fries)* • Knowledge, Belief and Aesthetic Sense
1324. Wissenschaft als Beruf *(M. Weber)* • Scholarship as a Profession
1325. Wissenschaft der Logik *(Hegel)* • Science of Logic
1326. Wissenschaft, Wahrnehmung und Realität *(Sellars)* • *orig.* Science, Perception and Reality
1327. Wissenschaft und Hypothese *(Poincaré), orig.* La science et l'hypothèse • Science and Hypothesis
1328. Wissenschaft und menschliches Verhalten *(Skinner)* • *orig.* Science and Human Behavior
1329. Wissenschaft und Metaphysik. Variationen zu Kantischen Themen *(Sellars)* • *orig.* Science and Metaphysics. Variations on Kantian Themes
1330. Wissenschaft und moderne Welt *(Whitehead)* • *orig.* Science and the Modern World
1331. Eine wissenschaftliche Theorie der Kultur *(Malinowski)* • *orig.* A Scientific Theory of Culture
1332. Wissenschaftliche Unterredungen oder Textzusammenstellung über den freien Willen *(Erasmus), orig.* De libero arbitrio diatribe sive collatio • Discourse on Free Will
1333. Wissenschaftslehre. Versuch einer ausführlichen und grösstenteils neuen Darstellung der Logik *(Bolzano)* • The Theory of Science. An Essay towards a Detailed and for the most Part New Exposition of Logic
1334. Die Wissenschaftslehre *(Fichte)* • The Science of Knowledge
1335. Die Wissensformen und die Gesellschaft *(Scheler)* • Problems of a Sociology of Knowledge
1336. Der Witz und seine Beziehung zum Unbewußten *(Freud)* • Jokes and Their Relation to the Unconscious

INDEX OF NAMES TO PHILOSOPHICAL TITLES

NAMENVERZEICHNIS PHILOSOPHISCHER WERKTITEL